HOW TO PAY ZERO TAXES, 2019

Also by Jeff A. Schnepper

How to Pay Zero Estate Taxes
Inside IRS
Professional Handbook of Business Valuation
New Bankruptcy Law
Can You Afford to Retire?

HOW TO PAY ZERO TAXES, 2019

THIRTY-SIXTH EDITION

Jeff A. Schnepper

New York Chicago San Francisco Athens London
Madrid Mexico City Milan New Delhi
Singapore Sydney Toronto

1 2 3 4 5 6 QVS 22 21 20 19 18

| ISBN | 978-1-260-14326-3 |
| MHID | 1-260-14326-0 |

| e-ISBN | 978-1-260-14327-0 |
| e-MHID | 1-260-14327-9 |

This publication is designed to provide accurate and authoritative information in regard to the subject matter covered. It is sold with the understanding that neither the author nor the publisher is engaged in rendering legal, accounting, securities trading, or other professional services. If legal advice or other expert assistance is required, the services of a competent professional person should be sought.

> —*From a Declaration of Principles jointly adopted by a Committee of the American Bar Association and a Committee of Publishers*

McGraw-Hill Education books are available at special quantity discounts to use as premiums and sales promotions or for use in corporate training programs. To contact a representative, please visit the Contact Us pages at www.mhprofessional.com.

This book is normally dedicated to my mogul,
Barbara, who taught me how to love, and to
my children, Brandy, Joshua, Allison, Mario,
and Jonelle, who gave me five more reasons why.

If I had the choice of doing it all over again,
I would begin by loving you again.

Also normally dedicated to the memory
of Frisco T. D. Schnepper, Tiger T. C. Schnepper,
Fred T. C. Schnepper, and to Bruno,
who now give me paws,

BUT

Forget it, guys . . . This one's
for my Bianca Rose Conlin,
and her brothers Drew Ethan Conlin, Tyler Evan Conlin,
Spencer Henry Conlin, and Owen Bae Alexander Conlin
and their cousins Dylan Simon Schnepper and Aubrey
Anne Schnepper, who have redefined my universe!

Contents

CHAPTER 6
"Above the Line" Deductions

A Deductions for Adjusted Gross Income

CHAPTER 9
Super Tax Shelters

Acknowledgments

I wish to thank Nancie Crook, Barbara Thomassian, Pat Berenson, Ronnie Smith, and Anne McVay, without whom this book could not have been written, and the U.S. Congress and the IRS, without whom this book wouldn't have been needed.

I also want to thank Sayes B. Block and Paul Malagoli, for their encouragement and professional guidance; Sandi Walker, April Napolitano, and Anne Rigney, for their typing and editorial assistance; my editors at McGraw-Hill, Mary Glenn, Jane Palmieri, Patricia Amoroso, Tania Loghmani, Zach Gajewski, Patricia Wallenburg, Maki Wiering, Amy Li, and Cheryl Ringer; and Sri Haran, CPA, Robert Doyle, Steve Leimberg, Jeff Kelvin, Michael Vassey, Joel Petchon, John McFadden, Kenn Tacchino, Bill Rotella, George Hasenberg, Frank Kesselman, John Oxley, Stephen D. Leightman, Noeleen McLoughlin, Julian Egnaczyk, Ed Caldwell, CPA, Al Blum, Brian Hans, Harry K. Sorenson, CPA, Patrick O'Rourke, CPA, S. Scott Davison, Rose Thompson, Lilly Thompson, Claire Davison, Allison Schnepper, Zulma Lombardo, Morris Abraham, Richard and Janice Schank, Mark S. Fineberg, CPA, Anthony Lyras, and Ron Campbell for their professional assistance; and Simba T.C. Schnepper Conlin, Bruno T.D. Conlin, and Fred T.C. Schnepper, who give me reason to paws. Special thanks to Stephanie Davison-Thompson and Brian Lance for research and editorial assistance, Bill Fox for his investment insights, Ray Palmucci for his guidance and care of my San Diego assets.

HOW TO PAY ZERO TAXES, 2019

HOW
TO PAY
ZERO
TAXES
2019

Tax Insanity

"Our income tax system is overly complex. It distorts investment decisions and encourages people to put money into schemes to reduce their tax bills instead of into enterprises to create jobs and help our economy grow."

BILL BRADLEY, New Jersey senator (1984)

"The words of such an act as the Income Tax... merely dance before my eyes in a meaningless procession: cross-reference, exception upon exception— couched in abstract terms that offer no handle to seize hold of—leave in my mind only a confused sense of some vitally important, but successfully concealed, purport, which it is my duty to extract, but which is within my power, if at all, only after the most inordinate expenditure of time. I know that these monsters are the result of fabulous industry and ingenuity, plugging up this hole and casting out the net, against all possible evasion; yet at times I cannot help recalling a saying of William James about certain passages of Hegel: that they were, no doubt, written with a passion of rationality; but that one cannot help wondering whether to the reader they have any significance save that the words are strung together with syntactical correctness...."

JUDGE LEARNED HAND, Thomas Walter Swan, 57 Yale L.J. 167, 169 [1947].

Q: What's the difference between Obama's cabinet and a penitentiary?

A: One is filled with tax evaders, blackmailers, and threats to society. The other is for housing prisoners.

—DAVID LETTERMAN

"I don't believe in a law to prevent a man from getting rich; it would do more harm than good."

ABRAHAM LINCOLN

"Politicians tax the middle class for the same reason some people rob banks. That's where the money is."

FORBES MAGAZINE
May 11, 1992

"If our current tax strucure were a TV show, it would either be 'Foul-ups, Bleeps and Blunders,' or 'Gimme a Break.' If it were a movie, it would be 'Revenge of the Nerds' or maybe 'Take the Money and Run.' And if the IRS ever wants a theme song, mabye they'll get Sting to do 'Every breath you take, every move you make, I'll be watching you.'"

PRESIDENT REAGAN, in remarks to students at
Northside High School, Atlanta, Georgia, June 6, 1985

2018 – A WHOLE NEW TAX SYSTEM

The Tax Cuts & Jobs Act of 2017, passed and signed in the last two weeks of December, 2017, is the biggest tax law change since the Economic Growth and Tax Relief Act of 2001. The IRS estimated that it will cost approximately $397 million and require hiring the equivalent of 1,734 full time employees over the next two years to implement the new rules. The details of the new law, and the strategies and techniques to maximize your benefits under it, are covered in Chapter 12 of **How To Pay Zero Taxes—2019**. But last year also saw the Bipartisan Budget Act, passed in February, 2018, which retroactively extended over thirty tax breaks into the 2017 tax year. That meant that every 1040 form filed for 2017 was incomplete and missed lines for allowable deductions. If you knew about the changes, you could write them in. If not, you missed them and have 3 years from the due date to amend your return.

Missing lines on their tax forms was not the only problem the IRS had last year. The IRS core systems computers went down on tax day (April 17th for 2017) and, as a result of this malfunctioning, the filing season had to be extended for an additional day. That Tax Day Glitch was not the only problem the IRS had in 2018. According to the Treasury Inspector General for Tax Administration (TIGTA) and the Government Accounting Office (GAO), last year revealed that:

- The Health Coverage Tax Credit is a refundable credit that covers 72.5 percent of the cost of qualified health insurance premiums for eligible individuals and their families. In tax year 2016, 9.5 percent (3,839 returns out of 40,227 filed for the credit) were erroneously processed.

- In the 2017 filing season, the IRS paid taxpayers $5.8 billion more in advanced premium tax credits than the law would allow.

- The Public Transportation Subsidy Program was created to encourage the use of public transportation when commuting to and from work. In 2016, 6,449 participants used almost $1.6 million more in transportation benefits than necessary for commuting to work or used benefits while on leave, while teleworking or while in a non-pay status.

- The GAO audits the IRS. For fiscal years 2016 and 2017, it found that the IRS' internal control over financial reporting contained continuing "material weakness" in internal control. And, they have a fit when *you* are missing a single receipt!

- The IRS won't get back a $21 million refund it erroneously issued to Starr International Co. Inc. because the agency failed to file suit within the allotted statute of limitations period.

- In fiscal years 2016 and 2017, the IRS issued more than $1.7 million in awards to 1,962 employees who had a disciplinary or adverse action during the 12 months prior to receiving their award. Such misconduct included unauthorized access tax return information, substance abuse, and sexual misconduct.

- In an October, 2017 study, the TIGTA found that the IRS had rehired more than 200 employees that were previously separated while under investigation for a substantial conduct or performance issue.

- IRS programing errors allowed the issuance of more than 227,000 Employer Identification Numbers (EIN) to individuals who already had an EIN or who were dead.

- In a review of IRS charge card use, the TIGTA found 42 instances totaling more than $15,000, of prohibited purchases being made.

- During the 2017 filing season, the IRS erroneously paid $2.8 billion in American Opportunity Tax Credits to 1.7 million ineligible taxpayers.

- During fiscal 2017, the IRS also improperly issued $16.2 billion (23.9%) in Earned Income Tax Credits.

- In a review of IRS procurement and grant transactions, the TIGTA found that "significant improvements" were needed to ensure the completeness, accuracy and overall quality of the information submitted. Over 97 percent had one or more data elements that were inaccurate.

- In a September, 2017 report, the TIGTA found that taxpayer data remains vulnerable to inappropriate and undetected use, modification, or disclosure. It found that three cybersecurity functions, Identify, Protect and Detect, were "not effective." Weaknesses in the IRS's Computer Security Incident Response Center program could prevent the timely detection, prevention, or reporting of unauthorized access and disclosure of taxpayer data. In a June, 2018 report, the TIGTA found that the IRS Cybersecurity Data Warehouse continues to need improved security controls.

- IRS controls for verifying and validating tax transcript requests failed to comply with government standards and did not protect taxpayers against unauthorized release of their tax information.

- A computer glitch resulted in the IRS failing to notify 458,658 victims of identity theft that somebody else was using their identity.

- The IRS's lack of a strategy for storing data online puts taxpayer data at risk.

- Special procedures are required before the IRS can Levy on a retirement account. TIGTA found that in a sample of 27 account levies, 11 were done without regard to those special procedures.

- It is important that taxpayers receive fair and balanced treatment from IRS employees when they attempt to collect taxes. TIGTA found violations including contacting taxpayers directly without the required consent of the taxpayer's power of attorney, harassing or abusing taxpayers, and using obscene or profane language with taxpayers during collection related activities.

- Seizures conducted by the IRS, did not adequately comply with the guidelines put in place to ensure taxpayer's rights were not violated.

- The IRS improperly withheld information 14.3 percent of the time when responding to Freedom of Information requests.

- The IRS could be missing out on as much as $60.9 million in unreported rental income because it is not spotting all nonresident aliens who owe the tax.

- Sixty-four percent of the IRS's information technology hardware infrastructure is beyond its useful life. These aged hardware failures may also have had a negative effect on IRS employee productivity, security of taxpayer information, and customer service.

- The IRS does not have an adequate tracking system to account for the records foreign countries send on a regular basis under the Automatic Exchange of information Program.

- The IRS's Criminal Investigation's Active Directory architecture lacks necessary logical security controls. For example, the operating system on the domain controllers are only 64 percent compliant with security requirements, and 295 service accounts and 1,751 user accounts are improperly configured.

- In November, 2017, according to Mary Beth Murphy, Commissioner of the Small Business/Self Employed Division of the IRS, the IRS received about 1 million cybersecurity threats a day. Also in November, 2017, according to the IRS Commissioner John Koskinen, "We get attacked four million times a day." Maybe they should get their statistics in line. . . . In May 2018, then IRS Commissioner David Kautter said the agency gets 2.5 million cyberattacks each day. Are they just making these numbers up?

- You have three years to file your return. If you did not file for 2014 in 2015, the statute of limitations expired in April, 2018. According to the IRS, refunds worth $1.1 billion were left on the table unclaimed and now lost.

- The cost of tax complexity? Over 8.9 billion hours to comply with IRS paperwork and more than $409 billion each year.

- As a result of the Tax Cuts and Jobs Act of 2018, the IRS will have to create and revise 450 new tax forms and reprogram approximately 140 interrelated return processing systems.

- Private debt collection in fiscal 2017 generated $6.7 million in taxpayer payments. But the program cost the government $20 million. Plan to make it up in volume?

- The IRS Criminal Investigation division returned $9.9 million to people whose property it determined had been seized erroneously. I guess that's why they're called the *Criminal* investigation division. . . .

- The IRS has suspended a program (Enterprise Case Management) because the software product the IRS had selected was not viable. That's $85.4 million and about two and a half years work down the drain.

There was some good news:

- Former Rep. Corrine Brown (D-FL) was sentenced to five years in prison for her role in a scheme involving a fraudulent educational charity and for tax obstruction and failing to disclose income.

- Those with the money are paying the taxes. The top 1% of taxpayers in 2015 (the 1.4 million filers with adjusted gross incomes of $480,930 or more) paid 39.0% of all federal income taxes. The top 5%, with incomes of $195,778, paid 59.6% and the top 10%, with income of $138,031 or more, paid 70.6%. Those in the bottom 50% only paid 2.8% of the total federal income tax take.

- Identity theft indicators continued their dramatic decline reports of identity theft were down 40 percent in 2017 from 2016; the number of tax returns with confirmed identity theft was down 32 percent from 2016 to 2017; and the inventory backlog of taxpayers who filed identity theft reports in 2017 was only 10 percent (34,000 cases) of that in 2013 (372,000 cases).

- The IRS issued a new strategic plan for 2018-2022 focusing on six goals to improve customer service:

1. Empower and enable taxpayers to meet their tax obligations.

2. Protect the integrity of the tax system by encouraging compliance through administering and enforcing the tax code.

3. Collaborate with external partners proactively to improve tax administration.

4. Cultivate a well-equipped, diverse, flexible and engaged workforce.

5. Advance data access, usability and analytics to inform decision making and improve operational outcomes.

6. Drive increased agility, efficiency, effectiveness and security in IRS operations.

2017 – POLITICS AGAIN TRUMPS ECONOMICS

2017 was the year when "facts" depended on who said it and in what context. It was also the year where the primary objective of each political party was to keep the other from achieving anything of value regardless of whether they agreed with the final objective . . . just make sure the other guy doesn't get any credit. In the middle of this chaos, President Trump proposed an outline for a major overhaul and simplification of our whole tax system . . . including a refocus of the IRS from enforcement to service.

Nevertheless, *How to Pay Zero Taxes, 2019* needs to step back from "wish it were so" to deal with the tax code, court cases, and regulations as they exist today. You can't play the game unless you know the rules and the agency that enforces them—the Internal Revenue Service. In that context, let's review the effectiveness of that agency as detailed by the Treasury Inspector General for Tax Administration (TIGTA) and the Government Accounting Office (GOA) during the last year:

- The IRS spent $12 million for subscriptions for a Microsoft enterprise e-mail system that, as it turned out, it could not use. The purchase was made without first determining project infrastructure needs, integration requirements, business requirements, security and portal bandwidth, and whether the subscriptions were technologically feasible for the IRS. . . . Really?

- IRS employees sent hundreds of unencrypted e-mails containing sensitive taxpayer information, and some used personal e-mail accounts for official agency business. I guess they thought it was OK as long as they were not running for president and the Russians didn't object.

- IRS examination function personnel did not always follow collectibility procedures, coordinate with the collection function, nor measure the collectibility of assessments.

- The IRS paid more than $27.2 million in potentially erroneous refunds or tax credits to 1,938 taxpayers who claimed *frivolous tax arguments* in tax year

2014. Frivolous tax arguments are those that have no basis in fact or in tax law. That's not too bad considering. . . .

- The IRS made about $25 billion in erroneous tax credit payments in 2016. Almost $17 billion of that was for the earned income credit.

- The IRS incorrectly disallowed about $54,000 in educator expense deductions and $1.5 million in residential energy credits in 2016 because of errors in the "process."

- The IRS's electronic record retention policies did not consistently ensure that records were retained and produced when requested.

- A June 2017 report revealed that more than 24,000 fraudulent returns with more than $1.3 billion in claimed refunds were filed with prisoner Social Security numbers.

- An estimated $4.3 billion in refundable tax credit payments were issued improperly during fiscal year 2016. At 5 percent interest, that's over $589,000 *per day*!

- The IRS Automated Non-Master File (ANFL), which contains roughly $4.5 billion in unpaid tax, penalties, and interest due from taxpayers, is subject to calculation errors and inefficient processing.

- In October of 2016, additional improvements were still needed to strengthen the IRS Electronic Authentication Process controls, which allowed fraudsters to gain access to about 724,000 taxpayer accounts in May of 2015.

- The IRS is vulnerable to the loss of laptop computers. Improved controls are also needed to account for the issuance and return of contractor employee laptop computers, which may contain sensitive taxpayer information.

- In 2016, TIGTA identified weaknesses within the IRS cybersecurity program in which three areas need significant improvement—Information Security Continuous Monitoring, Configuration Management, and Identify and Access Management. There were identified weaknesses in electronic authorization process controls, physical security controls, and backing up and restoring data.

- The IRS answered 79 percent of the telephone calls it received on its "Account Management" (AM) telephone lines that were routed to telephone assistors. That's up from 72 percent from 2016. In addition, time spent on hold declined from 11.1 minutes in 2016 to 6.5 minutes during the 2017 filing season.

- But, despite answering a higher percentage of calls, assistors actually answered 25 percent fewer calls in 2017 than in 2016. Had they received the same number of calls in 2017 as in 2016, the IRS would have answered only 54 percent of taxpayer calls. The fiscal year 2018 IRS budget projects that the agency will answer only 39 percent of calls routed to telephone helpers next year.

- The IRS only answered 40 percent of the 2.7 million calls it received in fiscal 2017 from taxpayers seeking to make payments, down from 36 percent the prior year. The wait time also increased from 11 minutes in 2016 to 47 minutes in 2017.

- Want to see a live IRS agent? You now need an appointment to receive any assistance at any of the 376 Taxpayer Assistance Centers (TACs) operated by the IRS. Call 844-545-5640 to schedule an appointment or you will be turned away.

- From January 2015 through March 2016, the IRS brought back more than 10 percent of the 2,000 employees who were terminated or separated from the agency while "under investigation for a substantiated conduct or performance issue."

- Taxpayers who go to the IRS Office of Appeals for collection due process issues are still misclassified and receive the wrong type of hearing.

- Up to 14 Fair Tax Collection Practices violations at the IRS were identified in 2015.

- Between fiscal 2015 and 2016, calculation errors caused the IRS to underpay 900 employees and overpay 600 more. Based on a sample of IRS employees who received salary increases of more than 10 percent for promotion into management positions between fiscal 2006 and 2015, 31 percent of sampled employees were not paid correctly.

- The IRS Whistleblower Office does not have appropriate controls in place for sufficient oversight of claims processing.

- $17.1 million was unlawfully seized by the IRS and forfeited to the government allegedly in violation of the Bank Secrecy Act. In a TIGTA civil forfeiture sample of 278 investigations, 91% of them were found to be businesses where the funds were obtained legally.

- During the 2016 filing season, the IRS doled out $1.2 million less in a property tax credit than taxpayers were owed. It was because the IRS failed to make computer program changes first highlighted in 2015. Because of

another computer problem, 5,600 direct deposits did not properly convert to paper checks.

- In 2016, the IRS's information security program was not fully effective due to program issues.

- Most people (57%) who claimed the *health coverage tax credit* on their 2015 returns did not qualify for that credit. Good news! The IRS correctly determined the amount of the allowable *premium tax credit* 93 percent of the time in 2015 and 97 percent of the time in 2016.

- The IRS failed to accurately impose a fee for failure to file a return for 85 accounts worth more than $1.7 million, overcalulated the penalty fee on 153 accounts totaling about $89,000, and underassessed the fee on 227 accounts, totaling about $354,000.

- About 1.1 million taxpayers were victims of employment-related identity theft—which happens when a taxpayer's identity is stolen to get a job—from February 2011 to December 2015. More than 800,000 victims were harmed just in 2015. Yet in June 2017 the IRS processes were still not sufficient to identify and assist all employment theft victims.

- As of September 30, 2016, the IRS had only 98 employees conducting education and outreach to the 62 million small business and self-employed taxpayers, and only 365 employees for the nearly 125 million individual taxpayers.

- A 2016 GAO report on IRS audits led House Ways & Means Chairman Brady and Oversight Subcommittee Chairman Roskam to conclude that the findings show that the agency "does not have protections in place to ensure that taxpayers are treated fairly when being selected for audits."

- The number of IRS employees working taxpayer correspondence cases and answering phone questions fell about 11 percent between fiscal years 2013 and 2015. This was despite taxpayer services funding increasing 9 percent, to $198 million, between fiscal years 2013 and 2016.

- Since 2001 to the end of 2016, there have been almost 5,900 legislative tax changes . . . more than one a day.

- In 2017, we spent close to $1 trillion more for taxes than for food, clothing, and housing combined.

- From the gang that couldn't shoot straight—one of the IRS' fabled successes is the takedown of gang leader Al Capone for tax evasion. The agency lent the new Mob Museum in Las Vegas a prized possession from its collection of historical artifacts—a handgun once owned by Mr. Capone. One small problem . . . it was the wrong gun!

- According to Ibis World, the U.S. tax preparation industry generates $8.9 billion in annual revenue. My children thank you!

- Interesting news! The Tax Revolution Institute has created a new website, AuditIRS.com, to collect personal experiences from taxpayers about their encounters with the IRS, and it plans to conduct an "audit" of the IRS's treatment of taxpayers.

- Good news! From January to April 2016, the IRS stopped $1.1 billion in fraudulent refunds claimed by identity thieves on more than 171,000 tax returns, compared to $754 million in fraudulent refunds claimed on 141,000 returns for the same period in 2015.

- Better news! During fiscal 2016, the IRS stopped more than $6.5 billion in fraudulent refunds on the 969,000 tax returns confirmed to be filed by identity thieves. Complaints of ID theft fell 46 percent in 2016 from the previous year, dropping to 376,500.

- Crazy news! Hope and belief beat out experience every time. That's why people keep getting married over and again—full disclosure—I have a sister-in-law who has been married ten times! After being discontinued twice before because of complaints about harassment of taxpayers and low success in collections, our Congress has reinstated a program to hire four private collection agencies to help collect unpaid federal income tax debts. The IRS has contracted with these collection agencies: Pioneer, in Horseheads, NY; Conserve, in Fairport, NY; Performant, in Livermore, CA; and CBE Group, in Cedar Falls, IA.

Who picked these debt collectors? In a letter to Pioneer, Senator Sherwood Brown (D-OH), Senator Benjamin Cardin (D-MD), Senator Jeff Merkley (D-OR), and Senator Elizabeth Warren (D-MA) expressed concerns that Pioneer may be:

1. failing to adequately protect taxpayers from criminals posing as IRS agents;

2. pressuring taxpayers into risky financial transactions;

3. violating the Fair Debt Collections Practices Act (FDCPA) and provisions of the Internal Revenue Code, and

4. violating IRS guidelines and provisions of Pioneer's contract.

The Senators were particularly concerned because Pioneer's parent company, Navient, abused federal student loan borrowers through its Education Department student loan servicing contracts.

In addition, this private collection program will surely be hampered by telephone scammers who pretend to be from the IRS in order to embezzle funds from unknowing taxpayers. Criminals impersonating IRS employees have stolen $55 million from more than 10,300 individuals in the last three years.

The IRS solution? TIGTA released a new flyer and a new poster warning taxpayers about potentially fraudulent calls from IRS imposter employees. You can always make an appointment to see them at any local IRS office . . . but don't try without an appointment.

IF YOU DO GET A CALL, ASK THEM TO SEND YOU A LETTER. THE REAL IRS NEVER MAKES A CALL UNTIL LETTERS HAVE BEEN SENT.

Call the TIGTA Hotline at 800-366-4484 for complaints and questions about IRS private debt collectors.

2016 – A NEW PRESIDENT AND CONTINUING CHAOS

2016 was the year we elected a new president, and now almost half the voters are contemplating moving out of the country. Throw in global warming and your best long-term investment may well be land in Canada.

2016 was also the year the House of Representatives Committee on Oversight and Government Reform voted to censure and impeach IRS Commissioner John Koskinen for lying to Congress. I'm not sure I understand. I thought the "inability to tell the truth" was a prerequisite to being a politician.

2016 was also the year in which the annual "extenders" game came to a halt. The extenders were a series of fifty some odd tax provisions that pretty much on an annual basis Congress would wait till the last minute to renew—and then renewed only for a short period of time. They included a group of

deductions such as the $250 "above the line" allowance for teachers' expenses, the deduction for state sales taxes, the mortgage insurance premium deduction, the tuition and fees deduction, the forgiven mortgage debt exclusion, the nonbusiness energy credits, etc. The Protecting Americans from Tax Hikes (the PATH Act), passed in the last two weeks of December 2015, extended several provisions through 2016 and made others permanent. See page 574 for details.

Here are some of the indignities suffered by the IRS in 2016 as revealed by the General Accounting Office (GAO) and the Treasury Inspector General for Tax Administration (TIGTA):

- Because of a programming error impacting more than 13,000 returns in 2013, over $27 million in refunds were erroneously issued.

- A computer programming error and the ineffective monitoring of potentially fraudulent tax returns resulted in the erroneous release of more than $46 million in refunds during 2014.

- In an analysis of 2011 data, it was found that the IRS failed to assess $200 million in fines and penalties for employer improper wage reporting. The IRS just didn't send out the bill!

- It was revealed that in 2011 the IRS paid out $3.6 billion in fraudulent refunds, growing to $5.8 billion in 2013. In June 2015, the IRS website got hit with thieves stealing information on about 100,000 taxpayers to generate $39 million in fraudulent refunds.

- The IRS Electronic Fraud Detection System was developed in 1994 and remains the IRS's main system for detecting fraudulent returns. The failure to phase out this old system with a developed new one could cost taxpayers an estimate additional $18 million per year to run both systems.

- Half of the IRS-approved *free* e-file services failed the IRS's security and privacy mandated standards. Among those who failed were 1040.com, 1040Now.net, FileYourTaxes.com, Free1040TaxReturn.com, Online Taxes at OLT.com, and Jackson Hewitt Online.

- IRS employee, Nakeisha Hall, who worked for the Taxpayer Advocate Service, where her job was to help taxpayers resolve their identity theft problems, pleaded guilty to identity theft. She got 9 years in prison.

- The new IRS fraud detection system failed to detect $313 million in fraudulent identity theft refunds in 2015.

- The IRS took an average of 70 days to accommodate requests by disabled employees. It should have been done in 15 days, absent extenuating circumstances.

- More than a dozen IRS employees misused their government-issued charge cards.

- The IRS is not ensuring that keys, identification badges, and other security items are collected from employees who leave the agency.

- By the end of 2016, the IRS plans to eliminate the walk-in option at Taxpayer Assistance Centers (TAC), migrating to an "appointment only" system.

- The IRS is conducting a pilot program under which it will not accept tax payments from walk-in taxpayers. Now you need an appointment to pay your bill!

- Nearly one third of the 4.6 million taxpayers who received an advanced premium tax credit for insurance coverage bought on a health care marketplace didn't report the credit on their returns.

- The IRS has failed to adequately test a database that will house all taxpayer information for the Affordable Care Act–related reporting requirements.

- The IRS's computer system miscalculated the allowable Premium Tax Credits for more than 27,000 taxpayers who received subsidies for health insurance under the Affordable Care Act in 2015.

- The IRS cannot adequately identify certain U.S. and foreign citizens who fail to pay Social Security taxes.

- The IRS allowed nearly $95 million in potentially improper foreign tax credits between tax years 2010 and 2012.

- Tax preparers who were given identification numbers by the IRS and allowed to practice in 2015 may have owed more than $367 million in taxes.

- Many of the special personal identification numbers issued by the IRS to protect victims of identity theft may have been stolen.

- About 724,000 taxpayer accounts were breached by hackers targeting the IRS's "Get Transcript" application, 390,000 more than the agency previously reported.

- The IRS failed to fully redact Social Security Numbers and Employer Identification Numbers from hundreds of its Offer in Compromise files that are available to the public.

- The IRS, which has 2,316 special agents, spent nearly $11 million on guns, ammunition, and military style equipment. That's nearly $5,000 in gear for each agent.

- Because of IRS failures, taxpayers received $572 million in excess Obamacare tax credits.

- The IRS needs to improve the management of its backup and restoration process.

- The IRS needs to strengthen certain internal controls for audit selection. Currently the IRS uses over 30 methods, called "workstreams," to identify and review tax returns that may merit an audit. The returns were initially identified through seven sources, which include referrals, computer programs that run filters, rules, or algorithms to identify noncompliant taxpayers.

- The IRS did not always follow its own procedures when selling some of the property it seized for unpaid taxes.

- The IRS's Automated Collection System lacks key controls for selecting which delinquent tax cases to pursue.

- Section 1204 of the IRS Restructuring and Reform Act of 1998 (RRA 98) mandates that managers evaluating employees not use any record of tax enforcement results (ROTER). Employees should not get promotions and awards based upon the amount of money they get from taxpayers at an audit. TIGTA found multiple instances in a 2015 report where these rules were not followed.

- In fiscal 2014, the IRS reported payments of $65.2 billion for the earned income tax credit (EITC). The IRS estimated that 27.2 percent, or $17.7 billion of those program payments were improper.

- During the 2015 filing season in 2016, the IRS estimated it may have paid $30 million to fraudsters who filed approximately 7,200 tax returns that passed through the Taxpayer Protection Program to identify fraudulent returns.

- The Taxpayer Protection Program (TPP) was set up to protect identity theft. Its false positive rate for 2015 was 36.6 percent, which means that 760,000 legitimate refunds were stopped.

- During the 2016 filing season, the TPP only answered 22.7 percent of more than 4.4 million calls. Nearly four out of five calls were not answered.

It wasn't just the IRS that had its problems. On April 6, 2016, former US Tax Court Judge Diane Kroupa and her husband were indicted for conspiracy to commit tax evasion and obstruction of an IRS audit.

There was some positive news:

- The GAO found that the IRS was generally successful in collecting delinquent taxes from current and retired federal employees. The IRS identified 304,665 federal employees and retirees who owed approximately $3.54 billion in unpaid taxes at the end of fiscal 2014.

- Federal income tax collection rose 10.5 percent in 2015. The $3.2 trillion collected from all federal taxes in 2015 was the highest on record.

- Good news if your identity has been stolen. The value of identity protection services provided by an entity whose data has been breached is NOT taxable income to the breach victim.

- During its pilot in calendar year 2014, the Return Review Program identified 10,348 identity theft cases, totaling $43 million in refunds and an additional 350,000 potentially fraudulent returns that were not detected by the existing fraud detection system.

- IRS spending on conferences, meetings, and events was only $22.2 million in fiscal 2014, down 87.5 percent from the prior year.

- From January through April 2016, the IRS stopped $1.1 billion in fraudulent refunds claimed by identity thieves on more than 171,000 tax returns. That compares to $754 million in fraudulent refunds claimed on 141,000 returns for the same period in 2015.

- Since January 2016, the IRS Identity Theft Victims Assistance function experienced a marked drop of 48 percent, which includes identity theft affidavits filed by victims.

- Because of low incomes or refundable credits, 44 percent of Americans paid no federal income tax.

2015 – EXTENDERS AGAIN AND A TOUGH YEAR FOR THE IRS

Insanity has been defined as doing the same thing over and over again and expecting different results. Yet year after year, we elect the same representatives back to Congress expecting them to legislate and govern and all they do is play politics (that's from the Greek *poli* meaning "many" and *tics* meaning "bloodsuckers").

Once again, the "extenders" expired only to be renewed in the last two weeks of the year. Last year's extender legislation had a shelf life of less than a carton of eggs. Signed into law on December 18, 2014, the provisions expired less than two weeks later. See page 570 for details on the 2014 extensions.

I Actually Felt Bad for the IRS in 2015

Clearly Congress is unhappy with the IRS. Clearly Congress has no idea what it is doing. There is no dispute that the IRS officials have acted inappropriately and potentially criminally in multiple occasions in the past. But, instead of coming down hard on the individuals responsible, Congress has punished the institution by severely slashing its budget at the same time the Affordable Care Act substantially increases its responsibilities. Less money to do more work. The results would be obvious to a fifth grader but maybe I'm giving our representatives too much credit.

Here are some of the indignities suffered by the IRS in 2015 as reported by the General Accounting Office (GAO) and the Treasury Inspector General for Tax Administration (TIGTA):

- Remember the 24,000 "missing" Lois Lerner e-mails tied to alleged IRS political targeting? More than 1,000 previously unreported e-mails have been recovered but as much as 23,000 more are still missing since backup data in 422 disaster recovery tapes were erased months after a preservation order and a subpoena to retain them were issued. "It's a destruction of evidence" according to House Oversight and Government Reform Committee Chairman Jason Chaffetz of Utah.

- The IRS bragged about preventing $24.2 billion in fraudulent identity theft refunds last year. But then it was revealed that the IRS did pay out $5.8 billion in fraudulent claims. That's more than twice my daughter's clothes budget for a year!

- The GAO noted that weaknesses remain in information security control that "could affect the confidentiality, integrity, and availability of financial and sensitive taxpayer data," as a result of which—

- Hackers broke through the security program used to protect taxpayer data on the IRS' Get Transcript Online System and stole past tax return information, including Social Security numbers, from more than 334,000 tax returns.

- If you are a victim of identity theft, go to www.IdentityTheft.gov for checklists as to what to do and file Form 8821-A. However, according to the TIGTA, the IRS has not always responded with accurate, timely information to requests from law enforcement officials to help identity theft victims.

- The IRS awarded $18.8 million in contracts to 17 corporations that owed back taxes in fiscal 2012 and 2013 despite a law specifically prohibiting such contracts with firms with unpaid tax debts.

- Identity theft fraudulent returns using TurboTax software caused its owner, Intuit, Inc., to suspend the filing of state tax returns. Massachusetts and Vermont actually suspended issuing tax refunds in "an abundance of caution."

- Between fiscal years 2010 and 2015, the IRS budget was reduced by more than $1.2 billion. This has resulted in a 21 percent reduction of Automated Collection Service (ACS) contact representatives and 28 percent of Field Collection revenue officers. The IRS is answering 25 percent fewer taxpayer telephone calls since 2011 and taxpayers who actually got through waited an average of eight minutes longer to speak with a representative. In fiscal 2014, 35.6 percent of phone calls to the IRS went unanswered and 50 percent of correspondence with the agency was not handled in a timely manner. During the 2015 tax filing season, the IRS' over-loaded phone system hung up on more than 8 million calls from taxpayers. According to a Ways & Means report, the time IRS employees spent on union activities would have allowed for an additional two million plus in taxpayer assisted phone calls. In fiscal 2014, revenue officers closed 34 percent fewer cases and collected $222 million (7 percent) less in revenue than in 2011. Fiscal year computer downtime reached 66,448 hours, the equivalent of losing 32 full-time employees for the year. The IRS currently employs about 90,000 people, of which only about 2,000 are under the age of 30, and about 650, less than 0.01 percent, were born after 1990—not a recipe for sustainment. More than half of the IRS work force is over age 50, and about 40 percent will be eligible to retire

in 2019. Because of budget cuts, the IRS will continue its hiring freeze and expects to lose through normal attrition approximately 3,000 additional full-time employees in fiscal year 2015. That would bring the total reduction in full-time staffing since fiscal year 2011 to over 18,000, while the amount spent on employee training for those left has been cut by 83 percent.

- While funding and employees have crumbled, over the past decade the number of individual tax returns have jumped 11 percent, business returns are up 18 percent, and phone calls to the IRS have soared 70 percent.

- According to the Treasury Department, every $1 cut from the IRS enforcement budget results in a loss of $6 in additional revenue.

- Adjusted for inflation, the IRS will have as much money as it did in 1998, when it processed 30 million fewer returns. According to IRS Commissioner John Koskinen, such budget cuts will result in the loss of $2 billion in revenue through enforcement cut backs.

- In 2015, budget prevented the IRS from distributing paper forms in libraries and most post offices. In fact, the IRS actually ran out of preprinted tax forms and reportedly didn't even have the extra blank paper to print out more forms.

- Computer upgrades will also suffer. According to the IRS Commissioner, "We still have applications that were running when John F. Kennedy was president."

- Nevertheless, the IRS managed to find $8.3 million to spend on market research, office furniture, fitness equipment, and nearly $4,000 for toy "give-away" items.

- Between October 2003 and September 2013, the IRS found that more than 1,500 employees were willfully not complying with our tax law. Over this period, 620 employees resigned, retired, or were terminated. However, others were rewarded with cash bonuses, promotions, and paid time off.

- In fiscal 2014, the IRS gave out $2.8 million in bonuses to employees who had conduct issues or owed back taxes.

- In fiscal 2012, the IRS handed out $5.6 billion in bogus education tax credits.

- Between fiscal years 2003 and 2013, the IRS paid out as much as $148 billion in improper Earned Income Tax Credits.

- Between 2011 and 2013, the IRS may have allowed $167.7 million in questionable fuel tax credits.

- IRS *ethics* attorney Takisha Brown was disbarred for intentionally misappropriating funds and making false statements. So much for IRS "ethics."

- In 2015, approximately 800,000 taxpayers received from the government incorrect tax information on their Form 1095-A relating to health insurance subsidies and couldn't correctly file their tax returns.

- GAO investigators filed 12 fraudulent applications for health insurance tax credits under the Affordable Care Act (ACA). Eleven of the twelve were approved!

- The IRS failed to maintain effective internal control over financial reporting because of continuing material weakness in internal control over unpaid tax assessments.

- According to a TIGTA audit of the agency, the IRS has failed to take adequate measures to safeguard tax information disclosed to other agencies.

- The IRS was also found to have failed to do background checks on some private contractors who handled confidential taxpayer information, exposing more than a million taxpayers to an increased risk of fraud and identity theft.

- The Centers for Medicare and Medicaid Services said in February 2015 that it had sent incorrect Forms 1095-A, Health Insurance Marketplace Statement, needed to reconcile subsidies with actual incomes on your 2014 tax return, to more than 800,000 people.

- The Internal Revenue Service's total tax debt inventory has increased 23 percent since 2009 to $380 billion, according to a 2015 GAO report, while the agency's collection staff has declined 23 percent after years of budget cuts.

- The study also found the IRS lacks adequate internal controls over its largely automated tax collection processes. The automated Inventory Delivery System, or IDS, categorizes and routes cases based on many factors, such as type of tax and amount owed.

MEMORIES OF 2014

I guess IRS now stands for *I*'m *R*eally *S*orry. In an age where every keystroke lives forever, it appears that what the agency called a "catastrophic failure" followed

by the routine recycling of backup tapes, wiped out 2 years' worth of e-mails belonging to former IRS official Lois Lerner, who has been under Congressional and Justice Department investigation. Try using that "the computer ate my records" defense at *your* next audit.

The IRS had other things to be sorry about:

- It was revealed that the IRS mailed out fraudulent refunds worth $3.6 billion in 2013. That was at least better than the $5.2 billion it paid out in 2012. I still have difficulty understanding how it could miss the half million dollars the agency mailed to a single address in Bulgaria used on 700 different income tax returns. Really, Bulgaria?

- It was also revealed that the IRS may have disclosed as many as 100,000 Social Security numbers (along with names and addresses) on its website. Oops. . . . On the other hand, more than 3,000 IRS employees are working on identity theft cases and the agency has assigned 35,000 more employees to work with taxpayers to look for warning signs and help victims.

- Forget calling the IRS for help. In fiscal 2013, only 61 percent of calls to IRS customer service representatives were answered with a 17.6-minute waiting time. The waiting time as of March 2014 was 16.8 minutes, better, but almost double the 8.8-minute hold in fiscal 2009. However, about 70 percent of calls were eventually answered in 2014. Thanks for waiting.

- Don't write either. More than 50 percent of written correspondence from taxpayers in fiscal 2013 was not answered within time frames set by the agency.

- Love getting letters from the IRS? Approximately 4,000 retirement plan sponsors received erroneous penalty notices. At least the Service sent out letters of apology. No sponsor, legal, or accounting fees were reimbursed.

- A National Small Business Association survey reported that more than half the businesses spend more than 40 hours per year dealing with federal taxes. Forty percent reported spending more than 80 hours, or 2 full weeks. More than a quarter of the respondents spend more than $10,000 per year on tax compliance.

- According to the American Action forum, compliance with IRS requirements takes 7.7 billion hours and costs $170.4 billion in labor each year.

- According to IRS estimates, more than 4,000 changes were made to the Internal Revenue Code just between 2000 and 2010.

Government agencies with IRS oversight were less than pleased as well. The Treasury Inspector General for Tax Administration (TIGTA) had the following issues:

- Taxpayer privacy? In one study, the TIGTA found that in more than half the cases taxpayers' authorized representatives were bypassed, unauthorized disclosures to third parties, or numerous processing errors were made.

- Amend your returns carefully. The TIGTA estimated that the IRS may have issued more than $439 million in potentially erroneous refunds claimed on 187,421 amended returns during fiscal 2012. The TIGTA estimated $2.1 billion in bad refunds over the next 5 years.

- Did you have your 2013 return prepared by the staff of the Internal Revenue Service's Volunteer Program? You were subject to a 49 percent inaccuracy rate based upon one audit. It's at least 2 percent better than the 47 percent inaccuracy rate for 2012 volunteer-prepared returns.

- Another audit exposed sensitive taxpayer information had been disclosed and taxpayer rights violated in 16.4 percent of Freedom of Information/ Privacy Act requests.

- The TIGTA found continuing difficulties in IRS handling of collection due process cases.

- Scanning of documents continues to plague the IRS. One audit found 24 percent of the documents scanned incomplete, illegible, or inaccurate.

- From 2003 to 2012, the IRS paid at least $110 billion and as much as $132.6 billion in improper earned income credits. That's at least $11 billion a year, or more than the $9.5 billion Congress will spend on the Department of Commerce in the 2013–2014 fiscal year.

- The TIGTA estimated another $11.4 billion potential loss over 5 years from fraudulent use of stolen Employer Identification Numbers (EINs).

- Almost 700 employees of companies contracting with the IRS owe $5.4 million in federal tax debt.

- The IRS may have forgone up to $1.5 billion in unassessed penalties for erroneous tax refund or credit claims from June 3, 2012, to May 2, 2013.

- The IRS now has responsibilities under the Affordable Care Act (ACA). Unfortunately, "the IRS's existing fraud detection system may not be capable of identifying ACA refund fraud or schemes prior to the issuance of tax return refunds."

- The IRS has failed to make adequate progress in allowing taxpayers to access their tax account information online as required by law.

- The IRS has failed to pursue up to $53 million in potentially improper claims for the Qualified Retirement Contributions credit.

- Nearly half the tax returns on which individuals claimed tax deductions for alimony payments did not match up with the former spouse's tax return showing an "alimony gap" of over $2.3 million in 2010 alone.

- Between October 1, 2010, and December 31, 2012, more than 2,800 IRS employees with recent substantiated conduct issues resulting in disciplinary action received more than $2.8 million in monetary rewards and more than 27,000 hours in time off awards. Among these, more than 1,100 IRS employees with substantiated federal tax compliance problems received more than $1 million in cash rewards and more than 10,000 hours in time off awards.

The Government Accountability Office (GAO) had its own concerns:

- An audit of the IRS's fiscal year 2013 financial statements revealed eight new internal control deficiencies.

- The IRS budget has been cut to below 2009 levels. While the IRS has taken short-term steps to address budget cuts, it doesn't have a strategy to operate in an uncertain budget environment over the long term or to stem declining performance.

- The IRS has been erroneously double charging some taxpayers for user fees in installment agreement arrangements, causing them to pay the same fee twice.

- The IRS is plagued by significant and material inaccuracies when it comes to financial reporting on unpaid tax assessments resulting in almost $11 *billion* in adjustments to its 2013 gross revenues balance. I had a client who was audited for being off $11 in dividend revenue, and they wanted a penalty. Don't look for fairness in the Internal Revenue Code.

- Sensitive taxpayer data remains at risk due to system weakness at the IRS. Such data is vulnerable to inappropriate and undetected use, modification and disclosure that could affect the confidentiality, integrity, and availability of financial and sensitive taxpayer data.

All was not bad. There was some positive news:

- Senate Minority Leader Mitch McConnell (R-Ky.) introduced a bill to allow parents who have baby cribs and other child care implements in their home offices to still claim the home office deduction despite failing the "exclusive use" test. As of this writing, the bill has not become law.

- The IRS now recognizes all same sex marriages nationwide. That allows for joint filing of returns and qualification for spousal benefits. Domestic partnerships and civil unions still do not qualify to be considered as married for federal tax purposes.

- In 2013, 78 percent of taxpayers were satisfied with their personal interactions with the IRS, up 2 percent from 2012.

- According to the Tax Policy Center, 43.3 percent of Americans had a zero or negative income tax liability for 2013, up from 41.8 percent the prior year.

EXTENDERS—AGAIN!

The 2014 filling season was pushed back to January 31 because of delays caused by the government shutdown the previous October. We had another problem in 2015 because Congress played politics with the "extenders" again. These are a group of deductions such as the $250 "above the line" allowance for teachers' expenses, the deduction for state sales taxes, the mortgage insurance premium deduction, the tuition and fees deduction, the forgiven mortgage debt exclusion, the nonbusiness energy property credits, etc., which expired after December 31, 2013, but which are traditionally extended for another 2-year period *after* the November elections. That means the IRS computers and all private tax preparation programs had to be redone, thereby creating additional costs and delays in filing. The provisions were extended on December 18, 2014.

See page 570 for details.

IN RETROSPECT, 2013 WASN'T THAT BAD

"April is the cruelest month"

T. S. ELIOT

It starts with laughter on April Fool's Day—but by April 15, nobody is smiling. The IRS had some issues in 2013:

- The Internal Revenue Service reportedly posted the Social Security numbers of tens of thousands of people on the Internet before taking it down when a whistleblower pointed out the mistake.

- The Treasury Inspector General for Tax Administration (TIGTA) found that IRS supervisors urged employees to ignore potential fraud when reviewing applications for Individual Taxpayer Identification Numbers (ITINs). The study showed 15,028 ITINs assigned to individuals with the same address in Dallas and $46.3 million in refunds sent to the same address in Atlanta. Another $7.3 million in refunds for allegedly 2,706 taxpayers went to the same single bank account.

- The TIGTA also found that the IRS revenue agents failed to follow procedures designed to protect taxpayer rights during the tax collection process, did not follow guidelines on contacting taxpayers with representatives, and were not efficiently or effectively processing information referrals, including identity theft claims. Identity theft has increased by more than 650 percent from fiscal 2008 to fiscal 2012. At the end of fiscal 2012, the IRS had nearly 650,000 identity theft cases in its inventory.

- Approximately 1.45 million taxpayers who qualified for relief from tax penalties totaling close to $181 million were never told they could get penalty abatement and never got it.

- The IRS could not provide documentation for $394,430 paid for labor hours. Point *that* out in your next audit!

- The IRS failed to save $527 million in erroneous tax credits for the Earned Income Credit and Additional Child Tax Credit due to inadequate IRS controls.

- For the second year in a row, the IRS failed to comply with the provisions of the Improper Payments Elimination and Recovery Act.

- Accounting errors by the IRS in calculating unpaid tax assessments created a risk of "a material misstatement of the IRS's financial statements."

- The American Civil Liberties Union released documents showing that the IRS criminal division had been reading taxpayers' e-mails without a warrant, in violation of the Fourth Amendment.

- And then there were the IRS *parties*. During one conference, more than $50,000 was spent on receptions, including 28 bottles of wine for 41 guests. Then there was the almost $4,000 spent on giveaway items, including footballs, $418 in Kazoos, bathtub toy boats, and other novelty decorations. IRS credit cards were used to purchase romance novels, steaks, diet pills, and unspecified items from merchants affiliated with online pornography . . . your tax money at work!

- The IRS spent about $50 million on 225 conferences during the 3 years between fiscal 2010 and 2012. The Small Business and Self-Employed division spent $4.1 million alone on a single conference in Anaheim, California. You should have been there. Speaker fees for presentations such as "how seemingly random combinations of ideas can drive radical innovation" totaled $135,350. One speaker was paid $17,000 to create six paintings. Three were donated to charity, two were given to conference attendees, and the sixth was lost. Then there were the videos that cost $50,107 to produce. They included a dance video showing IRS employees learning the "cupid shuffle" and a *Star Trek* parody, for which the set alone cost $2,400 and 11 hours of staff work (estimated to cost an additional $3,100). But, they did get a 1-minute finished video. We won't even talk about the IRS video parody of *Gilligan's Island* used to train 1,900 taxpayer assistance employees in 400 locations nationwide. As Maynard G. Krebbs would say, "WORK?" In addition to these large expenditures, the IRS spent $15,669 of your money on "brief bags" with free gifts and trinkets, $6,060 on lanyards and badge holders, $1,524 on engraved travel mugs and clocks, and $90 on sleeves for puzzle pieces.

- And then there were the *political issues*. The supposedly politically independent IRS was found to have targeted conservative groups seeking tax exemption for extra scrutiny. The TIGTA found the inappropriate conduct "inexcusable" and Attorney General Eric Holder announced that criminal

penalties may be sought in a Justice Department criminal investigation. Add that to the 24 IRS employees who were indicted for fraudulently obtaining more than $250,000 in government benefits and you have what some would call a rogue agency out of control.

There was some good news:

- The IRS *was* in compliance with restrictions on the use of enforcement statistics to evaluate employees.

- For fiscal 2012, the IRS collected $2.5 trillion but only spent about 48 cents for every $100 in revenue collected, which is the lowest cost since 2008.

- Among households with incomes of less than $50,000, 55 million or 59 percent didn't pay any federal income tax. Nonpayers made up 41 percent of all households.

- IRS firings for misconduct fell to the lowest level since 2002.

- Between fiscal 2009 and fiscal 2011, the total amount of outstanding taxes collected under the IRS Collection Program was 20 percent higher than before, with even fewer revenue officers on staff. Conversely, the IRS had grown slower in closing Offer-in-Compromise cases during the same period.

2012 WAS WHEN . . .

SHAMEFUL!

I don't want to get on a rant here but our Congress has all the character of an egg yolk frying on the asphalt road behind my grandfather's barn on a hot summer day. Since when did having a three-digit IQ disqualify someone from running for office? Are our choices limited only to the left-hand leg of the bell curve? As we crawl out of a recession, I'm reminded of my 92-year-old mother-in-law's comment, "Recession? I lived through the depression of the 1930s and this is a *depression*." Does anybody think a sane businessperson would take the risk and invest and expand when the tax rules keep changing (maybe) and the cost of employee healthcare is subject to a new law that nobody understands and few agree upon.

When I wrote this, we were approaching what some called a fiscal cliff and others refered to as tax Armageddon. If Congress did nothing, we faced the biggest tax increase in the history of the Internal Revenue Code. Between the

expiration of the Bush tax cuts (which were extended in 2010 for 2 years through 2012) and the expiration of the "extenders," deductions would be lost, rates would increase, credits would disappear, and the marriage penalty would return in full force. The maximum tax on dividends would jump from 15 percent to as much as 43.4 percent! According to the Tax Policy Center, four out of five U.S. households would face an average of $3,701 more in taxes. Add mandated spending cuts to this tax hike and on January 1, 2013, we were scheduled to suffer an *$8 trillion* hit!

Here's the part that really gets me angry. Everybody agreed on what should be done. But nobody in Congress had the backbone to do anything until *after* the November elections. So once again politics trumped economics and sanity. Once again hundreds of millions of dollars were wasted on reprogramming IRS computers and tax preparation programs at the last minute. More of your tax money was spent redoing IRS forms. It's hard to play the game if the rules keep changing. It's even harder if the rules change in December when the year is already up.

According to the Joint Committee on Taxation in March 2012, the prior cost of "kicking the can" down the road for tax cuts, extenders, estate tax, etc., through fiscal year 2012 was 967.7 billion in wasted dollars. Add to that decreased stability and the inability to properly budget into the future, and you had a framework for economic impotence.

Don't blame the IRS. Then Commissioner Doug Shulman warned, "If Congress can't act by the end of the year, and even starts to think about retroactive legislation of things like the AMT, which have already expired, you could have a real disaster in the filing season, where there is total confusion, where some people are filing under one law and others under another."

Congress finally passed the American Tax Relief Act of 2012 to address these issues. See Chapter 19 for details.

What else happened? Well, the IRS did have some issues:

- The IRS delayed tax refunds early this filing season for 7.8 million tax returns because of fraud detection problems with its computer system.

- It was revealed that the IRS paid $3.2 billion in erroneous American Opportunity Tax Credits during the first 5 months of 2010 to 2.1 million taxpayers.

- The Service either failed to notify or incorrectly notified 61,427 taxpayers about their need to start repaying the First-Time Home Buyer Credit.

- The Tax Inspector General for Tax Administration (TIGTA) reported that the IRS failed to "securely operate its computer network. . . ." The TIGTA also found that the IRS needed to gain tighter control over its wireless technology and improve security to protect data from computer attacker exploits. Weaknesses in the Internal Revenue Service's financial and tax processing systems continue to jeopardize the confidentiality, integrity, and availability of sensitive taxpayer information. No surprise that the number of fraudulent returns jumped to 2.2 million in 2011, up from just 457,369 in 2009.

- Somebody got the math wrong. The IRS sent out 8.6 million math error notices, but almost 138,000 taxpayers disputed the computer-generated adjustments.

- Tax returns that were incorrectly prepared by IRS volunteers, if filed, would have caused taxpayers to pay almost $10,000 more than they owed and would have kept them from receiving legitimate refunds of $4,000 according to a TIGTA study. Of the 36 returns audited, only 14 were prepared correctly.

- Another TIGTA study found more than $697 million in wrongly claimed investment theft deductions causing a revenue hit to the Treasury of over $41 million.

- The percentage of customer service phone calls that actually reached IRS representatives in fiscal year 2012 fell to 61 percent, down from 70.1 percent in 2011. That's what happens when Congress cuts the IRS budget by 2.5 percent, and the IRS responds by eliminating 3.1 percent of its full-time employees.

- TIGTA also found the IRS's new e-file system "error prone" and still unable to ensure the accurate processing of individual tax returns.

There was some good news:

- For 2011, the IRS scored a 73 percent on the American Customer Satisfaction Index survey, way up from only 32 percent in 1998.

- The IRS was ranked third out of 15 large agencies in the Best Places to Work in the Federal Government survey for 2011, up from eighth place as recently as 2008.

- Why is it so much fun to work at the IRS? It may have something to do with a forfeiture relating to a Nevada brothel. I guess the job with the Secret Service was already taken.

- According to the TIGTA, IRS inability to detect identity theft could result in the issuance of $21 billion in fradulent refunds over the next 5 years.

The best "tax tip" of the year? A Cleveland waitress received an erroneous tax refund of $434,712. She had requested a refund of only $754.

WE SURVIVED 2011

Senator Olympia Snowe (R-Maine) hit the nail on the head in 2011 when she said, "It's all political theater. It's not about legislating anymore. It's all for the next election that's coming very shortly." That pretty much described 2011. But we did have an interesting year:

- A Joint Tax Committee Report revealed that 51 percent of households not only owed no federal income tax for 2009, but that 30 percent of all households got back a check for their full income tax bill and more resulting from refundable credits.

- In January the IRS launched IRS2Go, a free application for the iPhone and Android market, an app that lets users check their refunds and access help lines over the phone.

- Having trouble keeping up with changes to the tax law? In April 2011, IRS Commissioner Shulman reported that there have been about 3,500 tax law changes since 2000.

- More than half of small businesses spend at least $5,000 and 40 hours per year just to file their taxes according to a National Small Business Association survey.

Our government tax enforcers are still having problems:

- The IRS improperly transferred hundreds of millions of dollars in taxpayer payments to its Excess Collections File.

- A March Government Accounting Office (GAO) report revealed that taxpayer data are at risk of being disclosed, modified, or destroyed because of material weaknesses in IRS internal control systems. About 74 percent of previously reported information security weaknesses still remained unresolved or unmitigated.

- A June 2011 report by the Treasury Inspector General for Tax Administration (TIGTA) found that IRS databases are increasingly being targeted by attackers and that the IRS needs to increase its security diligence.

- An August 2011 TIGTA report showed that only 19 percent of written inquiries from taxpayers received timely and accurate responses. In another study, the percent dropped as low as 8 percent.

- The TIGTA reported that the IRS has been doing a better job of detecting and preventing fraudulent returns. But, I guess that doesn't apply to prisoners and those with kids. The number of fraudulent tax returns filed by state and federal prisoners in the United States doubled from 18,103 in 2004 to 44,944 in 2009. That allowed $295.1 million in illegal tax refunds. The IRS reported that between 23 and 28 percent of earned income tax credits (EITCs) each year are issued erroneously. For 2009, that was $13 billion in improper payments.

- The IRS didn't do much better with cars or other credits. As much as 20 percent of the $163.9 million in credits claimed for electric and alternative motor vehicles was claimed in error according to a February TIGTA report. The IRS also allowed 125,762 individuals to erroneously receive $111.4 million in stimulus-related tax credits. If this is doing "better," how bad was it before?

- The TIGTA did find that the IRS needs to improve the security of a Web portal used by preparers to electronically file returns. I guess the IRS failed to show its security concerns when it awarded a tax processing contract to a company that admitted to having information on 1.5 million payment cardholders and 1.1 million Social Security numbers stolen by computer hackers.

- The TIGTA found that the IRS also divulged personal taxpayer records and information over the phone without properly authenticating taxpayer identity.

- Because of multiple use of taxpayer identification numbers, the IRS accepted $380 million in erroneous tax exemptions and tax credits in 2007.

- In July 2011, the TIGTA reported that the IRS may have violated over 32,000 taxpayers' tax lien rights with improper notifications.

- The IRS found over 245,000 identity theft incidents last year. Since 2004, there have been 470,000 incidents of identity theft affecting more than 390,000 taxpayers.

- TIGTA auditors found that taxpayers had to wait an average of one hour to receive assistance as per an August 2011 report.

- The good news—the IRS provides a special toll-free phone line for hearing and speech impaired taxpayers. The bad news—the IRS ignores most of the calls! Out of the 350,000 calls made to the special line, only 339 were responded to by the IRS.

- Really? The Center for Plain Language gave the IRS its Grand ClearMark Award for clear language in its simplified notices, as required under the Plain Writing Act signed in October 2010.

2010 WAS WHEN...

2010 was a great year for tax preparers. Congress "solved" any and all economic and social problems with multiple changes in the tax code while shamefully delaying any action on the estate tax and tax extenders by playing politics rather than providing clear and long-term rules for playing the tax game. But, we had fun:

- It's become harder and harder to reach executive level in government service if you actually pay your taxes. New York Congressional representative Charlie Rangel was forced to resign as Chairman of the House Ways and Means Committee, which writes all our tax rules, because he couldn't follow them. I guess anybody could forget to report $75,000 in rental income.

- Lael Brainard was nominated and approved to be undersecretary for international affairs despite late real estate tax payments, questionable home office deductions, late unemployment insurance payments for household employees, and questions as to their legal work status.

- You didn't have to be a senior executive to be bad. IRS employee Lattice Murray pleaded guilty to stealing cash and mail addressed to the IRS facility where she worked.

- IRS revenue officer Albert Bront threatened to kill tax agents who investigated his fraudulent returns and was hit with a 16-count indictment.

- IRS employee Colette Browne was charged with filing 32 fraudulent returns and embezzling over $100,000.

- While it helps, being on the government teat wasn't a prerequisite for cheating on your taxes. In April 2010, the Department of Justice and the IRS announced fraud charges against 26 New York City tax preparers.

And then there were the "successes" of the Internal Revenue Service itself:

- A report by the Treasury Inspector General for Tax Administration (TIGTA) found that errors in the Modernized e-Filing system limited its utility and caused it to erroneously reject tax returns. The $78 million MeF Release 6.1 was deployed in February 2010 and subsequently rejected 23 percent of the electronic returns filed.

- The TIGTA in July 2010 found security weaknesses in IRS contractors which placed "confidential information at risk of unauthorized access and disclosure."

- The IRS also failed to expeditiously process paper checks resulting in the loss of thousands of dollars in interest for the agency.

- The TIGTA also found $20 million in erroneous credits issued by the IRS under the Making Work Pay program.

- Then there was another $20 million in erroneous refunds issued to nearly 14,000 taxpayers as a result of dishonored and bounced checks for payments.

- Then our tax masters failed to make timely and appropriate lien determinations on more than $1.4 billion in delinquent taxes.

- IRS oversight could have been more focused. At least 130 companies that received federal funds under the Troubled Asset Relief Program (TARP) owed taxes totaling $530.8 million at the time they received government funding.

- The IRS didn't do much better with home buyer credits. A TIGTA study reported $636 million in bogus claims, including 500 people under age 18 and one "home buyer" only four years old. One hundred IRS employees filed dubious claims, and 256 filers took the credit for homes at just five addresses. That's your tax dollars at work with a computer system that won't work!

- Putting perpetrators in jail didn't appear to work. 1,295 prison inmates, including more than 200 serving life sentences, received $9.1 million in fraudulent home buyer tax credits. One home was used by 67 inmates to claim credits.

- Taxpayer security is still an issue. The Government Accounting Office (GAO) found control and processing weaknesses that "continue to jeopardize the confidentiality, integrity, and availability of financial and sensitive taxpayer information."

But, there was some good news:

- Laura Schultz, a house cleaner in the Denver area, received an erroneous $122,783 tax refund. Being honest, she voided the check and returned it to the IRS. Being a government agency, the IRS then billed her for $80 in taxes owed.

- IRS Commissioner Douglas Shulman revealed that nine out of ten taxpayers use either a tax preparer or third party software to complete their tax returns. Well, that's good news if you're a tax preparer or sell software.

- The IRS has established a global high wealth industry division to make sure high wealth taxpayers pay their share. These "wealth squads" will go after taxes on income from high net worth individuals regardless of its source or country of origin.

- I think the Tax Court got this one right: William C. Naylor, Jr., set up a foundation to store his sperm and, in conjunction with a sperm bank, distribute it to recipients of his choice. The Tax Court found that the foundation "did not promote health for the community" and denied the foundation status as a tax-exempt organization.

2009 WAS FINE

I'm beginning to understand now. The tax code *is* the Holy Grail—the answer to all our social and economic problems. If we have a problem, it can be solved through the tax code. Need to sell more cars? Simple! Make the sales tax on their purchase deductible, even for those taking the standard deduction, and create a "clunkers credit." But, then again, the government does own General Motors, doesn't it?

Still, I stand by my argument. Your house went down in value? Stimulate the real estate market by making real estate taxes on a principal residence deductible, again, even for those taking the standard deduction.

Oil prices getting too high again? Stimulate "green" energy alternatives with credits that reduce your taxes on a dollar-for-dollar basis.

On June 11, 2009, Rep. Carolyn Maloney (D-NY) introduced a bill that would give an employer a 50 percent tax credit on up to $10,000 for "qualified breast-feeding promotion and support expeditures." Talk about milking the system.

You can't say 2009 was a quiet year taxwise.

The Internal Revenue Service released a Taxpayer Attitude Survey on February 2, 2009, which found that 89 percent of Americans think it unacceptable for people to cheat on their taxes. The other 11 percent appear to be headed for the president's cabinet. President Obama's pick to lead the Department of Health and Human Services, former Senate Majority Leader Tom Daschle, apologized for owing $140,000 in back taxes and interest. In 1998, he was quoted as saying, "Make no mistake, tax cheaters cheat us all and the IRS should enforce our laws to the letter." The president's selection for the first Chief Performance Officer for the federal government, Nancy Killefer, failed to pay tax on her household help. Both had the good graces to withdraw from consideration. And then there was Ron Kirk, nominated to be the U.S. trade representative. He "forgot" to report $37,000 in speaking fees assigned to a charity, but he managed to remember taking a deduction for $7,500 of the donation. And then there was $7,400 in pro basketball tickets without a business purpose.

Cheating on his taxes didn't deter Timothy Geithner from becoming Treasury Secretary. His taxes were found to be underpaid in 2001, 2002, 2004, and 2005. (Nobody looked at 2003?) But then again, who better to put in charge of the IRS than someone who requests a ruling on the law and then ignores it? But, he did pay up, when caught.

President Trump continued the tradition by nominating Rep. Mick Mulvaney (R-SC) to be White House budget director. Mulvaney is a budget expert who "forgot" to pay the Social Security taxes for 5 years on a household worker.

Talking about the law, surprise, it changed again! The year started with the American Recovery and Reinvestment Act of 2009 passed on February 17. That was just the beginning. The details of these and other changes, and how to respond to their opportunities, are found in Chapter 18.

GOT STIMULATED IN 2008

Rebate, rebate, rebate!

That's all we heard in 2008. Once again Congress, in its infinite wisdom, decided that you could be trusted to spend your own money and spent many millions of your dollars to send some back to you—to stimulate the economy. The IRS estimated that the reallocation of hundreds of IRS collection staff members to answering taxpayer telephone calls about the stimulus payments alone would result in up to $565 million in foregone enforcement revenue. According to the Treasury Inspector General for Tax Administration, calculations of the economic stimulus payments by the IRS may have been wrong in nearly 400,000

cases. More than 100,000 self-employed taxpayers received larger checks than they were entitled to and 25,000 clergy members didn't get the rebates owed to them. The details of this give-back are covered in Chapter 17 as part of the Economic Stimulus Act of 2008.

Chapter 17 also discusses the tax aspects of three more tax law changes—both 2008's Housing Stimulus Bill and the Hero's Earnings Assistance and Relief Act, as well as the Mortgage Debt Relief Act of 2007, which was passed and signed into law on December 20, 2007. We also had the Emergency Economic Stabilization Act in October 2008 in response to our economic and financial meltdown.

Because of the last-minute changes in the law, more than 3 million and as many as 13.5 million taxpayers in 2008 were unable to even file their returns until February 11 because the forms were wrong—*again*! Let's not even think about the cost to update and correct all the tax preparation programs and educate the public. As noted by National Taxpayer Advocate Nina Olson, "When taxpayers do not claim tax benefits because they do not know about them, Congress's intent in providing the tax benefits is undermined and taxpayers understandably question the fairness of the tax system." She was referring to the last minute 2006 changes that resulted in 1.4 million fewer claims for deductions that were extended but weren't even on the forms that finally went out to confused taxpayers.

The IRS computer system remains a mess. The IRS still lacks adequate procedures to identify identify theft victims or adequate systems to even determine the number of tax-related identity thefts that occur. From 2002 to 2006, identity theft related to refund fraud rose by 396 percent, while employment related identity theft increased by 129 percent. Call 800-908-4490 if you have an identity theft issue.

2007 SUCKED BLOOD

I guess the IRS is a great training ground. First they want your money; now they want your blood! Former IRS Commissioner Mark W. Everson left that position in April 2007 to head the American Red Cross. In July, his successor, Kevin M. Brown, declared that he too was leaving the IRS to serve as chief operating officer for the American Red Cross. Unfortunately, Mr. Everson was caught in a tryst with one of his employees and the Red Cross wrote him off.

In December 2006, Congress passed an extenders package that gave renewed life to the research and development credits, deductions for college tuition, above-the-line deductions for teacher expenses, and the sales tax deduction. Unfortunately, the 2006 tax forms had already been printed *without*

these changes. The IRS incurred additional costs of $410,000 for printing and $1.3 million for postage for the new sales tax tables alone.

In 2007, the IRS eliminated the telefile program, a free telephone filing service. It had been used by about 2 million taxpayers in 2005. Half of those reverted to filing paper tax returns, slowing the refund process and increasing IRS processing costs. Those who paid tax preparers or purchased software spent nearly $24 million to file their taxes in 2006.

The Treasury Inspector General for Tax Administration revealed that of the 106 million refunds totaling $228 billion issued by the IRS to individual taxpayers in 2004, taxpayers voluntarily returned approximately 51,000 refunds totaling $302 million. The report estimated that about half of those erros were due to IRS mistakes!

It's a good thing the former IRS commissioner was a computer expert. In five weeks to April 13, 2007, the IRS sent upward of $300,000 worth of onetime $30 federal telephone tax refunds to a single JPMorgan Chase Bank account in Ohio. Personally, I would have called first. . . .

2007 was a tough year all around. More than 450,000 federal workers and retirees were revealed to owe the IRS a whopping $3 billion in back taxes. You didn't have to work for the government to get in trouble. More than 125 Jackson Hewitt tax preparation branches run by five franchises of the company were shut down for preparing fraudulent returns. That cost the government $70 million in lost revenue. Even Joseph Francis, the creator of *Girls Gone Wild*, was indicted for tax evasion!

2006 WAS NO PICNIC

DUH! Somebody give them a calendar. On May 17, *2006,* President Bush signed a tax bill into law. Its technical name is the Tax Increase Prevention and Reconciliation Act of *2005*! Maybe Congress was so impressed with corporate crooks back-dating options that it thought back-dating laws could generate back-dated votes?

We'll talk about what opportunities and traps that law offers in a later chapter.

The IRS building in Washington, D.C., was closed by a flood costing $13 million. It's almost biblical, isn't it? But, rather than wetting the bottoms of bureaucrats who are only struggling to do an impossible job, I suspect the flood was really a warning to those across the street in the Capitol who create the devilish complexity we call the tax law.

The General Accounting Office reported that the *lowest* available estimate of the cost of complying with federal tax code is $107 billion—a whopping 1 percent of the nation's gross domestic product. In January 2009, National

Taxpayer Advocate Nina Olson pegged the cost at $193 billion a year, 14 percent of the total taxes collected.

In 1969, the total number of pages of federal tax rules was 19,500. By 2009, it had increased to 70,320. Back in 1913, it was only 400 pages.

In 2006, the General Accounting Office visited alleged tax preparers at 19 outlets affiliated with major tax preparation chains. They were not happy with the results of their test returns. Nearly all of the returns were prepared incorrectly and were accompanied by "very bad tax advice." Errors ranged from incorrect refunds of almost $2,000 to a liability of $1,500.

Is the tax law complicated? H&R Block, the country's largest tax preparer, blew its own tax liability by $32 million! Couldn't it find someone to help with its taxes?

How about General Electric? In May 2006, it filed a 24,000-page tax return with the IRS.

By 2008, 62 percent of Americans were using professionals do their tax returns. In 2006, that included three of the four senior lawmakers on the Senate Finance and House Ways and Means Committees, the panels charged with writing our tax law. Another 22 percent purchased tax software. By 2010, 90 percent of the tax returns done were prepared by professionals or with computer software. Our code ain't simple!

A NATIONAL DISGRACE

I had a dream last night. I'd died and was taken by the devil down below to suffer my eternal torment. After all, I was an attorney. But, I couldn't believe my eyes. The place was a frozen wasteland, with huge mountains of ice and snow.

I was amazed. Congress had actually passed a *simple* tax law that helped taxpayers!

Then, I woke up. And I woke up mad!

Is the only difference between our government and the Mafia that the Mafia is organized?

If con is the opposite of pro, is Congress the opposite of progress?

Who was the prophetic visionary who designed all the streets in Washington, D.C. to go in circles?

Is *anybody* in charge here?

OUR TAX CODE

Our tax code is a disgrace! Thousands of words dancing without rhythm or connection, failing to make a point. As a tax attorney, I'm embarrassed.

According to former Treasury Secretary Paul O'Neill, ". . . the complexity of our Tax Code is the worst problem facing our society. . . ." Paul doesn't spend a lot of time in hospitals or hang with the homeless. But, I feel his pain.

I'm not the only one who's embarrassed. Rep. Steny Hoyer (D-MD), House Democratic Whip, saw it the same way. "Our tax system is an embarrassment that treats many taxpayers unfairly." His view on the code was no less frank. "The Internal Revenue Code is a Kafkaesque maze of complexity that confounds millions of Americans every single year."

To make sure we don't ever understand the code, Congress changes it each year. We've had over 52 *major* tax law changes in the last 55 years! Remember, it was Albert Einstein who said, "The hardest thing in the world to understand is the income tax." And, he said that way before it became a whopping 74,608-plus-page, 25-volume beast with more than 2.4 million words meandering in search of meaning.

WHY IT'S SO EASY TO MAKE MISTAKES

The tax code is long and complicated—and getting longer and more complex by the year.

Here are some 2017 return numbers directly from the IRS. The average taxpayer who files a Form 1040 needs 15 hours. Add a single rental property or

PAGES IN THE CCH STANDARD FEDERAL TAX REPORTER

'74 19,500

'84 26,300

'95 40,500

'04 60,044

'13 73,954

a Schedule C for your business and the hours jump to 21, and that's with over 91 percent filing with a computer.

In 2017, we spent more than 8.9 billion hours and over $409 billion complying with the tax code—just to figure out what we owe. That's equal to 4.3 million full-time workers doing nothing but tax return paperwork. That's more hours than are used to build every car, van, truck, and airplane manufactured in America. That's just your time.

Our government wants your money as well. According to the Tax Foundation, the average taxpayer had to work 109 days, until April 19, 2018, in order to earn enough to cover his federal, state, and local tax burden. If you include federal borrowing, the deficit inclusive tax freedom day is May 6, seventeen days later. They call it "Tax Freedom Day." I call it "Get Out of My Pocket Day." The group Americans for Tax Reform includes the cost of regulation. In its latest report, "Cost of Government Day" had us working for the government in 2014 until July 6, 2014!

THE TAX CODE IS DRIVING ME NUTS!

The tax code is driving me nuts! I've got two law degrees and an MBA in finance. I've been licensed by the New Jersey Board of CPAs. I've taught taxation for over two decades, both on an undergraduate and a graduate level. And I still have no idea what they're talking about half the time!

It's been claimed that the only difference between death and taxes is that death, on occasion, is allegedly painless. Wrong! Death doesn't become more complicated every time Congress meets.

Remember the Tax Foundation? If the average middle-income taxpayer's 2018 salary, starting from January 1, went to pay taxes, it would have taken 100 percent of the earnings until April 19 to meet all the federal, state, and local payments due. That's about one-third of the year, 109 days, or about 2 hours and 23 minutes of each 8 hours' earnings. In comparison, in 1930 it was only 57 seconds.

Here's some more of the stuff making me crazy:

- On average, Americans now spend more time working to pay their taxes than they spend working to provide food, clothing and housing combined.

- Secretary of State and former presidential candidate John F. Kerry illegally shaved $12,000 off his tax on his 2003 return. He sold a piece of art and reported the gain at the 15 percent rate. But, the profit on the sale of the art, as a collectible, should have been taxed at a 28 percent rate. If

the nominee of the Democratic Party for president, with 57 Heinz varieties of tax lawyers and CPAs, got it wrong, what can the IRS expect from the rest of us?

- The IRS audit rate for 2005 was 0.93 percent, up from 2004's 0.77 percent, up from 0.65 percent in 2003, and 0.57 percent in 2002. But who cares if they're auditing the wrong people? The percentage of no change audits grew from 14 percent in fiscal 2001 to 18 percent in 2003, a significant increase and a waste of time and resources. Why? Easy. Their formulas for selecting returns were way out of date. They hadn't been revised since the late 1980s. The IRS has updated its numbers. The data was reflected in IRS audit selection in 2006.

- The fiscal 2006 audit rate numbers showed an increase from 0.93 percent to a whopping 0.98 percent. For fiscal 2007, it grew to 1.03 percent and then dropped to 1.01 percent in 2008. In fiscal 2009, it rose to 1.03 percent and 1.11 percent in 2010 and 2011. I am not impressed. And then down to 1.03 percent in 2012, 0.96 percent in fiscal 2013, 0.86 percent for 2014, 0.84 percent in 2015, falling to 0.7 percent in 2016 and falling again in 2017 to 0.6 percent.

But, are they "real" audits? According to Senator Max Baucus (Mont.) on April 29, 2004, "I'm concerned that the IRS's audit priorities are misplaced. . . . IRS is trying to bolster its audit figures, not by going after those who are deliberately trying to cheat on their taxes, but by sending out more letters regarding mathematical errors or mismatching of taxpayer information."

In 2013, 75.5 percent of the audits were correspondence audits, done by mail, with no personal face-to-face contact. In 2014, about 1 million of the total 1.24 million individual audits, on almost 81 percent, were correspondence audits. In 2015, 961,041 out of 1,228,151 or 78 percent were correspondence audits. In 2016, the IRS did more than 190,000 fewer audits than the prior year. In 2017, 71 percent of individual audits were conducted by correspondence.

Our tax code is just too complex. Even the IRS agrees. Former Commissioner Mark Everson has remarked that "Frequent changes to the tax code and rising complexity are perhaps the greatest obstacles to reducing paperwork burden. . . . I am concerned that tax law complexity may discourage taxpayers and adversely impact voluntary self-assessment that is at the heart of our tax system."

Responding to a report of IRS employees incorrectly preparing 19 of 23 tax returns in a December 2003 survey, Everson replied, "Whatever you can do to simplify the code would really help us."

Guess what Commish? It would help the rest of us as well. If the code is too complex for the IRS and Jeff Schnepper, how about those of us who aren't supposed to be tax experts?!

But, let's not jump on the IRS. They don't write the code. It's those brain surgeons we send to Congress who have created this mess. In 1986, I was invited to the White House to consult on the proposed Tax Reform Act. I suggested that it include a provision requiring all members of Congress to do their own tax returns. I also suggested that all elections be held on April 16. Both my suggestions were rejected.

Since 1986, over 15,000 amendments were made to the U.S. tax code—and that doesn't include the 2012, 2013, 2014, 2015, 2016, 2017 and 2018 changes! From 2001 through 2012, there was more than one change per day.

As I said up front, the tax code is driving me nuts. But, let's see if I can add some sanity to your financial life. Tax planning is not for the timid. The laws are constantly changing and you have to keep up to minimize your tax liability.

You have to know the rules. That's what *How to Pay Zero Taxes* is for. If you don't know the rules, you can't win the game.

According to Jerold Rochwald, "Nuclear physics is much easier than tax law. It's rational and always works the same way."

For 2010, 51,980,000 taxpayers received a total of $160,185 billion in refunds, an average of $3,082 each. In 2011, the IRS paid out more than $288 billion in refunds to over 102 million taxpayers—an average of $2,704 each. For 2012 returns filed in 2013, almost $268 billion was refunded, averaging $2,651. In fiscal 2013, 118 million taxpayers received refunds of almost $312.8 billion. In 2014 the average refund was $2,686, totaling about $274.7 billion increasing to $2,711 and $273.4 billion for 2014 returns filed in 2015. For 2015 returns filed in 2016, the average refund was $3,120, for a total of nearly $375 billion. In fiscal 2017, the IRS processed $382.8 billion in refunds—an average of $2,895. For 2018, the average refund is projected to be $2,840. That's a huge, interest-free loan to the IRS.

The source of this nightmare—the Internal Revenue Code—is a quagmire so complicated that former Treasury Secretary Paul O'Neill disdained it as ". . . not worthy of an advanced society."

Even former IRS officials find the tax code confusing. "No, I don't do my own return," says Randolph Thrower, a former IRS commissioner. "It's much too complicated for me." In 1954, our tax code and related material fit into 14,000 pages in 9 volumes. By 1984, it was 26,300 pages in 14 volumes. By 2002, it grew to 52,310 pages in 25 volumes. As of 2009, it had grown to 70,320 pages

2017–2018 Tax Season – Average IRS and State Tax Refund

Rank	State	Average refund	Rank	State	Average refund
1	Connecticut	$3,126	26	Indiana	$2,572
2	Texas	$3,033	27	North Carolina	$2,566
3	New York	$2,963	28	Pennsylvania	$2,561
4	New Jersey	$2,959	29	Hawaii	$2,561
5	Mississippi	$2,944	30	Delaware	$2,560
6	Louisiana	$2,939	31	Kansas	$2,552
7	Florida	$2,843	32	West Virginia	$2,548
8	Illinois	$2,834	33	Missouri	$2,547
9	Alabama	$2,820	34	Rhode Island	$2,539
10	California	$2,809	35	Colorado	$2,539
11	Utah	$2,778	36	South Carolina	$2,532
12	Georgia	$2,767	37	North Dakota	$2,514
13	Oklahoma	$2,748	38	Nebraska	$2,502
14	Maryland	$2,748	39	New Hampshire	$2,496
15	Nevada	$2,738	40	Iowa	$2,486
16	Alaska	$2,721	41	Michigan	$2,481
17	Virginia	$2,692	42	Ohio	$2,465
18	Arkansas	$2,691	43	South Dakota	$2,463
19	Wyoming	$2,688	44	Idaho	$2,414
20	Tennessee	$2,687	45	Minnesota	$2,371
21	Massachusetts	$2,682	46	Oregon	$2,330
22	Arizona	$2,640	47	Wisconsin	$2,329
23	New Mexico	$2,603	48	Montana	$2,299
24	Kentucky	$2,601	49	Maine	$2,277
25	Washington	$2,588	50	Vermont	$2,254

Average Refund by State (Source: Business Insider)

and more than 3.7 million words! The tax code and regulations are now over 4 million words—many meandering without meaning. So much for tax simplification. . . .

This 2019 edition of *How to Pay Zero Taxes* will detail the new tax law changes, the hidden secrets of our tax code, and how you can take advantage of them to keep more of your hard-earned dollars.

According to the Tax Foundation, the United States passed a depressing milestone back in fiscal 1995. Total tax collections exceeded $2 trillion for the first time. That's a two and 12 zeros.

It is April 15, 2019, and the IRS is after your money again. To protect your hard-earned dollars, first turn to the new 2019 edition of *How to Pay Zero Taxes*. It contains all of the new laws, rules, regulations, and court cases to legally minimize your tax outlay. Remember, your objective should be to pay all of the taxes that are due, but not one penny more than the law requires. The law, however, is complicated, convoluted, and constantly changing. The new edition of *How to Pay Zero Taxes* is your guide through the minefield of these changes.

Three decades ago, on October 22, 1986, former president Reagan signed a sweeping revision of the tax code that touched the lives of all American taxpayers. The text of the Tax Reform Act of 1986 bulked 10 inches and weighed more than 33 pounds; it detailed changes in 2,704,000 subsections of the tax code, which cost the Internal Revenue Service an estimated $106,485,000 in fiscal year 1988 to implement. The act dramatically cut tax rates and paid for this decline by eliminating or reducing a vast array of tax breaks. The American tax structure for 2018 is vastly different from that in the past and will be different again in 2019.

Taxes have been likened to a plague of locusts on a field of wheat. Yet there are several individuals earning millions of dollars who pay little or no taxes and many more who earn hundreds of thousands of dollars each year whose tax bill is just as small. For the year 1998, filed in 1999, 2,085,211 individual tax returns were filed showing income of $200,000 or more. Of those, 0.07 percent, or about 1,467 returns, showed *no* U.S. tax liability. For 1999, filed in 2000, 1,605 returns with incomes of $200,000 or more showed *no* U.S. tax liability. For 2000, filed in 2001, 2,328 returns with incomes of $200,000 or more showed *no* U.S. tax, and 2001 returns, filed in 2002, without a tax liability increased to 2,959. The number for 2002 was 2,551 and for 2003, 2,416 returns showed no tax liability. In 2004, 2,833 filers had no tax liability. For 2005 the number jumped to 7,389 increasing to 8,252 in 2006. For 2007, the number was 13,412, jumping to 22,257 in 2008. In 2009, 1,470 people earned over $1 million and paid *zero* taxes

Historical Tax Freedom Day, 1900–2017

Year	Tax Freedom Day (Calendar)	Tax Freedom Day (Number of Days into Year)
1900	1/22	21.6
1901	1/21	21.0
1902	1/21	20.5
1903	1/20	19.5
1904	1/21	20.6
1905	1/20	19.8
1906	1/19	18.4
1907	1/19	18.6
1908	1/21	20.9
1909	1/19	18.0
1910	1/19	18.3
1911	1/20	19.2
1912	1/19	18.1
1913	1/19	18.9
1914	1/23	22.3
1915	1/25	24.4
1916	1/24	23.9
1917	1/24	23.2
1918	2/8	38.5
1919	2/7	37.1
1920	2/13	43.6
1921	2/22	53.0
1922	2/11	41.7
1923	2/4	34.7
1924	2/7	37.8
1925	2/4	34.9
1926	2/6	36.4
1927	2/8	38.9
1928	2/9	39.3
1929	2/8	38.9
1930	2/12	42.0
1931	2/15	45.5
1932	2/25	55.4
1933	3/6	64.4
1934	3/1	59.3
1935	2/27	57.7
1936	2/27	57.7
1937	3/4	62.7

(*continues*)

Historical Tax Freedom Day, 1900–2017 *(continued)*

Year	Tax Freedom Day (Calendar)	Tax Freedom Day (Number of Days into Year)
1938	3/6	64.7
1939	3/4	62.7
1940	3/7	65.1
1941	3/16	74.5
1942	3/18	76.6
1943	4/5	94.3
1944	3/29	87.9
1945	3/30	88.6
1946	3/30	88.8
1947	4/1	91.0
1948	3/27	85.2
1949	3/22	80.2
1950	3/31	89.9
1951	4/7	96.4
1952	4/7	96.7
1953	4/6	95.9
1954	4/1	91.0
1955	4/4	93.5
1956	4/7	96.0
1957	4/7	96.4
1958	4/5	94.1
1959	4/8	97.8
1960	4/12	101.1
1961	4/11	100.9
1962	4/12	101.1
1963	4/13	102.9
1964	4/9	98.2
1965	4/8	97.8
1966	4/11	100.3
1967	4/12	101.8
1968	4/18	107.6
1969	4/23	112.3
1970	4/19	108.1
1971	4/16	105.5
1972	4/20	109.6
1973	4/20	109.9
1974	4/23	112.1
1975	4/17	106.2
1976	4/19	108.7
1977	4/20	109.7

Historical Tax Freedom Day, 1900–2017 *(continued)*

Year	Tax Freedom Day (Calendar)	Tax Freedom Day (Number of Days into Year)
1978	4/20	109.4
1979	4/20	109.6
1980	4/21	110.6
1981	4/24	113.2
1982	4/21	110.9
1983	4/18	107.3
1984	4/17	106.2
1985	4/18	107.4
1986	4/19	108.2
1987	4/22	111.9
1988	4/21	110.8
1989	4/22	111.2
1990	4/21	110.8
1991	4/21	110.0
1992	4/19	108.9
1993	4/20	109.7
1994	4/22	111.2
1995	4/23	112.7
1996	4/25	114.4
1997	4/27	116.3
1998	4/29	118.5
1999	4/29	118.7
2000	5/1	120.4
2001	4/27	116.0
2002	4/17	106.4
2003	4/14	103.6
2004	4/15	104.3
2005	4/21	110.2
2006	4/24	114.0
2007	4/24	113.7
2008	4/18	107.2
2009	4/10	99.1
2010	4/11	100.2
2011	4/11	100.9
2012	4/13	102.7
2013	4/18	107.1
2014	4/21	110.6
2015	4/24	114.0
2016	4/22	114.0
2017	4/22	112.0
2018	4/19	109.0

and 20,752 taxpayers with incomes of $200,000 or more paid *zero* taxes. For 2010, the number fell to 19,003 "happy" returns, increasing to almost 33,000 in 2011. In 2012, more than 5 million individual tax returns showed income of $200,000 or more with 0.429 percent paying zero worldwide taxes. More than 70,000 households with income over $200,000 paid zero taxes in 2013. In 2014, 9,692 returns with incomes of $200,000 or more paid *zero worldwide* income taxes. These people are able to avoid paying taxes by the use of sophisticated tax strategies devised by high-priced and very professional tax planners, who guide their clients along the cracks in the federal tax code. Or, they read my book!

Many of those cracks have been put there intentionally by Congress as economic and social incentives. For example, to encourage capital spending and to support the U.S. auto industry, a combination of provisions in the tax code allows a knowledgeable average taxpayer to buy a $17,000 car at a net cash cost of only $6,412 (see page 356). If that car is run only 60,000 miles in its first 5 years, the net cash outlay for the car can be reduced to below *zero!* In effect, the taxpayer gets a free car; more important, his costless acquisition is completely legal. Exactly how to do this will be explained later in the book.

As the examples indicate, Congress has created a financial mechanism whereby certain actions substitute for tax payments. Rather than taking the taxpayers' money in taxes and then paying it out in direct support for certain activities, Congress has indirectly accomplished the same goal by granting taxpayers some credits and deductions if they make expenditures in certain defined areas. *How to Pay Zero Taxes* will expose these areas and detail how you, a now enlightened reader, can structure your transactions to benefit optimally from these completely legal strategies and techniques.

You first will learn how our tax system works and how the structure of the system provides opportunities to save money on your income tax. The crucial difference between tax deductions and tax credits will be explained, and the internal IRS chart detailing the average amount deducted for each tax bracket for each category of itemized deductions will be revealed.

You then will be transported into the netherworld of tax shelters and shown what to look for and what to avoid. The section on tax shelter strategies is followed by the fun part of the book—how to take tax deductions for your personal expenses and hobbies. Here you will be shown how to turn your normal living expenses into tax deductions. We all must pay housing and food costs, but *How to Pay Zero Taxes* will show you how to structure these costs to reduce your taxes. We all enjoy vacations—*How to Pay Zero Taxes* will show you how the federal government could pay part of their costs. If you have a hobby—stamp collecting, auto racing, etc.—*How to Pay Zero Taxes* will demonstrate how you can get the Internal Revenue Service to help finance it by converting it into a legitimate business.

Finally, *How to Pay Zero Taxes* will detail and explain those more sophisticated legal 2018 and 2019 tax techniques and instruments that have been developed for shifting income, deferring taxes, and avoiding payment completely. These techniques all have been court tested and approved. Most important, *How to Pay Zero Taxes* will not simply explain and document these tax savings strategies but will show you examples, provide you with guidelines and tax cases to support your deductions, and take you step by step through the creation of these money-saving instruments for your own use. Its objective is not merely to reveal and educate but to demonstrate and guide as well.

Taxpayers who can afford expensive professional tax planning don't pay high taxes. The goal of *How to Pay Zero Taxes* is to provide that planning and those techniques to middle-income taxpayers who are unknowingly overpaying. Supreme Court Justice Sutherland once remarked, "The legal right of a taxpayer to decrease his taxes or to altogether avoid them by means which the law permits cannot be doubted."[1] *How to Pay Zero Taxes* is dedicated to that ideal.

[1] *Gregory v. Helvering*, 35-1, USTC Par. 9043, 293 U.S. 463, 469 (1935).

Is It Legal?

"Taxation must not take from individuals what rightfully belongs to individuals."

HENRY GEORGE

In 2008, a record 51.6 million tax returns—36.3 percent of all returns filed—had no income tax liability because of the available credits and deductions in the tax code. For 2014, the number had risen to 46 percent. By 2015 it was 45.3 percent.

"The purpose of the IRS is to collect the proper amount of tax revenue at the least cost to the public, and in a manner that warrants the highest degree of public confidence in our integrity, efficiency, and fairness. To achieve that purpose, we will: Encourage and achieve the highest degree of voluntary compliance in accordance with the tax laws and regulations; Advise the public of their rights and responsibilities; Determine the extent of compliance and the causes of noncompliance; Do all things needed for the proper administration and enforcement of the tax laws; Continually search and implement new, more efficient and effective ways of accomplishing our Mission." (IRS statement of organization and functions, 39 Fed. Reg. 11,572, 1974)

It has been said that "the Internal Revenue Code is a remarkable essay in sustained obscurity . . . a conspiracy and restraint of understanding." (*All State Fire Insurance Company* [Ct. Cl.], 80-1 USTC-, 45 AFTR 2d, 80-1096)

For 2015 returns filed in 2016, individual taxpayers received almost $375 billion in refunds. That's a $375 billion interest-free loan to the IRS. At a 3 percent rate, that's $11.25 billion in lost interest—enough to cover my kids' spending for most of their teenage years!

When the modern income tax law was introduced in 1913, only one American in 271 was affected; the taxable incomes of the great majority did not exceed the exempt amount of $3,000 for individuals, $4,000 for couples. Those who were affected paid at the rate of 1 percent on taxable income up to $20,000 and, at most, 6 percent on income over that amount. The average tax rate for the 437,036 individual tax returns filed in 1916 was 2.75 percent. For the 2015 filing season, over 150 million individual income tax returns were filed and the IRS processed over two billion pieces of paper—which, if placed side by side, would stretch over 200 miles.

You pay too much in taxes, and it costs too much for you to do your tax returns. Here are a few "for instances:"

- Even after adjusting for inflation, the U.S. government collected twice as much income tax revenue in 2001 as it did in 1981.

- An increase of 250 million hours in the burden on the public of complying with the tax system during 2000 resulted in an overall increase of 180 million hours in the burden on the public of federal agencies' collection of information.

- Let's talk about complexity. By 2009, our tax rules needed 70,320 pages and it contained 3.7 million words. It now has over 4 million words. The epic book *War and Peace* has 1,444 pages and 660,000 words, while the Bible contains 1,291 pages and 774,746 words.

According to Daniel J. Mitchell of the Heritage Foundation:

- The paperwork received by the IRS would circle the globe 36 times.

- The IRS sends out 10,000,000 correction notices each year. 5,000,000 of them are wrong!

- The IRS has lost more than 6,400 computer tapes and cartridges.

- In 1948, the average American family with children paid 3 percent to the federal government in income and payroll taxes.

Time is money, and these dollars come out of your pocket and drain your ability to save and invest, while inflation compounds your financial concerns by draining your ability just to keep even.

Even if your earnings can keep even with inflation, you still lose. For example, assume you have a taxable income for 2018 of $82,500 and pay $14,090 in taxes. You have $68,410 left to spend (ignoring other taxes and deductions). With both inflation and a raise of 8 percent, you will now earn $89,100 and pay $15,674 in taxes, leaving you $73,426 to spend. But due to inflation, this $73,426 is worth only $67,552. In real dollars, the progressive nature of your tax structure and the purchasing power decay caused by inflation have together decreased your real buying power by $68,410 minus $67,552 equals $858 on a $6,600 increase in earnings! The impact of state and social security taxes further magnifies your financial dilemma.

What can you do? One simple answer is to try to reduce your taxes, and the rest of this book will tell you how to do so. Some of the techniques found in this book are the result of mixing complicated and convoluted tax code sections, but all of them are completely legal. Some are legal not because Congress intended them to be there but because both Congress and the Internal Revenue Service were lax in their homework and the tax code language allowing them is there. While Congress writes the tax law, that law is read and interpreted by the courts. Quite often the Internal Revenue Service and the courts differ in their interpretations of various code sections and their applications—the courts *always* win. Even if a tax effect is contrary to original congressional intent, the courts must and do support the language of the code. Such effects are the law and can be changed or eliminated only by congressional action. Until such action is taken, it is fully within the legal rights of the American taxpayer to use such code combinations to reduce, minimize, or even completely eliminate taxes. Each individual must pay taxes, but not one penny more than the law requires. If you want to make voluntary contributions to our federal Treasury, you'll have bought the wrong book.

On the other hand, most of the techniques detailed here have been intended by Congress. In many cases, legally reducing your income tax liability is both good for you and good for America. Certain kinds of receipts are intentionally excluded from gross income for tax purposes in order to achieve some economic or social objective. These provisions are frequently referred to as "tax incentives" and are specifically designed to encourage certain types of activity. Tax incentives have the same impact on the federal budget as direct expenditures because they represent revenues not collected by the federal government. These special tax provisions, therefore, have been labeled "tax expenditures" or "tax aids" by the Treasury Department.

These expenditures are revenue losses arising from provisions of the tax code that give special or selective tax relief to certain groups of taxpayers.

These provisions either encourage some desired activity or provide special aid to certain taxpayers. For example, the federal government seeks to encourage certain forms of investment. Thus business investment is encouraged by the accelerated rather than straight-line depreciation. This tax advantage has been legislated so that business will have additional capital to be able to expand. Tax advantaged investment helps create new businesses and new jobs. These new jobs produce more paychecks and these additional paychecks produce more taxes. In the long run, if everything works as it should, everyone wins.

Alternatively, other tax expenditure provisions have been adopted as "relief provisions" to ease "tax hardships" or to "simplify tax computations." For example, the elderly and the blind receive special financial benefits through a deduction called the "additional amount." The other tax benefits for the aged—the retirement income credit and the potential exclusion of social security annuity payments from taxable income—also fall into this "personal or tax hardship" category.

These revenue losses are called tax "expenditures" because they are payments or expenditures by the federal government made through a reduction of taxes rather than a direct grant. Just as a forgiveness of debt is equivalent to a payment, so a remission of tax liability is equivalent to an expenditure.

According to the Congressional Budget Office, in 1980 a total of 92 provisions were considered tax expenditures. These were estimated to cost $206 billion in fiscal year 1981, based on laws in effect at the start of 1980. 2016 individual tax expenditures were over $1.42 trillion, more than Congress appropriated to fund the entire federal government. The total cost of tax expenditures from 2016-2026 is projected at $18.4 *trillion*.

The financial benefits offered by tax expenditure provisions resemble those available through entitlement programs on the spending side of the budget. A tax expenditure provision can provide special tax relief in any of the following ways:

- *Special exclusions, exemptions, and deductions*, which reduce taxable income and thus result in a smaller tax liability—for example, tax-exempt municipal bond interest or the exclusion from taxable income of employee discounts or dependent care assistance programs.

- *Preferential rates*, which reduce liabilities by applying lower rates to all or part of the taxpayer's income—for example, the special reduced maximum tax rate on long-term capital gains income and qualifying dividends.

- *Special credits*, which are subtracted from the tax liability rather than from the income on which the taxes are figured—for example, the child tax credit or the foreign tax credit.

- *Deferrals of tax,* which generally result from allowing deductions that (according to standard accounting principles) are properly attributable to a future year—for example, accelerated depreciation allowances: The taxpayer, paying later rather than now, in effect receives an interest-free loan of the deferred liability.

Tax spending and direct spending are alternative methods of providing federal subsidies. Nearly any tax expenditure could be recast as a spending program, just as most spending programs could be replaced by tax expenditures. Thus, the choice between tax spending and direct spending is essentially a choice between alternative administrative mechanisms. Once it has been decided that a particular subsidy is worth providing, the question of the best method of providing that subsidy arises. In designing or evaluating any subsidy program, however, the following criteria have been applied:

- *Cost and efficiency.* How much does the program cost? How well targeted is the program—that is, does it reach those and only those it is intended to reach? Does it provide the incentive or benefit it was designed to offer? Does it achieve its goal at the least cost?

- *Fairness and equity.* Is the subsidy benefit fairly distributed?

- *Ease of administration.* How much does the program cost to administer? How quickly can the benefits be distributed? Can the benefits be distributed to those and only those for whom they are intended?

- *Budget visibility and control.* Is each program subject to periodic review by the Congress? Are its costs subject to control by the Congress?

In reality, though, many of these expenditures are the result of pressures applied by special interest groups seeking relief provisions for their own constituencies. For example, why is there an additional "standard deduction" amount for the blind and not for the deaf? The answer, I suggest, may have more to do with the political and lobbying power of the two groups than with any inherent difference between the hardships.

These special provisions also arise out of the political needs of our individual representatives in Congress. These are off-budget expenditures that show up as a reduction of revenues rather than as an increase in congressional spending. In effect they allow our representatives to increase our federal fiscal deficit, to spend more tax money, without appearing to do so. Arguments are made that these tax incentives are simple and involve far less government supervision and detail than direct expenditures. It has also been argued that these incentives encourage the private sector to participate in social programs

and promote private decision making rather than government-centered decision making.

Whether these asserted virtues of tax incentives are in fact valid or whether their defects outweigh their claimed advantages is not the subject of this book. The fact that they do exist is critical. In order to minimize or to eliminate your taxes completely, you must first accept the fact that the techniques to be detailed in this book are both legal and, for the most part, specifically intended by Congress. That they have not been publicized or made widely known by the Internal Revenue Service is not surprising. Despite publicity releases and continuous claims to the contrary, the Internal Revenue Service is a revenue collector. While the professed goal is a fair administration of the tax law, the service's job is to collect your tax money. No Internal Revenue agent ever received or ever shall receive a raise or promotion by suggesting to a taxpayer how to arrange a financial situation to reduce or eliminate taxes. To discover those techniques, you either have to pay thousands of dollars to a professional tax practitioner, attorney, or accountant—or you can turn to the next chapter.

How Our Tax System Works

"Kings ought to shear, not skin their sheep."

English poet ROBERT HERRICK shortly after the
execution of Charles I, who had imposed numerous
burdensome taxes on his subjects

*"The greater the number of statutes, the greater
the number of thieves and brigands."*

LAO-TZU

*"A fine is a tax for doing something wrong. A tax
is a fine for doing something right!"*

*"The 9,500 page tax code, with its endless
convolutions, is an abomination unworthy of our
society. Is it any surprise that some people run
from it? It undermines notions of law of, for, and
by the people, because even those who spend a
lifetime studying can barely understand it.
Certainly ordinary citizens cannot hope to figure
it out."*

Treasury Secretary PAUL O'NEILL, March 20, 2002

Now that you understand the legal foundation for our tax sheltering and eliminating techniques, it remains necessary first to uncomplicate our federal income tax structure so that you can see where each shelter technique fits into the whole picture. You pay taxes on your taxable income. Your taxable income is your gross income less certain deductions. It is necessary, therefore, to define your "gross" income.

Gross income means *all* income, from whatever source derived, including (but not limited to) the following items:

Compensation for services, including fees, commissions, and similar items
Gross income derived from business
Gains derived from dealings in property
Interest
Rent
Royalties
Dividends
Alimony and separate maintenance payments
Annuities
Income from life insurance and endowment contracts
Pensions
Income from discharge of indebtedness
Distributive share of partnership income
Income in respect of a decedent
Income from an interest in an estate or trust
Unemployment compensation

Income has been defined by the Supreme Court as "undeniable accession to wealth, clearly realized, over which the taxpayers have complete dominion" (348 U.S., 426 [1955]). Everything you receive for personal services must be included in your gross income. This includes wages, salaries, commissions, tips, and fees. You must report income in any form other than cash at the fair market value of the goods or services received.

Amounts withheld from your pay for income and social security taxes or savings bonds are considered received by you and must be included in your income in the year they were withheld. The same generally is true of amounts withheld for insurance and union dues.

If your employer uses your wages to pay your debt, or if wages are *attached* or *garnished,* the full amount is still considered received by you and must be included in your income. The same is true of fines or penalties withheld from your pay.

Vacation allowances paid to you from a vacation fund are wages and are also included in your income. Severance pay is taxable as well. A lump-sum payment for cancellation of your employment contract is income in the year you receive it.

Rewards and bonuses paid to you for outstanding work are income. These include such prizes as an all-expenses-paid vacation trip for meeting a sales goal and even prizes won on a TV quiz show. If a prize or award is in goods or services, you must include its fair market value in income. However, if your employer merely promises to pay you a bonus or award at some future time, it is not taxable until you receive it or it is made available to you.

If you buy property from your employer at a reduced price, you must normally include in your income as extra pay the excess of the property's fair market value over what you paid for it. If you receive a cash allowance from your employer for meals or lodging, you must include that cash allowance in your income. All tips you receive are also subject to federal income tax; they are not tax-free gifts. You must include in gross income the cash tips you receive directly from customers and the tips from charge customers that are paid to you by your employer.

Any interest that you receive or that is credited to your bank account is taxable income unless it is specifically exempt from tax. This is true even if that interest has not been entered in your bank book—it *has* been credited to you on the books of your bank. Certain distributions commonly referred to as dividends must be included in gross income as interest. You must report as interest the so-called dividends on deposits, withdrawals, or share accounts in:

Cooperative banks
Credit unions
Domestic building and loan associations
Federal savings and loan associations
Mutual savings banks
Money market accounts

In addition, the fair market value of gifts or services received for making long-term deposits or opening accounts in savings institutions is interest and should be reported as income in the year received.

Amounts you receive as rental income must also be included in your gross income. Rental income includes not only the amount you receive for the occupancy of real estate or for the use of personal property but other amounts as well. For example, advance rent must be included in your rental income in the year you receive it regardless of the period covered or the accounting method

used. Payments for the cancellation of a lease or the reduction in the principal of a mortgage (even on your home) if paid before due should normally also be included as income. So, too, are payments made directly by a tenant for any of *your* expenses. For example, if your tenant pays your heating bill in lieu of partial rent, that amount must be included as rental income.

You must also include in your gross income all fees for your services. Examples of these fees are payments you receive for services as:

A corporate director
An executor or administrator of an estate
A notary public
A member of a jury
An election precinct official
An accountant
An attorney
A medical practitioner

Income received in the form of property or services must be included in income at its fair market value on the dates received. If you receive the services of another in return for your services, and you both have definitely agreed ahead of time as to the value of the services, that value will be accepted as the fair market value unless the value can be shown to be otherwise. An exchange of property or services for your property or services is called bartering and should be included in your gross income.

Cancellation of debt is income. When you borrow money, there is an obligation to pay it back and therefore borrowed money is not income. But, if the debt is cancelled, you don't have to pay it back. That's why the cancellation of debt is income.

Finally, dividends, capital gain distributions, and all gains on the sale of property also are included in your gross income. Dividends are distributions paid to you by a corporation. You also may receive dividends through a partnership, an estate, a trust, or an association that is taxable as a corporation.

When all of your gains, all of your "accessions to wealth, clearly realized, over which you have complete dominion," are added together, you arrive at your gross income amount. From this amount you subtract your allowable deductions to arrive at your taxable income. Your tax is based on that taxable income. Therefore, in order to reduce or eliminate your tax, there are four possible avenues of attack:

1. You can reduce or minimize your gross income figure by converting income that normally would be included in gross income into certain forms of income that can be excluded from the gross. This means that amount of income will never even enter into the tax computation picture.

2. You can arrange your activities so that certain personal expenditures that you would normally make will be allowable as deductions, thus reducing both your gross income and your taxable income.

3. You can take advantage of special credits that the tax code allows as dollar-for-dollar offsets to your final tax liability.

4. You can reduce or eliminate your tax by attacking the progressivity of our tax rates structure through the allocation of family income to different family members and entities.

Chapter 9 discusses how this fourth very special and very sophisticated tax planning technique works.

The following chapters will take you through these tax sheltering and elimination approaches.

Exclusions— Tax-Free Money

"Thank God we don't get all the government we pay for."

WILL ROGERS

"When men get in the habit of helping themselves to the property of others, they cannot easily be cured of it."

"The history of our tax code, in economic terms, mirrors the course of most addictions: advancing dependence, diminished returns, and deteriorating health of the afflicted."

A 1909 EDITORIAL OPPOSING THE VERY FIRST
INCOME TAX
The New York Times

"When Congress talks of tax reform, grab your wallet and run for cover."

SENATOR STEVE SYMMS of Idaho

"You understand it, Stanley. I almost understand it. Now I must go out and teach it to 2,000 agents who have to apply it, and God help the millions of people who have to live with it."

AN INTERNAL REVENUE SERVICE COMMISSIONER,
in response to a technical proposal sponsored
by tax expert Stanley Surrey

In their infinite wisdom, Congress and the courts have decided that some income should not be taxed—that is, it should not even enter into the tax computation picture. The tax code and relevant case law therefore have provided that certain items received by you may be excluded from gross income for any one of the following four reasons:

1. The item may be excluded for constitutional reasons. For example, it has been argued that certain interest on state and municipal bonds is not subject to federal taxation because of the fear that "the power to tax is the power to destroy." Such interest, therefore, is constitutionally exempt from federal taxation.

2. The item received may not be true income but rather a return of cost. For example, when you lend money and then later collect it, the receipt of that money collected is merely a return of your original loan. Alternatively, when you sell property, part of the proceeds of the sale represents a return of your cost, and therefore only the excess of the proceeds over your original cost for that property represents true income.

3. Congress has from time to time seen fit to relieve certain items from taxation for equitable or other reasons. Each exclusion has its own legislative history and reason for enactment. Some exclusions are intended as a form of indirect welfare payments, as when certain injury or sickness payments are excluded from income. Other exclusions prevent double taxation of income or provide incentives for socially desirable activities. For example, scholarships for tuition may be excluded from the income of the recipient. Alternatively, other exclusions have been enacted by Congress to rectify the effects of judicially imposed decisions. For example, the value of improvements to property made by a lessee has been excluded from the lessor's income upon the termination of the lease in reaction to a Supreme Court decision that such value was taxable income.

4. Certain items have been excluded from gross income on the basis of administrative discretion and efficiency. For example, if you buy property from your employer at a reduced price, you normally must include in your income as extra pay the excess of the property's fair market value over what you paid for it. But if such employee discounts are generally available and are not part of negotiated compensation, the discounts are

not generally included in your gross income. This is because of the administrative difficulty the Internal Revenue Service would have in identifying and valuing such discounts. Other employee fringe benefits, such as free parking or nonbusiness use of your employer's facilities, would also be excluded from your gross income for the same reasons.

This chapter will detail those items that are not taxable and explain how you can use the availability of these items to reduce your income tax.

A Alternatives to "Earned Income"

The most important thing that you as a taxpayer can do to reduce your taxes to zero is to convert fully taxable income into excludable income. An exclusion is something that is not included in gross income. It is the best kind of revenue to receive. If you are in the 24 percent tax bracket (single, taxable income over $82,500), each dollar you convert to excludable income is the equivalent of getting a raise of 24 percent! Therefore, in negotiating compensation, you as an employee-taxpayer should examine the following forms of nontaxable remuneration for services rendered as alternatives to fully taxable cash income.

1 Hospitalization Premiums (Sec. 106)

Hospitalization premiums, including premiums for supplementary medical insurance (Medicare) paid by your employer, or your former employer if you are retired, are excludable from your income. However, if you have the *choice* when you retire either to receive continued coverage under your employer's group medical insurance plan or to receive a lump-sum payment and you choose the lump-sum payment, you must include the amount of the payment in your gross income at the time you make the choice to receive it. If you choose continued coverage, and if you qualify for itemization of deductions, you may deduct the amount you include in your income as a medical insurance premium.

For example, if you normally would purchase hospitalization insurance costing $500 a year, and you are in the 24 percent tax bracket, you would require pretax earnings of $657.89 in order to make that purchase. Of that

$657.89, 25 percent, or $157.89, would go to paying your taxes. In other words, having your employer pay the hospitalization premiums ($500) for you is the equivalent of receiving compensation of $657.89 from your employer and then paying your own hospitalization premiums. The savings of $157.89 to your employer can come back to you in *additional* alternative compensation.

2 Group Life Insurance Premiums (Sec. 79)

Group term life insurance coverage of $50,000 or less provided to you by your employer is excludable from your income. This rule applies even if you make an irrevocable assignment of your rights in the policy to another person who agrees to pay your part, if any, of the insurance premiums.

Group term life insurance is term life insurance protection (insurance for a fixed period of time) provided under a master policy or a group of individual policies. The policies must be life insurance contracts and form part of a plan of group insurance arranged for by an employer for all employees. The life insurance protection in a policy of permanent insurance (for example, a whole-life policy) is *not* term life insurance protection.

You are not taxed on the cost of group term life insurance protection of *more* than $50,000 if:

a) the coverage is provided after you have retired and are disabled;

b) your employer is the beneficiary of the policy for the entire period the insurance is in force during the tax year; *or*

c) the only beneficiary of the amount over $50,000 is a qualified charitable organization for the entire period the insurance is in force during the tax year. You do not make a deductible charitable contribution by naming a charitable organization as the beneficiary of your policy.

Where the policy provides only term insurance of $50,000 or less, the payment of premiums by your employer does not create any taxable income for you as an employee. The cost of insurance protection in excess of $50,000 paid by your employer is includable in your gross income according to the following table.

Table I

Uniform premiums for $1,000 of group term life insurance protection as of and after July 1, 1999 (Annual cost per $1,000 of protection)

Age	Amount Included in Income
Under 25	$ 0.60
25–29	$ 0.72
30–34	$ 0.96
35–39	$ 1.08
40–44	$ 1.20
45–49	$ 1.80
50–54	$ 2.76
55–59	$ 5.16
60–64	$ 7.92
65–69	$15.24
70 and above	$24.72

For example, assume you are 47 years old, hired July 1, 2018, and your employer carries a group policy that provides you with $60,000 of term life insurance. You must include only $9.00 ($1.80 × 10 divided by 6 months out of 12) in your income for your employer's payment of premiums. The rest of the premium paid for you is tax-free income. For 2019, you work the whole year and the amount is $18.00. Furthermore, any amount contributed by you toward the purchase of such group term life insurance reduces the amount of gross income that you realize. Had you contributed $9.00 in 2018 toward the purchase of the insurance, you would have had zero included in your income.

If two or more employers provide you with group term life insurance coverage, you must figure the amount of income from this source. Moreover, the cost of group term life insurance provided to you is the cost of life insurance provided to you during the tax year, regardless of when your employers pay the premiums.

For example, assume you are 51 years old and work for two employers. Both employers provide group term life insurance coverage for you. Your coverage with the first employer is $35,000 and with the second is $45,000. You pay premiums of $50 a year under the second employer's group plan. The amount to be included in your gross income is figured as follows:

First employer coverage	$35,000
Second employer coverage	+45,000
Total coverage	80,000
Minus exclusion	−50,000
Excess amount	30,000
Multiply cost per thousand, age 51 (from table)	×2.76
Cost of excess insurance for tax year	82.80
Minus premiums paid by you	−50.00
Amount included in income	$32.80

The cost of employer-provided group term life insurance must now be included in wages for FICA tax purposes to the extent that it is includable for income tax purposes. However, if you need life insurance, the use of this technique provides that insurance at either a tax-reduced or completely tax-free cost.

3 Group Legal Services Plans (Sec. 120)

Amounts paid by your employer for a qualified group legal services plan and the value of the benefits you receive under such a plan can no longer be excluded from your income. This exclusion expired July 1, 1992.

4 Accident and Health Plans (Sec. 105)

Although you realize no taxable income from the benefits of an accident and health policy on which you pay your own premiums, it may be more tax advantageous to have these policies paid by your employer. The general rule is that any benefits received by you as an employee under such policies are includable in your gross income.

There are, however, certain exceptions permitting you to exclude specific benefits that would otherwise be taxable under the general rule:

1. You may exclude benefits received directly or indirectly as reimbursement for medical expenses incurred for yourself, your spouse, or your dependents.

If you deducted such medical expenses in a prior year, however, the reimbursement for these expenses must be included in the current year's income.

2. You may exclude benefits received for the permanent loss or the loss of the use of a member or function of the body, or a permanent disfiguration of yourself or your spouse or dependents, so long as the benefits are not related to absence from work.

The value of the exclusion of accident and health benefits can be shown by the following example:

Assume you lost a leg in an automobile accident that was unrelated to your work and you collected $10,000 from an insurance policy carried by your employer. If the payments were computed with reference to the nature of the injury and were not related to the time period that you were absent from work, then the entire $10,000 would be excluded from your income. Furthermore, if you incurred $3,000 in medical expenses that were covered under an employer-sponsored hospitalization plan, those payments would also be excluded from your income.

5 Employee Death Benefits (Sec. 101)

Amounts received as death benefits by your family or by your estate could be excluded up to an aggregate amount of $5,000, whether paid directly or indirectly by your employer.

This exclusion could not be claimed for accrued salary, unused leave, or compensation for past services. Furthermore, it could be claimed for a nonforfeitable amount you had the right to receive before your death *only* if it was received as a lump-sum distribution from a qualified plan or under an annuity contract purchased by an employer that is a tax-exempt organization.

The Small Business Job Protection Act of 1996 repealed this exclusion for decedents dying after August 20, 1996.

6 Merchandise Distributed to Employees on Holidays

Merchandise distributed to you as an employee on holidays, such as Christmas or New Year's Day, is excludable from your income if it is not of substantial value and is given for substantially noncompensatory reasons.

A turkey, for example, or similar merchandise given to you by your employer on a holiday therefore will not be includable in your taxable income. Unfortunately, this does not apply to cash distributions such as bonuses.

7 "Expenses of Your Employer"

The law does not tax reimbursement expenses that are true reimbursements for expenses of your employer rather than income amounts truly compensatory in nature.

Under this category are such items as reimbursements for cab fares and the payment of supper money. Rather than being excludable on the basis of statutory or constitutional language, these items are truly nontaxable as the result of Internal Revenue Service recognition of the impossible administrative verification problems in auditing such expenses. For whatever reasons, therefore, they are nontaxable.

If you as an employee can arrange with your employer to work from 11 A.M. to 7 P.M. rather than from 9 A.M. to 5 P.M. and she agrees to provide you with supper money, these personal supper expenses therefore can be converted into nontaxable income. In effect, no matter what bracket you are in, you have arranged for the Internal Revenue Service to buy you dinner.

Here's another example. The IRS has indicated that iPads and other tablets will be treated like cell phones when employers provide them to employees. Thus, employees won't be taxed on the value of personal use, as long as the devices are provided primarily for business reasons rather than as a form of compensation. Similarly, reimbursements made by employers to employees for personally owned iPads generally should not be subject to tax when used primarily for business.

8 Meals and Lodgings (Sec. 119)

The value of meals and lodgings provided to you, your spouse, and your dependents without charge by your employer is not taxable income if the following three criteria are met:

1. The meals or lodgings are provided at your employer's place of business.

2. The meals or lodgings are provided for the convenience of your employer.

3. In the case of lodging (but not meals), you must accept the lodging at your employer's place of business as a condition of your employment. This means that you must accept the lodging to carry out the duties of your job properly, for example, if you must be available for duty at all times.

Lodging includes the cost of heat, electricity, gas, water, sewerage service, and similar items that are necessary to make lodging habitable.

With reference to meals, you may exclude from income the value of meals provided to you during working hours so that you can be available for emergency calls, or because the nature of your employer's business restricts you to a short meal period. For example, if you are the only receptionist at your place of work, you must be available "at all times." If your employer provides you with lunch every day, that lunch is not includable in your income. Furthermore, the Supreme Court has ruled that such lunches do not constitute "wages" for social security taxes. They are truly *tax-free* (see TAM 9829001 where meals provided by a casino to its food service and security employees were excluded from their income and *Boyd Gaming Corp. v. Commissioner*, 9th Cir., No. 98-70123, 5/12/99 where 100 percent of the expenses of a casino's employee cafeteria were allowable as *de minimis* fringe benefits).

However, if you receive a cash allowance from your employer for meals or lodging, you must include the cash allowance in your income. The solution, therefore, is to have your employer provide the food, not the dollars. The net effect is the same to you but the net cost is substantially less.

Situations in which meals and lodging are furnished for the convenience of the employer normally include the following:

- A waitress is required to eat her meals on the premises during the busy lunch and breakfast hours.

- A worker is employed at a construction site in a remote part of Alaska. The employer must furnish meals and lodging due to the inaccessibility of other facilities.

- A bank furnishes meals on the premises to limit the time tellers are away during the busy hours.

- A hospital provides a free cafeteria for its staff. The hospital's business purpose in providing the meals is to induce employees to stay on the premises in case an emergency arises. These meals are not includable in the income of the staff, even though staff members are *not* required to eat on the premises.

The 1998 Reform Act now provides that *all* meals furnished to employees at the employers place of business shall be treated as "for the convenience of the employer" if more than half of such meals are furnished for the convenience of the employer.

This technique should be used extensively when married couples run their own businesses or professions. For example, assume the situation where one spouse performs the services and the other runs the office. That second spouse needs to be available "at all times" to answer the phone, receive clients, etc.,

and therefore any meals provided to that spouse would be deductible by the business as an expense but not includable as income to the recipient. The spouse must truly be employed and must be required to be on the business premises during lunchtime or the deduction will be disallowed as a sham (*Weidmann*, 89-1 USTC ¶9197 [DC N.Y., 1989]). In effect, what we have done again is to convert a personal expense—a meal—into nontaxable compensation. Again, the Internal Revenue Service is put into the position of helping to pay for your dinner.

9 Employee Discounts

You need not include as taxable income the discounts or privileges of relatively small value that you, as an employee, receive, where such discounts are given primarily to provide good employee relations and do not take on the character of additional compensation. This exclusion includes the usual courtesy discounts allowed to employees in many retail stores. But the value of discounts beyond a mere courtesy discount would be taxable income to you. Furthermore, if you buy property from your employer at less than fair market value, the amount of that discount is income.

For example, if you pay $2,000 for one of your employer's company cars that has a fair market value of $6,000, you are considered to have earned $4,000 of income on the transaction.

10 Workers' Compensation (Sec. 104)

Workers' compensation received for sickness or injury is fully exempt from tax. If you turn over your workers' compensation payments to your employer, and all or part of your regular salary continues to be paid, the excess of the salary payments over the amount of workers' compensation is taxable income.

For example, assume you are hurt on the job and are out of work for 6 weeks. Your employer continues to pay your salary of $200 a week, or $1,200 for the time you are absent. You also receive $75 a week, or a total of $450, in workers' compensation. Under your employment contract, you turn over all your workers' compensation to your employer. The $75 a week is fully excludable from your income and the balance is taxable income.

11 "Cafeteria" Plans and Flexible Spending Accounts (Sec. 125)

Employer contributions under a written "cafeteria" plan, "salary deduction plan," or "flexible spending or benefit plan," permitting you as a participant to select between taxable and nontaxable benefits, are excludable from your income to the extent that you choose nontaxable benefits.

Nontaxable benefits include medical expenses including nonprescription drugs (but not vitamins), group life insurance (up to $50,000 coverage), disability benefits, dependent care, and accident and health benefits to the extent that such benefits are excludable from gross income.

Such employer contributions may be excluded if the following conditions are satisfied:

- Participation in the cafeteria plan must be restricted to employees.
- The same service requirement must apply to all participants.
- The participant chooses nontaxable benefits.
- The plan's eligibility requirements do not discriminate in favor of "highly compensated individuals."
- Employer contributions and employee benefits do not favor "highly compensated participants."

The deadline for the use of these funds has been extended to March 15 of the next year (Notice 2005-42), but the plan must allow it. Alternatively, the plan can (as of 2013) allow a carryover of unused amounts of up to $500 into the next year. But you can't have both the extension and the carryover.

As of January 1, 2011, over-the-counter drugs don't qualify. Payments from these plans are limited to prescription drugs and insulin. As of January 1, 2013, pay-ins to Health Flexible Spending Accounts will be capped at $2,500 a year.*

If you are covered by a flexible spending account you do not qualify for a health savings account contribution (Letter Ruling 201413005, 2/12/14). However, with a health flexible spending account, your full balance for the year is available to you immediately—even before you actually put the cash in the account.

12 Dependent Care Assistance Program (Sec. 129)

For tax years after 1981, the value of the dependent care assistance that an employer provides to employees under a dependent care assistance program is not generally includable in the employee's gross income. However,

*$2,600 for 2017 and $2,650 for 2018

if payments for child care expenses are made to someone who is a child of the employee under age 19 or who qualifies for a dependency exemption for the employee, the payments are not excludable. If the child is not under age 19 and is not claimed as a dependent, such payments *do* qualify (*Langlois,* T.C.M. 1988–415).

The value of dependent care assistance that you may exclude from your pay is limited. If you are an employee who is not married at the end of the tax year, the limit is equivalent to your earned income for that year. For married employees the limit is the lesser of: (a) the employee's earned income for the tax year; or (b) the employee's spouse's earned income for the tax year. The Tax Reform Act of 1986 put a $5,000 cap on dependent care expenses. Moreover, the Family Support Act of 1988 provides that any amount excluded under a dependent care assistance program reduces the amount of expenses otherwise eligible for the child care credit.

A dependent care assistance program is a plan written by the employer for the exclusive benefit of the employees and that meets the following requirements:

1. *Eligibility.* The program must benefit employees who qualify under a classification set up by the employer, and the Secretary of the Treasury must find it nondiscriminatory in favor of employees who are officers, owners, or highly compensated, or who are dependents of these employees. However, the employer does not have to include in this program employees who are covered by what the Secretary of Labor considers to be a collective bargaining agreement between employee representatives and one or more employers if there is evidence that the dependent care benefits were the subject of good faith bargaining between the representatives and the employer.

2. *Limitation on principal shareholders or owners.* Not more than 25 percent of the amounts paid or incurred by an employer for the dependent care assistance during the year may be for individuals who are shareholders or owners (or their spouses or dependents) each of whom—on any day of the year—owns more than 5 percent of the stock or of the capital or profit interest in the employer.

3. *Funding.* An employer is not required to fund a dependent care assistance program.

4. *Notification of availability.* An employer must provide all eligible employees with a reasonable notification of the availability and terms of the dependent care assistance program.

5. *Notification to participants.* The plan will give each employee, by January 31, a written statement showing the amounts paid for the expenses incurred by the employer in providing dependent care assistance to the employee during the calendar year.

13 Employer Educational Assistance (Sec. 127)

This provision excludes from an employee's gross income employer-provided educational assistance, regardless of whether or not the education is job-related. The provision did not apply to any payment for graduate-level courses (except for those taken in 1995 and those beginning prior to July 1, 1996) taken by an individual pursuing a program leading to an advanced academic or professional degree and is generally not available for any education involving sports, games, or hobbies. Employers are not required to withhold on educational assistance payments, but the exclusion is limited to $5,250 per individual per calendar year. Educational expenses that would be deductible by an employee as trade or business expenses if they had been paid by the employee are not subject to this $5,250 cap.

The plan must provide that not more than 5 percent of the benefits paid or incurred annually will be attributable to owners.

The 2001 Tax Relief Act made this exclusion permanent and it was extended to cover graduate education as of January 1, 2002. Every employer who maintains an educational assistance program must file a return showing the number of employees eligible to participate in the program; the number participating; the total cost of the program; the employer's name, address, and taxpayer identification number; and the type of business in which the employer is engaged.

In PLR 200339017, the IRS validated a law firm's plan for assisting its non-lawyer employees with the cost of attending law school.

14 Employee Awards (Sec. 274)

Under prior law, an employee award such as emblematic jewelry or an engraved plaque awarded an employee for job performance, which was not excludable as a scientific or other achievement award, was generally excludable from gross income if it qualified as a gift. If the employee award was includable in the employee's income, the employer was entitled to a deduction for the award as a business expense. If the award was excludable as a gift, the employer's deduction was limited to a maximum of $25 for the cost of gifts to any one employee in any one tax year.

If a gift of tangible personal property was awarded to an employee for length of service, safety achievement, or productivity, the deduction ceiling was raised from $25 to $400. If a length of service, safety, or productivity award was a *qualified plan award*, the ceiling on the employer's deduction was $1,600, provided that the average cost of all awards provided under the plan for qualified awards did not exceed $400. A qualified plan award was one awarded (a) under a permanent written program of the employer which (b) does not discriminate in favor of officers, shareholders, or highly compensated employees.

The Tax Reform Act of 1986 changed these rules. That law states specifically that employee awards will *not* be excludable from the employee's income as gifts. Since such awards will no longer be treated as gifts (and are therefore fully includable as income to the employee), the limitations described on employer deductions for business gifts will no longer apply. The entire amount of the award (assuming ordinary, necessary, and reasonable tests are met) will be deductible.

Employee awards generally will be includable in the income of the employee and will be deductible by the employer, subject to two limited exceptions. One exception applies to awards that are *qualified plan awards*.

The definition of a qualified plan award under new law is essentially the same as under prior law: one awarded (a) under a permanent written program of the employer which (b) does not discriminate in favor of officers, shareholders, or highly compensated employees. If an award is a qualified plan award, the award is excludable by the employee *and* deductible by the employer only to the extent that the cost to the employer of all such awards made to the employee during the taxable year (whether or not qualified plan awards) does not exceed $1,600. The $400 average cost limitation described for qualified plan awards has been retained: That is, awards will not be considered qualified plan awards unless the average cost limitation is met.

The second exception applies to certain awards that are not qualified plan awards. If the award is not a qualified plan award (for example, if it is awarded under an informal plan or in a discriminatory fashion), the award will be excludable by the employee *and* deductible by the employer only to the extent that the cost of all such awards that are not qualified plan awards provided to the employee during the taxable year does not exceed $400.

Under current law if the cost to the employer of the qualified plan award exceeds the limits just described, then the employee must include in income the *greater* of (a) the excess of the cost of the award over the amount allowable as a deduction (but not more than the award's value), or (b) the excess of the value of the award over the amount allowable as a deduction. If the employer's cost is *not* over the applicable limit, the employee may exclude the award regardless of its value.

Example: If an employer gave an employee one qualified plan award that cost the employer $2,000 and had a value of $1,900, the employee would have to include $400 (cost minus $1,600 limitation) in income. If the award cost $2,000 and had a value of $2,200, the employee would have to include $600 in income (its value minus the $1,600 limitation).

Furthermore, to be excludable under *either* of the exceptions just described, an award must be an *employee achievement award.* Only awards that are length of service awards or safety achievement awards will qualify as employee achievement awards. Professional, administrative, managerial, and clerical employees do not qualify for safety achievement awards for tax purposes. A significant change in the 1986 law is that awards for productivity will no longer qualify for an exclusion. Awards for productivity will simply be treated as compensation.

Also, the 1986 law specifically stated that employee achievement awards must be tangible personal property (not cash, securities, or life insurance). To the extent employee awards are excludable from income, they are also exempt from the Social Security and other employer withholding taxes.

After the 1986 law there would no longer be any need to make the subjective determination as to whether the employee award is a gift. No employee awards will be treated as gifts for income tax purposes.

However, the 1986 law created a double whammy with respect to employee achievement awards that are in excess of the applicable limits. They are not deductible by the employer and must be included in the gross income of the employee. Because of this double whammy, beginning in 1987 employers had to keep employee achievement awards for length of service and safety achievement within the applicable dollar amount limitations.

Example: An insurance company has a program of employee achievement awards provided to employees for length of service achievement, but the arrangement discriminates in favor of highly compensated employees. The company provides a top executive with a computer that cost the company $600. The computer has a value of $700. The cost of the computer is deductible by the employer only to the extent of $400. Since the computer's cost to the employer is more than $400, the executive must include the excess of its $700 value over the employer's $400 deductible portion in gross income. The reportable amount would be $300.

The 1986 law does make it easier to plan employee achievement award programs since the interest of the employer corresponds with the interest of the employee; that is, the employer receives a deduction under the same circumstances that the employee receives an exclusion. The 1986 law is less favorable with respect to employee awards in that the exclusion is not available for awards given for productivity of the employee.

The 1986 law does not change the rules for fringe benefits which are *de minimis* under Sec. 132(e). Under these rules employees may exclude from income employee awards that are of nominal value, such as holiday turkeys or employee picnics. However, the Senate Finance Committee's Report on the Tax Reform Act states that certain employee awards for length of service "such as a gold watch" may be treated under the *de minimis* provision! The rationale appears to be that such an award is the functional equivalent of several smaller gifts made over the course of many years of service. Or perhaps the committee has been too busy in recent years to follow the price of gold.

15 Clergy Housing Allowance (Sec. 107)

If you're a member of the clergy, you can exclude from taxes part of your income that's attributated to housing. The amount you exclude is equal to the fair market value of the property or the amount used to provide the home, whichever is less. But see *Gaylor,* DC-Wisc, 2017-2 U.S.T.C. ¶50,372 which struck down the clergy housing exclusion as unconstitutional. The same judge, in 2013, ruled it unconstitutional in *Freedom From Religion Foundation* but that decision was reversed by the 7th Circuit Court of Appeals based on standing in 2014. You no longer can have more than one house qualify if ministerial services are provided at both (*Driscoll v. Commissioner of IRS,* T.C. No. 1070-07, 135 T.C. No. 27, December 14, 2010, which was reversed by the 11th Circuit, on February 18, 2012.)

16 Miscellaneous Fringe Benefits

An employer can give discount fare cards, passes, or tokens to an employee who takes *public transportation* to work. If the subsidy provided is not worth more than $260 per month to an employee, it is considered to be a *de minimis* fringe benefit. As of 2018, the employer cannot deduct it, but you, as an employee, received it tax-free (Regulation Section 1.132-6T[d][1]). Note, however, that if the employer supplies you with more than $260 a month toward the public transportation commute, only the amount in excess of $260 is taxable as compensation income (Notice 94-3) (Rev. Proc. 2005-70).

Employer-provided free *parking*, up to a maximum value of $255 per month, is also excludable from income but no longer deductible.

An employer could designate $20 per month of your pretax earnings for expenses related to *bicycle commuting* in 2017. But if this occured, you could not claim the parking or transit benefits, which have the higher per month allowance. For 2018, this benefit is no longer available.

B Donative Items

17 Gifts, Bequests, and Inheritances (Sec. 102)

If you receive money or property by bequest, devise, or inheritance, that receipt does not constitute taxable income to you. (Any income produced by that money or property while in your hands, though, is taxable in the usual fashion.)

Only money and property received from a decedent or as a bona fide gift fall under this rule. For a transfer to constitute a gift, there must be a motive of "detached and disinterested generosity." The exclusion, though, applies only to the donee.

Here you must be careful. For purposes of taxation, a simple assignment of income is ineffective. For example, if you make a gift of salary receivable from your employer to your child, even though that check goes directly to your child, that income is still taxable to you. You were the one who earned it and therefore are the one who is taxed on that earning. Your child, however, will exclude the "gift" and not be taxed on its value.

But once property is conveyed, the impact of taxation does shift to the donee. Thus for example, if you are in the 24 percent bracket and own a bond

yielding $1,000 in interest, you must pay taxes of $240, leaving you only $760 of after-tax disposable income. Alternatively, if you transfer that bond to your child and allow your child to receive the income, the first $1,050 of interest to that child will be completely tax-free. In terms of net family disposable income, the total amount available will be increased by $240.

The advantages of interfamily income allocation will be discussed extensively later in the book. The important thing to recognize under this section is that the transfer of the bond to your child is not at all a taxable transaction—that is, your child will not be taxed on the value of the bonds received. This exclusion of gifts from the gross income of the recipient constitutes the foundation of the income allocation strategies and techniques to be discussed later.

18 Scholarships and Fellowships (Sec. 117)

Under prior law, if you received a scholarship or fellowship grant, you could exclude that amount from your gross income, subject to certain limits, depending upon whether you are a degree candidate. To qualify for this exclusion, the payment had to be made for your education and training. The payment did not qualify, however, if it was made to pay you either for past, present, or future services, or for studies or research conducted mostly for the grantor's benefit.

A scholarship generally means an amount paid for the benefit of a student at an educational organization, to aid in the student's pursuit of studies. An educational organization is any organization that normally maintains a regular faculty and curriculum and has a regularly organized body of students in attendance at the place where its educational activities are carried on. A fellowship is the same as a scholarship, but the individual receiving aid does not have to be enrolled at an educational institution, and research is usually the aim.

Under current law, the exclusion will be limited to scholarships or fellowship grants to individuals who are degree candidates at educational institutions that maintain a regular faculty and curriculum and have a regularly enrolled body of students. There will no longer be an exclusion available to nondegree candidates or for scholarships granted by organizations other than qualified educational institutions. In addition, the exclusion will be available only with respect to payments that are actually used for tuition, enrollment fees, books, supplies, and other equipment required for courses of instruction. Payments for teaching, research, or other services rendered to the institution by a degree candidate will no longer qualify for the exclusion.

The exclusion does apply to *qualified tuition reductions.* A qualified tuition reduction is a tuition reduction for the employees, spouses, and dependent children of employees of educational institutions for studies below the graduate level, under a plan that does not discriminate in favor of officers, owners, or highly compensated employees of the institution.

Amounts paid to help you in pursuing your studies or research are not excludable if the studies or the research is mostly for the benefit of the grantor. However, if the main purpose is to further your education and training, and the amounts are not payment for services, they would be excludable. This is true even if you must give progress reports to the grantor, or if the results of your studies or research may slightly benefit the grantor.

Payments for your past, present, or future services are not excludable, *but* there is a very important exception that must be kept in mind: If you work for pay for a research project, you generally must include that pay in income. Your pay is not a scholarship or fellowship grant merely because the research can be used for credit toward a degree. However, if similar services are required of all candidates for the degree, as a reasonable condition for it, you may exclude the pay from your gross income.

Your pay for services over and above those specifically needed for the degree must be included in your gross income. Interns, resident physicians, and registered nurses in training in a hospital therefore must include their pay in gross income. But tuition and work payments given to you under a work study program are considered scholarships if your college, under its educational philosophy, requires all students to take part in a work program. These payments, therefore, are excludable from your income. Alternatively, payments you receive for service *not* required by the work program must be included in your income. Furthermore, amounts paid by your employer to you when you are on educational leave also are not excludable.

The following example will demonstrate the value of the potential exclusion of scholarships and fellowship grants from your income: In a contest sponsored by a business firm, you receive a scholarship award of $5,000 that you can use only for tuition, books, and supplies when enrolled as a candidate for a degree at a certain college. You do not include any of the $5,000 award in your gross income if:

a) you are not employed by the firm at the time of the award;

b) you are not being paid for services you provided for the firm in the past; *and*

c) you are not required to provide future services for the firm.

If you are in the 24 percent bracket and desire to enroll as a candidate for a degree, you would have had to earn $6,578.95 before tax in order to have $5,000 after tax to pay for the college tuition and fees. The enormous financial advantage of the exclusion of scholarships and fellowships from taxable income thus becomes very clear. Remember, however, that the same after-tax effect can be achieved if your employer establishes an employee education assistance plan as discussed earlier.

Tax Treatment of Scholarship and Fellowship Payments

Payment for	Degree candidate	Not a degree candidate
Tuition	Tax free	Taxable
Fees	Tax free[1]	Taxable
Books	Tax free[1]	Taxable
Supplies	Tax free[1]	Taxable
Equipment	Tax free[1]	Taxable
Room	Taxable	Taxable
Board	Taxable	Taxable
Travel	Taxable	Taxable
Teaching	Taxable[2]	Taxable
Research services	Taxable[2]	Taxable
Other services	Taxable[2]	Taxable

[1] If required of all students in the course.

[2] Does not include amounts received under the National Health Service Corps Scholarship Program or the Armed Forces Health Professions Scholarship and Financial Assistance Program.

19 Prizes and Awards (Sec. 74)

Prior to 1987, prizes and awards received in recognition of past accomplishments—in religious, charitable, scientific, artistic, educational, literary, or civic fields—were excludable income if the winners were chosen without action on their part and were not expected to perform any future services. For example, if you received a Pulitzer or Nobel Prize or any other award and were selected for your past work, this award was not includable in your income. Under *current law,* the exclusion for scientific

and other achievement awards is repealed. The only exception to the repeal is when the recipient assigns the award to a governmental unit or charitable organization.

The provision in the current law which permits you to exclude the value of the prize or award if you assign it to the government or a charity is of limited benefit. Under prior law an excludable award could be contributed to charity and the recipient contributor could take a deduction for the contribution. Under new law you may exclude the prize or award if you contribute it to a charitable organization, but your contribution is disallowed. The end result is that you have simply given away what you received and have no extra income and no deduction. In effect, this is no different from your having included the prize or award in gross income and then taken a charitable deduction for contributing it.

In addition, if you win a prize in a lucky number drawing, a television or radio quiz program, a beauty contest, or some other event, that prize is taxable. So, too, are awards or bonuses given to you as an employee for your good work or for suggestions. These are not instances where the winners have been chosen without action on their part and are not expected to perform any future services.

Taxable prizes and awards in goods and services must be included in your income at their fair market value to you. This is very important. It is not the general fair market value but rather the fair market value of that prize *to you*. If you already have two attaché cases and win a third on a quiz show, the value of that third attaché case *to you* may be negligible. It clearly would not be its full retail selling price. However, when sold, the amount received for such prizes or awards is normally deemed to be equal to their fair market value. If, for example, you receive an award of a car that retails for $10,000 and immediately sell that car to a third party for $8,000, the amount to be included in your income would be the $8,000 figure rather than the $10,000 figure.

Be careful here. A bargain sale to a relative may be considered part sale, part gift. If you sold that $10,000 car to your brother for $5,000, the Internal Revenue Service might successfully argue that you received income of $10,000 and made a gift of the $5,000 difference to your brother. One technique that has been used to avoid this is to sell the car for $5,000 to an independent third party, who could turn around and resell the car to your brother for the

same $5,000. Watch the structuring of such three-party transactions. There must be no prearranged agreement for the third party to resell to your brother, and that third party must be truly independent. Otherwise, if the Internal Revenue Service catches on, it will collapse the two transactions, deem the first sale to be a sham, and successfully establish the true nature of the gift to your brother.

In October 2016, President Obama signed into law a bill that exempts the value of medals won and other prizes (cash) awarded by the U.S. Olympic Committee from athletes' taxable income but only if their income is under $1 million during that calendar year.

20 Qualified Charitable Distributions (QCDs)

A distribution from an IRA normally results in an increase in adjusted gross income (AGI). This higher AGI can reduce your medical expenses, miscellaneous deductions, total itemized deductions, exemptions, and your qualification for multiple credits.

Passed in 2006, and made permanent in 2015, QCDs allow a direct distribution to a charity without the inclusion amount being included in income. Requirements for a QCD are:

- The individual must be older than 70½ when the distribution is made.

- Charities must be eligible to receive tax-deductible charitable contributions.

- The maximum QCD is $100,000, although a spouse can also make a $100,000 QCD if the couple files a joint income tax return.

- The $100,000 maximum QCD does not apply to the overall charitable deduction limit. Individuals may make charitable contributions that exceed 50 percent of adjusted gross income.

- The distribution must be a direct transfer from the IRA to the charity.

- The distribution first comes from taxable funds, then from any nondeductible IRA contributions. Previously, distributions would have been allocated proportionately between deductible and nondeductible contributions.

C Investors

21

Interest on State and Municipal Obligations (Sec. 103)

You can exclude from gross income all interest earned on obligations of a state, territory, municipality, or any political subdivision, except in the case of arbitrage bonds issued after October 9, 1969.

An *arbitrage bond* is an obligation, the proceeds of which are reasonably expected to be used to acquire other securities or obligations that are expected over the term of the issue to yield a materially higher rate of return. This exception prohibits state and local governments from issuing bonds at a low interest rate because of their tax-exempt nature and using the proceeds to buy federal or industrial bonds returning a higher yield. Since the state or local government does not pay an income tax on the difference, this exception prevents the federal government from becoming an unintended source for financing state and local government operations.

If you are in a sufficiently high tax bracket, the advantages of purchasing a state or municipal bond can be substantial. If you are in a 24 percent bracket, a $6\frac{1}{2}$ percent yield on a municipal obligation is the equivalent of a 8.55 percent yield on a nonexempt security. Moreover, the risk factor on a state or municipal obligation will normally be far lower than that on an industrial security.

If Your Marginal Tax Rate Is:	And Your Tax-Exempt Investment Yields					
	4%	5%	6%	6.5%	7%	7.5%
	It Is the Equivalent of a Taxable Investment Yielding:					
12%	4.55	5.68	6.82	7.39	7.95	8.52
22%	5.13	6.41	7.69	8.33	8.97	9.62
24%	5.26	6.58	7.89	8.55	9.21	9.87
32%	5.88	7.35	8.82	9.56	10.29	11.03
35%	6.15	7.69	9.23	10.00	10.77	11.54
37%	6.35	7.94	9.52	10.32	11.11	11.90

The higher the tax bracket, the greater the attraction of a tax-exempt security. The preceding table shows the tax-exempt equivalent yield to a taxable investment at various marginal tax rates:

Click on www.investinginbonds.com to compare taxable and tax-free yields.

D Benefits for the Elderly

22 Public Assistance Payments

Benefit payments from a general welfare fund in the interest of the general public, such as payments to aid the indigent or the blind, or payments to crime victims, are excludable from your gross income. These welfare payments have been excluded by the Internal Revenue Service, because the IRS sees them in the nature of gifts.[1]

23 Social Security and Other Retirement Benefits

Social Security benefits under the federal Social Security programs may not be taxable. Social Security benefits received from foreign countries, however, are taxable unless they are specifically exempt by treaty.

Basic railroad retirement benefits are also not taxable. Railroad retirement lump-sum payments, commonly known as either the insurance lump-sum payment or the residual payment, are excluded from your gross income as well.

The Internal Revenue Service tax code does not specifically exclude Social Security benefits, but these benefits were declared not subject to tax by the Internal Revenue Commissioner.[2] According to the Internal Revenue Service, these payments are in part a return of the after-tax contributions made by the individual and in part a welfare or annuity payment from the government.

1. Rev. Rul. 71-425, 1971–2 CB 76.
2. Rev. Rul. 70-217, 1970-1 CB 12.

These welfare payments have been viewed by the Internal Revenue Service as essentially in the nature of gifts.[3]

Moreover, basic Medicare benefits received under the Social Security Act are also excluded from gross income since they are considered Social Security payments. So also are supplementary benefits covering costs of doctors' services and other items not covered under basic Medicare, as they are in the nature of medical insurance payments.

Note, however, that since January 1, 1984, part of your Social Security benefits have been subject to tax if your income exceeded a specified level determined by formula. There are three factors used in determining how much of your Social Security benefits, if any, will be included in taxable income: (1) your *income*, defined as your adjusted gross income for federal income tax plus any tax-exempt interest, plus any foreign source income you receive during the year; (2) your *half-benefit*, defined as half the Social Security income you (and, if you're married and filing jointly, your spouse) receive during the year; and (3) your *base amount*, which is $25,000 for a single taxpayer, $32,000 for a married couple filing jointly, and zero for a married couple filing separately (unless they have lived apart for the entire tax year, in which case they qualify for the $25,000 base amount).

The amount of Social Security income to be reported, if any, was 50 percent of the amount by which (1) your income plus (2) your half-benefit exceeds (3) your base amount. However, in no event will more than your half-benefit be reported as taxable income.

For example, assume a married couple filing jointly has an adjusted gross income of $20,000 plus tax-exempt interest of $8,000. They therefore have *income* of $28,000. If they have Social Security income of $12,000 they will report $1,000 of that benefit as taxable income as follows:

Income	$28,000
Half-benefit	+$6,000
Total	$34,000
Base Amount	−$32,000
Difference	$2,000
50% of difference	$1,000
Taxable S.S. benefit	$1,000

3. Rev. Rul. 71-425, 1971-1 CB 76.

Effective after December 31, 1993, the Omnibus Budget Reconciliation Act of 1993 created a second tier of Social Security benefit inclusion in gross income. Prior law now applies to *income* up to $34,000 for unmarried individuals and $44,000 for married individuals filing joint returns. For taxpayers with *income* above these amounts, the amount included in income shall be the *lesser* of:

1. 85 percent of your total Social Security benefit, or
2. the sum of:

 a) the smaller of (i) the amount included under prior law; or (ii) $4,500 (if unmarried) or $6,000 (if married filing jointly) [4]

 plus

 b) 85 percent of the excess of your *income* over the new applicable second tier threshold amounts ($34,000 and $44,000).

Use the table below to see if you are subject to tax. If your income, modified as above, is over the upper threshold up to 85 percent or your Social Security benefits may be taxed. Between the base amount and the upper threshold, only 50 percent would be taxed. Below the base amount, zero is taxed.

Taxes on Social Security Benefits

Filing Status	Base Amount	Upper Threshold
Single	$25,000	$34,000
Head of Household	$25,000	$34,000
Married Filing Jointly	$32,000	$44,000
Qualified Widow(er)	$25,000	$34,000

Now that Social Security payments may be taxable, recipients should find out whether their benefits are included as part of their adjusted gross income under the income tax laws of the states where they reside. Eleven states have, in the past, exempted from their income taxes Social Security benefits now included in federal adjusted gross income: Delaware, Hawaii, Idaho, Indiana, Maine, New Mexico, New York, South Carolina, Virginia, West Virginia, and Wisconsin. Minnesota has provided an exclusion from federal adjusted gross income for Social Security benefits in a portion of the calculation of the maximum income exclusion for pensions and retirement benefits. Other states, such as New Jersey, specifically exempt Social Security from taxation. Check your own state rules.

4. These amounts equal 50 percent of the difference between the prior and new thresholds: i.e., 50 percent of $34,000 − $25,000 = $4,500; 50 percent of $44,000 − $32,000 = $6,000.

24 Annuities (Sec. 72)

An annuity is a type of investment that requires you to pay a fixed amount in exchange for the right to receive periodic payments for your life or for some definite period. If the annuity payments are based on your life, or the life of another individual, the amounts of such payments are determined through the use of standard mortality tables.

When you receive the income from this annuity, part of what you are receiving represents a recovery of your initial investment. This recovery amount is fully excluded from income. The Internal Revenue Service provides tables with which you can compute your exclusion ratio. This exclusion ratio remains the same and continues to be applied to annuity payments even if you outlive your life expectancy.

For example, assume you have made principal payments into an annuity of $60,000 in return for payment of $500 per month for life. Also assume that the tables show that your life expectancy is 15 years from the annuity starting date. Your investment in the contract is $60,000 and your expected return is $6,000 per year times 15 years, or $90,000. You would exclude two-thirds of each payment ($6,000 × $\frac{2}{3}$) or a total of $4,000 yearly. That $4,000 is a nontaxable return of capital; the remaining $2,000 is taxable income.

In IRS Notice 88-18, the IRS came up with an easier way for some retirees to compute how much of their pension or annuity payments are tax-free. Under this IRS safe-harbor method, the expected number of monthly annuity payments is based on your age at the annuity's starting date, rather than on the life expectancy tables contained in Regulation Section 1.72-9. The same number is used for a single-life annuity or a joint and survivor annuity.

Age of Distributee	Number of Payments
55 and under	300
56 to 60	260
61 to 65	240
66 to 70	170
71 and over	120

For example, if you begin receiving payments at age 65, you would divide your total investment by 240 to find out how much of each payment is tax-free.

The Small Business Job Protection Act of 1996 provided that basis recovery on payments from qualified plan annuities generally will be determined under a method similar to the prior law simplified alternative method provided by the IRS above. The portion of each annuity payment that represents a return of basis is equal to the employee's total basis as of the annuity starting date, divided by the number of anticipated payments under the following table:

IRS Table V—One Life
Life Expectancies

Age	Years Remaining	Age	Years Remaining	Age	Years Remaining
5	76.6	42	40.6	79	10.0
6	75.6	43	39.6	80	9.5
7	74.7	44	38.7	81	8.9
8	73.7	45	37.7	82	8.4
9	72.7	46	36.8	83	7.9
10	71.7	47	35.9	84	7.4
11	70.7	48	34.0	85	6.9
12	69.7	49	34.0	86	6.5
13	68.8	50	33.1	87	6.1
14	67.8	51	32.2	88	5.7
15	66.8	52	31.3	89	5.3
16	65.8	53	30.4	90	5.0
17	64.8	54	29.5	91	4.7
18	63.9	55	28.6	92	4.4
19	62.9	56	27.7	93	4.1
20	61.9	57	26.8	94	3.9
21	60.9	58	25.9	95	3.7
22	59.9	59	25.0	96	3.4
23	59.0	60	24.2	97	3.2
24	58.0	61	23.3	98	3.0
25	57.0	62	22.5	99	2.8
26	56.0	63	21.6	100	2.7
27	55.1	64	20.8	101	2.5
28	54.1	65	20.0	102	2.3
29	53.1	66	19.2	103	2.1
30	52.2	67	18.4	104	1.9
31	51.2	68	17.6	105	1.8
32	50.2	69	16.6	106	1.6
33	49.3	70	16.0	107	1.4
34	48.3	71	15.3	108	1.3
35	47.3	72	14.6	109	1.1
36	46.4	73	13.9	110	1.0
37	45.4	74	13.2	111	.9
38	44.4	75	12.5	112	.8
39	43.5	76	11.9	113	.7
40	42.5	77	11.2	114	.6
41	41.5	78	10.6	115	.5

Age	Number of Payments
Not more than 55	360
56 to 60	310
61 to 65	260
66 to 70	210
More than 70	160

This provision was effective with respect to annuity starting dates beginning 90 days after the date of enactment (August 20, 1996). Therefore, if your annuity starting date is after November 18, 1996, you must use this new simplified method.

For annuity starting dates beginning after November 18, 1996, but before January 1, 1997, the total number of monthly annuity payments expected to be received is based on the primary annuitant's age at the annuity starting date. The same expected number of payments applies to an annuitant whether he or she is receiving a single life annuity or a joint and survivor annuity.

For annuity starting dates after December 31, 1997, the table used to determine the expected number of payments depends on whether payments are based on the life of more than one individual.

For joint and survivor annuities, the total number of monthly annuity payments expected to be received is based on the combined ages of the annuities at the starting date, IRS said. For annuities that are not based on life expectancies, the expected number of payments is the number of monthly annuity payments under the contract (Notice 98-2).

Whichever method you use, once you have received your investment back, your exclusion ratio expires. Although the total tax-free recoupment is the same with both methods, using the optional second method may reclaim your investment faster. For example, under a joint and survivor annuity, payments continue until the death of the second beneficiary. Since two beneficiaries have a longer life expectancy, and therefore more payments over which to recover the investment, using the regular IRS method results in a smaller portion of each payment coming back tax-free. With the optional method, it is irrelevant whether or not the joint and survivor annuity is elected.

The IRS optional second method could have been used for payments from annuities that began distributions after July 1, 1986. If you began receiving

payments before then, you must use the old method. New retirees will now use the new method as per the 1996 law.

25 Sale of Your Home (Sec. 121)

You may exclude from your gross income some or all of your gain from the sale or exchange of your main home, if you meet certain ownership and use tests at the time of the sale or exchange.

Prior to May 7, 1997, you could have expected to exclude from your gross income $125,000 (the maximum allowable) of gain on the sale or exchange of your main home *if:*

a) you were age 55 or older before the date of the sale or exchange;

b) you owned and lived in the property sold or exchanged as your main home for at least three years out of the five-year period ending on the date of the sale or exchange; *and*

c) you or your spouse never excluded gain on the sale or exchange of a home after July 20, 1981.

All three tests must be met by one taxpayer. For example, you may be age 55, and your younger spouse may have owned and lived alone in the property for the required 3 year period, but because you are not one taxpayer, you cannot take the exclusion.

These rules were *all* changed by the Tax Relief Act of 1997. *After May 6, 1997* joint filers can exclude, as often as every 2 years, as much as $500,000 ($250,000 for single filers) in gain on the sale of a principal residence occupied for 2 of the 5 years prior to sale. To qualify, you must have used the house as your principal residence for at least 2 out of the 5 years prior to the sale. However, the exclusion will be available once every 2 years, although there are exceptions to that rule too. Those close to retirement or whose children have moved out may be big winners here. They can now sell their old, big houses without the need to reinvest in new, more expensive homes to avoid taxation on the gains. They can now buy smaller residences, or even rent. The prior law provision under Section 1034 that deferred taxation upon a rollover of the sales proceeds into a new home has been repealed.

You can get a partial exclusion based on the time of use and ownership, but only if the sale is required because of a *change in place of employment, health*

reasons, or unforeseen circumstances. The IRS has been very flexible in defining "unforeseen circumstances." Even the birth of twins or the hostility of neighbors (PLR 200403049) will now qualify. See page 120 for details.

Unfortunately, the 1997 law was unclear if you owned the property for less than 2 years. The 1998 Act provided the answer. It provides partial relief based on a fraction of the *maximum exclusion,* rather than on the basis of your actual realized profit.

For example, assume you bought a house in 2017 for $250,000 and sell it in 2018 for a $25,000 profit. Because you are married, and lived there 1 year, you are eligible for half the $500,000 exclusion you would have been entitled to had you been there the full 2 years. Half the exclusion is $250,000, greater than the gain of $25,000, and therefore none of your gain is taxable. Had the alternative interpretation applied, you would have been able to exclude half your profit, and paid tax on the remaining $12,500.

Not everybody wins on this one. Miss Fortune bought her home in 2017 for $1.5 million and sold it 1 year later for a $400,000 profit. Since she is single and lived there only half the required 2 years, she gets to exclude $125,000, and pay tax on $275,000 of her gain. Had the alternative interpretation applied, she would have excluded half her $400,000 gain and only paid taxes on $200,000. Note that any "nonqualifying use," such as a rental, reduces your exclusion. See pages 119–121 for more details.

There is no age requirement for this exclusion and the exclusion can be claimed every 2 years. However, if you have a $250,000/$500,000 gain every 2 years, I want to meet your real estate broker!

E Miscellaneous Individual Exclusions

26 Carpool Receipts

If you form a carpool to carry passengers to and from work, the amounts received from these passengers are not included in your income. These amounts are considered reimbursement for transportation expenses incurred.

Although your cost of commuting back and forth to work has been subject to continually increasing costs as energy prices have risen, commuting costs are neither deductible nor normally excludable from income. But establishing a carpool can help you defray these expenses without incurring additional taxable income.

Therefore, what you should do is establish a carpool in which the passengers pay you amounts sufficient to cover the cost of your repairs, gasoline, and similar items used in connection with operating your car to and from work. In doing so, you convert personal nondeductible expenses into excludable income.

For example, if it has been costing you $100 a month to commute in the past, you have had to earn $131.58 (at the 24 percent tax bracket) in order to have the funds to pay for your commute. With a carpool arrangement in which your expenses are reimbursed, it costs you nothing. The establishment of a carpool, therefore, gives you an extra $131.58 in after-tax disposable income.

27 Damages (Sec. 104)

Damages received in settlement of a lawsuit or awarded by a court were normally excluded from income under the return of capital doctrine. Theoretically, damages awarded for personal wrong committed against you (for instance, breach of promise to marry, invasion of privacy, libel, slander, alienation of affection) replace the personal capital destroyed by these wrongful acts.[5] Defamation awards were also excludable.[6] Amounts received as damages for personal injury were excludable under both this doctrine and specific congressional mandate.[7] However, damages received as a substitute for income are generally taxable, since they represent a restoration of lost wages or profits that would have been taxable upon receipt.

Back pay and liquidated damages recovered under the Age Discrimination in Employment Act were not excludable from income.[8] These rules were modified by the Small Business Job Protection Act of 1996.

Under *prior law*, gross income did not include any damages received (whether by suit or agreement and whether as lump sums or as periodic payments) on account of personal injury or sickness. The exclusion from gross income of damages received on account of personal injury or sickness specifically did not apply to punitive damages received in connection with a case not involving physical injury or sickness. Courts differed as to whether the exclusion applied to punitive damages received in connection with a case involving a physical injury

5. Rev. Rul. 74-77, 1971-1 CB 33.
6. *Threlkeld,* 87 T.C. No. 76.
7. Internal Revenue Section 104(a) (2).
8. *Comm. v. Schleier,* US Sup Ct, No. 94-500, 6/14/95.

or physical sickness. Certain states provided that, in the case of claims under a wrongful death statute, only punitive damages may be awarded.

Courts have interpreted the exclusion from gross income of damages received on account of personal injury or sickness broadly in some cases to cover awards for personal injury that do not relate to a physical injury or sickness. For example, some courts have held that the exclusion applies to damages in cases involving certain forms of employment discrimination and injury to reputation where there is no physical injury or sickness. The damages received in these cases generally consist of back pay and other awards intended to compensate the claimant for lost wages or lost profits. The Supreme Court held that damages received based on a claim under the Age Discrimination in Employment Act could not be excluded from income.

CURRENT LAW

The 1996 law provides that the exclusion from gross income does not apply to any *punitive* damages received on account of personal injury or sickness whether or not related to a physical injury or physical sickness. Prior law continues to apply to punitive damages received in a wrongful death action if the applicable state law (as in effect on September 13, 1995 without regard to subsequent modification) provides, or has been construed to provide by a court decision issued on or before such date, that only punitive damages may be awarded in a wrongful death action.

The 1996 law also provides that the exclusion from gross income *only* applies to damages received on account of personal physical injury or physical sickness. If an action has its origin in a physical injury or physical sickness, then all damages (other than punitive damages) that flow therefrom are treated as payments received on account of physical injury or physical sickness whether or not the recipient of the damage is the injured party. For example, damages (other than punitive damages) received by an individual on account of a claim for loss of consortium due to the physical injury or physical sickness of such individual's spouse are and will be excludable from gross income. In Private Letter Ruling 200410022, the IRS defined "personal physical injuries" as "direct, unwanted or uninvited physical contacts resulting in observable body harms such as bruises or cuts." In addition, damages (other than punitive damages) received on account of a wrongful death continue to be excludable from taxable income as under prior law.

The 1996 law specifically provided that emotional distress is not considered a physical injury or physical sickness. Thus, the exclusion from gross income does not apply to any damages received (other than for medical

expenses as discussed below) based on a claim of employment discrimination or injury to reputation accompanied by a claim of emotional distress. Because all damages received on account of physical injury or physical sickness are excludable from gross income, the exclusion from gross income applies to any damages received based on a claim of emotional distress that is attributable to a physical injury or physical sickness. In addition, the exclusion from gross income also applies to the amount of damages received that is not in excess of the amount paid for medical care attributable to emotional stress in other cases. (See REG - 127270-06). Payments "only" for emotional distress are not excluded (*Sharp v. Commissioner,* T.C. No. 21332-12).

The above provisions generally are effective with respect to amounts received after the date of enactment (August 20, 1996). The provisions do not apply to amounts received under a written binding agreement, court decree, or mediation award in effect on or issued on or before September 13, 1995.

Amounts received to compensate for damages to property or to the goodwill of a business are also excludable up to the amount of the adjusted basis of the assets. Only receipts in excess of this basis will be taxable. For example, if your car, which cost you $500, is completely destroyed in an accident and you receive $600 as compensation for damages, the first $500 is nontaxable as a return of your capital; you include in your gross income only the $100 excess over your basis.

The difference between the taxable and excludable nature of alternative damages awarded provides an opportunity for sophisticated tax planning. For example, in arranging an out-of-court settlement of a suit involving personal injury and loss of income, you should be aware that damages from personal injury suits are excluded from income but the proportion representing loss of income is fully taxable (unless the income loss is a direct result of injury or sickness). Therefore, negotiate for a maximum allocation to the personal injury portion of the settlement.

In fact, it may be more advantageous to take less, totally, if the tax-free portion is increased. Assume you are in the 24 percent bracket and are offered $10,000 for personal injury and $20,000 for loss of income. That leaves you with $25,200 after taxes. A settlement of $25,000 for personal injury and $2,000 for loss of income would give you $26,520, or $1,320 more after taxes. At the same time, it saves the payer $3,000. In such a case, everybody wins—except the Internal Revenue Service.

SPECIAL NOTES

In 2006 the U.S. Court of Appeals for the D.C. Circuit held "unconstitutional" the tax on damages for loss of reputation and mental distress (*Murphy v. IRS*). The case was appealed and reversed. However, damages paid for wrongful imprisonment are tax free.

Tax and Reporting Treatment of Judgment/Settlement Payments to Employees

Payment Character	Income Taxable?	Wages (FICA and ITW)?	Reporting Requirement
Back pay (other than lost wages received on account of personal physical injury or physical sickness)	Yes	Yes[1]	W-2
Front pay	Yes[2]	Yes	W-2
Dismissal/severance pay	Yes	Yes	W-2
Compensatory or consequential damages paid on account of personal physical injuries or physical sickness	Generally, no	No	None
Compensatory damages not paid on account of personal physical injuries or physical sickness (e.g., emotional distress)	Generally, yes	No	1099-MISC, Box 3
Consequential damages not paid on account of personal physical injuries or physical sickness	Yes	No	1099-MISC, Box 3
Punitive/liquidated damages	Yes	No	1099-MISC, Box 3
Interest	Yes	No	1099-INT, Box 1 (if $600 or more)
Costs	Yes	No	1099-MISC, Box 3
Medical expenses	Generally, no	No	None
Overtime	Yes	Yes	W-2
Restoration of benefits: health premiums, TSP employee and employer contributions, and retirement contributions	To be determined	To be determined	To be determined
Taxes—employee income tax or employee portion of FICA	Yes	Yes. See Publication 15-A	W-2
Travel—if requirements of § 62(c) (accountable plan) are met	No	No	No
Travel—if requirements of § 62(c) are not met	Yes	Yes	W-2

[1] If the case is in the 8th Circuit and involves an illegal refusal to hire, contact CC:TEGE:EOEG:ET2 for guidance.

[2] If the case is in the 5th Circuit, contact CC:TEGE:EOEG:ET2 for guidance.

Tax and Reporting Treatment of Attorneys' Fees
Total Employer Payment Made Jointly to Attorney and Employee:

Nature of Payment	Income Taxable to Employee?	Reporting to Employee	Reporting to Attorney
Court award designating attorneys' fees[1]	Yes—attorneys' fees generally taxable to employee.	Attorneys' fees reportable in Box 3 of 1099-MISC (not W-2). Treas. Reg. § 1.6041-1(f)(1) and (2).	Box 14 of 1099-MISC in the amount of the check payable jointly to employee and attorney. Treas. Reg. § 1.6045-5(a), and (f) Ex. 1.
Court award without designation of attorneys' fees	Yes—attorneys' fees generally taxable to employee.	The total award is reportable, as appropriate (on 1099-MISC or W-2).	Box 14 of 1099-MISC in the amount of the the check payable jointly to employee and attorney Treas. Reg. § 1.6045-5(a), and (f) Ex. 1.
Settlement payment	Yes—attorneys' fees generally taxable to employee.	To be determined, based on the nature of the action. If wages, reportable on W-2. If not wages, reportable in Box 3 of 1099-MISC.	Box 14 of 1099-MISC in the amount of the check payable jointly to employee and attorney Treas. Reg. § 1.6045-5(a), and (f) Ex. 1.

[1] Workers' rights statutes, such as Title VII, generally include fee-shifting provisions.

Separate Employer Payments to Employee and to Attorney for Attorneys' Fees:

Nature of Payment	Income Taxable to Employee?	Reporting to Employee	Reporting to Attorney
Court award designating attorneys' fees[1]	Yes—attorneys' fees generally taxable to employee.	Attorneys' fees reportable in Box 3 of 1099-MISC (not W-2) even though paid separately to attorney. Treas. Reg. § 1.6041-1(f) (1) and (2).	Box 14 of 1099-MISC to attorney in the amount of check payable to attorney. Treas. Reg. § 1.6045-5(a), and (f) Ex. 3.
Court award without designation of attorneys' fees	Yes—attorneys' fees generally taxable to employee.	The total award is reportable, as appropriate (on 1099-MISC or W-2) even though attorneys' fees paid separately to attorney. Treas. Reg. § 1.6041-1(f)(1) and (2).	Box 14 of 1099-MISC to attorney in the amount of check payable to attorney. Treas. Reg. § 1.6045-5(a), and (f) Ex. 3.
Settlement payment	Yes—attorneys' fees generally taxable to employee.	To be determined, based on the nature of the action. If wages, reportable on W-2. If not wages, reportable in Box 3 of 1099-MISC.	Box 14 of 1099-MISC to attorney in the amount of check payable to attorney. Treas. Reg. § 1.6045-5(a), and (f) Ex. 3.

[1] Workers' rights statutes, such as Title VII, generally include fee-shifting provisions.

	Total Employer Payment to Employee:		
Nature of Payment	Income Taxable to Employee?	Reporting to Employee	Reporting to Attorney
Court award designating attorneys' fees[1]	Yes—attorneys' fees generally taxable to employee.	Attorneys' fees reportable in Box 3 of 1099-MISC (not W-2). Treas. Reg. § 1.6041-1 (f)(1) and (2).	None. See, e.g., Treas. Reg. § 1.6045-5(a), (d)(4), and (f) Ex. 4.
Court award without designation of attorneys' fees	Yes—attorneys' fees generally taxable to employee.	The total award is reportable, as appropriate (on 1099-and MISC or W-2).	None. See, e.g., Treas. Reg. § 1.6045-5(a), (d)(4), (f) Ex. 4.
Settlement payment	Yes—attorneys' fees generally taxable to employee.	To be determined, based on the nature of the action. If wages, reportable on W-2. If not wages, reportable in Box 3 of 1099-MISC.	None. See, e.g., Treas. Reg. § 1.6045-5(a), (d)(4), and (f) Ex. 4.

[1] Workers' rights statutes, such as Title VII, generally include fee-shifting provisions.

Total Employer Payment to Attorney:

Nature of Payment	Income Taxable to Employee?	Reporting to Employee	Reporting to Attorney
Court award under fee-shifting statute designated as attorneys' fees[1]	Yes—attorneys' fees generally taxable to employee.	Attorneys' fees reportable in Box 3 of 1099-MISC (not W-2). Treas. Reg. § 1.6041-1(f) (1) and (2).	Total amount of check reported on 1099-MISC, Box 14. Treas. Reg. § 1.6045-5(a) and (d)(4).
Court award without designation of attorneys' fees	Yes—attorneys' fees generally taxable to employee.	The total award is reportable, as appropriate (on 1099 or W-2).	Total amount of check reported on 1099-MISC, Box 14. Treas. Reg. § 1.6045-5(a) and (d)(4).
Settlement payment	Yes—attorneys' fees generally taxable to employee.	To be determined, based on the nature of the action. If wages, reportable on W-2. If not wages, reportable in Box 3 of 1099-MISC.	Total amount of check reported on 1099-MISC, Box 14. Treas. Reg. § 1.6045-5(a) and (d)(4).

[1] Workers' rights statutes, such as Title VII, generally include fee-shifting provisions.

28

Divorce and Separation Arrangements (Sec. 71)

Prior to July 18, 1984, alimony and support payments were taxable to the recipient spouse only if:

a) the payments qualified as periodic payments *and*

b) the payments were received under a decree of divorce or separate maintenance; *or*

c) the payments were received under a written separation agreement (provided the husband and wife were not living together and did not file a joint return).[9]

Alimony and support payments were termed periodic payments when no fixed total sum was established or when the cessation of payments was contingent upon the occurrence of some event, such as the death or remarriage of the divorced spouse or change in economic status of either spouse.

If you are the recipient spouse, you should be aware that lump-sum settlements are not taxed. Furthermore, where a fixed total sum is set and is payable in installments, the income is not taxable unless the sum was payable over a period of more than 10 years.

For arrangements prior to 1984, if a lump-sum settlement was payable in installments of more than 10 years, payments in each year up to 10 percent of the principal sum qualify as periodic payments and will be taxable to you. Ordinary periodic payments are taxable when received, whether received in advance or arrears. Under this same rule, the 10 percent limitation applied to advance payments but not to delinquent installment payments. For example, if under a decree of divorce you were to receive a total payment of $13,000 in 13 annual installments, each payment regularly received would be taxable as a periodic alimony payment. But if your spouse became delinquent in one year and paid $2,000 in the following year, the $2,000 was taxable when received. However, if your spouse paid $1,000 as a regular annual payment and paid an additional $1,000 in advance, the taxable amount would be only $1,300 (10 percent of the principal sum).

CURRENT LAW

The Tax Reform Act of 1984 made several significant changes in domestic relations taxation. Under prior law, gain generally was recognized on transfers of

9. A married couple living in the same house are not separated and living apart as a *matter of law*. See *Hertsch*, T. C. Memo 1982-109 Par. 57,684; also see *Washington*, 77 T.C. No. 44; but for a contrary decision in the 8th Circuit, see *Sydnes* 78-2 U.S.T.C. Par. 9487, 42 AFTR 2d 78-5143.

property in exchange for the release of marital claims. The Reform Act provides that transfers of property between spouses that are incident to divorce will generally be nontaxable, carryover basis transactions. This means that your spouse, who takes property from you incident to divorce, will have the same basis in that property that you had.

This provision of the Act applies to transfers after the date of the enactment (July 18, 1984), but not to transfers pursuant to instruments in effect on that date unless both parties elect to have the provisions apply. You and your spouse may, in addition, elect to have the provisions apply just to all transfers after December 31, 1983.

Moreover, the rules for taxation of *alimony* have been changed significantly for agreements executed after 1984. The section on alimony starting on page 179 details these provisions.

If the alimony is taxable to the recipient under the above rules, that same amount can be used by the payer as a deduction from adjusted gross income, even if you do not itemize deductions. Child-support payments are never deductible nor are they ever included in the gross income of the recipient. The amount of child support included in the payments should be clearly designated as such by the decree or written separation agreement. Note, however, that a payment, even one clearly delineated as alimony, will not be considered or treated as alimony if the payment is reduced (a) on the happening of a contingency relating to a child of the payer or (b) at a time that can clearly be associated with such a contingency. For this purpose, a contingency relates to a child of the payer if it depends upon any event relating to that child, regardless of whether such event is certain or likely to occur. Events that relate to a child of the payer include the following: the child's attaining a specified age or income level, dying, marrying, leaving school, leaving the spouse's household, or gaining employment.

There are two situations in which payments that would otherwise qualify as alimony or separate maintenance payments will be treated as arising out of a contingency relating to a child of the payer. The first situation is when the payments are to be reduced not more than 6 months before or after the date that the child is to attain the age of 18, 21, or local age of majority. The second situation is when the payments are to be reduced on two or more occasions that occur not more than 1 year before or after a different child of the payer spouse attains a certain age between the ages of 18 and 24, inclusive. The certain age referred to in the preceding sentence must be the same for each child, but need not be a whole number of years.

The presumption in the two situations that payments are to be reduced at a time clearly associated with the happening of a contingency relating to a child of the payer may be rebutted by showing that the time at which the

payments are to be reduced was determined independently of any contingencies relating to the children of the payer. The presumption in the first situation will be rebutted conclusively if the reduction is a complete cessation of alimony or separate maintenance payments during the sixth post-separation year or upon the expiration of a 72-month period. The presumption may also be rebutted in other circumstances, for example, by showing that alimony payments are to be made for a period customarily provided in the local jurisdiction, such as a period equal to one-half of the duration of the marriage.

For example, assume husband and wife are divorced on July 1, 2010, when their children—daughter (born July 15, 1995) and son (born September 23, 1997)—are 14 and 12, respectively. Under the divorce decree, husband is to make alimony payments to wife of $2,000 per month. Such payments are to be reduced to $1,500 per month on January 1, 2016, and to $1,000 per month on January 1, 2020. On January 1, 2016, the date of the first reduction in payments, daughter will be 20 years, 5 months, and 17 days old. On January 1, 2020, the date of the second reduction in payments, son will be 22 years, 3 months, and 9 days old. Each of the reductions in payments is to occur not more than 1 year before or after a different child of husband attains the age of 21 years and 4 months. Actually, the reductions are to occur not more than 1 year before or after daughter and son attain any of the ages of 21 years, 3 months, and 9 days through 21 years, 5 months, and 17 days. Accordingly, the reductions will be presumed to clearly be associated with the happening of the contingency relating to daughter and son. Unless this presumption is rebutted, payments under the divorce decree equal to the sum of the reductions ($1,000 per month) will be treated as fixed for the support of the children of husband and therefore will not qualify as alimony or separate maintenance payments.

Where payments constituting both alimony and child support are made but constitute less than the required amount each year, the payments are considered first to cover child support, with any excess deemed to be alimony.

The excludability of lump-sum alimony and child-support payments provides another avenue for sophisticated tax planning and negotiation. Remember, if the alimony payments are excludable, they are not deductible to the payer. The person making the alimony payments would clearly favor a divorce settlement that includes provisions for deductible alimony payments. On the other hand, the recipient would prefer that the payments do not qualify as includable income. If the payer is in a higher tax bracket than the recipient, both parties may benefit, after taxes, by increasing the payments and constructing them so that they qualify after taxes as "periodic."

For example, assume a husband and wife with no children are in the process of reaching a divorce agreement. If the wife is in a 12 percent tax bracket and the husband is in a 32 percent tax bracket, then $10,000 shifted

from property settlement to alimony would produce a net savings of $2,000 [$10,000 × (32 percent – 12 percent)]. Here again, the husband could pay the wife's taxes and share the $2,000 net savings, and both parties would still be ahead on an after-tax basis.

The same kind of planning can be used with child support. If the recipient is in a higher bracket than the payer, it is a good idea to negotiate for an increase in the amount designated as child support (excludable/nondeductible) in exchange for a reduction in periodic alimony payments (includable/deductible). If the payer is in a higher bracket, increase the amount of includable/deductible alimony in exchange for a reduction in child support.

As of January 1, 2019, the rules change again. For divorces entered into as of that date, alimony is no longer deductible nor included in the income of the recipient. There will be no tax difference between alimony and child support payments.

29 Life Insurance (Sec. 101)

Life insurance proceeds paid to you because of the death of the insured are not taxable unless the policy was purchased by you or transferred to you for a price. This is true even if the proceeds are paid under an accident or health insurance policy or an endowment contract.

If the death benefits are paid to you in a lump sum rather than at regular intervals, they are included in your gross income only if they are more than the amount originally specified as payable at the time of the insured person's death. If the benefit payable at death was not specified, you include the benefit payments in income when they are more than the present value of the payments at the time of death.

If you receive life insurance proceeds in regular installments, you may exclude part of each installment from your income. To determine the excludable part, you must divide the amount held by the insurance company (generally, the total lump sum, the principal, payable at the death of the insured party) by the number of installments that are to be paid. Anything over this excludable part must be included as interest income.

There was one special exception: If insurance proceeds were payable to you after the death of your spouse, and you received the proceeds in installments, you could have excluded up to $1,000 a year of the interest included in the installments in addition to the part of each installment that was excludable as a recovery of the lump sum payable at death. Even if you remarried, you could have continued to take the exclusion. This provision, however, was repealed by the Tax Reform Act of 1986, effective for deaths occurring after the date of enactment (October 22, 1986).

Under current law, if you leave the proceeds from life insurance on deposit with an insurance company under an agreement to pay interest only, the interest paid to you is taxable.

The Health Insurance Portability and Accountability Act of 1996 amended the above rules.

The change generally excludes "qualified accelerated death benefits" from income. If a contract meets the definition of a life insurance contract, gross income does not include insurance proceeds that are paid pursuant to the contract by reason of the death of the insured. However, recently many chronically or terminally ill individuals with short life expectancies have sold or assigned their life insurance policies to qualified viatical-settlement providers. These companies typically buy policies from people with life-threatening illnesses for a percentage of the policy's face value. Under prior law, recipients of viatical payments would owe federal income taxes on those payments. The 1996 law excludes these payments from income effective for amounts received after December 31, 1996.

There is an exception to the general rule that life insurance proceeds are excluded from income. This exception is applicable to a life insurance contract that has been transferred for a fee to another individual, who assumes ownership rights. Upon receipt of the proceeds, that individual must include as income the difference between the proceeds and the amount he or she paid for the contract, plus any premiums paid. For example, assume person A owns an insurance policy in the face amount of $10,000 upon the life of person B and subsequently sells the policy to you for $2,000. When B dies, you receive the proceeds of $10,000. The amount that you can exclude from gross income is limited to $2,000 plus any premiums you paid after the transfer.

There are, however, four exceptions to this rule. These are transfers to:

A partner of the insured
A partnership in which the insured is a partner
A corporation in which the insured is an officer or shareholder
A transferee whose basis in the policy is determined by reference to the transferor's basis

This last item translates into a basic exception for policies that are transferred as part of a tax-free exchange—for example, a transfer of insurance policies to a corporation by its controlling shareholders in exchange for the corporation's stock or securities.

One technique that has been suggested in order to qualify for the previous second exception is the creation of a partnership between shareholders

wherein that partnership would lease equipment to the co-owned corporation. Such a structure would avoid the transfer-for-value limitation that would normally be held to transfers between shareholders. In this case, the transfer is not merely between shareholders but between partners.

30 Qualified State Tuition (§529) Programs

Current law provides tax-exempt status to "Qualified State Tuition Programs." These are programs established by a state or a state agency under which you can (1) purchase tuition credits or certificates for the payment of education expenses or (2) make contributions into an account established to pay qualified education expenses, such as tuition, books, and fees, and for 2009, 2010, and 2015 forward, computers and computer technology.

The interest or other earnings from such accounts comes out federal and state tax-free! Several states (e.g., New York) have programs where you don't even have to go to school in that state to qualify. All 50 states have such a program. Following are some of the best. Don't miss this tax-advantaged way to finance your kid's college expenses and tuition for K–12 private schools, including religious schools, as allowed by the Tax Cuts and Jobs Act of 2017. Note that tax-free distributions for K–12 schools are capped at $10,000 per student per year.

Or, you can get really creative. Name yourself as beneficiary of a Section 529 account and save money for a 2- or 3-year sabbatical—tax-free as long as it involves education at an eligible institution! Not only can you use the money for books and tuition, but you can even pay for your apartment up to the amount specified in school guidelines.

Call toll-free at 877-277-6496 or check www.collegesavings.org or www.savingforcollege.com for more information.

As an alternative, check out the *Independent 529 Plan*. It lets you lock in current tuition rates at more than 200 private colleges.

It works like this. Suppose you contribute $10,000. Assume that's 50 percent of one year's tuition at school "x." When you or your child enrolls, you've got 50 percent of one year's tuition paid.

The deals vary per college. But the money invested grows tax free. If you don't go, you get a refund, plus or minus two percentage points each year, depending on how your investments fared.

Get details and enroll at www.independent529plan.org or 888-718-7878 (see LTR. RUL. 200311034).

State 529 Plans

Alabama	The Higher Education 529 Fund	866-529-2228	www.alabama529.com
Alaska	University of Alaska College Savings Plan	800-478-0003	www.uacollegesavings.com
	T. Rowe Price College Savings Plan	800-369-3641	www.price529.com
	John Hancock Freedom 529	866-626-8529	www.johnhancock-freedom529.com
Arizona	Fidelity Arizona College Savings Plan	800-544-1262	www.fidelity.com/arizona
	Arizona Family College Savings Program	602-258-2435	www.az529.gov
Arkansas	GIFT College Investing Plan	800-857-7301	www.thegiftplan.uii.upromise.com
California	ScholarShare Advisor College Savings Plan	800-544-9999	www.advisor.fidelity.com
Colorado	Stable Value Plus College Savings Plan	800-448-2424	www.collegeinvest.org
	Direct Porfolio Savings Plan	800-997-4295	www.collegeinvest.org
	Scholars Choice College Savings Plan	888-572-4652	www.collegeinvest.org
Connecticut	Connecticut Higher Education Trust	888-799-2438	www.aboutchet.org
Delaware	Delaware College Investment Plan	800-544-1655	www.fidelity.com/delaware
District of Columbia	DC College Savings Plan	800-987-4859	www.dccollegesavings.com
Georgia	Georgia Higher Education Savings Plan	877-424-4377	www.gacollegesavings.com

Hawaii	TuitionEDGE	866-529-3343	www.tutitionedge.org
Idaho	Ideal Idaho College Savings Program	866-433-2533	www.idsaves.org
Illinois	Bright Directions College Savings Program	866-722-7283	www.brightdirections.com
	Bright Start	877-432-7444	www.brightstartsavings.com
Indiana	Indiana College Choice 529 Investment Plan	866-400-7526	www.collegechoiceplan.com
Iowa	College Savings Iowa	888-672-9116	www.collegesavingsiowa.com
Kansas	Schwab 529 College Savings Plan	888-903-3863	www.schwab.com/529
	Learning Quest 529 Education Savings Program	800-579-2203	www.learningquestsavings.com
Kentucky	Kentucky Education Savings Plan Trust	877-598-7878	www.kysaves.com
Louisiana	START Savings Program	800-259-5626	www.startsavings.la.gov
Maine	NextGen College Investing Plan	877-463-9436	www.nextgenplan.com
Maryland	Maryland College Investment Plan	888-463-4723	www.collegesavingsmd.org
Massachusetts	U.Fund College Investment Plan	800-544-2776	www.fidelity.com/ufund
Michigan	Michigan Education Savings Plan	877-861-6377	www.misaves.org
Minnesota	Minnesota College Savings Plan	877-338-4646	www.mnsaves.com
Mississippi	Affordable College Savings Program	800-486-3670	www.collegesavingsms.org
Missouri	Missouri's 529 College Savings Plan	888-414-6618	www.missourimost.s.upromise.com

(*continues*)

Montana	Pacific Funds 529 College Savings Plan	800-722-2333	www.pacificlife.com
Nebraska	State Farm College Savings Plan	800-321-7520	www.statefarm.com
	AIM College Savings Plan	877-246-7526	www.aimvestments.com
	TD Ameritrade 529 College Savings Plan	877-408-4644	www.tdameritrade.com
	College Savings Plan of Nebraska	888-993-3746	www.planforcollegenow.com
Nevada	The Upromise College Fund	800-857-7305	www.uii.s.upromise.com
	Vanguard 529 College Savings Plan	866-734-4530	www.vanguard.com
New Hampshire	Fidelity Advisor 529 Plan	800-544-9999	www.advisor.fidelity.com
	UNIQUE College Investing Plan	800-544-1914	www.fidelity.com/unique
New Jersey	NJBEST College Savings Plan	877-465-2378	www.njbest.com
	Franklin Templeton 529 College Savings Plan	800-818-4030	www.franklintempleton.com
New Mexico	The Education Plan	877-337-5268	www.theeducationplan.com
	Scholar's Edge	866-529-7283	www.scholarsedge529.com
New York	New York's 529 College Savings Program	877-697-2837	www.nysaves.uii .upromise.com
North Carolina	National College Savings Program	800-600-3453	www.nc529.org
North Dakota	College SAVE	866-728-3529	www.collegesave4u.com
Ohio	College Advantage, A 529 Savings Plan	800-233-6734	www.collegeadvantage.com
Oklahoma	Oklahoma 529 College Savings Program	877-654-7284	www.okforsavings.org

Oregon	OppenheimerFunds 529 Plan	888-876-7529	www.opp529.com
	MFS 529 Savings Plan	866-637-7526	www.mfs.com
	Oregon College Savings Plan	866-722-8464	www.oregoncollegesavings.com
Pennsylvania	Pennsylvania College Savings Program	800-294-6195	www.pa529direct.s.upromise.com
	Pennsylvania 529 Direct Investment Plan	800-294-6195	www.pa529direct.com
	Pennsylvania 529 Guaranted Savings Plans	800-440-4000	www.tapfacts.com
Rhode Island	CollegeBoundfund	888-324-5057	www.collegeboundfund.com
South Carolina	Future Scholar 529 College Savings Plan	888-244-5674	www.futurescholar.com
South Dakota	CollegeAccess 529	866-529-7462	www.collegeaccess529.com
Tennessee	Tennessee's BEST Savings Plan	888-486-2378	www.tnbest.org
Texas	Tomorrow's College Investment Plan	800-445-4723	www.enterprise529.com
Utah	Utah Educational Savings Plan	800-418-2551	www.uesp.org
Vermont	Vermont Higher Education Investment Plan	800-637-5860	www.services.vsac.org
Virginia	Virginia Education Savings Trust	888-567-0540	www.virginia529.com
West Virginia	SMART529 College Savings Program	866-574-3542	www.smart529.com
Wisconsin	Tomorrow's Scholar	866-677-6933	www.tomorrowsscholar.com
	EdVest	888-338-3789	www.edvest.com

Source: August 2007 *Investment Advisor.*

State Tax Deductions for 529 Plan Contributions

529 plan tax benefits by state, as of May 2017

State	Maximum annual state income tax benefit	Who qualifies	Carry forward[1]	State tax rate[2]	State tax savings[3]
Alabama	$5,000[4], $10,000[5]	Any contributor		5.00%	$500
Arizona	$2,000[4], $4,000[5]	Any contributor		4.54%	$182
Arkansas	$5,000[4], $10,000[5]	Any contributor	4 years	6.90%	$690
Colorado	Full contribution amount, up to contributor's taxable income	Any contributor		4.63%	$463
Connecticut	$5,000[4], $10,000[5]	Any contributor	6 years	6.99%	$699
D.C.	$4,000[4], $8,000[5]	Acct owner only	5 years	8.95%	$895
Georgia	$2,000[4], $4,000[5]	Any contributor, per beneficiary		6.00%	$120
Idaho	$6,000[4], $12,000[5]	Any contributor		7.40%	$592
Illinois	$10,000[4], $20,000[5]	Any contributor		3.75%	$375
Indiana	20% tax credit on contributions up to $5,000; maximum credit is $1,000	Any contributor	Credit	3.30%	$1,000
Iowa	$3,239[4,6], $6,478[5,6]	Acct owner only, per beneficiary		8.98%	$582
Kansas	$3,000[4], $6,000[5]	Any contributor, per beneficiary		4.60%	$276
Louisiana	$2,400[4], $4,800[5,7]	Any contributor, per beneficiary	Unlimited	6.00%	$288
Maryland	$2,500	Any contributor, per beneficiary	10 years	5.75%	$575
Massachusetts	1,000[4]/2,000[5] through 2021	Any contributor		5.10%	$102
Michigan	$5,000[4], $10,000[5]	Any contributor		4.25%	$425
Mississippi	$10,000[4], $20,000[5]	Any contributor		5.00%	$500
Missouri	$8,000[4], $16,000[5]	Acct owner/spouse only		6.00%	$600
Montana	$3,000[4], $6,000[5]	Acct owner/spouse or custodian/parent		6.90%	$414
Nebraska	$10,000[4,5], $5,000 if married filing separately	Acct owner or parents/guardians of ugma/utma accounts		6.84%	$684

New Mexico	Full contribution amount	Any contributor		4.90%	$490
New York	$5,000[4], $10,000[5]	Acct owner only		8.82%	$882
North Dakota	$5,000[4], $10,000[5]	Any contributor		2.90%	$290
Ohio	$2,000[4,5]	Any contributor, per beneficiary	Unlimited	5.00%	$500
Oklahoma	$10,000[4], $20,000[5]	Any contributor	5 years	5.00%	$500
Oregon	$2,330[4,6], $4,660[5,6]	Any contributor	4 years	9.90%	$990
Pennsylvania	$14,000[4], $28,000[5]	Any contributor, per beneficiary		3.07%	$307
Rhode Island	$500[4], $1,000[5]	Acct owner only	Unlimited	5.99%	$599
South Carolina	Full contribution amount	Any contributor		7.00%	$700
Utah	5% tax credit on contributions up to $1,920[4,6], $3,840[5,6], maximum credit is $96[4,5,6], $192[5,6]	Acct owner only, per beneficiary[10]	Credit	5.00%	$190
Vermont	10% tax credit on contributions up to $2,500[4], $5,000[5]; maximum credit is $250[4], $500[5]	Acct owner only, per beneficiary	Credit	8.95%	$500
Virginia	$4,000[4,5]; fully deductible if age 70 or older	Acct owner only[9]	Unlimited	5.75%	$575
West Virginia	Full contribution amount	Any contributor		6.50%	$650
Wisconsin	3,100[1,4,5,6]	Any contributor, per beneficiary[9]	Unlimited	7.65%	$765

Source: BlackRock leveraging data from savingforcollege.com

The information provided should not be relied on for tax purposes. Consult your tax advisor for more information IL, VT, WI: Principal portion only of "rollover in" is deductible. DC, RI: "Rollover out" is taxed if moved to a qualified tuition plan within two years. CT, CO, DC, GA, IN, KS, LA, MO, MI, PA, RI: "Rollover in" (from another qualified 529 program) is not deductible. AL: Qualified withdrawals from non-AL plans are not excluded from AL state tax. AR, CO, IL, KS, LA, ME, MI, MN, NE, ND, NJ, OK, PA, RI, UT: Other monetary incentives exist, including grants. Review the applicable plan disclosure statements.

[1] Some states allow taxpayers who contribute above the maximum annual tax deduction to carry forward excess contributions to future state income tax returns. State tax savings reflect full deduction of $10,000 over the carry forward period.

[2] Assumes joint tax filers in the maximum state tax bracket for 2017 and $10,000 in 529 plan contributions.

[3] If you itemize, state tax savings must be claimed as income on the following year's federal tax return.

[4] Filing individually

[5] Filing Jointly

[6] Adjusted annually for inflation.

[7] Certain deductions may be claimed each year for an account opened for needy, non-related beneficiaries meeting eligibility requirements.

[8] Contributions are reduced by qualified withdrawals during the year for purposes of determining the amount that may be deducted.

[9] Contributions from non-account owners are deductible by the account owner.

[10] Beneficiary must be younger than age 19 when designated on account to claim tax credit or deduction.

When It Makes Sense to Switch

Should you cash out your child's custodial account pay the long-term capital gains tax bill and put the money in a state sponsored 529 college savings plan? Yes—if you have enough time to earn back the tax payment. Find the number of years before college on the table below then go down a line. A switch makes sense if your custodial account has had any gain up to the percentage shown.

Years to college	1	2	3	4	5	6	7	8+
Maximum gain (%)	30.6	50.8	64.4	75.5	84.0	91.9	99.2	Any amount

Assume the 529 contributions receive an annual state tax deduction of up to $2,500 and the 529 levies 0.3% more in fees than the custodial account.

Source: Data: T. Rowe Price Associates Inc.

Interest in Learning
A look at the different college savings plans available

	Tax Breaks	Contribution Limit	Income Restrictions	Federal Financial Aid Impact	Flexibility of Funds' Use
529 College Savings Plan	Qualified distributions tax-free. (Some states may also offer tax breaks.)	Up to total of about $300,000 for some plans; may pay gift taxes if more than $15,000 a year. Can donate up to $75,000 at one time.	None	Considered parent's assets, assessed up to 5.6%.	Tuition, fees, room, board, and graduate school.

Interest in Learning

A look at the different college savings plans available *(continued)*

	Tax Breaks	Contribution Limit	Income Restrictions	Federal Financial Aid Impact	Flexibility of Funds' Use
529 State Prepaid Plan	Qualified distributions tax-free. (Some states may also offer tax breaks.)	Maximum varies by state, but plans cover, in general, up to five years of college costs.	None	Considered student resource: Reduces aid eligibility dollar for dollar.	For most plans, tuition, fees, room, and board, books, and for 2009, 2010, and after 2014 computers and Internet access.
Independent 529 Plan	Qualified distributions tax-free.	Up to five years' tuition at the group's most expensive college (currently over $137,000).	None	Considered student resource: Reduces aid eligibility dollar for dollar.	Tuition fees. room and board, and for 2009, 2010 and, after 2014 computers and Internet access.
Coverdell Education Savings Account	Qualified distributions tax-free.	Up to $2,000 a year.	For single filers, $95,000– $110,000; for joint filers, $190,000– $220,000.	Considered student's assets, assessed at 35%.	Post-secondary costs; K–12 costs, some computers.

(continues)

Interest in Learning
A look at the different college savings plans available *(continued)*

	Tax Breaks	Contribution Limit	Income Restrictions	Federal Financial Aid Impact	Flexibility of Funds' Use
Custodial Accounts	For kids age 19 or older* earnings taxed at child's rate; under 19, earnings less than $1,050 are tax-free.	No total maximum, but may pay gift taxes if more than $15,000 a year.	None	Considered student's assets, assessed at 35%.	Anything that benefits the minor.
Savings Bonds	Interest earned is tax-free if used for qualified higher education purposes.	Annual limit of $20,000 per owner as of 2008.	For 2018, for single filers, $79,550–$94,550; for joint filers, $119,300–$149,300	Considered parent's assets, assessed up to 5.6%.	Tuition and mandatory fees.
Taxable Accounts	Up to 15% tax on capital gains and dividend income.	Unlimited	None	Considered parent's assets, assessed up to 5.6%.	Unlimited

*As of 2008, it's under age 19, or, if a full-time student, under age 24.
Source: The Wall Street Journal.

How Does the 529 College Savings Plan Compare?

	529 plans	UGMA/ UTMA	Coverdell Educational IRA	EE bonds	Prepaid QSTP	Regular investment account
Tax Deferral	Tax exempt	No (earnings taxed at beneficiary's rate)	Tax exempt until 1-1-11 sunset	Tax-exempt income	Varies by state	No
Maximum Annual Contribution	Up to $75,000 per child gift tax-free	None	$2000* per child under 18 per year	$20,000 per person	Varies by state	None
Maximum Income to Qualify	No limits	No limits	Phases out for single filers at $95,000 to $110,000; for joint filers at $190,000 to $220,000	Phases out for single filers at $79,550 to $94,550; for joint filers at $119,300 to $149,300	Varies by state	No limits
Who Controls Disbursement of Assets	Parent, guardian, or other donor	Custodian until child reaches 18, the child afterward	Parent or guardian	Registered owner	Parent or guardian	Registered owner
Ability to Transfer	In most instances, can be transferred to another member of the same family without penalty, including first cousins as of January 1, 2002	Not permitted	Can be transferred to another member of the same family without penalty	Can be transferred without penalty	Most plans require that the beneficiary is a resident of the offering state	Transfer is considered an asset sale and may trigger capital gains tax liabilities
Estate Planning Features	Assets are transferred out of the donor's estate, yet the donor retains control	Assets are transferred out of the estate	Limited	None	Assets are transferred out of the estate	None
Freedom to Choose Colleges	Can be used for any accredited post-secondary school in the U.S.	No restrictions	Can be used for any qualified educational expense. Must be used before beneficiary is age 30[†]	No restrictions	Usually restricted to participating schools, can only cover tuition and fees	No restrictions
Early Withdrawal	Earnings are taxed at donor's regular rate, plus a 10% penalty applies	None	Entire withdrawal taxed at donor's rate plus a 10% penalty	None	Fees or penalties vary by state. Typically, the donor gets principal back, plus a modest return	None
Investments Available	Fund or funds	Any legal security or valuable item	Any legal security	EE bonds	Government guarantee	Any legal security
Professional Management/ Asset Allocation	Yes	No	No	No	Yes	No

*$500 prior to January 1, 2002.
[†]As of January 1, 2002, the age limit does not apply to special needs students, and money can be used for elementary and secondary school expenses.

31 Your Home—the Mother of All Tax Shelters!

Want to invest in a tax shelter that puts a roof over your head? There are more tax advantages and exclusions with respect to your home than any other investment. It's the American way—Mom, apple pie, and owning your own home. Let's look at all the deductions and benefits you get when you pay homage to the mortgage gods and go into more debt than your parents earned in their lifetimes.

TAXES

First, you get to deduct all the real property taxes you pay.* That includes all state or local taxes for the general welfare. It does not count any trash or garbage collection fees, or homeowner association charges specifically stated and billed.

If you are escrowing for the taxes, you get the deduction when your bank makes the payment, not when you escrow with the bank. Even if you are a tenant shareholder in a co-op, you get to deduct your share of any property taxes paid.

There is no limit on the number of properties on which you can deduct taxes paid. If you have 10 homes, you can deduct the taxes on all 10.

Even if you took the standard deduction, you could have added to that amount $500 ($1,000 on a joint return) for taxes paid on your principal residence for 2008 and 2009.

INTEREST

Uncle Sam wants to put you in a home. Sorry, that does not sound right. How about Uncle Sam wants to put you in a house? We all know a house is not a home. In any case, our government wants to subsidize your home purchase. It does that by making your interest payments deductible.

Interest paid on the purchase of your principal residence is deductible. You can even finance the buy of additional land adjacent to your home and deduct the interest as qualified residence interest. You can also deduct the interest you pay to buy a second residence or vacation home.

There is a cap of one million dollars of acquisition indebtedness on which you can take a personal interest deduction. If you plan on spending more than $1 million for your house, call me and we will work something out.

You can also deduct the interest on as much as $100,000 worth of home equity debt. As long as the house has the equity and the debt is secured by that equity, the IRS does not care what you do with the borrowed money. You can use it for whatever you want, including vacations, or a party to celebrate your newfound deductions.

*As of 1/1/18, the total deduction for taxes, including real estate and state income taxes, is capped at $10,000.

If you are in the 24 percent bracket, that means that $100 in interest paid only takes $76 out of your pocket. Uncle Sam pays the other $24 in income taxes foregone. Not a bad deal!

For new mortgages taken out after December 31, 2017, the million dollar cap is reduced to $750,000. The $100,000 limit on home equity is included in the $750,000 cap and interest on home equity loans is allowed *only* if the borrowed money is used for home improvements.

GAIN EXCLUSION

Here is where the IRS "gave up the farm." The deal on this one is so good it makes my eyes glaze over (a.k.a. the MEGO effect).

Forget about having to roll over your gain into a new home. Forget about the $125,000 gain exclusion if you are age 55 or older. Both are now ancient history and no longer good tax law.

Here is the new rule . . . good no matter how old you are. If the property was your principal residence for any 2 of the 5 years prior to sale, you can exclude $250,000 in *gain* ($500,000 on a joint return)!

If you qualify under the 2 out of 5 rule, you normally sign an affidavit at settlement. If the house sold for less than $250,000/$500,000, the sale amount is not even reported to the IRS because you have no tax liability on that sale.

This is not a one-time exclusion. You do not have to buy a new house. You can even rent and you can get another full exclusion every 2 years, or whenever you qualify. But, if you have a $250,000/$500,000 gain every 2 years, I want to meet your real estate agent!

Note that the rule changes to only one out of five years if you can't care for yourself and have moved to a nursing home.

The full $500,000 exclusion will potentially be allowed even if the sale is within two years of the death of a spouse.

You can even get a *partial* exclusion based on the time of use and ownership. But you only get the partial exclusion if the sale is because of:

a) a change in place of employment, or

b) health reasons, or

c) unforeseen circumstances.

The partial exclusion is based on the maximum exclusion, not on the basis of your actual realized profit. So, say you bought a home for $250,000 and sold it for a $25,000 profit after only 1 year because of a job change.

Because the sale was covered by a change in employment, you get a partial exclusion. It was your principal residence for 1 year out of 2, so 50 percent of the maximum exclusion, up to $125,000 in gain, is excluded. Since that is more than the $25,000 gain, no tax is due on the sale. You exclude half the maximum

allowed, not half the $25,000 in gain. That is a major tax break. Not many properties are going to appreciate more than $125,000/$250,000 in 1 year.

The key is to qualify for the partial exclusion if possible. "Change in employment" covers anyone who lives in the household. They don't even have to be an owner of the property. The "change in employment" must be the *primary* reason for the move. There's a "safe harbor" which assumes that it was the primary reason if your new job is at least 50 miles farther from the residence sold than where you used to work.

If you do not meet the "safe harbor," all is not lost. You will just have to prove (if you are audited) that it was the primary reason for the move based on the facts and circumstances of your case.

Health reasons include advanced age-related infirmities, the need to move to care for a family member, or to obtain or provide medical or personal care for a qualified individual suffering from a disease, illness, or injury.

Unforeseen circumstances is where the IRS really became consumer friendly. Safe harbors here include divorce, death, multiple births from the same pregnancy, and even a change in employment or self-employment status that results in your inability to pay the costs and living expenses of your household. So, if your income goes down, or even if your spouse or other co-owner's income goes down, you can qualify for a partial or even a full exclusion.

Other unforeseen circumstances include an unexpected pregnancy (PLR 143156-04, PLR 200652041, 12/29/06) where unmarried taxpayers ended their relationship, sale of the property due to undisclosed noise from a nearby airport (PLR 200702032), where the owner married a new spouse with adolescent children had bought a new house with additional bedrooms (PLR 200725018), and even where you have a second child born after the purchase (PLR 200745011) or marry someone with children requiring a larger house (PLR 200826024).

Unforseen circumstances even includes a response to a criminal attack and the need to provide for the healthcare of a qualified individual.

And, even if you don't meet one of these "safe harbors," you might still qualify on the basis of your specific facts and circumstances.

Divorced or seperated spouses each can exclude up to $250,000 if *either one* uses the home for the qualifying period. That helps the spouse who has left the home. But, to qualify, there must be a court decree giving use to the other spouse.

However, for homes sold after the signing of the American Jobs Creation Act of 2004, if the house sold was acquired via a like kind swap and the home was sold within 5 years of the exchange, *no* gain will be excluded.

The Housing and Economic Recovery Act of 2008 changed the rules again. Prior to the Act, if a second home became a principal residence, after 2 years

the owner could sell it and exclude up to $250,000 in gain from income—or up to $500,000 for couples filing jointly. Now, gain from the sale of a principal residence home will no longer be excluded from gross income for periods that the home was not used as the principal residence ("nonqualifying use"). This new income inclusion rule applies to home sales after December 31, 2008, and is based only on nonqualified use periods that begin on or after January 1, 2009. A period of absence (for example, vacations) generally counts as qualifying use if it occurs after the home was used as the principal residence.

The amount of gain allocated to periods of nonqualified use is the amount of gain multiplied by a fraction, the numerator of which is the aggregate period of nonqualified use during which the property was owned by the taxpayer and the denominator of which is the period the taxpayer owned the property. Remember the "nonqualified use" for this computation does not include any use prior to 2009.

Say you bought a house on January 1, 2010, for $400,000 and rent it for 2 years, taking $20,000 in depreciation. On January 1, 2012, you move in as your principal residence.

You move out on January 1, 2014, and sell it for $700,000 on January 1, 2015.

The rental period (2010–2011) is nonqualifying use. All use post-December 31, 2011, qualifies, including 2014 when you moved out. You owned the property a total of 5 years (2010, 2011, 2012, 2013, 2014). Forty percent of the gain (2 years out of 5 owned) or $128,000 is taxable. The $20,000 gain attributable to depreciation is recaptured at rates as high as 25 percent. Up to $192,000 in gain can still be excluded.

HOME OFFICES

Here's where, in my opinion, the IRS actually crossed the line. But it was in favor of the taxpayer, so I'm not going to complain. Let's assume you use 20 percent of your house as a home office. In the past, when you sold your house, 20 percent of the gain wouldn't qualify for the exclusion because that 20 percent wasn't used as a "residence." It was used exclusively as your office.

New Rule—The IRS doesn't care! Even if you used your home 90 percent for business, as a home office, you can now exclude as much as 100 percent of your gain, up to the $250,000/$500,000 limit!

You're only going to be subject to tax on the gain to the extent of depreciation taken on the building since May 7, 1997.

Wow! That means that, if you qualify, there's no reason not to claim a home office.

I guess Dorothy was right in *The Wizard of Oz* . . . "There's no place like home!"

32 Disabled Veteran Payments

Payments under the Department of Veterans Affairs Compensated Work Therapy program are tax-free. Disabled veterans who paid tax on these benefits should file an amended return if they qualify under the statute of limitations.

33 Exclusion of Income for Volunteer Firefighters and Emergency Medical Responders

For tax years beginning after 2007 and before 2011, gross income did not include:

- Rebates or reductions of property or income taxes provided by a state or local government for providing services as a member of a qualified emergency response organization (defined below). Any such rebate or reduction reduces the amount of the income tax deduction for such taxes.

- Qualified payments made by a state or local government for providing services as a member of a qualified emergency response organization. The exclusion is limited to $30 multiplied by the number of months the member performs such services. A charitable deduction for expenses paid by the member in connection with performing such services must be reduced by any payment excluded from income.

A qualified volunteer emergency response organization is any volunteer organization organized and operated to provide firefighting or emergency medical services for persons in a state or local jurisdiction and required by written agreement with that state or local jurisdiction to furnish such services.

34 Unemployment Benefits

For 2009 only, The American Recovery and Reinvestment Act of 2009 made the first $2,400 in unemployment benefits received, per recipient, tax-free.

35 Homeowner Security

Afraid of losing your job and putting your home at risk? The federal government has a new Homeowner Affordability and Stability Plan to help

struggling homeowners modify their mortgages in order to avoid foreclosure. Under the plan, you can modify your loan and, if timely payments are received on the modified loan, can qualify for "pay for performance success payments" reducing the balance on your mortgage loan. Those who qualify can get principal reductions of up to $1,000 per year for up to 5 years. Best of all, these payments are tax-free!

36 Reimbursed Costs to Parents of Children with Disabilities

If a school district cannot provide adequate education for a child with disabilities, federal law requires that it must reimburse the parents for the costs of special education. Since the district is required to provide free education, such reimbursements are not taxable to either the parents or the child.

37 Wrongful Conviction and Incarceration

Compensation received from a state for wrongful conviction or incarceration that caused sickness, injuries, and related damages is now tax free (CCA 201045023).

38 Restitution Payments

Restitution payments under the Trafficking Victims Protection Act of 2000 are excluded from income. This law requires that a defendant convicted of a human trafficking offense make payments to the victim to compensate for costs for medical services, physical and occupational therapy or rehabilitation, transportation, temporary housing, child care expenses, lost income, attorneys' fees and other costs, as well as other losses the victim suffers as a proximate result of the offense.

39 Frequent-Flyer Miles

The IRS will continue to pass on taxing these miles even if earned on a business trip and used personally. But the IRS takes a different position on premiums awarded for opening a bank account or toasters given as incentives in the past. Such "incentives," even if given in the form of miles, are taxable.

40 Hurricane Sandy

Gross income does not include any amount received as a "qualified disaster relief payment," even cash or benefits from an employer to an employee, state program aid, or relief from a charitable organization. Such payments cover reasonable medical, temporary housing, and transportation expenses.

41 Cancellation of Indebtedness

Up to $2 million in cancellation of indebtedness income on your principal residence escaped taxation through 2017.

42 Medicaid Payments for Foster Care of Related Individuals

The IRS determined that state Medicaid waiver payments made to a home care provider for the care of a handicapped individual who is related to the care provider can be excluded from income as qualified foster care payments (Notice 2014–7, 2014–4 IRB, January 21, 2014). In the past, the IRS has opposed allowing an exclusion for the care of a related individual.

Code Section 131 excludes from income payments under a foster care program for the care of a qualified foster care individual in the home. It also excludes difficulty-of-care payments for the personal care of a handicapped individual in foster care.

A state may obtain a waiver to use Medicaid for the cost of personal care in the home for individuals who would otherwise have to be institutionalized. Code Section 131 does not address whether payments under Medicaid waiver programs are qualified foster care payments. The IRS concluded that Medicaid waiver programs and state foster care programs (especially difficulty-of-care payments) share similar oversight and purposes, particularly to prevent the institutionalization of individuals with physical, mental, or emotional handicaps.

The IRS treats Medicaid waiver payments received on or after January 3, 2014, as difficulty-of-care payments that are excludable from gross income,

whether for a related or unrelated individual. You can also file an amended return for any year the statute of limitations has not run out.

43 ABLE Accounts

The Achieving a Better Life Experience (ABLE) Act of 2014 created a tax-favored savings account for people under the age of 26 who are blind or disabled. Up to the amount of the gift tax exclusion (currently $15,000 per year) can be put into an account similar to a Section 529 account. There is no tax until distributions are made and no tax on those distributions if used for transportation, education, job training, or housing expenses. Nonqualified distributions would be subject to tax on their earnings portion plus a 10 percent penalty. Account owners would remain eligible for Medicaid, and balances of $100,000 or less wouldn't affect SSI benefits. ABLE accounts, like Section 529 accounts will be set up by each state. You can live in one state and establish accounts in other states. The Tax Cuts and Jobs Act of 2017 now allows ABLE beneficiaries to contribute to their own accounts and Section 529 money can now be rolled over into an ABLE account.

Here's what ABLE accounts can pay for:

- **Education**—Tuition for preschool through post-secondary education, books, supplies, and educational materials related to such education, tutors, and special education services.

- **Housing**—Expenses for a primary residence, including rent, purchase of a primary residence or an interest in a primary residence, mortgage payments, home improvements and modifications, maintenance and repairs, real property taxes, and utility charges.

- **Transportation**—Expenses for transportation, including the use of mass transit, the purchase or modification of vehicles, and moving expenses.

- **Employment Support**—Expenses related to obtaining and maintaining employment, including job-related training, assistive technology, and personal assistance supports.

- **Health and Wellness**—Expenses for health and wellness, including premiums for health insurance; mental health, medical, vision, and dental expenses; habilitation and rehabilitation services: durable medical equipment; therapy; respite care; long-term services and supports; nutritional management; com-

munication services and devices; adaptive equipment; assistive technology and personal assistance.

- **Assistive Technology and Personal Support**—Expenses for assistive technology and personal support with respect to any of the above.

- **Miscellaneous Expenses**—Financial management and administrative services, legal fees, expenses for oversight, monitoring, and funeral and burial expenses.

F Schedule of Excludable Items

Accident and health insurance premiums paid by your employer

Accident and health proceeds (under insurance purchased by you or under an employee-supported plan) not attributable to a previous medical expense deduction

Annuities (cost excluded over life expectancies)

Awards for noncompetitive achievements (if contributed)

Bequests and devises

Carpool receipts for transportation of fellow employees

Child-support payments received

Contributions paid by your employer to accident and health plans and to sickness and disability funds under sick-benefit laws

Damages for physical personal injuries or sickness

Dependent care, employer-provided services

Disability payments other than for loss of wages

Disability payments under employer-financed accident and health plans

Endowment policy proceeds until cost is recovered

Fellowship and scholarship grants (limited)

Frequent flier miles

Gain on sale of personal residence

Gifts

Group term life insurance premiums—if coverage is $50,000 or less or if employees' contribution premiums exceed the cost of coverage over $50,000

Health insurance proceeds not attributable to medical expense deductions in prior years

Inheritances

Interest on bonds of the state, city, or other political subdivision

Life insurance proceeds paid on the death of the insured under the terms of the contract, unless paid to a transferee

Medical care payments under employer-financed accident and health plans
Merchandise distributed to employees on holidays
Nobel Prize, Pulitzer Prize, and similar awards (if contributed)
Principal residences—up to $500,000
Qualified State Tuition (§529) Plans
Railroad passes to employees and their families
Restitution payments
Sickness and injury benefits equivalent to workers' compensation
Social Security and disability benefits (limited)
Supper money paid by employer
Tuition paid by employer (limited)
Unemployment benefits up to $2,400 for 2009 only
Viatical payments
Welfare payments

Credits— Dollar-for-Dollar Tax Reductions

"Taxing is an easy business."

EDMUND BURKE
Thoughts on the Cause of the Present Discontent
1770

"It will be of little avail to the people that the laws are made by men of their own choice if the laws be so voluminous that they cannot be read, or so incoherent that they cannot be understood."

The Federalist Papers

"Thousands of pages of pet rocks that have nothing to do with the national interest."

Former SENATOR SAM NUNN of Georgia
on the tax code

A *credit* is a dollar-for-dollar reduction in your tax; it is the best kind of expense to have. If you are in the 24 percent tax bracket, a deduction of $100 saves you $24.00 in tax, but a credit of $100 saves you $100 in tax. A credit, therefore, is a payment that counts in full as an offset to your tax liability. Because every dollar of credit is really an additional dollar in your pocket, it is imperative that you recognize those situations where credits are available and that you always claim them on your tax return. A lost or forgotten credit is money thrown away in tax dollars.

There are several areas in which potential credits are available. I shall examine each in turn and discuss the ways you can best take advantage of them. But first I want to detail two significant cash-saving techniques: estimating taxes and withholding exemptions.

A Estimated Tax and Withholding Exemptions

Significant savings can be realized by minimizing the amount of estimated tax payments or of taxes withheld from your income before they are actually due. You must pay estimated tax if your estimated total tax liability is more than $1,000 and you meet certain conditions (see below), but you still can minimize these payments. You should pay as little estimated tax as possible and therefore have the use and availability of these tax funds for as long as legally possible.

You need to pay estimated tax if your estimated net tax liability is more than $1,000.

Estimated tax normally is paid in quarterly installments. You need *not file* a declaration of estimated tax after 1982 but payments must still be made. There is a penalty, which cannot be deducted as interest, of about 5 percent (this rate changes every 3 months) per year for underpaying the estimated tax—unless the total of all payments ("including withholding") made by the due date of each quarter is at least as much as the smallest of the following figures:

- The amount that you would have paid if the estimated tax were the same as the previous year's tax liability, provided the preceding taxable year was a year of 12 months and you filed a return.

- The amount you would have paid if the estimated tax were 90 percent of the tax on your income up to the month in which the installment date falls. For this purpose, the income is *annualized* (computed at an annual rate), based upon taxable income before exemptions, if deductions are itemized, and the alternative minimum tax if applicable.

- If you retired after you became age 62, or are disabled, for that year, or the preceding year, no penalty will be imposed if the underpayment is due to "reasonable cause" and not "willful neglect."

The first exception is most advantageous when your current year's income is greater than that of the prior year. The last exception is most useful if the greater part of income is received in the later part of the year. In all cases the objective is to pay no more now than is required. Remember, while you may have to pay the tax on April 15, you will have had the use of the money and the interest earned on it during that interim period.

The rules were modified for those with an adjusted gross income in excess of $150,000 when the prior year's estimated tax safe harbor was changed to 100 percent for 1998, 105 percent for 1999, 108.6 percent for 2000, 110 percent for 2001, 112 percent for 2002, and 110 percent for 2003 through 2018.

For 2009 only, the safe harbor was reduced to 90 percent if

a) Your 2008 adjusted gross income was less than $500,000, and

b) More than 50 percent of your 2008 gross income was from a small business with an average of fewer than 500 employees during that year.

Anyone with income from a farming or fishing business may be able to avoid making any estimated tax payments by filing their 2018 return and paying the entire tax due on or before March 1, 2019. This rule generally applies if farming or fishing income was at least two-thirds of the total gross income in either 2018 or the preceding tax year.

This same pay-as-you-go aspect of the federal income tax system requires your employers to withhold income tax on compensation (salaries, wages, tips) paid to you as their employee. The amount of tax withheld by your employer depends upon the amount of salary or wages paid to you and the information you furnish on the W-4 form (the Employee's Withholding Allowance Certificate) that you file with your employer. If you had no income tax liability for the past year and expect to have no liability for the current year, you may claim exemption from withholding of income tax. If you are exempt, your employer will not withhold federal income tax from your wages. To claim exemption from withholding, you still must give your employer a completed W-4 form. On it you need to write "exempt" and no withholding will be taken from your wages.

The money-saving technique recommended here is the same as that with the estimated tax. The objective is to minimize the amount of withholding taken out of each paycheck so that you will have the use and interest on the money until the final tax payment is due. For 2018 returns, there is no penalty on underwithholding as long as the total amount withheld for the year is equal to either 90 percent of your final tax liability or 100/110 percent of your last year's tax liability, whichever is smaller.

Unfortunately, most Americans do not underwithhold; they actually *overwithhold*. While the Internal Revenue Service eventually returns all excess funds, the taxpayer loses the interest that the money would have generated during the time that it is in the hands of the government. This is no insignificant loss, especially when one considers that the average 2017 overwithholding was $2,895 per refund (2018 is estimated to be $2,840). That's a lot of interest-free money!

How then can you eliminate overwithholding—even better, how can you begin underwithholding? The first step is to get a W-4 form from your employer and see how many allowances you are currently claiming. Each allowance that you claim will reduce the amount that is withheld from your income.

Allowances are available for the following:

- You got an automatic allowance for each exemption you could have claimed on your tax return—for yourself, your spouse, and your dependents. With the 2018 elimination of the allowances of the exemption deduction, this will go away.

- You get a special withholding allowance if you are single and have only one employer, or if you are married and have only one employer and your spouse is not employed.

- You get additional withholding allowances for the estimated tax credits you expect to take. If you expect to take the earned income credit, credit for child and dependent care expenses, or credit for the elderly, these credits may lower your tax and therefore make you eligible for additional allowances.

- You get additional withholding allowances for employee business expenses, moving expenses, and if you qualify for the additional standard deduction for the aged or the blind.

- You get additional withholding allowances for estimated net losses from your business or profession, from capital losses, from losses on rental property, and from losses from farming expenses.

- You can get a special withholding allowance for potential contributions to an IRA.

- You can get additional withholding allowances if you expect to itemize your deductions and/or pay alimony during the year. (Section 3402 [F])

You can use creative accounting especially in these last areas. The key is expected, not actual, deductions, contributions, and losses. Additional allowances can always be claimed under the *expectation* of making charitable contributions, incurring higher medical expenses, or borrowing money and incurring an increase in interest expense. Additional withholding allowances

are permitted for anticipated tax credits as well. But be careful not to go overboard: If your total withholdings equal 100/110 percent of last year's taxes or 90 percent of this year's taxes, you are immune to any penalties or interest (see page 130). Under Reg. Sec. 31. 3420 (i)-2, employers must accede to an employee's request that withholding exemptions be increased. Note that as of 2005, if you have more than 10 withholding exemptions, your employer *no longer* must notify the IRS of the fact.

The advantages of reducing your withholdings can be significant. For example, if in 2018, one additional allowance claimed reduces the withholding taken from your salary by about $345.83 per month ($4,150 ÷ 12 = $345.83). That adds up to $4,150 a year. With five additional allowances, you have the use and interest on $20,750 every year.

You may file a new W-4 form at any time if you wish to change your withholding allowances for any reason. This gives you yet another opportunity for tax savings. Some sophisticated, tax-knowledgeable individuals significantly underwithhold on their income for the first 11 months of the year, file amended W-4 forms, and then significantly overwithhold in the final taxable month. A cooperative employer may even withhold your full final month's wages so that your total yearly withholding meets the 90 percent or 100 percent tests detailed above and you can avoid the penalty for underwithholding. In the meantime, you have had the use of and interest on the underwithheld amount. Sadly, the Internal Revenue Service does not pay any interest on any amount overwithheld. In effect, overwithholding is nothing more than granting an interest-free loan to the Internal Revenue Service. Better that the interest is in your pocket.

B Credits

The remainder of this chapter discusses specific credits that can be taken to reduce your taxes due. Please take advantage of them.

44 The Earned Income Credit (Sec. 32)

Certain eligible low-income workers are entitled to claim a refundable credit on their income tax returns. The amount of the credit an eligible individual may claim depends upon whether the individual has one, more than one, or no qualifying children and is determined by multiplying the credit rate by the taxpayer's earned income up to an earned income amount. The maximum amount of the credit is the product of the credit

rate and the earned income amount. For taxpayers with earned income (or adjusted gross income [AGI], if greater) in excess of the beginning of the phaseout range, the maximum credit amount is reduced by the phase-out rate multiplied by the amount of earned income (or AGI, if greater) in excess of the beginning of the phase-out range. For taxpayers with earned income (or AGI, if greater) in excess of the end of the phase-out range, no credit is allowed.

The parameters for the credit depend upon the number of qualifying children the individual claims. For 2018, the joint return parameters are given in the following table:

	Three or More Qualifying Children	Two Qualifying Children	One Qualifying Child	No Qualifying Children
Credit rate (in percent)	45.00	40.00	34.00	7.65
Earned income amount	$14,290	$14,290	$10,180	$6,780
Maximum credit	$6,431	$5,716	$3,461	$519
Phase-out begins*	$24,350	$24,350	$24,350	$14,170
Phase-out rate (in percent)	21.06	21.06	15.98	7.65
Phase-out ends*	$54,884	$51,492	$46,010	$20,950

*Married filing jointly.

For 2018, the refundable credit for families with three or more children is 45 percent of $14,290, for a maximum of $6,431.

For years after 2001, the credit rates and the phase-out rates will be the same as in the preceding table. The earned income amount and the beginning of the phase-out range are indexed for inflation; because the end of the phaseout range depends on those amounts as well as the phase-out rate and the credit rate, the end of the phase-out range will also increase if there is inflation.

In order to claim the credit, an individual must either have a qualifying child or meet other requirements. A qualifying child must meet a relationship test, an age test, an identification test, and a residence test. In order to claim the credit without a qualifying child, an individual must not be a dependent and must be over age 24 and under age 65.

To satisfy the identification test, individuals must include on their tax return the name and age of each qualifying child. Individuals must also provide a taxpayer identification number (TIN) for all qualifying children. An individual's TIN is generally that individual's Social Security number.

The Personal Responsibility and Work Opportunity Reconciliation Act of 1996 amended the above rules.

Individuals are not eligible for the credit if they do not include their taxpayer identification number and their spouse's taxpayer identification number on their tax return. If an individual fails to provide a correct taxpayer identification number, such an omission will be treated as a mathematical or clerical error under the new law and the taxpayer must be given an explanation of the asserted error and a period of 60 days to request that the IRS abate its assessment.

A second change relates to the disqualified income test for the earned income credit itself. Under prior law, an individual would not be eligible for the earned income credit if the aggregate amount of "disqualified income" of that taxpayer for the taxable year exceeded $2,350. This threshold was not indexed. Disqualified income was the sum of:

1. Interest (taxable and tax exempt)

2. Dividends

3. Net rent and royalty income

Under the new law, the following items are added to the definition of disqualified income: Capital gain net income and net passive income that is not self-employment income.

Moreover, the disqualified investment income threshold above which an individual is not eligible for the credit was reduced from $2,350 to $2,200 and that threshold is indexed for inflation after 1996 ($3,500 for 2018).

In addition, the 1996 law modified the definition of adjusted gross income used for phasing out the earned income credit by disregarding certain losses. The losses disregarded are:

1. Net capital losses

2. Net losses from trusts and estates

3. Net losses from nonbusiness rents and royalties

4. 50 percent of the net losses from businesses, computed separately with respect to sole proprietorships (other than in farming), sole proprietorships in farming, and other businesses.

For purposes of (4) above, amounts attributable to a business that consist of the performance of services by the taxpayer as an employee are not taken into account.

The Tax Relief Act of 1997 made several modifications to the earned income credit rule. It added compliance provisions, denied eligibility for prior acts of recklessness, required recertification where the credit was denied in the past, and created a due diligence requirement for paid preparers.

For the purpose of the EIC phase-out, you must now include in adjusted gross income any nontaxable distribution of IRAs, pensions, annuities, and tax-exempt interest, and an addback of 75 percent of business losses. However, the 1997 law provides that workfare payments do *not* qualify as earned income for purposes of the earned income credit.

The Internal Revenue Service (IRS) is required to provide notice to taxpayers with qualifying children who receive a refund on account of the EITC that the credit may be available on an advance payment basis. To prevent taxpayers from incurring an unexpectedly large tax liability due to receipt of the EITC on an advance payment basis, the amount of advance payment allowable in a taxable year is limited to 60 percent of the maximum credit available to a taxpayer with one qualifying child.

The earned income credit represents dollars in your pocket, but it must be claimed to be received. In effect, it is a form of negative income tax—that is, a refundable credit for taxpayers who do not even have a tax liability.

45 Excess Social Security Tax

If you work for two or more employers during the tax year, too much Social Security tax may be withheld from your wages. You may claim this excess amount as a credit against your income tax. The tax consists of two parts: (1) old-age, survivor, and disability insurance (OASDI) and (2) Medicare hospital insurance (HI). For 2018 the rate on OASDI is 6.20 percent (12.4 percent if self-employed), and on HI it is 1.45 percent (2.90 percent if self-employed). Starting 2013, there is a 0.9 percent Medicare surtax for those with *earned* income of more than $200,000 ($250,000 on a joint return) on the excess over these amounts. For 2011 and 2012 only, the employee part of your OASDI tax was cut by 2 percent with potential savings of as much as $2,136 (2 percent of $106,800) and $2,202 (2 percent of $110,100).

Your Social Security tax obligation is computed each year by applying a fixed rate to your wages. There is, however, a maximum wage base* (which is subject to change) to which this tax may be applied. For example, in 2018, all wages in excess of $128,400 will not be subject to OASDI Social Security tax. There is no cap on

*The maximum in 1937 was $3,000, with a 1% rate, creating a maximum $30 tax!

HI. Therefore, if you work for two employers, earning $128,400 (maximum projected to go to $132,300 for 2019) from each, both employers will take the maximum OASDI (6.2 percent × $128,400, or $7,960) from your wages. But because you are only liable for a maximum payment of $7,960, you can have a credit against your income tax for the additional $7,960 subtracted from your wages. This is money you should get back. Even if you owe no taxes, excess Social Security payments will be refunded to you.

46 The Child and Dependent Care Credit

Congress has attempted to ease the tax burden of those citizens who must pay for dependent care while earning a living by allowing a child care credit. If, in order to work, you incur expenses in connection with the care of certain dependents, you are permitted a credit for those expenses. This credit, unlike the earned income credit or excess Social Security payments, cannot reduce your tax liability below zero—that is, it is not refundable.

To qualify for this credit:

1. Your child and dependent care expenses must be incurred to allow you to work, full-time or part-time, whether for others or in your own business or partnership. "Work" even includes actively looking for work. Furthermore, your spouse is considered to have worked if he or she:

 a) was a full-time student for five months during the tax year; *or*

 b) is physically or mentally unable to function without supervision or aid.

 This rule applies to only one spouse for any one month.

2. You must have income from work during the year. Unpaid volunteer work or work for a nominal salary does not qualify.

3. You must maintain a home in which you and one or more qualifying persons live. This means that you (and your spouse, if you are married) pay more than half the cost of maintaining your principal residence. If you are married, you and your spouse must live together.

Upkeep expenses normally include property taxes, mortgage interest, rent, utility charges, home repairs, insurance on the home, and food costs. Excluded from upkeep are payments for clothing, education, medical treatment, vacations, life insurance, transportation, mortgage principal, or the purchase, improvement, or replacement of property. For example, the cost of replacing a water heater is not considered upkeep, but the cost of repairing a water heater can be included.

A qualifying person is:

a) Your qualifying child who is your dependent and who was under age 13 when the care was provided,

b) Your spouse who was not physically or mentally able to care for himself or herself and lived with you for more than half the year, or

c) A person who was not physically or mentally able to care for himself or herself, lived with you for more than half the year, and either:

 i. Was your dependent, or

 ii. Would have been your dependent except that:

 (*a*) He or she received gross income of $4,150 or more,

 (*b*) He or she filed a joint return, or

 (*c*) You, or your spouse if filing jointly, could be claimed as a dependent on someone else's 2018 return.

Dependent defined. A dependent is a person, other than you or your spouse, for whom you could have claimed an exemption. To be your dependent, a person must be your qualifying child (or your qualifying relative).

Qualifying child defined. To be your qualifying child, a child must live with you for more than half the year and meet other requirements.

The physical or mental incapacity must be disabling: People who are not able to dress, clean, or feed themselves because of physical or mental problems or who require constant attention to prevent them from injuring themselves or others qualify.

Qualification is determined on a daily basis when the disability lasts for less than a calendar month. For example, if a dependent or spouse for whom you paid work-related expenses no longer qualifies on September 16, you may include in your computation all work-related expenses through September 15.

CHILD CARE CREDITS FOR CHILDREN OF DIVORCED OR SEPARATED PARENTS

Expenses for the care of children of divorced or separated parents are also allowed for the child care credit under certain conditions. If you are divorced, legally separated under a decree of divorce or separate maintenance, or separated under a written separation agreement, and you have custody of your child for a longer time during the calendar year than the other parent, your child qualifies if certain conditions are met.

To qualify, *all* these criteria must be met:

1. The child must be under age 13 or unable to care for himself or herself.

2. The child must be in the custody of one or both of the parents for more than half the year.

3. One or both of the parents must provide more than half of the child's support during the year.

4. You must normally file a joint return if you are married. If you are legally separated from your spouse under a decree of divorce or separate maintenance, you are not considered married and can file for the child care credit. The credit may be claimed on a separate return. If you are still married and want to file a separate return, you will not be considered married if:

 a) your home is the home of a qualifying person for more than half the tax year; *and*

 b) you pay more than half the cost of keeping up your home for the tax year; *and*

 c) your spouse does not live in your home for the last 6 months of the year.

5. You must pay someone other than your spouse or a person you can claim as a dependent for the child's care. You may count payments made to relatives who are not your dependents, even if they live in your home.

Only work-related expenses qualify for the child or dependent care credit, and your expenses must be for the well-being and protection of a qualifying person. Expenses are considered to be work-related if they allow you (and your spouse, if married) to work, not if you incur them while you are working. However, whether the purpose of the expenses is to allow you to work depends upon the facts. Work-related expenses may include the following:

HOME EXPENSES

This covers the cost of ordinary services done in and around your home that are necessary to maintain the well-being and protection of a qualifying person. The services of a housekeeper, maid, or cook usually are considered necessary to run your home if performed at least partly for the benefit of the qualifying person. Payments for the services of a chauffeur or gardener are not included. The expense of food, clothing, education, or entertainment for the qualifying person is not included.

CHILD CARE EXPENSES

These expenses are not limited to services performed in your home. You may include expenses for nursery school or day care for preschool children, or even summer camp (*ZOLTAN* 79 T.C. 1982) if these expenses allow you to work. The Revenue Act of 1987 excludes overnight camp expenses, but summer day camp expenses are still allowable. That's even for special camps for the study of computer science, theater, or soccer and camps that improve reading or study skills. Amounts you pay for food, clothing, or schooling are not child care expenses. However, if a nursery school or day care center provides these as part of its service, the entire cost is treated as child care. Schooling in the first grade or higher is not treated as part of child care. Neither is the cost of getting your child to and from the center, whether by bus, subway, taxi, or private car, unless the cost is included in the tuition and is not billed separately (IRS Letter Ruling 8303037). Half-day, but not full-day, kindergarten can qualify.

DISABLED SPOUSE OR DEPENDENT CARE EXPENSES

Expenditures for out-of-home, noninstitutional care of a disabled spouse or dependent who regularly spends at least 8 hours a day in your home are eligible for the credit. Under prior law, services outside the home qualified only if they involved the care of a child under 13 years of age.

Meals and lodging provided for housekeepers may be added to your child care expenses, and also any added expenses for lodging your housekeeper. For example, if you have moved to an apartment with an extra bedroom for a housekeeper, you may include the added rent and utility expenses for this bedroom.

The *child care credit*, whether for married, divorced, or separated parents, provides a significant opportunity for effective tax planning. For example, if you have an elderly parent whom you wish to help support, money that you give for food may result in a gift tax liability for you. But if you have this parent babysit for your children so that you can work, not only will you avoid a potential gift tax penalty on the money you pay that parent, but you will also receive an income tax credit. Furthermore, if that parent eats at your home while providing child care services, you will receive a tax credit for the value of the food eaten—and the value of that food will *not* be taxable income to your parent.

For example, assume you have your mother provide child care to your son so that you may work, and your mother eats $100 worth of food per week. Even if you pay her nothing in dollars, her income tax is unaffected, your gift tax is unaffected, but your income tax will be reduced by a $20–$35 credit for each week she qualifies.

There are limits on the amount of work-related expenses you may use to figure your credit. These are the earned income limit and the dollar limit.

1. *The earned income limit.* If you are single at the end of your tax year, the amount of work-related expenses that you may use to figure your credit may not be more than your earned income for the tax year. If you are married at the end of your tax year, the amount of work-related expenses may not be more than your earned income or the earned income of your spouse, whichever is *less.*

 If you are married and, for any month, your spouse is either a full-time student or not able to provide self-maintenance, your spouse is considered to have an earned income of $200 a month (if there is one qualifying person in your home) or $400 a month (if there are two or more qualifying persons in your home). That disabled spouse is counted as a qualifying person, along with a dependent child. This rule applies to only one spouse for any one month.

 Earned income is all wages, salaries, tips, other employee compensation, fees for professional services, and net earnings from self-employment. It is reduced by any net loss in earnings from self-employment. It does not include pensions, annuities, or payments for your services that were distributions of earnings and profits, other than a reasonable amount for your work for a corporation. In addition, it does not include amounts received under accident or health plans that are not included in your gross income.

2. *The dollar limit.* Prior to 2003, the child and dependent care credit was computed on a three-tier basis. First, if you had an adjusted gross income of $10,000 or less, you were entitled to a credit equal to 30 percent of your work-related expenses. Then, the credit was reduced by one percentage point for each $2,000 of adjusted gross income (or fraction thereof) above $10,000. Finally, if you had an adjusted gross income of over $28,000, the credit was equal to 20 percent of the work-related expenses you paid during your tax year.

The maximum amount of work-related expenses to which you could apply the credit was $2,400 for one qualifying child or dependent, or $4,800 if more than one was involved. Thus, the maximum credit for one qualifying individual ranged from $720, if your income was below $10,000 ($2,400 × .30), to $480 if your income exceeded $28,000 ($2,400 × .20). Similarly, the maximum credit for two or more qualified individuals ranged from $1,440 to $960.

These figures were yearly limits. You used the $2,400 limit if you had one qualifying person at *any time* during the year. You used $4,800 if you had more than one at *any time* during the year. It was not based on the length of time during the year that your dependent qualified. However, include only the expenses you had for a qualifying person *during the time the person is qualified*. For example, if your child turned 13 in April, you were eligible for the entire $2,400 limit, but only the expenses you had before your child's 13th birthday can be used. If you had expenses of less than $2,400 during that time, only the smaller amount could be used.

The Family Support Act of 1988 amended previous rules. For tax years beginning after 1988, a child of the taxpayer is a qualified individual only if the child is under age 13 (rather than 15, as under prior law). Moreover, the dollar amount of expenses eligible for the credit is reduced, dollar for dollar, by the amount of expenses excludable under a dependent care assistance program provided by an employer. In addition, effective for returns whose due date is after 1989, the taxpayer must identify with name, address, and taxpayer identification number (Social Security number) each person or each institution providing the child care.

Effective January 1, 2003, the Tax Relief Act of 2001 increased the maximum credit to 35 percent and the reduction in the credit amount (phasedown) will begin at adjusted gross income of $15,000 rather than $10,000. The *minimum* 20 percent credit was applied to taxpayers with adjusted gross incomes over $43,000.

The amount of qualified expenses is increased from $2,400 to $3,000 per child. With two children, you can then get a maximum credit of $6,000 × 35 percent, or $2,100, or a minimum credit of $6,000 × 20 percent, or $1,200.

The following example shows you how the child care credit is computed. Assume you are a widow and that you maintain a home for yourself and your two preschool children, whom you claim as dependents. You had an earned income of $44,000 for the year and you incurred work-related expenses of $4,000 (for a housekeeper to care for your children in your home) and $2,200 (for child care at a nursery school).

Your credit is computed as follows:

1. In-home child care expenses	$4,000
2. Plus outside child care expenses	+2,200
3. Total work-related expenses	$6,200
4. Maximum allowable expenses for two qualifying children	6,000
5. Multiply by credit rate	× .20
6. Amount of credit	$1,200

Alternatively, assume you are married and have two children. You have an earned income of $44,000, and your spouse was a full-time student from January 2 through May 31 only. If you paid a housekeeper $450 a month from January 2 to May 31 (a total of $2,250) to look after your children, prepare meals, and do housework as time allowed, your credit was figured in this way:

1. Total work-related expenses $ 2,250
2. Your earned income 44,000
3. Income considered earned by
 your spouse ($500*/month for 5 months) ($2,500 limited to $2,250)
4. Multiply by credit rate × .20
5. Allowable credit $ 450

Remember: Work-related expenses cannot exceed either the $3,000 (for one child)/$6,000 (for two or more) limit *or* your own or your spouse's earned income, and you must use the smaller earned income in your computations.

The 2001 law also created, as of January 1, 2002, a credit to employers of 25 percent of qualified expenses for employee child care and 10 percent for qualified expenses for child care resources and referral services. The maximum annual credit is capped at $150,000.

47 Credit for the Elderly or Permanently and Totally Disabled

To compensate for tax exclusions offered to recipients of Social Security benefits, this tax credit is offered to those taxpayers who are not covered by Social Security and spend their retirement years living off past savings and investments. In this way, the credit attempts to help place all elderly taxpayers on a par.

Prior law provided that individuals aged 65 or over, or under 65 with income from a public retirement system, were eligible for a credit equal to 15 percent of the base amount. *Beginning in 1984,* the law increased the base amounts and limits the credit for those under age 65 to individuals with a permanent and total disability who received disability income from public or private employers on account of that disability. You are considered permanently and totally disabled if (1) you are not able to engage in any "substantial gainful activity" because of your

*$250 for one child.

physical or mental condition, and (2) your condition has lasted or can be expected to last continuously for 12 months or more, or lead to your death.

"Substantial gainful activity" usually refers to paid work that requires the performance of significant duties over a reasonable period of time. Nonproductive make-work activities will not be treated as "substantial gainful activity." However, if you work full-time or part-time at your employer's convenience for at least the minimum wage, you will usually be treated as engaging in substantial gainful activity. If you do a type of work as a volunteer that is generally done for pay, you may be considered to have a gainful activity even though you receive no "gain."

Disability income is the total taxable amount you are paid under your employer's accident or health plan or pension plan for the time you are absent from work because of your disability and that is included in your income as wages (or payments in lieu of wages). For purposes of the credit, disability income does not include any amount you receive from your employer's pension plan after you reach your employer's mandatory retirement age.

If you are claiming disability, you must have a physician certify that you are permanently and totally disabled and you must attach that certification to your return. If the certification states your condition will not improve, you will not have to file certifications in subsequent years. The change in base amounts is as follows:

Description	Prior Law	Current Law
Married with one spouse eligible or unmarried	$2,500	$5,000
Married, joint return, both spouses eligible	$3,750	$7,500
Married, filing separately	$1,875	$3,750

These base amounts *are reduced*, however, by the following:

- Pensions or annuities received under Social Security, Railroad Retirement, and certain other pensions, disability benefits received, and annuities otherwise excluded from gross income; *and*

- One-half of adjusted gross income over:
 $ 7,500—single return
 $10,000—married, joint return
 $ 5,000—married, separate return

In the case of an individual under age 65, the base amount is limited in any event to the amount of his or her disability income. Note that under the Social Security Amendments in 1983, for a married disabled individual filing jointly, one spouse eligible, all disability income will be taxable and no tax credit will be available if adjusted gross income is $20,000 or more.

There are few tax-planning strategies that can be employed with the retirement income credit except to note its existence and the fact that it must be claimed to be received. Any failure to recognize or to claim it represents little more than cutting a hole in your wallet and allowing your tax dollars to float freely in the wind.

C Special Credits

In the past, Congress provided a number of tax incentives to encourage employment or investment in research.

48 Work Opportunity Credit (Formerly Targeted Jobs Tax Credit) (Sec. 51)

The *targeted jobs tax credit* was available to employers on an elective basis for hiring individuals from several targeted groups. The targeted groups consist of individuals who are either recipients of payments under means-tested transfer programs, economically disadvantaged, or disabled. Included are "high-risk" youths, qualified veterans, and families receiving food stamps, and, as of 2009, unemployed veterans and disconnected youth—those between the ages of 16 and 25 who have not worked or gone to school in the past 6 months.

The credit generally was equal to 40 percent of up to $6,000 of qualified first-year wages paid to a member of a targeted group.

The Small Business Job Protection Act of 1996 amended the above rules.

It replaced the *targeted jobs credit* with a "work opportunity tax credit." The new credit was available on an elective basis for employers hiring individuals from one or more of nine targeted groups. The credit generally was equal to 40 percent of qualified first-year wages up to $6,000 ($12,000 for qualified veterans). The maximum credit was $2,400. For employees who work at least

120 but less than 400 hours, the credit falls to 25 percent of the first $6,000, or a maximum of $1,500.

No credit was allowed for wages paid unless the eligible individual was employed by the employer for at least 120 hours in the first year of employment. The credit applied to employees who started work after September 30, 1996 and before January 1, 2008. The credit did not apply to wages paid to a relative, dependent, or prior employee.

The Work Opportunity Tax Credit (WOTC) was extend through 2011. While the WOTC sunset at the end of 2011, Congress passed a new Returning Heroes Tax Credit and Wounded Warriors Tax Credit for the hiring of military veterans after November 21, 2011 through December 31, 2012. The credit was extended once by the Tax Relief Act of 2012 through December 31, 2013 and again in 2013 through 2014. The credit may be as much as $9,600 per qualified veteran.

The Tax Relief and Health Care Act of 2006 combined this credit with the Welfare to Work Credit below for employees who start work after December 31, 2006.

The Protecting Americans from Tax Hikes Act of 2015 (the PATH Act) retroactively allows eligible employers to claim the Work Opportunity Tax Credit (WOTC) for all targeted group employee categories that were in effect prior to the enactment of the PATH Act, if the individual began or begins work for the employer after December 31, 2014, and before January 1, 2020. For tax-exempt employers, the PATH Act retroactively allows them to claim the WOTC for qualified veterans who begin work for the employer after December 31, 2014, and before January 1, 2020. The PATH Act also added a new targeted group category to include qualified long-term unemployment recipients.

NEW TARGETED GROUP—QUALIFIED LONG-TERM UNEMPLOYMENT RECIPIENT (HIRED ON OR AFTER JANUARY 1, 2016)

The PATH Act expanded the targeted groups of individuals to include qualified long-term unemployment recipients. A qualified long-term unemployment recipient is any individual who on the day before the individual begins work for the employer, or, if earlier, the day the individual completes Form 8850, Pre-Screening Notice and Certification Request for the Work Opportunity Credit, is in a period of unemployment that is (i) not less than 27 weeks and (ii) includes a period (which may be less than 27 weeks) in which the individual received unemployment compensation under state or federal law.

The 10 categories of WOTC-eligible workers now include:

- Qualified IV-A Temporary Assistance for Needy Families (TANF) recipients
- Unemployed veterans, including disabled veterans
- Ex-felons
- Designated community residents living in Empowerment Zones or Rural Renewal Counties
- Vocational rehabilitation referrals
- Summer youth employees living in Empowerment Zones
- Food stamp (SNAP) recipients
- Supplemental Security Income (SSI) recipients
- Long-term family assistance recipients
- Qualified long-term unemployment recipients (for people who begin work after 2015).

Eligible businesses claim the WOTC on their income tax return. The credit is first figured on Form 5884 and then becomes a part of the general business credit claimed on Form 3800.

PRE-SCREENING AND CERTIFICATION

An employer must obtain certification that an individual is a member of the targeted group, before the employer may claim the credit. An eligible employer must file Form 8850, Pre-Screening Notice and Certification Request for the Work Opportunity Credit, with their respective state workforce agency within 28 days after the eligible worker begins work (see above).

Employers should contact their individual state workforce agency with any specific processing questions for Form 8850.

LIMITATIONS ON THE CREDITS

The credit is limited to the amount of the business income tax liability or Social Security tax owed.

A taxable business may apply the credit against its business income tax liability, and the normal carry-back and carry-forward rules apply. See the instructions for Form 3800, General Business Credit, for more details.

For qualified tax-exempt organizations, the credit is limited to the amount of employer Social Security tax owed on wages paid to all employees for the period the credit is claimed.

CLAIMING THE CREDIT

Qualified tax-exempt organizations will claim the credit on Form 5884-C, Work Opportunity Credit for Qualified Tax-Exempt Organizations Hiring Qualified Veterans, as a credit against the employer's share of Social Security tax. The credit will not affect the employer's Social Security tax liability reported on the organization's employment tax return.

TAXABLE EMPLOYERS

After the required certification is secured, taxable employers claim the tax credit as a general business credit on Form 3800 against their income tax by filing the following:

- Form 5884

- Form 3800

- Your business's related income tax return and instructions (i.e., Forms 1040, 1041, 1120, etc.)

TAX-EXEMPT EMPLOYERS

Qualified tax-exempt organizations described in IRC Section 501(c) and exempt from taxation under IRC Section 501(a), may claim the credit for qualified veterans who begin work on or after December 31, 2014, and before January 1, 2020.

After the required certification (Form 8850) is secured, tax-exempt employers claim the credit against the employer Social Security tax by separately filing Form 5884-C, Work Opportunity Credit for Qualified Tax-Exempt Organizations Hiring Qualified Veterans (PDF).

File Form 5884-C after filing the related employment tax return for the period that the credit is claimed. The IRS recommends that qualified tax-exempt employers do not reduce their required deposits in anticipation of any credit. The credit will not affect the employer's Social Security tax liability reported on the organization's employment tax return.

QUALIFIED VETERANS

A qualified veteran is a veteran certified as any of the following:

- A member of a family receiving assistance under the Supplemental Nutrition Assistance Program (SNAP) (food stamps) for at least 3 months during the first year of employment.

- Unemployed for a period totaling at least 4 weeks (whether or not consecutive) but less than 6 months in the one-year period prior to the date of hire.

- Unemployed for a period or periods totaling at least 6 months (whether or not consecutive) in the one-year period ending on the date of hire.

- Entitled to compensation for a service-connected disability and hired not more than one year after being discharged or released from active duty in the U.S. Armed Forces.

- Entitled to compensation for a service-connected disability and unemployed for a period totaling at least 6 months (whether or not consecutive) in the one-year period that ended on the date of hire.

See IRS Notice 2012-13 for more detailed information.

49 Welfare to Work Credit (Sec. 51)

This was a credit of 35 percent of the first $10,000 of eligible wages paid to recipients of long-term family assistance in the first year of employment and 50 percent of the first $10,000 of eligible wages paid in the second year. The maximum credit was $8,500 per qualified employee. This credit has been combined with the Work Opportunity Credit above. Use Form 5884, Work Opportunity Credit, to claim a credit for an employee who begins work for an employer after December 31, 2006.

50 Research Tax Credit (Sec. 41)

A research tax credit equal to 20 percent of the amount by which a taxpayer's qualified research expenditures for a taxable year exceeds its base amount for that year is allowed.

The 20 percent research tax credit also applied to the *excess* of (1) 100 percent of corporate cash expenditures (including grants or contributions)

paid for basic research conducted by universities (and certain nonprofit scientific research organizations) *over* (2) the sum of (a) the greater of two minimum basic research floors and (b) an amount reflecting any decrease in nonresearch giving to universities by the corporation as compared to such giving during a fixed base period, as adjusted for inflation. This separate credit computation was commonly referred to as "the university basic research credit."

Start-up businesses with gross receipts of less than $5 million may take the credit against payroll taxes.

51 Orphan Drug Tax Credit

Prior to January 1, 1995, a 50 percent nonrefundable tax credit was allowed for qualified clinical testing expenses incurred in testing of certain drugs for rare diseases or conditions generally referred to as "orphan drugs." The Small Business Job Protection Act of 1996 extended the orphan drug tax credit for 11 months, that is, for the period July 1, 1996, through May 31, 1997. The Tax Relief Act of 1997 extended it permanently.

52 Adoption Assistance

OLD LAW

Prior law did not provide a tax credit for adoption expenses nor did it provide an exclusion from gross income for employer-provided adoption assistance. The Federal Adoption Assistance Program provides financial assistance for the adoption of certain special needs children. Specifically, the program provides assistance for adoption expenses for those special needs children receiving federally assisted adoption assistance payments as well as special needs children in private and state funded programs. The maximum federal reimbursement is $1,000 per special needs child. Reimbursable expenses include those nonrecurring costs directly associated with the adoption process such as legal costs, social services review, and transportation costs.

The Small Business Job Protection Act of 1996 provided taxpayers with a maximum nonrefundable credit against income tax liability of $5,000 per child ($6,000 in the case of special needs adoptions) paid or

incurred by the taxpayer. Any unused adoption credit may be carried forward by the taxpayer for up to five years. Qualified adoption expenses are reasonable and necessary adoption fees, court costs, attorney's fees, and other expenses that are directly related to the legal adoption of an "eligible child."

In the case of an international adoption, the credit is not available unless the adoption is finalized. Credits for domestic adoptions are earned when the expenses are paid—even if the adoption failed. An "eligible child" is an individual (1) who has not attained age 18 as of the time of the adoption, or (2) who is physically or mentally incapable of caring for himself or herself. No credit is allowed for expenses incurred (1) in violation of state or federal law, (2) in carrying out any surrogate parenting arrangement, or (3) in connection with the adoption of a child of the taxpayer's spouse. The credit was phased out ratably for taxpayers with modified adjusted gross income a bove $75,000 and is fully phased out at $115,000 of modified adjusted gross income.

Note that the credit for non–special needs adoptions was not available for expenses paid or incurred after December 31, 2001. Moreover, special needs foreign adoptions were limited to a maximum credit of $5,000 (rather than $6,000) for qualified adoption expenses until December 31, 2001, at which time the credit for special needs foreign adoptions was also repealed. The credit for special needs domestic adoptions ($6,000) was permanent.

With respect to the exclusion from income, a maximum exclusion of $5,000 ($6,000 in the case of special needs adoptions) was available for specified certain adoption expenses provided by an employer. The limit was a per-child limit, not an annual limitation. The exclusion was phased out ratably for taxpayers with modified adjusted gross income above $75,000 and was fully phased out at $115,000 of modified adjusted gross income. No credit was allowed for adoption expenses paid or reimbursed under an adoption assistance program.

Note that the exclusion was not available for expenses paid or incurred after December 31, 2001, and that special needs foreign adoptions are limited to a maximum exclusion of $5,000 (rather than $6,000) for qualified adoption expenses.

CURRENT LAW

Effective as of January 1, 2002, the Tax Relief Act of 2001 modified the preceding rules.

The 2001 law permanently extended the adoption credit for children other than special needs children. The maximum credit was increased to $10,000* per eligible child, including special needs children. A $10,000* credit is provided in the year a special needs adoption is finalized, whether you have qualified adoption expenses or not. The beginning point of the income phaseout range was increased to $150,000† of modified adjusted gross income. The adoption credit is allowed against the alternative minimum tax permanently. The credit was refundable for 2010 and 2011.

The 2001 law permanently extended the exclusion from income for employer-provided adoption assistance. The maximum exclusion was increased to $10,000* per eligible child, including special needs children. In the case of a special needs adoption, the exclusion is provided, whether you have qualified adoption expenses or not. The beginning point of the income phase-out range was increased to $150,000† of modified adjusted gross income. The 2001 law generally is effective for taxable years beginning after December 31, 2001. The provisions that extend the tax credit and exclusion from income for special needs adoptions, whether you have qualified adoption expenses or not, are effective for taxable years beginning after December 31, 2002.

53 Hope Scholarship Credit

The Tax Relief Act of 1997 created this new *per-child* credit for qualified tuition and fees paid during the *first 2* years of post-secondary or certificate education after 1997. Room and board did not qualify.

The credit was equal to:

100% of the first $1,200 in tuition and fees	$1,200
50% of the next $1,200 in tuition and fees	600
for a maximum Hope Credit of	$1,800

*$13,810 for 2018
†$207,140–$247,140 for 2018.

This credit was phased out for 2012 between adjusted gross income of $80,000–$90,000 for singles and $160,000–$180,000 for joint returns. For all intents and purposes, this credit was replaced by the new American Opportunity Education tax credit for 2009 through 2017.

54 American Opportunity Tax Credit

The American Recovery and Reinvestment Act of 2009 and several extensions provide taxpayers with an "American Opportunity" tax credit of up to $2,500 of the cost of tuition and related expenses paid during the taxable year. You will receive a tax credit based on 100 percent of the first $2,000 of tuition and related expenses (including course materials and books) paid during the taxable year and 25 percent of the next $2,000 of tuition and related expenses paid during the taxable year. Forty percent of the credit will be refundable. This tax credit is subject to a phase-out for taxpayers with adjusted gross income of $80,000–$90,000 ($160,000–$180,000 for married couples filing jointly).

This credit is available for each of the four years of college. Graduate students are not eligible.

The credit can't be claimed against the following sources:

a) 529 plans

b) Tax-free scholarships

c) Pell grants

d) Coverdell education savings account (ESA)

e) Employer-provided education assistance

f) Military educational assistance

g) Any other tax-free educational assistance

Only one of these credits/deductions can be selected per student:

a) The $2,500 American Opportunity Education tax credit

b) The $2,000 Lifetime Learning tax credit

c) The $4,000 above-the-line deduction for education expenses

Since 40 percent of the credit is refundable, you can get as much as $1,000 from the IRS even if you have no tax liability.

The American Opportunity Education tax credit is the best of these three because it is a higher credit than the Lifetime Learning tax credit and a $4,000 deduction provides at most $1,480 in relief in the 37.0 percent bracket.

55 Lifetime Learning Credit

The Tax Relief Act of 1997 created this *per-family* credit for tuition and fees up to $5,000 ($10,000 after December 31, 2001) for undergraduate OR *graduate* level and professional degree courses paid after June 30, 1998. Room and board do not qualify.

The maximum credit is now 20 percent of up to $10,000 of qualified tuition and fees or $2,000. It is a per-family, not per-child (as is the Hope Scholarship/American Opportunity Credit)), credit. The 2018 phase-out is $57,000–$67,000 ($114,000–$134,000 for a joint return). As of 2016, you need a 1098 T form from the college to claim either the Lifetime Learning Credit or the American Opportunities Credit.

56 Child Tax Credit

Present law provides a $2,000 tax credit for each qualifying child under the age of 17. Your child becomes 17 on the anniversary of his or her date of birth (Rev. Rul. 2003-72). A qualifying child is one you claim as a dependent. The $2,000 credit may be partially refundable up to $1,400.

As of 2018, you get a $500 non-refundable credit for dependents who are not qualifying children—such as aged parents.

The 2018 credit is phased out on a joint return earning more than $400,000 and for singles earning more than $200,000. For every $1,000 or part thereof earned, the credit is reduced by $50. If you have only one qualifying child, for a joint return earning more than $439,000, the credit would have been eliminated completely.

The 2001 Tax Relief Act made the child credit refundable to the extent of 10 percent of your earned income in excess of $10,000 for calendar years 2001–2004. The percentage was increased to 15 percent for calendar years 2005 and thereafter. The $10,000 amount is indexed for inflation beginning in 2002 and was lowered to $8,500 by the Emergency Economic Stabilization

Act of 2008. Families with three or more children are allowed a refundable credit for the amount by which your Social Security taxes exceed your earned income credit (the present-law rule), if that amount is greater than the refundable credit based (before the law changed) on your earned income in excess of $12,050 for 2009. The American Recovery and Reinvestment Act of 2009 reduced the threshold to the excess over $3,000, reduced to $2,500 by the Tax Cuts and Jobs Act. The law provides that the refundable portion of the child credit does not constitute income and shall not be treated as resources for purposes of determining eligibility or the amount or nature of benefits or assistance under any federal program or any state or local program financed with federal funds. The credit is not refundable if you claim the foreign earned income exclusion.

The 2001 law provided that the refundable child tax credit will no longer be reduced by the amount of the alternative minimum tax. In addition, the 2001 law allows the child tax credit to the extent of the full amount of your regular income tax and alternative minimum tax.

57 Disability Credits

This credit was created in 1990 specifically for businesses with gross revenues of $1,000,000 or less, or 30 or fewer full-time employees. The credit is intended to cover Americans with Disabilities Act (ADA)–related business access costs. Anything that helps access or communication is covered, including:

- Provision of readers for customers or employees with visual disabilities

- Provision of sign language interpreters

- Purchase of adaptive equipment

- Production of accessible formats of printed materials (i.e., Braille, large print, audiotape, computer diskette)

- Removal of architectural barriers in facilities or vehicles (alterations must comply with applicable accessibility standards)

- Fees for consulting services (under certain circumstances)

- Provision for access to the Internet for those with disabilities

The credit can't be used for new construction, only for adapting existing facilities. The first $250 doesn't count.

The credit is 50 percent of eligible expenditures per year, worth a maximum expenditure of $10,250. Therefore, the maximum annual credit is $5,000.

58 Health Insurance Credit

On August 6, 2002, President Bush signed a trade bill that gave you a health insurance subsidy if you lost your job "as a result of shifts in imports or exports, or because . . . companies shift production overseas."

You got a 65 percent subsidy in the form of an advanceable, refundable tax credit to cover the costs of maintaining your health insurance.

59 Saver's Credit

In order to stimulate savings, Congress gives you a credit of up to 50 percent on the first $2,000 you sock away in a traditional or Roth IRA, 401(k), or other qualified retirement plan. So if you contribute $2,000, you'll get a $1,000 credit. That's in addition to the minimum $200 that the $2,000 deduction will save you in taxes (at the 10 percent bracket).

Unfortunately, to get the *50 percent credit*, your adjusted gross income can't be more than $19,000. If you then subtract a $12,000 standard deduction, your taxable income is capped at $7,000. The maximum *tax* on that is $700, not the $1,000 promised by Congress.

On a joint return, the numbers limit the credit to $1,400, rather than the promised $2,000*. It's not available for those under age 18, full-time students, or dependents claimed on another tax return.

The saver's credit rate is based on your adjusted gross income for the taxable year for which the credit is claimed, as follows:

*$38,000 − 24,000 = $14,000 × 10% = $1,400

Adjusted Gross Income

Married Filing Jointly	Head of Household	All Other Filers	Credit
$0–$38,000	$0–$28,500	$0–$19,000	50% of contribution
$38,001– $41,000	$28,501– $30,750	$19,001– $20,500	20% of contribution
$41,001– $63,000	$30,751– $47,250	$20,501– $31,500	10% of contribution
Over $63,000	Over $47,250	Over $31,500	Credit not available

Want to push the envelope? Make a $4,000 joint return contribution December 31 into a Roth IRA for 2018 and then take a distribution in January for 2019. Only the income during that period would be taxed and you can get a credit as much as $2,000. But you can only do this once.

Additional information can be obtained toll-free from the IRS at 877-829-5500.

60 Small Employer Credit

The Tax Relief Act of 2001 created a new, nonrefundable income tax credit if you have a small business that adopts a defined benefit or defined contribution plan [including a 401(k) plan], a SIMPLE plan, or a SEP. The credit is 50 percent of the first $1,000 of administrative and retirement-education expenses incurred for the plan for each of the first three years the plan is in existence. Expenses offset by the credit may not be claimed a deduction for those expenses.

The credit may be claimed by an employer that did not employ more than 100 employees with compensation in excess of $5,000 in the preceding year. To qualify for the credit, the employer's plan must cover at least one nonhighly compensated employee [IRC Sec. 45E]. The credit may be claimed for costs paid or incurred in tax years after December 31, 2001, with respect to plans established after that date.

61 Electric Vehicle Credit

Form 8834 was used to get a refundable credit of 10 percent of the cost of a qualified electric vehicle that was placed in service after June 30, 1993, and before 2012. The maximum credit was $4,000 per qualified electric vehicle. The portion of the cost of a qualified electric vehicle that was expensed under code Sec. 179 is ineligible for the credit.

The credit applied to a motor vehicle powered primarily by an electric motor drawing current from rechargeable batteries, fuel cells, or other portable sources of electric current. The original use of the vehicle must commence with the taxpayer. For vehicles placed in service in 2004 through 2006, the credit was reduced 25 percent each year. The basis of a qualified electric vehicle was reduced by the amount of the credit allowed.

The credit was extended with a $2,500 maximum for vehicles purchased after February 17, 2009, and before 2012. See pages 164–167 for *current* vehicle credits.

The Energy Tax Incentive Act of 2005 added several new credits including:

62 Credit for Residential Energy Efficient Property

You could take a 30 percent nonrefundable credit for the cost of *solar* systems to heat air or water, but not pools or hot tubs. It also covers small wind, fuel cell, and geothermal heat pump property. This credit was good for second homes as well as primary residences. You could get 30 percent on a new home furnace and another 30 percent on a water heater. The dollar cap was $2,000 for *each* system and this credit was good only for 2006 through 2008.

The 2008 Energy Improvement and Extension Act extended these credits for 8 years, through 2016. It was extended again in 2018 to cover 2017. And except for fuel cell property (which remains subject to a maximum credit of $500 per half-kilowatt), the American Reinvestment and Recovery Act (ARRA) repealed the dollar caps that had applied to these renewable energy items. ARRA also repealed the limitation on "subsidized energy financing," including assistance provided under a federal, state, or local program designed to promote energy production or conservation.

This credit was nonrefundable and the depreciable basis of the property was reduced by the amount of the credit.

Heating stoves that use renewable biomass fuel—wood, pellets, plants— qualified for the tax credit.

Business could get a separate 30 percent credit for renewable energy property such as solar heating systems and for fuel cells used to generate electricity. As of January 1, 2009, the $4,000 limit on the 30 percent tax credit for small wind energy property and the limitaion on property financed by subsidized energy financing was repealed.

63 Energy Saving Home Improvement Credit

This 10 percent credit applied to the cost of skylights, outside doors, windows, pigmented roofs, and high-efficiency furnaces, water heaters, and central air conditioners installed in a *primary home* in 2006 and 2007. The top credit was $500, with no more than $200 attributable to windows. Check out www.energytaxincentives.org for details. Claim the credit on Form 5695.

The American Recovery and Reinvestment Act of 2009 increased the energy tax credit for homeowners who make energy-efficient improvements to their existing homes. The 2009 law increased the credit rate to 30 percent of the cost of all qualifying improvements and raises the maximum credit limit to $1,500 for improvements placed in service in 2009 and 2010. For 2011, the credit was cut to 10 percent up to $500 (reduced by any credit claimed since 2006) with a cap of $50 to $300 on fans, furnaces, hot water heaters, heat pumps, and central air-conditioning and a $200 cap on windows.

The credit applies to improvements such as adding insulation, energy-efficient exterior windows, and energy-efficient heating and air-conditioning systems. The credit does not count the labor costs for installation.

This credit has been renewed several times through 2017.

What Was Included in the Energy Saving Tax Credit?

Tax Credit: 10 percent of cost up to $500 or a specific amount from $50–$300

Expired: December 31, 2017

Details: Must be an existing home and your principal residence. New construction and rentals **do not** qualify.

Biomass stoves

Heating, ventilating, air conditioning (HVAC)

Insulation

Roofs (Metal & Asphalt)

Water heaters (nonsolar)

Windows and doors

Tax Credit: 30 percent of cost with no upper limit

Expired: December 31, 2017

Details: Existing homes and new construction qualify. Both principal residences and second homes qualify. Rentals **do not** qualify.

Geothermal heat pumps

Small wind turbines (residential)

Solar energy systems

Renewable Energy Tax Credits

Under the Bipartisan Budget Act of 2018, the renewable energy tax credits for fuel cells, small wind turbines, and geothermal heat pumps now feature a gradual step down in the credit value, the same as those for solar energy systems.

Tax Credit:

- 30% for systems placed in service by 12/31/2019
- 26% for systems placed in service after 12/31/2019 and before 01/01/2021
- 22% for systems placed in service after 12/31/2020 and before 01/01/2022

Expires: December 31, 2021

Details: Existing homes and new construction qualify. Both principal residences and second homes qualify. Rentals **do not** qualify.

Geothermal heat pumps

Small wind turbines (residential)

Solar energy systems

Fuel cells (residential fuel cell and microturbine system)

64 Hybrid Vehicles Credit

For cars bought in 2006 through 2014, you could get a *conservation credit* of between $250 and $1,000 and an additional *fuel economy* credit of between $400 and $2,400, based on estimated lifetime fuel savings and on overall fuel economy. The credit was claimed on Form 8910.

The fuel economy credit was based on the following efficiency gains over model year 2002 baselines.

- 125%–149%: $400
- 150%–174%: $800
- 175%–199%: $1,200
- 200%–224%: $1,600
- 225%–249%: $2,000
- 250%+: $2,400

How it's calculated The conservation credit increases the fuel economy credit based on the following lifetime fuel savings:

- 1,200%–1,799 gal: $250
- 1,800%–2,399 gal: $500
- 2,400%–2,999 gal: $750
- 3,000 gal+: $1,000

Heavy-duty hybrid vehicles were subject to the following incremental cost limitations:

- <14,001 GVWR: $7,500
- 14,001–26,000 GVWR: $15,000
- 26,001+ GVWR: $30,000

Qualifying criteria To qualify for the credits, the vehicles must meet at least Bin 5 standards if they are up to 6,000 lb GVWR, or Bin 8 standards if the vehicles are 6,001 lb–8,500 lb GVWR.

Those who waited–lost. The credit phased out quickly. The phase-out period was triggered when an auto manufacturer sold its 60,000th hybrid vehicle. That's the total per manufacturer, not 60,000 per model. Once the cap was reached, the phase-out started at the beginning of the second subsequent calendar quarter.

For the next two quarters, buyers could claim only half the credit.

In the 6 months after that . . . 25 percent of the full credit. So if Honda's cap was reached say, in August 2010, buyers of Honda hybrids would get 100 percent of the credit through December 31, 50 percent for those purchased in January 2011 through June 2011, and 25 percent for any bought in the remainder of the year. After that, zero.

See pages 164–167 for *current* credits on Electric Drive Vehicles.

65 Telephone Tax Refund

If you paid a long distance telephone tax, you got a refund on your 2006 tax return. You could have claimed either the tax you paid or a standard refund amount of $30 if you claim one exemption, $40 if you claim two, $50 for three, and $60 for four or more.

66 First-Time Home Buyer Credit

The Housing and Economic Recovery Act of 2008 gave first-time home buyers a refundable tax credit of 10 percent of the purchase price, up to $7,500 ($3,750 for married people filing separately). The credit began to phase out at the $150,000 adjusted gross income level for joint filers ($75,000 for other filers) and was not available for joint filers with income above $170,000 ($95,000 for other filers). It also was not available to non-resident aliens, those who qualified for a similar District of Columbia credit, or those whose financing came from tax-exempt mortgage revenue bonds. The credit was effective for homes purchased on or after April 9, 2008, and before July 1, 2009. But this credit must be paid back, in equal installments for 15 years. So if you got the full $7,500, you'd pay an additional "tax" of $500 each year. Payments start 2 years after the year in which the residence is purchased or earlier, if you sell the house or if it is no longer your principal residence. You qualify as a "first-time home buyer" if neither you nor your spouse had any ownership interest in a principal residence during the 3-year period before the new home is purchased. The best news: is that if you die, you don't have to pay back the credit.

The American Recovery and Reinvestment Act of 2009 changed the rules for those buying a principal residence after January 1, 2009, and before December 1, 2009. It increased the credit to $8,000 and eliminated the obligation to repay (unless the house was sold within 3 years of purchase).

The phase-out to qualify remained the same. You still could not buy from a relative, and multiple buyers could allocate the credit in any "reasonable" way. Whether or not you qualified was determined on the date of closing. So, if you qualified and closed and then married someone who didn't qualify, you still got the credit. If you purchased in 2010, you could have amended your 2009 return and would have received the credit refund before filing your 2010 return in 2011. This provision not only got your money faster, but it allowed you to qualify on the basis of 2009 income if your 2010 income was too high. A copy of your settlement sheet attached to the amended return proved your eligiblity.

If you bought in 2008 and financed with tax-exempt mortgage revenue bonds, you didn't qualify. This restriction was removed for post-2008 purchases.

This credit was extended again to include contracts signed by April 30, 2010, which closed by September 30, 2010. Also added was a credit of up to $6,500 for new buyers who owned a principal residence for at least 5 consecutive years of the 8-year period ending on the date of the new purchases. File Form 5405 to claim this credit.

These new rules raised the income limits for purchases after November 6, 2009. You got the full credit with income up to $125,000 ($225,000 on a joint return) phasing out at $145,000 ($245,000 on a joint return).

Dependents were no longer eligible nor was a home costing more than $800,000. The buyer must be at least age 18 on the day of closing. Members of the armed forces and certain federal employees serving outside the United States for at least 90 days during 2009 and 2010 had an extra year to buy and qualify.

67 "Making Work Pay" Tax Credit

This provision of the American Recovery and Reinvestment Act of 2009 cut taxes for more than 95 percent of working families in the United States. For 2009 and 2010, the provision provided a *refundable* tax credit of up to $400 for working individuals and $800 for working families. This refundable tax credit was calculated at a rate of 6.2 percent of earned income, and phased out for taxpayers with adjusted gross income in excess of $75,000 ($150,000 for married couples filing jointly). You could receive this benefit through a reduction in the amount of income tax that was withheld from your paycheck, or through claiming the credit on your tax return using Schedule M.

	Phase-out	
	Unmarried taxpayer (maximum credit)	
MAGI	**Credit before Phase-out**	**Credit after Phase-out**
$75,000	$400	$400
$80,000	$400	$300
$85,000	$400	$200
$90,000	$400	$100
$95,000	$400	$0

	Married taxpayer (maximum credit)	
MAGI	**Credit before Phase-out**	**Credit after Phase-out**
$150,000	$800	$800
$160,000	$800	$600
$170,000	$800	$400
$180,000	$800	$200
$190,000	$800	$0

If you had no other earned income but were receiving Social Security, SSI, or railroad retirement or veteran disability compensation benefits, your credit was $250. A retired federal employee also qualified for the $250 credit ($500 on a joint return if both spouses are eligible). Both the Social Security and retired government employee benefits were one-shot deals, while the regular "making work pay" credit was available in both 2009 and 2010.

For 2011, this credit was not available, but the loss was offset by a one-year 2 percent reduction in employee (and self-employed) Social Security payroll taxes, extended into 2012, but for the employee side only.

The American Recovery and Reinvestment Act of 2009 added the following new energy credits.

68 Plug-in Electric *Drive* Vehicle Credit (Sec. 1141)

The 2009 law modified the 10 percent credit for qualified plug-in electric drive vehicles purchased or leased after December 31, 2009. To qualify, vehicles must be newly purchased or leased, have four or more wheels, have a gross vehicle weight rating of less than 14,000 pounds, and draw propulsion using a battery with at least 4 kilowatt hours that can be recharged from an external source of electricity. The minimum

amount of the credit for qualified plug-in electric drive vehicles is $2,500, and the credit tops out at $7,500, depending on the battery capacity. The full amount of the credit will be reduced with respect to a manufacturer's vehicles after the manufacturer has sold at least 200,000 vehicles. Two quarters after that, the credit drops to $3,750 and two quarters later it is halfed again, and it is gone half a year later. Only one credit per vehicle. Note, *this credit is based on energy savings rather than cost.*

There is no income limitation for this $7,500 tax credit. Plus you can still claim this credit even if you are subject to the Alternative Minimum Tax. Here is a list from the IRS regarding which cars qualify:

Which Vehicles Currently Qualify for the Federal Credit?

Here's the list, as of April 2016:*

Electric Vehicles	Federal Tax Credit
BMW i3	$7,500
Chevrolet Spark EV	$7,500
Fiat 500e	$7,500
Ford Focus Electric	$7,500
Kia Soul EV	$7,500
Mercedes-Benz B-Class EV	$7,500
Mitsubishi i-MiEV	$7,500
Nissan Leaf	$7,500
Smart Fortwo EV	$7,500
Tesla Model S**	$7,500
Tesla Model X**	$7,500
Tesla Model 3**	$7,500
Volkswagen e-Golf	$7,500

*Go to http://fueleconomy.gov/feg/taxevb.shtml for latest updates
**Start phasing out after December 31, 2018.

Plug-In Hybrid	Federal Tax Credit
Audi A3 e-tron	$4,168
BMW i3 (with range extender)	$7,500
BMW i8	$3,793
BMW X5 xDrive40e	$4,668
Cadillac ELR	$7,500
Chevrolet Volt	$7,500
Ford C-Max Energi	$4,007
Ford Fusion Energi	$4,007
Hyundai Sonata Plug-In Hybrid	$4,919
Mercedes-Benz S500e	$4,042
Porsche Cayenne S E-Hybrid	$5,335
Porsche Panamera S E-Hybrid	$4,751
Porsche 918 Spyder	$3,667
Toyota Prius Plug-In	$2,500
Volvo XC90 T8	$4,545

200,000 CAR LIMIT

Like with the Hybrid Car Tax Credit, this credit will begin to phase-out on some of the more popular models. To level the playing field for each manufacturer, the allowable tax credit starts to disappear for a manufacturer once they sell 200,000 plug-in electric vehicles, as follows:

- The full credit is allowed through the end of the quarter following the quarter during which the manufacturer sells its 200,000th plug-in electric vehicle.

- The credit is cut in half for the subsequent two quarters.

- The credit is then cut to a quarter of the original credit for the subsequent two quarters.
- No credit is allowed for vehicles purchased from that manufacturer thereafter.

Use Form 8936 to claim this credit.

69 Plug-in Electric Vehicle Credit (Sec. 1142)

The 2009 law also created a special tax credit for two types of plug-in vehicles—certain low-speed electric vehicles and two- or three-wheeled vehicles. Think golf carts. The amount of the credit is 10 percent of the cost of the vehicle, up to a maximum credit of $2,500 for purchases made after February 17, 2009, and through 2013 (extended by subsequent laws). To qualify, a vehicle must be either a low- speed vehicle propelled by an electric motor that draws electricity from a battery with a capacity of 4 kilowatt hours or more or be a two- or three-wheeled vehicle propelled by an electric motor that draws electricity from a battery with the capacity of 2.5 kilowatt hours. A taxpayer may not claim this credit if the plug-in electric *drive* vehicle credit is allowable. Only one credit per vehicle. Note, *this credit is based on cost.*

70 Conversion Kits (Sec. 1143)

The 2009 law also provided a tax credit for plug-in electric drive conversion kits. The credit is equal to 10 percent of the cost of converting a vehicle to a qualified plug-in electric drive motor vehicle and placed in service after February 17, 2009. The maximum amount of the credit is $4,000. The credit does not apply to conversions made after December 31, 2011. A taxpayer may claim this credit even if the taxpayer claimed a hybrid vehicle credit for the same vehicle in an earlier year. Claim the credit on Form 8910.

71 Treatment of Alternative Motor Vehicle Credit as a Personal Credit Allowed Against AMT (Sec. 1144)

Starting in 2009, the 2009 law allows the alternative motor vehicle credit, including the tax credit for purchasing hybrid vehicles, to be applied against the alternative minimum tax. Prior to the 2009 law, the alternative motor vehicle credit could not be used to offset the AMT. This means that

the credit could not be taken if a taxpayer owed AMT or was reduced for some taxpayers who did not owe AMT.

72 Small Business Health Insurance Credit

Many small businesses and tax-exempt organizations that provide health insurance coverage to their employees now qualify for a special tax credit.

This is designed to encourage small business employers to offer health insurance coverage for the first time or maintain coverage they already have. In general, the credit is available to small business employers that pay at least half the cost of single coverage for their employees.

The maximum credit was 35 percent of premiums paid by eligible small business employers and 25 percent of premiums paid by eligible employers that are tax-exempt organizations. In 2014, this maximum credit increases to 50 percent of premiums paid by eligible small business employers and 35 percent of premiums paid by eligible employers that are tax-exempt organizations.

The credit is specifically targeted to help small businesses and tax-exempt organizations that primarily employ low- and moderate-income workers. It is generally available to employers that have fewer than 25 full-time equivalent (FTE) employees (not more than 10 gets you the maximum credit) and that are paying wages averaging less than $52,400 (in 2017) per employee per year. Because the eligibility formula is based in part on the number of FTEs, not the number of employees, many businesses will qualify even if they employ more than 25 individual workers.

The maximum credit goes to smaller business employers—those with 10 or fewer FTEs—paying annual average wages of $26,200 (in 2017) or less.

73 Small Business Health Care Credit

If you are an employer, you might be eligible for the Small Business Health Care Tax Credit. To be eligible for the credit, you must

- have purchased coverage through the Small Business Health Options Program—also known as the SHOP marketplace
- have fewer than 25 full-time equivalent employees
- pay an average wage of less than $53,200 a year (indexed)
- pay at least half of employee health insurance premiums

For tax years beginning in 2014:

- The maximum credit increases to 50 percent of premiums paid for small business employers (35 percent of premiums paid for small tax-exempt employers).

- To be eligible for the credit, you must pay premiums on behalf of employees enrolled in a qualified health plan offered through a Small Business Health Options Program Marketplace or qualify for an exception to this requirement.

- The credit is available to eligible employers for two consecutive taxable years. Even if you did not owe tax during the year, you can carry the credit back or forward to other tax years. Also, since the amount of the health insurance premium payments is more than the total credit, you can still claim a business expense deduction for the premiums in *excess* of the credit.

You can benefit from the credit even if you forgot to claim it on a prior tax return; there's still time to file an amended return. Generally, a claim for refund must be filed within three years from the time the return was filed or two years from the time the tax was paid, whichever of such periods expires later. For tax years 2010 through 2013, the maximum credit was 35 percent of premiums paid for small business employers (25 percent of premiums paid for small tax-exempt employers such as charities).

You use Form 8941, Credit for Small Employer Health Insurance Premiums, to calculate the credit. Include the credit as part of the general business credit on your income tax return.

74 Foreign Tax Credit

You can get a credit for foreign income taxes you pay. If the amount totals not more than $300 ($600 on a joint return), you do *not* have to file Form 1116 to claim the credit.

75 The Premium Tax Credit

If you get your health insurance coverage through the Health Insurance Marketplace, you may be eligible for the Premium Tax Credit. This tax credit can help make purchasing health insurance coverage more affordable for people with moderate incomes. The open enrollment period to purchase health insurance coverage through the Marketplace for 2019 runs from November 1, 2018, through December 15, 2018.

The Department of Health and Human Services administers the requirements for the Marketplace and the health plans they offer. For more information

about your coverage options, financial assistance, and the Marketplace, visit www.HealthCare.gov.

ELIGIBILITY

You may be eligible for the credit if you meet all of the following:
- buy health insurance through the Marketplace;
- are ineligible for coverage through an employer or government plan;
- are within certain income limits;
- do not file a Married Filing Separately return*; and
- cannot be claimed as a dependent by another person.

HOW THE PREMIUM TAX CREDIT WORKS

- Household income must be between 100 percent and 400 percent ($48,560 for singles and $65,840** for couples in 2018***) of the federal poverty level.
- Covered individuals must be enrolled in a "qualified health plan" through an Affordable Insurance Exchange.
- Covered individuals must be legally present in the United States and not incarcerated.
- Covered individuals must not be eligible for other qualifying coverage such as Medicare, Medicaid, or affordable employer-sponsored coverage.

CREDIT AMOUNT

- The credit amount is generally equal to the difference between the premium for the "benchmark plan" and your "expected contribution."
- The expected contribution is a specified percentage of your household income. The percentage increases as income increases, from 2 percent of income for families at 100 percent of the federal poverty level (FPL) to 9.5 percent of income for families at 400 percent of the FPL. (The actual amount a family pays for coverage will be less than the expected contribution if the family chooses a plan that is less expensive than the benchmark plan.)
- The benchmark plan is the second-lowest-cost plan that would cover the family at the "silver" level of coverage.

*MFS permitted for domestic abuse victims. Learn more at www.IRS.gov/aca.
**Higher if family size is more than 2.
***$60,720 and $82,320 for Alaska and $55,840 and $75,720 for Hawaii.

- The credit is capped at the premium for the plan the family chooses (so no one receives a credit that is larger than the amount they actually pay for their plan).

IT'S YOUR CHOICE

If you are eligible for the credit, you can choose to:

- **Get It Now:** have some or all of the estimated credit paid in advance directly to your insurance company to lower what you pay out-of-pocket for your monthly premiums during 2018; or
- **Get It Later:** wait to get the credit when you file your 2018 tax return in 2019.

REPORT CHANGES IN CIRCUMSTANCES

If you receive advance payment of the Premium Tax Credit to help pay for your insurance premiums, you should report changes such as income or family size to your marketplace when they happen in 2018. Reporting changes will make sure you get the correct amount of the advance payment of the credit. Receiving too much or too little in advance can affect your refund or balance due when you file your 2018 tax return in 2019.

CLAIM THE CREDIT

Whether you choose to get the credit now or later, you must claim it by filing a federal income tax return.

When you file your 2018 tax return in 2019, you will use form 8962 to subtract the total of any advance payments you received during the year from the amount of the Premium Tax Credit calculated on your tax return. This may affect your tax refund or balance due. If you are entitled to more credit than you have already received, this will either increase your refund or lower your balance due. Find out more about the Premium Tax Credit at www.IRS.gov/aca.

PENALTY FOR NO HEALTH INSURANCE

You will pay a penalty if you don't have health insurance, in the higher of two amounts. The *basic penalty* for 2016 was $695 a person ($347.50 for each family member under age 18) with a family ceiling of $2,085 or the *income-based* penalty of 2.5 percent of household income over the filing threshold for 2016. In 2017 and 2018, the *basic penalty* stayed at $695. So you paid the higher of 2.5 percent of income or $695 per person ($347.50 per child) with a cap or $2,085 per family. But, in no case could the penalty tax exceed the cost of a bronze-level exchange plan, $13,000 in 2016 and $13,100 in 2017. As of January 1, 2019, the shared responsibility mandate disappears and, with it, the penalty for no health insurance.

76 Employer Credit for Family and Medical Leave Benefits

You can get a credit of 12.5% for qualified wages paid to an employee while on family or medical leave. The credit increases 0.25% for each percentage point paid to a qualifying employee that exceeds 50% of his or her wages, up to a maximum of 25%. Wages *required* to be paid by state or local law do not count.

- To claim the credit, employers must have a written policy that meets certain requirements:
 - Employers must provide at least two weeks of paid family and medical leave annually to all qualifying employees who work full time. This can be prorated for employees who work part time.
 - The paid leave must be not less than 50 percent of the wages normally paid to the employee.

- A qualifying employee is any employee who:
 - Has been employed for one year or more.
 - For the preceding year, had compensation that did not exceed a certain amount. For 2018, the employee must not have earned more than $72,000 in 2017.

- For purposes of this credit, "family and medical leave" is leave for one or more of the following reasons:
 - Birth of an employee's child and to care for the newborn.
 - Placement of a child with the employee for adoption or foster care.
 - To care for the employee's spouse, child, or parent who has a serious health condition.
 - A serious health condition that makes the employee unable to perform the functions of his or her position.
 - Any qualifying event due to an employee's spouse, child, or parent being on covered active duty – or being called to duty – in the Armed Forces.
 - To care for a service member who is the employee's spouse, child, parent, or next of kin.

- The credit is generally effective for wages paid in taxable years of the employer beginning after December 31, 2017. It is not available for wages paid in taxable years beginning after December 31, 2019.

"Above the Line" Deductions

"Take it off. Take it all off. . . ."

GYPSY ROSE LEE

INCOME TAX RATES

Year	Maximum Individual Rate	Year	Maximum Individual Rate
1914	7%	1990	28/33%
1916	15	1991	31
1917	67	1992	31
1918	77	1993	36/39.6
1920	65	1994	36/39.6
1921	50	1995	39.6
1924	40	1996	39.6
1926	25	1997	39.6
1934	63	1998	39.6
1936	79	1999	39.6
1941	81	2000	39.6
1942	88	2001	39.1
1944	94	2002	38.6
1945	91	2003	35
1951	92	2004	35
1954	91	2005	35
1964	77	2006	35
1970	70	2007	35
1981	50	2008	35
1987	38.5	2009	35
1988	28/33	2010	35
1989	28/33	2011	35
		2012	35
		2013	44.3*
		2014	44.3*
		2015	44.3*
		2016	44.3*
		2017	44.3-*
		2018	41.7**

*39.6% + 0.9% additional payroll tax on *earned* income + 3.8% additional payroll tax on *unearned* income.
**37.0% + 0.9% additional payroll tax on *earned* income + 3.8% additional payroll tax on *unearned* income.

Our tax system is founded on a multistep computation. You begin with gross income. This is all income, all accession to wealth, clearly realized, over which you have dominion, less those items defined earlier as tax exclusions. From gross income you then subtract a certain category of expenses called by tax practitioners *adjustments* or *above the line deductions*. A deduction is a reduction of your taxable income—the income base on which your tax is imposed. *Above the line deductions* include trade and business deductions, alimony, moving expenses, student-loan interest, self-employment, tuition tax deduction, IRA, Keogh, and SEP deductions, certain education expenses, the deduction for contributions to a health savings account, and employee business expenses of performing artists.

Gross income less adjustments (*above the line deductions*) gives your adjusted gross income. From adjusted gross income, you then subtract the greater of your itemized deductions (*below the line deductions*) or your standard deduction. The standard deduction is basically similar to the old zero bracket amount. It is different from the zero bracket amount in that it is a deduction from adjusted gross income and not a tax bracket.

Unlike pre-1987 law, if you itemize your deductions you will not be required to reduce your itemized deductions by the amount of the standard deduction (zero bracket amount). Instead, you will deduct 100 percent of your itemized deductions and not take the standard deduction. Therefore, you will only itemize deductions if they exceed the amount of your standard deduction.

For 2016, 2017, and 2018 the standard deduction amounts are as follows:

	2016	2017	2018
Married taxpayers filing jointly	$12,600	$12,700	$24,000
Heads of households	9,300	9,350	18,000
Single taxpayers	6,300	6,350	12,000
Married taxpayers filing separately	6,300	6,350	12,000

For 2008 and 2009, those who did not itemize could add real estate taxes paid up to $500 ($1,000 on joint returns) plus the motor vehicle sales tax deduction to their standard deduction.

Prior to 1987, an additional personal exemption was available if you were 65 or older or blind. For 2018 tax returns, a taxpayer is deemed to be 65 or older if his or her 65th birthday falls on January 1, 2019, or earlier*; one is legally blind if one's central visual acuity does not exceed 20/200 in the better eye with corrective lenses, or if the diameter of one's visual field subtends an angle of

*For dependency exemptions, the child care credit, the adoption credit, and the child tax credit, you don't get older until your actual birthdate.

20 degrees or less. This additional personal exemption has been replaced by an increased standard deduction called *the additional amount*. If you or your spouse qualified for the age or blindness exemptions under prior law, you will qualify for these additional amounts. The additional amounts are as follows:

1. $1,600 for individuals who are single or head of household

2. $1,300 each for all other taxpayers

These additional amounts, if available, will be added to the regular standard deduction and treated in the same way as the standard deduction. However, any taxpayer who is the dependent of another taxpayer for purposes of the dependency exemption will have a limited standard deduction. Such a taxpayer's standard deduction will be the greater of either $1,050 or that individual's earned income plus $350 up to the amount of the regular standard deduction.

Prior to 2018, your tax computation continued with a subtraction for your personal exemptions, leaving a figure called your taxable income. Your tax is based on your taxable income. After December 31, 2017, personal exemptions are eliminated.

Without personal exemptions, the calculation should stop with "taxable income." However, our intellects in Congress decided to allow a new pass through deduction for those receiving income from partnerships, trusts, Subchapter S corporations, rental and self-employment. See chapter 12 for details on the new provision. But now, your tax is not based on "taxable income" but on taxable income less the pass through deduction. But shouldn't *that* be called "*taxable income*"? That's how I show it below.

In summary, the process appears as follows:

Gross Income
− Adjustments ("above the line" deductions)

Adjusted Gross Income
− Itemized ("below the line") Deductions or Standard Deduction

− Pass through deduction

Taxable Income

To reduce your tax you must reduce your taxable income. One of the most important things to do, therefore, is to recognize and claim all available deductions. The chart that follows shows the value of every dollar of deductions in terms of dollars saved for each taxpayer classification.

Dollar Values of Deductions Claimed

2018 Old Law						New—2018 After the Tax Cuts and Jobs Act				
Seven-bracket progressive rate income tax with a top marginal rate of 39.6 percent.						Retains seven brackets, but at reduced rates, including a top marginal rate of 37 percent. Provisions sunset at end of 2025.				
Rate	Single	HoH	Joint		Savings per $1 Deduction	Rate	Single	HoH	Joint	Savings per $1 Deduction
10%	$0–9,524	$0–13,599	$0–19,049		.10	10%	$0–9,524	$0–13,599	$0–19,049	.10
15%	$9,525	$13,600	$19,050		.15	12%	$9,525	$13,600	$19,050	.12
25%	$38,700	$51,800	$77,400		.25	22%	$38,700	$51,800	$77,400	.22
28%	$93,700	$133,850	$156,150		.28	24%	$82,500	$82,500	$165,000	.24
33%	$195,450	$216,700	$237,950		.33	32%	$157,500	$157,500	$315,000	.32
35%	$424,950	$424,950	$424,950		.35	35%	$200,000	$200,000	$400,000	.35
39.6%	$426,700	$453,350	$480,050		.396	37%	$500,000	$500,000	$600,000	.37

Note that the higher your taxable income, the more valuable the dollar amount of deductions. This is the result of our progressive tax structure. I will use this structure later to show you how you could reduce your taxes by shifting income from the 37.0 percent bracket (where you keep only 63¢ from each additional dollar you earn) to the 10 percent bracket (where you keep 90¢ from each additional dollar you earn). But first you must recognize and understand the concept of tax-deductible expenses. To do that, you must understand the basic difference between deductions *for* adjusted gross income (above the line deductions) and deductions *from* adjusted gross income (below the line deductions).

A Deductions for Adjusted Gross Income

There are several categories of deductions for adjusted gross income that you must be aware of to minimize your taxes. We will take each in turn:

77 Trade and Business Deductions

All "ordinary and necessary expenses" paid or incurred by you during your taxable year in carrying on any trade or business are allowed as above the line deductions.

Here it is very important to understand that the words "ordinary and necessary" are words of art. For an expense to be deductible, it need not be absolutely necessary in the sense that you cannot conduct your trade without incurring such an expense. The courts have interpreted the words "ordinary and necessary" to mean "reasonable and customary," and this interpretation has been accepted by the Internal Revenue Service. Therefore, any expenses that you might incur in your business that are reasonable and customary for that business, even if not in any sense necessary, are deductible.

This provides you with an excellent opportunity to convert what would normally be nondeductible personal expenses into deductible business expenses. For example, assume that you have your own trade or business in New York and want to take a vacation in Miami. Alternatively, you could live in Miami and want to vacation in California. Almost all businesses have professional associations or trade groups who conduct seminars or hold meetings in resort areas. If you could schedule your vacation in these areas at the same time as the professional meeting and attend that professional meeting, your

travel expenses, subject to the limits discussed in Chapter 9, would be converted from personal expenses into allowable, deductible business expenses. While attendance at these conventions or trade shows might not be necessary to your business, it would be reasonable and customary. Later in the book I will discuss more of these extensive tax advantages for those who own their own businesses.

78 Employee Business Expenses of Actors and Other Performing Artists

Employee business expenses of actors and other performing artists are deductible in arriving at adjusted gross income. In order to qualify, the performing artist must have performed services in the performing arts as an employee for at least two employers during the year. For this purpose, a nominal employer (i.e., one from whom less than $200 was received for the performance of such services during the year) is excluded.

Moreover, the allowable expenses in connection with the performance of the services must be more than 10 percent of the taxpayer's gross income from the services, and the individual's adjusted gross income for the year, before deducting these expenses, cannot be more than $16,000.

A performing artist who is married at the end of the taxable year must file a joint return with his/her spouse to qualify for the above the line deduction unless both husband and wife live apart at all times during the year. In the case of a joint return, the two-employer requirement as well as the requirement that the expenses be more than 10 percent of gross income are applied separately with respect to each spouse. However, the $16,000 adjusted gross income test is applied to the combined adjusted gross income of both spouses. In effect, such performing artists are allowed the deductions as if they were independent contractors rather than employees.

Such deductions would be allowable above the line and would include all ordinary and necessary expenses incurred by you during your taxable year. These expenses are detailed in the section on Miscellaneous Trade and Business Deductions of Employees on page 347.

79 Employee Business Expenses

Unreimbursed employee business expenses normally could have been deducted only as miscellaneous itemized deductions and thus were subject to the 2 percent adjusted gross income floor on such deductions.

In Rev. Rul. 77-350, the Internal Revenue Service had held that, in certain circumstances, an employee could claim an above the line deduction for certain expenses incurred pursuant to "nonaccountable plans." Congress became concerned that the 2 percent floor could be circumvented by restructuring the form of an employee's compensation so that the salary amount is decreased but the employee receives an equivalent nonaccountable expense allowance.

Effective for tax years beginning after 1988, employee business expenses paid or incurred under nonaccountable plans were deductible by an employee *only* as an itemized deduction subject to the 2 percent floor. These are arrangements under which the employee is *not* required to substantiate the expenses covered by the arrangement to the person providing the reimbursement, or the employee has the right to retain amounts in excess of the substantiated expenses covered under the arrangement. Otherwise allowable employee business expenses are deductible above the line as reimbursed expenses *only* if they were incurred pursuant to a reimbursement or other expense allowance arrangement that *requires* the employee to substantiate expenses covered by the arrangement to the person providing the reimbursement. The expense must be business-connected, and any excess payment must be returned to the employer. Such "*accountable*" plans yield no income to the employee, and a deduction to the employer. An employee who receives a per diem or other fixed allowance from an employer will be considered as substantiating the amount of expenses covered by the arrangement up to amounts that have been specified by the IRS.

As of January 1, 2018, employee business expenses are no longer allowable as miscellaneous itemized deductions. That is why an accountable plan becomes so important–deducted by the employer and no income to the employee. The key is effective record keeping.

80 Alimony

Certain payments that constitute "alimony" may be taken as above the line deductions by the payer. Such alimony payments may be made from

husband to wife or from wife to husband. For illustration purposes, I will refer to payments coming from husband to wife.

The Internal Revenue Service tax code provides that periodic payments received by a wife in discharge of her husband's obligation of support arising out of the marital or family relationship are deductible if any one of the following situations is true:

1. The payments are made in discharge of a legal obligation incurred under a court order, decree of divorce, or legal separation, where the spouses are either divorced or legally separated.

2. The payments are made under a written separation agreement where the spouses are separated, living apart, *and* do not file a joint return.

3. The payments are made under a court order or decree for the spouse's support or maintenance where the spouses are separated, living apart, *and* do not file a joint return.

PRE-TAX REFORM ACT OF 1984 LAW

Such payments were deductible by the husband and would therefore also be included in the wife's income. If any of the payments were fixed, in terms of a total amount of money or of payment for the support of minor children, they would not be deemed alimony and were neither taxed to the wife nor deductible by the husband. Prior to the Tax Reform Act of 1984, to qualify as child support payments rather than periodic alimony, the amounts must have been designated specifically as child support and not left to determination by inference or conjecture. Any amounts paid will be applied first to child support if such amounts are less than the total required to be paid. To be child support, though, the payments must be used for the support of minor children of the payer, the age of majority to be determined by applicable state law.

Periodic alimony payments will be deductible by the payer as an above the line deduction for adjusted gross income. In order to be deductible, the payments must be periodic rather than installment payments of a principal sum. Whether the payments are made at regular intervals is irrelevant; the key is whether they are periodic or principal sum payments, and the distinction between these two is whether there is a total amount to be paid that can be computed with certainty. If this is the case, the payments are *not* periodic. If the payments are contingent on death, remarriage of the wife, or a change in the

economic status of either spouse, they *are* deemed to be periodic. This contingency may be a result of the decree or the separation agreement, or may be imposed by local law.

There is an exception to this general rule: If the principal amount payable under the terms of the divorce or separation decree is to be paid over more than 10 years from the date of the decree, then the payments *will* be considered periodic, but only the portion that equals 10 percent of the principal amount. For example, in a settlement of $300,000 to be paid over 15 years, with a first payment of $40,000, the recipient must include as gross income $30,000; the remainder is excludable. This limitation does not apply to late payments, but it does apply to advance payments. Late payments are treated as if they were made on time, and since both parties are deemed to be cash-basis taxpayers, these payments will be deductible when paid.

A payer may establish a trust or use an existing trust to discharge an obligation created by the decree of separation or divorce. All periodic payments from this kind of trust will be taxable to the recipient. Payments made by the trust will not be deductible by the payer, but an amount of the trust income that is equal to what is paid to the recipient will be excludable from the payer's gross income. An equal inclusion and deduction therefore result.

Other payments may or may not be deductible as periodic alimony. Payments for medical or dental insurance or direct medical or dental expenses for the spouse, even though made at irregular intervals, would be periodic. If the parties hold property jointly, any payments made that equal the recipient's interest in the property will be deductible by the payer—except where there is a right of survivorship. In that case, the payer will get a deduction only if the recipient is personally liable on the underlying debt or realizes an ascertainable increase in the value of the property that would be received as a survivor. No payments that are allocatable to the payer's interest in the property can be deducted by the payer or included in the recipient's income.

If the recipient resides in the home, utility expenses and repairs will be deductible regardless of ownership because the recipient is receiving a direct economic benefit. Capital expenditures must be capitalized rather than deducted. Periodic payments of life insurance premiums will also constitute deductible alimony payments if the recipient receives an economic benefit and is the absolute owner. Premium payments are not deductible if the policy is merely a security device, or if the recipient interest is contingent upon not remarrying or upon surviving the payer or the children who are the primary beneficiaries of the policy. In these cases, no present economic benefit to the recipient is ascertainable.

Property settlements, moreover, will not constitute periodic alimony. The intent of the parties, as determined by all of the facts and circumstances, will be the controlling factor here, rather than the label used. Property settlements *not* made out of the marital or family obligation of support will therefore be neither deductible nor includable. You should be aware, though, that if appreciated property is transferred in exchange for your spouse's inchoate marital rights, you will realize a gain equal to the full fair market value of the property less your cost or other basis. The character of the gain will be determined by the nature of the property you transfer. The spouse receiving the property will have a stepped-up basis and realize no gain. The amount realized there is deemed to be equal to what is exchanged.

If the property exchanged has depreciated in value, *never* make the transfer until the marriage has been dissolved. Otherwise, the loss will not be recognized. An alternative route to avoid this tax trap would be to sell the property to a third party and give the proceeds to your spouse. Be aware, though, that the rules do *not* apply in a community property state where all divisions are considered to be partitions of jointly owned property. There, taxable income will not be realized unless the division is clearly unequal in value.

POST–TAX REFORM ACT OF 1984 LAW

The Tax Reform Act of 1984 made significant changes both to the alimony rules and to property transfers incident to a divorce. With reference to property transfers incident to a divorce, the transfer will be treated in the same manner as a gift and therefore no capital gain or loss will be recognized for tax purposes. This rule applies to all transfers made after the date of enactment of the Act, or if both parties elect, to both transfers made between December 31, 1983 and the date of enactment as well as to transfers made after the date of enactment pursuant to instruments in effect before that date.

With reference to the rules governing alimony, the 1984 Act requires that alimony be paid in cash and terminate at the death of the payee spouse (if the decree or agreement does not specifically state that the payments terminate at the death of the payee spouse, it is not alimony and not deductible [*Crabtree* T.C. Memo 2015-163]), that the parties may not be members of the same household at the time the payment is made, and that no amount will be deductible as alimony to the extent the payment is contingent on the status of a child (for example, if the payment terminates when a child marries, dies, or reaches maturity). Furthermore, under the 1984 Act, if payments in any year exceed $10,000, no part of such payments will be deductible unless the agreement provides that the payments be made for at least 6 years (unless the spouse dies or the payee spouse

remarries), and a decline in excess of $10,000 in payments between any two successive years will cause a recapture of the excess amount. The effective date of the rules was January 1, 1985 for divorce or separation agreements executed on or after that date. The provisions apply to divorce or separation agreements executed before January 1, 1985 but modified on or after such date if the modification expressly provides that these provisions will apply.

The Tax Reform Act of 1986, however, amended the 6-year rule. Under the new law, amounts that are considered "excess alimony payments" will be included in taxable income of the payer in the *third* postseparation year. This inclusion will eliminate the benefit of the previous deduction for such payments. The payee will also be permitted a deduction corresponding to the amount includable in the payer's income in that third year.

Excess alimony payments are determined as follows:

- For the first postseparation year the excess alimony payment is that amount that exceeds the average of alimony payments in the second and third years plus $15,000. The excess alimony payment for the second year is that amount that exceeds the payment in the third year by more than $15,000. For example, a divorce agreement provides that the husband will pay his former wife alimony over a 3-year period as follows:

1st year	$35,000
2nd year	10,000
3rd year	20,000

- To calculate the excess alimony payment for the first year, the average of the second- and third-year payments must be computed. This average is $15,000 ([$10,000 + $20,000] ÷ 2). The excess alimony payment for the first year is therefore $5,000 ($35,000 – [$15,000 + $15,000]). In the third year the husband will have to include the $5,000 excess alimony payment in income, and the ex-wife will receive a corresponding deduction of $5,000.

The formula is as follows:

$$\text{Excess payments} = \text{alimony paid in 1st year} - \left[\$15,000 + \frac{\text{alimony paid in 2nd year} - \text{excess payments in 2nd year} + \text{alimony paid in 3rd year}}{2} \right]$$

- To complete the computation, the second-year excess amount must be determined first.

 The excess payment for the second postseparation year is the excess of the second-year alimony paid over the sum of third-year alimony paid plus $15,000; i.e.,

$$\text{Excess payment} = \text{alimony paid in 2nd year} - \left(\text{alimony paid in 3rd year} + \$15{,}000 \right)$$

- If alimony consists of one payment of $30,000 in the first postseparation year, and no alimony is paid thereafter, the amount recaptured is $15,000:

$$\$30{,}000 - \left[\$15{,}000 + \frac{(0-0)+0}{2} \right]$$

- If alimony paid in the first postseparation year is $50,000, in the second is $25,000, and in the third is zero, the second-year excess payment is $10,000:

$$\$25{,}000 - (0 + \$15{,}000)$$

- The first-year excess payment is $27,500:

$$\$50{,}000 - \left[\$15{,}000 + \frac{(\$25{,}000 - \$10{,}000)+0}{2} \right]$$

- The recapture amount is $37,500, the sum of the first- and second-year excess payments. If $25,000 had also been paid in the third year, the recapture amount would be $10,000, the amount of the first-year excess payment, as there is no second-year excess payment:

$$\$50{,}000 - \left[\$15{,}000 + \frac{(\$25{,}000 - 0)+\$25{,}000}{2} \right]$$

The objective is to allow alimony payments as deductible if they are made in as few as 3 years. However, if the first payment is made in December of year 1, the second in January of year 2, and the third in January of year 3, the alimony will be deductible even though the payments are in fact spread over only 13 or 14 months.

Moreover, recapture is not required if alimony ceases when death or remarriage occurs before the end of the third postseparation year. Payments under temporary support agreements are also excluded from the recapture rules. In addition, the 1986 Act clarified that payments will not be disqualified from being treated as alimony simply because the divorce or separation agreement does not specifically state that the payments will terminate at the death of the recipient

and, finally, that payments contingent on the fluctuating earnings of a business or property or from employment will also not result in recapture, if the obligation to pay extends for at least 3 years. These 1986 amendments apply to divorce or separation instruments executed after December 31, 1986, and divorce or separation instruments executed before that date if modified on or after such date to expressly state that the new provisions will apply.

The Tax Reform Act of 1984 also changed the rules with respect to which divorced parent receives the dependency exemption for a child. Beginning in 1985, the custodial parent is entitled to the exemption unless:

a) the custodial parent releases the exemption for the year, by written declaration on Form 8332, to the noncustodial parent. This form must be signed by the custodial parent and attached to the noncustodial parent's return, *or*

b) a decree of divorce or separate maintenance or a written agreement was executed before 1985, under which the custodial parent released the exemption to the noncustodial parent. In this event, the noncustodial parent can claim the exemption if he or she provides at least $600 annually for the child's support. However, the parties can expressly modify the document to render this exception inapplicable, *or*

c) a multiple support agreement is in effect.

Note also that under the 1984 Act, support by a remarried parent's new spouse was considered support furnished by that parent, and children of divorced were treated as *both* parents' dependents for medical deduction purposes. Hence, a parent could deduct medical expenses paid for a child even though the other parent got the dependency exemption for that child.

Furthermore, a custodial parent who releases a dependency exemption will be considered as retaining that exemption when determining marital and head of household status, the earned income credit, and the child and dependent care credit. If otherwise eligible, such a parent could still qualify for unmarried and head of household status and those credits. For example, to claim head of household status, an individual must maintain a household as his or her home, which is also the principal place of abode for more than half a year for:

1. Any person whom you can claim as a dependent. But do not include:
 a) Your qualifying child whom you claim as your dependent because of the rule for *Children of divorced or separated parents* (see below).
 b) Any person who is your dependent only because he or she lived with you for all of 2018 or
 c) Any person you claimed as a dependent under a multiple support agreement.

2. Your unmarried qualifying child who is not your dependent.

3. Your married qualifying child who is not your dependent only because you can be claimed as a dependent on someone else's 2018 return.

4. Your child who, even though you are the custodial parent, is neither your dependent nor your qualifying child because of the rule for *Children of divorced or separated parents*.

Temporary absences by you or the other person for special circumstances, such as school, vacation, business, medical care, military service, or detention in a juvenile facility, count as time lived in the home.

The status is also available, as before, if a household is maintained for a taxpayer's dependent parents for a full year. The parent does not have to live with you.

The Working Families Tax Relief Act of 2004 modified some rules. A *noncustodial* parent may claim the exemption if awarded it under a decree of divorce or separate maintenance or under a written separation agreement. As of 2005, The Working Families Tax Relief Act of 2004 allows a written release to shift the dependency exemption. The shift should be documented in the formal divorce or separation paperwork. Form 8332 should be signed by the custodial parent and attached to the return of the noncustodial parent claiming the exemption. Without an executed Form 8332, the non-custodial parents cannot get the dependency exemption (*Cappel v. Com.*, T.C. No. 4920-15, T.C. Memo 2016-150, August 10, 2016).

In Rev. Proc. 2008-48, the IRS ruled that a child of divorced or separated parents or of parents living apart would be qualified as a "dependent" of both parents for purposes of employee fringe benefits, including medical expense reimbursement, accident and health plans, the deductibility of medical expenses, and distributions from medical savings accounts and health savings accounts to pay medical expenses.

Several additional tax planning strategies present themselves based upon the rules. If a separation rather than a divorce is desired, you should be aware that while a *decree* of separate maintenance will prevent the filing of a joint return, mere physical separation will not. Physical separation, though, combined with a written separation agreement, will make any periodic payments "alimony," and deductible as such. Therefore, your first tax consideration must be to weigh the benefits of a joint return against an alimony deduction. Depending upon the marginal tax brackets of each party, a limited amount of shifting the tax burden may also occur here. Trade-offs, in terms of higher receipts in exchange for the filing of a joint return, may also be made by sophisticated and aware taxpayers.

You must carefully consider the character of any payments to be made—that is, whether they are for child support or alimony. Child support is neither includable nor deductible. Here again a certain amount of tax shifting is possible.

If any payment for child support is not specifically designated as such, it potentially may be taxed or deducted as alimony. If the recipient is in a lower tax bracket than the payer, any increase in "alimony" from child support will be taxable at a lower marginal rate and deductible at the payer's higher marginal rate. Because of this tax savings, the payer can afford to pay a larger amount of "child support," enough to offset the recipient's increased tax burden, plus a little more.

For example, assume that a husband-payer has a marginal tax bracket of 28 percent and his recipient-wife has a marginal tax bracket of 15 percent. The husband plans to pay periodic alimony of $10,000 and child support of $10,000 per year. The wife has agreed. This agreement would cost the husband $17,200 per year:

Child support (no deduction)	$10,000
Alimony [$10,000 × (1 − 0.28)]	+7,200
	$17,200

The wife would keep $18,500 per year:

Child support (no inclusion)	$10,000
Alimony [$10,000 × (1 − 0.15)]	+8,500
	$18,500

If the husband converted the whole $20,000 to alimony, it would cost him only $14,400:

$$\text{Alimony } [\$20,000 \times (1 - 0.28)] = \$14,400$$

He therefore would save $2,800 over the original agreement. The wife would now have:

$$\text{Alimony } [\$20,000 \times (1 - 0.85)] = \$17,000$$

which is a loss of $1,500. But this loss could be offset by the $2,800 saved by the husband. All he would have to do is increase the alimony payments to $22,500:

$$\text{Cost to husband } [\$22,500 \times (1 - 0.28)] = \$16,200$$
$$\text{Wife keeps } [\$22,500 \times (1 - 0.15)] = \$19,125$$

The result of this plan is that the husband would save $1,000 ($17,200 − $16,200) over the first plan. The wife's position would also be better—by $625 ($19,125 − $18,500)!

Another tax planning strategy involves post-1984 separations. If a husband transfers stock that has appreciated in value from $10,000 to $100,000, the 1984

law relieves him of the tax on the gain and gives it to his wife instead. This presents another alternative strategy for shifting income from a high bracket taxpayer (husband) to a lower bracket taxpayer (wife). To offset this incidence of taxation, the recipient wife should again negotiate an increased payout to absorb, or reduce, the husband's net tax savings on the transfer of appreciated, rather than nonappreciated, property.

CHANGES DUE TO THE TAX CUTS AND JOBS ACT OF 2017

1. As of January 1, 2018, there no longer is a deduction for personal exemptions. The issue as to who gets the exemptions for the children is now moot.
2. For divorces after December 31, 2018, alimony will no longer be deductible nor includable in income. It will be treated just like child support for tax purposes.
3. For divorces prior to January 1, 2018, the old rules apply.

81 Interest on Qualified Education Loans

Interest paid on qualified education loans was deductible above the line for payments made during the first 60 months in which payments are required. After December 31, 2001, the 60-month limit is eliminated.

The maximum amount of this deduction was $1,000 for 1998, $1,500 for 1999, $2,000 for the year 2000, and is $2,500 for tax years 2001 and after.

The deduction is phased out for taxpayers with modified adjusted gross income between $65,000 and $80,000 for single filers, and between $135,000 and $165,000 for joint returns.

You must be legally obligated to make the payments (sign the note) and you can't be claimed as a dependent if you want to qualify for this deduction.

82 Retirement Plan Payments

As you get older, it is important that you carefully provide for sufficient retirement funds. The same consideration must also be given to sheltering current income from the painful bite of our progressive tax system. The above the line deduction for retirement plan payments allows you to satisfy both of these needs.

If you are self-employed, which includes being an owner or a partner of an unincorporated business, you may provide for your retirement by setting up either

a Keogh plan (H.R. 10 Plan), an individual 401(k) plan, or an Individual Retirement Plan, as described below. Under the Self-Employed Individual's Tax Retirement Act of 1962 (also called the Keogh Act and H.R. 10), you are permitted to put a portion of your yearly earned income, on a tax-deferred basis, into a fund that can earn tax-deferred income until it starts paying out at retirement.

You are eligible for an individual retirement account (IRA) if you or your spouse are employed, self-employed, or even covered by a corporate pension plan. You may have an IRA in addition to a Keogh plan. But, there will be limits as to what you can deduct.

Under both a traditional IRA and a Keogh plan, a portion of your income is sheltered from current taxation; there is no tax on the earnings of the fund until postretirement distribution; there is no tax on income contributed to the fund until post-retirement distribution; and qualified contributions made by employers to provide employees with retirement benefits are deductible by the employers. Keogh plans, individual 401(k)s, and IRAs allow the self-employed owner of a business to shelter current earned income and allow that income to accumulate and earn currently nontaxable income until postretirement distribution.

The primary difference between a Keogh plan and an IRA is the amount of earnings that may be sheltered. Under an IRA, as much as 100 percent of compensation—up to a normal limit of $5,500 a year—may be put aside, and that amount, subject to the limits detailed below, is deductible. If you have a non-employed spouse, both of you are age 50 or older, and your modified adjusted gross income is under $121,000, the potential contribution maximum increases to $13,000. With a Keogh plan, the contribution limits are 25[1] percent of earned income or $55,000 for 2018, whichever is less. Defined benefit plans allowed an amount computed to yield a maximum annual benefit of $220,000 for 2018. A special type of IRA called a Simplified Pension Plan will also allow contributions—the lesser of $55,000 or 25 percent for 2018 of earned income. The major constraint for both the Simplified Pension Plan and the Keogh plan is that in both cases the owner (considered an employee as well under certain plans) may be forced to make contributions for other employees as well; however, these contributions will be deductible. The ultimate decision as to whether to establish an IRA or Keogh plan or both should be made on the basis of which has the greatest cash savings after tax.

If you are an employer, you may set up an Individual Retirement Account for yourself without setting up a similar one for your employees. With a Keogh plan you must cover your employees.

1. For owner-employees only, this is 25 percent of income after the Keogh deduction. This really equals about 20 percent of pre-Keogh earned income. The actual number is a multistep calculation (see worksheet). I will be using the 20 percent figure as an estimate for examples and discussion.

For a Single Profit Sharing Plan or a Single Money Purchase Plan

Use this worksheet to calculate your annual Keogh contribution if you have a single Profit Sharing or Money Purchase Plan.

		Example	Yourself
1.	**Net Business Profits** (From Schedule C, C-EZ, or K-1)	$250,000	
2.	**Deduction for Self-Employment Tax** (From IRS Form 1040)	$9,969	
3.	**Adjusted Net Business Profits** (Subtract Line 2 from Line 1)	$240,031	
4.	**Actual Contribution Percentage (expressed as a decimal)** (Desired contribution percentage of earned income—for Money Purchase Plan, 3–25%; for Profit Sharing Plan, 0–25%)	.25	
5.	**Contribution Factor** (Add 1.00 to Line 4)	1.25	
6.	**Adjusted Earned Income** (Divide Line 3 by Line 5)	$192,025	
7.	**Maximum Earned Income** (Enter $275,000 for 2018)	$275,000	
8.	**Final Earned Income** (The lesser of Line 6 and Line 7)	$192,025	
9.	**Preliminary Contribution Amount** (Multiply Line 4 by Line 8, round down to closest dollar)	$48,006	
10.	**Maximum Dollar Contribution Amount** (Enter $55,000)	$55,000	
11.	**Contribution Amount** (The lesser of Line 9 and Line 10)	$48,006	

IRA PLAN[2]

There are several advantages to an IRA. An IRA allows the owner of a business to shelter personal earned income for retirement *without* the requirement to make contributions for employees. As a taxpayer eligible for an IRA, you would be allowed to contribute for a nonemployed spouse and the contribution maximum would increase ($2,000 each for years after 1996, increased to $3,000 each in 2002, $4,000 each in 2005, and to $5,500 each in 2008 and after, plus a $500 catch-up contribution [$1,000 for 2006 and after] if you're age 50 or older). The purpose of this is to provide retirement income for nonemployed homemakers. Contributions are deposited into separate accounts for you and your non-employed spouse or into one account with subaccounts for each. No one account, however, may have attributed to it more than $5,500 in contributions per year (plus catch-up). In case of divorce, the homemaker keeps his or her share of the money. Of course, if both spouses are employed and are eligible, each can set aside 100 percent of earnings, up to $5,500 each year, in separate IRAs.

The tax deduction for the IRA contribution is available as an above the line deduction. Taxes on both contributions to and earnings of the account may be deferred until the funds are withdrawn as retirement benefits. At that time you may be in a lower tax bracket than previously and may qualify for retirement income credits. At age 65 you are entitled to the additional standard deduction (now called "additional amounts"). So during the period you receive your IRA funds, you may be paying a smaller percentage of your income for taxes than you did in earlier years. Benefits from IRA plans can be drawn without penalty anytime after reaching age 59½. Distribution normally begins no later than April 1 in the year following the year you attain age 70½. This rule was modified by the Small Business Protection Act of 1996.

The 1996 law modified the rule that requires all participants in qualified plans to commence distributions by age 70½ without regard to whether the participant is still employed by the employer. Under the 1996 law, distributions are generally required to begin by April 1 of the calendar year following the later of the calendar year in which the employee attains age 70½ *or* the calendar year in which the employee retires. However, in the case of a 5 percent owner of the employer, distributions are required to begin no later than April 1 of the calendar year following the year in which the 5 percent owner attains age 70½. This does not apply to SEPs—see below.

In addition, in the case of an employee (other than a 5 percent owner) who retires in a calendar year after attaining age 70½, the 1996 law requires the employee's accrued benefit to be actuarially increased to take into account the period after age 70½ in which the employee was not receiving benefits under

2. Note that for tax years beginning after 1997, the Tax Relief Act of 1997 created new IRAs and modified the phase-out rules for old IRAs.

the plan. Thus, under the 1996 law, the employee's accrued benefit is required to reflect the value of benefits that the employee would have received if the employee had retired at age 70½ and had begun receiving benefits at that time. However, this actuarial adjustment rule does not apply in the case of a defined contribution plan.

Earnings eligible for IRA contributions include wages, salaries, or professional fees and other amounts received for personal services actually rendered, including (but not limited to) commissions paid to sales personnel, compensation for services on the basis of a percentage of profits, commissions on insurance premiums, tips, and bonuses. Retroactive to 2004, even tax exempt combat pay now qualifies. All contributions must be made in cash. No deductions are allowable for contributions of property other than cash.

If you receive payment from an IRA before you reach age 59½ or before you become disabled, the payment will normally be considered a premature distribution. That amount received is included in your gross income in the tax year of receipt. In addition, your income tax liability for that year will be increased by an amount equal to 10 percent of the premature distribution includable in gross income. This penalty can be avoided by withdrawing substantially equal annual amounts over your life expectancy, until age 59½ or for five years, whichever comes later. For example, if you are 58, you must make withdrawals through age 63. However, if you are age 45, you must continue making withdrawals through age 59½. Once you finish making the *required withdrawals* they may be modified or stopped.

As discussed previously, amounts withdrawn from an individual retirement account (IRA) are includable in income (except to the extent of any nondeductible contributions). In addition, a 10 percent additional tax applies to withdrawals from IRAs made before age 59½ and unless the withdrawal is made on account of death or disability or is made in the form of annuity payments.

A similar additional tax applies to early withdrawals from employer-sponsored tax qualified pension plans. However, the 10 percent additional tax does not apply to withdrawals from such plans to the extent used for medical expenses that exceed 7.5 percent of adjusted gross income.

The Small Business Job Protection Act of 1996 extended the exception to the 10 percent tax for medical expenses in excess of 10 percent (now back to 7.5 percent for 2017 and 2018) of adjusted gross income to withdrawals from IRAs. In addition, it provides that the 10 percent additional tax does not apply to withdrawals for medical insurance (without regard to the 10 percent of adjusted gross income) if the individual (including a self-employed individual) has received unemployment compensation under federal or state law for at least 12 weeks, and the withdrawal is made in the year such unemployment compensation is received or the following year. If a self-employed individual is not eligible for unemployment compensation under applicable law, he or she is treated as having received unemployment compensation for at least 12 weeks if the individual would

have received unemployment compensation but for the fact the individual was self-employed. You also avoid 10 percent penalty if you're age 55 or older and are "separated from service"—fancy legal talk for "lost your job."

The Taxpayer Relief Act of 1997 extended the exception to the 10 percent penalty to *first time home purchases* and *qualified higher education expenses.*

A first-time home buyer is an individual (and/or spouse) who has had no present ownership interest in a primary residence during the 2-year period ending on the date of acquisition (see following) of the principal residence. A first-time home buyer under these rules does not necessarily mean a person buying a home for the first time. For example, individuals could be buying their fifth home yet qualify as "first-time" home buyers if they have had no ownership interest in a primary residence for the past two years. *Both* spouses must qualify, and, if so, *both* may withdraw $10,000 from each IRA.

A date of acquisition is the date when a binding contract to purchase a principal residence is executed or the date when construction or reconstruction of a principal residence begins.

Qualified acquisition cost is the cost of acquiring, constructing, or reconstructing a residence.

The amount withdrawn for the purchase of a principal residence is required to be used within 120 days of the date of withdrawal. You are limited to a $10,000 lifetime withdrawal. Even though withdrawals made from traditional IRAs for first-time home purchases are penalty-free, they may be subject to regular income taxes. (Withdrawals from a Roth IRA, discussed in the following, can be both penalty *and* tax-free if the 5-year requirement is met.)

The 1997 tax law also allows you to make penalty-free withdrawals from traditional IRAs for higher education expenses, such as tuition at an eligible postsecondary education institution, room and board, fees, books, supplies, and equipment required for enrollment or attendance. Expenses for graduate-level courses also are covered. You can use your IRA distribution to pay for these expenses incurred by you, your spouse, your children, your spouse's children, your grandchildren, or your spouse's grandchildren. Please note that this type of withdrawal is not an income-tax-free distribution.

SUMMARY OF PREMATURE DISTRIBUTION RULES

Many taxpayers mistakenly fail to pay the additional 10 percent tax due on premature distributions. Premature distributions (sometimes called early withdrawals or early distributions) are subject to an additional 10 percent tax. The definition of premature distributions are amounts that are withdrawn from traditional individual retirement accounts (IRAs) or annuities before the individual reaches the age of 59½.

In certain circumstances, the additional penalty tax does not apply to premature distributions from an IRA or annuity even though they are made prior to reaching the age of 59½.

There are exceptions for:

- Effective only through December 31, 2007, those in the military, including the Reserve and National Guard, who were on active duty for at least 180 days after September 11, 2001.

- Certain unemployed individuals to pay health insurance premiums. To qualify, you must receive unemployment benefits for 12 consecutive weeks and tap the IRA either in the year that the benefits are paid or in the following year. The 10 percent penalty won't apply even if the medical premiums are paid before the withdrawal is made from the IRA (*Davis*, TC Summ. Op. 2009-61).

 Note that the distributions are still subject to income tax, except in the case of a Roth IRA. Contributions from Roth IRAs usually can be withdrawn free of tax.

- Certain medical expenses (beginning after December 31, 1996)

- Disability

- Death

- Annuity distributions

- Qualified higher education expenses (beginning after December 31, 1997)

- Qualified first-time home buyer (beginning after December 31, 1997 $10,000 lifetime limitation)

- IRS levy on IRA (beginning after December 31, 1999)

- Distributions under an "eligible automatic contribution arrangement," to wit, a qualified deferred compensation plan, See IRC 414(w)(1)(B).

The additional tax is equal to 10 percent of the premature distribution that must be included in gross income. The tax is in addition to any regular income tax that is due. It does not include tax-free rollovers. For more information regarding the additional 10 percent tax, see Publication 590, Individual Retirement Account Arrangements (IRAs) including Roth IRAs and Education IRAs.

Taxable distributions from an individual retirement account are taxed as ordinary income regardless of their source. They are not eligible for capital gains treatment or the special averaging rules that apply to lump-sum distribution from qualified employer plans (which were available only through December 31, 1999).

Under *old* minimum distribution rules, if you died before receiving the entire interest on your individual retirement account, the remaining interest had to be distributed to your beneficiary within 5 years after death, or be applied

Exception to 10% Additional Tax

Type of Distribution	401(k) and Other Qualified Retirement Plans	IRA/SEP, SIMPLE IRA and SARSEP Plans	Internal Revenue Code
After participant/IRA owner reaches age 59½	Yes	Yes	§72(t)(2)(A)(i)
After *death* of the participant/IRA owner	Yes	Yes	§72(t)(2)(A)(ii)
Total and permanent *disability* of the participant/IRA owner	Yes	Yes	§72(t)(2)(A)(iii)
Series of substantially equal payments	Yes	Yes	§72(t)(2)(A)(iv)
Separation from service during or after year employee reaches age 55 (age 50 for public safety employees)	Yes	No	§§72(t)(2)(A)(v) and 72(t)(10)
Dividend pass through from an ESOP	Yes	N/A	§72(t)(2)(A)(vi)
Because of an IRS levy of the plan	Yes	Yes	§72(t)(2)(A)(vii)
Amount of your *unreimbursed medical expenses* (> 7.5% AGI)	Yes	Yes	§72(t)(2)(B)
To an alternate payee under a *Qualified Domestic Relations Order*	Yes	No	§72(t)(2)(C)
Payment of health insurance premiums made while unemployed	No	Yes	§72(t)(2)(D)
Qualified higher education expenses	No	Yes	§72(t)(2)(E)
Qualified first-time homebuyers up to $10,000	No	Yes	§72(t)(2)(F)
Certain distributions to qualified military reservists called to active duty	Yes	Yes	§72(t)(2)(G)
Corrective distributions (and associated earnings) of excess deferrals, excess contributions, and excess aggregate contributions made timely	Yes	N/A	§§401(k)(8)(D), 401(m)(7), and 402(g)(2)(C)
Excess IRA contributions if withdrawn by extended due date of return	N/A	Yes	§408(d)(4)
Earning on *excess* IRA contributions distributed	N/A	No	§408(d)(4)
Permissive *withdrawals* from a plan with auto enrollment features	Yes	Yes for SIMPLE IRAs and SARSEPs	§414(w)(1)(B)
Rollovers	Yes	Yes	§§402(c), 403(a)(4), 403(b)(8), 408(d)(3), and 408A(d)(3)(A)

Governmental 457(b) distributions are not subject to the 10% additional tax except for distributions attributable to rollovers from another type of plan or IRA.

to purchase an immediate annuity for the beneficiary payable over the life or for a period not exceeding the life expectancy of that beneficiary. Any annuity contracts so purchased had to be distributed immediately to the beneficiary. A spousal beneficiary may roll the distribution into his or her own IRA account.

NEW MINIMUM DISTRIBUTION RULES

On January 11, 2001, the Internal Revenue Service proposed regulations (REG-130477-00, REG-130481-00) to simplify the minimum distribution rules for qualified plans and individual retirement accounts.

The rules would:

- Provide a uniform table to determine lifetime required minimum distributions regardless of age
- Permit a beneficiary to be determined up to the end of the year following an employee's death
- Allow life expectancy at the time of death to be taken into account in the calculation of postdeath minimum distributions.

The IRS said the regulations would affect qualified plans, individual retirement plans, tax code Sec. 457 plans, tax code Sec. 403(b) annuity contracts, custodial accounts, and retirement income accounts. The rules would be permissable for determining required minimum distributions for calendar years beginning on or after January 1, 2001, and must be used for distributions after December 31, 2001. However, they could *not* be used for calculating 2000 distributions deferred and made during the 3-month grace period—ending April 1, 2001—available to IRA owners who turned 70½ during 2000.

The regulations provide a uniform distribution period for all employees of the same age, calculated by the minimum distribution incidental benefit divisor table. The MDIB table—based on the joint life expectancies of an individual and a survivor 10 years younger at each age beginning at 70—would allow employees to determine their required minimum distribution each year based only on current age and current account balance, IRS said.

There are now only two calculation choices to be made:

1. **Uniform Distribution Table, Recalculated Life Expectancy.** This method will be used by all IRA owners with one exception, as noted in No. 2. IRA owners will obtain their life expectancy factor from the Uniform Distribution Table. The Uniform Distribution Table [referred to in IRS Publication 590 as the Table for Determining Applicable Divisor for MDIB (Minimum Distribution Incidental Benefit)] assumes that RMDs are based on the lives of an IRA owner and a beneficiary who is 10 years younger than the IRA owner. The IRA owner will refer back to the Uniform (MDIB) Distribution

Table each calendar year and use the factor that appears next to the IRA owner's age on his or her birthday during that year. This method should be used whether an individual or a nonliving entity (such as a charity, trust, or estate) is named as the primary beneficiary of the IRA account.

2. **Joint Life Expectancy, Recalculating Both Life Expectancies.** This is the one exception to the Uniform Distribution Table rule in No. 1: If an IRA owner has named his or her spouse as the *sole primary beneficiary for the entire calendar year and the spouse is more than 10 years younger than the IRA owner,* the IRA owner can choose to use the Joint Life Expectancy Tables. The IRA owner refers back to the Joint Life Expectancy Tables each calendar year and uses the factor that appears at the intersection of the ages of the IRA owner and younger spouse as of their birthdays in that year.

The amount of the Required Minimum Distribution (RMD) is determined by taking the IRA account balance as of the end of the prior year (December 31 value), and then dividing it by the life expectancy factor for that year.

December 31 prior-year balance/life expectancy factor = RMD

The minimum distribution rules were waived for 2009, but returned for 2010 and after.

Note that RMDs must be calculated separately and distributed separately from each employer-sponsored account. But RMDs for IRAs can be aggregated, and the total can be withdrawn from one or multiple IRAs.

CALCULATING IRA REQUIRED MINIMUM DISTRIBUTIONS

Use the following table to compute your required minimum distribution. Take the account balance on December 31 of the previous year and divide it by the figure next to your age. If a spouse beneficiary is more than 10 years younger than you are, use the joint-life-and-last-survivor table in IRS Pub. 590.

The minimum distribution rules were amended in 2014 to make room for *"longevity" annuities,* deeply deferred income annuities, by providing that if the annuity is payable not later than age 85 and meets certain conditions, it's taken out of the equation for calculating the minimum distribution amount. (See T.D. 9673.) A Qualified Longevity Annuity Contract is called a *"QLAC"*

The maximum permitted investment you can use to purchase qualifying longevity annuity contracts without worrying about noncompliance with the age 70½ minimum distribution requirements is 25 percent of your account balance, or $125,000, whichever is less. The $125,000 limit will increase with inflation in $10,000 increments.

IRA Required Minimum Distributions

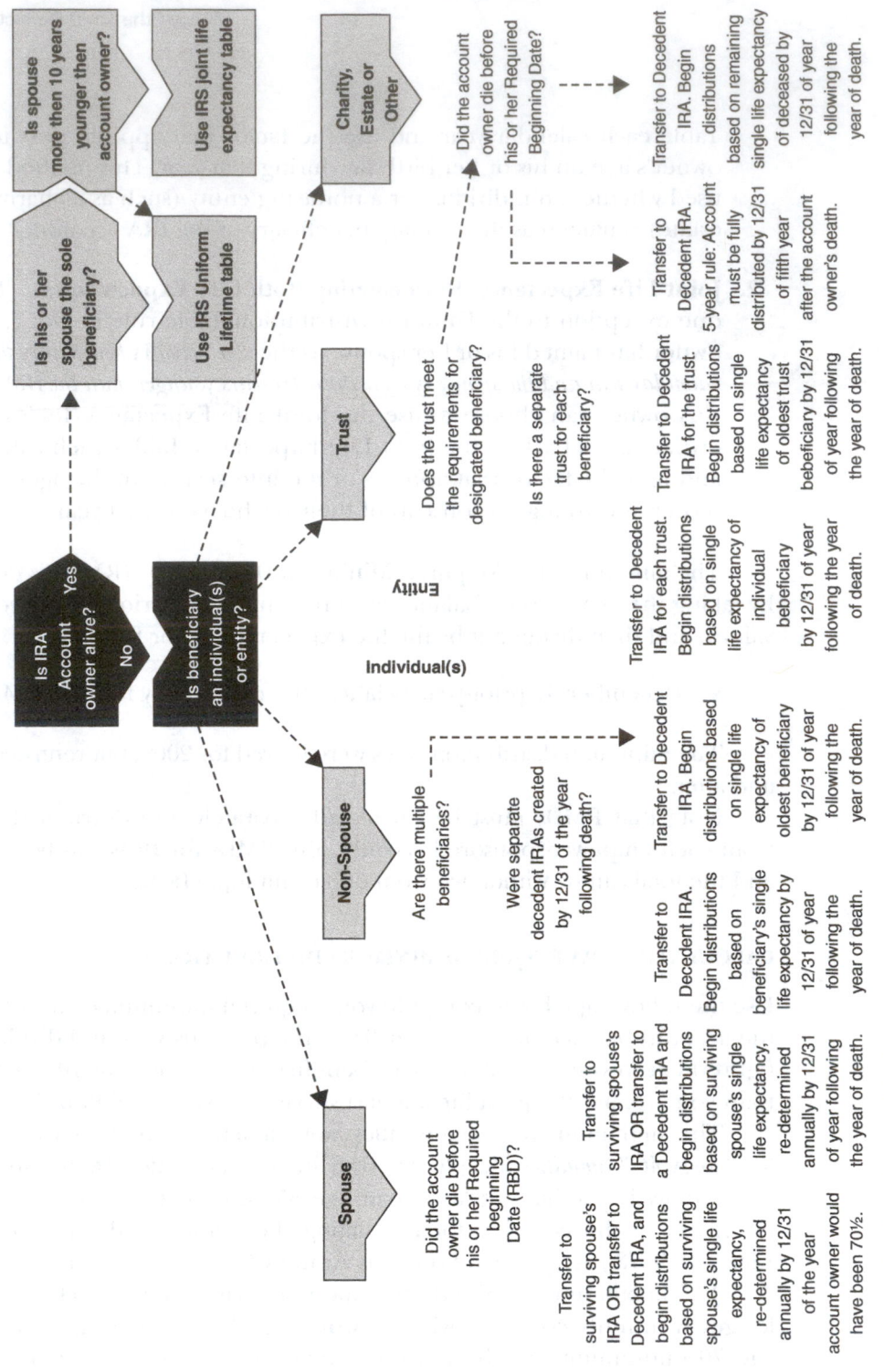

Source: Stephen D. Leightman of RBC Management

Uniform Distribution Table

This table is the new life expectancy table to be used by all IRA owners to calculate lifetime distributions (unless your beneficiary is your spouse who is more than 10 years younger than you). In that case, you would not use this table, you would use the actual joint life expectancy of you and your spouse based on the regular joint life expectancy table. The Uniform Distribution Table is never used by IRA beneficiaries to compute required distributions on their inherited IRAs.

Age	Distribution Period	Age	Distribution Period	Age	Distribution Period	Age	Distribution Period / Life Expectancy
70	27.4	81	17.9	92	10.2	103	5.2
71	26.5	82	17.1	93	9.6	104	4.9
72	25.6	83	16.3	94	9.1	105	4.5
73	24.7	84	15.5	95	8.6	106	4.2
74	23.8	85	14.8	96	8.1	107	3.9
75	22.9	86	14.1	97	7.6	108	3.7
76	22.0	87	13.4	98	7.1	109	3.4
77	21.2	88	12.7	99	6.7	110	3.1
78	20.3	89	12.0	100	6.3	111	2.9
79	19.5	90	11.4	101	5.9	112	2.6
80	18.7	91	10.8	102	5.5	113	2.4
						114	2.1
						115 & over	1.9

Single Life Expectancy Table for Inherited IRAs*

(to be used for calculating post-death required distributions to beneficiaries)

Designated beneficiaries use this single life expectancy table based on their age in the year after the IRA owner's death. That factor is reduced by one for each succeeding distribution year. Spouse beneficiaries who do not elect to roll the IRA over or treat it as their own, also use the single life table, but they can recalculate each year.

Age	Life Expectancy	Age	Life Expectancy	Age	Life Expectancy	Age	Life Expectancy
10	72.8	29	54.3	48	36.0	67	19.4
11	71.8	30	53.3	49	35.1	68	18.6
12	70.8	31	52.4	50	34.2	69	17.8
13	69.9	32	51.4	51	33.3	70	17.0
14	68.9	33	50.4	52	32.3	71	16.3
15	67.9	34	49.4	53	31.4	72	15.5
16	66.9	35	48.5	54	30.5	73	14.8
17	66.0	36	47.5	55	29.6	74	14.1
18	65.0	37	46.5	56	28.7	75	13.4
19	64.0	38	45.6	57	27.9	76	12.7
20	63.0	39	44.6	58	27.0	77	12.1
21	62.1	40	43.6	59	26.1	78	11.4
22	61.1	41	42.7	60	25.2	79	10.8
23	60.1	42	41.7	61	24.4	80	10.2
24	59.1	43	40.7	62	23.5	81	9.7
25	58.2	44	39.8	63	22.7	82	9.1
26	57.2	45	38.8	64	21.8	83	8.6
27	56.2	46	37.9	65	21.0	84	8.1
28	55.3	47	37.0	66	20.2	85	7.6

*partial table – full table can be found in IRS Publication 590 – www.IRS.gov

These annuities can provide a "return of premium" feature that allows beneficiaries of a deceased owner to recapture the difference between premiums paid and benefits received.

BENEFICIARY RULES

You no longer have to name a beneficiary for your account by April 1 of the year after you reach age 70½. Failing to do so used to trigger a demand that the IRA be paid out over your relatively brief single-life expectancy. Now, you'll use the uniform life expectancy table even if you don't name a beneficiary. You can name—and change—your beneficiaries at any time, without worrying that a post-70½ switch will speed up required withdrawals.

In most cases, after your death, your beneficiary will use his or her own life expectancy (as shown in Publication 590 and Publication 590 Sup) to figure distributions.

If there are multiple beneficiaries to a single account, the payout is based on the oldest beneficiary's life expectancy. To expand the payout time, you might consider multiple accounts with a single beneficiary for each. This method gives your heirs the longest possible period of tax deferral and is best guaranteed by naming a designated beneficiary on your IRA.

Forced lump-sum distributions are gone. Under the new rules, your heirs will never face the tax consequences of being forced to empty the IRA in a single year.

If you die *after* required distributions begin and *without a designated beneficiary,* the distribution period for your heirs will generally be your remaining life expectancy at the end of the year after your death.

If you die *before* mandatory payouts begin and *without a designated beneficiary,* at worst the IRS will allow your heirs up to 5 years to withdraw the money and pay taxes.

BENEFICIARY DISTRIBUTION OPTIONS

	BENEFICIARY	DISTRIBUTION OPTIONS
Death Before Required Beginning Date	**Spouse**	1. Transfer or roll to own IRA. • RMDs must begin at 70½. 2. Decedent IRA—Distributions are required to begin by 12/31 of the year the account owner would have been 70½. • Distributions are based on the single life expectancy of the surviving spouse, redetermined annually. • No 10% penalty. 3. Lump Sum Distribution.
	Non-Spouse— Designated Beneficiary	1. Decedent IRA—Annual distributions must begin by 12/31 of the year following the year of the account owner's death. • Separate beneficiary accounts are established.

BENEFICIARY DISTRIBUTION OPTIONS *(continued)*

	BENEFICIARY	DISTRIBUTION OPTIONS
Death After Required Beginning Date		• Distributions are based on the single life expectancy of the beneficiary, reduced by one for each subsequent year. 2. Five-year death rule. • Discretionary payouts until 12/31 of fifth year after the account owner's death. Account must be fully paid out by this date.
	Non-Spouse—No Designated Beneficiary	1. Five-year death rule. • Discretionary payouts until 12/31 of fifth year after the account owner's death. Account must be fully paid out by this date.
	Spouse	1. Transfer or roll to own IRA. • RMDs must begin at 70½. 2. Decedent IRA—Annual distributions must begin by 12/31 of the year following the year of the account owner's death. • Distributions are based on the single life expectancy of the surviving spouse, redetermined annually. • No 10% penalty. 3. Lump Sum Distribution.
	Non-Spouse— Designated Beneficiary	1. Decedent IRA—Annual distributions must begin by 12/31 of the year following the year of the account owner's death. • Separate beneficiary accounts are established. • Distributions are based on the single life expectancy of the beneficiary, reduced by one for each subsequent year or the hypothetical remaining life expectancy of the deceased account owner, whichever is longer. 2. Five-year death rule. • Discretionary payouts until 12/31 of fifth year after the account owner's death. Account must be fully paid out by this date.
	Non-Spouse—No Designated Beneficiary	1. Decedent IRA—Annual distributions must begin by 12/31 of the year following the year of the account owner's death. • Distributions are based on hypothetical remaining life expectancy of the deceased account owner, reduced by one for each subsequent year.

Source: Stephen D. Leightman RBC Wealth Management

A beneficiary who is a surviving spouse can roll over the dollars into his or her own IRA. This allows the spouse to use the uniform Distribution Table and to name beneficiaries that can further extend the payout life of the account.

Under the new RMD rules, non-spousal beneficiaries (e.g., a child) can "stretch" out payments over his or her own life expectancy as well! This results in longer tax defined compounding inside the IRA and much greater family wealth creation.

An excellent MDR calculation can be found at Professor Stephen A. Leimberg's www.Leimbergservices.com.

Also see the following websites for more details:

- www.ataxplan.com
- www.irahelp.com
- www.stretchira.com

Avoiding Rollover Penalties

You can now self-certify that you qualify for a waiver of the 60-day rollover rule. The rollover must be completed within 30 days after the reason for failing to timely do it in the first place ceases (Rev. Proc. 2016-47). Use the following letter* provided by the IRS:

Example of the Certification for Late Rollover Contribution (included in Rev. Proc 2016-47)
Certification for Late Rollover Contribution

> *Name*
> *Address*
> *City, State, ZIP Code*
> Date:_____

Plan Administrator/Financial Institution
Address
City, State, ZIP Code

Dear Sir or Madam:

Pursuant to Internal Revenue Service Revenue Procedure 2016–47, I certify that my contribution of $ [ENTER AMOUNT] missed the 60-day rollover deadline for the reason(s) listed below under Reasons for Late Contribution. I am making this contribution as soon as practicable after the reason or reasons listed below no longer prevent me from making the contribution. I understand that this certification concerns only the 60-day requirement for a rollover and that, to complete the rollover, I must comply with all other tax law requirements for a valid rollover and with your rollover procedures.

Pursuant to Revenue Procedure 2016–47, unless you have actual knowledge to the contrary, you may rely on this certification to show that I have satisfied the conditions for a waiver of the 60-day rollover requirement for the amount identified above. You may not

*You send the letter to your IRS trustee or retirement plan administrator, not the IRS.

rely on this certification in determining whether the contribution satisfies other requirements for a valid rollover.

Reasons for Late Contribution

I intended to make the rollover within 60 days after receiving the distribution but was unable to do so for the following reason(s) (check all that apply):

— An error was committed by the financial institution making the distribution or receiving the contribution.

— The distribution was in the form of a check and the check was misplaced and never cashed.

— The distribution was deposited into and remained in an account that I mistakenly thought was a retirement plan or IRA.

— My principal residence was severely damaged.

— One of my family members died.

— I or one of my family members was seriously ill.

— I was incarcerated.

— Restrictions were imposed by a foreign country.

— A postal error occurred.

— The distribution was made on account of an IRS levy and the proceeds of the levy have been returned to me.

— The party making the distribution delayed providing information that the receiving plan or IRA required to complete the rollover despite my reasonable efforts to obtain the information.

Signature

I declare that the representations made in this document are true and that the IRS has not previously denied a request for a waiver of the 60-day rollover requirement with respect to a rollover of all or part of the distribution to which this contribution relates. I understand that in the event I am audited and the IRS does not grant a waiver for this contribution, I may be subject to income and excise taxes, interest, and penalties. If the contribution is made to an IRA, I understand you will be required to report the contribution to the IRS. I also understand that I should retain a copy of this signed certification with my tax records.

Signature:_____

You can call the IRS toll-free at 1(877)-829-5500 if you have a question on retirement plans.

Trusts As Beneficiary

Trusts offer asset protection against third-party claims. Remember, *inherited* IRAs do not have creditor protection. But normally if a trust is a beneficiary, the withdrawal period is shortened to only 5 years.

You can get around this problem by using a "designated beneficiary trust" or "look through trust." Then, the lifespan of the oldest beneficiary becomes the lifespan of the trust, if:

1. The trust is valid under state law
2. The trust is irrevocable, or becomes so at the death of the IRA owner
3. The beneficiaries of the trust are limited to people and are identifiable.
4. A copy of the trust is given to the IRA custodian by October 31st of the year immediately following the year in which the IRA owner died.

CONTRIBUTIONS

Tax-deductible contributions to an IRA must be made through:

a) an individual retirement account at a bank, federally insured credit union, or savings and loan association, or with certain applicants, any of whom, under temporary regulations, may act as a trustee or custodian;

b) an individual retirement annuity of a life insurance company;

c) individual retirement bonds purchased from the U.S. government; *or*

d) a trust account established by an employer or employee association.

The following transactions with IRA money are prohibited by law:

1. You cannot borrow money from your IRA.
2. You cannot use money in an IRA as collateral for a loan.
3. You cannot transfer property to an IRA in exchange for money.
4. You can put only cash into an IRA. For example, you cannot put stock that you currently own into an IRA account. You must sell the stock first, put the cash from that sale into your IRA, and then purchase the stock again if you want to have that stock in the IRA account.

While not specifically prohibited, note that an IRA investment in a limited partnership interest where business income is passed through would trigger an IRA tax on "unrelated business income" (IRS Letter Ruling 9703026). Any debt-financed property inside a qualified plan will trigger this unrelated business tax (UBT).

You can, however, invest your IRA funds in real estate—from raw land to rental property. While you can't manage the property, your trustee can hire a third party to do so. Moreover, the property must remain in the IRA trust until distribution at retirement and the property can't be mortgaged. Based on *Swanson v.*

Commissioner, 106 T.C. 76 (1996), some advisors suggest forming a limited liability company wherein the IRA accountholder is named the manager of the LLC. The accountholder instructs the IRA custodian to deposit the IRA assets into the newly formed LLC. If you want real estate in your IRA, check out Steve Berman and Jay Suttenberg at the Laurel Group, 856-857-2859, www.realestate4IRA.com, or see independent IRA custodians, independent IRA administrators, and IRA advisors www.sterling-trust.com or call toll-free 1-800-955-3434.

Other custodians who take IRAs with unconventional assets, such as real estate or business interests, include:

Fiserv Investment Support Services (recent rollup of Lincoln Trust, First Trust, Resources Trust, Retirement Accounts): 800-525-2124, www.fiserviss.com

Pensco Trust: 415-274-5600, www.pensco.com

Millennium Trust: 800-258-7878, www.mtrustcompany.com

Quads: 800-435-7024, www.quadsweb.com

Trust Administration Services: 800-455-9472, www.trustlynk.com

Moreover, you should note that any stock in an IRA account that is sold loses the capital gains treatment. This means that when you withdraw your money from the IRA, gains cannot be offset by capital losses.

ELIGIBILITY

Starting with 1987, the Tax Reform Act of 1986 made substantial changes in IRA eligibility. Under the prior law, IRA deduction is retained for returns of taxpayers who meet *either* of the following requirements:

1. The taxpayer is not an active participant in certain specified retirement arrangements for any part of the plan year ending with or within the taxpayer's tax year. Active participation status is determined without regard to whether a taxpayer has a vested right to any benefits under a plan and may depend upon the type of plan in which an individual participates or is eligible to participate. For example, for defined benefit plans, a person who is not excluded under the plan's eligibility provisions for any part of the plan year ending with or within the taxpayer's tax year is an active participant. Therefore, even if you elect not to participate in a plan or fail to make an employee contribution required to accrue a benefit attributable to employer contributions, you nevertheless are an active participant in the plan. For defined contribution plans, a taxpayer is an active participant if employer or employee contributions or forfeitures are required to be allocated to his account for a plan year ending with or within the taxpayer's tax year.

According to the IRS, a taxpayer may be an active participant even if a required contribution for the plan year is not actually made. However, unlike defined benefit plans, an individual who does not meet the hours of service requirements of a defined contribution plan is not considered an active participant unless contributions or forfeitures have been allocated to her account. For a married individual filing a joint return, neither the individual taxpayer nor the taxpayer's spouse may be an active participant. Moreover, retirement arrangements not only include traditional qualified plans, annuity plans, and trusts, but also include simplified employee pensions and 401(k) plans. For 401(k) plans however, you are usually not an "actual participant" until pay-ins are made to the plan.

2. The taxpayer has adjusted gross income that does not exceed the "applicable dollar amount." For a married couple filing jointly, combined income may not exceed the applicable dollar amount. The applicable dollar amount *was* (a) $25,000 for an individual, (b) $40,000 for a married couple filing a joint return, and (c) $0 for a married couple filing separately.

$$\frac{\$10,000 - \text{excess adjusted gross income}}{\$10,000} \times \begin{array}{c} \text{the maximum permissible} \\ \text{dollar deduction defined} \\ \text{as the lesser of 100} \\ \text{percent of compensation} \\ \text{or \$2,000 (\$2,250 for} \\ \text{spousal IRAs)} \end{array} = \begin{array}{c} \text{adjusted dollar} \\ \text{deduction limit} \end{array}$$

Active participants whose adjusted gross incomes exceed the applicable dollar amount by no more than $10,000 are still entitled to deduct IRA contributions, but only in a reduced amount calculated according to the following formula provided by the IRS:

Note that for this purpose, adjusted gross income includes Social Security benefits and passive income or losses, but not IRA contributions.

For example, assume in 1997 that you and your spouse earned $25,000 and $20,000 in adjusted gross income (total $45,000) and that your spouse was a participant in a qualified pension plan. Your maximum permissible dollar deduction would have been $4,000 ($2,000 for you and $2,000 for your spouse). Your maximum deductible IRA, however, would be computed as follows:

Maximum IRA		$4,000
Less: Phase-out over $40,000		
$\dfrac{(\$45,000 - \$40,000) \times \$4,000}{\$10,000}$	=	$2,000
Tax-deductible IRA		$2,000

Your maximum tax-deductible IRA would therefore be only $2,000. Taxpayers not above the phaseout maximum are permitted a minimum IRA deduction of $200. Moreover, prior to the Tax Reform Act of 1986, a spousal IRA of $250 was allowed only if the spouse had no compensation. Under current law, an individual may elect to be treated as if he or she had no compensation for the taxable year. This means, for an otherwise qualifying couple, the annual deduction contribution has increased from $2,000 to $2,250 ($4,000 for years after 1996, becoming $6,000 for 2002 and $8,000 for 2005, and $10,000 for 2008 through 2012, and $11,000 for 2013 and after).

The Taxpayer Relief Act of 1997 changed the rules again. We now have three kinds of IRAs. The first is the current deductible IRA. The 1997 law raised the phase-out income limits on these front-loaded IRAs for those covered by a qualified plan. Note that the law allows a nonworking spouse to contribute a fully deductible $5,500, even if the other spouse participates in a qualified retirement plan, with a phase-out of $189,000–$199,000 in 2018. The following table summarizes the changes in phase-out rules:

	Joint (in thousands)	Single (in thousands)
1997	$40–50	$25–35
1998	50–60	30–40
1999	51–61	31–41
2000	52–62	32–42
2001	53–63	33–43
2002	54–64	34–44
2003	60–70	40–50
2004	65–75	45–55
2005	70–80	50–60
2006	75–85	50–60
2007	83–103	52–62
2008	85–105	53–63
2009	89–109	55–65
2010	89–109	56–66
2011	90–110	56–66
2012	92–112	58–68
2013	95–115	59–69
2014	96–116	60–70
2015	98–118	61–71
2016	98–118	61–71
2017	99–119	62–72
2018	101–121	63–73

ROTH IRA

The second kind of IRA is the *Roth IRA*. Here, contributions will not be deductible but, if the IRA is held for at least 5 years (the 5-year period starts on the first day of the year for which a contribution is made or in which the first conversion contribution is made) and the account holder is at least 59½ years old, then all withdrawals will be tax-free! Moreover, more people will be eligible to fund these accounts. The 2018 income limits phased out at from $120,000–$135,000 for single taxpayers and from $189,000–$199,000 for couples. However, the combined contributions to these two types of accounts are limited to $5,500 per year for each taxpayer. You could roll a regular IRA into a Roth IRA account but some taxes would be assessed upon the rollover. These taxes were spread over 4 years, if done in 1998, to minimize the impact of the change. I think it was a reasonable toll charge to avoid all future taxes on the account. After 1998, the 4-year spread is not available. Whether you should convert to a Roth is a function of your age and the expected return on the account. The older you are, the less advantageous the conversion becomes. See page 244 for current conversion opportunities.

More than two dozen financial services companies offer Roth IRAs for minors. Here are some examples:

- **American Century Investments:** 800-345-2021

- **Franklin Templeton Investments:** 800-632-2301

- **Strong Financial:** 800-368-1030

- **T. Rowe Price:** 800-638-5660

- **Vanguard Group:** 800-662-7447

Note that distributions from Roth IRAs that are not qualified distributions are generally treated as a recovery of basis first, and then as taxable distributions.

Roth 401(k) and Roth 403(b) distributions that are not qualified distributions are treated differently—they are generally taxed on a pro rata basis.

The Tax Increase Protection and Reconciliation Act of 2005, passed in 2006, eliminated the income limits on conversions of traditional IRAs to a Roth for years starting January 1, 2010. But, you did not have to wait till then. You could have contributed to nondeductible IRAs before 2010 if your income was too high. Then, convert those dollars to a Roth. You pay tax only on the gain, and that tax was spread over 2 years, 2011 and 2012 if you converted in 2010. You can't do this back door Roth contribution once you are age 70½. That's because you can't make any traditional IRA contributions once you reach that age.

The new rule on *after-tax* contributions is much more liberal than the one that governs a conversion from a traditional IRA to a Roth IRA. In that case, the

tax-free portion of the rollover is determined by the ratio of nondeductible pay-ins to the total amount in all of your IRAs. So if your $60,000 IRA contains $6,000 in nondeductible contributions ("after-tax money") and you convert that $6,000 to a Roth IRA, just $600, or one-tenth of the converted amount, would escape income tax. The remaining $5,400 would be taxed at your regular income tax rate. But under the new rules (IRS Notice 2014-54) for after-tax money in *401(k)s and 403(b)s and 457 plans,* the full $6,000 would escape taxes if you use separate accounts for taxable and nontaxable amounts. Plus, there is no limit on how much you may convert.

You can even use the new *non*pro rata rules to pocket your contributions from a designated Roth account, which have already been taxed, while doing a tax-free rollover of your earnings from that account into another Roth IRA. Take your principal—roll your earnings!

What if you convert an IRA to a Roth and the value goes down? Consider using separate Roth IRAs for different asset classes. For the ones that go down in value, you can escape tax on the higher value by recharacterization to a traditional IRA before the due date of the return (plus extensions—normally until October 15). Then, if you want, you can reconvert to a Roth at the new lower value, at a lower tax cost.

For more information about firms that offer Roths, try the Investment Company Institute's Website, at www.ici.org.

MILITARY SURVIVORS ROLLOVER

Under the Heroes Earning Assistance and Relief Tax Act (HEART Act) of 2008, the entirety of a service member's $400,000 life insurance policy, plus an additional $100,000 for a combat-related fatality, can be rolled directly into a Roth. You take tax-free proceeds and put them into a tax-free investment account. But you have only one year to put the money into the Roth.

COVERDELL EDUCATION IRAs

The 1997 law created a new *Education IRA,* also called *Education Savings Accounts.* As of July 26, 2001, they are called *Coverdell Education Accounts.* Contributions could be made of up to $500 per child under age 18 into an Education IRA, with a *then* income limit of from between $95,000 and $110,000 for singles and $150,000 and $160,000 for couples. These IRAs are *nondeductible,* but the earnings are tax-free. There is no penalty if they are used for educational purposes (including tuition, fees, room and board), regardless of your age. Any unused portion of an Education IRA can be rolled over to another child but, if the children do not attend college, the amounts must be paid out when the last child turns 30. Even if you don't qualify because of income limits, your parents may qualify to set up an account for their grandchildren. With an Education IRA, the donor doesn't even have to be related to the beneficiary!

Provision	Traditional IRA	Roth IRA
Eligibility Requirements	Contributions can be made through an individual's 69½ year as long as that individual, or their spouse, has earned income.	Contributions can be made at any age as long as the contributor, or their spouse, has earned income and your modified-adjusted gross income (MAGI) does not exceed (for 2013):

	Full Contribution	Partial Contribution	Not Eligible Contrib.
Single Filers	up to $119,999	$120,000–$134,999	$135,000 or more
Joint Filers	up to $188,999	$189,000–$198,999	$199,000 or more
Married, Filing Separately	up to $9,999	Not eligible	$10,000 or more

Provision	Traditional IRA	Roth IRA
Maximum Contribution Limits	• For 2018, the maximum contribution limit is $5,500. • In 2018 an individual age 50 or older may contribute an additional $1,000. • Annual total contribution limit between Traditional IRA and Roth IRA in 2018, is $5,500 (or $6,500 if age 50 or over).	Same as Traditional IRA, subject to restrictions on MAGI as noted in Eligibility Requirements above.
Contribution Deadline	Tax Filing Deadline not including extensions (generally April 15).	Tax Filing Deadline not including extensions (generally April 15).
Key Tax Advantage	Tax-deferred growth. Contribution may be tax deductible.	Federally tax-free growth.
Deductibility of Contributions	Yes, subject to retirement plan participation and MAGI limits: Single filer, retirement plan participant with MAGI of: 2018 **Fully Deductible** $63,000 or less **Partially Deductible** $63,001–$72,999 **Nondeductible** $73,000 or more Single filer, no retirement plan participation: Fully deductible Married, filing separately, retirement plan participant with MAGI of: 2018 **Partially Deductible** $0–$10,000 Married, filing a joint return, retirement plan participant with MAGI of: 2018 **Fully Deductible** $101,000 or less **Partially Deductible** $101,001–$120,999 **Nondeductible** $121,000 or more	All contributions are nondeductible.

Provision	Traditional IRA	Roth IRA
	Joint filer, no retirement plan participation (but spouse is participant) with MAGI of: **2018** **Fully Deductible** $188,999 or less **Partially Deductible** $189,000–$198,999 **Nondeductible** $199,000 or more **Joint filer, neither spouse is a retirement plan participant: Fully deductible**	
Required Distributions	Minimum distributions must begin by Required Beginning Date which is April 1 following 70½ year.	No minimum distributions required at any age.
Taxation of Distributions	• Taxes are deferred until distributions are made. All earnings and deductible contributions are taxed as ordinary income upon withdrawal. • If nondeductible contributions have been made each withdrawal is taxed proportionately. You use IRS Form 8606 to calculate your tax-free portion. Non-taxable distributions are also not subject to the 10% premature penalty.	**Qualifying Distributions** are tax and penalty free if your initial contribution to your Roth IRA was made at least five years ago and one of the following exceptions apply: • Attainment of age 59½ or older • Disability • Qualified first time home purchase • Distribution is made to an (lifetime limit of $10,000) account beneficiary **Non-Qualified Distributions** • *Annual contributions* can be withdrawn tax and penalty free at any time. • Distributions from a *conversion amount* must satisfy a five-year investment period to avoid the 10% penalty, unless an exception applies. The conversion amount is not subject to taxation. • Distributions from *earnings* will be taxed as ordinary income unless they are a qualifying distribution. They also will be subject to the 10% penalty unless an exception applies. The exceptions are the same as those for Traditional IRAs.
Exceptions to 10% Premature Penalty	Distributions taken on or after age 59½ or on account of: • Death • Substantially Equal Periodic Payments • Disability • Medical expenses in excess of 7½% AGI • Higher education expenses • Involuntary distributions due to an IRS levy • Insurance premiums paid by certain unemployed individuals • Qualified acquisition costs of a first time home buyer (lifetime limit of $10,000)	Distributions taken on or after age 59½ or on account of: • Death • Substantially Equal Periodic Payments • Disability • Medical expenses in excess of 7½% AGI • Higher education expenses • Involuntary distributions due to an IRS levy • Insurance premiums paid by certain unemployed individuals • Qualified acquisition costs of a first time home buyer (lifetime limit of $10,000)
Death Distributions	Regardless of when the owner dies: • Spouse can transfer directly to own IRA. • If beneficiary is non-spouse living person or qualifying trust: ♦ Generally, distributions must commence by 12/31 of the year following the year of death over the single declining life expectancy of the designated beneficiary; or, ♦ Exception: the 5-year rule.	Regardless of when the owner dies: • Spouse can transfer directly to own IRA. • If beneficiary is non-spouse living person or qualifying trust: ♦ Generally, distributions must commence by 12/31 of the year following the year of death over the single declining life expectancy of the designated beneficiary; or, ♦ Exception: the 5-year rule.

(continues)

2018 Options At-a-Glance *(continued)*

Provision	Traditional IRA	Roth IRA
Conversions	• Conversion from Traditional IRA, Simple IRA, SEP IRA or qualified plan to Roth IRA is allowed regardless of income. • The amount converted is taxed as ordinary income, but no 10% penalty applies.	• Conversion from Traditional IRA, Simple IRA,[1] SEP IRA or qualified plan to Roth IRA is allowed regardless of income. • The amount converted is taxed as ordinary income, but no 10% penalty applies.
Transfers	• Assets can be transferred to another Trustee/Custodian. • A transfer may not be made between a Traditional IRA and a Roth IRA (however, a distribution from a Traditional IRA and subsequent conversion to a Roth IRA may be made).	• Assets can be transferred to another Trustee/Custodian. • A transfer may not be made between a Traditional IRA and a Roth IRA (however, a distribution from a Traditional IRA and subsequent conversion to a Roth IRA may be made).
Rollovers	• Traditional IRA, SEP IRA, SARSEP or Simple IRA1 to Traditional IRA • With Triggering Event • Qualified Plan to Traditional IRA • 403(b) Plan to Traditional IRA • Governmental Thrift Savings Plan to Traditional IRA • Governmental 457(b) to Traditional IRA	• Roth IRA to Roth IRA

[1]Simple IRA rollovers and conversions to non-Simple IRA accounts are not allowed in the first two years of participation

2018 Retirement Plan Options At-a-Glance

Feature	SEP	SIMPLE IRA	Money Purchase	Profit Sharing	Safe Harbor 401(k)	401(k)	Defined Benefit
Eligible Employer	Any Employer	Employers who, on any day during the preceding year, have 100 or fewer employees earning $5,000 or more in compensation. No other plan may be maintained at the same time.	Any Employer	Any Employer	Any Employer	Any Employer	Any Employer
Establishment Deadline	Employer tax filing deadline, including extensions.	October 1 current year.	Last day of employer's taxable year.	Last day of employer's. taxable year	New plans must be established 3 months prior to plan year-end. Existing plans must be amended by 1st day of plan year.	Last day of employer's taxable year.	Last day of employer's taxable year.
Eligible Employees	May be less restrictive, but cannot exclude those who exceed: • 21 years of age • Employed 3 of the last 5 years • $600 annual income Requires 100% participation of eligible employees.	Employees who receive $5,000 in compensation in *any* two preceding years *and* are expected to receive $5,000 in the current year are eligible. These requirements may be less restrictive.	May be less restrictive, but cannot exclude those who exceed: • 21 years of age • Completion of one year of service. (1,000 hours in 12 months.) May be 2 years if 100% immediate vesting.	May be less restrictive, but cannot exclude those who exceed: • 21 years of age • Completion of one year of service. (1,000 hours in 12 months.) May be 2 years if 100% immediate vesting.	May be less restrictive, but cannot exclude those who exceed: • 21 years of age • Completion of one year of service. (1,000 hours in 12 months.) May be 2 years if employer contribution if 100% immediate vesting.	May be less restrictive, but cannot exclude those who exceed: • 21 years of age • Completion of one year of service. (1,000 hours in 12 months.) May be 2 years for employer contributions if 100% immediate vesting.	May be less restrictive, but cannot exclude those who exceed: • 21 years of age • Completion of one year of service. May be 2 years if 100% immediate vesting. • 1,000 hours of service per year.
Contribution Limits Employers	Employer's discretion up to 25% of employee's compensation with a maximum of $55,000 for 2018. Contributions may continue beyond age 70½.	Employer must make matching contributions up to 3% of employee compensation or contribute 2% of total eligible employee compensation. Total employer contribution may not exceed $12,500 per year for 2018.	As specified in plan. Up to 25% of eligible payroll with a maximum of $55,000 for 2018. Contributions may continue beyond age 70½.	Employer's discretion up to 25% of eligible payroll. Maximum allocation per employee is $55,000 for 2018. Contributions may continue beyond age 70½.	Employer must make dollar-for-dollar matching contributions up to 3% of employee compensation and 50 cents on the dollar for the next 2% of employee compensation or contribute 3% of total eligible employee compensation. Additional discretionary profit-sharing contributions allowed. Total employer contributions may not exceed 25% of eligible payroll.	Employer's discretion up to 25% of eligible payroll. Can be made as a matching or a profit-sharing contribution may continue beyond age 70½.	Actuarially computed based on age, compensation and years of service. Maximum benefit at age 65 is $220,000 for 2018 or 100% of average 3 years highest salary.
Deadline for Employer Contribution	Employer tax filing deadline, including extensions.	Employer tax filing deadline, including extensions.	Employer tax filing deadline, including extensions.	Employer tax filing deadline, including extensions.	Employer tax filing deadline, including extensions.	Employer tax filing deadline, including extensions.	Employer tax filing deadline, including extensions.

(continues)

2018 Retirement Plan Options At-a-Glance (*continued*)

Feature	SEP	SIMPLE IRA	Money Purchase	Profit Sharing	Safe Harbor 401(k)	401(k)	Defined Benefit
Contributions Limits of Employee	Employee can contribute a traditional IRA contribution of up to $5,500, 2018 limit, $6,500 for 2018 if 50 or older, to their SEP account in addition to the employer's SEP contribution.	Employees can defer up to $12,500 per year for 2018 or 100% of compensation, whichever is less. Employees who are 50 or older can defer an additional $3,000 in 2018.	N/A	N/A	Employees can defer up to $18,500 for 2018. Employees who are 50 and older can defer an additional $6,000 in 2018. Employee and employer contributions per employee cannot exceed $55,000 for 2018.	Employees can defer up to $18,500 for 2018. Employees who are 50 and older can defer an additional $6,000 in 2018. Employee and employer contributions per employee cannot exceed $55,000 for 2018.	N/A
Deductions and Deferrals	Deduction for employer. Tax-deferred for employee.	Employer contributions deductible to employer. Tax-deferred for employee. Employee contributions are pre-tax and tax-deferred.	Deduction for employer. Tax-deferred for employee.	Deduction for employer. Tax-deferred for employee.	Employer contributions deductible to employer. Tax-deferred for employee. Employee contributions are pre-tax and tax-deferred.	Employer contributions deductible to employer. Tax-deferred for employee. Employee contributions are pre-tax and tax-deferred.	Deduction for employer. Tax-deferred for employee.
Vesting	100% vested immediately.	100% vested immediately.	Several permissible vesting schedules.	Several permissible vesting schedules.	100% vested immediately on Safe Harbor contributions. Vesting schedule allowed on non-safe harbor profit sharing contributions.	Several permissible vesting schedules.	Several permissible vesting schedules.
Loan Provisions[1]	None	None	Yes	Yes	Yes	Yes	Yes
Testing	Generally not subject to top-heavy testing.	No testing.	Subject to top-heavy testing.	Subject to top-heavy testing.	Plan will pass 401(k) ADP and ACP tests if Safe Harbor rules are followed and will also meet top-heavy test requirements.	Subject to ADP, ACP, and top-heavy testing.	
Distributions	Same as IRA. 10% premature distribution penalty may apply. Must begin distributions at age 70½. In-service distributions allowed.	10% premature distribution penalty may apply; penalty is increased to 25% during first 2 years. Must begin distributions at age 70½. In-service distributions allowed.	10% premature penalties may apply. Must begin distributions at age 70½ unless still employed.[2] In-service distributions not allowed.	10% premature distribution penalties may apply. Must begin distributions at age 70½ unless still employed.[2] In-service distributions available if plan document allows.	10% premature distribution penalties may apply. Must begin distributions at age 70½ unless still employed.[2] In-service distributions available if plan document allows.	10% premature distribution penalties may apply. Must begin distributions at age 70½ unless still employed.[2] In-service distributions available if plan document allows.	10% premature distribution penalties may apply. Must begin distributions at age 70½ unless still employed.[2] In-service distributions not allowed.

[1]Loan Limits: maximum of 50% of vested balance up to $50,000. Payments must be made at least quarterly with level amortization.

[2]Owners of 3% or more of a company must start distributions at age 70½.

The 2018 Chart: Retirement Plan Options for a SELF-EMPLOYED INDIVIDUAL with No Employees At-a-Glance

Feature	SEP	SIMPLE IRA	Owner-Only 401(k)	Defined Benefit Pension
Key Advantage	Easy to set up and maintain.	Salary reduction plan with less administration.	Often allows for larger contribution than a SEP or SIMPLE IRA.	Highest contribution allowed by IRS
Establishment Deadline	Business' tax-filing deadline, including extensions.	October 1 of current year.	Last day of business' taxable year.	Last day of business' taxable year.
Contribution Limits	Flexible contributions up to 25% of compensation with a maximum of $55,000 for 2018.	*Two sources of contributions*—Salary deferrals up to $12,500 per year, 2018 limit, or 100% of compensation, whichever is less. Individuals who are 50 or older can defer an additional $3,000 for 2018. Must make matching contribution up to 3% of compensation (maximum of $12,500 in 2018) or contribute 2% of compensation.	*Two sources of contributions*—Flexible contributions up to 25% of compensation. Salary deferrals up to $18,500 per year (2018). Individuals who are 50 or older can defer an additional $6,000 in 2018. Total contribution cannot exceed $55,000.	Actuarially computed based on factors such as compensation, age, and years of service. Maximum benefit at age 65 is $220,000 for 2018 or 100% of the average highest 3 years of salary.
Employer Deduction/ Contribution Deadlines	Business' tax-filing deadline including extensions	If business is incorporated, salary deferrals must be made through payroll withholding. Deferrals must be deposited into a Simple IRA no later than the last day of the month following the month they were withheld. If business is sole proprietor or partnership salary deferrals must be made by business' tax-filing deadline, including extensions. Deadline for employer matching or non-elective contribution is business' tax-filing deadline, including extensions.	If business is incorporated, salary deferrals must be made through payroll withholding. Deferrals must be deposited to the plan as soon as administratively feasible. If business is sole proprietor or partnership salary deferrals must be made by business' tax-filing deadline, including extensions. Deadline for employer contributions is business' tax-filing deadline, including extensions.	Business' tax-filing deadline, including extensions. Quarterly deposits of plan contributions are required. However, to avoid a funding deficiency excise tax of 10% of the under funded amount a contribution must be made no later than 8 months after the close of the plan year.
Funding Requirements	Flexible	Flexible	Flexible but requires consistent funding.	Annual minimum funding requirements.
Catch-up Provisions	None	Yes	Yes	None
Administrative Responsibilities	Minimal, no employer tax filings.	Minimal, no employer tax filings.	Some administrative requirements – tracking of contributions, loans. IRS 5500 - EZ filing required when plan assets exceed $250,000 and annually thereafter.	Administrator required for contribution calculation, tracking of contributions, loans. IRS 5500-EZ filing required when plan assets exceed $250,000 and annually thereafter.
Distributions	Withdrawals permitted anytime subject to ordinary income taxes, 10% premature distribution penalty may apply.	Withdrawals permitted any time subject to ordinary income taxes, 10% premature distribution penalty may apply; penalty is increased to 25% during first two years.	Permitted after a specified event occurs (e.g. retirement, plan termination etc.). Distributions subject to ordinary income taxes. In-service distributions may be allowed. 10% premature distribution penalty may apply.	Payments of benefits or distribution permitted after a specified event occur (e.g., retirement, plan termination etc.). Distributions subject to ordinary income taxes. In-service distributions are not allowed. 10% premature distribution penalty may apply.
Loan Provisions[1]	No	No	Available	

[1]Loan Limits: maximum of 50% of vested balance up to $50,000. Payments must be made at least quarterly with level amortization. Please note, the plan document must be drafted to allow loans.

2018/2017 Dollar Limitations for Retirements Plans

Account Types		2018 Limit	2017 Limit
IRA	Traditional and Roth IRA Contribution Limit	$5,500	$5,500
	Catch-Up Limit for individuals age 50 and older	$1,000	$1,000
SIMPLE IRA	Elective Deferral Limit	$12,500	$12,500
	Catch-Up Limit for individuals age 50 and older	$3,000	$3,000
SEP IRA	Maximum SEP Contribution	$55,000	$54,000
	SEP Compensation Exclusion	$600	$600
401(k), SARSEP, 403(b) and 457(b)	Elective Deferral Limit	$18,500	$18,000
	Catch-Up Limit for individuals age 50 and older	$6,000	$6,000
Profit Sharing, 401(k) and Money Purchase Pension	Defined Contribution Limit (415(c) limit)	$55,000	$54,000
Profit Sharing, 401(k), SEP and Money Purchase Pension	Employee Annual Compensation Limit	$275,000	$270,000
401(k), SARSEP, 403(b) and 457(b)	Highly Compensated Employee (no requirement for 5% owner)	$120,000	$120,000
Profit Sharing, 401(k) and Money Purchase Pension	Top-heavy Plan Key Employee Compensation Limit	$175,000*	$175,000*
Defined Benefit	Defined Benefit Limit	$220,000	$215,000
Social Security	Social Security Taxable Wage Base	$128,400	$127,200
	Maximum Earnings for Individuals under Normal Retirement Age before Social Security Benefits are reduced. One dollar in benefits will be withheld for every $2 in earnings above the limit.	$17,040	$16,920

* $150,000 for more than 1% owners
 $1 for more than 5% owners

Retirement Planning 2018/2017 Key Numbers

While an increasing number of retirement plan and IRA limits are indexed for inflation each year, most of the limits eligible for a cost-of-living adjustment (COLA) did not adjust upward. Some of the key numbers for 2017 are listed below, with the corresponding limit for 2018.

Elective Deferral Limits	2018	2017
401(k) plans, 403(b) plans, 457(b) plans, and SAR-SEPs[1] (includes Roth contributions)	Lesser of $18,500 or 100% of participant's compensation	Lesser of $18,000 or 100% of participant's compensation
SIMPLE 401(k) plans and SIMPLE IRA plans[1]	Lesser of $12,500 or 100% of participant's compensation	Lesser of $12,500 or 100% of participant's compensation

IRA Contribution Limits	2018	2017
Traditional IRAs	Lesser of $5,500 or 100% of earned income	Lesser of $5,500 or 100% of earned income
Roth IRAs	Lesser of $5,500 or 100% of earned income	Lesser of $5,500 or 100% of earned income

Retirement Planning 2018/2017 Key Numbers (*continued*)

Additional "Catch-up" Limits (individuals age 50 or older)	2018	2017
401(k) plans, 403(b) plans, 457(b) plans, and SAR-SEPs[2]	$6,000	$6,000
SIMPLE 401(k) plans and SIMPLE IRA plans	$3,000	$3,000
IRAs (traditional and Roth)	$1,000	$1,000

Defined Benefit Plan Annual Benefit Limits	2018	2017
Annual benefit limit per participant	Lesser of $220,000 or 100% of average compensation for highest three consecutive years	Lesser of $215,000 or 100% of average compensation for highest three consecutive years

Defined Contribution Plan Limits (qualified plans, 403(b) plans, and SEP plans)	2018	2017
Annual addition limit per participant (employer contributions; employee pretax, after-tax, and Roth contributions; and forfeitures)	Lesser of $55,000 or 100% (25% for SEP) of participant's compensation	Lesser of $54,000 or 100% (25% for SEP) of participant's compensation

Retirement Plan Compensation Limits	2018	2017
Maximum compensation per participant that can be used to calculate tax-deductible employer contribution (qualified plans and SEPs)	$275,000	$270,000
Compensation threshold used to determine a highly compensated employee	$120,000 (when 2018 is the look-back year)	$120,000 (when 2017 is the look-back year)
Compensation threshold used to determine a key employee in a top-heavy plan	$1 for more-than-5% owners $175,000 for officers $150,000 for more-than-1% owners	$1 for more-than-5% owners $175,000 for officers $150,000 for more-than-1% owners

(*continues*)

Retirement Planning 2018/2017 Key Numbers *(continued)*

Retirement Plan Compensation Limits	2018	2017
Compensation threshold used to determine a qualifying employee under a SIMPLE plan	$5,000	$5,000
Compensation threshold used to determine a qualifying employee under a SEP plan	$600	$600

Income Phase-out Range for Determining Deductibility of Traditional IRA Contributions for Taxpayers:	2018	2017
1. Covered by an employer-sponsored plan and filing as:		
Single/Head of household	$63,000–$73,000	$62,000–$72,000
Married filing jointly	$101,000–$121,000	$99,000–$119,000
Married filing separately	$0–$10,000	$0–$10,000
2. Not covered by an employer-sponsored retirement plan, but filing joint return with a spouse who is covered by a plan	$189,000–$199,000	$186,000–$196,000

Income Phase-out Range for Determining Ability to Fund a Roth IRA for Taxpayers Filing as:	2018	2017
Single/Head of household	$120,000–$135,000	$118,000–$133,000
Married filing jointly	$189,000–$199,000	$186,000–$196,000
Married filing separately	$0–$10,000	$0–$10,000

[1] Must aggregate employee deferrals to all 401(k), 403(b), SAR-SEP, and SIMPLE plans of all employers; 457(b) contributions are not aggregated. For SAR-SEPs, the percentage limit is 25% of compensation reduced by elective deferrals (effectively a 20% maximum contribution).

[2] Special catch-up limits may also apply to 403(b) and 457(b) plan participants.

The preceding rules were modified by the Tax Relief Act of 2001:

The 2001 law increased the annual limit on contributions to Coverdell Education Accounts from $500 to $2,000. The law expanded the definition of qualified education expenses that may be paid tax-free from an education IRA to include elementary and secondary school expenses. The law increased the phase-out range for married taxpayers filing a joint return so that it is twice the range for single taxpayers. Thus, the phaseout range for married taxpayers filing a joint return is $190,000 to $220,000 of modified adjusted gross income. However, you don't need *earned income* to contribute to an education IRA. If you make too much, gift the dollars to your child and have the child make the contribution.

The 2001 law provided that various age limitations do not apply to special needs beneficiaries. You are limited to only one rollover from a single account per individual per year.

The 2001 law clarified that corporations and other entities (including tax-exempt organizations) are permitted to make contributions to education IRAs, regardless of the income of the corporation or entity during the year of the contribution.

The 2001 law allows you to claim a HOPE credit or Lifetime Learning credit for a taxable year and to exclude from gross income amounts distributed (both the contributions and the earnings portions) from a Coverdell Education Account on behalf of the same student, as long as the distribution is not used for the same educational expenses for which a credit was claimed.

The 2001 law repealed the excise tax on contributions made by any person to a Coverdell Education Account on behalf of a beneficiary during any taxable year in which any contributions are made by anyone to a qualified state tuition program on behalf of the same beneficiary.

The 2001 law allows a rollover of unused Coverdell Education Account funds to other family members, provided that they are under age 30, without penalty. If you invest $2,000 a year at 7 percent into a Coverdell Education Account for 18 years, you will have $36,758 in tax-free income and a total account valued at $72,758.

The provisions modifying Coverdell Education Accounts are effective for taxable years beginning after December 31, 2001.

For bankruptcy filings after October 16, 2005, creditors cannot touch pay-ins to state tuition plans or Coverdell Education Accounts that are made more than 720 days before the bankruptcy filing date. The exclusion falls to $5,000 for pay-ins made more than 365 days but less than 721 days before the filing date, and to zero for any pay-ins made within 365 days.

The tables from Steve Leightman of RBC Wealth Management on pages 210–218 compare the various kinds of IRAs and other retirement plans. The table on page 221 details the rules for the Roth IRA.

How Your Money Could Grow

- ◆ $500 invested today and each year thereafter for a newborn child
- ◆ Grows for 17 years at 8% with no taxes due

End of Year

■ Tax free ▨ Taxable (28% tax bracket)

Since 1987, *nondeductible* contributions to an IRA may be made up to the maximum deduction, reduced by any deductible contributions. Therefore, even if your contribution deduction is reduced under the adjusted gross income limitation, you can contribute the difference without deducting it. The earnings on such contributions are not taxed until distribution. Any nondeductible contribution must be indicated on your tax return for the contribution year.

If nondeductible contributions are made, withdrawals from IRAs must be divided between taxable and nontaxable segments. The Tax Reform Act of 1986 used an averaging approach to accomplish this task. For purposes of the computations, all of a taxpayer's IRAs are considered to be one single IRA and all withdrawals made during the year are added together and considered as one withdrawal. The percentage of an IRA withdrawal treated as a return of a nondeductible contribution, and therefore not taxable, is represented by a ratio whose numerator is the sum of all nondeductible contributions made to any of the taxpayer's IRAs and whose denominator is the sum of the balances in the taxpayer's IRAs at the end of the tax year plus withdrawals made during the year.

Tables 3 to 6, on pages 222–223, developed by Jerrold J. Stern of the Graduate School of Business, Indiana University, show break-even points at various tax and interest rates for deductible IRA contributions and nondeductible

Roth IRA

CONTRIBUTIONS

Maximum	$5,500 per year of W-2 or Schedule C earnings (contributions allowed after age $70\frac{1}{2}$).
	Contributions amount is limited if AGI is between:
	• $120,000 and $135,000 for individual returns
	• $189,000 and $199,000 for joint returns
	$5,500 maximum combined contribution into Roth IRA or traditional IRA per individual, per year.
Provisions above AGI limits	Cannot participate if AGI exceeds stated limits (see "Maximum" subsection).
Tax deductibility	Contributions are not tax deductible.

ACCUMULATIONS

Interest, dividends, and capital gains	Grow tax-deferred and distributed income tax-free as long as you abide by withdrawal rules (see "Distributions" section).
Suitable investments	CDs; common and preferred stocks; unit investment trusts; government, corporate, and mortgage-backed bonds; mutual funds; private money managers.

DISTRIBUTIONS

When allowed	May withdraw up to original contribution amount at any time (may not apply to converted balances)
Taxation	Withdrawal of earnings after age $59\frac{1}{2}$ are income tax-free as long as investments have been in the account for 5 consecutive years.
	Before age $59\frac{1}{2}$ and meeting the 5-consecutive-year requirement, earnings may be withdrawn income tax-free if one of the following qualifications is met:
	• Death.
	• Disability.
	• First-time home purchase up to $10,000 (once-in-a-lifetime use).
When penalty applies	10% IRS penalty (in addition to ordinary income tax rates) applies to investment earnings withdrawn before reaching age $59\frac{1}{2}$ regardless of the 5-year investment period (unless certain exceptions apply as described below or withdrawal qualifies as "special purpose," also described below).

ROLLOVERS CONVERSIONS

Exceptions to 10% IRS Penalty	• First-time home purchase up to $10,000 (once-in-a-lifetime use).
	• Qualified higher education expenses.
	• Death.
	• Disability.
	• Substantially equal payments (annuitization).
	• Medical expenses exceeding 10%/7.5% of AGI.
	• Health insurance premiums when receiving unemployment compensation for longer than 12 months.
Mandatory distributions	No required minimum payments at any time.
Qualifications	Taxpayers may roll over a Roth IRA to another Roth IRA without incurring income or penalty taxes.
	Rollovers must follow the 60-day rules.

TABLE 3. Years before Break-Even: Deductible IRA Contributions

| Interest | Marginal Tax Rates | | |
Rates	15%	28%	33%
4%	22	14	13
6	15	10	9
8	12	8	7
10	10	6	6
12	8	5	5

TABLE 4. Years before Break-Even: Nondeductible IRA Contributions, Taxable Percentage of Principal = 0%

| Interest | Marginal Tax Rates | | |
Rates	15%	28%	33%
4%	37	26	24
6	25	18	17
8	20	14	13
10	16	11	11
12	14	10	9

TABLE 5. Years before Break-Even: Nondeductible IRA Contributions, Taxable Percentage of Principal = 100%

| Interest | Marginal Tax Rates | | |
Rates	15%	28%	33%
4%	50	45	44
6	34	30	30
8	26	23	23
10	21	19	19
12	18	16	16

TABLE 6. Years before Break-Even: Nondeductible IRA Contributions, Taxable Percentage of Principal = 50%

Interest Rates	Marginal Tax Rates		
	15%	28%	33%
4%	45	38	38
6	31	26	26
8	24	20	20
10	19	17	16
12	17	14	14

Calculating Deductibility of Your Traditional IRA Contribution*

	2018	
	Single	**Joint**
AGI limit	$73,000	$121,000
Your modified AGI	– _____	– _____
AGI limit less your modified AGI	_____	_____
Divide remainder by†	$10,000	$10,000
Percentage of your contribution eligible	_____%	_____%
Multiply by $5,500	× $5,500	× $5,500
Amount you can deduct	$_____	_____

Calculating Eligibility for a Roth IRA Contribution*

	2018	
	Single	**Joint**
AGI limit	$135,000	$199,000
Your modified AGI	– _____	– _____
AGI limit less your modified AGI	_____	_____
Divide remainder by†	$15,000	$10,000
Percentage of your contribution eligible	_____%	_____%
Multiply by $5,500	× $5,500	× $5,500
Amount you can contribute	$_____	_____

*Maximum combined contribution may not exceed $5,500 per individual, per year.
†These numbers are determined by the range between minimum and maximum AGI for partially deductible contributions to the traditional IRA and for eligible contributions to the Roth IRA.

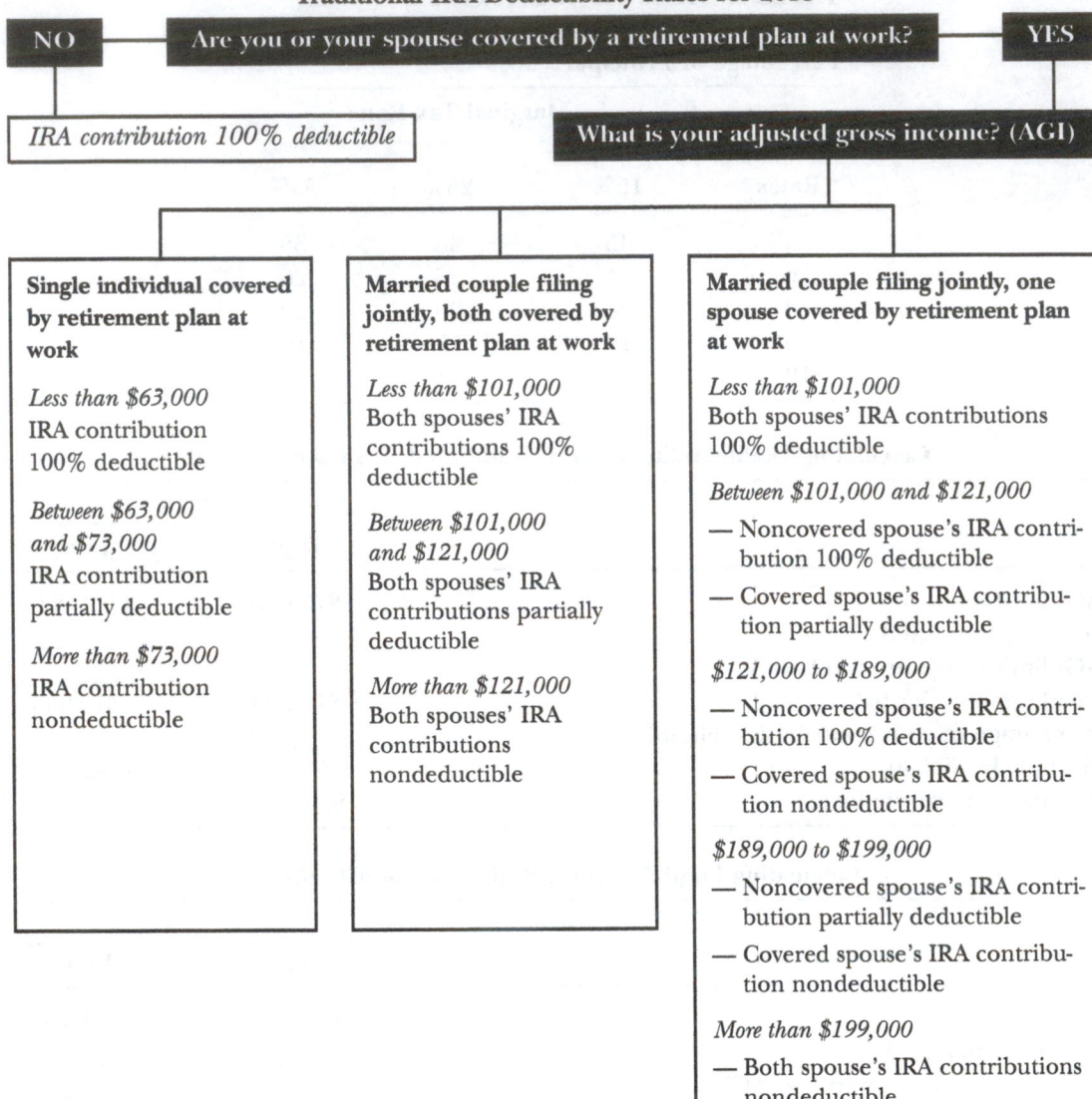

Traditional IRA Deductibility Rules for 2018

| NO | Are you or your spouse covered by a retirement plan at work? | YES |

IRA contribution 100% deductible

What is your adjusted gross income? (AGI)

Single individual covered by retirement plan at work

Less than $63,000
IRA contribution 100% deductible

Between $63,000 and $73,000
IRA contribution partially deductible

More than $73,000
IRA contribution nondeductible

Married couple filing jointly, both covered by retirement plan at work

Less than $101,000
Both spouses' IRA contributions 100% deductible

Between $101,000 and $121,000
Both spouses' IRA contributions partially deductible

More than $121,000
Both spouses' IRA contributions nondeductible

Married couple filing jointly, one spouse covered by retirement plan at work

Less than $101,000
Both spouses' IRA contributions 100% deductible

Between $101,000 and $121,000
— Noncovered spouse's IRA contribution 100% deductible
— Covered spouse's IRA contribution partially deductible

$121,000 to $189,000
— Noncovered spouse's IRA contribution 100% deductible
— Covered spouse's IRA contribution nondeductible

$189,000 to $199,000
— Noncovered spouse's IRA contribution partially deductible
— Covered spouse's IRA contribution nondeductible

More than $199,000
— Both spouse's IRA contributions nondeductible

IRA contributions. Note that the tables include a 10 percent penalty on withdrawals prior to age 59½ and that the rates used were those prior to the Tax Cuts and Jobs Act of 2017. Where the taxable percentage of the principal is zero, the tables assume that tax and penalty are paid only on the interest earned, and that the principal contribution (for example, $5,500) withdrawn is received tax-free.

Remember that if a taxpayer and spouse have 2018 joint income in excess of $101,000 and if even only one spouse is covered by a retirement plan, joint return deductions for payments to individual retirement accounts are phased out for the covered employee. But if the modified adjusted gross income limits are met ($189,000–$199,000), the noncovered spouse may make deductible contributions (see pages 205–207 and 224).

Certain investments are off limits to IRA holders. They include investments in collectibles, such as rare books; rugs; artworks; metals, such as gold, silver, and platinum; antiques; stamps; coins; alcoholic beverages; and any other forms of tangible personal property. In addition, life insurance, as opposed to annuities offered by life insurance companies, is also off limits to IRA investors. Under the Tax Reform Act of 1986, however, you may invest in gold and silver coins issued by the United States. This provision is effective for coins acquired after 1986.

The deadline for making contributions to an IRA is April 15, the date for filing the taxpayer's return. An extension to file is not an extension to contribute to an IRA. Taxpayers who establish an individual retirement account or annuity are required to file Form 5239, Return for Individual Retirement Savings Arrangements, with their income tax return if they owe IRA penalty taxes (for instance, on excess contributions, premature distributions, or the failure to distribute at age 70½).

In Private Ruling 8527082 the IRS affirmed that you may deduct interest paid on money borrowed to put into an IRA. Note, however, that the Tax Reform Act of 1986 makes interest potentially nondeductible as "consumer interest" (although, I would argue that it was investment interest, but as long as the Roth yields tax-free income, the deduction would still be lost). Moreover, the IRS has ruled that the separate payment by an IRA beneficiary or trustee of administration fees for the IRA will not reduce the amount the beneficiary would otherwise be entitled to treat as a deductible contribution to the IRA, and is deductible as an expense incurred for the production or collection of income (Rev. Rul. 84-146). However, no separate deduction is allowed for brokers' commissions paid by IRAs or even qualified plans. Brokers' commissions are not recurring administrator or overhead expenses, such as trustee or actuary fees, incurred in connection with the maintenance of the trust or plan. Brokers' commissions rather are intrinsic to the value of a trust's assets—buying commissions are a part of the cost of the securities purchased and selling commissions are an offset against the sales price. Therefore, the Internal Revenue Service has ruled that

contributions to reimburse for brokers' commissions are not deductible (Rev. Rul. 86-142, 1986-48 I.R.B. 4).

Under the 2015 PATH Act, the 10% penalty will not apply to distributions from a defined benefit government plan to qualified public safety employees who have separated from service after attaining age 50.

Under the Tax Cuts and Jobs Act of 2017, all miscellaneous itemized deductions are disallowed as of January 1, 2018 . . . including IRA administrative fees.

TAX-FREE CHARITABLE CONTRIBUTIONS FROM IRAs

The Pension Protection Act of 2006 allowed taxpayers age 70½ or older to exclude from gross income otherwise taxable distributions ("qualified charitable distributions," or QCDs) from their IRA that were paid directly to a qualified charity. Taxpayers were able to exclude up to $100,000 in both 2006 and 2007. The law was extended through 2009 by the Emergency Economic Stabilization Act of 2008, extended again, through 2011, by the Tax Relief, Unemployment Insurance Reauthorization, and Job Creation Act of 2010 (the Tax Relief Act), and again by the Tax Relief Act of 2012 through 2013 and again through 2014. It was made permanent in 2015.

You must be 70½ or older in order to make QCDs. You direct your IRA trustee to make a distribution directly from your IRA (other than SEP and SIMPLE IRAs) to a qualified charity. The distribution must be one that would otherwise be taxable to you. You can exclude up to $100,000 of QCDs from your gross income. If you file a joint return, your spouse can exclude an additional $100,000 of QCDs. You don't get to deduct QCDs as a charitable contribution on your federal income tax return—that would be double dipping.

QCDs count toward satisfying any required minimum distributions (RMDs) that you would otherwise have had to receive from your IRA, just as if you had received an actual distribution from the plan. However, distributions that you actually receive from your IRA (including RMDs) that you subsequently transfer to a charity cannot qualify as QCDs.

SIMPLIFIED EMPLOYEE PENSION PLANS

Under a normal IRA, your deduction is limited to the lesser of 100 percent of earned income or $5,500 ($11,000 in the case of spousal IRAs) for contributions made. Under the Simplified Pension Plan, the exclusion limitation for all contributions to this type of IRA is now the lesser of $55,000 or 25 percent of compensation. In the case of a self-employed individual or owner-employee in a noncorporate plan, "compensation" is defined to mean net earnings from self-employment, less excludable contributions to the plan made on his or her own behalf. This effectively reduces the self-employed maximum contribution

percentage from 25 to 20 percent. Moreover, if an employer maintains another qualified plan, the maximum amount that can be contributed to that plan for any employee is reduced by all amounts contributed to the SEP. There is a 25/20 percent limitation on deductible contributions to more than one qualified plan [Internal Revenue Code Section 404(h)(3)].

The intent of this type of plan is to establish a simpler mechanism by which employers can make employer-deductible contributions to provide employees with retirement benefits. It offers the owner-employee the opportunity to increase the maximum contributions that may be made to a personal plan, but it does so at the cost of requiring contributions for certain other employees as well.

Contributions made to an SEP by the employer or by a self-employed individual are deposited into individual IRAs in the name of the plan member. Employer contributions to an SEP are not includable in an employee's gross income. The employer contribution must be a specified percentage of the employee's total compensation up to $275,000 for 2018, and the same percentage rate must be used for all employees. That rate may be specified in the plan or set by the employer annually by a written resolution. Unlike profit-sharing plans, an SEP does not require employers to make recurring contributions to the plan to remain qualified.

The five requirements for the establishment of a Simplified Pension Plan are as follows:

1. The IRA must be maintained solely by the individual employee. This means that all employees, including the owner as an employee, must maintain their own individual IRA accounts.

2. Employer contributions must be made pursuant to a written allocation formula.

3. The program must provide for contributions for each employee who has attained age 21, has performed services for the employer during any part of three of the immediately preceding 5 calendar years, and receives compensation of at least $600 during the current year (indexed). Employees under collective bargaining agreements and nonresident aliens may be excluded; part-time employees, however, must be covered.

4. Employer contributions must not discriminate in favor of officers, shareholders, or highly compensated employees. Generally, discrimination will not exist if the contributions bear a uniform relationship to the first $275,000 for 2018 of each employee's total compensation. Employer contributions may be reduced by the amount of the employer's share of the Social Security tax.

5. No limitations may be imposed by the employer on the employee's right of withdrawal.

Unlike the Keogh plan, an SEP can be set up after the end of the calendar year so long as the contribution is made by April 15 of the year following (*plus extensions*). Moreover, there are no annual reporting requirements for SEPs, so long as each individual who participates in the plan receives a copy of the plan agreement and a written document from the employer each year informing that individual of the amount of contributions made on his or her behalf by the employer. An employer can create an SEP by using an unmodified Model Form (Form 5305-SEP), which is available from the Internal Revenue Service. An employer who follows the instructions on this two-page form will automatically satisfy IRS reporting and disclosure requirements.

Additional advantages of an SEP include the following:

- **Unlike regular contributions to an IRA, contributions can be made to a SEP even if you are 70½ or older, even if you are self-employed. Participants age 70½ or over must also take required distributions.**
- Low start-up costs compared to the cost of establishing regular pension or profit-sharing plans
- No need to pay contributions to the SEP every year (similar to a profit-sharing Keogh)
- Portability of benefits—that is, participants who end their employment can take their benefits with them in the form of individual retirement accounts
- Low administrative costs
- Reduced fiduciary responsibility, because participants choose their own vehicle when they establish an IRA

SARSEP

A salary reduction SEP, known as a SARSEP, was available for firms with 25 or fewer workers. Under a SARSEP, each worker chose how much he or she wanted to set aside through regular payroll deductions. The 2018 maximum is $18,500.

With a SARSEP, 50 percent of all eligible employees must participate and no more than 60 percent of contributions can be made by highly compensated employees. If a firm fails the latter test, called the *top-heavy rule*, the IRS will require the firm to contribute a minimum of 3 percent of salary into employee accounts.

The amounts put into a SARSEP are not currently taxed and therefore you will get tax-free compounding on your investment until the money is withdrawn.

Under SARSEPs, which are not qualified plans, employees could elect to have contributions made to the SARSEP or to receive the contributions in cash. The amount that an employee elected to have contributed to the SARSEP was not

currently included in income. Under the Small Business Job Protection Act of 1996, SARSEPs are repealed for years beginning after December 31, 1996, unless the SARSEP was established before January 1, 1997. Consequently, an employee is not permitted to establish a SARSEP after December 31, 1996. SARSEPs established before January 1, 1997 can continue to receive contributions under prior law rules, and new employees of the employer who are hired after December 31, 1996 can participate in the SARSEP in accordance with such rules.

PLANNING WITH IRAs

As noted, the deadline for making IRA contributions is April 15, but what if you don't have the necessary cash at the moment? One possible solution to this problem is to use an old IRA for the funds required for the current IRA contribution.

There are no immediate tax consequences when an individual withdraws part or all of his or her interest in an IRA and within 60 days deposits the amount withdrawn into another IRA. Therefore, if you have an IRA account established in an earlier year, you can withdraw $5,500 from it and use it for your subsequent year's contribution. So long as the deposit is completed within 60 days, there is no problem.

Question: Where do you get the money to cover your original withdrawal? *Solution:* It is hoped that you get it with the refund you will get from your tax return as filed with the additional IRA deduction. *Worst case theory:* If you cannot find the $5,500 to cover within the 60-day period, then you are still entitled to the deduction for the current contribution year, but you have to include the $5,500 withdrawn (with penalty) on your next year's tax return.

Rather than wait for the last minute, you should make your IRA contribution as early as possible. When you delay, you lose not only the tax-free interest for the year but the interest that would have been compounded on it in future years.

The table below lists how much you lose by making a contribution at the last minute. It assumes that *only* $2,000 is placed annually into an IRA earning 10 percent interest, and it shows the interest forfeited after a given number of

Number of Years	Interest Lost
5	$ 1,500
10	$ 4,000
15	$ 8,000
20	$ 14,000
30	$ 41,000
40	$112,000

years when the contributions are regularly made as late as possible (April 15), as opposed to as early as possible (on January 1 of the preceding year).

In 1985, the Internal Revenue Service ruled that a jobless widow could add to her own IRA for the year her husband died. The decedent had created a spousal IRA for his unemployed wife in 1982 and 1983. He died on February 23, 1984, after earning over $2,250 but before adding to either IRA for that year. The taxpayer's spouse earned no wages in 1984 but wanted to make and deduct a $2,000 payment from the decedent's 1984 income to her spousal IRA for 1984. In Private Ruling 8527083, the Internal Revenue Service said that she could so long as she had no earned income of her own, filed a joint return, and showed that no 1984 payment was made to the decedent's IRA.

SIMPLE RETIREMENT PLANS

The Small Business Job Protection Act of 1996 created a simplified retirement plan for small businesses called the Savings Incentive Match Plan for Employees (SIMPLE) Retirement Plan. A SIMPLE plan can be adopted by employers who employ 100 or fewer employees with at least $5,000 in compensation for the current and any 2 preceding years. Employers who no longer qualify are given a 2-year grace period to continue to maintain the plan. A SIMPLE plan can be either an IRA for each employee or part of a qualified cash or deferred arrangement (401(k)) plan. If established in IRA form, a SIMPLE plan is not subject to the nondiscrimination rules generally applicable to qualified plans (including the top-heavy rules) and simplified reporting requirements apply. Within limits, contributions to a SIMPLE plan are not taxable until withdrawn.

A SIMPLE plan can also be adopted as part of a 401(k) plan. In that case, the plan does not have to satisfy the special nondiscrimination tests applicable to 401(k) plans and is not subjected to the top-heavy rules. The other qualified plan rules continue to apply.

A SIMPLE retirement plan allows employees to make elective contributions to an IRA or 401(k). Employee contributions for a SIMPLE 401(k) or IRA have to be expressed as a percentage of the employee's compensation and cannot exceed $12,500 for 2018. Employer matching can yield as much as $25,000 per year into your SIMPLE account.

All contributions to an employee's SIMPLE account have to be fully vested. Contributions to a SIMPLE account generally are deductible by the employer. Early withdrawals from a SIMPLE account generally are subject to the 10 percent early withdrawal tax applicable to IRAs. However, withdrawals of a contribution during the 2-year period beginning on the date the employee first participated in the SIMPLE plan are subject to a 25 percent early withdrawal

tax, rather than 10 percent. The provisions relating to SIMPLE plans are effective for years beginning after December 31, 1996.

KEOGH PLAN

The alternative to an IRA or IRA/SEP is the Keogh plan. Since 1962, self-employed individuals and their employees have been eligible to receive qualified retirement benefits under what is known as an H.R. 10 or Keogh plan. These qualified pension, annuity, profit-sharing, or bond purchase plans must meet the following qualifications:

1. They must be in writing.

2. They must be effective within the tax year for which a qualification is sought.

3. They must be established by an owner for the benefit of employees or their beneficiaries. Self-employed individuals will be treated as employees under these plans.

4. They must be funded plans (that is, a trust or custodial account, an insured plan, or a bond purchase plan).

5. They must benefit a stipulated percentage of employees, or alternatively, the owner may establish a classification of employees that is found by the Internal Revenue Service not to discriminate in favor of highly paid employees.

6. They may not discriminate in favor of highly paid employees for contributions or benefits.

7. In the case of a plan that provides contributions or benefits only for owner-employees, contributions made on behalf of any owner-employee may not exceed the amount deductible by the individual. This means that an owner cannot contribute into a personal plan, in an attempt to defer taxes, an amount in excess of what is deductible for employees.

8. When an owner-employee covered under the plan, alone, or in conjunction with another employee, controls the trade or business for which the plan is established, any transaction between that owner-employee and the trust-forming part of the plan is prohibited. Transactions between the members of the owner-employee's family and the trust are deemed to be transactions between the owner-employee and the trust. Furthermore, even if the owner-employee does not control the trade or business, a transaction between the trust and that owner-employee is prohibited.

Generally, a disqualified person who engages in a prohibited transaction by contributing property to the trust is subject to a 5 percent excise tax

on the amount involved in the transaction. An additional tax of 100 percent of the amount involved is imposed if the prohibited transaction is not corrected within 90 days from the mailing of a notice of deficiency.

9. A plan that covers an owner-employee must also cover all employees age 21 or older (whether or not U.S. citizens) of the trade or business who have completed two or more years of service. A year of service is a 12-month period, beginning on the date of hire, during which an employee has provided at least 500 hours of service (1,000 hours if it is the first year the employee qualifies). In addition, the employees' rights to contributions in their behalf must be 100 percent vested when the contributions are made.

 If eligibility to participate is shortened to one year, employees can be made to wait for a longer time before being able to leave with benefits. A plan can be set up so that an employee with fewer than 5 years of plan participation is not entitled to any benefit whatsoever. This relieves an employer from the expense of paying retirement benefits to all but true long-term employees. Note, however, that if the plan is "top-heavy"—if more than 60 percent of the benefits are for the owners, officers, and more highly paid employees—plan participants' benefits must vest immediately, or 20 percent after two years and 20 percent thereafter, with full vesting after 6 years [Section 416 (b)(1)].

 The following employees are not required to be covered under a self-employed retirement plan, even though they have completed one or more years of service:

 • Employees included in a unit covered by a collective bargaining agreement, if there is evidence that retirement benefits were subject to good faith bargaining between employee representatives and the employer.

 • Nonresident alien employees who do not have earned income from a U.S. source.

10. If the employer is a partnership, each partner is considered the employee of that partnership. The partners must mutually consent to the establishment of the plan, which means that one partner cannot establish a plan for individual services to that partnership. But each owner-employee can decide whether to be covered under the plan, so a partner who is an owner-employee can agree to the plan and still not participate in it.

Under a Keogh plan, both the maximum contribution permitted on behalf of owner-employees and the deduction allowed self-employed individuals is limited to:

a) 25 percent of the earned income from the trade or business for which the plan is established, limited to

b) $55,000 for 2018

Note that a Keogh plan may be structured either as a *money-purchase pension* plan or as a *profit-sharing* plan, or as a combination of both. An owner-employer must reduce his or her compensation base by the contribution made. Under old law this effectively translated into a limit for *profit-sharing* plan-based deductions of 13.0435 percent and a limit for *money-purchase pension* or combination *money-purchase pension/profit-sharing* deductions of 20 percent of earned income.

With a money-purchase pension plan, the employer is locked into making the contributions every year, unless granted a limited reprieve. Contributions can be the lesser of 25 percent of compensation or $55,000. Note that the 25 percent figure is reduced to 20 percent for an owner-employer making contributions for himself or herself.

The *profit-sharing* plan is the simplest type of defined contribution plan. Contributions can be discretionary with respect to both amounts and whether they are made at all. Deductible contributions for nonowner-employers were as much as 15 percent of compensation, up to the maximum each year for each participant.

Combination plans used to typically contribute a fixed 10 percent each year to the money-purchase plan, and, if the cash is available, up to 15 percent to the profit-sharing plan. Note that plan contributions can be reduced to account for an employer's contribution to Social Security made on an employee's behalf. This is known as Social Security integration. Note, however, that if a plan is top-heavy, a minimum 3 percent annual contribution must be made for nonkey employees, and the employer must fund a benefit of at least 2 percent of compensation per year of service for the first 10 years of service. These requirements limit the cost savings sought by Social Security integration.

As of 2002, the Tax Relief Act of 2001 increased the maximum *profit-sharing* contribution to 25 percent. This should eliminate or at least minimize the use of money-purchase plans or combination plans where a fixed minimum contribution is required.

The contribution maximums were computed under what is known as a *defined contribution plan,* in which the limits are delineated on the basis of how much may be contributed. A self-employed individual may choose instead to establish what is known as a *defined benefit plan,* in which the limits are based on payable benefits. This type of plan permits a self-employed individual to state the retirement benefits desired and contribute amounts necessary to provide those benefits. In addition, a defined benefit plan permits yearly contributions to a plan without regard to profits. For 2018, the maximum annual defined benefit amount is increased to $220,000.

Warning! Everyone will tell you that you have until the due date of your return, plus extensions, to make your Keogh contributions. That is what the tax law says, and extensions are allowed up to October 15.

But, these plans are considered "qualified pension plans" under ERISA. That law requires contributions by September 15. If you contribute after that, it doesn't qualify.

The solution? Use a defined contribution profit-sharing plan. Such plans now allow the maximum 25 percent contribution rate and are not subject to the earlier funding date requirement. That allows funding up to October 15 again.

INDIVIDUAL 401(k)

The 2001 tax law created a new individual 401(k) for businesses in which you and your spouse are the only employees. A 401(k) is simply a profit-sharing plan that allows employee elective deferrals.

The plan must be established by year-end, the contributions are all discretionary each year, and they vest in full immediately.

Big advantage—you can borrow up to 50 percent of your account balance, with a maximum loan of $50,000. You can't borrow from an IRA.

For 2018, the maximum contribution is the sum of A, B, and C below:

A. Employer contribution—up to 25 percent of compensation
B. Salary deferral contribution—up to $18,500
C. If you're age 50 or older, a catch-up contribution of $6,000

A plus B cannot exceed $55,000 or 100 percent of compensation.

If you have no other employees, hire your spouse. Pay your spouse $1,000 per month as reasonable compensation. Give her a $6,500 Christmas bonus. Your spouse can elect to defer $18,500 into the 401(k).

Your family has a $18,500 investment, you have a $18,500 deduction, and your spouse has an additional *zero* in taxable income. Sounds like a great deal to me! Your only downside is that 401(k) deductions are still subject to FICA (Social Security/Medicare) taxes.

ROTH 401(k)

As of January 1, 2006, we now also have Roth 401(k)s. The standard 401(k) limits apply, with a $18,500 maximum (plus an additional $6,000 catch-up) for 2018.

You get no deduction, but qualified distributions come out tax-free.

Pay-ins are subject to the nondiscrimination rules. But there are *no income limitations* (unlike the $189,000–$199,000 adjusted gross income limit for traditional Roth accounts). This is a fantastic investment opportunity for the well-to-do to increase their wealth on a *tax-free* basis.

DB(k) PLANS

A DB(k) plan is a combination of a defined contribution 401(k) plan and a defined benefit plan. It's available only to small business employers, those with at least 2 but no more than 500 employees. The defined benefit is equal to at least 1 percent of final average pay for each year of service up to 20 years. Employees are automatically enrolled in the 401(k) portion with 4 percent of compensation contributed unless the employee opts otherwise. The employer must match at least half the 4 percent.

DB(k)s have minimal paperwork and are exempt from "top heavy" rules, which is an inducement to highly paid employees.

CASH BALANCE PLANS

A cash balance plan is a defined benefit plan that defines the benefit in terms that are more characteristic of a defined contribution plan. In other words, a cash balance plan defines the promised benefit in terms of a stated account balance.

In a typical cash balance plan, your account is credited each year with a "pay credit" (such as 5 percent of compensation from your employer) and an "interest credit" (either a fixed rate or a variable rate that is linked to an index such as the 1-year Treasury bill rate). Increases and decreases in the value of the plan's investments do not directly affect the benefit amounts promised. Thus, the investment risks and rewards on plan assets are borne solely by the employer.

When you become entitled to receive benefits under a cash balance plan, the benefits that are received are defined in terms of an account balance. For example, assume that you have an account balance of $100,000 when you reach age 65. If you decide to retire at that time, you would have the right to an annuity. Such an annuity might be approximately $7,000 per year for life. In many cash balance plans, however, you could instead choose (with consent from your spouse) to take a lump-sum benefit equal to the $100,000 account balance.

In addition to generally permitting you to take your benefit as a lump-sum benefit at retirement, cash balance plans often permit you, if vested, to choose (with consent from your spouse) to receive your accrued benefit in a lump sum if you terminate employment prior to retirement age. Traditional defined benefit pension plans do not offer this feature as frequently. If you receive a lump-sum distribution, that distribution generally can be rolled over into an IRA or to another employer's plan if that plan accepts rollovers.

Cash balance plans are defined benefit plans. In contrast, 403(b) and 401(k) plans are a type of defined contribution plan. There are four major differences between typical cash balance plans and defined contribution plans.

(a) Participation. Participation in typical cash balance plans generally does not depend on the workers, contributing part of their compensation to the plan; however, participation in a 403(b) or 401(k) plan does depend, in whole or in part, on an employees choosing to make a contribution to the plan.

(b) Investment risks. The investments of cash balance plans are managed by the employer or an investment manager appointed by the employer. The employer bears the risks and rewards of the investments. Increases and decreases in the value of the plan's investments do not directly affect the benefit amounts promised to participants. By contrast, 403(b) or 401(k) plans often permit participants to direct their own investments within certain categories. Under 401(k) plans, participants bear the risks and rewards of investment choices.

(c) Life annuities. Unlike many 401(k) plans, cash balance plans are required to offer employees the ability to receive their benefits in the form of lifetime annuities.

(d) Federal guaranty. Since they are defined benefit plans, the benefits promised by cash balance plans are usually insured by a federal agency, the Pension Benefit Guaranty Corporation (PBGC). If a defined benefit plan is terminated with insufficient funds to pay all promised benefits, the PBGC has authority to assume trusteeship of the plan and to begin to pay pension benefits up to the limits set by law. Defined contribution plans are not insured by the PBGC.

The Tax Relief Act of 2001 made significant changes to the retirement vesting rules.

VESTING SCHEDULES

Under prior law, a plan was not a qualified plan unless benefits vested at least as rapidly as under one of the minimum vesting schedules.

1. A plan satisfied the first schedule if a participant acquired a nonforfeitable right to 100 percent of the accrued benefit from *employer contributions* after completing 5 years of service.

2. A plan satisfied the second schedule if at least 20 percent of accrued benefits vested after 3 years, 40 percent after 4 years of service, 60 percent after 5 years, 80 percent after 6 years, and 100 percent after 7 years of service.

Faster Vesting. Under current law, faster vesting schedules apply to employer matching contributions. The contributions will be required to vest at least as rapidly as under one of the following two alternative schedules:

1. A plan satisfies the first schedule if 100 percent of employer matching contributions vest after 3 years of service.

2. A plan satisfies the second schedule if matching contributions vest at the rate of 20 percent each year starting with the participant's second year of service. The contributions will be 100 percent vested after 6 years of service.

The new vesting schedule generally applies to contributions for plan years beginning after December 31, 2001. In applying the new vesting schedule, service before the effective date is taken into account.

CREDITOR PROTECTION

Any IRA money can now be rolled over into a qualified plan. If you get deep in debt, this may save your retirement dollars. Although some states do not insulate IRA accounts from creditors, qualified money [such as a 401(k), Keogh, profit sharing plan, money purchase plan, 403(b)] is subject to ERISA and is therefore exempt from creditors' claims, even if you declare bankruptcy.

The Bankruptcy Act of 2005 insulated up to $1,000,000[†] (not counting rollovers) of IRA money from creditors in a bankruptcy action. This covers traditional plus Roth IRAs.[‡] It does *not* apply to inherited IRAs. See www.wealth defense.com/irachart.htm for individual state IRA insulation.

[†]$1,283,025 as of 2016. It adjusts every 3 years.
[‡]If filing for bankruptcy, you must have funded the account at least 2 years prior to filing.

NEW RETIREMENT PLAN PROTECTIONS

Type of Plan	Exemption
Single business owner/business owner and spouse (such as Keogh plan and single-owner corporate plan)	Unlimited
Contributory IRA (funded with annual contributions, as opposed to rollovers from qualified plans)	$1 million (Indexed)*
Rollover IRA	Unlimited
Roth IRA	$1 million (Indexed)* if a contributory IRA; unlimited if a rollover IRA was converted to a Roth
SEP-IRA	Unlimited
Simple	Unlimited

*$1,283,025 as of 2016.

MINIMUM DISTRIBUTION

If you're not a 5 percent holder of an interest in the business, and you continue to work, you are not subject to the minimum distribution rules when you reach age 70½. If the money was held in an IRA, you would be subject to those rules.

All required regular distributions from IRAs and qualified plans were suspended for 2009. The suspension did not apply to defined benefit plans or deferred 2008 withdrawals. It was only for 2009.

HOW LONG WILL YOUR MONEY LAST

RATE OF RETURN

WITHDRAW	1%	2%	3%	4%	5%	6%	7%	8%	9%	10%	11%	12%
12%	7	8	8	8	8	9	10	10	11	11	12	13
11%	8	8	9	9	9	10	10	11	12	13	14	15
10%	9	9	10	10	10	11	12	13	14	15	17	19
9%	10	10	11	11	12	13	14	15	16	18	21	26

8%	11	11	12	13	14	15	16	18	20	24	30	*
7%	12	13	14	15	16	18	20	22	27	36	*	*
6%	14	15	16	18	19	22	25	31	44	*	*	✓
5%	17	18	20	22	24	29	36	*	*	*	✓	✓
4%	20	22	25	28	33	42	*	*	*	✓	✓	✓
3%	25	28	33	39	*	*	*	*	✓	✓	✓	✓
2%	35	40	50	*	*	*	*	✓	✓	✓	✓	✓
1%	*	*	*	*	*	*	✓	✓	✓	✓	✓	✓

SOURCE: Deena Katz, Evensky, & Katz/Foldes Financial, Coral Gables, Fla.

NOTE: This table assumes that you'll Increase the amount you withdraw after the first 3% per year to account for inflation.

*—Money will never be reduced

✓—Original investment will never be reduced

LOANS

As of January 1, 2002, retirement plan loans can be made to sole proprietors, partners, and shareholders of an S corporation. The loans must be made from a qualified plan (IRA loans are still prohibited), and the plan must allow, or be amended to allow, such loans.

BENEFITS OF RETIREMENT PLANS

It is almost always financially superior to adopt either an individual retirement account or a qualified pension plan rather than have no plan at all. Both the IRA and the Keogh plan allow you to shelter current earnings and allow those earnings to appreciate without making that appreciation currently taxable. There may be an extraordinary situation in which having no plan would be superior. Such a situation would exist if the after-tax cash remaining from funds not invested in an IRA or Keogh plan could be invested in a project whose yield would exceed, after taxes, both the amount that could be earned on the qualified retirement investment and the amount initially lost in taxes. Remember, all income that comes out of retirement accounts is taxed at your highest marginal bracket. The maximum tax rate on nonqualified long-term gains for 2018 is capped at 20 percent with a potential 3.8 percent surcharge for a total of 23.8 percent.

Assume you could put $1,000 in an individual retirement account that would yield 5 percent interest, or $50 a year. For simplicity, assume that your present tax bracket is 20 percent, so that if you do not adopt the individual retirement account, you would have only $800 to invest. But this $800 could be invested in a project yielding 25 percent, or $200 a year. After taxes (at 20 percent) the project

would allow you to keep $160 a year. At the end of 2 years you would therefore have, after taxes, $800 + $160 + $160 = $1,120. (The example has been simplified by excluding compound interest on the investment yield.) Under the IRA, you would have only $1,000 + $50 + $50 = $1,100, and that $1,100 would be taxable at a later date, when withdrawn from the individual retirement account. In this case, the decision not to adopt any plan would clearly be superior.

To evaluate a Keogh plan compared to an IRA, you must consider the following questions:

1. How much money can you afford to surrender the present use of? If not over $5,500 ($11,000 if you have an unemployed spouse), consider an IRA.

2. What will be the tax savings on your contributions to each plan?

3. Must you make contributions for your employees?

4. What will be the after-tax cost of those contributions?

5. Compare the net after-tax savings from an individual retirement account a Keogh plan.

For example, assume you are in the 31 percent bracket* and are making $200,000 a year. You plan to retire in 10 years. You can adopt a Keogh plan, yielding 5 percent. Under the Keogh plan, assume you contribute $15,000 at the end of each year.

Under the Keogh plan, you would contribute $150,000 plus earnings on these contributions, for a total untaxed accumulation of $188,668. You would defer $58,487 in taxes.

But with a Keogh plan qualified employees must also be covered. If you have qualified employees, you would have to contribute 7.5 percent of their earnings (as you contribute 7.5 percent of your own earnings) each year. If you have one qualified employee earning $20,000, you would have to contribute an additional $1,500 per year ($20,000 × 7.5 percent), or $15,000 over the 10-year period. If you have four qualified employees, the contributions would rise to $60,000.

But you are in the 31 percent bracket. Therefore, this would involve an after-tax cost to you of only $41,400. But remember, Keogh saving is merely

*Federal plus state.

a tax *deferral*, not a savings. Therefore, the real question is whether the $41,400 after-tax outflow can be justified by a deferral of the taxes of $58,487!

Under the Keogh plan you would accumulate $188,668. If you expected to be in the 15 percent bracket after you retire, the difference between your marginal tax today and your post-retirement marginal tax would be .16 (31 percent – 15 percent).[3] Therefore, your true net savings on the Keogh plan would be the difference in your tax bracket (.16) times the accumulations under the Keogh plan ($188,668), or a net savings of the present value of $30,187. Thus the determining question is whether the present value of $30,187 is greater than the present value of the after-tax outflow for the contributions you would have to make for your employees.

With a single employee, the cash outflow cost would be the present value of 31 percent of $15,000, or the present value of $4,650. Here the net savings of $30,187 would be greater than the incremental cost of $4,650, and therefore the Keogh adoption would still be superior. If there were four employees, the decision model would compare the present value of $30,187 with the present value of 69 percent of $15,000 × 4, or $41,400. Here the IRA would be financially superior.

Keogh accounts, like all ERISA qualified plans, are exempt from creditor attacks. IRA accounts vary in creditor protection. (As noted above, IRAs up to $1 million [indexed] are now protected from creditors in a bankruptcy.) See www.mosessinger.com/resources/protecting.shtml to check your state. (Exemption for annuities and life insurance can be found at www.mosessinger.com/resources/creditprotec.shtml.)

Finally, you must consider whether the employee Keogh contributions would merely replace alternative additional compensation that would be paid to the employee in any case. If so, then the Keogh penalty for employee payments must be reduced by this amount.

DISTRIBUTIONS & ROLLOVERS

On July 3, 1992 then President Bush signed the Unemployment Compensation Amendments Act of 1992 primarily to extend unemployment benefits.

3. The numbers have been simplified for purposes of this example. You would not be in the 15 percent bracket with a lump-sum distribution of $188,668.

Nevertheless, you need to be aware of several significant changes to the pension rules relating to rollovers and withholding on distributions from such qualified plans as profit sharing, money purchase, 401(k), defined benefit, and tax-sheltered annuities [403(b) plans]. *The new rules do not apply to IRAs.*

These provisions affect all qualified plans that make lump-sum distributions or allow in-service withdrawals. The changes are effective for distributions made after Dec. 31, 1992 (except for a delayed effective date for certain tax-sheltered annuities of state and local governments). The provisions include:

- *Optional Direct Transfer of Distribution.* A participant has 60 days to roll over an eligible distribution from a qualified plan to an IRA or another qualified plan to avoid current taxation. At the time of the distribution, the participant may elect to have federal income taxes withheld or not.

 The 1992 legislation requires a qualified plan sponsor to provide participants who are eligible to receive a rollover distribution the option of making a direct transfer to an IRA or a new employer's qualified plan. However, a qualified plan is not required to accept transfers.

 Even though the participant does not actually receive the money, such a direct trustee-to-trustee transfer is considered a distribution under the current law. Therefore, the spousal consent rules, if applicable, and other beneficiary protection rules will continue to apply.

- *Withholding on Nonperiodic Distributions.* To encourage plan participants to use this direct transfer option, the 1992 law imposes a *mandatory* 20 percent income tax withholding on any amount distributed to the participant. If a participant wants to avoid withholding on the distribution, the participant needs to instruct the employer to transfer the amount directly to another retirement plan or an IRA. Plan participants can no longer elect out of this withholding.

- *Partial Distribution Rules Repealed.* The 1992 Act also changed the situations in which partial distributions can be rolled into an IRA. Under prior law, partial distributions can only be rolled over when:

 - the distribution represents 50 percent or more of the balance to the credit of the employee;

 - the distribution is not one of a series of periodic payments;

- the distribution is made because of death, disability, or separation from service;

- the employee elects rollover treatment.

The 1992 rules allow *any part* of the taxable portion of a qualified plan distribution to be rolled over to an IRA, qualified annuity, or another qualified plan unless the distribution is:

- one of a series of substantially equal periodic payments made over the life expectancy (or joint life expectancies) of the participant and the designated beneficiary;

- one of a series of substantially equal periodic payments made for a specified period of 10 years or more;

- required as a result of the mandatory distribution rules at age 70½ under Section 401(a)(9) of the IRS code;

- after-tax employee contributions, which are not eligible for rollover.

Despite prior IRS rulings to the contrary, you can have only one rollover per year from an individual retirement account to another IRA, rather than one rollover per IRA per year (*Bobrow v. Comm.*, T.C. Memo 2014-21). Remember, with a "rollover" you have 60 days to put the money in the new IRA. Avoid the limitation with a direct "rollover"—e.g., as a broker-to-broker moving of your IRA assets.

Or, you can try this technique from Steve Hedeker, CPA, JD in Lincolnshire, Ill. While you can only have one IRA rollover per year, the one-year limitation doesn't apply to Roth conversions. Assume you are a business owner who needs $50,000 to cover payroll obligations for your company. You would begin by taking money out of your IRA and using it to cover your cash-flow needs, just as with a traditional rollover. But rather than putting $50,000 back into the IRA within 60 days, you would create a Roth IRA and fund the new account with $50,000. That is what is known as a Roth conversion.

To avoid triggering taxes, the final step is to re-characterize that conversion on or before the due date of the tax return for the year of the conversion. That effectively undoes the Roth conversion and transfers the $50,000 (plus any growth accumulated during that year) back into the traditional IRA. From a tax

perspective, it is as if the money never left the account. But, you have had a short-term, interest-free "loan" of the funds, and there is no limit to the number of times you can do this.

Unfortunately, the Tax Cuts and Jobs Act of 2017 makes a conversion to a Roth irreversible as of January 1, 2018. That eliminates the above strategy to return the money to the traditional IRA.

Note that to qualify for a direct rollover, you must be alive at the time of the actual asset rollover (PLR 200204038).

TRADITIONAL V. ROTH IRA

Which should *you* use? That depends on the benefits you want to get and your current and projected tax brackets.

The younger you are, the better the Roth IRA appears. If you start early, the Roth allows more years of tax-free accumulations. The younger you are, presumably, the better the chances you are in a lower bracket, therefore reducing the benefit of its deduction with the traditional IRA.

Alternatively, if you are older and in a higher bracket, the better the traditional IRA looks. Additional elements that must be examined or projected are the yields you expect to earn, whether you want to make contributions after age 70½, and the marginal bracket you expect to be in when the dollars are withdrawn.

There are no simple answers. Every brokerage account out there has computer programs that will find you an "answer" based on your assumptions. I have even found different answers with the same input, depending on when the computer assumes the money is invested. Pen your own numbers and relax—your decision is between the better of two strategies, both of which are winners!

CONVERTING A TRADITIONAL IRA TO A ROTH IRA

Should you convert your traditional IRA into a Roth IRA and change from *tax deferral* to *tax-free* accumulations? The answer here also depends on a number of factors.

You can roll all or part of a traditional IRA into a Roth IRA at any time, even if you have started to take withdrawals. However, when you do, you owe income tax on the money you move. If you made the rollover in 2010, you spread that extra income, and tax, over 2 years—2011 and 2012. But the tax rate then may be higher.

Your first consideration should be where you get the money to pay the tax on the rollover. It can't come from the regular IRA or there will be a premature distribution with a penalty because those dollars are not going into the Roth.

Once you have funded your rollover, the considerations are the same as between a traditional and Roth IRA—your age and years to retirement, your bracket now and at retirement, do you want to contribute after age 70½, and will this impact on the taxability of your Social Security. (Traditional IRAs require annual distributions \which could increase the taxability of your Social Security receipts. You *don't* have to ever take money out of your Roth although your beneficiaries are subject to minimum distribution rules.) The big difference here is the immediate reduction of your wealth from taxes paid on the rollover, reducing your liquidity for future investments. Again, all of the major brokerage and mutual fund houses offer computer programs which will give you an "answer," based on the assumptions you input. As of January 1, 2018, such Roth conversions are irreversible.

COMPANY STOCK ROLLOVERS

"Never" roll over *company stock* in your 401(k) into an IRA. If you do, all distributions will be ordinary income.

If you place the stock into a regular brokerage account instead, you will be taxed, at ordinary income rates at *only* the cost-basis of that stock. That's the value when your employer put the stock in your account.

The difference between the cost-basis and the market value of the stock at the time of distribution, called the net unrealized appreciation (NUA), isn't taxed until you sell the stock, and, at that time, at a rate no greater than the 15/20 percent maximum long-term capital gains rate.

How much "company stock" you want to keep in your retirement savings is another issue.

*my*RA—A REALLY SIMPLE RETIREMENT ACCOUNT

Former President Obama asked the U.S. Department of the Treasury to develop a *my*RA ("My Retirement Account") program, offering a new retirement savings account for individuals looking for a simple, safe, and affordable way to start saving. Savers will be able to open an account with as little as $25 and contribute $5 or more every payday. *my*RA balances will never go down, and there will be no fees. *my*RAs will be initially offered through employers and will be backed by the full faith and credit of the United States.

Q. Who will *my*RAs be for?

A. *my*RAs will be Roth IRA accounts available to anyone who has an annual income of less than $131,000 a year for individuals and $193,000 for couples. *my*RAs will be for savers who either do not have access to an

RETIREMENT PLAN ROLLOVER CHART

This is a chart of what the Internal Revenue Service regards as permissible when rolling funds over from one type of retirement account to another. This chart is for informational purposes only and is not legal, tax and investment advice. Always check with a tax advisor before rolling funds between plans.

Roll From \ Roll To	Roth IRA	Traditional IRA	SIMPLE IRA	SEP IRA	Governmental 457(b) Plan	Qualified Plan[1] (pre-tax)	403(b) Plan (pre-tax)	Designated Roth Account (401(k), 403(b) or 457(b))
Roth IRA	Yes[2]	No	No	No	No	No	No	No
Traditional IRA	Yes[3]	Yes[2]	Yes[2,7], after 2 years	Yes[2]	Yes[4]	Yes	Yes	No
SIMPLE IRA	Yes[3], after 2 years	Yes[2], after 2 years	Yes[2]	Yes[2], after 2 years	Yes[4], after 2 years	Yes, after 2 years	Yes, after 2 years	No
SEP IRA	Yes[3]	Yes[2]	Yes[7], after 2 years	Yes[2]	Yes[4]	Yes	Yes	No
Governmental 457(b) Plan	Yes[3]	Yes	Yes[7], after 2 years	Yes	Yes	Yes	Yes	Yes[3,5]
Qualified Plan[1] (pre-tax)	Yes[3]	Yes	Yes[7], after 2 years	Yes	Yes[4]	Yes	Yes	Yes[3,5]
403(b) Plan (pre-tax)	Yes[3]	Yes	Yes[7], after 2 years	Yes	Yes[4]	Yes	Yes	Yes[3,5]
Designated Roth Account (401(k), 403(b) or 475(b))	Yes	No	No	No	No	No	No	Yes[5]

1. Qualified plans include, for example, profit-sharing, 401(k), money purchase, and defined benefit plans.
2. Only one rollover in any 12-month period.
3. Must include in income.
4. Must have separate accounts.
5. Must be an in-plan rollover.
6. Any nontaxable amounts distributed must be rolled over by direct trustee-to-trustee transfer.
7. Applies to rollover contributions after December 18, 2015.

employer-sponsored retirement savings plan or are looking to supplement a current plan. They will be designed for savers who want an investment with a low opening amount.

Q. How will *my*RAs work?

A. *my*RAs will earn interest at the same variable rate as the Government Securities Investment Fund in the Thrift Savings Plan for federal employees. Savers may voluntarily roll over *my*RAs to private-sector retirement accounts at any time. Once a saver's *my*RA reaches $15,000, or after 30 years, the balance will be rolled over to a private-sector retirement account. The Treasury will finalize rollover procedures when it launches the *my*RA program later this year.

Q. How will I sign up for a *my*RA?

A. Once the accounts are available, employees of participating employers will start by signing up for *my*RA online. Then they will set up an initial automatic payroll direct deposit with their employers for a minimum contribution of $25. Employees will then elect to have a portion of their paychecks—as little as $5—directly deposited into their *my*RAs automatically every payday.

Simple

- Automatic payroll deduction.
- Portable—not tied to a single employer.
- Your contributions can be withdrawn tax free at any time; earnings generally can be withdrawn tax free after age 59½.

Safe

- Account balances will never go down.
- The same variable interest rate as a low-risk account available to federal government employees.
- Individual information will be private and secure.
- Backed by the U.S. Department of the Treasury.

Affordable

- Only $25 to open an account and contributions as low as $5 every payday.
- No fees.
- Tax advantages of Roth IRA.

Q. When will *my*RAs be available?

A. Treasury expects to begin rolling out *my*RAs in late 2014.

Q. How will employers participate?

A. *my*RAs will be free and easy for employers to offer. Employers may distribute *my*RA information but will not administer employee accounts or contribute to them. On payday, employers will send a direct deposit to each participating employee's *my*RA.

For additional information, visit www.treasurydirect.gov/readysavegrow or call 1-800-553-2663. The program officially rolled out in 2016. In July 2017, President Trump called for the termination of the program. Accounts would be rolled over tax free into Roth IRAs.

83 Self-Employment Tax

Beginning in 1990, if you had income from self-employment and you owe self-employment tax, you may deduct one-half of that tax above the line. Note that this deduction reduces your income base for Keogh and SEP deductions as previously discussed.

84 Health Insurance Deduction for Self-Employeds

The deduction for health insurance of self-employed individuals is 100 percent since 2003. This special deduction for health insurance is not subject to the floor of 10 percent of adjusted gross income for medical expense deductions.

Certain limitations apply to this new health insurance deduction. No deduction is allowed to the extent that health insurance payments exceed your earned income for the taxable year. Nor is any deduction allowed for any month for which you are eligible to participate in a subsidized accident-and- health plan provided by an organization that employs (whether on a full- or part-time basis) either you or your spouse. Moreover, no deduction is allowed unless you provide coverage under one or more accident or health plans for all of your employees, should you have any. Those plans must also satisfy nondiscrimination rules.

This deduction is available even though you do not itemize your deductions. This deduction did reduce your earnings for the computation of self-employment tax as of the Small Business Jobs Act of 2010, but only for 2010. In addition, it is available for greater than 2 percent partnerships and S corporation owners (Rev. Rul. 91-26).

85 Moving Expenses—Old Law

Moving expenses incurred if you change job locations or if you start a new job are generally deductible if you meet certain requirements. For moves made after 1993, your new job location must be at least 50 miles from your former job location, you must make your move within 1 year from the date you start your new job, and you must work full-time for a specified period of time. For moves in 1994 or after, expenses are above the line deductions. (Pre-1994, the mileage was 30 miles and the expenses were itemized deductions.)

You may take a moving expense deduction, subject to dollar limits explained later, for the following expenses:

- Travel for yourself and family to your new job location, including lodging but not meals.
- Moving your household goods and personal items.
- House-hunting trips before you move (pre-1994 only).
- Temporary living expenses at the new location (pre-1994 only).
- Expenses incurred in disposing of your former home and acquiring your new one (pre-1994 only).

You may qualify for such deductions whether you are self-employed or an employee. These expenses, though, must be in connection with starting work at a new job location. You will be able to deduct your moving expenses if you meet the requirements of certain tests.

THE DISTANCE TEST

You may now deduct your moving expenses if your new principal job location is at least 50 miles farther from your former home than was your former principal job location. In addition, the distance from your new home to your new job location must not be longer than the distance from your old home to the new job location. Your home is your primary residence; it may be a house, apartment, condominium, houseboat, housetrailer, or similar dwelling. It does not include other homes owned or kept up by you or members of your family, or a seasonal home (such as a beach cottage).

The distance between two points is measured by the shortest of the most commonly traveled routes between the points. If your old job was 3 miles from your former home, your new job must be at least 53 miles from that home.

If you did not have an old job location, your new job location must be at least 50 miles from your former home.

For example, assume your old job was 3 miles from your former home. Your new job is 55 miles from that home. You qualify because the difference (52 miles) is over the minimum of 50 miles. Your new home may be less than 50 miles from your former home, but it must be at least as close to your new job as your former home. If so, you have met the distance test. See the chart below for an example of how you qualify even if the distance between old and new homes is less than 50 miles.

Your principal job location is usually the place where you do most of your work and spend most of your time. A new principal job location is a new place where you will work on a permanent or indefinite basis rather than on a temporary basis. However, you may have a principal job location even if there is no one place where you spend a substantial part of your work and time. In this case, use the distance to the place where your work is centered—for example, where you report for work or otherwise have the "base" for your work.

		55 miles				
Old Job	3 miles	Old Home	49 miles	New Home	6 miles	New Job

New Job to Old Home	= 55 miles	Old Home to New Job	= 55 miles
Old Home to Old Job	= −3 miles	New Home to New Job	= 6 miles
Qualifying distance	= 52 miles	New Home is at least as close to new job as Old Home to new job	

If you work for a number of employers on a short-term basis, or get work under a union hall system (such as in construction and the building trades), use the distance between your home and the union hall.

TIME TEST

To deduct your moving expenses you also must meet one of the following time tests:

1. If you are an employee, you must work full-time at least 39 weeks during the 12-month period following your arrival in the general area of your new

job location. You do not have to work for one employer for the 39 weeks; you do not even have to work 39 weeks in a row. But you must work full-time within the same general commuting area. Whether you are employed full-time depends upon the custom for your type of work. For example, a schoolteacher on a 12-month contract who teaches on a full-time basis for more than six months is considered a full-time employee for the entire 12 months. Any week that you work full-time is used to satisfy the 39 week full-time work test. If the work is seasonal, you are considered to be working full-time during the off-season weeks if your contract or agreement covers an off-season of less than 6 months. You are considered to be working during any week you are temporarily absent from work because of illness, strikes, natural disasters, or the like. You are also considered to be a full-time employee during any week you are absent from work for leave or for vacation that is provided for in your work contract or agreement.

2. If you are self-employed, you must work full-time for at least 39 weeks during the first 12 months and a total of 78 weeks during the 24 months after your arrival in the area of your new job location. Whether you perform services full-time during any one week depends upon the custom of your type of work in your area.

Despite these restrictions, you may deduct your moving expenses even if you have not met the time test by the time your return is due. You may do this if you *expect* to work for 39 weeks by the end of the next year, or for 78 weeks by the end of the second year. Furthermore, you do not have to meet the time test at all if any one of the following situations applies:

- You are in the armed forces and your move is due to a permanent change of stations.

- You move to the United States because you retire or are the survivor of a person who dies while living and working outside the United States.

- Your job ends because of disability, transfer for the employer's benefit, or layoff other than for willful misconduct. The time test does not have to be met in case of your death. If you are transferred, you are expected to meet the test at the time you start the job.

THE START OF WORK TEST

In general you must have moving expenses within 1 year from the time you first report to your job or business at the new location, and the move must be

in connection with the start of work at the new location. If you do not move within 1 year, the expenses are ordinarily not deductible unless you can show that certain circumstances prevented the move within that time period. For example, if your family moved more than a year after you started work at the new location in order to allow your child to complete junior high school in the same school, your allowable moving expenses are deductible.

A move is considered closely related to the start of work if:

a) you are required to live at the new location as a condition of employment; *or*

b) you will spend less time or money commuting from the new home to the new job.

It is important that you understand and recognize all of the possible expenses that are deductible under this category. You can deduct expenses of moving your possessions, traveling to your new home, looking for a new home (pre-1994), living temporarily in a new area (pre-1994), selling and buying a home (pre-1994), or settling and signing a lease (pre-1994).

If you use your car to take yourself, your family, or your things to your new home, or for house hunting, you figure your expenses in either of two ways:

1. You may deduct your actual expenses such as gas, oil, and repairs (but not depreciation) for the use of your car, if you keep an accurate record of each expense.

2. You may deduct 18.0¢ a mile for 2018 instead of the actual costs if you can prove the mileage traveled. You may deduct parking fees and tolls you pay in moving no matter which way you figure your expenses.

Not only may you deduct the expenses of moving your own possessions, but you may also deduct the costs for transporting the possessions of the members of your household. This includes the actual cost of transportation or hauling from your former home to your new one. The cost of packing and crating, in-transit storage, and insurance is included. Expenses of storing and insuring household goods and personal effects are in-transit expenses if incurred within 30 consecutive days after your things are moved from your former home and before they are delivered at your new one.

Prior to 1994, moving expenses also included the cost of transportation, lodging for yourself and members of your household while traveling to your new home, and 80 percent of the cost of meals while moving. This included expenses for the day you arrive, and any meals and lodging expenses incurred in your old neighborhood within one day after your former home becomes

uninhabitable because your furniture has been moved out. You could deduct expenses for only one trip to your new home for yourself and each member of your household. However, all members do not have to travel together.

Prior to 1994, deductions were allowed as well for premove house-hunting expenses. House-hunting expenses include the cost of transportation, meals, and lodging for yourself and members of your household while traveling to and from the area of your new job and while you are there. You could deduct these expenses only if you begin your trip *after* you get the job in the new area and if you go primarily to look for a new place to live. Your house hunting did not have to be successful to qualify for this deduction. You and members of your household could travel separately. Furthermore, you were not limited in the number of trips you or members of your household may take.

Prior to 1994, you also could deduct the cost of temporary living expenses. These expenses include not only the cost of lodging in the area of your new job but the cost of meals as well.

HOME SALE, PURCHASE, OR LEASE EXPENSES

In addition, pre-1994, home sale, purchase, and lease expenses also were deductible. You therefore could deduct the costs of selling your home or settling your lease in the former area and buying or leasing a home in the new area.

When you sold or exchanged a home, you could deduct real estate commissions, attorney's fees, title fees, escrow fees, points or loan placement charges you were required to pay, state transfer taxes, and similar expenses connected to the sale or exchange. You could not, however, deduct the cost of physical improvements intended to improve the condition or appearance of your former home. When you bought your new home, you could again deduct attorney's fees, escrow fees, appraisal fees, title fees, points and loan placement charges that did not represent payment or prepayment of interest, and similar expenses connected to the purchase. When you lease a new home, you cannot deduct payments or prepayments of rent.

There are certain dollar limits that you must remember. Deductions for the costs of moving household goods and traveling to your new home are not limited to any amount. For premove travel, meals, and lodging expenses, temporary living expenses, and home sale, purchase, or lease expenses, you could not deduct more than $3,000. Deductions for house-hunting trip costs and temporary living expenses together could not be more than $1,500.

If you are a homeowner, you should have claimed the costs of premove house-hunting expenses and temporary living expenses before you claimed the costs of selling and buying your home as moving expenses. However, within the dollar limits you may choose to deduct any combination of these expenses. If you have expenses from selling or buying a home that you cannot deduct as

moving expenses because of the $3,000 limit, you should use these expenses to reduce the gain on the sale of your former home or to increase the basis of your new home.

The following items cannot be deducted as moving expenses:

Home improvements to help sell your home
Loss on the sale of your home
Mortgage penalties
Losses from the disposing of memberships and clubs
Any part of the purchase price of your new home
Real estate taxes
Car tax for the state you move to
Driver's license for the state you move to
Refitting carpets and draperies
New security deposits on a new lease
Security deposits on an old lease because the vacated space needed cleaning
 or redecorating when the lease ended

However, you may deduct a security deposit that you give up if the lease is broken as a result of the move.

CHANGED LAW

The Omnibus Budget Reconciliation Act of 1993 made several substantial changes in the moving expense deduction—effective for expenses incurred after December 31, 1993. As of 1994, the Act excludes from the definition of moving expenses: (1) the costs related to the sale of (or settlement of an unexpired lease on) the old residence, and the purchase of (or acquisition of a lease on) the new residence in the general location of the new job and (2) the costs of meals consumed while traveling and while living in temporary quarters near the new job. It also contains the following additional modifications:

1. The cost of premove house-hunting trips is excluded from the definition of moving expenses.

2. The cost of temporary living expenses for up to 30 days in the general location of the new job is excluded from the definition of moving expenses.

3. The mileage limit is increased from 35 miles to 50 miles.

4. Moving expenses not paid or reimbursed by the taxpayer's employer are allowable as a deduction in calculating adjusted gross income.

5. Moving expenses paid or reimbursed by the taxpayer's employer are excludable from gross income. *Moving expenses* are now defined as the reasonable costs of

 a) moving household goods and personal effects from the former residence to the new residence, including no more than 30 days of storage expenses (*Parameter*, TC Summ. Op 2015-75); and

 b) traveling (including lodging during the period of travel) from the former residence to the new place of residence.

 Moving expenses do not include any expenses for meals.

EMPLOYER-PAID MOVING EXPENSES

Moving expenses are excludable from gross income and wages for income and employment tax purposes to the extent paid for by the taxpayer's employer (whether directly or through reimbursement). Moving expenses are not excludable if the taxpayer actually deducted the expenses in a prior taxable year. The 1993 law intends that the employer treat moving expenses as excludable unless it has actual knowledge that the employee deducted the expenses in a prior year. The employer has no obligation to determine whether the individual deducted the expenses. Rules similar to the rules relating to accountable plans will apply to reimbursed expenses.

MOVING EXPENSES NOT PAID FOR BY THE EMPLOYER

Moving expenses are deductible in computing adjusted gross income to the extent not paid for by the taxpayer's employer (whether directly or through reimbursement). Allowing such a deduction will treat taxpayers whose expenses are not paid for by their employer in a comparable manner to taxpayers whose moving expenses are paid for by their employer.

TAX STRATEGIES

The availability of the moving expense deduction allows you several very sophisticated tax planning strategies.

One strategic tax move may come about if you are considering retirement and a move to a different—warmer—climate. If you make the move in connection with a change in employment and satisfy the 39-week work requirement, you get a deduction for your moving expenses. The tax effect of this deduction will, in effect, increase your compensation for the 39 weeks of work and perhaps make it worthwhile to postpone your actual retirement. Note that included in the definition of moving expenses are all of your "personal effects." See, for example,

John R. Fogg, 89 T.C. No. 27 (decided in 1988), wherein a marine officer's moving expense deduction included the cost of moving his boat.

You should recognize that the deductibility of your moving expenses is in effect a tax subsidy of those expenses. So, for example, if you think it may be too expensive to hire a moving company, your decision to save money by moving your household goods yourself may be modified by considering the tax effect of the deduction for moving expenses. Moving company charges of $3,000 actually would represent a cash outflow of only $2,250 if you are single and have taxable income over the $37,950 level ($3,000 × .025 = $750 in tax savings).

CURRENT LAW

Unfortunately, the Tax Cuts and Jobs Act of 2017 now limits the deduction to active military personnel. Worse, if your employer reimburses you for your moving expenses, that amount is now added to your income.

86 Clean Fuel Vehicles

If you were the original owner, you could have gotten a deduction of up to $2,000 of the cost of a clean fuel vehicle. That's a vehicle that uses a significant source of energy other than gasoline.

You got the $2,000 deduction if the car was placed in service in 2004 or 2005. Now, you'll use the Hybrid Vehicles Credits found on pages 161–162.

You got the deduction for the year you started driving the car. The IRS has validated *hybrid cars* for this deduction. A hybrid combines an electric motor with a gas-fueled internal combustion engine. (See the Ford Escape, the Toyota Prius and Highlander, and Honda's Insight and Hybrid Civic, among others.) U.S. automakers will focus on sport utility vehicles and pickup trucks rather than passenger cars. If you qualified, the IRS contributed to the cost of your new car. You took the deduction on Line 33 of your Form 1040 by writing in "clean fuel."

87 Deduction for Qualified Higher Education Expenses—Tuition and Fees

The 2001 Tax Act created an above-the-line deduction for qualified higher education expenses you pay. Qualified higher education expenses are defined in the same manner as for purposes of the HOPE credit. Room and board do *not* count.

In 2002 and 2003, if you had an adjusted gross income that did not exceed $65,000 ($130,000 in the case of married couples filing joint returns) you were entitled to a maximum deduction of $3,000 per year. Taxpayers with adjusted gross income above these thresholds didn't get the deduction. Since 2004, taxpayers with adjusted gross income that did not exceed $65,000 ($130,000 in the case of married taxpayers filing joint returns) were entitled to a maximum deduction of $4,000 and taxpayers with adjusted gross income that does not exceed $80,000 ($160,000 in the case of married taxpayers filing joint returns) were entitled to a maximum deduction of $2,000. This deduction was allowable through 2009 and was renewed by Congress through 2017.

The tuition and fees deduction of up to $4,000 was available to help parents and students pay for postsecondary education. Below are 10 important facts about this deduction every student and parent should know.

1. You do not have to itemize to take the tuition and fees deduction. You claim a tuition and fees deduction by completing Form 8917 and submitting it with your Form 1040 or Form 1040A.

2. You may be able to claim qualified tuition and fees expenses as either an adjustment to income, a Hope, American Opportunity, or Lifetime Learning credit, or, if applicable, as a business expense.

3. You cannot take the tuition and fees deduction on your income tax return if your filing status is married and you're filing separately.

4. You cannot take the deduction if you are claimed, or can be claimed, as a dependent on someone else's return.

5. The deduction is reduced or eliminated if your modified adjusted gross income exceeds certain limits, based on your filing status (see above).

6. You cannot claim the tuition and fees deduction if you or anyone else claims the Hope, American Opportunity, or Lifetime Learning credit for the same student in the same year.

7. If the educational expenses are also allowable as a business expense, the tuition and fees deduction may be claimed in conjunction with a business expense deduction, but the same expenses cannot be deducted twice.

8. You cannot claim a deduction or credit based on expenses paid with tax-free scholarship, fellowship, grant, or education savings account funds such as a Coverdell education savings account, tax-free savings bond interest, or employer-provided education assistance.

9. The same rule applies to expenses you pay with a tax-exempt distribution from a qualified tuition plan except that you can deduct qualified expenses you pay only with that part of the distribution that is a return of your contribution to the plan.

10. IRS Publication 970, Tax Benefits for Education, can help eligible parents and students understand the special rules that apply and decide which tax break to claim. The publication is available at IRS.gov or by calling 800-TAX-FORM (800-829-3676).

This deduction expired at the end of 2017. But you can still file an amended return if you failed to claim it and qualify.

88 Legal Fees

Fees and court costs you pay to your attorney on settlements or awards for *unlawful discrimination*—sex, race, or age—after the signing of the American Jobs Creation Act of 2004 on October 22, are now allowed as above the line deductions. These deductions are not subject to the alternative minimum tax, nor to the 2 percent floor on miscellaneous itemized deductions.

89 Classroom Materials

You get an above the line deduction of up to $250 annually for expenses paid for books, supplies, computer equipment, professional development and enhancement, and supplementary materials if you're an eligible educator. An eligible educator is a kindergarten through grade 12 teacher, aide, instructor, counselor, or principal in a school for at least 900 hours during the school year. If both spouces qualify, that's a $500 above-the-line deduction.

90 Medical Savings Accounts (Archer Medical Savings Accounts)

Under law prior to the Health Insurance Portability and Accountability Act of 1996, self-employed individuals were entitled to deduct 30 percent of the amount paid for health insurance for the self-employed individual and his or her spouse or dependents. (It's now 100 percent.) Any individual who itemized tax deductions could deduct unreimbursed medical expenses (including expenses for medical insurance) paid during the year

to the extent that the total of such expenses exceeded 7.5 percent of the individual's adjusted gross income. Prior law did not contain any special rules for medical savings accounts.

A medical savings account (MSA) is a trust or custodial account created exclusively for the benefit of the account holder and is subject to rules similar to those applicable to individual retirement accounts. Within limits, contributions to a medical savings account are deductible if made by an eligible individual and are excludable if made by an employer of an eligible individual. Moreover, earnings on amounts in a medical savings account are not currently taxable and distributions from a medical savings account for medical expenses will also not be taxable.

Since 1997, medical savings accounts have been available to employees covered under an employer-sponsored high-deductible plan of a small employer and to self-employed individuals. An employer is a small employer if it employed on an average no more than 50 employees during either the preceding or second preceding year. In order for an employee of an eligible employer to be eligible to make medical savings account contributions (or to have the employer contributions made on his or her behalf), the employee must not be covered under any other health plan. In the case of an employee, contributions can be made to a medical savings account either by the individual or by the individual's employer. However, an individual is not eligible to make contributions to a medical savings account for a year if any employer contributions are made to a medical savings account on behalf of the individual for the year.

Similarly, in order to be eligible to make contributions to a medical savings account, a self-employed individual must be covered under a high-deductible health plan and no other health plan is allowed (except certain permitted coverages). With both self-employed individuals and employees, medical savings accounts are allowable if the taxpayer has another health plan that provides *only* certain limited permitted coverage for accidents, disability, dental care, vision care, or long-term care. This coverage may be by insurance or otherwise and permitted insurance includes: (1) Medicare supplemental insurance; (2) insurance if substantially all of the coverage provided under such insurance relates to (a) liabilities incurred under Workers' Compensation Law, (b) tort liabilities, (c) liabilities relating to ownership and use of property (e.g., auto insurance), or (d) such other similar liabilities as the Secretary of the Treasury may prescribe by regulations; (3) insurance for a specified disease or illness; and (4) insurance that provides a fixed payment for hospitalization.

Individual contributions to a medical savings account are deductible (within limits) above the line. In addition, employer contributions are excludable within the same limits.

In the case of a self-employed individual, the deduction cannot exceed your earned income from the trade or business with respect to which the high-deductible plan is established. In the case of an employee, the deduction cannot exceed your compensation attributable to the employer sponsoring the high-deductible plan in which you are enrolled.

The maximum annual contribution that can be made to a medical savings account for a year is 65 percent of the deductible under the high-deductible plan in the case of individual coverage and 75 percent of the deductible in the case of family coverage. No other dollar limits on the maximum contribution apply. The annual contribution limit is the sum of the limits determined separately for each month, based upon the individual's status and health plan coverage as of the first day of the month.

A high-deductible plan for 2018 is a health plan with an annual deductible of at least $2,300 and no more than $3,450 in the case of individual coverage and at least $4,550 and no more than $6,850 in the case of family coverage. In addition, the maximum out-of-pocket expenses with respect to allowed cost (including the deductible) must be no more than $4,550 in the case of individual coverage and no more than $8,400 in the case of family coverage. Since 1999, these dollar amounts have been indexed for inflation in $50 increments based on the Consumer Price Index.

Earnings on amounts in a medical savings account are not currently included in income, and distributions from a medical savings account for the medical expenses of an individual and his or her spouse or dependents generally are excludable from income.

The medical savings account plan was a trial plan. The number of taxpayers benefiting annually from a medical savings account contribution is limited to a threshold level (generally, 750,000 taxpayers). If it is determined in a year that the threshold level has been exceeded then, in general, for succeeding years during the four-year pilot period, 1997–2000, only those individuals who (1) made a medical savings account contribution or had an employer medical savings account contribution for the year or a preceding year or (2) are employed by a participating employer, would be eligible for a medical savings account contribution.

If you have a medical savings account, you attach Form 8853 to your tax return. During 1997–2000, the Department of the Treasury evaluated medical savings account participation and the reduction in federal revenues due to such participation and made reports of such evaluations to Congress. As a result, Congress has voted to expand MSAs.

Few Archer MSAs will be set up after 2005. The reason—Health Savings Accounts. (See IRS Announcement 2007-44.)

91 Health Savings Accounts

I love it! Tax deductible when going in. *And* no tax when you take it out! You can't get much better than that.

I'm talking about the new Health Savings Accounts (HSAs) that were created as part of the Medicare Act of 2003.

The concept is easy. Congress wants to put you in charge of your own health costs. So, if you buy their special ticket, you'll be able to set up a magical account. You'll put money into that account and be able to deduct it. There's no tax while the money is held by the account. And, if you take the dollars out for the right reasons, there's no tax ever.

Technically, it's a bit more complicated. Let's start with the special ticket.

In order to qualify to open a Health Savings Account, you have to be covered by a high-deductible health plan. It must be your only health plan. (There are some exceptions—e.g., workers' compensation, coverage under an auto policy, etc.)

A high-deductible health plan is one with an annual deductible of not less than $1,350 for 2018 and 2019 for individual coverage and not less than $2,700 for 2018 and 2019 for family coverage. That means you pay for the routine medical visits, tests, eyeglasses, and the like. Remember, the bigger the deductible, the smaller the premium you have to pay.

In addition, the sum of the annual deductible and other out of pocket expenses required to be paid under the plan can't exceed $6,650 for 2018 ($6,750 for 2019) for individual coverage, and $13,300 for 2018 ($13,500 for 2019) for family coverage.

Can your employer offer a high-deductible plan? Sure. In fact, many supporters of the concept expect large employers to offer the option before long.

If you've got this special ticket, what does it let you do? If you have a high-deductible health plan, you can now set up your own Health Savings Account.

Where do you get the money? How about from the premiums you saved by switching to a *high-deductible* health plan!?

Technically, the HSA is a trust. For 2018 and 2019, you can contribute to that trust and *take a tax deduction of* $3,450 ($6,900 with family coverage). For 2019, the numbers are reset to $3,500 and $7,000.

If you're age 55 or older, you can make additional $1,000 deductible contributions.

You can pretty much invest the money any way you want, similar to an IRA. In fact, IRA funds can now be rolled over into an HSA, saving the tax and any 10 percent penalty.

You can dip into this pot at any time. Any dollars used for medical expenses come out tax-free. You can use the HSA for routine doctor visits, lab tests, eyeglasses, dental care, or even cosmetic surgery. Anything left over at the end of the year rolls back into the pot. So, if you're young and healthy, you could built up a nice pot of cash in case of major medical problems years later.

You can't use your HSA to buy health insurance. But, payments for long-term care insurance count. You can also use the money for temporary health insurance while you're unemployed and collecting unemployment, or for COBRA continuation insurance.

If you withdraw for nonmedical purposes, you pay tax, plus a 20 percent penalty (10 percent before 2011), on the nonqualified amount.

Similar accounts, the Archer Medical Savings Accounts, have been around for a while. But, the Archer MSAs were limited to small businesses and the self-employed. They were also temporary and scheduled to potentially terminate after a trial period. That really didn't encourage insurance companies to develop the appropriate policies on a mass basis. The Health Savings Accounts are designed to be permanent and can be used by anybody!

HSAs can be offered to employees as part of a cafeteria plan. Contributions can be made by both employers and employees. Whoever puts the dollars in gets the deduction. However, if you have a health Flexible Spending Account (FSA), even if your balance is solely from a prior year carryover, you don't qualify for an HSA. You can contribute to an HSA even if your spouse is covered with insurance, so long as you are not covered by the policy (Rev. Rul. 2005-25).

You can even fund your HSA with a transfer from your IRA. It's a onetime transfer. See IRS Notice 2008-51 for details.

Here's how the numbers might work. A 38-year-old couple with two children could buy a health policy with a $5,950 deductible for $250 a month, or $3,000 a year. A plan with a $500 deductible would cost $600 a month, or $7,200 a year.

With the $3,000 plan, they save $4,200 in premiums. That $4,200 can be used to fund an HSA and would be fully deductible.

Now, you're in charge. First you've got the tax savings. In the 37 percent bracket, that's an additional $1,554 in your pocket. But even more important, you now have control over your own medical expenditures. For a $10 co-payment, it was easy to visit the doctor. But, now it's *your* money that's being spent. That should help put a break on runaway health costs.

The one downside is that you can no longer make additional HSA contributions once you sign up for Medicare, but you still can make withdrawals.

If you're young, healthy, or wealthy, this is a deal you don't want to pass up. I know of no other vehicle where you get a deduction with a deposit and no tax with a withdrawal. That's my kind of tax shelter!

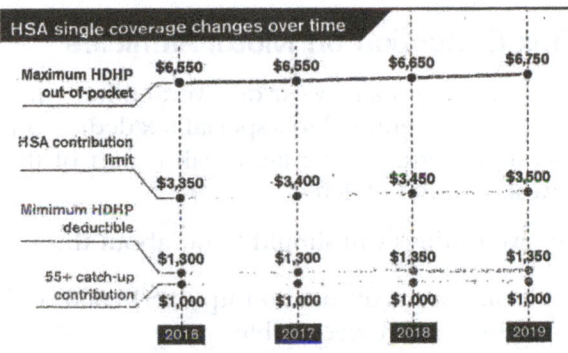

HSA single coverage changes over time

	2016	2017	2018	2019
Maximum HDHP out-of-pocket	$6,550	$6,550	$6,650	$6,750
HSA contribution limit	$3,350	$3,400	$3,450	$3,500
Mimimum HDHP deductible	$1,300	$1,300	$1,350	$1,350
55+ catch-up contribution	$1,000	$1,000	$1,000	$1,000

HSA family coverage changes over time

	2016	2017	2018	2019
Maximum HDHP out-of-pocket	$13,100	$13,100	$13,300	$13,500
HSA contribution limit	$6,750	$6,750	$6,900	$7,000
Mimimum HDHP deductible	$2,600	$2,600	$2,700	$2,700
55+ catch-up contribution	$1,000	$1,000	$1,000	$1,000

HSA contribution changes over time

	2016	2017	2018	2019
Family coverage	$6,750	$6,750	$6,900	$7,000
Single coverage	$3,350	$3,400	$3,450	$3,500
55+ catch-up contribution	$1,000	$1,000	$1,000	$1,000

HSA limit changes: Family HDHP coverage

2015	2016	2017	2018	2019
$6,650	$6,750	$6,750	$6,900	$7,000

92 Sales Tax Deduction on Motor Vehicles

Taxpayers who bought a new car or several other types of motor vehicles in 2009 may have been entitled to a special tax deduction when they filed their 2009 federal tax returns. The tax break is part of the American Recovery and Reinvestment Act of 2009.

Here are seven things you should know about this old deduction:

1. State and local sales taxes paid on up to $49,500 of the purchase price of qualifying vehicles were deductible.

2. Qualified motor vehicles generally included new (not used) cars, light trucks, motor homes, and motorcycles.

3. Purchases must have occurred after February 16, 2009, and before January 1, 2010.

4. This is an above-the-line deduction and can be taken regardless of whether or not you itemize other deductions on your tax return.

5. Taxpayers will claim this deduction when filing their 2009 federal income tax return. File an amended return, Form 1040X, if you missed it.

6. The amount of the deduction was phased out for taxpayers whose modified adjusted gross income was between $125,000 and $135,000 for individual filers and between $250,000 and $260,000 for joint filers.

Note that there was no separate line to take this deduction. It was added to your standard deduction (like the extra deduction for real estate taxes paid) using Schedule L.

If your state doesn't have a sales or excise tax, you could have deducted other fees or taxes imposed by the state or local government based on the vehicle's sales price or a per-unit fee.

PLAN COMPARISON

	Flexible Spending Account	Health Savings Account	Health Reimbursement Arrangement
Initial Legislator or Regulation	Revenue active 1978	Medicare active 2003	U.S. Department of the Treasury Revenue Ruling 2002
Date Effective	January 1, 1979	January 1, 1997	June 26, 2002
Eligibility	All employees except self-employed	All employers	All employers
Qualified Medical Expenses	Unreimbursed medical care expense as defined by Internal Revenue Code, Section 213	Any qualified medical expense permitted under tax law	Unreimbursed medical expenses as defined by the Internal Revenue Code 213
Nonqualified Medical Expenses	Expenses not under Internal Revenue Code 213. Health insurance premiums under a continuation or coverage arrangement. Health insurance premiums when receiving unemployment compensation	Expenses not under Internal Revenue Code 213	Expenses not under Internal Revenue Code 213
Must Be Covered by Health Insurance Plan	No	Yes, a high-deductible health plan	No
Contributor	Employee, employer or both	Employee, employer or both	Employer
Contribution Limits	$2,650 salary reduction	Up to the amount of the high-deductible health plan but no more than $3,450 for self-coverage and $6,900 for family coverage	No statutory limit. Limit may be set by employer.
Funds Carried Over to Next Year	Extension to March 15 or $500 carryover	Yes	Yes
Portability	Account cannot be maintained if employee is no longer working for the employer. Continued access to unused account balance if the employee is no longer working for the employer	Completely portable	At employer's discretion

Source: Benefits Selling, October 2005.

	Health Savings Accounts (HSAs)	Medical Savings Accounts (MSAs)
Contribution source	Individual (or by a family member on behalf of the individual) and/or employer	Either individual or employer (not both)
Tax-deductible contribution	Up to 100 percent of deductible with a maximum cap determined by the Internal Revenue Service each year: Single coverage: $3,450 Family coverage: $6,900	Single: 65 percent of deductible Family: 75 percent of deductible
Deductible ranges	For 2018: minimums = $1,350 for single; $2,700 for family	For 2018: $2,300–$3,450 for single; $4,450–$6,850 for family
Maximum out of pocket*	For 2018: maximums = $6,650 for single; $13,300 for family	For 2018: maximums = $4,550 for single; $8,400 for family
Who is eligible?	Individual or employer of any size that has established a qualified high-deductible health plan (HDHP); individual must be below Medicare eligibility age (65), not covered by any non-HDHP; and not listed as a dependent on another's tax return	Self-employed and small employers (under 50 employees); individuals must be covered by a qualified HDHP
Is there a "catch-up" contribution provision for older workers?	Individuals between the ages of 55 and 65 may contribute an additional $1,000.	No
Effective date	Must be established on or after January 1, 2005.	Must have been established by December 31, 2003, and before January 1, 2006; rollovers into an HSA are allowed.
Do employers need to make comparable contributions?	Yes, but under HSA legislation both employers and employees can contribute.	Yes

* Includes deductible and any expenses incurred once deductible is met.

Source: MSA Bank (HAS Bank).

"Below the Line" Deductions

"I am proud to be paying taxes in the United States. The only thing is—I could be just as proud for half the money."

ARTHUR GODFREY

"About 510,000 taxpayers who claimed tax standard deductions on their 1998 income tax returns would have saved an average $610 by itemizing their deductions."

General Accounting Office April 13, 2001

"About 948,000 taxpayers in the year 1998 failed to itemize their deductions, even though they qualified to do so, resulting in a $473 million overpayment in taxes."

General Accounting Office April 11, 2002

"Our tax system is complicated and unfair, and it must be eliminated."

RICHARD K. ARMEY (R-Tex.) Former Majority
Leader of the House of Representatives and
BILL ARCHER (R-Tex.) Former Chairman
of the House Ways & Means Committee

"Congress has a lot of respect for logic—they use it so sparingly."

JEFF SCHNEPPER

Your itemize deductions only if they exceed the amount of your standard deduction.

For 2018 the standard deduction amounts are as follows:

If your filing status is:	2018
Single	$12,000
Married, filing jointly, or a qualifying widow or widower	$24,000
Married, filing separately	$12,000
Head of household	$18,000

For 2008 and 2009, nonitemizers could have deducted up to $500 ($1,000 for joint returns) for real estate taxes paid, plus, for 2009, your standard deduction was also increased by the sales tax deduction on motor vehicles discussed on page 264.

The personal tax exemption was $4,050 for 2017 but is zero for 2018, and the added standard deduction for the aged or blind is $1,300 each on a joint return and $1,600 for a single for 2018.

A The Importance of Filing Status

Your filing status is determined on the last day of each year. This affords you another opportunity for sophisticated tax planning. The rates for married individuals, filing either jointly *or* separately, are much lower than those for single, unmarried taxpayers. For example, for 2018, on taxable income of $82,500, a single person pays a marginal tax rate of 22 percent and a total tax of $14,090. On the other hand, a married taxpayer with a spouse who has no income would pay a marginal rate of 22 percent and a total tax of only $10,029. If you are planning a New Year's wedding, advancing it only a few days to Christmas would therefore save you $4,061—enough to pay for your honeymoon.

Alternatively, if both married partners work, there may be, in effect, a tax on the marriage. In 2018, two individuals earning $500,000 in taxable income would each pay $150,689 in taxes for a total outlay of $301,379. If they got married before the year-end, their total income would be $1,000,000, and they would have filed either a joint return or a return as married, filing separately— either way mandating a total tax payment of $309,379, $8,000 more than what they would have paid had they remained unmarried!

Marriage Penalties and Bonuses on Income Tax

An April 1999 Treasury Department study shows that nearly as many couples receive a "marriage bonus" as pay a "marriage penalty." In many cases, the average bonus is greater than the average penalty.

1999 Adjusted Gross Income	Percent of Couples Penalized	Average Penalty	Percent of Couples Who Get a Bonus	Average Bonus	Percent Getting Neither
$0–15,000	7.4%	$302	33.4%	$418	59.2%
$15,001–30,000	40.2%	$607	49.5%	$528	10.3%
$30,001–40,000	52.5%	$792	45.7%	$662	1.8%
$40,001–50,000	57.3%	$578	40.0%	$952	2.7%
$50,001–60,000	48.8%	$535	44.3%	$1,299	6.9%
$60,001–75,000	50.6%	$798	41.4%	$1,537	8.0%
$75,001–100,000	64.9%	$1,384	34.4%	$1,960	0.7%
$100,001–200,000	65.0%	$1,926	34.9%	$2,580	0.1%
$200,001 and more	48.5%	$5,688	50.0%	$3,428	1.5%

Source: Treasury Department.

To compute your marriage penalty/bonus, go to www.taxpolicycenter.org/taxfacts/marriagepenaltycalculator.cfm

Same-sex couples can now file jointly on their *federal* and *state* returns. Registered domestic partnerships civil unions, and similar formal relationships are not treated as marriage for *federal* purposes.

The extraordinary penalty on marriage is the result of previous congressional actions that attempted to correct apparent inequities in the old tax structure. Prior to 1948, husbands and wives in community property states could each claim half of their household income for tax purposes even if only one of them actually earned all of the income. The law of the individual state attributed half of the income ("property") to the other spouse. For example, if only the husband worked, earning $30,000, both he and his wife would have reported $15,000 in income. Given our progressive tax rate, where each additional dollar earned is taxed at a higher rate, this was a substantial advantage. In 1948, the federal income tax code was amended to allow this benefit to all married taxpayers—including those in non–community property states. This was done by doubling the income brackets for married taxpayers associated with each rate. For example, if the first

$500 of income was taxed at 11 percent for a single person, the first $1,000 of income for married couples would have also been taxed at 11 percent.

While those who were married rejoiced, single taxpayers making the same income as married couples were subject to much higher tax rates. In 1970, for example, single taxpayers could have been liable for as much as 42 percent more in taxes than a married couple earning an equivalent income. In response to this harsh inequity, Congress in 1971 changed the rates for single taxpayers to reduce this differential to a 20 percent maximum. The Tax Reform Act of 1986 reduced the differential even further. However, according to the Congressional Budget Office, 21 million couples filing jointly in 1996 suffered the marriage penalty averaging around $1,400 each! According to Senator Hutchison of Texas, that $1,400 marriage penalty number was still valid in March of 1999. The Tax Cuts and Jobs Act of 2017 further reduced the potential penalty.

In the past, the tax penalty on marriage when both husband and wife work was compounded by the standard deduction. The Jobs and Growth Tax Relief Reconciliation Act of 2003 remedied this by making the standard deduction for joint returns twice that offered to singles. It also increased the standard deduction for married filing separately to the same as singles.

In addition, high-income earners who married also lost write-offs for personal exemptions faster than their single counterparts. The 2017 exemption of $4,050 was phased out for singles with taxable incomes above $261,500, but the phase-out for a married couple started at $313,800, 60 percent of the income amount for two single persons. For 2018, the personal exemption is gone.

Marriage may also wipe out potential IRA deductions. If two taxpayers with incomes of $60,500 each marry and both are covered by an employer plan, neither could write off an IRA contribution. They would lose $11,000 in deductions and pay as much as $2,420 more in total tax.

Because your marital status for the entire year is based upon your status as of December 31, many individuals have been advised to fly to a Caribbean divorce haven, such as the Dominican Republic, for a quickie divorce before the year ends and to remarry in January. The tax savings can often more than offset the cost of legal fees and the Caribbean "vacation."

The Internal Revenue Service has reacted to this situation, declaring: "If you obtain a foreign divorce for the sole purpose of enabling you and your spouse to qualify as unmarried individuals eligible to file separate returns, and if you then remarry each other early in the next tax year, you and your spouse must file as married individuals."

This response has been tested in the Tax Court with interesting results. The Tax Court has ruled that it will not recognize such quickie divorces solely on the basis of the fact that the state in which the taxpayers are domiciled will not recognize such divorces. (The Fourth Circuit Court of Appeals ruled in 1981 that there may be a sham even if your state does recognize the divorce [668 F 2d. 1238]. This ruling is not universally accepted—see *Wake Forest Law Review*, Volume 18, pages 881–901, 1982.) But many states *do* recognize such divorces; by implication, therefore, if you reside in such a state, a quickie divorce and a remarriage could save you substantial tax dollars. Your divorce, though, must be real, with significant economic consequences—for example, loss of rights under a will—and not merely a sham. (See *Felt Estate v. Commissioner*, T.C. Memo 1987-465, September 16, 1987, in which a divorce decree obtained by a husband in the Dominican Republic was recognized for federal income tax purposes.)

In cases where divorces or legal separations would be either impractical or unwanted, you could at least make a substantial initial tax savings by postponing your original Christmas wedding until New Year's. This several days' wait may be worth several thousand tax dollars.

Can same-sex couples now file joint federal and state income tax returns? They can now! The Defense of Marriage Act has been held unconstitutional by the Supreme Court. Legally married same-sex couples should file amended federal and state refund claims for all open tax years if they would benefit tax-wise from joint filing. More than joint filing is affected. Gifts between same-sex spouses now get the unlimited gift tax marital deduction. Bequests to surviving spouses are not subject to estate tax, and the survivor is entitled to use any unused estate tax exemption of the deceased spouse. And employer-provided health coverage for same-sex spouses is tax-free.

Being single may also be an advantage in qualifying for excess itemized deductions. For example, assume your spouse has total below the line deductions of $24,000. As you are married and don't exceed the amount of the joint standard deduction, none of these deductions give you any tax benefits. The single standard deduction would be only $12,000.

Filing separately may sometimes help, but a husband and wife filing separate returns must use the same method of claiming deductions: If one itemizes, the other must itemize as well. This could result in a situation in which one spouse who itemizes has an allowable itemized deduction in excess of the standard deduction by, say, $4,000, but the other spouse who has no itemized deductions would have no "below the line" deductions.

In July 2000, the IRS ruled (S.C.A. 200030023) that (1) if a married individual files a separate return with head of household status and elects to itemize deductions, and if the other spouse continues to file as a married individual filing a separate return, then that other spouse is not eligible for the full standard deduction, but (2) if the other spouse who files as married filing separately elects to itemize deductions, then the spouse who files a separate return with head of household status may still use the full standard deduction available for head of household status.

Married filing separately may be profitable if the spouse who has itemized deductions is in a higher tax bracket. For example, if one is in the 32 percent bracket and the other is in the 10 percent bracket, the first would save $1,280 ($4,000 × .32) at a cost to the second of only $1,200 (married filing separately standard deduction of $12,000 × .10), or a net gain of $80.

However, this advantage may be dissipated by the greater advantage of the married tax schedule over the potentially more costly schedule for married filing separately. For example, filing jointly, a husband with a taxable income of $165,000 and a wife with $10,000 would pay $30,579 in taxes on a total income of $175,000. Filing separately, the husband would owe $34,890 and the wife $1,010, a total of $35,900 and a net *loss* of $5,321! Note that as the rates are condensed, the potential net loss is reduced.

The usual instance in which filing separately is advantageous is when substantial excess itemized deductions can be picked up. For example, as you will see later, medical expenses must be reduced by 7.5 percent of your adjusted gross income before they can be included in your itemized deduction computation. Assume one spouse has $6,000 in medical expenses and an adjusted gross income of $10,000, while the other spouse has no medical expenses and an adjusted gross income of $50,000. Filing separately would require a reduction of only $750 (7.5 percent of $10,000) rather than $4,500 (7.5 percent of $60,000)—a net additional itemized deduction of $3,750. In this case, depending upon the other itemized deductions and specific credits available to each spouse, it might pay to file separately. In any case, if you are married and both parties earn income, it is always to your advantage to prepare your return each way to see which provides the lower tax.

B Tax Planning with Itemized Deductions

There are a number of general strategies that should be implemented when planning for your itemized deductions. The most important of these is the timing of your deductions. Many deductions can be shifted from one year to the next.

You might want to implement such shifting if your itemized deductions are close to the standard deduction amount. Your aim should be to bunch your deductions for expenses so that they exceed the full value of your standard deduction amount. For example, assume that you have itemized deductions of $24,000 each year, of which $3,000 can be accelerated or deferred. With a standard deduction amount of $24,000, none of these deductions would be allowed as excess. What you do, therefore, is to time the expenses you can control so as to itemize deductions of $27,000 in the alternate years ($24,000 + $3,000). This strategy allows you an extra deduction of $3,000 every second year, and if you are in the 32 percent bracket, it saves you $960 in taxes each time.

For you to be able to claim all of your available itemized deductions and to time them appropriately, we must examine and dissect each one in turn.

93 Medical Expenses

You may deduct certain medical and dental expenses not only for yourself but for your spouse and your dependents as well. Medical expenses are payments that you make for the diagnosis, cure, relief, treatment, or prevention of disease. They also include payments for treatment affecting any part or function of the body. Expenses for transportation for needed medical care are included in medical expenses. Payments for insurance that provide medical care for you, your spouse, and your dependents are also included in medical expenses.

The following list shows those items that are generally deductible as medical expenses:

- Fees for doctors, surgeons, dentists, ophthalmologists, optometrists, chiropractors, osteopaths, chiropodists, podiatrists, psychiatrists, psychologists, and Christian Science practitioners.

- Fees for hospital services, therapy, nursing services (including nurses' meals while on duty), ambulance hire, and laboratory, surgical, obstetrics, diagnostic, dental, and X-ray services.

- Meals and lodging provided by a hospital during medical treatment, and meals and lodging provided by a center during treatment for alcoholism or drug addiction.

- Medical and hospital insurance premiums.

- Special equipment such as motorized wheelchairs, hand controls on a car, and special telephones for the deaf.

- Special items, including false teeth, artificial limbs, eyeglasses, hearing aids, bandages, crutches, and guide dogs for the blind or deaf.
- Transportation for needed medical care.
- Insulin and prescription medicines and drugs, including special foods and drinks your doctor prescribes specifically for the treatment of an illness, and pills, birth control items, and vitamins and iron *your doctor prescribes*. Imported prescription drugs are *not* deductible because the importation of foreign drugs is against the law.
- Expenses for diagnostic tests are allowed even if you exhibit no symptoms or sickness (Rev. Rul. 2007-72). This includes electronic scans, pregnancy tests, and physical exams.
- Under certain conditions, medical deductions may be allowed for boarding school expenses. In Letter Ruling 8447014, the IRS ruled that a psychiatrically oriented boarding school is a special school. Thus, the taxpayer was able to deduct, as a medical expense, tuition as well as transportation expenses to and from the school. In Info 2004-0090, the IRS allowed private school tuition as a medical expense when a doctor recommended special education to correct a medical condition.
- The cost of special school programs for children with Attention Deficit Hyperactivity Disorder (PLR 9852015).
- The cost of programs and prescriptions to help you stop smoking (but not over the counter patches and gums) (Rev. Pub. 99-28).
- Radical keratotomy surgery to correct vision is deductible (Ltr. Rul. 9625049) but, so far, even medically prescribed marijuana, even in a state where it is legal, is not (Rev. Rul. 97-9).
- While drugs (except insulin) must be prescribed the cost of needles to inject them does not (see INFO 2005-0008).
- Health club membership fees incurred primarily for the purpose of preventing or alleviating obesity (IRS information letter 2002-0077).
- Nursing home expenses if the principal purpose is the availability of medical care (IRS INFO 2002-0169).
- Weight loss to treat a *specific disease*, but not for appearance or general health (see Rev. Rul. 79-151). Weight loss programs, but not the cost of diet foods, would also qualify (see Rev. Rul. 2002-19).
- The cost of alterative treatment to heal illness (*Malev*, Tax Court Order, 2017)
- The cost of a *prescribed* special diet to the extent that it exceeds the cost of a regular diet (see INFO 2001—0075, 0085, 0086, and 0088).

- The cost of cayenne pepper to treat Raynaud's disease (see INFO 2001-0297).
- Expenses related to obtaining a donated egg for fertilization (PLR 200318017) including egg donor fee, agency fee, insurance and legal fees.
- Breast reconstruction surgery after a mastectomy (Rev. Rul. 2003-57).
- Vision correction surgery (Rev. Rul. 2003-57).
- Egg donor fees and related legal expenses (see INFO 2005-0102), but not the cost of using a surrogate mother (see INFO 2004-0187).
- Tuition costs for kids with learning problems who need special education (PLR 200704001, PLR 200729019, and Ltr. Rul. 200521003).
- Lactation equipment such as breast pumps (Announcement 2011-14).
- The cost of a caregiver for a dementia patient or anyone unable to perform two of the six activities of daily living: eating, toileting, transferring (general mobility), bathing, dressing, and continence.
- Acupuncture (INFO 2011-45).

Amounts paid to whiten teeth discolored as a result of age were *not* allowed as medical expenses.

Costs for male to female gender reassignment surgery were also not allowed (C.C.A. 200603025) according to the IRS. But the tax court in the 2010 *O'Donnabhain* case allowed medical deductions for sex reassignment surgery and hormone therapy. The IRS agreed in AOD No. 2011-03.

In Rev. Rul. 2003-58, the IRS ruled that non-prescription drugs, even if recommended by a doctor, are not allowed as medical expenses. But, in IR 2003-108, the IRS announced that over the counter drugs *would* be covered by Health Care Flexible Spending Accounts (Rev. Rul. 2003-102). Effective for expenses incurred in 2011, the Pension Protection Act requires distributions from health saving accounts, Archer medical savings accounts, and flexible spending accounts *only* for prescribed drugs or insulin. They also ruled in Rev. Rul. 2003-43 that debit cards can be used for Health Reimbursement Arrangements.

Medical expenses paid for a surrogate mother and unborn child also do not qualify (Info 2002-0291) unless this surrogate qualifies as your dependent. In *Morrissey v. United States*, DC-Fla., 2017–1, the expenses related to *in vitro* fertilization were found to be the expenses of the egg donor and the surrogate, not the taxpayer or a dependent. They were therefore not allowed.

Payments for prostitutes and pornography, which are *not* a part of prescribed sex therapy, were also denied as medical expenses to attorney William Halby by the Tax Court in 2010. Lesson learned? Get a prescription from your doctor first!

There are certain limitations on the amount you may deduct. For 2018, you may deduct only that part of your medical and dental expenses that is more than 7.5 percent of your adjusted gross income. Drug expenses, which include *only* prescription drugs and insulin, are included in this 7.5 percent pool.

As of 1983, the separate deduction for one-half of medical insurance premiums up to $150 was eliminated. All medical insurance premiums are now included in the 7.5 percent pool.

Medical care includes a wide array of services. It includes payments for a legal abortion as well as payments for an operation legally performed to make a person unable to have children. It no longer includes payments for purely cosmetic surgery, such as a face-lift, but does cover charges for medical care that are included in the tuition fee of a college or private school, as long as the breakdown of the charges is included in the bill given by the school.

Payments for acupuncture and payments to a treatment center for drug addicts or alcoholics, including meals and lodging provided by the center during the treatment, are also deductible. So too are payments for surgical, hospital, laboratory, and transportation expenses by an actual or possible donor of a kidney or other body organ.

Wages for an attendant who provides nursing services and any out-of-pocket amounts you pay for the attendant's meals are also deductible. Divide the food expense among the household members to find the cost of the attendant's food. If you had to pay additional out-of-pocket amounts for household upkeep because of the attendant, this extra amount you paid is deductible as well. This includes items such as extra rent you paid because you moved to a larger apartment to provide space for the attendant, or the extra cost of utilities for the attendant. If the attendant also provided personal and household services, costs for these must be separated from costs for the nursing, since only the amount spent for nursing services is allowable as a deduction. Remember, though, that even the part of the Social Security (FICA) tax you pay for a worker who provides medical care is deductible.

You may also deduct payments for psychiatric care mainly for relieving a mental illness or defect. You may include the cost of supporting a mentally ill dependent at a specially equipped medical center where the dependent receives medical care, as well as your transportation expenses for regular visits that are recommended as part of that dependent's treatment.

MEDICAL INSURANCE PREMIUMS

Medical insurance premiums are deductible within the limits described earlier. The premiums you pay for medical insurance are for medical care, whether the insurance company pays the provider of the care (hospital, doctor, etc.) directly or reimburses you for payments you've made. Medical

insurance premiums you pay may be included in your medical expenses if the premiums are for:

a) policies that pay for hospitalization, surgical fees, and other medical expenses;

b) policies that pay only for prescription drugs including Medicare Part D;

c) policies that replace lost or damaged contact lenses;

d) the medical part in policies that provide more than one type of payment, if the medical charge is reasonable and is stated separately in the insurance contract or is given to you in a separate statement;

e) membership in an association furnishing cooperative, "free choice" medical service, or group hospitalization clinical care;

f) Medicare B, supplementary medical insurance for the aged (check the information you receive from the Social Security Administration to find out your premium rate and the amount of your deduction);

g) Medicare A, the part of Social Security that covers basic Medicare (you may deduct premiums you voluntarily pay for Medicare A coverage if you are 65 or older and are not entitled to Social Security benefits; Medicare A premiums are not deductible if they are paid as part of your Social Security tax); *or*

h) prepaid insurance premiums you pay before you are 65 for medical care coverage—for yourself, your spouse, or dependents—after you are 65. These are deductible when paid if they are paid in equal installments yearly or more often. The payments must be made for 10 years or more; if paid until you reach 65, the payments must be made for a minimum of 5 years.

You may not deduct premiums paid for life insurance policies or for policies providing repayment for loss of earnings or for the accidental loss of limb, life, sight, etc. Nor can you deduct premiums for a policy that guarantees a specified amount each week (for a specified number of weeks) if you are hospitalized for sickness or injury.

LONG-TERM CARE INSURANCE AND SERVICES

Prior to 1996, the Internal Revenue Code did not provide explicit rules relating to the tax treatment of long-term care insurance contracts or long-term care services. Beginning in 1997, the Health Insurance Portability and Accountability Act of 1996 provides that qualified long-term care insurance premiums will count toward itemized medical expenses and, to the extent that such expenses exceed 7.5 percent of adjusted gross income, a tax deduction will be available.

There is a cap on the amount of premium that can be applied to the medical expense deduction. See below.

For taxable years beginning after 1997, these dollar limits have been indexed for increases in the medical care component of the Consumer Price Index. Moreover, long-term care insurance premiums will now qualify for the self-employed health insurance deduction (100 percent in 2003 and thereafter).

Long-Term Care Deduction Caps

Attained Age at the End of the Tax Year	2018 Maximum Deduction
Not more than 40	$420
More than 40 but not more than 50	$780
More than 50 but not more than 60	$1,560
More than 60 but not more than 70	$4,160
More than 70	$5,200

Under the Pension Protection Act of 2006, as of January 1, 2010, there's no federal tax on the proceeds of an annuity if those proceeds are used to pay for long-term care coverage.

HOSPITAL MEALS AND LODGING

Meals and lodging are also deductible if they are furnished by a hospital or similar institution as a necessary part of medical care and if the main reason for your being in the hospital is to receive that medical care. The cost of your meals or lodging while you are away from home for medical treatment, or for the relief of a specific condition, however, is not deductible if you are not at a hospital or similar institution, even if the trip is made on the advice of your doctor. Under the Tax Reform Act of 1984, a deduction of up to $50 per day per individual for lodging expenses, but not for meals, for the patient and certain accompanying individuals away from home to receive outpatient care at hospitals or certain outpatient clinics is allowed. For example, treatment in an outpatient clinic, such as the Mayo Clinic, that provides substantially similar services to those provided by a hospital would qualify. Moreover, although food costs are not deductible, presumably if they are included in the cost of the lodging, no allocation is necessary and the full cost will be deductible subject to the $50 per day per person limit. (See Letter Ruling 8516025.)

Alternatively, if an individual is in a nursing home or a home for the aged because of a physical condition, and the main reason for being there is to get medical care, the entire cost, including meals *and* lodging, may be included as a deductible medical expense.

TRANSPORTATION EXPENSES

Transportation payments necessary for medical care also qualify as a deductible medical expense. Assume that you have been ill with a bad heart condition and you live in an area that has extremely cold winters, which makes your condition worse. Your doctor advises you to spend the winter in a warmer place, and you and your family spend the winter in a rented house in Florida. The trip is made for a specific medical reason, and although none of your expenses for food and lodging while on your way to Florida or during your stay there are deductible, your share of the transportation expenses between your home and Florida *is* deductible.

Transportation expenses include the following:

- Amounts paid for bus, taxi, train, or plane fare, or for ambulance hire.

- Out-of-pocket expenses for your car, such as gas and oil. You may not deduct any part of general repair or maintenance expenses. If you do not wish to deduct your actual expenses, you may use the 2018 *standard rate* of 18¢ a mile for each mile you use your car for medical reasons, and add to that any parking fees and tolls that you pay.

- Transportation expenses of a parent who must accompany a child needing medical care.

- Transportation expenses of a nurse familiar with injections, medications, and other treatments required by a patient who is traveling to get medical care but cannot travel alone.

CARE FOR THE HANDICAPPED

Special care may be needed for handicapped individuals. You may include the following payments for this care in your deductible medical expenses:

1. Payments to a special school for mentally or physically handicapped individuals, if the main reason for going is the school's means for relieving the handicap. The cost of sending a blind child to school to learn braille, or a deaf child to learn lip reading, is a medical expense. If you pay for remedial language training to correct a condition caused by a birth defect of the brain, you may deduct these payments as medical expenses.

Tuition or tutoring expenses you pay on your doctor's advice for a child who has severe learning disabilities caused by a nervous system disorder are also medical expenses. So too are the costs of meals, lodging, and ordinary education supplied by the special school, but only if the main reason for the child's attendance is the availability of medical care.

2. The cost of keeping a mentally retarded individual, at the advice of a psychiatrist, in a specially chosen home that is not the home of a relative; for example, a "halfway" house to help in the adjustment from life in a mental hospital to community living.

3. Payments to a nonprofessional individual for giving "patterning" exercises (coordinated physical manipulation of the individual's limbs to imitate crawling and other normal movements) to a mentally challenged child.

4. Advance payments to a private institution for the lifetime care, treatment, and training of your physically and mentally handicapped dependent in the event that you die or become unable to care for your dependent. The payments must be required as a condition for the institution's future acceptance of your dependent and cannot be refundable.

5. Expenses paid for the care of your invalid spouse in your home. Only amounts spent for care to relieve your spouse's illness are deductible. The cost of household services, such as cooking and cleaning, is not deductible as a medical expense but may be eligible for the credit for household and dependent care expenses.

6. The cost and upkeep of service dogs for those with either mental or physical handicaps.

SPECIAL MEDICAL EQUIPMENT

Moreover, you may also deduct payments for special items and equipment. This includes payments for:

1. False teeth, artificial limbs, eyeglasses, hearing aids, and crutches, or the cost and care of guide dogs for the blind and deaf. Such expenses are medical, not business, even if you use the dog in carrying on your business.

2. The part of the cost of braille books and magazines that is more than the price for regular books and magazines.

3. The cost and repair of special telephone equipment that enables a deaf person to communicate over a regular telephone.

4. Amounts paid for oxygen equipment and oxygen to relieve problems in breathing due to a medical condition.

5. The cost of special attachments, such as a motorized wheelchair or autoette or special hand controls that are installed in a car for the use of a physically handicapped driver.

6. The amount you pay for a special design of a car to hold a wheelchair, as well as the cost of operating and keeping up an autoette or wheelchair used mainly for the relief of sickness or disability.

7. The cost of removing lead-based paints from walls, woodwork, etc., in your home to prevent a child who has lead poisoning (or who has had lead poisoning) from eating the paint. This must be on the advice of a doctor, and it must be determined that the paint contains lead. The areas covered with lead-based paint have to be in poor repair (peeling or cracking) or within the child's reach. The cost of painting the scraped area is not a deductible medical expense.

Payments for special equipment installed in a home, or similar improvements made for medical reasons, may be deductible even if they are capital improvements. If these expenses are for permanent improvements that increase the value of the property, only the amount in excess of the increase in value may be deducted as a medical expense. For example, assume you have a heart ailment, and on your doctor's advice you install an elevator in your home so that you will not need to climb stairs. The elevator costs $1,000. According to competent appraisals, the elevator increases the value of your home by $700. The $300 difference is a medical expense. If the elevator did not increase the value of your home, the whole cost would have been a medical expense.

If a capital expense qualifies as a medical expense, any amount paid for operation or upkeep also qualifies as a medical expense, as long as the medical reason for the capital expense still exists. These expenses are deductible even if none or only part of the original expense was deductible.

Amounts paid by a handicapped individual to buy and install special plumbing fixtures in a rented house are also deductible medical expenses. For example, assume you are handicapped with arthritis and a bad heart condition. You cannot climb stairs or get into a bathtub. On your doctor's advice, you install a bathroom with a shower stall on the first floor of your two-story rented house. The landlord does not pay any of the cost of buying or installing the special plumbing and does not lower your rent. The whole amount you pay for this bathroom is a deductible medical expense. A medical expense deduction is also available for the cost of special equipment used to display subtitles on the television set of a hearing impaired individual (Rev. Rul. 80-340).

In 1987, the IRS released a list of 13 such deductible home improvements. If these improvements are made to accommodate yourself or a family member with a physical handicap, they count in full toward the 7.5 percent deduction floor (Rev. Rul. Section 7-106, I.R.B. 1987-43).

The improvements on the IRS list are the following:

1. Constructing entrance or exit ramps to the home
2. Widening doorways and entrances or exits to the home
3. Widening or otherwise modifying halls and interior doorways
4. Installing railings, support bars, or other modifications to bathrooms
5. Lowering or making other modifications to kitchen cabinets and equipment
6. Altering the location of or otherwise modifying electrical outlets and fixtures
7. Installing porch lifts or other forms of lifts (this does not include elevators, as they may increase the value of the home)
8. Modifying fire alarms, smoke detectors, and other warning systems
9. Modifying stairs
10. Adding handrails and grab bars, whether or not in bathrooms
11. Modifying hardware on doors
12. Modifying areas in front of entrance and exit doorways
13. Grading of ground to provide access to the home

Note that just because an improvement is not on the list, this does not necessarily mean that such an improvement is not a fully deductible expense.

COMPUTING YOUR MEDICAL EXPENSES

Computing your medical expenses is a simple process. Your allowable drugs, your medical insurance premiums, plus all of your other medical expenses, are reduced by 7.5 percent of your adjusted gross income.

If you and your spouse live in a community property state and file separate returns, any amount you paid for medical expenses out of community funds is divided equally. Each of you may deduct half of the expenses. If medical expenses are paid out of the separate funds of one spouse, only the spouse who paid the medical expenses may deduct them.

If you and your spouse do not live in a community property state and you file separate returns, each of you may deduct only the medical expenses you actually paid. Any medical expenses paid out of a joint checking account in which you and your spouse have the same interest are considered to have been paid equally by each of you, unless you can show otherwise. Furthermore, you must reduce your total medical expenses for the year by the total reimbursements (repayments) you receive from insurance or other sources for those expenses during the year. This includes payments you receive from Medicare A and Medicare B. The reimbursement may be paid directly to you or to the doctor or hospital.

The actual computation of your medical expense deduction can be demonstrated by the following example. Assume you and your spouse paid the following medical expenses:

a) $595.60 for hospital insurance, $80.40 for medical and surgical insurance, $125 for allowable medicines and drugs, $238 for hospital bills, $39 for doctor bills, and $20 for transportation;

b) $2,000 for doctors and $75 for medicines and allowable drugs for your spouse's dependent mother;

c) $350 for doctors and $100 for medicines for your sister, whom you claim as your dependent.

The hospital and doctor expenses cited have already been reduced by repayment from your insurance company. Your adjusted gross income is $20,000. The deductible amount is computed as follows:

Medicines and drugs	
You and spouse	$ 125.00
Spouse's mother	75.00
Sister	+100.00
Total medicines and drugs	$ 300.00
Insurance:	
Hospitalization	$ 595.60
Medical and surgical	+ 80.40
Total insurance	$ 676.00
Other medical expenses:	
You and spouse (doctors)	$ 39.00
Spouse's mother (doctors)	2,000.00
Sister (doctors)	350.00
You and spouse (hosp.)	238.00
Transportation	+ 20.00
	$ 2,647.00
Total medical expenses [medicine plus insurance plus other expenses ($300.00 + 676.00 + 2,647.00)]	$3,623.00
Minus 7.5 percent exclusion ($20,000 × .7.5)	–1,500.00
Total deduction	$2,123.00

Not only must you reduce your total medical expenses by the total reimbursements you have received from insurance and other sources for those expenses, but if you receive payment under an accident insurance contract, you must also reduce your medical expenses by that part of the payment set aside for hospitalization and medical care. However, you need not reduce medical expenses by any repayments you have received for loss of earnings or damages for personal injury. But you must also reduce medical expenses by that amount received in settlement of a damage suit for personal injuries that has been set aside for future medical expenses. Medical expenses paid this year and in future years because of these injuries must be reduced until the amount received in settlement has been completely used. Any amount you pay after that may be deductible.

Even if you fail to file a claim under an insurance policy that would have covered your medical expenses, those expenses that you pay are still deductible (*Weaver*, TCM 1984-634).

If you are reimbursed for medical expenses you deducted in an earlier year, you must report as income the amount of the reimbursement that is equal to or less than the amount you previously deducted as medical expenses. For example, assume you had an adjusted gross income in year A of $10,000, and during that year you paid medical insurance premiums of $300 and incurred medical expenses of $800. No amount was included for medicine and drugs. You deducted $100, figured as follows:

Medical expenses	$ 800
Plus insurance	+300
Total medical expenses	$1,100
Minus 7.5 percent of adjusted gross income	750
Total deduction	$ 350

In year B you collected $50 under your insurance policy as reimbursement for part of your year A medical expenses. If you had collected in year A, your deduction for medical expenses would have been only $50, figured as follows:

Medical expenses	$ 800
Plus insurance	+300
Total medical expenses	$1,100
Minus insurance reimbursements	−50
Balance	$ 1,050
Minus 7.5 percent of adjusted gross income	−750
Total deduction	$ 300

Since the $50 reimbursement is less than the $100 deduction, you should include $50 in income in year B.

If you did not deduct a medical expense in the year you paid it, either because you did not itemize deductions or because your medical expenses were not more than the 7.5 percent limitation, you should not include in income the reimbursement for this expense that you received in a later year. For example, assume in year C you paid $150 for medical insurance premiums and $400 for medical expenses, but you could not deduct the $550 because it was under the 7.5 percent limitation. If in year D you were reimbursed for any of the $400 medical expenses, you would also not include the reimbursement in your gross income because you received no tax benefit for it in the earlier year.

There are a number of sophisticated tax planning strategies that you can utilize when claiming medical expense deductions. First, you must recognize that these expenses are deductible only in the year that they are paid. If you charge medical expenses to your credit card, these expenses are deducted in the year the charge is made—it does not matter when you paid the amount charged. But expenses for eyeglasses, dental work, hearing aids, elective surgery, and year-end doctor visits can often be juggled as to the year in which they are actually paid. Since these medical expenses must exceed 7.5 percent of your adjusted gross income before you can begin taking deductions, it may pay to bunch expenses in one year if that will get you over the hump. You currently cannot deduct a mere prepayment of a possible future bill, however. There must be an actual bill or at least an actual scheduling of services.

Medical expense shifting can be demonstrated by the following example. Assume your adjusted gross income is $30,000. Late this year your doctor bills you $2,000. Your other medical expenses amount to only $250. If you can, pay in January of next year. You will get no deduction in this year, anyway (7.5 percent of $30,000 is $2,250), so deferring the expense until next year will give you another chance of exceeding the 7.5 percent floor.

Alternatively, if you have already met your 7.5 percent floor, you should accelerate the payment of your medical expenses. Payments in December of this year will reduce your taxes and increase your cash balance, and the potential earnings on it, for all of next year. If you wait till January to make the payment, the deduction and its attendant tax benefit will be deferred for an additional year (even assuming that you meet the percent limit in the second year).

For example, assume you have exceeded the standard deduction amount and the 7.5 percent floor for deducting medical expenses. Further assume that in mid-December you have a $1,000 doctor bill due in 30 days. If you are in the 32 percent bracket and pay the bill in December, you save $320 in taxes, *and*

you have an additional $320 on which you can earn interest throughout the next tax year. If you wait until January to make the payment, you will lose the interest on the saved $320 in taxes and may lose the deduction completely if you cannot both pass the percent floor test and exceed your standard deduction amount for excess itemized deductions. The solution in this case, clearly, is to make the payment on December 31.

Effective in 2013, the old 7.5 percent threshold was increased to 10 percent. This increase was delayed until 2017 if you or your spouse had attained age 65 before the close of the tax year. The Tax Cuts and Jobs Act of 2017 retained the 7.5 percent floor for 2017 and 2018. For 2019, it goes back to 10%.

TAX STRATEGIES

Sophisticated tax planning also involves knowing how to structure your personal deductions so that they qualify as allowable medical expenses. Many expenditures that do not readily appear to be deductible are allowable as medical expenses. For example, elastic stockings qualify as medical expenses if needed by an infirm or elderly person. In one case, the cost of a sacroiliac belt prescribed by a doctor was deductible, as was the cost of high blood pressure medication and a blood sugar test. In another instance, a deduction was allowed for a device installed to add fluoride to a home water supply at a controlled rate; it was represented that fluoride is a chemical that strengthens the dental enamel as the teeth grow, making them more resistant to decay, and that the only purpose of the installation and use of the device was to prevent tooth decay. Travel to Alcoholics Anonymous meetings, based on medical advice, is a deductible medical expense (Rev. Rul. 63-273).

Deductions have been allowed for extraordinary forms of medical equipment. For example, the costs of oxygen equipment and oxygen to alleviate breathing difficulty *and* of a reclining chair recommended by a doctor for a person with a cardiac condition have qualified as medical deductions. So, too, have special mattresses and certain thicknesses of plywood boards prescribed for an individual who had arthritis of the spine. In one instance, a wig purchased to avoid mental upset to a patient who had lost her hair was deductible!

Super medical deductions can be obtained if your doctor can find an ailment in yourself, your spouse, or your dependents that would require you to have a whirlpool for baths, or central air conditioning to provide you or your dependents with pure, dehumidified air. Even the expense of a swimming pool may be deducted if it is installed because of a physician's recommendation and if that facility in any way alleviates your physical condition (see *Cherry*, T.C. Memo 1983-470 and Rev. Rul. 63-273, 1963-2 C.B. 112). If such a swimming pool is used

for a specific medical purpose—for example, to provide hydrotherapy—then not only is a deduction allowed for the installation, but a deduction is also allowed for the cost of upkeep, including chemicals, cleaning, water, and utilities. Note, though, that the installation is a capital expenditure and therefore only the excess cost over the added value to your property is deductible. (See Rev. Rul. 83-33 and Letter Ruling 822-1128 and 832-6095.)

One of my own favorite medical deductions is the cost of an overseas trip for medical or dental work. For example, it has been established that the cost of extensive dental work is far less expensive in Europe than in the United States. Therefore, even adding the transportation costs to go to an overseas dentist, your total cash outlay is lower than having such work performed locally. On this basis, such transportation costs have been allowed as deductible medical expenses. One woman consulted three different dermatologists in the United States, but none was able to improve her skin condition. Finally, she was treated success-fully as an outpatient in a foreign country. The IRS agreed that her expenses were deductible (Letter Ruling 812-6044).

In 1991, the Tax Court let Alex L. and Earlene Polyak of Trenton, Michigan, deduct $1,124 for 1984 transportation to Palm Beach Gardens as essential to her care for heart and lung ailments and arthritis. Her doctors advised her to winter in warmer climates.

You potentially can write off your child's private school tuition as a medical expense. The IRS, in a private ruling, found that one family's dyslexic children required special education that could be deemed medical care.

Take these steps to ensure your deduction:

- Make sure the school offers special education aimed at helping the student overcome a diagnosed handicap. The school should have staff available to design a curriculum aimed at your child's particular handicap, and that should be why the child attends that school.

- Get the school to write a statement about its program.

- Remember that as a legitimate medical expense, it's still not deductible until it exceeds 7.5 percent of your adjusted gross income. Given the cost of most private schools today, that won't be a problem.

Furthermore, amounts paid for "medical care" may be deductible even if they are for purposes that do not have the sanction of the medical profession or even if the payments are made to persons without medical qualifications. For example, amounts paid to such practitioners as psychotherapists are categorized for tax purposes as fees for medical care, even though those who perform the

services may not be licensed, certified, or otherwise qualified to perform these services, and even if certification is required by law. In other words, payments to unlicensed practitioners are deductible if the type and quality of their services are not illegal and if such services may be deemed to fall within the parameters of medical care. In fact, in IRS Letter Ruling 8442018, the Internal Revenue Service allowed as a deductible medical expense electrolysis performed by a nonlicensed technician as "medical care." Remember, *medical care* means any amounts paid for the diagnosis, cure, mitigation, treatment, or prevention of disease or for the purpose of affecting any structure or function of the body. (In Rev. Rul. 82-111, the IRS had ruled that hair removal through electrolysis performed by a state licensed technician was deductible as a medical expense.)

Note that, effective for tax years beginning after December 31, 1990, expenses for unnecessary cosmetic surgery are no longer deductible as medical care expenses, except when the surgery is necessary to correct a deformity due directly to a congenital abnormality, a personal injury resulting from an accident or trauma, or a disfiguring disease.

The law further defines cosmetic surgery as any procedure that is directed at improving the patient's appearance and does not meaningfully promote the proper function of the body or prevent or treat illness or disease.

The definition of cosmetic surgery is quite broad and seems to bar the deductibility of many procedures that are not strictly surgical. Orthodontic work should qualify, but other dental procedures may be considered strictly cosmetic.

A second category of below the line deductions is the taxes that you pay during your tax year. Such taxes fall under three classifications, which will be discussed separately.

94 Income Taxes

You may deduct some state and local income taxes, including taxes on interest income that is exempt from federal income tax. You may not deduct state and local taxes on any other exempt income. For example, the part of state income tax on a cost-of-living allowance that is exempt from federal income tax is not deductible.

State and local taxes are those imposed by the 50 states or any of their political subdivisions (such as a county or city) and by the District of Columbia. You may deduct state, local, or foreign income taxes withheld from your salary, as well as estimated payments made under a pay-as-you-go plan of a state or local government. You also may deduct payments made on taxes due but not paid in

an earlier year in the year they were actually withheld or paid. In sum, to be deductible the tax must be paid during your tax year. You may deduct only those taxes paid during the calendar year for which you file a return.

If you receive a refund of these taxes in a later year, you must include the return as income in the year you receive it. This would include refunds resulting from taxes that were overwithheld, not figured correctly, or figured again as a result of an amended return. If you did not itemize your deductions in a previous year, you do not have to include the refunds. Furthermore, the amount included in your income is limited to the tax benefit you received in the earlier years. For example, assume you deducted $500 in taxes and received a refund of $100; your total itemized deductions exceeded your standard deduction amount by only $50. The only tax benefit you received, therefore, was the $50 excess itemized deduction. On this basis you need only include $50 of the refund in your income for the subsequent year. If you were hit by the Alternative Minimum Tax (AMT) in the prior year, then you had zero benefit from your deductions for taxes and include zero.

You also may deduct amounts required to be withheld from your wages for certain state disability benefit funds that provide against loss of wages. These payments to the disability fund are deductible as state income taxes. Furthermore, employee contributions to a state fund that provides indemnity coverage for the loss of wages caused by unemployment resulting from business contingencies are also deductible as taxes. Employee contributions to private disability plans, however, are not deductible.

Foreign taxes include those taxes imposed by a foreign country, a U.S. possession, or any of their political subdivisions.

Foreign income taxes that you pay may either be deducted as an itemized deduction or claimed as a credit against your U.S. tax.

SALES TAXES

Since 2004, *instead* of deducting income taxes, you have the option of deducting state and local *sales* taxes (including compensating use taxes) instead of state and local *income* taxes. Use the actual taxes you pay, or see Publication 600 for optional sales tax tables. You can add to the table amounts any sales taxes paid on a motor vehicle (including leased vehicles), aircraft, boat, home, and home building materials.

This is a great deal for those in low or no income tax states such as Texas, Washington, Tennessee, Wyoming, South Dakota, Alaska, Nevada, or Florida.

Any sales tax paid on business items would be allowed on the business schedules rather than as itemized deductions.

95 Real Property Taxes

Real property (real estate) taxes are any state, local, or foreign taxes on real property levied for the general public welfare. Local benefit taxes are deductible if they are for maintenance or repair, or for interest charges related to these benefits. If only a part of the tax is for maintenance, repair, or interest, you must be able to show the amount of that part to claim the deduction. If you cannot determine what part is for maintenance or repair, none of it is deductible.

If you are a tenant shareholder in a cooperative housing corporation, you may deduct the amounts you pay to that corporation that represent your share of the real estate taxes the corporation pays or incurs on the property. If the corporation leases the land and buildings and is required to pay the real estate taxes under the terms of the lease agreement, however, your part of the taxes is not deductible. Moreover, if your landlord increases your rent in the form of a tax surcharge because of increased real estate taxes, you cannot deduct that increase as taxes either.

Real property taxes also do not include trash and garbage collection fees or homeowners association charges you may pay for the recreation, health, safety, and welfare of residents and for maintaining common areas.

If real estate is sold during the tax year, the real estate taxes must be divided between the buyer and seller. These taxes must be divided according to the number of days in the real property tax year (the period to which the imposed tax relates) that each owns the property. The seller pays the taxes up to the date of the sale, and the buyer pays the taxes beginning with the date of the sale, regardless of the lien dates under local law. If you use the cash method and do not deduct taxes until they are paid, and the buyer of your property is personally liable for the tax, you are considered to have paid your portion of the imposed tax at the time of the sale. This permits you to deduct the portion of the tax to the date of sale even though you did not actually pay for it.

For example, assume that your real property tax year is the calendar year, with payment due on August 1. Your tax on your old home, sold May 5, was $300, and your tax on your new home, bought on May 3, was $200. You are considered to have paid a proportionate share of the real estate taxes on the old home even though you did not actually pay them to the taxing authority. On the other hand, you may claim only the proportionate share of the taxes you paid on your new property even though you paid the entire amount.

Because you held the old property for 125 days (January 1 to May 4, the day before the sale), you are entitled to a deduction of 125/365 of $300, or $102.73.

You owned the new home for 243 days (May 3 to December 31, including the date of the purchase), so your taxes on the new home are 243/365 of $200, or $133.15. Your real estate tax deduction is therefore $102.73 + $133.15, or $235.88.

If you and your spouse held property jointly, and you file separate returns, each of you may deduct only the taxes each of you paid on the property.

For 2008 and 2009, nonitemizers could have deducted up to $500 ($1,000 on a joint return) for real estate taxes paid as additions to their standard deduction.

96 Personal Property Taxes

Some personal property taxes are also deductible, subject to certain requirements:

1. The tax must be based only on the value of the personal property. For example, assume your state charges a yearly motor vehicle registration tax of 1 percent of value plus 40¢ per hundredweight. You pay $28.60 based on the value ($1,500) and weight (3,400 pounds) of your car. You may deduct $15 as a personal property tax, since it is based on the value. The remaining $13.60, based on the weight, is not deductible.

2. The tax must be charged on a yearly basis, even if it is collected more or less often than once a year.

3. The tax must be charged on personal property. A tax is considered charged on personal property even if it is for the exercise of a privilege. A yearly tax based on value qualifies as a personal property tax although it is called a registration fee—that is, for the privilege of registering motor vehicles or using them on the highways.

THE TAX CUTS AND JOBS ACT OF 2017 LIMITS THE *TOTAL* ITEMIZED DEDUCTION FOR STATE AND LOCAL INCOME/SALES TAXES PLUS REAL ESTATE TAXES TO $10,000. THOSE IN HIGH TAX STATES SUCH AS NY, NJ, AND CA, ARE NOT HAPPY.

97 Interest

Some interest payments qualify as below the line deductions. The type of deduction you may take depends on whether the money was borrowed for personal use, for rental or royalty property, or for your business.

Interest payment on a loan for income-producing rental or royalty property, on a business loan, and on farm business loans are above the line deductions. Interest of a personal nature, such as home mortgage interest, is a below the line deduction; normally, so is interest paid on margin accounts held with your broker. Interest on these accounts is considered paid when the broker is paid or when the interest becomes available to the broker through your account.

To deduct interest on a debt, you must be legally liable for that debt. No deduction will be allowed for payments you make for someone else if you are not legally liable to make them. Note that the Tax Court has allowed the deduction even if you don't have title but do have "the benefits and burdens of ownership." See *Adams v. Commissioner* T.C. No. 2563-08, T.C. Memo 2010-72 (April 13, 2010). Also see *Qui Van Phan v. Commissioner* (Docket No. 162-02-35 filed on January 12, 2015) and *Wainwright*, T.C. Memo. 2017-70 where the taxpayer was found to be an "equitable owner" and deduction allowed. Both the lender and the borrower must intend that the loan be repaid.

For example, assume you make a loan to your son, hoping to be repaid when he is able. If no true debtor-credit relationship is created, he is not legally liable to pay the debt and will not be able to deduct any interest paid. Here he should sign a note and make scheduled repayments to ensure his interest deduction. Alternatively, if you cosign a note for a loan made by a bank to your son, even if your son is a student, and if both you and your son are jointly liable on the note, you may deduct any interest you pay on the loan in the year you pay it.

Make sure you follow through on any mortgage note to ensure your deduction. In *Christopher DeFrancis and Jennifer Gross v. Commissioner*, Docket No. 24282-11S, November 6, 2013, the court found that the couple was not entitled to deduct payments made to a relative as qualified residence interest because they did not record the mortgage note with the appropriate county recorder of deeds or any other public office and did not otherwise establish that the loan was a secured debt. The couple signed a mortgage note, which set a rate of interest and payment terms, and a mortgage, which granted, conveyed, and assigned the property to the relative. The mortgage document was not notarized, however, and failed to satisfy the requirements to be a "secured loan."

In *Yong J. Dong and Lijun Weng v. Commissioner*, Docket No. 23204-12S, January 9, 2014, married taxpayers were not entitled to a mortgage interest deduction with respect to payments they made to relatives under a loan agreement that was secured by the taxpayers' principal residence. The agreement was not recorded or otherwise perfected and, thus, under applicable state (New York) law, it was not a secured debt because it was not valid against third parties that did not have actual notice of it.

You must normally pay the interest before you may deduct it. But if you use the accrual method of accounting, you may deduct interest over the period it accrues regardless of when it is paid. To show how this works, suppose you borrow $1,000 in September, *payable in 90 days* at 12 percent interest. In December you make the payment with a new note for $1,030 due the following March. If you use the cash method of accounting, that $30 is not deductible in the year you give the new note, since you do not actually pay the interest. However, if you pay the $30 and give a new note for $1,000, the interest is deductible. If you are on the accrual method, the $30 is deductible in either case. If you pay interest in advance for a period that goes beyond the end of the tax year, you must spread the interest over the tax years to which it belongs. You may deduct in each year only the interest that belongs to that year.

The following items are generally deductible as interest:

Mortgage interest
"Points," if you are a buyer (see explanation that follows)
Interest on a business loan
Installment plan interest (unless consumer interest)
Investment interest

The following items normally are *not* deductible as interest:

"Points," if you are a seller (potentially deductible by *buyer* under Rev. Proc. 94-27)
Service charges
Credit investigation fees
Loan fees
Interest relating to tax-exempt income
Interest paid to carry single-premium life insurance
Premium on a convertible bond
Interest owed to related taxpayers, unless there is an actual debtor-creditor relationship
Purchaser mortgage insurance (PMI), except for rental properties where it would be allowed as "insurance."

But, nonrental PMI was deductible (as interest) for 2007 through 2017 *only.* It is allowed only for insurance issued after 2006, so prior homeowners do not qualify. This deduction was phased out for joint returns with adjusted gross income more than $100,000 ($50,000 for singles).

Effective Interest Rates on Mortgages with Points

Stated Rate (%)	Points				
	1	2	3	4	5
Assuming 30-year mortgage held to maturity					
5	5.09	5.18	5.27	5.36	5.46
6	6.09	6.19	6.29	6.29	6.48
7	7.01	7.20	7.30	7.41	7.52
8	8.11	8.21	8.32	8.44	8.55
9	9.22	9.23	9.34	9.46	9.58
10	10.12	10.24	10.37	10.49	10.62
11	11.13	11.26	11.39	11.52	11.66
12	12.13	12.27	12.41	12.55	12.70
Assuming 30-year mortgage paid off in 15th year					
5	5.11	5.22	5.33	5.44	5.56
6	6.11	6.23	6.35	6.46	6.58
7	7.12	7.24	7.36	7.49	7.61
8	8.12	8.21	8.32	8.44	8.55
9	9.13	9.26	9.40	9.53	9.67
10	10.14	10.28	10.42	10.56	10.70
11	11.14	11.29	11.44	11.59	11.74
12	12.15	12.30	12.46	12.61	12.77
Assuming 30-year mortgage paid off in 7th year					
5	5.18	5.36	5.55	5.73	5.92
6	6.18	6.37	6.56	6.75	6.95
7	7.19	7.38	7.57	7.77	7.97
8	8.19	8.39	8.59	8.79	8.99
9	9.20	9.40	9.61	9.81	10.02
10	10.20	10.41	10.62	10.83	11.05
11	11.21	11.42	11.64	11.86	12.08
12	12.22	12.44	12.66	12.88	13.11
Assuming 30-year mortgage paid off in 3rd year					
5	5.37	5.74	6.12	6.50	6.89
6	6.37	6.75	7.13	7.52	7.91
7	7.38	7.76	8.15	8.54	8.93
8	8.38	8.77	9.16	9.56	9.96
9	9.39	9.78	10.18	10.58	10.98
10	10.39	10.79	11.19	11.60	12.01
11	11.40	11.80	12.21	12.62	13.04
12	12.40	12.81	13.22	13.64	14.06

One of the most usual types of personal interest expense is the interest on your mortgage. You may deduct only the interest part of your mortgage payment. If your records do not show the interest paid, get a statement showing that information from the lender who holds your mortgage. If you are a cash method taxpayer, you may deduct the full amount of interest paid during the year. If you are an accrual method taxpayer, you may deduct the amount accrued each year.

A point is equal to 1 percent of the loan amount, so on a $100,000 mortgage each point would cost you $1,000. If you pay off a mortgage over 30 years, each point on a 12 percent loan adds 0.13 percentage points to the interest rate. Thus on a 12 percent loan with four points charged, the effective interest rate is 12.52. On a 14 percent, 30-year loan, each point adds 0.15 percentage points. On a 16 percent loan, it is 0.17 percentage points. Keep in mind that these figures apply only if the mortgage is paid off over the full 30-year term. If you sell the property and pay off the loan sooner, the effective interest is higher, since those extra dollars paid up front are spread over fewer years of borrowing.

The term *points* is sometimes used to describe the charges paid by a borrower. They are also called loan origination fees, maximum loan charges, or premium charges. If the payment of any of these charges is solely for the use of money, then it is considered interest.

In one case, the Tax Court allowed a taxpayer to deduct interest he paid on a mortgage on his residence, even though the title to the home was held in the name of his corporation. The court reasoned that the taxpayer had always treated the home as his own and the mortgage indebtedness therefore was his (*Lang, Jr.*, T.C. Memo 1983-318). In *USLU v. Commissioner*, T.C. Memo 1997–551, 12/16/97, the Tax Court ruled that a person who lived in a house and made all the payments for it could deduct mortgage interest even though legal title and financing was obtained by the person's brother. All the facts established equitable and beneficial ownership of the house. Also see *Odosada*, T.C. Summ. Op. 2012-17 where beneficial ownership was found again.

The amount you pay in points is deductible in full in the year of payment only if it is paid to buy or improve your main home and if the loan is for that home. The charging of points has to be an established business practice in your area. The deduction may not be more than the number of points generally charged in your area. If these conditions are not met, points are treated as prepaid interest. They must be spread over the life of the mortgage and are considered as paid and deductible over that period. Moreover, in IRS Notice 86-68, May 13, 1986, the Internal Revenue Service ruled that points paid on refinancing a home mortgage are not *currently* deductible. Thus, they could only be deducted over the loan period. For example, assume that $2,400 of points is paid in connection with refinancing a mortgage that is to run for another 20 years (i.e., 240 monthly payments remain to be paid). These points are deductible over the term of the loan, $10 per monthly payment. The IRS reaffirmed this position in Rev. Rul. 87-22, as did the Tax Court in 1988. Points paid

in a refinancing, therefore, must be amortized over the life of the loan, unless the money is used to improve the home (*Huntsman,* T.C. 1988, reversed), or unless the refinancing is an integral part of the original purchase of the property.

Points charged for specific services by the lender for the borrower's account (such as a lender's appraisal fee, the cost of preparing the mortgage note or deed of trust, settlement fees, or notary fees) are not interest. Points charged in connection with getting a V.A. loan were not interest until 1992, retroactive to 1991. For example, assume you get a loan from a bank to buy your main home. The loan was insured by the Veterans Administration and you pay the bank a loan origination fee. This fee is 1 percent of the amount of the loan and is charged in addition to the maximum rate of interest permitted. The amount of the 1 percent loan origination fee (one point) is now interest and may be deducted.

Alternatively, assume you got a loan of $48,000 to buy a $60,000 home. In addition to interest, you paid the lender a loan processing fee of $1,440 (three points). None of the fee was for specific services. The charging of points was an established business practice in the area and the number of points was not more than that generally charged in the area. This loan processing fee to purchase a principal residence is interest and is deductible in full in the year of payment. [See Section 461(g)(2) and *Schubel,* 77 T.C. No. 701 (1981).] [See also *Pacific First Federal Savings and Loan Association,* 79 T.C. No. 33 where points were found to be interest where the fee was for the use or forebearance of money and bore no relation to the actual cost to underwrite the loan.] It was best to exchange checks with your bank rather than just reduce the amount received on your mortgage. In the past, unless you formally exchanged checks, the Internal Revenue Service argued a lack of "payment." However, in IRS Notice 90-70, the separate check for points was ruled as unnecessary as long as you provide a down payment, escrow deposit, or other closing funds "at least equal to" the points charged. This means points are now deductible even if the lender finances them if your cost payments are at least equal to the points charged. [See also Rev. Proc. 92-12.]

The term *points* is also used to describe loan placement fees that the seller may have to pay to the lender to arrange financing for the buyer. Prior to 1994, you could *not* deduct these amounts as interest. See Revenue Procedure 94-27 below to see if you may qualify now. (However, these charges are a selling expense that reduces the amount realized by the seller.) Furthermore, if you pay off your mortgage early, you may have to pay a penalty. This amount is deductible as interest, as is any amount you pay as a tenant stockholder in a housing cooperative for the interest on the cooperative's debt, or for points required in the year you became a tenant-stockholder.

In Rev. Proc. 87-15, I.R.B. 1987-14, the Internal Revenue Service set forth the method for determining the amount of points allocable to each tax year

during the term of an indebtedness in a situation where points charged to a taxpayer in respect of the indebtedness are required to be deducted over the period of indebtedness. Such points may be deductible on an internal rate of return basis—i.e., considering the time value of money with the bulk of the deduction being taken in the earlier years—or, alternatively, as a matter of administrative convenience, the Internal Revenue Service will allow a taxpayer consistently to allocate the points ratably over the indebtedness. For example, if $3,600 in qualified points were paid on a 30-year (360-month) loan, $10 per payment would be allowed as deductible point interest ($3,600 divided into 360 monthly payments).

Note that the points must be paid at the time the indebtedness is incurred. In *Schubel*, 77 T.C. 701 (1981), the Tax Court held that points withheld by a lender from loan proceeds may not be deducted by a borrower in the year the points are withheld, because the withholding did not constitute payment within that tax year. Note IRS Notice 90-70 discussed above.

The above rules were modified by Revenue Procedure 94-27 and IRS News Release 94-28 wherein it was ruled that home *buyers will* be able to deduct *seller*-paid points on mortgages so long as the purchase price of the home is reduced by the amount of the seller's payment. This rule does not apply to improvement (rather than acquisition) loans or to loans not for your principal residence.

Other payments also constitute interest. When you buy property on the installment plan, you may deduct your interest payments if they are separately stated, or if they can be determined and proved. Finance charges added to your monthly credit card statements also constitute deductible interest, as do one-time charges made on new cash advances and new check and overdraft advances added to your bank credit card account balance. No part of these one-time charges, though, can be a service charge, loan fee, credit investigation fee, or similar charge.

When you buy personal property such as clothing, jewelry, furniture, or appliances on the installment plan using a revolving charge account, there is usually a separately stated finance charge. The total amount of these finance charges was deductible as interest, subject to the consumer interest deduction phase-out discussed below. For example, if you buy a refrigerator for $300 from the American Department Store and charge it to your revolving charge account, there will be no extra charge if you pay the balance within 30 days after you are billed. But if you make installment payments, your account will be charged the finance charge of 1.5 percent on the unpaid balance each month. These finance charges were previously deductible as interest.

Sometimes when you borrow money the interest is subtracted from the face amount of the note and you receive the balance. If you use the cash method, you may deduct the interest only in the year you make payments. Alternatively, if you use the accrual method, you may deduct the interest as it accrues.

For example, assume you sign a note for $1,200 on March 27, agreeing to pay it in 12 equal installments beginning on April 28. The interest is $1,200 × 12 percent = $144 and is subtracted from the face value of the note so that you receive only $1,056. If you use the cash method, the interest is considered to be repaid in 12 installments of $12 each. Your deduction for the first year is $108 ($12 × nine payments). If you miss two payments in the first year and made only seven payments, your deduction is $84. If you use the accrual method, the deduction is determined by prorating interest over the period in which it accrues. You may therefore deduct $108 (9/12 × $144) in the first year and $36 (3/12 × $144) in the following year.

Interest often is "hidden" in other payments, such as in judgments and personal loans. If you make a late payment of taxes, or if you must pay additional taxes at a later date, part of the amount will usually be for interest. This interest is no longer deductible (see personal interest limitations below). Penalties, in addition, are not deductible. Furthermore, you may not deduct interest on any money you borrow to buy tax-exempt securities or to buy a single-premium life insurance endowment or annuity contract. A single-premium contract includes policies on which you pay almost all the premiums within four years from the date you buy the contract; it also includes policies for which you deposit an amount with the insurer for the payment of future premiums. Also, you may not deduct interest on a loan that is used to buy stock if the collateral on the loan is a single-premium annuity contract.

However, according to Rev. Rul. 83-51, the Internal Revenue Service holds that the "contingent interest" portion of a shared appreciation mortgage (SAM) loan used by a cash-basis individual taxpayer to finance the purchase of a personal residence is deductible as interest when paid. The ruling deals with three situations. In each, the taxpayer purchases a home by securing a SAM from a financial institution. The SAM provides for a fixed interest annual rate and "contingent interest" equal to 40 percent of the appreciation in the value of the residence, payable when the SAM terminates. Termination is to occur at the earliest of (1) prepayment of the entire outstanding balance of the SAM, (2) sale of the residence, or (3) 10 years from the SAM loan. The taxpayer also has the option to refinance the mortgage balance and contingent interest due at the prevailing interest rate. The SAM agreement provides that it creates no more than a debtor-creditor relationship.

In the first situation provided for under the ruling, the taxpayer sells the residence at a profit and uses a portion of the sales proceeds to pay the remaining SAM principal balance and the contingent interest. In the second situation, the taxpayer prepays the outstanding principal balance and contingent interest with funds not obtained from the SAM lender. In the third situation, the taxpayer

refinances the principal balance and contingent interest due on maturity of the SAM by obtaining a conventional 30-year mortgage from the SAM lender. The Internal Revenue Service holds that in the first and second situations, the taxpayer can deduct the contingent interest in the year the SAM is paid off, on the grounds that interest, to be deductible, need not be computed at a stated rate. All that is required is that a definitely ascertainable sum be paid for the use of borrowed money pursuant to a loan agreement. In the first and second situations, the contingent interest is ascertainable. In the third situation, however, the taxpayer cannot deduct contingent interest, because merely executing a new note does not constitute payment. But payments on the new note to the extent allocable to the contingent interest will be deductible in the year paid. In all three situations, the taxpayer can deduct the fixed interest when paid.

To ensure that you have a debtor-creditor relationship and that the SAM does not in substance create an equity arrangement, the SAM agreement should provide, in addition to stating that only a debtor-creditor relationship is intended, that:

a) the mortgage secures only the indebtedness;

b) the mortgagor can sell, transfer, improve, and encumber the property without the mortgagee's consent;

c) the mortgagee is not liable for any decrease in the value of the property; *and*

d) the mortgagor is solely responsible to pay real estate taxes, insurance premiums, and other charges relating to ownership.

The following table, from Patrick O'Rourke, CPA, in Washington, DC, summarizes the tax treatment of various line items at a real estate closing:

Closing Statement Deductions

The closing statement to a real estate purchase contains many potential tax deductions. Treatment of closing statement line items differs depending on whether the property is business (rental) property or used for a personal residence.

We have summarized typical tax treatment of major line items of the often used HUD-1 closing statement. However, there may also be certain items that are treated differently depending on your particular situation. There are differences in tax treatment depending on whether the property is used as a personal residence or rented out. A notation of "basis" refers to costs that become part of the total capitalized cost of the property and not currently deductible; however, these costs can be deducted at the time of sale, or earlier via *depreciation* if they relate to rental property.

	Purchaser (Borrower) HUD-1 Closing Statement		
HUD-1 Line #	Closing Statement Description	Tax Treatment— Personal Residence	Tax Treatment— Rental Property
101	Contract sales price	Basis—is relevant if property is later sold or rented	Basis—building portion eligible for depreciation
102	Personal property	Basis—is relevant if property is later sold or rented	Basis—eligible for accelerated depreciation
103	Settlement charges	See Lines 700–1305	See Lines 700–1305
104–105	Miscellaneous	Varies	Varies
106	City/town taxes (See Line 210)	Deductible as itemized deduction on Form 1040 Schedule A*	Deductible as rental expense*
107	County taxes (See Line 211)	Deductible as itemized deduction on Form 1040 Schedule A*	Deductible as rental expense*
108	Assessments (See Line 212)	LID assessments are part of basis; other assessments are typically non-deductible	LID assessments are part of basis; other assessments are typically deductible*
109–112	Miscellaneous	Varies	Varies
210	City/town taxes (See Line 106)	* This credit reduces deductible taxes on Line 106	* This credit reduces deductible taxes on Line 106
211	County taxes (See Line 107)	* This credit reduces deductible taxes on Line 107	* This credit reduces deductible taxes on Line 107
212	Assessments (See Line 108)	* This credit reduces assessments on Line 108	* This credit reduces assessments on Line 108
213–216	Miscellaneous	Varies	Varies
700–703	Sales and Realtors' commissions	Basis	Basis

	Purchaser (Borrower) HUD-1 Closing Statement *(continued)*		
HUD-1 Line #	**Closing Statement Description**	**Tax Treatment— Personal Residence**	**Tax Treatment— Rental Property**
801	Loan origination fee	Deductible as itemized deduction ("points") on Form 1040 Schedule A	Amortized over term of mortgage
802	Loan discount	Deductible as itemized deduction ("points") on Form 1040 Schedule A	Amortized over term of mortgage
803	Appraisal fee	Basis	Basis
804	Credit report	Nondeductible	Basis
805	Inspection fee	Basis	Basis
806	Mortgage insurance fee	Nondeductible	Amortized over term of mortgage
807	Assumption fee	Nondeductible	Amortized over term of mortgage
808–811	Miscellaneous	Varies	Varies
901	Prorated interest	Deductible as itemized deduction—this interest is typically included in year-end interest statement (Form 1098)	Deductible as rental expense—this interest is typically included in year-end interest statement (Form 1098)
902	Mortgage insurance	Nondeductible except for 2007 through 2010	Amortized over term of mortgage
903	Hazard insurance	Nondeductible	Deductible as rental expense
904–905	Miscellaneous	Varies	Varies
1001	Hazard insurance	Nondeductible	Reserves—deductible when paid from escrow
1002	Mortgage insurance	Nondeductible	Reserves—amortizable when paid from escrow
1003	City property taxes	Reserves—deductible as itemized deduction when paid from escrow	Reserves—deductible when paid from escrow

(continues)

	Purchaser (Borrower) HUD-1 Closing Statement *(continued)*		
HUD-1 Line #	Closing Statement Description	Tax Treatment—Personal Residence	Tax Treatment—Rental Property
1004	County property taxes	Reserves—deductible as itemized deduction when paid from escrow	Reserves—deductible when paid from escrow
1005	Assessments	Varies	Varies
1006–1008	Miscellaneous	Varies	Varies
1101	Settlement fees	Basis	Basis
1102	Abstract or title search	Basis	Basis
1103	Title examination	Basis	Basis
1104	Title insurance binder	Basis	Basis
1105	Document preparation	Basis	Basis
1106	Notary fees	Basis	Basis
1107	Attorneys' fees	Basis	Typically part of basis; if tenant-related, may be amortized over term of lease(s)
1108–1110	Title insurance	Basis	Basis
1111–1113	Miscellaneous	Varies	Varies
1201	Recording fees	Basis	Basis
1202	City/county tax stamps	Basis	Basis
1203	State tax/stamps	Basis	Basis
1204–1205	Miscellaneous	Varies	Varies
1301	Survey	Basis	Basis
1302	Pest inspection	Basis	Basis
1303–1305	Miscellaneous	Varies	Varies

The above table summarizes tax treatment for *buyers* of properties. For sellers, these costs (including remaining basis) are deducted at the time of sale, with the exception of costs that are specifically noted as nondeductible. Of course, capital gains may not be recognized if the property is a personal residence and you qualify.

LIMITATIONS

There are certain limitations on the amount of interest that you can deduct.

The deduction for investment interest incurred or continued is limited to net investment income to purchase or carry *property held for investment*. Disallowed investment interest can be carried forward indefinitely and allowed to the extent of future net investment income.

Investment income and investment expenses do not include any income or expenses taken into account when computing income or loss from a passive activity, including any interest paid or accrued on debt to acquire or carry an interest in a passive activity. However, it does include portfolio income from passive activities.

DEFINITIONS

Net investment income means the excess of *investment income* over *investment expenses*. Investment income is defined as income from interest, dividends, rents, royalties, short-term capital gains arising from the disposition of investment assets, and certain recapture amounts (but only if the income is not derived from the conduct of a trade or business), except that all gain (not just short-term gain) attributable to the disposition of property held for investment may be included. The Omnibus Budget Reconciliation Act of 1993 complicated the deductibility of investment interest. The Act provides that long-term capital gains qualify as investment income only if the investor volunteers to have them taxed at the same rate as personal income. "Dividends" taxed at the reduced 0 percent–20 percent rate do not qualify as investment income.

The calculations can get complicated. If you have a long-term gain of $50,000 and $50,000 of investment interest, with no other investment interest, with no other investment income, you could effectively avoid the tax on the gain by opting to treat it as ordinary income. The savings would be (if you were in a 32 percent bracket) 32 percent of $50,000 or $16,000 (or $7,500 if you qualified for the 15 percent maximum capital gains tax).

However, if you expect $50,000 in investment income the next year, and you pay the $16,000 in this year, you could carry the deduction forward and

potentially save $18,500 in income tax at the 37 percent rate in the second year—a net 2-year savings of $2,500. *Investment expenses* are deductible expenses (other than interest) directly connected with the production of investment income. Investment expenses should be considered as those allowed after application of the 2 percent floor for miscellaneous itemized deductions (see page 347). In computing the amount of expenses that exceed the 2 percent floor, expenses that are not investment expenses are disallowed before any investment expenses are disallowed. Note that as of 2018, all miscellaneous itemized expenses, including investment expenses, and no longer deductible.

Property held for investment includes property that produces interest, dividends, annuities, or royalties plus any interest held by a taxpayer in an activity involving the conduct of a trade or business that is not a passive activity and in which the taxpayer does not materially participate. A passive activity is defined as an activity that involves the conduct of a trade or business in which the taxpayer does not materially participate. The only activity excluded from this definition is a working interest in an oil and gas property that a taxpayer holds directly or through an entity that does not limit the liability of the taxpayer with respect to that activity. However, regulations may be issued that could broaden the class of activities that are excluded under the definition of a passive activity, and the class of activities so excluded would thereby be considered property held for investment.

THE DISALLOWANCE OF DEDUCTION FOR PERSONAL INTEREST

Taxpayers other than corporations are no longer allowed to deduct personal interest paid or accrued during the taxable year. Personal interest means any interest other than (1) interest paid or accrued on indebtedness incurred or continued in connection with the conduct of a trade or business, (2) any investment interest, (3) any interest taken into account when computing income or loss from a passive activity of the taxpayer, (4) any qualified residence interest, and (5) interest payable on extensions of time for payment of estate tax on the value of reversionary or remainder interests in property or where an estate consists largely of interests in a closely held business. In other words, virtually all personal or consumer interest (including interest on underpayment or late payment of taxes) that was allowable as a deduction without limit under prior law may no longer be deducted with the exception of qualified residence interest.

The term *qualified residence interest* means any interest that is paid or accrued during the taxable year on indebtedness secured by any property that (at the time such interest is paid or accrued) is a qualified residence of the

taxpayer. The term *qualified residence* means the principal residence of the taxpayer and one vacation home.

Note that interest on income tax deficiencies arising from the conduct of a trade or business *is* personal interest (the Tax Court in *Redlark*, 106 T.C. No. 2, 1/11/96, said it *was* deductible as did the District Court in *Allen v. U.S.,* DC ENC, No. 5:96-CV-909-F, 12/1/97, in North Carolina, but it was later reversed by the 4th Cir. Court of Appeals, No. 98-1401 on 4/20/99, while the Eighth Circuit says it *is not, Miller v. U.S.,* No. A3-92-183, 11/5/93, reversed by the Eighth Circuit, No. 94-3225, 9/7/95). However, the Ninth Circuit also reversed *Redlark* on 4/10/98 (CA-9, No. 96-70398) and was supported by *Stecher v. U.S.,* P. Colo., No. 97-WY-1892-AJ, 6/18/98 and *McDonnell v. U.S.,* 6th Cir., No. 98-5383, 5/27/99. In *Robinson v. Commissioner,* T.C. No. 9574-99, 119 T.C. No. 4, on September 5, 2002, the Tax Court agreed that interest on income tax underpayments was *not* deductible. Interest on tax deficiencies of partnerships and S corporations must be taken *below* the line (*True v. U.S.,* No. 91-CV-1004-J, 7/30/93) as opposed to above the line business entity deductions.

Interest on a credit card used to pay your tax is personal interest and therefore not deductible. Also not deductible were any fees paid to the credit card company to charge the tax (SCA-2001-15032). This position was reversed by IR 2009-37 and such fees were allowed as miscellaneous itemized deductions, until 2018 when all miscellaneous deductions disappear.

LIMITATION ON THE AMOUNT OF INTEREST DEDUCTIBLE AS QUALIFIED RESIDENCE INTEREST

The amount of interest that may be deducted on a debt secured by a qualified residence is limited in the following manner: Interest is deductible only to the extent that the indebtedness does not exceed the lesser of (1) the fair market value of the qualified residence or (2) the taxpayer's basis in the qualified residence (adjusted only by the cost of any improvements to such residence). However, as of August 16, 1986, if the aggregate amount of outstanding indebtedness secured by a qualified residence exceeded the taxpayer's basis in the property at that time, the amount of indebtedness at that time would substitute for the taxpayer's basis in the qualified residence when determining qualified residence interest.

The limitation on the deductibility of personal interest may encourage many taxpayers to seek other ways of financing consumer purchases. Two immediate methods of converting what would otherwise be nondeductible personal interest into deductible interest are (1) to borrow against marginable securities (or property held for investment) or (2) to borrow against a qualified residence. Each of these techniques presents potential problems.

USING HOME EQUITY

Originally, interest paid on debt secured by a home could be deductible only to the extent that the debt does not exceed the lesser of (1) the fair market value of the home or (2) the taxpayer's adjusted basis in the home (or if the debt secured by the home exceeded the basis on August 16, 1986, that amount of debt).

Many homeowners who have owned their homes for many years or who have acquired new homes in recent years after rolling over gains from the sale of a previous home have relatively low bases in their homes. In addition, they may have debt secured by these homes that already exceeds their bases. Consequently, the opportunity to increase interest-deductible borrowing in many cases may be limited. Even in cases where the potential to tap home equity exists, in many cases it may be unwise to risk the loss of a home to finance consumer purchases since circumstances could evolve that preclude repayment of the debt.

However, taxpayers who have sufficient equity in their homes and untapped borrowing capacity under the qualified residence interest rules may wish to finance new consumer purchases or consolidate consumer loans by increasing qualified residence borrowing.

Some homeowners could consider selling their homes, using the $250,000/$500,000 gain exclusion, and purchasing a new home. The proceeds from the sale of the home could be used to purchase the new home. They would have potential interest-deductible borrowing capacity equal to the cost of their new homes.

The Revenue Act of 1987, signed in December 1987, modified the above rules on home equity indebtedness but introduced further—and more favorable—limitations for home acquisition indebtedness. Indebtedness that was incurred on or before October 13, 1987, and that was secured by a qualified residence on such date or on any date thereafter is classified as acquisition indebtedness. Such debt will not be subject to the new acquisition indebtedness limitation in 1988 or after. Therefore, interest that was associated with indebtedness incurred on or before October 13, 1987, and that exceeded the limitations under the 1986 Tax Reform Act, will not exceed the limitations under the 1987 Act. The related interest will be viewed as qualified residence interest for 1988 and thereafter.

Under the latest rules, the aggregate amount treated as acquisition indebtedness for any period cannot exceed $1,000,000 (or $500,000 in the case of a married individual filing a separate return). Also, refinancing of indebtedness after October 13, 1987, is considered acquisition indebtedness, but only to the extent of the refinanced indebtedness. If a qualified residence is refinanced for more than the existing indebtedness, the excess amount may qualify in total, in part, or not at all as acquisition indebtedness. **AS OF 2018, FOR PURCHASES AFTER 2017, THE LIMIT IS REDUCED TO $750,000 FROM $1 MILLION.**

Home equity indebtedness is *now* defined as any indebtedness (other than acquisition indebtedness) secured by a qualified residence to the extent that the aggregate amount for any period does not exceed the lesser of (1) $100,000 (or $50,000 for a married individual filing separately), or (2) the fair market value of such qualified residence less the amount of acquisition indebtedness with respect to the residence.

Note that in *Sophy v. Commissioner,* Dec. 58, 965, 138 T.C. No. 8 (2012), the Tax Court held that unmarried co-owners of two personal residences were **not** each allowed to deduct interest on $1.1 million of acquisition and home-equity indebtedness because the debt limitations are *residence based,* rather than *tax-payer based.* Instead, each taxpayer could only deduct a proportionate share of interest paid on a total of $1 million of acquisition indebtedness plus $100,000 of home-equity indebtedness. This was reversed by *Voss vs. Commissioner,* 2015 BL 254104, 9th Cir., No 12-73257 on August 7, 2015. The correct view is *taxpayer* rather than *residence-*based for unmarried taxpayers.

Example 1: Assume that you bought a house for $1,000,000 prior to 2018 and borrowed $800,000 to finance the purchase. You reduce your debt to $600,000 by making payments over several years. You refinance and take out a new mortgage for $700,000. Your acquisition debt will still be $600,000. However, if you used $100,000 to substantially improve your home, the $100,000 would be added to acquisition debt. Alternatively, the interest may qualify as home equity debt.

Example 2: Assume that you bought your home 15 years ago for $50,000. You have completely paid off your mortgage, and the property is now worth $200,000. In 2017, you took out a $120,000 home loan. You used $110,000 to make additions to the home and $10,000 to buy a car. Interest on the entire loan is deductible: $110,000 of the loan is acquisition debt, and the balance qualifies as home equity debt.

Example 3: Assume that you have an unpaid balance of $90,000 on your home, which is valued at $300,000. You obtain a *second mortgage* of $110,000 in 2017 and use the proceeds to help your parents buy a home and to buy personal assets. Interest on $100,000 of the new mortgage was deductible as qualified home equity interest. Interest on the $10,000 balance was personal interest.

THE TAX CUTS AND JOBS ACT OF 2017 CHANGED THE RULES AGAIN. YOU CAN STILL USE UP TO $100,000 IN HOME EQUITY, BUT TO DEDUCT THE INTEREST, THE MONEY MUST BE USED TO IMPROVE YOUR HOME. HOME EQUITY INTEREST FOR OTHER THINGS, SUCH AS BUYING A CAR, IS NO LONGER ALLOWABLE.

Note that the 1987 limits on acquisition indebtedness make it very important not to overlook many elements of the cost of a house besides the amount paid to the seller. These would include appraisal fees, title search, transfer taxes, survey fees, bank or lender fees, legal fees, mortgage taxes, brokers' commissions (if paid by the buyer), and other nondeductible closing costs. Note that the cost of the home and improvements does not include painting and routine maintenance and repairs. However, it does include additions to the home and improvement or replacement of equipment that is part of the home. Such improvements include landscaping; resurfacing the driveway; installing a swimming pool; constructing a new roof; finishing an attic or basement; replacing or making a major improvement to heating, air conditioning, or plumbing systems or to a water heater; or adding on a room or garage.

Can you finance the purchase of additional land, adjacent to your home, and deduct the interest as qualified residence interest? In Private Letter Ruling 8940061, the IRS said yes! In the ruling, a family built a home on 15 acres and later bought five more adjacent acres that will be cleared, landscaped, and incorporated into the family compound. The loan to finance the extra land is secured by both the new land and the original 15-acre tract. The family told the IRS it had no plans to separately develop the five acres.

The IRS said that the loan to buy the five acres was purchase debt, and since total purchase debt didn't exceed the then $1 million limit, all of the interest paid was deductible in full.

USING DEBT SECURED BY INVESTMENT PROPERTY

The major advantage of borrowing against a home rather than against property held for investment is that qualified residence interest is not subject to the investment interest expense limitation. When borrowing against property held for investment, care must be taken not to generate investment interest expense in excess of net investment income (plus excess amounts allowed under the phase-in rules for investment interest), or the interest deductions will be disallowed in the year paid or incurred. However, any excess may be carried forward indefinitely and deducted in later years when investment income exceeds investment interest expense paid or incurred in that year. Therefore, carryovers of investment interest will still generally be preferable to personal interest, which is no longer deductible.

PASSIVE ACTIVITIES WITH PASSIVE INCOME

Individuals who own passive activities that are earning passive income may wish to increase borrowing against that activity even if they do not wish to finance consumer purchases. The proceeds could be used to acquire investment assets with appreciation potential that could as well be leveraged up to their respective

margin limits, thereby creating investment interest deductions to offset the current income from the portfolio.

The interest on debt used to acquire or carry an interest in a passive activity is not subject to the investment interest expense limitation. Such interest is fully deductible against passive income from the passive activity. However, if the interest expense exceeds the passive income from the passive activity, the excess interest will be treated as a passive loss. That loss may be deducted only against passive income from other passive activities or, on disposition of that passive activity, against gains on the disposition, passive income from other passive activities, and any active income or gain of the taxpayer, in that order.

OTHER INTEREST PLANNING TIPS

To the extent that a loan finances an asset used partially for business and partially for personal purposes, it appears that interest would have to be prorated between the two uses.

Example 1: Ms. Agent, an insurance agent, finances a new automobile to be used 75 percent for business and 25 percent for personal purposes. She would treat 75 percent of the interest as deductible business interest and 25 percent as nondeductible consumer interest.

Example 2: In example 1, Ms. Agent was treated as a self-employed individual. If she was an outside salesperson and an employee, rather than a self-employed individual, apparently all the interest she would pay on her automobile loan would be treated as consumer interest and would not be deductible as interest, even if she used the automobile 95 percent of the time in her employer's business. In that case, get an accountable plan reimbursement from your employer—even if you have to reduce your salary to get it!

Under current law, it may be more advantageous to have a business-use vehicle owned by the employer rather than by the employee, even though the employee must include the value of any personal use as compensation income.

The term *residence* as used in the qualified residence interest exception includes, in addition to houses, condominium units and cooperative housing units and any other property that the taxpayer uses for personal purposes as a dwelling unit, which generally includes a mobile home, a motor home, or a boat with living accommodations. A taxpayer who owns a boat that is large enough to live aboard for short periods, a mobile home, or a motor home may be able to treat it as a second residence for purposes of the residential interest deduction. You need to have kitchen and bathroom facilities as well as a place to sleep to qualify.

Taxpayers who are planning to purchase a new home might consider having appliances and various options such as a deck, fencing, and landscaping installed by the builder and included in the sales price. The interest on these items would then qualify as fully deductible residential interest. Otherwise the interest will be treated as nondeductible consumer financing and will be deductible only to the extent permitted under the phase-in rule.

The use of interest-free and other below-market-rate loans is affected by the interest deduction limitation. An individual borrower's imputed interest deduction will no longer fully offset the imputed interest income. Both borrowers and lenders who are party to employment-related or gift-type interest-free loans should reconsider whether these types of arrangements are still suitable.

Taxpayers with excess investment interest expense should consider recognizing capital gains by selling property held for investment.

There are a number of tax strategies that you should employ in planning your interest deductions. First, you must consider the timing of your actual interest payments in relation to both exceeding your standard deduction amount and determining your subsequent year's income. This technique has been discussed in detail under medical expenses and taxes. Second, you must recognize that unlike many other forms of expenditure, interest expenses need not be reasonable to be deducted. If you borrow money at an exorbitant rate, that interest is deductible regardless of what it has been labeled in order to circumvent a state law on maximum percentages.

Interest is also deductible if paid to a related party for a bona fide indebtedness. This means that if you actually have a legal debtor-creditor relationship with your spouse, for example, you may deduct interest paid to that spouse. In fact, parents may legitimately deduct interest paid on money borrowed from their minor children as long as there is an effective debtor-creditor relationship. This means that you sign a note, arrange for a repayment schedule, and meet that repayment schedule. Substantial savings can be accrued by paying legitimate interest to a child in a lower tax bracket. For example, assume that you paid $2,100 in interest to your dependent child (who has no other income) and you are in the 32 percent bracket. The first $1,050 of that interest is not taxable to the child because of the standard deduction. Therefore, the child pays only $105 on the interest received ($1,050 × 10 percent). But if you are in the 32 percent bracket, you saved $672 in taxes—a net savings of $567!

STUDENT LOAN INTEREST DEDUCTION

The Tax Relief Act of 1997 provided a new *above the line* deduction of up to $1,000 for any interest on any qualified education loan in 1998, $1,500 in 1999, $2,000 in 2000, and up to $2,500 per year in 2001 and thereafter during the first 60 months in which interest payments are required. This deduction phased out at a modified

adjusted gross income level of $60,000 to $75,000 for joint filers and $40,000 to $55,000 for all others. These limits were also indexed for inflation.

The Tax Relief Act of 2001 eliminated the 60-month limitation, and increased the phaseout to between $100,000 and $130,000 for joint returns and between $50,000 and $65,000 for single returns, both as of January 1, 2002.*

A qualified education loan is a loan used to pay the costs of attendance at an eligible educational institution for a student enrolled at least half-time in a program leading to a degree, certificate, or other recognized educational credential. The student must be the taxpayer, the taxpayer's spouse, or the taxpayer's dependent at the time the loan was taken.

98 Mortgage Insurance

Private Mortgage Insurance premiums were deductible *only* for 2007 through 2017 and *only* for policies issued after 2006. If you prepaid, the insurance was treated as interest and deducted over the shorter of the term of the loan or 84 months.

This deduction was phased out for joint filers with adjusted gross income between $100,000 and $110,000 ($50,000–$55,000 for singles).

This is the insurance you pay if your down payment is less than 20 percent. If your equity is 20 percent or more, notify your lender to eliminate this additional cost.

99 Charitable Contributions

A charitable contribution is a gift to a qualified charitable organization. (To be deemed as making a gift, the taxpayer must have "donative intent"—that is, a detached and disinterested generosity. There must be no *quid pro quo* expected or received. That's why payments for religious education don't count. That's also why state plans to avoid the $10,000 limit on itemized deduction taxes with real estate tax credits for charitable contributions probably won't work.) The tax law allows charitable contributions to reduce taxable income, and therefore the actual cost of the donation will be reduced by your tax savings. As your income tax bracket increases, the real cost of your charitable gift will therefore decrease, making contributions more attractive for those in the higher brackets.

*For 2018, the numbers are $135,000–$165,000 for joint returns and $65,000–$80,000 for singles.

Regardless of the accounting method you use, contributions are usually deducted in the year in which they are paid. A contribution is paid when you unconditionally deliver or mail your gift to the recipient or to a designated agent or when you make a completed gift of property. A contribution made by a credit card is deductible immediately even if payment to the credit card company is made in a different year.

You can obtain an itemized deduction for your charitable contributions, but these deductions are limited to a maximum of 50 percent of your adjusted gross income for the year (60% as of 2018). These contributions may consist of gifts to public charities and certain private foundations.[*] If the 60 percent limit is not exhausted, you can deduct contributions to other entities subject to a more restrictive constraint of 20 percent of your adjusted gross income.[†]

Appreciated capital gain property generally is further subjected to an additional 30 percent limit. These limits will be detailed in the analysis under planning considerations.

Charitable contributions can take numerous forms. Though cash and property are the main ones, there are others that must be considered. Unreimbursed costs incurred for charity contributions, dues, admission charges, and other payments may be deductible, but not if they are made in exchange for benefits or property you receive. The amount deductible is usually the property's fair market value, yet for gifts of appreciated property this value may be reduced under special rules. Cancelled checks and receipts offer the best proof to the contributor. When a charitable deduction is taken you must be able to state the name of each charity and the amount and date of each gift. The *charitable mileage deduction* is 14¢/mile for 2018.

PLANNING CONSIDERATIONS

Qualified Donees

You can deduct charitable contributions only if they are made to or for the use of a "qualified donee." No charitable contribution deduction is allowed for

[*]The following types of foundations qualify: 1. private operating foundations; 2. all other private foundations that distribute all their contributions to public charities within $2\frac{1}{2}$ months after the year-end; and 3. pooled community foundations.

[†]The Tax Reform Act of 1984 increased the limits on contributions to tax-exempt private *nonoperating* foundations from 20 percent to 30 percent of adjusted gross income, for gifts of cash or ordinary income property. It also provided that excess post-1984 contributions can be carried forward for 5 years. The Act, in addition, provided a deduction at full fair market value for contributions of up to 10 percent of the stock of a corporation to a private *nonoperating* foundation, provided the stock is publicly traded and is long-term capital gain property. These provisions are effective for contributions made after the enactment of the Act.

gifts to other kinds of organizations, even if those organizations are exempt from U.S. income tax.

Organizations that provide sellar funded down-payment assistance to home buyers do *not* qualify as tax exempt charities (Rev. Rul. 2006-27).

The gift must be made directly to an organization to qualify for the deduction. However, in the case of *Rockefeller*, 76 T.C. 178 (1981), the court held that unreimbursed expenses incurred in rendering services to a qualified charitable organization constituted deductible contributions made "to" the charitable organization. The IRS has acquiesced in this decision (Rev. Rul. 84-61, I.R.B. 1984-17). No deduction to an individual or individuals is allowed by the IRS unless that individual or group is acting as an agent for a qualified organization. This rule is necessary because there is no guarantee that the money given to an individual will be forwarded to the charity. Payments to individual ministers have been disqualified as charitable contributions when there was no evidence that the money ever went to the minister's religious organization.

The Treasury Department publishes IRS Publication 78, which lists the organizations to which contributions are deductible, identifies each by type, and states their corresponding limit of deductibility. This list is updated annually. Three cumulative supplements listing only new additions are published every quarter. A list informing the public of organizations that no longer qualify as charitable organizations is published monthly.

Deductions are allowed for contributions given to or for the use of the following qualified organizations:

1. A state or possession of the United States, or the District of Columbia, if the contribution or gift is made for public purposes only.

2. A corporation, trust, or community chest, fund, or foundation if created in the United States and organized and operated exclusively for religious, charitable, scientific, literary, or educational purposes, or to foster national or international amateur sports competition (but not to help provide athletic equipment or facilities), or for the prevention of cruelty to children or animals. No part of the net earnings can benefit any private shareholder or individual. The organization must not be disqualified for tax exemption due to influencing legislation, and must not take part in any political campaign.

3. A post or organization of war veterans, if organized in the United States and if no part of the net earnings benefits any private shareholders or individual. Any dues, fees, or assessments paid by members of these organizations do not qualify for deductions.

4. A domestic or fraternal society, order, or association, operating under the lodge system, if the gift is to be used exclusively for religious, charitable, scientific, literary, or educational purposes, or to foster national or international amateur sports competition, or for the prevention of cruelty to children or animals. Dues to offset sickness or burial costs are deductible.

5. A nonprofit cemetery company whose funds are totally devoted to the continuous upkeep of the cemetery.

You can only deduct contributions to charities created or organized in the United States. But qualifying domestic charities that support foreign charities may be deductible, depending on specific circumstances (INFO 2009-0026).

If an organization qualifies as a church for tax purposes, it need not be required to seek exemption and has no filing requirements. Since Congress did not define the term *church*, the common meaning and usage of the term have been applied. In making this decision, the IRS utilizes the following 13 characteristics of a church:

A distinct legal existence
A recognized creed and form of worship
A definite and distinct ecclesiastical government
A formal code of doctrine and discipline
A distinct religious history
A membership not associated with any other church or denomination
A complete organization of ordained ministers chosen after completing prescribed courses of study
Literature of its own
Established places of worship
Regular congregations
Regular religious services
Sunday schools for religious education of the young
Schools to prepare their ministers

Not all of the above characteristics must be satisfied, and no single factor is given controlling weight. By listing these characteristics as a rough outline, the IRS gives guidelines for its determination as to whether an organization may qualify as a "church."

Contributions to foreign governments, charities, and private foundations are disallowed. Gifts to Communist-ruled organizations are also disallowed. The Treasury Department does not allow tax-exempt status for private schools that

practice racial discrimination, and any donations to them will not qualify as charitable contributions.

No charity can take part in any political activity. Charity status is lost by an organization if any substantial segment of its activities is devoted to formulating propaganda or otherwise trying to influence legislation. However, an organization (other than a church) may qualify as a charity and still perform some of these activities by keeping its political expenditures to an "insubstantial" part of its activities. Furthermore, donations to needy individuals are not deductible under the law.

ADDITIONAL PLANNING CONSIDERATIONS

Donation Limitations

Only if you contribute more than 20 percent of your adjusted gross income to a qualified charity is it necessary to be knowledgeable about donation limitations. Contributions up to this limit are automatically deductible if you itemize. For those who give more than 20 percent, certain rules apply.

If the contributions are all made to maximum deduction organizations (see the list that follows), the deduction ceiling is 60 percent of the contribution base (except that contributions of appreciated capital gain property are subject to a 30 percent ceiling, unless a special election is made). The contribution base is defined as adjusted gross income computed without regard to any net operating loss carryback to the taxable year.

To qualify for the 60 percent ceiling, the contribution must be made "to" one of the maximum deduction organizations (as opposed to "for the use of" an organization). If the contributions are not "to" 60 percent charities but rather are "for the use of" any charities, the deduction limit is 30 percent. Contributions of appreciated capital gain property to nonoperating foundations are limited to 20 percent. For contributions subject to the 20, 30, and 60 percent limits, the amount not deductible in the contribution year may be deductible in a future year as a carryover.

On a joint return, these limits apply to the aggregate contribution base.

You are allowed a 60 percent ceiling on contributions to any of the following maximum deduction organizations:

1. *Churches.*

2. *Tax-Exempt Educational Organizations.* The educational organization should maintain a regular faculty and curriculum and have a regularly enrolled body of students in attendance at the place where its educational activities are regularly conducted.

An organization set up for the benefit of certain state and municipal colleges and universities can also be included if it is organized and operated exclusively to receive, hold, invest, and administer property and to make expenditures to or for the benefit of an acceptable college or university.

The educational organization must be engaged entirely in educational activities (although noneducational activity incidental to the educational activities is allowable). Tuition payments are not deductible, and contributions made under circumstances where you or those related to you benefit may be examined to see if personal benefit is the purpose of the payment.

3. *Tax-Exempt Hospitals and Certain Medical Research Organizations.* Hospitals, in this case, do not include homes for children or the aged or institutes that provide vocational training for the handicapped. The medical research organization must be engaged primarily and directly in the continuous active conduct of medical research. In addition, it must be committed to spending each contribution received on such active conduct of medical research before January 1 of the fifth calendar year after the date the contribution is made.

4. *A Government Unit* as referred to in the Internal Revenue Code Section 170(c)(1) (such as a state or a political subdivision of a state).

5. *A "Publicly Supported" Organization* (such as a community chest). This type of organization normally receives a substantial part of its support (exclusive of operating income) from a governmental unit or from direct or indirect contributions from the general public.

6. *Certain Private Nonoperating Foundations.* These distribute all contributions they receive to public charities within 2½ months after the foundations' fiscal year-end.

7. *A Privately Operating Foundation.* This type of private foundation is one that pools all of its donations in a common fund. Any substantial contributor (or spouse) can annually direct the foundation as to which public charity shall receive the principal from his or her contribution and the interest from that principal.

8. *Certain Membership Organizations.* Only those in which more than one-third of their support comes from the general public are allowable.

The Public Support Test

To determine whether an organization is "publicly supported," you must apply the public support, or mechanical, test. An organization will be considered to be a publicly supported organization for its current taxable year and for the immediately succeeding taxable year if, for the four taxable years immediately preceding the current taxable year, the total amount of the support the organization received from governmental units, from donations made directly or indirectly by the public, or from a combination of the two equals 33.33 percent or more of the total support of the organization. In addition, contributions made by individuals, trusts, or corporations during the four taxable years may not exceed 2 percent of the organization's total support. The 2 percent limitation does not apply to support from governmental units or from other publicly supported organizations.

The Facts and Circumstances Test

A corporation, trust, or community chest, fund, or foundation that does not qualify as a "publicly supported" organization under the mechanical test may qualify on the basis of the facts and circumstances test. There are several requirements, but only requirements 1 and 2 below must be met on an aggregate basis. However, a substantial number of the remaining ones must also be met in the 4 taxable years preceding the current taxable year.

1. *10 Percent of Support Limitations.* The percent of support "normally" received by an organization from governmental units, from the public, whether direct or indirect, or from a combination of these sources must be substantial. The amount of this support must equal at least 10 percent of the total support.

2. *Attraction of Public Support.* An organization must be so organized and operated as to attract new and additional public or governmental support on a continuous basis. It must maintain a continuous program for canvassing funds from the general public, community, or membership groups involved, or it must carry on other activities to attract support.

3. *Percent of Financial Support.* The percent of public support received will be considered. The higher the percent, the lesser will be the burden of establishing the publicly supported nature of the organization.

4. *Sources of Support.* A large number of different contributors is preferred. In determining what a "representative number of persons" is, consideration

will be given to the type of organization involved, the length of time it has been in existence, and any restrictions it practices.

5. *Representative Governing Body.* The fact that the organization has a governing body that represents the broad interest of the public will also be considered in determining whether an organization is publicly supported.

6. *Availability of Public Facilities for the Benefit of the Public.* Public participation in programs or policies will also be reviewed.

7. *Additional Factors.* Pertinent to membership organizations are answers to the following questions:

 a) Is the organization designed to enroll a substantial number of persons in a particular field?

 b) Are dues set at fixed rates to be affordable by a broad cross section of the interested public?

 c) Are the activities of the organization likely to appeal to persons with a broad range of interests, or do they focus on a particular purpose?

Those factors relevant to each case and the weight given to each factor may change depending upon the nature and function of the organization.

Contributions shall be considered as support from the *general public* only if the total amount of all contributions, direct and indirect, does not exceed 2 percent of the organization's total support for a set period, except as provided by the *exclusion of unusual grants.* The 2 percent limit does not apply to support received from governmental units. (The donation is included in full in the denominator but will only be included in the numerator of such a fraction to the extent that it does not exceed 2 percent of the denominator. Any unusual grants may be excluded entirely from the fraction.) The unusual grant exclusion is generally intended to apply to substantial contributions or bequests from disinterested parties whose contributions or bequests:

 a) are attracted by reason of the publicly supported nature of the organization;

 b) are in unusual or unexpected amounts; *or*

 c) would, by reason of size, adversely affect the status of the organization as normally being publicly supported.

Support does *not* include the following:

- Any amounts received by an organization from the exercise or performance of its functional purpose, which comprises the basis for its exemptions

- Contributions of services for which there is no deduction

Both of the above must be excluded from the numerator and the denominator.

An organization dependent on gross receipts from related activities will not satisfy either the mechanical test or the facts and circumstances test. The condition for public support will also not be met if an insignificant amount of the organization's support comes through governmental units from contributions made directly or indirectly by the general public. Support from a governmental unit includes any amount received from a governmental unit, which covers donations, contributions, and amounts received in connection with an agreement with a governmental unit for either the execution of services or for a governmental research grant. However, such amounts will not count as support from a governmental unit if they are for the performance of the organization's exempt activity, and if the reason for the payment is to enable the organization to offer a facility for the direct benefit of the public, rather than to serve only its members.

To summarize the tests involved in determining whether organizations qualify as publicly supported: The organization must normally receive in excess of 33.33 percent of its support from a governmental unit and from direct and indirect donations from the general public to qualify under the mechanical test; or, alternatively, at least 10 percent of its support must come from governmental units and public donations, and most, if not all, of points 3 through 7 of the facts and circumstances test must apply.

COMMUNITY TRUSTS

Community trusts have been established to invite large donations of a capital or endowment nature for the benefit of a certain community. Each has a governing body consisting of representatives of the community it serves. The contributions are often kept in the form of separate trusts or funds subject to changing degrees of control by the governing body.

A community trust must also meet the mechanical test or be able to attract sources on a continuous basis from the government and public in order to meet the facts and circumstances test. This test will usually be satisfied if the trust attracts a broad range of donors from the community served.

Another point concerning community trusts is the treatment of them as single entities. Any organization that meets the requirements described in points 2 through 5 below will be treated as a single entity; all funds linked with an organization that meets the requirements of point 1 will be considered as component parts of that organization.

1. The organization must be established by a gift, bequest, legacy, devise, or other transfer to a community trust that is considered a single entity, and it may not be subjected by the transferor to any restraints.

2. The organization must be recognized as a community trust, fund, or foundation to support charitable events in the community it serves.

3. All funds of the organization must be subject to common governing instruments.

4. The organization must have a common governing body that administers the fund.

5. Periodic financial reports must be prepared to show that all of the funds held by the community trust are funds of the organization.

A few final words on 60 percent limit contributions: Gifts made "for the use of" public charities or 60 percent limit private foundations do not qualify for the 60 percent limit. You must make the gift "to" a 60 percent charity to qualify for the donation. A charitable gift to a fraternal lodge that then contributes a gift to a 60 percent charity does not qualify for the 60 percent limit. A donation of an *income interest* is considered as made for the use of the recipient organization. Thus, you do not get the 60 percent limit. But a gift of a *remainder interest* is treated as made to the donee charity, thus enabling you to reach the 60 percent ceiling.

LIMITS ON DEDUCTION

There is a 20 percent ceiling on deductions for any contributions of appreciated capital gain property to 30 percent charities—i.e., charitable organizations except those listed previously (e.g., a nonoperating foundation). For years beginning with 1987, the amount of your deduction is limited to your basis. Any excess over the ceiling can be carried over to the 5 succeeding tax years.

For example, assume you have a painting with a basis of $15,000 and a $20,000 fair market value. You have an adjusted gross income of $100,000. You

want to contribute the painting to a veterans organization (a nonpublic charity). Your charitable deduction will be $15,000, because your basis does not exceed your ceiling of $20,000 (20 percent of $100,000). There is, however, a special rule for gifts of stock. If you contribute *qualified appreciated stock* to a *private non-operating foundation,* you may take as a charitable deduction, subject to the above 20 percent ceiling limit, the full fair market value of the stock. Qualified appreciated stock is any stock of a corporation that (a) has price quotations readily available from an established securities market and (b) if sold would produce a long-term capital gain. This provision does not apply to the gift of any stock or portion of stock that exceeds 10 percent of the ownership interest in a corporation.

This special rule for stock was in effect through 1994 and was extended by the Small Business Job Protection Act of 1996 for gifts made July 1, 1996 through May 31, 1997, extended in 1997 to June 30, 1998, and made permanent in 1998.

If you give property that, if sold, would result in a long-term capital gain (appreciated capital assets or Section 1231 Property),* and the charity is a 60 percent donee, then you are subject to a 30 percent ceiling. If the contributions of capital gain property exceed 30 percent of your contribution base, the excess amount can qualify for a 5-year carryover. Charitable contributions with 30 percent limitations paid during the taxable year are considered after all other charitable contributions.

Donation of a 30 percent capital gain property is defined as the charitable contribution of a capital asset that, if sold by the donor at its fair market value at the time of the contribution, would result in long-term gain; also, the amount of such a contribution must not be required to be reduced under Section 170(3)(1)(B) (this covers tangible personal property used by a donee in a function unrelated to the basis for its exemptions, and contributed "to" or "for the use of" certain private foundations).

You can make a special election to qualify for the 60 percent adjusted gross income limit on this property. In doing so, the deduction for the contribution is limited to your basis. If the election is made, it applies to all donations of capital gain property made during the year as well as to prior-year carryovers of appreciated capital gain property. The election must be made by the due date of the return and cannot be made on an amended return.

*Section 1231 Property is real or personal property used in a trade or business that would normally produce ordinary gains or losses upon sale or exchange. Gains on such property are capital gains and losses are ordinary losses.

For example, assume that you have some stock that you would like to give to a public charity. You have held the stock for a number of years and your adjusted gross income is $100,000. The stock has a basis of $45,000 and a fair market value at the time of the donation of $50,000. If you do not make the 60 percent election, your charitable contribution deduction is limited to $30,000 (30 percent of $100,000) with the remaining $20,000 carried over. If you do make the election, you would get a deduction of the full $45,000 basis. Note that in exchange for getting the full $45,000 in the current year, you lose $5,000 of your deduction.

When making this special election, you are actually exchanging a reduced deduction on each separate contribution of appreciated capital gain property for the more generous 60 percent limit. The election of the 60 percent deduction ceiling is made by attaching to the original return for the election year a statement that the election is being taken. The following guidelines should be used in deciding whether the election should be taken:

1. If your long-term capital gain property contributions to 60 percent charities will not total more than 30 percent of your contribution base, do not make the election.

2. If you give long-term capital gain property in excess of the 30 percent ceiling to 60 percent charities, consider the following factors:

 a) any excess over the 30 percent limit, which can be carried over;

 b) your income for the current year, which should be compared with what you expect to earn in the following years; *and*

 c) the amount of unrealized long-term capital gain included in the value of the property.

Where long-term appreciated property consists of *tangible personal property*, such as works of art, the amount of the deduction *depends upon its use* by the charitable organization. If its use by the charity is unrelated to the charity's exempt function, then the amount of the deduction is limited to your basis.

For example, you own a work of art that you have held for more than one year and then you donate that work to a museum. If the donation is used by the museum for display, it is deemed related to the museum's exempt purpose.

Therefore, if the work of art has a fair market value of $24,000 on the date of donation, that donation gives you a deduction of $24,000.

If the donation is made to a hospital, however, the amount of the deduction is limited to your basis. If the basis of the property is $4,000, then the deduction is limited to $4,000.

CARRYOVERS TO OTHER TAX YEARS

If the amount of contributions to 60 percent organizations made within a taxable year exceeds 60 percent of your contribution base for that year, the excess may be carried over for the next 5 succeeding taxable years. Current contributions must first be considered before any carryover is applied. Contributions that are carried over, plus the current year's contributions, must fall within the 60 percent limit. Five-year carryovers are also available for excess 20 percent and 30 percent contributions.

The charitable contribution deduction must be specially computed when taxpayers with carryovers change their filing status. Note that an unused carryover of a deceased spouse can be used on a return for the year the spouse dies; otherwise it is lost.

ORDER OF DEDUCTIBILITY

The amount that you should deduct in any year is determined in the following order:

1. Gifts for the year to 60 percent charities

2. Carryover of gifts to 60 percent charities from the preceding 5 years, from the earliest year first

3. Gifts for the year to 30 percent charities

4. Carryover of gifts to 30 percent charities from the preceding 5 years, from the earliest year first

5. Gifts that are limited by the 20 percent ceiling

Your total deduction for any year cannot exceed 60 percent of your contribution base for that year and cannot exceed the amount actually contributed currently and in the past. Where 60 percent of your contribution base income exceeds the amount of your gifts, any carryovers from prior years are deductible, in order of

time, to the extent of this excess. Any carryovers not used up may be carried forward to later years until exhausted or until the 5-year period for each excess contribution runs out.

Contributions to which the 20 percent limitation would apply should be avoided when gifts are made of 30 percent limit property to 60 percent limit organizations that surpass your 30 percent limit. In this situation, you should consider the special election to reduce the 30 percent limit items and receive the 60 percent ceiling on them. This especially applies if a carryover of such a contribution exists from a prior year. Prior years' deductions are not influenced by this special election.

FORM OF THE GIFT

The deduction for a contribution of property is normally equal to the fair market value of the property at the time the donation is made. For a great program to value your contributions, see itsdeductible.com or try bigwriteoff.com. No gain is normally realized on a charitable contribution of appreciated property. You have an advantage when you contribute appreciated property because you get a deduction for the full fair market value of the property contributed, including both your basis and your unrealized paper profit. You are not taxed on this profit, so in effect you receive a deduction for an amount that you need not report as income.

If the fair market value of the property donated is below its basis, no loss is recognized on this donation. In such a case it would be better to sell the property first, realize the loss for tax purposes, and then make a gift of the proceeds. Using this approach, a deduction is allowed for the entire basis of the property.

The deduction for certain contributions of appreciated property must be reduced in some cases, depending on the type of appreciated property or the character of the donee. The amount of deduction for appreciated property must be reduced below its fair market value by the sum of ordinary income or short-term capital gain that would result if the property were sold at the time of the gift. Both a capital asset held for not more than 12 months and property subject to recapture of depreciation would result in ordinary income. Any appreciation in excess of the recapture amount is handled as a contribution of capital-gain property. The above rule applies regardless of the type of donee. Other examples of property that would result in ordinary income are letters, memoranda, and works of art created by the donor. Note that the Tax Increase

Ordering of Deductions to Charity*

	Deduct All:	Up to This % of Contribution Base
First—	Cash contributions to public charities	60%
Second—	Carryover of prior years' cash contributions to public charities	60%
Third—	Cash contributions to private foundations	30%
Fourth—	Carryover of prior years' cash contributions to private foundations	30%
Fifth—	Capital gain property contributions to public charities	30%
Sixth—	Carryover of prior years' capital-gain property contributions to public charities	30%
Seventh—	Qualified appreciated stock contributions to private foundations	20%
Eighth—	Carryover of prior years' qualified appreciated stock contributions to private foundations	20%

*When contributions reach the indicated percentage, any excess must be carried over to the next year. If contributions in any tier are below the indicated percentage in any taxable year, contributions in the next lower tier may be deducted.

Prevention Act of 2005, enacted in 2006, provided that self created music works now qualify when sold, for capital gain treatment. Under prior law, such sales were taxed as ordinal income.

For example, if an artist contributed a personal piece to a charity, there would be no charitable deduction. This portrait would generate ordinary income if it were sold by the artist at fair market value. Therefore, the

deduction would be reduced to zero by the subtraction of this ordinary income component.

Except for "qualified appreciated stock" gifted to a private nonoperating foundation, if appreciated long-term capital gain property is donated to a private foundation that is not a 60 percent limit donee, then its value must be reduced by 100 percent of that long-term capital gain. Your deduction is limited to your basis. The deduction for contributed capital gain property that is tangible personal property is reduced in the same manner as when the use of the property is dissimilar to the donee's exempt status.

You will sometimes sell property to a charity for less than the property's fair market value, intending the "bargain" portion as a charitable contribution. Except in the case of ordinary income property sold for its adjusted basis, the seller may treat the amount of the bargain (fair market value minus purchase price) as a charitable donation for deduction reasons.

The donor usually also realizes taxable gain on the bargain sale; thus you must divide your basis (original cost) in the property between the part of the property sold and the part given. Your gain is determined only by that portion of your total cost that the bargain selling price (amount received) bears to the fair market value. The following formula can be used to calculate the adjusted basis of the property sold:

$$\frac{\text{Selling Price}}{\text{Fair Market Value}} \times \text{Property Basis} = \text{Adjusted Basis}$$

You must allocate this figure to the property sold and determine your taxable gain. For example, assume you have 100 shares of appreciated long-term capital gains stock with a tax basis of $4,000 and a fair market value of $10,000. You want to give $6,000 to the American College and you therefore sell this stock for your basis, or $4,000. Your realized gain is shown on the following page.

The rules for determining basis that apply to bargain sales also apply when mortgaged property is donated and the charity assumes the mortgage. The transfer is treated like a sale, with the purchase cost being the mortgage that the charity agrees to pay. In the case of both bargain sales and mortgaged property, the bargain sale rule does not apply unless the exchange produces a charitable deduction.

Fair market value of stock		$10,000
Minus sale proceeds		−4,000
Charitable contribution		$ 6,000
Sale proceeds		$ 4,000
Tax basis in property sold:		

$$\text{Sale price } \frac{\$4{,}000}{\text{Fair value } \$10{,}000} \times \text{basis of } \$4{,}000$$

		−1,600
Gain realized		$ 2,400

The courts have allowed owners of closely held corporations to withdraw funds from their firms tax-free by means of charitable contributions followed by a redemption: The owner gives stock to charity and at a later date the corporation redeems the stock. The donor is allowed a charitable contribution deduction, even though an understanding exists between the donor and donee that the stock will be redeemed shortly after contribution, where redemption is not required.

The valuation for the gift of stock is the average of the high and low sales price reported on the date of the gift.

EASEMENTS ON BUILDINGS IN HISTORIC DISTRICTS

You cannot claim a deduction for a contribution of an easement on a building in a registered historic district made after July 25, 2006, unless the contributed interest includes restrictions preserving the entire exterior of the building (including front, sides, rear, and height) and prohibiting any change to the exterior of the building inconsistent with its historical character. If you claim a deduction for this type of contribution in a tax year beginning after August 17, 2006, you must include with your return a qualified appraisal, photographs of the building's exterior, and a description of all restrictions on development of the building.

FILING FEE FOR EASEMENTS ON BUILDINGS IN HISTORIC DISTRICTS

A new $500 filing fee must be paid for each qualified conservation contribution after February 12, 2007, that is an easement on a building in a registered historic district, if the claimed deduction is more than $10,000. See Form 8283-V, Payment Voucher for Filing Fee.

ATHLETIC EVENTS

In Rev. Rul. 86-63, 1986-1 C.B. 6, the IRS ruled that if you make a contribution to an educational institution where athletic games are regularly sold out in advance and in return receive the right to buy tickets to those games, you cannot take a charitable contribution deduction for the amount contributed. This has been congressionally overruled.

Retroactive to tax years beginning after December 31, 1983, 80 percent of the cost of the right to obtain preferred seating at athletic events of a college or university was deductible. No amount paid for the purchase of *tickets*, whether paid separately or as part of a lump-sum payment that includes the right to purchase tickets, is deductible as a charitable contribution. The Tax Cuts and Jobs Act of 2017 eliminated the 80% deduction as of January 1, 2018. Booster clubs are not happy.

CONTRIBUTION OF SERVICES

No deduction exists for the contribution of your services. However, unreimbursed expenses incurred during the rendering of free services for a qualified charity are deductible as charitable contributions.

Any cost incurred in traveling from your house to where you served is deductible. *A standard mileage rate* of 14¢ per mile is allowed if you use your car. Or you can choose to deduct your actual unreimbursed expenses for gas and oil. Parking fees and tolls are also deductible. No deduction is given for depreciation, insurance, or repairs on the car. Donating blood is considered the contribution of services and thus no deduction is allowed.

A deduction for reasonable outlays for meals and lodgings is also allowed if incurred while away from home. In addition, deductions have been allowed for the cost of baby-sitting services for children whose parents were performing services for charitable organizations.

UNIFORMS

A deduction is allowed for the cost of uniforms used while performing charitable services as long as the clothing isn't suitable for everyday wear. *Classic examples*: you can write off the cost of Boy Scout or Girl Scout uniforms, Salvation Army uniforms, Santa Claus suits for charitable events, etc.

CONSERVATION EASEMENTS

A conservation easement is a binding agreement between a landowner and a nonprofit group called a land trust that places development restrictions on the

property. The reduction in value is deductible up to 50 percent of your AGI, with a 15-year carryforward for unused contributions.

LIFE INSURANCE POLICIES AND OTHER DONATIONS

If full rights of ownership are contributed, a gift of a life insurance policy is acceptable as a charitable gift. Any subsequent payments of premiums by the donor will also qualify as charitable contributions. Even a single premium whole life payment for the benefit of a charity would be allowed (PLR 200209020). The amount of the deduction for this type is its fair market value (LTR. RUL. 9147040).

Dues, admission charges, etc., where you receive property or benefits can only be deducted if they exceed the value of the benefits received for them. Amounts paid for raffle tickets, bingo, or similar chance games and losses on games of chance are not deductible charitable contributions.

Where amounts are paid in connection with admission to fund-raising affairs for charity, you must show that a clearly identifiable segment of the payment is a gift, and only this amount will qualify. The same rule applies whether or not the tickets are actually used. If you have no intention of using the tickets, you should give them back and make a gift of the purchase price. Using this approach, you will get the full amount as a deduction.

Donations of less than your entire interest in property are not deductible, but there are certain exceptions to this rule. For example, the transfer of a remainder interest in a personal residence or a farm is deductible. Also, the contribution of an undivided portion of your entire interest in property will qualify for the deduction. But a gift of one week's use of a vacation property to a charity yields no deduction for rental value—it was less than the entire interest.

A charitable remainder gift made during your lifetime is also deductible, based upon the value of the remainder interest. The Internal Revenue Service tax code requires that a fixed percentage be paid to one or more persons for a specified term of years (not to exceed 20) or for the life or lives of the income beneficiaries, with an irrevocable remainder to be paid to the charitable organization. If the remainder interest to the charity is subject to a contingency, it is not deductible. In addition, the value of the gift must be readily determinable.

CHARITABLE REMAINDER TRUSTS

The ability to take a deduction today for a gift of a remainder interest to a charity has led to the creation of charitable remainder trusts. You would contribute appreciated property (stocks, real estate, etc.) to the trust in exchange for an income stream over your lifetime—either a fixed amount each year (an annuity trust) or a given percent of the value of the trust annually (a unitrust).

The value of what is projected to go to the charity at your death (you can use multiple lives) is deductible today!

This value is a function of your age and life expectancy (based on IRS tables), the income stream you are receiving, and the assumed rate of return that the trust is expected to generate (the "applicable federal rate" which is published monthly by the IRS).

The advantages of the CRT are:

1. You and the trust pay no tax on the sale of the appreciated asset.

2. Therefore, you get a potentially much higher income stream during your life.

3. You get an immediate tax deduction even though you keep the income stream.

4. You can use the tax savings from the immediate tax deduction to purchase a life insurance policy to replace the value of the asset that goes to the charity at your death.

5. Structured correctly, life insurance can be removed from your estate. Your heirs after the estate tax may have more wealth go to them from a $500,000 life insurance policy not in your estate, than from $800,000 assets had you not transferred them into the CRT.

PROOF

You are required to provide information in support of all of your deductions; therefore, you should be able to prove all charitable contributions through receipts, canceled checks, etc. If a contribution is made in property other than money, you should state the kind of property contributed, the method used in ascertaining the fair market value of the property at the time the contribution is made, and whether the amount of the contribution is reduced because the property is either ordinary income or capital-gain property.

If you contribute property other than money valued in excess of $500, you must attach Form 8283 to the income tax return with the following information:

a) the name and address of the donee organization;

b) the date of the actual contribution;

c) a description of the property;

d) the manner of acquisition;

e) the fair market value of the property at the contribution time and the method utilized in determining the fair market value; *and*

f) the cost or other basis of the property.

Salvation Army Valuation Guideline

Ladies Clothing	Low	High
Blouse	$2.50	$12.00
Bathrobes	2.50	12.00
Boots	2.00	5.00
Bras	1.00	3.00
Bathing Suits	4.00	12.00
Coats	10.00	40.00
Dresses	4.00	19.00
Evening Dresses	10.00	60.00
Fur Hats	7.00	15.00
Fur Coats	25.00	400.00
Foundation Garments	3.00	8.00
Handbags	2.00	20.00
Hats	1.00	8.00
Jackets	4.00	12.00
Nightgowns	4.00	12.00
Pant Suits	6.50	25.00
Socks	.40	1.25
Suits	6.00	25.00
Shoes	2.00	25.00
Skirts	3.00	8.00
Sweaters	3.00	15.00
Slips	1.00	6.00
Slacks	3.50	12.00

Men's Clothing	Low	High
Jackets	$7.50	$25.00
Over Coats	15.00	60.00
Pajamas	2.00	8.00
Pants-Shorts	3.50	10.00
Raincoat	5.00	20.00
Suits	15.00	60.00
Slacks	5.00	12.00
Shirts	2.50	12.00
Sweaters	2.50	12.00
Shoes	3.50	25.00
Swim Trunks	2.50	8.00
Tuxedo	10.00	60.00
Undershirts	1.00	3.00
Undershorts	1.00	3.00
Belts Ties	3.00	8.00

Children's Clothing	Low	High
Blouses	$2.00	$8.00
Boots	3.00	20.00
Coats	4.50	20.00
Dresses	3.50	12.00
Jackets	3.00	25.00
Jeans	3.50	12.00
Pants	2.50	12.00
Snowsuits	4.00	19.00
Shoes	2.50	8.75
Skirts	1.50	6.00
Sweaters	2.50	8.00
Slacks	2.00	8.00
Shirts	2.00	6.00
Socks	.50	1.50
Underwear	1.00	3.50

Dry Goods	Low	High
Blankets	$2.50	$8.00
Bedspreads	3.00	24.00
Chair Covers	15.00	35.00
Curtains	1.50	12.00
Drapes	6.50	40.00
Pillows	2.00	8.00
Sheets	2.00	8.00
Throw Rugs	1.50	12.00
Towels	.50	4.00

Furniture (Complete Sets)	Low	High
Bedroom Set	$250.00	$1000.00
Dining Room Set	150.00	900.00
Kitchen Set	35.00	170.00
Bed Complete (dbl)	50.00	170.00
Bed Complete (sgl)	35.00	100.00

Furniture	Low	High
Air Conditioner	$20.00	$90.00
Bar	30.00	75.00
Bar Stools	10.00	20.00
Bed (dbl) Complete	50.00	170.00

Furniture (Continued)	Low	High
Bed (sgl) Complete	$35.00	$100.00
Bicycles	15.00	65.00
Chest	25.00	95.00
Clothes Closet	15.00	50.00
China Cabinet	85.00	300.00
Convertible Sofa (w/Mattress)	85.00	300.00
Crib (w/Mattress)	25.00	100.00
Carriage	5.00	100.00
Chair (Upholstered)	25.00	75.00
Coffee Table	15.00	65.00
Dresser w/Mirror	20.00	100.00
Desk	25.00	140.00
Dryer	45.00	90.00
Electric Stove (Wkg)	75.00	150.00
End Tables (2)	10.00	50.00
Figurines (Lg.)	50.00	150.00
Fireplace Set	30.00	90.00
Floor Lamps	7.50	40.00
Folding Beds	20.00	60.00
Gas Stove	50.00	125.00
Heaters	7.50	22.00
High Chair	10.00	50.00
Hi Riser	35.00	75.00
Kitchen Table	25.00	60.00
Kitchen Cabinets	25.00	75.00
Kitchen Chair	2.50	10.00
Mattress (dbl)	35.00	75.00
Mattress (sgl)	15.00	35.00
Organ Console	75.00	200.00
Piano	75.00	200.00
Pictures and Paintings	5.00	200.00
Ping-Pong Table	15.00	40.00
Play Pen	15.00	30.00
Pool Table	20.00	75.00
Record Player (Stereo)	30.00	90.00
Record Player (Components)	30.00	200.00
Rugs	20.00	90.00
Refrigerator (Wkg)	75.00	250.00

Furniture (Continued)	Low	High
Radio	$7.50	$50.00
Secretary	50.00	140.00
Sofa	35.00	200.00
TV (B/W Wkg)	25.00	60.00
TV (Color Wkg)	75.00	225.00
Trunk	5.00	70.00
Wardrobe	20.00	100.00
Washer (Wkg)	50.00	150.00
Waterbed Frame	15.00	40.00
Waterbed Headboard	30.00	90.00
Waterbed (Complete)	150.00	325.00

Sporting Goods	Low	High
Bicycles	$15.00	65.00
Fishing Rods	5.00	25.00
Ice/Roller Skates	10.00	40.00
Skis	15.00	100.00
Sleds	5.00	20.00
Tennis Rackets	5.00	40.00
Toboggans	15.00	90.00

Miscellaneous	Low	High
Adding Machine	$20.00	$75.00
Christmas Trees	15.00	50.00
Broiler Oven	15.00	25.00
Copier	100.00	200.00
Home Computer	150.00	500.00
Mimeograph Machine	100.00	200.00
Mixer	5.00	20.00
Mannequins	25.00	200.00
Mower (Riding)	100.00	250.00
Mower (Auto)	10.00	100.00
Power Edger	5.00	25.00
Rototiller	25.00	90.00
Sewing Machine	15.00	75.00
Snow Blower	50.00	150.00
Telephone Ans. Mach.	25.00	75.00
Typewriter	7.50	35.00
Vacuum Cleaner (Wkg)	20.00	60.00
Wigs	5.00	25.00

Wkg = Working

My favorite valuation source is itsdeductible.com. It's a great way to prove your deductions. Another excellent third-party valuation guideline can be downloaded from www.salarmychicago.org/frames/extd_your_help/donations .htm or check out bigwriteoff.com. For a vast database on charities, see www.guidestar.org.

Expert witnesses are frequently brought in during Tax Court cases to evaluate contributed property. The burden is on the individual to establish the value of the contribution.

An appraisal may be your best method to avoid an audit, especially if the property is difficult to value and a substantial contribution is involved. An added attraction is that the appraiser's fees are also deductible.

For other gifts, have the charity value the gift and send you a receipt. This will establish the proof necessary for a gift and may avoid valuation difficulties. Taking out an insurance policy reflecting the property's value might also be a useful technique for establishing the true value of the property.

Furthermore, for tax years beginning after 1982, IRS Proposed Regulation Section 1.170 A-13 (a) would require an individual taxpayer (or a corporation) making a charitable contribution of money to maintain a cancelled check, a receipt, or other reliable written evidence showing the amount of the charitable contribution, the date contributed, and the name of the donee. In the absence of a cancelled check or receipt, the reliability of the other written evidence will depend on the facts and circumstances of the particular case but, in all events, the burden would be on the taxpayer to establish reliability. Factors indicating that such other written evidence is reliable include, but are not limited to, the contemporaneous nature of the writing evidencing the contribution, the regularity of the taxpayer's recordkeeping procedures, and, in the case of the contribution of a small amount, any other written evidence from the donee charitable organization evidencing receipt of a donation that would not otherwise constitute a receipt.

For charitable contributions of property other than money for which the taxpayer claims a deduction in excess of $500, the taxpayer would be required to maintain additional records regarding the manner of acquisition of the property and the property's cost or other basis if it was held for one year or less prior to the date of contribution. For property held for more than one year preceding the date of contribution, cost or other basis information should be maintained by the taxpayer if it is available. Fill in and file the appropriate forms. *In RERI Holdings LLC*, TC, Dec. 60, 954, the failure to fill in the space for the donor's cost or other basis lost the deduction. But you deduct fair market value.

The Tax Reform Act of 1984 mandated the Internal Revenue Service to issue regulations, by December 31, 1984, which would impose appraisal and information reporting requirements on charitable contributions by individuals, closely held corporations, and personal service corporations. Appraisals will be required for each item with a claim value in excess of $5,000 ($10,000 for privately held stock). Similar items are to be added in determining the dollar threshold.

This provision would not apply to publicly traded securities. When the rules apply, the donor must obtain a written appraisal of the property's fair market value from a qualified independent appraiser, and a summary of the appraisal must be attached to the donor's tax return.

If the donee charity sells, exchanges, or otherwise transfers donated property valued in excess of $5,000 within 2 years, the donee must furnish an information report to the IRS, with a copy to the donor. These provisions apply for contributions made after December 31, 1984.

Note that if a taxpayer contributes works of art with an aggregate value of at least $20,000, the taxpayer must attach a complete copy of the signed appraisal. In addition, an eight-by-eleven-inch color photograph, or a color transparency no smaller than four by five inches, must be submitted. For donations made after 1987, the submission of the appraisal is mandatory. It was optional for art donated before 1988.

For this purpose, the definition of art includes paintings, watercolors, prints, drawings, sculptures, ceramics, antique furniture, decorative arts, textiles, carpets, silver, rare manuscripts, historical memorabilia, and other similar objects. It does not include gems, jewelry, or books.

These requirements are intended to assist the IRS Art Advisory Panel, which is composed of art dealers, curators, museum directors, and other experts, in checking the valuation of artwork for tax purposes. An evaluation of $20,000 or more must be referred to the panel.

The Internal Revenue Service said that its Art Advisory Panel accepted just 36 percent of the taxpayer art appraisals it reviewed in 2007, a drop of 2 percent from the 38 percent acceptance rate in 2006, according to the agency's annual summary of the panel's closed-door meetings. Nearly half the artwork donated/gifted was found to be misvalued by the panel in 2010, 51 percent misvalued in 2012.

Taxpayers claimed their artwork was worth nearly $279 million for tax purposes; the panel recommended $94.5 million in adjustments across 131 cases.

The Omnibus Budget Reconciliation Act of 1993 changed the substantiation and disclosure rules for charitable contributions. Effective for years after December 31, 1993, no deduction will be allowed for a separate contribution of $250 or more unless you have written confirmation from the charity. E-mail acknowledgments by the charity are acceptable. A cancelled check alone will not be enough. If the contribution is to a religious organization solely for an intangible religious benefit, written substantiation is still required but the charity need not value that benefit. All other contributions of cash must describe the estimated fair market value of any goods or services given in exchange for that contribution. Charities, however, are not required to value noncash contributions if you, as the taxpayer, are required to obtain from the charity a receipt that describes the donated property.

Moreover, any *quid pro quo* contributions of more than $75 solicited will require the charity to tell you in writing how much is deductible; e.g., a charitable dinner ticket costing $90 for a dinner worth $60 will give you a deduction of $30.

In *Rolfs v. Commissioner of Internal Revenue* (T.C. No. 9377-04, 135 T.C. No. 24, November 4, 2010), a taxpayer donated his house to a fire department tox burn down as part of a training exercise. (See below for details.) The Court disallowed a deduction because the taxpayer received the benefits of the destruction of the house in exchange for the donation. In this case, the value of the demolition was more than the fair market value of the house. Any "quid pro quo" will kill the deduction to the extent of the benefit received.

NEW RECORD KEEPING REQUIREMENTS

As of January 1, 2007 you will need a receipt or cancelled check for all donations. For clothing and household items donated after August 17, 2006, no write off will be allowed unless an item is in good condition or better. If the value of an item is more than $5,000, a deduction cannot be taken without an appraisal.

An interesting technique exists for obtaining a charitable deduction before a cash outlay. This can be done by establishing an irrevocable banker's letter of credit in favor of the charity. The full amount of the letter of credit will be deductible by you in the year in which it is established, even if the charity does not draw upon the credit until the next year. The charity, however, must have the absolute right to draw down the entire amount of the letter of credit immediately. This technique could present an important planning opportunity when you can reasonably expect that the charity would not draw down the funds immediately. For example, when the letter of credit will finance a construction project, it is reasonable to expect the charity to draw down those funds over the various phases of the construction, rather than immediately.

The tax saved from a charitable donation reduces the cost of donating. As the marginal tax rates increase, the actual cost of donating decreases. The actual cost to a person in the lowest tax bracket (10 percent) for a $1 charitable deduction is 90¢. For a person in the highest tax bracket (37.0 percent), the actual cost is only 63.0¢ on the dollar.

BEWARE

Any contributions to a *nonexempt* organization will not be allowed. In *United Cancer Council v. Commissioner,* Docket No. 2008-91X, 109 T.C. No. 17, 12/2/97, the court ruled that the charity's use of a professional fundraiser resulted in inurement of the organization's net earnings to the fundraiser and the IRS did not abuse its discretion in *retroactively revoking* the exempt status of the organization. Fortunately, this decision was reversed by the Seventh Circuit on February 10, 1999.

Beware once more: The IRS is currently focusing on "overvalued" contributions of autos. If you take the deduction, be prepared to fully substantiate the value.

AUTOS/BOATS

The American Jobs Creation Act of 2004 changed the rules for contributions of autos and boats of more than $500. Effective as of January 1, 2005, the charity receiving the donated vehicle must tell you the actual price it sold for—and your donation is limited to that amount. The charity must give you a 1099-C within 30 days of the sale. You attach it to your return. This may be far different than the Bluebook value usually deducted. If the auto is used by the charity (e.g. a car used for Meals on Wheels), then you get to deduct the full fair market value.

DON'T GET BURNED

Taxpayers who demolished their lakefront home to make way for the construction of a new home by donating it to the local fire department to conduct firefighter training exercises benefited from the home's destruction and cannot claim a charitable deduction, the U.S. Court of Appeals for the Seventh Circuit held February 8, 2012 (*Rolfs v. Commissioner,* 7th Cir., No. 11-2078, 2/8/12).

The value *gifted* was found to be less than the benefit received. The value *gifted* was reduced by the "must destroy" limitation.

"No one disputes that $76,000 worth of home value was lost in the fire," wrote the court. "The disagreement concerns the portion of that value, if any, that was actually transferred to the fire department as a gift. By deciding to destroy the house and then making that demolition a condition of their gift, the taxpayers themselves became responsible for that decrease in value, even if the fire department provided the mechanism to accomplish it. None of the value of the house, as a house, was actually given away."

The solution? Gift the house with no limitations.

SCHNEPPER CONTRIBUTION

Want to donate money to a charity and make a profit? Check out the *Schnepper Contribution* on page 458.

PARTIAL INTERESTS

Want to donate the right to use your vacation home for a week? You get no deduction, because you gave only a partial interest in the property . . . and the buyer gets no deduction either unless the cost was in excess of the fair market value of the week.

100 Casualty Losses

A *casualty* is the damage or destruction of property resulting from an identifiable event that is sudden, unexpected, or unusual in nature. Casualty losses can be used to lower your taxes.

Deductible casualty losses may result from a number of different causes, including but not limited to:

Automobile accidents
Civil disturbances
Drought
Earthquakes
Explosions
Fires
Flood
Freezing rain
Hurricanes
Ice and snow
Lightning
Mine cave-ins
Shipwrecks
Smog
Sonic booms
Storms
Vandalism
Winds and tornadoes

A reduction in your property's value because it is in or near an area that suffered a casualty or that might again suffer a casualty is usually not deductible. A neighbor of O. J. Simpson was denied a deduction for the reduction in value of his property due to its proximity to the murder. However, in *Finkbohner, Jr.*, 86-1 USTC para. 9393, 57 AFTRO 2d 86-1400 (CA-11, 1986), a permanent decline in market value due to buyer resistance was includable in the amount of a casualty loss deduction. There, the court refused to follow the prevailing view in two other circuits that limited the deduction to actual physical loss. In the *Finkbohner* case, the taxpayers' residence was unharmed, but 7 of the 12 houses in the neighborhood had to be razed after a flood. The court ruled that the removal of most of the homes in the neighborhood was a permanent change. The diminished market value reflected more than a fear of future flooding, since the residence was above maximum flood levels. They concluded that the fair market value after the casualty would have to reflect such permanent loss of value. A loss is allowed only for the actual casualty damage to your property.

The partial or complete destruction of property must be the result of an identifiable event that is either sudden, unexpected, or unusual. For example, if your spouse, while washing the dishes, inadvertently knocks a diamond ring that you put in a glass next to the sink down the drain and activates the garbage disposal unit, thus destroying the ring, this unusual event will qualify as a deductible casualty. So, too, will the loss of a diamond ring if your spouse slams

the car door on your hand. Both of the events were sudden and unusual, therefore allowing the casualty deduction. However, a loss due to the accidental breakage of articles such as glassware or china under normal conditions is not a casualty loss. Neither is a loss due to damage done by a family pet.

The event must be one that is sudden—that is, swift, not gradual or progressive. If a steadily operating cause from a normal process damages your property, it is not considered a casualty. So, for example, the steady weakening of a building due to normal wind and weather conditions will not qualify as a casualty. On the other hand, the rust and water damage to rugs and drapes caused by the bursting of a water heater will qualify—but not the deterioration and damage to the water heater itself. The IRS has ruled that a decline in the value of a house due to chinese drywall is eligible for casualty loss treatment.

If trees, shrubs, or other plants are damaged or destroyed by a fungus, disease, insects, worms, or similar pests, the loss is not deductible as a casualty loss. However, a sudden, unexpected, or unusual infestation by beetles or other insects may result in a casualty loss. If trees and shrubs are damaged by a storm, flood, or fire, the loss is also a deductible casualty loss.

Normally a loss from an accident to your car is deductible. This is not true, though, if your willful negligence or willful act causes the accident, or if it is caused by the willful act or willful negligence of someone acting for you.

If you do have an accident, you must file a claim with your insurance company. If you do not file the claim, you will not be entitled to a casualty loss deduction for the damage done to your car. Casualty loss deductions are allowed only for losses not compensated for by insurance or otherwise. But "not compensated for" doesn't just mean actual payment. When a collectible insurance claim *can* be filed, a deliberate election not to file will not give rise to a casualty loss deduction. Your loss can be "compensated for."

Yet in a 1981 case the Tax Court allowed a theft loss deduction despite a refusal to make an insurance claim predicated on a fear of increased premiums.* The court concluded that *compensated* did not mean *covered* and that since no *compensation* was received, a deduction could be allowed. This ruling was confirmed in the case of *Dixon F. Miller v. Commissioner* on May 2, 1984; the Sixth Circuit joined the Eleventh Circuit and the Tax Court in taking the above position. The Tax Reform Act of 1986, however, imposed a new precondition on the allowance of casualty losses. Any loss that is covered by insurance is taken into account only if the taxpayer files a timely insurance claim. This new limitation applies only to the extent that the insurance policy would have provided reimbursement if a claim had been filed (IRC § 165[a][4][i]).

For example, if you sustain $800 worth of damage for an insured loss with a $500 deductible, if no claim is made $300 of your loss will not be allowable

H.L. Hills, 76 T.C. No. 42.

as a deduction. The $500 balance will count as a loss, subject to the $100 and 10 percent adjusted gross income floors.

You should deduct your casualty loss in the year of occurrence. This timing rule is modified, though, when insurance enters the picture. In such a case, the loss deduction is limited to the part of the damage that is not reimbursed that year. If you deduct a casualty in the year of occurrence and receive insurance reimbursement in a later year, you should not amend the earlier return. Instead, the portion of the reimbursement that exceeds the original estimate of recovery should be taken back into income in the later year.

For example, you suffered a $6,000 deductible loss in 2017 and estimated an insurance recovery of $5,000, and you took a $1,000 casualty loss deduction in that year. In 2018, however, your insurance company pays the full $6,000. What you must do on your 2018 return is include the extra $1,000 as income. Note, though, that you must have received a tax benefit for the casualty loss in 2017. If you did not itemize your deductions in that year, you received no benefit and therefore have no additional taxable income when the insurance company repays the full $6,000 in 2018.

The amount of loss from a casualty that can be deducted is generally the lesser of the following two amounts:

a) the decrease in the fair market value of the property as a result of the casualty; *or*

b) your basis in the property before the casualty.

In the case of business property, if the fair market value of the property immediately before the casualty is less than the adjusted basis, the amount of the adjusted basis is deemed to be the amount of the loss. Alternatively, the loss may be measured by the cost of repairing the damage. In a case of nonbusiness (or personal use) property, the deduction is the amount by which the casualty loss exceeds 10 percent of your adjusted gross income plus $100.

The fair market value must be based on a valid judgment of the selling price of the property at the time of the casualty. An appraisal is the best way to do this. The appraisal should be made by an experienced and reliable appraiser. Several factors are important in evaluating the accuracy of the appraisal:

- The appraiser's familiarity with your property before the casualty
- Sales of comparable properties
- Conditions in the area of the casualty
- The method used in making the appraisal

When available, photographs should be used in making the appraisal and in determining the extent of damage from a casualty. The costs of photographs

obtained for this purpose are not a part of the loss but can be taken as a miscellaneous deduction. They are an expense of determining your tax liability. Furthermore, you may deduct as a miscellaneous deduction the amount you must pay for the appraisal itself, since it also is an expense of determining your tax liability.

The cost of cleaning up or making repairs after a casualty may be used as a measure of the decrease in fair market value if:

a) the repairs are necessary to restore the property to its condition before the casualty;

b) the amount spent for repairs is not excessive;

c) the repairs do no more than take care of the damage;

d) the value of the property after the repairs is not, as a result of the repairs, more than the value of the property before the casualty.

The cost of restoring landscaping to its original condition may also be taken as an indication of the decrease in fair market value. You may be able to measure your loss by what is spent on the following:

- Removing destroyed or damaged trees and shrubs, minus any salvage you receive

- Pruning and other measures taken to preserve damaged trees and shrubs

- Replanting that is necessary to restore the property to its approximate value before the casualty

The incidental expenses you have due to a casualty, such as expenses for the treatment of personal injuries, for temporary housing, or for a rental car, are not deductible as casualty losses. Moreover, the cost of protecting your property against a potential casualty is not deductible. For example, you cannot deduct what you spend on insurance or to board up your house against a storm. Expenses like these are only deductible by businesses as business expenses. If you make a permanent improvement to your property to protect it against a casualty, the cost should be added to your basis in the property. An example would be the cost of a dike to prevent flooding.

THE TAX CUTS AND JOBS ACT OF 2017, AS OF JANUARY 1, 2018, LIMITS CASUALTY LOSSES TO THOSE IN PRESIDENTIALLY DECLARED DISASTER AREAS UNDER SECTION 401 OF THE ROBERT T. STAFFORD DISASTER RELIEF AND EMERGENCY ASSISTANCE ACT.

101 Theft Losses

A *theft* is the unlawful and intentional removal of money or property from its rightful owner. It includes, but is not limited to, larceny, robbery,

and embezzlement. If money or property is taken as the result of extortion, kidnapping for ransom, or blackmail, it may also be a theft. The simple disappearance of money or property does not constitute a theft. However, an accidental loss or disappearance of property may qualify as a casualty if it results from an identifiable event that is sudden, unexpected, or unusual in nature. The lost diamond ring in the example given in the previous section constitutes such a deductible casualty.

The amount of loss from a theft that can be deducted is generally the lesser of the following two amounts:

a) the decrease in the fair market value of the property as a result of the theft, *or*

b) your basis in the property before the theft.

The fair market value of property immediately after a theft is considered to be zero. That is, a theft loss deduction is either the full fair market value of the stolen property or its basis, whichever is less. If you get your stolen property back, however, your loss is measured like a casualty loss from vandalism. You must consider the actual fair market value of the property when you get it back in order to compute your loss.

The decrease in the fair market value must be based on a judgment of the actual price you could have asked if your property had been sold. Sentimental value is not a factor in determining the amount of the loss. Any loss from the theft of a family portrait, heirloom, or keepsake must be based on its actual market value apart from any sentiment. An appraisal is the best way to make this judgment. This appraisal must recognize the effect of any general market decline that may occur so that any deduction is limited to the actual loss resulting from deprivation of the property. See the preceding section on casualty losses for more information on appraisals.

The cost of any theft-preventive equipment, such as burglar alarm systems or theft insurance, is not deductible. If a protective device increases the value of your property, however, the cost may be added to your basis.

Investors *cannot* deduct the decline in the value of their stock portfolio as a theft loss, even if due to corporate misconduct (IRS Notice 2204-27). You get the deduction when you sell.

MADOFF DEDUCTION

If you suffered losses as a result of the Bernard L. Madoff "Ponzi" scheme, they are allowable as "investment" theft and are not subject to either the 10 percent or $100/$500 reductions (see page 539).

DEDUCTION LIMITS

The limits and computations for determining both casualty and theft loss deductions are very similar, so they are now grouped together for ease of discussion.

After you have figured the amount of your casualty or theft loss, you must figure how much of the loss you can deduct. There are three ways that you may adjust the casualty or theft loss before you can deduct it:

1. If you receive insurance or another type of reimbursement for your loss, you must subtract the reimbursement from the amount of the loss before you figure your deduction. As noted above, if you expect to get a reimbursement but have not yet received payment, you must still subtract the expected reimbursement from the loss. In a business situation, though, the cost of repairs made for business purposes *is* deductible, even if insurance recovery later is likely. The amount of the final recovery that is attributable to previously deductible items will be taxable in the later year.*

2. If the stolen, destroyed, or damaged property was for your own or your family's personal use, you must reduce each loss by an additional $100,† because the first $100 of a casualty or theft loss on personal use property is not deductible. However, if you used the stolen, destroyed, or damaged property in your business or for investment purposes, this $100 limit does not apply.

3. For nonbusiness losses, you must reduce the *total* amount of the losses by 10 percent of your adjusted gross income. This is done after the $100 reduction in adjustment 2 above and after any reimbursement from insurance. Note that under the Tax Reform Act of 1984, for purposes of computing the 10 percent floor, the casualty loss deduction (adjusted gross income) is determined without regard to the application of Section 1231 to gains or losses from involuntary conversions arising from a casualty or theft. Gains and losses from these personal casualties (without regard to the period the property was held) will be netted. If the recognized gains exceed the recognized losses from these transactions, then all such gains and losses will be treated as gains and losses from the sale or exchange of a capital asset, and the losses will not be subject to the 10 percent floor. (The amount of any recognized loss will be subject to the $100 floor before netting.) If the recognized losses exceed the recognized gains, all gains and losses will be ordinary. Losses to the extent of gains will be allowed in full. Losses in excess of gains will be subject to the 10 percent adjusted gross income floor.

*R.R. Hensler, Inc. v. Commissioner, T.C. 317 (1979).
†For 2009 casualty losses *only*, the $100 floor increased to $500.

For example, assume you have $100,000 of adjusted gross income without regard to casualty gains and losses, $50,000 of such casualty gains, and $40,000 of such casualty losses (after applying the $100 floor) for a taxable year. All your personal casualty gains and losses for that year will be treated as capital gains and losses. The 10 percent floor will not be applicable. Assume, however, that your losses for the year are $70,000 rather than $40,000. The gains and losses will all be treated as ordinary. $60,000 of losses will be allowed as a deduction [$50,000 plus the $10,000 excess of the remaining $20,000 over the $10,000 (10 percent of $100,000) adjusted gross income floor].

If an insurance company reimburses you for any of your living expenses after you lose the use of your home because of a casualty, the insurance payments are not considered a reimbursement reducing your casualty loss. Any part of these payments that covers normal living expenses that you and your family would have during this period anyway must be reported as income on your tax return, but any insurance payments that cover a temporary increase in your living expenses should *not* be reported as income. The same rule applies if you are denied access to your home by government authorities due to the threat of a casualty. Generally, the amount you do not have to report is the amount of your extra expenses for renting suitable housing and for transportation, food, utilities, and miscellaneous services during the period you are unable to use your home because of the casualty.

For example, assume that as a result of a fire you vacated your apartment and moved to a motel. You normally pay $200 a month rent, but none was charged for the month the apartment was vacated. Your motel rent for this month was $275, but you received only $240 in reimbursement for rental expenses from your insurance company. Part of that reimbursement, $75, covers the difference between your actual rent and your normal rent. You do not have to report this amount as income, but the balance of the reimbursement, $165, must be reported as income.

As mentioned, the first $100 of a casualty or theft loss of personal use property is not deductible. This limit applies *after* all reimbursements have been subtracted. Furthermore, a single $100 limit applies to each individual casualty or theft, no matter how many pieces of property are involved. Generally, events closely related in origin are considered a single casualty or theft, as when your summer home suffers wind damage and flood damage caused by a hurricane. A single casualty may also damage two or more widely separate pieces of property.

Remember, though, that the $100 exclusion does not apply if the loss is on business property, property that earns you rent or royalty income, or other investment property. Furthermore, if a husband and wife each sustain a loss from the same casualty or theft and they file a joint return, only one $100 limit applies. It does not matter whether the property involved is jointly or separately owned. If they file separate returns, however, each is subject to a separate $100 limit for the loss, regardless of whether the property is jointly or separately

owned. A husband and wife who file separate returns and have a casualty loss on property they own together may deduct one-half of the loss on each return, or either spouse may claim the entire deduction on a separate return.

COMPUTING THE DEDUCTION

The way to figure a deduction for a casualty or theft loss depends upon the kind of property involved. The rules for personal use property are different from those for business and investment property. The rules for real estate property, such as a house, differ from those for personal property, such as a car or furniture.

In figuring a loss to real estate property that you own for personal use, all improvements, such as buildings and ornamental trees, are considered together. A single loss is figured for the entire property. The amount of the loss is either the decrease in fair market value of the entire property or its adjusted basis, whichever is less. From this amount you must subtract any insurance or other reimbursement you receive or expect to receive. The amount remaining that is more than $100 is your personal casualty loss deduction.

As an example, assume that several years ago you bought a house that you then lived in as your home. You paid $5,000 for the land and $20,000 for the house itself; you also paid $1,000 for landscaping. This year, when your adjusted gross income was $10,000, your home was totally destroyed by fire. Competent appraisers said that before the fire the property as a whole had a fair market value of $36,000 but that its value after the fire was only $6,000. Shortly after the fire, the insurance company paid you $20,000 for the loss. Your casualty loss deduction is figured as follows:

Value of entire property before fire	$36,000
Minus value of entire property after fire	– 6,000
Decrease in value of entire property	$30,000
Basis (cost for entire property)	$26,000
Casualty loss (in this case basis)	$26,000
Minus insurance reimbursement	–20,000
Casualty loss before the $100 limit	6,000
Minus: $100 nondeductible amount	– 100
10% of adjusted gross income	– 1,000
Casualty Loss Deduction	$ 4,900

Personal property is generally any property that is not real estate. If your personal property is stolen or is damaged or destroyed by a casualty, you must figure your loss separately for each individual item of property.

For example, assume a fire in your home damaged an upholstered chair and completely destroyed a rug and an antique table. You do not have fire insurance to cover your loss. The chair cost you $150, and you establish that it had a fair market value of $75 just before the fire and $10 just after the fire. The rug cost you $200 and had a value of $50 just before the fire. You bought the table at an auction for $15 before discovering it was a valuable antique. It was appraised at $350 before the fire.

The loss on the chair is limited to the difference in fair market value before and after the fire, or $65, since that decrease is less than its basis ($150). The loss on the rug is limited to its value of $50 just before the fire, because this amount is also less than its basis ($200). The table, on the other hand, had a value just before the fire that was greater than your basis in it. Your loss on the table, therefore, is its basis, $15. Your total loss from the fire is $130, and after subtracting the $100 limit, your deduction is $30 before the reduction for 10 percent of your adjusted gross income.

When a casualty involves both real and personal property, a single $100 limit applies to the total loss, but you must figure the amount of the loss separately for each type of property, as discussed above. Remember, a loss on business property, property that earns you rent or royalty income, or other investment property is *not* subject to the $100 limit. For business and investment property, you must figure your loss separately for each item that is stolen, damaged, or destroyed. If casualty damage occurs to a building and to trees on the same piece of property, the loss is measured separately for each.

If you have business or investment property that is completely lost because of a casualty or theft, your deductible is your basis in the property minus any salvage value and minus any insurance or other reimbursement that you receive or expect to receive. For example, suppose you owned a building that you rented out, and your basis in it, not including land, was $20,000 before it was completely destroyed by fire. Its fair market value just before the fire was only $15,000.

Since this was investment property and since it was completely destroyed, the deduction is your basis in the building, $20,000, decreased by salvage value and by any insurance or other reimbursement. Fair market value is not considered when figuring your loss, even though it is less than your basis in the building.

If business or investment property is damaged but not completely destroyed in a casualty, the loss is the decrease in value because of the casualty, or your basis in the property, whichever is less. From this amount you must subtract any insurance or other reimbursements you receive or expect to receive.

After you take a casualty or theft loss deduction, you must subtract from your basis in the damaged, destroyed, or stolen property the amount of your deduction and the amount of any reimbursement you receive. The result is a new, lower total for your basis in the property. In some cases, this lower basis will carry over to any property you get to replace the property that is stolen or destroyed.

PROOF OF LOSS

To take a deduction for casualty or theft loss, you must be able to show that there was actually a casualty or theft, and you must be able to support the amount you take as a deduction. For a casualty loss, you should be able to show:

a) the nature of the casualty and when it occurred;

b) that the loss was a direct result of the casualty; *and*

c) that you were the owner of the property; or, if you leased the property from someone else, that you were contractually liable to the owner for the damage.

For a theft, you should be able to show:

a) the date on which you found that the property was missing;

b) that your property *was* stolen; *and*

c) that you were the owner of the property.

To qualify for a theft loss deduction, the taking of your property must be illegal under the laws of the state where it occurred. If a theft loss is not reported promptly to the police, you must offer as a substitute the testimony of anyone who witnessed the event or its aftermath. If records were burglarized, steps must be taken to reconstruct the records by gathering substitutes.

Proof of the amount of a theft loss is difficult in the case of cash, where there is little likelihood that there is any documentation of how much you had on your person or in your home. Deductions will be allowed in full when you have evidence of why you had such a large amount of money with you. One theft loss deduction was allowed because the records showed that the victim was on his way to complete the closing on the acquisition of a house.

You do not have to be virgin-pure to qualify for a theft loss deduction. Even if you were naive or greedy and that naïveté or greed resulted in your being the victim of a theft, you may still receive a deduction for that theft. "Indeed," according to one court, "gullibility or cupidity of the victim is often a crucial factor that enables the swindler to succeed in his fraud."*

For both casualty losses and theft losses you must be able to give evidence supporting the amount you deduct. You should have supporting evidence in the following three areas:

1. *Basis.* The purchase contract or deed can show your original basis (its cost) in real estate. Improvements to the property that increase basis should be supported by checks, receipts, and similar items.

Perry A. Nichols et al., T.C. 842 (1965).

2. *Decrease in Fair Market Value.* Appraisals should be used where possible. Photographs of your property before it was damaged or stolen will be helpful in showing its condition and value before the casualty or theft. Photographs taken after a casualty will be helpful in establishing the condition and value of the property after it was damaged. Photographs showing the condition of the property after it was repaired, restored, or replaced may also be helpful.

3. *Insurance and Other Types of Reimbursement.* Keep records of all you receive or expect to receive.

PLANNING CONSIDERATIONS

Ordinarily, a casualty loss is deductible in the year the event took place. However, the tax code permits a special election to take "disaster area" loss deductions in the year prior to occurrence. To qualify, the President must declare the region a "disaster area" eligible for federal relief under the Disaster Relief Act of 1964. Go to www.fema.gov to see if your area qualifies. Once this is done you can make an irrevocable election to treat the entire disaster loss as having occurred in the prior tax year. This allows you to get an immediate tax benefit for the loss rather than forcing you to wait until the subsequent year to claim it.

For example, assume you suffered a casualty loss in 2018. In order to get the tax benefit for that loss, it would have to be claimed as a deduction from your 2018 taxes, payable in April 2019. But if you elected and qualified for the optional disaster relief provision, you could take the disaster loss deduction on your 2017 return, by filing an amended 2017 return. Alternatively, if your income increased in 2018 and put you in a higher bracket, you could decline to make the election and take the higher valued deduction on your 2018 return.

If you were in a federally declared disaster area, for 2009 nonitemizers could have added their casualty losses to Schedule L as an increase in their standard deduction. Those who itemized could have claimed the deduction without the 10 percent adjusted gross income reduction in Schedule A.

As explained above, expenses to prevent a casualty are not normally deductible as casualty losses. Such expenditures are likely to involve the acquisition of property with an estimated useful life of more than one year. But a tax deduction *can* be claimed if the preventive measures do not add to the value of the property. In one case a plant had sustained cave-ins under its flooring, and further trouble of the same sort was anticipated. The drilling and grouting undertaken to forestall this was a deductible business expense. In another case, an individual used temporary dikes to protect his personal residence as well as his business property from flooding. The dikes were constructed of earth and sand

bags and were removed immediately after the floodwater receded. While the cost of constructing and removing the temporary dikes was not allowed as a casualty loss with respect to either the business or the nonbusiness property, the cost of constructing and removing the dikes to protect business property was deductible as an ordinary and necessary business expense. In a third case, an expense that had been incurred to prevent an accident—and *was* held to be a different kind of deduction—was the cost of a vasectomy! The moral here is simple: What you may think of only in terms of a casualty loss expense may qualify as a deduction under a noncasualty classification—for example, as an ordinary and necessary business expense or as a medical expense.

102 Miscellaneous Trade and Business Deductions of Employees

THE TAX CUTS AND JOBS ACT OF 2017, AS OF JANUARY 1, 2018, SUSPENDS ALL MISCELLANEOUS ITEMIZED DEDUCTIONS SUBJECT TO THE 2% FLOOR. THIS SUSPENSION ENDS ON DECEMBER 31, 2025. BECAUSE THE DEDUCTIONS ARE SCHEDULED TO RETURN IN 2026, THEY ARE PRESENTED AND DISCUSSED BELOW.

Prior to the Tax Reform Act of 1986, if you were an employee who had travel, entertainment, or gift expenses in connection with your employment, you would be entitled to deduct the amounts you spent in those areas as above the line deductions. For years after December 31, 1986, all trade and business deductions of employees must be taken as miscellaneous itemized deductions. As of January 1, 1987, miscellaneous itemized deductions have been allowable only to the extent that they exceed 2 percent of your adjusted gross income.

This 2 percent floor does not apply to impairment-related work expenses for handicapped employees; to gambling losses to the extent of gambling winnings; and to certain actors who are allowed to report their income and expenses from acting as if they were independent contractors, if they had two or more employers in the acting profession during the tax year, and if the expenses relating to their acting profession exceeded 10 percent of their gross income and their adjusted gross income (before deducting expenses related to acting) did not exceed $16,000. The 2 percent floor does apply to investment advisor fees for trusts (Knight vs. Com., January 16, 2008). But in Private Ruling 9316003, the IRS ruled that a partner may deduct in full (not subject to the 2 percent rule) any expenses that a partnership agreement requires him to pay.

103 Job Loss Insurance

Premiums paid by employees on job loss insurance policies can be written off as employee business expenses to the extent the cost and other miscellaneous expenses exceed 2 percent of adjusted gross income. If the employer pays for the coverage, the premiums are a tax-free working-condition fringe benefit. No matter who pays the premiums, benefits are subject to the income tax but not employment taxes.

104 Travel Expenses

If you are an employee, you may deduct as miscellaneous itemized deductions all the ordinary and necessary travel expenses, in excess of reimbursements, that you have in connection with your work.

"Ordinary and necessary" has been translated as "reasonable and customary." Travel expenses are those expenses incurred in traveling away from home for your business, profession, or job. Your tax home, for travel expense purposes, is your principal place of business or employment or your station or post of duty, regardless of where you maintain your family residence. The entire city or general area in which your business or work is located is your tax home.

For example, assume you live with your family in Chicago, but work in Milwaukee. You stay in a Milwaukee hotel and eat in a restaurant during the week and return to Chicago every weekend. You may not deduct any of your expenses for traveling back and forth, or for your meals and lodging in Milwaukee, because Milwaukee is your tax home and the travel over the weekends is not for a business reason.

If you regularly work in two or more separate areas, your principal tax home is the general area where your principal work or business is located. The main factors in determining your principal place of business or work are:

a) the total time ordinarily spent in performing your duties in each area;

b) the degree of your business activity in each area; *and*

c) the relative amount of your income from each area. (See *Bowles*, 85-1 USTC Para. 9244, 55 AFTR 2d, 85-1113 [DC Va. 1984], in which the place of the taxpayers' minor business in terms of income was held to be their tax home, since that was where they spent the majority of their time and effort.)

For example, assume you live in Miami where you have a seasonal job for 8 months and earn $15,000, and you work the remaining 4 months in Cincinnati, also at a seasonal job, and earn $4,000. Miami is your principal place of work because you spend most of your time there and earn most of your income there.

You are considered "away from home" when you are on a *temporary* (rather than indefinite or permanent) job that takes you away from your regular or principal place of business. Temporary employment must be temporary in contemplation, and its termination must be foreseeable at the time of acceptance. (See Rev. Rul. 60-189, 1960-1 C.B. 60, Rev. Rul. 60-314, 1960-2 C.B. 48, and *Flowers*, 326 US 465 [S. Ct., 1946].)

In Rev. Rul. 83-82 the Internal Revenue Service stated that employment is temporary "only if its termination can be foreseen within a reasonably short period of time." Where a taxpayer anticipates employment to last for less than 1 year its status will be determined on the basis of the facts and circumstances. Where the taxpayer anticipates employment of 1 year or more, but less than 2 years, and it in fact falls within this range, there is a rebuttable presumption that the employment is "indefinite." An expected or actual stay of 2 years or longer is considered "indefinite" regardless of other facts and circumstances.

To rebut the 1- to 2-year presumption you must (1) clearly demonstrate by objective factors that you realistically expected that the employment in question would last less than 2 years and that you could then return to your claimed tax home, and (2) show that the claimed tax home is your regular place of abode in a real and substantial sense.

The following three factors may be used to determine if point (2) is met: (1) whether you have used the claimed abode as lodging while working in that vicinity immediately before the claimed temporary employment and you continue to maintain work contacts there; (2) whether your living expenses at the claimed abode are duplicated because of your work away from such abode; and (3) whether you (a) have a family member or members (marital or lineal only) currently residing at the claimed abode or (b) continue to currently use the claimed abode frequently for lodging.

If you satisfy the expectation test and all three of the abode tests the IRS will deem the work assignment temporary. If only two of the three abode tests are met, then all the facts and circumstances will be subject to close scrutiny to determine if the assignment is temporary or indefinite. If only one of the abode tests is met the IRS will regard the assignment as indefinite.

These rules were modified in Notice 93-29, where the IRS ruled that travel expenses paid or incurred in 1993 while away from home for a period or more than *1 year* in pursuit of a trade or business will be *non*deductible even if such period began in 1992. This Notice, pursuant to the Energy Policy Act of 1992, now

even more clearly defines the difference between temporary and indefinite. (See also Rev. Rul. 93-86.)

But, in *Senulis*, TC Summ. Op. 2009–97, the court ruled that because a worker reasonably expected that a job's duration would be less than 1 year when he took it, his living expenses (meals, lodging, and travel) were deductible even though the job actually lasted 13 months!

You may also be considered as *traveling* away from home when you work in the same city in which you and your family live. Suppose your family residence is in Pittsburgh, where you work for 12 weeks a year. The remainder of the time you work for the same employer in Baltimore, where you eat in restaurants and sleep at a rooming house. Your salary is the same whether you are in Pittsburgh or Baltimore. Since you spend most of your working time and earn most of your salary in Baltimore, that city is your tax home and you may not deduct any expenses incurred for meals and lodging there. However, when you go to work in Pittsburgh, you are away from your tax home even though you stay at your family home. Therefore, you may deduct the cost of your round trip between Baltimore and Pittsburgh and that part of your family living expenses for meals due to your living in Pittsburgh while working there.

Deductible travel expenses include the following:

Air, rail, and bus fares

Operation and maintenance of your automobile

Taxi fares or other costs of transportation between the airport or station and your hotel, from one customer to another, or from one place of business to another

Transportation from the place where you eat and sleep to your temporary work assignment

Baggage charges and transportation costs for sample and display material

Meals (limited to 50 percent of cost) and lodging when you are away from home on business

Cleaning and laundry expenses

Telephone and telegraph expenses

Public stenographer's fees

Operation and maintenance of house trailers

Tips that are incidental to any of these expenses

Similar expenses incident to qualifying travel

You are considered traveling away from home if your duties require you to be away from the general area of your tax home for a period substantially longer than an ordinary day's work. It is not necessary, however, to work the full time. It is reasonable for you to need and to get some sleep or rest to meet the

demands of your work or business. This does *not* mean napping in your car to make sure you qualify for the full period. You need not be away from your tax home for an entire 24 hours or from dusk to dawn so long as your relief from duty (rest period) while you are traveling constitutes a sufficient period of time in which to get necessary sleep or rest.

For example, assume you are a railroad conductor and you leave your home terminal on a regularly scheduled round trip between two cities, returning home 16 hours later. During the run you are released for 6 hours at your turnaround point, where you eat two meals and rent a hotel room to get necessary rest before starting the return trip. You are considered to be away from home for tax travel purposes and may deduct the expenses you incur.

Alternatively, assume you are a truck driver. You leave your terminal and return later the same day. You are released at your turnaround point for 1 hour in order to eat. Since you are not released to obtain necessary sleep and the brief interval of release does not constitute an adequate rest period, you are not away from home.

Here again the opportunity for sophisticated tax planning presents itself. You may deduct all those travel expenses you incur in attending a convention if you can show that your attendance benefits or advances the interest of your own work or business, as distinguished from the business or work of another. If the convention is for political, social, or other purposes unrelated to your business or work, the expenses are not deductible. But the agenda of the convention need not deal specifically with your official duties. It is sufficient if the agenda is related to your duties and responsibilities in such a way that attendance for a business purpose is indicated.

Regardless of whether the primary purpose of your trip is business or pleasure, all expenses incurred at your destination that are properly attributable to your trade or business are deductible. So if you make a trip primarily for business and, while there, you extend your stay for nonbusiness reasons, make a nonbusiness side trip, or engage in other nonbusiness activities, the travel expenses to and from your destination are still deductible. Furthermore, you may even deduct the expenses you paid or incurred in attending *foreign* conventions in a tax year. Here, however, the allowable expenses of attending the foreign convention must be extensively substantiated: You must make a schedule for the part of the total days of the trip devoted to business-related activities and even the number of hours of business activity you attend each day, which will limit the deduction.

No deductions are allowed for any travel expenses, including meals and lodging while away from home, for any expenses generally considered entertainment, amusement, or recreation expenses, including expenses for facilities used in connection with such activities, or for any gift expenses, unless you substantiate certain elements.

For *travel* you must prove *all* of the following elements:

- The amount of each separate expenditure for travel away from home, such as the cost of your transportation or lodging. The daily cost of your breakfast, lunch, and dinner and any incidental elements of such travel may be totaled if they are listed in reasonable categories, such as meals, gasoline and oil, and taxi fares.

- The dates of your departure and return for each trip, and the number of days spent on business away from home.

- The destination or locality of your travel, described by name of city, town, or similar designation.

- The business reason for your travel or the business benefit derived or expected from your travel.

Furthermore, an *employee* who receives reimbursement from an employer for travel expenses is excused from the normal recordkeeping and substantiation requirements if the standard reimbursement and allowance rules are satisfied. Under these rules, reimbursement for actual subsistence or travel away from home—lodgings, meals, and incidentals—(exclusive of transportation to and from the destination) is limited to an amount based on your locality or the maximum per diem rate for U.S. government employees in the locality in which travel is performed. If you elect to use the optional allowance, it must be used in computing the deduction for *all* meal expenses for the year (Rev. Proc. 83-71, 1983-39 I.R.B. 19). (See Rev. Proc. 93-21, Publication 1542, Rev. Proc. 93-50, Rev. Proc. 94-77, Rev. Proc. 96-28, Rev. Proc. 96-64, Rev. Proc. 97-59, Rev. Proc. 98-64, Rev. Proc. 2000-9, Rev. Proc. 2001-47, and Rev. Proc. 2002-63.) These rates will be updated every October 1st, and you can get the latest rates at www.policyworks.gov/perdiem, or you could order a copy of Pub. 1542 from the IRS at 1-800-829-3636. The IRS updates its rates on www.irs.gov/pub/irs-pdf/p1542, or for rates outside the continental United States, including Alaska, Hawaii, Puerto Rico, and foreign countries, see www.state.gov/m/a/als/prdm/2018.

If you are *self-employed,* you can use the per diems *only* for meals. You must substantiate lodging separately.

The Tax Reform Act of 1986 further limited deductions for luxury water travel. Luxury water travel consists of travel by ocean liner, cruise ship, or other form of luxury water transportation. This rule applies, for example, in the case of a taxpayer who has business reasons for traveling from New York City to London and who travels by ocean liner. The deduction allowable for luxury water travel cannot exceed twice the highest amount generally

allowable with respect to a day of travel for employees of the executive branch of the federal government while away from home but serving the United States, multiplied by the number of days the taxpayer was engaged in luxury water travel. For example, if during a particular taxable year the applicable federal per diem amount is $75, a taxpayer's deduction for a 6-day trip cannot exceed $900 ($150 per day times 6 days). The applicable per diem amount generally is the highest travel amount applying for an area in the conterminous United States.

Moreover, after the 1986 Reform Act, no deduction is allowed for travel as a form of education. This rule applies when a travel deduction would be allowable only on the ground that the travel itself serves an educational purpose (for example, in the case of a teacher of French who travels to France in order to maintain general familiarity with the French language and culture). This disallowance does not apply, however, when a deduction is claimed with respect to travel that is a necessary adjunct to engaging in an activity that gives rise to a business deduction relating to education. (For example, when a scholar of French literature travels to Paris to do specific library research that cannot be done elsewhere or to take courses that are offered only at the Sorbonne.)

The Tax Reform Act of 1986 also amended the rules on charitable travel. As of January 1, 1987, no deduction will be allowed for transportation and other travel expenses incurred in performing services away from home for a charitable organization (whether paid directly by the individual or indirectly through a contribution to the organization) unless there is no significant element of personal pleasure, recreation, or vacation in the travel away from home.

The Tax Reform Act of 1986 also provided that travel and other costs of attending a convention or seminar for investment purposes (i.e., not for trade or business purposes) are not deductible.

All of the foregoing provisions of the Tax Reform Act of 1986 are applicable for tax years beginning after December 31, 1986.

Note, in addition, that the IRS has ruled in Doc. 9237014 that a deduction *would be allowed* for Saturday travel expenses incurred to take advantage of reduced air fares.

105 Transportation Expenses

Transportation expenses, which must be differentiated from *travel* expenses, sometimes can be deducted. Transportation expenses include the cost of traveling by air, rail, bus, taxi, etc., and the cost of operating and maintaining your car, but *not* the cost of meals and lodging.

Commuting expenses, those expenses incurred between your principal or regular place of work and your home, are not part of deductible transportation expenses. This is true regardless of the distance between your home and your regular place of work or of whether you are employed at different locations on different days within the same city or general area. If you work at two places in a day, however, whether or not for the same employer, you may deduct the expense of getting from one to the other. These expenses are part of your allowable transportation deduction. Furthermore, if you have a temporary or minor assignment beyond the general area of your tax home and return home each evening, you can deduct the expenses of the daily round-trip transportation.

If you use your car in your work, and you use it exclusively for that purpose, you may deduct the entire cost of its operation. Included among the deductible items are the cost of gas, oil, repairs, insurance, depreciation, interest to buy the car, taxes, licenses, garage rents, parking fees, tolls, etc.

If you use your car for both personal and business purposes, you must divide your expenses between business and personal use. For example, if you drive your car 20,000 miles during the year, 8,000 for business and 12,000 for personal use, only 40 percent (8,000 ÷ 20,000) of the cost of operating your car may be claimed as a work expense.

Furthermore, if you lease a car that you use in your business, you may deduct any lease payments that are for your business. You may not deduct any part of the lease payments for commuting or other personal use of the car, and any advance payments must be apportioned over the entire lease period. In addition, you may not deduct any payments you make toward the purchase of a car even if the payments are lease payments. They must be capitalized and recovered through a deduction for depreciation.

Instead of deducting your actual itemized automobile transportation costs, you may deduct a standard mileage rate. You must:

a) own the car;

b) not use the car for hire, for example, as a taxi (prior to 2011 only);

c) not operate a fleet of cars, using more than four at the same time;*

d) not have claimed depreciation using any method other than the straight-line method (equal depreciation over the life of the asset); *and*

e) not have claimed additional first-year depreciation on the car.

In addition to the standard mileage rate, you can also deduct any tolls, interest, taxes, and parking fees paid. Of the standard rate for 2018, 25¢ a mile constitutes an allowance for depreciation, reducing your basis in the car.

*Prior to Rev. Proc. 2003-76, the rule was more than one.

Standard Mileage Rates, 2002–2017

Year	Rate
2002	36.5¢
2003	36.0¢
2004	37.5¢
2005	40.5¢/48.5¢ (after Sept. 1)
2006	44.5¢
2007	48.5¢
2008	50.5¢/58.5¢ (after July 1)
2009	55.0¢
2010	50.0¢
2011	51.0¢/55.5¢ (after July 1)
2012	55.5¢
2013	56.5¢
2014	56.0¢
2015	57.5¢
2016	54.0¢
2017	53.5¢
2018	54.5¢

In *Wicker* (TCM 1986-1), a nurse-anesthetist maintained an automobile for travel between her office in the cellar of her home and the hospital where she performed anesthesia services. Although she served as head of the Department of Anesthesiology, no office space was provided to her at the hospital. She practiced exclusively at the hospital. The court found that her home office was her principal place of business and that her travel between her home office and the hospital was, therefore, business travel, rather than commuting. The expenses incurred in such travel were deductible.

In 2013, the U.S. Tax Court held that a music professor and jazz musician was allowed to deduct his vehicle expenses for travel to performance activities as business or unreimbursed employee expenses because the expenses were ordinary and necessary (*Scully v. Commissioner*, T.C., No. 17784-10, T.C. Memo. 2013-229, September 30, 2013).

If you are reimbursed or receive an allowance for your car expenses, you may use the standard mileage rate to determine the cost of operating your car. However, only the cost so figured that is more than your reimbursement or allowance may be deducted.

If you and your spouse have separate cars, *each* one of you can compute the deduction by claiming 54.5¢ per mile (Notice 2014-79). You can use the optional mileage rate even if you do not own the vehicle (Section 1.274(d) IT).

Moreover, the Internal Revenue Service has stated that depreciation will be considered to have been allowed for standard mileage property at the following rates per mile:

1980–1981	7.0¢
1982	7.5¢
1983–1985	8.0¢
1986	9.0¢
1987	10.0¢
1988	10.5¢
1989–1991	11.0¢
1992–1993	11.5¢
1994–1999	12.0¢
2000	14.0¢
2001–2002	15.0¢
2003–2004	16.0¢
2005–2006	17.0¢
2007	19.0¢
2008–2009	21.0¢
2010	23.0¢
2011	22.0¢
2012–2013	23.0¢
2014	22.0¢
2015	24.0¢
2016	24.0¢
2017	25.0¢
2018	25.0¢

This per mile rate, according to the IRS, will be the "depreciation" used to adjust the basis of standard mileage property.

Most important, a car you acquire will qualify for the depreciation expense if it is used in your work or business. The deduction for transportation expenses may in effect reduce your net cash outlay for a new car to less than half its cost!

For example, assume you are in the 35 percent bracket and you bought a $17,000 car in 2018 that you used 100 percent for business. You elected to expense and depreciate the first $3,160 of the car's cost. You elected 5-year class recovery life for the car. If you ran the car 30,000 miles in its first year, your net cost for the acquisition of the car can be reduced to almost half of its cost as follows:

Cost of car		$17,000
Minus 2018 election to expense and depreciation		
$18,000 × .35		−6,300
Net cost of car		$10,700
Minus expenses:		
30,000 miles @ 15 mpg =		
2,000 gallons @ $2.75/gal	$5,500	
Repairs, oil, and upkeep	900	
Insurance	1,210	
Garage rent, license, & registration	2450	
Tolls, parking, interest on auto loan, etc. ($6/day)	2,190	
Total expense	$12,250	
Tax saving ($12,250 × .35)		−4,288
Final Net Cost ($10,929 − $4,288)		$6,412

Let's still assume that you are in the 35 percent bracket. Let's see what would happen if you run the car only 60,000 miles over the first 5 years. Employing the appropriate tax-saving strategy above, your net cost would be zero!

Cost of car		$17,000
Minus: election to expense and depreciation ($17,000 × .35)		−5,950
Net cost of car (end of fifth year)		$11,050
Minus expenses:		
60,000 miles @ 15 mpg =		
4,000 gallons @ $2.75/gal	$11,000	
Repairs, oil, and upkeep	3,285	
Insurance	6,050	
Garage rent, licenses, and registrations	12,250	
Tolls, parking, interest on auto loan etc. ($6/day)	+10,950	
Total expenses	$43,535	
Tax savings ($43,535 × .35)		−$15,237
Net cash *saved*		$4,187
After car cost *below* zero		

As the cost of gas goes up, so does your tax savings. But, your net cash flow would be hurt by the increased cost. Also note that this is a generic example.

106 Meals and Entertainment Expenses

THE TAX CUTS AND JOBS ACT OF 2017 ELIMINATES THE DEDUCTION FOR ENTERTAINMENT AS OF JANUARY 1, 2018. MEALS (NOT PART OF ENTERTAINMENT) ARE STILL ALLOWABLE, AS BELOW:

Not only can you deduct the above travel and transportation expenses, but you can also take as additional miscellaneous deductions certain entertainment expenses. Entertainment expenses may be deducted if you can show that the entertainment of prospects has a direct effect on and can reasonably be expected to increase or maintain earnings or your commissions.

These entertainment expenses must be ordinary and necessary (reasonable and customary) and must be incurred in the course of your work. You may deduct entertainment expenses only if you can show that your employer required or expected you to have such entertainment expenses in connection with your work.

You must prove *all* the following elements for entertainment deductions:

- The amount of each separate expenditure for entertaining, except for incidental items such as taxi fares and telephone calls that may be totaled on a daily basis
- The date the entertainment took place
- The name, address or location, and type of entertainment, such as dinner or theatre, if the information is not apparent in the name or designation of the place
- The reason for the entertainment or the business benefit derived or expected to be gained from entertaining and, except for certain business meals, any business discussion or activity that took place
- The occupation or other information about the person or persons entertained, including the name, title, or other designation sufficient to establish the business relationship to you

Effective January 1, 1987, *entertainment expenses* were allowed only to the extent of 80 percent of what was spent. Exceptions allowing full deductibility include (a) expenses reimbursed by an employer (in which case the employer is subject to the percent rule); (b) traditional employer-paid recreational expenses for

employees (e.g., holiday parties); (c) items given as compensation to the recipient that are excludable from income as *de minimis* fringe benefits; (d) items made available to the general public (e.g., as promotional activities); and (e) tickets to certain charitable fund-raising sports events. Ticket costs in excess of face value are not deductible, except with regard to tickets for charitable fund-raising sports events. Moreover, deductions for the rental or other use of a sky box at a sports arena are disallowed, to the extent in excess of the cost of regular tickets, if the box is used by the taxpayer for more than one event. This sky box disallowal of deductibility was subject to a 3-year phase-out starting January 1, 1986.

The Tax Reform Act of 1986 also reduced to 80 percent the amount of deductions otherwise allowable for *business meal expenses,* including meals away from home and meals furnished on an employer's premises to its employees. Exceptions allowing full deductibility include (a) employee meal expenses reimbursed by the employer (in which case the employer is subject to the percent rule); (b) employer-furnished meals that are excludable from the employee's income as *de minimis* fringes (including subsidized eating facilities); (c) meals taxed to employees as compensation; and (d) items sold to the public (such as the cost of food to restaurants) or furnished the public as samples or for promotion. Moreover, the meals, to be deductible at all, must be directly related to or associated with a business discussion—i.e., "quiet" business meals are no longer deductible.

The Omnibus Budget Reconciliation Act of 1993, effective for years beginning after December 31, 1993, reduced the 80 percent deduction to 50 percent. The Act also eliminated, after December 31, 1993, all deductions for club dues, including airline and hotel clubs. Club meals may still be deducted if they satisfy the above standards for deductibility.

107 Gifts

You may deduct ordinary and necessary (reasonable and customary) expenses for business gifts made directly or indirectly to any individual. The total value of business gifts to any one individual during the tax year cannot be more than $25. If a gift is not intended for the eventual personal use or benefit of a particular individual or a limited class of individuals, the gift is not considered to be made to an individual.

A gift to the spouse or child of an individual with whom you are doing business is a gift to that individual. However, if one spouse has an independent bona fide business connection with you, such a gift generally will not be considered a gift to the other spouse unless it is intended for that spouse's eventual use or benefit.

An item costing $4 or less on which your name is clearly and permanently imprinted and which is one of a number of identical items distributed by you is not subject to the $25 rule. This includes such items as pens, desk sets, plastic bags, and cases. In addition, incidental costs, such as jewelry engraving or packaging, insuring, and mailing or other delivery costs, are not generally included in determining the cost of a gift for the $25 rule.

A related cost will be considered incidental only if it does not add substantial value to the gift. For example, although the cost of gift wrapping will be considered an incidental cost, the purchase of an ornamental basket for packaging fruit will not be considered an incidental cost of packaging if the basket has a value that is substantial in relation to the value of the fruit.

Furthermore, it must be remembered that we are dealing here with gift, entertainment, travel, and transportation expenses of *employees*. Any of these expenses incurred by employers may be deductible for adjusted gross income as trade or business deductions.

You must prove *all* the following to be allowed a deduction for business gifts:

- The cost

- The date of the gift

- A description of the gift

- The reason for giving the gift or any business benefit derived or expected to be gained from giving it

- The name, title, occupation, or other information about the person receiving the gift, or some other designation sufficient to establish the business relationship to you

KEEP PROOF OF EXPENSES

Substantiation of travel, meals, entertainment, and business gift expenses should be kept in an account book, diary, statement of expense, or similar record, supported by adequate documentary evidence that together can support each element of an expenditure. For example, entries on a desk calendar, not supported by evidence, are not proper proof. The simple rule here, therefore, is to keep receipts and records. For example, if you take a business associate out to dinner, simply jot the associate's name and the general topic of discussion on the back of the receipt given to you by the restaurant.

Note that under DOC 9805007, faxed or e-mailed documents qualify as documentary evidence for meal and entertainment substantiation.

In the area of such deductions there is no such thing as too much documentation. If these deductions are questioned by the Internal Revenue Service, the only things an audit agent will look for are receipts. Therefore, *always* remember to get a receipt, note the cost of the expenditure, the person to whom it relates, and your business relationship. A total of 30 seconds of effort may guarantee you $100 of unquestioned deductions. If your 2018 taxable income is more than $82,500, you're in at least the 24 percent bracket and that 30 seconds of effort would have saved you $24 in taxes—that's the equivalent of $2,880 an hour—even more than most tax attorneys make!

108 Reimbursable Employee Business Expenses

Normally, when reimbursement is available to an employee for a business expense incurred, if the employee does not obtain that reimbursement, no deduction is allowed [*Podems,* 24 T.C. 21 (1955)]. However, in *Kessler* (T.C. Memo 1985-254), the court ruled that if a taxpayer can establish that reimbursement, though nominally available, is unavailable as a practical matter, then out-of-pocket business expenses should be allowable as a deduction. (See also *Jetty,* T.C. Memo 1982-378.) The Tax Court's position was reinforced and supported by the Internal Revenue Service in Action on Decision 1986-011, on January 8, 1986, wherein a recommendation was made that the IRS acquiesce in *Kessler.*

109 Educational Expenses

Educational expenses incurred to maintain or improve your skills in your current position are deductible as a miscellaneous itemized expense. In a private letter ruling (PLR 8706048), the IRS held that a financial consultant may deduct the cost of obtaining a Master of Science degree in financial planning. The taxpayer was a financial consultant and the degree was sought in order to maintain and improve the taxpayer's financial planning skills. If the education will qualify you for a new trade or business or is a minimum requirement for your current job, that education expense is not deductible. In the private letter ruling the Internal Revenue Service held that a master's degree in financial planning was not a minimum requirement for the taxpayer's job as a financial consultant and did not qualify the taxpayer for a new trade or business. Therefore, the taxpayer's expenses for tuition and books incurred

in obtaining the degree in financial planning were deductible as ordinary and necessary expenses.

As a general rule, however, if you earn a degree that makes you eligible for a new trade or business, there is no deduction for tuition. The real key is your intent at the time you take the course. For example, in one case, after 23 years in the accounting field, a CPA attended law school at night. He took all the tax courses he could at law school, intending to improve himself as an accountant. He did not intend to go into the practice of law and in fact did not. His purpose was not to obtain a new position or advancement in position. His only intent was to improve his skills as an accountant. The expense of going to law school in this case was deductible (*Berry*, T.C. Memo 1971-110). In *Singleton-Clarke*, T.C. Summ. Op. 2009-182, the court allowed a $15,000 MBA tuition deduction for a registered nurse. She met the criteria.

Alternatively, the U.S. Tax Court held that a pharmaceutical salesman who was unemployed for part of the tax year couldn't deduct as an unreimbursed employee expense his tuition for a master of business administration program, because he wasn't carrying on a trade or business (*Hart v. Commissioner*, T.C. Docket No. 23893-12, T.C. Memo 2013-289, December 23, 2013).

Judge Kathleen Kerrigan said that being qualified to engage in a trade or business wasn't the same as "carrying on" a trade or business for the purpose of deducting an expense under tax code Section 162.

The taxpayer, Adam Edward Hart, claimed a deduction for $17,138 for an MBA program tuition for the 2009 tax year. Hart enrolled in the program in January 2009 and also was employed with a pharmaceutical distribution company from January through April 2009. Hart became unemployed in May, began working in August as an account manager with a nonpharmaceutical business, was briefly unemployed in October, and then began working as an entry-level professional with Walgreen Co.

Kerrigan found that Hart wasn't in a trade or business because he had graduated from college only 2 years prior to beginning the MBA program, worked for the pharmaceutical company for only 4 months while he was enrolled in the program, and failed to link his position at Walgreen Co. to cancer pharmaceutical sales. In my opinion, this was a poor decision by the court.

Another poor decision, in my opinion, was *Czarnecki v. US*, US Court of Federal Claims 2017-2 U.S.T.C ¶50,378 (Oct. 13, 2017) where the court ruled that education that "could" lead to a new trade or business was enough to deny the deduction even if there was no intent or other requirements were necessary to enter the field. I don't think that was the intent, or the wording, of the law.

110 Limit on Itemized Deductions

Under the Omnibus Budget Reconciliation Act of 1990 (OBRA), a new limit was put on itemized deductions. For regular tax purposes, the new law establishes a floor that you must exceed before your itemized expenses are deductible. The 2009 floor for all taxpayers, regardless of filing status (except married filing separate, where it was 1 percent* in excess of $83,400), was 1 percent of the amount of your adjusted gross income (AGI) exceeding $166,800 (indexed for inflation). Medical expenses, casualty and theft losses, and investment interest expenses were not subject to the floor, and the deduction cannot reduce by more than 80 percent your otherwise allowable deductions.

Example: If your 2009 AGI was $266,800, you had to knock $1,000 ($100,000 × 1 percent) off the bottom line of your Schedule A. So each thousand dollars of excess income lops off $2.80 of tax benefits in the 28 percent bracket or $3.50 in the 35 percent bracket.

However, the slicer would not cut your itemized deductions by more than 80 percent (and does not apply at all when computing AMT). Better yet, the 80 percent stopper did not include deductions for medical expenses, investment interest, and casualty or gambling losses.

Note that this reduction applied after the other deduction limits, e.g., 10 percent medical and 2 percent miscellaneous.

There was no reduction for 2010, 2011, or 2012. In 2013, the limits returned as per below:

Phase-out Threshold	2013	2014	2015	2016	2017
Married filing jointly	$300,000	$305,050	$309,900	$311,300	$313,800
Head of household	$275,000	$279,650	$284,050	$285,350	$287,650
Unmarried	$250,000	$254,200	$258,250	$259,400	$261,500
Married filing separately	$150,000	$152,525	$154,950	$155,650	$156,900

Your total itemized deductions were now reduced by 3 percent of the excess of your AGI over the above numbers. You can't lose more than 80 percent of your total. Medical expenses, investment interest, casualty losses, and all other gambling losses were exempt from this cutback.

* The 1 percent figure for 2008 and 2009 was 2 percent for 2007. For 2017, it was 3 percent.

This cutback added up to 1.19 percent to your marginal rate.
**THE TAX CUTS AND JOBS ACT OF 2017 SUSPENDED THIS LIMIT ON
ITEMIZED DEDUCTIONS UNTIL JANUARY 1, 2026.**

C Schedules of Deductions

111 Medical Deductions

Abortion
Acupuncture
Advances for lifetime care
Ambulance hire
Apartment rent
Artificial teeth or limbs
Autoette wheelchair
Automobile expenses
Birth control pills
Braille books and magazines
Capital expenditures in excess of
 property's increased value
Central air conditioning
Clarinet lessons
Commutation costs
Computer medical data bank
Contact lens insurance
Cosmetic surgery (limited)
Crutches
Dental care
Diagnostic services
Drug or alcohol therapy centers
Education aids
Elastic stockings
Employee medical plans
Eyeglasses
Guide dogs
Guide for blind individual
Handrails

Hearing aids and component parts
Hospital care
Invalid spouse
Iron lung
Kidney transplants
Laetrile
Last illness expenses
Lip reading
Massages
Mattresses and boards
Meals and lodging if part of
 hospital or treatment charge
Meat diet
Medical insurance premiums
Medical transportation
Medical travel
Medicare B
Medicinal liquors, if prescribed
Medicines and drugs
Nonlocal medical transportation
 costs
Nurse's transportation expenses
Nursing homes and homes for the
 aged
Nursing services
Operations affecting childbearing
Operations and treatments in
 general
Organic foods

Outdoor elevator
Oxygen and oxygen equipment
Paint removal
Patterning exercises
Physician's fees
Prepaid medical insurance
Prosthetic devices
Psychiatric or psychoanalytic care
Reclining chair
Remedial reading
Retirement homes
Salt-free diet
School for the physically or
 mentally handicapped
Sexual therapy
Smoke-ending program, if to
 cure specific disease
Special foods or beverages
Special home for mentally
 retarded

Special plumbing fixtures
Specially designed automobiles
Swimming pool
Telephone equipment
Throat treatment
Transporting patient's relative
Tutoring fees
University medical plan, if charges
 separately stated
Unlicensed practitioners
Vasectomy
Vitamins, if prescribed
Voluntary payments for
 Medicare A
Water fluoridation device
Wheelchair
X-ray treatment

112 Deductible Taxes

Taxes imposed by state, city, and
 possessions of the United States
Auto registration (to the extent
 that it is based on value)
Income (except where claimed as
 credit)
Personal property
Real property
Foreign taxes
Income, war profit, excess profit
 (unless claimed as credit)
Real estate

*If paid or accrued in connection
 with business or for the
 production of income,* you can
 also deduct these taxes:
Federal taxes
 Excise
 Import duties
 Liquor
 Railroad Retirement
 (employers)
 Social Security (employers)
 Tobacco
 Unemployment (employers)

State and local taxes
 Admission
 Auto registration
 Beverages
 Cigarettes
 Cosmetics
 Driver's license fees
 Excise
 Liquors
 Mortgage
 Occupancy
 Sales/Use
 Stamp
 Stock transfer
 Tobacco
 Transfer (except estate, inheritance, legacy, succession, and gift taxes)
 Unemployment

113 Charitable Deductions

Aid to evacuees
Artwork contributed by owner
Automobile expenses
Bargain sales to charity
Benefit performances
Book samples
Charitable travel
Church bonds, if donated after purchase
Church building funds
Church dues
Church repairs
Civil Defense volunteer's out-of-pocket expenses
Community chests
Credit card contributions
Delegate's expenses
Domestic fraternal societies
Essays
Excess rent
Eyeglass donations
Films and tape recordings
Foster parent's expenses
Future interest in tangible personal property
Government contributions
Home for elderly
Hospital fees
Installment notes
Insurance policies
Inventory donated
Legal expenses donated
Maintaining student in home
Medical equipment
Membership in art or fine arts association
Music manuscripts
Ordinary income property
Out-of-pocket charitable expenses
Partial interest in property
Patents donated
Promissory notes
Property donated
Rent in excess of fair rental value
Scenic easement
Tickets donated for resale

Uniforms
Unmarried pregnant women
 programs

Volunteer fire companies
Volunteer income tax assistance
War veterans' organizations

114 Casualty and Theft Loss Deductions

Accidents
Airplane, train, and other
 transport crashes
Appraisal fees
Automobile damage
Bomb damage
Casualty and theft losses of
 investment property
Chinese drywall
Cleanup and repair costs
Confiscation by foreign
 government
Disaster area losses
Driveway breakup
Earthquake or earth slide
Explosion
False representation or pretenses
Fire
Flood
Freeze
Hurricane
Insect and disease damage to trees
 and shrubs, if sudden

Lightning
Loss of property used partly for
 rental and partly for personal
 purposes
"Madoff" thefts
Mine cave-ins
Razing
Shipwrecks
Smog
Snow
Sonic boom
Storms
Swindles
Theft of business property
Theft of personal property
Thin ice
Tornado
Vandalism
Water damage (as from burst water
 heater)

115 Miscellaneous Deductions

Attorney fees paid by spouse to
 secure taxable alimony
Bad debts
Bar examination fee (amortizable)
Bond premium amortization
Gambling losses (to extent of
 gambling gains)
Job-hunting expenses

Labor union dues and assessments
 for noninsurance purposes
Physician's hospital privilege fee
 (amortizable)
Tax counseling costs
Tax litigation expenses
Tax return preparation
Uncollectible debts
Uncollectible loans

116 Employee Miscellaneous Deductions

Automobile expenses (allocatable
 to business)
 Depreciation
 Garage rent
 Gasoline and oil
 Insurance
 Parking fees
 Repairs for business cars
 State inspection and registration
 fees
 Taxes
 Tolls
 Washing
Briefcase
Christmas gifts to customers
 (limited)
Convention expenses

Dues (except "Club Dues")
 Business association
 Labor unions
 Professional societies
Educational expenses (limited)
Employment agency fees
Entertainment expenses
Fidelity bond costs
Gifts to customers and prospects
 (limited)
Insurance premiums
 Automobile (to extent of
 business use)
 Bonds (fidelity, etc.)
 Malpractice
Job-hunting expenses

Labor unions, initiation fees, dues, fines, assessments for pension funds

Laundry and cleaning while traveling away from home

Legal fees to protect future employment*

Meals or lodging while traveling away from home

Office furnishings†

Outside sales business expenses

Passport fees for business travel

Reimbursed expenses (if reimbursement included in income)

Safety equipment

Subscriptions to professional journals and magazines

Tax return preparation

Technical periodicals

Telephone

Tips

Tools

Transportation expenses

Traveling expenses

 Baggage charges

 Fares

 Laundry and cleaning while away from home

 Meals and lodging while away from home

 Passport fees, if for business

 Sample rooms

 Taxis

 Telephone and telegraph messages

 Tips

Tuition fees

Uniforms not adaptable to general wear

Work clothes

117 Investor Deductions

Investors can deduct expenses incurred to produce or collect income and to conserve, manage, or maintain income-producing property. Anyone who owns securities, rents real estate, or owns other investments should not overlook the typical deductions in the following list.

*Renkiewicz, et ux. v. Commissioner, T.C. Memo 2001-1.

†For example, office furnishings bought by an executive with his own funds to maintain his image as a successful district sales manager (Leroy Gillis, T.C. Memo 1973-96).

Accounting fees
Advertising expenses
Alterations and repairs
Attorneys' fees
Auditing expenses
Bad debts
Bookkeeping expenses
Collection of rent costs
Custodian fees
Damages paid for breach of
 contract or lease
Depreciation
 Buildings
 Furniture and fixtures
Exchange of asset losses
Expenses of successfully resisting
 condemnation of property
Fire insurance premiums
Franchise taxes
Heat and light
Interest
Investment counseling costs
Leasehold improvements
Leases
 Amortization of improvements
 by lessee
 Amortization of lease acquisition
 costs
 Rentals paid
 Repairs made by lessee
 Taxes paid by lessee
Legal expenses
License taxes and fees (limited)
Losses (to extent not covered by
 insurance)
 Abandonment of worthless
 interest in real estate
 Bad debts
 Demolition of building

Forced sales
Foreclosure
Forfeitures
Property sales
Property seized by government
Maintenance of property costs
Management expenses
Mortgage foreclosure losses
Moving expenses of machinery
 and equipment
Night protection services
Office rent
Porter and janitor services
Recordkeeping costs
Redecoration costs
Refuse and waste removal expenses
Repairs
Safe-deposit boxes
Salaries
Sales of assets losses
Stationery and supplies
Tax counseling costs
Tax return preparation
Taxes (state)
 General sales (add to basis)
 Gross income
 Income
 License fees (limited)
 Motor fuel
 Personal property
 Real estate
 Stamp
 Stock transfer (adjust basis)
 Transfer of property (except
 estate, inheritance, legacy, gift,
 etc.) (adjust basis)
Traveling expenses
Worthless bonds and stocks

Traditional Tax Shelters

"As a citizen, you have an obligation to the country's tax system, but you also have an obligation to yourself to know your rights under the law and possible tax deductions. And to claim every one of them."

DONALD ALEXANDER
former Commissioner of the Internal
Revenue Service under three presidents

"The tax laws reflect a continuing struggle among contending interests for the privilege of paying the least."

LOUIS EISENSTEIN
The Ideologies of Taxation

"When Congress talks of tax reform, grab your wallet and run for cover."

Senator STEVE SYMMS of Idaho

The art of sophisticated tax planning requires you to understand the elements of tax-sheltered investments. These investments allow you to offset certain "artificial losses"—noneconomic losses, but losses that are available as deductions under the present tax laws, and not only against the income from those investments but also against your other income from your regular business or professional activity.

Often, tax shelters have been described by the unsophisticated as gimmicks or "loopholes." Nothing could be further from the truth. These laws were adopted by Congress after careful deliberation, with the purpose of serving some major economic or social goal. Therefore, when you utilize these techniques you are not only improving your financial position, but you are also furthering a legitimate national economic goal. For example, the allowance of percentage depletion for oil and other tax provisions for mineral development have been effective incentives to investments in petroleum exploration and discovery. These attractive tax benefits have encouraged other taxpayers to provide the risk capital needed to bring into production many useful sources of oil that would otherwise go untapped. Special tax benefits for equipment leasing and life insurance also serve national economic and social goals.

The Internal Revenue Service, in a manner of speaking, sometimes finds itself involved in a shelter. For example, all of the staff at the regional IRS headquarters in New York are in a shelter. It seems the office building housing the Internal Revenue Service in New York was sold to a tax shelter syndicator.

Among those who have invested in tax shelters are former Attorney General William French Smith and former Internal Revenue Service Commissioner Roscoe Egger, Jr. Clearly, tax shelters are investments that you should consider if appropriate.

THE TAX REFORM ACT OF 1986

The Tax Reform Act of 1986 significantly affected the attractiveness of traditional tax shelters. The 1986 Reform Act effectively limits losses from passive trade or business activities (limited partnership tax shelters, etc.), generally to offset passive income. What this means is that, effectively, tax shelter losses can be used only to offset tax shelter gains. Passive income does not include portfolio income—e.g., dividends on stocks and interest on bonds—or gain from the sale of stocks and bonds, nor does it include income from the rental of property to an entity in which you materially participate. You can't claim passive income from renting personally owned equipment to a partnership you manage. (But see Chapter 9 to learn how to use a trust for your kids to accomplish the same thing.)

The following discussion explains the Tax Reform Act and details the remaining potential alternative tax shelter vehicles.

The passive loss rules are sweeping provisions that in general deny any individual, estate, trust, closely held C corporation, or personal service corporation the use of losses or credits generated in "passive activities" to offset other income such as salary, interest, dividends, and active business income. Deductions from passive activities may offset income from passive activities. Credits from passive activities generally are limited to the tax attributable to income from passive activities.

Disallowed losses and credits are carried forward and treated as deductions and credits from passive activities in the next taxable year. Suspended losses from an activity are allowed in full when the taxpayer disposes of his entire interest in the activity in a fully taxable transaction. Suspended credits may not be claimed in full in the year in which the taxpayer disposes of the interest in the passive activity. Rather, they are carried forward until used to offset tax liability from passive income. However, upon a fully taxable disposition of a passive activity, taxpayers may elect to increase the basis of property immediately before the transfer by an amount equal to the portion of any suspended credit that reduced the basis of the property for the taxable year in which the credit arose.

If a closely held C corporation (other than a personal service or S corporation) has "net active income" for any taxable year, the passive activity loss for the taxable year will be allowable as a deduction against net active income. A similar rule applies in the case of any passive activity credit of the taxpayer. The term *net active income* means the taxable income of the taxpayer for the taxable year determined without regard for any income or loss from a passive activity and any *net portfolio income*.

PASSIVE ACTIVITY DEFINED

In general, the term *passive activity* means any activity that involves the conduct of any trade or business and in which the taxpayer does not *materially participate*.

It also includes any rental activity of either real or tangible personal property regardless of whether the individual materially participates. With respect to equipment leasing, short-term rental to various users (where the lessor provides substantial services) is an active business rather than a passive activity.

In general, working interests in any oil or gas property that the taxpayer holds directly or through an entity that does not limit the taxpayer's liability with respect to such interests will be treated as an active trade or business and will not be subject to the passive loss rules.

The passive activity limitations *do not apply* to real estate if you're in the "real property business" that requires substantial activity. Just owning a rental

property doesn't put you in the "real property" business. You must spend over 50 percent of your time and at least 750 hours per year to qualify.

MATERIAL PARTICIPATION DEFINED

In general, a taxpayer will be treated as materially participating in an activity only if the taxpayer is involved in the operations of the activity on a regular, continuous, and substantial basis.

All limited partnership interests are treated as not materially participating.

Management decision making by an individual may constitute material participation if such services are substantial and bona fide. For example, when management services are rendered on a full-time basis, and the success of the activity depends on the exercise of an individual's business judgment, such services constitute material participation. The test applies regardless of whether an individual owns an interest in the activity directly or through a pass-through entity such as a general partnership or an S corporation.

Taxpayers who own working interests in oil and gas properties through a limited partnership will be subject to the passive loss rules with respect to that interest. That is notwithstanding the special exclusion for working interests in oil and gas properties.

In 1988, the IRS attempted to clarify the definition of "material participation" and provided special standards for limited partners. A taxpayer who is not a limited partner is a material participant in an activity during the tax year if one of the following tests is met:

1. The taxpayer participates for more than 500 hours.

2. The taxpayer's participation represents substantially all participation in the activity by individuals (including nonowners).

3. The taxpayer participates for more than 100 hours, and no other individual's participation in the activity exceeds that of the taxpayer.

4. The activity is a significant participation activity for the tax year, and the taxpayer's total participation in all significant participation activities for the year exceeds 500 hours.

5. The taxpayer has materially participated in the activity for 5 of the 10 preceding years.

6. The activity is a personal service activity in which the taxpayer has materially participated for any 3 preceding years.

7. In light of the facts and circumstances, the taxpayer participates in the activity on a regular, continuous, and substantial basis. To satisfy this

facts-and-circumstances test, the taxpayer must have at least 100 hours of participation.

Limited partners materially participate in an activity only if they meet one of tests 1, 5, or 6, above.

A *significant participation* activity is a new concept created by the Internal Revenue Service's temporary regulations. It is any trade or business activity in which the taxpayer has more than 100 hours of participation during the tax year but fails to satisfy all the material participation tests (other than test 4, above, relating to significant participation activities).

This concept is important for taxpayers involved in several trades or businesses, because it allows them to satisfy the material participation test by *aggregating* hours of participation in different businesses. However, if the taxpayer enjoys *net income* from significant participation activities during the year, that income is considered *nonpassive* and cannot be used to offset losses from other passive activities. If the significant participation activities produce a net loss, the loss is considered *passive* and must be suspended unless there is sufficient income from other passive activities to offset the loss.

NEW TEST FOR LIMITED PARTNERS

Taxpayers will not be treated as limited partners under new Internal Revenue Service rules (REG-109369-10) if they have the right to manage under either a partnership agreement or under state law, an agency official said January 10, 2012.

The right to manage includes the right to bind.

NET PORTFOLIO INCOME

In general, net portfolio income will not be included when determining the income or loss from any passive activity. Net portfolio income means gross income from interest, dividends, annuities, or royalties not derived in the ordinary course of a trade or business less expenses (other than interest) that are clearly and directly allocable to such gross income, less interest expense properly allocable to such gross income, plus gain or less loss attributable to the disposition of property held for investment or producing income such as interest, dividends, or royalties.

Any income, gain, or loss that is attributable to an investment of working capital will not be treated as income or loss from a passive activity.

This provision prevents taxpayers from placing property that would otherwise be producing active portfolio income into an entity that is subject to the passive loss rules, thereby using losses from passive activities to offset active portfolio income.

Income earned for personal services will not be taken into account in computing the income or loss from a passive activity for any taxable year. For example, if a limited partner is paid for performing services for the partnership (whether by way of salary, guaranteed payment, or allocation of partnership income), these payments cannot be sheltered by passive losses from the partnership or from any other passive activity.

TREATMENT OF FORMER PASSIVE ACTIVITIES

If an activity is a former passive activity for any taxable year and has suspended losses or credits from prior years when the activity was passive, the suspended losses may be offset against the income from the activity for the taxable year. Suspended credits allocable to such activity may be offset against the regular tax liability allocable to that activity for the taxable year. Any remaining suspended losses or credits continue to be treated as arising from a passive activity.

It appears that suspended losses and credits from a passive activity may be used to offset active income from the activity in the year in which the activity changes from passive to active and in later years. Any remaining suspended losses or credits will also be allowed as a deduction to income or credit against tax attributable to other passive activities.

If a taxpayer ceases for any taxable year to be a closely held C corporation or personal service corporation, suspended losses and credits will continue to be treated in the same manner as if the taxpayer continued to be a closely held C corporation or personal service corporation, whichever is applicable.

DISPOSITIONS OF ENTIRE INTERESTS IN PASSIVE ACTIVITY

If during the taxable year a taxpayer disposes of his entire interest in any passive activity (or former passive activity) and all gain or loss realized on such disposition is recognized, any suspended losses from the activity are no longer treated as passive activity losses and are allowable as a deduction against the taxpayer's income in the following order:

- Income or gain from the passive activity for the taxable year (including any gain recognized on the disposition)

- Net income or gain for the taxable year from all passive activities

- Any other income or gain

However, if the person acquiring the interest is a related party to the taxpayer, then any suspended losses will not apply against the taxpayer's active income

until the taxable year in which such interest is acquired by another person unrelated to the taxpayer. However, such suspended losses may be offset by income from other passive activities of the taxpayer.

To the extent that any loss recognized upon a disposition of an entire interest in a passive activity is a loss from the sale or exchange of a capital asset, the capital loss is limited to the amount of gains from the sale or exchange of capital assets plus $3,000 (in the case of individuals). The limitation on the deductibility of capital losses is applied before the determination of the amount of losses allowable upon the disposition under the passive loss rule.

For example, if a taxpayer has a capital loss of $10,000 upon the disposition of a passive activity that has $5,000 of suspended losses, the $5,000 of suspended losses are allowed, but the capital loss deduction is limited to $3,000 for the year (assuming the taxpayer has no other gains or losses from the sale of capital assets for the year). The remainder of the capital loss from the disposition is carried forward and allowed in accordance with the provisions determining the allowance of such capital losses.

PARTIAL DISPOSITION OF AN INTEREST IN A PASSIVE ACTIVITY

The 1986 law made no provision for the allowance of part or all of the suspended losses and credits attributable to a passive activity when an individual makes a partial or incomplete disposition of an interest in that passive activity. All losses and credits apparently remain suspended until offset by income from the individual's remaining interest in that passive activity or other passive activities, or until the individual completes the disposition of his entire interest in that passive activity.

DISPOSITION AT DEATH

If an interest in an activity is transferred due to the taxpayer's death, suspended losses may be deducted against income to the extent such losses are greater than the excess (if any) of the basis of such property in the hands of the transferee, over the adjusted basis of such property immediately before the death of the taxpayer. Any unused suspended losses as a result of this limitation are not allowed as a deduction for any taxable year.

For example, assume Mother owns rental real estate with a market value of $70,000, an adjusted basis of $50,000, and $25,000 of suspended losses. Mother dies and leaves the property to Daughter. The basis is stepped up to $70,000 in the hands of Daughter. Only $5,000 of the suspended losses are deductible on the income tax return of the estate. The remaining $20,000 of suspended losses (equal to the step-up in basis) is lost forever.

DISPOSITION BY INSTALLMENT SALE

If an individual disposes of an entire interest in an activity in an installment sale, suspended losses are allowed each year based on the ratio of gain recognized each year to the total gain on the sale.

DISPOSITION BY GIFT

If an interest in a passive activity is disposed of by gift, the basis of the interest immediately before the transfer is increased by any suspended passive losses allocable to the interest. Suspended losses that are added to the basis because of the gift of an interest are not allowed as deductions for any taxable year.

Moreover, the specific language of the statute appears to imply that gain on the sale of an interest in a passive activity cannot be offset with passive losses and credits from other passive activities. Only suspended or current year losses and credits from the passive activity may be used to offset gains realized on the disposition of that activity.

For example, an individual has interests in two separate limited partnerships, A and B, which are separate passive activities. Assume the following facts apply:

	A	B
Current year loss	($30,000)	($10,000)
Prior suspended losses	($70,000)	($25,000)

Assume that the individual sells his interest in B for a gain of $40,000. The full amount of the losses from partnership B, $35,000, may offset this gain. However, it appears that none of the current or suspended losses from partnership A may offset the remaining $5,000 gain.

SPECIAL RULE FOR RENTAL REAL ESTATE ACTIVITIES

In the case of rental real estate activities in which an individual actively participates, up to $25,000 of losses (and credits in a deduction-equivalent sense) from all such activities are allowed each year against nonpassive income of the taxpayer. The $25,000 amount that is allowed under this special provision is reduced by 50 percent of the amount by which the taxpayer's adjusted gross income for the taxable year exceeds $100,000. Any losses that this provision disallows in the year incurred and that carry over as suspended passive losses to later years may not be used under the $25,000 allowance in later years.

For example, an individual has $30,000 of net losses from rental real estate activities in which she actively participates. Her adjusted gross income, without regard to the net losses from the rental real estate activity, is $120,000. First, only $25,000 of her net losses are eligible for the special allowance. Second, the amount of the net loss she may deduct against active income (her adjusted gross income before deductions for net losses from rental activities)

must be reduced by $.50 for each dollar of adjusted gross income over $100,000, or by $10,000. Therefore, she may deduct $15,000 of these net losses from her adjusted gross income when computing her taxable income. The remaining $15,000 of net losses are carried forward.

The $25,000 allowance is applied by first netting income and loss from all of the taxpayer's rental real estate activities in which he actively participates. If there is net loss for the year from such activities, net passive income (if any) from other activities is then applied against it in determining the amount eligible for the $25,000 allowance.

For example, assume that a taxpayer has $45,000 of losses from a rental real estate activity in which he actively participates. If he also actively participates in another rental real estate activity from which he has $40,000 of passive income, resulting in a $5,000 net loss from rental real estate activities in which he actively participates, then only $5,000 is allowed under the $25,000 allowance for the year.

In the case of rehabilitation and low-income housing credits, the phase-out of the $25,000 allowance does not begin until the adjusted gross income of the taxpayer for the taxable year exceeds $200,000.

In the case of taxable years of an estate ending less than 2 years after the date of the decedent's death, the $25,000 allowance for rental real estate activities applies to all rental real estate activities with respect to which such decedent actively participated before his death.

Married individuals filing separate returns and living apart from their spouses at all times during the taxable year each qualify for half the $25,000 allowance. The phase-out begins for each at $50,000 rather than $100,000 for rental real estate activities other than low-income housing, and at $100,000 rather than $200,000 for low-income housing. If married taxpayers filing separate returns do not live apart from their spouses at *all* times during the taxable year, neither may use the $25,000 allowance for rental real estate activities.

If you are a "real estate professional," you may treat your real estate activities as nonpassive. Real estate agents may qualify but mortgage brokers do not (CCA 2015 04010). But even "real estate professionals" must meet the material participation tests before taking a write-off for rental losses (*Gragg*, 9th Cir. 2016). In AOD 2017-7, the IRS said it would *not* follow a federal district court's ruling that an employee and shareholder of a property management company was a "real estate professional" for tax purposes (*Stanley v. US*. W.D. Ark. 2015). To satisfy material participation, over 500 hours must be spent in the rental activity . . . or just 100 hours as long as no one else, including nonowners, puts in more time (see page 374).

RENTAL ACTIVITY

A rental activity is any activity from which gross income is derived primarily from payments for the use of tangible property. In addition, an activity may

qualify as a rental activity if the property is held out for rent, even though no rental income is received in a tax year.

There are six exceptions to the general rule. An activity involving the use of tangible property is not a rental activity in any tax year if *any one* of the following situations exists:

1. If the average rental period is 7 days or less, the activity is not considered a rental activity. This exception would exclude many resort properties from the rental category. However, the activity may remain passive if the owner does not materially participate, so the owner must be involved in the day-to-day management or operations of the activity—Treasury Reg. 1.469-5T(f)(2)(ii).

 The passive loss rules are strict for short-term rentals of real estate— average rentals of seven days or less. A couple rented out several property units, and each had rental periods averaging seven days or less. They used the companies that managed the properties to obtain tenants, collect rents, perform maintenance, and the like. They visited occasionally to buy items for the units and make repairs.

 The Taxpayers must materially participate in the units to deduct their losses, the Tax Court says. The easier-to-satisfy active participation test (see below) does not apply in the case of short-term rentals. So to deduct their rental losses, the owners must put in at least 100 or more hours a year on each unit, and their participation must be more than anyone else's. Or they must work over 500 hours on each rental. In this case, the couple did not satisfy either test (*Jende*, T.C. Summ. Op. 2011–82).

2. If the average rental period is 30 days or less and significant personal services are provided to the customers, the activity is not considered a rental activity.

3. The activity is not treated as a rental activity if extraordinary services are provided to the customers in connection with the use of the property. In order for the services to be "extraordinary," the use of the property by customers must be incidental to the receipt of such services. For example, providing a hospital room to patients would not be considered a rental activity, because the use of the room is incidental to the receipt of medical services.

4. The activity will not be treated as a rental activity if the rental is incidental to nonrental activity. For example:

 a) The property is held to realize gain for appreciation, and the gross rental income is less than 2 percent of the lesser of the unadjusted basis or fair market value of the property. This is the only situation in which rental property will be treated as property held for investment.

b) The property is generally used in a trade or business owned by the individual, and the gross rental income is insubstantial. This exception applies to property that was predominantly used in the trade or business either in the current year or in at least two of the five preceding tax years. The 2 percent test described above is used to test the substantiality of the rental income.

c) If the property is held for sale to customers in the ordinary course of business, the rental of the property will not be rental activity if the property is sold during the year.

d) Lodging rented to an employee for the convenience of the employer is not rental property.

5. If property is customarily made available for nonexclusive use by various customers during specific business hours, the activity is not a rental activity. For example, a golf course where customers either pay daily fees or purchase passes for a longer period is not considered a rental activity regardless of the average period of customer use.

6. If an owner of an interest in a partnership or S corporation provides property to be used in a nonrental activity of the entity, the partner or shareholder is not treated as being engaged in a rental activity if the property is provided in the owner's capacity as a partner or shareholder and no rent is charged.

ACTIVE PARTICIPATION DEFINED

To qualify for the $25,000 allowance for rental real estate activities, an individual must actively participate in the rental activity. Individuals will not be treated as actively participating for any period if, at any time during such period, their ownership interest (including any interest of the individual's spouse) is less than 10 percent (by value) of all interests in such activity. The degree of participation that is required once this 10 percent or more ownership threshold is met is unclear. The Conference Report suggests that the degree of participation required to meet the active participation test is less than the material participation standard.

A limited partnership interest in rental real estate does not meet the active participation requirement (except as described below for rehabilitation and low-income housing credits).

What happens to the $25,000 deduction when you have several rental real estate properties? To the extent that the aggregate loss from several active participation rental real estate activities does not exceed $25,000, the entire loss is deductible. However, where the aggregate net loss exceeds $25,000, the loss

must be allocated among activities on a pro rata basis with respect to the losses from each loss activity. For example, if a taxpayer who qualifies for the full $25,000 allowance has $10,000 of losses from one activity and $40,000 of losses from a second activity, then $5,000 is treated as allowed from the first activity and $20,000 is treated as allowed from the second activity.

This allocation is necessary in part because the suspended losses from a specific activity (those that are not deducted) are allowed in full when the taxpayer disposes of his or her interest in that activity.

Note that the IRS does not permit pro rata allocation between pre- and post-October 1986 investments. (See below for the phase-in of disallowance of losses and credits for interests held before October 23, 1986.) Where there were losses from both old (pre-October) activities and new (post-October) activities, the $25,000 allowance is applied to old activities first—that is, without proration. This generally results in a smaller amount of the loss being allowed.

For example, assume that you were an active participant in two rental real estate activities. In 1987, the loss from each was $50,000. One of the activities was acquired before October 23, 1986, and the other after. The following is a comparison of the Internal Revenue Service approach and the pro rata approach:

	IRS		**Pro Rata**	
	Pre-October 1986	*Post-October 1986*	*Pre-October 1986*	*Post-October 1986*
Loss	$50,000	$50,000	$50,000	$50,000
Allowed under $25,000 rule	$25,000	$0	$12,500	$12,500
Balance subject to 65% phase-in rule	$25,000		$37,500	
65% phase-in	$16,250		$24,375	
Total	$41,250		$49,375	

Note that the IRS method yielded an allowable loss for 1987 of $41,250 ($25,000 plus $16,250). The pro rata method would permit $49,375 of the loss to be deducted in 1987 ($12,500 plus $12,500 plus $24,375).

The following example shows you how losses are carried forward. Assume that you have invested in three separate passive activities. Activity A is an interest acquired in 1985; Activity B is an interest in a rental activity acquired in 1987; and Activity C is an interest in rental realty acquired in 1987. Also assume that your gross income is under $100,000.

	Activity A	Activity B	Activity C
	$10,000	($50,000)	($100,000)
1987 results:			
Net passive activity loss			($140,000)
Net losses from B and C			
offset against A income:			
B = $10,000 × $50,000/$150,000 =			($3,333)
C = $10,000 × $100,000/$150,000 =			($6,667)
Net loss from B offset			
against active and portfolio income			($25,000)
Loss carryforward to 1988:			
B = $50,000 − $3,333 − $25,000 =			($21,667)
C = $100,000 − $6,667 =			($93,333)
			($115,000)

Assume the following activity in 1988:

	Activity A	Activity B	Activity C
	$110,000	($20,000)	($40,000)
1988 results:			
Net passive activity loss:			
($60,000 + $115,000 NOL carryover −			
$110,000 income) =			($65,000)
Net losses from B and C			
offset against A income:*			
B = $110,000 × $41,667/175,000 =			$26,190
C = $110,000 × $133,333†/175,000 =			$83,810
			($110,000)
Net loss from B offset			
against A income:			
($21,670 + $20,000 − $26,190) =			($15,480)

Loss carryforward to 1989:

	Activity A	Activity B	Activity C
	-0-	-0-	($49,520)

*$21,667 + $20,000
†$93,333 + $40,000

REHABILITATION AND LOW-INCOME HOUSING CREDITS

In the case of the rehabilitation and low-income housing credits (but not losses), the $25,000 allowance applies on a credit-equivalent basis. This is so regardless of whether the individual claiming the credit actively participates in the rental real estate activity, including participation as a limited partner. After December 31, 1989, investors in low-income housing projects must actively participate to claim the low-income housing credit against the $25,000 allowance. However, if the property is placed in service after December 31, 1989, but before January 1, 1991, an investor will still not have to meet the active participation standard with respect to the low-income housing credit if at least 10 percent of the costs of such property are incurred before January 1, 1989.

The credit equivalent of the $25,000 allowance is $8,000 of passive credits for an individual in the 32 percent tax bracket. However, where a taxpayer has more than $250,000 of adjusted gross income, the taxpayer will generally receive no current benefit from the rehabilitation or low-income housing credit.

PLANNING

The overall effect of the passive activity loss limitation is not to *disallow* the tax benefits of a loss but to *defer* the timing of those benefits until the taxpayer recognizes income from passive activities, or until the taxpayer disposes of the entire interest in a fully taxable transaction. Consequently, the current value of any investment in a passive loss activity, relative to the value of the same investment made under the prior law, is diminished by the time value of the deferred losses.

You will have to plan carefully when evaluating any new tax-sheltered investment opportunity. The economics of the investment will be critical, as it always should have been. "Investment" planning will now be composed of two separate packages of investments: portfolio investments and passive activities.

Prospective investments in rental real estate should be evaluated primarily on their potential economic return, especially by taxpayers whose adjusted gross income exceeds $100,000 (the level at which the $25,000 allowance begins to phase out). However, rental property that qualifies for rehabilitation credits or low-income housing credits may still offer some tax benefits to taxpayers with adjusted gross incomes between $100,000 and $200,000. Income-producing limited partnerships, such as nonleveraged rental real estate, will become a popular vehicle to offset passive losses from other activities. Individuals with passive activity losses and no offsetting passive activity income

may find it advantageous to convert income from an active business into passive activity income by reducing the level of involvement in the business. Conversely, individuals with passive activity losses and little or no passive activity income could attempt to convert the passive activity into an activity in which they materially participate. The potential for this would be greatest for passive S corporation shareholders who have invested in a business but who have only marginally participated in its operation.

An alternative avenue of attack would be to attempt to generate passive income from a passive income generator (PIG). One suggestion for creating a controllable passive activity income with which to absorb passive losses is to lease real estate or equipment to a closely held corporation. That rental income will be passive and will offset passive tax-shelter losses. However, if you lease real estate or equipment to a partnership or an S corporation, such rental income, unless paid under a binding lease in effect before February 19, 1988, is recharacterized to active income, which is ineligible to offset tax-sheltered losses. The opportunity to create controllable passive activity income still exists, however, with a rental to a regular or C corporation.

Many taxpayers who actively participate in rental real estate activities may not realize that their effective marginal tax rate for income over $100,000 is considerably higher than 30 percent. The phase-out of the $25,000 allowance for income over $100,000 increased a taxpayer's effective marginal tax rate on income between $100,000 and $150,000 to 42.9 percent in 1988, 46.8 percent in 1989, 47.85 percent in 1990, and over 49 percent in 1991 and later years.

The following example computes the effective marginal tax rate resulting from the passive loss limitation by comparing two situations that are identical except for an additional income of $20,000 in 1988.

Example: In 1988, Mr. and Mrs. Couple had adjusted gross income of $120,000, not counting $25,000 of losses from rental real estate activities in which Mrs. Couple actively participated. Under the passive loss limitation rules, $19,000 of the real estate losses could be used to offset their other income. (The $120,000 of income phases out $10,000 of the loss that would be allowed under the rental real estate allowance. However, the amount disallowed under the $25,000 allowance phase-out was then subject to the more general passive loss rule under which only 60 percent was disallowed in 1988. Therefore, they were allowed $15,000 of losses under the $25,000 allowance rule and $4,000 under the general passive loss rule.) Consequently, their adjusted gross income was $101,000. After itemized deductions and personal exemptions, their taxable income was $90,000. Their tax liability is $22,237.

Mr. and Mrs. Family had an identical income pattern except for the fact that they had an additional $20,000 of capital gains. Under the $25,000 allowance phase-out rule, only $5,000 of their real estate losses was deductible (the $140,000 of income causes $20,000 to be phased out). Of the remaining $20,000 of loss, the general passive loss rule permitted $8,000 to be deducted ($20,000 reduced by 60 percent). This produced $127,000 of adjusted gross income. With the same itemized deductions and personal exemptions, their taxable income was $116,000, and their tax liability was $30,817.

Summary: Mr. and Mrs. Family's tax $30,817

 Mr. and Mrs. Couple's tax $22,237
 Tax on marginal income $ 8,580

 Effective tax rate $ 8,580
 on marginal income = --------- = 42.9%
 $20,000

A Deferral and Leverage

There normally are three elements that make up the typical tax shelter arrangement. One or more of these elements will be found in almost all tax shelters. The first is the *deferral concept,* in which deductions are accelerated in order to reduce the tax liability of an individual in the early years of the transaction instead of matching those deductions against the income that is eventually generated from the investment. This deferral of tax liability from the earlier years to the future years results, in effect, in an interest-free loan by the federal government, repayable when the investment either produces net taxable income, is sold, or is otherwise disposed of.

The other element of a typical tax shelter is *leverage,* in which borrowed funds are used in a taxpayer's investments to pay the expenses for which accelerated deductions are received. Your position is enhanced when the borrowing is on a nonrecourse basis, which means that you are not *personally* liable to repay loans and your personal investment risk is limited to your equity investment. Unfortunately, recent tax laws and Internal Revenue Service rulings have limited the availability of tax shelter investments with a nonrecourse-loan basis.

A third tax shelter element for many investments is the *conversion* of ordinary income to capital gains at the time of the sale or other disposition of the investment. Long-term capital gains are taxed at a *maximum* 20 percent rate

(23.8 percent in 2013 and after with the 3.8 percent surcharge on unearned income). For those in the 37 percent or lower brackets, the rate is not more than 15 percent. Conversion occurs when the portion of the gain reflecting the accelerated deductions taken against ordinary income is taxed as a capital gain. If you are in a lower income tax bracket in the later years, you effectively convert the tax rate as well.

The rest of this chapter will discuss several of the traditional tax shelters and examine and analyze their elements, advantages, and disadvantages. I will focus on traditional tax shelter investments—real estate, oil and gas, equipment leasing, etc. In the next chapter, I will unveil those super-sophisticated, nontraditional tax shelters that can bring your effective tax liability down to zero.

118 Real Estate

"It'd take a genius to invest in real estate and pay taxes": House Ways and Means Committee member Fortney H. (Pete) Stark, D-Calif., on the committee's decisions regarding the taxation of real estate, 1986. Of the various forms of investments available to you that involve possible tax incentives, the most widely used is real estate. Historically, real estate has been sold as an investment for income and long-term gain, as well as a hedge against inflation. Real estate can be purchased in the form of shopping centers, warehouse net leases, apartment buildings, residential housing, and even raw land.

In the decade before reform, one of the major reasons for the high degree of tax shelter investment in real estate was that the "at risk" rules introduced by the Tax Reform Act of 1976 did not apply to any partnership in which the principal activity was investing in real estate. The "at risk" rules limited your tax deductions to the amount you invested plus the amount of borrowed funds for which you were personally liable. Real estate tax shelters were exempt from this requirement until January 1, 1987 (Tax Reform Act of 1986).

Prior to 1987, the law provided an at-risk limitation on losses from business and income-producing activities other than real estate and certain active corporate business activities applicable to individuals and to certain closely held corporations. Taxpayers could deduct losses from an activity only to the extent of the amount they had at risk in the activity. The amount at risk is generally the sum of (1) the taxpayer's cash contributions to the activity; (2) the adjusted basis of other property contributed to the activity; and (3) recourse debt (amounts borrowed for use in the activity with respect to which the taxpayer has personal liability or has pledged property not used in the activity). Nonrecourse

debt (amounts borrowed for use in the activity for which none of the participants assumes personal liability and which is secured only by the assets of the activity) is not considered an amount at risk in the activity. The amount at risk is generally increased (or decreased) each year by the taxpayer's share of income (or losses and withdrawals) from the activity.

The Tax Reform Act of 1986 applied the at-risk rules to the activity of holding real property, with an exception for *qualified nonrecourse financing*. In general, taxpayers will be considered at risk with respect to their share of any *qualified nonrecourse financing* that is secured by real property used in the activity. The term qualified nonrecourse financing means any financing that is borrowed by the taxpayer (1) with respect to the activity of holding real property; (2) from a *qualified person*, or represents a loan from a federal, state, or local government, or is guaranteed by any federal, state, or local government; (3) except to the extent provided in regulations, with respect to which no person is personally liable for repayment; and (4) which is not convertible debt.

In the case of a partnership, a partner's share of any qualified nonrecourse financing of the partnership will be determined on the basis of the partner's share of liabilities incurred in connection with the financing of the partnership.

Borrowing from a "qualified person" means (1) the loan is taken from an unrelated commercial lender, or is from or guaranteed by certain government entities; (2) the property is acquired from an unrelated person; (3) the lender is unrelated to the seller; (4) the lender or a related person does not receive a fee with respect to the taxpayer's investment in the property; (5) debt is not convertible; and (6) the nonrecourse debt does not exceed 80 percent of the credit base of the property. However, nonrecourse debt acquired from related persons may still be qualified nonrecourse financing if the financing from the related person is "commercially reasonable and on substantially the same terms as loans involving unrelated persons."

An analysis of the nontax advantages of real estate investments follows.

LEVERAGE

Leverage is the use of borrowed funds with the anticipation that the property will increase in value at a rate greater than the cost of borrowing, so that a profit will be realized not only on the investor's own money but also on the use of someone else's money. For example, if you make an investment of $100, putting up $10 in cash and borrowing $90 at an interest rate of 10 percent, at the end of the first year you will have a net cash outflow of $19 (your $10 initial investment plus $9 interest on the $90 borrowed). Assume your property increases in value 20 percent

during that same period and then you sell it, paying off your $90 debt. You receive a total of $120; subtract the $99 ($90 in principal plus $9 in interest), and you have a net gain of $21. On your initial cash investment of $10, this represents a 210 percent return. You can often use borrowed capital in a real estate purchase to finance as much as 80 percent of the total cost of the property.

INFLATION HEDGE

The supply of real estate is clearly limited. For this reason, many people believe that investments in well-selected real estate can be expected to at least keep up with inflation, and perhaps even increase in value faster than inflation.

CASH FLOW

In many cases, good income-producing real property will generate a favorable cash flow. This cash flow can be augmented by increased income tax savings due to the shelter aspects of real estate investments.

EQUITY BUILDUP

Income-producing real estate may create increased liquidity. Debt reduction plus inflation may create equity that can be the source of new or additional financing.

ABILITY TO POOL CAPITAL

Syndicates or partnerships enable investors to pool their capital in order to acquire large, select properties they would not be able to buy individually.

DEDUCTIBLE EXPENSES

There are basically five different categories of expenses that are deductible on a real estate deal:

1. *Mortgage interest,* that portion of debt service payments represented by deductible interest costs.

2. *Depreciation,* an accounting adjustment that reflects the theoretical wear and tear and economic obsolescence of the property. It is the deduction for the investment you made—both borrowed and out of pocket. Because of this, a portion of the income you receive is considered a return of your capital investment and not subject to tax.

3. *Operating expenses,* which include property management, maintenance, insurance, garbage removal, real estate taxes, common area utilities, etc.

4. *Construction period expenses,* deductible expenses incurred before the building is occupied, such as real estate taxes, interest on the construction loan, etc. These costs are not deductible when incurred, but must be amortized over a period of years.

5. *Fees,* a portion of the purchase price that, frequently, the seller of the property agrees to take as payment for services, resulting in an immediate deduction—for instance, guarantees for "rent up," completion, financing, etc.

Note that you can rent living space to a relative at below the fair market rate and still treat the activity as a business entitling you to deduct depreciation, utilities, insurance, and other business expenses. The Tax Court has validated this reduced rate despite a tax code requirement that relatives be charged a "fair" rent. This is because there is less risk involved in renting to a relative than to a stranger, so the relative is entitled to a discount. In one case, the court suggested that a discount of 20 percent would be reasonable (*Lee Bindseil,* T.C. Memo 1983-411).

The tax advantage of real estate results from the possibility that your deductible expenses for tax purposes may exceed your cash outflow. Only operating expenses and mortgage interest are paid in cash from property operations. As a result, your taxable income—for instance, your rental income from the property minus the expenses listed above—does not reflect the cash flow from property operations. Your true cash flow, therefore, is your taxable income or loss plus construction period expenses and fees and depreciation minus mortgage principal payments. Construction period expenses and fees are those costs normally paid when incurred from the limited partner capital contribution or from the mortgage proceeds (but not from property operations). Depreciation is, of course, not a cash expense but rather a bookkeeping entry. Mortgage principal payments are not deductible for tax purposes because they have been included in your basis of the property and are reflected for tax purposes in your depreciation deductions.

Although land itself cannot be depreciated, many land improvements may be. In Rev. Rul. 65-256, 1965-2 C.B. 52, the Internal Revenue Service ruled that the excavating, grading, and removal costs "directly associated" with the

construction of buildings and paved roadways are depreciable. Such directly associated costs have included:

1. Grading and graveling of a private road to provide customers with access to a store and warehouse

2. Plank road and filling in and grading of swampland on which a new lumberyard was constructed

3. Expenditures for slag and for grading and building up swampland to make a level racetrack and to create roads and parking space for customers

4. A tunnel constructed under a public road between two business buildings used by a taxpayer

5. The cost of sidewalks, gutters, and drains constructed on a taxpayer's private property in a mill village

Although real estate must now be depreciated over either 27.5 years (for residential) or 39 years (31.5 years for property placed in service before May 14, 1993 unless placed in service before January 1, 1994 and there was either a binding contract or construction started before May 13, 1993), taxpayers can write off *land improvements* over just 15 years, using 200 percent declining-balance depreciation. There is no deduction for the cost of the *land*.

The following computations show a hypothetical tax income statement loss and its conversion into a cash flow gain:

Tax Income Statement		
Rental Income		$500
Less:		
operating expenses	$150	
mortgage interest	250	
construction period expenses	80	
fees	25	
depreciation	+175	
	$680	
		−680
Tax Income (loss)		($180)

Cash Flow

Tax Income (loss)		($180)
Add back:		
construction period expenses	$ 80	
fees	25	
depreciation	+175	
	$280	
		$100
Minus mortgage principal payments		– 25
Cash Flow from Property Operations		$ 75

At a 32 percent marginal tax bracket you would save $57.60 in taxes and have a positive total cash flow of $132.60 ($57.60 + $75).

Moreover, the normal real estate tax shelter is usually structured so that any actual cash losses in the first years will be provided, or paid for, by the limited partners' capital contribution or the proceeds of the mortgage itself. This item is referred to as "rent-up loss"—the operating deficit during the period before the property is fully rented.

SUMMARY OF BENEFITS

As the preceding statements indicate, there are a number of benefits achieved from real estate tax shelter investing. The bottom line of the tax income statement shows your taxable loss. Multiply this figure by your tax bracket to determine your tax savings.

The cash flow statement represents the cash distributions you will be paid from the property's operations. Add to this the cash in pocket from the above tax savings and that yields your net cash increase in wealth.

An additional benefit that investing in real estate tax shelters will yield is equity buildup. This is the amount of the mortgage principal that you are paying off each year. Even if the property value merely remains flat with no appreciation, your equity interest in that property will increase each year by the principal payoff.

The final benefit from such an investment is the potential appreciation in the property itself. Building costs are rising with inflation, so it is likely that in 10 years the replacement cost of real estate will be much higher than construction

costs today. If a property is well located and well maintained, its cash flow should expand over the years and its value should increase.

Before investing in a shelter you must recognize that real estate projects fall into three major categories:

Commercial
Residential
Government-supported housing

REHABILITATION—CERTIFIED HISTORICAL CREDITS

Each category of investment has its own rules and deduction limits for tax purposes. For example, rehabilitation costs on low-income housing and certified historic structures can still qualify for investment tax credits. For a building in service before 1936 (other than a certified historic structure), the credit is 10 percent; for a certified residential or commercial historic structure, the credit increases to 20 percent! This means that you get the equivalent of one-fifth off your rehabilitation expenses. If you use the rehabilitation credit, however, you must use straight-line depreciation, reduce the base by the full amount of its credit, and make a substantial rehabilitation of the building. This means that the qualifying expenditures of the tax year and the preceding tax year must exceed the adjusted basis of the property or $5,000, whichever is larger. For rehabilitations completed in phases, the 24-month measuring period is extended to 60 months. In addition, to qualify for the credit one of the following three tests must be met:

a) at least 50 percent of the external walls are retained as external walls;

b) at least 75 percent of the external walls are retained as either external or internal walls; *and*

c) at least 75 percent of the internal structural framework is retained in place.

Under government-sponsored housing, you can deduct construction loan interest and taxes immediately; with other real estate you must amortize them over 4 years. Furthermore, an owner of a subsidized housing project may defer any taxes due on the sale of the project if it is sold to a tenant cooperative and the proceeds reinvested in another subsidized housing project within 1 year.

The rehabilitation credit may be used to offset tax on up to $25,000 of non-passive income, regardless of whether the individual actively participates, subject to a phase-out between $200,000 and $250,000 of adjusted gross income.

Parties interested in obtaining further information on historic preservation opportunities and procedures should contact the various agencies and organizations listed below.

Copies of historic preservation standards and guidelines set forth by the government for certifying historic structures and a current list of state historic preservation offices are available by writing to the following address:

> Tax Reform Act
> Office of Archaeology and Historic Preservation
> Department of the Interior
> Washington, DC 20240

The following is the address of the historic preservation agency that administers the Department of the Interior's preservation tax incentive program:

> Historic Preservation Tax Incentives
> Archaeology and Historic Preservation
> National Park Service
> Washington, DC 20240

The following regional offices of the National Park Service review certification applications:

Regional Office	States Administered for Tax Certification Purposes
Mid-Atlantic 143 South Third Street Philadelphia, PA 19106 (215)597-7013	Connecticut, Delaware, District of Columbia, Maine, Maryland, Massachusetts, New Hampshire, New Jersey, New York, Pennsylvania, Rhode Island, Vermont, Virginia, West Virginia
Southeast 75 Spring Street, NW Atlanta, GA 30303 (404)242-2635	Alabama, Florida, Georgia, Kentucky, Mississippi, North Carolina, Puerto Rico, South Carolina, Tennessee

Midwest
Federal Building
200 East Liberty Street
Ann Arbor, MI 48107
(313)378-2035

Illinois, Indiana, Iowa, Kansas,
Michigan, Minnesota, Missouri,
Nebraska, Ohio, Wisconsin

Rocky Mountain
P.O. Box 25287
Denver Federal Center
Denver, CO 80225
(303)234-2915

Colorado, Montana, North Dakota,
South Dakota, Utah, Wyoming

Southwest
5000 Marble Street, NE
Room 211
Albuquerque, NM 87110
(505)474-3514

Arkansas, Louisiana, New Mexico,
Oklahoma, Texas

West
450 Golden Gate Avenue
P.O. Box 36063
San Francisco, CA 94102
(415)556-7741 or 556-7090

Arizona, California, Hawaii, Nevada

Pacific Northwest
Westin Building, Room 1920
2110 Sixth Avenue
Seattle, WA 98121
(206)399-0791

Idaho, Oregon, Washington

Alaska
1011 East Tudor Street
Suite 297
Anchorage, AK 99503
(907)277-1666

Alaska

The National Trust for Historic Preservation, a private, nonprofit membership organization, provides advice on preservation issues and techniques. For more information on membership, write:

National Trust for Historic Preservation
1785 Massachusetts Avenue, NW
Washington, DC 20036

The regional offices of the National Trust are as follows:

Regional Office	States and Territories Administered
Northeast 100 Franklin Street, 7th Floor Boston, MA 02110 (617)223-7754	Connecticut, Maine, Massachusetts, New Hampshire, New York, Rhode Island, Vermont
Mid-Atlantic 1600 H Street, NW Washington, DC 20006 (202)673-4203	Delaware, District of Columbia, Maryland, New Jersey, Pennsylvania, Puerto Rico, Virgin Islands, Virginia, West Virginia
South 456 King Street Charleston, SC 29403 (803)724-4711	Alabama, Arkansas, Florida, Georgia, Kentucky, Louisiana, Mississippi, North Carolina, South Carolina, Tennessee

Regional Office	States and Territories Administered
Midwest 407 South Dearborn Street Number 710 Chicago, IL 60605 (312)353-3419 or 353-3424	Illinois, Indiana, Iowa, Michigan, Minnesota, Missouri, North Dakota, Ohio, South Dakota, Wisconsin
Southwest/Plains 210 Colcord Building Oklahoma City, OK 73102 (405)231-5126	Colorado, Kansas, Nebraska, New Mexico, Oklahoma, Texas
West 681 Market Street, Number 859 San Francisco, CA 94105 (415)556-2707	Alaska, Arizona, California, Guam, Hawaii, Idaho, Micronesia, Montana, Nevada, Oregon, Utah, Washington, Wyoming

The combination of first-year accelerated depreciation and heavy start-up costs may produce tax deductions exceeding the size of your initial cash investment when 80 percent of the cost of that investment is financed with borrowings. What that means is that if you are in the 32 percent bracket, your net initial cash outlay may be reduced to zero! However, with any tax shelter, as with any

investment, *never* invest just on the basis of tax deductions alone. You must always consider the total expected cash flow from the property. The advantages of a real estate tax shelter are that the risks are normally minimal and the total cash flow is normally augmented in the early years by substantial tax savings. Furthermore, a good shelter should be structured to give you substantial cash rental income that is either minimally taxed or not taxed at all due to offsetting depreciation expense deductions even in the middle years. These depreciation deductions are pencil transactions that do not involve any real cash outflow, and they arise out of basis created by borrowed money. In effect, with a properly structured transaction you get to eat your cake and keep it too.

LOW-INCOME HOUSING CREDITS

The Tax Reform Act of 1986 created a new low-income housing credit. This housing credit is claimed annually over a 10-year period with percentages set so that over that 10-year period, the credits will equal a present value of 70 percent of the basis of a new building which is not federally subsidized and 30 percent of the basis of an existing building or federally subsidized new building. The credit applies only to expenditures on the low-income units, and rehabilitation expenditures will qualify for the credit only if they exceed $2,000 per unit.

A building will qualify for the credit if either at least 20 percent of the units are occupied by individuals with incomes of 50 percent or less of area median income, or if at least 40 percent of the units are occupied by individuals with incomes of 60 percent or less of area median income. Furthermore, the rent charged to tenants may not exceed 30 percent of the applicable qualified income, which will vary depending on family size.

If a building is placed in service in 1987, the credit percentages are 9 percent annually over 10 years (that equates to the 70 percent present value credit), and/or 4 percent over 10 years (that equates to the 30 percent present value credit).

If a building is placed in service after 1987, the credit percentages will be adjusted monthly by the Treasury to reflect the present values of 70 percent and 30 percent at the time the building is placed in service. In a project consisting of two or more buildings placed in service in different months, a separate credit percentage may apply to each building.

One additional word on real estate tax shelters. The Senate Report on the Tax Reform Act of 1986 (S. Rep. at 742) states that hotel and motel properties ("transient rentals") are not considered to be rental activities, and thus are not per se designated as passive. Consequently, if a real estate investor holds hotel and motel property either through a general partnership interest or ownership in an S Corporation, and if that investor actively manages the property, it may be

possible to have these properties designated as active businesses. In this case, the investor would be able to utilize losses from the property to offset other income. In order to qualify as an active manager, you must "materially participate" in the running of the hotel business. You should attempt to do each of the following:

1. Make frequent visits to the hotel for on-site inspections and consultations with the firm managing your condo.

2. Regularly establish room rental rates.

3. Set up and review hiring and other personnel policies.

4. Review and approve periodic financial reports.

5. Participate in budgeting operating costs and establishing capital expenditures.

6. Establish the need and level of financial resources.

7. Select the bank depository for rental proceeds and reserves.

8. Assist in off-site business promotion activities.

Alternatively, if the hotel or motel is producing taxable income, holding such property through a limited partnership interest would characterize the income generated therefrom as passive. By eliminating hotel or motel properties from the rental income classification, the Tax Reform Act presents a unique planning opportunity with respect to such properties. Such ownership gives you, the investor, the opportunity to classify the activities as either active or passive, depending upon which planning approach you choose to undertake.

Watch out for fees in many limited partnership deals. A typical limited partnership will pay 7 to 10 percent of equity in sales commissions; 1 to 3 percent or more of the equity raised for legal, accounting, and paperwork expenses; and up to 15 percent of the equity for organization and mortgage finding fees. Later, sponsors may take 5 to 6 percent of the cash flow in property management fees. After the property is sold, 3 to 6 percent of the sales price may go for commissions, and an additional 10 to 33 percent of any profit on the sale may go to the sponsors. Clearly, the greater the front-end fee, the less money is left to invest in property. According to Arnold G. Rudoff, who analyzes partnerships for the accounting firm of Price Waterhouse in San Francisco, real estate front-end fees should be under 20 percent.

According to a survey by the accounting firm of Coopers & Lybrand, privately offered real estate partnership transactions showed the following fees and structure:

	Typical	Range
Partnership participation		
Cash flow	10%	1–10%
Tax benefits	10%	1–10%
Refinancing/disposition (subordinated)	20%	15–30%
Initial fees (as % of equity raised)		
Sales commission	8%	6–10%
Acquisition and ancillary fees	30%	15–60%
Operating period (as % of revenues)		
Property management	4%	3–6%
Partnership management	Modest	Modest
Reimbursable expenses	Modest	Modest
Disposition fees		
Real estate commission	3%	Competitive
Participation in residual value	20%	15–30%

Reprinted with permission of Coopers & Lybrand © March 1985 Coopers & Lybrand (USA)

One measure of the fairness of offering terms is how the various fees relate to the North American Securities Administrators Association (NASAA) guidelines. These guidelines appear in the next section.

119 Fees in Public Real Estate Partnerships

Front-end fees include sales commissions for the broker/dealer, offering and organization costs, and property acquisition fees paid to the general partner and unaffiliated third parties. The NASAA front-end fee standard is 20 percent of limited partner capital contributions for unleveraged properties, 28.1 percent for 50 percent leveraged properties, and 33 percent for 80 percent leveraged properties.

Operational phase fees are typically paid to the general partner from cash flow (earnings) of the real estate as compensation for management of the day-to-day operation of the partnership and the properties. NASAA approves "property management fees" equal to 6 percent of gross revenues for residential properties and 3 percent of gross revenues for commercial properties, plus a "promotional" interest of 10 percent of annual cash flow (if the liquidation phase fee from net proceeds, explained below, is limited to 15 percent).

Liquidation phase fees are payable to the general partner upon resale or refinancing of the properties. These fees consist of a real estate commission and a percentage of the net proceeds from the sale or refinancing of the property. Normally, these fees are subordinated (not paid to the general partner) until the return of the limited partners' investment, plus a minimum return. NASAA approves a real estate commission to all parties, not to exceed 3 percent. The promotional or incentive fee is limited to 15 percent if the sponsor also received 10 percent of annual cash flow, or 25 percent otherwise. The real estate commission and the appreciation percentage are "subordinated" to the return of limited partner capital, plus a minimum return of 6 percent per annum on initial capital reduced by periodic cash distributions.

120 Oil and Gas

Petroleum and gas are important sources of energy throughout the world. Accordingly, Congress has determined that certain types of investments in oil and gas are deductible. Former Attorney General Smith invested in an oil and gas partnership. An investment in an oil and gas program is probably your most advantageous single-year tax-advantaged investment if the economics are viable.

The tax advantage in an oil and gas deal is the ability to deduct, as a current expense, the investments in capital expenditures known as intangible drilling and developing costs, or IDCs. The income tax regulations define *intangibles* as any cost incurred that has no salvage value and is "incident to and necessary for the drilling of wells and the preparation of wells for the production of oil and gas." This definition includes the hours worked by the drilling crew and the cost of the installation of tangible equipment placed *in the well*, although the cost of such equipment must be capitalized and recovered through depreciation. Expressly excluded from classification as *intangibles* are expenditures incurred in connection with equipment, facilities, or structures (including installation charges) that are not incident to or necessary for the drilling of oil or gas wells but are used in operations after the oil or gas is produced (for instance, structures for storing and treating oil or gas).

Essentially, then, nearly all costs of drilling and completing a well, except for the bare cost of the lease, the cost of tangible equipment and labor, and the geological and geophysical costs incurred prior to the selection of a drill site, are deductible in the year incurred. Without this special break accorded to

intangible drilling and development costs, you would be unable to deduct them until drilling was either abandoned or the product was actually being extracted from the wells.

In the first year you are able immediately to deduct 70 percent to 80 percent of productive-well costs as intangible expenses, and 100 percent of dry well costs. In many public tax shelter programs, you pay for only intangible costs and can therefore immediately deduct up to 100 percent of the amount you invest.

There is a catch: with gas and oil deals the Internal Revenue Service will not permit deductions in excess of your personal cash investment, or "at risk" basis. In the past, however, it did permit the year-end deduction of all the intangible costs of wells even if those wells were not actually to be drilled until the following year. (Thus promoters of oil and gas shelters tried to "front load" deductions in the initial year of the shelter by prepayment of intangible costs.) In all other tax shelters, legislation has ruled out retroactive allocations of losses for year-end investments; it also no longer allows immediate deductions for many expenses that are incurred prior to actual operations—for example, cattle feeding programs—unless there is a clear business purpose. And on St. Patrick's Day, 1980, the Internal Revenue Service asserted that prepaid intangible drilling costs *also* must be disallowed as a deduction in the year paid—unless the taxpayer can demonstrate the existence of some commercial exigency making it advisable to prepay the costs.*

In an Eighth Circuit 1984 Court of Appeals Case (*Keller,* 84-1 USTC Par. 9194, 53 AFTR2d 84-663), the Court found that prepayments for intangible costs served no business purpose and materially distorted the taxpayer's income. The taxpayer's deduction, therefore, was deferred until the subsequent year.

The Keller case, however, did not involve a "turnkey" contract. In fact, the Court found that with a "turnkey" contract, where the amounts expended could not be refunded, a prepayment would be deductible in the year paid. This was a validation of the general rule that intangible drilling and development costs under a "turnkey" agreement were deductible in the year paid (*Ruth,* T.C. Memo 1983-586).

Furthermore, the Tax Reform Act of 1984 provided that "tax shelters" (other than forming syndicates), whether on the cash or accrual method, will not be able to deduct prepaid expenses until both economic performance occurs and the expenses actually paid are incurred. A deduction, however, will

*Rev. Rul. 80-71, I.R.B. 1980-11, 7.

be allowed for prepaid expenses where economic performance occurs after the end of the year under the following conditions:

a) Economic performance occurs within 90 days after the end of the taxable year;

b) the deduction is limited to the cash investment made by the person (i.e., not paid for with any recourse or nonrecourse liabilities); *and*

c) the requirements of present laws are met.

For purposes of this exception in the case of intangible drilling expenses, economic performance occurs when the well is "spudded." If oil and gas prepayments do not meet the requirements of the 90-day exception, economic performance will occur as the drilling services are provided. If drilling is commenced in the year of prepayment (and the above exception is not met), only that portion of the intangible drilling cost attributable to drilling prior to the end of the year will be deductible in that year. This provision applies for prepayments made after March 31, 1984, and enhances the potential significance of a "turnkey" contract.

Note, in addition, that working interest in any oil or gas property that you hold directly or through an entity that does not limit your liability with respect to such interest will be treated as an active trade or business and will not be subject to the passive loss rules.

TAX SHELTER STRATEGIES

A sophisticated shelter will sustain the current deductibility of an intangible drilling cost prepayment by the following techniques:

- The prepayment requirements should be set forth in the contract.

- The contract should set forth the particular well to be drilled and provide for a definite commencement date.

- If it is a co-owner situation, the same prepayment requirement should be imposed on other co-owners.

- The contract should be with the actual driller, if possible, and not with an intermediary.

- There should be a business benefit to be derived from the prepayment requirement (that is, the price might be lower if the driller is paid in advance).

- The contract should be binding on the driller.

- Prepayment should not be more than a reasonable estimate of the amount to come due to the driller.

- The payments should actually be made prior to the end of the year, and the driller's access to the funds should not be restricted (that is, payment into an escrow account may not constitute a valid prepayment).

Additional tax shelter is still available through your ability to take 200 percent declining-balance depreciation on the remaining 20 to 30 percent of the costs of the wells (capitalized costs). A statutory depletion deduction (one that is provided by law), which is 15 percent of your gross income from the well before expenses, also is available.

After the development of the property and the drilling are completed, the program will begin to receive cash from oil or gas sales, if any successful wells are drilled. If receipts exceed operating and overhead costs as well as depletion and depreciation, you will have taxable income.

The depletion allowance you are allowed to claim is the *greater* of cost depletion or percentage depletion.

COST DEPLETION

Cost depletion is computed by dividing the estimated total units (barrels of oil or thousand cubic feet of gas) recoverable from the property into its adjusted tax basis in order to obtain the per-unit depletion allowance, and then multiplying the per-unit depletion allowance by the number of units sold during the year. Cost depletion is then compared to percentage depletion on a property-by-property basis to determine the amount to be deducted.

PERCENTAGE DEPLETION

Percentage depletion for up to 1,000 barrels of average daily production of oil or 6 million cubic feet of domestic natural gas is allowed to "independent producers and royalty owners" at the rate of 15 percent of gross revenue. This depletion allowance is limited to 50 percent of the net income from the property. The allowance calculated is further limited to 65 percent of your taxable income (prior to taking the depletion allowance). The 65 percent limitation and average daily production limitation are calculated at the individual investor or partner level.

Both cost and percentage depletion are computed separately for *each* property in which you have an interest. Percentage depletion at the applicable

statutory rate is computed on *gross* income from the property before deductions of any kind, including production or windfall profit taxes, operating expenses, or depreciation. Accordingly, the benefit obtained is significantly more than the statutory rate as a percentage of net (taxable) income.

The Supreme Court has ruled, in *Commissioner v. Engle et ux.*, S. Ct. Docket 82-599, that lessors of interests in mineral deposits are entitled to percentage depreciation allowances on any bonus or advanced royalties whether or not there is actual production of the underlying mineral in the year of payment. Production, therefore, has been found not to be a prerequisite for claiming percentage depletion deductions on lease bonus and advanced royalty income.

Percentage depletion is almost always larger than cost depletion. For example, if a well is drilled on a lease that cost $2,000 and yields an estimated 100,000 barrels of recoverable reserves, the rate of cost depletion for that property would be 2¢ per barrel of oil produced. This is far less than percentage depletion at the applicable rate. Fifteen percent of the gross income of oil selling at $65 per barrel is $9.75. The net impact of the depreciation and depletion deductions is that, with normal operating expenses, from about a quarter to a third of your income from the well is tax-free.

Oil and gas drilling tax shelter programs break down into three types:

1. *Wildcatting,* also known as exploratory drilling, which involves drilling operations in search of a yet-undiscovered pool of oil or gas, or with the hope of greatly extending the limits of a pool already developed. It is an attempt to find new fields where the probability of success for an individual well may be 10 percent and the chances of "proving," or discovering, a big field are about 1 percent to 2 percent.

2. *Development drilling,* which involves drilling an additional well to a reservoir that supports an already-producing well on a lease or on an offset lease that is usually close to or adjacent to the producing well. Development wells can have success rates of from 75 percent to 100 percent, but real fortunes are made only by "proving" a big field and selling or developing it.

3. *Balanced or combination programs,* which involve both exploratory and development drilling, therefore promising up-side potential with limited down-side risk. Unfortunately, most balanced programs combine wildcatting's delayed significant cash flow (3 years can be common) with a development program's low multiple cash return (on average, 2.5 × the cash investment).

Unlike most investments, investments in oil and gas exploration may result in a complete loss. Industry statistics reflect that about 1 out of 10 wildcat wells is productive and that many of the productive wells do not have sufficient reserves to cover the drilling, equipping, and operating costs of the wildcat venture. Approximately 1 out of 200 wildcat wells discovers a medium-size field, and only 1 out of 1,000 discovers a large field. As indicated by the statistics, investments in oil and gas exploration should be spread over a sufficient number of prospects to provide you with a reasonable expectation of a return on your investment.

If you are interested in entering the oil business, there are several ways to participate, including the following:

- Participation with an oil operator on a selective basis for fractional interest in a number of oil and gas prospects

- Participation with several different oil operators for a fractional interest in selected oil and gas prospects

- Investments in a limited partnership with one or more oil and gas prospects

- Various combinations of these

NONTAX CONSIDERATIONS

In addition to the tax considerations discussed above, you must examine the following nontax considerations if you want to get involved with oil and gas.

Management

Management in the oil business is of primary importance. The ability to operate an oil and gas investment program successfully consists basically of two skills: technical expertise and administrative competence. The organization must have the technical expertise to assemble prospects, select drilling sites, supervise the drilling and completion of wells, operate productive wells, and market the output. The competence of the technical staff is extremely difficult to evaluate on a short-run basis, since entirely new prospects are assembled and drilled each year.

Program Size

There is no optimum program size. However, the size of the technical and administrative staffs will dictate certain minimum and maximum projects that can be undertaken. The program should have enough capital to drill a sufficient number of prospects for a reasonable spread of the risks; also, a minimum

amount of capital must be raised to be used for administrative costs associated with offering the program and other administrative matters.

The area in which operations will be conducted is also important. A $5 million program that will explore an area where the average well costs $400,000 could offer a satisfactory spread of risk. A $5 million program exploring in areas where the average well costs $1.5 million may *not* offer an adequate spread. The geographic area in which the technical staff has expertise should also be considered. A technical staff with operating experience in Colorado and Wyoming may not be qualified to conduct operations in Texas and Louisiana.

Past Performance

One of the most important nontax considerations that you must examine is the drilling company's past record of performance. You should measure and compare the net future revenues from proven oil and gas reserves in relation to limited partner capital contributions. Use only proven reserves, not what are called probable or possible reserves. Examine the price escalation figures and use only formulas provided by an independent reserve engineering firm.

Do not focus on past performance success ratios or cash distribution tables. The success ratio is the percent of all wells drilled that are completed as producing wells. A better success ratio does not necessarily mean a better economic result. For example, drilling in the Appalachian Basin (Ohio and West Virginia) should be successful 90 percent of the time, while drilling in Louisiana may be successful only perhaps 30 percent or 40 percent of the time. Why then should you invest in a project that drills in Louisiana? The answer is more abundant reserves and a potentially greater return on investment.

The cash distribution tables show the cash actually paid out to the investor. These can be deceiving in that some types of wells pay (or produce) over 50 percent of all that they will ever pay out in the first 2 years of their productive life; after the first 4 years, they do not produce any significant revenues. Other types of wells produce a lower percentage in their earlier life but continue to produce for as long as 20 to 30 years.

Management Costs

An additional nontax risk of oil and gas deals is the overpricing of the leases so that various parties in the promotional and marketing chain can realize this compensation from the initial capital invested. As compensation, the general partner and/or operator may receive up to 25 percent of the revenues earned by the limited partners after paying oil and gas royalties to the land owner and other promotional interests. In addition, there is usually a first-year management fee of about 5 percent of the amount of the investment.

Generally, you should expect to hold your interest in the well for its lifetime. Your investment is a capital asset and if sold should produce capital gains. But if the well is sold, then a portion of the intangible drilling costs deducted during the developmental phase of the shelter may be "recaptured" and treated as ordinary income, as may some of the depreciation taken. Many public programs offer buy-back provisions after 2 or 3 years of operation, but generally you will receive a better return if you wait 5 to 7 years. With a successful shelter, you might well be advised to retain your interest in the shelter, collect the cash flow from the sale of the oil, and shelter this income with percentage depletion. It is not normally recommended that you buy the interest of an original investor as a tax shelter. This is because although percentage depletion is available to investors who are in a successful oil deal during the developmental phase, an investor who purchases the interest of the original investor in the deal is purchasing a "proven property" and therefore is not entitled to percentage depletion deductions.

Compensation

If you are interested in involving yourself as an active developer of oil and gas properties, you should note that compensation paid in oil rights potentially can be tax-free. In Letter Ruling 813-7006, the Internal Revenue Service held that a consultant who contributed only services to the pool of capital, acquiring in return an interest in the minerals (oil) in place, is not required to include that interest in his income. The same reasoning has been extended to accountants, lawyers, geologists, petroleum engineers, and lease brokers who receive an interest in an oil or gas drilling venture in return for services rendered. The contributors are not viewed as performing services for compensation but are viewed as acquiring capital interests through making a contribution to the pool of capital that is necessary for development (see Rev. Rul. 77-176, 1977-1 C.B. 78, and G.C.M. 22730, 1941-1 C.B. 214, but see Rev. Rul. 83-46, where overriding royalty interest to a corporate promoter, an attorney, and an employee were found to be includable in gross income at fair market value immediately. See also Rev. Proc. 93-27, 6/9/93, where a partnership profit interest received for services was not a taxable event).

STRUCTURING A SUCCESSFUL OIL OR GAS TAX SHELTER

Assume that you are in the 43 percent bracket, including not only federal taxes but state and local income taxes as well. You invest $50,000 in an oil program in which 80 percent of your investment is deductible as intangible drilling costs.

The remaining 20 percent is depreciated and deducted on a 10-year straight-line basis. Assume in addition that the well produces a lifetime total income of only $50,000.

First Year

IDC deduction (80% of $50,000)	$40,000
Plus depreciation deduction (1/10 of 20% of $50,000)	+ 1,000
	41,000
First-year net cost [$50,000 – ($41,000 × .43)]	$32,370

Subsequent Years' Total

Total income		$50,000
Depletion sheltered (15% × $50,000)	$ 7,500	
Plus depreciation (9/10 of 20% of $50,000)	+ 9,000	
Nontaxable cash income	$16,500	
Plus after-tax cash from taxable income [$33,500 – (.43 × $33,500)]	+19,095	
After-tax return		$35,595
Minus first-year net cost		–32,370
Net Cash Return		$ 3,225

Note that while no allowance for discounting future income to present value is made in the above analysis, if your oil or gas investment returns a total income at least equal to your initial cash investment, it will be at least marginally successful. Any excess return over your initial investment will substantially multiply your yield on that investment, especially on an after-tax basis.

SELF-EMPLOYMENT TAX TECHNIQUES

The Tax Reform Act of 1986 made purchasing a working interest in oil and gas wells a popular technique by allowing a working interest owner to escape the passive loss rules and claim drilling costs against other income, such as salaries, interest, or dividends. An interesting opportunity has recently been created with respect to self-employment tax on oil and gas income. The IRS has taken

the position that a working interest constitutes a trade or business for purposes of the self-employment (Social Security) tax. It is irrelevant whether operations were conducted by the working interest owner or by a third party. In that case, the IRS viewed the third-party operator as acting as the agent for the owner (Rev. Rul. 58-166). The position of the Internal Revenue Service, therefore, was that any income from a working interest in a gas or oil well constituted self-employment income. Such income or such losses were therefore added or subtracted if the taxpayer was not over the Social Security maximum with compensation from other employment and the like. Such income, however, would qualify for a Keogh contribution.

In *Howard W. Hendrickson,* T.C. Memo 1987-566, November 12, 1987, the Tax Court ruled that a salesman who had no experience in the oil and gas industry and who purchased a 21.875 percent interest in a gas well, as well as similar interest in two other wells, was not in the trade or business of producing oil and gas and therefore was not subject to self-employment tax.

These conflicting opinions allow you the following choice. If you are under the Social Security maximum and have losses from a working interest in a gas or oil well, the IRS position should be adopted to further reduce your potential self-employment taxes. However, if you have gains from a working interest and are not at the Social Security maximum, and *if you fit within the parameters* of the *Hendrickson* case, you should adopt the position of the Tax Court and not increase your self-employment income for Social Security tax purposes. [Note that the Tax Court, in *Cokes,* 91 T.C. 222 (1988), *Perry,* T.C. Memo 1994-215, *Methvin,* T.C. Memo 2015-81, and *Methvin,* 10th Circuit, 2016-1 came to a conclusion in opposition to *Hendrickson.* The facts in those cases, however, were different.]

121 Equipment Leasing

Leasing, as a method of financing capital assets for industry, has grown tremendously in recent years and can be a good tax shelter. According to the National Association of Securities Dealers, equipment leasing deals have been the fastest growing category of direct placement programs (tax shelters). Capital assets frequently financed by leasing include computers, airplanes, railroad rolling stock, ships, pollution control equipment, and industrial machinery.

A lease contract allows the lessee to use the equipment for a specified length of time in return for periodic rental payments. While a variety of lease

contracts have been developed, such contracts will normally be classified either as finance (full-payout) leases or as operating (non-full-payout) leases.

Finance leases provide the lessor with recovery of the cost and a reasonable profit from rentals and tax benefits over the original noncancelable lease term. These leases may be leveraged or nonleveraged. A leveraged lease is one in which the lessor has financed a significant portion (typically up to 80 percent) of the equipment purchased from third-party lenders. In the case of a non-leveraged lease, the lessor provides 100 percent of the equipment cost, either entirely through equity or by a combination of equity and recourse debt (a debt on which you are personally liable). Finance leases are almost invariably net leases—that is, the lessee is obligated to pay for most of the expenses, such as maintenance and property taxes associated with the equipment and insurance.

Operating leases do not provide the lessor with a return of cost over the initial noncancelable lease term. In order to realize a profit, lessors rely on their ability to sell or re-lease the equipment profitably at the end of the initial lease term. An operating lease may or may not be a net lease. It is not unusual for lessors writing operating leases to provide other services, such as maintenance and repair, along with the equipment.

The typical format of an equipment leasing transaction includes the following:

- Purchase of the equipment by a limited partnership (or direct ownership by the investor) for a cash down payment plus financing (either recourse or nonrecourse) for the balance of the purchase price.

- The equipment is then typically leased as either a full-payout finance lease or an operating lease.

- The lease may grant an option to purchase the equipment at a specified price at its fair market value.

- The lease may contain renewal options.

NONTAX CONSIDERATIONS

As an investor-owner, you must be aware of several nontax considerations. First, with a normal financing lease, you are in effect making a loan to the lessee of the purchase price of the equipment. Under an equipment leasing deal, you normally will have a greater economic return than you could realize on a conventional loan transaction.

Alternatively, since you are the owner of the equipment, you must take the risk of technological improvements—for instance, the obsolescence of the equipment. This risk can be modified by leasing on what is known as a "hell and high water" basis. Under such an arrangement, the lessee is obligated to make lease payments whether or not continued use of the equipment is desired. In effect, you are shifting the risk of obsolescence to the lessee. But as a result of that shift, you will receive reduced lease payments.

In addition, you must face a credit risk. Will the lessee be financially able to meet the lease payments? If not, your cash flow will be terminated and you will have to find another lessee.

There is also an interest risk. You as a lessor are essentially extending credit throughout the lease term at a fixed rate, while at the same time you may obtain your funds at variable rates—usually from banks at the prime rate or higher. In addition, your total annual debt service cost can be quite a bit higher than the interest charge alone because of the repayment of principal. If the interest rates on your borrowing increase, they can completely eliminate your return. When the cost of debt service exceeds the cash flow from the property, you have what is known as "negative leverage." Under these circumstances, your only real alternative is to repay the debt.

Finally, the residual value risk must be considered. Will the property be worth the anticipated amount at the end of the lease term? If not, your return could be significantly reduced.

There are also some nontax considerations for the lessee. Normally, the lessee will be making lease rental payments in amounts less than the direct purchase price of the equipment, even if paid on an installment basis.

In many cases, the lessee is cash poor or has limited borrowing capacity, and an equipment leasing arrangement reduces short-term cash outlay. In some cases, equipment leasing tax shelters may be structured in a sale leaseback format: The lessee originally owns the equipment but sells it to meet an immediate cash need. Under the terms of sale, the lessee turns around and leases the equipment from the buyer-lessor. Such a transaction will immediately augment the lessee's short-term cash position.

TAX BENEFITS

The key tax benefit that results from equipment leasing is deferral, which is a means of postponing a tax liability until a later and more convenient time. In years when your tax liability is high, you can invest in an equipment leasing program. You deduct a large amount of depreciation in the first year, along with

miscellaneous front-end expenses and interest on the borrowed capital. After the first 3 to 5 years, the lease will begin generating taxable income because depreciation and interest will have been reduced. Be aware, though, that there may not be any cash income paid to you because of the debt service payments due on the borrowed money. However, you should note that by the time you start receiving taxable income prior to sufficient tax-flow generation, you will have had the use and yield on the considerable tax savings for a significant period of time.

DEPRECIATION

The deferral advantage of equipment leasing discussed above comes mainly from depreciation. The accelerated depreciation rate is 200 percent of straight-line depreciation. Furthermore, what is known as "the half-year convention" is automatically imputed in the ACRS depreciation tables. The half-year convention allows a person who puts equipment into service anytime during the year to depreciate that equipment as though that person had had it for half the entire year. However, the Tax Reform Act of 1986 provides that a mid-quarter convention be applied to all property that is more than 40 percent of all property placed in service by a taxpayer during the last 3 months of the taxable year. This mid-quarter convention treats all property placed in service during any quarter of a taxable year as placed in service on the midpoint of such quarter. Moreover, if the leasing constitutes a trade or business, you now have the option of expensing up to $1 million (for 2018) in personal property immediately rather than over time through depreciation deductions.

In addition, as an investor, you should recognize that you would normally need a long-term, full-recourse loan to help buy the equipment. Otherwise, the depreciation that you take will quickly exceed your cash basis, and you will not be able to take any further deductions. What this means is that you should be extremely careful in leasing the equipment. Your major risks are residual value and that the lessee will default, so a good equipment leasing program will involve major corporations with superior credit ratings. With such programs, your effective risk is minimal.

SUMMARY OF ADVANTAGES

By taking accelerated depreciation on the equipment over a life shorter than your loan repayment period, you can obtain substantial cash-flow benefits from federal income tax deferrals over the first few years of ownership. The

total cash required to be put up is normally only about 20 percent of the cost of the equipment. These funds become available due to the tax deductions resulting from the purchase. Your tax deductions in each of the first few years of the transaction will be a significant multiple of the cash invested in that year. Substantial deductions will also normally be enjoyed for several more years.

You will enjoy an interest-free loan as a result of the transaction. If a reasonable value is attributed to the use of the funds produced by the interest-free loan, you will normally secure a return of your original investment in the equipment even if the equipment has less than the originally anticipated residual value at the end of the lease. An economic return over and above the profits earned on the interest-free loan is normally provided from re-lease revenues generated by the equipment at the end of the initial lease and by full payment of your bank debt.

122 Single-Premium Life Insurance

Prior to the Technical and Miscellaneous Revenue Act of 1988 (TAMRA), single-premium life insurance was one of the last remaining quality tax shelters. With single-premium life insurance, for a single lump sum, which may range from $1,000 to $5 million, a policyholder receives a little insurance protection and a big tax-deferred investment account. Single-premium life insurance offers a tax-free buildup of cash along with life insurance. Unlike universal life, the policy carries just enough insurance to qualify for tax-free status under the Internal Revenue Code. Therefore, more of the premium goes toward earning tax-deferred interest rather than buying insurance.

In fact, some experts have said that the insurance is a "free" bonus, since most single-premium policies quote a net rate of return. There are no fees or up-front commissions. That means that all of your cash immediately starts growing at the full rate quoted.

In the case of single-premium whole life, there was usually a 4 percent minimum guaranteed return. With an investment in single-premium variable life, like other variable products, there are no guaranteed rates of return, but the policyholder can pick his investments and move between alternative investments.

One suggested technique to avoid the limitations on Clifford trusts and the kiddie tax on children under 14 years of age was to purchase a single-premium

policy on the life of the parent with a young child as owner and beneficiary. The income can accumulate inside the policy until the child reaches 14 or college age. At that point the child has two options: he can take out the income and be taxed at his own, lower bracket, or he can simply borrow it. Prior to TAMRA, if he borrowed the money, there were no tax consequences. Policyholders can normally borrow against the amount of their initial deposit, in some cases at no interest, and in other cases with interest charges of 2 or 3 percent. They can borrow their accumulated interest typically at a rate equal to what the policy is then currently earning—i.e., at a net zero cost.

If the parent dies, the child receives the death benefit, and because the child is the owner of the policy, it does not go into the parent's estate. If the parent lives, the child is able to pay for his education with pre-tax dollars. The proceeds of the insurance policy are tax-free anyway, the parent has leveraged his investment, and the child's wealth has been magnified by compounding. If the loan is not repaid—it need never be—it is subtracted from the death benefit.

For example, a 35-year-old male pays $25,000 for a single-premium variable life insurance policy. He then can choose his own investment options and switch between different investments. For the $25,000, he would get a death benefit only of approximately $80,000 to $85,000 on a typical policy. While he could possibly buy the same protection for only $100 a year, the life insurance is not the real objective.

Assume the taxpayer is able, through a combination of stocks, bonds, and other investments, to achieve a return of 12 percent a year on the investment portion of his policy. At the end of 15 years, when he is 50 years old, the death benefit would be typically in excess of $230,000 and the policy would have a cash surrender value of $100,000.

If the taxpayer then cashes in the policy, he pays taxes at that time. Alternatively, he could have borrowed over $22,000 tax-free each year for four years to put his child through college. This would bring the death benefit down to between $160,000 and $170,000 with a cash surrender value of approximately $30,000.

If the taxpayer did not touch his policy until he retired at age 65, his 12 percent rate of return would give him a death benefit of approximately $650,000 with a cash surrender value in excess of $400,000. At that time he could cash in his policy and pay tax on the money. Alternatively, he could annuitize part of the policy when he retires by rolling over part of the cash surrender value into an annuity that would pay him income for life, leaving enough money in the policy to keep it in force and provide a tax-free benefit to his spouse. There would be no taxes due on the money rolled over into the annuity.

This would allow the taxpayer to buy a cheaper annuity on his own life only, while he is providing insurance benefits for his spouse.

There are innumerable creative ways of using single-premium life insurance policies. For example, assume, prior to TAMRA, you have $1 million in bank certificates of deposit paying 10 percent and you are in the 33 percent tax bracket. After tax you get $67,000 in earnings. If you were to put the $1 million into a single-premium whole-life policy, also earning 10 percent, it would, in the past, throw off $100,000 in tax-free income through policy loans. Assume, to make the numbers simple, that you are also paying $100,000 in tax-deductible alimony. If you keep your $1 million in a taxable investment, remember you get to keep only $67,000 after tax. Alternatively, if you used your insurance policy $100,000 to pay the alimony, you would have, prior to TAMRA, reduced your tax bill by $33,000 (33 percent of $100,000).

Single-premium life insurance policies are not without their disadvantages. If you cash in your policy, every penny earned inside the policy over however many years you have held it is taxed as ordinary income. In addition, most insurance companies impose a surrender charge in the first few years of the policy, although the charge usually shrinks year by year.

Single-premium life insurance was too good to last in the above form. In order to discourage the purchase of life insurance as a tax shelter investment vehicle, TAMRA altered the federal tax treatment with respect to a class of life insurance contracts that are statutorily defined as "modified endowment contracts." If a contract is a modified endowment contract:

a) amounts received under the contract are treated first as income, and then as recovered basis;

b) loans under the contract (and loans secured by a modified endowment contract) are treated as amounts received under the contract; *and*

c) an additional 10 percent income tax is imposed on certain amounts that are includable in gross income.

Policies entered into before June 21, 1988, have been grandfathered and will not be affected by the TAMRA changes unless they undergo a material change. TAMRA changes the tax treatment of any policy entered into on or after June 21, 1988, in which the aggregate premiums paid during the first 7 years of the contract exceed 7 times the annual net level premium of a 7-paid policy. This is called the "7-pay test."

For example, if the annual net level premium for a $100,000 7-pay policy is $4,500, then any $100,000 policy for the same insured on which the

aggregate premiums exceed $4,500 during the first year, $9,000 during the first 2 policy years, $13,500 during the first 3 policy years, $18,000 during the first 4 policy years, $22,500 during the first 5 policy years, $27,000 during the first 6 policy years, or $31,500 during the first 7 years of the policy will be considered and treated as a modified endowment contract.

If the aggregate premiums paid during the first 7 years are less than the aggregate premiums that would have been paid on a level annual premium basis using the net level premium amount ($4,500 a year in this example) for a 7-paid policy for the same insured, the policy will *not* be a modified endowment contract and will receive the same tax treatment previously applicable to all policies.

Under these new rules, single-premium policies have lost their potential for use as a strictly investment-oriented, tax-deferred vehicle. If a policyholder is forced to borrow from a modified endowment contract, he or she will have taxable income for the portion of the loan that represents internal gain on the policy. For example, a policy with a $50,000 single premium that has a $60,000 cash value would have a maximum of $10,000 gain that could be taxed. A policy loan of $15,000 ($10,000 of taxable income plus a $5,000 nontaxable portion) would generate $10,000 of taxable income plus a 10 percent penalty if the policy holder is under age 59½. The penalty is applied only to the taxable portion of the loan. In this case the penalty will be 10 percent of $10,000, or $1,000. If you are in the 28 percent bracket, this loan would cost you a total of $3,800 ($10,000 × 28% plus $1,000 penalty).

Single-premium policies may still be viable and desirable for other reasons. They provide a mechanism to pass assets to others without subjecting them to the costs, delays, and uncertainties of probate. Attacks on or elections against an insured's will are avoided, as are any claims of potential creditors. Such policies also provide a way to fully prefund future debts or pledges with discounted tax-advantaged dollars. Moreover, at death they are still income tax-free and can be arranged to be both estate and inheritance tax-free.

In shopping for single-premium life insurance, the following considerations should be evaluated:

1. Does the life insurance company offering the policy have a rating of A or better from AM Best Corporation, the authoritative source on financial stability in the industry?

2. What is the current net interest being paid on the policy? Does this take into consideration the mortality charge—i.e., has that charge been taken out of the rate that is quoted?

3. Is the net rate guaranteed, and if so for what period of time?

4. Is there any minimum interest rate guaranteed over the life of the policy?

5. Is there a bailout provision under which you can get out of the policy if rates fall below a certain level?

6. What is the surrender charge if you cash in the policy?

7. Does the surrender charge decrease over a period of time?

8. What is the rate at which you can borrow the accumulated interest?

9. What is the rate at which you can borrow against your original premium?

10. Is there a minimum guaranteed death benefit?

11. Can you make additional payments, and if so what are the time and quantity limitations?

123 Cattle Feeding Programs

A cattle feeding program can enable you to spread income earned in one year over a number of years so that it can be taxed at lower rates. There are no capital gains or depreciation opportunities. You buy calves in the spring or early summer and deduct the cost of feeding them for the remainder of the year. When they reach commercial weight the following year, you will sell them and pay ordinary income taxes. You have, in effect, deferred income from one year to the next, unless beef prices have fallen in the interim.

Feeding programs seek to convert grain (or grass) into beef, at the same time offering a short-term tax deferral and an opportunity for substantial profit or loss. If the cost of converting feed to beef is less than the per-pound cost of the beef added, the cattle feeding program results in a profit to you. If the cost of feeding the cattle is more than the price of beef, you lose.

A 1979 IRS ruling made prepaid feed deductions difficult for tax shelter schemes.* Under the prior rule, a prepaid feed expense had to meet three criteria:

1. It could not be on "deposit"—you had to own the feed and bear the economic risk of price fluctuations.

*Rev. Rul. 79-229, 1979 C.B. 2.

2. The purchase of the feed had to be for a "valid" business purpose.

3. The deduction could not result in a "material distortion of income."

Under the 1979 rule, these three criteria are retained, but in addition the Internal Revenue Service looks at the substantive purpose behind the transaction. According to the latest ruling, a motive based on the income tax advantages of prepayment is *not* a valid business purpose, and if you lack other motives, your deduction will be disallowed.

Moreover, the Tax Reform Act of 1984 included statutory language to include any arrangement with the principal purpose of tax avoidance within the definition of what constitutes a farm syndicate. According to the Conference Committee Report, "The prepaid expense provisions will apply to individual taxpayers engaged in farming activities with the principal purpose of tax avoidance. The conferees intend that marketed arrangements in which individuals carry on farming activities utilizing the assistance of a common managerial or administrative service may be presumed under certain circumstances to have the principal purpose of tax avoidance. If under such arrangements, taxpayers prepay a substantial portion of their farming expenses with borrowed funds, they should generally be presumed to have a principal purpose of tax avoidance."

The Internal Revenue Service could argue that all feed lot customers are tax shelters because they use the high leverage customary to the industry and feed cattle through a custom feed yard. If so, then the 1984 provisions would effectively limit all deductions for commercial cattle feeders to consumed feed. There would be no allowance of prepayments for feed, seed, fertilizer, or other farm supplies unless the taxpayer were "actively participating in the management." In addition, if the above provisions were to apply, they would preempt and eliminate the 90-day allowance rule on prepayments as contained in Section 461(i). Therefore, if you want to receive the benefits of a cattle feeding program, you must be able to document "active participation," establish a substantial business purpose, and prove that your principal purpose is not tax avoidance, in order to still be eligible to deduct valid prepayments for your farm expenditures.

A typical cattle feeding tax shelter will provide for the purchase of very young calves (or feeders) in the summer or fall. The animals are generally raised in feed yards for which you will be charged a fee in addition to the cost of the feed. The cattle are usually sold the following year, when they reach their commercial weight. If you meet the "valid business purpose" test just described by

proper timing of feeder-cattle purchases and sales, you should be able to deduct your expenses in the first year and pick up this amount, plus or minus the profit or loss, in the following year. You should be able to meet the "valid business purpose" test if you can establish a legitimate expectation of higher feed costs in the future—that is, it is cheaper to buy the feed now than to wait—and a legitimate expectation of profit on the ultimate sale of the cattle.

Moreover, under the Tax Reform Act of 1986, farmers using the cash method of accounting will not be allowed to deduct any amount paid for feed, seed, fertilizer, or other supplies prior to the year in which such items are used or consumed to the extent that they exceed 50 percent of expenses for which economic performance has occurred. This provision is effective for prepayments made on or after March 1, 1986. Since most investors in cattle feeding will not have other farm expenses, they will not be entitled to deduct prepaid feed costs. Except for investors in other farming ventures who may have such expenses and who will therefore be entitled to the deduction within the specified limits, cattle feeding as a tax deferral for non-full-time farmers is no longer an effective tax shelter.

124 Cattle Breeding Programs

Cattle breeding programs seek to increase herd size. Prior to ultimate sale, the cattle breeding program offers substantial tax deductions of a long-range deferral nature.

In a cattle breeding program, you might purchase a herd of 50 to 100 cows, which should triple in 3 to 4 years. Over a 5-year period your average annual outlay of cash on a 100-cow herd can be about $12,000. This outlay may be offset by tax deductions of $6,000 a year.

Expenses normally are deducted as incurred. This includes amounts paid for feed, seed, fertilizer, or other similar supplies. The provision that expenses are deducted as incurred normally prevents the allowance of current deductions for prepaid expenses. If use or consumption of the supplies during the taxable year is prevented on account of fire, storm, flood, or other casualty, however, the items may then be taken as an expense in the current period.

The cattle usually are bred in the summer or fall, so the calf crop will be born in warm weather. A calf crop of 75 percent to 95 percent can be expected. After the calves are weaned, the steers are sold and the heifers are retained to build up

the breeding herd. The new crop of heifers is generally bred after 2 years. Each year, certain animals are culled from the breeding herd and sold.

After 5 to 7 years, the entire herd is usually sold. You can take depreciation on your breeding cattle, but gain equal to the depreciation taken will be recaptured as ordinary income upon their sale. Depreciation can be taken over a 5-year period using the 200 percent declining-balance method.

Prior to 1986, you were also entitled to the investment tax credit in a breeding operation. That was a credit against your tax bill of 10 percent of the purchase price, not just your investment. For example, if you bought a herd for $20,000 in 1985, putting in $2,000 in cash and borrowing the additional $18,000, you got an investment tax credit of 10 percent of the total $20,000, or $2,000. In effect, therefore, your initial net cash investment was zero. The Tax Reform Act of 1986 eliminated the investment tax credit as of January 1, 1986.

You can get into the breeding business with as little as 10 percent equity. With feeders, you can get in with as little as 5 percent equity. Up to 90 percent or 95 percent of the purchase price can be borrowed from the feedlot operator, the rancher, or a bank. You can therefore heavily leverage your investment, but this leverage must be based upon full-recourse financing.

The economics of breeding and feeding cattle can be seriously affected by the cyclical market price of cattle. Conditions such as increased costs (feed grains and supplies), price controls, reduced consumption due to high beef prices, and large supplies of available fat cattle have, at times, forced many one-way ventures into economic losses.

Diversification into combined feeding and breeding provides for a longer-lasting investment. The yearly cycle of feeding is extended to a period that provides for the building of herds in hope of a rising demand. In both feeding and breeding programs, management compensation is normally 5 percent to 10 percent of the herd value in the first year, and 5 percent to 10 percent of the operating expenses in subsequent years. Both activities are subject to the "at risk" limitation, and you will be personally liable for any loans if you finance your investment to obtain added tax leverage in order to take the full deductions available.

One very real advantage of cattle breeding is the flexibility that it extends to tax planning. Just as you can defer the recognition of income in a cattle feeding program by continuing to reinvest the proceeds of the sale of cattle, you can also pick the date on which you wish to realize the majority of the income from the sale of your breeding herd. Similarly, depreciation of the purchased cattle, the cost of their maintenance, and interest on any debt create additional deductions

until the herd is sold. Remember, though, this flexibility, while useful in tax planning, does not ensure that when the herd is eventually sold, it will be sold at a profit. Furthermore, cattle breeding is a long-term investment. You can expect little, if any, cash flow from the breeding venture for a substantial period of time. But the potential gains are there. Prior to 1987, all gain on the raised portion of the herd that had been held for more than 24 months and any gain on purchased animals in excess of prior depreciation would receive long-term capital gain treatment. And throughout the breeding and raising period, you would have been taking ordinary income deductions for your expenses. By eliminating the long-term capital gains deduction, however, the 1986 Reform Act significantly impaired the tax advantage of cattle breeding programs. Cattle breeding programs still give you the advantage of tax deferral.

125 Tax Straddles

A commodity tax straddle is designed to defer short-term capital gain into your next year or to convert it into long-term capital gain. Straddling involves a simultaneous purchase and *short sale* (the sale of a security you do not currently own) of two futures contracts—that is, agreements first to buy and then to sell stated amounts of the same commodity at set prices and times in the future.

To offset the short-term capital gain, you straddle a very volatile commodity (such as copper, silver, or pork bellies) near year-end, hoping for significant price movement—up *or* down—before December 31. If prices rise, you cover your short position at a loss; if prices fall, you liquidate the long position. Either way, the short-term capital loss from commodities offsets your short-term capital gain from other sources. After year-end you liquidate the profitable position. This moves your short-term gain into the next year or (depending on how you hold the contract) converts it to a long-term capital gain. According to former IRS Commissioner Jerome Kurtz, the worst that can happen is that you "receive the equivalent of an interest-free loan from the government for the period of deferral." But if the price does not move, or if it turns around before you can liquidate the profitable position, you will have a loss.

Straddles can be used not only with commodities but with government securities, such as treasury bills, bonds, or "Ginnie Maes," or with options on those securities as well. The objective is the same—to create a loss that will

reduce your taxable income for one year while you also set the stage to cover that loss with a capital gain in the next year. If the year works out right, you get a current tax benefit and come close to breaking even on the transaction itself.

Prior to 1987 it was possible through straddling to reduce your tax rate by as much as 30 percent. Ordinary income, which was taxed up to 50 percent, was converted into long-term capital gains, which were taxed at a maximum of 20 percent. Moreover, unlike other investments, commodity investments could qualify for long-term capital gain treatment after only 6 (rather than 12) months.

Treasury bills were a favorite vehicle for straddles because, unlike most securities, they are not classified as capital assets. Under tax rules, any gain or loss from the sale of Treasury bills was treated as ordinary income. These bills are sold at a discount of face value and appreciate to *par* (face value) at maturity. Because the bills are such safe collateral, margin requirements on these straddles are low, as little as 3 percent of the bills' face value. The following example shows you how a Treasury bill straddle might have worked.

Assume that on December 17 you sell short $1 million in Treasury bills due December 26, and you buy $1 million in Treasury bills due the following March 26, which you intend to sell on January 2. The March maturity date allows for what is generally considered a reasonable period of market risk. But for purposes of this example, assume that between December 26 and January 2 interest rates are high. The result is that you don't receive the full $1 million face value because the bills due December 26 have 9 days to go until maturity. Assuming a discount of 16.83 percent, the purchase price is $995,793. On the maturity date, you have to cover the sale of borrowed securities. This will cost $1 million, giving you a loss on the transaction of $4,027 for the year.

The $1 million in bills due March 26 that you buy after making the short sale have 99 days to maturity. Assuming a discount of 16.30 percent, the purchase price is $955,175. When you sell those bills on January 2, you collect $962,419, for a gain of $7,244.

After commission costs of approximately $1,200, the net economic gain on the two transactions is $1,837. This gain is reduced by any interest charges on a margin account. In terms of the tax deduction, the straddles saved an investor in the 50 percent bracket (including state, federal, and local taxes) $2,103.50 in taxes for the first year ($4,027 × .50).

Such commodity straddles appear to be no-lose situations. In fact, though, they may turn out to be no-win situations. The Internal Revenue Service views

these transactions as "wholly tax motivated and without any real economic substance." Internal Revenue Service staff members who screen and classify returns are being trained to recognize "straddle" returns and are targeting them for audit. According to the IRS, "taxpayers claiming tax benefits from these transactions will face a substantial likelihood of having their return selected for audit and their claims of artificial losses disallowed on examination."

The bottom line on commodity tax straddles is that until they have been court approved as legitimate tax strategies, they should be avoided. The Economic Recovery Tax Act has made this shelter a dead issue by requiring you to "mark to market"—i.e., close all your positions even if they are not sold at year-end. Moreover, the Tax Reform Act of 1986 eliminated the capital gains deduction (the tax on long-term gains is now capped at 23.8 percent). There is little reason, therefore, to use a tax straddle as a tax shelter. Stay away from straddles. There are too many *legal* tax shelters for you to buy into this kind of audit *dis*allowance.

126 Art Reproduction

Art reproduction is another tax shelter that you should forget. Almost all lithograph shelters are going to be disallowed by the Internal Revenue Service. Under a lithograph shelter, you will be asked to purchase a lithograph plate that the artist uses to make a limited number of prints (50 to 500). An estimate of revenues available from sales is used to value the plates, from which investment tax credits and depreciation could be obtained.

In a typical shelter, you would give an artist $30,000 cash, say, plus a promissory note for $170,000 and assume the entire responsibility for marketing the prints. Prior to 1986, you would then seek a 10 percent investment tax credit and a first-year depreciation of 25 percent. At a 50 percent tax rate, you would reduce your tax payments by $43,750 [(200,000 – 10,000) × .25 = $47,500 in depreciation, or a tax savings of $23,750 at a 50 percent rate, plus an additional $20,000 from the 10 percent investment tax credit]. You would therefore be $13,750 ahead. However, the Internal Revenue Service would view the personal promissory note as a sham unless there was a real compulsion to pay it and would argue that the actual investment was only $30,000. In fact, most of these deals are marketed with the assumption that the full

risk of the personal promissory note will be paid only out of the proceeds from the sale of the prints. In effect, they are really nothing but shams.

Out of the $30,000 cash paid, $7,500 might go for printing, advertising, and sales; $7,500 to accountants and lawyers; $6,000 to the promoter; and $9,000 to the artist. You must either market the prints yourself or hire the promoter's "marketing" firm to do so for you. In one case, an investor sought to claim depreciation deductions and investment tax credit as a result of the purchase of a lithographic plate "master" and prints made from the "master."* According to the Internal Revenue Service, no depreciation could be claimed because the master was a nondepreciable work of art with a life of less than 3 years. The bottom line on this shelter is: Stay away.

127 Noncash Gift Shelters

This is another that you should avoid unless you are anxious to be part of an audit. The noncash gift shelter works as follows: You are asked to buy property such as books, Bibles, gemstones, etc., that are supposed to appreciate in value. You hold these objects for a period longer than 12 months and then contribute these "investments" to a charity. In return, you will get a charitable contribution deduction equal to the fair market value of the property.

For example, assume that you purchase rare Bibles at a cost of $5,000, and one year later they "appreciate" to a value of $30,000. You then contribute those Bibles to a church, claiming a deduction of their alleged fair market value of $30,000. If you are in the 35 percent bracket, this saves you $10,500 in tax—a $5,500 profit over your cost.

This is another shelter that the Internal Revenue Service considers nothing more than a sham. In one case a taxpayer-investor purchased limited-edition art books at a volume discount and then donated them to charity. The Internal Revenue Service ruled that the investor's activity was tantamount to that of an art dealer and that the investor's charitable deduction had to be reduced by the amount of gain that would not have been long-term capital gain had the investor sold the books.† In other words, the deduction was limited to only the cost basis.

*Rev. Rul. 70-432, I.R.B. 1979-53, 20.
†Rev. Rul. 79-419, I.R.B. 1979-52, 9.

Internal Revenue Service auditors have been instructed to look for non-cash gift deductions exceeding $5,000, particularly for deductions of well over the property's cost or basis, and especially if the property was held for less than 2 years. They will consistently challenge any determination of fair market value and try to disallow all of these shelters that they catch.

I question the validity of the Internal Revenue Service's position where it applies to true investments (for instance, gemstones) that may appreciate substantially over a year's period. However, in *Anselmo*, 80 T.C. No. 46, the Tax Court concluded that gems without settings would not be sold at retail, but rather sold to jewelers who would set the gems into rings or other jewelry. Since the jewelers are the consumers of gems, such stones should be valued on the basis of what the jeweler would pay to a *wholesaler* to obtain comparable gems.

Nonetheless, even if your shelter were to be allowed as a matter of law, you would be buying an audit on the question of valuation. The courts have consistently ruled against the taxpayer in these situations. I therefore recommend avoiding these types of shelters.

128 Municipal Bond Swaps

A municipal bond swap is an intriguing tax idea that allows you to maintain your equivalent current investment and yet at the same time take a tax-deductible loss on it. The swap lets you write off current paper losses and keep the advantage of owning municipal bonds as a shelter from federal income taxes, and possibly from state and local taxes as well. When interest rates increase, municipal bonds will normally be traded at substantially less than their face value. To do a swap, you merely sell your devalued bonds. This gives you a tax deduction for the current year. Then you reinvest the proceeds in other municipals of comparable yield and quality.

If you are contemplating any kind of swap, you must be aware of—and *avoid*—the "wash sale": You can deduct the realized loss on your current federal income tax return by selling your devalued bonds any time right up through December 31. But the Internal Revenue Service will call it a wash sale—and disallow the current loss deduction—if you turn around and buy the same bonds, or "substantially identical" ones, without waiting a full 30 days. That's 30 days either before or after the loss sale.

"Substantially identical" has never really been clearly defined. If the issuer is different, there should be absolutely no problem. But if the bonds you are

selling and the bonds you are buying are from the same issuer, the farther apart they are in maturity or interest rate the safer you will be. At a minimum, you should look for a five-year difference in maturities, or a spread of at least 50 *basis points* (0.5 percent difference in yields to maturity).

If you hold the original bonds for a year or less, you have a short-term loss, which can be used to offset, dollar for dollar, gains from the sale of other assets. Likewise, long-term losses can be used to offset gains dollar for dollar.

Any loss up to $3,000 that isn't absorbed can be deducted from your ordinary income. Losses in excess of gains plus $3,000 can be carried over to future years.

B How to Analyze a Tax Shelter

The most important part of a tax shelter offering is the prospectus. It summarizes the deal, details the history of the participants, and gives you a lawyer's opinion as to the projected tax consequences. Read it carefully! The summary and introduction in the front of most prospectuses are a good starting point, but make sure that you go beyond them. Look at the section on sources and uses of the proceeds very carefully. This will indicate who gets what and how much of the proceeds are going to the promoters and their affiliates, as opposed to being invested in the main objective of the partnership. Read the tax risks and considerations section equally carefully, as this should explain in detail the various tax considerations that might affect you as an investor.

Choose carefully the lawyer or accountant who will evaluate the deal. An unfamiliar lawyer or accountant who brings a deal to your attention at a social gathering may simply be representing the promoters. Find out whether your lawyer or accountant will be receiving a commission from the promoters if the deal is sold. On the other hand, it could also be unwise to rely on your own lawyer or accountant in evaluating a deal. Lawyers and accountants are prejudiced in the other direction, since if the deal goes sour, they could lose you as a client. They therefore have very little incentive to recommend anything with any risk.

Make sure that the deal evidences an intent to make a profit. If a shelter is based on deductions of interest and depreciation, with only a remote possibility of the receipt of revenues, it stands a greater risk of being disallowed by the Internal Revenue Service. For example, a 1985 shelter that marked up a $10 product to $100, took a 10 percent investment tax credit to make the $10 initial

contribution, and then took depreciation on the whole $100 was a high risk and unlikely to be approved if questioned in an audit.

Always invest in a tax shelter on the basis of economic returns. For example, the phase-out rule with respect to actively managed real estate could also produce a devastatingly high marginal tax rate as you approach the phase-out point. For example, assume you have $102,000 of adjusted gross income. You can claim up to $24,000 of losses from actively managed real estate. If you have $104,000 of adjusted gross income, then you claim $23,000 of deductions from such real estate activities. Assume instead that you had $1,000 of such losses from actively managed real estate activities and adjusted gross income of $148,000. Clearly the $1,000 is fully deductible. But, if you get a $2,000 raise, your adjusted gross income would rise to $150,000 and the $1,000 deduction would be disallowed. As a result, an extra $2,000 of gross income would be taxed at an effective rate of 36 percent. There would be a tax of $720 (24 percent of $3,000 increase in taxable income based on the extra $2,000 salary plus the $1,000 loss deduction), when your adjusted gross income rose only $2,000. This $720 increase in taxes on a $2,000 increase in your tax base produces a marginal rate of 36 percent.

Many shelters appear to give high write-offs on the basis of interest expense accrued according to the Rule of 78's. The Rule of 78's computes interest in a manner analogous to the sum of the year's digits methods for depreciation. The interest is ascertained by applying a fraction to the total interest due, the numerator of which is the number of payment periods remaining and the denominator of which is the sum of the periods. In Rev. Rul. 83-84, I.R.B. 1983-23, 12, the IRS ruled that it would no longer recognize interest deductions computed under that rule which exceeded the "economic accrual of interest." An exception was made for short-term consumer loans in Rev. Proc. 83-40, I.R.B. 1983-23, 22.

Determine the actual profit potential—that means measure the potential *after-tax return* against the *after-tax cost*. This allows a comparison of the cost of the tax shelter investment with other alternatives, such as stocks and bonds acquired with after-tax dollars. Make sure that you take into consideration how long it will take to get the yield from the after-tax dollars. For example, a three-to-one return ($3 of cash received for each $1 invested) looks better than a two-to-one return at first, but it will not be better if it takes several years longer to realize the full profit.

Examine the promoter's past history. What kind of track record does the person have? Have past deals been successful? Examine the financial statements of the general partner and evaluate them to ascertain that person's strength and

staying power in the face of adversity. What are the sharing arrangements and front-end fees of the general partner? That person's share of revenues should be reasonably related to the services he or she renders to the program. Fees, commissions, and other front-end-loaded charges should be reasonable, too.

Does the program provide for additional assessments? You must be told (a) the maximum amount of additional capital that the general partner can assess for unexpected expenses, (b) when the assessment can be made, (c) the tax consequences of meeting the assessment, and (d) the penalty if you fail to comply.

Carefully examine the forecast figures provided in the prospectus. Review even more carefully the footnotes accompanying the forecast, which explain the assumptions involved in putting that forecast together.

Review your state of mind. Probably the most important consideration that you must ponder before entering into a traditional tax shelter is your own personal tax-comfort level. Many people are not temperamentally suited to invest in projects that increase the possibility that they may be audited. It is important, therefore, for you to decide whether you can live comfortably with this added potential risk.

129 Getting Out of the Tax Shelter

Tax shelters, by definition, are long-term investments. However, there may come a time when you need to get out of the shelter immediately because of pressing cash requirements. There are four major firms that purchase partnership units:

- Liquidity Fund (1900 Powell Street, Emeryville, California 94608; 415-652-1462) buys public and private real estate programs, with the exception of government-subsidized housing partnerships.

- MacKenzie Securities (650 California Street, San Francisco, California 94108; 800-854-8357; in California, 800-821-4252) buys only public and private real estate deals that are at least 3 years old and have current cash flow. The firm won't buy private programs if the investor still owes payments to the sponsors.

- Equity Resources Group (1776 Massachusetts Avenue, Cambridge, Massachusetts 02140; 617-876-4800) deals only in private real estate programs. It turns down programs with more than half the investment unpaid.

- Livon Oil (220 Bush Street, San Francisco, California 94104; 415-781-6427) buys units in public and private oil and gas drilling and income programs. It also won't purchase partnerships from investors who still owe payments to the sponsors.

Other such firms include the following:

- Raymond James Limited Partnership
 Trading Desk
 140 66th Street North
 St. Petersburg, FL 33710
 1-800-237-7591

- National Partnership Exchange
 P.O. Box 578
 Tampa, FL 33601
 1-813-222-0555

- Investors Advantage Corp.
 The Fountains Financial Center
 US 19 North
 Suite 302
 Palm Harbor, FL 33563
 1-800-282-5865

- Partnership Securities Exchange
 1814 Franklin Street
 Suite 820
 Oakland, CA 94612
 1-415-763-5555

- Realty Repurchase, Inc.
 50 California Street
 Suite 1300
 San Francisco, CA 94111
 1-800-233-7357

- Oppenheimer & Bigelow
 489 Fifth Avenue
 New York, NY 10017
 1-800-431-7811

In addition, the Chicago Partnership Board, Inc. (800-272-6273) and the Partnership Exchange (10051 Fifth Street, North, Box 21438, St. Petersburg, Florida 33742; 800-356-2739; in Florida, 800-336-2739) match buyers and sellers of private and public real estate, oil and gas, equipment leasing, and cable TV partnerships.

130 Master Limited Partnerships

A master limited partnership is not a tax shelter. It is merely a vehicle or form in which an investment can be made. A master limited partnership is a large publicly registered limited partnership that is the principal or sole owner of multiple assets or partnerships that themselves may have been structured as tax shelters.

Master limited partnerships can pass through income and losses like traditional limited partnerships but provide investors greater liquidity. Units in numerous master limited partnerships are listed for trading on national securities exchanges, and master limited partnerships generally have the ability to issue additional units in the future.

There are two basic forms of master limited partnerships. The first is the roll-up, in which multiple assets or small limited partnerships are consolidated into a large single master limited partnership. The second is the roll-out, in which the apparent entity, like a corporation, spins off some of its assets into a separate master limited partnership. A third form is known as a roll-in. In this form new assets are put into a master limited partnership with the promise to add additional assets in the future.

Master limited partnerships may be attractive as passive income generators to shelter passive losses from other activities. For example, dividends distributed by real estate investment trusts (REITs) are classified as portfolio income, which cannot be sheltered by passive losses. However, income distributed by real estate master limited partnerships will be treated as passive income.

Another advantage of the master limited partnership is that it can pass through to investors a greater portion of each dollar of operating income than a corporation since the master limited partnership itself is not subject to taxation. Moreover, unlike REITs, a master limited partnership can actively engage in real estate activities, and they are entitled to more favorable depreciation. The master limited partnership structure, however, increases the difficulty of complying with the new partnership allocation rules because of the large number of investors and constant trading of partnership interests.

The Revenue Act of 1987 had a substantial impact on master limited partnerships. Such partnerships, falling under the classification of publicly traded partnerships (PTPs), will be treated as corporations for tax years after 1987. An exception is made, however, for those partnerships whose gross income is predominantly (90 percent or more) "qualifying income." Qualifying income consists of the following:

1. Interest: This category does not include interest derived in the conduct of a financial or insurance business, nor does it include amounts contingent on profits.

2. Dividends.

3. Real property rents: This category generally includes rents from interest in real property, charges for services customarily furnished in connection with the rental of real property, and rental income attributable to personal property in connection with the lease of real property. Amounts contingent on income or profits are not generally treated as rents from real property.

4. Gain from the sale or other disposition of real property.

5. Income or gains from the exploration, development, mining or production, refining, transportation, or marketing of any mineral or natural resource.

6. Any gain from the sale or other disposition of a capital asset or Section 1231 asset held for the production of any type of income described in 1 through 5, above.

7. Income and gains from commodities (other than those held for sale to customers in the ordinary course of business) and futures, options, or forward contracts with respect to other commodities.

Moreover, although the general corporate treatment applies for tax years beginning after 1987, in the case of an "existing partnership" it applies to tax years beginning only after 1997. An existing partnership is any one of the following:

1. A partnership that was publicly traded on or before December 17, 1987.

2. A partnership for which a registration statement was filed with the Securities and Exchange Commission on or before December 17, 1987.

3. A partnership for which an application was filed with a state regulatory commission on or before December 17, 1987, seeking permission to restructure a portion of a corporation as a publicly traded partnership.

These "grandfathered" partnerships have been given the opportunity to remain partnerships by the Tax Relief Act of 1997. The price, however, is a 3.5 percent tax on gross income, or on gross receipts minus cost of goods sold. Those that choose not to pay will be taxed as corporations, and face the 35 percent corporate tax rate. In the case of publicly traded partnerships that are not treated as corporations, the passive loss rules are to be applied separately for the items attributable to each PTP. The net losses of a partner from each PTP are to be suspended at the partner level and carried forward and netted against the partner's share of the nonportfolio income of that PTP in a later year or years. Generally, these losses may not be applied against passive income from other activities. Similarly, a partner's share of the credits is to be suspended, carried forward, and applied against the tax liability of a subsequent year or years attributable to that PTP. Generally, these credits may not be applied against tax liability attributable to other activities. Moreover, a partner's share in the net income of a PTP (both portfolio and business income) will generally not be treated as income from a passive activity; that is, it will generally be treated as portfolio income. However, a partner's share of the net business (nonportfolio) income of a PTP will be treated as passive income for carryover purposes. This means that a partner's share of a PTP's net business income may be offset by any suspended business losses of that PTP carried forward from an earlier year, but a partner's share of portfolio income may not be offset by any other current or carryover losses from other passive activities.

131 Abusive Shelters

In May 2002, the General Accounting Office reported that offshore and abusive tax shelters cost the Treasury an estimated $25 billion to $45 billion in lost revenue each year. Those are the tax shelters that Yale professor Michael J. Graetz defines as "a deal done by very smart people that, absent tax considerations, would be very stupid."

The IRS is now targeting all forms of abusive shelters. *Stay away!* I've discussed and suggested avoiding those kinds of investments. The Health Care and Education Reconciliation Act passed on March 30, 2010, makes it easier to stay away from "bad" shelters. Now you have to prove that any transaction had a substantial nontax business purpose and that it leads to a meaningful change in economic position.

Acting Assistant Attorney General John A. DiCicco said it best, "Those who promote tax fraud schemes will be investigated, prosecuted, and convicted, and they will also face substantial prison sentences."

A strict liability penalty of as much as 40 percent, will be applied to understatements arising out of undisclosed transactions, reduced to 20 percent for disclosed transactions. But don't let that stop you from investing in the economically based and completely legal structures explained earlier.

Super Tax Shelters

"When more of the people's sustenance is exacted through the form of taxation than is necessary to meet the just obligations of government . . . , such exaction becomes ruthless extortion and a violation of the fundamental principles of a free government."

GROVER CLEVELAND
Second Annual Message
December 1886

"As to the astuteness of taxpayers in ordering their affairs so as to minimize taxes, it has been said that the very meaning of a line in the law is that you intentionally may go as close to it as you can if you do not pass it."

Superior Oil Co. v. Mississippi, 280 U.S. 390, 395–96

"This is so because nobody owes any public duty to pay more than the law demands; taxes are enforced exactions, not voluntary contributions."

J. FRANKFURTER
Atlantic Coast Line v. Phillips, 322 U.S. 168, 172–73 (1947)

"Only feeble minds are paralyzed by facts."

ARTHUR C. CLARKE
Science fiction author

This is the chapter that alone is worth more than a hundred times the cost of this book. Each of the following shelters is completely legal and has been sold to sophisticated taxpayers for thousands of dollars. These shelters have been worth the cost—they have saved those taxpayers many multiples of their acquisition price in taxes not paid. Each of these supershelters will be presented, explained, and structured in detail. Study them well. They will show you how legally and painlessly to reduce your own taxes to zero.

A Family Shifts

The first rule of income taxation is that a tax liability for personal service income may not be avoided by the earner of that income by assignment or other transfer before the income is realized. If you perform services that earn monetary reward, that income will be taxed to you. The second law of income taxation, however, is that income earned from *property* belongs to the owner of that property. Therefore, the first key to reducing your taxes is to transfer income-producing property to a family member in a lower bracket. If you make a bona fide transfer of income-producing property that you own, you have effectively shifted all future income from that property. After the transfer, the future income and all income tax due on that income will belong to the new owner in the lower tax bracket.

Part of your solution to the problem of reducing your tax, therefore, is to get your current income taxed to lower-bracketed family members. This strategy is based on the premise that a family is an economic and social unit and that it is immaterial to the welfare of the family as a whole which member derives income or owns property. From a tax perspective, however, it is extremely material.

For example, assume you are in the 32 percent bracket and transfer $1,000 of annual income to your son so that it is taxable to him instead of to you. Immediately you save $320 in taxes. Furthermore, the whole $1,000 will come tax-free to a child who has no other income, even if the $1,000 represents unearned income (for instance, interest, dividends, or rents). Moreover, not only can the savings be multiplied by the number of children involved, but if your son is under age 17 you can get a $2,000 credit for him on your tax return.

The shift does not have to be made to a child. Suppose you are supporting a parent out of your current income. You might save an enormous amount of taxes if you could transfer some of that income so that the tax would be shifted from you directly to your lower-bracketed parent. For 2018, your parents, if over age 65, get a standard deduction of $24,000 + ($1,300 × 2). Thus, if you are paying $26,600 a year of your after-tax income to your parents, you could save $8,512 a year in taxes if you are in the 32 percent bracket. Such a shift of income can be accomplished through a direct gift of income-producing property or by using one of a number of trusts that will be examined later in this chapter.

The standard deduction now permits the tax-free transfer of $1,050 of investment income to a child or other member of your family who has no other income. Alternatively, if the child is of sufficient age to work, that child can earn up to $17,500 ($12,000 standard deduction plus $5,500 IRA*) a year in income and still pay zero taxes. Remember, however, that the objective is not necessarily that the family member pay zero taxes, but rather that the taxes paid be less than what you would pay if the income were taxed directly to you. For example, even if that family member is in the 10 percent bracket, a shift of $1,000 in income from you in the 32 percent bracket would result in a net savings of $220.

There are a number of ways to effect an income shift within the family. Remember, when transactions among family members are genuine, they must be given full legal effect for tax purposes.

Note, however, that the Tax Reform Act of 1986 limited the availability of certain income-shifting techniques to children under age 14, increased to under age 18 as of January 2006. In 2007, Congress upped the age limit to as high as under age 24.

NEW RULES

For 2007:

The Tax Increase Prevention and Reconciliation Act of 2006 expanded the kiddie tax to children under age 18 who earn more than $1,700 in interest, dividends, capital gains, and other unearned income.

The first $850 ($900 for 2008, $950 for 2009 through 2012, $1,000 for 2013 and 2014, and $2,050 for 2015) is taxed at a zero rate, with the next $850 ($900 for 2008, $950 for 2009 through 2012, $1,000 for 2013 and 2014, and $1,050 for 2015 and 2016) taxed at the child's rate, currently 10 percent (as low as zero percent for long-term capital gains). Any unearned income in excess of $1,700 ($1,800 for 2008, $1,900 for 2009 through 2012, $2,000 for 2013 and 2014, and $2,100 for 2015 and 2016) will be taxed at the parents' highest marginal rate, now as much as 39.6 percent.

It gets worse.

For 2008 and after:

The Small Business and Work Opportunity Act, signed into law May 25, 2007, changed the rules again.

If your child is under age 19, he or she is subject to the kiddie tax, *unless* his or her earned income is more than half his or her support.

*Many companies, including Merrill Lynch, Charles Schwab, and TD Waterhouse, will establish IRA accounts for children. However, at this age, a nondeductible Roth IRA may be preferable.

If your child is a full-time student, *unless* his or her earned income is more than half his or her support, the kiddie tax applies up to age 24. A child is generally considered a full-time student if he or she attends school full-time for at least five months during the year.

At age 24, the child would be taxed at his or her own rate. For 2018, that would subject the first $9,525 to a 10 percent rate and the next $29,175 to a 15 percent hit. Long-term capital gains and qualified dividends would be taxed as low as 0 (zero) percent for income up to $38,600—that is, *after* all deductions.

The kiddie tax will apply only if:

a) the child is not married and does not file a joint return; *and*

b) at least one of the child's parents is alive at year-end.

The child's age is determined by his or her age on December 31. Note that the kiddie tax only applies to unearned income. Earned income from a job or self-employment is exempt from the kiddie tax.

The tax payable by the child on net unearned income was essentially the additional amount of tax that the parent would have had to pay if the net unearned income of the child were included in the parent's taxable income.

If parents had two or more children with unearned income to be taxed at the parent's marginal tax rate, all of the children's applicable unearned income would be added together and the tax calculated. The tax was then allocated to each child based on the child's pro rata share of unearned income.

The Tax Cuts and Jobs Act of 2017 changed the rules. Now, the child will pay based on the schedule for estates or trusts, rather than on their parents'. Not good—the top 37% rule based on the schedule for estates or trusts kicks in at $12,500. For a parent, it would not hit until taxable income of over $600,000.

The intent of the law is to create three stages:

1. There will be no tax on the first $1,050 of unearned income because of the child's standard deduction. The standard deduction for a dependent in 2018 is the greater of $1,050 in *unearned* income or the sum of $350 plus any *earned* income, with a total of $12,000.

2. The next $1,050 of unearned income will be taxed to the child at the child's bracket.

3. Unearned income in excess of the first $2,100 will be taxed to the child at the appropriate estate or trust rate.

The term *unearned income* means income from sources *other* than wages, salaries, professional fees, and other amounts received as compensation for personal services actually rendered.

The parent whose taxable income was taken into account was the custodial parent of the child in the case of unmarried parents. In the case of parents who were married but filing separately, the individual with the greater taxable income would be the parent whose taxable income is used in these calculations.

The parent of a child subject to the kiddie tax receiving unearned income was required to provide that child with the parent's taxpayer identification number (TIN). That number (typically the parent's Social Security number) had to be included in the child's tax return.

Upon written request a parent's return had to be disclosed to the child or the child's legal representative to the extent necessary for the child's return to be properly filed.

PLANNING SUGGESTIONS

Note that the so-called *kiddie tax* rules discussed above apply regardless of who gave the children the income-producing property. They apply even if the cash or other property generating the income was transferred prior to 1987. So income from existing custodial accounts and income distributed from existing nongrantor trusts may be taxable to children at the parent's rates regardless of when the account or trust was created.

It may appear that the advantage of shifting income was eliminated by the reduction in bracket spreads (until 1987 the spread from the top bracket of 50 percent to the bottom bracket of 11 percent was 39 percentage points, then the spread was from 39.6 percent to 10 percent, a 29.6 percentage point difference, and it is now between 10 percent and 37 percent, a 27 percentage point difference). But this is an oversimplification. Once a child becomes 19, all earned and unearned income is potentially taxed at the child's rate. So dropping $10,000 a year of income from the 37 percent bracket to the 10 percent bracket will save 27 percent per year of the amount of income shifted. In 10 years that amounts to $27,000 in tax savings!

132 Unearned Income of Minor Children

Beginning in 1989, the parent whose marginal tax rate would be applied in calculating the tax on the new unearned income of a child subject to the

kiddie tax could have elected on Form 8814 to include the child's net unearned income on his or her own return. The election could have only be made if:

a) the child has gross income only from interest or dividends;

b) such gross income is more than $1,050 and less than $10,500; *and*

c) no estimated tax payments for such year are made in the name and taxpayer identification number of such child, and no amount of tax has been withheld.

If the election was made, the child would not have to file a tax return, and the parent's gross income would be increased by the amount of the child's net income over $2,100. The parents' tax will also normally be increased by $105 (10 percent of the $1,050 that would have been taxed to the child).

There could have been two advantages to a parent in directly including a child's income on his or her own return. First, it avoided the filing of an additional return. Second, and perhaps even more important, if the parent was subject to a limit on the amount of investment interest that he or she could have deducted the inclusion of the child's investment income on the parent's return could obviate this interest expense limitation to the extent of additional investment income. However, to the extent that the parent's adjusted gross income was a factor in computing certain itemized deductions—such as the miscellaneous itemized, medical expense, and casualty loss deduction—such inclusion may actually reduce the deductions on the parent's return. According to Rev. Proc. 2018-18 (March 5, 2018), parents can still include a child's income on their joint return. But that income, subject to this kiddie tax, would be taxed at the estate and trust rate. You should weigh the administrative savings and the savings on tax preparation fees against any potential additional cost.

As of 2018, the use of the estate and trust rates simplifies this issue.

There are still many ways to shift both wealth and income and save taxes.

WHAT SHOULD YOU DO NOW?

If your kids are not currently subject to the kiddie tax, but would be next year, you have a small window of opportunity. Give long-term appreciated assets to the kids to sell now. The tax on any gain would fall from your 15/20 percent rate to as low as 0 (zero) percent, a 15/20 percent differential in your family pocket.

You can gift as much as $15,000 in securities to each child without even filing a gift tax return. With two kids, and two parents, that's as much as $60,000 that can be transferred gift tax-free. If it is more than that amount, Form 709, the gift tax return, must be filed. But, in addition to the $15,000 annual per donee exclusion,

each donor has a lifetime $11.18 million exclusion for 2018. So, even if you do have to file the return, you probably won't be liable for any gift tax.

Consider using a Section 529 plan to invest for your child. If the money is used for qualified college expenses, all income comes out tax-free.

For financial aid purposes 20 percent of the money held in your child's name is considered fair game to pay for his or her tuition. But, only 5.6 percent of money held in a parents' name counts. Even though the 529 plan benefits the child, it is considered an asset of the parents for aid determination.

Also consider converting current UGMA accounts in the child's name to 529 accounts. Under both umbrellas, the hit to financial aid is the same. But, at least with the 529 account, the kiddie tax slam is avoided.

What else can you do?

1. Give a Series EE U.S. Savings Bond that will not mature until after the donee-child is age 19 (24 for full-time students, in all examples below as well). No tax will be payable until the bond is redeemed. At that time the gain will be taxed at the child's relatively lower tax bracket. Remember that this strategy will not work if the child already owns Series EE bonds and is already reporting each year's interest accrual as income. Once the election to report income currently is made, it is irrevocable. But, if the total interest is not more than $1,050 per year, you may want immediate recognition at a zero tax cost!

2. Give growth stocks (or growth stock mutual funds) which pay little or no current dividends. The child will therefore pay no tax currently and can hold the stock until reaching age 19. Upon a sale the child will be taxed at the child's bracket.

3. Give *deep discount* tax-free municipal bonds that mature on or after the child's 19th birthday. The bond interest will be tax-free to the child and the discount (face less cost basis) will be taxed to the child at the child's bracket when the bond is redeemed at maturity.

4. Employ your children. Pay them a reasonable salary for work they actually perform. Remember that the standard deduction for children is the greater of (a) $1,050 or (b) earned income plus $350 in unearned income (up to a 2018 $12,000). You could pay an additional tax-free $5,500 if they open a traditional deductible IRA. Regardless of how much is paid to the child, the business will have a deduction at its tax bracket, and the amount will be taxable to the child at the child's bracket. Alternatively, the child could establish a Roth IRA to shelter income forever.

5. Sell all nonappreciated property (be sure to consider brokerage costs and time value of money) and purchase tax-free municipals for the child.

6. Consider the multiple advantages of a *term of years* charitable remainder trust for children over age 19—so the income will be taxed to the child, but the grantor will receive an immediate income tax deduction.

7. In making gifts to your children consider support obligation cases such as *Braun, Sutliff,* and *Miller.* Parents who can with ease meet the support needs of even an adult college-age child may be considered obligated to provide support. If UGMA (the Uniform Gifts to Minors Act) or 2503(c) trust funds are used to send a child to college, will the parent be taxed? Worse yet, do these cases mean the UGMA custodian (or 2503(c)) trustee violates a fiduciary duty by using such funds to pay for a college education when it's the parent's duty (thus making such funds unavailable for the very purpose for which they were intended)?

 Assuming the support problems addressed above are not applicable, judicious use of a 2503(c) trust (but not a UGMA account) will allow significant income shifting. The trust can accumulate income while the beneficiary is under age 19 and avoid the kiddie tax.

8. Life insurance and annuity policies that stay within statutory guidelines (ask for a written guarantee from the home office) for life insurance should be particularly attractive, assuming *loading* costs are relatively low and/or backended. This includes universal, variable, and traditional whole life of the single-, annual-, and limited-payment types. In the case of the SPWL (Single-Premium Whole Life) the entire single premium paid at purchase starts earning the declared interest rate immediately. The cost of insurance and expenses is recovered by the insurer from the difference between the declared interest rate and the rate the insurer actually earns. If surrendered, any unrecovered expenses are deducted from the policy's cash values. The owner can obtain cash values at any time by (1) surrender (gain over cost is taxable) or (2) loan (loan interest is probably nondeductible). But note the limitations and new penalties imposed by TAMRA in 1988. Interest is charged at about the same rate credited on borrowed sums and is free of current tax. Earnings compound free of current taxation. Unlike tax-free municipal bonds there is no market risk, and SPWL is highly liquid. A parent can purchase the product on his or her own life which makes college education for the children more likely, and the parent does not have to give up control or make a gift.

9. Concentrate on gift and estate tax savings devices such as the annual exclusion. Parents should consider gifting $15,000–$30,000 a year of non-income-producing assets to a minor's trust or custodial account, which could be converted into income-producing assets slowly after the child turns age 19.

The fund can become self-liquidating and exhaust itself by the time the child finishes college/graduate school.

10. We still have limited shifting of income to children under the age of 19 with the 2018 $1,050 minimum standard deduction and the special rule taxing the first $1,050 of unearned income at the child's marginal tax rate. Assuming that the parent is in the highest marginal tax rate (37.0 percent), the first $1,050 of income shifted to the child would result in $388.50 of tax savings ($1,050 × .37), and the next $1,050 of transferred income would result in $283.50 of tax savings [$1,050 × (.37 − .10)] for a total of $672.

Over a period of years, the tax savings generated by shifting $2,100 of income to the child can be significant. For example, if the annual tax savings were invested at 8 percent for a 18-year period, the total tax savings and interest would be $27,180. Furthermore, the one-time gift necessary to generate the $2,100 of unearned income would closely approximate the $30,000 annual gift tax exclusion for both parents, so that little, if any, of their estate tax exclusion is used.

The above limitations apply only to the shifting of unearned income—e.g., interest, dividends, rents, etc. For those shifts discussed later in this chapter, assume that whenever there is a reference to shifting unearned income to children, those children are not under age 18. The following techniques can be used to shift income to lower-income members of your family.

133 Outright Gifts

A gift of income-producing property to members of your family is perhaps the most common method of splitting income to gain a tax advantage. The simplest way to transfer money, tax-free, is by gifts in relatively small lumps. You can give an annual gift of $15,000 per person to any number of family members—$30,000 if the gift is made jointly with a spouse—without incurring any gift liability. In order to qualify for the $15,000 or the $30,000 exclusion in the year the gift is made, it must be a gift of a *present interest* (current benefit). A gift tax return is required for any gifts in excess of these amounts to any recipient in any year if the gift is one of a present interest. A gift tax return is required for a gift of any amount if it is of a future interest. A gift is a completed transfer of the entire legal and beneficial interest in the property given. There is no gift *tax paid* until you use up your annual $15,000 exclusion plus your $11.18 million lifetime exclusion.

For a gift to your spouse, there is now an unlimited gift tax marital deduction. If the family members to whom you wish to give gifts are adults, then normally there are no problems. This is *not* true if the objects of your income shifting are minor children, who lack full legal capacity. In consequence, legal difficulties are often encountered in connection with their ability to manage and dispose of the property that they acquire. Furthermore, they normally lack full maturity and it is often less desirable from a practical standpoint to give them control over property.

Certain types of property are more suited than others to practical ownership by minors. Securities that require no management control can be put in the name of a minor when there is no desire to dispose of them before majority. If there is such a desire, the securities should be in bearer form or registered in the name of an adult nominee who may dispose of them at the direction of the minor. Under such circumstances you should file a Form 1087 putting the Internal Revenue Service on notice as to the true ownership of the stock. Alternatively, savings bonds may be purchased and registered in the sole name of a minor and may be redeemed at the option of the minor or a parent.

Cash is the simplest thing to give to a minor. It may be kept in a savings account by the parent in trust for the child. If you want to give cash to a family member but must sell appreciated stock to do so, it is normally cheaper to give your family member the securities and *then* have them sold. Any gain realized will be taxed at the lower marginal tax bracket rate of that person if he or she is 19 or older.

It is very important to note that under no circumstances should funds transferred to a minor be used to satisfy a parent's legal obligation of support (see *Sutliff v. Sutliff,* 489 A.2d 764 [Super. Ct. PA 1985], subsequently invalidated by a later ruling by the Pennsylvania Supreme Court, and *Braun v. Commissioner,* T.C. Memo 1984-285). If funds are so used, the income will be taxed to the parent!

GUARDIANS

Many of the practical and legal difficulties inherent in dealing with minors can be alleviated either by having a guardian appointed for the minor or by creating a trust for the benefit of the minor. A guardian must be appointed by the state court having jurisdiction over such matters. There is normally little difficulty in securing the appointment on the petition, with the consent of both parents. Once appointed, the guardian usually becomes responsible to the

appointing court for the proper and faithful performance of any duties. The judiciary standards governing a guardian's investment powers are those set by state law. A guardian is not allowed a choice or discretion beyond standards that are usually quite conservative. There are, however, a number of problems in using a guardian. The guardian is usually required by state law to furnish a bond for the faithful performance of duties. If sureties are required on the bond, the guardian is further restricted by the supervision exercised by the sureties. Furthermore, the guardian may be required to get court approval and certification that any actions—for instance, a sale of securities—are in the best interest of the ward.

Each state has its own standards and requirements detailing the duties and responsibilities of a guardian. For example, some statutes require that annual or periodic accounts be presented for approval by the courts. On the other hand, many of these provisions are often disregarded in a parent-guardian situation where harmony prevails within the family. This is because, as a practical matter, the courts usually do not take any action except on a complaint of a party in interest.

TRUSTS

Many of the technical and legal difficulties of guardianship can be eliminated through the use of a trust for the benefit of the minor. The standards governing the investment and management powers of the trustee may be as broad or narrow as the creator of the trust desires. If the trust that is created comes into being during your lifetime (*inter vivos* trust), that trust usually is under no direct court supervision. Furthermore, if you should so provide, no bond will be required by the trustee for faithful performance of duties and no court approval will be necessary for the disposal of trust assets in the usual course of the trustee's administration of that trust. Furthermore, while it is usually preferable to have an independent trustee, it is legally permissible for you as a parent to act as trustee.

You should be aware, however, that there are certain limits and dangers in the use of the trust for income shifting:

1. The income must not be "applied or distributed for the support or maintenance of a beneficiary (other than the grantor's spouse) whom the grantor is legally obligated to support or maintain." You have the legal obligation to support your minor children. If the income or principal of a trust you create is used to discharge this obligation, it is regarded as your income and taxable to you. The solution here is to use the funds for non-support purposes. For example, in most states a college education would

not constitute a legal obligation that would fall under the umbrella of "support." In the case of *Frederick C. Braun, Jr, et al. v. Commissioner* (T.C. Memo 1984-285) however, the Tax Court found that under New Jersey law, financially able parents have the legal obligation to provide their children with a college education. The court therefore ruled that to the extent that income from two trusts was used to pay for tuition, room, and board for Braun's children, the income was taxable to Braun. The solution here would have been to distribute the income directly to the children and have them pay for their own college expenses. Structured that way, the income would not have been taxable to the parents. (See also the Pennsylvania case of *Sutliff v. Sutliff*, 489 A.2d 764, 1986, wherein the Appellate Court held that a parent may not use Uniform Gifts to Minors Act [UGMA] funds for a child's support. The import of this case, which arose out of a divorce situation, is that the court ruled that the parental duty of support may extend to providing a college education, even though the child has attained an age of majority under general state law but not under UGMA. This case was later invalidated by a subsequent ruling by the Pennsylvania Supreme Court. See also *Stone*, T.C. Memo 1987-454, wherein the Tax Court again ruled that trust payments for private school tuition are within a parent's legal support obligation; thus, such payments are taxable to the grantor/parent instead of the minor trust beneficiary. *Stone* involved only the payment of private school tuition to minor beneficiaries, thus avoiding the more difficult question of the support obligation in regard to payments of college expenses for adult children. These cases follow the analysis in *Braun* with reference to a college education constituting parental support, and its solution should be approached in the same manner—i.e., distributing the income directly to the children and having them pay for their own education expenses.)

2. The trust must *not* be set up so that it could be considered to be carrying on a business or as having sufficient attributes of a corporation to make it taxable as a corporation by the federal government. An ordinary, valid, and legal trust is not an association taxed as a corporation.

3. The property contributed to the trust by gift must not be deemed a gift of a future interest. If it is, the gift will not be entitled to the benefits of the annual exclusion for gift tax purposes. A gift to a minor, in trust or otherwise, will *not* be considered a gift of a future interest (and the annual exclusion will be available) if:

a) the property and income may be used for the benefit of the minor; *and*

b) any amount not so used will pass to the minor at age 21, or to that person's estate, or to any testamentary appointee in the event of an early death. A gift of an income interest that meets this test is considered a present interest.

4. The trust must be irrevocable or, if the transfers to the trust were made prior to March 2, 1986, irrevocable for at least 10 years, and you as a grantor cannot retain powers that, in the eyes of the tax law, constitute a beneficial interest in the property.[1] I will examine these 10-year trusts under the section on Clifford Trusts.

To simplify the procedures for making gifts to minors of securities and other specified property, all states have enacted what is known as the Uniform Gift to Minors Act. The effect of this act is to permit such gifts to be made through a custodian, and to permit a subsequent transfer without the appointment of a guardian or the creation of a trust. Under the Act, securities can be transferred to minors by registering them in the donor's name, in the name of an adult member of the minor's family, or in the guardian's name, as *custodian* for the minor, and delivering the securities to the custodian. If the donor is the custodian, registration constitutes delivery. Securities in bearer form can be given by delivery to an adult member of the minor's family (other than the donor) or to the guardian as custodian for the minor, together with the deed in statutory form.

The custodian gets the managerial power a guardian would have, and the minor gets absolute legal title to the securities. The custodian can sell and reinvest, and can collect income and accumulate it or apply it for the minor's benefit. When the minor reaches the age of majority (21 or, in some states, 18), the custodian must turn over the securities and any accumulated income. If the minor dies before then, the securities and the income are part of the estate. Remember, however, that any income from the transfer that is used to discharge, in whole or in part, the legal obligation to support and maintain a minor is *pro tanto* taxable to the person who made the transfer. Furthermore, you should note that if you are the donor and name yourself as custodian of the securities or succeed to custodianship, your death before the minor reaches the age of majority will throw the securities into your estate.

1. Internal Revenue Code, Section 676.

134 Clifford Trusts

Prior to March 2, 1986, as an alternative to a completed gift, you could have considered the creation of a temporary trust commonly known as a Clifford Trust. Clifford or temporary trusts to shift taxable income from a high-bracket taxpayer to a low-bracket taxpayer were extensively used in the past.

The Tax Reform Act of 1986 effectively eliminated the use of Clifford Trusts. Except for transfers made prior to March 2, 1986—with another exception under which the 10-year rule of prior law would continue to apply to certain trusts created pursuant to certain binding property settlements entered into before March 1, 1986—Clifford Trusts are taxed as grantor trusts as of January 1, 1987. That means that the income of the trust is taxed at *your* higher marginal tax bracket.

135 Interest-Free Loans

Because of the limits imposed on the transfer of funds to a Clifford Trust free of gift tax, an alternative planning strategy was devised. As an alternative or a supplement to transferring funds to a Clifford Trust, you could have made an unlimited interest-free loan to your lower-bracketed family member.

Unfortunately, the use of interest-free loans as a method to allocate income to lower-bracketed taxpayers was effectively eliminated by the Tax Reform Act of 1984. Under that Act, foregone interest on a loan is treated as a gift from the lender to the borrower and is subject to the gift tax. Moreover, the lender (parent) is deemed to have interest income if the loan is more than $100,000. For loans from a corporation to a shareholder, the interest element is treated as if a dividend includable in income was paid by the corporation to the shareholder. A loan to a person providing services results in the foregone interest being treated as compensation.

136 The Schnepper Shelter: Gift Leasebacks

An alternative technique used to increase income-shifting potential is the gift-leaseback transaction. In the typical situation, the taxpayer, usually a professional such as a doctor, attorney, accountant, or even a shareholder in a

closely held corporation, establishes a trust for any children. Then business property, such as an office building, furniture, equipment, autos, trucks, or machinery, is transferred to the trust, which agrees to lease it back to the taxpayer. The lease payments are then deductible by the high-bracketed taxpayer and reported as income by the low-bracketed trust beneficiary.

In effect, the taxpayer has relinquished title in exchange for significant income shifting. There is no depreciation recapture on such transfers,[2] nor should there be any investment credit recapture.[3] In addition, not only is the first $1,050 of the shifted income to each child exempt from tax,[4] but the parent-taxpayer could, prior to 2018, continue to be entitled to a personal exemption for each child until each is 19 or as long as each is a full-time student if more than half of each child's total support is received from the parent.[5]

The Tax Court has approved the gift-leaseback technique as a legitimate means of reducing your tax liability. It has developed four requirements that must be satisfied before it will permit a grantor to deduct the lease payments.[6] These requirements are as follows:

1. The grantor must not retain substantially the same control over the property that was held before making the gift. This requirement can be satisfied by appointing an independent trustee. The Tax Court has recognized both commercial banks[7] and personal attorneys[8] as independent trustees. In no case should the grantor-taxpayer become the trustee[9]; neither should the spouse.[10]

2. See I.R.C. Section 1245(b)(1) and (3) and Section 1250(d)(1) and (3). Potential recapture is deferred until a subsequent disposition of the property—see *Rainier Companies, Inc. v. Comm.,* 61 T.C. 68 (1973), acq., 1974-1 C.B.2.

3. Reg. Section 1.47-3(g) provides that the recapture provisions will not apply where qualified property is disposed of and, as part of the same transaction, is leased back. The regulation is directed at sales but "disposed of" should incorporate and apply as well to gifts in trust situations.

4. I.R.C. Section 63(b)5.

5. See I.R.C. Section 152, Section 151(e)(1)(B) and Section 151(e)(4).

6. See *Mathews v. Comm.,* 61 T.C. 12 (1973), rev'd, 520 F.2d 323, 75-2 USTC Par. 9734, 36 AFTR2d 75-5965 (CA-5, 1975) *cert. den.* See also *Rosenfeld v. Comm.,* (CA-2, 1983), 51 AFTR 2d 83-1251 (May 2, 1983), and *May v. Comm.,* 76 T.C. 7 (1981) (CA-9, 1984), 53 AFTR 2d 84-626, where a gift leaseback was found valid despite an oral lease!

7. See *Serbousek,* TCM 1977-105.

8. See *Lerner,* 71 T.C. 290 (1978).

9. See *Penn,* 51 T.C. 144 (1968); *Van Zandt,* 40 T.C. 824 (1963), aff'd, 341 F.2d 440, 65-1 USTC Par. 9236, 15 AFTR2d 372 (CA-5, 1965) cert. den.

10. See *Larry Benson,* T.C. 86, for problems created with a spouse trustee. See also *Rosenfeld,* T.C. Memo 1982-263 re: control.

2. The leaseback should normally be in writing and must require payment of a reasonable lease rental. The trustee should have the trust property appraised[11] and find out the lease price of similar property to justify the reasonableness of the lease rental. A payment schedule should be established and adhered to.[12] Moreover, the trustee's powers detailed in the trust instrument should be broad enough to maintain independence. One suggested technique to ensure the court's recognition of the trustee's independence is to make the initial term of the lease less than the term of the trust. In doing so the trustee is forced to exercise independent power to renegotiate renewal agreements.[13]

3. The leaseback (as distinguished from the gift) must have a bona fide business purpose. This requirement can be easily satisfied, since the trust property is business property intended to be used again in the taxpayer's business. Certain circuits of the U.S. district court, however, require a bona fide business purpose for *both* the leaseback *and the gift*. Merely to place trust property beyond the reach of creditors has been held to be insufficient as a business purpose for the gift.[14] One suggested business purpose would be to get managerial expertise in the control and operation of the property.[15] This would be especially effective, for example, if the taxpayer were a doctor, the property an office building, and the trustee an attorney expert in real estate.

4. The taxpayer must not possess a disqualifying "equity" in the property. Once the property is transferred, the taxpayer possesses only a reversionary interest in the trust property. The Tax Court holds that a reversionary interest is not a disqualifying equity, since its enjoyment is realized only after the trust expires.[16] Unfortunately, the Internal Revenue Service does not accept this position.[17] One way to avoid litigation on this matter would be to create a remainder interest that passes to the taxpayer's spouse or children, or to a corporation set up for the purpose, at the termination of the trust.[18]

11. Supra, note 13.
12. Supra, note 14.
13. See *Mathews,* supra, note 11, and *Quinlivan,* TCM 1978-70 aff'd 599 F.2d 269, 79-1 USTC Par. 9396, 44 AFTR2d 79-5059 (CA-8, 1979) cert. den.
14. See *Butler,* 65 T.C. 327 (1975).
15. See *Skemp,* 8 T.C. 415 (1947), rev'd, 168 F.2d 598, 48-1 USTC Par. 9300, 36 AFTR 1089 (CA-7, 1948).
16. See *Oaks,* 44 T.C. 524 (1965) and *Serbousek,* supra, note 12.
17. See Rev. Rul. 54-9, 1954-1 C.B. 20.
18. See supra, note 13 and supra, note 10.

Once the gift-leaseback trust is established, the benefits can be substantial. For example, assume a married taxpayer in the 30 percent federal and state tax bracket established a trust for three children by transferring business property valued at $84,000 into the trust. No gift taxes are payable on such a transfer.[19] Assume further that this is property that has been fully depreciated and that therefore no further deductions are available to the taxpayer if the property is retained. The fair rental for such property, though, is $250 per month.

The higher-bracket taxpayer therefore pays lease rentals of $3,000 per year and takes that amount as a business deduction. This saves $900 in taxes.[20] The three children each include $1,000 in their income, less their share of the trustee's management fee. Ignoring that fee for illustrative purposes and assuming no other income, the three children may pay zero taxes and retain $3,000. As a result of a transfer of $3,000, total family wealth has increased by $3,900, for a net increase of $900.[21]

If the property were still subject to depreciation by the original taxpayer, the above benefits would be reduced by the tax savings from depreciation deductions foregone in the transfer. These deductions, though, would be available to the children-beneficiaries. Any maintenance or upkeep expenses incurred for the property can still be deducted by the lessee-taxpayer, if so provided in the lease agreement. Note that in this example the $1,000 retained by each child can be used to pay that child's college expenses.[22] If the trust were not used, to accumulate $3,000 for tuition would require the 30 percent taxpayer to earn an incremental $4,286 in pretax dollars.[23]

Furthermore, if the property that you're contemplating transferring into trusts for your children is subject to a mortgage, you should be aware that the Garn Act lists certain property transfers that should never trigger loan acceleration under a due on sale clause. These exceptions apply to all loans— to loans originated by state chartered institutions and by federal lending institutions, regardless of the date of their origination. Included in these safe harbor transfers is a transfer in which a spouse or *children* of the borrower receive ownership of the property.

Note that the Tax Reform Act of 1986 eliminated the viability of Clifford Trusts for tax savings. The above trust-leaseback technique, however, would still

19. Split gift ($14,000 × 2) × 3 = $84,000 exclusion.
20. The lease payments would be deductible as ordinary and necessary business expenses under I.R.C. Section 162—$3,000 × .30 = $900 reduction in taxes at that bracket level.
21. $3,000 retained plus $900 saved in taxes = $3,900.
22. Or any other nonsupport expenses. See supra, note 8.
23. $4,286 at a marginal 30 percent rate leaves $3,000 after taxes.

be viable using an irrevocable trust. All of the other provisions, as discussed above, would apply.

Trust leasebacks have been specifically validated in at least the following 23 states: Alaska, Arizona, Arkansas, California, Delaware, Hawaii, Idaho, Illinois, Indiana, Missouri, Montana, Nebraska, Nevada, New Jersey, New York, North Dakota, Oregon, Pennsylvania, Rhode Island, South Dakota, Vermont, Washington, and Wisconsin.

The IRS will no longer litigate gift-leaseback cases where the lessee is a taxable entity separate from the grantor. This position was announced in an Action on Decision on April 23, 1984. By separate taxable entity, the IRS means a regular corporation, rather than a partnership or a Subchapter S corporation. Two-party gift-leaseback arrangements have been upheld not only by the Tax Court but by the following circuits: the Second (*Rosenfeld*, 706 F. 2d 1277, 83-1 USTC para. 9341 [CA-2, 1983], see *Use of gift leaseback to shift income given substantial boost by new decision*, 12 TL 128 [Sep/Oct 1983]); the Third (*Brown*, 180 F. 2d 926, 50-1 USTC para. 9219; 39 AFTR 155 [CA-3, 1950]); the Seventh (*Skemp*, 168 F. 2d 598, 48-1 USTC para. 9300, 36 AFTR 1089 [CA-7, 1948]); the Eighth (*Quinlivan*, 599 F. 2d 269, 44-2 AFTR 2d 79-5059 [CA-7, 1979]), and the Ninth (*Brooke*, 468 F. 2d 1155, 72-2 USTC para. 9594, 30 AFTR 2d 72-5284 [CA-9, 1972]). However, they have been held invalid in the Fourth and Fifth Circuits (*Perry*, 520 F. 2d 235, 75-2 USTC para. 9629, 36 AFTR 2d 75-5500 [CA-4, 1975], and *Van Zandt*, 341 F. 2d 440, 65-1 USTC para. 9236, 15 AFTR 2d 372 [CA-5, 1965]). In the circuits where gift leasebacks have been held invalid, however, the transactions only involved two parties; i.e., there was no corporation involved, but instead the lessee was the individual grantor.

An interesting twist on this technique has been developed by Schnepper Associates of Cherry Hill, New Jersey. Assume the children in the preceding example are too young for college and that the taxpayer has a current need for the funds being paid out in lease rentals. The Schnepper Shelter directs the taxpayer to make the lease payments and then to borrow back the money at a fair rate of interest.[24] The interest may be fully deductible, depending on what the money is used for.

To use the above example, the taxpayer would make payments of $3,000 and borrow back $3,000 for use in business, paying $300 in interest yearly (10 percent). Each child aged 19 or older would pay approximately an additional $10 in taxes on the interest payments, a total of an additional $30, but the taxpayer would save

24. Note that the interest expense need not be limited to the prime rate. In fact, "there is no requirement ... that deductible interest be ordinary and necessary or even that it be reasonable." *Dorzback v. Collison*, 52-1 USTC Par. 9263, 195 F.2d 69, 72 (3d Cir. 1952). An interest payment as high as 60 percent to the taxpayer's *mother* has been upheld. *Raymond J. Barton*, 38 TCM 934 (1979).

an additional $90 in taxes (30 percent of $300)—a difference of $60 per year or $300 over 5 years. Of course, as its lease rentals increase, so too do tax savings. For 2018, up to $9,525 in taxable income can be taxed to a nonstudent child aged 19 (age 24 for a student) or older at the 10 percent rate, and the next $29,175 would be taxed at 15 percent.

When the children begin college and tuition is due, the taxpayer would then repay the borrowed money, in effect getting a current income tax deduction for future cash payments for the children's tuition. If the taxpayer dies before repayment is made, any remainder value in the trust is included in the estate,[25] but that estate (and therefore any tax due on it) is reduced by any debts owed to the trust—further magnifying the benefits of the Schnepper Shelter.[26]

While the Schnepper Shelter also appears to be contrary to congressional intent to eliminate assignment of income among family members, all of its components have been court tested and accepted. Here again, as long as the trustee is truly independent, the separate entity identity of the trust protects the legality and validity of a properly structured transaction. If such a shelter is to be eliminated, it too must be done through congressional action. Until such action, the Schnepper Shelter is a viable technique that should be considered in your planning to reduce your taxes to zero.

Moreover, the leaseback technique can provide substantial advantages to a taxpayer whose passive losses have been reduced or eliminated by the Tax Reform Act of 1986. For example, let's say a doctor owns a corporation that he does not materially participate in, which needs additional equipment, furniture, etc. Instead of buying that equipment through his or her corporation, the doctor will buy the equipment personally and lease it to the corporation. The lease rental payments made by the corporation would be extensively sheltered by the depreciation taken on this "leased business" equipment. Any net profits over and above the depreciation sheltered cash flow could be sheltered as passive income by the doctor's excess passive losses. By utilizing this technique, the doctor is able to take money out of the corporation at a zero tax cost. The cash flow is sheltered by previously unused passive losses and by the depreciation on the new equipment. Moreover, the corporation is entitled to a tax deduction for the "nontaxable" lease rental payments made to the doctor! This technique only works if the taxpayer doesn't materially participate in the activities of the corporation (Reg. Section 1.469-2(f)(6). Otherwise, the income is considered nonpassive.

25. See I.R.C. Section 2033. The value of that reversionary interest is determined by actuarial tables. See *Comm. v. Henry's Estate (Biddle)*, (3 Cir: 1947), 161 F2d 574, 35 AFTR 1252 aff'g 4 T.C. 423.
26. See I.R.C. Section 2051; Section 2053 (a)(3) and Section 2053 (a)(4).

Remember that the Tax Reform Act of 1986 effectively eliminates the use of Clifford Trusts as planning devices. Therefore, in order to effectively use the gift-leaseback technique, rather than a Clifford Trust, you should create an irrevocable trust. With an irrevocable trust, the property is transferred to the trust (beneficiaries) irrevocably. Unlike the Clifford Trust, you will not get it back after 10 years. However, if you are leasing back personal property—e.g., business furniture, equipment, etc.—that has been fully depreciated, that equipment would normally be over 15 years old when it would be returned using a Clifford Trust. The value of that equipment then would be minimal. Had you been gift-leasebacking an office building, however, the Tax Reform Act of 1986 forces you to relinquish present and future ownership of an asset with substantial value. If this is a strategy to be employed, the loss of that value is the price that must be paid.

137 The Schnepper Deep Shelter

Another alternative for shifting income to a lower-bracketed family member is to transfer rental property, excluding the building, to a trust for your children and rent the land back from the trust. The donor parent would still get all of the depreciation on the building, and the trust beneficiary children would be taxed on the lease rental income received. That lease rental income, however, would be a deductible investment expense by the parent. In effect, the parent would be paying lease rental income to the children, deducting that rent expense in the higher bracket and having it taxed to the children at the lower bracket. Moreover, this transfer of family wealth could take place without any gift tax consequences. In *Stanley J. Wolfe*, T.C. Memo 1984-446, this arrangement was validated with a sale leaseback of land to an irrevocable 10-year trust. The leaseback had a bona fide business purpose, and the lease payments were determined to be reasonable rent. Here again, the Tax Reform Act of 1986 would require the use of an irrevocable trust if this technique were to be used effectively.

138 Family Partnerships

If you are an individual business owner, the use of a family partnership can play an important role in your income tax planning. By giving or selling an interest in your business to members of your family (particularly to your

children), you can decrease your personal income tax payments and thereby increase your family unit's spendable income and capital.

For this arrangement to work, however, the establishment of the partnership must be genuine. This has been simplified by an IRS tax code section that specifically allows you to set up a family partnership by gift or purchase even though the family partners render no services.[27] Therefore, in those cases where capital is a material income-producing factor for the partnership, significant income shifting to lower-bracketed family members can be accomplished through the establishment of family partnerships.

A family partnership can be established in any of the following ways:

- Take into the partnership any child or relative who can contribute capital.

- Make a gift of a partnership interest to children or other relatives.

- Sell a partnership interest to children or other relatives. This sale can be substantially on credit, to be paid out of subsequent partnership income.

- Accept into partnership any child or other relative who can be expected to perform important work in the business on a regular basis.

139 Family Trusts

A family trust should be very carefully differentiated from a family partnership. A family trust is a trust to which you transfer "the exclusive use of your lifetime services and all the currently earned remuneration therefrom."

The problem with family trusts is that they do not work. A basic rule of taxation is that income must be taxed to the person who earned it. The transfer of your lifetime services and the income earned through the performance of those services is simply an assignment of income, and therefore ineffective in shifting the tax burden from you to the trust. *You cannot shift income earned through personal service.* A family trust, therefore, is nothing more than a tax avoidance scheme.[28] Do not, however, confuse a family trust with a trust to which income-earning *property* is transferred. When property is transferred, the income from that property *can* be shifted.

27. Section 704(e) of the Internal Revenue Code.
28. *Hailey, Jr.,* 73 T.C. No. 99 (1980).

140 The Schnepper Malagoli Super Shelter

This one is going to get me into *lots* of trouble!

How would you like to take money out of one pocket, deduct it as a business expense, and then put it in your other pocket tax-free? Even better, how would you like to do it completely legal?!

Follow me on this. It's really very simple once you get the basic idea. Let me give you the concept. Here's how it works. . . .

For this technique to work, you need a legitimate business. Assume you have a legitimate business and rent a suite in a hotel for a business meeting. You actually have and can document the meeting as a business event.

Clearly, the rent you pay is an allowable business deduction. Both small and big businesses do this all the time. Nothing new here . . . yet.

The other side of the coin is that the hotel has taxable rental income.

Now, instead of your business renting a suite in a hotel, you rent my home. Once again, if you actually use it for business purposes, and can document the business use, there's no reason why you shouldn't get the same "rental" deduction on your tax return.

The other side of the coin is that I should have rental income, right?

Wrong!

I want you to think Olympics, Super Bowl, and World Series.

Many years ago, Congress recognized that there were going to be situations where someone might rent out his or her home on a short-term basis. Rather than require an allocation of heat, electric, utilities, depreciation, interest, taxes etc. over the short-term rental, Congress actually came up with a reasonable solution.

The short-term landlord gets zero additional deductions for the "rental" expenses. But none of the income is taxable!

The code section—because everyone's going to look it up—is Section 280A (g). It specifically states that if you rent out your home for less than 15 days during the calendar year, none of the income is taxable.

Be careful when you read the code section. The general rule is that you get no deduction with respect to the use of your home for a business.

There are several exceptions, one of which is for the rental of the house. The Internal Revenue Code is full of general rules, exceptions, and exceptions and limitations to the exceptions.

If you're an employee of the business that rents the house, then there's an exception to the exception. You get no deductions for the rental of your house to your employer.

But, we're not talking about the deductions you, as the landlord, are getting for the rental of your house. You're getting none of those deductions anyway. What we're excited about is the deduction your company (the short-term tenant) gets for renting your house. That's not the subject of these limitations. Just the deductions for your expenses as the landlord are denied. And, I'll trade them any day for the tax-free income!

Let's get creative. If you have a regular corporation (the tax pros call it a "C corporation"), the corporation gets the deduction and you get tax-free income rather than taxable dividends or compensation. That's the easy one.

Now, let's assume you have what the tax pros call an "S corporation." That's a corporation that passes through its expenses and income to the owners. It's taxed similar to a partnership.

If your S corporation rents and uses your home for business, then it gets the expense and the deduction is passed through directly to you, reducing your personal income tax liability. And, if you don't rent out the home for more than 14 days, none of the income is taxable to you.

Take it out of one pocket—deduct it—and put it in the other pocket tax-free!

What if you're self-employed? What if you don't have a corporation?

Remember the old Wall Street adage, "Bulls make money; bears make money; pigs get slaughtered." You can push the envelope. But, don't be a pig.

If the house is in your name, that may be the pig position. But, what if the house is in the name of your spouse? Arguably, that should work. Remember, the Internal Revenue Code will exclude the landlord's deductions for the rental of the house. But we're not getting them anyway. We're after the deduction for the tenant and the tax-free income.

Alternatively, if I rent Charley's house, and Charley rents your house, and you rent my house, we're clearly within the four corners of the law.

What arguments can the IRS make? As long as the space is used for business, there should be no issue as to the legitimacy of the deduction. You just have to prove the business use. The tax pros call that the business "nexus."

Prove the business use with specific documentation. If you have a monthly meeting (last time I looked, 12 was less than 15, so monthly meetings should qualify for the tax-free treatment), keep the minutes. Craft the minutes with the reason why you're having the meeting outside your normal business location. The standard reason is so that you're not bothered by the interruptions of your normal business setting.

Prove the reasonableness of the rental charge by getting a letter from a local hotel. If the Four Seasons is charging $500 a day for a suite for a meeting, a note from them should be sufficient substantiation for your $500 a day rental expense. On a monthly basis, that's a $6,000 deduction (saving as mach as $2,376 in tax each year) plus $6,000 in tax-free income.

So long as you can substantiate the business connection and the reasonableness of the charge, the deduction should be allowed.

As for the tax-free receipt of the rental income—the Internal Revenue Code clearly states that it's *not* taxable as long as you rent it for less than 15 days during the year. The IRS really has no argument here.

Is this an aggressive strategy? Absolutely! Is it reasonable? Yes, because it's based on the clear meaning in the tax code.

Was this part of the Congressional intent when the Code was drafted? Absolutely not!

But just because Congress didn't think about it when they drafted the law, that doesn't mean it doesn't work under the law that was passed.

Use this technique now to reduce your taxable income. Once it becomes known and used by many, I strongly suspect Congress will move to change the law.

SCHNEPPER CONTRIBUTION

Let's get really creative here. Contribute $6,000 to a charity. Let the charity rent your house for monthly meetings for $5,000 for 12 meetings. You now have $5,000 in tax-free cash plus a deduction of $6,000. In the 24% bracket, that saves you $1,440. You are now up $5,000 + $1,440 (in tax savings) for a total of $6,440—$440 *more* than your $6,000 contribution. The charity is up $1,000 even after paying rent. Everybody wins except the IRS.

141 Employing Members of the Family

If you are an individual business owner, a simple and effective method of splitting your income with a family member is to employ that family member in your business and pay compensation. The employment must be bona fide and the salary paid must be reasonable in relation to the services rendered. Even a young child can be compensated for the reasonable value of such services as cleaning your office, mailing your letters, or opening your mail. A 1982 tax court decision allowed a $1,200 deduction for a 7-year-old child who performed a variety of services—maintenance and office work—for a mobile-home-park operator.[29] Be aware, however, that wages actually used by your children for their own support can affect your claim for their dependency exemptions. When in doubt, have your children bank their wages, thereby saving the exemption and teaching them the virtue of thrift as well.

29. See *Eller,* 77 T.C. No. 66. See also *James A. Moriarty,* T.C. Memo 1984-249, where a doctor was allowed to deduct salaries he paid his teenage children for handling business correspondence, insurance forms, etc., and for keeping patient files in order.

If your business is not incorporated, services performed by your child under the age of 18 are excluded from Social Security coverage. (Prior to the Revenue Act of 1987, the exclusion was for a child under the age of 21, and payments to your spouse were also exempt.) This means that you can deduct the value of the services that you pay to your children from your income tax without the added expense of paying Social Security taxes on that compensation. Services performed in the employ of a corporation, however, are not within this exclusion. But all is not lost if you are in a corporate firm. If your spouse is a bona fide employee of your corporation, such tax breaks as Social Security, workmen's compensation, tax-free sick pay, pension or profit-sharing plan benefits, stock option plans, group life insurance, and many others are open to you. According to IRS regulations, services performed in the employ of a partnership are also not within the exclusion unless the requisite family relationship exists between the employee and each of the partners comprising the partnership. Although wages paid to a child under age 18 by an unincorporated business are exempt from Social Security and federal unemployment taxes (up to age 21), wages paid to a parent are exempt from federal unemployment taxes but not from Social Security taxes.

Furthermore, if your spouse works for you, you may be able to deduct all your medical expenses. (If you hire your spouse, make sure that you can substantiate the payments that are made. Keep records or a journal of hours worked, and make payments with a check. No record keeping means no substantiation. No substantiation means no deduction [L.T.R. 8753003].) Normally, the deduction for medical expenses is limited to expenses that exceed 10 percent of your adjusted gross income. If you have your own business, however, you can install a written medical reimbursement plan for your employees. As a sole proprietor, you would not be considered eligible because you do not qualify as a common-law employee. Your spouse, however, would qualify. *You* would qualify as well if the plan included all employees, the dependent children, and the employee's *spouse!* With such a plan, your cost for insurance coverage and for the medical reimbursement plan would be deductible in full as a business expense. (See *Frahm*, T.C. Memo 2007-351.) Payments from the plan, of course, would be tax-free to you and your spouse. To achieve the anticipated tax results, the plan must be a welfare plan for all employees (Rev. Rul. 71-588; see also Doc. 9409006).

In C.C.A. 2005 24001, the IRS ruled that a self-employed individual who is a sole proprietor may deduct the medical care insurance costs of the sole proprietor and his or her family from the earned income of his or her trade or business when the health insurance policy purchased by the sole proprietor is issued in his or her individual name and not in the name of the sole proprietor's trade or business.

HRAs

On June 26, 2002, the IRS established a new Health Reimbursement Arrangement (HRA) that bypasses the complex limitations of Health Flexible Spending Accounts (FSAs) or cafeteria plans and sets up a simple structure for health cost coverage.

These plans must be funded 100 percent by the employer. The big new advantage is that dollars under these plans don't disappear at the end of the year under the "use it or lose it" FSA rules (under a 2005 ruling, amounts left over in an FSA at year-end may be carried over for 2½ months before they are forfeited or, as of 2014, you can carry over up to $500, if the plan allows). Any unused amounts carried over from year to year or maintained following termination or retirement are excluded from the income of the employee. HRAs for employees with fewer than 50 workers can reimburse up to $4,950 ($10,000 for a family policy) for an individual health policy-without being subject to group health plan requirements. This new arrangement makes it easy to hire your children and deduct 100 percent of their medical costs—above the line!

The children's work need not be full-time and can even be done during their summer vacations. Furthermore, provided that you continue to furnish more than one-half of your child's support and your child is younger than 19 or is a full-time student under age 24 for part of each of 5 months during the year, prior to 2018 you could have continued to claim a personal exemption deduction for that child. Remember, a child with earned income in 2018 pays *zero* taxes on the first $12,000 worth of earned income. That means if you are in the 24 percent bracket and pay each of your three children $12,000 for services rendered, their tax is zero, the money remains within the family group, and your tax savings is $8,640! Note that another $5,500 could be paid tax-free to each child if placed in an IRA. That could produce a total tax saving of $12,600 ([$12,000 + $5,500] × 3 × 0.24).*

Want to push the envelope? Under the new 401(k) rules, you can hire your child and pay up to the 401(k) contributor limit—$18,500 for 2018.

Put the $18,500 in the child's 401(k) individual account and you get:

1. A deduction of $18,500 to the employer parent

2. No current taxation to the child

Now let's change the numbers. Pay $12,000 plus $18,500 or $30,500 in reasonable salary to each of your three children—a total of $91,500—and in the

*But normally a nondeductible Roth IRA would be a better way to go for your children. The following companies have Roth IRAs for minor children: American Century Investments (1-800-345-2021), Franklin Templeton Investments (1-800-632-2301), Strong Financial (1-800-368-1030), T. Rowe Price (1-800-638-5560), and Vanguard (1-800-662-7447).

24 percent bracket, you save $21,960 in income tax. If you're not above the Social Security maximum ($128,700 for 2018), you save an additional 15.3[†] percent or $14,000 for a total tax savings of $35,960! Even if you're above the Social Security maximum, you'll still save the 2.9 percent Medicare tax for an additional $2,653 in tax savings. Your children pay zero tax!

142 Author's Delight

An interesting income allocation technique was made possible by an Internal Revenue Service ruling (Ltr. 8217037). A writer signed a contract with a publisher for royalties based on sales of a completed book. The contractual rights owned were then transferred to trusts for the benefit of minor children.

The IRS ruled that this was not a transfer of income, but rather of income-producing property. As long as the income was not used to meet the support obligations of the parents, such income would be taxed only to the trusts/children! In Letter Ruling 8444073, an author assigned to his child all royalties and interest in his publishing contract within 10 days after completing the book. The IRS again ruled that the author's child, not the author, would be taxed on the book royalties. Be careful, however: If an author assigns less than the entire contract, the IRS could assert the assignment of income doctrine to tax the income [see *Lewis*, 45-2 USTC Para. 9348, 34 AFTR 124 (CA-3, 1945)]. Both the contract and the royalties must be assigned: An assignment of the royalty income alone would not be a complete assignment of all of the author's property.

Note, however, that in IRS Letter Ruling 8444073, the IRS ruled that if the author was required in the contract to make revisions to the book, and no additional compensation were received for such revisions, the royalties would represent, in part, compensation for the author's services and would be taxable to that author. The measure of the compensation would presumably be what the publisher paid someone else to do the revisions. The solution to this problem is to have a separate contract or agreement specifying additional or different compensation for revisions. In addition, note that the rule that expenses incurred by an author in writing a book after 1986 must be capitalized and deducted over the life of the income stream of that book (Section 23[b] of the Tax Reform Act of 1986) has been repealed. The IRS had ruled that an author could deduct 50 percent of those expenses in the first year and 25 percent in each of the subsequent 2 years, in lieu of total income stream capitalization (Notice 88-62, 1988-22 I.R.B.). That ruling is now obsolete.

[†]13.3 percent for 2011 and 2012.

B Running Your Own Business

One of the important and effective techniques to reduce your taxes to zero is to convert your personal expenses to deductible *business* expenses. In order to do that you must own your own business. This is not complicated, expensive, or difficult to do, and incorporation is *not* needed. I will, however, detail the extensive tax benefits available if a corporate form of business is used.

To be in business, you merely declare yourself to be so. If you want to operate in a noncorporate form under a name different from your own, you can do that as well. In some states, however, if you are operating under an assumed name, you must file what is known as a "DBA" (Doing Business As) form with your local county clerk. Basically, this is merely a statement containing your name, address, and the assumed name under which you are doing business. For example, a form might merely say, "Jeff A. Schnepper is doing business under the name of 'Super Tax Savings Associates.'"

Moreover, your business need not make a profit in order for your expenses to be allowable deductions. All you need to do is establish a "profit motive." Under the Internal Revenue Service tax code, a "profit motive" is presumed if you earn any net income in any 3 out of 5 business years (2 out of 7 for horse racing and breeding). In the early loss years you can insist that the Internal Revenue Service defer challenge until the 5-year period is up (Form 5213). Furthermore, in fact, you need *never* have to actually show a profit if you can show a *profit motive* (*Melvin Nickerson*, CA-7, No. 82-1323; see also *Paul Farrell*, T.C. Memo, 1983-542 where farming expenses were held deductible despite 5 straight years of losses. See also *Churchman*, 68 T.C. No. 59, where despite 20 years of losses, the court found a profit objective and allowed deductions of business losses in full, *Frazier*, T.C. Memo 1985-61, *Dennis*, T.C. Memo 2010-216, *Blackwell v. Commissioner of Internal Revenue*, T.C. No. 29287-09, T.C. Memo 2011-188, August 8, 2011, and *Crile v. Commissioner*, T.C., No 9713-10, T.C. Memo 2014-202 decided October 2, 2014 where an art professor was found to be in the business of being an artist and losses allowed in 18 of the past 20 years.) In *Metz v. Commissioner*, T.C. Memo 2015-54, a taxpayer was found to be "in business" despite $14.6 million in losses over an 11-year period.

The test for deductibility is whether you have an actual and honest profit *objective*—you need not even have a reasonable expectation of profit (Treasury Regulation Section 1.183-2(a); *Dreicer v. Commissioner*, 78 T.C. 642, 1982). While the Tax Court requires a primary or dominant profit motive (*Lemmen*, 77 T.C. 1326 [1981]), in *Johnson*, 86-2 U.S.T.C. Par. 9705, 58 AFTR 2d 86-5894, the U.S. Claims Court held that having a reasonable chance to make a reasonable profit, apart from tax considerations, would suffice. Although the ultimate question is

whether or not you have an intent to make a profit, the determination of your motive is made by reference to objective standards, taking into account all of the facts and circumstances. The facts that will be taken into consideration include the following:

1. The manner in which you carry on the activity
2. The expertise of yourself and your advisors
3. The time and effort expended by you in carrying out this activity
4. The expectation that assets used in your business may appreciate in value
5. Your success in carrying on similar or dissimilar activities
6. Your history of income or losses with respect to the activity
7. The amount of occasional profits, if any, that are earned
8. Your financial status
9. The elements of personal pleasure or recreation ("Suffering has never been made a prerequisite for deductibility."—*Jackson v. Commissioner,* 59 T.C. 312)

The fact that you are employed full-time elsewhere will not bar a finding of your being in a separate trade or business. (See *Watson,* T.C. Memo 1988-29. See also *Riddle,* 205 F.2d 357, 62-2 USTC para. 9261, 10 AFTR 2d 5042 [DC Colo., 1962], wherein a full-time government employee was held to be in the trade or business of a consultant, despite the fact that he couldn't deal with anyone who had a government contract; *Estes,* 69-1 USTC para. 9261, 23 AFTR 2d 69-903 [DC Ala., 1969], wherein another full-time government employee was held to be in the lapidary business, so that his expenses were deductible; and *Christensen,* T.C. Memo 1988-484.)

One effective tax planning strategy, therefore, is to convert your personal hobby into a business. For example, one of my clients raced stock cars as a hobby. When he came to me, I converted that hobby into a business. He had cards and stationery printed. He ran ads looking for a sponsor. He gave his "hobby" the image and appearance of a "business," and he demonstrated a real profit motive. This client had a salary income of $40,000. When his new "business" expenses were deducted, not only did he pay zero taxes, but because he qualified for the earned income credit, the Internal Revenue Service paid him money!

Two years later he was audited on that year's return. The law requires that you prove your business expenses, with receipts, checks, or a log book that is updated daily. Unfortunately, he had not kept a log or any receipts for his expenses for the first year. His expenses, though, were legitimate, and he had receipts for the subsequent 2 years. On the basis of the receipts for the 2 subsequent years not in question, this taxpayer with $40,000 in other income and

no receipts, after an IRS audit, paid less than $100 in taxes, including interest and penalties! Had he kept receipts for the first year, he would have paid zero.

To be allowable, your business expenses must be:

a) ordinary and necessary;

b) paid or incurred during the taxable year; *and*

c) connected with the conduct of a trade or business.

"Ordinary and necessary" has been interpreted by the courts and the Internal Revenue Service as "reasonable and customary" and this really depends upon your specific business and the business customs in your locale. In fact, an "ordinary" expense is one that is customary or usual. It need not be customary or usual for you, provided that it is customary or usual for your particular trade, industry, or community. The Supreme Court has held that even a one-time outlay falls within the definition (*Welch v. Helvering*, 290 US 111, 1933). Similarly, the Second Circuit Court of Appeals defined "necessary" as "appropriate" and "helpful," rather than necessarily essential to a taxpayer's business (*Blackmer v. Commissioner*, 70 F.2d 255).

For example, in one case a husband and wife produced, exhibited, and sold their sculptured works. The expenses incurred by them in doing so were held to be ordinary and necessary business expenses.[30] In another case, a breeder and raiser of bird dogs tried to develop an outstanding dog so that he could reap profits from sales and stud fees. Some years were profitable and some showed losses, yet all of the business expenses were found to be deductible.[31] In a third, a coal miner operated a kennel for bird dogs. Despite the fact that he sustained 11 years of losses, there was sufficient evidence of an ever-present profit motive for all of his expenses to be allowed as deductible.[32] In fact, in *Donald C. Kimbrough*, T.C. Memo 1988-185, a high school teacher's golfing activity was engaged in "for profit," resulting in his losses being allowed as deductible expenses. In *Harrison*, T.C. Memo 1996-509, the Tax Court found a profit motive and allowed gold-hunting expenses as deductible. In the 2003 case of *William Whitehurst*, the Tax Court validated bowling with a profit motive as a business and allowed his deductions. In 2005, in *Morrissey et ux. v. Commissioner*, T.C. Summ. Op. 2005-86, losses from drag racing activities were allowed as business expenses.

Owning your own business, therefore, affords you the opportunity to convert a great many of your personal expenses into allowable business deductions. The rest of the section will detail some of the most important reservoirs of deductible expenses.

30. *Road*, 184 F. Supp. 791.
31. *Sloan*, T.C. Memo 1956-36.
32. *Sasso*, T.C. Memo 1961-216.

143 Your Home

Probably the most significant conversion of a personal expense into a business expense occurs when you use your home for your business. (This can apply to a primary *or* secondary business.) To be deductible, these home business expenses must be allowable under the Internal Revenue Service tax code.

The code states that no deduction for any business expenses attributable to an at-home office will be allowable unless these expenses are attributable to a portion of the home used "exclusively and on a regular basis" as:

a) the principal place of business; *or*

b) a place of business that is used by patients, clients, or customers in meeting or dealing with you in the normal course of your business.

Watch out for "exclusive." IRS auditors may question the amount you use your office computer for "business as opposed to investment." Is it 90 percent–10 percent or 50 percent–50 percent. The question is a trap! If you say anything less than 100 percent, you have failed the "exclusive" test and lose all your home office deductions. (Basic rule of thumb—never represent yourself at your own audit. You don't know what *not* to say and can never plead ignorance to a difficult question.)

In *Miller,* T.C. Summ. Op. 2014-74, the taxpayer met the exclusive test even though she had to walk through her office to get to her bedroom each night.

While the Code requires that any office at home constitutes your principal place of business, this does not mean that it must be your *single* principal place of business, where all of your businesses are considered together. The test according to the courts is "whether with respect to a particular business conducted by a taxpayer, the home office [is] his principal place for conducting that business." Also, your home office can qualify if it is the principal place of your first *or* second business. (See *Jones,* TCM 1984-544 and *Green,* TCM 1989-599.)

There have been many rulings on this important question. In *Drucker et al. v. Commissioner,* 52 AFTR 2d 83-5804, for example, the Second Circuit Court of Appeals allowed concert musicians home office deductions for the business use of their apartments because they spent most practice time at home and their employers did not provide the musicians with space for the essential task of private practice.

In *Weissman v. Commissioner,* 84-4031, December 20, 1984, the U.S. Court of Appeals for the Second Circuit ruled that a college professor may deduct the expenses of maintaining a home office used exclusively to do most of the research and writing expected of him as a condition of retaining his teaching position. The Court found that the college professor's principal place of business was not necessarily the college at which he teaches any more than a

musician's principal place of business is necessarily the concert hall at which he performs. However, the Tax Court, in *Neville Bardsley Dudley et ux.*, T.C. Memo 1987-607, ruled that a full-time business professor at the downtown campus of Wayne County Community College in Detroit was provided office space at the college, was not required to maintain an office in his home, and had no substantial out-of-classroom responsibilities such as research and publication. The Court concluded that Dudley's deduction for home office expenses was legitimate only if his home office was indeed the principal place of business. It was not, so Dudley was denied his deduction.

In *John Meiers et ux. v. Commissioner*, No. 85-1209 (Seventh Cir., January 14, 1986), the Seventh Circuit found that the "principal place of business" must be determined by looking at both hours worked and functions performed. The Court found that the Meierses, who each day spent an hour in the laundromat and two hours at their home office devoted exclusively to administrative work on behalf of the laundry, were entitled to the claimed deductions for the home office. This was another reversal of the Tax Court's "focal point" test. Under that test, the principal place of business has been held to be that place where goods and services are provided to customers or clients or where income is produced.

The 9th Circuit Court of Appeals, in *Pomarantz v. Commissioner*, No. 87-7151, decided on November 7, 1988, that a physician's principal place of business was the hospital where he spent more of his time and treated patients, not his home where he studied medical journals and kept records of patients but treated no patients; therefore, no home office deduction was allowable. Here the court chose not to adopt a specific standard, but found that under any of these tests, the hospital, rather than the home, was the doctor's principal place of business. The doctor consistently spent more time on duty at the hospital than at home. The court found the essence of his profession to be the hands-on treatment of patients, which he did only at the hospital, never at home. Finally, the court found that the doctor had generated income only by seeing patients at the hospital, not by studying or writing at home.

In another example, the taxpayer was a dermatologist, and the hospital was his principal place of business. But he also owned and managed 6 rental units, and he had set aside a room in his residence used exclusively for managing that activity. The court found that in this case the managing of rental property was a trade or business and that his home office expenses *were* deductible.[33] This decision was codified in PL 97-119 on December 28, 1981, when President Reagan signed into law an act specifically allowing a deduction for business use of a home for activities other than a taxpayer's primary occupation. (The Black Lung

33. *Edwin R. Curphey*, T.C. 61.

Benefits Revenue Act of 1981 [including other tax provisions adopted], Public Law No. 97-119, Section 113(c), 95 Stat. 1642 [1980].) Furthermore, these changes were made retroactive to years beginning after 1975. Moreover, on November 19, 1982, the Court of Claims ruled that investment activities can constitute a trade or business and therefore allowed home office deductions for taxpayers who managed large investment portfolios full-time (*Moller*, 82-2 USTC Par. 9694, 51 AFTR 2d 83-369). Unfortunately, on November 18, 1983 the Claims Court was overruled by the Federal Circuit Court of Appeals (721 F. 2d 810).

In *Anthony J. Ditunno* [80 T.C. No. 12 (February 7, 1983)], the Tax Court overruled prior precedent and provided a new definition and set of criteria for determining whether a taxpayer is engaged in a trade or business for tax purposes. The Court broadened the meaning of the phrase "trade or business" by replacing the previous "goods and services" test with a "facts and circumstances" test which requires a subjective determination to be made in each instance by "an examination of all the facts involved in each case." Despite a Second Circuit Court of Appeals decision to return to the "goods and services" test in *Gajewski*, 84-1 U.S.C. Par. 9116, 53, AFTR 2d 84-386 (CA-2, 1983), and the *Estate of Dan B. Cole*, No. 83-1601 (6th Circuit, October 23, 1984), where the Appeals Court ruled that one must hold oneself out to others as a provider of goods or services to be in a trade or business, the Tax Court has reaffirmed its "facts and circumstances" test in *Robert P. Groetzinger v. Commissioner*, 82 T.C. No. 61 (May 24, 1983) where it ruled that Groetzinger's trade or business under the Code was gambling. However, on May 23, 1985, the Tax Court revised its decision and deferred to the Second Circuit when it ruled that Gajewski was not in a trade or business (*Gajewski*, 84 T.C. No. 63). *Groetzinger*, however, *was* affirmed by the 7th Circuit Court of Appeals on August 21, 1985 (No. 84-2507). These conflicting decisions were resolved when the Supreme Court, on February 24, 1987, again affirmed *Groetzinger* (480 U.S. 23, 28 (1987)], ruling that the taxpayer, who made gambling his full-time livelihood "with continuity and regularity," was in a trade or business. See also *Linda M. Myers v. Commissioner*, T.C. Summ. Op. 2007–194 (November 19, 2007); *Michael Ferguson v. Commissioner*, T.C. Summ. Op. 2007–30 (February 28, 2007); *Merkin v. Commissioner*, T.C. Memo 2008–146 (June 5, 2008); *Crawford v. Commissioner*, T.C. No. 10413-08, T.C. Memo 2010-54 (March 22, 2010); *J. F. Chow Estate*, T.C. Memo 2014-49, and *Boneparte v. Commissioner*, T.C., No. 2452, T.C. Memo 2015-128, July 13, 2015, where the facts failed to support the taxpayer. But the taxpayer won in *Le*, T.C. Summ. Op. 2010–94 and *Mayo*, 136 T.C. No. 4, 2011.

Furthermore, in *Morley v. Commissioner*, No. 40685-84, 87 T.C. No. 69, decided on November 19, 1986, the court ruled that a taxpayer's purchase, for the first time, of property that he intends to resell, followed promptly by bona fide efforts to resell the property, constituted a trade or business. Here, even the single purchase of a parcel of real estate, with the requisite intent, constituted a trade or business.

In 1982, the Tax Court ruled that an employee who was required by his employer to take frequent after-office-hours telephone calls from clients could deduct the cost of maintaining his at-home office used exclusively and regularly for that purpose. The Tax Court agreed with the Internal Revenue Service that the taxpayer had failed to prove it was "his principal place of business." But a majority of the Court, siding with the taxpayer, held that his office met the alternative test "as a place of business in which patients, clients, or customers meet or deal with the taxpayer in the normal course of the taxpayer's business." The significance of this decision is that the Court found no requirement "that such meetings or dealings are limited to physical encounters."[34] This decision, however, was reversed upon appeal to the Ninth Circuit on May 31, 1983, and the reversal was affirmed by the Tax Court in *Frankel*, 82 T.C. No. 26 on February 28, 1984. But in the case of *Feldman v. Commissioner*, 14126-82, 84 T.C. No. 1, on January 8, 1985, the Court allowed a taxpayer the costs of maintaining space in his home that he *leased* to his corporate employer for his use as a home office. Here Feldman maintained an office in his home that was rented to his employer for his own use. The employer, of which the taxpayer was a shareholder and director, paid $5,400 designated as rent to Feldman in 1979. The taxpayer reported the rental income and deducted his costs of maintaining the leased space, which he calculated as 15 percent of his home. The Court found, to the extent that the payments were reasonable, that they constituted rent and that the costs of producing that rental income may be deducted. By using the rental strategem, the taxpayer was able to create an allowable home office without "physical encounters." (But see below under depreciation for 1986 Tax Reform Act limits.) Moreover, in Rev. Rul. 86-148, the IRS allowed a deduction for a monthly fee to a security service for a home office used as a dental practice.

In *Soliman*, 94 T.C. No. 3 (March 27, 1990), the Tax Court changed the rules again. An anesthesiologist spent approximately 30 percent of his work time at his home office. He kept office equipment there, as well as a telephone, insurance and patient records, and his medical library. He never saw patients at his home, however. For a deduction, Section 280A(c)(1)(A) requires a portion of the home to be used exclusively and regularly as the principal place of a trade or business. Under the "focal point" test previously used by the Tax Court, a home office is a principal place of business if that is where goods and services are provided to customers and revenues are generated. Noting that the test had been questioned by the Second, Seventh, and Ninth Circuits, the Tax Court now states that "where a taxpayer's occupation requires essential organizational and management activities that are distinct from those that generate income, the place where the business is

34. *John W. Green*, 78 T.C. No. 30.

managed can be the principal place of business." The court also concluded that such an administrative location of the business need not be where the taxpayer spends most of his work time. The time spent there need only be substantial and the activities conducted there must be essential to the business as a whole. The focal point test is now replaced by a "facts and circumstances" test—as per the wisdom of *Soliman*. This was affirmed in *Kahaku*, TCM 1990-34.

Unfortunately, *Soliman* was reversed by the U.S. Supreme Court No. 91-998 (January 12, 1993), which ruled that a home office must achieve preeminence in a comparative analysis of the various locations of your trade or business in order for that office to be your "principal place of business." Two primary factors must be examined:

1. The relative importance of the activities performed at each business location; *and*
2. the amount of time spent at each location.

In Rev. Rul. 94-24, the IRS ruled that a comparison of the relative importance of the activities performed at each location depends on characteristics of each business, and if the business requires a taxpayer to meet with clients or to deliver goods or services to clients, the place where the contact occurs must be given great weight in determining where the most important activities of the business are done.

The IRS also said in the ruling that time spent on business at home must be compared to time spent on business at other locations and that the time test becomes more important if the relative importance test provides no definitive answer to the principal place of business.

The revenue ruling also holds that the relative importance test will be applied first to determine whether an office in the home is the taxpayer's principal place of business and if no definitive answer is reached, the IRS will apply the time test. In some cases, the application of both tests may result in a finding that there is no principal place of business.

The IRS provided four examples of how they would apply the ruling—a self-employed author who uses a home office to write, a self-employed retailer of costume jewelry, a self-employed plumber, and a teacher who grades papers at home.

In the example concerning the self-employed author, who spent approximately 30 to 35 hours per week in the home office to write, and 10 to 15 hours a week at other locations conducting research or meeting with publishers or attending promotional events, the IRS said that the essence of the author's home office is the principal place of business and the author can deduct expenses for the business use of the home, the IRS concluded.

The IRS said a self-employed plumber who works 40 hours at customer locations and spends 10 hours per week at a home office talking with customers on the telephone, deciding what supplies to order, and reviewing the books, could not deduct expenses for the business use of the home.

Even though the plumber employs a nonrelated, part-time employee in the home office to schedule appointments, order supplies, and keep books, the essence of the plumber's business requires the plumber to work at the homes or offices of customers and the fact that the plumber has an employee working in the home office does not alter the result, the IRS said.

In the case of the jewelry retailer, the most important activity of the business—sales to customers—is conducted at a number of locations, including craft shows and consignment shops. In this case, the amount of time spent at each location assumes particular significance, the IRS said. Because the retailer spent more time per week in the home office, expenses for business use of the home are deductible.

In the case of the teacher, the IRS said the principal place of business is clearly the school, and although work done at home is essential and time-consuming, expenses cannot be deducted for business use of the home.

Purely administrative or billing activities alone would not normally be determinative. In *Crawford v. Commissioner,* No. 1380-90, T.C. Memo 1993-192, April 29, 1993, the Tax Court applied the *Soliman* test to deny a home office deduction to a doctor who did follow-up patient work at home and who worked as an independent contractor for several Dallas hospitals.

Current rules. The Tax Relief Act of 1997 reversed *Soliman* for tax years beginning after December 31, 1998. *Now* home offices will be allowed for purely administrative or management activities if you have no other fixed place of business for those activities.

On April 17, 2001, the Ninth Circuit joined U.S. Second Circuit in allowing a concert and recording musician a home office deduction for a portion of her apartment used exclusively for practice (*Popov v. Commissioner,* 9th Cir., No. 99-70749).

Note that in *Lynn Crawford,* T.C. Memo 1993-192, the Tax Court ruled that the IRS could not add penalties to your tax bill when it disallows a home office deduction that was supported by the Tax Court's decision at the time it was taken.

Another option is available to qualify space for a home office deduction—if that space is used as a storage unit. The Small Business Job Protection Act of 1996 clarified that the special rule contained in prior law, Section 280A(c)(2), permits deductions for expenses relating to a storage unit in a taxpayer's home regularly used for inventory or product samples (or both) of the taxpayer's trade or business of selling products at retail or wholesale provided that the home is the sole fixed location of such trade or business. Such deductions will

now be allowed for business expenses related to a space within a home that are used on a regular *(even if not exclusive)* basis as a storage unit.

Unfortunately, however, the Tax Reform Act of 1986 provided that when an *employee* leases a portion of his home to his employer, no net losses would be allowable. Get around this by making the home office a condition of your employment and have your employer reimburse you for expenses under an "accountable plan" (see pages 179 and 480).

The following expenses for your home office will be allowable:

1. *Depreciation on Your Office Furniture and Equipment.* This would include any desks, chairs, couches, lamps, etc., that you put into your office. In *Liddle*, No. 94-7733, 9/8/95, a professional musician was allowed depreciation on his violin. Moreover, in *Zeidler*, T.C. Memo 1996-157, the court ruled that a computer used in a home office for business was deductible even without records of usage. Don't be a tax case—keep records.

2. *Depreciation on Your "Office Building."* If your home is owned, you can depreciate the portion of the acquisition cost and improvements allocable to your home office. Note that in *Weightman*, T.C. Memo 1981-301, the Tax Court held that a taxpayer need not have an entire room as an office but could set aside an area for exclusive business use. Therefore, one part of a room could be used for personal reasons without affecting the deduction for the business use of another part of the room.

3. *Rent.* If your home is rented, you can deduct an allocatable portion of that rent for your home office.

4. *Homeowner's Insurance.* If you own your home, an allocatable portion of your homeowner's insurance is deductible.

5. *Electric Utilities.* An allocatable portion of your electric bill for providing current and light to your home office is also deductible.

6. *Heating and Air Conditioning.* An allocatable portion for heating your home office in winter or air conditioning your home office in summer would also be an allowable, ordinary, and necessary business expense. In addition, if you put in an air conditioner that does not become a structural part of the building—a window or portable air conditioner—that air conditioner's cost can be recovered through depreciation or expensed under Section 179.

7. *Lawn Care and Landscaping.* "In *Hefti* (T.C. Memo 1988–22), the Tax Court even permitted a deduction for an allocable share of lawn care and landscaping expenses where the taxpayer "had clients visiting on a regular basis and the appearance of the residence and the grounds would be of significance" to the taxpayer's business operations.

8. *Phone.* The use of your home phone would also normally be an ordinary and necessary business expense. You can either deduct an allocatable portion of your regular phone bill or insert a separate line exclusively for the use of your "business." Even part of the basic charge for a home phone, when used for business, was deductible (*Robert H. Lee,* T.C. Memo 1960-58) until January 1, 1989. Thereafter, deductible costs for business use of a phone at home are still allowable for:

a) Long-distance calls

b) Equipment rental

c) Call waiting

d) Call forwarding

e) Charges for a second phone line

Moreover, you should determine whether basic local service includes charges for local message units. If not, then a proportionate part of these would also be deductible.

The following example demonstrates the available tax advantage of having a home office: Assume that you have a five-room home costing $150,000, with $50,000 allocatable to land and $100,000 allocatable to the building. The home has a 39-year recovery life, because the "office space" is not *residential* rental space. You purchase $20,000 in furniture with a 7-year recovery life for your one-room home office and incur the following total costs over the year:

	Allowable Deductions
Heat and air conditioning ($2,400 × 1/5) =	$ 480
Electricity ($1,200 × 1/5) =	240
Second phone (50 percent business) ($1,200 × 1/2) =	600
Depreciation on furniture:*	
Election to expense	20,000
Depreciation on home (39 years)	
[(100,000 ÷ 5) × .02461]	492
Total Deductions	$21,812
Tax savings in the 24 percent bracket	$ 5,235

* Depreciation on furniture and equipment is a "direct" expense, allowable without the home office limitations.

Under IRS regulations, these "indirect" deductions are allowable only if they do not exceed the amount of gross income derived from the use of your home for your trade or business reduced by the deductions that are allowed without regard to their connection with your trade or business—that is, interest and taxes. Note that in addition to the expenses deducted above for your home office, you can also deduct an allocatable portion of the interest on your mortgage and your home taxes. These deductions are allowable as "above the line" business deductions even if you do not qualify to itemize your deductions.

The limitation on home office deductions can be shown by the following example. Assume the same deductions as in the previous case, but in addition, assume that you pay $3,000 in real estate taxes and $10,000 in mortgage interest. Furthermore assume that you have gross revenue of $23,000 from your "business." Your deductions are limited as follows:

Gross revenue (income)	$ 23,000
Minus direct expenses (furniture depreciation)	−20,000
Minus allocatable portion of interest in taxes [1/5 × ($10,000 + $3,000)]	−2,600
Limit on remaining expenses	$ 400
Remaining expenses (from above)	$ 1812
Deductible expenses (lesser of actual expenses or limit)	$ 400

The $1,412 is carried forward as a deduction to offset income in the subsequent year.

Several additional factors should be noted. First, the Internal Revenue Service instructions talk about gross income, not gross revenue. They are equivalent. I am talking here about total inflow of dollars before *any* expenses. Second, with such high expenses in relation to income, you should elect straight-line depreciation over an extended life period. Third, note that even though your home office expenses are limited, there is no limitation on other expenses—for instance, travel, entertainment (prior to 2018), supplies, etc.—for your business. Note that these examples do not contain *all* of the possible home office deductions. Anything that relates to your home office per se would be a potential deduction. For example, add any allocatable water charges, sewer charges, repairs, depreciation on such improvements as painting, aluminum siding, etc. In Rev. Rul. 86-148, the IRS allowed a deduction of a proportionate share of the monthly fee for a home security system, as well as depreciation deductions on that system, to a homeowner who used one-sixth of his house as office space. Your deductions are limited only by your imagination and your ability to relate your expenditures to your business.

Although the above limitations on home office deductions are contained in the Internal Revenue Service regulations, in the Tax Court case of *Scott v. Commissioner*, No. 18916-82, 84 T.C. No. 45, decided on April 15, 1985, Judge Simpson and the Court ruled that those regulations were invalid. According to the Judge, Section 280A(c)(5) limits the deductions allocable to the use of a home office to the gross income derived from such use. For purposes of this limitation, "gross income is not reduced by the other deductions attributable to the . . . businesses carried on in the building." What this means is that in the above example, the deductions would be limited not to $400, but to the gross revenue of $23,000 (allowable, of course, to the actual remaining expenses incurred). While *Scott* was specifically overruled by the Tax Reform Act of 1986 for years after 1986, the Internal Revenue Service National Office has held that it would apply for open years prior to 1987 (TAM 8640001).

If you fear taxable recapture of depreciation upon sale of your house note that in Rev. Rul. 82-26 (February 8, 1982) the IRS ruled that the *prior* business use of a residence would not require the recognition of gain when the residence is sold. The IRS looked to the use of the residence at the time of the sale (Rev. Rul. 59-72). Thus, if the entire house was used as the principal residence in the year of sale, the entire gain on the sale would have been eligible for tax-deferral, regardless of prior use. [See IRC Sections 1234 and 1250(d)(7)(A).] Unfortunately, the Tax Reform Act of 1997 now requires the recapture of any depreciation taken after May 7, 1997, upon sale, and this depreciation may be taxed up to a 25 percent rate. However, you still have the time value of the tax savings. Moreover, while any depreciation will be recaptured to the extent of the gain, real appreciation recognized on the sale can *now* be sheltered by the $250,000/$500,000 exclusion if you qualify. See page 92.

In Rev. Proc. 2005–14, the IRS validated the combination of the $250,000/$500,000 home sale exclusion with a like kind swap. First you apply the gain exclusion to the primary home. Then the tax-free swap rules can exclude gain on the business portion—including depreciation after May 6, 1997, which would be otherwise taxed. To qualify, you'd need a new home office in the new home.

SIMPLE OPTION

In Rev. Proc. 2013, the IRS announced a new simplified, optional method of claiming a home office deduction. Under the new procedure, a significantly simplified form is used. The new optional deduction is limited to $1,500 per year based on $5 per square foot for up to 300 square feet. Homeowners using the new option will not be able to depreciate the portion of their home used in a trade or business. However, they will be able to claim allowable mortgage interest, real estate taxes, and casualty losses on the home as itemized deductions on Schedule A of Form 1040. The new option is available beginning with year 2013 return.

Simplified Option	Regular Method
Deduction for home office use of a portion of a residence allowed only if that portion is exclusively used on a **regular basis** for business purposes	Same
Allowable square footage of home use for business (not to exceed 300 square feet)	Percentage of home used for business
Standard $5 per square foot used to determine home business deduction	Actual expenses determined and records maintained
Home-related itemized deductions claimed in full on Schedule A	Home-related itemized deductions apportioned between Schedule A and business schedule (Sch. C or Sch. F)
No depreciation deduction	Depreciation deduction for portion of home used for business
No recapture of depreciation upon sale of home	Recapture of depreciation on gain upon sale of home
Deduction cannot exceed gross income from business use of home less business expenses	Same
Amount in excess of gross income limitation may **not** be carried over	Amount in excess of gross income limitation may be carried over
Loss carryover from use of regular method in prior year may not be claimed	Loss carryover from use of regular method in prior year may be claimed if gross income test is met in current year

To prove a home office, photograph it, have it on your business cards and stationery, and keep a log of whom you see, when you use the office, and what you work on.

In addition, travel expenses between your home office and job sites are deductible. For example, one taxpayer operated a home-repair business using his home as a business headquarters where he received inquiries for possible contracting services. He claimed a deduction for the expenses of traveling between his home and job sites. The deduction was allowable because his home was the sole fixed location of his business and was essential to his business operations (*Adams*, TCM 1982-223). In fact, in *Carl F. Worden*, T.C. Memo 1981-366, a home office had the effect of converting a personal residence into a job site. In that case, the Tax Court found that the insurance salesman's home was his

place of business. Therefore, *all* his travel costs were allowable as business deductions. See also 76 T.C. No. 72, *Wisconsin Psychiatric Services, Limited,* where Wess R. Vogt, a psychiatrist, established that his home office was his principal office and therefore that trips to and from his home were business trips and not nondeductible commuting expenses; *Wicker,* TCM 1986-1, wherein the court ruled that a home office that was the principal place of business for a nurse-anesthesiologist enables her to deduct the costs of going from there to the hospital where she was associated and where she practiced exclusively, but without office space; and *Ronald Carey,* SD, OH, No. C-3-80-422, where a salesman who worked out of his home was able to deduct the cost of his daily sales trips because the salesman's home was his principal place of work.

In *Walker v. Comm.,* No. 20919-19, 101 T.C. No. 36, 12/13/93, the court applied Revenue Ruling 90-23 and held that a self-employed taxpayer could deduct truck expenses paid for traveling to various locations in a national forest where he worked as a logger. It found that his residence was a "regular place of business" and that transportation expenses between a "regular place of business" and a "temporary work location" were deductible. The advance in *Walker* was that the residence did *not* qualify as a home office—such as the principal place of business under *Soliman.*

In Revenue Ruling 94-37, the IRS ruled that *Walker* would be followed only if one of two other conditions apply.

Under the first condition, if the taxpayer has one or more regular work locations away from the taxpayer's residence, the taxpayer may deduct daily transportation expenses incurred in going between the taxpayer's residence and a *temporary* work location in the same trade or business, regardless of the distance.

Under the second condition, if the taxpayer's residence is the taxpayer's principal place of business, the taxpayer may deduct daily transportation expenses incurred in going between the residence and another work location in the same trade or business, regardless of whether the other work location is *regular or temporary* and regardless of the distance.

In 1999, the IRS modified the rule again. Issued January 15, 1999, Revenue Ruling 99-7 now provides three exceptions to the general rule that transportation expenses between a residence and a place of business or employment are not deductible. Now you *can* deduct:

a) expenses incurred in going from your residence and a temporary work location outside the metropolitan area where you live and normally work;

b) expenses incurred going between your residence and a temporary work location in the same trade or business in which you have one or more regular work locations away from this residence; *and*

c) expenses incurred going between your home office (principal place of business) and another work location in the same trade or business, regardless of the distance or whether the work location is regular or temporary.

A work location is "temporary" if employment there is realistically expected to last—and does in fact last—for 1 year or less. But, in *Senulis*, T.C. Summ. Op. 2009–97, the taxpayer who took on a 9-month project that actually lasted 13 months was allowed to deduct away-from-home expenses—meals, lodging, and travel. The worker "reasonably" expected that the job's duration would be less than a year when he took it.

Note that if you file a separate income tax from your spouse, an additional income-shifting opportunity is available. In Rev. Rul. 74-209, the Internal Revenue Service ruled that rent paid by a husband to his wife for the use of the jointly owned Wisconsin real estate that the husband used in his business is deductible as a business expense on the husband's separate income tax return. For this strategy to be successful, you should compare the net results on a joint return to those on separate returns. It is a technique that should be considered where appropriate.

Moreover, additional tax savings can be found if you have a home office that requires a secretary or a receptionist to be present at all times during business hours and the only person available is a member of your family. In the previous section we discussed the advantages of employing members of your family in your business as an income-shifting device. In this case, any member of your family, including your spouse, can reap enormous tax-saving advantages. The tax code excludes from gross income the value of any meals furnished to an employee by the employer for the convenience of the employer if the meals are furnished on the business premises of the employer.[35] If your spouse, for example, is required as your employee to be on your business premises—that is, your home office—as a receptionist, telephone operator, etc., then any meals (for instance, lunch) provided are not compensation that your spouse would include in gross income, but they are a *deductible* business expense to you! By structuring your first or second business in this manner, you can effectively and *legally* deduct the cost of your spouse's or children's lunches. Your spouse must truly be employed and required to be on business premises during lunchtime or the deduction will not be allowed (*Weidmann*, 89-1 USTC ¶9197 [DC N.Y. 1989]). Given the price of food today, this is an enormous benefit that can result in substantial tax savings. Moreover, no Social Security payments are due on such lunches. At $20 per lunch, five times a week for 50 weeks, your total deductible expense would be $5,000. In the 24 percent bracket, this saves you $1,200 in taxes!

35. Section 119 of the Internal Revenue Code.

144 Your Car

Automobile expenses incurred in your business travel are deductible either as a travel expense (if away from home on business) or as a transportation expense (even if you are not away from home). Remember, transportation expenses are not normally deductible unless they are incurred in a business or investment situation. To get the deduction here, there must be a direct connection between the use of the car and your trade or business or some income-producing activity—for instance, to check on your investments. If you have one car that you use both for personal and for business use, only the portion of your car expenses directly attributable to business use is deductible.

In allocating your car expenses between business and personal use, there are a number of methods that you can use. One simple method is known as the mileage cost basis. Using this method, you multiply your business mileage by a standard mileage rate that the IRS allows in lieu of the operating and fixed costs of your car, along with parking fees, interest, taxes, and tolls.

Standard Mileage Rates

2008	50.5¢ January–June/58.5¢ July–December
2009	55.0¢
2010	50.0¢
2011	51.0¢ January–June/55.5¢ July–December
2012	55.5¢
2013	56.5¢
2014	56.0¢
2015	57.5¢
2016	54.0¢
2017	53.5¢
2018	54.5¢

So, for example, if you drive your car 24,000 business miles over the year, you will deduct 24,000 × .545 for a total of $13,080. In addition to this $13,080 deduction, you will be allowed all of your expenses for parking fees, interest, taxes, and tolls.

As an alternative to the standard mileage cost basis, you can use the mileage percentage basis. Under the mileage percentage method, you simply divide your business mileage by your total mileage and take that percentage of your total expenses as a deduction.

Included in such auto expenses, when using the mileage percentage method, are not only your parking fees and tolls (at 100 percent) but also depreciation on your car, interest, taxes, registration and license fees, and gas,

oil, and repair expenses. Given the cost of gasoline, it would probably be to your advantage to keep receipts and records of your actual expenditures. Whereas the Internal Revenue Service allows you a deduction of 54.5¢ per mile under the mileage cost basis, studies by auto-renting firms have established that actual mileage costs may be two to three times greater than that allowance.

There is a special tax planning strategy that you can use if you have two cars in your family. Assume that you have been using one car exclusively for business and the other exclusively for personal family use and that you put 36,000 miles each year on your business car and only 12,000 miles a year on your family car. Normally you can deduct only the costs of using the business car. Now, suppose you switched the use of each car every 6 months. The combined mileage of both cars in the original example is 48,000 miles per year. By rotating your cars equally between business and family use, each car will be driven 24,000 miles a year, 75 percent of which will be business miles (36 ÷ 48). Therefore, 75 percent of your depreciation and other costs on *each* car will be deductible. This can be a lot more than simply deducting all of the costs on one car and nothing on the other.

A taxpayer cannot normally deduct commuting expenses. However, if you have a regular place of business, you *can* deduct daily transportation expenses from your *home* and a *temporary* work location (Rev. Rul. 90-23, 1990-11 I.R.B. Rev. Rul. 94-37, and Rev. Rul. 99-7).

What is a temporary place of business? For purposes of determining whether daily transportation expenses are deductible business expenses or nondeductible commuting expenses, a regular place of business is any location at which the taxpayer works or performs services on a regular basis, and a temporary place of business is any location at which the taxpayer performs services on an *irregular or short-term* (i.e., generally a matter of days or weeks) basis. A taxpayer may be considered as working or performing services at a particular location on a regular basis whether or not the taxpayer works or performs services at that location every week or on a set schedule. For example, daily transportation expenses incurred by a doctor in going between the doctor's residence and one or more offices, clinics, or hospitals at which the doctor works or performs services on a regular basis are nondeductible commuting expenses. However, daily transportation expenses incurred by the doctor in going between a clinic and a hospital or between the doctor's residence and a temporary work location are deductible business expenses.

Under this rule, a doctor's expense of travel from home to a patient's home for a house call is deductible.

An executive or salesperson may make calls on customers or clients. If these visits are on an infrequent basis, the client's office would be a temporary place of business. The cost of travel from home to client's office is deductible.

The rule is not limited to prospective application. Thus, it applies retroactively to open years (see also Rev. Rul. 99-7 discussed above).

If the taxpayer is an employee, the deduction for these expenses can only be claimed as a miscellaneous itemized deduction. As such, it is subject to the 2 percent of adjusted gross income floor on such deductions.

The IRS warns that if an audit shows a clear pattern of abuse by the taxpayer in claiming a business expense deduction for daily transportation expenses paid or incurred in going between the taxpayer's residence and asserted temporary work locations without proof of a valid business purpose, the IRS will disallow any deduction for those expenses and impose appropriate penalties.

Employer reimbursement. In some cases, an employer may reimburse an employee for otherwise deductible daily transportation expenses. The IRS says that the employee doesn't have to include such reimbursement if it is paid under an *accountable plan*, i.e., one that (a) requires the employee to substantiate expenses covered by the arrangement to the person providing the reimbursement, and (b) requires the employee to return any amount above the substantiated expenses. Reimbursement that is paid under a nonaccountable plan must be included by the employee in gross income. In turn, the employee can deduct the deductible daily transportation expenses as a miscellaneous itemized deduction.

Employer reporting. An employer is not required to report on the employee's Form W-2, or to withhold payroll taxes on, amounts paid as a reimbursement or other expense allowance for daily transportation expenses that are paid under an accountable place. However, reporting and withholding are required for amounts paid as reimbursement or other expense allowance for daily transportation amounts that are paid under a nonaccountable plan.

145 Meals and Entertainment

THE TAX CUTS AND JOBS ACT OF 2017 ELIMINATES THE DEDUCTION FOR ALL ENTERTAINMENT AFTER DECEMBER 31, 2017. THIS PROVISION DOES *NOT* SUNSET AFTER 2025.

The below discussion relates to the entertainment deduction prior to 2018. If you missed a deduction, you have 3 years to amend your return.

Wouldn't it be great to have the Internal Revenue Service pay part of the cost of your meals and entertainment? When you have your own business, you can have the Internal Revenue Service split the bills for these expenses with you.

In order to deduct any expenses for travel, meals, entertainment, gifts, or listed property, you must have a receipt or other documentary evidence for any expenditure of $75 or more. For expenditures incurred prior to October 1, 1995, the $75 amount was $25. (Internal Revenue Service Notice 95-50, issued September 29, 1995.)

Any expenses for food and drink furnished under circumstances of a type generally considered conducive to a business discussion, and when a business discussion is held, are deductible business expenses. Therefore, the custom of plying business clients or potential business clients with food and drink in restaurants and hotels will be deductible if they meet the requirements of an ordinary and necessary expense. When you go out with friends or relatives for a meal or drink, do you ever pick up their check? If they are or *could be* potential clients or customers for your business, and if you discussed business with them, then that expense would be deductible. Alternatively, if they are in business and they pay your expenses for meals at a restaurant, those expenses would be deductible for them.

Note that under the Tax Reform Act of 1986, no deduction would be allowed with respect to entertainment, amusement, or recreation unless the taxpayer establishes that the item was directly related to or, in the case of an item directly preceding or following a substantial and bona fide business discussion, that such item was associated with the active conduct of the taxpayer's trade or business. Meals as part of entertainment, e.g., hot dogs at a ballpark, are treated as entertainment, and are no longer deductible after 2017. A meal expenditure is associated with the active conduct of a trade or business if the taxpayer establishes a clear business purpose in making the expenditure. The meal must directly follow or precede a substantial and bona fide business discussion. The directly follow or precede standard is satisfied if the meal occurs on the same day as the business discussion.

The directly related test would be satisfied if any one of the following four tests is satisfied:

1. The taxpayer had more than a general expectation of deriving some business benefit; the taxpayer actively engaged in a business meeting, negotiation, or other bona fide business transaction; the principal character or aspect of the meal was the active conduct of the taxpayer's business; and the expenditure was allocable to the taxpayer and persons with whom the taxpayer engaged in the active conduct of business.

2. The expenditure occurred in a clear business setting, directly in furtherance of the taxpayer's trade or business.

3. The expenditure was made directly or indirectly for the benefit of an individual (other than an employee), and if such expenditure was in the nature of compensation for services rendered or paid as a prize or award, that is required to be included in gross income.

4. The expenditure was made with respect to a facility used by the taxpayer for the furnishing of food or beverages in an atmosphere conducive to business discussion.

However, even if one of the four directly related tests is satisfied, expenditures will not be directly related to the active conduct of a trade or business if incurred under circumstances where there is little or no possibility of engaging in the active conduct of a trade or business.

You should have receipts specifying the name of the restaurant, the amount, and the date. The relationship of your guest to your business activity should also be noted. Recognize, however, that no actual business need come from the meeting so long as you discuss business at the restaurant. In this area be careful not to simply alternate days in which you and your friend pick up the check. Any "regular" exchange of meal checks, if caught by the Internal Revenue Service, will be disallowed as a sham in an audit and subject you to fraud penalties.

Moreover, not only can you deduct meals, but you could, prior to 2018, also deduct business entertainment expenses. Amounts spent for business entertainment, amusement, or recreation were allowable if you could show that the expense was:

a) for entertainment directly preceding or following a substantial bona fide business discussion (including business meetings at a convention that was associated with your trade or business); *or*

b) directly related to the active conduct of your trade or business.

Examples of entertainment, amusement, or recreation included entertaining guests at nightclubs, theaters, football games, prizefights, and on hunting, fishing, and vacation trips. In *Detko v. Commissioner,* No. 14790-81, T.C. Memo 1987-99, February 18, 1987, an anesthesiologist was found to be entitled to deductions for entertainment expenses and depreciation in connection with a fishing boat on which he entertained doctors who were his referral source!

In applying the "directly related" or "associated with" tests, remember these points:

1. The entertaining must have been to further your trade or business. So, for example, if you entertained at a time when you already had more business than you could possibly handle, your deduction would be disallowed.

2. Expenses that violate public policy or local law—for instance, providing "call girls" for clients or serving liquor where it is against local law—would not be deductible.

3. Entertainment, amusement, or recreation expenses that were considered lavish or extravagant under the circumstances would be deductible *only* up to a reasonable amount. What a "reasonable amount" is depended upon all of the facts and circumstances; given the current business and entertainment climate, it was very difficult to exceed a "reasonable amount."

The Tax Reform Act of 1986 limited deductions for most meals and entertainment to 80 percent of cost. After December 31, 1993, the limit fell to 50 percent. Moreover, expenditures qualify as business meals or business entertainment only if business is actually discussed. Business transportation (airfare, taxis, etc.) remains fully deductible, but travel to *investment* seminars or *investment* conventions is not. The chart below summarizes these rules.

Type of Expense	Deductible
Lunch with customer/client; business before, during, or after the meal	50%
No business discussed	None
Cab fare to restaurant	100%
Air fare to Philadelphia to call on customer/client	100%
Lodging in Philadelphia	100%
Meals in Philadelphia (alone)	50%
Meals with customer/client; no business discussed:	
a. Your meal	50%
b. Customer's/client's meal	None
Air fare to New York for dentist to attend dental convention	100%
Meals in New York	50%
Air fare to Dallas for investment seminar	None
Lodging in Dallas	None
Tickets to ball game for taxpayer and customer/client; business discussed	None*
Taxi fare to game	100%
Food and drink at game	None*
Complimentary theater tickets for customer/client; taxpayer *not* present (note possible deduction as a gift)	None
Lunch at service organization as member	50%
Tickets to charity golf tournament run by volunteers	None*
Greens fees, carts, food and beverages consumed while hosting customer/client; business discussed	None*

Note that some meal and entertainment expenses remain fully deductible:

- expenses treated by the employer as compensation to an employee (the 50 percent reduction applies at the employee level if the employee claims the deduction);

* 50% prior to 2018.

- expenses reimbursed under an "accountable plan" (fully deductible to the person receiving the reimbursement, *if* reported in income with the deduction applying to the person making the reimbursement);

- meals served as an employer-operated eating facility, such as a cafeteria. This was changed by the Tax Cuts and Jobs Act of 2017 to 50% as of 2018 and zero after 2025.

- expenses incurred for recreational or social activities provided by the employer for the benefit of its employees (e.g., holiday parties, summer outings, etc.); *and*

- expenses for goods, services, and facilities made available by the taxpayer to the general public, such as promotional tickets or customer samples;

- food or beverage expenses excludable under the "de minimis fringe benefit" rules; eg. coffee and tea.

On June 26, 2017 the U.S. tax court in *Jacobs v. Commissioner,* 148 T.C. No. 24, T.C. No. 19009-15, ruled that the Boston Bruins could deduct the full amount spent on meals for players and staff at hotels during away games. This may make it easier for singers, authors, actors, and others to claim full-meal expense deductions while on the road if meals were part of their work travel schedule.

The court allowed the deduction under the de minimis fringe exception, finding that the meals were provided in a facility on or near the employer's business premises and were provided immediately before, during, or after the employee's workday. Depending upon the circumstances, it appears that "premises" may be portable.

But the Tax Cuts and Jobs Act of 2017 has modified this deduction. The case hinged on the court's agreeing that the hotel where the team ate was an "employer operated eating facility." As of 2018, only 50% of such expenses are allowed dropping to zero after 2025.

For years after December 31, 1997, the business meal deduction will be increased by 5 percent every other year to 80 percent *for persons subject to the federal hours of service limitation.*

With entertainment as well as with meals, your expenses had to be substantiated. You needed a receipt detailing the amount paid, the client you entertained, the business relationship, the date, and the place. The deductions for meals and entertainment allowed you substantial opportunities to convert your personal expenditures into allowable business deductions. Do not fail to claim them and do not fail to keep them because of lack of adequate substantiation. In the 24 percent tax bracket, a $100 business meal costs you $76. No

matter how much money you are making, it would be worth $24 in tax savings to spend thirty seconds noting the name of your business client on the back of the tab. That's the same as earning, tax-free, $2,880 an hour!

146 Travel and Vacation

There is no law prohibiting you from combining a business trip and a vacation. The Internal Revenue Service concedes that you are entitled to a deduction for attending a business convention. While such attendance must benefit or advance your business to be a deductible expense, there is no reason why such a convention cannot coincide with your vacation. If a business purpose can be established, the expenses of your spouse may also be deductible (Rev. Rul. 56-168; see also *Bank of Stockton*, TCM 1977-24). Note, however, that such business conventions or seminars must relate to your specific business. For example, in IRS Letter Ruling 8451027 and Rev. Rul. 84-113, 1984-31 I.R.B. 5, the Internal Revenue Service ruled that investment seminars in resort locations and a financial planning seminar dealing with general planning strategies were not deductible because they did not relate specifically to the taxpayer's activities.

The Omnibus Budget Reconciliation Act of 1993, effective after December 31, 1993, denies a deduction for travel expenses paid or incurred with respect to a spouse, dependent, or other individual accompanying a person on business travel, unless (1) the spouse, dependent, or other individual accompanying the person is a bona fide employee of the person paying or reimbursing the expenses, (2) the travel of the spouse, dependent, or other individual is for a bona fide business purpose, and (3) the expenses of the spouse, dependent, or other individual would otherwise be deductible.

WITHIN THE UNITED STATES

If the business-vacation trip is within the United States, the transportation expenses will be deductible only if the trip is primarily for business. If the trip is primarily for pleasure, no transportation expenses can be taken as a deduction. This means that you have to establish a primary business motive for making the trip—for instance, a convention located in that city, or a client or potential client that you want to see at that location. It would be advisable under such a situation to write to this person and receive in return a letter requesting you to visit her or him to discuss business matters. The amount of time that you spend on business as opposed to pleasure will be a

factor in answering the "primarily" question. For example, if you spend 5 days conducting business and 3 days sightseeing and seeing shows, the trip will be deemed primarily for business (5 days vs. 3 days) and the transportation will be deductible. Alternatively, if you conducted business for 2 days and vacationed the remaining 6, the trip will most likely be found primarily personal, and no transportation expenses will be allowed.

Even if the trip is found to be primarily personal, any expenses incurred at the destination that are properly allocable to business—meals, lodging, and incidental expenses during your "business days"—will be deductible.

OUTSIDE THE UNITED STATES

If the business-vacation trip is outside the United States, Canada, certain other Caribbean countries,[36] Mexico, and the Pacific Islands Trust Territories, special rules apply. If you were out of the country for 7 days or less, or if less than 25 percent of the time was for personal purposes, no allocation of transportation expenses need be made. Furthermore, no allocation is required if you had no substantial control over the trip arrangements and if the desire for a vacation was not a major factor in taking the trip. Alternatively, if the trip was primarily for pleasure, none of the transportation expenses will be deductible. In all other cases, all travel expenses must be allocated between business and personal expenses, and days devoted to travel are considered business days.

For example, assume that you took a trip from New York to London primarily for business purposes. You were away from home from July 20 through July 29 and spent 3 days vacationing and 7 days conducting business (including 2 travel days). Your fare was $500 and your meals and lodging amounted to

36. The Caribbean Basin Initiative (CBI) was enacted on August 5, 1983, authorizing preferential tax measures for Caribbean Basin countries and territories. The Act allows deductions for business expenses incurred while attending conventions and meetings in a designated Caribbean Basin beneficiary country, if that country enters into an agreement with the United States to provide for the exchange of certain tax information. The following countries have been eligible and qualify for the benefits of the CBI: Antigua and Barbuda, Aruba, the Bahamas, Barbados, Belize, Bermuda, Costa Rica, Dominica, the Dominican Republic, El Salvador, Grenada, Guatemala, Haiti, Honduras, Jamaica, Montserrat, the Netherlands Antilles, Panama, St. Christopher-Nevis, St. Vincent, and Trinidad and Tobago. As of 2007, the countries that remain eligible but have not yet qualified for the benefits of the CBI are Anguilla, The British Virgin Islands, the Cayman Islands, Guyana, Nicaragua, St. Lucia, Surinam, and the Turks and Caicos Islands (see Rev. Rul. 2007-28). Updates to the list of qualifying countries can be obtained by calling 1-202-287-4851.

$75 per day. You can deduct 70 percent of your transportation expenses (7 days out of 10) and $75 per day for 7 business days, as you were away from home for more than 7 days and more than 25 percent of your time was devoted to personal purposes.

If you find your trip is subject to the allocation rule, there is a planning strategy to maximize your tax deductions. When booking your flight, arrange for a stopover within the United States at the point closest to your destination. That way, the portion of the trip between your home and the stopover point will be fully deductible. You will have to allocate only the cost of the remainder of the trip.

For example, assume that you live in New York and will be attending a 3-day business convention in the Bahamas that will be followed by a 6-day vacation. If you fly directly to the Bahamas from New York, only one-third of the cost of your round-trip flight is deductible (3 business days out of 9 days total). However, if you fly from New York to Miami, conduct business in Miami, then take another flight to the Bahamas, the entire cost of the trip from New York to Miami would be deductible—as well as one-third of the cost of the trip from Miami to the Bahamas and back.

FOREIGN CONVENTIONS

No deduction will be allowed for expenses attributable to a foreign convention/vacation unless it is "reasonable for the convention to be held outside North America." "North America" means the countries below and on the next page including the Pacific Islands Trust Territories. Under Rev. Rul. 94-56*, 1994-36 I.R.B. 10, for purposes of claiming deductions for expenses incurred in connection with a convention, seminar, or similar meeting, the following areas are included in the "North American Area":

1. The fifty states of the United States and the District of Columbia;
2. The possessions of the United States, which for this purpose are American Samoa, Baker Island, the Commonwealth of Puerto Rico, the Commonwealth of the Northern Mariana Islands, Guam, Howland Island, Jarvis Island, Johnston Island, Kingman Reef, the Midway Islands, Palmyra Atoll, the U.S. Virgin Islands, Wake Island, and other U.S. islands, cays, and reefs not part of the fifty states or the District of Columbia;
3. Canada;

* Updated by Rev. Rul. 2016-16.

4. Mexico;

5. The Republic of the Marshall Islands;

6. The Federated States of Micronesia;

7. The Republic of Palau;

For expenses incurred in attending a convention that began on or after:

8. Antigua and Barbuda, February 10, 2003

9. Aruba, September 13, 2004

10. Bahamas, January 1, 2006

11. Barbados, November 3, 1984

12. Bermuda, December 2, 1988

13. Costa Rica, February 12, 1991

14. Curaçao, December 23, 2013

15. Dominica, May 9, 1988

16. Dominican Republic, October 12, 1989

17. Grenada, July 13, 1987

18. Guyana, August 27, 1992

19. Honduras, October 10, 1991

20. Jamaica, December 18, 1986

21. Panama, April 18, 2011

22. Saint Lucia, May 5, 2014

23. Trinidad and Tobago, February 9, 1990

In other words, there is no deduction if it is more reasonable to have the convention within rather than outside of North America. Three factors must be considered in determining the reasonableness of the convention location:

1. The purpose of the meeting and the activities taking place at the meeting

2. The purpose and activities of the sponsoring organization or groups

3. The residence of the active members of the sponsoring organization or groups and places where other meetings of the sponsors have been or will be held

CRUISE CONVENTIONS

In addition, there is no limit on the number of foreign conventions/vacations that yield deductible expenses, but no deductions will be allowed for conventions, seminars, or other meetings held on cruise ships, except if:

a) the convention or meeting is directly related to your trade or business;

b) the cruise ship is U.S. registered; *and*

c) all ports of call are located in the United States or its possessions. Only the following ports qualify as possessions: The U.S. Virgin Islands (St. Thomas, St. John, St. Croix), American Samoa, Guam, the North Mariana Islands, and Puerto Rico.

Even under these circumstances, the maximum deduction is $2,000 for each taxpayer (Highway Revenue Act of 1982) and you must attach two written statements to your return. The first statement, signed by you, must include information as to the number of days that were devoted to scheduled business activities, a program of the scheduled business activities, and such other information as may be required by regulations. The other statement, signed by a representative of the sponsoring organization, must include a schedule of the business activities each day, the number of hours you attended such scheduled activities, and such other information as may be required by regulations. Business seminars on cruise ships that are U.S. registered are now being offered by United States Line and American Hawaii Cruises (to Hawaii) and Delta Line Cruises (on the Ohio and Mississippi Rivers). In addition, American Cruise Lines and the Clipper Cruise Line, which operates a variety of voyages in intercoastal waters from New England to Florida, are also operating under the seminar restrictions.

WATER TRANSPORTATION

Note that the Tax Reform Act of 1986 limits the deduction for expenses incurred for transportation by water to twice the highest federal government per diem allowance (for employees traveling away from home but serving in the United States) times the number of days in transit. These rates are changed annually and are found in Publication 1542 available free from the IRS. In addition, according to Notice 87-23, the 50 percent limitation on meals is applied prior to the above maximum per diem limitations. If meal expenses are not separately stated, the amount deductible under the luxury water or travel limitation is not subject to the 50 percent rule.

Ship travel, however, can be an asset on a combined business-vacation trip. Days spent in transit count as business days in the allocation formula. For example, assume a 2-day business meeting in London followed by a 2-week British vacation. If you fly (1 day each way), only 22 percent of your travel excluding transportation is deductible—2 business days plus 2 days of travel out of a total of

18 days away. But if you sail (5 days each way), 46 percent is deductible—2 business days plus 10 days of travel out of a total 26 days away.

Remember, the key to being able to deduct your vacation as a business expense is prior planning. Make sure that you can substantiate your business purpose for the trip and your expenses. Properly planned and substantiated expenses will allow you to deduct the cost of your transportation, food, meals, lodging, entertainment, cleaning, etc. I have found that perhaps the easiest way to maintain a substantiation record is to keep a diary or account book of such expenses. Combined with appropriate receipts, such a diary will help reduce your taxes to zero.

147 Gifts

Ordinary and necessary expenses for business gifts you make directly or indirectly to any individual will be allowed as deductible expenses. However, the total value of business gifts during the tax year to any one individual cannot be more than $25, and in addition, gifts from a husband and wife are treated as coming from one donor in applying this limitation. Incidental costs, such as packaging, mailing or other delivery, and insuring the gifts, are not included in this limitation.

The following items are not subject to the $25 limitation:

1. Items of a clear advertising nature that cost $4 or less

 a) on which your name is permanently printed; *or*

 b) which are among a number of identical items generally distributed by you.

2. Signs, display racks, or other promotional material given by you as a producer or wholesaler to a retailer for use on the business premises of the retailer

3. Employee awards

Here again you must provide substantiation for your expenses in order to make them allowable. While the price of allowance is increased record keeping,

the benefit now is that gifts to friends, relatives, etc., who are or may become business clients or associates have been converted from nondeductible personal expenses to allowable income tax deductions. Every time you convert a personal expense to a deductible business expense you take one more step on the road to reducing your taxes to zero.

148 Advertising

The Tax Court allowed the sponsor of an amateur basketball team to deduct the costs of the team as an advertising expense. The taxpayer used the team sponsorship as the main form of advertising for his rental housing and commodity brokerage businesses. Before games, the taxpayer would meet with customers to discuss business. The Court said that, while there was an element of personal satisfaction, the team sponsorship promoted the taxpayer's business at low cost. *James C. Bower*, T.C. Memo 1990-16.

149 Deductible Clothes

The costs of buying and maintaining a uniform are deductible business expenses only if the uniform is (1) specifically required to be worn as a condition of employment and (2) is not adaptable for general or continued use. Uniforms that can be worn as ordinary clothing don't meet this second test and can't be considered ordinary and necessary business expenses.

Uniforms worn by police officers, fire fighters, nurses, bus drivers and railway workers have been held to meet this two-part test [Rev. Rul. 70-474, C.B. 1970-2, 34], as have commercial fishermen's protective clothing [Rev. Rul. 55-235, C.B. 1955-1, 274]. But work clothing worn by painters (white shirts, caps, bib overalls, and work shoes) did not qualify, even though the clothing was required by a union [Rev. Rul. 57-143, C.B. 1957-1,89].

Note, however, that ordering clothes imprinted with the name of your business may be deductible as *advertising*—it keeps your business name before the public and enhances your customer base.

150 Creative Deductions—Busting the IRS

In Green Bay, Wisconsin, a stripper got a tax deduction for surgically enlarged breasts. Then she put her deductions on display and called it a victory for all exotic dancers.

"It is simply a stage prop we are carrying around to make money," Cynthia Hess said before appearing at the Bamboo Room.

Hess, otherwise known as "Chesty Love," and her husband, Reginald R. Hess of Fort Wayne, Ind., claimed a $2,088 deduction on the implants that enlarged her bust size to 56FF.

The Internal Revenue Service turned it down.

But Hess found an ally in Special Trial Judge Joan Seitz Pate, who ruled that the breasts did increase her income, and at 10 pounds each, were so cumbersome that she couldn't derive personal benefit from them.

151 Medical Premiums

Section 162(m), added by the Tax Reform Act of 1986, permits self-employed individuals to deduct a percentage of their health insurance premiums (including Medicare payments). For 1998, the percentage was 45 percent; it increased to 60 percent in 1999, went to 70 percent in 2002, and is 100 percent in 2003 and after. The amount of this deduction is limited to your self-employment income and is not available on a month-by-month basis, if you or your spouse is eligible to participate in any subsidized health plan maintained by any employer of either you or your spouse. The deduction is also not available unless the premium is paid under a nondiscriminatory health plan. The premium paid is an "above the line" deduction. That means that it is deductible even if you do not itemize your deductions.

152 Borrowing from Your Company

If your own business is in a corporate form, you have a special opportunity for tax savings. This opportunity is the supersophisticated technique of borrowing from your own corporation or from your corporate pension

plan. This can be done as long as the loan bears a reasonable rate of interest—that is, the prime rate, give or take a percentage point.

This extraordinary technique allows you to borrow money, pay yourself interest, deduct the interest you pay (see Chapter 7 for limitations), and receive the same interest tax-free. It normally is done by having a qualified profit-sharing or pension plan make a loan to you as one of its participants. This technique was approved by the Internal Revenue Service for a qualified plan even with *single* participant.[37]

This technique will be approved by the Internal Revenue Service for a qualified plan that has a loan provision *if* the loan:

a) is available to all participants and beneficiaries on an equal basis;

b) is not made available to highly compensated office employees, officers, or shareholders in a percentage amount greater than that available to other employees;

c) is made in accordance with specific provisions regarding such loans set forth in the plan;

d) bears a reasonable rate of interest; *and*

e) is adequately secured.

The vested portion of your account (for a profit-sharing or money purchase plan) can be used as security for the loan. Moreover, loans from such plans can exceed the vested amount in your account without the plan's risking disqualification as long as:

- The loans are adequately secured by other than the nonvested portion of the plan.

- The loans bear a reasonable interest rate.

- The loans are repaid within a specified period of time.

- The loan payments are made on a level basis, at least quarterly.

Loan security for a defined benefit pension plan can be provided up to an amount equal to the actuarial equivalent, or present value, of your accrued

37. Letter Ruling 800-8059.

benefit. Furthermore, the arrangement must be an actual loan. There must be evidence that a true debtor-creditor relationship exists; otherwise the "loan" will be labeled by the Internal Revenue Service as an "advance distribution," making such funds taxable income to you.

The Tax Equity and Fiscal Responsibility Act of 1982 restricts borrowing against the vested benefits of your plan. Effective with respect to loans made after August 13, 1982, the law allows loans up to the lesser of $50,000 or 50 percent of the value of your vested employee benefit, but not less than $10,000. Additionally, the loan must be repaid within 5 years. But a loan used to acquire, construct, or rehabilitate your personal residence or the residence of a member of your family would not be subject to the 5-year repayment rule.

The extraordinary savings from this technique can be demonstrated by the following example:

Your vested share in a profit-sharing plan	$100,000
Amount borrowed to purchase a home	$50,000
Interest rate	20%
Tax-free interest you pay into the plan	$10,000
Amount deducted	$10,000
Tax savings at 24 percent tax bracket	$2,400
New value of your profit-sharing plan	$60,000

In effect, you pay yourself $10,000 and, by virtue of your tax deduction, come out ahead by $2,400!

The Tax Reform Act of 1986 eliminated this benefit for key employee loans made after December 31, 1986. Effective for loans made after that date, the top loan is limited to $50,000 less the outstanding loan balance of plan loans on the date of the loan *and* less the excess of the highest outstanding loan balance from the plan during the 1-year period ending on the day before the date of the loan over the outstanding loan balance of plan loans on the date of the loan. For example, assume you have a balance of $150,000 in your profit-sharing plan and have never made any loans from the plan. On January 1, 2018, you borrow $35,000. On May 1, 2018, the loan balance is $30,000. On November 1, 2018, the loan balance is $25,000. At that time you would like to borrow an additional amount without having to include it in income. The maximum amount you may borrow on that date is $15,000 ($50,000 – $25,000 – [$35,000 – $25,000]).

Moreover, the former 5-year repayment period has been tightened. Effective for loans made after December 31, 1986, the 5-year period may be

extended only in the case of a loan made to purchase the principal residence of the plan participant. The extension of the 5-year period is not permitted in the case of refinancing a principal residence. In addition, the repayment of loans made after December 31, 1986, must be made in level payments. The use of balloon payment arrangements is no longer permitted. Such payments must be made no less frequently than quarterly.

Finally, no interest is deductible for any post-1986 loan to a key employee. This means that even if you use the funds to purchase a principal residence, if you are a key employee, no interest will be deductible, even though all interest would have been fully deductible had you secured normal financing of the home.

A key employee was defined as a plan participant who at any time during the plan year or the preceding 4 plan years was (1) an officer of the company, (2) an employee owning one of the 10 largest interests in the company, (3) a 5 percent owner of the company, or (4) a 1 percent owner of the company earning more than $150,000 per year (IRC § 416)(i)(1)(A).

The Tax Relief Act of 2001 redefined a *key employee* as (1) an officer with compensation in the prior year of more than $130,000,[38] (2) a more than 5 percent owner, or (3) a more than 1 percent owner with prior-year compensation of more than $150,000.

Note also the limitations on the deduction of interest discussed on page 303.

153 Miscellaneous Corporate Advantages

There are a number of other miscellaneous tax saving strategies that owning your own company in a corporate form will allow you. They include the following:

1. The corporation can purchase for you $50,000 of group term life insurance with tax-deductible dollars. Term life insurance in excess of $50,000 is also available at a negligible after-tax cost to you. For example, assume that you are 39 years old and the corporation purchases $100,000 in term life insurance for you. The premium would be 100 percent deductible to the corporation, and you would have to report only $54 per year of additional income. In the 24 percent bracket, this would cost only an additional $1,296.

38. $175,000 for 2018.

2. The corporation can accumulate dividend income or other income at the maximum rate of 21 percent. That's a whole lot better than the pre-2018 top rate of 35 percent.

3. IRA plans absolutely prohibit owner-employees from borrowing money from the plan. But all plan participants *may* borrow their money from a corporate retirement plan. The advantages of such a provision have already been detailed.

 Remember, the interest earned on such loans will not be taxed to either the corporation or the plan and may be deductible by you on your personal income tax return. In the process, it will increase the amount of money accumulating tax-deferred in the plan, as well as your total financial wealth.

4. Prior to the Tax Reform Act of 1984, a current deduction for future college costs could have been allowed. The corporation could have set up an educational benefit plan in which a trust was established to which the corporation contributed funds to provide a given amount per year for each employee's child enrolled in an accredited college or university, without regard for financial need or academic achievement. In the case of *Greensboro Pathology Associates,* Federal Circuit, December 15, 1982, the Court ruled that the contributions to the trust were deductible when made by the corporation and only taxable income to the employees when the money was withdrawn. This can be a significant deferral tax advantage if the children are relatively young. In such a situation, the company can receive its deductions several years before the employees must pick up the income.

 In determining that this was a welfare plan rather than a plan of deferred compensation wherein the corporate deduction would have been deferred until the employee recognized the income, the court looked at the following questions:

 a) Is the plan concerned with the employees' well-being?

 b) Are the benefits based on the earnings of the employees?

39. Seventy percent if the corporation does not own at least 20 percent of the dividend-paying corporation. In order to qualify for the dividends-received deduction, the stocks must have been held by the corporation for at least 46 days. The holding period is 91 days for cumulative preferred stock in arrears for more than 366 days. Borrowing to purchase equities by corporate investors will reduce the amount of the dividends-received deduction.

c) Are benefits based on the length of service?

d) Are benefits available to all employees?

e) Are benefits really a substitute for salaries?

f) Does the plan serve its stated purpose, or is it a sham?

g) Does the employer lose control of the funds contributed?

h) Can the funds revert to the company or its shareholders?

i) Is the plan administered by someone independent of the company?

The court said that if items b and c were present, there was a strong presumption that the plan was a form of deferred compensation—no deduction allowed until funds were distributed. It also said that item d, availability to all employees, was essential if the plan was to qualify for current deductions.

The passage of the Tax Reform Act of 1984 appears, however, to effectively overrule the *Greensboro* case as to the immediate deductibility of plan contributions. The Tax Reform Act of 1984 provides that contributions to a funded welfare benefit plan will not be deductible under Section 162 but will now be governed by new Section 419. Section 419 provides that a contribution made to a funded welfare plan will be deductible in the year of contribution only to the extent that it would have been allowable as a deduction if the employer had paid the benefits directly and the employer used the cash-basis method of accounting. In essence, unless the plan is distributing benefits, no immediate deduction is allowable for fund contributions by the employer. Section 419, however, does provide for a carryover of contributions in excess of deductibility to the succeeding taxable year. Moreover, these new rules on plan contribution deductions apply not only to formal welfare benefit plans but to any method of employer contributions having the effect of a plan.

5. A final advantage of the corporate form of business is the elimination of the danger of vicarious liability that exists in a professional partnership. For example, assume that Dr. Smith and Dr. Jones operate as a partnership. Dr. Jones is on a vacation on the day that her partner, Dr. Smith, creates a potential malpractice problem in the operating room. Under the vicarious liability rules that apply to partnerships, Dr. Jones is just as responsible for the malpractice as is Dr. Smith, who is directly involved. In a corporate setting, Dr. Smith and the corporation are liable. Dr. Jones is personally off the hook.

SIMPLE RECORD KEEPING

In Notice 2015-82, the IRS raised the safe harbor threshold for deducting certain capital items that could arguably be depreciated from $500 to $2,500 ($5,000 if you had audited financial statements).

SPECIAL DEPRECIATION DEDUCTIONS

The Tax Cuts and Jobs Act of 2017 created a bonus depreciation deduction of 100 percent for 2018 for purchases of qualified property, effective for items bought and placed in service after September 27, 2017. This allows full expensing of items that would normally have to be depreciated. Beginning in 2023 the 100 percent allowance falls to 80 percent and is reduced by 20 percent each following year.

Investment Planning to Save Taxes

"If Patrick Henry thought that taxation without representation was bad, he should see how bad it is with representation."

OLD FARMER'S ALMANAC

"There's nothing more dangerous than the U.S. Congress with an idea."

E. PATRICK MCGUIRE of the Conference Board
Opening a Conference Examining Tax Incentives

"How do I say it? When Congress enacts a law, it isn't always well thought out."

FREDRIC GRUNDEMAN
former Treasury Department attorney

"The alternative minimum tax is a 'perfect example' of a lack of common sense in the tax code. . . ."

NINA OLSON
National Taxpayer Advocate

The first key to investment planning for 2018 tax purposes is finding out the ever-changing status of the capital gains tax on sales of capital assets. Capital assets include such things as stock, securities, real estate held as an investment, and most properties held for personal purposes. In fact, all property except the following is included under the umbrella of capital assets:

- Stock in trade, inventory, and other property held primarily for sale to customers in the ordinary course of business

- Depreciable property used in a trade or business and real property used in a trade or business

- Accounts and notes receivable acquired in the ordinary course of a trade or business for services rendered or from the sale of stock in trade, inventory, or other property held for sale to customers

- A copyright or a literary, or artistic composition (not musical) held by a person whose personal efforts created it, or held by a taxpayer whose basis is determined by reference to the creator's basis (e.g., by gift)

- A letter or memorandum or similar property held by a person for whom the property was prepared or produced, or held by a taxpayer whose basis is determined by reference to the first person's basis (e.g., by gift)

- Obligations of the federal or a state government or one of its political subdivisions that are issued on a discount basis and payable without interest at a fixed maturity date not exceeding one year from the date of issue

- Free U.S. government publications

If you go after your investment advisor and get a settlement for recovery or long-term capital losses, that portion of the award is treated as long-term capital gain PLR 200724012.

OLD LAW

Prior to 1987, an individual could deduct from gross income 60 percent of *net long-term capital gain* (the excess of net long-term capital gain over any net short-term capital loss), leaving only 40 percent taxable. Since the maximum regular income tax rate was 50 percent, the deduction meant that net capital gain was taxed at a maximum rate of 20 percent (50 percent × 40 percent).

Capital losses were allowed in full against capital gains. Capital losses were also allowed against up to $3,000 of ordinary income; however, only one-half of

the excess of long-term capital loss over net short-term capital gain was allowed for this purpose. Unused capital losses could be carried forward indefinitely.

The Tax Reform Act of 1986 repealed the net long-term capital gain deduction. However, the maximum rate on long-term capital gains of individuals was made 28 percent.

The 1986 law did not change the character of gain as ordinary or capital, or as long- or short-term capital gain. Capital losses are allowed in full against capital gain, as under prior law.

Capital-loss treatment also was changed by the 1986 law. Capital losses continue to be fully offset by capital gains. The overall deduction limit of $3,000 per year (against ordinary income) still applies. Losses over that amount can be carried over to future years. Short-term capital losses continue to be fully deductible against ordinary income, up to this $3,000 limit. Long-term capital losses also continue to be fully deductible against up to $3,000 of ordinary income. Beginning in 1987, both short-term and long-term capital-loss carry-forwards can be used to offset ordinary income on a dollar-for-dollar basis up to a $3,000 limit.

Note that the difference between long-term and short-term capital gains and losses still exists under current law. A gain from the sale or exchange of an asset acquired after December 31, 1987, will not be treated as long-term capital gain unless you held it for more than 1 year. The holding period was more than 6 months for assets acquired after June 22, 1984, and before January 1, 1988. Recognize that the longer holding period still has an impact, beyond the maximum rate, in that it affects charitable contributions of certain property. For example, a deduction normally cannot exceed 50 percent of your adjusted gross income. The equivalent limit for contributions to a private nonoperating foundation is 30 percent. For contributions of long-term capital gain property, however, the limit is 30 percent of the contribution base, or 20 percent if the contribution is made to a private nonoperating foundation.

Capital gain property includes only property that would have produced long-term capital gain if it had been sold at the time of the contribution. With the longer holding period, it would be that much longer before assets acquired after 1987 fall into that definition and within the lower percentage limits.

Moreover, the otherwise allowable deduction for a charitable contribution of property has to be reduced by the amount of gain that would not be long-term capital gain if the contributed property has been sold at the time of the contribution. That covers the amount of hypothetical gain that would have been recaptured in an actual sale (e.g., depreciation). However, it also covers all the hypothetical gain on an asset acquired after 1987 and not held for more

than 1 year. Thus, the deduction for contributions of such post-1987 capital gain property would be limited to the property's adjusted basis.

In post-1986 tax years, if the sale of the property would have produced long-term gain, the difference between the allowable deduction for the contributed property and its adjusted basis was a preference item for alternative minimum tax purposes. The rule did not apply, however, to contributions of tangible personal property beginning in 1991 and all property, real, personal, and intangible, after December 31, 1992.

The Tax Relief Act of 1997 changed the above rules. Retroactive to May 7, 1997, the law cut the top capital gains tax rate from 28 percent to 20 percent for investments (excluding collectibles such as art, stamps, or coins which will retain a maximum 28 percent rate) held for at least 18 months (12 months if the investment was sold before July 29, 1997). The top rate dropped further to 18 percent for assets purchased after 2000 and held for 5 years or longer. Gains on real estate, to the extent of Section 1250 depreciation recapture, will be taxed at a maximum 25 percent rate. Capital assets held for more than 12 months but less than 18 months retained the maximum 28 percent rate.

For those in the lower brackets, the rate would fall to as low as 10 percent on investments held more than 18 months. That rate would drop to 8 percent for assets held for 5 years or longer regardless of when the asset was acquired.

The 1998 Reform Act changed the rules again. As of January 1, 1998, the long-term holding period is again 12 months!

The impact of the change? Enormous! The difference between short-term and long-term gains was then the difference between 38.6 percent and as low as 18 percent, which was 20.6 percent. On a $100,000 gain, that was $20,600 in your pocket.

CURRENT LAW

The 2003 Tax Act cut the long-term capital gains rates again. The maximum capital gains rate for long-term sales on or after May 6, 2003 was 15 percent. For those in the 10 or 15 percent bracket, the rate had been slashed to 5 percent! For 2008 and after that rate went to ZERO!

The American Taxpayer Relief Act of 2012 raised the maximum long-term capital gains rate to 20 percent for those in the top tax bracket (now 39.6%). The Tax Cuts and Jobs Act of 2017 changed the rules again. *Now, your capital gains tax rate is based on set income thresholds,* which will be adjusted annually for inflation. For 2018, the 0% rate applies to taxpayers with taxable income under $38,600 on single returns, $51,700 for head of household, $2,600 for estates and trusts, and $77,200 on joint returns. The 20% rate starts at $425,800 for singles and $479,000 for jointly filed returns. The 15% rate is for filers with taxable incomes between

the 0% and 20% break points. The actual top capital gains rate is 23.8 percent. That includes 3.8 percent surtax on unearned income discussed below.

The rate reduction hurts tax-deferred investments. All payments out of retirement plans (except for Roth IRA plans discussed in Chapter 6) are taxed at ordinary income rates. The advantage of tax deferral disappears when you could have paid a 0–20 percent capital gains tax and end up paying ordinary income tax at the 39.6 percent rate. If you are close to retirement and expect to remain in the higher brackets, tax deferral may even work against you.

3.8 PERCENT MEDICARE SURTAX ON INVESTING INCOME

The Patient Protection and Affordable Care Act imposes a 3.8 percent surtax on investment income starting in 2013. It hits those with modified adjusted gross income of over $200,000 ($250,000 for joint returns). You will use new Form 8960 to report this tax.

The tax is 3.8 percent of the lessor of

1. Net investment income, or

2. The amount by which your modified adjusted gross income exceeds the $200,000/$250,000 thresholds.

Net investment income includes interest, dividends, royalties, rents, net gains from the disposition of property (capital gains), and nonqualified annuities. Qualified annuities, pensions, IRA distributions, and alimony are specifically exempt from the tax.

The tax also applies to passive income, which is income from a trade or business that is a passive activity under Code Sec. 469. An activity is passive if it involves the conduct of a trade or business in which you do not materially participate. Very generally, material participation exists if you are involved in the operations of the activity on a *regular, continuous,* and *substantial* basis. Accordingly, if you materially participate in the entity's business, the tax on net investment income does not apply to income from the entity. If you do not materially participate, the income is characterized as passive and may be subject to the tax. You must put in 750 hours per year to "materially participate."

How to minimize the impact? See if you can qualify as a "real estate professional" by putting in 750 hours on your rental activity. Any net rental income won't count. Consider a charitable remainder trust (see pages 329–330). The gain on the sale would be exempt and the 3.8 percent tax on that gain would go away. Time your income to fall under the thresholds. Use installment sales, tax-free income, and deferred income to avoid the surtax hit. Note that the tax applies to any gain on the sale of a second home, and any gain *in excess* of the potential $500,000 exclusion on the sale of your principal residence.

Also consider direct IRA donations to a charity (if you qualify) or charitable contributions of appreciated property. Let's keep that adjusted gross income down!

The following tax planning strategies and techniques are suggested to optimize the advantages of favored capital gains rates at the end of the year:

Planning Year-End Securities Transactions

Results to Date	Unrealized Portfolio Gains and Losses	Possible Action to Be Taken Before Year-End
Short-term	Losses and gains	Cover short-term gain by taking losses. Take additional loss to offset ordinary income.
Short-term gain only	No losses	Taxwise, nothing need be done.
Short-term loss	Gains only	Generally no advantage to realizing additional gains, except gains can be realized tax-free to extent of losses.
Long-term gain	Losses and gains	Cover long-term gain by taking losses. Take additional losses to offset ordinary income.
Long-term gain	Gains only	Taxwise, nothing need be done.
Long-term loss	Gains only	Generally nothing further need be done. Long-term loss will offset ordinary income. Remainder will carry forward. Opportunity exists to realize gains at no tax cost to extent of losses.
Long-term loss	Losses only	Nothing need be done.
None	Losses and gains	Generally no advantage to realizing gains except to extent of losses. Consider taking loss to offset ordinary income.

CAPITAL GAINS BREAK FOR INVESTING IN SMALL CORPORATIONS

If you buy stock in a C corporation with assets of $50 million or less directly from the company after Sept. 27, 2010, and hold it for more than five years, you can exclude 100% of your gain when you sell. The gain is exempt from the AMT, too. The exclusion is capped at the greater of 10 times share basis of $10 million. Stock of companies in certain lines of business is not eligible for this tax break. Those lines include banking, insurance, leasing, farming, restaurants, oil and gas, and personal services such as law, health, architecture, consulting and accounting.

154 Short Sales

In a short sale, you contract to sell stock that you do not own or intend to make available for delivery upon sale. The securities are borrowed for delivery to the buyer. The sale must eventually be covered by the purchase of the securities in the market or by the delivery of securities owned at the time of the short sale. The taxable event occurs when the securities are delivered to the lender (usually your brokerage firm) by the seller to close the short sale.

Whether capital gain or loss on a short sale is long- or short-term will generally be determined by how long the seller held the stock used to close the short sale. However, special rules exist regarding short sales where substantially identical property is held by the short seller at the time of the short sale. These rules prevent the conversion of a short-term gain into a long-term gain or the conversion of a long-term loss into a short-term loss.

The definition of substantially identical is a question of fact. Securities of different corporations are not substantially identical. However, a convertibility feature or an impending reorganization under which such securities will be exchanged for one another could lead to a different conclusion. Bonds of different issuers, or with a difference in maturity of at least 20 percent, or a difference in coupon of at least 30 percent would not be substantially identical.

A short sale could have been used to defer the recognition of a capital gain into the next taxable year. For example, an investor selling "short against the box" will lock in the selling price but can defer recognition of the gain until the position is closed, which can be in the next taxable year. Here you are selling short securities that you already own to lock in gain but defer recognition.

Unfortunately, the Tax Relief Act of 1997 closed this area of tax planning. Generally, for all short sales made after June 8, 1997, such sales are considered "constructive sales" and are taxable in the year made.

The Internal Revenue Service issued a revenue ruling concerning the tax treatment of "short sales." It clarified the timing of gains or losses. Timing is critical when doing year-end tax planning and in determining the holding period of the stock for gain or loss purposes. Two common scenarios were addressed.

In the first, the taxpayer directs his broker to borrow shares in January of year 1. On December 31, the broker is directed to purchase shares (which have increased in value) to close the position. The shares are delivered on January 4 of year 2. The IRS ruled that the sale is not complete until the shares are delivered in year 2. Accordingly, the loss is realized in year 2.

In the second, the facts are the same, but the stock has decreased in value and the short sale results in a gain. The taxpayer is considered as having entered into a constructive sale position and realized a gain in year 1.

155 Broad-Based Index Options and Regulated Futures Contracts (RFCs)

Broad-based index options and RFCs are subject to special rules. Those open at year-end must be marked to market, and unrealized gains and losses are taxed as if the position had been closed at year-end. Under these special rules, 60 percent of the capital gain or loss is treated as long-term and 40 percent is treated as short-term, irrespective of the actual holding period.

156 Wash Sales

The wash sale rule applies only to losses. A wash sale occurs when an investor who sells a security at a loss purchases (or acquires an option to purchase) securities that are substantially identical to those sold within the 61-day period, beginning 30 days before the sale and ending 30 days after the sale.

A current deduction is denied for losses realized under those circumstances. Instead, the disallowed loss is added to the basis of the substantially identical securities acquired. The holding period of the securities sold at a loss is added to the holding period of the newly acquired securities.

A wash sale may be avoided by purchasing an equivalent amount of the same security, holding both lots for 31 days, and then selling the original security at a loss. Alternatively, you could reinvest in securities that are not substantially identical, such as those of another company in the same industry.

Rev. Rul. 2008-5 applies the wash sale limitation even if you have your IRA purchase the identical stock.

157 Premiums on Taxable and Tax-Exempt Bonds

At your option, the premium on a taxable bond may be amortized and deducted each year (with a corresponding reduction in cost basis) over the remaining life of the bond.

Otherwise, upon sale or maturity, the premium may result in a capital loss that would be deductible at that time. For bonds acquired before October 23, 1986, the amortized amount of premium is considered a miscellaneous itemized deduction not subject to the 2 percent floor. For bonds acquired after October 22, 1986, and before 1988, the deduction for amortized bond premium is treated as interest expense, subject to the investment interest expense limitations.

However, effective for bonds acquired after 1987 or, if elected, for obligations acquired after October 22, 1986, amortizable bond premium is treated as an offset to interest income on the bond rather than as a separate interest deduction (and therefore not subject to investment interest expense limitations).

On tax-exempt bonds, the premium must be amortized over the life of the bond or to the earliest call date. The premium cannot be deducted because it is an expense of earning tax-exempt interest. The basis of the tax-exempt bond is reduced by the amount of premium attributable to the period for which the bond is held. If the bond is held to maturity, no capital loss will result from the purchase of a tax-exempt bond at a premium.

158 Original Issue Discount (OID)—Taxable Bonds

OID interest on government bonds issued after July 1, 1982, and on corporate bonds issued after May 28, 1969, accrues and must be reported annually for tax purposes even though it is not payable until sale or maturity of the instrument. For corporate bonds issued before July 2, 1982, OID is computed on a straight-line monthly accrual basis. For corporate and government bonds issued after July 1, 1982, OID is computed on a constant-interest-rate method based on the original issue price and yield-to-maturity.

159 Original Issue Discount (OID)—Tax-Exempt Bonds

Tax-exempt OID is calculated under two different methods, depending on when the bond was issued. OID on a tax-free municipal bond is treated as

tax-exempt interest income and is not included in taxable income. However, calculating OID on tax-exempt bonds is necessary for purposes of adjusting basis in order to determine whether there is a capital gain or loss on sale or redemption prior to maturity and for determining whether Social Security benefits are taxable.

For tax-exempt OID securities issued prior to September 4, 1982, or acquired prior to March 2, 1984, OID is calculated on a straight-line basis. For tax-exempt OID securities issued after September 3, 1982, and acquired after March 1, 1984, OID is calculated under the constant-rate method.

160 Market Discount

A market discount occurs when you buy a bond in the secondary market for a price *below* a certain value. For most bonds, that value is par (usually $1,000). In the case of original issue discount (OID) bonds (e.g., zero coupon bonds), the measuring stick is the bond's current "accreted" value. This is the increased value of the bond due to the pro rata accretion of the discount while you hold the bond. If an old bond is bought for less than its accreted value, it becomes a market discount bond. The discount, therefore, is normally the difference between acquisition price and par or accreted value.

In the past, when market discount bonds were sold, called, or matured, the excess of the redemption or sales price over the purchase price was treated as capital gain rather than ordinary income. Market discount bonds *purchased after* April 30, 1993 will now have the difference taxed as ordinary income.

161 Municipal Bond Swaps

Municipal bond swaps are transactions in which municipal bonds in a given portfolio are sold and the proceeds of the sale are then used to purchase other municipal bonds of like quality, coupon, par value, and yield.

Traditionally, this "tax swap" is the favorite method among individual investors to reduce their tax liabilities. Municipal bond market prices characteristically move up or down uniformly. Therefore, in most cases, if your bonds have depreciated in value, all other issues have as well, because interest rates have risen. The result is that by effectuating a swap, you merely establish paper

losses for tax purposes. Your capital loss is the difference between your adjusted cost (or book value) and the current selling price of the bonds. The proceeds of a sale can be used to purchase other bonds, which should differ from those sold in coupon, maturity, or issuer. In most cases, tax swapping can be accomplished with a small adjustment (extension) of maturity to overcome market spreads.

Correctly done, a timely tax swap can provide you with the following benefits:

- Equal or greater income from your investments

- Equivalent quality and/or maturity in bond portfolios

- Continued participation in a favored security, or realizing tax losses that reduce your tax

- Meaningful tax savings to offset both capital gains taken in your current year and up to $3,000 of other income, by using capital losses realized through the tax swap

The mechanics of a tax swap are relatively simple. If you want to establish a capital loss for tax purposes, sell a bond for less than you paid for it. If at the same time you want to maintain your portfolio, buy a similar bond. There is no actual loss. At maturity the bond pays its face amount. If you buy one bond at $900 and sell it at $850, and then buy another at $850 and hold it to $1,000 maturity, you still make the $100 difference between your original purchase price and maturity; the intermediate sale and purchase do not matter. If you have a portfolio of bonds, therefore, you should contact your broker at year-end to arrange for an appropriate tax saving swap. If structured correctly, whether you do it with municipal bonds or with regular bonds, you should be a tax winner.

162 Employee Options—Nonqualified

Another investment tax saving strategy involves the handling of employee stock options. The grant of a nonqualified stock option results in no compensation to you as an employee. But exercising your option does result in compensation, measured by the difference between the option price and the fair market value at the time of the exercise.

For example, the *grant* of an option to buy 1,000 shares at $20 per share when the market value is $25 per share results in no income to you. If you *exercise* the option later when the market value is $40, you will recognize compensation

income of $20,000 ($40,000 – $20,000). This taxable income plus the cash investment necessary to exercise the option are the major disadvantages of non-qualified stock options. In order to exercise the option in the above example, you must raise $26,400 in cash—$20,000 to buy the stock and as much as $6,400 to pay the tax in the 32 percent bracket.

The Internal Revenue Service has ruled that if full or partial payment for stock acquired upon exercise of a nonqualified stock option is made by transferring identical shares in the employer company, it will not result in any gain to you on the shares used to pay for the stock option.[1] The following example shows how you can take advantage of this ruling. Assume you own 1,000 shares of stock of your employer, acquired for $10 per share. You exercise a nonqualified option to acquire 2,000 shares of identical stock at an option price of $25 per share ($50,000 total). At the time of exercise, the market value of the stock is $50 per share ($100,000 total value).

If your employer agrees, you can pay for the 2,000 new shares by transferring to that employer the 1,000 shares of identical stock you already own. Since the value of the stock surrendered equals the option price, no cash is needed to buy the stock. In this way, you defer recognition of gain on the transfer of the 1,000 old shares, but you enjoy the full appreciated value by converting 1,000 shares of stock into 2,000 shares.

Using this technique, the cash required has been reduced to $15,000, the amount necessary to pay the tax on the $50,000 of compensation in a 30 percent federal and state bracket. Without this technique, you would also need $50,000 more to pay for the stock. Thus, the total cash outlay has been reduced from $65,000 to only $15,000. Of course, a proportionate reduction in the number of shares or the value of the shares would result in a proportionate reduction in the amount of cash that you actually would have to lay out.

163 Incentive Stock Options (Sec. 422A)

The Economic Recovery Tax Act of 1981 provided for a new type of stock option, called an "incentive stock option." No tax consequences result from the grant of an incentive stock option or from the exercise of an incentive stock option by an employee. You, the employee, will be taxed when you sell the stock. Furthermore, you must normally be an employee from the date of granting the option until 3 months before the date of exercise.

1. Revenue Ruling 80-244.

In its simplest form, a stock option is the right to buy a company's stock sometime in the future for a fixed priced. An option granted in 2010 to buy stock at $10 a share by 2018 yields a $5-a-share profit if the stock rose to $15 a share by then and the owner exercises the option and sells the stock.

Summary of Incentive Stock Option Features

Typically granted to	Executives; senior management.
Option price	Must be granted at a price that at least equals the stock's market value at the time of the grant.
Taxation	
When granted	None
At exercise	None but the spread between the exercise price and the fair market value may be subject to alternative minimum tax.
After sale of the stock	If you hold your shares for more than one year after exercise, the entire spread between the sale price and your cost basis is characterized as a long-term capital gain and taxed at a maximum of 15%/20%.
	If you hold your shares for less than a year, you "disqualify" your ISO shares, and the difference between the fair market value at the time of exercise and the option price is taxed as ordinary income. The fair market value of the stock at the time of exercise becomes your cost basis, and the difference between the cost basis and the price at which you sell the stock is taxed as a short-term capital gain.
Vesting	May be subject to a graduated or cliff vesting schedule, according to the terms set forth in the option agreement.
Expiration	Typically 10 years following the grant date, as set forth in the option agreement.
Remember	If the gain on the stock granted through an ISO qualifies for special long-term capital gains treatment, the spread between the option price and the stock's fair market value at the time of exercise is a preference item for alternative minimum tax (AMT) purposes. Consult your tax advisor to determine if and how the AMT may affect you.

Summary of Nonqualified Option Features

Typically granted to	All employees.
Option price	May be lower than the value of the stock on the date of the grant, making it instantly "in-the-money."
Taxation	
When granted	None.
At exercise	In the year of the exercise, ordinary income tax is due on the spread between the fair market value of the stock on the date you exercise and the exercise price.
After sale of the stock	In the year of the sale, capital gains tax is due on the difference between your cost basis (the fair market value of the stock on the date you exercise your NSO) and the price at which you sell the stock. If you sell within one year of exercise, the gain will be characterized as short-term.
Vesting	May be subject to a graduated or cliff vesting schedule, according to the terms set forth in the option agreement.
Expiration	Typically 10 years following the grant date, as set forth in the option agreement.
Remember	Your employer must report the income you realize when you exercise your options on your W-2 and withhold income and employment taxes. Usually, you must pay your employer the amount of any withholding along with the exercise cost of your options.

The tax-favored treatment of capital gains adds to the usefulness of incentive stock options for stock-based executive compensation. Moreover, incentive stock options still retain an advantage for an employee over *nonqualified options* (those options that do not qualify under Sec. 422A—for example, an option that is exercisable 11 years after the date it is granted). The recipient of an incentive stock option will continue to avoid regular income tax on the exercise of such an option. However, the *open* spread by which the fair market value of the incentive stock option, at time of option exercise, exceeds the stock's option price is a tax preference under the alternative minimum tax rules.

In contrast, upon *exercise* of a nonqualified option, the excess of the nonqualified option stock's fair market value over the option price is treated as

additional compensation and taxed at regular income tax rates. Thus, an employee who exercises a nonqualified option must find the funds to pay tax as well as to pay for the stock.

Example: Assume an executive in the 32 percent tax bracket exercised an *incentive* stock option to acquire stock worth $150 for $100. His total *cost* for the stock ranges from $100 (if he is not subject to the alternative minimum tax) to a maximum of $113 ($100 option price plus 26 percent minimum tax on the $50 spread). In contrast, if the stock was acquired through the exercise of a *nonqualified* option, the cost to the executive to buy the stock would be $116 ($100 option price plus 32 percent tax on the $50 spread).

The employer is not entitled to a deduction for the benefit realized by the executive on an incentive stock option exercise. Since a deduction continues to be available when a nonstatutory option is exercised, nonstatutory options retain the employer's tax advantage over incentive stock options after 1986.

Therefore, incentive stock options continue to provide better tax advantages to employees than nonstatutory options, and since the current corporate tax rates reduce the employer's tax benefits from nonstatutory options, incentive stock options will continue to offer advantages for executive compensation packages.

Under the 1998 Reform Act, when you sell your ISO shares, the entire profit (the spread at exercise plus subsequent appreciation) can qualify for the maximum rate on long-term capital gains. This beneficial deal applies only when you sell the ISO shares more than 2 years after the option grant date (the date you received the option) and more than 12 months after you actually bought the shares by exercising your ISO.

Gains from ISO shares sold more than 2 years after the grant date and more than 12 months—but not more than 18 months—after the exercise date were taxed at a maximum 28 percent rate in 1997. Now the holding period is back to 12 months.

Example: On January 2, 2017, you received an ISO giving you the right to purchase 100 shares of employer stock for $10 a share. You exercised that right on February 1, 2018, when the market price was $16. Your per-share basis is $10 (exercise price). You sell on February 2, 2019, for $25 a share. The sale date is more than 2 years after the January 2, 2017 grant date and more than 12 months after the February 1, 2018, exercise date. Therefore, your entire $1,500 profit was treated as a long-term capital gain qualifying for the 15/20 percent rate.

Now what if you meet the above rules but sell your ISO shares at a price that's either below the market value on the exercise date or (even worse) below the exercise price? In this case, your basis in the shares is the exercise price, so when the sale price exceeds that number, you have a gain that qualifies for the maximum rate. If your sale price is below the exercise price, you've got a long-term capital loss.

An interesting twist on the incentive stock option concept is the junior stock plan, which works as follows. The employer corporation issues special "junior" nonvoting common stock, paying dividends. These shares can be exchanged by holders for regular common stock, share for share, at a specified date if the holders meet certain conditions. The junior shares are sold to employee executives at a bargain price—for example, $20 while the regular common is trading at $30. Each executive pays taxes on the original price differential—the $10 price spread. At the end of the term, with the employer common stock trading at, for example, $80, the executives swap the junior stock for the common in a tax-free exchange. On sale of the common stock, the executive has a tax basis of $30—the $20 paid for the junior shares plus the $10 on which he was taxed. Thus he has a gain of $50 per share—$80 less $30—taxed at a maximum percent rate.

This technique adds several breaks not available under normal incentive stock option rules. For example, junior stock lets an executive effectively buy the company's shares at a price far below the market. This allows far easier financing of a purchase of a block of shares.

164 Year-End Stock Sales

The Internal Revenue Service had ruled that gains from stocks sold in a year's last week come under the installment sales law. That allowed you to choose—at leisure—to incur the tax in either the current year or the next. Prior to 1982, a gain on stocks sold through a broker in one year for payment in the next was considered taxable in the payment year; to make it taxable in the year of sale, you had to allow 5 business days for settlement. Under the installment sales law, however, an installment sale is one where any payment is made in a later year. That makes gain taxable in the later year unless you elect not to use the installment method; in that case, the gain is taxable in the sale year. You did not have to make an election to choose the year in which to incur the tax until the due date for your sale-year return, including the automatic 4-month extension. This means that if you expected your income to increase, it may have been advisable for you to recognize the gain earlier, in the lower-bracketed year.

Effective January 1, 1987, taxpayers who sell stock or securities *on an established securities market* are *not* permitted to use the installment method to

account for such sales. The trade date is considered the date of tax recognition (see also Rev. Rul. 93-84).

165 Fund Strategies

When a mutual fund sells stock inside the fund, your proportional share of the gain is taxable to you. To minimize this tax, some advisors have recommended either index funds or exchange traded funds (ETF).

Like index funds, ETFs aim to match the performance of a stock market benchmark. But ETFs don't redeem shares or issue new shares depending on the buying and selling of individual investors. Instead, they are traded like regular stock.

That means that the underlying shares of stock never have to be sold in response to a wave of redemptions. Anything that reduces volatility reduces your potential "inside" gain or the investment.

HOLDRS (Holding Company Depository Receipts) aren't technically funds. They are a fixed portfolio of securities which allow an investor to exchange his HOLDRS for the underlying stocks (tax free) and sell the "losing" shares to offset gain elsewhere in his portfolio. They're another arrow in your quiver of tax minimization techniques.

166 Dividends

The 2003 Tax Act changed the rules on the taxation of dividends.

Under prior law, dividends were taxed at a rate as high as 38.6 percent and long-term capital gains were subject to a maximum tax of 20 percent.

The 2003 law reduced those rates substantially. For those in the 15 percent bracket or less the tax rate on dividends and long-term capital gains had been slashed to only 5 percent. For 2008 and after, the rate changed to ZERO!

After the Tax Cuts and Jobs Act of 2017, qualified dividends are now taxed just like long term capital gains. For 2018, the 0% rate applies if your taxable income is below $38,600 ($77,200 on joint returns) and the 20% rate hits at $425,800 for singles ($479,000 for joint returns).

Regardless of your income, the maximum rate on qualified dividends has been capped at 15 percent, 20 percent as of 2013, not counting the 3.8 percent surtax.

Great news for the retired and elderly. AARP (American Association of Retired Persons) estimated that 75 percent of dividends paid go to investors over the age of 50.

Be careful, everything called a "dividend" really isn't a "dividend" and won't qualify. A qualifying dividend is a distribution of a corporation's earnings and profits, which has already been taxed to the corporation. Let's look at some examples where there may be some confusion.

1. Mutual funds have, in the past, reported short-term capital gains as "dividends." Both were taxed at ordinary rates rather than at the lower capital gains rates. Now, such distributions must be separated out. That's because short-term capital gains don't qualify for the lower rates.

2. Do you have a margin account with your broker? If so, then you may have a problem. Your broker often lends out securities in such accounts to other investors who sell short using your stock. These borrower investors receive the dividends and they reimburse you for what they receive. You end up with the same dollars but these "payments in lieu of dividends" don't qualify as "dividends" and could be taxable at rates as much as 37.0 percent!

 The rate reduction on dividends is retroactive to January 1, 2003. So, if earlier in the year your broker lent out your securities, and a dividend was paid, that dividend didn't qualify for the lower rate. SURPRISE!

3. Dividends paid by Regulated Investment Companies (RICs) and Real Estate Investment Trusts (REITs) *do* qualify.

4. You just bought a stock and the company declares and pays a dividend. Then you sell the stock. Is your dividend subject to the maximum rate? Maybe!

Here's why: Congress wants you to invest for the long-term. In order to get the lower rate, you needed to have held the stock for 61 days during the 121-day period beginning 60 days before the ex-dividend date. So, if you don't hold the stock a minimum of 61 days, there's no way you're going to qualify for the lower rates. Even if you hold the stock for 61 days, it has to be within that 121-day window to qualify.

Remember, "Simplification" wasn't ever even suggested for the title of this new law!

What to do? Focus on long-term rather than short-term gains. Consider preferred stock and stock that has a high dividend payout, such as utilities. Income investing and focusing on dividends now becomes more attractive.

Companies with lots of free cash become buys. Those are the companies that have the ability to pay more out in tax advantaged dividends. And because they are "buys," they also should generate capital appreciation as more taxpayers

seek their tax advantages. This creates a double benefit as both dividends and capital gains are now tax favored.

Municipal bonds and tax shelter investments become less attractive compared with other investments. That's because the tax versus tax free gap has been reduced.

Those in the higher brackets should consider investment leverage. Borrow money at interest rates that are deductible at 37 percent and invest where the return is taxed at only 15 percent.

You can even make out if your yield is *lower* than your cost of money. For example, if you borrow $10,000 at 5 percent your interest is $500. At a 35 percent tax rate, your deduction reduces your net after tax cost to only $325 (65 percent of $500).

If your $10,000 investment only yields 4.5 percent, you have $450 in income. After tax at a maximum 15 percent rate, you have $382.50 left (85 percent of $450). That's $57.50 more in your pocket on an investment that yields less than your cost of money!!!

But there's a trap here. First, you have to itemize your deductions to get the deduction for investment interest. Then, that investment interest deduction is limited to your investment income.

But the law says that dividends that qualify for the 15/20 percent maximum rate don't qualify as investment income for the investment interest deduction. So, if your only investment income is the dividends, you don't get the deduction for the interest you paid.

In order for this investment leverage to work, you need other investment income (such as interest, rents, etc.) to offset the interest expense. Otherwise, you're borrowing at a higher net marginal cost than your marginal revenue. And you ain't gonna make it up with volume!

6 REASONS WHY DIVIDENDS ARE BETTER THAN CAPITAL GAINS

I'm a financial professional. I've spent a good part of the last four decades practicing tax alchemy—trying to convert ordinary income into capital gains. That's because ordinary income has been taxed at rates as high as 39.6 percent and capital gains as low as zero. That's been a gap of 39.6 percent!

The Tax Relief Act of 2003 blessed dividends with a 15 percent maximum rate (now 20 percent). Even though both are taxed at the same maximum rate, I think dividends are better than capital gains. Here's why:

1. *Keep Your Investment.* You get capital gains when you sell a capital asset. Your capital gain is the excess of what you get over what's technically called your

basis, normally the cost of the asset you sold. You're only taxed on that difference.

If you don't sell the asset, say shares of stock, you don't have any gain. But, if you don't sell the stock, you don't have any additional dollars either. So, to have capital gains, you have to liquidate your position.

That's not true with dividends. You still get to keep your original shares of stock. This is incremental money in addition to your shares of stock. In fact, in many cases, you can use your dividend dollars to buy more shares without a broker's commission on the purchase.

2. *Stock Returns to Predividend Level.* Yes, theoretically the value of the stock should decrease by the dividends paid. But, in the real world, that's not always the case. That allows you to eat a piece of your cake, and keep the whole cake too. Yummy!!

3. *Ask Any Senior Citizen—Regularity Is Good!* Remember, capital gains require you to liquidate your position. It's a one-time cash inflow.

That may not be appropriate in all situations. An investor may be looking for a relatively predictable regular cash flow each year. Baby boomers seeking income-producing investments for retirement cash flow are going to be attracted to dividend-paying securities. Americans over age 65 have equity portfolios with an average yield of 2.6 percent compared to only 0.8 percent for those under 65.

Remember, AARP estimated that 75 percent of dividends paid go to investors over the age of 50.

4. *Bunching Is Bad.* Even adjusting for the time value of money, there's a gazango difference between receiving $100,000 in capital gains in a single year, and receiving $10,000 yearly in dividends over 10 years.

While both may be taxed at the same rate, the one-year additional $100,000 could substantially thin your wallet. That's because many deductions and exemptions are reduced and or eliminated as your adjusted gross income (AGI) increases. For example:

- Medical expenses are reduced by 10 percent of AGI.

- Prior to 2018, miscellaneous itemized expenses were reduced by 2 percent of AGI.

- Your deduction for student loan interest is eliminated if your modified AGI is $80,000 or more ($165,000 on a joint return).

- Your deduction for IRA contributions is phased out as your modified AGI goes from $63,000 to $73,000 ($101,000 to $121,000 on a joint return).

- Hope and Lifetime Learning credits, the earned income credit, the American Opportunity credit, the first-time home buyers credit, the exclusion of savings bond interest used to pay educational expenses, the adoption assistance exclusion, and even your total itemized deduction are all phased out as your AGI increases.

- As a cherry on the cake, the single-year $100,000 capital gain also increases your exposure to the Alternative Minimum Tax (AMT) by phasing out your AMT exclusion.

5. *Shorter Holding Period.* To qualify for the maximum rate on capital gains, you have to hold the stock for more than one year.

 To qualify for the maximum rate on dividends, your holding period may be as little as 61 days. But, it has to be 61 days during the 121-day period beginning 60 days before the ex-dividend date. That's the date on which, even if you buy the stock and the dividend is paid after your buy, you still don't get the dividend dollars. That's because there wouldn't be enough time after your purchase for the corporation to change its records to show you as the owner

 You must hold the stock during that window, or you don't qualify.

6. *No Broker's Commission.* If you're gonna sell stock, you're gonna pay a commission. That's gonna suck some dollars out of your pocket, even with a low cost on line broker.

 There are no brokers' commissions on dividends. That's more money for you!

167 Tax-Exempt Income

A final word should be said about tax-exempt income. In the investment context, tax-exempt income results primarily from nontaxable interest from municipal securities. The table shown here indicates the equivalent rate of return that fully taxable income, such as rents or taxable interest, would have to yield in order to produce net income equivalent to that produced by various tax-exempt returns at the same tax rates.

Based on federal income tax brackets (also see page 83).

Tax-Exempt/Taxable Yield Equivalents

Tax Bracket	24%	32%	35%	37%
Tax-Exempt Yield	Taxable Yield Equivalents			
1.00%	1.32%	1.47%	1.54%	1.59%
2.00%	2.63%	2.94%	3.08%	3.17%
2.50%	3.29%	3.68%	3.85%	3.99%
3.00%	3.95%	4.41%	4.62%	4.76%
3.50%	4.61%	5.15%	5.38%	5.56%
4.00%	5.26%	5.88%	6.15%	6.35%
4.50%	5.92%	6.62%	6.92%	7.14%
5.00%	6.58%	7.35%	7.69%	7.94%
5.50%	7.24%	8.09%	8.46%	8.73%
6.00%	7.89%	8.82%	9.23%	9.52%
6.50%	8.55%	9.56%	10.00%	10.32%
7.00%	9.21%	10.24%	10.77%	11.11%
7.50%	9.87%	11.03%	11.54%	11.90%
8.00%	10.53%	11.76%	12.31%	12.70%

THE VALUE OF TAX-FREE YIELDS

Munis make the most sense for people whose tax-equivalent yield on a tax-free bond or bond fund would be greater than the yield from a similar taxable alternative. Here are two equations to determine whether the tax-exempt yields are right for you.

For tax-equivalent yields:

$$\frac{\text{Tax-Free Yield}}{(1 - \text{Tax Rate})} = \text{Tax-Equivalent Yield}$$

For combined effective federal/state tax rates (if you're considering buying bonds or funds with bonds issued in your home state):

$$\text{State Rate} \times (1 - \text{Federal} = \text{Effective State Rate})$$

$$\frac{\text{Effective}}{\text{State Rate}} + \frac{\text{Federal}}{\text{Rate}} = \frac{\text{Combined Effective}}{\text{Federal/State Tax Rate}}$$

See www.investinginbonds.com to compute equivalents.

At a 37 percent marginal tax rate, you would need to earn 9.52 percent in taxable interest to have the same after-tax return as 6 percent tax-free.

To find the equivalent taxable income return for a tax-exempt return not given in the table, multiply the tax-exempt return rate by the figure in the 1 percent column next to the applicable tax rate. For example, at a 37 percent tax rate, a taxable investment would have to yield 13.52 percent to produce the same amount of after-tax income that is produced by a tax-exempt investment that yields a 8.5 percent return (8.5 percent × 1.59 = 13.52 percent).

To find the tax-free income equivalent to a given taxable income, divide that taxable income by the figure in the 1 percent column next to the given rate. For example, at a 35 percent tax rate, $2,000 in taxable income yields $1,300 ($2,000 ÷ 1.54).

Note, in addition, that state taxation of interest income should be taken into consideration in computing total yield. For example, most states do not tax interest on municipal bonds issued within their own state. Thus, a New Jersey tax-free municipal bond held by a New Jersey investor would be exempt both on the federal and on the New Jersey tax return. In many states there is no difference in the state tax treatment of in-state versus out-of-state bonds. The chart below summarizes state bond taxation as of 1993. If appropriate, check the current position of your own state.

States That Tax Their Own and Other States' Bonds

Illinois	Iowa
Oklahoma	Wisconsin

States That Tax Other States' Bonds but Not Their Own

Alabama	Louisiana
Arizona	Maine
Arkansas	Maryland
California	Massachusetts
Colorado	Michigan[§]
Connecticut	Minnesota
Delaware	Mississippi
Georgia[§]	Missouri
Hawaii	Montana
Idaho	Nebraska
Kansas	New Hampshire
Kentucky[§]	New Jersey

New Mexico	Rhode Island
New York	South Carolina
North Carolina§	Tennessee
Ohio	Vermont
Oregon	Virginia
Pennsylvania	West Virginia

States That Do Not Tax Their Own or Other States' Bonds

Alaska†	South Dakota†
District of Columbia	Texas†
Florida§	Utah
Indiana	Washington†
Nevada†	Wyoming†
North Dakota††	

† Alaska, Florida, Nevada, South Dakota, Texas, Washington, and Wyoming do not currently levy an income tax.

†† North Dakota does not tax its own or other states' bonds when the "piggyback" method is used to compute state income tax liability.

§ These states also subject municipal interest income on out-of-state bonds to state intangibles taxes.

168 Old Prices

You can find stock prices back to 1971 at bigcharts.com if you have the date of purchase.

169 Alternative Minimum Tax for Individuals

The Alternative Minimum Tax (AMT) is a heartbreaker. You compute your tax and are entitled to a major refund—until you compute the AMT. The Alternative Minimum Tax is an *alternative* formula to compute your liability. It gives you no credit for personal exemptions, taxes, miscellaneous itemized deductions, and your AMT exemption amount dissolves as your income increases. It hurts people with kids (no deduction for exemptions) and those who live in high tax states like California, Massachusetts, and New York (no deduction for state income taxes paid).

To compute the AMT, you add certain items called "preferences" to your income. Those are the deductions/profits that you got under the normal tax computation that are not allowed under the AMT computation—such as those state taxes.

That sum is reduced by an exemption amount, which itself is wiped out if your new AMT income is too high. That new total is then subject to a flat tax of either 26 percent or 28 percent … unless you had qualified dividends or capital gains.

You compare your tax computed this way with the normal computation, and pay the *higher* amount.

For certain preferences, individuals could elect for regular tax purposes to take a deduction ratably over 10 years (3 years in the case of circulation expenses) and thereby avoid an AMT preference.

Preference Items and Adjustments after 1986

The items of preference adjustment after the 1986 Tax Reform Act included the following:

- Accelerated depreciation on real property placed in service after 1986 will be considered a preference item to the extent that it exceeds depreciation computed on a 40-year straight-line basis. For personal property the preference item will be the excess of accelerated depreciation over the depreciation computed using the 150 percent declining-balance method (switching to straight line in the year necessary to maximize the deduction). However, the preference does not apply to property that is expensed under Sec. 179.

- Depreciation with respect to property placed in service prior to 1987 is treated as a preference only to the extent that it constituted a preference under prior law. Also, for property placed in service after 1986 with respect to which the alternative depreciation system is used, no AMT preferences will arise.

 Under the revised AMT, the alternative depreciation system is substituted for the accelerated cost recovery system (ACRS). This system permits *netting*. If the AMT depreciation exceeds the ACRS with respect to real or personal property for that year, the amount of the preference is reduced. Since the AMT uses the alternative depreciation system, separate depreciation basis adjustments must be made for AMT purposes. Therefore, the amount of gain on disposition may differ for AMT and regular tax purposes.

- As under prior law, the rapid amortization for pollution-control facilities, the excess of allowable depletion over the adjusted basis of the property (determined without regard to the depletion deduction), mining exploration and development costs, circulation expenditures, research and development costs, the amount by which the fair market value of a share of stock at the time of exercise of an incentive stock option exceeds the option price, and

intangible drilling costs (except that the net income offset is reduced from 100 percent to 65 percent) are all still tax preference items.

The 1986 law also added the following new preference items and adjustments:

- Tax-exempt interest on nongovernmental purpose bonds issued after August 7, 1986. Exceptions are provided for bonds issued on behalf of certain tax-exempt organizations and certain bonds issued before September 1, 1986. However, no exceptions are provided for industrial development bonds.

- For any long-term contract entered into by the taxpayer after March 1, 1986, use of the completed contract is not permitted for AMT purposes. Instead, the taxpayer is required to use the percentage-of-completion method for AMT purposes.

- For dispositions after March 1, 1986, the use of the installment-sale method is not permitted for AMT purposes by dealers and others subject to proportionate disallowance of the installment method (sales of trade or business or rental property when the purchase price exceeds $150,000).

- Charitable contributions of appreciated property. Prior to 1993, a tax preference existed to the extent of the unrealized appreciation of contributed capital gain property. Therefore, for minimum tax purposes, the charitable-contribution deduction was limited to the property's adjusted basis. In calculating the amount of the preference, unrealized gains on appreciated property were offset by unrealized losses. The amount of preference was determined by disregarding any amount that was carried forward to another taxable year for regular tax purposes. This preference was eliminated by the Omnibus Budget Reconciliation Act of 1993.

- Passive activity losses that are allowed under the passive loss phase-in rules must be added back to taxable income in computing the AMT with the following revisions: (1) the amount of losses that otherwise would be added back for the current taxable year is reduced by the amount of the taxpayer's insolvency; (2) in calculating passive losses, minimum tax measurements of items of income and deduction will be used rather than regular tax measurements; and (3) the amount added back is reduced by other items of tax preference to prevent double counting.

 Because of these calculations the amount of suspended passive losses relating to a passive activity may differ for AMT and regular tax purposes.

However, it appears that after the 5-year phase-in of the regular tax passive loss rules, differences should be minimal.

- Passive farm losses from a tax-shelter farming activity are treated like passive activity losses with the revisions discussed immediately above (for passive activity losses) and with the following special provisions: (1) each farm is treated as a separate activity—no netting between farming activities is allowed; (2) the preference applies to personal service corporations; and (3) loss from a disposition of a tax-shelter farm activity shall be allowed for minimum tax purposes and not treated as a loss from a tax-shelter farm activity.

- The standard deduction must be added back to taxable income when computing the AMT.

- Non-AMT itemized deductions used in computing taxable income must be added back in computing the AMT.

- The $100 ($200 joint filing) exclusion for dividends and the net capital gain deduction have both been deleted as items of tax preference because they are no longer applicable for regular tax purposes.

AMT Itemized Deductions

In general, the AMT itemized deductions are the same as under prior law and include the following:

- Theft, casualty, and wagering losses

- Charitable contributions

- Medical expenses, except the floor is 10 percent of adjusted gross income instead of 7.5 percent, as used for regular tax purposes in the past

- Qualified interest expenses (which include interest paid or incurred on debt to acquire, construct, or substantially rehabilitate the taxpayer's principal or qualified dwelling and other investment interest to the extent it does not exceed the taxpayer's qualified net investment income for the taxable year)

- The deduction for estate taxes for recipients of income in respect of decedents

The definition of investment interest is the same as under the current law for regular tax purposes. No AMT deduction is allowed for consumer interest. Disallowed investment interest deductions may be carried forward. Interest paid on a refinanced loan is treated as qualified residence interest if it qualified under

the original loan and the amount of the loan was not increased. Also refunds of state and local taxes are not included in alternative minimum taxable income.

Carryover of Tax Credits

As under prior law, nonrefundable credits are not allowed against minimum tax liability. Refundable credits that do not benefit the taxpayer because of the minimum tax can be carried back or forward to other taxable years. The recomputed foreign income tax credit is allowed against AMT.

Minimum Tax Credit

Under prior law minimum tax incurred by a taxpayer in one year had no effect on regular tax liability in other years.

The current law creates a minimum tax credit for prior-year minimum tax liability that may offset regular tax in later years. The AMT tax credit is equal to the excess of the AMT tax liability attributable to *deferral preferences* over the regular tax liability for the year. Deferral preferences are essentially all tax preferences except those relating to percentage depletion, tax-exempt interest, the appreciated-property charitable deduction, and regular tax itemized deductions that are not allowed for AMT purposes. The AMT credit can be carried forward (but not back) indefinitely.

Example: Ms. Fortunate has a regular tax liability of $35,000 after taking into account $15,000 of passive losses attributable to accelerated depreciation deductions on leased equipment that were deductible under the phase-in of the passive loss limitation. Her AMT is $39,000. She must pay tax of $39,000 but has a minimum tax credit to the extent that her AMT was attributable to the accelerated depreciation deferral preferences. The minimum tax credit is $3,150 ($39,000 AMT – $35,850 adjusted net minimum tax).

If Ms. Fortunate has a regular tax liability of $28,000 and an AMT of $26,000 in the next year, $2,000 of the minimum tax credit may be applied in that year. The remaining $1,150 of credit carries forward to the following year and, if necessary, later years.

Net Operating Losses (NOLs)

For AMT purposes a separate computation of NOLs and NOL carryovers will be required. In general, the AMT NOL, which cannot offset more than 90 percent of AMT income, is computed in the same manner as the regular tax NOL, except for two special rules. The items of tax preference arising during the taxable year are added back to taxable income, and only AMT itemized deductions are taken into account.

Example: In year 1 a taxpayer has $10,000 of income and $35,000 of losses, of which $10,000 are preference items. The AMT NOL for year 1 is $10,000.

Regular Tax Elections

Under the new law taxpayers may still elect for regular tax purposes to deduct ratably over 10 years (3 years for circulation expenditures) certain expenditures (IDCs and mining exploration and development expenditures) that are otherwise currently deductible and thus avoid treatment of the items as minimum tax preferences.

CREDITS

Starting in 1998, nonrefundable personal credits (the dependent care credit, the credit for the elderly and disabled, the adoption credit, the child tax credit, the credit for interest on certain mortgages, residential energy efficient property credits, nonbusiness energy property credits, personal use portion of the alternative motor vehicle credit, and the Hope Scholarship and Lifetime Learning credits) are allowed to offset your regular tax in full. These credits can now also reduce your alternative minimum tax.

IMPACT OF THE TAX RELIEF ACTS OF 2001, 2003, AND AFTER

The 2001 law increased the individual alternative minimum tax exemption amount by $2,000 for single taxpayers and by $4,000 for married taxpayers filing joint returns for 2001 through 2004, but only through 2004. No big deal! With the reduction of the marginal rates, more people will be hit by the AMT. Many taxpayers making between $72,000 and $627,000—especially those with large families, big medical bills, or homes in higher-tax states like New York, New Jersey, Connecticut, Massachusetts, Illinois, and California—saw perhaps two-thirds of their Bush income tax cuts taken away by the alternative minimum tax.

About 1.5 million Americans were hit by the AMT in 2001, About 4.25 million tax returns were hit by the AMT in 2011.

The 2001 law also allowed the child credit and the adoption credit to be claimed against both the regular tax and the alternative minimum tax on a permanent basis. In addition, the refundable credits will no longer be reduced by a taxpayer's AMT.

In 2003, Congress again voted to reduce, but not eliminate, the AMT. As amended in 2004, for 2003, 2004, and 2005, the AMT exemption increased to $58,000 for joint returns and $40,250 for single taxpayers—up from $49,000 and $35,750.

AMT victims who get hit because of incentive stock options may recoup some or all of their AMT payments through an "AMT Credit." This credit can reduce your regular tax bill to what it would be under the AMT in years when your regular tax bill is higher.

Beginning in 2007 and for each year through 2012, a taxpayer with unrecovered AMT credits more than 3 years old can claim a refundable credit equal to either $5,000 of his old credit or 20% of his old credit, whichever is greater. A taxpayer with old AMT credits of $1 million would get $200,000 back. If he otherwise owed $50,000 in 2007 taxes, the credit would wipe those out, and the IRS would cut him a $150,000 check. In 2008 he'd have $800,000 in old, unused credit left and get another 20 percent—in this case, $160,000—back.

This break phased out for couples with adjusted gross incomes above $239,950 (over $159,950 for singles).

Congress tinkered once more in 2006 and 2007, raising the exemption level to $62,550 for joint returns and $42,500 for single filers in 2006 and to $66,250/$44,350 for 2007 only. For 2008 Congress raised the exception to the $46,200/$69,950. It also increased the 20 percent rate to 50 percent. This is a BIG change! Use Form 8801 to claim your credits.

The following credits are now allowed against the AMT:

1. Child tax credit (up to $1,000 per child)
2. Hope Scholarship education tax credit (up to $1,800) and Lifetime Learning education tax credit (up to $2,000)
3. Child and dependent care tax credit
4. Adoption tax credit
5. Retirement saver's tax credit
6. Tax credit for certain energy-saving equipment installed in your residence
7. Tax credit for elderly and disabled individuals
8. Mortgage tax credit
9. First-time D.C. home buyer tax credit

Another provision in the 2008 law allowed you to walk away from any unpaid AMT bills that were outstanding on October 3, 2008, if they were caused by your exercising incentive stock options before 2008. You could also walk away from any related interest and penalty charges assessed by the IRS. If you already paid some interest and penalty charges, you could recover them over two years under the new and improved refundable AMT credit rules.

Congress increased the exemption amounts yearly. The table below summarizes 2017 and 2018 changes:

Maximum AMT exemption amount	2018	2017
Married filing jointly or surviving spouse	$109,400	$ 84,500
Single or head of household	$ 70,300	$ 54,300
Married filing separately	$ 54,700	$ 42,250
AMT income exemption phaseout threshold	**2018**	**2017**
Married filing jointly or surviving spouse	$1,000,000	$160,900
Single or head of household	$ 500,000	$120,700
Married filing separately	$ 500,000	$ 80,450
AMT tax rate (26% rate applies to AMTI at or below amount; 28% applies to AMTI above amount)	**2018**	**2017**
All taxpayers except married filing separately	$191,100	$187,800
Married filing separately	$ 95,550	$ 93,900

The Tax Cuts and Jobs Act of 2017 substantially increased the exemption allowed and phaseout thresholds. It also eliminates the deduction for miscellaneous itemized deductions and caps the tax deduction for state and local taxes at $10,000. All of these changes will reduce your exposure to the AMT.

PLANNING CONSIDERATIONS

In general, middle- and high-income individuals will have to pay even more attention to the alternative minimum tax. There are many changes. The AMT rate has been raised from 20 to 24 to as high as 28 percent, and the exemption amounts are phased out as AMT income increases. The passive loss rules apply for AMT purposes, except that the preference is reduced by the amount, if any, of the taxpayer's insolvency. In addition, passive losses are reduced to the extent attributable to tax preference, since those preferences are added in elsewhere.

Tax planning for the AMT will involve many of the techniques applicable under prior law. In years when the AMT is inevitable, a taxpayer's objective should be to *accelerate* income and *defer* deductions. A taxpayer's marginal tax rate while subject to the AMT is as high as 28 percent for all additional income realized until the AMT is used up. The taxpayer's tax rate jumps to the marginal rate for regular tax purposes as soon as the AMT is used. If a taxpayer is subject to the alternative minimum tax, non-AMT itemized deductions provide no tax benefit. Additional alternative minimum tax itemized deductions provide a tax deduction rate only equal to the AMT rate. Additional tax preferences, like non-AMT itemized deductions, provide no benefit when the taxpayer is subject to the AMT.

Methods taxpayers may wish to consider for accelerating income when subject to the AMT include:

- Take prepayments of salary and bonuses.

- Declare and pay corporate dividends from closely held corporations. This may also have a potentially positive effect on the corporation if it has a problem with the accumulated earnings tax.

- Consider redeeming Series EE U.S. savings bonds, or elect to report all the accrued interest on the bonds in the current year.

- Redeem certificates of deposit.

- Make early sales of U.S. T-bills.

- Make early sales of investment certificates.

- Recognize gains on portfolio securities.

- Elect out of the installment method for any installment sales (under Sec. 453(d)).

- Consider converting tax-free municipal investments into taxable investments.

- Sell stocks acquired by incentive stock options (ISOs) within a year after the ISOs are exercised. Under Sec. 422(a)(1) this is a disqualifying transaction that makes the gains taxable as ordinary income (even if the transaction takes place in a taxable year subsequent to the year the ISOs were exercised). In addition, this transaction eliminates the tax preference if the transaction takes place in the same taxable year as the exercise of the options. By so doing, you can possibly zero out the AMT (with no additional tax paid because the regular tax is increased while the AMT is reduced). You can immediately repurchase the stocks and effectively step up the basis in the stock and avoid the tax that would otherwise be realized sometime in the future.

- Withdraw funds from IRAs in some circumstances if subsequent withdrawals are anticipated at tax rates greater than 36–38 percent (26–28 percent AMT plus 10 percent penalty).

Taxpayers may also benefit by deferring deductions, especially non-AMT itemized deductions.

Taxpayers subject to the AMT should also try to capitalize otherwise deductible expenses. For example, they should not expense any part of the cost of a depreciable business asset. They should consider electing 10-year write-offs on any portion of currently deductible expenses that constitute tax preferences (which also eliminates the preference). The items to which this applies are research and experimentation expenditures, mining exploration and development costs, and intangible drilling costs. In addition, magazine circulation expenses may be capitalized and written off over a 3-year period. Taxpayers with research and experimentation expenditures for their own business should consider electing to amortize those expenditures over 60 months or longer. This will both shift deductions out of the current year and reduce AMTI. Taxpayers acquiring new depreciable property should consider electing depreciation under the alternative recovery system, which will defer deductions and reduce AMTI.

Here are some ways to beat the AMT and keep more tax dollars in your pocket:

1. REDUCE YOUR GROSS INCOME

The lower the income you report, the less likely you're gonna be hit by the AMT. It's the core base for AMT measurement. That doesn't mean earn less—just report a lower net number before your standard or itemized deductions. The smaller your gross income, the more of the AMT exclusion you get to keep, reducing your potential AMT liability.

Reduce your gross income by:

- Participating in your employer's 401(k) plan
- Investing in a deductible IRA
- Investing in appropriate tax free bonds
- Accepting alternative forms of compensation (qualified employee benefits) that are not taxable in lieu of straight salary increases
- Invest in a health savings account
- Invest in a self-employed SEP, SIMPLE, or qualified retirement plan
- Pay increased alimony (deductible) in lieu of child support (not deductible) for divorces prior to 2019

2. MOVE TO A STATE WITH NO INCOME TAX

The AMT gives you no credit for taxes paid. So, if you're in a state with no income tax, you minimize your exposure. Such states as Alaska, Florida, Nevada, South Dakota, Texas, Washington, and Wyoming currently have no state income tax. Additionally, New Hampshire and Tennessee limit their state income taxes to dividends and interest income only.

Note that the deduction for sales tax in lieu of income tax reduces the coverage of this AMT shield strategy. But, it's no surprise that the AMT is most prevalent in states with the highest income taxes.

3. USE AN ACCOUNTABLE PLAN FOR EMPLOYEE BUSINESS EXPENSES PRIOR TO 2018

An accountable plan is a special provision that allows an employer to reimburse you on a tax-free basis for your employee business expenses. You provide the substantiation to your employer who then takes the deduction.

If you expect, say, to incur $10,000 in employee business expenses, arrange with your employer to reduce your salary by $10,000 in exchange for agreeing to reimburse you for up to $10,000 for such expenditures.

Your employer will spend the same dollars, but will actually make money on the deal because it escapes payroll taxes on the $10,000 taken out of salary. The Social Security/Medicare savings alone could be as much as $765 each year.

- You're out of pocket the same $10,000 (less the same payroll taxes that **you** have to match),
- The $10,000 never shows up as a miscellaneous itemized deduction so you don't lose 2 percent of your adjusted gross income with the deduction, and
- Since your miscellaneous itemized deductions are added back to your income for AMT purposes, your exposure to the AMT was reduced.

After 2017, miscellaneous itemized deductions, including employee business expenses, are no longer allowable and therefore irrelevant to the AMT.

4. USE INSTALLMENT SALE STRUCTURING TO REPORT A GAIN

Several years ago, I sold an apartment building and took back a mortgage for part of the purchase price. Since I was on the cash basis, I only reported gain on the cash I received, as I received it.

By not reporting the full gain in a single year, I minimized my gross income and limited the reduction in my AMT exclusion. Any interest income received increased my potential deduction for the investment interest expense deduction.

By using the installment sale structure, I not only reduced my current regular tax liability, but also decreased my potential exposure to the dreaded AMT.

On the other hand, if the gain is big enough, make sure that the addition of the yearly installments doesn't subject you to the AMT each subsequent year. In that case, it may be preferable to take the hit in a single year, rather than be AMT fodder for several.

5. DEFER INCOME

Deferring income has the same impact on the AMT as reducing gross income. Your AMT exclusion is reduced as your reported income increases. The more of the exclusion you're able to retain, the less you're exposed to the AMT.

Consider investing in tax-deferred annuities or cash value life insurance. Both provide potential investment gains that escape current taxation. With cash value life insurance, you can take cash withdrawals as loans, and never report the "income." And, if structured correctly, the insurance proceeds can avoid both the income tax and the estate tax. Such insurance may be more than appropriate if you're a high-income taxpayer with an estate that is sufficiently large enough to be subject to the estate tax. Few alternative investments can provide fully tax-free immediate liquidity when most needed.

6. TAKE STRAIGHT LINE DEPRECIATION

Accelerated depreciation is a tax preference item for the AMT. For property placed in service after 1998, if you used the 200 percent declining balance method for regular tax purposes for business or investment equipment/furnishings, etc., you must use the 150 percent declining balance method for the AMT. The difference between them is a tax preference item that increases your AMT income, potentially reduces your AMT exclusion, and clearly increases your exposure to the AMT itself.

Consider using straight line depreciation. It may increase your current tax because the yearly deduction is reduced. But, you'll get bigger deductions in the later years to make up for it. Or, if you qualify, expense the items under Section 179. In either case, such deductions don't increase your potential AMT hit.

You may be hit with the alternative minimum tax even if you don't have one single dollar of tax preferences. For example, assume that you had an adjusted gross income of $150,000. In 1987 you paid $25,000 in state and local income taxes (including your April 1987 payment for your 1986 taxes) and $22,000 in property taxes on raw land you own as an investment. You paid $6,000 in interest on home equity loans you took out to pay college

Alternative Minimum Tax Preference Items Under Pre-1986 Law and Post-1986 Law

| Tax Preferences | Individual | | Description of Tax Preference |
	Prior Law	Post-1986 Law	
Long-term contracts	No	Yes	Income must be calculated on the percentage-of-completion method for new contracts
Certain tax-exempt interest	No	Yes	Interest income on certain private-activity tax-exempt bonds issued after August 7, 1986
Appreciated property charitable deduction	No	Yes prior to 1993	Unrealized appreciation on long-term capital gain property
Passive activity losses	N/A	Yes	Net losses from passive activities
Accelerated depreciation on new property	N/A	Yes	Depreciation for AMT is calculated using the Alternative Depreciation System except that the preference for personal property is based on the 150 percent DB method
Premodified ACRS and pre-ACRS depreciable leased personal property	Yes	Yes	Excess of accelerated over straight-line deductions
Mining exploration and development costs	Yes	Yes	Excess over amount allowable if amortized ratably over 10 years
Circulation expenditures	Yes	Yes	Excess over amount allowable if amortized ratably over 3 years

Alternative Minimum Tax Preference Items Under
Pre-1986 Law and Post-1986 Law *(continued)*

| Tax Preferences | Individual | | Description of Tax Preference |
	Prior Law	Post-1986 Law	
Research and experimental costs	Yes	Yes	Excess over amount allowable if amortized ratably over 10 years
Depletion	Yes	Yes	Excess of depletion over adjusted basis in property
Incentive stock options	Yes	Yes	Excess of fair market value over option price at date of exercise (basis of stock adjustment for AMT)
Dividend exclusion from income	Yes	N/A	Amount of dividends excluded
Capital gains	Yes	N/A	Under present law full LTCG deduction is no longer a preference
Intangible drilling costs	Yes	Yes	Excess over amount allowable if amortized ratably over 120 months over 65% of net income from oil and gas
Pollution-control facilities	Yes	Yes	Excess of amortization over allowable depreciation
Individual itemized deductions	Yes	Yes	Certain itemized deductions not allowed
Alternative tax net operating loss	Yes	Yes	NOLs with certain adjustments
Installment method accounting	No	Yes	Installment method generally not allowed for AMT purposes

expenses for your children and had $8,000 in other itemized deductions, including $2,000 for investment expenses in excess of 2 percent of your adjusted gross income. Assume further that you had absolutely no tax preferences.

Because your itemized deductions for purposes of the alternative minimum tax were not the same as your itemized deductions for your regular tax, your alternative minimum tax was $260 higher than your regular tax. Therefore, you paid an extra $260 in taxes for 1987. As the regular tax rates fell in 1988, however, the chance of being hit with the alternative minimum tax increased, and your potential alternative minimum tax bill got bigger. For example, on these same facts, you would have owed an alternative minimum tax of more than $2,400 in 1988! What this means is that you should watch your itemized deductions as they may, by themselves, subject you to the AMT. Because personal exemptions are not allowed in computing the AMT, you can be hit by it just because you have "too many" children!

170 U.S. Savings Bond Exclusion (Sec. 135)

To help finance qualified higher educational expenses, Congress has created an incentive to purchase U.S. savings bonds. Under prior law, interest that accrues on certain U.S. savings bonds need not be reported until the bond is redeemed, unless you elect to report the increase in redemption value annually.

For years after 1989, you can potentially exclude all or a portion of the interest that accrues on the bond. In order to qualify for the exclusion, you must:

a) purchase a qualified U.S. savings bond;

b) pay qualified higher educational expenses in the year of redemption;

c) not be married and filing separately; *and*

d) not have income over a certain amount.

If your modified adjusted gross income exceeds $60,000 (indexed) in case of a joint return and $40,000 (indexed)[2,3] in all other cases, there is a phase-out of the benefit. For joint filers, the entire benefit was phased out once modified

2. $119,300 and $149,300 for 2018.
3. $79,550 and $94,550 for 2018.

adjusted gross income exceeds $95,250. For all other taxpayers, the phase-out was completed at $58,500. There is a proportional phase-out of the benefit for income within the phase-out range. For example, if modified adjusted gross income on a joint return was $80,000, then approximately two-thirds of the total benefits would be phased out.

A qualified U.S. savings bond is any bond issued after 1989 at a discount to an individual who has attained age 24. Bonds acquired in the names of minor children will not qualify for the exclusion. Moreover, the exclusion is not available to the individual who is the owner of a Series EE bond (Series E bonds issued in June 1950 stopped paying interest in June 2010) that was purchased by another individual other than a spouse. The bond should therefore not be purchased by a parent and put in the name of a child or another dependent, even if such a child or dependent is 24 years of age at the time of the purchase. Nor should bonds be bought by a relative, such as a grandparent, and gifted to a parent or child if the exclusion is desired. If you bought "wrong," you can file a reissue form PDF 4000 with the Bureau of Public Debt, Parkersburg, WV 26106-1328 and plead your case. You can get bonds commission-free from Treasury Direct at 1-800-722-2678 or at www.savingsbonds.gov. See also www.investinginbonds.com, www.treasurydirect.gov, and www.treasuryhunt.gov for the current value of your bond.

If you paid for your bonds with a credit card, you could have picked up some frequent flyer mileage or cash back. Not anymore. Uncle Sam will no longer accept credit cards for savings bond purchases.

The Impact of Inflation on Yields

Rate of Inflation	Interest Rate Needed to Break Even in Following Tax Brackets:		
	15%	24%	35%
1%	1.18%	1.32%	1.54%
2%	2.35	2.63	3.08
3%	3.53	3.95	4.62
4%	4.71	5.26	6.15
5%	5.88	6.58	7.69
6%	7.06	7.89	9.23
7%	8.24	9.21	10.77
8%	9.41	10.53	12.31

(continues)

The Impact of Inflation on Yields *(continued)*

Rate of Inflation	Interest Rate Needed to Break Even in Following Tax Brackets:		
	15%	24%	35%
9%	10.59	11.84	13.85
10%	11.76	13.16	15.38
11%	12.94	14.47	16.92
12%	14.12	15.79	18.46
13%	15.29	17.11	20.00
14%	16.47	18.42	21.54
15%	17.65	19.71	23.08

In the past you could buy up to $15,000 worth of EE bonds (purchase price, *not* face value) each year, per owner. That's a $30,000 face value. Starting January 1, 2008, that dropped to $20,000 in face value—$10,000 in paper bonds bought at a bank and another $10,000 in an online Treasury Direct account. Note that there is no direct tracing of the redeemed bond proceeds to the payment of tuition. However, the qualified higher education expense must equal or exceed the redeemed proceeds for the full exclusion to apply. See www.treasurydirect.gov.

The Bureau of the Public Debt announced that as of January 1, 2012, *paper* savings bonds will no longer be sold at financial institutions. But savings bonds, introduced in 1935, are not going away. Series EE and I electronic savings bonds will remain available for purchase in TreasuryDirect accounts. You can also buy up to $5,000 in bonds with your refund by using Form 8888. Persons currently holding paper savings bonds can continue to redeem them at financial institutions. Bonds that have not matured, but were lost, stolen, or destroyed, can be reissued in paper or electronic form.

Now may be a good time to review your bond holdings to ensure they are still earning interest. All Series E bonds have reached final maturity and no longer earn interest. Series EE bonds, first issued in 1980, reach "final maturity" 30 years from the date of issue.

The Treasury has a variety of online tools for evaluating U.S. savings bonds at http://savingsbonds.gov/indiv/tools/tools.htm, or call 844-284-2676.

171 Madoff Losses

In Revenue Ruling 2009–9, the IRS ruled that investors who suffered Ponzi scheme losses could claim the losses as investment thefts. The ruling provides that:

- You can claim investment theft losses, which are not subject to the usual tax code limits on personal theft losses that are 10 percent of adjusted gross income plus $100;

- Investment theft losses are deductible in the year in which the fraud is discovered, unless you have a reasonable prospect of recovering the investment assets in a later year;

- You can claim theft loss deductions for the net amount you invested and for the fictitious income that the promoter credited to your investment accounts and that you reported as income before discovering the fraudulent scheme; and

- Investment theft losses that create a net operating loss can be carried back and forward, as prescribed by law, to generate a refund of taxes paid in other taxable years.

- Revenue Procedure 2009–20 allows investors to deduct 95 percent of their "Madoff" investment minus any recoveries from insurance, the Securities Investor Protection Corp., or lawsuits.

- Use Form 4684 to claim your losses.

172 Collars—Tax Free Lock in Your Gain

Assume you own one hundred shares of a stock with a current share price of $5. You could construct a collar by buying one put with a strike price of $3 and selling one call with a strike price of $7. The collar would ensure that the gain on the portfolio will be no higher than $2 and the loss will be no worse than $2 (before deducting the net cost of the put option, i.e., the cost of the put option less what is received for selling the call option).

There are three possible scenarios when the options expire:

- If the stock price is above the $7 strike price on the call he wrote, the person who bought the call from you will exercise the purchased call; you

effectively sell the shares at the $7 strike price. This would lock in a $2 profit for you. You *only* make a $2 profit (minus fees), no matter how high the share price goes. For example, if the stock price goes up to $11, the buyer of the call will exercise the option and you will sell the shares that he bought at $5 for $11, for a $6 profit, but must then pay out $11 − $7 = $4, making the profit only $2 ($6 − $4). The premium paid for the put must then be subtracted from this $2 profit to calculate the total return on this investment.

- If the stock price drops below the $3 strike price on the put then you may exercise the put and the person who sold it is forced to buy your 100 shares at $3. You lose $2 on the stock but can lose *only* $2 (plus fees) no matter how low the price of the stock goes. For example, if the stock price falls to $1 then you exercise the put and have a $2 gain. The value of your stock has fallen by $5 − $1 = $4. The call expires worthless (since the buyer does not exercise it) and the total net loss is $2 − $4 = −$2. The premium received for the call must then be added to reduce this $2 loss to calculate the total return on this investment.

- If the stock price is between the two strike prices on the expiry date, both options expire unexercised and you are left with the 100 shares whose value is that stock price (×100), plus the cash gained from selling the call option, minus the price paid to buy the put option, minus fees.

What you get on the sale of the call offsets the cost of the put. But your underlying stock portfolio was never sold while you used the collar to "lock in" your gain.

Last-Minute Tax Planning

"Potius sero quam numquam." (Better late than never.)

TITUS LIVIUS, 59 B.C.–A.D. 17

"You cannot help the poor by destroying the rich. You cannot lift the wage earner by pulling down the wage payer."

ABRAHAM LINCOLN

"The reward of energy, enterprise, and thrift is taxes."

WILLIAM FEATHER

"The current tax system is very unstable."

JOHN BUCKLEY
Majority chief tax counsel for the House Ways and
Means Committee, November 6, 2007

"Enough is enough, folks"

President GEORGE W. BUSH,
April 16, 2001

While effective tax planning is basically a year-round proposition, certain techniques are still available even if you buy this book during the last week in December. This chapter will explain those last-minute tax strategies that can help you reduce your overall tax burden.

173 Defer Taxes

Certain kinds of investments allow you to postpone paying taxes from the year in which the income is earned to a later year. At that point, you may be in a lower tax bracket, or you will at least have had the use and yield on the tax savings in the interim.

Series EE savings bonds offer this feature, as do deferred annuity contracts. Interest on savings bonds is normally not taxed until the bonds are cashed. As with an annuity, you postpone taxes on the interest until the income is actually paid out. Series EE savings bonds sold after May 1, 1995 no longer have a *minimum* guaranteed yield of 4 percent (7.5 percent if purchased between November 1, 1982, and October 31, 1986) even if the bonds are held for at least 5 years. When alternative investments are yielding amounts equal to or less than the Treasury rate, the investment attractiveness of Series EE bonds is magnified even more. The interest on these bonds is tax free on state tax returns. The limit on Series EE bonds that can be purchased in the name of one person as of January 1, 2008, is $20,000 face amount (or $10,000 issue price) in any one calendar year.

The interest on Series EE bonds accrues monthly and compounds every 6 months.

Series EE Savings Bonds issued on and after May 1, 2005, will earn fixed rates of interest. The fixed rate will apply for the 30-year life of each bond, which includes a 10-year extended maturity period, unless a different rate or rate structure is announced and applied at the start of the extension period.

Rates for new issues will still be adjusted each May 1 and November 1. Series EE bonds issued prior to May 1, 2005, will continue to be governed by the terms in effect when they were issued.

A current listing of redemption values for all savings bonds—Form PD 3600—is available free from the Bureau of the Public Debt. Values are shown for 6 months, so an investor who follows a bond across the six columns can figure out the two months of the year in which the value rises.

Meanwhile, two useful one-page listings are available by writing the public affairs office of the U.S. Savings Bonds Division, Department of the Treasury, Washington, D.C. 20226 (202-377-7715). One sheet shows the current guaranteed minimum interest rates for Series EE and E bonds and Savings Notes

bought *prior* to May 1, 1995. Holders get the higher of those minimum rates, which range from 4 percent to 8.5 percent, or variable rates that are based on market conditions.

The second sheet, dubbed "Table of Interest Accrual Dates," shows the two months a year in which Series E and EE bonds rise in value.

Savings bond holders can also call their nearest Federal Reserve Bank for savings bond information. Another option is an information service offered by Mr. Pederson, the former Federal Bank of Chicago official. His Savings Bond Informer Inc. in Detroit (313-843-1910) sells computer printouts listing key dates, interest rates, and redemption values for an investor's bonds. The cost for between 26 and 75 bonds: $22.50. Alternatively, if you are on-line, you can get the value of a Series EE bond from www.execpc.com/nmmrsoft or from the Bureau of Public Debt at www.publicdebt.treas.gov/sav/sav.htm.

Taxes are also deferred on income that builds up in Individual Retirement Account, corporate pension, and Keogh plans. Furthermore, as discussed earlier, if you qualify for these plans, you also can deduct from your current income the amount you contribute to your plan each year.

One old tax planning strategy for taxpayers close to retirement was to buy Series EE savings bonds (which stop paying interest after 30 years) today and, when they retire, exchange those bonds for HH bonds, which were available only through such an exchange. This would have allowed you to defer tax on the interest the EE bonds earned before the exchange until you redeem the HH bonds. In the meantime, you will get a check for interest on the HH bonds every 6 months. That interest rate is fixed, however, and is taxable. There is no limit to the dollar amount of HH bonds that may be acquired through the exchange process. It is important though that you compare the after-tax cash flows from the bonds and alternative investments. It may be better to pay the tax and reinvest the net proceeds at a higher yield than the HH bonds for a higher net after- tax cash return.

Unfortunately, as of August 31, 2004, the Treasury no longer issues Series HH bonds. If you buy certain 6-month bank certificates of deposit (CDs) now, you can defer paying part of the tax on the interest until you file your return in the subsequent year. The CD must be the type on which the interest is neither credited to your account nor made available to you without substantial penalty before the maturity date. In addition, an investment in U.S. Treasury bills provides a similar tax benefit. This is because interest on them is not recognized until the bills are redeemed. Note, furthermore, that Treasury bill (also called T-bill) interest is not subject to state or local tax; however, taxable short-term CDs may yield a higher rate of interest.

You also can defer your taxes on fees and compensation. For example, a binding agreement to delay until January the grant of a bonus otherwise

payable in December defers taxation on that bonus until the subsequent year. But this agreement must be entered into before the bonus is "constructively received." Deferring fees or service compensation is easy. All you need to do is delay billing until late December. You will not receive payment—therefore, no taxable income either—until the next year.

A final alternative strategy for delaying your tax payments is to delay your receipt of income with an installment sale. You should consider postponing part or all of the profit from a big gain to next year or later. Not only could an installment sale keep this year's tax cost down (you pay tax only on the share of the profit you receive during the year), but it could also allow you to avoid a big bulge in income that could force you into a higher bracket.

174 Accelerate Expenses

You may have a great deal of flexibility in the timing of a number of your expenses. For example, any of your medical expenses not reimbursed are deductible in the year they are paid. An effective tax reducing strategy, therefore, would be to concentrate as many expenses as possible in a year when it appears that the percent medical expense deduction limit will be exceeded. If, at year-end, it is apparent that no deduction will be available, defer payment of medical bills until the following year when the situation may be otherwise. In a year when the deduction is probable, make sure that all medical needs are satisfied and paid for in that year.

For example, eye examinations, new glasses, and dental work may be accelerated by a month or two to permit a deduction; the remaining balance on your children's orthodontic work may be paid immediately in full. Note, however, that a deduction *is* available in the current year for medical needs charged to your credit card before the year-end, even if payment is not actually made until the subsequent year.

Tax payments can also be accelerated. The principal categories here are real estate taxes, personal property taxes, and state and local income taxes. Amounts withheld for income taxes are deductible in the year withheld. If your state or city income tax exceeds your withholding, estimated tax payments are probably required. The last installments of these taxes should be paid before the end of the current year even though they may not be due until the next year. This will accelerate your deduction into the current year. Moreover, prepayments of real estate taxes are deductible in the year paid—if they are not merely advance deposits paid before the tax becomes a liability. Each of these accelerated payments represents a current deduction from your income tax liability. But watch out for the Alternative Minimum Tax (AMT).

Charitable contributions are also susceptible to acceleration. Sometimes it is feasible to make a large contribution in a high-income year in order to satisfy a charitable commitment extending over a number of years. Do not make a contribution on January 1 that you could have made on December 31. Remember, however, that contributions are deductible subject to certain limitations based upon your adjusted gross income. Contributions that exceed these limitations should *not* be made.

Moreover, contributions of appreciated capital gain property, such as securities held over 12 months, will allow you a tax deduction equal to their full market value. Therefore, a gift of appreciated securities has the advantage of a market value deduction without the payment of a tax. Conversely, you should never make charitable donations of securities that have declined in value below cost, since you would forfeit the tax loss. In those situations, it is better to sell the securities, take the tax loss, and contribute the cash proceeds.

175 Accelerate Special Deductions

The election to expense allowance is available for depreciable personal property used in your business and acquired after 1981. This is a deduction against your business income. This accelerated expense is *in addition* to your regular depreciation (on the reduced basis) and is as much as $1 million for 2018. And, again, it does not matter how late in the year the property is put into service.

176 Dependents and Personal Exemptions

A dependent is someone related to you or a "qualifying relative" who need not be related if he or she is a member of your household for whom you provide more than half the support. Until 2018, you could have claimed a dependency exemption of $4,050 for each person who met *all* exemption tests, with certain exceptions. For example, the gross income test did not apply if your child is a full-time student under age 24 or a nonstudent under age 19 or any age if permanently and totally disabled and if the income of such person is for services performed at a sheltered workshop. Also, special support rules applied to children of divorced parents and to those dependents being claimed under multiple support agreements. Furthermore, whether the dependent is born or dies during the year is irrelevant. If you pass the tests for the portion of the year during which the dependent was alive, you could have received the full $4,050 exemption.

The following tests had to be met with respect to the person in question in order to qualify you for a dependency exemption:

1. *Support.* You must furnish over one-half of the total support of the person in the calendar year in which your tax year begins. Support includes amounts spent for food, shelter, clothing, medical and dental care, education, church contributions, child care expenses, wedding apparel and receptions, capital items (a car or a TV set), and the like. It does *not* include the value of services performed for a dependent, or scholarships received by a dependent student. Also, support is what is spent, not what is available. This means that even if your child earns $10,000 and banks $5,000 of it, as long as you contribute $5,001 in support, you have contributed more than one-half.

 Several tax-saving strategies present themselves in this area. A year-end budgeting of support expenditures can produce substantial tax benefits and thus reduce the out-of-pocket cost of supporting a dependent. For example, assume that you are unmarried and live with your mother. By December 1, your mother has spent $4,000 of her nontaxable Social Security payments for her own support and you have contributed $2,000 for her support. During the rest of the year, you provide for all of your mother's support at a cost of $800 and give her a $1,400 television set for her exclusive use in her room. Consequently, you provide more than 50 percent of your mother's total support (that is, $4,200 of a total of $8,200) for this year. Thus, you could have claimed the $4,050 dependency exemption for your mother.

 When two or more persons furnish the support of a dependent, one of the contributing group is entitled to take the deduction for the dependent if:

 a) no one person contributes more than half of the dependent's support;

 b) each member of the group, were it not for the support test, would be entitled to claim the individual as a dependent;

 c) the one claiming the deduction gives more than 10 percent of the dependent's support; *and*

 d) every other person who gives more than 10 percent of the dependent's support files a written relinquishment of the claim to the exemption in the same calendar year.

2. *Relationship of Dependent.* The person supported must be your relative or a "qualifying relative," which includes a nonrelated member of your household. Your relatives include your children, grandchildren, great-grandchildren, and step-children; foster children; brothers, sisters, half-brothers, half-sisters, step-brothers, and step-sisters; parents, grandparents, great-grandparents,

step-mother, and step-father; nephews, nieces, uncles, and aunts; and sons-in-law, daughters-in-law, fathers-in-law, mothers-in-law, brothers-in-law, and sisters-in-law. A legally adopted child or one placed with you for adoption is considered a child by blood. Furthermore, on a joint return, this condition is satisfied if the qualifying relationship exists between the person claimed as a dependent and either you *or* your spouse.

If a person is not one of your relatives, that person may qualify as a dependent if he or she is a member of your household. A member of your household is one who, during your entire tax year, or during part of it, uses your home as the principal dwelling. By tax magic, a member of your household may now qualify as your "Qualifying Relative."

But it must not be an illegal relationship. In states with statutes forbidding sexual relations between unmarried people (and there have been a bunch, including Florida, Michigan, Virginia, North Carolina, Idaho, Mississippi, North Dakota, and West Virginia), the IRS could disallow exemptions for live-ins. Residents of those states who claim such exemptions were exposed to a fight with the IRS. But, in light of recent Supreme Court decisions, I doubt the IRS would bring the issue to the courts. The IRS clearly won't balk at exemptions claimed by residents of states without such statutes—if, again, they meet the basic requirements.

Dependent Exemption Summary

A. To claim a dependency *exemption* for a qualifying child, all of the qualifying child dependency tests must be met:
- Dependent taxpayer test
- Joint return test
- Citizenship test
- Relationship test
- Age test
- Residency test
- Support test

B. To claim a dependency *exemption* for a qualifying relative, the person must meet the following tests:
- Dependent taxpayer test
- Joint return test
- Citizenship test
- Not a qualifying child test
- Member of household or relationship test
- Gross income test
- Support test

3. *Dependent's Gross Income.* Your dependent's gross income for the calendar year in which your tax year begins had to have been less than $4,050. This did not apply to children who are students under age 24 or nonstudents under age 19 and certain income earned by those permanently and totally disabled. A child is a student if, during each of any 5-months of the calendar year in which your tax year begins, he or she (a) is in full-time attendance at an educational institution or (b) is taking a full-time course of institutional or farm training.

 In figuring your dependent's gross income, you exclude any type of exempt income. This includes Social Security benefits, tax-exempt interest, etc. Remember, though, that if your dependent has used these tax-exempt benefits for support, generally the benefits *will be* considered in determining whether the support test has been met.

4. *Joint Return.* Generally, you lost an exemption for a married dependent who files a joint return. This rule did not apply, however, if neither the dependent nor his or her spouse was required to file a return but they filed a joint return solely to claim a refund of tax withheld. Here you should examine the advantage to your dependent in terms of tax savings from filing a joint return as opposed to the tax cost to you from losing the exemption. In many cases it would pay for you to compensate your dependent for a tax loss and claim the deduction for the exemption. For example, assume that you are in the 28 percent bracket and that the tax loss to your married dependent from filing a separate as opposed to a joint return is $200. The $4,050 personal exemption would save you $1,134 in taxes in your tax bracket. In this case, it would pay for you to give $200 to your dependent for this "loss." After taxes, you would still be ahead $934.

5. *Citizenship or Residency.* A dependent, to qualify you for an exemption, must be a U.S. citizen or a resident of the United States, Canada, or Mexico at some time during the calendar year in which your tax year begins.

The above rules and tests are used to determine whether your dependent qualifies you for the $4,050 exemption deduction. If you fail the gross income test—that is, your dependent has a gross income of $4,050 or more—but you pass the other four tests, you may have what I call a *nondeductible* dependent. This still affords several significant advantages. For example, a nondeductible dependent could qualify an unmarried taxpayer to use the more advantageous head of household rate schedule; likewise, a married but separated taxpayer with a nondeductible dependent child could also use the more advantageous single taxpayer or head of household rate schedule. Moreover, any payments made by you for a nondeductible dependent's medical expenses can qualify as a medical expense deduction on your return. These rules were modified in 2005 (see below).

For example, assume that your 60-year-old mother and father, who have no taxable income, reside in a nursing home, primarily to obtain medical care. Therefore, the entire cost of their maintenance (including meals and lodging) at the home qualifies as a medical expense. You pay your parents' nursing home bills, totaling $36,000 yearly, and thereby provide over half of their support. Furthermore, assume that you are single, that you have an adjusted gross income of $100,000, and that, after all deductions except those relating to your parents, you are in the 32 percent bracket.

You can now claim a medical expense deduction of $28,500 ($36,000 − 7.5% of $100,000). In the 32 percent bracket, this will save you $9,120 in taxes [$28,500 × 0.32). Moreover, you can probably reduce your taxes even further because you are now entitled to compute your tax as head of household instead of single taxpayer.

Note, however, that an individual who is eligible to be claimed as a dependent by another is not eligible for his or her own personal exemption. For that reason it becomes very important to examine the potential tax consequences to your parents. The loss of the dependency exemption may cause them to pay taxes in excess of your own tax savings. In all situations, therefore, a comparative analysis should be made to maximize the tax savings to all parties.

The above rules were too simple. So Congress went to work confusing this issue for 2005 and future years. Under the new rules a "qualifying child" does not have to pass the gross income test to be a "dependent" but a "qualified relative" does.

Your potential "dependent" must be either a "qualifying child" or a "qualified relative"—which includes a *nonrelated* member of your household.

For a qualify relative you need to provide more than half his/her support. But for a qualifying child, the rule is that the child can not provide more than half his/her own support.

THE TAX CUTS AND JOBS ACT OF 2017 ELIMINATED THE DEDUCTIBLE FOR EXEMPTIONS AS OF 2018. BUT, THEY ARE SCHEDULED TO RETURN AFTER 2025.

177 Phase-out of Exemptions

As part of the 1990 Tax Reform Act, Congress mandated a phase-out of personal exemptions for high income taxpayers. When adjusted gross income (AGI) exceeded the following thresholds, the 1990 law began to reclaim the tax savings from personal exemptions:

- $100,000 for singles (indexed)
- $150,000 for joint returns (indexed)

- $75,000 for marrieds filing separately (indexed)
- $161,150 for head of household

Every time AGI exceeded the threshold by another $2,500 ($1,250 for marrieds filing separately), 2 percent was cut off the dollar amount of personal exemptions. *Example:* If your AGI exceeded the threshold by $25,000, you lost 20 percent of your personal exemptions ($25,000 ÷ $2,500 =10; 10 × 2% = 20%). At $122,500 ($61,250 for marrieds filing separately) above the threshold, all claimed exemptions were wiped out.

For 2009, even after the phase-out, your minimum exemption amount was $2,433.

This translated into a marginal-rate increase of about one-half of 1 percent for each exemption claimed. Thus, parents of two children with sufficient taxable income might really be paying almost 37 percent. Add the effect of the itemized deduction cap and that marginal rate nears 38 percent.

There was no phase-out of exemptions for 2010, 2011, or 2012. But it is back for 2013, 2014, 2015, 2016 and 2017 as per below:

Personal Exemption Amount

Amount	2013	2014	2015	2016	2017
Personal exemption amount	$ 3,900	$ 3,950	$ 4,000	$ 4,050	$ 4,050
Married filing jointly	**2013**	**2014**	**2015**	**2016**	**2017**
Phase-out threshold amount	$300,000	$305,050	$309,900	$311,300	$313,800
Completed phase-out amount after	$422,501	$427,550	$432,400	$433,800	$436,300
Head of household	**2013**	**2014**	**2015**	**2016**	**2017**
Phase-out threshold amount	$275,000	$279,650	$284,050	$285,350	$287,650
Completed phase-out amount after	$397,501	$402,150	$406,550	$407,850	$410,150
Unmarried	**2013**	**2014**	**2015**	**2016**	**2017**
Phase-out threshold amount	$250,000	$254,200	$258,250	$259,400	$261,500
Completed phase-out amount after	$372,501	$376,700	$380,750	$381,900	$384,000
Married filing separately	**2013**	**2014**	**2015**	**2016**	**2017**
Phase-out threshold amount	$150,000	$152,525	$154,950	$155,650	$156,900
Completed phase-out amount after	$211,251	$213,775	$216,200	$216,900	$218,150

The loss of personal exemptions added as much as 1.05 percent per exemption to your true tax rate. You lost 2 percent for each $2,500 or part above the adjusted gross income threshold amounts.

The Tax Cuts and Jobs Act of 2017 eliminated exemptions, and the relevance of the phase-out.

178 Timing Strategies

We have already discussed timing strategies in terms of accelerating expenses and deferring income. Remember, you can take deductions on items paid for by check in the current year, even if you mail the check on New Year's Eve, as long as there is no impediment to cashing the check in the ordinary course of business in early January. If you mail a check covering a large deductible item in late December, use certified mail so that you will receive a date-stamped receipt as proof that you actually mailed the payment in the earlier year.

Furthermore, wherever possible you should charge deductible items on credit cards. Deductible items charged in the current year on nonspecific store credit cards can be deducted in that year, even if you do not actually pay (or receive) the credit card bill until next year. Credit card charges also provide excellent proof as to the amount and nature of expenses—especially travel and entertainment expenses. (In addition, credit card charges have been known to get lost. Lost credit card charges do not reduce your taxes but do provide you with free goods and services.)

179 Retirement Plans

If you participate in a qualified retirement plan of your employer, you receive a number of tax advantages—especially if you are your own employer. The employer is entitled to deduct payments to the plan immediately. As an employee, you do not have to recognize current income from the contributions; rather, you will be taxed only when you receive distributions from the plan. Since distributions are normally made after you retire and have less taxable income, these distributions may be taxed at lower rates. Moreover, the retirement plan itself is exempt from tax. This means that your earnings will accumulate tax-deferred at a faster rate.

If you are self-employed, you have the option of two basic forms of noncorporate qualified retirement plans, discussed in the next two sections.

180 Individual Retirement Plans (IRAs)

Even if you are covered by an employer retirement plan, and if you do not exceed the appropriate income limits, you may establish an IRA for your own retirement. You are eligible for an IRA deduction even if you have a Keogh, but cannot exceed the contribution limits. The maximum allowable IRA deduction is the lesser of $5,500 ($6,500 if age 50 or older) or earned income. In order to generate an IRA deduction, the contribution must be made (and the plan established) by the due date (*not including extensions*) for filing your return. According to the IRS national office, you should make the contribution prior to filing the return—i.e., you cannot take the deduction and file on March 1 and make the contribution on April 15.

For married persons, the maximum deduction is computed separately for each individual who has compensation. An eligible individual with a nonemployed spouse may make deductible contributions to IRA accounts of up to $11,000 ($5,500 each).

Furthermore, in a 1983 Private Letter Ruling 832-9049 the IRS has held that a separate payment to an IRA for custodian fees does not constitute an excess contribution and such a payment is deductible as an itemized expense under Section 212. Moreover, according to IRS Letter Ruling 843-2109, the amount that you can contribute to an IRA is not diminished by the *separate payment* of brokerage commissions or other fees. Accordingly, the payment of brokerage commissions and other fees, such as administrative and service fees that are separately billed and paid, will not be considered additional contributions to your IRA.

181 H.R. 10 or Keogh Plans

In general, the maximum annual deduction for self-employed retirement plans is the lesser of 20 percent of earned income, less your deduction for half your self-employed payroll tax, before the deduction, or $55,000. (This equates to 25 percent of net earned income after the deduction.) Under certain circumstances, a defined benefit type of self-employed retirement plan may allow a contribution in excess of the usual limits.

Individuals who have part-time self-employment income, such as directors and consultants, are allowed to establish such a plan. Thus, even if you are covered

by your employer's qualified retirement plan, you might also establish a Keogh plan with any outside fees or other income that you receive. If your self-employment income is from a business that has employees, they must also be included under the plan.

With a Keogh plan you may deduct contributions made *after* the end of the taxable year, if paid by the due date for filing your return including extensions. The plan must be established before the end of the tax year.

There are substantial tax advantages to either of these plans. You obtain an immediate tax deduction for the contribution; earnings accumulate on the contributions free of current taxes; and when distributed, the plan benefits may be taxed at a lower rate.

A number of considerations are involved in deciding whether to establish a retirement plan and selecting between IRAs and Keogh plans. For example, the amount that may be contributed under a Keogh plan is greater than the amount allowable under an IRA. Alternatively, using an IRA rather than a Keogh plan will allow you to restrict the retirement plan to cover only yourself, which can mean a substantial tax savings if you have a lot of employees. All of these factors must be considered and discussed with your tax advisor.

182 Marital Status

Whether you are single or married can have a substantial impact on your tax bill. Speeding or delaying the ceremony can yield you an enormous one-time tax savings.

In general, marriage will cut taxes only if one spouse works or earns almost all of the income. Alternatively, if both spouses work and earn relatively good salaries, marriage will substantially boost your taxes. This is because holy wedlock will push your combined income into a higher tax bracket.

If you are planning an end of the year/New Year's Day wedding, it would be well worth your while to compute your taxes both singly and jointly. You may find that the savings from deferring (or accelerating) your wedding date could be enough to pay for your honeymoon vacation.

In conclusion, recognize that the focus of this chapter has been to reduce your current year's income tax. Due to inflation, any tax liability deferred to a later year will be paid with cheaper dollars. Moreover, a deferral of income to a later year is the equivalent of an interest-free loan because it enables you to use the funds that you would otherwise have to pay toward your tax liability. Be aware, however, that this might not always be the correct planning strategy.

If you expect your income to go up substantially in later years, you do not want to bunch more income into those years, because the graduated rates could bring about a greater total aggregate tax liability over the years involved. Furthermore, you should *always* take into consideration the political climate for tax changes. If tax rates are expected to go down in the future, then income deferral and expense acceleration is the right strategy. Alternatively, if rates go in the other direction, you will want to recognize your income now and defer your expenses until later.

183 The Goldinger Deferral

An interesting tax deferral technique was developed by Jay Goldinger in Beverly Hills. He has suggested the acquisition of a one- or two-month bank certificate of deposit by putting up 1.5 percent of the purchase price and borrowing the rest from your broker. The deal is close to a wash. Assume the certificates would pay about 9.25 percent, and the loan would cost 9 percent, including the broker's markup. But by paying the interest on or before December 31, you could deduct the expense from your current year's income. If the certificate of deposit is from a sound bank, your risk is low.

To swing such a deal on a one-month $1 million certificate of deposit, the smallest negotiable denomination, you would need $24,000—a $15,000 down payment and about $9,000 for interest on the loan. In January of the next year, when the certificate matures, you would repay the loan and collect the income on the certificate of deposit. That income would be taxable in the new year, but you would have a $9,000 deduction allowable in the earlier year.

Be aware of the limits on personal and investment interest deductions here. You should have sufficient other investment income to cover the investment interest expense.

Also be aware that the courts have disallowed "straddle" transactions where the primary motivation was to generate tax benefits and not realize profits (*Ewing v. Commissioner,* 91 T.C. 396, 1988). Be careful that you document your motive here.

More Tax Changes

"Tax simplification is complicated stuff."

PAM OLSON
Deputy Assistant Treasury Secretary for Tax Policy

"It's all political theater. It's not about legislating anymore. It's all for the next election that's coming up shortly."

Senator OLYMPIA SNOWE (R-Maine)
August 2010, before the Congress congressional recess

"Today we are creating an IRS where the American taxpayer comes first and customer service is second to none."

Treasury Secretary ROBERT RUBIN and
Commissioner of Internal Revenue
CHARLES O. ROSSOTTI

"In the last decade, taxes have been raised four times explicitly for deficit reduction. In the year following each hike, the deficit actually increased."

Senator DAN COATS 1993

"I don't make jokes. I just watch the government and report the facts."

WILL ROGERS

*"Suppose you were an idiot.
And suppose you were a member of Congress. . . .
But then I repeat myself."*

MARK TWAIN

"Taxation is the art of plucking the chicken so as to get the maximum number of feathers with the minimum amount of squawking."

LOUIS RÉNN from Peter Vico, CPA

> Note that the following chapters represent the law as it was passed. Subsequent changes have already been incorporated in the prior chapters.

Congress manages to pass tax changes each year. Here's a summary of the most important new laws and how to use them to keep more money in your pockets.

A The Patient Protection and Affordable Care Act

This massive bill, signed into law on March 23, 2010, has provisions effective from 2010–2018. Here's what's scheduled:

2010

- Adoption credit—made refundable and extended through 2011; credit increased to $13,170 for 2010.
- 10 percent excise tax imposed on indoor tanning services effective July 1, 2010.
- Economic substance required for transactions mandated. Now a transaction must have a substantial nontax business purpose creating a meaningful change in economic position to be tax recognized.
- Student debt forgiven for medical professionals working in "underserved" areas escape taxation for years after December 31, 2008.

Many small businesses and tax-exempt organizations that provide health insurance coverage to their employees now qualify for a special tax credit. This is designed to encourage small business employers to offer health insurance coverage for the first time or to maintain coverage they already have. In general, the credit is available to small business employers who pay at least half the cost of single coverage for their employees.

The maximum credit is 35 percent of premiums paid in 2010 by eligible small business employers and 25 percent of premiums paid by eligible employers that are tax-exempt organizations. In 2014, this maximum credit increases to 50 percent of premiums paid by eligible small business employers and 35 percent of premiums paid by eligible employers that are tax-exempt organizations.

The credit is specifically targeted to help small businesses and tax-exempt organizations that primarily employ low- and moderate-income workers. It is generally available to employers who have fewer than 25 full-time equivalent (FTE) employees and who are paying wages averaging less than $50,000 per employee per year. Because the eligibility formula is based in part on the number of FTEs, not the number of employees, many businesses will qualify even if they employ more than 25 individual workers.

The maximum credit goes to smaller business employers—those with 10 or fewer FTEs—paying annual average wages of $25,000 or less.

Eligible small businesses can claim the credit as part of the general business credit starting with the 2010 income tax return they file in 2011. For tax-exempt employers, the IRS will provide further information on how to claim the credit.

2011

- Businesses must report the value of health-care benefits on employees' W-2.

- Money in health savings accounts, flexible spending accounts, and other health reimbursement arrangements can be used only for *prescribed* over-the-counter medicines or face a 20 percent penalty. Solution? Talk to your doctor.

- The 10 percent penalty for nonqualified use of funds from health savings accounts doubles to 20 percent.

2012

- New 1099 reporting mandated for all businesses making payments of over $600 over the course of a year to a corporation.

2013

This is when the major changes take effect:

- A 3.8 percent tax will be imposed on *unearned* (investment) income of individuals with incomes of more than $200,000 ($250,000 for joint filers). This would apply to rents, interest, dividends, royalties, capital gains, and so on and *only* to amounts in excess of those floors. Distributions from retirement accounts would not be taxed as unearned (investment) income nor would life insurance proceeds, municipal bond interest, and veterans benefits count.

The 3.8 percent Medicare surtax won't apply to all home sale profits after 2012. Most gains on sales of primary residences will be exempt. Only the portion of profits that exceeds the $250,000 or $500,000 exclusion will be subject to the tax.

But profits on sales of rental properties and second homes will be hit by the surtax, assuming that the seller's adjusted gross income is large enough.

What should you do? Consider Roth accounts because Roth withdrawals don't increase your income. Also consider installment sales to keep your income below the floors. Life insurance becomes more attractive as you can borrow against it without increasing your income and the proceeds are not subject to the tax.

- The normal 1.45 percent Hospital Insurance (HI) payroll tax on wages or earnings will be increased by 0.90 percent to 2.35 percent for individuals with income of more than $200,000 ($250,000 on a joint return). Again, only the excess over the floor would be subject to the added tax. Employers will still pay only 1.45 percent. Self-employed individuals who pay the additional 0.90 percent will not be able to deduct any part of the increase.

- The floor for claiming medical expenses increases from 7.5 percent of adjusted gross income to 10 percent. For those aged 65 or over the floor stays at 7.5 percent until 2016.

- Contributions to health-care flexible spending accounts limited to $2,500. This cap will be indexed to consumer price inflation beginning in 2014.

2014

- You will be required to have health insurance or face a tax of as much as 2.5 percent of taxable income. Those without coverage pay a tax penalty of the greater of $695 per year up to a maximum of three times that amount ($2,085) per family or 2.5 percent of household income. The penalty will be phased in according to the following schedule: $95 in 2014, $325 in 2015, and $695 in 2016 for the flat fee or 1 percent of taxable income in 2014, 2 percent of taxable income in 2015, and 2.5 percent of taxable income in 2016. Beginning after 2016, the penalty will be increased annually by the cost-of-living adjustment. Exemptions will be granted for financial hardship, religious objections, American Indians, those without coverage for less than 3 months, undocumented immigrants, incarcerated individuals, those for whom the lowest cost plan option exceeds 8 percent of an individual's income, and those with incomes below the tax filing threshold.

- Assess employers with more than 50 employees who do not offer coverage and have at least one full-time employee who receives a premium tax credit of $2,000 per full-time employee, excluding the first 30 employees from the assessment. Employers with more than 50 employees who offer coverage but have at least one full-time employee receiving a premium tax credit will pay the lesser of $3,000 for each employee receiving a premium credit or $2,000 for each full-time employee. Employers with 50 or fewer employees are exempt from any of the above penalties.

- Require employers who offer coverage to their employees to provide a free choice voucher to employees with incomes less than 400 percent of the federal

poverty level whose share of the premium exceeds 8 percent but is less than 9.8 percent of their income and who choose to enroll in a plan in the exchange. The voucher amount is equal to what the employer would have paid to provide coverage to the employee under the employer's plan and will be used to offset the premium costs for the plan in which the employee is enrolled. Employers providing free choice vouchers will not be subject to penalties for employees who receive premium credits in the exchange.

2018

- A 40 percent excise tax on high-cost insurance plans goes into effect based on the amount of premium in excess of $10,200 ($27,500 for families). The tax is paid by the insurers or self-insured firms.

According to the tax policy center, 85 percent of the tax burden under the new law will be shouldered by the top 1 percent of taxpayers.

B Small Business Jobs Act of 2010

Signed into law by President Obama on September 27, 2010, the SBJA makes the following changes:

1. The Act extends the additional 50 percent first-year depreciation deduction through 2010. Fifty percent of the basis of the property can be deducted in the first year with the other 50 percent under normal depreciation rules. Let's take an example of a new (used doesn't count) SUV with a loaded weight of over 6,000 pounds costing $50,000 and used 100 percent for business. The first $25,000 is expensed, the maximum for the vehicle. Half the remaining cost of $25,000 ($12,500) is claimed as bonus depreciation. Normal depreciation is 20 percent of the $12,500 balance or $2,500. That's a total first-year deduction of $40,000 on a $50,000 purchase!

 For assets put in use after September 8, 2010, and before January 1, 2012, the bonus depreciation is 100 percent, allowing an immediate expense of assets with a useful life of 20 years or less, including machinery, land improvements, and mixed-purpose farm buildings.

2. Effective for 2010 and 2011, the maximum you can *expense under Section 179* is increased to $500,000. This number is reduced if capital expenditures exceed $2 million.

3. If you're self-employed, your *health insurance costs* have been deducted above the line. Starting 2010, your HI premiums will now also reduce your income subect to self-employment taxes. If your net self-employment income is more than $106,800, that's an additional 15.3 percent saved. So if you pay premiums of $10,000 and are in the 28 percent bracket, you save $2,800 in income taxes and an additional $1,530 in Social Security and Medicare taxes. See Schedule SE for this deduction.

4. The Act *delists cell phones* and other communications devices from "listed property." This removes the strict substantiation of use requirement and the limit on depreciation deductions.

5. The amount of *start-up expenses* that can be deducted is increased from $5,000 to $10,000.

6. The Act eliminates 100 percent of both the regular tax and the AMT on the sale of *small business stock* acquired at original issue after September 27, 2010, and before January 1, 2011 provided you hold the stock for at least 5 years.

7. If you pay anybody $600 or more for *rental property services* (e.g., plumbers, painters, etc.), you will now have to file a Form 1099 MISC to report that income paid. (Repealed in 2011.)

8. Small businesses will now be able to *carry back general business credits* up to 5 years (as opposed to only 1) and offset both regular and AMT tax liabilities. A small business is a non–publicly traded corporation, partnership, or sole proprietorship with gross receipts of $50 million or less each year.

9. If your 401(k) offers a *Roth* option, you can now move funds from the regular 401(k) to the Roth so that future earnings will be tax-free. The same rule applies to Section 403(b) and Section 457(b) plans. Such *rollovers* are allowed, but any untaxed money will be subject to tax—but you can defer the tax until 2011 and 2012 if you convert in 2010.

The conversion is optional and your plan must allow it. It must be an eligible rollover distribution, such as resulting from termination, disability, death, or reaching age 59½. Certain distributions, such as the hardship distribution and minimum required distributions, are not eligible rollover distributions and are not eligible for conversion.

This provision is for distributions after September 27, 2010.

C The Tax Relief, Unemployment Insurance Reauthorization, and Job Creation Act of 2010

It was almost mid-December 2010 when Congress finally passed the Tax Relief, Unemployment Insurance Reauthorization, and Job Creation Act of 2010 (2010 Tax Relief Act). It basically said, "never mind." Extending provisions for just 2 years up through 2012, the Act sets up a major issue for the 2012 presidential election and merely postpones final decision making. Here's what's been extended and what's new.

INDIVIDUAL CHANGES

Tax Rates. The 2010 Tax Act extends all individual tax rates at 10, 15, 25, 28, 33, and 35 percent through December 31, 2012.

Capital Gains/Qualified Dividends. The Act also extends the maximum 15 percent rate (0 percent for those in the 10 and 15 percent tax bracket) for long-term capital gains and qualified dividends through December 31, 2012. Dividends from regulated investment companies (RICs), real estate investment trusts (REITs), and other qualified pass-through entities continue to qualify.

Itemized Deduction (Pease) Limitations. The Act repeals this reduction in itemized deductions based on income through December 31, 2012.

Person Exemption Phase-out. Prior to 2010, taxpayers with incomes above a certain level were subject to a reduction in their personal exemptions. The Act extends the repeal of this deduction reduction through December 31, 2012.

Marriage Penalty Relief. Prior legislation reduced the marriage penalty by increasing the basic standard deduction for a married couple to twice that of a single filer. The Act extends this marriage penalty relief through December 31, 2012.

Child Tax Credit. The Act extends the $1,000 child care credit through December 31, 2012. It was scheduled to fall to $500.

Earned Income Credit. The Act extends the enhanced earned income credit through December 31, 2012.

Adoption Credit/Exclusion. Prior legislation increased the dollar limitation for the adoption credit and increased the exclusion for employer-provided assistance to $10,000 increased by another $1,000 by the Patient Protection and Affordable Care Act for 2010 and 2011. The 2010 Act extends the enhancements to the credit and exclusion through December 31, 2012. However, the PPACA is not available after 2010.

Dependent Care Credit. The 2010 Act extends the enhanced dependent care credit through December 31, 2012.

Employer-Provided Child Care. Employers who provide child care facilities have been able to claim a 25 percent tax credit for qualified expenses and a 10 percent tax credit for qualified resource and referral services. The Act extends these credits through December 31, 2012.

Mortgage Insurance Premiums. Under current law, certain qualified mortgage insurance premiums are potentially allowable deductions. The 2010 Act extends this deduction for one year.

American Opportunity Tax Credit. The 2010 Act extends this four-year credit through December 31, 2010.

Educational Assistance Exclusion. The 2010 Act extends this exclusion of up to $5,250 in employer-provided education assistance through December 31, 2012.

Student Loan Interest Deduction. The 2010 Act extends through December 31, 2012, the elimination of the 60-month rule and the expanded income phase-out amount for this potential $2,500 deduction.

Coverdell Education Savings Accounts. Scheduled to fall back to $500, the maximum $2,000 annual contribution has been extended through December 31, 2012.

Annual Extenders. The following individual benefits and deductions have been extended for 2 years, 2010 and 2011. That means Congress will have to revisit them again next year:

- State and local sales tax deduction

- Higher education tuition deduction

- Teacher's $250 above the line classroom expense deduction

- Charitable contribution deduction of appreciated property for conservation purposes.

- Charitable contribution of IRA proceeds. Here the IRS has allowed direct contributions made in January 2011 to count for 2010.

Alternative Minimum Tax. The 2010 Act patches the AMT with higher exemption amounts for 2010 and 2011. Without the changes, an estimated 21 million more taxpayers would be subject to the AMT. The new exemption amounts are:

	2010	2011
Single	$47,450	$48,450
Joint/Surviving Spouse	$72,450	$74,450
Married Filing Separately	$36,225	$37,225

Payroll Tax Cut. This one is new. The 2010 Act cuts the 2011 employee share of the Social Security tax from 6.2 to 4.2 percent. This 2 percent cut can potentially save you as much as $2,136 (2 percent of $106,800). Self-employed individuals will calculate the above the line deduction for employment taxes without regard to the temporary rate reduction.

Transit Benefits. Employer-provided transit benefits (transit passes and van-pool benefits) may be tax-free to employees. For 2010, the ceiling is $230. The 2010 Act extends these benefits for one year, through 2011.

Energy Incentives. The 2010 Act extends energy credits through 2011. But the total maximum $1,500 credit for 2009 and 2010 has been reduced to pre-2009 Recovery Act limits ($500) for 2011.

BUSINESS CHANGES

100 percent Bonus Depreciation. The 2010 Act increases bonus depreciation from 50 percent to 100 percent for qualified investments made after September 8, 2010, and before January 1, 2012. It also makes 50 percent bonus depreciation available for qualified property placed in service after December 31, 2011, and before January 1, 2013.

Code Section 179 Expensing. To encourage business spending, Congress increased the amount that can be expensed and the investment limit to $500,000 and $2 million, respectively, for 2010 and 2011. For 2012, the numbers are $125,000 and $500,000, both indexed for inflation.

Research Tax Credit. This credit was renewed for 2 years, 2010 and 2011.

Work Opportunity Credit. Scheduled to expire after August 31, 2011, the 2010 Act extends this credit through the end of 2011. But, the Act does not extend this credit for unemployed veterans and disconnected youth beyond 2010.

Small Business Stock. The 2010 Act extends the 100 percent exclusion of gain from the sale of qualified small business stock by noncorporate taxpayers to stock acquired before January 1, 2012. The stock must be held for more than 5 years, and the amount excluded is limited to the greater of $10 million or 10 times your basis in the stock.

Business Energy Incentives. These incentives, such as the credits for biodiesel fuel, refined coal facilities, and so forth, have been extended for 2 years.

FEDERAL ESTATE TAX

The 2010 Act revives the Estate Tax for 2011 with a $5 million exclusion and a top marginal bracket of 35 percent. Step-up basis is returned. For those dying in 2010, estates have the option of using the 2010 rules with no tax and a limited step up, or the new 2011 rules with a full step up in basis and the $5 exclusion.

Big Change! The exclusion is now portable between spouses. So if a husband dies and uses up $2 million of his $5 million exclusion, the surviving spouse has an exclusion of $5 million plus the unused $3 million from the husband's estate for a total $8 million exclusion. If the surviving spouse is predeceased by more than one spouse, the exclusion amount available is limited to the lesser of $5 million or the unused exclusion of the last deceased spouse.

Gift Taxes: For gifts made after 2010, the gift tax is reunified with the estate tax with a top gift tax rate of 35 percent and a maximum exclusion amount of $5 million.

Tax Relief Act of 2010: Quick Guide

The Tax Relief, Unemployment Insurance Reauthorization, and Job Creation Act of 2010 was signed into law on December 17, 2010. Here's quick guide to some of the changes.

Tax Rates

	Before Act	After Act
Federal income tax brackets	Five 2011 tax brackets: 15%, 28%, 31%, 36%, 39.6%	Six 2010 tax brackets extended to 2011 and 2012: 10%, 15%, 25%, 28%, 33%, 35%
Maximum tax rate on long-term capital gains	Starting in 2011: 20% (10% for individuals in the 15% tax bracket)[1]	2010 rates extended to 2011 and 2012: 15% (0% for individuals in the 10% or 15% tax brackets)
Tax on qualifying dividends	Taxed as ordinary income starting in 2011	2010 treatment extended to 2011 and 2012: 15% (0% for individuals in the 10% or 15% tax brackets)
Alternative minimum tax (AMT)	Exemption amounts 2010: • $45,000 (married joint) • $33,750 (single) • $22,500 (married separate)	Exemption amounts 2010: • $72,450 (married joint) • $47,450 (single) • $36,225 (married separate) Exemption amounts 2011: • $74,450 (married joint) • $48,450 (single) • $37,225 (married separate)
	Personal tax credits not allowed against AMT beginning in 2010	Personal tax credits allowed against AMT in 2010 and 2011

Tax Relief Act of 2010: Quick Guide *(continued)*

Estate Tax

	Before Act	After Act
Top estate tax rate	No estate tax for 2010 (modified carryover basis rules applied), estate tax would return in 2011 with top rate of 55%	Estate tax retroactively reinstated for 2010; top rate of 35% applies to 2010, 2011, and 2012
Estate tax exemption equivalent amount (basic exclusion amount, formerly called applicable exclusion amount)	No estate tax for 2010 (modified carryover basis rules applied), estate tax would return in 2011 with $1 million applicable exclusion amount	$5 million basic exclusion amount applies to 2010, 2011, and 2012[2]; ($5 million amount will be indexed for inflation in 2012)
Portability of exemption amount	N/A	For 2011 and 2012, when one spouse dies, any unused portion of that spouse's estate tax exemption equivalent amount may be transferred to the surviving spouse

Gift and Generation-Skipping Transfer Tax

	Before Act	After Act
Gift tax	For 2010: $1 million lifetime exemption equivalent, top rate of 35% For 2011: $1 million lifetime exemption, top rate of 55%	For 2011 and 2012, there will be a $5 million lifetime exemption equivalent, estate tax rates (top rate of 35%) applies
Generation-skipping transfer tax (GSTT)	No GSTT for 2010, $1 million exemption for 2011 with tax rate of 55%	GSTT exemption amount for 2010, 2011, and 2012 is $5 million; 0% rate applies for 2010; tax rate of 35% applies for 2011 and 2012

(continues)

Tax Relief Act of 2010: Quick Guide *(continued)*

Business/Self-Employed Individuals

	Before Act	After Act
"Bonus" depreciation	50% additional first-year depreciation allowed for 2010, no bonus depreciation beginning in 2011	100% bonus depreciation for property acquired and placed in service after 9/8/10 and before 1/1/12, 50% bonus depreciation allowed for property acquired and placed in service after 12/31/11 and before 1/1/13
IRC Section 179 expensing	For 2010 and 2011, $500,000 expense limit, reduced by amount by which cost of qualifying property placed in service during the year exceeds $2 million; beginning in 2012, limit would be reduced to $25,000 with $200,000 phase-out threshold	2010 and 2011 unchanged; for 2012, the limit will be set at $125,000, reduced by amount by which cost of qualifying property placed in service during the year exceeds $500,000 ($125,000 and $500,000 amounts indexed for inflation)
Tax credit for research and experimentation expenses	Expired at the end of 2009	Retroactively reinstated for 2010 and extended through 2011
New markets tax credit	Expired at the end of 2009	Retroactively reinstated for 2010 and extended through 2011
Indian employment tax credit	Expired at the end of 2009	Retroactively reinstated for 2010 and extended through 2011

Source: Steve Leightman of RBC Wealth Management.

[1] Slightly lower rates would apply to qualifying property held for 5 or more years.

[2] For individuals who died in 2010, an election can be made to choose the estate tax provisions in effect prior to the Act.

D American Tax Relief Act of 2012

Finally passed on January 1, 2013 (Congress still can't get the year right), the new law provides for the following:

1. INCOME TAX RATE INCREASE?

Not for you unless you make more than $400,000 ($450,000 for joint returns). If you're part of the 2 percent that may get hit with this extra tax, suck it up! It's only another 4.6 percent and that only applies to the excess over the $400,000 ($450,000). So, a couple making $500,000 would pay an extra $2,300 ($50,000 × 4.6%). The rest of us are still paying under the old Bush rates.

2. PAYROLL TAX INCREASE

Even if your rates stay the same, your check is going to be smaller. Facing a projected shortage in future funds to pay benefits, fiscal fools in Congress had cut the employee half of the Social Security tax from 6.2 percent to 4.0 percent. Those self-employed also enjoyed a 2 percent reduction in their obligation. This payroll tax holiday ended in 2012. For 2013, you'll pay an additional 2 percent on as much as $113,700, or as much as $2,274.

3. DIVIDENDS

Qualified dividends are still taxed at a reduced rate. For those at the $400,000/$450,000 income levels, the top rate was increased from 15 to 20 percent. That's still a lot lower than the 39.6 percent dividend rate originally proposed by the Obama administration. "Qualified dividends" are those held for an extended period. Technically, you start with the ex-dividend date, the date on which the company looks at its books for a list of shareholders who will get the dividend. Go back 60 days and forward 60 days. If you held the stock for any 60 days during that 121 day period, the dividends are "qualified" for the lower rate.

4. CAPITAL GAINS

The top tax on net long-term capital gains also jumped from 15 to 20 percent, but only for those at the $400,000/$450,000 income levels. To qualify as "long term," the asset must have been held for more than 1 year. It must be *more* than 1 year. Exactly 1 year defines your gain as short term, subject to a rate as high as 35 percent, and up to 39.6 percent for those at the $400,000/$450,000 levels.

For those in the 10 or 15 percent tax brackets, both qualified dividends and long-term capital gains continue to be taxed at a *zero* rate.

5. 3.8 PERCENT MEDICARE SURTAX

This wasn't part of the fiscal cliff deal, but you better be aware of it if you earn more than $200,000 ($250,000 for joint filers). To the extent your investment income (interest, dividends, rents, royalties, distribution from nonqualified annuities, income from passive activities, etc.) exceeds these levels, you're hit with an additional 3.8 percent Medicare surtax. So, if you're a single filer with $230,000 in income of which $30,000 is investment income, you're hit with an additional tax of $1,140 ($30,000 × 3.8%). That brings the potential tax on short-term dividends for high-income taxpayers to as much as 43.40 percent (39.6% + 3.9%).

6. PERMANENT AMT FIX

This awfully mean tax is a required alternative minimum tax computation that claws back certain deductions such as taxes paid and miscellaneous itemized deductions, denies you any deductions for personal exemptions, gives you an exemption deduction that disappears as your income increases, and applies a flat 26/28 percent rate on the balance. You pay the higher of the AMT or your regular tax.

The exemption amount was scheduled to fall to $33,750 ($45,000 on joint returns). Had that happened, as much as an additional 100 million taxpayers would have been hit with an AMT created tax increase. The new deal increases the exemption to $50,600 ($78,750 for joint returns) and indexes it for inflation for future years ($51,900 for individuals, $80,750 on joint returns, for 2013).

7. STATE AND LOCAL SALES TAX DEDUCTION

You can elect to deduct state and local sales taxes in lieu of income taxes as an itemized deduction on your Schedule A. This is a great benefit for taxpayers living in states without a state income tax, such as Alaska, New Hampshire, Tennessee, Florida, South Dakota, Washington, Nevada, Texas, and Wyoming.

The new tax deal extends this expired deduction for 2 years, 2012 and 2013.

8. TEACHER'S TAX DEDUCTION

From January 1, 2002, through 2011, you got an above-the-line deduction (you didn't have to itemize to get this) of up to $250 for expenses paid for books, supplies, computer equipment, and supplementary materials if you qualified as an eligible educator. That's a kindergarten through grade 12

teacher, aide, instructor, counselor, or principal in a school for at least 900 hours during the year.

The new tax deal extends this deduction for 2 years, 2012 and 2013.

9. BENEFITS

The new law makes permanent the $5,250 exclusion for employer-provided education assistance for college and graduate school education. It also extends through 2013 the monthly exclusion from income for employer-provided mass transit benefits from $125 to $240, and it makes permanent the $10,000 tax exemption for adoption expenses paid by your employer. Also made permanent was the $10,000 tax credit (a credit is a dollar-for-dollar reduction in your tax) for families that pay for their own adoption expenses.

10. ESTATE TAXES

Scheduled to drop to $1 million, the estate tax exclusion was raised to $5 million with a 40 percent top rate (the top rate for 2012 was 35 percent). Portability of a spouse's unused exclusion amount was made permanent. That means that there is now zero federal estate tax on a married couple unless their combined estate is more than $10 million.

Unless indicated otherwise, all of the above changes are made permanent. Note also that when the law refers to "income" here, it means taxable income, after all deductions.

11. EXTENSIONS

The new deal extends for 5 years the $1,000 child tax credit (which would have dropped to $500), the earned income tax credit, and the $2,500 American Opportunity Tax Credit for college tuition. It also permanently allows a $2,000 contribution to Coverdell Education Accounts, which otherwise would have fallen to $500, and permanently excludes as much as $5,250 in employer-provided education assistance.

The $2 million exclusion of cancellation of indebtedness on your principal residence income was extended through 2013.

The Work Opportunity Tax Credit, the Individual Energy Efficient Residence Improvement Tax Credit ($500 total, $200 for windows and skylights), and the Renewable Resources Tax Credit for facilities that produce energy from wind were all extended through 2013.

The deduction for mortgage insurance premiums as interest and the above-the-line deduction for tuition and fees were both extended through 2013.

It also extends for 2 years (2012 and 2013) the tax-free distribution of direct charitable donations of IRA assets up to $100,000 for taxpayers age 70½ or older. That means such distributions are not even included in income and don't reduce deductions that must exceed a percent of your adjusted gross income to be allowable—e.g., the 10 percent floor for medical expenses and the 2 percent floor for miscellaneous itemized deductions.

12. LIMITATIONS

The new law revives the "Pease" *limitations on itemized deductions* for singles with incomes of $250,000 or more and joint returns showing income of $300,000 or more.

It also restores the *personal exemption phase-out* for individuals with the same income thresholds.

13. BUSINESS PROVISIONS

For 2012 and 2013, Code Section 179 expensing limits were raised to $500,000 with a $2 million investment limit.

The 50 percent bonus depreciation was extended through 2013.

E Tax Increase Prevention Act of 2014

What do you call an organization that waits until there's two weeks left in the year to pass a law (affecting multiple sections of the Tax Code) that expires at the end of that same year? Here, we call it the U.S. Congress.

In an amazing display of ineptitude, our representatives finally passed the Tax Increase Prevention Act of 2014, which extended more than 50 provisions of the Tax Code that had expired on December 31, 2013, until December 31, 2014. But, the Tax Increase Extension Act of 2014 had a shorter shelf live than a carton of eggs! Signed by President Obama on December 18, the law retroactively reinstates what we call the "extenders," because they constantly expire and are then renewed at the last minute by Congress.

Among the most popular, all retroactively extended *only through 2014*, are:

1. STATE AND LOCAL SALES TAX DEDUCTION

You can continue to elect to deduct state and local sales taxes in lieu of income taxes as an itemized deduction on your Schedule A. This is a great benefit for taxpayers living in states without a state income tax, such as

Alaska, New Hampshire, Tennessee, Florida, South Dakota, Washington, Nevada, Texas, and Wyoming.

2. TEACHER'S TAX DEDUCTION

This is the above the line deduction (you don't have to itemize to get this) of up to $250 for expenses paid for books, supplies, computer equipment, and supplementary materials if you qualified as an eligible educator. That's a kindergarten through grade 12 teacher, aide, instructor, counselor, or principal in a school for at least 900 hours during the year.

3. BENEFITS

The law extended through 2014 the monthly exclusion from income for employer-provided mass transit benefits to $250, on "parity" with the exclusion for employer-provided parking.

4. MISCELLANEOUS INDIVIDUAL EXTENSIONS

The $2 million exclusion of *cancellation of indebtedness* on your principal residence income was extended through 2014, as was the provision allowing the deduction of *mortgage insurance premiums* as interest.

The above the line deduction for *tuition and fees* and the *non-business energy credit* were both extended through 2014.

The new law also extended the tax-free distribution of *direct charitable donations of IRA* assets up to $100,000 for taxpayers age 70½ or older. That means such distributions are not even included in income and don't reduce deductions that must exceed a percent of your adjusted gross income to be allowable—e.g., the 10 percent floor for medical expenses and the 2 percent floor for miscellaneous itemized deductions. Such contributions also count against your minimum distribution requirements.

5. BUSINESS PROVISIONS

Code Section 179 *expensing limits* were retroactively raised to $500,000 with a $2 million investment limit through 2014.

The 50 percent *bonus depreciation* was extended through 2014. For auto depreciation, this increased the maximum first-year deduction from $3,160 to $11,160, an $8,000 difference.

The *research tax credit* and the *Work Opportunity tax credit* were both extended through 2014.

Suggestion for our elected representatives: When you got back from "recess" (all children need recess), it would have been both reasonable and appropriate for you to have passed the "extenders" in January at least through 2015 so some appropriate financial planning could be done. Once again you failed to do so as this book is being written, the extenders have not yet been renewed. It's real hard to plan if you don't know the rules.

F The ABLE Act

Also passed at the end of the year was the Achieving a Better Life Experience (ABLE) Act of 2014. Starting in 2015, it creates a tax favored savings account for people under the age of 26 who are blind or disabled. Up to the amount of the gift tax exclusion (currently $14,000 per year) can be put into an account similar to a Section 529 account. No tax until distributions are made and no tax on those distributions if used for transportation, education, job training, or housing expenses. Nonqualified distributions would be subject to tax on their earnings portion plus a 10 percent penalty. Account owners would remain eligible for Medicaid and balances of $100,000 or less wouldn't affect SSI benefits. ABLE accounts, like Section 529 accounts will be set up by each state. You can live in one state and establish accounts in other states.

Here's what ABLE accounts can pay for:

- **Education**—Tuition for preschool thru post-secondary education, books, supplies, and educational materials related to such education, tutors, and special education services.

- **Housing**—Expenses for a primary residence, including rent, purchase of a primary residence or an interest in a primary residence, mortgage payments, home improvements and modifications, maintenance and repairs, real property taxes, and utility charges.

- **Transportation**—Expenses for transportation, including the use of mass transit, the purchase or modification of vehicles, and moving expenses.

- **Employment Support**—Expenses related to obtaining and maintaining employment, including job-related training, assistive technology, and personal assistance supports.

- **Health and Wellness**—Expenses for health and wellness, including premiums for health insurance; mental health, medical, vision, and dental expenses; habilitation and rehabilitation services; durable medical

equipment; therapy; respite care; long-term services and supports; nutritional management; communication services and devices; adaptive equipment; assistive technology; and personal assistance.

- **Assistive Technology and Personal Support**—Expenses for assistive technology and personal support with respect to any of the above.

- **Miscellaneous Expenses**—Financial management and administrative services, legal fees, expenses for oversight, monitoring, and funeral and burial expenses.

G More Changes

a) On December 18, 2014, President Obama signed legislation (HR 2591) to give certain airline employees the option to contribute bankruptcy settlements to retirement accounts without incurring a penalty. This provision was made available to employees of airlines following their bankruptcies but expired before American Airlines sought bankruptcy protection in 2011.

Sen. James Inhofe, R-Okla., introduced Sen 2614 on July 16, with Sen. Sherrod Brown, D-Ohio, chairman of the Senate Finance Subcommittee on Social Security. The House passed the bill on December 11 and the Senate on December 13.

"The bankruptcy caused those employed by American Airlines to suffer the loss of their earned pensions, and this legislation will give them the opportunity to rebuild their future without penalty from the federal government," said Inhofe. *The Worker, Retiree, and Employer Recovery Act of 2008* (P.L. 110-458) allowed employees of air service providers, who filed bankruptcy prior to 2007, to roll up to 90 percent of airline bankruptcy settlements into an individual retirement account without paying tax penalties through April 15, 2013. American Airlines did not declare bankruptcy until November 29, 2011, and had not yet emerged from bankruptcy by April 15, 2013.

b) On May 22, 2015 President Obama signed the *Don't Tax Our Fallen Public Safety Heroes Act*, which makes contributions to the families of public safety workers (police officers, paramedics, firefighters, etc.) who are killed or disabled in the line of duty exempt from federal income tax. The exclusion applies to payments from the Bureau of Justice Assistance and similar state-run benefit programs.

Retirement plan withdrawals by public safety workers at age 50 will now be exempt from the 10 percent penalty tax after December 31, 2015.

c) *Protecting Americans from the Tax Hikes Act of 2015:* The PATH Act
Somebody please buy them a calendar. Once again our Congress waited until the last two weeks in December 2015 to pass a new extenders bill. But, this time they extended some provisions through 2019 and actually made others permanent.

Some provisions will still expire at the end of 2016, however, and they will need to be revisited. The following provisions were extended through 2016:

- The exclusion of up to $2 million in mortgage debt cancellation on a principal residence from income.

- The treatment of mortgage insurance premiums as deductible qualified residence interest.

- The above-the-line deduction for tuition and related expenses.

- The 10 percent residential energy property credit capped at $500. Over a dozen other incentives for energy production and conservation were also modified and extended.

The following provisions were extended and modified through 2019:

- The Work Opportunity Tax Credit, modified and enhanced for employers who hire long term unemployed individuals (unemployed 27 weeks or more) to 40 percent of the first $6,000 in wages.

- Bonus depreciation, at 50 percent for 2015–2017 phased down to 40 percent in 2018 and 30 percent in 2019.

- The New Markets Tax Credit.

The following provisions were made *permanent:*

- The Research & Development credit.

- The Section 179 expensing limit of $500,000 (now indexed for inflation beginning in 2016).

- The exclusion of 100 percent of gain on certain small business stock.

- The reduced earned income threshold amount of $3,000 to qualify for the child tax credit. This $1,000 per child credit may be refundable to the extent of 15 percent of your earned income in excess of $3,000.

- The American Opportunity Tax credit.

- The increase in phase-out amount for joint filers and the increased credit percentage for taxpayers with three or more qualifying children under the Earned Income Credit.

- The up to $250 (indexed beginning in 2016) above the line deduction for certain expenses of elementary and secondary school educators. As of 2016, professional development expenses qualify.

- Parity for exclusion from income for employer-provided mass transit and parking benefits. Both are inflation adjusted at $255 for 2016. The exclusion for qualified bicycle reimbursement is unchanged at $20 per month.

- The deduction of state and local sales taxes in lieu of deducting state and local income taxes.

- The maximum $100,000 exclusion for charitable distributions from an IRA for those aged 70½ or older.

- The 15-year straight line recovery for qualified leasehold improvements to retail and restaurant property.

- The employer wage credit for employees who are active duty member of the uniformed services.

- Business charitable deduction for the contributions of food inventory.

- Under Section 529 plans, the purchase of computer equipment and technology are now qualified expenses.

- Section 529 accounts may now be rolled over into ABLE accounts. ABLE accounts now need not be established only in the state of residence of the ABLE account owner.

Finally, two Obamacare taxes were delayed or given a temporary moratorium.

1. The 40 percent excise tax on employer-sponsored Cadillac health plans will now begin in 2020, a two-year delay from the original 2018 effective date.

2. The 2.3 percent tax on medical device sales was suspended for 2016 and 2017.

On October 7, 2016, then President Obama signed into law H.R. 5946—*United States Appreciation for Olympians and Paralympians Act of 2016*. In general, effective for prizes and awards received after December 31, 2015, gross income

does not include the value of any medal awarded, or any prize money received from the U.S. Olympic Committee on account of competition in the Olympic Games or Paralympic Games. This gross income exception does not apply if the taxpayer's adjusted gross income exceeds $1 million ($500,000 for MFS) for the year of the prize.

In December, former President Obama signed the *21st Century Cures Act* (P.L. 114-255). The new law allows certain small businesses to use qualified small business health reimbursement accounts (HRAs) without risking penalties under the Affordable Care Act. Certain limits to the accounts would apply, including an annual cap of $4,950 per year ($10,000 for families).

Obama also signed in December the *Combat-Injured Veterans Tax Fairness Act of 2016* (P.L. 114-292). The measure is intended to refund money that was improperly withheld for tax purposes from severance payments to certain veterans of the U.S. Armed Forces. Generally, severance payments for veterans separated from the armed forces because of combat-related injuries are not income. The law extends the time for filing a claim to remedy the improper withholding.

The *Disaster Tax Relief and Airport and Airway Extension Act of 2017* signed September 29, 2017 gave relief to victims of Hurricanes Harvey, Irma and Maria. **For taxpayers affected** it:

- Raised the casualty subtraction from $100 to $500 but eliminated the 10 percent of adjusted gross income subtraction. But, you can claim the loss back to your 2016 tax return.

- Eliminated the 10 percent penalty for premature retirement plan distributions up to $100,000 from IRA or qualified retirement plans.

- Allowed recontributions of qualified hurricane retirement plan distributions within 3 years (rather than 60 days).

- Allowed the income from qualified hurricane retirement plan distributions to be spread over 3 years.

- Allowed distributions received between March 1, 2017 and September 20, 2017 to buy or build a principle residence in the hurricanes locations that did not go through because of the storms to be recontributed tax free between August 23, 2017 and February 28, 2018.

- Allowed charitable contributions for storm relief to be deducted up to 100 percent of your adjusted gross income (normally limited to 50 percent).

- Allowed the use of 2016 rather than 2017 income for computing the Earned Income Tax Credit (EITC) and Child Tax Credit (CTC).

- Allowed the claiming of storm casualty losses even if you don't itemize.
- Allowed qualified plan loans up to the lessor of $100,000 or 100 percent of your account balance (normally limited to the greater of $50,000 or 50 percent).

H The Tax Cuts and Jobs Act of 2017

President Trump got his Christmas present. With less than two weeks left in the year, the more than 500 page Tax Cuts and Jobs Act was passed by Congress on December 20, 2017 creating massive and sweeping changes to out Tax Code. The IRS will create or revise approximately 450 forms, publications, and instructions as well as modify about 140 information technology systems. Some changes are permanent . . . others, mostly the individual tax cuts, expire at the end of 2015.

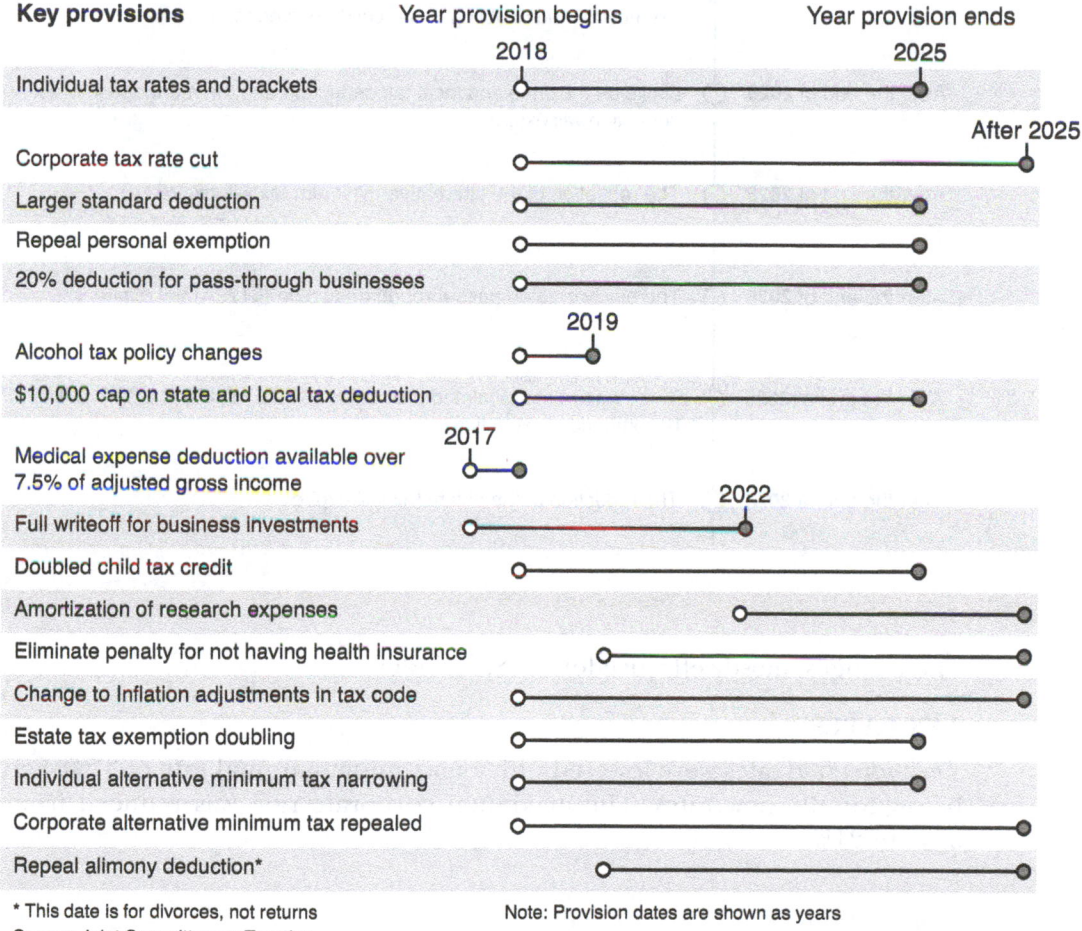

Key provisions	Year provision begins	Year provision ends
	2018	2025
Individual tax rates and brackets		
Corporate tax rate cut		After 2025
Larger standard deduction		
Repeal personal exemption		
20% deduction for pass-through businesses		
Alcohol tax policy changes	2019	
$10,000 cap on state and local tax deduction		
Medical expense deduction available over 7.5% of adjusted gross income	2017	
Full writeoff for business investments		2022
Doubled child tax credit		
Amortization of research expenses		
Eliminate penalty for not having health insurance		
Change to Inflation adjustments in tax code		
Estate tax exemption doubling		
Individual alternative minimum tax narrowing		
Corporate alternative minimum tax repealed		
Repeal alimony deduction*		

* This date is for divorces, not returns
Note: Provision dates are shown as years
Source: Joint Committee on Taxation

TIMELINE

After the end of **2018**	Businesses will be required to deduct re-search and experimentation costs over five years, rather than immediately
After the end of **2021**	The deduction for business net interest expense will be limited to 30% of EBIT, rather than 30% of EBITDA
After the end of **2021**	Full expensing for short-life business investments will begin phasing out
After the end of **2022**	The reduction of individual income tax rates will expire
After the end of **2025**	The increase in the standard deduction, elimination of the personal exemption, and doubling of the child tax credit will expire
After the end of **2025**	Limits on the state and local tax deduction and the mortgage interest deduction will expire
After the end of **2025**	The reduction of the alternative minimum tax will expire
After the end of **2025**	The newly created pass-through deduction (§199A) will expire
After the end of **2025**	Three international-related provisions (GILTI, FDII, and BEAT) will become more restrictive
After the end of **2025**	The reduction of the estate tax will expire

The changes, mostly effective for 2018, include:

TAX RATES

The individual rates were lowered with a maximum marginal rate of 37%. See below for the new rates. The maximum corporate rate was reduced from 35% to 21%.

Individual Income Taxes

Old Law				The Tax Cuts and Jobs Act			
Seven-bracket progressive rate income tax with a top marginal rate of 39.6 percent.				Retains seven brackets, but at reduced rates, including a top marginal rate of 37 percent. Provisions sunset at end of 2025.			
Rate	Single	HoH	Joint	Rate	Single	HoH	Joint
10%	$0–9,524	$0–13,599	$0–19,049	10%	$0–9,524	$0–13,599	$0–19,049
15%	$9,525	$13,600	$19,050	12%	$9,525	$13,600	$19,050
25%	$38,700	$51,800	$77,400	22%	$38,700	$51,800	$77,400
28%	$93,700	$133,850	$156,150	24%	$82,500	$82,500	$165,000
33%	$195,450	$216,700	$237,950	32%	$157,500	$157,500	$315,000
35%	$424,950	$424,950	$424,950	35%	$200,000	$200,000	$400,000
39.6%	$426,700	$453,350	$480,050	37%	$500,000	$500,000	$600,000

INDEXING

Changed from Traditional CPI to Chained CPI to measure inflation. Results in a smaller percentage growth factor and higher taxes than otherwise would have been due.

ABOVE THE LINE DEDUCTIONS

Moving expenses are GONE except for active military personnel. If reimbursed by your employer, that's taxable income to you. For divorces after 2018, *alimony* will be treated like child support – not deductible by the payer nor income to the payee. *Tuition and fees* deduction allowed to expire (subsequently extended through 2017 – see below). Other above the line deductions retained, including the deduction for educators and student loan interest and the graduate school tuition waiver.

PERSONAL EXEMPTION

GONE! Would have been $4,150 for 2018.

STANDARD DEDUCTION

Doubled! $12,000 for singles; $18,000 for head of household; and $24,000 for joint returns. The additional standard deduction for the elderly and blind was retained. More people will claim the standard deduction but the benefit of the

increase, net of the loss of the personal exemption deduction, may be minimal. (the Joint Committee on Taxation projects a 61.35, decrease in those who itemized in 2018). For example, a couple with two 17 year old children would have had a standard deduction of $13,000 plus $4,150 times 4 ($16,600) for a total deduction of $29,600. Now, they only get $24,000 for a loss of $5,600.

ITEMIZED DEDUCTIONS

Lots of changes here. *The medical floor* of 7.5% is retained for 2017 and 2018 then returning to 10%. *Mortgage interest* is limited to $750,000 in acquisition/improvement debt for primary and secondary homes. Existing mortgages grandfathered with a $1 million limit. No deduction for any interest on debt in excess of the $750,000 and home equity for non-home improvements disallowed. You can no longer borrow against your home to purchase a car or go on vacation and deduct the interest paid. The total allowed for *state and local taxes* (or sales taxes) plus real estate taxes is capped at $10,000. The law specifically prohibits the prepayment of a future year's income tax but there's no reason why your fourth quarter estimated state income tax and first quarter real estate taxes can't be prepaid in December on alternate years when your total itemized deductions are close to your standard deduction. The 50% of adjusted gross income limit for public *charity* deductions is raised to 60%, but you no longer get any deduction for money paid for rights to tickets to athletic events. *Casualty losses* limited to those in Presidentially declared disaster areas under Section 401 of the Robert T. Stafford Disaster Relief and Emergency Assistance Act.

All other *miscellaneous deductions* – GONE!

No more deductions for employee business expenses, union dues, safe deposit fees, personal tax preparation, investment expenses or tax and investment planning. However, the reduction in total itemized deductions for high income taxpayers is repealed.

The elimination of the employee business expense deduction creates a significant burden on employees but comes with a unique opportunity. Employees can no longer deduct business expenses on their personal return. If your employer grants you a flat stipend to cover business expenses, that is taxable income. Consider what the IRS calls an "Accountable Plan". An accountable plan (see page 480) must be supported by employee provided business expense documentation. Employees provide this detailed business expense documentation to employers who then reimburse employees tax free. Then the employer takes the business deduction. Even in a worst-case scenario, have your employer reduce your salary by the amount of your businesses expenses. Then you get the equivalent of the benefit of business

expense deduction, because reimbursement under an accountable plan is not included in your income. As an employee you are better off than previous tax year calculations because you are no longer must reduce your employee business deduction by 2% of your adjusted gross income. Also, as an employee you are not subject to payroll taxes on income not received, nor income tax on those payroll taxes that would have been paid. There is more money in your pocket after tax. Your employer gets to deduct the expenses directly in lieu of salary and saves on payroll taxes. Both employee and employer win, but only by providing the necessary and appropriate documentation to the essential accountable plan.

If you want to deduct you must substantiate. Like all expenses, business expenses for use of mobility devices and networks need to be accumulated, categorized and recorded. This is not only important for employees, but for any business that uses gig workers or independent contractors and reimburses them for their directly related business expenses. The issue is identifying the *business* expenses. Only with the required supporting detailed documentation of actual business expenses incurred will a company reimburse its employees, gig workers and independent contractors.

I recommend a U.S. patented solution from mobilityView, Inc. (http://www.mobilityView.com) which automates the separation of business versus personal use of mobile devices and services. mobilityView's Mobile Cost Management (MCM) solution works on every mobile/wireless operator in the world and on Android and iOS. It provides the necessary documentation (in near real time) down to the penny for each call, SMS, and megabyte of data in local and roaming situations. It clearly separates business versus personal for both use and cost. Essentially you now need a mileage book for your smartphone just like you need a mileage book for your car to denote business and personal mileage. You can find one here: http://www.mobilityview.com/align The MCM solution is a critical tool providing governance and documentation to substantiate to the satisfaction of the IRS.

It also protects employers from any claims of under reimbursement of mobile usage. There have been cases in a variety of states where the courts have required employee reimbursement for legitimate business usage (see *Cochran v. Schwan's Home Services, Inc.* in California and *Mohammedi v. Nwabuis* in Texas).

Full disclosure—I was so impressed with mobilityView's ability to provide optimum personal privacy, mobile cost management and productivity insights, that I became a consultant to the company. Email: howtopayzerotaxes@mobilityview.com and mention *How To Pay Zero Taxes*, to receive a free 60 day trial! For more personal service contact Bob.Bonocore@mobilityView.com or call him at 856.220.4157 on U.S. East Coast time.

CREDITS

The $1,000 credit for each child under age 17 has been increased to $2,000 per child, with as much as $1,400 being refundable. There is also a new $500 credit for each dependent who is not a qualifying child – e.g. an elderly parent or a disabled adult child. The adjusted gross income phase-out begins at $400,000 for joint returns and $200,000 for all others (up from $110,000 and $75,000 in 2017).

SECTION 529 ACCOUNTS

Expanded to cover tuition for students in K-12 private schools, including religious schools.

ENTERTAINMENT EXPENSES

DEAD as of 2018. You no longer can deduct the cost of football games or theater tickets to entertain clients. President Trump's revenge on the NFL? Company picnics and holiday parties are still 100% allowed as employee benefits.

New Entertainment Rules

1. Coffee, tea, bottled water provided in the break room—50%.*

2. Breakfast, lunch, and dinner—50%.*

3. Air travel for golf or other entertainment event—0%.

4. Entertainment and meals during *employee* or *stockholder business* meetings—50% for meals, 100% for non-meal entertainment.

5. Clients or customer restaurant meals—0% if part of entertainment, if not, 50% deductible.

6. Company cafeteria—pre-2026 meals 50%.* Post 2025, cafeteria meals and operating expenses are 0% deductible.

ALTERNATIVE MINIMUM TAX

Corporate AMT is gone. . . . personal AMT retained with higher exemption and phaseout thresholds (for joint filers, the exemption goes to $109,400 with a phaseout threshold of $1 million).

* If part of non-discriminatory employee social or recreational activity—100% deductible.

Type of Expense	Percentage Deductible		
	100%	50%	0%
MEALS			
Recreational employee meals Holiday Party Employee Picnics	X		
Meals provided to an employee at work		X	
Meals provided to the public to foster business Open House	X		
Food and beverage expense directly related to business leagues Chambers Of Commerce Business Leagues Boards of Trade Real Estate Boards		X	
Meals when traveling overnight on business		X	
Meals with a business prospect, customer or employee where business is discussed Mentor Lunches Trade Shows Client/Customer Seminars External/Internal Referral Lunches Parties With Clients Meals Before/After Entertainment Shareholder/Employee Meetings		X	
Meals with a business prospect, customer or employee where no business is discussed		X	
Lavish or extravagant meals			X
ENTERTAINMENT			
Entertaining a client or customer whether or not business is discussed Golfing All Entertainment Activities Meals At Games/Entertainment Facility			X
Tickets to a sporting event where business is discussed Hockey/Football/Baseball Games			X
Tickets for a sporting event that you did not attend			X
Lavish or extravagant entertainment expenses Club dues/Membership Fee's Country Club Social Club Fees Athletic and Sporting Club/Organization			X
Skybox lease fees or other entertainment facility fees such as hunting facility fees			X
TRAVEL			
Local travel for business purposes	X		
Out of town travel for business purposes	X		
Non-business travel			X

COMMUTER BENEFITS

Starting in 2018, employers can no longer deduct the $260 parking and transit pass fringe benefit for employees. Employees can still receive the benefits tax free but the employer can not deduct them. Bicycle commuting reimbursements are still deductible. But as of 2018, the reimbursement is included in your income.

ROTH CONVERSIONS

In the past, you could undo a conversion to a ROTH IRA by October 15th of the following year. Starting in 2018, such conversions are irreversible.

INVESTORS

The capital gain rates remain the same. . . .and the LIFO proposal did NOT make it into the final bill. But, you lost your deduction for investment fees and expenses, and LIKE KIND EXCHANGES are now limited to real estate ONLY!

KIDDIE TAX

Such income was taxed at the parents' marginal rate . . . now taxed at the same rate as trusts and estates. On a 2018 joint return, the top 37% rate kicks in at $600,000. For trusts and estates, that top rate hits income over $12,500.

INTELLECTUAL PROPERTY

Sales of self-created property (or property acquired with a substituted or transferred basis from the creator) such as an invention, patent, design or secret formula would be taxed as ordinary income. Music composers and copyright holders can continue to treat such sales as sales of capital assets.

INDIVIDUAL MANDATE

Still technically alive for 2018 . . . but the penalty for failure to comply is $0 in 2019.

ABLE ACCOUNTS

ABLE beneficiaries can now contribute into their own ABLE accounts and money in a Section 529 account can now be rolled over into an ABLE account (but this counts toward the $15,000 annual limit).

401(k) BORROWERS

If you borrowed from your 401(k) plan and lost your job, you had to repay the loan within 60 days or it would be considered additional income. The new law extends the repayment date to the due date for their tax return for the year.

MARRIAGE PENALTY

Still around. Two singles can deduct $10,000 each in state and local taxes but only a single $10,000 deduction is allowed on a joint return; the top 37% rate

applies to income of $600,000 or above on a joint return, singles get to earn $500,000 each before that rate applies.

BUSINESS EXPENSING

Full expensing of *new* and *used* capital investment through 2022. As of 2023, the 100% allowance would be phased down 20% each year. Section 179 expensing increased to $1 million. (This is known as "Bonus Depreciation".)

Bonus Depreciation Percentage

Placed in Service Year	Qualified Property in General/Specified Plants	Longer Production Period Property and Certain Aircraft
Portion of Basis of Qualified Property Acquired before Sept. 28, 2017		
Sept. 28, 2017–Dec. 31, 2017	50 percent	50 percent
2018	40 percent	50 percent
2019	30 percent	40 percent
2020	None	30 percent
2021 and thereafter	None	None
Portion of Basis of Qualified Property Acquired after Sept. 27, 2017		
Sept. 28, 2017–Dec. 31, 2022	100 percent	100 percent
2023	80 percent	100 percent
2024	60 percent	80 percent
2025	40 percent	60 percent
2026	20 percent	40 percent
2027	None	20 percent
2028 and thereafter	None	None

LISTED PROPERTY

Computers and peripheral equipment removed from the definition of listed property. . . no longer subject to enhanced substantiation requirements.

ESTATE AND GIFT TAXES

Exclusions doubled . . . $11.18 million per person in 2018.

LOBBYING

Business expenses for lobbying local governments are no longer deductible.

SEXUAL HARASSMENT

Settlement payouts and legal fees relating to sexual harassment will not be allowable if the payments are subject to a non-disclosure agreement.

EMPLOYEE ACHIEVEMENT AWARDS

To clarify current law, such awards would not be qualified if the award was really compensation—e.g. cash, gift cards, vacations, meals, lodgings, theater or sports tickets, etc.

PAID LEAVE CREDIT

Employers who pay their employees 50% of their wages while they are on family or medical leave will receive a credit for 12.5% of wages paid . . . increased by 0.25% to as much as 25%, for each percentage point that the wages paid exceed 50% or normal earnings. The credit is available for as much as 12 weeks and is available for 2018 and 2019.

- A qualifying employer is one who:
 - Allows all qualifying FT employees at least two weeks of annual paid FMLA leave (and a prorata amount for non-FT employees); and
 - Has a leave program providing for at least 50% of normal wages.

- A qualifying employee is one who:
 - Has been employed for at least one year; and
 - Who had compensation in the previous year below 60% of the highly compensated threshold. The highly compensated threshold in 2018 is $120,000, meaning the compensation to be a qualifying employee for purposes of the credit is $72,000 for 2018.

ORPHAN DRUG CREDIT

Reduced from 50% to 25%.

CARRIED INTEREST

The holding period for long term capital gains is increased to three years with respect to certain partnership interests transferred in connection with the rendering of services.

QUALIFIED OPPORTUNITY ZONES

The Tax Cuts and Jobs Act of 2017 allows a temporary deferral of capital gains taxation if reinvested in a qualified opportunity fund and the permanent exclusion of capital gains from investments in a qualified opportunity fund. The designation

of census tracts as opportunity zones is made by a state's Governor with the number of tracts capped by statue. No election for deferral of gain allowed after 12/31/2026.

You have 180 days from the date of disposition to reinvest. The qualified opportunity fund must hold 90% of its assets in qualified opportunity zones property. If you hold the interest in the fund for at least five years, you receive a basis increase in the investment that equals 10 percent of the deferred gain that you invested in the fund. If you hold your interest in the fund for an additional two years (or, seven years total), you receive an additional increase in your basis that equals 5 percent of the deferred gain invested in the fund. If you are still holding the interest in the fund on Dec. 31, 2026, then, regardless of if you continues to hold the interest in the fund, you are required to recognize and pay taxes on the deferred gain on that day, subject to any increases in basis that you may have received for holding the property for five years or more.

If you continue to hold the interest in the fund after Dec. 31, 2026, for at least a total of 10 years, you receive a step up in basis in the interest so that your basis equals the fair market value. Therefore, you are not taxed on any appreciation in your interest. In order to receive a 10 percent increase in basis, you must invest in a fund by 2021 and in order to receive an additional 5 percent increase in basis, you must make an investment in a fund by 2019. Lastly, the business cannot be a private or commercial golf course, country club, massage parlor, hot tub facility, suntan facility, racetrack or other facility used for gambling, or any store the principal business of which is the sale of alcoholic beverages for consumption off premises." Tax Code Section 1400Z-2(d) (3) (iii).

AUTO DEPRECIATION CAPS

The limits on business depreciation deductions for autos was increased to $10,000 year one (was $3,160), $16,000 the second (was $5,100), $9,600 for the third year (up from $3,050) and $5,760 for each subsequent year (up from $1,875). Over the first four years, that's a total deduction of $41,360 compared to $13,185 under 2017 law. These numbers are before bonus depreciation which adds $8,000 to the limit.

PASS THROUGH DEDUCTION

This is a big one. About 90% of U.S. businesses are organized as pass-throughs. For 2018 through 2025, sole proprietorships, partnerships, limited liability companies and S corporations get a deduction of 20% of their domestic qualified business income. It applies to both service and non-service businesses. Specified service businesses are subject to limitations and a potential phaseout of the deduction if the taxpayer's taxable income exceeds $157,500 ($315,000 on a joint return). The phaseout is $50,000, $100,000 on a joint return.

Specified service businesses include those in health, law, consulting, athletics, financial services, brokerage services, or any trade or business where the principal asset of such trade or business is the reputation or skill of one of its employees or owner, or which involves the performance of services that consist of investing and investment management, trading, or dealing in securities, partnership interests, or commodities. Engineering and architecture services are specifically excluded from the definition. Real estate and insurance brokers were excluded from the definition by treasury department rules and will get the deduction.

If your taxable income is greater than the threshold amounts above, the deduction is limited to the greater of (a) 50% of the W-2 wages paid by the business, or (b) the sum of 25% of the W-2 wages paid or 25% of the wages plus 2.5% of the *unadjusted* basis of all qualified property. Qualified property is the tangible property of the business that is subject to depreciation.

Assume you are subject to the limit (exceed the taxable income threshold), have no employees, and bought a machine (your only business asset) for $100,000. Your deduction is limited to 2.5% of your original acquisition cost, or $2,500.

Alternatively, if you were not subject to the limit, your deduction on $100,000 in business income would be $20,000.

The ideal sweet spot for percentage of W2 wages versus overall income is 28.571428571, rounded to 28.57%. For example, assume you had $1,000,000 in qualified business income before the deduction. If you take wages of 28.57% of $1,000,000, the qualified business income is reduced by $285,700 to $714,300.

$$\$285,700 \times .50 = \$142,500$$
$$\$714,300 \times .20 = \$142,500$$

Total Taxable Income (e.g. similar to Line 43 of 2018 Form 1040)	Not exceeding threshold Single: $157,500 Joint: $315,000	Threshold plus Phase Outlin Single: $157,501- $207,500 Joint: $315,001- $415,000	Over Threshold Single: $207,501 Joint: $415,001
Specified Service trade or business (e.g. , accounting law, consulting)	Full 20% Deduction No W-2 Limit applied	20% Deduction subject to phase-out. W-2 Limit phased in	No 20% Deduction at all permitted, so W-2 Limit irrelevant
Non-specified Service trade or business (e.g. rental)	Full 20% Deduction No W-2 Limit applied	20% Deduction subject to phase-in of W-2 Limit	20% Deduction permitted but fully subject to W-2 Limit

Dividends from cooperatives and real estate investment trusts (REITs) and income from publicly traded partnerships would qualify. Income from agricultural and horticultural cooperatives and income from businesses conducted by trusts could also qualify.

The 20% deduction is not allowed in computing adjusted gross income but is instead is allowed as a deduction reducing taxable income. So, it does not affect limitations based on AGI. The deduction is available to both itemizers and those who take the standard deduction.

The IRS released proposed regulations on the pass-through deduction on August 8, 2018.

Winners: (not included as a "specific service trade or business") included retail bankers and insurance companies, health clubs, health spas, real estate agents and brokers, analysts, economists, mathematicians, and statisticians not engaged in analyzing or assessing the financial costs of risk or uncertainty of events, and analytics firms not offering financial risk-related insights.

Losers: (included under the umbrella as a "specific service trade or business") include investment bankers, financial advisors, managers of private equity or hedge funds, and wealth planners. Celebrities selling their names and likenesses as commodities and also ineligible.

Planning

1. You must be in a trade or business. How about renting out vacation homes or Airbnb transactions? Cases have validated a single rental as a "trade or business," but you must be involved in the activity with "continuity and regularity" to reach that standard.

2. Consider the use of multiple trusts as long as the beneficiaries of each trust are different. Set up a separate trust for each child. Contribute vacation property to gain the new $10,000 cap on the state and local tax deduction. Contribute investments generating passive income to absorb the real estate taxes paid.

3. The proposed technique known as "crack and park," where an entity "cracks apart" its "specified service" trade or business income from other income, "parking" everything it can into the side that qualifies for the deduction, was specified DENIED by the IRS—won't work!

4. The proposed technique to credit specified charitable donations for real estate taxes due on a local level is before the courts as this is written. *My prediction is that it won't work!* To get a charitable deduction, you need to

have made the donation with "detached and disinterested generosity." Such real estate tax substitution payments don't meet that criterion.

5. If your business has a small amount of service income, there is a de *minimus* exception:

If a business has gross receipts of $25 million or less, the rules disregard specified service income if it constitutes less than 10 percent of those gross receipts. For an owner with more than $25 million in gross receipts, the 10 percent threshold falls to 5 percent.

The Budget Deal Passed on February 9, 2018

The budget deal passed on February 9, 2018 contains several provisions that affected your 2017 tax return and were not reflected on your 2017 tax forms. Over 30 tax breaks were retroactively extended through 2017. Don't blame the IRS. It's not easy to print forms correctly if Congress changes the law after the year is over and people have already started filing their returns.

The following provisions were extended through 2017 unless otherwise noted:

- exclusion from gross income of discharge of qualified principal residence indebtedness;
- mortgage insurance premiums treated as qualified residence interest;
- above the line deduction for qualified tuition and related expenses;
- Indian employment tax credit;
- railroad track maintenance credit;
- mine rescue team training credit;
- classification of certain race horses as three-year property;
- seven-year recovery period for motorsports entertainment complexes;
- accelerated depreciation for business property on an Indian reservation;
- election to expense mine safety equipment;
- special expensing rules for certain productions;
- deduction allowable with respect to income attributable to domestic production activities in Puerto Rico;
- special rule relating to qualified timber gain;

- empowerment zone tax incentives;
- American Samoa economic development credit;
- nonbusiness energy property credit;
- nonresidential energy property credit (extended through 2021 and modified);
- new qualified fuel cell motor vehicles credit;
- credit for alternative fuel vehicle refueling property;
- credit for 2-wheeled plug-in electric vehicles;
- second generation biofuel producer credit;
- biodiesel and renewable diesel incentives;
- production of credit for Indian coal facilities (extended to a 12-year period);
- credits with respect to facilities producing energy from certain renewable resources;
- credit for energy-efficient new homes;
- energy credit (extended through 2021 and modified);
- special allowance for second generation biofuel plant property;
- energy efficient commercial buildings deduction;
- special rule for sales or dispositions to implement FERC or state electric restructuring policy for qualified electric utilities;
- excise tax credits relating to alternative fuels;
- oil spill liability trust fund financing rate;
- temporary increase in limit on cover over rum excise taxes to Puerto Rico and the Virgin Islands;
- waiver of limitations with respect to excluding from gross income amounts received by wrongfully incarcerated individuals (extended through December 18, 2018); and
- carbon dioxide sequestration credit (enhanced, modified and generally extended through 2023).

How to Avoid/Survive an IRS Audit

"Where deductions are based on a number of small items not susceptible to complete documentary substantiation, reasonable determinations should be made at the district examination level. Consideration will always be given to the reasonableness of the taxpayer's claimed deductions."

Policy Statement P4-39

"If we don't change our system of collecting taxes, it will break down . . . Our traditional approach cannot sustain an acceptable level of compliance."

IRS Commissioner SHIRLEY PETERSON
to the Annual Meeting of the
New York State Bar Association's Tax Section
(January 31, 1993)

"Citing a survey showing that taxpayers annually spend more than 5 billion hours dealing with the tax system, former IRS Commissioner Fred Goldberg said, 'American people have every right to demand a tax system they can live with.'"

October 10, 1991

"The objective of the Internal Revenue Service is to 'encourage and achieve the highest degree of voluntary compliance with the tax laws and regulations and to maintain the highest degree of public confidence in the integrity and efficiency of the IRS.'"

IRS statement of organization and functions,
39 Fed. Reg. 11,572, 1974

"A taxpaying public that does not understand the law is a taxpaying public that cannot comply with the law."

Former IRS Commissioner LAWRENCE B. GIBBS,
March 2, 1987

"Some agents 'need more training in how to be courteous.'"

Former IRS Commissioner LAWRENCE B. GIBBS,
April 14, 1987

"The examiner has a responsibility to the taxpayer and to the government to determine the correct tax liability and to maintain a fair and impartial attitude in all matters relating to the examination. . . . The fair and impartial attitude of an examiner aids in increasing voluntary compliance. An examiner must approach each examination with an objective point of view."

Internal Revenue Manual 4015.3(1)

"The IRS cannot do some of the basic accounting and recordkeeping tasks it expects American taxpayers to do."

GAO, March 1, 1999

". . . You don't have to be nasty to people to collect money."

CHARLES O. ROSSOTTI, IRS Commissioner,
May 17, 2001

"I think the complexity of our Tax Code is the worst problem facing our society. . . . We wouldn't have either evasion or avoidance if we didn't have 10,000 pages of Tax Code it takes a machine to understand."

Treasury Secretary PAUL O'NEILL,
March 14, 2002

"The function of the Internal Revenue Service is to administer the Internal Revenue Code. . . . Administration should be both reasonable and vigorous. It should be conducted with as little delay as possible and with great courtesy and considerateness. It should be reasonable within the bounds of law and sound administration. It should, however, be vigorous in requiring compliance with the law and it should be relentless in its attack on unreal tax devices and fraud." (Rev. Proc. 64-92)

"There is little debate today: The Internal Revenue Code is a Kafkaesque maze of complexity that confounds millions of Americans every single year," says Rep. Steny Hoyer, a Maryland Democrat and the House Democratic Whip. "Our tax

system is an embarrassment that treats many taxpayers unfairly."

July 15, 2004

"The IRS needs to do a better job of educating taxpayers and tax preparers. . . ."

Treasury Inspector General
for Tax Administration,
J. RUSSELL GEORGE
March 15, 2007

"The abuse this been inflicted on American citizens by the IRS is inexcusable."

Rep. Judy Hice (R-GA)
May, 2017

Dear Taxpayer:

This is to inform you that we, at the Internal Revenue Service, have lost your file. Unless we find it within thirty (30) days, you will face a $10,000 fine and a jail sentence of not less than five (5) years. Please advise.

"I don't think you can take the tax system seriously anymore."

CHRISTOPHER S. RIZEK
former Associate Tax Legislative Counsel

IRS TERROR

The letter on the preceding page is, of course, a phony. At least I thought it was a phony until an equivalent letter reached my grandson Owen in 2015. The IRS lost his return and threatened interest and penalties if he didn't send a new signed copy. They didn't lose his check, though. Rather than submit a less than two-year-old to an audit, my daughter sent a second copy. In fact, the Internal Revenue Service has lost about 2 million tax returns or related documents from its files each year, according to an in-house study. It lost over 40,000 documents and $1.2 billion in payments in Pittsburgh alone in 2001—not to mention 2,300 computers and several firearms that somehow disappeared. The checks' in the Bay—in 2005, 30,000 estimated payment to the IRS were dumped into San Francisco Bay after an auto accident. "It's very embarrassing to tell a taxpayer, 'I am disallowing all of your losses,' and then ask them to provide a copy of their return because we can't find their original return," said one IRS employee quoted in an agency study. The report drew on questionnaires, interviews, and a random sample of 15,000 requests for tax documents in 1987. "In most federal record centers, we found Forms W-2 scattered on the floor," it stated. The report estimated that 21 percent of taxpayers who paid the fee for photocopies of tax returns got their money back because the document could not be found within 90 days.

It's not surprising that to most American taxpayers, receiving correspondence from the Internal Revenue Service is on a par with spending three weeks in a dentist's chair or two hours in a locked room with an encyclopedia salesperson. Greetings from the IRS means one thing: the ultimate curse of a civilized society—a tax audit.

The Internal Revenue Service defines an audit as "an impartial review of the taxpayer's return to determine its completeness and accuracy." Former Senator Edward V. Long of Missouri didn't agree. He compared the Internal Revenue Service to a "Gestapo preying upon defenseless citizens." His Senate committee found the audit and investigative techniques of the IRS to include defying court orders, picking locks, stealing records, illegally tapping telephones, intercepting and reading personal mail, using hidden microphones to eavesdrop on the private conversations of taxpayers with their lawyers, employing undercover agents with assumed identities, and using sexual entrapment.

In an April 26, 1982, hearing before the House Ways and Means Subcommittee on Oversight, Representative George Hansen of Idaho alleged the existence of "IRS Hit Lists, Snooping and Spying Operations, political retaliatory audits . . . and arbitrary assessments and seizures for punitive rather than tax collection purposes" The case against the Internal Revenue Service, however, was presented more strikingly by the alleged victims of Internal Revenue Service brutality, who methodically testified to individual confrontations with

the service in great detail, including descriptions of forced detention, physical force, and the use of weapons for intimidation.

One taxpayer's wife, stricken with polio, needed an iron lung to keep her alive. An IRS agent threatened to seize the iron lung unless taxes claimed to be due were immediately forthcoming. The panicked taxpayer paid the claimed deficiency immediately.

IRS terrorists show no fear. In Kansas City, police officer Paul Campbell stopped a speeder and started to write a ticket. The offending driver, after making the usual objections, identified himself as an agent for the Internal Revenue Service. When Officer Campbell continued to write, the agent sneered, "We'll just have to check out your taxes." Soon after Campbell filed his next tax return, he was ordered to report to the Internal Revenue Service for an audit. It took four months of agency interrogations, repeated phone calls, and constant letter writing before the IRS finally admitted that Campbell owed it nothing.

In *Richman*, 78-1 U.S.T.C. Par. 9331, 41 AFTR 2d 78-1072 (DC Ill., 1978), the court was outraged at the lengths to which the IRS went to collect and keep some $5,000 to which, it turned out, it was not entitled. The IRS agents had padlocked the door to the taxpayer's place of business and discussed with the taxpayer the various sources from which he might beg or borrow the money in a conversation "distressingly like those between 'juice loan' debtors and creditors." The court found that the "conduct of the IRS agents was almost beyond belief."

In another case, senator Nancy Kassebaum of Kansas remarked, "They should not be hit with outlandish penalties for failing to memorize the Federal Tax Code." She was talking about a $50 penalty against an 84-year-old Kansas City woman who underpaid her income tax by $0.60! According to the *Washington Post*, on July 11, 1984, one couple was assessed $205 when they were found to be one cent shy after paying taxes of nearly $9,000!

In a 1977 incident, several IRS collection agents bashed in the side window of a Volkswagen owned by a woman in Alaska who owed some taxes, then dragged her from the car and seized it as a payment for the money she owed. A photographer caught the incident on film; otherwise, it would have gotten little national notice.

In March 1989, then Senator, now former Vice President Albert Gore of Tennessee revealed that IRS tax examiners in the Memphis Service Center "have been instructed to remain silent" when they uncover legitimate deductions that taxpayers failed to take. "For example, retirees and those laid off from their jobs who failed to claim withholding on pensions in lump sum distributions are not given

credit, even if tax examiners catch the mistakes." The IRS attributed the embarrassment to "procedures used in the informationdocument matching program for tax year 1987." However, it was not explained where those procedures and the policy behind them originated. Moreover, one then-current IRS employee claimed that examiners had been *instructed* to let withholding errors in the IRS's favor go uncorrected.

According to Beryl Abbin, then Director of Federal Tax Services for Arthur Andersen and Company, "On the local IRS level, you have some very bad apples out there—agents who try to push their way and intimidate."

In one study of the Internal Revenue Service, almost half the agents surveyed said they are hesitant to reveal their occupation to people they meet. Their general attitude is, "People don't trust us." Understandably so. As Internal Revenue Service agent Thomas Mennitt so succinctly put it in public testimony, "I violate laws at all times; it's part of my duties."[1] On June 28, 1987, the *Washington Post* reported three instances of the IRS intercepting first-class mail and altering checks that were made out to third parties. These allegations followed an earlier report about a San Francisco man whose $1,300 mortgage check to a bank was intercepted by the IRS in July 1986. The words "Internal Revenue Service" were stamped over the bank's name, and the check was then cashed. According to Ronald Noll of the Pennsylvania Society of Public Accountants, testifying before a House subcommittee in Congress, "The IRS has sunk so low in public opinion that a responsible accountant honestly believes he needs a hood to protect himself from IRS retaliation." IRS agents have been authorized to pose as doctors, lawyers, journalists, and clergy to conduct undercover investigations.

As former senator from Kansas and former Chairman of the Senate Finance Committee, Bob Dole blasted the IRS as an "intrusive" and "oppressive" presence in American life. "We don't need the IRS; we can get rid of the IRS," he vowed. Dole suggested that we abandon what he called "the whole twisted wreck of federal tax law." He decried what he called "KGB-like" audits that allow the government to snoop into a citizen's style of life.

Moreover, despite Internal Revenue Service National Office policy against collection quotas, IRS regional managers continued to instruct their revenue agents to make collections at almost any cost. According to a June 22, 1987, hearing before the Senate Finance Subcommittee on IRS Oversight, there was considerable competition among revenue officers and almost a daily comparison of what they have collected. Management challenged employees to "go

1. Jeff A. Schnepper, *Inside IRS* (New York: Stein and Day, 1978), p. 187.

out and make seizures . . ." and ". . . intimidation, and [the] abusiveness and harshness . . . is passed down to [the] taxpayers."

Things were no better in 1998. First, the IRS sent out apologies to 20,000 taxpayers for mistakes it made in handling their accounts. Then, the IRS sent 1 million taxpayers tax packages with the wrong bar code, making them unusable because of zip code errors.

Things then got worse. Kenneth L. Steen of Chattanooga, Tennesee, expected a refund of $513. Instead, he received a letter from the IRS demanding the payment of $300,000,007.57! An IRS official reported 3,000 people around the nation got similar erroneous notices.

Then things got really bad. The IRS itself issued a detailed report of 12 of the agency's 33 districts.

It found that the IRS had increasingly relied in recent years on numerical goals—such as the dollars that each revenue officer collects or the number of properties seized by a certain office—in enforcing tax laws, and that an obsession with such goals has raised the possibility of overzealous collections.

Though Congress outlawed the use of numerical goals almost two decades ago in 1988, high-profile Senate hearings in 1997 and an IRS report released in December, 1997 showed that the practice remained common.

It was found that more than a third of the IRS front line collection managers were evaluated based on enforcement statistics and that a fourth of all collection officers "feel pressure to achieve enforcement goals and take enforcement actions."

Things *are* getting better. The Treasury Inspector General, in a March 2003 study, concluded that the IRS "is generally compliant" with the restriction on using statistics to evaluate employee performance. In a 2005 study, the Inspector General found the IRS "complying" with legal guidance to evaluate employees on taxpayer treatment, rather than enforcement quotas. A 2007 investigation again found that the IRS continued to be "compliant." A July 27, 2010, TIGTA report concluded that the IRS "had complied well overall" with the evaluation guidelines.

Apparently, no one is immune from foul-ups by the Internal Revenue Service. In the summer of 1987, the Internal Revenue Service acknowledged that it had accidentally placed an erroneous $338.85 lien against then President and Mrs. Reagan. Although the lien was discovered and rescinded, it will remain a permanent entry in the County Court record system where it had been filed.

As the 1998 IRS report and Roth hearings demonstrate, IRS horror stories are not just in the far past. As a 1993 Tax Court decision noted, an IRS

agent contacted Chicago businessman Vince Han and his wife to arrange an audit. At the second meeting—at Mr. Han's house—the agent's supervisor arrived on the premises and shouted: "You have to pay $70,000 now—if you don't pay it, you are going to jail!" Actually, Mr. Han owed the government nothing. The IRS auditor didn't bother reading key documents Mr. Han provided and instead merely asserted that Mr. Han "was not an honest taxpayer." It took a 4-year legal struggle for Mr. Han to clear his name and recover some of the heavy legal costs he incurred.

The horror continued. In 2007 an Arkansas federal court found that the "extortionary" conduct of two IRS agents amounted to fraud or malfeasance and penalties against them justified (*Barry J. Jewell v. U.S.* No. 4:06-CV-684 November 19, 2007).

More horror—in 2014 the IRS seized and emptied the bank account of Khalid Quran, because he made multiple cash deposits of legally earned receipts from his convenience store near a local airport. The forfeiture laws were designed to catch illegal drug money but, according to the Institute for Justice, there were some 600 forfeitures imposed by the IRS on legal funds before the IRS issued guidance in October 2014 stating that it would "no longer pursue the seizure and forfeitures of funds" associated with "legal source" deposits, except in exceptional circumstances—i.e., they will now obey the law . . . we will see.

Fear of the Internal Revenue Service *is* justified. All too often IRS agents are arbitrary, antagonistic, and capricious. According to a study commissioned by the Federal Administrative Conference, the Internal Revenue Service has been found to be "whimsical, inconsistent, unpredictable, and highly personal" in dealing with those caught in its machinery. The study concluded, among other things, that different IRS districts follow different rules and that the same district can be either easy or tough depending upon whether it is ahead or behind its acknowledged "quota" for recoveries.

For example, according to the conference, a New Yorker's chances of being audited averaged 1:39, compared to 1:78 in New Mexico. IRS audit negotiators in Brooklyn averaged 32¢ on the dollar in settling disputes, while those in Baltimore extracted 74¢. In Albany, New York, 6 of every 10 delinquent accounts led to tax seizures, but only 3 of 10 did in New Mexico. The Federal Administrative Conference also found that the higher the deficiency the Internal RevenueService claimed, the lower the percentage it finally accepted in settlement. The conference suggested that this was due to the ability of rich taxpayers to hire lawyers to argue their cases while poorer taxpayers had no choice but to pay up.

Odds of IRS District Tax Audit 2000 All 1040/10140A Returns Filed by Individuals

Region	District	Average Adjusted Gross Income Reported	Rank	Percent Audited	Rank
	United States	42,917	–	0.20	–
Northeast Region	Brooklyn	46,252	16	0.29	7
Northeast Region	Connecticut-Rhode Island	59,576	2	0.18	16
Northeast Region	Manhattan	66,191	1	0.37	5
Northeast Region	Michigan	48,251	9	0.11	31
Northeast Region	New England	51,448	5	0.16	19
Northeast Region	New Jersey	58,295	3	0.10	33
Northeast Region	Ohio	42,121	27	0.10	32
Northeast Region	Pennsylvania	45,198	17	0.13	29
Northeast Region	Upstate New York	42,394	25	0.14	22
Southeast Region	Delaware-Maryland	50,972	6	0.13	26
Southeast Region	Georgia	44,284	21	0.11	30
Southeast Region	Gulf Coast	36,256	31	0.20	12
Southeast Region	Indiana	43,951	23	0.14	25
Southeast Region	Kentucky-Tennessee	39,342	30	0.13	27
Southeast Region	North Florida	39,923	29	0.14	23
Southeast Region	North-South Carolina	40,472	28	0.16	20
Southeast Region	South Florida	46,562	14	0.23	9
Southeast Region	Virginia-West Virginia	46,308	15	0.13	28
Midstates Region	Arkansas-Oklahoma	35,625	33	0.21	11
Midstates Region	Houston	47,493	10	0.22	10
Midstates Region	Illinois	50,679	7	0.14	24
Midstates Region	Kansas-Missouri	43,231	24	0.16	18
Midstates Region	Midwest	44,540	19	0.19	14
Midstates Region	North Central	47,259	11	0.47	2
Midstates Region	North Texas	44,529	20	0.19	15
Midstates Region	South Texas	36,061	32	0.17	17
Western Region	Central California	50,117	8	0.29	6
Western Region	Los Angeles	44,215	22	0.48	1
Western Region	Northern California	52,650	4	0.41	4
Western Region	Pacific Northwest	46,993	12	0.15	21
Western Region	Rocky Mountain	44,709	18	0.20	13
Western Region	Southern California	46,563	13	0.47	3
Western Region	Southwest	42,180	26	0.29	8

Source: Transactional Records Clearinghouse, Syracuse University.

Average Yield of an IRS Audit

United States	$5,330
IRS Region	
Southwest (SW)	$7,883
North Atlantic (NA)	$7,606
Mid-Atlantic (MA)	$5,013
West (W)	$4,441
Southeast (SE)	$4,401
Midwest (MW)	$3,665
Central (C)	$3,424
States and IRS Districts	
1. Colorado (SW)	$17,614
2. Texas (all) (SW)	$9,780
Austin District	$4,002
Dallas District	$1,665
Houston District	$6,789
3. Alaska (W)	$8,973
4. Maryland[a] (MA)	$7,532
5. Oklahoma (SW)	$7,382
6. Arkansas (SE)	$7,218
7. Florida (all) (SE)	$7,136
Fort Lauderdale District	$8,980
Jacksonville District	$5,826
8. Nevada (W)	$6,566
9. New Jersey (MA)	$6,341
10. Idaho (W)	$6,295
11. New York (all) (NA)	$6,216
Albany District	$3,846
Brooklyn District	$6,216
Buffalo District	$3,846
Manhattan District	$8,414
12. Massachusetts (NA)	$5,642
13. California (all) (W)	$5,608
Laguna Niguel District	$4,735
Los Angeles District	$9,538
Sacramento District	$4,138
San Francisco District	$3,884
San Jose District	$3,884

(continues)

Average Yield of an IRS Audit *(continued)*

14. Oregon (NW)	$5,561
International[b]	$5,391
15. Illinois (all) (MW)	$5,176
Chicago District	$5,590
Springfield District	$3,422
16. Kansas (SW)	$4,825
17. Pennsylvania (all) (MA)	$4,572
Philadelphia District	$5,089
Pittsburgh District	$3,550
18. Utah (SW)	$4,372
19. Michigan (C)	$4,315
20. Arizona (SW)	$4,290
21. Tennessee (SE)	$4,178
22. Wyoming (SW)	$4,154
23. Louisiana (SE)	$4,140
24. New Hampshire (NA)	$3,957
25. Connecticut (MA)	$3,889
26. Hawaii (W)	$3,882
27. Delaware (MA)	$3,756
28. Georgia (SE)	$3,727
29. Kentucky (C)	$3,713
30. Virginia (MA)	$3,640
31. New Mexico (SW)	$3,590
32. Ohio (all) (C)	$3,534
Cincinnati District	$3,057
Cleveland District	$3,765
33. Wisconsin (MW)	$3,382
34. North Carolina (SE)	$3,286
35. South Carolina (SE)	$3,209
36. Washington (NW)	$3,188
37. Indiana (C)	$3,180
38. Maine (NE)	$3,069
39. Iowa (MW)	$3,049

Average Yield of an IRS Audit *(continued)*

40. Rhode Island (NE)	$2,965
41. Minnesota (MW)	$2,949
42. Missouri (MW)	$2,922
43. Nebraska (MW)	$2,728
44. South Dakota (MW)	$2,629
45. Mississippi (SE)	$2,529
46. Alabama (SE)	$2,513
47. West Virginia (SE)	$2,375
48. Montana (MW)	$2,181
49. Vermont (NE)	$2,095
50. North Dakota (MW)	$1,825

Source: Derived from statistics in the 1987 Commissioner's Annual Report.

[a]Includes the District of Columbia.

[b]Returns filed in Puerto Rico and from abroad.

States with the most IRS audits

1. California
2. Colorado
3. Nevada
4. Vermont
5. Missouri
6. New Mexico
7. Arizona
8. Massachusetts

The rankings were based on the percentage of 2013 TaxAudit.com Audit Defense users that were audited in 2014.

Taxpayers in North Dakota were the least likely to be auditing by the IRS.

CONGRESS RESPONDS

In response to these problems, Congress passed a Taxpayer's Bill of Rights in 1988. The creation of Senator David Pryor of Arkansas, it consists of procedural safeguards and penalties to help clarify and ensure the rights and obligations of a taxpayer and the IRS during an audit or appeal, as well as during the refund and collection processes. As then Finance Committee Chairman Lloyd Bentsen put it, the bill's provisions counter the "bully mentality" that many taxpayers

perceive behind IRS tax law enforcement. The focus of the bill was to create a more balanced relationship between the tax agency and the citizenry. The details of the bill can be found on page 708 and following. A second Taxpayer Bill of Rights was passed in 1996, and a third in 1998.

In 1997, the IRS received two additional hits. Responding to reports of unauthorized inspection of tax return information by IRS employees, Congress passed the Taxpayers Browsing Protection Act, which imposes both civil and criminal penalties for the unauthorized inspection of tax returns and return information. Between late 1994 and April 1997, more than 700 IRS employees were punished for improperly accessing agency information.

Moreover, in March 1997, Rep. Bill Archer and Sen. William Roth, the then Chairmen of the House Ways and Means and the Senate Finance Committees, respectively, agreed to investigate allegations that the IRS was conducting politically targeted audits of exempt organizations.

Responding to serious IRS deficiencies, the National Commission on Restructuring the IRS, in a June 25, 1997 report, recommended sweeping changes for the agency.

The key recommendations in the commission's report called for:

- creating a seven-member board of directors for IRS, with five members from the private sector, appointed (and removable) by the president and confirmed by the Senate;
- consolidating congressional oversight of IRS by creating a joint committee of leaders of the multiple committees that now oversee IRS on Capitol Hill;
- stabilizing the IRS' budget for the next 3 years so it can plan for modernization;
- giving IRS and Treasury more flexibility to hire the qualified personnel they need to implement modernization;
- giving IRS more input into the administrability of tax laws before they are enacted; *and*
- requiring IRS to provide taxpayers with compensation for damages incurred as a result of wrongful actions by IRS, among other taxpayer rights provisions.

Many of these issues were addressed again in the 1998 Reform Act. Things *were* changing. On August 5, 1999, the IRS issued T.D. 8830 to establish a balanced measurement system for employees. Specifically, the new rules measure employee performance and implement requirements that all employees be evaluated on the basis of "providing fair and equitable treatment to taxpayers." The use of records

of tax enforcement results to evaluate or to impose or suggest goals for any employee of the IRS is barred.

But as then IRS Commissioner Charles O. Rossotti stated in July 1999, "Frankly, we haven't yet succeeded in building an IRS that accomplishes, or is ever capable of accomplishing, our goals at an acceptable level."

Yet things *were* changing in 2000. More than one-fifth of IRS employees, the equivalent of nearly 21,000 people working full-time, were assigned to customer service, up from 12,000 4 years ago by one measure and nearly 18,000 by another. By either measure there were thousands fewer workers available to conduct audits and collect overdue taxes.

The IRS culture was also changing. "Don't aggravate taxpayers—that's what our managers are telling us," the *New York Times* quoted an IRS agent in a December 1999 article. As he spoke six colleagues nodded in agreement and offered similar comments from their bosses.

A revenue agent in Florida said his manager told him: "Don't probe deeply. Just find three or four obvious items and close the case."

An IRS worker in Nashville said anyone there could get a tax case resolved favorably if the taxpayer had enough influence to get a senator or congressman to complain to the IRS. "We just collapse," the 14-year veteran said.

"Please don't call us tax collectors in the newspaper," one longtime revenue officer in New York said. "We don't collect taxes anymore. We aren't allowed to."

The chief of IRS operations, John Dalrymple, said "none of these comments shock me."

The pendulum has now swung in the other direction. Former IRS Commissioner Everson declared enforcement, rather than service, to be the new priority. "The agency will not brook arguments by taxpayers that the IRS is abusing its enforcement powers." "The law is that if you make money, you have to pay taxes."

As the Congressional Research Services noted in an August 23, 2007 report, the proposed IRS budget for fiscal year 2007 "continues a trend, several years in the making, of putting greater stress on enforcement at the expense of the modernization effort and, to a lesser extent, taxpayer service."

They really mean it. In March 2010 *The Week* reported that two dark-suited IRS agents showed up at a California car wash, hand-delivering the owner an unpaid tax bill of 4 cents. Aaron Zeff, of Harv's Metro Car Wash in Sacramento, says the agents were "deadly serious" about the $0.04 bill from 2006, which had accrued $202.31 in late fees and taxes. "It's hilarious," said Zeff, who paid the bill. "I think (the IRS) may have a problem with priorities."

UNDERSTANDING THE SYSTEM

Short of adopting a vow of poverty and hiding in a monastery or joining the ever-growing army of illegal tax evaders, what can *you* do? The best defense is a good offense. If you know how the service works internally and where it is vulnerable, you can at least better your odds of winning when the tax man calleth.

Making your return indistinguishable from the "average" individual return can lessen your chances of facing an audit. Once you have prepared and signed your return, you mail it to the IRS Regional Service Center for your geographical area. The center checks some of the figures and transfers all information to magnetic tape, which then goes to the IRS computer center in Martinsburg, West Virginia. Here it becomes part of a master file for the Internal Revenue Service's complex automatic data processing system. With the master file, the Internal Revenue Service can locate people who fail to file returns and taxpayers who do not report such income as dividends or bank interest. Each tax return is assigned a document locator number (DLN) by the local Service Center. To better understand the document locator system, let us "decode" a hypothetical DLN: 3414133300134. Working from left to right, the digits indicate the following:

34	=	the IRS district (viz., the Cleveland District)
1	=	the tax class (viz., withholding tax)
41	=	the document code (viz., Form 941)
333	=	the control date (the numeric day of the year remittance was made)
001	=	the block number
34	=	the serial number of the specific DLN

An understanding of the document locator number system can help you better understand the communication process of the Internal Revenue Service.

In addition to printing out notices and letters to advise you of a tax refund due, to request information, or to report actions taken on returns already filed and the status of your account, the system is programmed to check returns for three basic mistakes.

First, all returns are examined for mathematical errors. Mistakes in arithmetic or in transferring figures from one schedule to another—for example, the total of itemized deductions to the Form 1040—result in an immediate correction notice. If the error leads to a tax deficiency, you automatically receive a bill for that amount. If you overpaid, the excess is applied to future taxes, credited, or refunded at your request. You cannot appeal such corrections, but you can ask in writing that they be reviewed. Errors in arithmetic alone rarely lead to a full audit.

The Internal Revenue Service's second computer check also provides for automatic adjustments to your return before any audit is made. This Unallowable Items Program is designed to catch clearly illegal deductions, such as claiming an exemption for a spouse who is filing separately. Under this program, the computer

cross-checks reported income against the W-2 forms received from your employer. The dividends and interest reported by banks, brokerage houses, and other financial institutions are cross-checked in over 99 percent of the cases. As a result of this cross-checking, the Internal Revenue Service sends out notices for taxes and interest on overdue taxes or for income or other payments that were not reported. Unfortunately, however, according to the General Accounting Office, about half of the ten million correction notices the IRS issues each year have been "incorrect, unresponsive, unclear, or incomplete." If you get an incorrect notice, follow the appropriate procedures to contest it, or contact your local Problem Resolution office, now known as the Office of the Taxpayer Advocate, at 1-877-777-4778.

Statistics revealed in June 2017 showed that unless there are "significant" discrepancies, most mismatches are ignored. Out of the about 25 million annual mismatches, the IRS issues only 4 to 5 million notices (Form CP2000). But the IRS refuses to reveal what level of mismatch constitutes "significant."

Another common mistake picked up by this program is a claim for a deduction that exceeds limits set by the Internal Revenue Service tax code. For example, not all medical expenses may be claimed. You may itemize and write off only those medical expenses that exceed 7.5 percent of adjusted gross income. The Unallowable Items Program is also likely to catch excessive deductions for charitable contributions or failure to reduce a "casualty loss" by $100, as required by the tax code. When an adjustment is made, you receive a letter allowing you to explain or protest. If you accept the change, you are asked to sign the "correction notice."

Unless the mistakes are extensive, these automatic adjustments do not usually lead to a full audit. However, basic errors like these should be avoided: Anytime your return is made to stand out, *for any reason*, it increases your chances for a full audit, with all the corresponding consequences.

Another IRS program for checking tax returns is the Questionable Items Program. Here, your whole return or a part of it is subjected to a detailed investigation. You are, in effect, being challenged rather than corrected. You must justify each deduction to the last penny, and to the satisfaction of the examining agent.

IRS computer programs use three techniques to decide which returns to review under this program: random selection, "discriminant function" selection, and special target selection.

Your income, claimed deductions, and profession are irrelevant when returns are selected at random. A student earning only $6,000 a year at part-time jobs may be invited to the local IRS office for a tax audit only to find a business executive making $600,000 in the same situation.

Once the return is in the computer, you are at the mercy of the second selection criterion—"discriminant function" *(DIF)* analysis. Based on previous experience, the Internal Revenue Service has created a number of composite

hypothetical "taxpayers." These composite "norms" are determined by interviewing a random selection of taxpayers. Unfortunately, this can be a horror for the taxpayer selected as a "norm": The IRS agent asks questions about every single item on the return; the taxpayer has to produce a birth certificate, marriage certificate—the works. Each item is checked, and the results are fed into the computer. In a "discriminant function" analysis, the characteristics of these "average" taxpayers are given different weights and compared to a return selected for audit. Of the 1.1 million closed books and records audits received in 1992, 1993, and 1994, 59 percent were selected on the basis of "*DIF*" scores.

Average taxpayers were determined by the IRS Taxpayer Compliance Measurement Program (TCMP). One research audit covered 54,000 personal returns for 1988. The IRS planned to TCMP audit about 153,000 returns of all types for 1994 to be picked randomly in 1995 to represent 25 business sectors, 5 personal income groups, and 30 geographic areas. Budget constraints put these audits on hold.

But, they're back, now called National Research Program (NRP) audits. The IRS scheduled these audits for late fall 2002 and 2003. Here's how they set it up:

- 8,000 returns were reviewed without the taxpayers being contacted.
- 9,000 taxpayers got letters asking questions about their returns.
- 30,000 returns were subject to "limited"-scope face-to-face audits.
- 2,000 others were to be subject to the audit from hell, where they'll be required to back up every line on their returns. These audits are technically called *Calibration Audits*.

By summer of 2005, the IRS had selected nearly 90 percent of the returns to be audited. They put the new audit formulas in place in 2006. Your odds of winning the Powerball lottery in 2002 were 1 in 80 million. Your odds of facing an audit from hell were 1 in 65,000. As Kevin McCormally commented, "A grateful nation appreciates your sacrifice."

These NRP audits continue. On June 6, 2007, the IRS announced plans to launch a new study, the first of an ongoing series of annual individual studies using an innovative multiyear rolling methodology. The study started in October 2007 and examined about 13,000 randomly selected tax year 2006 individual returns. Similar sample sizes will be used in subsequent tax years.

An advantage of using this method, which combines results over rolling three-year periods, is that the IRS will be able to make annual updates to compliance estimates and develop more efficient workload plans on an annual basis, after the initial three annual studies. Previous studies started from scratch, drew tax returns from a single tax year, and involved examinations of more than 45,000 taxpayers.

A September 2009 TIGTA report found that examination productivity is improving for individual returns selected by the updated DIF scores.

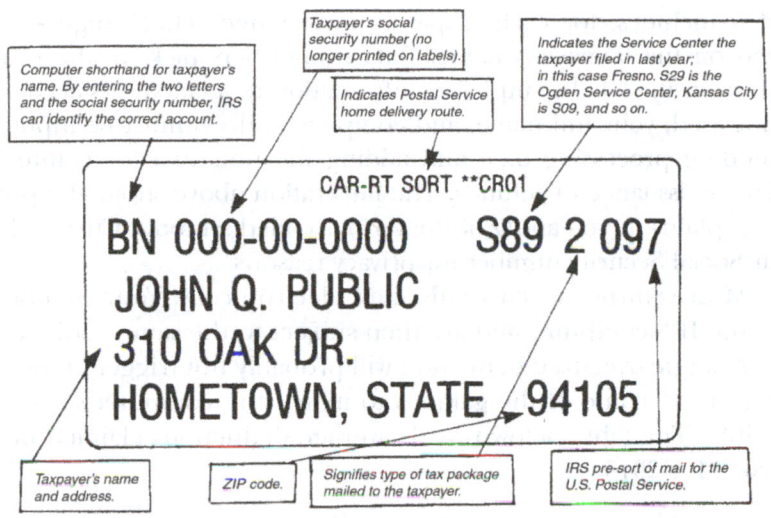

Computer shorthand for taxpayer's name. By entering the two letters and the social security number, IRS can identify the correct account.

Taxpayer's social security number (no longer printed on labels).

Indicates Postal Service home delivery route.

Indicates the Service Center the taxpayer filed in last year; in this case Fresno. S29 is the Ogden Service Center, Kansas City is S09, and so on.

CAR-RT SORT **CR01

BN 000-00-0000 S89 2 097

JOHN Q. PUBLIC

310 OAK DR.

HOMETOWN, STATE 94105

Taxpayer's name and address.

ZIP code.

Signifies type of tax package mailed to the taxpayer.

IRS pre-sort of mail for the U.S. Postal Service.

Let's see how the DIF score works. First, the deductions on the selected returns are added up and weighed for what is called the "discriminant function" score. The computer then recommends audits for significantly differing returns. The computer is also programmed to notice special deviations. For example, it may recommend an audit if all your deductions turn out to be nicely rounded even numbers. It will also compare your deductions to your job. A person who works as a construction laborer will rarely have a need for a home office deduction. The computer model-match takes into account income level, profession, number of dependents claimed, whether your spouse works, and even your address: A Beverly Hills zip code with a ghetto-level reported income will immediately signal for an audit. According to former IRS Commissioner Roscoe L. Egger, Jr., two-thirds of the audited returns were selected on the basis of the IRS discriminant function formula. The rest were chosen on the basis of tax-avoiding trends, such as abusive tax shelters.

You should also understand the bar-coded envelopes and peel-off labels that come with your returns. Some taxpayers believe that the coding somehow triggers an audit. In fact, the coding simply allows the IRS to process the mail on their automatic sorting machine, which reads the bar codes and separates the mail by type of return (i.e., 1040A, 1040EZ, 1040), thus expediting processing. Uncoded mail must be sorted by hand, which is much more time-consuming and slows up processing, which slows up refunds.

The coded numbers on the preprinted address label affixed to your tax package also speed up processing of returns and expedite refunds. Again, the label coding has no relationship to audits. It assures the IRS that the name is valid

and it includes, for each taxpayer, an assigned "check digit"—two characters based on the taxpayer's name. Data transcribers pick up the two-stroke check digit from the label to input tax information to a taxpayer's account. If the label is not used, your full name, and complete address must be input—significantly extending processing time and adding the potential for common errors that delay the issuance of refunds. The illustration above shows the preprinted label and explains the meaning of the various coded symbols. Current labels leave off your Social Security number for privacy reasons.

Most returns are currently filed electronically. Your numbers go directly into the IRS computer and are then subject to the same audit criteria.

A single oversized deduction will probably not trigger an immediate audit. For you the name of the game is to match the computer's norm as closely as possible. The table below reveals average deductions claimed on returns filed in 2016 for 2015.

Average Itemized Deductions, Individual Income Tax Returns for 2015

Adjusted Gross Income	Taxable Income	Interest Expense	Taxes Paid Deduction	Charity	Medical Expenses Deducted	Total Itemized Deductions
Under $15,000	$2,568	$6,397	$3,667	$1,533	$9,210	$15,624
$15,000–$29,999	9,340	6,571	5,497	2,483	8,646	17,826
$30,000–$49,999	21,741	6,357	4,026	2,812	8,761	16,026
$50,000–$99,999	48,362	7,382	6,323	3,244	9,426	19,050
$100,000–$199,999	102,480	8,905	11,052	4,155	11,305	25,300
$200,000–$249,999	177,355	11,370	17,711	5,779	17,624	35,369
$250,000 & above	599,755	16,580	51,906	21,769	37,031	81,394

Source: Statistics of Income Internal Revenue Service, Publication 1136

COMPUTER CHAOS

A dual expansion of IRS computer operations was substantially completed in 1985. First, the major equipment replacement program, with a new UNIVAC 1100 System, was made operational in all service centers. This system tripled the capacity and speed of the old equipment. Second, administration of office examinations was computerized and operates from the service centers. As District appointments become available, the computer selected cases by priority and generated both appointments and taxpayer notification letters. These letters detailed the time and place of the examination, the issues to be resolved, what to bring, etc. The system

also identified whether the taxpayer has other years under examination and automatically routed the examination to the same agent. In 1994, the IRS spent an additional $689 million to upgrade its computer system. Unfortunately, it still didn't work properly. After spending $8 billion on new computer systems, even a top agency official, in 1997, admitted that the systems "do not work in the real world."

A 7-year program to upgrade and modernize the agency's system at a cost of almost $4 billion received a scathing review from the General Accounting Office. Among the problems: cost overruns, failure to move toward a more efficient system, and continued inability of IRS employees to get current and accurate information on taxpayer returns.

The computer systems and processes did not interact with each other. The result was a problem that may be resolved by one IRS office, but another department showed the issue is still open. The taxpayer thinks the matter is closed . . . but not every IRS office is necessarily in agreement. Steps were taken to develop a centralized system that will allow all existing computers and systems to communicate with each other.

The then Commissioner of Internal Revenue, Charles O. Rossotti, was not an attorney nor an accountant—he was a computer systems expert. Rossotti said that reforming the IRS could take the better part of a decade; the computer modernization program also was likely to extend into the next century.

Moving to the new millennium didn't help. In April 2000, on technological modernization, Rossotti admitted the IRS still depended on a "very, very old . . . frankly unacceptable system" as the backbone to the administration function. Sometimes, embarrassingly, the IRS has been forced to ask a taxpayer for information it should be able to get but simply cannot find or extricate. This is akin, he said, to a bank not knowing exactly, at any one time, the balance of some of its customers, which is unacceptable.

In May 2001, the IRS project to replace the agency's 1960s database with a comprehensive modern computer framework was delayed again to "ensure its functionality."

It seems to be working better. In 2001 taxpayers who called phone numbers in two IRS publications were referred to adult chat lines—progress?

According to the General Accounts Office (GAO) in January 2003, the IRS's compliance programs, modernization, and financial management continued to be "high risk" activities. By June 2003 things had not improved.

The Internal Revenue Service is facing ongoing challenges and problems in the massive effort to overhaul its antiquated computer systems, the Treasury Inspector General for Tax Administration said in a semiannual report.

"IRS's major modernization projects continue to experience delays, cost increases, management difficulties, and reductions in deliverables," according to the report, which covers October 1, 2002, through March 1, 2003.

In July 2003, the Internal Revenue Service announced the delay of the first phase of the program to modernize its taxpayer master files, the Customer Account Data Engine (CADE), until the 2004 filing season. The first group of taxpayers, approximately 6 million 1040 EZ filers, was originally scheduled to move to the new system in 2001.

"This most recent setback is a serious matter," said then IRS Commissioner Mark W. Everson.

Everson also announced the IRS has launched an independent review of the program to evaluate its progress and determine whether any changes are needed. Following up on a commitment he made when becoming Commissioner in May 2003, Everson announced the selection of Software Engineering Institute of Carnegie Mellon University to conduct the study and report back to the IRS in 60–90 days.

When fully operational, CADE will be a modern database that will house tax information for more than 200 million individual and business taxpayers. It replaces the antiquated, magnetic tape-based system that came into use 4 decades ago. The system, called the Master File, takes a week to update its records, creating delays in providing accurate account information for taxpayers. When completed, CADE will provide a variety of benefits to taxpayers, such as faster refunds along with daily postings of transactions and updating of accounts.

Or, alternatively, you could always go back to the adult chat lines. . . .

By 2004, things had not gotten a lot better. Then IRS Commissioner Everson conceded that the Business Management System (BMS) "has failed" on the CADE project, the new Master File system, and the new IRS financial systems. The BMS alone had suffered cost overruns of $290 million since 1999.

Moreover, the GAO has found "significant computer security weakness" at the IRS. According to the GAO in a February 2004 report, the IRS has blamed delays on improving its computer system on the costs and resources used to implement the advanced child tax credit payments. Maybe they were too focused on the adult chat lines. . . .

As of July 2005, the GAO concluded that "incremental improvements" had been made, but long-term problems associated with cost overruns and schedule delays remain a concern. In April 2006, the Government Accountability Officer (GAO) concluded that the IRS's ambitious program to modernizing its outdated tax administration and financial systems still lacks adequate policies and procedures to ensure program success.

In an earlier 2005 report, the GAO found that "significant" weaknesses in the security of the IRS information systems continues to threaten the confidentiality, integrity, and availability of key financial and tax data.

In July 2006, the Treasury Inspector General for Tax Administration report found the IRS Business Systems Modernization (BSM) program "faulty" and it

concluded that the IRS Customer Account Data Engine (CADE) was "not fully developed to provide a foundation for IRS current and planned modernization systems." The CADE system was designed for managing taxpayer accounts.

In an August 2006 Treasury Inspector General for Tax Administration report, it was revealed that about $318 million in erroneous tax refunds were issued as a result of a computer based foul up that left the IRS without any fraud detection program for the 2006 filing season. Another bad sign.

As of August 2007, things weren't a lot better. Sixty percent of Internal Revenue Service employees were duped into giving control of their passwords to unauthorized callers, according to an inspection report that found lingering problems with computer security years after they were supposed to have been corrected.

Sixty-one of 102 employees telephoned by the Treasury Inspector General for Tax Administration were fooled by undercover inspectors posing as computer support help desk representatives. The inspectors asked for help with correcting a computer problem and requested the employees to provide their user names and temporarily change their passwords to the ones suggested by the inspectors.

The majority of them complied. Only eight of the employees reported the incident to either the audit team, TIGTA's Office of Investigations, or the IRS's own computer security people as they were supposed to do.

As for the CADE project, it still wasn't where it should have been, despite the IRS spending more than $230 million to right it over the last few years. By June 2008 the program was in its 10th year, and $2.5 billion into contract court costs and $310 million in internal expenses. Another $267 million was budgeted for fiscal 2008, and the program still fails to give the appropriate level of service taxpayers expect, according to the TIGTA.

And even what worked needed better supervision. In 2007, Senate Finance Committee Chairman Max Baucas (D-Mont) reported that the IRS's failure to follow procedures put the integrity of the electronic filing program at risk and exposed a greater probability of inaccurate returns, fraud, and identify theft. The TIGTA in 2008 found IRS security controls "inadequate." In 2009, the TIGTA concluded that cost overruns and schedule delays had increased with the IRS's returns system modernization program. In July 2010 the TIGTA found IRS data "at risk" for unauthorized access or disclosure.

As of February 2011, the GAO still found the IRS Business Systems Modernization (BSM) a high-risk area. Progress is slow, and the TIGTA even found that the IRS's Modernized e-File (MeF) system was not performing to expected levels. "Due to recent events at IRS facilities and the potentially expanding role of the IRS, security has replaced modernization as the top challenge facing the IRS," said Treasury Inspector General for Tax Administration J. Russell George, in December 2010.

Good news! In October 2011, the GAO found the Business Systems Modernization "on good track." In fact, in December 2011, the TIGTA upgraded the

modernization effort all the way up from "Material Weakness" to "Deficiency." That's after spending nearly $20 billion on information technology over the last decade. I for one feel so much better!

2012 was a much better year. The IRS Oversight Board took note of milestones achieved by the IRS in fiscal 2012 in a number of key areas, such as technology, enforcement and issue resolution. Most notable was the successful launch of the Customer Account Data Engine 2, or CADE 2, in January 2012, allowing the IRS to migrate from a weekly to a daily processing cycle for individual taxpayer accounts.

The CADE 2 dataplace deployment system was delayed, causing costs to rise by an estimated 74 percent to $83 million. The TIGTA recommended that the IRS not move ahead until problems were resolved and, as of December 2013, still regarded the program as "a major risk." We hope for the best.

We did not get it. As of March, 2017, a new technology designed to help the IRS detect tax fraud remains in limbo. The Return Review Program (RRP) has been in development for 8 years but has yet to come online. Current completion date is now estimated for 2022.

A June 2018 report found the IRS cybersecurity data warehouse program continued to "need improved security controls."

AUDIT HOT BUTTONS

After these computers have "graded" income tax returns to determine their "audit worthiness," the returns with the highest scores are screened by humans. The following characteristics are what these human screeners look for:

- Insufficient income to support claimed deductions
- Refunds out of line with gross income and exemptions
- Possibility of unreported income
- Profit from business or profession below the "norm"
- Investment yield or profits below the interest income that would have been earned if the funds had been deposited in savings accounts

Other Internal Revenue Service guidelines used in choosing returns to be audited include:

- Comparative size of the item—a questionable expense item of $5,000 when expenses total $25,000 would be significant; however, if total expenses were $250,000, the item ordinarily would not be significant.
- Absolute size of the item—despite the comparability factor, size itself may be significant. For example, a $60,000 item may be significant even though it represents a small percentage of taxable income.

- Inherent character of the item—although the amount of an item may be insignificant, the *nature* of the item may be significant. For example, airplane expenses claimed by a carpenter may be significant.

- Evidence of intent to mislead—this may include missing, misleading, or incomplete schedules, or showing an item incorrectly on the return.

- Beneficial effect of the manner in which an item is reported—expenses claimed on a business schedule rather than claimed as itemized deductions may be significant.

- Relationship to other items—the absence of a deduction for interest expense when real estate taxes are claimed may be significant. Similarly, the lack of dividends reported when the return shows sales of stock may also be significant.

According to a declassified handbook, the IRS looks for the following in selecting returns for an audit: exemptions claimed by noncustodial parents; losses claimed on rental property recently converted from a residence; and high receipt, low net profit business schedules for nonitemizers. The above deductions are listed as higher priority items than large medical expenses of large families or older taxpayers, home mortgage interest, auto expenses of users of the standard mileage rate, or transportation expenses of construction workers who work at more than one job site for more than one employer (*The Classification Handbook*, IRMO 41(12)0).

In September 2002, the Internal Revenue Service announced it was shifting its audit priorities to concentrate on "key areas" of tax law noncompliance by high-income taxpayers.

As part of a broader, agency-wide plan, the IRS said it will place "top priority on pursuing promoters of abusive schemes, shelters and trusts" and on identifying participants in the schemes.

The IRS increased audit resources, starting in fiscal year 2003, and used all available tools, the agency said, including "summons enforcement, injunctions and criminal investigation of promoters" and "civil audits of participants."

The strategy focused on six key areas of noncompliance:

- offshore credit card users,

- high risk, high-income taxpayers,

- abusive schemes and promoter investigations,

- high-income nonfilers,

- unreported income, *and*

- the National Research Program, the agency's compliance study involving 50,000 tax returns.

The Internal Revenue Service expects its management to use employee time productively. Therefore, each year, top administrators will "target" taxpayers in specific professions or with incomes from unusual sources where the highest potential monetary recovery may be found. For example, dentists, doctors, lawyers, and even accountants may receive much of their income in cash payments. The Internal Revenue Service believes that this permits them to "forget" to report all of their receipts. The Service also believes that the incentive to underreport would be greatly dulled if these professionals knew that, as a class, they were more likely to be audited. Therefore, as a class, they *are* more likely to be audited.

The IRS audit manual, *The Policies of the Internal Revenue Service Handbook,* set as the "primary objective" in selection of tax returns "*the highest possible revenue yield from the examination man hours expended,* and the examination of as many returns as is feasible for the maintenance of a high degree of voluntary taxpayer compliance" (author's italics).

Our federal income tax rates are imposed on a graduated progressive schedule. When you earn $1 more than the top of the previous bracket, a higher percentage of that *additional* dollar will be taken as taxes. Therefore, the more money you earn, the higher the potential return is likely to be on the time invested by the Internal Revenue Service in the case. If an agent denies a $100 deduction to a taxpayer in the 35 percent bracket, the United States Treasury receives $35, as opposed to only $10 from a taxpayer in the 10 percent bracket.

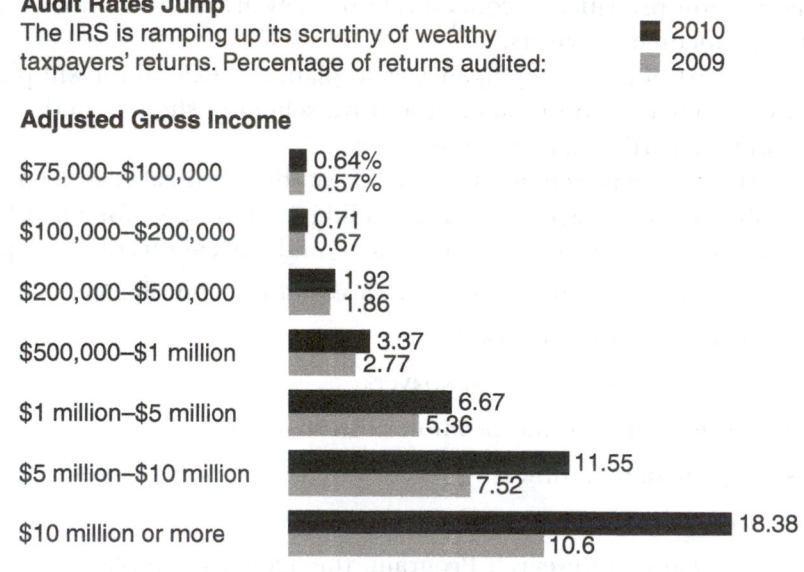

Audit Rates Jump
The IRS is ramping up its scrutiny of wealthy taxpayers' returns. Percentage of returns audited:

■ 2010
■ 2009

Adjusted Gross Income

Adjusted Gross Income	2010	2009
$75,000–$100,000	0.64%	0.57%
$100,000–$200,000	0.71	0.67
$200,000–$500,000	1.92	1.86
$500,000–$1 million	3.37	2.77
$1 million–$5 million	6.67	5.36
$5 million–$10 million	11.55	7.52
$10 million or more	18.38	10.6

Source: 2010 IRS Data Book

One out of every twelve individuals with $1 million or more in total positive income was audited in fiscal year 2010. For 2011 and 2012, it jumped to one out of eight, falling to only 10.9 percent or about one out of nine in 2013. In 2014 7.5 percent of those with million-dollar incomes were audited, increasing to almost 10 percent in 2015 but dropping to 5.83 percent in 2016 and 4.4% in 2017.

The Internal Revenue Service has found that returns filed by people who make over $100,000 provide fertile grounds for audit reviews. Other groups watched closely include taxpayers with a second or sideline business, those who report hefty capital gain income, and all who might be involved in a partnership tax shelter.

The IRS has adopted a more efficient system for classifying individual taxpayers of similar economic circumstances in order to select returns for an audit. In the past, returns were selected on the basis of adjusted gross income. Under that old system, individuals were selected for audit by separating business and non-business returns, grouping them into examination classes according to adjusted gross income, and running each class through the mathematical "discriminant function" formula to identify returns with high audit potential.

This system had definite drawbacks from the Internal Revenue Service's perspective, because adjusted gross income is determined *after* deductions and adjustments, which are of primary interest to auditors. A return showing a high gross income but large offsetting deductions (as from tax shelters) would present a relatively low adjusted gross income. Therefore, it would be assigned to a low adjusted gross income examination class, would generally receive light audit coverage, and would be scored under a "discriminant function" formula not geared to test its true audit potential.

The IRS's new classification system is based upon total positive income, relying on the total income of a taxpayer *before* adjustments or deductions. This is the sum of all positive items on your return. Any negative items—for instance, losses from tax shelters—are treated as zero. As a result of this reclassification, suspicious deductions and adjustments will not escape notice in, or distort the voluntary compliance level of, an examination class designed for lower-income taxpayers.

RATTING TO THE IRS

There is an additional reason why your return might be chosen for an audit. While the Internal Revenue Service does not publicly encourage tax informers, its representatives admit that many investigations could not be successfully conducted without the use of paid informants or the direct purchase of evidence. Most informers are former employees of a business that has been underreporting its income. A disgruntled employee who does not "rat" on the business itself may "rat" on its owner, or on a disliked manager.

But a neighbor who objects to your loud stereo at midnight or becomes jealous of your new car each year may just as quickly turn informer. These unofficial "agents" are used extensively in cases where the taxpayer under investigation is allegedly engaged in illegal activity. Tax informers were normally rewarded with up to 10 percent of the additional tax collected up to a $75,000, 5 percent of the next $25,000, and 1 percent of any additional amount. The maximum reward was $10 million. Informants fill out Form 211 which they can get by calling 1-800-TAX FORM. Rewards can be paid to any person, other than a present or former federal employee. Even payments to police officials are allowed. The IRS does not divulge the identity of its informants, (see *Whistleblower 14106–10 W v. Commissioner,* 2011), but such rewards are fully taxable. However, the grant of a reward was discretionary, not mandatory (*Krug v. U.S. Fed Ct.,* No. 96-62IT, 5/27/98). In fact, the IRS's denial of an award to an informant is not even reviewable by a court (*Destefano v. U.S.,* 2002), *Cooper v. Commissioner of Internal Revenue,* 136 T.C. 30 (2011).

Since the late 1960s, only about 8 percent of claims from tipsters has been judged worthy of a reward. To informers, though, the money is often secondary to revenge. You should, therefore, keep two rules in mind:

1. Never cheat on your income taxes.
2. If you do, never anger anyone who might know about it.

The Tax Relief and Health Care Act of 2006 changed the rules to encourage more reports. Now we have two tiers of rewards—the old discretionary system above and a new mandatory system. Here are the rules for mandatory rewards:

Q. What is the maximum reward you can receive?

A. Under the new law, which was effective as of December 26, 2006, for cases involving $2 million in taxes, penalties, fines, and interest (and, as of 2018, criminal fines and civil forfeitures), there is no longer a cap on the maximum reward that can be obtained. For cases in which less than $2 million is at issue, there is a $10 million cap on rewards.

Q. What is the reward based upon?

A. The IRS reward is based upon the taxes, reduction in overpayment credits, civil and criminal fines, penalties, and civil forfeitures that the IRS collects as a result of the information provided to it. See *Whistleblower 21276-13W v. Commissioner* T.C. No. 21276–13W, 147 T.C. No. 4, 8/13/16.

Q. What percentage of the IRS collection will you receive?

A. Under new law, which was effective as of December 26, 2006, for cases involving $2 million in taxes, penalties, fines, and interest and at least $200,000 in gross income (if an individual), the IRS will pay **between 15 percent and 30**

percent of the monies recovered. For cases in which less than $2 million is at issue the percentage of the reward will vary from 1 percent to 15 percent depending upon how much the information provided assists the IRS in its investigation.

Q. What determines the percentage of the Reward that you will receive?

A. The quality and specificity of the information and how helpful your information was to the IRS in its investigation determines in large part the percentage of the reward. The more specific your evidence and the more compelling your presentation of an IRS violation, the higher the reward will generally be. If the IRS is already aware of the violation, the less the reward will typically be.

Q. Will your name be kept confidential by the IRS?

A. The IRS keeps the name of the individual providing information confidential and will not disclose your name at anytime during its investigation. However, there are some exceptional circumstances under which the whistleblower's identity could be revealed. You should discuss these circumstances with your lawyer.

Q. Will the IRS use your information in a criminal or civil case?

A. Your information could be used in a civil or criminal case or both, depending upon the type of IRS violations and the type of information provided.

Q. What determines whether the IRS will use your information to conduct an investigation?

A. The quality of the information determines in large part whether the IRS will use your information to start an investigation. The more specific your evidence and the more compelling your presentation of an IRS violation, the more likely the IRS will use your evidence to conduct an investigation.

Q. Does the IRS have to pay a Reward if it uses your information?

A. Prior to the new legislation enacted on December 26, 2006, the IRS had the discretion to determine whether a reward should be paid and whether the reward should be anywhere from 1 percent to 15 percent. The new law provides that if the IRS uses your information in matters involving $2 million or more in taxes, penalties, fines, and interests, the IRS must pay a reward between 15 percent and 30 percent.

The new system seems to be working. For fiscal year 2009 the IRS received leads on 1,900 taxpayers, up from 1,246 in fiscal year 2008. Dozens of the tips involve purported tax losses of $100 million or more. In fiscal year 2010, the IRS collected $464.6 million as a result of tips, more than twice what it col-

lected in the prior year. A CPA was awarded $4.5 million by the IRS on April 7, 2011, for a tip on a Fortune 500 company.

However, whistleblowers and their attorneys complained that the IRS has been slow to process whistleblower claims and in many cases refused to acknowledge them. The IRS paid fewer than 100 whistleblowers in 2011, about half the number it paid 2 years earlier, even though it received more than twice the number of whistleblower cases.

As of April 2011, about 66 percent of the claims submitted in fiscal 2007 and 2008 were still in process. Pressured by Senator Grassley, who held up the confirmation of high Treasury officials, the IRS got the hint and paid over 90 awards between October 2011 and the end of July 2012. In September 2012, whistleblower Bradley Birkenfeld was awarded $104 million by the IRS. In 2013, collections were $367 million, and $53 million was paid to informants. In 2014, collections dropped to $310 million and $52 million was paid out. For 2015, the IRS collected $501.3 million and paid out over $103 million. But as of December, 2015, the GAO found the IRS whistleblower program still "plagued by delays, vague procedures, overpayments, and under payments."

In fiscal 2016, 418 awards totaling $465 million were paid out. Typically the IRS does not determine awards for at least 5 to 7 years after a claim is filed, because payment cannot be made until there is a final determination of tax.

Total Claims Related to Awards and Average Days to Process Awards by Claim Type, Fiscal Years 2015 to 2017

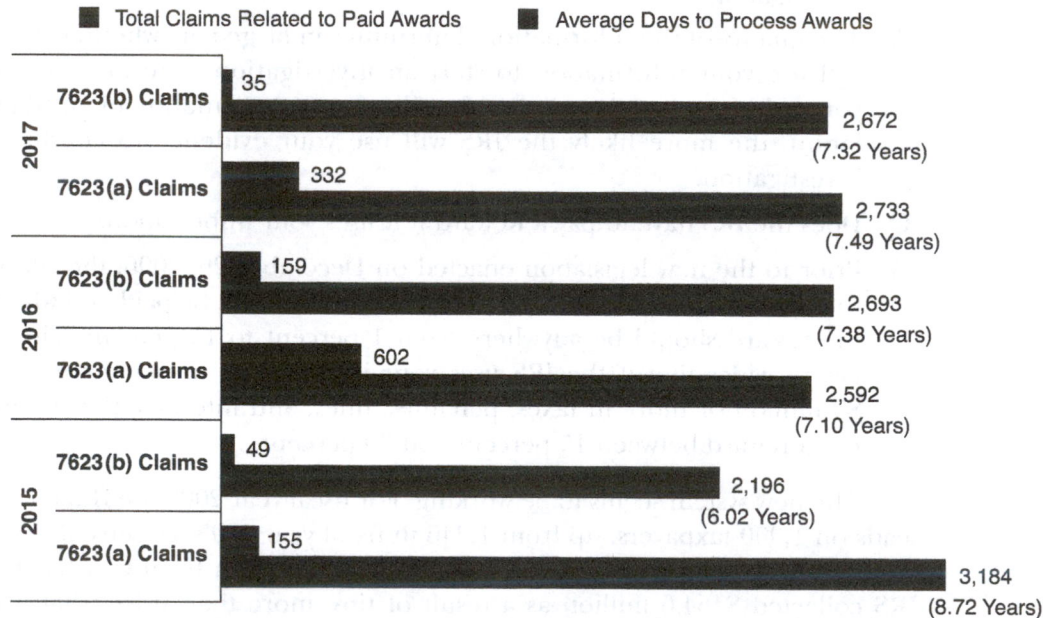

■ Total Claims Related to Paid Awards ■ Average Days to Process Awards

2017	7623(b) Claims	35
		2,672 (7.32 Years)
	7623(a) Claims	332
		2,733 (7.49 Years)
2016	7623(b) Claims	159
		2,693 (7.38 Years)
	7623(a) Claims	602
		2,592 (7.10 Years)
2015	7623(b) Claims	49
		2,196 (6.02 Years)
	7623(a) Claims	155
		3,184 (8.72 Years)

Common Initial Review Rejection / Denial Reasons

- No specific or credible tax issue,
- Claim is missing information,
- Claim is purely speculative,
- Insufficient Assessment Statute, or
- Assessment Statute Expired

Whistleblower

Files Form 211 with Whistleblower Office

Intake / Initial Review
(Generally 30–90 Days)

Subject Matter Expert (SME)
Submission evaluation
(Generally 90 days)

Initial Review Rejection / Denial

No action taken
or
No adjustments

Field Examination
(Generally 1-3 years)

Taxpayer does not agree

Claims rejected or denied as a 7623(b) claim have an administrative proceeding and are eligible to be petitioned to the tax court

Issue Rejection or Denial Letter(s)
(Generally 30–90 days)

Taxpayer agrees w/ Exam

Appeals / Court
(Generally 3–10 years)

All adjustment(s) reversed

Whistleblower's information did not contribute to the examination or Ineligible Whistleblower

Preliminary Award Recommendation
(Generally 60 days)

All or some adjustments upheld

No collected Proceeds

Monitoring for Payment
(May take up to the full collection statute of 10 years)

Taxpayer paid in full or
Taxpayer made partial payment and collection statute is expired

Award Determination
(Generally 60 days)

Start Administrative Proceeding – Issue Preliminary Award Recommendation Letter (PARL)

Monitoring Refund Statute Expiration
(Generally 2 years from the date of payment)

Agreed to PARL

Unagreed or No response

Whistleblower disagrees with determination and petitions tax court

Issue Final Determination
(Generally 30 days)

Award Payment Processing
(Generally 5–10 days)

Whistleblower does not petition Tax Court

Tax Court
(Generally 3–6 years)

Whistleblower

AWARDS PAID, FISCAL YEARS 2009 TO 2016

The table below includes data on awards paid and collections attributable to whistleblower information in those cases. The year in which an award is paid is generally not the year in which the collections occurred, because the IRS must wait until the taxpayer appeal rights have been waived or exhausted. All awards paid through FY 2010 were paid under section 7623(a), the pre-amendment law governing award claims. FY 2011 through FY 2013 awards paid include nine awards paid under 7623(b). In fiscal year 2014, the IRS

Amounts Collected and Awards Paid Under Section 7623, FY 2009–2013

	2009	2010	2011	2012	2013
Awards Paid	110	97	97	128	122
Collections over $2,000,000	5	9	4	12	6
Total Amount of Awards Paid	$5,851,608	$18,746,327	$8,008,430	$125,355,799	$53,054,302
Amounts Collected	$206,032,872	$464,695,459	$48,047,500	$592,498,294	$367,042,420
Awards Paid as a Percentage of Amounts Collected	2.8%	4.0%	16.7%	21.2%	14.6%

Amounts Collected and Awards under Section 7623, Fiscal Years 2014 to 2017

	FY 2014	FY 2015	FY 2016	FY 2017
Total Claims Related to Awards	240	204	761	367
Total Number of Awards[1]	101	99	418	242
Total IRC 7623(b) Awards		19	18	27
Collections over $2,000,000[2]	9	11	16	19
Total Amount of Awards[3]	$52,281,628	$103,486,236	$61,390,910	$33,979,873
Amounts Collected	$309,990,568	$501,317,481	$368,907,298	$190,583,750
Awards as a Percentage of Amounts Collected	16.9%	20.6%	16.6%	17.8%

[1] For Table 1, "Total Number of Awards" reflects the number of payments to whistleblowers. In some cases, awards can include proceeds from multiple taxpayers, which are reflected in the "Total Claims Related to Awards."

[2] This row includes pre-enactment section 7623(a) claims that were greater than $2 million and section 7623(b) claims.

[3] The "Total Amount of Awards" is prior to sequestration reductions.

made 101 awards totaling almost $52.3 million and more than $103 million in 2015.

If you see tax fraud, please call the IRS Tax Fraud Hotline at 1-800-829-0433. It takes an average of 5 to 7 years to collect.

THE OTHER SIDE OF THE STORY

Despite its image as a bureaucracy of terror, in all fairness another side of the IRS story must be told. Staff turnover has been one of the IRS's biggest problems, according to the internal study mentioned at the start of this chapter. More than 50 percent of the agency's file clerks had less than 12 months of experience in their positions, and 36 percent of managers had been in their jobs less than 1 year. Moreover, many employees were in the lowest civil service pay grades, and, as one IRS employee quoted in the study put it, "We lose them to Hardee's," the fast-food franchise.

In 1999, the IRS reported losing more than 15,000 people over the prior 5 years and was still losing about 450 tax examiners a year! In one 4-year period, the IRS hired just 28 new revenue agents—total!

An April 2001 study conducted by the Syracuse University Transactional Records Access Clearinghouse (TRAC) found that the IRS's permanent staff, after reaching a high of 119,000 in 1988, declined 31 percent to 82,000 in 2000. At the same time, the study noted, corporate and individual tax returns increased 20 percent, returns of individuals with $100,000 of income had quadrupled, and returns of the largest corporations had doubled.

As of April 2002, the IRS was operating with 15,000 fewer staff members than it had in the early 1990s. Processing had to be maintained, so cuts went to auditing and collection.

Between 1996 and 2002, the number of revenue agents, revenue officers, and criminal investigations personnel declined by 25 percent.

The attrition rate among revenue agents for 2006 was 20 percent. But the IRS has replaced bodies to stop the bleed. In fiscal 2006, it hired 670 auditors for the Large and Mid-Size Division alone.

But experienced auditors were leaving, and many of those left were needed to train new agents.

Even before the so-called Tax Simplification Act of 1978, the Service was responsible for interpreting and administrating codes, regulations, and revenue manuals that filled over 32 shelf-feet with an incredible 40,000 pages of the most arcane, unintelligible gobbledygook ever written. There have been many "tax reform" bills since 1978. The law is so complex, so convoluted, that it is incomprehensible. As former Citicorp Chairman Walter B. Wriston pointed out: "All the Congress, all the accountants and tax lawyers, all the judges and a convention of wizards cannot tell for sure what the income tax law says." Between 1985 and 1996 Congress changed more than 3,000 sections of the tax code and

Enforcement Revenue Collected[1]

(Dollars in Billions)	FY 2005	FY 2006	FY 2007	FY 2008	FY 2009	FY 2010	FY 2011	FY 2012	FY 2013	FY 2014
Collection	$26.6	$28.2	$31.8	$31.1	$26.9	$29.1	$31.10	$30.44	$31.40	$33.20
Examination	$13.8	$13.0	$15.2	$15.8	$12.6	$16.9	$12.40	$10.20	$9.83	$12.51
Appeals[2]	$ 3.9	$ 4.3	$ 8.3	$ 4.8	$ 4.8	$ 6.7	$ 6.50	$ 4.20	$6.83	$ 6.47
Document Matching	$ 3.1	$ 3.3	$ 3.9	$ 4.7	$ 4.6	$ 4.9	$ 5.20	$ 5.27	$ 5.29	$ 4.97
Total[3]	$47.3	$48.7	$59.2	$56.4	$48.9	$57.6	$55.20	$50.20	$53.35	$57.15

Staffing for Key Enforcement Occupations[4]

	FY 2006	FY 2007	FY 2008	FY 2009	FY 2010	FY 2011	FY 2012	FY 2013	FY 2014	FY 2015
Revenue Officers	5,627	5,662	5,492	5,451	6,042	5,619	5,186	4,748	4,439	3,995
Revenue Agents	12,778	12,816	12,599	12,958	13,888	13,867	13,021	12,234	11,629	10,840
Special Agents	2,780	2,709	2,631	2,650	2,780	2,698	2,661	2,549	2,475	2,373
Total	21,185	21,187	20,722	21,059	22,710	22,184	20,868	19,531	18,543	17,208

Notes:

[1] Enforcement revenue collected in a fiscal year includes tax, interest, and penalties from multiple tax years. Some enforcement activities can take more than a year to close and may generate revenue over several years, so it is generally inappropriate to compare revenue collected in a given fiscal year to the staffing available for that same year.

[2] Includes any revenue collection attributable to IRS Appeals activities.

[3] Includes the Information Reporter Program (IRP) and the Automated Underreporter (AUR) Program.

[4] Enforcement staffing levels presented in Full Time Equivalents (FTE). FTE funded directly by the Enforcement appropriation and by reimbursements are included.

IRS Funding

IRS funding has dropped nearly $1 billion between FY2010 and FY2015.
FY 2007, $10.6 billion
FY 2008, $11.9 billion
FY 2009, $11.6 billion
FY 2010, $12.15 billion
FY 2011, $12.12 billion
FY 2012, $11.82 billion
FY 2013, $11.20 billion
FY 2014, $11.29 billion
FY 2015, $10.9 billion;
FY 2016, $11.2 billion.

created more than 100 new forms. Asked to perform an impossible function, it's not surprising that the IRS agent often fails. In December 1990, former IRS Commissioner Lawrence B. Gibbs noted that the numerous complex changes in the Internal Revenue Code in recent years have resulted in "confusion and frustration within the IRS and among taxpayers and their representatives." In November 2002, IRS National Taxpayer Advocate Nina Olson found taxpayers to be "frustrated" and "confused." Surprise!

That may account for an average of 16 percent of the total IRS workforce dropping out of the agency every year as revealed in June 2008. A TIGTA report from about the same time forecast the loss of 51 percent of the agency's executives and managers by 2010.

In 2009, the TIGTA reported that the IRS had made a significant effort to recruit new employees. But with an attrition rate for mission critical operations of 6.8 percent throughout the agency over the last several years, the agency has been unable to replace all the employees being lost.

In 2009, the IRS hired 1,600 new revenue agents, 1,100 revenue officers, and 400 tax compliance officers. But as reported, roughly 20 percent of IRS employees in managerial roles became eligible to retire in 2010. To keep up, the IRS will have to recruit one manager a day for the next 10 years according to the TIGTA.

In 2010 the IRS added nearly 1,300 revenue agents and tax compliance officers. But the increased hiring did not make up for the growing IRS workload or pace of attrition.

Budget cuts and mission creep continued to weaken the IRS. Recent tax changes have expanded the IRS's role in administrating social, non-tax-related programs. Each dollar cut from the IRS budget costs as much as $200 in lost revenue. As of the end of 2011, more than half of IRS employees and managers have reached 50 years old and 39 percent of IRS executives and 20% of managers were already eligible for retirement.

The IRS budget for 2014 was almost $1 billion less than 2010, despite the increased responsibility from combating identity theft and implementing new laws. The Service was nearly 10,000 employees below in 2013 where it was during the 2010 filing season. Key enforcement jobs dropped 6 percent from 2012 to 2013 and more than 3,000 IRS employees were then working on identity theft—double the figures from the prior year. Forty percent of IRS staff becomes eligible for retirement in the next 5 years said the TIGTA in February 2013.

By January 2014, the IRS had lost 21,000 people in the previous 3 years, 11,000 in the last year alone. Compared to the prior fiscal year (2012), the number of revenue officers fell from 5,186 to 4,748. The number of revenue agents dropped from 13,021 to 12,234 while the number of special agents decreased from 2,661 to 2,549. As a result of these cuts, the IRS will undertake 100,000 fewer audits, and the number of collection activities will drop

by 190,000 in fiscal year 2014. Budget cuts in 2015 caused a hiring freeze. Since 2010, the IRS budget has been pared by more than $1.2 billion.

From 2010 though 2016, IRS employees have seen their ranks shrink by over 17,000—more than 5,000 in enforcement alone. The IRS had 17,208 enforcement employees in 2015, down 24 percent from 2010. According to the National Tax Employees Union (NTEU), between 2011 and 2016, the IRS lost 22,808 full- and part-time employees—a 21 percent staffing cut. By the end of 2016, the IRS expected the total number of employees in the Office of Appeals to drop below 1,500.

In 2016, the IRS announced plans to hire up to 700 more enforcement agents. Even with the new hires, the agency was still down more than 2,000 employees for the year.

According to the IRS, lack of personnel costs the government $5 billion a year in cost revenues. In 2016, 41 percent of IRS frontline managers and 61 percent of IRS executives were retirement eligible. Finding qualified people will be a problem.

From 2010 to 2016, the IRS lost 17,000 employees because of budget cuts. That works out to be a loss of around 50 employees every week for about 350 weeks. Between fiscal 2011 and 2016, the IRS annual appropriations declined by $900 million. Collection staff since 2010 is down by 50 percent, and by 2015, more than 40 percent of closed cases were closed by shelving rather than by a revenue officer working the case. Add brain drain and retirement, and the IRS has major difficulties. As of April 2017 over 30 percent of the IRS's workforce was at retirement age and the agency had only 122 workers under the age of 26.

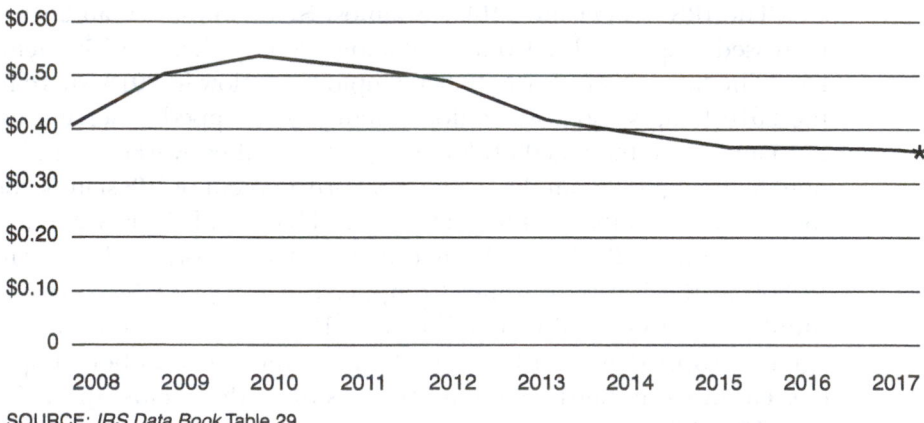

Cost of Collecting $100 of Revenue, Fiscal Years 2008–2017

SOURCE: *IRS Data Book* Table 29

*34 ¢

Experienced examiners and managers continue to retire or go into the private sector . . . and there is no money in the budget to replace them.

A January 2018 report revealed that the IRS's staffing in key taxpayer-facing positions had "declined precipitously" and its employee-training budget cut by almost 75% since fiscal 2009. In 1992, the IRS had 116,673 full-time positions. By 2016, it had dropped to only 77,924.

As former IRS Commissioner Koskinen has said, "If the agency fails and people are looking for fault, they can look to Congress if there is not adequate funding. It is a question of fault. It is a question of responsibility. I am blaming Congress."

The impact of budget cuts on IRS personal has been devastating!

Locations With Specified Employees in the Last Pay Period of the Fiscal Year

Number of Locations, Employees, or Visitors	2011	2012	2013	2014	2015	2016	2017
IRS Offices (Cities)	541	523	510	499	479	470	454
Appeals Officers (AOs)	1,129	1,058	958	881	795	739	737
Revenue Officers (ROs)	4,402	4,035	3,703	3,441	3,191	3,072	2,962
Revenue Agents (RAs)	8,652	8,638	8,520	8,418	8,329	8,557	8,502
Stakeholder Liaison Outreach Employees (Communication Liaison Outreach Employees in FY 2017)	137	123	119	110	105	98	105
Stakeholder Partnerships, Education and Communication Outreach Employees (SPEC)	522	475	444	405	386	365	311
Taxpayer Assistance Centers (TACs)	401	401	398	382	378	376	371
TAC Service Reps	1,639	1,515	1,484	1,520	1,423	1,267	1,121
Taxpayer Advocate Service, Case Advocates	996	945	919	862	784	726	683

IRS EVALUATED—CONFUSION AND COMPLEXITY

Such confusion has been documented by Ralph Nader's Tax Reform Research Group. They prepared 22 identical tax reports based on the fictional economic plight of a married couple with one child, and these 22 identical copies were submitted to 22 different IRS offices around the country. Each office came up with an entirely different tax figure. The results varied from a refund of $811.96 recommended in Flushing, New York, to a tax-due figure of $52.14 derived by the tax office in Portland, Oregon.

In 1983, *USA Today* took an informal telephone survey of IRS tax-assistance offices in 15 major cities across the United States. Seven questions were picked that private tax consultants agreed were common and difficult but fair. For each question, interviewers called 10 IRS telephone tax assistants—70 phone calls in all. In 20 cases—28.6 percent of the time—the Internal Revenue Service's answers were wrong. In 5 more cases, the Internal Revenue Service's answers were only partly correct, bringing the total of incorrect or incomplete answers to 35.7 percent.

Furthermore, getting through to the Internal Revenue Service by phone was close to impossible. In the *USA Today* study, it was found that the IRS telephone line was busy 9 times out of 10 in New York City. When it did ring, the phone often went unanswered. On one try it rang 48 times before being picked up, and twice it rang 25 times to no avail.

On February 12, 1985, the *Wall Street Journal* asked the same four tax law questions of 17 IRS offices. Two questions, involving the casualty loss deduction and one-time diesel credit, were answered correctly most of the time. The other two, involving the medical expense deduction and the wash sale rules, resulted in totally or partially wrong answers most of the time. Walter M. Alt, Director of the IRS Taxpayers' Services Division, told the *Journal* that he was "dismayed and unhappy" about the errors. IRS advice is not binding—whether oral or in print. In fact, the IRS is not bound by statements contained in its own publications, including *Your Federal Income Tax*, the IRS's free instruction booklet (*Thomas R. Underwood*, T.C. Memo 1983–99; *Harvey Richard Bennett*, T.C. Memo 1983–183; see also *Sundermeier*, T.C. Memo 1987–50, wherein taxpayers were not permitted to rely on an IRS publication, even though their local IRS office advised them that there was no other information available).

According to U.S. District Court Judge Michael M. Mihm, in his opinion in *Sinn Oil Company, et al. v. United States:* "The case law has girded the Internal Revenue Service with a nearly impregnable shield against the people it serves. Beginning with a Code which in its complexity is well nigh unfathomable to the average citizen...the judicial coup de grace is executed with the insistence that, if the taxpayer could find the relevant section and if he could be assured that there is not some supervening or nullifying regulation elsewhere and if he could then read and understand it, his reliance on the verbal representations of an agent [is] unreasonable."

The General Accounting Office did a study of its own: It checked out a sample of 2,543 tax returns in which the Internal Revenue Service had found 3,720 errors in arithmetic. Unfortunately, the General Accounting Office noted that the Internal Revenue Service itself had made nearly two-thirds of the errors. The General Accounting Office said that 33 million errors were found

on the 94 million individual income tax returns processed in the fiscal year 1981, of which 37 percent were made by taxpayers and *63 percent* were made by employees of the IRS!

Another General Accounting Office survey in February and March of 1987 also faulted the accuracy of the IRS taxpayer telephone assistance program. The GAO found that taxpayers who called the Internal Revenue Service with tax law questions got inaccurate or incomplete answers more than one-third of the time. The survey showed that the IRS assistors provided correct answers to basic questions posed by callers from the General Accounting Office 63 percent of the time, correct but incomplete answers 15 percent of the time, and incorrect answers 22 percent of the time.

One year later things had not improved. A 1989 GAO report found that more than one-third of the answers that IRS telephone assistors provided were inaccurate. The GAO said that assisters provided the correct answer to a group of 20 questions only 64 percent of the time. According to House Ways and Means Committee Oversight Subcommittee Chairman J. J. Pickle of Texas, "Calling the IRS for tax advice is a real crap shoot."

Things didn't get better in 1999. In a GAO report issued in December, 1999, they reported that despite having assistors available 24 hours a day, 7 days a week, "The service did not improve. Instead it deteriorated."

Things were no better when the IRS took the time to write. A GAO review dated May 24, 1988, found that IRS centers issued incorrect, incomplete, unresponsive, or unclear correspondence half the time. The GAO considered IRS errors in 30 percent of this correspondence critical; these letters each contained at least one instance in which the Adjustment/Correspondence Branch either provided incorrect information, failed to address all the taxpayer's questions, or acted incorrectly in adjusting or failing to adjust the taxpayer's account.

Things had improved in 1990 when 77 percent of the telephone questions were answered correctly compared to 64 percent in 1989. However, while the questions asked by taxpayers were answered correctly more often than in 1989, fewer taxpayers were able to reach IRS personnel for assistance. IRS answered about 34 percent of the calls it received in 1990, while the balance either reached busy signals or hung up after being placed on hold, GAO said. In 1989, 58 percent of the incoming calls were answered.

The IRS's performance in handling calls from taxpayers deteriorated in 1992, according to the General Accounting Office. About 7 out of every 10 calls to the IRS between January 1 and April 25 went unanswered, the congressional watchdog agency says. That was up from 6 out of 10 calls in 1991. On the bright side, IRS helpers correctly answered 85 percent of questions posed by anonymous IRS test callers, up from 84 percent the prior year.

The "most significant" decline was in the timeliness with which IRS filled GAO's test mail and phone orders, the report noted. For example, GAO received only 33 percent of the mail-ordered items within IRS' 14-day goal, as compared to 74 percent the previous year, the report said.

However, Internal Revenue Service data, as of April 8, 1992, showed that 9 out of the 10 IRS service centers had met or exceeded IRS' 98 percent refund accuracy goal, and that all 10 service centers met IRS' goal of issuing taxpayers refunds in an average of 40 days or less, GAO said in the report (*Tax Administration: IRS' 1992 Filing Season Was Successful but Not without Problems*, GAO/GGD-92-132).

According to the GAO, taxpayers who called the IRS in 1993 had only a one in four chance of getting through—worse than in 1992. It found IRS efforts to communicate with taxpayers by mail littered with "delayed, inaccurate, incomplete, and confusing responses" to taxpayer questions.

In 1995, according to IRS data, telephone assistors answered 11 percent more calls than the IRS anticipated and provided accurate answers to 91 percent of the questions asked. However, the General Accounting Office reported that the IRS received many more calls than it was able to answer—only about 9 percent of the calls made during the study period were answered. In 1996, as a result of 119 million fewer calls, the IRS increased its rate of calls answered to 20 percent.

Moreover, the IRS, the auditor of us all, failed its own audit. The General Accounting Office in 1995 reported that it could not verify the reliability of the IRS's internal financial statements for 1993 and 1994 because of "poor accounting practices." They could not even verify either total revenue collected nor tax refunds paid!

In 1997, the GAO reported that at several facilities it inspected, the IRS could not account for about 6,400 missing tapes, cartridges, and other magnetic storage devices that could contain taxpayer data.

In a 1999 GAO audit, the IRS was found to continue to suffer from "serious financial management system deficiencies and internal control weaknesses. . . ."

Things weren't much better in March 2000, when the GAO reported that the "IRS cannot complete some of the basic accounting and recordkeeping tasks it expects from American taxpayers."

The good news in 1998 was that the GAO found that the IRS "met or exceeded most" of its 1997 tax-filing season goals, such as making it easier for taxpayers to reach the agency by phone. Perhaps the tide is beginning to turn. Perhaps not—in 1999, the chances of a taxpayer actually getting through to the IRS were only 54 percent, lower than in 1998, and, according to Commissioner Rossotti, "May not improve in 2000." Why?—Budget limitations!

In a May 2001 report by the Treasury Inspector General for Tax Administration, IRS employees charged with helping taxpayers at walk-in sites (now

called Taxpayer Assistance Centers) around the United States provided incorrect or insufficient answers 73 percent of the time. The report found that taxpayers seeking help were sometimes denied service, told to return at another time or another day, had to wait excessive lengths of time to obtain help, and were occasionally subjected to IRS practices that may have confused, embarrassed, or angered them. Another report, released in July 2002, showed a vast improvement, but 20 percent of the answers were still incorrect.

In a January 2001 report, the General Accounting Office noted that major problems continued to persist. "Longstanding material weaknesses" remain in the IRS's systems and internal controls, says the report that focuses on fiscal 1999. Among the problem areas: "fundamentally deficient operational and financial systems" and "inadequate internal controls, policies, and procedures."

On May 15, 2002, the Federal Performance Project gave the IRS an overall grade of B minus in assessing the agency's management. In February, the GAO had issued an unqualified audit opinion for the second consecutive year on the IRS's financial statements. In addition, the GAO found, in May that five of the six IRS compliance programs and both of the IRS's collection programs have suffered "large and pervasive" declines.

According to then-Commissioner Rossotti, on September 24, 2002, the IRS was "winning the battle but losing the war." Rossotti reported that over the previous 5 years, the number of income tax returns increased by 12 million, while 19 tax bills were passed that changed 292 tax code sections and required 575 changes to forms and instructions.

Moreover, fixing IRS mistakes can take a long time. In one case, the IRS wrongly entered a taxpayer's $4,668 adjusted gross income as $466,800. "As a result, the taxpayer was assessed over $160,000 in taxes when he was actually due a refund," the GAO said. "It took 18 months for IRS to abate this erroneous assessment even though documentation in the case file indicated that IRS personnel believed the assessment was erroneous 10 months before they corrected the report." An IRS official says the agency agrees "on the whole" with the GAO report's recommendations for improvement.

By 2003, things were still mixed. The General Accounting Office concluded in reviewing the 2002 tax filing season, that "... IRS's performance included issuing almost all refunds on time, providing more accurate telephone service than 2001, and meeting many of its 2002 performance goals in all areas." The IRS customer service representatives answered 1.6 million more calls than in 2001. But, that was 2.6 million less than service's 2002 goal.

A December 2003 report from the Treasury Inspector General revealed that during a survey of assistance sites across the country, IRS employees incorrectly prepared 19 of 23 tax returns.

Some things did get better in 2003 when the GAO found that the IRS improved its filing season performance in key areas involving returns processing, refunds, electronic services, and taxpayer assistance. The IRS even improved its phone service—providing 872,000 more toll-free services than the prior year. But, 6.7 million taxpayers got disconnected.

So, how are they doing now? Since then, government studies have found:

- The IRS is not always following guidelines when conducting seizures. In 2007, 17 of the 50 cases it studied had violations.
- The time needed to resolve a taxpayer problem by the Taxpayer Advocate Service more than doubled from fiscal 1998 to 2003, from 37 to 76 days. This was despite no decrease in staff or increase in workload.
- The IRS Centralized Authorization file contained incomplete or incorrect information in about 40 percent of the records reviewed.
- The IRS system designed to uncover unauthorized access to IRS electronic data continues to malfunction.
- The IRS failed to release tax liens on nearly 23,000 taxpayers with no liability (32 percent of all liens).
- 21 percent of taxpayers were not at all satisfied with IRS customer service in 2004, up from 19 percent in 2003.
- A 2005 study concluded that the IRS had "serious weaknesses" in its ability to protect sensitive taxpayer and financial data.
- A 2006 TIGTA report found a 27 percent error rate at IRS taxpayer assistance centers. That might explain a 2007 study showing visits to such centers down by more than 1.9 million, a 22 percent decrease.
- The IRS system that is used to detect fraudulent returns had "significant security vulnerabilities" in a 2007 TIGTA study.
- Telephone inquiries were inaccurate as much as 10 percent of the time in 2006 as per a GAO study.

But there was some "good" news.

- For the 2004 filing season, the IRS gave taxpayers complete and accurate information regarding their accounts during 94 percent of all monitored calls. So 6 percent still got their accounts wrong.
- The accuracy of answers to tax questions at IRS offices improved to 67 percent in 2004. Still, 33 percent wrong?!
- In 2005 questions were answered correctly 66 percent of the time. That's still 34 percent wrong.
- But phone accuracy in 2005 jumped from 79.5 percent the year before to 89.5 percent. It surged to almost 90 percent in 2006.
- That's better if you can get through. Unfortunately phone accessibility slidded to 82 percent—18 percent couldn't even connect to ask a question.

- In 2006 telephone answers were still wrong about 10 percent of the time.
- In 2007 telephone answers were wrong only 9 percent of the time.
- Customer satisfaction for 2007 was up to 94 percent, at least for the 82 percent that actually got through.
- A 2009 TIGTA study found errors and legal violations in nearly half the IRS property seizures it studied.
- The IRS still needs help with the phone. In 2009, 5 million taxpayers received busy signals, and almost 18 million callers hung up before getting through.
- The GAO in 2009 found the IRS computer network still vulnerable to internal threats.
- After another 2009 study by the TIGTA, it was concluded that unauthorized and insecure Web servers placed both the computers and the entire IRS network at risk of unauthorized access to taxpayer and personally identifiable information.
- The IRS spent nearly 2 years and $19.5 million to develop its new Web portal, but it cancelled the project 6 months before its scheduled completion date.
- As of December 2008, the IRS had implemented only 81 percent of the security settings mandated by the Office of Management and Budget.
- The level of services on toll-free lines in 2009 was 71 percent, up from 53 percent in 2008. That's still 29 percent of calls not answered.
- A 2010 TIGTA report found that the IRS failed to follow statutory taxpayer rights when filing tax liens.
- Let's not even think about how the IRS handled the home buyer credit. The TIGTA identified more than 19,000 electronic returns claiming credit in excess of $139 million for homes not yet bought and 580 taxpayers under age 18 who reported to be first-time home buyers.
- In 2010, the TIGTA concluded that the IRS had lost $695,115 in interest due to slow processing of paper checks.
- Another 2010 TIGTA report found that the IRS was not authenticating taxpayers who called toll-free assistance lines before giving out confidential tax account information.
- IRS employees did not work well with others. Two Covington, Kentucky, service center workers were charged with stealing money orders, and a California IRS agent was indicted for filing false tax returns, helping others to file false tax returns, and threatening to kill tax agents who were investigating him.
- Even volunteers had it rough, with a government audit finding that on 3.5 million returns filed, there was an accuracy rate of only 59 percent, in 2009, down from 69 percent in 2008.

- With the new IRS2Go 2.0 smartphone app, you can apply for a transcript, get the latest IRS news, or watch IRS YouTube videos.
- They are happy. Seventy-five percent of IRS employees were either "very satisfied" or "satisfied" with their jobs in 2011, up from 74 percent in 2010 and 55 percent in 2002. The fact that they actually had jobs may have been an influence.
- We are happy. In September 2011, TIGTA found IRS management in compliance with the law on employee evaluation standards. It found that the IRS did *not* use quota or tax enforcement results records to evaluate employee performance.
- In fiscal 2012, the IRS detected 3 million fraudulent returns totaling $20 billion, up from $14 billion in the prior year.
- The accuracy rate for the IRS Volunteer Program increased to 49 percent in 2012, up from 39 percent in 2011. That's still 51 percent wrong!
- The TIGTA in March 2013 found the IRS information technology system more than 2 years behind schedule, leaving taxpayers' information vulnerable to hackers.
- The IRS telephone service level in 2012 declined to 68 percent and 40 percent of the paper correspondence received by the IRS failed to be responded to within 45 days of receipt.
- In fiscal 2012, IRS employees used 573,319 hours on union activity, equivalent to 23,888 days!
- In fiscal 2012 and 2013, the IRS spent over $1 million on travel expenses for union activity.
- The IRS spent over $4.8 million in fiscal 2011 and $4.7 million in fiscal 2012 for executive travel.
- In a 2012 study, the TIGTA found that the IRS did not comply with legal seizure guidelines in 15 cases out of a random sampling of 50 seizures.
- According to TIGTA, the IRS is doing a poor job with identity theft reports. Many identity theft victims, including some visitors to IRS assistance centers, incorrectly used Form 3949-A to notify the IRS. That form is supposed to be used to report suspected fraudulent tax activity of individuals and businesses. Adding insult to injury, the Service destroyed about 3,000 forms filed by identity theft victims. If you believe you might be a victim of identity theft, call the IRS at 800-908-4490.
- In fiscal 2013, the IRS could only answer 61 percent of calls from taxpayers seeking to speak with an IRS customer service representative (CSR). That's down from 87 percent 10 years earlier, with half the decline occurring since FY 2010. In FY 2013, 39 percent of calls (some 20 million) simply did not get through.

2015 Tax Season:

Percent of calls answered by IRS assistors for various phone lines

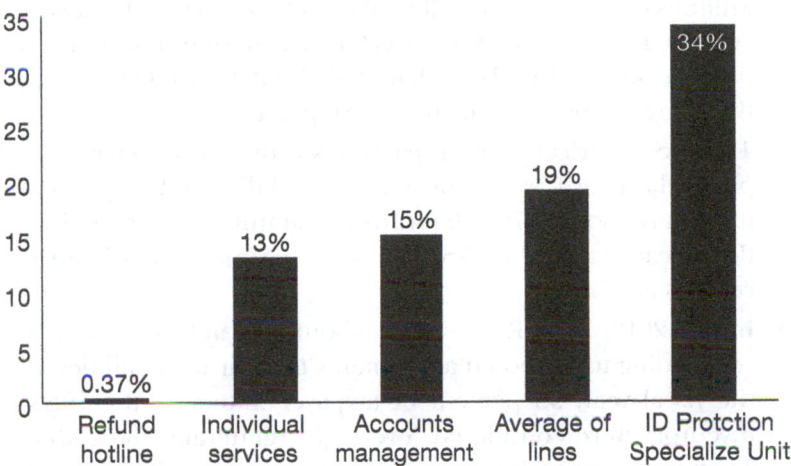

IRS phone responsiveness for taxpayers and tax pros

The IRS didn't play favorites—they may have answered a higher percentage of practitioners' calls than of taxpayers', but only after they waited an average of 22 minutes longer.

- Taxpayers who did get through had to wait on hold approximately 17.6 minutes before speaking with a CSR. That's up from 2.6 minutes 10 years earlier, a nearly sixfold increase, with nearly half the increase occurring since FY 2010.

- Millions of taxpayers visit IRS walk-in sites each year for assistance. Ten years ago, the IRS answered some 795,000 tax law questions in the sites during the filing season. In FY 2013, it handled about 110,000 tax law questions during the filing season—a reduction of 86 percent.

- The IRS historically has prepared tax returns for taxpayers seeking its help, particularly for low income, elderly, and disabled taxpayers. Ten years ago, it prepared some 476,000 returns. That number declined significantly over the decade, and the IRS recently announced it will no longer prepare returns at all.

- In FY 2013, the IRS received about 8.4 million letters from taxpayers responding to proposed adjustments to their tax liabilities. As of the end of the fiscal year, 53 percent of taxpayer letters in the IRS's "adjustments" inventory were considered "over age" (generally, more than 45 days old). That compares with "over age" percentages of 12 percent 10 years earlier and 28 percent in FY 2010.

- In 2013, the IRS announced it will only answer "basic" tax law questions on its telephone lines and in its walk-in sites during the upcoming filing season, and it will not answer any tax law questions after the filing season, including questions from the millions of taxpayers who obtain filing extensions and prepare their returns later in the year.

- Good news! The IRS has decided not to audit a taxpayer for more than 5 consecutive years. On the other hand, you may qualify for Examination Technique Code 4. That's where an audit can be closed after the initial appointment with a taxpayer.

During the 2015 filing season:

- The IRS processed 126.1 million individual tax returns (compared with 125.6 million in 2014) and issued 91.8 million refunds (compared with 94.8 million in 2014). The average refund amount was $2,711 (compared with $2,686 in 2014).

- The IRS answered only 37 percent of taxpayer calls routed to customer service representatives overall, and the hold time for taxpayers who got through averaged 23 minutes. This level of service represents a sharp drop-off from the 2014 filing season, when the IRS answered 71 percent of its calls and hold times averaged about 14 minutes.

2016 & 2017 Filing Season Statistics for Selected Toll-Free Telephone Lines[45]

Telephone Line	2016				2017				Percent Change	
	Dialed Attempts	Assistor Calls Answered	Average Speed of Answer (Minutes)	Level of Service	Dialed Attempts	Assistor Calls Answered	Average Speed of Answer (Minutes)	Level of Service	ASA Percentage Change	LOS Percentage Change
Accounts Management (AM) [SUM of 29 Lines]	50,197,902	13,156,402	11.1	72.1%	36,853,126	9,872,802	6.5	79.1%	-41%	10%
Refund Hotline 800-829-1954	16,609,333	166,703	11.4	65.7%	13,155,827	138,167	5.4	74.9%	-52%	14%
Individual Income Tax Services 800-829-1040	8,835,528	2,641,875	12.2	72.1%	8,121,605	2,238,786	5.1	81.3%	-58%	13%
Transcript 800-908-9946	1,172,769	75,533	11.7	71.0%	2,073,759	159,197	6.0	86.6%	-49%	22%
Wage & Investment IMF Customer Response 800-829-0922	2,101,600	676,708	11.7	64.3%	1,818,893	749,240	5.1	80.5%	-56%	25%
Refund Call Back 800-829-0582	2,953,193	709,417	12.8	68.7%	1,787,379	539,793	6.6	74.9%	-48%	9%
Business & Specialty Tax Services Line 800-829-4933	1,372,748	709,392	11.0	77.0%	1,440,368	719,092	10.3	77.0%	-7%	0%
Identity Protection Specialized Unit (IPSU) 800-908-4490	1,574,881	841,261	14.9	76.5%	1,079,399	663,230	8.3	82.8%	-44%	8%
Self Employed IMF Customer Response 800-829-8374	976,523	312,337	11.1	64.0%	864,595	338,973	5.1	79.3%	-54%	24%
ACA Hotline 800-919-0452	1,180,112	803,046	13.5	71.8%	737,028	495,149	8.5	76.7%	-37%	7%
Tax Law 866-883-0217	717,876	421,941	9.4	70.2%	718,472	459,566	10.5	71.8%	12%	2%
PPS 866-860-4259	549,037	391,037	7.3	83.5%	683,674	487,346	6.9	81.0%	-6%	-3%
BMF Customer Response 800-829-0115	850,033	600,333	11.6	81.1%	683,239	486,811	10.0	82.1%	-13%	1%
International 8775 (855-790-8775)	254,332	154,487	6.9	74.3%	223,201	140,284	4.4	78.8%	-37%	6%
Tax Exempt and Government Entities (TE/GE) 877-829-5500	201,179	117,552	10.4	72.8%	199,771	122,162	8.4	74.0%	-19%	2%
Individual Taxpayer Identification Number (ITIN) 800-908-9982	123,905	74,091	10.0	71.1%	189,254	121,148	7.6	73.6%	-24%	4%
NTA 877-777-4778	266,438	138,647	5.1	73.7%	175,879	91,629	2.7	77.2%	-48%	5%
VITA Location 800-906-9887	58,150	39,681	2.9	75.6%	53,428	35,390	3.3	74.4%	11%	-2%
TAC Appointment 844-545-5640	961,103	630,594	5.4	75.9%	2,188,336	1,514,657	4.8	80.3%	-11%	6%
Installment Agreement/Balance Due	2,463,090	1,864,816	11.3	75.7%	2,656,759	1,071,182	46.8	40.3%	31.3%	-47%
Taxpayer Protection Program 800-830-5084	4,543,631	1,053,121	10.3	23.7%	1,368,598	879,273	7.4	77.8%	-28%	229%

(Continued)

2016 & 2017 Filing Season Statistics for Selected Toll-Free Telephone Lines45 (continued)

Telephone Line	2016				2017				Percent Change	
	Dialed Attempts	Assistor Calls Answered	Average Speed of Answer (Minutes)	Level of Service	Dialed Attempts	Assistor Calls Answered	Average Speed of Answer (Minutes)	Level of Service	ASA Percentage Change	LOS Percentage Change
Forms Order Line 800-829-3676 (800-TAX-FORM)	1,081,589	651,142	4.0	80.2%	886,921	554,807	1.6	90.9%	–59%	13%
Amended Return Hotline 866-464-2050	706,250	427,956	11.8	74.6%	518,197	337,970	7.4	78.4%	–37%	5%
Enterprise Total (Includes AM, Compliance, Forms Order Line, ASK TAS, and EPSS)	**55,341,769**	**15,725,909**	**11.8**	**71.3%**	**44,327,213**	**13,176,265**	**11.6**	**70.7%**	**–2%**	**–1%**

45 IRS, JOC, *Snapshot Reports: Enterprise Snapshot* (Apr. 22, 2017) (source of AM and Enterprise Total data); IRS, JOC, *Snapshot Reports: Product Line Detail* (Apr. 22, 2017) (source of all other data except the Taxpayer Protection Program (TPP) line); IRS, JOC, *FY 2016 Weekly TPP Snapshot Report* (Apr. 22, 2017) (source of TPP line data). Data from Jan. 1–Apr. 22, 2017. Dialed attempts, sometimes called Net Attempts, is the number of callers intended for a given product line. Dialed attempts excludes callers who dialed the number, but should have dialed another number, and includes callers who dialed another number but should have dialed this number. IRS, *FY17 Snapshot & ELS Reporting Guidelines*, Version 2017.02 (Mar. 3, 2017).

- The IRS answered only 39 percent of calls from taxpayers seeking assistance from TAS on the National Taxpayer Advocate (NTA) toll-free hotline, and hold times averaged 19 minutes. TAS serves as the IRS's "safety net" for taxpayers who are experiencing a financial or systemic hardship as a result of IRS action or inaction.

- The IRS answered only 17 percent of calls from taxpayers who called after being notified that their tax returns had been blocked by the Taxpayer Protection Program (TPP) on suspicion of identity theft, and the hold times averaged about 28 minutes. In three consecutive weeks during the filing season, the IRS answered fewer than 10 percent of these calls.

- The IRS answered only 45 percent of calls from practitioners who called the IRS on the Practitioner Priority Service line, and hold times averaged 45 minutes.

- The number of "courtesy disconnects" received by taxpayers calling the IRS skyrocketed from about 544,000 in 2014 to about 8.8 million this filing season, an increase of more than 1,500 percent. The term "courtesy disconnect" is used when the IRS essentially hangs up on a taxpayer because its switchboard is overloaded and cannot handle additional calls.

- The decline in telephone performance can be attributed largely to three factors: The number of taxpayer calls routed to telephone assistors increased by 41 percent, the number of calls answered by telephone assistors decreased by 26 percent, and the average call duration increased by 10 percent.

- The IRS sharply restricted the availability of paper copies of forms and publications, imposing burden on taxpayers without Internet access or online literacy. The IRS's own Taxpayer Assistance Centers (TACs) and its Tax Form Outlet Partners such as libraries and post offices did not receive forms until February 28, almost halfway through the filing season. Once a TAC ran out of forms or publications, it could not order more.

For the 2016 filing season, Congress added $250 million in funding specifically for tax payer service, identity theft and cyber security. That helped fund the hiring of 1,000 additional customer service representatives to answer the toll-free help lines. In 2015, only about 37 percent of callers actually got through. For 2016, IRS Commissioner Koskinen expected that at least 60 percent of taxpayers will be able to reach a representative. He should be proud—for the 2016 filing

season, the IRS answered nearly 73 percent of all customer service calls with an average wait time of 11 minutes.

Yet, according to House Ways and Means Committee Chairman Kevin Brady (R-Texas), "reaching an IRS employee often seems as unlikely as winning Powerball."

If the congressman thinks he has trouble reaching the IRS on the phone, it would be no better in person at one of the Taxpayer Assistance Centers (TACs). The IRS maintains approximately 362 (after closing 9 in 2018) TACs around the country that collectively serve more than 5 million taxpayers annually. Historically, the TACs were known as "walk-in sites," but the IRS has eliminated virtually all walk-in service and requires that taxpayers schedule advance appointments in all TAC locations as of the end of 2016. This requirement will cause particular harm to (i) taxpayers who do not know the TACs have shifted to appointment-only scheduling and travel sometimes considerable distances to seek personal assistance and (ii) taxpayers who need assistance urgently and cannot wait to obtain an appointment. Under a pilot program testing appointment-only service, 20 percent of taxpayers had to wait between 13 and 41 days to obtain an appointment and 5 percent had to wait more than 41 days. Those wait times are too long for taxpayers with urgent needs. At several TACs, the IRS went so far as to refuse to accept tax payments or returns this filing season.

There were other 2016 filing season problems. Both on its phone lines and in its TACs, the IRS continued recent restrictions on answering tax-law questions. During the filing season, the IRS answered only "basic" questions, deeming more complex questions "out of scope." After the filing season, the IRS is not answering any tax-law questions at all, even though many taxpayers obtain legally authorized extensions of time to file. In 2015, nearly 15 million returns were submitted after the filing season.

The law is so complicated that it is difficult to fault the IRS on their incorrect answers, even when a taxpayer call goes through. In a 1988 study done by *Money* magazine, 50 tax professionals, including attorneys and CPAs, were asked to complete a tax return for a hypothetical family. The results were "unnerving"—no two preparers computed the same tax due and, worse, the answers varied by as much as 50 percent! In a second study by *Money*, done one year later, the answers were even more off the mark. Again, each participant computed a different tax for the family. And the bottom line ranged astonishingly from a low of $12,539 to a high of $35,813. The *Money* studies have continued each year with different bottom lines computed each year. The *minimum* spread was 50 percent in 1988; it was nearly 1,000 percent in 1991.

A 2006 GAO undercover investigation revealed poor performance at 19 tax-prep chain operations. Among the problems were micalculated refunds resulting in unwarranted extra refunds or incorrectly figured losses; unreported business income; faulty calculation of earned income credit; failure of preparers to take the most advantageous post-secondary education tax benefit; and improper itemization of deductions or failure to claim all available deductions.

The complexity and its confusion continue. Tax Analysts created a fictitious profile for a taxpayer in 2009 and filled out several free file tax returns. Each company calculated a different refund amount for the taxpayer, ranging from $1,201 to $3,400! Personally, I'd file the return with the $3,400 refund. The IRS's office of professional responsibility has revealed that even tax practitioners who have been convicted of *tax crimes* continued to represent entities before the IRS. In a statistical survey, it was found that 4.5 percent of practitioners were noncompliant regarding their own individual tax obligations.

For fiscal year 2017, the IRS answered 95,618,714 calls with a 77.1% answer/call rate. But the number of answered calls was down by 21,861,267 from the prior year. Customer satisfaction was up 2% to 90.0% – but that only counts those that actually got through. They might have gotten a different score had they included the opinions of the 28.4 million who did NOT get through.

Thankfully, former IRS Commissioner Lawrence Gibbs, in a hearing of the Senate Finance Committee on Private Retirement Plans and IRS Oversight, stated that the IRS would not impose penalties on taxpayers who relied on incorrect information supplied by IRS telephone taxpayer assistance personnel. Nevertheless, the tax itself would not be forgiven, and the taxpayer would have the burden of maintaining a record of the name of the IRS employee who supplied the incorrect information as well as the date of the conversation.

Even though the Internal Revenue Service may not always be accurate, it strives always to be prepared. The IRS has revised IRM 1(16)00—Physical, Document, and Computer Systems Security—to include two former policy statements, P-1-165 and P-1-166. Both statements cover national emergency operations. The first statement discusses the function of the "IRS in the Event of a National Emergency—Especially Resulting from a Nuclear Attack." In case of an emergency, the primary duty of the IRS "is to support the Secretary of the Treasury." To this end, the duties of the IRS "will consist of analyzing and reporting on emergency tax legislation, prescribing regulations in forms, and issuing rulings and technical information of an emergency nature." The second statement specifies that, in the event of an emergency, the IRS will focus on operations that, given the circumstances, would yield the greatest revenue. "On the premise that the collection of

IRS STRATEGIC PLANNING FRAMEWORK

MISSION

Provide America's taxpayers top quality service by helping them understand and meet their tax responsibilities and by applying the tax law with integrity and fairness to all.

GUIDING PRINCIPLES

- Understand and solve problems from taxpayer's point of view

- Enable managers to be accountable — knowledge, responsibility, authority, action

- Align measures of performance at all organizational levels.

- Foster open, honest communication

- Insist on total integrity

- Demonstrate effective stewardship of assets and information entrusted to the IRS

STRATEGIC GOALS and OBJECTIVES

Service to Each Taxpayer
- Make filing easier
- Provide first quality service to each taxpayer needing help with his or her return or account
- Provide prompt, professional, helpful treatment to taxpayers in cases where additional taxes may be due

Service to All Taxpayer
- Increase fairness of compliance
- Increase overall compliance

Productivity through a Quality Work Environment
- Increase employee job satisfaction
- Hold agency employment stable while economy grows and service improves

MODERNIZATION PROGRAMS

Fundamental long-term improvement in way IRS works

MAJOR STRATEGIES

How IRS will achieve goals in near term (2–3 years)

Organizational Modernization

- Customer-focused organizational structure
- Clear management roles and responsibilities

Business Systems Modernization

- Develop enterprise vision and architecture
- Revamp all major business practices
- Reengineer technology

Balanced Measures

- Align with strategic goals

Operational Priorities

- Specific areas of emphasis to achieve strategies and goals

Improvement Projects

- Focused, near-term improvements in business practices and technology

Strategic Measures

- For major taxpayer segments
- Agency as a whole

Operational Measures

- For each operational program or activity

Program Plans

- Program activities and resources
- Operational measures

Modernization Projects

IRS MISSION

Provide America's taxpayers top-quality service by helping them understand and meet their tax responsibilities and by applying the tax law with integrity and fairness to all.

STRATEGIC GOALS AND OBJECTIVES

Service to Each Taxpayer	Service to All Taxpayer	Productivity through a Quality Work Environment
• Make filing easier • Provide first quality service to each taxpayer needing help with his or her return or account • Provide prompt, professional, helpful treatment to taxpayers in cases where additional taxes may be due	• Increase fairness of compliance • Increase overall compliance	• Increase employee job satisfaction • Hold agency employment stable while economy grows and service improves

IRS Balanced Measures System

SERVICEWIDE and MAJOR CUSTOMER SEGMENT STRATEGIC MEASURES

• Overall customer satisfaction • Burden	• Payment compliance • Filing compliance • Reporting compliance	• Overall employee satisfaction • Productivity/Workload index

OPERATING UNIT OPERATIONAL MEASURES

• Customer satisfaction with specific products and services	• Quality of work products and services produced • Quality, accuracy and timeliness of products and services provided	• Organizational unit and Work group employee satisfaction

DIAGNOSTIC and WORKLOAD INDICATORS

• Diagnostic data that is helpful in understanding what influences and impacts operational and strategic measures

• Workload data used to project expected levels of activity for an organizational unit or program

Organizational Performance

INDIVIDUAL MEASURES

• Performance plans or agreements for executives, managers, and management officials aligned with strategic goals and balanced measures of customer satisfaction, employee satisfaction, and business results

• Critical job elements for front-line employees aligned with the goals of balanced measures

delinquent accounts would be most adversely affected, and in many cases would be impossible in a disaster area, the Service will concentrate on the collection of current taxes," the manual said. Given the real possibility of a nuclear attack, I, for one, feel a lot more comfortable.

Or, at least it did until a June 2017 TIGTA report that found the IRS lacks adequate support to recover remittance, tax returns, and refund data after a tech-related disaster or emergency.

THE AUDIT

Internal Revenue Code Section 7605(a) gives the IRS the authority to fix the time and place of an audit as is reasonable under the circumstances. The Internal Revenue Manual states that IRS examiners should endeavor to make appointments at a time and place convenient for the taxpayer (IRM 4261.2). (See also Temp Reg. Section 301.7605-IT.)

Generally, the office that handles your audit will be determined by your domicile—where you live. However, the Internal Revenue Service will approve a request for a transfer of an audit if your domicile has changed before or during the examination or if you have died and your legal representative is in another district. The following rules for audit location generally apply:

1. A request for a transfer to a district closer to your residence will normally be approved.

2. If you live in one district, work in another, and are not represented by a Power of Attorney, you will be examined in the district where you reside.

3. If you are called for an audit in one district but live in another district that is within commuting distance (not defined) of the first, and are represented by a Power of Attorney within that distance, the audit will normally take place in the district where you reside.

4. If you live in one district and are represented by a Power of Attorney doing business in another district that is within commuting distance of the first, you will be audited in the district where you live.

5. If you live in another district outside commuting distance of the district where your return is scheduled for audit and are represented by a Power of Attorney in the other district, you will have a transfer request approved.

6. If you reside in the district where the audit is scheduled and are represented by a Power of Attorney in a district outside commuting distance of the first, you may obtain a transfer if the receiving district agrees.

Each IRS district office is made up of four divisions. Each division is subdivided into branches, the titles of which describe what is done in each branch. The four divisions are Administration, Collection, Audit, and Intelligence.

The Administration Division handles such matters as personnel, training, and facilities management of all types—from selection of the site of the office to ordering pens and paper.

The Collection Division is the bill-collecting arm of the Internal Revenue Service. It is represented in the field by Revenue Officers and in the Office Branch. The Collection Division also has a section known as the Taxpayer Service Section, which is a year-round information center manned by Taxpayer Service Representatives.

The Intelligence Division is the branch of the Internal Revenue Service that handles criminal investigations. It is staffed with Special Agents, who are enforcement officers and whose work is primarily technical. The main objective of an investigation by a Special Agent is to determine whether or not there should be criminal prosecution—as contrasted with an Internal Revenue Agent's objective, which is to determine the proper tax to be paid.

The Audit Division is charged with verifying the accuracy of tax returns filed, regarding both the substance of the law and the validity of the amounts reported. The major branches of the Audit Division are Field Audit, Office Audit, Review, and Audit Service. They have been renamed Examinations Branch. Field Audit employs Internal Revenue Agents and Estate Tax Examiners, and they are charged with auditing the more complex tax returns filed. Office Audit is staffed with Tax Auditors, who primarily audit individual returns. The Review staff is composed of former Field Agents and Tax Auditors, who check the accuracy of the audits made by the examining officers. Audit Service maintains the files on prior reports by examining officers and is a control center for cases under audit or cases that have been audited.

The charts on pages 644 and 645 detail the 2001 IRS strategic planning framework.

Victims of IRS errors now have a form on which to claim reimbursement. Such a claim is allowable under 31 U.S.C. Section 3732 but is limited to $1,000 and must be submitted within 1 year of its accrual. Filers of new Form 8489, Claim for Reimbursement for Expenses Incurred Due to Service Error, are instructed to submit substantiating documentation and are cautioned not to claim expenses for telephone calls, mileage or parking, lost wages, postage, or other nonreimbursable costs of the kind that are common to any disputed bill.

The scope of an audit will depend on various factors, but according to a recent addition to the IRS Manual, there are four items that *must* be reviewed by an agent:

1. Income probes, including bank statement analysis, bartering schemes, sale of assets, prizes, alimony, pensions, income tax refunds, etc.

2. Determination of the results of previous audits, including when the last took place, the results, and any recent correspondence the taxpayer may have had with the IRS.

3. Examination of subsequent and prior years' returns to make sure whether they were filed on time, where similar adjustments to the year under examination are necessary, and whether there are other issues that should be probed.

4. Determination of whether penalties have been previously assessed and whether they should be assessed as a result of the current examination.

The IRS Manual instructs the agents to comment on these items in their workpapers or to document the reasons why they were not examined.

According to IRS guidelines, unless specific recordkeeping requirements must be met, statements by the taxpayer, or others, may serve as adequate evidence in an audit. The IRS Manual notes that adequate evidence does not require complete documentation (IRM 4231, Audit Guidelines for Examiners, 330[2]).

Because the law is so vague in spots and so complicated, an intensive review and appeals procedure is available to you. Once your audit has been completed, the agent will present a Revenue Agent's Report stating recommendations and advising of any additional tax you owe. You will then be asked to sign a waiver indicating that you agree with the assessment. At this point you have three choices:

1. You can accept the adjustments, sign the waiver, and pay the tax.
2. You can pay the tax and file for a refund of the disputed amount.
3. You can request a conference with the IRS Appellate Division.

Prior to October 2, 1978, you could have taken a dispute with a revenue agent to a district conference. If an agreement was not reached there, a second hearing was available at the appellate division level. Alternatively, you could have elected to go directly to the appellate division. Under the present system the Internal Revenue Service maintains appeals offices at all locations where full-time district conferees and regional appellate offices were formerly located. The theory of eliminating the district conference is that, according to the Internal Revenue Service, the two-level system of administrative review was a costly duplication, for both the taxpayer and the Service.

It is almost universally agreed that it is best to settle at the agent level, if possible. If the tax deficiency involved is small, it may not justify the cost in time and dollars of pursuing your case to a higher level. Moreover, if the agent has

missed items that you don't want questioned, your best approach may be to pay the deficiency and run. But *never* settle or concede any issue until the audit is completed. When the agent's cards are on the table, you have more leeway in planning your negotiation strategy.

For a psychological advantage, where appropriate, you may wish to tape-record the audit proceedings. The Internal Revenue Service has revised the table of contents for, and added new text to, IRM 7600, Processing Determination Letter Applications. The new text, IRM 7610, Verbatim Recording of Conversations during Determination Proceedings, provides that verbatim recordings of Determination Proceedings will be permitted ordinarily with group manager approval (Manual Transmittal 7600-50 [11-18-83]; *Mott*, 214 F. Supp. 20 [N.D. Cal. 1963]; 1 Audit, CCH Internal Revenue Manual 4245). The absolute right to audiorecord a taxpayer interview was codified in Section 7520, enacted as part of the Omnibus Taxpayer Bill of Rights (you can even record an appeals hearing, *Keene v. Commissioner*, July 9, 2003), but see *Huehne*, 83-2345 (October 23, 1983), wherein the Court ruled that the taxpayer did not have a right to videotape the audit. However, in 2012, Taxpayer Advocate Nina Olson recommended that the IRS set up the technology to conduct virtual face-to-face audits via video-conference.

If you disagree with the agent's assessment, you will receive a copy of the revenue agent's report with a preliminary note advising you that you have 30 days to appeal. If you ignore this letter, you will then receive a "90-day" letter advising you to pay or to petition the tax court for redetermination.

After receiving the 30-day letter, but before receiving the 90-day letter, you may request a hearing by notifying your IRS regional appeals office. If the original audit was conducted by a tax auditor at an IRS office or by correspondence, you do not have to file a written protest to begin the appeal process. In the past, if the disputed amount was $2,500 or less, the same was true of a field examination conducted at your place of business; and if your field audit resulted in a disputed amount over $2,500, a written protest was necessary. These rules were changed by the IRS. Now, a written protest is required for field examinations only if the amount at issue for any tax year exceeds $25,000. (If the amount at issue does not exceed $25,000 but exceeds $2,500, a brief written statement of disputed issues is required [IA-85-91, 9/17/93].) As under prior law, no brief written statement or written protest is required to obtain an appeals office conference, in-office interview, or correspondence examination. An oral request will still suffice. The protest should be filed in duplicate and should contain the following:

a) your name and address;

b) the date and case reference symbols on the letter from the Internal Revenue Service transmitting the findings that you are protesting;

c) the tax years or periods involved;

d) an itemized schedule of adjustments or findings with which you do not agree;

e) a statement that you want to appeal the findings of the revenue agent;

f) a statement of factual evidence supporting your position in the contested issues, which should be sworn to as true, under penalties of perjury; *and*

g) a statement outlining the law or other authority upon which you are relying.

In response to your protest, an appellate conferee will meet with you at the regional office to discuss the disputed issues. While such a hearing is an informal procedure, you must remember that the burden of proof is still on you to provide clear and convincing evidence that the revenue agent's report should be amended. While oral statements and evidence will be considered, the best evidence is documentary—books, records, worksheets, journals, and so forth.

To help you with the appeals process, the IRS has created an appeals customer service program. You can call the following numbers to get help with any appeals matter:

Telephone Directory—National (Toll-Free) 877-457-5055
Appeals Customer Service Representation

Office (Location)	Customer Service Representatives (Not a Toll-Free Number)
NORTHEAST REGION	
Brooklyn *(Hempstead)*	516-539-6259
Connecticut-Rhode Island *(East Hartford)*	860-390-4055
Manhattan *(New York City)*	212-298-2430
Michigan *(Detroit)*	313-226-2314 ext. 62344
New England *(Boston)*	617-565-7962
New Jersey *(Newark)*	973-645-6288
Ohio *(Cleveland)*	216-623-2047
Pennsylvania *(Philadelphia)*	215-597-2177 ext. 160
Upstate New York *(Buffalo)*	716-551-5330 ext. 21
SOUTHEAST REGION	
Delaware-Maryland *(Baltimore)*	410-962-9354
Georgia *(Atlanta)*	404-338-7335
Gulf Coast *(New Orleans)*	504-558-3177
Indiana *(Indianapolis)*	317-226-6778
Kentucky-Tennessee *(Nashville)*	615-250-5613

Office (Location)	Customer Service Representatives (Not a Toll-Free Number)
North Florida *(Jacksonville)*	904-665-0962
North-South Carolina *(Greensboro)*	336-378-2309
South Florida *(Ft. Lauderdale)*	305-982-5377
Virginia-West Virginia *(Richmond)*	804-771-2302 ext. 19
MIDSTATES REGION	
Oklahoma-Arkansas *(Oklahoma)*	405-297-4941
Houston *(Houston)*	281-721-7255
Illinois *(Chicago)*	312-886-5736 ext. 652
Kansas-Missouri *(St. Louis)*	314-612-4652
Midwest *(Milwaukee)*	414-297-4120
North Central *(St. Paul)*	651-290-3867 ext. 351
North Texas *(Dallas)*	972-308-7329
South Texas *(Austin)*	512-499-5650
WESTERN REGION	
Central California *(San Jose)*	408-817-4622
Los Angeles *(Los Angeles)*	213-894-4700 ext. 129
Northern California *(San Francisco)*	415-744-9255
Northern California *(San Francisco)*	415-744-9255
Pacific Northwest *(Seattle)*	206-220-6054
Southern California *(Laguna Niguel)*	949-360-6380
Southwest *(Phoenix)*	602-207-8167
Rocky Mountain *(Denver)*	303-844-1951

For additional information, contact:

National Office *(Washington, DC)*

Office of Alternative Dispute Resolution and Customer Service Progrmas: Tom Louthan (202) 694-1842, Frederick L. Gavin (616)235-1280 or Darlene Marshall (202)694-1875

Regional Coordinators

Northeast Region (New York City): Ellen Wassong (212)298-2361

Southeast Region (Atlanta): Janell Gadd (404)338-7706

Midstates Region (Dallas): Leonard Horton (972)308-7495

Western Region (San Francisco): Dennis Malone (415)575-7313

The informality of the conference hearing is designed to save time and trouble for all parties. You may represent yourself, or you may be represented by an attorney, CPA, or an enrolled agent, an individual licensed to practice before the Internal Revenue Service. The aim of this stage of the appeals process is to resolve the issues with as little difficulty as possible. The objective

here is to *settle!* In fiscal 1979 IRS agents at this level proposed to assess $1,900,124,000 in added tax and penalties. They *closed* these cases for $1,161,977,000—about 61 percent of the proposed assessments. In 1982, appeals officers heard more than 50,000 cases covering an estimated 150,000 separate tax returns in over 500 locations. According to Howard T. Martin, director of the Appeals Division, "Appeal officers have more flexibility, and we never give up the idea of resolving a case." A 1982 survey by the General Accounting Office found that extra taxes and penalties were reduced or eliminated in 84 percent of the cases in appeals. Unlike agents at the audit level, Appeals Officers can settle cases based on "hazards of litigation." Thus, in Appeals, it is possible to split or trade issues.

The Internal Revenue Service tells its Appellate personnel to negotiate settlements "on a basis which is fair to both the Government and the taxpayer. Strive to close on an agreed basis the highest possible number of cases." They are to maintain an overall agreement rate of at least 85 percent in cases not yet docketed for trial in the Tax Court except for certain tax shelter, protestor, and similar cases. In docketed cases, the Internal Revenue Service wants to "maximize" settlements, with the aim to maintain or improve the agreement rate achieved in the previous year.

In July 2007, the IRS revealed that of the roughly 100,000 appeals cases reviewed each year, 80 percent were successfully resolved.

On December 29, 1999, the IRS announced a two year test when the taxpayer and the IRS can request binding arbitration on *factual* issues in dispute with Appeals (Announcement 2000-4). Legal issues are not allowed. Mediation for appeals cases was expanded by announcement 2001-9 through January 2002. This arbitration process is no longer a pilot program, but rather "business as usual" (IR 2006-163).

The Internal Revenue Service Small Business/Self-Employed Division (SB/SE) has available Fast Track Mediation, a new service to assist you in resolving disputes that arise from examination or collection actions.

Fast Track Mediation can be offered even with disputes not yet before a court. The program is designed to assist in resolving tax disputes arising from an examination, an offer in compromise, a Collection Due Process, or a trust fund recovery penalty.

You can choose either fast track mediation or the normal appeals process. You don't forgo any appeal rights during mediation and can withdraw from mediation. If you withdraw from mediation, the dispute would follow the normal appeals process. Either you or the IRS can request mediation, but both must agree to mediate. On average, the mediation

process should be started and completed within about 30–40 days. The normal appeals process can take months.

A specially trained IRS mediator from the Appeals Division will conduct the mediation session at a mutually agreed upon site. The mediator will discuss the dispute with both sides and can request additional information from either side. The mediator will not decide anything regarding the dispute. The mediator cannot impose a resolution and will not have settlement authority. The mediator will work to resolve the dispute between you and the IRS. You and IRS must both agree to any proposed resolution.

Fast track mediation was made permanent in June of 2003 (IR-2003-72 and Rev. Proc. 2003-41). Call (972)308-7330 for further details and how to initiate the process.

In July 2013, IRS Appeals Chief Sheldon Kay said that Appeals is developing new processes, such as the Rapid Appeals Process (RAP), to accelerate the resolution of cases in Appeals. Appeals is also stressing a more quasi-judicial approach to cases to ensure that Appeals employees do not act as investigators or examiners and do not raise new issues, according to Kay. He noted that the current cycle time for the largest cases in Appeals is 700 days, almost 2 years.

The IRS Appeals Arbitration Program was terminated in 2015 (Revenue Procedure 2015-44). Don't live near an IRS office? As of August 1, 2017, the IRS appeal office will be providing Web-based virtual conferences in a pilot program.

If you want to stop the running of interest on any potential deficiency, you are entitled to make what is known as a "deficiency deposit." Such a deposit should be made before the mailing of a deficiency notice and designated in writing as a "deposit in the nature of a cash bond." If you request a part or all of your deficiency deposit to be returned before the assessment of any tax, the request will be granted—unless the Internal Revenue Service determines that the deposit should be applied against a jeopardy assessment or another tax liability. No interest will be paid or allowed with respect to an amount returned to you.

There's one additional avenue of administrative redress for taxpayer problems. In 1977, the IRS instituted "problem resolution offices" (PROs) (now under the National Taxpayer Advocate's Office) to handle problems that have not been resolved through normal channels. Such problems include not only complaints by disgruntled taxpayers but lost, stolen, or delayed refund checks, billing errors, and hardship situations. The following table lists the addresses and telephone numbers of the Taxpayer Advocate Offices (TAO). For each district, address correspondence to the Taxpayer Advocate Officer, Internal Revenue Service.

ALABAMA
Birmingham Office
Taxpayer Advocate
801 Tom Martin Dr.
Birmingham, AL 35211
205-912-5631

ALASKA
Anchorage Office
Taxpayer Advocate
949 East 36th Ave.,
Stop A-405
Anchorage, AK 99508
907-271-6877

ARIZONA
Phoenix Office
Taxpayer Advocate
210 E. Earll Drive,
Stop 1005-PHX
Phoenix, AZ 85012
602-207-8240

ARKANSAS
Little Rock Office
Taxpayer Advocate
700 West Capitol St.,
Stop 1005-LIT
Little Rock, AR 72201
501-396-5978

CALIFORNIA
Laguna Niguel Office
Taxpayer Advocate
24000 Avila Road-
Room 3362
Laguna Niguel, CA 92677
949-389-4804

Los Angeles Office
Taxpayer Advocate
300 N. Los Angeles St.
Stop 1005-LA Room 5119
Los Angeles, CA 90012
213-576-3140

Oakland Office
Taxpayer Advocate
1301 Clay St. # 1540S
Oakland, CA 94612
510-637-2703

Sacramento Office
Taxpayer Advocate
4330 Watt Ave.
N. Highlands, CA 95660
916-974-5007

San Jose Office
Taxpayer Advocate
55 S. Market St.,
Stop HQ000-4
San Jose, CA 95113
408-817-6850

COLORADO
Denver Office
Taxpayer Advocate
600 17th St.,
Stop 1005-DEN
Denver, CO 80202-2490
303-446-1012

CONNECTICUT
Hartford Office
Taxpayer Advocate
135 High St., Stop 219
Hartford, CT 06103
860-756-4555

DELAWARE
Wilmington Office
Taxpayer Advocate
1352 Marrows Rd.
Newark, DE 19711-5445
302-286-1643

DISTRICT OF COLUMBIA
Baltimore Office
Taxpayer Advocate
31 Hopkins Plaza
Baltimore, MD 21201
410-962-2082

FLORIDA
Ft. Lauderdale Office
Taxpayer Advocate
7850 SW 6th Court
Plantation, FL 33324
954-423-7677

Jacksonville Office
Taxpayer Advocate
841 Prudential Dr.,
Suite 100
Stop: TA:SE/INT:JAX
Jacksonville, FL 32207
904-665-1000

GEORGIA
Atlanta Office
Taxpayer Advocate
401 W. Peachtree St., NW,
Summit Building
Stop 202-D
Atlanta, GA 30308
404-338-8099

HAWAII
Honolulu Office
Taxpayer Advocate
Stop H-405
300 Ala Moana Blvd.,
#50089
Honolulu, HI 96850
808-539-2870

IDAHO
Boise Office
Taxpayer Advocate
550 West Fort St., Box 041
Boise, ID 83724
208-387-2827

ILLINOIS
Chicago Office
Taxpayer Advocate
230 S. Dearborn St.
Stop 1005-CHI
Chicago, IL 60604
312-566-3800

Springfield Office
Taxpayer Advocate
320 W. Washington St.
Stop 1005-SPD
Springfield, IL 62701
217-527-6382

INDIANA
Indianapolis Office
Taxpayer Advocate
575 N. Pennsylvania St.,
Stop TA770
Indianapolis, IN 46204
317-685-7840

IOWA
Des Moines Office
Taxpayer Advocate
210 Walnut St.,
Stop 1005-DSM
Des Moines, IA 50309
515-564-6888

KANSAS
Wichita Office
Taxpayer Advocate
271 W. 3rd St., North
Stop 1005-WIC
Wichita, KS 67202
316-352-7506

KENTUCKY
Louisville Office
Taxpayer Advocate
600 Dr. MLK Jr. Place
Federal Building-Room 622
Louisville, KY 40202
502-582-6030

LOUISIANA
New Orleans Office
Taxpayer Advocate
600 South Maestri Pl.,
Stop 2
New Orleans, LA 70130
504-558-3001

MAINE
Augusta Office
Taxpayer Advocate
68 Sewall St., Room 313
Augusta, ME 04330
207-622-8528

MARYLAND
Baltimore Office
Taxpayer Advocate
31 Hopkins Plaza
Baltimore, MD 21201
410-962-2082

MASSACHUSETTS
Boston Office
Taxpayer Advocate
25 New Sudbury St.
Boston, MA 02203
617-316-2690

MICHIGAN
Detroit Office
Taxpayer Advocate
McNamara Federal
Building
477 Michigan Ave. -
Room 1745
Detroit, MI 48226
313-628-3670

MINNESOTA
St. Paul Office
Taxpayer Advocate
Stop 1005-STP
316 North Robert St.
St. Paul, MN 55101
651-312-7999

MISSISSIPPI
Jackson Office
Taxpayer Advocate
100 W. Capitol St.,
Stop JK31
Jackson, MS 39269
601-292-4800

MISSOURI
St. Louis Office
Taxpayer Advocate
Robert A. Young Building
1222 Spruce Street,
Stop 1005-STL
St. Louis, MO 63103
314-612-4610

MONTANA
Helena Office
Taxpayer Advocate
Federal Building
301 S. Park, Stop 1005-HEL
Helena, MT 59626-0023
406-441-1022

NEBRASKA
Omaha Office
Taxpayer Advocate
1313 Farnam St.,
Stop 1005-OMA
Omaha, NE 68102
402-221-4181

NEVADA
Las Vegas Office
Taxpayer Advocate
110 City Parkway Blvd.
Stop 1005-LVG
Las Vegas, NV 89106
702-868-5179

NEW HAMPSHIRE
Portsmouth Office
Taxpayer Advocate
Federal Office Building
80 Daniel St.
Portsmouth, NH 03801
603-433-0571

NEW JERSEY
Springfield Office
Taxpayer Advocate
955 S. Springfield Ave.
Springfield, NJ 07081
973-921-4043

NEW MEXICO
Albuquerque Office
Taxpayer Advocate
5338 Montgomery Blvd.
N.E.
Stop 1005-ALB
Albuquerque, NM 87109
505-837-5505

NEW YORK
Albany Office
Taxpayer Advocate
Leo O'Brien Federal
Building
1 Clinton Square
Albany, NY 12207
518-427-5413

Brooklyn Office
Taxpayer Advocate
10 Metro Tech Center
625 Fulton St.
Brooklyn, NY 11201
718-488-2080

Buffalo Office
Taxpayer Advocate
201 Como Park Blvd.
Buffalo, NY 14227
716-686-4850

Manhattan Office
Taxpayer Advocate
290 Broadway - 7th Floor
New York, NY 10007
212-436-1011

NORTH CAROLINA
Greensboro Office
Taxpayer Advocate
320 Federal Place,
Room 125
Greensboro,
NC 27401
336-378-2180

NORTH DAKOTA
Fargo Office
Taxpayer Advocate
657 2nd Ave, N.,
Stop 1005-FAR
Fargo, ND 58102
701-239-5141

OHIO
Cincinnati Office
Taxpayer Advocate
550 Main St.,
Room 3530
Cincinnati,
OH 45202
513-263-3260

Cleveland Office
Taxpayer Advocate
1240 E. Ninth St.,
Room 423
Cleveland,
OH 44199
216-522-7134

OKLAHOMA
Oklahoma City Office
Taxpayer Advocate
55 N. Robinson,
Stop 1005-OKC
Oklahoma City,
OK 73102
405-297-4055

OREGON
Portland Office
Taxpayer Advocate
1220 S.W. 3rd Ave.,
Stop O-405
Portland, OR 97204
503-326-2333

PENNSYLVANIA
Philadelphia Office
Taxpayer Advocate
600 Arch St.
Philadelphia,
PA 19106
215-861-1304

Pittsburgh Office
Taxpayer Advocate
1000 Liberty Ave.
Pittsburgh,
PA 15222
412-395-4769

RHODE ISLAND
Providence Office
Taxpayer Advocate
380 Westminster St.
Providence,
RI 02903
401-525-4200

SOUTH CAROLINA
Columbia Office
Taxpayer Advocate
1835 Assembly St.
MDP 03
Columbia, SC 29201
803-253-3029

SOUTH DAKOTA
Aberdeen Office
Taxpayer Advocate
115 4th Ave.
Southeast
Stop 1005-ABE
Aberdeen, SD 57401
605-226-7248

TENNESSEE
Nashville Office
Taxpayer Advocate
801 Broadway,
Stop 22
Nashville, TN 37203
615-250-5000

TEXAS
Austin Office
Taxpayer Advocate
300 E. 8th St.,
Stop 1005-AUS
Austin, TX 78701
512-499-5875

Dallas Office
Taxpayer Advocate
1114 Commerce St.
10th Floor MC1005
Dallas, TX 75242
214-413-6500

Houston Office
Taxpayer Advocate
1919 Smith St.,
Stop 1005-HOU
Houston, TX 77002
713-209-3660

UTAH
Salt Lake City Office
Taxpayer Advocate
50 South 200 East,
Stop 1005-SLC
Salt Lake City,
UT 84111
801-799-6958

VERMONT
Burlington Office
Taxpayer Advocate
Courthouse Plaza
199 Main St.
Burlington,
VT 05401
802-859-1052

VIRGINIA
Richmond Office
Taxpayer Advocate
400 North 8th St.
Richmond, VA 23240
804-916-3501

WASHINGTON
Seattle Office
Taxpayer Advocate
915 2nd Ave.,
Stop W-405
Seattle, WA 98174
206-220-6037

WEST VIRGINIA
Parkersburg Office
Taxpayer Advocate
425 Juliana St.
Parkersburg, WV 26101
304-420-8695

WISCONSIN
Milwaukee Office
Taxpayer Advocate
211 West Wisconsin Ave.
Stop 1005-MIL
Milwaukee, WI 53203
414-231-2390

WYOMING
Cheyenne Office
Taxpayer Advocate
5353 Yellowstone Rd.
Stop 1005-CHE
Cheyenne, WY 82009
307-633-0800

National
877-777-4778
Toll-free

**TAXPAYER ADVOCACY
PANEL REPRESENTATIVE**
888-912-1227
Toll-free

**TAXPAYERS LIVING
ABROAD OR IN U.S.
TERRITORIES**
A/C International
Taxpayer Advocate
7 Tabonuco Street
San Patricio Office
Building
Room 200
Guaynabo, Puerto Rico
00966

or
P.O. Box 193479
San Juan, Puerto Rico
00919-3479
787-622-8940 English
787-622-8930 Spanish

CENTERS
Andover Center
Taxpayer Advocate
P.O. Box 9055, Stop 121
Andover,
MA 01810-9055
978-474-5549

Atlanta Center
Taxpayer Advocate
P.O. Box 48-549,
Stop 29A
Doraville, GA 30362
770-936-4500

Austin Center
Taxpayer Advocate
P.O. Box 934,
Stop 1005-AUSC
Austin, TX 78767
512-460-8300

Brookhaven Center
Taxpayer Advocate
P.O. Box 960, Stop 102
Holtsville, NY 11742
631-654-6686

Cincinnati Center
Taxpayer Advocate
P.O. Box 1235,
Stop 11-G
Cincinnati,
OH 45201-1235
859-292-5316

Fresno Center
Taxpayer Advocate
P.O. Box 12161,
Stop 01
Fresno, CA 93776
559-442-6400

Kansas City Center
Taxpayer Advocate
333 W. Pershing
Stop 1005
Kansas City, MO 64108
816-291-9000

Memphis Center
Taxpayer Advocate
P.O. Box 30309 AMF,
Stop 13M
Memphis, TN 38130
901-395-1900

Ogden Center
Taxpayer Advocate
P.O. Box 1640
Stop 1005
Ogden, UT 84402
801-620-7168

Philadelphia Center
Taxpayer Advocate
11601 Roosevel Blvd.
Stop SW-820
Philadelphia, PA 19154
215-516-2499

An Internal Revenue Manual Supplement (MT 1279-57, May 25, 1988) provides complete guidelines for the operation of the program at all levels of the agency. The IRS adopted 11 separate categories of rights to which taxpayers are entitled. Some of these categories include:

- the right to prompt, courteous, and impartial treatment that includes the assumption that "each taxpayer wants to comply" with the tax code;
- the right to a reasonable amount of time to produce requested documentation;
- the right to receive copies of their returns from IRS Service Centers and any other tax information, such as examination, criminal investigation, and collection division work papers; *and*
- generally, the right to have a case transferred to a specific district office.

DEFICIENCY NOTICES

When the Internal Revenue Service determines that a deficiency exists, it must first send you a notice of the deficiency determination. You are then allowed a specific period—normally 90 days, beginning with the mailing of the notice—in which to file a petition for redetermination with the Tax Court. At that point the Internal Revenue Service is prohibited, with certain exceptions, from undertaking any assessment or collection activity until the deficiency notice has been mailed, the specified period has expired, and, if a Tax Court petition has been timely filed, the decision has become final [Section 6213(a)]. During the time this prohibition is in force, it is expressly provided that any assessment or collection activity by the IRS is subject to injunctive relief, notwithstanding the Anti-Injunction Act.

An *assessment* is, in essence, a bookkeeping notation that occurs when the IRS establishes an account against a taxpayer on the tax rolls. Technically, the assessment is made by an assessment officer for the district or regional service center by signing the summary record of assessment, which, through supporting records, provides the taxpayer's identification, the type of tax and taxable period, and the amount of the assessment. The date of the assessment is the date of the signing.

As soon as practical, and within 60 days after making the assessment, the IRS must give you notice of the unpaid amount and demand its payment by leaving the notice at your dwelling or usual place of business or by mailing it to your last known address. If you neglect or refuse to pay within 10 days after notice and demand, the IRS can proceed to collect the amount owed by levy. A *levy* includes the power of distraint and seizure by any means [IRC Section 6331(b)]. Ordinarily, a levy requires written notice of intent to levy at least 30 days prior to the day of levy, either in person or by leaving it at the dwelling or

usual place of business or by certified or registered mailing to the last known address of the taxpayer [IRC Section 6331(d)(1), (2)]. In circumstances where you neglect or refuse to pay the tax after demand, a lien is created in favor of the United States on all property owned by you. The lien arises from the date of the assessment and is effective as against certain persons upon proper filing of a notice of lien. The Internal Revenue Service possesses additional power, subject to certain limitations, to sell property that it has seized (see IRC Sections 6335 and 6336). Remember, however, that a petition to the Tax Court, timely filed, will prevent the Internal Revenue Service from proceeding with any of these potential administrative actions.

If you are not satisfied at the administrative level, you must go to court. Even if the law is probably in favor of the Internal Revenue Service, it may pay for you to move a case into the judiciary if the dollar amount is large enough. This is because it provides an additional opportunity for you to compromise the case. When you go to court, the case is removed from the jurisdiction of the Internal Revenue Service district office, which started the investigation, and placed in the hands of the regional counsel. While agents in the district office are primarily concerned with the letter of the law, the regional counsel's staff is more concerned with disposing of cases. Remember, it costs the Internal Revenue Service time and money to litigate a case, just as it costs you. If there is no special reason, such as emphasizing an IRS stand on a particular issue for contesting a case, the regional counsel may offer a settlement just to save the trouble of going to court. Even if the offer is only 10 percent of an amount that the district office disallowed completely, you may still come out ahead.

The general rule is that a taxpayer will lose who attempts to sue an IRS agent for harrassment. In *Pope v. Organ*, 82-2 USTC Par. 9613, 50 AFTR 2d 82-5273 (DC Texas, 1982), the court held that an agent would be immune from prosecution if both of the following conditions were met: (1) the action was taken with the belief that it was lawful and without malicious intent to cause deprivation of constitutional rights, and (2) given the discretion of the official and the circumstances, it was reasonable to believe that there was a right to take the action.

However, on April 11, 1983, the U.S. Court of Appeals for the Fifth Circuit ruled that a taxpayer *could sue* an IRS agent as a federal official, acting under color of federal law when he allegedly violated taxpayers' constitutional rights to due process by willfully and maliciously assessing them for taxes they did not owe and harrassing them into paying those taxes *(Rutherford* 83-1 USTC Par. 9289, 51 AFTR2d 83-1084). The Court allowed suit for compensatory damages for mental anguish and for the legal fees incurred in resisting the government's claim as well as punitive damages in retribution for the agent's abuses of authority. (See also *Miklautsch v. Commissioner*, No.

A89-291 Civil, 11/6/90 where it was held that the taxpayers have the right to bring action for unreasonable actions taken by IRS employees.) In 1998, Elvis E. "Johnny" Johnson was awarded $3.5 million when the IRS improperly publicized details of his tax situation.

EMPLOYEE DISCIPLINARY ACTION

The IRS has recognized the problem of employees' misconduct and has responded. IRS workers and the public may call 800-366-4484 to report IRS employee misconduct. Calls also may go to 800-826-0407 to reach the Treasury Inspector General's Office, which investigates senior IRS managers. In 1997, 172 IRS employees were fired or otherwise separated from the agency due to "administrative actions related to employee violations"—i.e., as a result of complaints, misuse of position or authority, or rude or discourteous conduct. In 1998, the IRS investigated 3,100 complaints against IRS employees. Of those one-third led to disciplinary action, including 200 criminal prosecutions.

Between July 1998 and September 2002, the IRS fired 71 employees after investigating 3,512 allegations and finding 419 violations. Other employees faced penalties or resigned. For fiscal 2007, the IRS took disciplinary action against more than 2,000, or 2.3 percent of its employees.

WHAT GETS AN IRS EMPLOYEE FIRED?

In general, the Commissioner of Internal Revenue shall terminate any IRS employee if there is a final administrative or judicial determination that, in the performance of official duties, such employee committed any misconduct violations outlined as follows. Such termination shall be a removal for cause on charges of misconduct. Misconduct violations include:

- Willfully failing to obtain the required approval signatures on documents authorizing the seizure of a taxpayer's home, personal belongings, or business assets;

- Providing a false statement under oath with respect to a material matter involving a taxpayer or taxpayer representative;

- Violating, with respect to a taxpayer, taxpayer representative, or other employee of the IRS, any right under the Constitution of the United States, or any civil right established under Title VI or VII of the Civil Rights Act of 1964; Title IX of the Education Amendments of 1972; Age Discrimination in Employment Act of 1967; Age Discrimination Act of 1975; Section 501 or 504 of the Rehabilitation Act of 1973; or Title 1 of the Americans With Disabilities Act of 1990;

- Falsifying or destroying documents to conceal mistakes made by any employee with respect to a matter involving a taxpayer or taxpayer representative;

- Committing assault or battery on a taxpayer, taxpayer representative, or another employee of the IRS, but only if there is a criminal conviction or a final judgment by a court in a civil case with respect to the assault or battery;

- Violating the Internal Revenue Code of 1986, as amended (the Code), the Department of the Treasury regulations, or policies of the IRS (including the Internal Revenue Manual) for the purpose of retaliating against or harassing a taxpayer, taxpayer representative, or other employee of the IRS;

- Willfully misusing provisions of §6103 of the Code for the purpose of concealing information from a congressional inquiry;

- Willfully failing to file any return of tax required under the Code on or before the date prescribed therefore (including any extensions), unless such failure is due to reasonable cause and not to willful neglect;

- Willfully understating Federal tax liability, unless such understatement is due to reasonable cause and not to willful neglect; and

- Threatening to audit a taxpayer for the purpose of extracting personal gain or benefit.

OFFERS IN COMPROMISE

Before you go to court (or even afterward), you have one more alternative option. An offer in compromise is a contract (Form 656) with the Internal Revenue Service whereby you recognize your liability but offer to satisfy it for less than its full amount. Such offers will be entertained only when there is doubt regarding either the taxpayer's liability or the collectibility of the amount assessed. Offers based on "equity and hardship factors" are also accepted for "effective tax administration."

According to the IRS District Director's letter, before the IRS will accept an offer in compromise, it will almost always require the taxpayer to enter into a collateral agreement to make payments from future income. Where liability has been established by a valid court judgment, the IRS will not compromise the liability. An offer in compromise is made on Form 656 and must be accepted in writing by the Internal Revenue Service.

The advantages of an offer in compromise are:

1. You may be able to satisfy the liability by paying less than the full amount.
2. You can defer payment over a number of years, thus reducing the immediate tax burden.
3. Making an offer will delay collection action, even if the offer is not accepted.
4. The compromise offer fixes your liability for the period once it is accepted.
5. If the offer is accepted, and you live up to it, there will be no surprise collection action by the IRS.
6. If you enter into a collateral agreement to make payments from future income, the IRS normally will release any tax liens that have been filed on your property.

Alternatively, the rejection of an offer can result in immediate collection action by the IRS. In addition, the offer requires the submission of detailed financial statements, which will aid the IRS Collection Division should the offer not be accepted; the offer requires a waiver of the statute of limitations; and when an offer is made, you will usually be required to make a cash deposit. This deposit will not draw interest, and it is subject to collection in case the offer is rejected.

In May 2004, National Taxpayer Advocate Nina Olson called the IRS OIC program "inflexible" and "mechanistic," with taxpayers treated as "inventory."

If the debt can be paid in 15 years, it's considered a "full pay" case. She discussed the case of a 75-year-old man who was ill. He was turned down for an OIC because he was deemed a full pay case!

The backlog of offers kept increasing. The number of unresolved offers tripled from 32,300 to 94,900 cases between fiscal 1997 and 2001. It took, on average, 10 months to get a determination. According to the IRS in 2002, 37 percent of offers were settled within 6 months, and 74 percent within 1 year. By 2005, settlement time dropped to an average of 6 months for a single offer and about 22 months for repeat offers. As of October 25, 2011, there were 7,472 *unassigned* offers in the holding queues waiting to be looked at. Why? More offers and less IRS personnel.

As of January 1, 2014, the IRS charges a $186 "user fee" ($300 as of Februrary 27, 2017) to process offers. The fee will be waived for offers based "solely" on doubt as to liability and for offers from "low income" taxpayers. A "low income" taxpayer is one with income at or below 250 percent of the poverty guidelines set by the Department of Health and Human Services. Get current levels from www.atdn.org/access/property.html.

The fee will be applied to your offer or refunded if:

- an offer is accepted to promote effective tax administration, *or*
- there is doubt as to collectability, and collecting an amount greater than the offer would create economic hardship.

The Tax Increase Protection Act of 2005 changed the rules again. Effective for all offers received starting July 16, 2006, you must make a 20 percent nonrefundable upfront payment for lump sum offers.

Taxpayers submitting requests for periodic-payment OICs must include the first proposed installment payment with their application. A periodic payment OIC is any offer of payments made in six or more installments. The taxpayer is required to pay additional installments while the offer is being evaluated by the IRS. All installment payments are nonrefundable.

Under the new law, taxpayers qualifying as low-income or filling an offer based solely on doubt as to liability qualify for a waiver of the new partial payment requirements.

If the IRS cannot make a determination on an OIC within two years, then the offer will be deemed accepted. If a liability included in the offer amount is disputed in any court proceeding, that time period is omitted from calculating the two-year timeframe.

See T.D. 9086 dated August 15, 2003 and IR-2006-106, dated July 11, 2006 for further details.

In 2012, the IRS made qualifying for the OIC program more flexible by:

- Revising the calculation for a taxpayer's *future income*. The IRS will now look at only 1 year (instead of 4 years) of future income for offers paid in 5 or fewer months; and 2 years (instead of 5 years) of future income for offers paid in 6 to 24 months. All OICs must be paid in full within 24 months of the date the offer is accepted.

- Allowing taxpayers to repay their *student loans*. Minimum payments on student loans guaranteed by the federal government will be allowed for the taxpayer's post–high school education. Proof of payment must be provided.

- Allowing taxpayers to pay *state and local* delinquent *taxes*. When a taxpayer owes delinquent federal and state or local taxes and does not have the ability to fully pay the liabilities, monthly payments to state taxing authorities may be allowed in certain circumstances.

- Expanding the *Allowable Living Expense* allowance. Standard allowances incorporate average expenses for basic necesssities for citizens in similar geographic areas. These standards are used when evaluating installment agreements and offer-in-compromise requests. The *National Standard* miscellaneous allowance has been expanded. Taxpayers can use the allowance to cover expenses such as credit card payments and bank fees and charges.

In FY 2017, taxpayers proposed 62,000 offers in compromise to settle existing tax liabilities for less than the full amount owed. IRS accepted 25,000 offers, amounting to almost $256.0 million, during the year.

Offers in Compromise, Percentage Accepted, Fiscal Years 2008–2017

SOURCE: *IRS Data Book* Table 16

For instructions on making an offer in compromise, go to www.irs.gov/prod/ind_info/oic/index.html.

It is important to recognize that *oral* compromise agreements and unsigned settlements will not bind the Internal Revenue Service (see *Boulez*, 87-1 USTC Par. 9177, 59 AFTR 2d 87-608 [CA-D.C., 1987] and *Estate of Oman*, TCM 1987-71).

INSTALLMENT AGREEMENTS

A negotiated agreement to pay in monthly installments over a lengthy period of time is now within the recognized policy guidelines of the IRS. IRS Policy Statement P-5-14 (approved on March 3, 1976) states: "Although there is no specific authority for allowing a taxpayer to liquidate a delinquent account by installment payments, installment agreements are to be considered, and may be entered into, when appropriate." IRM 5223: (4)(g) states that "the amount to be paid monthly on an installment agreement payment will be the difference between the taxpayer's net income and allowable expenses rounded down to the nearest $5.00 increment." The 1998 Tax Reform Act, however, made installment agreements mandatory under certain circumstances if the liability, with interest and penalties, is not more than $10,000. However, the IRS generally will accept installment offers on tax debts up to $50,000, and have gone higher. You can actually get an agreement online—with no financial statements needed—at www.irs.gov up to $50,000 if you can pay in full within 72 months. If you owe $25,000 or less, you don't ever have to provide financial statements.

The IRS is currently testing a new streamlined processing criteria as follows:

For individual taxpayers who have filed all required returns and have an assessed balance of tax, penalties, and interest of $50,000 or less,

CURRENT Streamlined CRITERIA	TEST CRITERIA
Payment Terms Up to 72 months—or—the number of months necessary to satisfy the liability in full by the Collection Statute Expiration date, whichever is less	**Payment Terms** None. This criteria is unchanged.
Collection Information Statement Verification of ability to pay required in event of an earlier default for assessed balances of $25,001 to $50,000	**Collection Information Statement** Not required.
Payment Method Direct debit payments or payroll deduction required for assessed balances of $25,001 to $50,000	**Payment Method** Direct debit payments or payroll deduction is preferred, but not required.
Notice of Federal Tax Lien Determination not required for assessed balances up to $25,000. Determination is not required for assessed balances of $25,001–$50,000 **with** mandatory use of direct debit or payroll deduction agreement. Note: If taxpayer does not agree to direct debit or payroll deduction, then they do not qualify for Streamlined IA over $25,000.	**Notice of Federal Tax Lien** No change in criteria for assessed balances up to $25,000. Determination is not required for assessed balances of $25,001–$50,000 **with** the use of direct debit or payroll deduction agreement. Note: If taxpayer does not agree to direct debit or payroll deduction, then they do qualify for Streamlined IA over $25,000, but a Notice of Federal Tax Lien determination will be made.

The test criteria discussed above also applies to all out of business debts up to $25,000 and all out of business sole-proprietorship debts up to $50,000. For in-business taxpayers, test criteria apply to income tax only debts up to $25,000.

An application for an installment agreement will stop the IRS from levying against your property. But, the IRS *can* issue a notice of intent to levy.

For individual taxpayers who have filed all required returns and have an assessed balance of tax, penalties and interest between $50,001 and $100,000,

CURRENT CRITERIA	TEST CRITERIA CHANGES
None—Streamlined processing criteria currently does not apply to assessed balances of tax between $50,001 and $100,000	**Payment Terms** Up to 84 months—or—the number of months necessary to satisfy the liability in full by the Collection Statute Expiration date, whichever is less **Collection Information Statement** Not required if the taxpayer agrees to make payment by direct debit or payroll deduction **Payment Method** Direct debit payments or payroll deduction is not required; however, if one of these methods is not used, then a Collection Information Statement is required. **Notice of Federal Tax Lien** Determination is required.

The test criteria discussed above also applies to all out of business sole-proprietorship debts between $50,001 and $100,000.

When you are unable to pay all of your taxes on time, you should file Form 1127. It's called "Application for Extension of Time for Payment of Tax" and it will give you up to 6 months from the due date to pay the tax you owe. In order to qualify, you must be able to show that you cannot borrow money to pay your tax bill except under terms that would cause severe loss and hardship. If you are granted an extension, all late payment penalties will be excused. However, you will still owe the IRS interest on the late-paid tax. In addition, the IRS now charges a $120 user fee ($225 as of January 1, 2017) for entering into a non-direct-debit installment agreement ($52 for direct-debit agreements, increasing to $107 as of January 1, 2017 or $43 if your income is within poverty guidelines)

and a $50 user fee ($89 as of January 1, 2017) for restructuring or reinstating an installment agreement (IR 94-118). If you request the agreement online and agree to a direct debit, you only pay $31.

Pay less than you owe

Measure/Indicator	FY 2015	FY 2016	FY 2017
Offer in Compromise (OIC): Number of Offers Submitted[a]	66,600	64,479	62,243
OIC: Percentage of Offers Accepted[b]	42.5%	42.5%	38.1%
Installment Agreements (IA): Number of Individual & Business IAs[c]	2,986,121	3,115,404	2,924,780
Streamlined Installment Agreements Number of Individual & Business IAs[d]	2,567,623	2,630,811	2,236,434
Installment Agreements Collection Field Function (CFf): Number of Individual & Business IAs[e]	52,053	42,978	35,449
Streamlined Installment Agreements (CFf): Number of Individual & Business IAs[f]	10,679	8,477	6,936
Number of OICs Accepted per Revenue Officer[g]	7.4	7.7	7.6
Number of IAs Accepted per Revenue Officer[h]	14.0	12.0	10.6
Percentage of Cases in the Queue (Taxpayers)[i]	15.7%	15.5%	13.9%
Percentage of Cases in the Queue (Modules)[j]	24.7%	23.9%	21.8%
Percentage of Taxpayer Delinquent Accounts (TDAs) reported Currently Not Collectible – Tolerance[k]	16.3%	16.9%	32.3%
Age of Delinquencies in the Queue[l]	4.5 years	4.5 years	4.5 years
Percentage of Modules in Queue prior to three tax years ago[m]	79.2%	78.7%	78.2%
Percentage of cases where the taxpayer is fully compliant after five years[n]	44%	48%	48%

[a] IRS, Collection Activity Report No. 5000–108, FY 2015 (Oct. 4, 2015), FY 2016 (Oct. 7, 2016), and FY 2017 (Oct. 2, 2017).

[b] *Id.*

[c] IRS, Collection Activity Report No. 5000–6, FY 2015 (Dec. 9, 2015), FY 2016 (Oct. 3, 2016), and FY 2017 (Oct. 1, 2017).

[d] *Id.*

[e] *Id.*

[f] *Id.*

[g] *Id.* See also IRS Human Resources Reporting Center – number of revenue officers in Small Business/Self Employed as of the end of FY 2015, FY 2016, and FY 2017 (pay period 19).

[h] *Id.*

[i] IRS, Collection Activity Report No. 5000–2, FY 2015 (Dec. 5, 2015), FY 2016 (Oct. 3, 2016), and FY 2017 (Oct. 1, 2017).

[j] *Id.*

[k] *Id.* For FY 2017, the IRS shelves cases prior to potential transfer for the Private Collection Initiative.

[l] Accounts Receivable Dollar Inventory. Age of cases in the collection queue as of cycle 37 of 2015, 2016, and 2017.

[m] IRS, Collection Activity Report No. 5000–2, FY 2015 (Dec. 5, 2015), FY 2016 (Oct. 3, 2016), and FY 2017 (Oct. 1, 2017).

[n] Calculation by TAS Research. Percentage of taxpayers with tax delinquent accounts in 2010, 2011, and 2012, respectively, and who have no new delinquencies five years later. IRS, CDW, Individual Master File (IMF).

GOING TO COURT

In entering the judiciary, you have three basic options:

1. *The U.S. Tax Court.* The U.S. Tax Court was first established in 1923. It is made up of 19 judges who travel around the country and hear cases in major cities on a regular basis. Currently, about 30,000 cases are filed each year, double the filing rate in 2000. It handles only tax litigation and consists exclusively of tax experts. The major advantage of choosing this court is that it will decide the case **before** you have to pay the tax. When you receive the 90-day letter, if you file a petition with the U.S. Tax Court within 90 days of the date of the letter, the Internal Revenue Service may not initiate any further tax collection mechanics until after the case is decided. Be careful: Your letter must be postmarked within 90 days after the *date* of the IRS letter, not after you receive it.

 To get complete instructions on how to file a petition, write to the Clerk, United States Tax Court, 400 2nd Street, N.W., Washington, DC 20217, or call 202-376-2754. Although you may represent yourself at the Tax Court, it is best to have an attorney specializing in taxation to handle the case.

 If the disputed tax is $50,000 or less for any taxable year, a simplified alternative procedure is now available. Here you may want to represent yourself. Upon your request and with approval of the Tax Court, your case can be handled by the Small Claims Division, under the small tax case rules, at little cost to you in time or dollars. Cases in the Small Claims Division are heard by "special trial judges." If you want to use this procedure, write to the previously given address and ask that the clerk send you the small tax case division filing form, Petition, Form 2. You must file the original and two copies of the petition, a copy of the 90-day letter, and a fee of $60, along with your pick of one of the more than 100 cities in which the Small Claims Division of the Tax Court sits. The fee for cases that are not small claims cases is also $60. The case is heard informally by a trial judge and the formal rules of evidence do not apply. One special caveat, however: If you lose your case before the Small Claims Division, you cannot appeal. Their decision is final and binding.

 Several final comments must be made about the Tax Court. First, while the disputed tax is not paid until after the trial, or until the case is settled, any tax found due will be paid with interest. This interest, however, is no longer tax deductible. Second, remember that the Tax Court consists exclusively of expert judges. There are no jury trials

before the Tax Court. Therefore, if you have a case where the equities are strongly on your side, but the law itself is against you, you might be better advised to stay out of the Tax Court. Finally, don't expect quick action if you file a case in the Tax Court. The court is struggling to cope with a massive and ever-growing backlog of pending cases at a time when it also faces financial woes. Taxpayers in some large cities must now wait as long as a year and a half for their cases to come to trial. Furthermore, experts have predicted the problem will intensify, reflecting the complexity of new laws and confusing tax shelter controversies.

In Rev. Proc. 82-42, the Internal Revenue Service announced new procedures for processing Tax Court cases in an attempt to facilitate earlier disposition through trial or settlement. Docketed cases will be referred by district counsel to the Appeals Division for settlement unless counsel determines it unlikely that even a partial settlement will be reached there. Cases involving deficiencies of more than $10,000 (including tax and penalties for a period) will then be promptly returned to counsel when it appears that no progress toward a settlement has been made, unless counsel agrees to extend the period for the Appeals Division's consideration. Cases involving deficiencies of $10,000 or less (including small claims cases) will stay in the Appeals Division for 6 months or until receipt of notice of trial in regular cases, or 15 days before the trial calendar call in small claims tax cases if that is earlier. Again, counsel may extend the period in Appeals Division if it appears that a settlement may be reached.

2. *The U.S. District Court.* The U.S. District Court, which is part of the federal judiciary system, is the only place where a jury trial is available. These courts hear all kinds of litigation involving federal laws and any kind of law, state or federal, if the litigants are citizens of different states. You can represent yourself in a district court, but the judges frown upon it. The advantages of going to the district court include the availability of a sympathetic jury and the fact that the judge may be more sympathetic to the equities of your case than to the letter of the tax law. To get into a U.S. District Court, however, you must first pay your tax deficiency and then file a claim for a refund with the Internal Revenue Service. Though the Internal Revenue Service has 6 months to act on your claim, chances are it will reject the claim promptly and you can then file suit for a refund in your district court. You can obtain

information about the procedures for filing suit in a U.S. District Court by calling or writing the Clerk of the Court in the district in which you reside. See page 679 for the address of your area's office.

3. *The U.S. Claims Court.* The U.S. Claims Court is a special court that hears all sorts of claims against the United States, including the claim of overpaying taxes and wanting the money back with interest. Here, too, the tax has to be paid in advance. The major advantage of the claims court is that it does not have to follow the same precedents as do the Tax Court and district courts. If the other courts appear unfavorable, this may be your best avenue of appeal.

Currently, judges of the claims court usually hear case argument only in Washington, DC. However, before the argument, there is a fact-finding hearing before a trial judge of the claims court. This hearing will be conducted by the trial judge in a city near where you live. The trial judge will file the findings and the recommended decision. If either you or the Internal Revenue Service disagree, the case will come on for arguments before the full court in Washington. Legal briefs, which must be printed, are also required of both parties. Here the major disadvantage is the substantial expense of litigation. For information on filing suit here, contact the Clerk of the Court of Claims, 1717 Madison Place, N.W., Washington, DC 20005.

Appeals from both the Tax Court and the U.S. district courts go to the U.S. courts of appeals. The United States is divided geographically into 12 judicial circuits, each with its own court of appeals. District and tax court decisions in each circuit must follow the precedents of that circuit's court of appeals. Note, however, that decisions of the claims court do not have to follow such precedents. Furthermore, the courts of appeals in different circuits do not have to agree with each other. And if one circuit's court of appeals has not ruled on an issue, the lower courts may disagree among themselves. This means that a supereffective tax planning strategy for tax appeals is to file your case, whenever possible, in a judicial circuit whose precedents support your position.

Appeals from U.S. courts of appeals go directly to the Supreme Court. In addition, if you lose in the claims court, your appeal is directed first to the Federal Circuit Court of Appeals, then the Supreme Court, which may or may not accept such an appeal. As a practical matter, it accepts very few tax appeals from the claims court, or from appeals courts. Usually, it will

only agree to do so where two U.S. courts of appeals have reached opposite results on a similar issue of fact and law.

One final note about going to court: Under Internal Revenue Code Section 7430, enacted by Section 292(a) of the Tax Equity and Fiscal Responsibility Act of 1982, Public Law 97-248 (September 3, 1982), the Tax Court is enabled to award *reasonable litigation costs* to a prevailing party who establishes that the position of the IRS commissioner was unreasonable. That means if you exhaust administrative remedies, go to court, and win, and the position of the Internal Revenue Service was not "reasonable," your costs, including what you have to pay to your attorney, will be reimbursed by the Treasury. The Tax Reform Act of 1986 changed the "not reasonable" requirement to one where the taxpayer must establish that the government's position was "not substantially justified." The 1996 Taxpayer's Bill of Rights 2 reversed the burden. If you win in court, the IRS must now prove that *it* was "substantially justified." These awards are now being given—see *Ashburn*, D.C. Alabama, June 15, 1983 and *Marlar Inc. v. U.S.*, W.D. Wash., No. C95–0729L, 5/18/99. In the case of *David Kaufman v. Roscoe Egger*, on March 19, 1985, the First Circuit Court of Appeals ruled that "unreasonable" IRS conduct, even prior to a suit, can be considered. Examining the underlying congressional committee reports, the Court concluded "that Congress intended IRS' liability to be triggered by unreasonable IRS conduct regardless of which stage in the proceedings such conduct occurs." Moreover, the purpose of the provision would be frustrated if the Internal Revenue Service, "after causing the taxpayer all kinds of bureaucratic grief at the administrative level, could escape attorney's fee liability by merely changing its tune after the initiation of a suit by the taxpayer." These litigation costs can be awarded without limit at a rate of $110 per hour[2] (indexed for inflation after 1996) (unless the court finds justification for a higher rate)! Moreover, this provision applies to suits not only in the District Court but also in the Tax Court (suits in the U.S. Claims Courts are covered only between February 28, 1983, and December 31, 1985—see the Tax Reform Act of 1984, Section 714[c]).

Section 7430(a)(1) now permits the recovery of reasonable administrative costs incurred in an administrative proceeding with the IRS in connection with the determination, collection, or refund of any tax, interest, or penalty. Such costs, under Prop. Reg. 301.7430-4, include the following:

2. $180 per hour for 2012, $190 for 2013 and 2014, and $200 for 2015, 2016, 2017 and 2018.

1. A representative's fee
2. IRS administrative fees or similar charges
3. Costs of studies, analyses, etc., incurred in preparing the taxpayer's case

A taxpayer must meet the following conditions to be eligible for an award of administrative costs:

1. The underlying issues are not now, and were never, before a court.
2. The taxpayer is the prevailing party.
3. The taxpayer did not unreasonably prolong the portion of the proceeding for which recovery of costs is sought.
4. The application procedures of the Proposed Regulations were followed.

To be a prevailing party, you must:

1. Establish that the Service's position was not justified.
2. Substantially prevail in the dispute.
3. Meet certain size and net worth limitations.

Administrative awards are available to estates and individuals only if their net worth is not over $2 million ($4 million for joint returns as per the Tax Relief Act of 1997) (based on cost, not fair market value, *Swanson v. Comm.*, No. 21203-92, 106 T.C. No. 3, 2/14/96) on the administrative proceeding date. Businesses, whether incorporated or not, and most other organizations cannot have a net worth of more than $7 million and 500 employees.

The procedures for claiming an award are detailed in Prop. Reg. 301.7430-2(c).

In general, a request must be made within 90 days of the mailing of the Service's final decision.

The claim must be filed with the Service employee who decided that issue, or the district office that considered the matter, if the employee's identity is unknown. The request must contain the following provisions:

1. A statement that neither the underlying issue or issues nor the claim for reasonable administrative costs is, or has been, before a court
2. A clear and concise assertion as to why the Service's position was not substantially justified
3. A declaration that the taxpayer prevailed with respect to the amount in controversy or the most significant issue or set of issues
4. A statement that the taxpayer did not unreasonably prolong the proceeding
5. An affidavit giving the nature and amount of each recovery item and a copy of the representative's billing records, if fees are requested

6. Another affidavit stating that the taxpayer meets the net worth and size limitations

7. An address where the taxpayer may be located

If your request is denied, you can appeal to the Tax Court.

The IRS Office of Chief Counsel issued a notice (CC-2010-007) dated April 2, 2010, that explained, under the "qualified offer rule," a taxpayer who meets certain net worth requirements and has used all of his administrative remedies may recover reasonable administrative and litigation costs from the IRS if the taxpayer's liability in a court proceeding is equal to or less than the liability the taxpayer would have had if the IRS had accepted the taxpayer's qualified offer.

One effect of the qualified offer rule, the notice explained, is that it eliminates the IRS's defense that its position was substantially justified.

CRIMINAL SANCTIONS

To survive an audit you must be able to document all deductions and you should demand the audit agent to document any claims of fact or law alleged. Alternatively, some tax practitioners have advised, "When in doubt, deduct." The rationale behind this perspective is that even if your deductions are disallowed, your maximum exposure is to pay the tax you would have paid originally plus about 5 percent interest (this rate will change every 6 months; the next change is scheduled for January 1, 2019). Remember, however, that your focus must be on tax avoidance rather than tax evasion. The focus of this book, as well, has been on avoidance—the completely legal objective of minimizing your taxes. You should *never* intentionally attempt to defraud the government with reference to your taxes. Such actions can bring about *criminal* penalties. In fact, a competitive writer, the author of *Pay No Income Taxes without Going to Jail*, went to jail. He also lost a big Tax Court case in which it was found that he treated employees as independent contractors, wrote checks in nonphotocopiable ink, did not report all his income, and did not file returns for several years (*Fry*, T.C. Memo 1991-51). However, the Internal Revenue Service has told its agents not to pursue criminal prosecution of most tax cheaters unless the underpayments average at least $2,500 a year for 3 straight years. Under these guidelines, a married person earning $20,000 a year and not itemizing deductions could file no return at all and not risk a felony prosecution, although civil penalties would probably be sought.

Further IRS internal guidelines with reference to criminal penalties include the following:

- Do not recommend felony prosecution in complex tax evasion schemes requiring difficult methods of proof unless the total amount of unpaid taxes is at least $10,000, including at least $3,000 for any single year.

- Do not recommend felony prosecution for willful failure to file or for filing a false return unless the average yearly unpaid tax involved is at least $2,500 over a 3-year period.
- Do not recommend misdemeanor prosecution for delivery or disclosure of false returns or documents unless the unpaid tax involved is more than $500.

The preceding guidelines contain exceptions for "flagrant or repetitious conduct," which would allow IRS agents to ignore the minimum dollar amounts. These exceptions are more likely to be used against celebrities whose prosecution would be covered by the news media and therefore serve as a deterrent to others. If a doctor were to be prosecuted, for example, they would probably select one who had just written a popular diet book. Alternatively, if they were to look at an attorney, they would want someone well known, particularly a tax lawyer.

In going criminal, the amount of tax itself is only one factor. Other egregious facts, such as misrepresenting information in an audit or outright lying to an IRS agent could elevate the case to the criminal level. Generally the IRS is looking at cases where more than $40,000 in taxes is due, but that will fluxuate based on geography.

By 2018 the numbers had increased: "Typically we're not going to look at anything that's not in excess of $100,000," Troy Caldron, an Internal Revenue Service Criminal Investigation (CI) special agent based in San Antonio, Texas, said June 6. "If there's some type of scenario with a high profile individual, perhaps a public official or something like that, it could require a little more scrutiny on our part," he said.

Taxpayers in some communities are 10 times more likely to face criminal charges by the Internal Revenue Service than those living in others, but IRS recommends such action for only 17 per million taxpayers,* according to an analysis of internal government records released April 13, 1996 by Syracuse University's Transactional Records Access Clearinghouse (TRAC).

TRAC said it found the chances of facing IRS criminal charges were higher in the federal judicial districts of Tulsa and Oklahoma City, Louisville, Wheeling, and Charleston, W.Va., New York's Manhattan and Bronx boroughs and northern suburbs, Pittsburgh, Miami, and Indianapolis. Among the least active, it added, were Madison, Wis., Montgomery, Ala., Topeka, Kan., Detroit, Boston, Milwaukee, St. Louis, Philadelphia, Houston, and Des Moines, Iowa.

See the table on pages 676–678 for a summary of prosecutions and investigations in prior years.

* Falling to 9.2 per million in fiscal 2015 due to budget cuts.

Fiscal 2015, Criminal Investigation Program, by Status or Disposition

Criminal Investigation's highest priority is to enforce our country's tax laws and support tax administration. The Fiscal Year 2015 investigative priorities were:

- Identity Theft Fraud
- Return Preparer Fraud & Questionable Refund Fraud
- International Tax Fraud
- Fraud Referral Program
- Political/Public Corruption
- Organized Crime Drug Enforcement Task Force (OCDETF)
- Bank Secrecy Act and Suspicious Activity Report (SAR) Review Teams
- Asset Forfeiture
- Voluntary Disclosure Program
- Counterterrorism and Sovereign Citizens

FY 2016 Business Results:

	FY 2016	FY 2015	FY 2014	FY 2013
Investigations Initiated	3,395	3,853	4,297	5,314
Prosecution Recommendations	2,744	3,289	3,478	4,364
Informations/Indictments	2,761	3,208	3,272	3,865
Convictions	2,672	2,879	3,110	3,311
Sentenced*	2,699	3,092	3,268	2,812
Percent to Prison	79.9%	80.8%	79.6%	80.1%

- Conviction rate is the percentage of convictions compared to the total number of convictions, acquittals, and dismissals. The conviction rate for FY 2015 was 93.2 percent, 0.02 percent less than the FY 2014 rate (93.4 percent).

* Sentence includes confinement to federal prison, halfway house, home detention, or some combination thereof.
A fiscal year runs from October 1 through September 30.
Data Source: Criminal Investigation Management Information System.
How to Interpret Criminal Investigations Data: Actions on a specific investigation may cross fiscal years; the data shown in investigations initiated may not always represent the same universe of investigatons shown in other actions within the same fiscal year.

Conviction rate is the percentage of convictions compared to the total number of convictions, acquittals, and dismissals. The conviction rate for FY 2015 was 93.2 percent, compared to 93.4 percent in 2014 and 93.1 percent in 2013.

As of September 30, 2016, IRS-CI had 2,217 special agents, a 4.3 percent decrease compared to the number of special agents at the conclusion of FY 2015. Professional staff personnel were 907, reflecting a decrease of 3.3 percent compared to FY 2015 Total CI Staffing in FY 2016 was 3,124, a 4.0 percent decrease compared to FY 2015. Over the past five years (FY 2011–FY 2016), staffing levels for special agents and professional staff have decreased by 522 and 251 respectively representing 19.1 percent and 21.7 percent reductions respectively.

Criminal Investigation Program, by Status or Disposition, Fiscal Year 2017

Status or disposition[1]	Total	Legal source tax crimes[2]	Illegal source financial crimes[3]	Narcotics-related financial crimes[4]	Identity theft[5]
	(1)	(2)	(3)	(4)	(5)
Investigations initiated	3,019	1,188	1,096	735	374
Investigations completed	3,089	1,235	1,162	692	524
Referrals for prosecution	2,251	795	875	581	403
Investigations completed without prosecution	838	440	287	111	121
Indictments and informations[6]	2,294	827	882	585	484
Convictions	2,300	927	822	551	n.a
Sentenced	2,549	1,062	872	615	550
Incarcerated[7]	2,043	852	656	535	481
Percentage of those sentenced who were incarcerated[7]	80.1	80.2	75.2	87.0	87.5

n.a.—Not available due to current system constraints. There are insufficient data available to provide the number of identity theft convictions.

[1] Investigations may cross fiscal years. An investigation initiated one fiscal year may not be indicted, convicted, or sentenced until a subsequent fiscal year. Therefore, the disposition (completions, indictments/informations, convictions, sentences) of investigations shown in this table may be related to investigations initiated in prior fiscal years.

[2] Under the Legal Source Tax Crimes Program, IRS Criminal Investigation identifies, investigates, and assists in the prosecution of crimes involving legal industries, legal occupations, and, more specifically, legally earned income associated with the violation of Title 26 (tax violations) and Title 18 (tax-related violations) of the U.S. Code. The Legal Source Tax Crimes Program also includes employment tax cases and those cases that threaten the tax system, such as Questionable Refund Program cases, unscrupulous return preparers, and frivolous filers/nonfilers who challenge the legality of the filing requirements.

[3] Under the Illegal Source Financial Crimes Program, IRS Criminal Investigation identifies, investigates, and assists in the prosecution of crimes involving proceeds derived from illegal sources other than narcotics. These encompass all tax and tax-related violations, as well as money laundering and currency violations under the following statutes: Title 26 (tax violations); Title 18 (tax-related and money laundering violations); and Title 31 (currency violations) of the U.S. Code. The utilization of forfeiture statutes to deprive individuals and organizations of illegally obtained assets is also linked to the investigation of criminal charges within this program.

[4] Under the Narcotics-Related Financial Crimes Program, IRS Criminal Investigation seeks to identify, investigate, and assist in the prosecution of the most significant narcotics-related tax and money laundering offenders. The IRS derives authority for this program from the statutes for which it has jurisdiction: Title 26 (tax violations); Title 18 (tax-related and money laundering violations); and Title 31 (currency violations) of the U.S. Code. IRS Criminal Investigation also devotes resources to high-level multiagency narcotics investigations warranting Organized Crime Drug Enforcement Task Force (OCDETF) designation in accordance with OCDETF Program reimbursable funding.

[5] The data highlighted in gray are a subset of total IRS Criminal Investigations (CI) and include cases from all CI programs: Legal source tax crimes, Illegal source financial crimes, and Narcotics-related financial crimes. IRS CI detects and investigates tax fraud and other financial fraud related to identity theft. Identity theft is often found through the Questionable Refund Program (QRP). The QRP involves the detection of false returns which may have used stolen identities to claim fraudulent tax refunds. Additional areas involving identity theft include employment tax cases, abusive return preparer schemes, and narcotics and money laundering investigations.

[6] Both "indictments" and "informations" are accusations of criminal charges. An "indictment" is an accusation made by a Federal prosecutor and issued by a Federal grand jury. An "information" is an accusation brought by a Federal prosecutor without the requirement of a grand jury.

[7] The term "incarcerated" may include prison time, home confinement, electronic monitoring, or a combination thereof.

SOURCE: Criminal Investigation, Communications and Education Division.

For more information about Criminal Investigation, visit: https://www.irs.gov/pub/fola/ig/ci/2017_criminal_investigation_annual %20report.pdf

Past Criminal Investigations

Prosecutions Recommended

By Source	FY 2002	FY 2003	FY 2004	FY 2005	FY 2006	FY 2007	FY 2008	FY 2009	FY 2010	FY 2011	FY 2012
Tax and Tax Related	991	1,336	1,439	1,434	1,343	1,423	1,293	1,269	1,511	1,622	1,846
Nontax (illegal)	483	521	719	658	756	866	804	769	864	989	1,073
Narcotics	659	684	879	767	621	548	688	532	659	799	782
Total	**2,133**	**2,541**	**3,037**	**2,859**	**2,720**	**2,837**	**2,785**	**2,570**	**3,034**	**3,410**	**3,701**

	FY 2002	FY 2003	FY 2004	FY 2005	FY 2006	FY 2007	FY 2008	FY 2009	FY 2010	FY 2011	FY 2012
Overall Conviction Rate	91.5%	91.5%	92.2%	91.2%	91.5%	90.20%	92.30%	87.20%	90.2%	92.70%	93.00%

	FY 2002	FY 2003	FY 2004	FY 2005	FY 2006	FY 2007	FY 2008	FY 2009	FY 2010	FY 2011	FY 2012
Average Sentence[1]	19	19	21	22	22	22	24	24	27	25	32

	FY 2002	FY 2003	FY 2004	FY 2005	FY 2006	FY 2007	FY 2008	FY 2009	FY 2010	FY 2011	FY 2012
Investigations initiated	3,906	4,001	3,917	4,269	3,907	4,211	3,749	4,121	4,706	4,720	5,125
Information & indictments[2]	1,924	2,128	2,489	2,406	2,319	2,323	2,547	2,335	2,645	2,998	3,390

[1] Average sentence in months for tax and tax-related cases.

[2] Both "information" and "indictments" are accusations. "Information" means an accusation made by law enforcement without the intervention of a grand jury, whereas an "indictment" is an accusation made by a prosecutor and issued by a grand jury.

Federal District Courts

ALABAMA

Northern District
104 Federal Courthouse
Birmingham, AL 35203

Middle District
P.O. Box 711
Montgomery, AL 36101

Southern District
P.O. Box 2625
Mobile, AL 36652

ALASKA
Federal Building
701 C Street
Anchorage, AK 99513

ARIZONA
Room 1400
U.S. Courthouse
 & Federal Building
230 N. 1st Avenue
Phoenix, AZ 85025

ARKANSAS

Eastern District
P.O. Box 869
Little Rock, AR 72203

Western District
P.O. Box 1523
Fort Smith, AR 72902

CALIFORNIA

Northern District
U.S. Courthouse
P.O. Box 36060
San Francisco, CA 94102

Eastern District
2546 U.S. Courthouse
650 Capitol Mall
Sacramento, CA 95814

Central District
U.S. Courthouse
312 N. Spring Street
Los Angeles, CA 90012

Southern District
940 Front Street
San Diego, CA 92189

COLORADO
Room C-145
U.S. Courthouse
1929 Stout Street
Denver, CO 80294

CONNECTICUT
141 Church Street
New Haven, CT 06510

DELAWARE
Lockbox 18
Federal Building
844 King Street
Wilmington, DE 19801

DISTRICT OF COLUMBIA
U.S. Courthouse
3rd & Constitution
 Ave., N.W.
Washington, DC 20001

FLORIDA

Northern District
110 East Park Avenue
Tallahassee, FL 32301

Middle District
P.O. Box 53558
Jacksonville, FL 32201-3558

Southern District
301 N. Miami Avenue
Miami, FL 33128-7788

GEORGIA

Northern District
75 Spring Street, S.W.
2211 U.S. Courthouse
Atlanta, GA 30335

Middle District
P.O. Box 128
Macon, GA 31202

Southern District
P.O. Box 8286
Savannah, GA 31412

GUAM
6th Floor
Pacific News Building
238 O'Hara Street
Agana, Guam 96910

HAWAII
P.O. Box 50129
Honolulu, HI 96850

IDAHO
U.S. Courthouse
P.O. Box 039
550 West Fort Street
Boise, ID 83724

ILLINOIS
Northern District
U.S. Courthouse
219 South Dearborn St.
Chicago, IL 60604

Central District
P.O. Box 315
Springfield, IL 62705

Southern District
U.S. Courthouse &
 P.O. Building
P.O. Box 677
Benton, IL 62812

INDIANA
Northern District
Federal Building
Rm 305, 204 S. Main St.
South Bend, IN 46601

Southern District
U.S. Courthouse
Room 105
46 East Ohio Street
Indianapolis, IN 46204

IOWA
Northern District
Federal Building
P.O. Box 4411
Cedar Rapids, IA 52407

Southern District
U.S. Courthouse
Room 200
E. 1st & Walnut Streets
Des Moines, IA 50309

KANSAS
204 U.S. Courthouse
401 N. Market
Wichita, KS 67202

KENTUCKY
Eastern District
P.O. Box 741
Lexington, KY 40586

Western District
230 U.S. Courthouse
601 West Broadway
Louisville, KY 40202

LOUISIANA
Eastern District
U.S. Courthouse
500 Camp Street
Chambers C-151
New Orleans, LA 70130

Middle District
Room 139, 707 Florida Ave.
Federal Building &
 U.S. Courthouse
Baton Rouge, LA 70801

Western District
106 Joe D. Waggonner
 Federal Building
500 Fannin Street
Shreveport, LA 71101

MAINE
P.O. Box 7505 DTS
Portland, ME 04112

MARYLAND
U.S. Courthouse
101 W. Lombard Street
Baltimore, MD 21201

MASSACHUSETTS
1525 Post Office &
 Courthouse Building
Boston, MA 02109

MICHIGAN
Eastern District
U.S. Courthouse
Room 133
Detroit, MI 48226

Western District
458 Federal Building
110 Michigan Street, N.W.
Grand Rapids, MI 49503

MINNESOTA
708 Federal Building
316 N. Robert Street
St. Paul, MN 55101

MISSISSIPPI
Northern District
P.O. Box 727
Oxford, MS 38655

Southern District
P.O. Box 769
Jackson, MS 39205

MISSOURI
 Eastern District
 U.S. Court & Custom
 House
 1114 Market Street
 St. Louis, MO 63101

Western District
 U.S. Courthouse
 811 Grand Avenue
 Room 201
 Kansas City, MO 64106

MONTANA
 Rm 5405, Federal Bldg.
 316 N. 26th Street
 Billings, MT 59101

NEBRASKA
 P.O. Box 129
 Downtown Station
 Omaha, NE 68101

NEVADA
 300 Las Vegas Blvd., S.
 Las Vegas, NV 89101

NEW HAMPSHIRE
 P.O. Box 1498
 Concord, NH 03301

NEW JERSEY
 U.S. Post Office &
 Courthouse
 P.O. Box 419
 Newark, NJ 07102

NEW MEXICO
 P.O. Box 689
 Albuquerque, NM 87103

NEW YORK
 Northern District
 Box 950
 Albany, NY 12201

Southern District
 U.S. Courthouse
 Foley Square
 New York, NY 10007

Eastern District
 U.S. Courthouse
 225 Cadman Plaza East
 Brooklyn, NY 11201

Western District
 604 U.S. Courthouse
 Buffalo, NY 14202

NORTH CAROLINA
 Eastern District
 P.O. Box 25670
 Raleigh, NC 27611

Middle District
 P.O. Box V-1
 Greensboro, NC 27402

Western District
 P.O. Box 92
 Asheville, NC 28802

NORTH DAKOTA
 P.O. Box 1193
 Bismarck, ND 58501

NORTHERN MARIANA
ISLANDS
 P.O. Box 687
 Saipan, 96950

OHIO
 Northern District
 102 U.S. Courthouse
 201 Superior Avenue, NE
 Cleveland, OH 44114

Southern District
 328 U.S. Courthouse
 85 Marconi Blvd
 Columbus, OH 43215

OKLAHOMA
 Northern District
 411 U.S. Courthouse
 333 W. 4th Street
 Tulsa, OK 74120

Eastern District
 P.O. Box 607
 U.S. Courthouse
 Muskogee, OK 74401

Western District
 Room 3210
 U.S. Courthouse
 Oklahoma City, OK 73102

OREGON
 516 U.S. Courthouse
 620 S.W. Main Street
 Portland, OR 97205

PENNSYLVANIA
 Eastern District
 2609 U.S. Courthouse
 Independent Mall West
 601 Market Street
 Philadelphia, PA 19106

Middle District
P.O. Box 1148
Scranton, PA 18501

Western District
P.O. Box 1805
Pittsburgh, PA 15230

PUERTO RICO
P.O. Box 3671
San Juan, PR 00904

RHODE ISLAND
119 Federal Building
& U.S. Courthouse
Providence, RI 02903

SOUTH CAROLINA
P.O. Box 867
Columbia, SC 29202

SOUTH DAKOTA
Room 220
Federal Building &
U.S. Courthouse
400 South Phillips Ave.
Sioux Falls, SD 57102

TENNESSEE
Eastern District
P.O. Box 2348
Knoxville, TN 37901

Middle District
800 U.S. Courthouse
801 Broadway
Nashville, TN 37203

Western District
950 Federal Building
167 North Main Street
Memphis, TN 38103

TEXAS
Northern District
U.S. Courthouse
1100 Commerce Street
Room 15C22
Dallas, TX 75242

Southern District
P.O. Box 61010
Houston, TX 77208

Eastern District
309 Federal Building &
U.S. Courthouse
211 W. Ferguson Street
Tyler, TX 75702

Western District
Hemisfair Plaza
655 E. Durango Blvd.
San Antonio, TX 78206

UTAH
P.O. Box 45390
Salt Lake City, UT 84145

VERMONT
P.O. Box 945
Burlington, VT 05402

VIRGINIA
Eastern District
307 U.S. Courthouse
600 Granby St.
Norfolk, VA 23510
Western District
P.O. Box 1234
Roanoke, VA 24006

VIRGIN ISLANDS
P.O. Box 720
Charlotte Amalie
St. Thomas, VI 00801

WASHINGTON
Eastern District
P.O. Box 1493
Spokane, WA 99210

Western District
308 U.S. Courthouse
Seattle, WA 98104

WEST VIRGINIA
Northern District
P.O. Box 1518
Elkins, WV 26241

Southern District
P.O. Box 2546
Charleston, WV 25329

WISCONSIN
Eastern District
Room 362
U.S. Courthouse
Milwaukee, WI 53202

Western District
P.O. Box 432
Madison, WI 53701

WYOMING
P.O. Box 727
Cheyenne, WY 82001

The following table provides IRS-CI's Identity Theft statistics for fiscal years 2011–2014:

	FY 2014	FY 2013	FY 2012	FY 2011
Investigations Initiated	1063	1,492	898	276
Prosecution Recommendations	970	1,257	544	218
Indictments/Informations	896	1,050	494	165
Sentenced	748	438	223	80
Incarceration Rate	87.7%	80.6%	89.2%	100.0%
Average Months to Serve	43	38	48	44

Staffing

- As of September 30, 2014, IRS-CI had 2,465 special agents on board, a 3.0 percent decrease compared to the 2,541 of special agents at the conclusion of FY 2013.

- Professional staff assigned at the conclusion of FY 2013 was 1,029, a 5.0 percent decrease from 1,083 professional staff at the end of FY 2013.

- By the end of 2016, the number of criminal agents is projected to fall by 21 percent since 2011.

Agent Strength

In fiscal 2017 there was a nearly 35% drop in initiated investigations on identity theft, a 9.6% decrease in money laundering investigations, a 23% drop in corporate fraud investigations, a 30% decline in financial institution fraud probes, and a 43% decrease in investigations of potential crimes related to the Questionable Refund Program.

Why? The IRS had about the same number of special agents – around 2,200, as they did 50 years ago.

2015–2017 IRS Criminal Investigation Results

FY 2017 Combined Results

	2017	2016	2015
Investigations Initiated	3019	3395	3853
Prosecution Recommendations	2251	2744	3289
Informations/Indictments	2294	2761	3208
Sentenced	2549	2699	3092
Incarceration Rate	80%	80%	81%
Average Months to Serve	42	41	40

Abusive Tax Schemes

	2017	2016	2015
Investigations Initiated	77	56	68
Prosecution Recommendations	38	35	58
Informations/Indictments	44	35	51
Sentenced	48	47	77
Incarceration Rate	69%	77%	68%
Average Months to Serve	24	25	21

Corporate Fraud

	2017	2016	2015
Investigations Initiated	48	62	75
Prosecution Recommendations	42	59	35
Informations/Indictments	46	49	29
Sentenced	25	33	43
Incarceration Rate	80%	97%	81%
Average Months to Serve	54	37	35

Abusive Return Preparer Program

	2017	2016	2015
Investigations Initiated	304	252	266
Prosecution Recommendations	200	174	238
Informations/Indictments	169	204	224
Sentenced	194	202	204
Incarceration Rate	75%	73%	80%
Average Months to Serve	26	22	27

Bank Secrecy Act (BSA)

	2017	2016	2015
Investigations Initiated	499	504	613
Prosecution Recommendations	391	411	519
Informations/Indictments	390	399	533
Sentenced	409	449	557
Incarceration Rate	78%	75%	72%
Average Months to Serve	38	36	31

Employment Tax

	2017	2016	2015
Investigations Initiated	162	137	102
Prosecution Recommendations	59	77	80
Informations/Indictments	60	71	87
Sentenced	77	87	62
Incarceration Rate	78%	70%	77%
Average Months to Serve	21	14	24

Financial Institution Fraud

	2017	2016	2015
Investigations Initiated	46	66	84
Prosecution Recommendations	37	53	69
Informations/Indictments	35	46	73
Sentenced	51	64	160
Incarceration Rate	67%	75%	81%
Average Months to Serve	53	37	44

Identity Theft

	2017	2016	2015
Investigations Initiated	374	573	776
Prosecution Recommendations	403	566	774
Informations/Indictments	484	649	732
Sentenced	550	613	790
Incarceration Rate	88%	88%	85%
Average Months to Serve	34	40	38

Money Laundering

	2017	2016	2015
Investigations Initiated	1096	1201	1436
Prosecution Recommendations	886	1010	1301
Informations/Indictments	845	979	1221
Sentenced	720	668	691
Incarceration Rate	84%	84%	84%
Average Months to Serve	67	62	65

Healthcare Fraud

	2017	2016	2015
Investigations Initiated	124	127	122
Prosecution Recommendations	94	101	91
Informations/Indictments	89	90	79
Sentenced	92	46	64
Incarceration Rate	86%	85%	83%
Average Months to Serve	67	41	54

International Operations

	2017	2016	2015
Investigations Initiated	283	221	186
Prosecution Recommendations	176	221	168
Informations/Indictments	211	187	166
Sentenced	152	154	148
Incarceration Rate	80%	83%	78%
Average Months to Serve	43	45	43

Narcotics

	2017	2016	2015
Investigations Initiated	735	788	955
Prosecution Recommendations	581	684	897
Informations/Indictments	585	721	872
Sentenced	615	635	580
Incarceration Rate	87%	86%	85%
Average Months to Serve	80	69	71

Non-Filter	2017	2016	2015
Investigations Initiated	206	206	223
Prosecution Recommendations	113	137	164
Informations/ Indictments	106	157	166
Sentenced	159	159	167
Incarceration Rate	84%	80%	83%
Average Months to Serve	37	38	36

Questionable Refund Program	2017	2016	2015
Investigations Initiated	280	495	775
Prosecution Recommendations	328	514	780
Informations/ Indictments	390	594	767
Sentenced	555	669	839
Incarceration Rate	85%	85%	84%
Average Months to Serve	30	34	34

Public Corruption	2017	2016	2015
Investigations Initiated	75	84	68
Prosecution Recommendations	60	59	68
Informations/ Indictments	63	61	69
Sentenced	54	57	60
Incarceration Rate	74%	81%	73%
Average Months to Serve	34	29	25

Terrorism	2017	2016	2015
Investigations Initiated	28	42	18
Prosecution Recommendations	19	33	6
Informations/ Indictments	16	19	5
Sentenced	14	1	16
Incarceration Rate	71%	100%	75%
Average Months to Serve	9	84	42

WHAT ARE YOUR CHANCES?

The odds of facing criminal charges by the IRS depend on where you live. Of the 90 IRS offices, these are the top and bottom five by number of referrals to prosecutors in 1994 per million population.

According to Mark E. Matthews, Deputy Assistant Attorney General in the Tax Division, ". . . the certainty of prison time is generally faced only when the loss amount exceeds $40,000." This is not ". . . a realistic threat to many taxpayers." Do NOT, however, take this as a license to cheat up to $40,000!

You can access the IRS criminal investigation website at www.treas.gov/irs/ci for fraud and scam alerts.

REFUNDS

If you are due a refund and if you file by April 15, that refund must be paid by June 1 or else the IRS must pay you interest. Interest on your refund

IRS District Office	Per Capita Referrals
Washington, DC	71
Tulsa, Okla.	65
Louisville, Ky.	60
Oklahoma City	55
Charleston, W. Va.	45
Topeka, Kan.	5
Montgomery, Ala.	4
Madison, Wis.	4
Concord, N.H.	4
Burlington, Vt.	3

Source: Transactional Records Access Clearinghouse, Syracuse University.

starts accruing 45 days after the return's due date or the date on which you actually filed, whichever is later, and ends accruing 30 days before the date on which the IRS makes out a check to you. The status of a refund may be checked by calling the IRS during regular business hours on a special number available in 27 cities. Under this system, 10 weeks after the return is filed, you may dial the special automated service, then dial your Social Security number and the amount of the expected refund. You will then be advised when to expect a check. The numbers to call are listed below:

New Jersey	1-800-0-554-4477	St. Louis, MO	314-241-4700
Phoenix, AZ	602-261-3560	Newark, NJ	201-624-1223
Los Angeles, CA	213-617-3177	Brooklyn, NY	212-858-4461
Oakland, CA	415-839-4245	Buffalo, NY	716-856-9320
Denver, CO	303-592-1118	Manhattan, NY	212-406-4080
Washington, DC	202-628-2929	Cincinnati, OH	513-684-3531
Jacksonville, FL	904-353-9579	Cleveland, OH	216-522-3037
Atlanta, GA	404-221-6572	Portland, OR	503-294-5363
Chicago, IL	312-886-9614	Philadelphia, PA	215-592-8946
Indianapolis, IN	317-634-1550	Nashville, TE	615-242-1541
Baltimore, MD	301-244-7306	Dallas, TX	214-767-1792
Boston, MA	617-523-8602	Houston, TX	713-850-8801
Detroit, MI	313-961-4282	Seattle, WA	206-343-7221
St. Paul, MN	612-224-4288	Milwaukee, WI	414-886-1615

You can also check the status of your refund on the IRS website, www.irs.gov, or by calling 1-800-829-1954, or after 4 weeks, 800-829-4477.

COLLECTIONS

If you have not read this book carefully, you may lose an audit and have to go into Collections. As of September 1, 1995, the IRS has implented new procedures which provide a consistent framework for evaluating a taxpayer's maximum ability to pay. The procedural changes center around allowable expenses—specifically, the types and amounts of expenses that are allowed.

The new procedures establish national standards for reasonable amounts for five necessary expenses: (1) food, (2) housekeeping supplies, (3) apparel and services, (4) personal care products and services, and (5) miscellaneous. All standards, except miscellaneous, are derived from the Bureau of Labor Statistics (BLS) Consumer Expenditure Survey. The miscellaneous standard has been established by the Service.

Local standards will be established for housing and transportation. Utilities are included under housing. "Other" expenses, not covered under the national or local standards (e.g., health care, job-related education), will be allowed if they meet the necessary expense test.

CONCLUSION

In conclusion, it is important to reiterate that this book has not taught you how to evade taxes but rather how legally, within the full ambit of our tax code, to reduce your taxes to zero. According to a 1987 report issued by the American Bar Association's Commission on Taxpayer Compliance, one-third of all taxpayers deliberately fail to claim tax deductions to which they believe they are entitled. (Reasons for not taking these deductions include concern that they might not be correct, ignorance or forgetfulness, insufficient records, perceptions that the deduction was too trivial or too complicated, and fear of audits.) If you want to pay more in taxes than the law requires, you may. In 1983, 3,500 taxpayers voluntarily coughed up a total of $300,000 in voluntary donations to the Internal Revenue Service in an attempt to reduce the national debt. In fiscal 1984, the government received 2,513 gifts, totaling $405,007. Through July 27, 1985, the Internal Revenue Service counted an additional 2,205 voluntary—and deductible—gifts, totaling $350,394, to help Uncle Sam reduce the public debt. Americans donated

Collections

	FY 2006	FY 2007	FY 2008	FY 2009	FY 2010	FY 2011	FY 2012	FY 2013	FY 2014	FY 2015
Levies	3,742,276	3,757,190	2,631,038	3,478,181	3,606,818	3,748,884	2,961,162	1,855,095	1,995,987	1,464,026
Liens	629,813	683,659	768,168	965,618	1,096,376	1,042,230	707,768	602,005	535,580	515,247
Seizures	590	676	610	581	605	776	733	547	432	426

Criminal Investigation

Prosecutions Recommended

By Source	FY 2006	FY 2007	FY 2008	FY 2009	FY 2010	FY 2011	FY 2012	FY 2013	FY 2014	FY 2015
Tax and Tax Related	1,343	1,423	1,293	1,269	1,511	1,622	1,846	2,500	2,075	1,762
Nontax (illegal)	756	866	804	769	864	989	1073	976	669	630
Narcotics	621	548	688	532	659	799	782	888	734	897
Total	2,720	2,837	2,785	2,570	3,034	3,410	3,701	4,364	3,478	3,289

	FY 2006	FY 2007	FY 2008	FY 2009	FY 2010	FY 2011	FY 2012	FY 2013	FY 2014	FY 2015
Overall Conviction Rate	91.5%	90.20%	92.30%	87.20%	90.2%	92.70%	93.00%	93.1%	93.4%	93.2%

	FY 2006	FY 2007	FY 2008	FY 2009	FY 2010	FY 2011	FY 2012	FY 2013	FY 2014	FY 2015
Average Sentence[1]	22	22	24	24	27	25	32	31	31	31

1 Average sentence in months for Tax and Tax Related cases.

	FY 2006	FY 2007	FY 2008	FY 2009	FY 2010	FY 2011	FY 2012	FY 2013	FY 2014	FY 2015
Investigations Initiated	3,907	4,211	3,749	4,121	4,706	4,720	5,125	5,314	4,297	3,853
Information & Indictments	2,319	2,323	2,547	2,335	2,645	2,998	3,390	3,865	3,272	3,208

Both "information" and "indictments" are accusations. "Information" means an accusation made by law enforcement without the intervention of a grand jury, whereas an "indictment" is an accusation made by a prosecutor and issued by a grand jury.

$1,697,366 to the Bureau of the Public Debt in fiscal 1986 for the Debt Reduction Fund. Of this amount, $1.1 million came via the Internal Revenue Service, thanks to a note in tax return instructions. An additional $719,516 arrived in the 6 months ending March 31, 1987, bringing the then-to-date total since 1961 to $13,138,462. Through fiscal 1993, the total was $38.6 million. In fiscal 2016, donors chipped in just over 2.7 million. These payments qualify as charitable contributions. Give online at Pay.gov or send a check with a note to the Bureau of Fiscal Service. If you want to pay more taxes, you therefore have the opportunity to do so. See the following chart showing donations made to pay off the national debt.

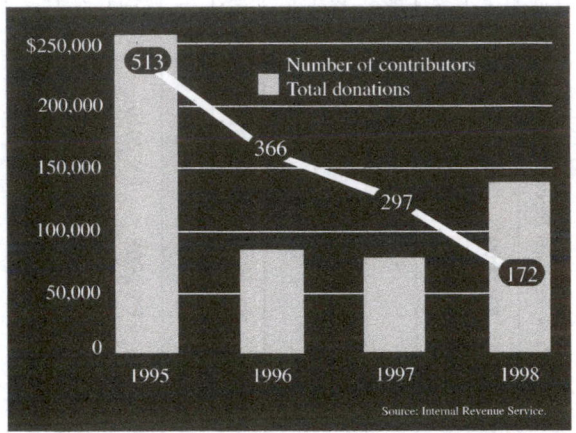

A great deal has been written and said on the question of the morality of tax saving in general, and on those who save taxes in particular. Perhaps the best statement on tax avoidance—the legal minimization of your tax liability—was written by Judge Learned Hand:

> If I understand the Commissioner, he wishes us to consider that these deeds may have been a preliminary step in a reprehensible scheme to lessen . . . income taxes. There is not the faintest ground for imputing any such purpose to the parties at bar; and if there were, it ought not to count. Over and over again courts have said that there is nothing sinister in so arranging one's affairs as to keep taxes as low as possible. Everybody does so, rich or poor; and all do right, for nobody owes any public duty to pay more than the law demands; taxes are enforced exactions, not voluntary

contributions. To demand more in the name of morals is mere Cant. (*Commissioner v. Neuman*, 159 F. 2d 848.)

<div align="right">February 20, 1947</div>

CHANCES OF AN AUDIT

Here's a quick and dirty on your chance of being audited.

The IRS audited 0.6 percent of all individual income tax returns filed in CY 2016. The IRS conducted the majority of Fiscal Year (FY) 2017 audits, 70.8 percent, via correspondence. The remaining 29.2 percent were conducted in the field.

Number of Returns Examined, Fiscal Years 2012—2017

SOURCE: *IRS Data Book* Table 9a

Of the almost 1.1 million examinations of tax returns, more than 24,000 taxpayers did not agree with the IRS examiner's determination, totaling to an unagreed recommended additional tax of almost $11.5 billion.

During fiscal year 2017, the IRS collected more than $3.4 trillion, processed more than 245 million tax returns and other forms and issued more than 121 million individual income tax refunds totaling almost $437 billion.

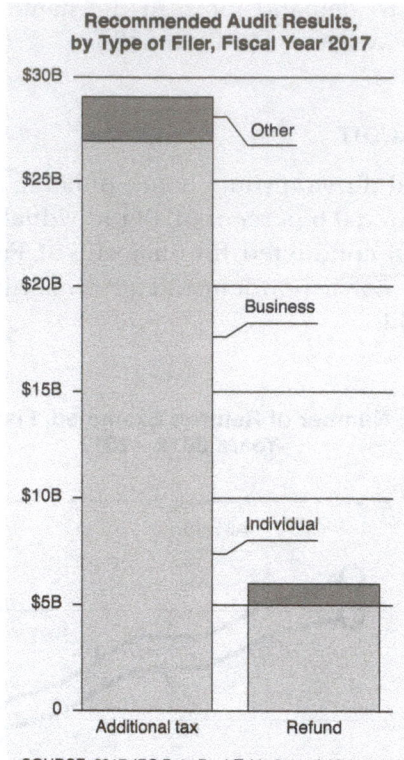

Recommended Audit Results, by Type of Filer, Fiscal Year 2017

SOURCE: 2017 *IRS Data Book* Table 9a and 12

Compared to the prior year, there were fewer audits and collection actions during fiscal year 2017. The IRS audited almost 934,000 individual income tax returns during the fiscal year, the lowest number of audits since 2003. The chance of being audited fell to 0.6 percent, the lowest coverage rate since 2002.

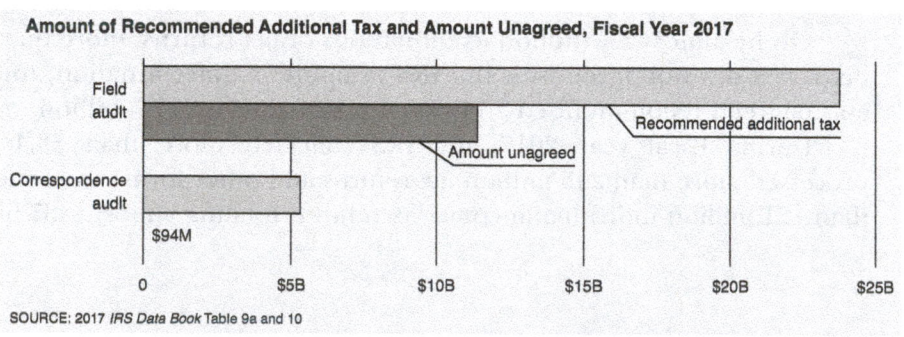

Amount of Recommended Additional Tax and Amount Unagreed, Fiscal Year 2017

SOURCE: 2017 *IRS Data Book* Table 9a and 10

On average, the IRS spent 34 cents to collect $100 in tax revenue during fiscal year, 2017.

The IRS audited about 1 in every 167 returns filed.

Here are your 2017 odds for an audit:

Examination Coverage: Individual Income Tax Returns Examined, by Size of Adjusted Gross Income, Fiscal Year 2017

Size of adjusted gross income[1]	Returns filed in Calendar Year 2016 (percent of total)[2]	Examination coverage in Fiscal Year 2017 (percent)[3]
All returns [4]	100.00	0.62
No adjusted gross income[5]	1.69	2.55
$1 under $25,000	36.47	0.71
$25,000 under $50,000	23.33	0.49
$50,000 under $75,000	13.26	0.48
$75,000 under $100,000	8.59	0.45
$100,000 under $200,000	12.19	0.45
$200,000 under $500,000	3.60	0.70
$500,000 under $1,000,000	0.58	1.56
$1,000,000 under $5,000,000	0.26	3.52
$5,000,000 under $10,000,000	0.02	7.95
$10,000,000 or more	0.01	14.52

[1] Adjusted gross income is total income (including losses), as defined by the Internal Revenue Code, less statutory adjustments—primarily business, investment, and certain other deductions.

[2] Calendar Year (CY) 2016 data are presented because, in general, examination activity is associated with returns filed in the previous calendar year. The total number of individual income tax returns filed in CY 2016 was 149,919,416. See Table 9a for additional details.

[3] Represents returns examined in Fiscal Year 2017 for each adjusted gross income (AGI) class, as a percentage of the total number of returns filed in Calendar Year 2016 for that AGI class.

[4] In addition to examinations of returns filed, the IRS examined more than 62,800 cases in which no return was filed. These nonfiler cases were referred for examination by the Collections Program and the Automated Substitute for Return (ASFR) Program, the IRS uses information returns from third parties (such as Forms W-2 and 1099) to identify tax return delinquencies, constructs tax returns for certain nonfilers based on that third-party information, and assesses tax, interest, and penalties based on the substitute returns. These nonfiler cases are excluded from the examination data in this table. See Table 14 for information on the ASFR Program.

[5] Includes returns with adjusted gross income of less than zero. AGI may be less than zero when a taxpayer reports losses or statutory adjustments that exceed total income.

NOTE: This table shows examination coverage of individual income tax returns classified by size of adjusted gross income, while Tables 9a and 10–12 report examination coverage by size of total positive income. Total positive income is the sum of all positive amounts shown for the various sources of income reported on the individual income tax return and therefore excludes losses. By comparison, adjusted gross income includes losses, such as farm losses.

SOURCE: Research, Applied Analytics, and Statistics.

Total Amount of IRS Audits on Individual Tax Returns

	FY 2014	FY 2015	FY 2016	FY 2017
Total Returns Filed Prior CY	145,236,429	146,861,217	147,964,324	149,919,416
Total Audits Conducted	1,242,479	1,228,117	1,034,955	933,785
Percentage Audited	0.85%	0.84%	0.7%	0.6%

IRS Audit Rates by Income Level for Individuals (2017)

	Percentage of Total Returns Filed in Year 2016	Percentage of Returns Audited
No adjusted gross income	1.69%	2.55%
$1–$24,999	36.47%	0.71%
$25,000–$49,999	23.33%	0.49%
$50,000–$74,999	13.26%	0.48%
$75,000–$99,999	8.59%	0.45%
$100,000–$199,999	12.19%	0.47%
$200,000–$499,999	3.60%	0.70%
$500,000–$999,999	0.58%	1.56%
$1,000,000–$4,999,999	0.26%	3.52%
$5,000,000–$9,999,999	0.02%	7.95%
$10,000,000+	0.01%	14.52%

	Returns FY 2017 Filed (Prior Calendar Year)	Returns Audited	Percentage Audited
Small Corporation	1,771,641	12,157	0.7%
Large Corporation	77,709	6,109	7.9%
S Corporation	4,808,833	15,869	0.3%
Partnership	3,862,691	13,448	0.3%
Individual	149,919,416	933,785	0.6%

Examination Coverage: Recommended and Average Recommended Additional Tax After Examination, by Type and Size of Return, Fiscal Year 2017

Type and size of return	All returns filed in Calendar Year 2016[1,2]	Returns examined in Fiscal Year 2017[1]				Percentage of returns examined with no change		Recommended additional tax (thousands of dollars)			Average recommended additional tax per return (dollars)	
		Total	Percentage covered	Field[3]	Correspondence	Field[3]	Correspondence	Total	Field[3]	Correspondence	Field[3]	Correspondence
	(1)	(2)	(3)	(4)	(5)	(6)	(7)	(8)	(9)	(10)	(11)	(12)
United States, total	195,614,161	1,059,924	0.5	309,062	750,862	[4]	[4]	28,991,634	23,893,558	5,098,076	[4]	[4]
Taxable returns:												
▲ Individual income tax returns, total	149,919,416	[5]933,785	0.6	214,582	719,203	8	10	[6]9,028,417	4,703,305	4,325,112	21,918	6,014
△ Returns with total positive income under $200,000[7]:												
▲ Nonbusiness returns without Earned Income Tax Credit:												
Without Schedule C, E, F, or Form 2106[8]	81,474,839	154,310	0.2	24,510	129,800	9	10	892,600	377,358	515,242	15,396	3,970
With Schedule E or Form 2106[9]	15,818,718	112,792	0.7	32,054	80,738	5	9	765,756	484,834	280,922	15,126	3,479
▲ Business returns without Earned Income Tax Credit:												
Nonfarm business returns by size of total gross receipts[10]:												
Under $25,000	11,005,284	98,952	0.9	26,382	72,570	4	9	493,741	218,686	275,055	8,289	3,790
$25,000 under $100,000	3,305,637	44,484	1.3	20,910	23,524	6	4	605,703	378,763	226,940	18,114	9,647
$100,000 under $200,000	914,814	18,994	2.1	13,612	5,382	5	7	388,711	258,096	130,615	18,961	24,269
$200,000 or more	719,214	13,307	1.9	10,757	2,550	8	19	301,119	290,855	10,264	27,039	4,025
Farm returns	1,244,590	5,454	0.4	2,379	3,075	8	20	24,451	14,799	9,652	6,221	3,139
▲ Business and nonbusiness returns with Earned Income Tax Credit by size of total gross receipts[10,11]:												
Under $25,000	25,948,509	[12]361,360	1.4	18,513	342,847	9	9	1,742,741	118,026	1,624,715	6,375	4,739
$25,000 or more	1,909,631	[12]19,909	1.0	11,949	7,960	9	14	272,541	235,156	37,385	19,680	4,697
△ Returns with total positive income of at least $200,000 and under $1,000,000[7]:												
Nonbusiness returns	4,873,138	40,521	0.8	17,114	23,407	12	24	878,551	441,310	437,241	25,786	18,680
Business returns	2,001,954	31,471	1.6	16,265	15,206	10	21	859,436	529,702	329,734	32,567	21,684
△ Returns with total positive income of $1,000,000 or more[7]	519,406	22,704	4.4	11,087	11,617	14	34	1,783,111	1,336,524	446,587	120,549	38,443
△ International returns[13]	183,682	9,577	5.2	9,050	527	2	4	19,956	19,196	760	2,121	1,443

(Continued)

Examination Coverage: Recommended and Average Recommended Additional Tax After Examination, by Type and Size of Return, Fiscal Year 2017

(continued)

Type and size of return	All returns filed in Calendar Year 2016[1, 2]	Returns examined in Fiscal Year 2017[1]				Percentage of returns examined with no change		Recommended additional tax (thousands of dollars)			Average recommended additional tax per return (dollars)	
		Total	Percentage covered	Field[3]	Correspondence	Field[3]	Correspondence	Total	Field[3]	Correspondence	Field[3]	Correspondence
	(1)	(2)	(3)	(4)	(5)	(6)	(7)	(8)	(9)	(10)	(11)	(12)
▲ Corporation income tax returns, except Form 1120-S, total[14]	1,906,645	18,962	1.0	17,962	1,000	31	43	17,718,475	17,020,575	697,900	947,588	697,901
▷ Returns other than Forms 1120-C and 1120-F[15]:												
▲ Small corporations	1,771,641	12,157	0.7	11,803	354	27	31	624,977	555,503	69,474	47,065	196,255
No balance sheet returns	414,636	2,527	0.6	2,459	68	16	37	131,860	130,483	1,377	53,064	20,243
Balance sheet returns by size of total assets:												
Under $250,000	849,698	4,370	0.5	4,278	92	27	43	211,543	145,530	66,013	34,018	717,538
$250,000 under $1,000,000	302,052	3,221	1.1	3,157	64	34	16	126,306	124,360	1,946	99,392	30,406
$1,000,000 under $5,000,000	169,366	1,587	0.9	1,495	92	31	25	68,034	67,934	100	45,441	1,087
$5,000,000 under $10,000,000	35,889	452	1.3	414	38	35	29	87,234	87,196	38	210,617	1,006
▲ Large corporations	77,709	6,109	7.9	5,659	450	36	48	16,989,101	16,360,786	628,315	2,891,109	1,396,255
Balance sheet returns by size of total assets:												
$10,000,000 under $50,000,000	42,992	1,676	4.0	1,585	91	40	37	158,539	157,494	1,045	99,365	11,479
$50,000,000 under $100,000,000	9,141	930	10.2	887	43	50	42	75,333	75,327	6	84,923	134
$100,000,000 under $250,000,000	9,031	897	9.9	842	55	47	69	80,355	80,256	99	95,316	1,807
$250,000,000 under $500,000,000	5,529	550	9.9	483	67	40	57	102,312	101,675	637	210,507	9,508
$500,000,000 under $1,000,000,000	4,127	462	11.2	413	49	27	57	320,069	319,695	374	774,080	7,635
$1,000,000,000 under $5,000,000,000	5,293	810	15.3	737	73	22	52	1,734,213	1,727,235	6,978	2,343,602	95,589
$5,000,000,000 under $20,000,000,000	1,580	424	26.8	381	43	18	33	3,456,110	3,454,706	1,404	9,067,470	32,652
$20,000,000,000 or more	616	360	58.4	331	29	14	21	11,062,170	10,444,398	617,772	31,554,072	21,302,483
▷ Form 1120-C returns[15]	9,303	40	0.4	d	d	d	d	24,169	d	d	d	d
▷ Form 1120-F returns[15]	47,992	656	1.4	d	d	d	d	80,228	d	d	d	d
▲ Estate and trust income tax returns[16]	3,187,535	3,284	0.1	953	2,331	3	24	50,895	37,460	13,435	99,308	5,764
▲ Estate tax returns, total[17]	35,042	2,876	8.2	2,876	0	19	N/A	798,898	798,898	N/A	277,781	N/A
▷ Size of gross estate:												
Under $5,000,000	23,013	570	2.5	570	0	16	N/A	25,296	25,296	N/A	44,274	N/A
$5,000,000 under $10,000,000	8,095	1,086	13.4	1,086	0	23	N/A	91,292	91,292	N/A	84,063	N/A
$10,000,000 or more	3,934	1,220	31.0	1,220	0	17	N/A	682,370	682,370	N/A	559,320	N/A
▲ Gift tax returns	244,974	1,886	0.8	1,886	0	35	N/A	439,458	439,458	N/A	233,011	N/A
▲ Employment tax returns	30,582,806	53,716	0.2	37,137	16,579	13	5	721,367	661,873	59,494	17,822	3,589
▲ Excise tax returns	1,000,648	13,961	1.4	12,256	1,705	26	20	197,980	196,728	1,252	16,052	734
▲ Other taxable returns[18]	[4]	335	[4]	143	192	10	3	36,144	35,261	883	246,578	4,597

Nontaxable returns[19]:

▶ Partnership returns	3,978,262	15,275	0.4	9,005	6,270	43	56	N/A	N/A	N/A	N/A	N/A
▶ S corporation returns[20]	4,808,833	13,448	0.3	12,169	1,279	29	33	N/A	N/A	N/A	N/A	N/A
▶ Other nontaxable returns[21]	[4]	2,306	[4]	93	2,303	14	36	N/A	N/A	N/A	N/A	[4]
Income, estate, gift tax, and nontaxable returns, total	164,080,707	991,912	0.6	259,526	732,386	12	11	28,036,143	22,999,696	5,036,447	N/A	[4]

d—Not shown to avoid disclosure of information about specific taxpayers. However, the data are included in the appropriate totals.

N/A—Not applicable.

[1] Excludes excise tax returns filed with U.S. Customs and Border Protection and the Alcohol and Tobacco Tax and Trade Bureau. Also excludes returns of tax-exempt organizations, Government entities, employee retirement benefit plans, and tax-exempt bonds; and excludes information returns (e.g., Forms 1098, 1099, 5498, W-2 and W-2G, and Schedule K-1).

[2] Calendar Year 2016 data are presented because, in general, examination activity is associated with returns filed in the previous calendar year.

[3] Field examinations are generally performed in person by revenue agents, tax compliance officers, tax examiners, and revenue officer examiners. However, some field examinations may ultimately be conducted through correspondence in order to better serve the taxpayer.

[4] Not tabulated.

[5] Includes a total of 327,805 returns selected for examination on the basis of an Earned Income Tax Credit (EITC) claim.

[6] Includes a total of $1,551,646,733 in recommended additional tax (accounting for the effect of Earned Income Tax Credits) on returns selected for examination on the basis of an EITC claim.

[7] In general, total positive income is the sum of all positive amounts shown for the various sources of Income reported on the individual income tax return, and thus excludes losses.

[8] Includes Forms 1040 without a Schedule C (nonfarm sole proprietorship), Schedule E (supplemental income and loss), Schedule F (profit or loss from farming), or Form 2106 (employee business expenses).

[9] Includes Forms 1040 with a Schedule E (supplemental income and loss) or Form 2106 (employee business expenses) but without a Schedule C (nonfarm sole proprietorship) or Schedule F (profit or loss from farming).

[10] Total gross receipts is the sum of gross receipts from farm and nonfarm businesses. It is calculated by adding the positive values of gross receipts and other income from Schedule C and gross income (which can be positive or negative) from Schedule F. Schedule C is used to report profit or loss from nonfarm sole proprietorships. Schedule F is used to report profit or loss from farming. If a taxpayer reports both farm and nonfarm income, the return is classified by the larger source of Income.

[11] Includes all Forms 1040, those with and without business income, reporting an Earned Income Tax Credit claim. These returns are classified by size of total gross receipts. Business returns have total gross receipts reported on Schedule C (nonfarm sole proprietorship) or Schedule F (profit or loss from farming). Nonbusiness returns, those with no Schedules C or F, are reported in the "Under $25,000" classification.

[12] These returns were selected on the basis of an Earned Income Tax Credit (EITC) claim.

[13] Includes Forms 1040-PR (self-employment income tax return for Puerto Rico residents) and 1040-SS (self-employment income tax return for U.S. Virgin Islands, Guam, American Samoa, and the Northern Mariana Islands residents).

[14] Includes the Form 1120 series as follows: 1120 (corporation income tax return); 1120-C (income tax return for cooperative associations); 1120-F (foreign corporation income tax return, except foreign life insurance company, foreign property and casualty insurance company, or foreign sales corporation); 1120-H (homeowner association income tax return); 1120-L (life insurance company income tax return); 1120-ND (return for nuclear decommissioning funds); 1120-PC (property and casualty insurance company income tax return); 1120-REIT (real estate investment trust income tax return); 1120-RIC (regulated investment company income tax return); and 1120-SF (income tax return for settlement funds). Excludes certain other types of corporation returns, which are included in "Other taxable returns" described in footnote 18.

[15] Forms 1120-C are filed by cooperative associations. Forms 1120-F are filled by foreign corporations with U.S. income, other than foreign life insurance companies (Form 1120-L); foreign property and casualty insurance companies (Form 1120-PC); or foreign sales corporations (Form 1120-FSC).

[16] Includes taxable Form 1041 (income tax return for estates and trusts) and Form 1041-N (income tax return for electing Alaska Native Settlement Trusts).

[17] Includes Form 706 (estate and generation-skipping transfer tax return).

[18] Includes Forms 1120-FSC (foreign sales corporation income tax return); 1120-S for S corporations reporting a tax (see footnote 20); 1065-B for partnerships reporting a tax; 8288 (withholding tax return for disposition by foreign persons of U.S. property interests); and 8804 (return of withholding tax on foreign partner's share of effectively connected income).

[19] Nontaxable returns are filed for entities that generally do not have a tax liability but pass through any profits and losses to the underlying owners, who include these profits or losses on their income tax returns. The examination of partnership, S corporation, and other nontaxable returns affects the amount of recommended additional tax for these associated income tax returns.

[20] Includes most Forms 1120-S, which are filed by qualifying S corporations electing to be taxed through shareholders. Under certain conditions, S corporations are subject to tax and are included in "Other taxable returns" in this table. See footnote 18.

[21] Includes the following nontaxable returns: Form 1120-IC-DISC (domestic international sales corporation return); Form 1041 (income tax return for estates and trusts); and Form 1066 (real estate mortgage investment conduit income tax return). Under certain circumstances, estates and trusts (Form 1041) are not subject to tax and are reported as nontaxable. See Estate and trust income tax returns for taxable Forms 1041.

NOTES:

Detail may not add to totals because of rounding.

This table includes information on examinations of all individual income tax, corporation income tax, estate and trust income tax, estate tax, gift tax, employment tax, excise tax, and other taxable returns, as well as partnership, S corporation, and other nontaxable returns.

SOURCE: Small Business/Self-Employed, Examination, Performance Planning and Analysis Examination, Small Business Exam Data Management.

Examination—Individual Return Closures and Coverage Rates

Total Individual Returns	FY 2006	FY 2007	FY 2008	FY 2009	FY 2010	FY 2011	FY 2012	FY 2013	FY 2014	FY 2015
Field	302,785	311,339	310,429	326,249	342,762	391,621	359,750	344,152	291,643	267,076
Correspondence	981,165	1,073,224	1,081,152	1,099,639	1,238,632	1,173,069	1,122,216	1,060,779	950,836	961,041
Total Examinations	1,283,950	1,384,563	1,391,581	1,425,888	1,581,394	1,564,690	1,481,966	1,404,931	1,242,479,	1,228,117
Coverage	0.97%	1.03%	1.01%	1.03%	1.11%	1.11%	1.03%	0.96%	0.86%	0.84%

Income Under $200,000	FY 2006	FY 2007	FY 2008	FY 2009	FY 2010	FY 2011	FY 2012	FY 2013	FY 2014	FY 2015
Field	266,726	267,699	256,854	269,865	284,241	313,229	290,015	270,636	234,758	214,678
Correspondence	929,666	1,011,315	1,003,976	1,010,870	1,144,178	1,076,607	1,012,898	962,336	848,451	851,255
Total Examinations	1,196,392	1,279,0141	260,8301	280,7351	428,4191	389,8361	302,9131	232,9721,	083,2091	065,933
Coverage	0.93%	0.98%	0.95%	0.96%	1.04%	1.02%	0.94%	0.88%	0.78%	0.76%

Income $200,000 and Higher	FY 2006	FY 2007	FY 2008	FY 2009	FY 2010	FY 2011	FY 2012	FY 2013	FY 2014	FY 2015
Field	36,059	43,640	53,575	56,384	58,521	78,392	69,735	73,516	56,885	52,398
Correspondence	51,499	61,909	77,176	88,769	94,454	96,462	109,318	98,443	102,385	109,786
Total Examinations	87,558	105,549	130,751	145,153	152,975	174,854	179,053	171,959	159,270	162,184
Coverage	2.57%	2.68%	2.94%	2.89%	3.10%	3.93%	3.70%	3.26%	2.71%	2.61%

Income $1 Million and Higher	FY 2006	FY 2007	FY 2008	FY 2009	FY 2010	FY 2011	FY 2012	FY 2013	FY 2014	FY 2015
Field	9,459	12,259	12,233	15,730	16,509	20,475	17,826	19,167	15,029	13,781
Correspondence	4,728	10,941	9,641	12,619	15,985	15,947	23,139	20,254	19,332	25,972
Total Examinations	14,187	23,200	21,874	28,349	32,494	36,422	40,965	39,421	34,361	39,753
Coverage	5.25%	6.84%	5.57%	6.42%	8.36%	12.48%	12.14%	10.85%	7.50%	9.55%

* CY = calendar year.
n/a = not available

Examination—Business Return Closures and Coverage Rates[1]

	FY 2006	FY 2007	FY 2008	FY 2009	FY 2010	FY 2011	FY 2012	FY 2013	FY 2014	FY 2015
Total Returns Examined	52,149	59,516	59,823	58,144	58,067	62,445	70,265	61,020	57,211	61,677
Returns Filed in Prior CY	8,722,410	9,072,828	9,530,662	9,951,648,	9,941,289	9,869,358	9,950,784	9,938,483	10,044,551	10,236,183
Coverage	0.60%	0.66%	0.63%	0.58%	0.58%	0.63%	0.71%	0.61%	0.57%	0.60%
Small Corporation Returns (Assets Under $ 10 Million)										
Returns Examined	17,849	20,020	20,580	18,298	19,127	19,697	21,164	17,604	17,257	16,460
Coverage	0.80%	0.92%	0.95%	0.85%	0.94%	1.02%	1.12%	0.95%	0.95%	0.92%
Large Corporation Returns (Assets $10 Million and Higher)										
Returns Examined	10,578	9,644	9,406	9,536	10,207	10,459	10,752	9,876	7,858	7,410
Coverage	18.6%	16.8%	15.26%	14.55%	16.58%	17.64%	17.78%	15.84%	12.23%	11.15%
Subchapter S Returns (Form 1120-S)										
Returns Examined	13,970	17,657	16,634	17,455	16,327	18,519	21,658	18,670	16,317	18,595
Coverage	0.38%	0.45%	0.40%	0.40%	0.37%	0.42%	0.48%	0.42%	0.36%	0.40%
Partnership Returns (Form 1065)										
Returns Examined	9,752	12,195	13,203	12,855	12,406	13,770	16,691	14,870	15,779	19,212
Coverage	0.36%	0.42%	0.42%	0.38%	0.36%	0.40%	0.47%	0.42%	0.43%	0.51%

[1] Business Returns include Small and Large Corporation Returns and Subchapter S and Partnership Pass-Through Returns.

* CY = Calendar Year.

Examination—Large Corporation Return Closures and Coverage Rates

Assets $10 Million and Higher	FY 2006	FY 2007	FY 2008	FY 2009	FY 2010	FY 2011	FY 2012	FY 2013	FY 2014	FY 2015
Total Returns Examined	**10,578**	**9,644**	**9,406**	**9,536**	**10,207**	**10,459**	**10,752**	**9,876**	**7,858**	**7,410**
Returns Filed in Prior CY*	56,877	57,357	61,641	65,546	61,570	59,291	60,489	62,347	64,261	66,484
Coverage	18.6%	16.8%	15.3%	14.5%	16.6%	17.6%	17.78%	15.84%	12.23%	11.15%

By Asset Class	FY 2006	FY 2007	FY 2008	FY 2009	FY 2010	FY 2011	FY 2012	FY 2013	FY 2014	FY 2015
$10 Million <$50 Million										
Returns Examined	4,218	4,473	3,833	3,473	4,307	4,059	3,266	2,240	2,065	2,000
Coverage	14.2%	15.0%	11.7%	10.1%	13.4%	13.3%	10.48%	6.98%	6.18%	5.77%
$50 Million <$100 Million										
Returns Examined	999	801	893	1,158	1,259	1,442	1,543	1,206	882	913
Coverage	13.8%	11.4%	11.7%	14.3%	16.2%	18.9%	20.74%	15.51%	11.18%	11.31%
$100 Million <$250 Million										
Returns Examined	1,085	946	1,026	1,134	1,191	1,289	1,854	1,589	1,084	1,185
Coverage	14.0%	12.1%	12.8%	13.6%	14.7%	16.6%	23.19%	19.43%	13.10%	14.25%
$250 Million and Higher										
Returns Examined	4,276	3,424	3,654	3,771	3,450	3,669	4,089	4,841	3,827	3,312
Coverage	35.2%	27.2%	27.4%	25.7%	25.3%	27.6%	29.41%	33.88%	26.10%	21.45%

* CY = Calendar Year.

Examination—Tax-Exempt Organization Return Coverage

	FY 2006	FY 2007	FY 2008	FY 2009	FY 2010	FY 2011	FY 2012	FY 2013	FY 2014	FY 2015
Total Returns Examined	7,079	7,580	7,861	10,187	11,449	11,699	10,743	10,575	8,084	6,392
Returns Processed in Prior Calendar Year	849,227	867,696	888,412	823,087	776,300	858,865	798,903	771,675	765,395	787,339
Coverage	0.83%	0.87%	0.88%	1.24%	1.47%	1.36%	1.34%	1.37%	1.06%	0.81%

Taxpayer Service

Electronic Filing (e-File) Rate—Individual Returns

FY 2006	FY 2007	FY 2008	FY 2009	FY 2010	FY 2011	FY 2012	FY 2013	FY 2014	FY 2015
54%	57%	58%	66%	69%	77%	81%	82.50%	84%	85%

Toll-Free Assistor Level of Service

FY 2006	FY 2007	FY 2008	FY 2009	FY 2010	FY 2011	FY 2012	FY 2013	FY 2014	FY 2015
82%	82%	53%	70%	74%	70%	68%	60.50%	64%	38%

Toll-Free Tax Law Accuracy

FY 2006	FY 2007	FY 2008	FY 2009	FY 2010	FY 2011	FY 2012	FY 2013	FY 2014	FY 2015
91%	91%	91%	93%	93%	93%	93%	95.70%	95%	95%

Toll-Free Customer Satisfaction Rating

FY 2006	FY 2007	FY 2008	FY 2009	FY 2010	FY 2011	FY 2012	FY 2013	FY 2014	FY 2015
94%	94%	93%	93%	92%	94.0%	92%	92%	89%	87%

Web Page Visits on IRS.Gov (in millions)

FY 2006	FY 2007	FY 2008	FY 2009	FY 2010	FY 2011	FY 2012	FY 2013	FY 2014	FY 2015
193.9	214.9	347.8	296.3	304.8	319.3	372.5	456.2	437.1	490.5

Online Refund Status Checks Through 'Where's My Refund' (in millions)

FY 2006	FY 2007	FY 2008	FY 2009	FY 2010	FY 2011	FY 2012	FY 2013	FY 2014	FY 2015
24.7	32.1	39.2	54.30	66.9	78.0	132.3	197.4	189.1	234.7

The result of cuts in the IRS budget? Traditional face-to-face IRS representative to taxpayer contact is replaced by online and third-party interaction. As for audits, New York CPA Fred Slater, hit it on the head: "The audit division being told to close cases in a set amount of time and not having enough qualified personnel had repeatedly refused to negotiate or try and resolve their cases. They had told taxpayers and their representatives, we don't care what you say, we are denying all arguments and amending the return to what we think. So the Appeals Division repeatedly was doing the audit."

PENALTIES AND INTEREST

In 1955 there were 14 civil penalties in the tax code. By 2017, there were more than 170, many of which are rarely assessed. Here are some of the most important.

Late Filing of a Return: There is a penalty of 5 percent of the unpaid tax for each month or fraction thereof that the return is late, up to a maximum of 25 percent. For example, assume you owe $10,000 on your Form 1040, which you file on April 20 (5 days late). The late filing penalty is $500. There is a minimum late *filing* penalty of the lesser of $210 or the tax due if the return is not filed within 60 days of the prescribed due date.

Understatement of Taxes: In IRS Ruling 8802003, the Internal Revenue Service ruled that a taxpayer was liable for a 25 percent substantial understatement penalty even though his tax liability had been satisfied through withholding or estimated payments. In this case, the tax returns for more than 3 years were filed only after numerous contacts and inquiries by IRS personnel. The IRS ruled that the substantial underpayment penalty is imposed if an underpayment of taxes is attributable to an understatement that exceeds the greater of 10 percent of the tax required to be shown on the return or $5,000. An understatement is generally the excess of the amount of tax required to be shown on a tax return over the actual amount of tax shown on the return. The IRS concluded that for this purpose, the amount of tax shown on the return did not include any additional tax shown on a return filed *after* the Internal Revenue Service had contacted the taxpayer about the liability for the year. Moreover, the amount of tax required to be shown on the return is the tax *without* regard to any payments of tax or estimated tax by the taxpayer.

However, the Tax Court has held that the 25 percent penalty on a tax underpayment attributable to a substantial understatement of tax applies to the unpaid amount of tax after reduction by the amount of federal taxes withheld from a taxpayer's wages. (See *W.A. Woods, II,* C.C.H. Dec. 44903 91 T.C., No. 11.) The substantial understatement penalty is now 20 percent.

Negligence: There is a negligence penalty of 5 percent of the underpaid tax, plus 50 percent of the interest due on the portion of the underpayment attributable to negligence or intentional disregard. This 50 percent of the interest charge is a penalty and cannot be deducted from federal taxes.

Moreover, in Technical Advice Memorandum 8527012, the Internal Revenue Service ruled that a 5 percent negligence penalty may be imposed in the case of a taxpayer who was entitled to a refund on a late-filed return where the late filing was due to negligence or intentional disregard of the rules and regulations. According to the TAM, "the failure to file a timely tax return in itself can constitute the negligence or intentional disregard of rules and regulations." Whether this Technical Advice Memorandum can withstand the test of judicial scrutiny, however, is arguable.

Late Payment of Tax: There is a penalty of .5 percent (increasing to 1 percent on the tenth day after the date a notice of levy is given) of the tax due for each month or fraction thereof that the payment is late, up to a maximum of 25 percent. For example, assume you owe $2,000 on your Form 1040, which you filed timely, but did not pay the tax due until April 30. The late *payment* penalty is $10. In the event that the return is neither timely *filed* nor timely *paid*, both penalties will apply for the first 5 months, but the combined monthly penalty cannot exceed 5/(5.5) percent. After the 5-month period, the late payment penalty continues at .5 percent per month until the maximum 25 percent is reached. Obviously, if you are short of cash and cannot pay the tax due at the filing date, you should still file the return. Remember that an extension of time avoids a penalty for failure to file but does not extend the time to pay the tax. These penalties apply to most types of returns, such as income, payroll, and fiduciary tax returns. They will be waived only if the failure to file or failure to pay is due to "reasonable cause," such as illness or incapacity. If you enter into an installment agreement with the IRS, the 0.5 percent penalty falls to 0.25 percent per month.

To assist those in need, the IRS granted a 6-month grace period from the failure to pay penalty for tax year 2011 only if the tax, interest, and any other penalties were fully paid by October 15, 2012.

The penalty relief was available to two categories of taxpayers:

- Wage earners who have been unemployed at least 30 consecutive days during 2011 or in 2012 up to the April 17 deadline for filing a federal tax return in 2012.
- Self-employed individuals who experienced a 25 percent or greater reduction in business income in 2011 due to the economy.

This penalty relief was subject to income limits. A taxpayer's income must not exceed $200,000 if he or she files as married filing jointly or not exceed $100,000 if he or she files as single or head of household. This penalty relief was also restricted to taxpayers whose calendar year 2011 balance due did not exceed $50,000.

Taxpayers meeting the eligibility criteria needed to complete Form 1127A to seek the 2011 penalty relief.

Interest: In addition to the penalties, interest will compound daily on any taxes and penalties due until they are paid. The current interest rate, about 5 percent, will change on January 1, 2019. The rate is adjusted quarterly and calculated on the basis of the short-term federal rate plus 3 percent as of the first month of each quarter, effective as of the *following* calendar quarter.

For example, assume the short-term federal rate during January 2019 is 2 percent. Therefore, an underpayment rate of 5 percent will be established for the calendar quarter beginning April 1, 2019. Note that rates of interest paid by the IRS to corporate taxpayers for overpayments are always 1 percent lower than the rates paid to the Internal Revenue Service for underpayments. For noncorporations, the rates are the same. The personal interest paid and the penalties are both now not deductible.

Failure to File Information Returns: There is a $50 penalty for failure to timely file required information returns and statements with the IRS.* There is an additional $50 penalty for failure to provide a copy to the payee. Thus, a failure *both* to file the information return with the IRS and to provide a copy to the payee results in a penalty of $100 per failure. Every person engaged in a trade or business (including nonprofit organizations) must file an information return for payments of employees' salaries, rent and royalties, nonemployee compensation (independent contractors), interest, and dividends. Information returns are required if payments to a single individual total $600 or more, except for interest and dividends, where the limit is $10. Of course, all employee wages and salaries are reported on Form W-2 regardless of amount paid.

Stopping Interest: Interest on taxes owed is compounded daily, and charging interest on interest is allowed. In Revenue Proclamation 84-58, I.R.B. 1984-33, 9, the IRS detailed the steps that should be taken to stop the running of interest on a contested IRS determination. You may stop the running of interest by prepaying the amount contested, without jeopardizing your right to contest the issue, or by posting a cash bond. The prepayment would draw interest and the bond would not. However, the bond could be withdrawn at any time before assessment. Note, however, that a payment response to a proposed liability—e.g., as a result of a revenue agent's report—will be treated as a payment of tax, rather than a cash bond, unless you specifically designate the remittance as a "deposit in the nature of a cash bond." A remittance that is made before liability is proposed, however, will be

* If your gross receipts are $5 million or less. As of 2017 the penalty per return is as much as $260 ($530 if intentional disregard) with a calendar year maximum of $1,064,000 (no limit if intentional disregard).

treated as a cash bond. If the cash bond exceeds the amount of tax ultimately determined, you may have it applied against other liabilities, either assessed or unassessed. Furthermore, you may make a partial payment, but you must designate the part of the liability that is proposed to be satisfied. If the IRS cannot tell whether the payment is a partial payment of tax or a cash bond, it will treat it as being in the latter category. Moreover, the bond must include interest to date in order to stop the further running of interest on any interest accrued.

Partial Payments: If you do not pay the entire amount owed to the Internal Revenue Service, a partial payment generally will be applied first to tax, then to penalty, and finally to the interest that is owed.

Frivolous Tax Penalty: A frivolous tax penalty of up to $25,000 can be assessed on a taxpayer who institutes a Tax Court proceeding primarily to delay payment or for frivolous reasons. Moreover, a $25,000 penalty can be imposed upon any taxpayer who, in furtherance of a frivolous position or with a prima facie intent to delay or impede administration of the tax law, files a purported return that fails to contain information from which the correctness of a reported tax liability can be determined, or that clearly indicates that the tax liability shown must be substantially incorrect.

In fact, the IRS can assess a penalty against a taxpayer who files a return that it deems frivolous even when no taxes are owed and a return is not required to be filed. For example, in *Bradley v. U.S.* (No. 85-2445, May 22, 1987, CA9), the taxpayer wrote a statement to the IRS saying that he refused to pay taxes because of the government's intervention in Central America and filed that statement with his Form 1040. The taxpayer owed no tax and was not required to file a return. However, a notice was sent to Bradley informing him that he had filed a frivolous return and that a penalty was being assessed. The court upheld the penalty because the Form 1040 that Bradley returned purported to be a tax return but lacked the information on which the substantial correctness of the self-assessment could be judged and took a frivolous position.

Interest on Erroneous Refunds: Normally, if you receive an erroneous refund, the Internal Revenue Service will require that you pay it back with interest. However, in Delegation Order No. 231, published in *The Federal Register* on July 11, 1988, the IRS delegated authority to district service center directors to determine administratively that interest is not due on erroneous refunds under certain circumstances. These circumstances include the following:

1. Documentation is present that leaves no doubt that an IRS error caused the erroneous refund to be issued.

2. Documentation is present that substantiates that repayment of the refund has been made in full.

3. The official is satisfied—after considering the relative size of the erroneous refund, the amount of the interest involved, the circumstances surrounding any delay in the repayment of the refund, and the handling and collection cost that would be entailed—that a waiver would be fair and equitable to the government and the taxpayer.

PENALTY ABATEMENT

You may be entitled to penalty abatement, if the IRS follows the rules.

The TIGTA found that many taxpayers did not receive an abatement of the failure to file (FTF) and failure to pay (FTP) penalties even though they qualified under the *First-Time Abate* (FTA) criteria. The IRS waives the FTF and FTP penalties for some taxpayers who have demonstrated full compliance over the prior 3 years in the FTA program to reward past compliance and promote future compliance. However, many taxpayers with compliant tax histories were not offered and did not receive the FTA waiver. The unabated penalties totaled more than $181 million. You must request the abatement to get it.

GET COPIES OF PRIOR YEAR TAX RECORDS

If you need a copy of your tax return, you should file Form 4506, Request for Copy of Tax Return. The usual fee per copy is $50. However, the IRS will waive this fee if you are a victim of a federally declared disaster. If you just need information that shows most line items from your tax return, you can request a free transcript. The quickest way to get a copy of your tax transcript is to use the Get Transcript application. You can also get it if you call 1-800-908-9946. Two other options are to file Form 4506T-EZ, Short Form Request for Individual Tax Return Transcript, or Form 4506-T, Request for Transcript of Tax Return.

STATE TAXES

To aid in the filing of state tax returns, see pages 714–716 for a list of telephone numbers and addresses for obtaining out-of-state income tax forms.

CREDIT CARD PAYMENTS

If you want to pay your tax with a credit card, call either 800-272-9829 or 888-255-8299. Any mileage earned could offset any fees charged, but, after 2017, the fees are no longer deductible.

THE TAXPAYER'S BILL OF RIGHTS

The Technical and Miscellaneous Revenue Act of 1988 (TAMRA) created a consolidated statutory system that addressed a wide range of procedural subjects, including extensive changes in collection procedures. The intent of the Taxpayer's Bill of Rights is to provide a better balance between taxpayers' rights and the IRS's authority in administering the federal tax system. The Bill enhanced many safeguards and remedies previously available to taxpayers and established several new restrictions on the procedures governing the assessment and collection of taxes by the Internal Revenue Service.

The provisions of the Bill included the following: The Internal Revenue Service must provide taxpayers with a written statement of taxpayer rights and the obligations of the Internal Revenue Service during audit, repeals, refund, and collection processes when taxpayers are contacted regarding determinations or collections of tax.

Within 1 year after November 10, 1988, the IRS must prescribe standards for selecting a reasonable time and place for taxpayer interviews. These regulations should provide that it is not reasonable to require an interview at a service office other than the one closest to the taxpayer's home. Moreover, it is unreasonable for the IRS to audit a taxpayer at his or her place of business if the business is so small that doing so effectively requires the taxpayer to close the business, except where facts, such as inventory, must be verified by a direct visit.

The Internal Revenue Service must prescribe procedures for a taxpayer to make an audio recording of an interview at his or her own expense. The IRS can also record an interview, provided that the taxpayer is given advance notice and a transcript or copy of the recording upon request and payment of costs. These changes largely codify existing practices.

The IRS must notify a taxpayer that an interview may be suspended at any time if the taxpayer clearly states the desire to consult with an authorized representative—that is, an attorney or accountant. Moreover, the IRS cannot require a taxpayer to accompany an authorized representative to an interview unless it issues an administrative summons.

The IRS must abate any portion of penalties on tax attributable to erroneous written advice provided by the IRS. However, the Bill does not require abatement of interest on deficiencies arising from such erroneous advice. The new provision applies (1) if the advice was given in response to a specific written request made after 1988, (2) if the advice was reasonably relied upon, and (3) if the penalty or addition did not result from the taxpayer's failure to provide full and accurate information to the IRS.

The Bill extended the time period within which levies can be issued by the IRS and within which banks must respond to a levy. The required

minimum period of time between the IRS's issuance to a taxpayer of a notice of levy and the actual levy was increased from 10 to 30 days. Similarly, banks must now wait 21 days before surrendering deposits in response to a levy. The amount to be surrendered includes any interest that accrues during the escrow period.

Any notice of levy must contain a statement describing the statutory provisions and administrative procedures relating to the levy, sale and redemption of property, the administrative appeals available to contest the levy, and the alternatives available to the taxpayer (including an installment payment agreement) for preventing the use of a levy. This statement must be written in simple and nontechnical terms.

The Bill prohibits the use of a levy if the IRS estimates that the expenses that will be incurred for the levy and sale of the property will exceed the property's fair market value at the time of the levy.

Moreover, the Bill expanded the types and amounts of property exempt from levy. The exemption for wages and salary was increased from $75 plus $25 for each dependent, per week, to a weekly amount equal to the taxpayer's standard deduction and allowable personal exemptions, divided by 52. The exemption for fuel, provisions, furniture, and personal effects was also increased from $1,500 to $1,550 in 1989 and $1,600 thereafter. Similarly, the exemptions for books, tools, and personal effects was increased from $1,000 to $1,050 in 1989 and $1,100 thereafter. A new exemption was created for the principal residence of a taxpayer, except in jeopardy cases or where the district director or assistant district director personally approves the levy in writing. New exemptions were also created for certain public assistance and job training partnerships payments.

The Bill directed that the IRS provide an accelerated appeals process to determine whether any seized personal property used in a trade or business should be released from levy on any appropriate statutory grounds. Such grounds would include the taxpayer's entering into an installment agreement with respect to the liability or an IRS determination that the levy "is creating an economic hardship due to the financial condition of the taxpayer."

The owner of seized property now has the right to request that that property be sold within 60 days after such a request.

The Bill required the IRS to issue regulations under which taxpayers may obtain a review of a publicly filed notice of lien. The taxpayer will be able to correct erroneous filings—for example, when the underlying tax liability has been satisfied or the assessment was untimely or improperly made.

Regardless of whether a taxpayer challenges the lien, the IRS is required to issue a special certificate of release whenever a lien is found to be erroneously filed. The certificate must be filed expeditiously—"if practicable, within 14 days"—after the error is determined. It must also include a statement that the filing of the notice was erroneous.

The Bill codified the current IRS practice of entering into installment agreements when taxpayers are unable to satisfy a tax delinquency in full. However, the IRS is given the authority to alter, modify, or terminate an agreement if it determines that the financial condition of the taxpayer has significantly changed. The IRS must give the taxpayer at least 30 days' notice prior to the action and must provide the reason for its determination.

The Bill allows the IRS's taxpayer ombudsman to issue taxpayer assistance orders (TAOs) that may include releasing taxpayers from levies of property and directing the IRS to cease collection attempts, though such orders can be modified or rescinded by certain other IRS officials. The issuance of a TAO will suspend any applicable period of limitation from the date of the taxpayer's application until the date of the ombudsman's decision on the application.

The Bill expanded the jurisdiction of the Tax Court to intercede when the IRS decides to seize taxpayer property immediately if a taxpayer petition has been filed with the court. Effective November 10, 1988, the Tax Court has concurrent jurisdiction with the taxpayer's local district court to enjoin the assessment or collection of a tax that is the subject of a timely filed petition with the Tax Court. Note that taxpayers who are the subject of a premature assessment or collection activity but who have not yet filed a petition with the Tax Court must still pursue their injunctive remedy in a district court.

Moreover, the Tax Court now has jurisdiction, upon motion by a taxpayer, to order a refund if the IRS has failed to make a refund within 120 days after the court's decision becomes final. This provision is effective for overpayments not refunded by February 8, 1989.

In addition, the Tax Court is granted limited jurisdiction to consider disputes concerning the interest due on deficiencies that it has determined. The jurisdiction of both the Tax Court and the district courts to hear certain causes of action arising from jeopardy assessments and levies has also been expanded.

The Bill created a new cause of action for damages against the United States in district courts for the reckless or intentional disregard of the Code or Regulations by an IRS employee in connection with the collection of any tax. However, to be eligible for a recovery, a taxpayer must exhaust all administrative remedies. This civil action must be commenced within 2 years after the date the right of action accrued, and the liability of the government under this provision is limited to the lesser of $100,000 or the sum of the "actual, direct economic damages, sustained as a proximate cause" of the reckless or intentional actions of the employee, plus the costs of the action.

Note that the court has the right to assess damages up to $10,000 against a taxpayer who the court determines to have instituted or maintained a frivolous or groundless action under this provision.

The Bill also created a new cause of action for damages against the United States in a federal district court for an IRS failure to release a lien after 1988. Both the exhaustion of administrative remedies and the period of limitations are the same as the above newly created cause of action.

Reasonable litigation costs were available to prevailing taxpayers prior to the Bill. TAMRA creates an expanded remedy to permit taxpayers to recover reasonable administrative costs incurred for certain administrative proceedings. Such costs include costs incurred on or after the earlier of (1) the date the taxpayer receives a notice of deficiency or (2) the date the taxpayer received the decision notice from the IRS Office of Appeals. In order to collect, the taxpayer must be a "prevailing party," and the taxpayer retains the burden of proof that the position of the government was not substantially justified. "The position of the U.S." means the position taken by the IRS after the dates referred to above. If neither date is applicable, then the position of the United States is the position taken in litigation.

The Bill contained provisions that prevent temporary regulations from remaining in effect longer than 3 years.

The Bill contained provisions preventing the IRS from using tax enforcement results as a basis for evaluating its employees or for imposing or suggesting production goals or quotas for its employees to meet. Each district director must certify quarterly, in a letter to the commissioner, that tax enforcement records are not being used in a prohibited manner.

The Bill provided for a statutorily required position as second assistant commissioner responsible for Taxpayer Services.

The Bill created a new civil penalty against tax return preparers who disclose any information obtained in preparing a return or who use such information for any purpose other than preparing a return. This penalty was $250 for each such disclosure, up to a maximum of $10,000 per calendar year. The criminal penalty for such disclosures is modified to apply only when the prohibited disclosure is done knowingly or recklessly.

The creation of the Taxpayer's Bill of Rights represented a significant advance in the direction of tax equity and fairness. Further advances were achieved by the Taxpayer's Bill of Rights 2 passed in 1996, which created what is now the Office of the Taxpayer Advocate, and 3, passed in 1998, which provided enhanced "innocent spouse" relief.

Original Income Tax Return, 1913

Form 1040.

INCOME TAX.

THE PENALTY

FOR FAILURE TO HAVE THIS RETURN IN THE HANDS OF THE COLLECTOR OF INTERNAL REVENUE ON OR BEFORE MARCH 1 IS $20 TO $1000.

(SEE INSTRUCTIONS ON PAGE 4.)

UNITED STATES INTERNAL REVENUE.

RETURN OF ANNUAL NET INCOME OF INDIVIDUALS.

(As provided by Act of Congress, approved October 3, 1913.)

RETURN OF NET INCOME RECEIVED OR ACCRUED DURING THE YEAR ENDED DECEMBER 31, 191___

(FOR THE YEAR 1913, FROM MARCH 1 TO DECEMBER 31.)

Filed by (or for) .. of

(Full name of individual.)

in the City, Town, or Post Office of State of

(Street and No.)

(Fill in pages 2 and 3 before making entries below.)

1. GROSS INCOME (see page 2, line 12)		$		
2. GENERAL DEDUCTIONS (see page 3, line 7)		$		
3. NET INCOME		$		

Deductions and exemptions allowed in computing income subject to the normal tax of 1 per cent.

TO BE FILLED IN BY COLLECTOR.

List No.

......... District of

Date received

TO BE FILLED IN BY INTERNAL REVENUE BUREAU.

File No.

Assessment List

Page Line

4. Dividends and net earnings received or accrued, of corporations, etc., subject to like tax. (See page 2, line 11) $

5. Amount of income on which the normal tax has been deducted and withheld at the source. (See page 2, line 9, column A)

6. Specific exemption of $3,000 or $4,000, as the case may be. (See Instructions 3 and 19)

Total deductions and exemptions. (Items 4, 5, and 6) $

7. TAXABLE INCOME on which the normal tax of 1 per cent is to be calculated. (See Instruction 3). $

8. When the net income shown above on line 3 exceeds $20,000, the additional tax thereon must be calculated as per schedule below:

	INCOME		TAX
1 per cent on amount over $20,000 and not exceeding $50,000	$		$
2 " " 50,000 " " 75,000			
3 " " 75,000 " " 100,000			
4 " " 100,000 " " 250,000			
5 " " 250,000 " " 500,000			
6 " " 500,000			
Total additional or super tax			$
Total normal tax (1 per cent of amount entered on line 7)			$
Total tax liability			$

713

State Tax Departments

ALABAMA
205-262-1112
State Dept. of Rev
 Income Tax Division
P.O. Box 327410
Montgomery, AL
 36132-7410

ALASKA
907-465-2302
Dept. of Rev.
S.O.B. Box SA
Juneau, AK 99811

ARIZONA
602-542-4260
Dept. of Rev.
Attn: Forms
1600 W. Monroe
Phoenix, AZ 85007

ARKANSAS
501-682-7255
Dept. of Finance and
 Administration
Rev. Division
P.O. Box 3628
Little Rock, AR 72203

CALIFORNIA
916-635-8023
Franchise Tax Board
Tax Forms Request
P.O. Box 942840
Sacramento, CA
94240-0070

COLORADO
303-534-1408
Dept. of Rev.
1375 Sherman Street
Denver, CO 80261

CONNECTICUT
203-566-8520
State Tax Dept.
Dept. of Rev. Services
92 Farmington Avenue
Hartford, CT 06105

DELAWARE
302-571-3300
Dept. of Finance
Division of Rev.
Delaware State Building
820 N. French St.
Wilmington, DE 19801

FLORIDA
904-487-3107
Dept. of Rev. Supply Dept.
501 S. Calhoun St.
Tallahassee, FL
323/99-0100

GEORGIA
404-656-4293
Income Tax Unit
Dept. of Rev.
Trinity-Washington Bldg.
Atlanta, GA 30334

HAWAII
808-548-3270
First Taxation District
830 Punch Bowl St.
P.O. Box 259
Honolulu, HI 96809

IDAHO
208-334-7660
State Tax Commission
700 W. State St.
P.O. Box 36
Boise, ID 83722

ILLINOIS
217-782-3336
Dept. of Rev.
101 W. Jefferson
Springfield, IL 62708

INDIANA
317-232-2189
Dept. of Rev.
100 N. Senate Ave.
Room 113
Indianapolis, IN
46204-2253

IOWA
Dept. of Rev.
Hoover State Office
 Building
Des Moines, IA 50319

KANSAS
913-296-305
Dept. of Rev.
Division of Taxation
Box 12001
Topeka, KS 66612-2001

KENTUCKY
502-564-3658
Rev. Cabinet
Property and Mail Service
Frankfort, KY 40620

LOUISIANA
504-925-7532
Dept. of Rev.
P.O. Box 201
Baton Rouge, LA 70821

MAINE
207-289-3695
Bureau of Taxation
Income Tax Section
Station 24
Augusta, ME 04333

MARYLAND
301-974-3117
Comp. of the Treasury
Income Tax Division
Annapolis, MD 21401

MASSACHUSETTS
617-727-4392
Income Tax Bureau
Services and Supplies
 Section
100 Cambridge Street
Boston, MA 02204

MICHIGAN
517-335-1144
Dept. of Treasury
Treasury Building
430 W. Allegan St.
Lansing, MI 48922

MINNESOTA
612-296-3781
Minnesota Dept. of Rev.
Tax Division
Mail Station 4451
St. Paul, MN 55145

MISSISSIPPI
601-359-1105
State Tax Commission
P.O. Box 960
Jackson, MS 39205

MISSOURI
314-751-4866
Dept. of Rev.
P.O. Box 3022
Jefferson City, MO 65102

MONTANA
406-444-2981
Income Tax Division
Sam Mitchell Building
Helena, MT 59620

NEBRASKA
402-471-2971
Dept. of Rev.
Box 94818
Lincoln, NE
 68509-4818

NEVADA
702-885-4892
Dept. of Taxation
Capitol Complex
Carson City, NV 89710

NEW HAMPSHIRE
603-271-2191
Dept. of Rev.
61 S. Spring St.
P.O. Box 457
Concord, NH 03302

NEW JERSEY
609-292-6400
Division of Taxation
50 Barrack St.
Trenton, NJ 08646-0269

NEW MEXICO
505-827-0700
Rev. Division
P.O. Box 630
Santa Fe, NM 87509-0630

NEW YORK CITY
718-935-6000
Dept. of Finance
Forms Information
25 Elm Place, 3rd Floor
Brooklyn, NY

NEW YORK STATE
518-457-2772
Dept. of Taxation and
 Finance
Taxpayer Service
Harriman Campus
State Office Building
Albany, NY 12227

NORTH CAROLINA
919-733-3991
Dept. of Rev.
Box 25000
Raleigh, NC 27640

NORTH DAKOTA
701-224-3450
State Tax Commission
State Capitol
Bismarck, ND 58505

OHIO
614-433-7750
Dept. of Taxation
Forms Request
P.O. Box 2679
Columbus, OH 43270

OKLAHOMA
405-521-3108
Income Tax Division
2501 Lincoln Blvd
Oklahoma City, OK
 73194-0020

OREGON
503-3-371-2244
Dept. of Rev.
955 Center St., N.E.
Salem, OR 97310

PENNSYLVANIA
717-986-4621
Dept. of Rev.
Bureau of Admin.
 Services
Dept. 281200
Harrisburg, PA
 17128-1200

RHODE ISLAND
401-277-3934
Division of Taxation
289 Promenade St.
Providence, RI 02908

SOUTH CAROLINA
803-737-5000
Tax Commission
Individual Income Tax
 Division
P.O. Box 125
Columbia, SC 29214

SOUTH DAKOTA
605-773-3311
Dept. of Rev.
700 Governors Dr.
Pierre, SD 57501-2276

TENNESSEE
615-741-3133
Dept. of Rev.
Andrew Jackson
State Office Bldg.
Room 807
500 Deaderick St.
Nashville, TN 37242

TEXAS
512-463-4600
Comptroller's Office
Capitol Station
Austin, TX 78774

UTAH
801-530-6306
Heber Wells Building
160 East, 300 South
Salt Lake City,
UT 84134

VERMONT
802-828-2545
Pavillion Office Bldg.
Dept. of Taxes
Montpelier,
VT 05602

VIRGINIA
804-367-8055
Dept. of Taxation
P.O. Box 1317
Richmond, VA
23210-1317
Attn: Forms Request
Unit, P.O. Box 3784

WASHINGTON
206-753-5540
Dept. of Rev. AX-02
Olympia, WA 98504

WASHINGTON, D.C.
202-727-6104
District of Columbia
Finance Office Rev. Div.
Room 1046
300 Indiana Ave., N.W.
Washington, D.C. 20001

WEST VIRGINIA
304-348-3333
State Tax Dept.
Taxpayer Service Division
P.O. Box 3784
Charleston, WV
25337-3784

WISCONSIN
608-266-1961
Dept. of Rev.
P.O. Box 8903
Madison, WI 53708

WYOMING
307-777-7378
The State of Wyoming
 Secretary of State
Capitol Building
Cheyenne, WY
 82002-0020

In 2014, the IRS came out with its own Taxpayer's Bill of Rights:

1. **The Right to Be Informed**
 Taxpayers have the right to know what they need to do to comply with the tax laws. They are entitled to clear explanations of the laws and IRS procedures in all tax forms, instructions, publications, notices, and correspondence. They have the right to be informed of IRS decisions about their tax accounts and to receive clear explanations of the outcomes.

2. **The Right to Quality Service**
 Taxpayers have the right to receive prompt, courteous, and professional assistance in their dealings with the IRS, to be spoken to in a way they can easily understand, to receive clear and easily understandable communications from the IRS, and to speak to a supervisor about inadequate service.

3. **The Right to Pay No More Than the Correct Amount of Tax**
 Taxpayers have the right to pay only the amount of tax legally due, including interest and penalties, and to have the IRS apply all tax payments properly.

4. **The Right to Challenge the IRS's Position and Be Heard**
 Taxpayers have the right to raise objections and provide additional documentation in response to formal IRS actions or proposed actions, to expect that the IRS will consider their timely objections and documentation promptly and fairly, and to receive a response if the IRS does not agree with their position.

5. **The Right to Appeal an IRS Decision in an Independent Forum**
 Taxpayers are entitled to a fair and impartial administrative appeal of most IRS decisions, including many penalties, and have the right to receive a written response regarding the Office of Appeals' decision. Taxpayers generally have the right to take their cases to court.

6. **The Right to Finality**
 Taxpayers have the right to know the maximum amount of time they have to challenge the IRS's position as well as the maximum amount of time the IRS has to audit a particular tax year or collect a tax debt. Taxpayers have the right to know when the IRS has finished an audit.

7. **The Right to Privacy**
 Taxpayers have the right to expect that any IRS inquiry, examination, or enforcement action will comply with the law and be no more intrusive than necessary and will respect all due process rights, including search and seizure protections, and will provide, where applicable, a collection due process hearing.

8. **The Right to Confidentiality**
 Taxpayers have the right to expect that any information they provide to the IRS will not be disclosed unless authorized by the taxpayer or by law. Taxpayers have the right to expect appropriate action will be taken against employees, return preparers, and others who wrongfully use or disclose taxpayer return information.

9. **The Right to Retain Representation**
 Taxpayers have the right to retain an authorized representative of their choice to represent them in their dealings with the IRS. Taxpayers have the right to seek assistance from a Low Income Taxpayer Clinic if they cannot afford representation.

10. **The Right to a Fair and Just Tax System**
 Taxpayers have the right to expect the tax system to consider facts and circumstances that might affect their underlying liabilities, ability to pay, or

ability to provide information timely. Taxpayers have the right to receive assistance from the Taxpayer Advocate Service if they are experiencing financial difficulty or if the IRS has not resolved their tax issues properly and timely through its normal channels.

IRS PICKS UP SPEED ON INFORMATION SUPERHIGHWAY

With a computer and a modem, you can get federal tax forms and information online.

"This is another way the IRS is keeping its promise to serve our customers more efficiently and change the way we do business," said Bob Wenzel, IRS Chief of Strategic Planning and Communications.

The address for the IRS homepage on the World Wide Web is www.irs.gov. To check the status of a refund, call 800-829-1954 or 800-829-4477.

To pay your taxes using the Internet, go to www.eftps.com or call 800-555-4477 or 800-945-8400.

To get an extension, call 888-796-1074.

For the Tax Practioners Priority Service for correspondence audits, call 866-860-4259.

YOU CAN NOW VIEW YOUR TAX ACCOUNT AND PAYMENT HISTORY ONLINE

IRS continues to improve and expand taxpayer services by adding new features to your tax account online. You can now view 18 months of your payment history along with your federal tax account balance. It's safe and secure, and you can access your account through the IRS.gov/payments page.

While viewing your account, you can also pay with IRS Direct Pay, a debit or credit card, or apply for an installment agreement.

Before accessing your tax account online, you must authenticate your identity through the Secure Access process. This is a two-step authentication process, which means that if you are a returning user, you must use your credentials (username and password) and request a new security code (sent via text) each time you log in. If you already have a user name and password from Secure Access for Get Transcript Online or Identity Protection PIN, you may use the same username and password.

To register for the first time, you must have:

- an email address
- a text-enabled mobile phone in your name
- specific financial information such as a credit card number or specific loan number

As part of the security process, the IRS will send verification, activation or security codes via email and text. The IRS will not initiate contact via text or email asking for log-in information or personal data. The IRS texts and emails will only contain one-time codes.

Your balance will update no more than once every 24 hours, usually overnight. After making an electronic payment, allow at least two business days for it to appear in your payment history. Allow two weeks if you are paying by mail.

In the future, you will be able to view your tax records online, download full account transcripts and use other IRS online tools within your tax account.

Having access to your tax account online expands IRS self-service options by providing you with a secure, interactive online capability. It allows convenient service, assistance and improves compliance.

State Tax Department Internet Sites

Alaska Department of Revenue	www.revenue.state.ak.us/
Arizona Department of Revenue	aspin.asu.edu/aztax/
California Franchise Tax Board	www.ftb.ca.gov/
Colorado Department of Revenue	www.state.co.us/gov_dir/revenue_dir/home_rev.html
Delaware Division of Revenue	www.state.de.us/govern/agencies/revenue/revenue.htm
Florida Department of Revenue	fcn.state.fl.us/dor/revenue.html
Hawaii Department of Taxation	www.hawaii.gov/icsd/tax/tax.html
Idaho State Tax Commission	www.state.id.us/apa/idapa35/taxindex.htm
Illinois Department of Revenue	www.revenue.state.il.us/
Indiana Department of Revenue	www.state.in.us/sic//HTML/revenue.html
Iowa Department of Revenue and Finance	www.state.ia.us/government/drf/index.html
Kansas Department of Revenue	www.ink.org.public/kdor/
Kentucky Revenue Cabinet	www.state.ky.us/agencies/revenue/rev.home.htm
Louisiana Department of Revenue Taxation	www.rev.state.la.us/
Maine Bureau of Taxation	www.state.me.us/taxation

(*continues*)

State Tax Department Internet Sites *(continued)*

Maryland Comptroller of the Treasury	www.inform.umd.edu:8080/ UMS+State/MD_/Resources/COT/
Massachusetts Department of Revenue	www.magnet.state.ma.us/dor/
Michigan Department of Treasury	info.migov.state.mi.us/depts/ treasury/treasury.html
Minnesota Department of Revenue	www.state.mn.us/ebranch/mdor/
Missouri Division of Taxation and Collection	www.state.mo.us/dor/tax
Nebraska Department of Revenue	www.nol.org/home/NDR/
Nevada Department of Taxation	www.state.nv.us/inprog.htm
New Hampshire Department of Revenue	www.state.nh.us/agency/drabbs.htm
New Jersey Division of Taxation	www.state.nj.us/treasury/taxation/
New Mexico Taxation and Revenue Department	www.state.nm.us/tax/
New York State Department of Taxation and Finance	www.tax.state.ny.us/forms/
North Carolina Department of Revenue	www.dor.state.nc.us/DOR/
Ohio Department of Taxation	www.odh.ohio.gov/tax/
Oklahoma Tax Commission	www.state.ok.us/~tax/
Oregon Department of Revenue	www.dor.state.or.us/
Pennsylvania Department of Revenue	www.revenue.state.pa.us/
South Carolina Department of Revenue	www.state.sc.us:80/dor/
South Dakota Department of Revenue	www.state.sd.us/state/executive/ revenue/revenue.html
Tennessee Department of Revenue	www.state.tn.us/revenue/
Texas Comptroller of Public Accounts	www.window.texas.gov/
Utah State Tax Commission	txdtm01.tax.ex.state.ut.us/
Virginia Department of Taxation	www.state.va.us/tax/tax.html
Washington Department of Revenue	www.wa.gov/DOR/wador.htm
Wisconsin Department of Revenue	badger.state.wi.us/agencies/dor/
Wyoming Department of Revenue	www.state.wy.us/state/government/ state_agencies/text_revenue.html

STATE-BY-STATE SUMMARY OF ELECTRONIC FILING OPPORTUNITIES

State	Tax[1]	Website
Alabama	Personal Income Sales and Use Withholding	www.ador.state.al.us
Alaska	None	www.revenue.state.ak.us
Arizona	Personal Income	www.revenue.state.az.us
Arkansas	Personal Income Sales and Use Motor Fuel Corporate Franchise Tax	www.accessarkansas.org/dfs
California	Personal Income Sales and Use Withholding Motor Fuel	www.ftb.ca.gov
Colorado	Personal Income Sales and Use	www.taxcolorado.com
Connecticut	Personal Income Sales and Use Business Use Withholding	www.drs.state.ct.us
Delaware	Personal Income Gross Receipts Withholding (S Corporation)	www.state.de.us/revenue
District of Columbia	Personal Income Corporate Franchise Sales and Use Withholding Personal Property	www.cfo.dc.gov/etsc/ main.shtm
Florida	Sales and Use Motor Fuel Withholding Intangible Personal Property Communication Services	sun6.dms.state.fl.us/dor

(continues)

STATE-BY-STATE SUMMARY OF ELECTRONIC FILING OPPORTUNITIES *(continued)*

State	Tax[1]	Website
Georgia	Personal Income	www2.state.ga.us/ Departments/DOR
Hawaii	Personal Income Corporate Income Sales and Use Withholding	www.state.hi.us/tax/tax.html
Idaho	Personal Income Sales and Use Withholding Motor Fuel	www2.state.id.us/tax/index.html
Illinois	Personal Income Sales and Use	www.revenue.state.ll.us
Indiana	Personal Income Corporate Income Sales and Use Withholding (Fuel Tax available soon)	www.state.in.us/dor
Iowa	Personal Income	www.state.la.us/tax
Kansas	Personal Income Sales and Use Withholding Motor Fuel	www.ink.org/public/kdor
Kentucky	Personal Income	www.state.ky.us/agencies/ revenue
Louisiana	Personal Income Sales and Use Withholding	www.rev.state.la.us
Maine	Personal Income Sales and Use Withholding	www.state.me.us/revenue
Maryland	Personal Income Sales and Use (telefile) Withholding (telefile)	www.comp.state.md.us

STATE-BY-STATE SUMMARY OF ELECTRONIC FILING OPPORTUNITIES *(continued)*

State	Tax[1]	Website
Massachusetts	Personal Income Corporate Estimated Income Sales and Use (telefile) Withholding (telefile)	www.dor.state.ma.us
Michigan	Personal Income Motor Fuels Tax Single Business	www.treas.state.mi.us
Minnesota	Personal Income Sales and Use Withholding	www.taxes.state.mn.us
Mississippi	Personal Income	www.mstc.state.ms.us
Missouri	Personal Income Sales and Use Withholding	www.dor.state.mo.us
Montana	Personal Income Withholding	discoveringmontana.com/ revenue/css/default.asp
Nebraska	Personal Income Sales and Use Withholding	www.revenue.state.ne.us/ index.html
Nevada	None	www.tax.state.nv.us
New Hampshire	In development	www.state.nh.us/revenue
New Jersey	Personal Income Sales and Use	www.state.nj.us/ treasury/taxation
New Mexico	Personal Income	www.state.nm.us/tax
New York	Personal Income Sales and Use Withholding Motor Fuel Petroleum Business	www.tax.state.ny.us
North Carolina	Personal Income Sales and Use Withholding in 2003	www.dor.state.nc.us

(continues)

STATE-BY-STATE SUMMARY OF ELECTRONIC FILING OPPORTUNITIES *(continued)*

State	Tax[1]	Website
North Dakota	Personal Income Sales and Use Withholding Oil and Gas	www.state.nd.us/taxdpt
Ohio	Personal Income Natural Gas	www.state.oh.us/tax
Oklahoma	Personal Income Sales and Use Withholding	www.oktax.state.ok.us
Oregon	Personal Income	www.dor.state.or.us
Pennsylvania	Personal Income Corporate Estimated Income Sales and Use Withholding Fuel Tax	www.revenue.state.pa.us
Rhode Island	Personal Income Sales and Use Withholding	www.tax.state.ri.us
South Carolina	Personal Income Corporate Estimated Income Withholding Sales and Use (telefile)	www.sctax.org
South Dakota	Sales and Use Contractor's Excise	www.state.sd.us/revenue/ revenue.html
Tennessee	Sales and Use Hall Income Tax (on dividends and interest)	www.state.tn.us/revenue
Texas	Sales and Use Withholding Motor Fuel Natural Gas International Fuel Tax Agreement	www.window.state.tx.us

STATE-BY-STATE SUMMARY OF ELECTRONIC FILING OPPORTUNITIES *(continued)*

State	Tax[1]	Website
Utah	Personal Income Sales and Use Withholding IFTA	www.tax.ex.state.ut.us
Vermont	Personal Income	www.state.vt.us/tax
Virginia	Personal Income Sales and Use Withholding	www.tax.state.va.us
Washington	Sales and Use Business Excise Taxes	www.dor.wa.gov
West Virginia	Personal Income	www.state.wv.us/taxdiv
Wisconsin	Personal Income Sales and Use Motor Fuel (EFT)	www.dor.state.wi.us
Wyoming	Sales and Use Mineral Tax	revenue.state.wy.us

[1] This chart does not include less significant taxes such as lodging or tourism tax. Also, many states, including those that do not offer e-filing, allow payment of business taxes, such as withholding and motor fuels tax, through electronic funds transfer.

Tax-Related Websites

www.aicpa.org—	The AICPA's website, rated highly by professionals and non-CPAs alike. This site gives AICPA Tax Division members access to the online version of *The Tax Advisor.*
www.taxsites.com— or www.el.com/elinks/taxes	Probably the only other tax website you'll really need, since either is a "metasite" (a site whose sole purpose is to provide links to other websites of the same topic).
www.irs.gov—	Homesite of the Internal Revenue Service, helpful for accessing and downloading Federal forms, instructions, and other IRS materials.
www.ssa.gov—	The Social Security Administration's website, which includes the text of totalization agreements the U.S. has with various foreign countries.

(continues)

Tax-Related Websites *(continued)*

www.mtc.gov—	This site is a must for practitioners who service multistate clients. Here, the Multistate Tax Commission keeps you informed on the state uniformity of nexus issues.
www.ipl.org—	Even the Internet has a public library, and this is it. A great source for links to background information and numerous online publications.
The Big Six and national firms sites—	Although designed to market the firm's products and services, these sites offer useful information with their respective tax pages and links:

www.arthurandersen.com	www.bdo.com	www.ey.com
www.colybrand.com	www.gt.com	www.pw.com
www.us.deloitte.com	www.kpmg.com	

Other sites—	The larger firms aren't the only ones in the game; some smaller practitioners are offering their own blend of creative and informative tax sites. Some to try: www.taxman.com; www.taxwizard.com

Governmental Sites

Internal Revenue Service: *www.irs.gov*

Joint Committee on Taxation: *www.house.gov/jct*

Department of Treasury: *www.ustreas.gov*

Federal Register reflecting latest information on pending legislation: *www.access.gpo.gov/su_docs/aces/aces140.html*

Supreme Court and appellate court cases: *law.house.gov/6.htm*

IRS Bulletins: *www.fedworld.gov*

Highlights of latest revenue rulings, court opinions, legislation, and other tax topics: *www.ppcinfo.com/5-min.htm*

Tax Code Online: *www.law.cornell.edu/uscode*

Federal Web Locator: *www.law.vill.edu/Fed-Agency/fedwebloc.html*

Library of Congress: *lcweb.loc.gov/homepage/lchp.html*

SEC database of corporate information: *www.sec.gov/edgarhp.html*

General Accounting Office: *www.gao.gov*

U.S. Tax Court: *www.ustaxcourt.gov*

Criminal activity: *www.treas.gov/irs/ci*

IRS appeals: *www.irs.gov/prod/indinfo/appeals*

IRS telephone directory: The main directory is located at www.irs.gov/prod/bus_info/tax_pro/iod/index.html; the state-by-state directory at www.irs.gov/prod/where_file/index.html; the practitioner hotline directory at www.irs.gov/prod/bus_info/tax_pro/prac-htln.html; and the Centralized Authorization File (CAF) Unit fax directory at www.irs.gov/prod/bus_info/tax_pro/caf.html. The filing locations by processing site are available at www.irs.gov/prod/bus_info/tax_pro/svc-cntr2001.html; and find the service center directory at www.irs.gov/prod/bus_info/tax_pro/svc-cntrstate.html.

SPECIAL REPORT—TAXES AND TERRORISM

Special tax consideration has been voted on for victims of terrorism, even those outside of the immediate disaster areas:

The Victims of Terrorism Relief Act of 2001 provided a 1-year exemption from federal income taxes for individuals who were killed or who died as a result of a terroristic attack.

For specific questions, call the IRS toll-free at 866-562-5527.

For donation questions, go to www.abanet.org/tax or www.guidestar.org.

See also IRS Pub. 3920 and Pub. 3991 for additional details. Both can be downloaded from www.irs.gov.

Mission Statement

"The Internal Revenue Service has adopted a new mission statement:

Provide America's taxpayers top quality service by helping them understand and meet their tax responsibilities and by applying the tax law with integrity and fairness to all.

Taxpayers have the right to be treated fairly, professionally, promptly and courteously by Internal Revenue Service employees. Our goal at the IRS is to protect the rights of taxpayers and ensure the highest confidence

in the integrity, efficiency and fairness of our tax system. To make sure that taxpayers always receive such treatment, you should know about the many rights you have at each step of the tax process.

1. Receive an explanation of the examination and collection processes and taxpayers' rights under these processes before or at the initial interview for the determination or collection of tax.

2. Have representation at any time during these processes by a person who may practice before the IRS, except in certain criminal investigations.

3. Make an audio recording or receive a copy of such a recording of an interview for the determination or collection of tax.

4. Reasonably rely on written advice of the IRS that was provided in response to a specific written request.

5. File an application for relief with the IRS National Taxpayer Advocate or Local Taxpayer Advocate in a situation in which the taxpayer is suffering or about to suffer a significant hardship as a result of the manner in which the IRS is administering the tax laws.

6. Receive a written notice of levy, no less than 30 days prior to enforcement, that explains in nontechnical terms the levy procedures and the administrative appeals and alternatives to levy that are available."

April 19, 1999

"Activities engaged in by a citizen to prevent the Government from confiscating the fruits of his labor are the noblest endeavors of man."

BENJAMIN FRANKLIN

Appendix A

Cost Recovery/Depreciation

The Tax Reform Act of 1986 created a new accelerated depreciation system, which grouped property in the following classes:

- 3-year class—asset depreciation range (ADR) midpoints of 4 years and less, except that automobiles and light trucks are excluded and present law for horses that are in the 3-year class is retained. The method is 200 percent declining balance, switching to straight line.

- 5-year class—ADR midpoints of more than 4 years and less than 10 years, adding automobiles, light trucks, qualified technological equipment, computer-based central office switching equipment, renewable energy and biomass properties that are small power production facilities, and research and experimentation property. The method is 200 percent declining balance.

- 7-year class—ADR midpoints of 10 years and more but less than 16 years, adding single-purpose agricultural and horticulture structures and property with an ADR midpoint that is not classified elsewhere. The method is 200 percent declining balance.

- 10-year class—ADR midpoints of 16 years and more but less than 20 years. The method is 200 percent declining balance.

- 15-year class—ADR midpoints of 20 years and more but less than 25 years, including sewerage treatment plants and telephone distribution plants and related equipment used for the two-way exchange of voice and data communications. The method is 150 percent declining balance.

- 20-year class—ADR midpoints of 25 years and more, other than real property with an ADR midpoint of 27.5 years and more, and including sewer pipes. The method is 150 percent declining balance.

- 27.5 years—residential real property. The method is straight line.

- 31.5 years—nonresidential real property (real property that is not residential rental property and does not have an ADR midpoint of less than 27.5 years). The method is straight line.

To find appropriate ADR class lives, see Rev. Proc. 87-56, 1987-2 C.B. 674.

For personal property, both the first and last depreciation allowances for an asset reflect the one-half-year convention. The prior law mid-month convention applies to real property, and a midquarter convention applies to taxpayers who place more than 40 percent of their property in service during the last quarter of the taxable year.

Generally, the effective date for all depreciation provisions is for property placed in service on or after January 1, 1987. However, the Act allowed taxpayers to start using the new system for property placed in service after July 31, 1986

Note that OBRA '93 changed nonresidential real estate from a 31.5-year basis to a 39-year basis for property placed in service on or after May 13, 1993 unless there was a binding contract or construction began prior to May 13, 1993.

The following tables list percentages for property in the 3-, 5-, 7-, 10-, 15-, and 20-year classes.

TABLE 1. General Depreciation System
Applicable Depreciation Method: 200 or 150 Percent
Declining Balance Switching to Straight Line
Applicable Recovery Periods: 3, 5, 7, 10, 15, 20 Years
Applicable Convention: Half-Year

If the Recovery Year Is:	and the Recovery Period Is:					
	3-Year	5-Year	7-Year	10-Year	15-Year	20-Year
	the Depreciation Rate Is:					
1	33.33	20.00	14.29	10.00	5.00	3.750
2	44.45	32.00	24.49	18.00	9.50	7.219
3	14.81	19.20	17.49	14.40	8.55	6.677
4	7.41	11.52	12.49	11.52	7.70	6.177
5		11.52	8.93	9.22	6.93	5.713
6		5.76	8.92	7.37	6.23	5.285
7			8.93	6.55	5.90	4.888
8			4.46	6.55	5.90	4.522
9				6.56	5.91	4.462
10				6.55	5.90	4.461
11				3.28	5.91	4.462
12					5.90	4.461
13					5.91	4.462
14					5.90	4.461
15					5.91	4.462
16					2.95	4.461
17						4.462
18						4.461
19						4.462
20						4.461
21						2.231

TABLE 2. General Depreciation System
Applicable Depreciation Method: 200 or 150 Percent
Declining Balance Switching to Straight Line
Applicable Recovery Periods: 3, 5, 7, 10, 15, 20 Years
Applicable Convention: Mid-Quarter
(Property Placed in Service in First Quarter)

If the Recovery Year Is:	and the Recovery Period Is:					
	3-Year	5-Year	7-Year	10-Year	15-Year	20-Year
	the Depreciation Rate Is:					
1	58.33	35.00	25.00	17.50	8.75	6.563
2	27.78	26.00	21.43	16.50	9.13	7.000
3	12.35	15.60	15.31	13.20	8.21	6.482
4	1.54	11.01	10.93	10.56	7.39	5.996
5		11.01	8.75	8.45	6.65	5.546
6		1.38	8.74	6.76	5.99	5.130
7			8.75	6.55	5.90	4.746
8			1.09	6.55	5.91	4.459
9				6.56	5.90	4.459
10				6.55	5.91	4.459
11				0.82	5.90	4.459
12					5.91	4.460
13					5.90	4.459
14					5.91	4.460
15					5.90	4.459
16					0.74	4.460
17						4.459
18						4.460
19						4.459
20						4.460
21						0.557

TABLE 3. General Depreciation System
Applicable Depreciation Method: 200 or 150 Percent
Declining Balance Switching to Straight Line
Applicable Recovery Periods: 3, 5, 7, 10, 15, 20 Years
Applicable Convention: Mid-Quarter
(Property Placed in Service in Second Quarter)

If the Recovery Year Is:	and the Recovery Period Is:					
	3-Year	5-Year	7-Year	10-Year	15-Year	20-Year
	the Depreciation Rate Is:					
1	41.67	25.00	17.85	12.50	6.25	4.688
2	38.89	30.00	23.47	17.50	9.38	7.148
3	14.14	18.00	16.76	14.00	8.44	6.612
4	5.30	11.37	11.97	11.20	7.59	6.116
5		11.37	8.87	8.96	6.83	5.658
6		4.26	8.87	7.17	6.15	5.233
7			8.87	6.55	5.91	4.841
8			3.33	6.55	5.90	4.478
9				6.56	5.91	4.463
10				6.55	5.90	4.463
11				2.46	5.91	4.463
12					5.90	4.463
13					5.91	4.463
14					5.90	4.463
15					5.91	4.462
16					2.21	4.463
17						4.462
18						4.463
19						4.462
20						4.463
21						1.673

TABLE 4. General Depreciation System
Applicable Depreciation Method: 200 or 150 Percent
Declining Balance Switching to Straight Line
Applicable Recovery Periods: 3, 5, 7, 10, 15, 20 Years
Applicable Convention: Mid-Quarter
(Property Placed in Service in Third Quarter)

If the Recovery Year Is:	and the Recovery Period Is:					
	3-Year	5-Year	7-Year	10-Year	15-Year	20-Year
	the Depreciation Rate Is:					
1	25.00	15.00	10.71	7.50	3.75	2.813
2	50.00	34.00	25.51	18.50	9.63	7.289
3	16.67	20.40	18.22	14.80	8.66	6.742
4	8.33	12.24	13.02	11.84	7.80	6.237
5		11.30	9.30	9.47	7.02	5.769
6		7.06	8.85	7.58	6.31	5.336
7			8.86	6.55	5.90	4.936
8			5.53	6.55	5.90	4.566
9				6.56	5.91	4.460
10				6.55	5.90	4.460
11				4.10	5.91	4.460
12					5.90	4.460
13					5.91	4.461
14					5.90	4.460
15					5.91	4.461
16					3.69	4.460
17						4.461
18						4.460
19						4.461
20						4.460
21						2.788

TABLE 5. General Depreciation System
Applicable Depreciation Method: 200 or 150 Percent
Declining Balance Switching to Straight Line
Applicable Recovery Periods: 3, 5, 7, 10, 15, 20 Years
Applicable Convention: Mid-Quarter
(Property Placed in Service in Fourth Quarter)

If the Recovery Year Is:	and the Recovery Period Is:					
	3-Year	5-Year	7-Year	10-Year	15-Year	20-Year
	the Depreciation Rate Is:					
1	8.33	5.00	3.57	2.50	1.25	0.938
2	61.11	38.00	27.55	19.50	9.88	7.430
3	20.37	22.80	19.68	15.60	8.89	6.872
4	10.19	13.68	14.06	12.48	8.00	6.357
5		10.94	10.04	9.98	7.20	5.880
6		9.58	8.73	7.99	6.48	5.439
7			8.73	6.55	5.90	5.031
8			7.64	6.55	5.90	4.654
9				6.56	5.90	4.458
10				6.55	5.91	4.458
11				5.74	5.90	4.458
12					5.91	4.458
13					5.90	4.458
14					5.91	4.458
15					5.90	4.458
16					5.17	4.458
17						4.458
18						4.459
19						4.458
20						4.459
21						3.901

The following tables show recovery percentages for residential and non-residential real property.

TABLE 6. General Depreciation System
Applicable Depreciation Method: Straight Line
Applicable Recovery Period: 27.5 Years
Applicable Convention: Mid-Month

Recovery Year Is:	and the Month in the First Recovery Year the Property Is Placed in Service Is:											
	the Depreciation Rate Is:											
	1	2	3	4	5	6	7	8	9	10	11	12
1	3.485	3.182	2.879	2.576	2.273	1.970	1.667	1.364	1.061	0.758	0.455	0.152
2	3.636	3.636	3.636	3.636	3.636	3.636	3.636	3.636	3.636	3.636	3.636	3.636
3	3.636	3.636	3.636	3.636	3.636	3.636	3.636	3.636	3.636	3.636	3.636	3.636
4	3.636	3.636	3.636	3.636	3.636	3.636	3.636	3.636	3.636	3.636	3.636	3.636
5	3.636	3.636	3.636	3.636	3.636	3.636	3.636	3.636	3.636	3.636	3.636	3.636
6	3.636	3.636	3.636	3.636	3.636	3.636	3.636	3.636	3.636	3.636	3.636	3.636
7	3.636	3.636	3.636	3.636	3.636	3.636	3.636	3.636	3.636	3.636	3.636	3.636
8	3.636	3.636	3.636	3.636	3.636	3.636	3.636	3.636	3.636	3.636	3.636	3.636
9	3.636	3.636	3.636	3.636	3.636	3.636	3.636	3.636	3.636	3.636	3.636	3.636
10	3.637	3.636	3.637	3.637	3.636	3.637	3.636	3.636	3.637	3.636	3.636	3.637
11	3.636	3.637	3.636	3.636	3.637	3.636	3.637	3.637	3.637	3.637	3.637	3.637
12	3.637	3.636	3.637	3.637	3.636	3.637	3.636	3.636	3.636	3.636	3.636	3.636
13	3.636	3.636	3.636	3.636	3.636	3.636	3.637	3.637	3.637	3.637	3.637	3.637

14	3.637	3.637	3.637	3.637	3.637	3.637	3.636	3.636	3.636	3.636	3.636	3.636
15	3.636	3.636	3.636	3.636	3.636	3.636	3.637	3.637	3.637	3.637	3.637	3.637
16	3.637	3.637	3.637	3.637	3.637	3.637	3.636	3.636	3.636	3.636	3.636	3.636
17	3.636	3.636	3.636	3.636	3.636	3.636	3.637	3.637	3.637	3.637	3.637	3.637
18	3.637	3.637	3.637	3.637	3.637	3.637	3.636	3.636	3.636	3.636	3.636	3.636
19	3.636	3.636	3.636	3.636	3.636	3.636	3.637	3.637	3.637	3.637	3.637	3.637
20	3.637	3.637	3.637	3.637	3.637	3.637	3.636	3.636	3.636	3.636	3.636	3.636
21	3.636	3.636	3.636	3.636	3.636	3.636	3.637	3.637	3.637	3.637	3.637	3.637
22	3.637	3.637	3.637	3.637	3.637	3.637	3.636	3.636	3.636	3.636	3.636	3.636
23	3.636	3.636	3.636	3.636	3.636	3.636	3.637	3.637	3.637	3.637	3.637	3.637
24	3.637	3.637	3.637	3.637	3.637	3.637	3.636	3.636	3.636	3.636	3.636	3.636
25	3.636	3.636	3.636	3.636	3.636	3.636	3.637	3.637	3.637	3.637	3.637	3.637
26	3.637	3.637	3.637	3.637	3.637	3.637	3.636	3.636	3.636	3.636	3.636	3.636
27	3.636	3.636	3.636	3.636	3.636	3.636	3.637	3.637	3.637	3.637	3.637	3.637
28	1.970	2.273	2.576	2.879	3.182	3.485	3.636	3.636	3.636	3.636	3.636	3.636
29	0.000	0.000	0.000	0.000	0.000	0.000	0.152	0.455	0.758	1.061	1.364	1.667

TABLE 7. General Depreciation System
Applicable Depreciation Method: Straight Line
Applicable Recovery Period: 31.5 Years
Applicable Convention: Mid-Month

Recovery Year Is:	and the Month in the First Recovery Year the Property Is Placed in Service Is:											
	1	2	3	4	5	6	7	8	9	10	11	12
	the Depreciation Rate Is:											
1	3.042	2.778	2.513	2.249	1.984	1.720	1.455	1.190	0.926	0.661	0.397	0.132
2	3.175	3.175	3.175	3.175	3.175	3.175	3.175	3.175	3.175	3.175	3.175	3.175
3	3.175	3.175	3.175	3.175	3.175	3.175	3.175	3.175	3.175	3.175	3.175	3.175
4	3.175	3.175	3.175	3.175	3.175	3.175	3.175	3.175	3.175	3.175	3.175	3.175
5	3.175	3.175	3.175	3.175	3.175	3.175	3.175	3.175	3.175	3.175	3.175	3.175
6	3.175	3.175	3.175	3.175	3.175	3.175	3.175	3.175	3.175	3.175	3.175	3.175
7	3.175	3.175	3.175	3.175	3.175	3.175	3.175	3.175	3.175	3.175	3.175	3.175
8	3.175	3.174	3.175	3.174	3.175	3.174	3.175	3.175	3.175	3.175	3.175	3.175
9	3.174	3.175	3.174	3.175	3.174	3.175	3.174	3.175	3.174	3.175	3.174	3.175
10	3.175	3.174	3.175	3.174	3.175	3.174	3.175	3.174	3.175	3.174	3.175	3.174
11	3.174	3.175	3.174	3.175	3.174	3.175	3.174	3.174	3.174	3.175	3.175	3.174
12	3.175	3.174	3.175	3.174	3.175	3.174	3.175	3.174	3.175	3.174	3.175	3.174
13	3.174	3.175	3.174	3.175	3.174	3.175	3.174	3.175	3.174	3.175	3.174	3.175

14	3.175	3.174	3.175	3.174	3.175	3.174	3.174	3.175	3.174	3.175	3.175	3.174
15	3.174	3.175	3.174	3.175	3.174	3.175	3.175	3.174	3.175	3.174	3.174	3.175
16	3.175	3.174	3.175	3.174	3.175	3.174	3.174	3.175	3.174	3.175	3.175	3.174
17	3.174	3.175	3.174	3.175	3.174	3.175	3.175	3.174	3.175	3.174	3.174	3.175
18	3.175	3.174	3.175	3.174	3.175	3.174	3.174	3.175	3.174	3.175	3.175	3.174
19	3.174	3.175	3.174	3.175	3.174	3.175	3.175	3.174	3.175	3.174	3.174	3.175
20	3.175	3.174	3.175	3.174	3.175	3.174	3.174	3.175	3.174	3.175	3.175	3.174
21	3.174	3.175	3.174	3.175	3.174	3.175	3.175	3.174	3.175	3.174	3.174	3.175
22	3.175	3.174	3.175	3.174	3.175	3.174	3.174	3.175	3.174	3.175	3.175	3.174
23	3.174	3.175	3.174	3.175	3.174	3.175	3.175	3.174	3.175	3.174	3.174	3.175
24	3.175	3.174	3.175	3.174	3.175	3.174	3.174	3.175	3.174	3.175	3.175	3.174
25	3.174	3.175	3.174	3.175	3.174	3.175	3.175	3.174	3.175	3.174	3.174	3.175
26	3.175	3.174	3.175	3.174	3.175	3.174	3.174	3.175	3.174	3.175	3.175	3.174
27	3.174	3.175	3.174	3.175	3.174	3.175	3.175	3.174	3.175	3.174	3.174	3.175
28	3.175	3.174	3.175	3.174	3.175	3.174	3.174	3.175	3.174	3.175	3.175	3.174
29	3.174	3.175	3.174	3.175	3.174	3.175	3.175	3.174	3.175	3.174	3.174	3.175
30	3.175	3.174	3.175	3.174	3.175	3.174	3.174	3.175	3.174	3.175	3.175	3.174
31	3.174	3.175	3.174	3.175	3.174	3.175	3.175	3.174	3.175	3.174	3.174	3.175
32	1.720	1.984	2.249	2.513	2.778	3.042	3.175	3.174	3.175	3.174	3.174	3.175
33	0.000	0.000	0.000	0.000	0.000	0.000	0.132	0.397	0.661	0.926	1.190	1.455

Table 8 lists depreciation rates for nonresidential real property placed in service after 5/13/93, unless there was a binding contract prior to that date.

TABLE 8. Depreciation Rates for Nonresidential Real Property Placed in Service After May 13, 1993, Unless There Was a Binding Contract Prior to May 13, 1993

Mid-Month Convention

Straight Line—39 Years

Year	Month Property Placed in Service											
	1	2	3	4	5	6	7	8	9	10	11	12
1	2.461%	2.247%	2.033%	1.819%	1.605%	1.391%	1.177%	0.963%	0.749%	0.535%	0.321%	0.107%
2–39	2.564	2.564	2.564	2.564	2.564	2.564	2.564	2.564	2.564	2.564	2.564	2.564
40	0.107	0.321	0.535	0.749	0.963	1.177	1.391	1.605	1.819	2.033	2.247	2.461

Appendix B

Business Use of "Listed Property"

Prior to 1984, computers, automobiles, and other types of personal property were eligible for annual depreciation deductions with accelerated rates and recovery periods. Where such property was partly used for business purposes and partly used for personal purposes, the allowable amount of the otherwise available depreciation deduction was determined on the basis of the proportion of business use.

In 1984, Congress drew a sharp distinction between property used more than 50 percent for business purposes as compared to property having business use of 50 percent or less. Furthermore, for automobiles, additional restrictions have been imposed upon the maximum amount of yearly depreciation deductions.

The property covered by the stricter rules is referred to as "listed property" and includes the following:

a) passenger automobiles weighing 6,000 pounds or less,

b) other transportation property,

c) property used for entertainment, recreation, or amusement,

d) computers and peripheral equipment,* *and*

e) "other" property to be specified by regulations.

For *all* categories of the above listed property used 50 percent or less for business purposes, depreciation is to be determined on the straight-line method over a period of years that is longer than the minimum period otherwise provided.

In addition, satisfaction of the 50 percent test will be determined solely with reference to the use of the property in a *trade or business*. Use of the property in connection with the production of investment income is not taken into account for this purpose. Once it is determined, however, on the basis of business use, whether the property is to be treated under the more than 50 percent or the 50 percent or less rule, the use of the property in investment activities will be taken into account in determining the proportion of the tax benefits that are allowable.

For example, assume a computer was used 40 percent in the conduct of a trade or business and 30 percent for investment activities. The more than 50 percent business use test is *not* satisfied. Depreciation will be determined on

*Removed as listed property (by the Tax Cuts and Jobs Act of 2017) if placed in service after 2017

the straight-line method. However, *70* percent of that depreciation so determined will be allowable.

Except for *automobiles*, the depreciation deductions for listed property used *more* than 50 percent in a trade or business will be determined under prior law. The accelerated rates and periods under 1987 modified ACRS may be used to determine depreciation and then the percentage of business use will be combined with the percentage of use in investment activities to determine the portion of the total amount of depreciation that will be allowable.

For automobiles, however, including those with more than 50 percent business use, there are additional restrictions and limitations. Depreciation deductions are limited for each year. These fixed limitations apply to all depreciation deductions, not just depreciation under the accelerated method.

If business use is less than 100 percent, you are entitled to claim the portion of the depreciation deduction allowable which corresponds to your business use percentage.

Moreover, leasing an automobile will not avoid the limitations. Lessees of property will be subject to restrictions on lease payments. These restrictions are comparable to the limitations on depreciation that would apply if the automobile were owned instead of leased. The percentage of lease payments allowable will be calculated pursuant to tables published by the Treasury. These restrictions, however, do not apply to the tax benefits available under prior law to the lessors of property regularly engaged in the business of leasing property.

Employees

If you are an employee, the rules are even more stringent. *No* depreciation will be allowable for listed property owned by employees unless the property is:

a) required for the convenience of the employer, *and*

b) required as a condition of employment.

These requirements will *not* be satisfied merely by an employer's statement that the property is required as a condition of employment. It is intended that the property must be required in order for an employee to properly perform the duties of his/her employment.

Furthermore, if in years subsequent to the year of purchase, there is a reduction of the percentage of business use, that reduction could have triggered an investment credit recapture. If the business use declines to 50 percent or less of the use of the property in the subsequent year, the *entire* amount of the investment credit was recaptured. However, the Treasury can provide a rule that a *de minimus* reduction in the business use of the property will not trigger any recapture.

In addition to the existing rules governing the recapture of depreciation, the law requires recapture in the event property used more than 50 percent for

business in the year it is placed in service declines to 50 percent or less of business use in a subsequent year. The amount of the recapture will be based upon the difference between the depreciation allowed in prior years and the amount that would have been allowed if the applicable accelerated rate and period of ACRS had not been available in such years. The Treasury has been instructed to provide for comparable recapture requirements applicable to lessees whose business use declines in subsequent years.

In IRS Letter Ruling 8615024, the IRS ruled that an employee's use of a personal computer did *not* meet the convenience of the employer and condition of employment tests. In denying any deduction or credit, the Internal Revenue Service said that to meet the convenience of the employer test, the employee must be *required* to purchase the computer to properly perform the duties of her employment. In that case, the taxpayer was not "required" to purchase the computer to properly perform her duties. Although the benefits of the taxpayer's use of the computer may inure to her employer, the purchase of a computer was clearly not required as a condition of employment. The facts of the case suggested that computer use, although work-related, was not inextricably related to proper performance of the taxpayer's job. Moreover, there appeared no evidence in the facts that those employees who did not purchase a computer were professionally disadvantaged. See *Mulne v. Commissioner*, T.C. Memo 1996-320 for an example of how to meet both tests.

In IRS Letter Ruling 871009, this position was reiterated. Here the Internal Revenue Service held that an insurance agent's use of a portable computer as an aid in selling financial products did not meet the convenience of the employer test. They concluded that the taxpayer, who used the computer exclusively for business purposes, must be required to purchase the computer to properly perform the duties of his employment in order to take the deduction. The com-puter purchase was optional rather than mandatory. "The facts indicate that computer use, although work-related, is not inextricably related to the proper performance of 'the taxpayer's' job. Further, there appears no evidence that those employees who do not purchase computers are professionally disadvantaged." (See also Rev. Rul. 86-129, 1986-45 IRB 4 and Letter Rul. 8725067.) I doubt whatever these rulings (almost three decades old) are applicable in today's Internet-based business environment.

As of January 1, 2010, the Small Business Jobs Act of 2010 removed cell phones as "listed property."

The IRS has informally indicated that iPads and other tablets will be treated like cell phones when employers provide them to employees. Thus, employees won't be taxed on the value of personal use, as long as the devices are provided primarily for business reasons rather than as a form of compensation. Similarly, reimbursements made by employers to employees for personally owned iPads generally should not be subject to tax when used primarily for business.

Luxury Cars

The Tax Reform Act of 1986 defined a *passenger automobile* as any four-wheeled vehicle that is manufactured primarily for use on public streets, roads, and highways and is rated at 6,000 pounds *unloaded* gross vehicle weight or less. For *trucks* or *vans*, the rule becomes *loaded* gross vehicle weight—its maximum recommended weight for the vehicle, fuel, passengers, and all cargo. Sport Utility Vehicles (SUVs) are classified under trucks. The Act requires that fixed limitations on automobile deductions be conformed to the new recovery period, so that the price range of affected cars is unaffected. Depreciation deductions are limited for each year. These fixed limitations apply to all depreciation deductions, not just depreciation under the accelerated method.

Limitations on Luxury Auto Depreciation Deductions

Date of Purchase	Yearly Maximum			
	1	2	3	4 and After
6/19/84 to 4/2/85[a]	$4,000 (25%)	$6,000[b] (38%)	$6,000[b] (37%)	$6,000[b]
4/3/85 to 12/31/86[a]	3,200 (25%)	4,800 (38%)	4,800 (37%)	4,800
1987 to 12/31/88[c]	2,560 (20%)	4,100 (32%)	2,450 (19.2%)	1,475 (11.52%)
1989 to 12/31/90[c]	2,660 (20%)	4,200 (32%)	2,550 (19.2%)	1,475 (11.52%)
1991[c]	2,660 (20%)	4,300 (32%)	2,550 (19.2%)	1,575 (11.52%)
1992[c]	2,760 (20%)	4,400 (32%)	2,650 (19.2%)	1,575 (11.52%)
1993	2,860 (20%)	4,600 (32%)	2,750 (19.2%)	1,675 (11.52%)
1994	2,960 (20%)	4,700 (32%)	2,850 (19.2%)	1,675 (11.52%)
1995	3,060 (20%)	4,900 (32%)	2,950 (19.2%)	1,775 (11.52%)
1996	3,060 (20%)	4,900 (33%)	2,950 (19.2%)	1,775 (11.52%)
1997	3,160 (20%)	5,000 (33%)	3,050 (19.2%)	1,775 (11.52%)
1998	3,160 (20%)	5,000 (33%)	2,950 (19.2%)	1,775 (11.52%)
1999	3,060 (20%)	5,000 (33%)	2,950 (19.2%)	1,775 (11.52%)
2000	3,060 (20%)	4,900 (33%)	2,950 (19.2%)	1,775 (11.52%)
2001	3,060 (20%)[d]	4,900 (33%)	2,950 (19.2%)	1,775 (11.52%)
2002	3,060 (20%)[d]	4,900 (33%)	2,950 (19.2%)	1,775 (11.52%)
2003	10,710 (20%)[e]	4,900 (33%)	2,950 (19.2%)	1,775 (11.52%)

[a]Year of disposition: zero.

[b]The limit is $6,200 if placed in service after 12/31/84 and before 4/3/85.

[c]Year of disposition: half-year.

[d]The first-year writeoff limit is increased by $4,600 for a total of $7,660 for cars placed in service after September 10, 2001 and before September 11, 2004.

[e]Including first-year bonus depreciation of $7,650—i.e., $3,060 + $7,650 = $10,710—as per the 2003 Tax Act.

THE 2004 LIMITS

Depreciation Limitations for Passenger Automobiles (That Are Not Bonus Depreciation Passenger Automobiles, Trucks, Vans, or Electric Automobiles) Placed in Service by the Taxpayer During Calendar Year 2004

Tax Year	Amount
1st tax year	$2,960
2nd tax year	$4,800
3rd tax year	$2,850
Each succeeding year	$1,675

Depreciation Limitations for Trucks and Vans That Are Bonus Depreciation Passenger Automobiles Placed in Service by the Taxpayer During Calendar Year 2004

Tax Year	Amount
1st tax year	$10,910
2nd tax year	$5,300
3rd tax year	$3,150
Each succeeding year	$1,875

Depreciation Limitations for Bonus Depreciation Passenger Automobiles (That Are Not Trucks, Vans, or Electric Automobiles) Placed in Service by the Taxpayer During Calendar Year 2004

Tax Year	Amount
1st tax year	$10,610
2nd tax year	$4,800
3rd tax year	$2,850
Each succeeding year	$1,675

Depreciation Limitations for Electric Automobiles (That Are Not Bonus Depreciation Passenger Automobiles) Placed in Service by the Taxpayer During Calendar Year 2004

Tax Year	Amount
1st tax year	$8,880
2nd tax year	$14,300
3rd tax year	$8,550
Each succeeding year	$5,125

Depreciation Limitations for Trucks and Vans (That Are Not Bonus Depreciation Passenger Automobiles) Placed in Service by the Taxpayer During Calendar Year 2004

Tax Year	Amount
1st tax year	$3,260
2nd tax year	$5,300
3rd tax year	$3,150
Each succeeding year	$1,875

Depreciation Limitations for Electric Automobiles That Are Bonus Depreciation Passenger Automobiles Placed in Service by the Taxpayer During Calendar Year 2004

Tax Year	Amount
1st tax year	$31,830
2nd tax year	$14,300
3rd tax year	$8,550
Each succeeding year	$5,125

THE 2005 LIMITS:

Depreciation Limitations for Passenger Automobiles Placed in Service by the Taxpayer During Calendar Year 2005

Tax Year	Amount
1st tax year	$2,960
2nd tax year	$4,700
3rd tax year	$2,850
Each succeeding year	$1,675

THE 2006 LIMITS:

Depreciation Limitations for Passenger Automobiles Placed in Service by the Taxpayer During Calendar Year 2006

Tax Year	Amount
1st tax year	$2,960
2nd tax year	$4,800
3rd tax year	$2,850
Each succeeding year	$1,775

Depreciation Limitations for Trucks and Vans Placed in Service by the Taxpayer During Calendar Year 2005

Tax Year	Amount
1st tax year	$3,260
2nd tax year	$5,200
3rd tax year	$3,150
Each succeeding year	$1,875

Depreciation Limitations for Trucks and Vans Placed in Service by the Taxpayer During Calendar Year 2006

Tax Year	Amount
1st tax year	$3,260
2nd tax year	$5,200
3rd tax year	$3,150
Each succeeding year	$1,875

Depreciation Limitations for Electric Automobiles Placed in Service by the Taxpayer During Calendar Year 2005

Tax Year	Amount
1st tax year	$8,880
2nd tax year	$14,200
3rd tax year	$8,450
Each succeeding year	$5,125

Depreciation Limitations for Electric Automobiles Placed in Service by the Taxpayer During Calendar Year 2006

Tax Year	Amount
1st tax year	$8,980
2nd tax year	$14,400
3rd tax year	$8,650
Each succeeding year	$5,225

THE 2007 LIMITS:

Depreciation Limitations for Passenger Automobiles Placed in Service by the Taxpayer During Calendar Year 2007

Tax Year	Amount
1st tax year	$3,060
2nd tax year	$4,900
3rd tax year	$2,850
Each succeeding year	$1,775

Depreciation Limitations for Trucks and Vans Placed in Service by the Taxpayer During Calendar Year 2007

Tax Year	Amount
1st tax year	$3,260
2nd tax year	$5,200
3rd tax year	$3,050
Each succeeding year	$1,875

Note: Expanded Limits for electric cars expired on December 31, 2006.

Depreciation Limitations for Passenger Automobiles (that are not trucks or vans) Placed in Service by the Taxpayer in Calendar Year 2007, for which the 50 percent additional first-year depreciation deduction does not apply

Tax Year	Amount
1st tax year	$2,960
2nd tax year	$4,800
3rd tax year	$2,850
Each succeeding year	$1,775

THE 2008 LIMITS:

Depreciation Limitations for Passenger Automobiles (that are not trucks or vans) Placed in Service by the Taxpayer in Calendar Year 2008, for which the 50 percent additional first-year depreciation deduction applies

Tax Year	Amount
1st tax year	$10,960
2nd tax year	$4,800
3rd tax year	$2,850
Each succeeding year	$1,775

Depreciation Limitations for Trucks and Vans Placed in Service by the Taxpayer in Calendar Year 2008, for which the 50 percent additional first-year depreciation deduction does not apply

Tax Year	Amount
1st tax year	$3,160
2nd tax year	$5,100
3rd tax year	$3,050
Each succeeding year	$1,875

Depreciation Limitations for Trucks and Vans Placed in Service by the Taxpayer in Calendar Year 2008, for which the 50 percent additional first-year depreciation deduction applies

Tax Year	Amount
1st tax year	$11,160
2nd tax year	$5,100
3rd tax year	$3,050
Each succeeding year	$1,875

THE 2009 LIMITS:

Depreciation Limitations for Passenger Automobiles (that are not trucks or vans) Placed in Service by the Taxpayer in Calendar Year 2009, for which the 50 percent additional first-year depreciation deduction does not apply

Tax Year	Amount
1st tax year	$2,960
2nd tax year	$4,800
3rd tax year	$2,850
Each succeeding year	$1,775

Depreciation Limitations for Trucks and Vans Placed in Service by the Taxpayer in Calendar Year 2009, for which the 50 percent additional first-year depreciation deduction does not apply

Tax Year	Amount
1st tax year	$3,060
2nd tax year	$4,900
3rd tax year	$2,950
Each succeeding year	$1,775

Depreciation Limitations for Passenger Automobiles (that are not trucks or vans) Placed in Service by the Taxpayer in Calendar Year 2009, for which the 50 percent additional first-year depreciation deduction applies

Tax Year	Amount
1st tax year	$10,960
2nd tax year	$4,800
3rd tax year	$2,850
Each succeeding year	$1,775

Depreciation Limitations for Trucks and Vans Placed in Service by the Taxpayer in Calendar Year 2009, for which the 50 percent additional first-year depreciation deduction applies

Tax Year	Amount
1st tax year	$11,060
2nd tax year	$4,900
3rd tax year	$2,950
Each succeeding year	$1,775

THE 2010 LIMITS:

Rev. Proc. 2010-18 Table 1

Depreciation Limitations for Passenger Automobiles (That Are Not Trucks or Vans) Placed in Service in Calendar Year 2010

Tax Year	Amount
1st tax year	$ 3,060
2nd tax year	$ 4,900
3rd tax year	$ 2,950
Each succeeding year	$ 1,775

Rev. Proc. 2010-18 Table 2

Depreciation Limitations for Trucks and Vans Placed in Service in Calendar Year 2010

Tax Year	Amount
1st tax year	$ 3,160
2nd tax year	$ 5,100
3rd tax year	$ 3,050
Each succeeding year	$ 1,875

THE 2011 LIMITS:

Rev. Proc. 2011-21 Table 1

Depreciation Limitations for Passenger Automobiles (that are not trucks or vans) Placed in Service in Calendar Year 2011, for which the §168(k) additional first-year depreciation deduction applies

Tax Year	Amount
1st tax year	$11,060
2nd tax year	$4,900
3rd tax year	$2,950
Each succeeding year	$1,775

Rev. Proc. 2011-21 Table 2

Depreciation Limitations for Trucks and Vans Placed in Service in Calendar Year 2011, for which the §168(k) additional first-year depreciation deduction applies

Tax Year	Amount
1st tax year	$11,260
2nd tax year	$5,200
3rd tax year	$3,150
Each succeeding year	$1,875

Rev. Proc. 2011-21 Table 3

Depreciation Limitations for Passenger Automobiles (that are not trucks or vans) Placed in Service in Calendar Year 2011, for which the §168(k) additional first-year depreciation deduction does not apply

Tax Year	Amount
1st tax year	$3,060
2nd tax year	$4,900
3rd tax year	$2,950
Each succeeding year	$1,775

Rev. Proc. 2011-21 Table 4

Depreciation Limitations for Trucks and Vans Placed in Service in Calendar Year 2011, for which the §168(k) additional first-year depreciation deduction does not apply

Tax Year	Amount
1st tax year	$3,260
2nd tax year	$5,200
3rd tax year	$3,150
Each succeeding year	$1,875

Rev. Proc. 2011-21 Table 7

Depreciation Limitations for Passenger Automobiles (that are not trucks or vans) Placed in Service in Calendar Year 2010, for which the §168(k) additional first-year depreciation deduction applies

Tax Year	Amount
1st tax year	$11,060
2nd tax year	$4,900
3rd tax year	$2,950
Each succeeding year	$1,775

Rev. Proc. 2011-21 Table 8

Depreciation Limitations for Trucks and Vans Placed in Calendar Year 2011 for which the §168(k) additional first-year depreciation deduction applies

Tax Year	Amount
1st tax year	$11,160
2nd tax year	$5,100
3rd tax year	$3,050
Each succeeding year	$1,875

THE 2012 LIMITS:

Rev. Proc. 2012-23 Table 1

Depreciation Limitations for Passenger Automobiles (that are not trucks or vans) Placed in Service in Calendar Year 2012, for which the §168(k) additional first-year depreciation deduction applies

Tax Year	Amount
1st tax year	$11,160
2nd tax year	$5,100
3rd tax year	$3,050
Each succeeding year	$1,875

Rev. Proc. 2012-23 Table 2

Depreciation Limitations for Trucks and Vans Placed in Service in Calendar Year 2012, for which the §168(k) additional first-year depreciation deduction applies

Tax Year	Amount
1st tax year	$11,360
2nd tax year	$5,300
3rd tax year	$3,150
Each succeeding year	$1,875

Rev. Proc. 2012-23 Table 3

Depreciation Limitations for Passenger Automobiles (that are not trucks or vans) Placed in Service in Calendar Year 2012, for which the §168(k) additional first-year depreciation deduction does not apply

Tax Year	Amount
1st tax year	$3,160
2nd tax year	$5,100
3rd tax year	$3,050
Each succeeding year	$1,875

Rev. Proc. 2012-23 Table 4

Depreciation Limitations for Trucks and Vans Placed in Service in Calendar Year 2012 for which the §168(k) additional first-year depreciation deduction does not apply

Tax Year	Amount
1st tax year	$3,360
2nd tax year	$5,300
3rd tax year	$3,150
Each succeeding year	$1,875

THE 2013 LIMITS:

Rev. Proc. 2013-21 Table 1

Depreciation Limitations for Passenger Automobiles (that are not trucks or vans) Placed in Service in Calendar Year 2013, for which the §168(k) additional first-year depreciation deduction applies

Tax Year	Amount
1st tax year	$11,160
2nd tax year	$5,100
3rd tax year	$3,050
Each succeeding year	$1,875

Rev. Proc. 2013-21 Table 2

Depreciation Limitations for Trucks and Vans Placed in Service in Calendar Year 2013, for which the §168(k) additional first-year depreciation deduction applies

Tax Year	Amount
1st tax year	$11,360
2nd tax year	$5,400
3rd tax year	$3,250
Each succeeding year	$1,975

Rev. Proc. 2013-21 Table 3

Depreciation Limitations for Passenger Automobiles (that are not trucks or vans) Placed in Service in Calendar Year 2013, for which the §168(k) additional first-year depreciation deduction does not apply

Tax Year	Amount
1st tax year	$3,160
2nd tax year	$5,100
3rd tax year	$3,050
Each succeeding year	$1,875

Rev. Proc. 2013-21 Table 4

Depreciation Limitations for Trucks and Vans Placed in Service in Calendar Year 2013, for which the §168(k) additional first-year depreciation deduction does not apply

Tax Year	Amount
1st tax year	$3,360
2nd tax year	$5,400
3rd tax year	$3,250
Each succeeding year	$1,975

THE 2014 LIMITS:*

Rev. Proc. 2014-21 Table 1

Depreciation Limitations for Passenger Automobiles (that are not trucks or vans) Placed in Service in Calendar Year 2014

Tax Year	Amount
1st tax year	$11,600
2nd tax year	$5,100
3rd tax year	$3,050
Each succeeding year	$1,875

Rev. Proc. 2014-21 Table 2

Depreciation Limitations for Trucks and Vans Placed in Service in Calendar Year 2014

Tax Year	Amount
1st tax year	$11,460
2nd tax year	$5,500
3rd tax year	$3,350
Each succeeding year	$1,975

THE 2015 LIMITS:

Rev. Proc. 2015-19 Table 1

Depreciation Limitations for Passenger Automobiles (that are not trucks or vans) Placed in Service in Calendar Year 2015

Tax Year	Amount
1st tax year	$3,160***
2nd tax year	$5,100
3rd tax year	$3,050
Each succeeding year	$1,875

Rev. Proc. 2015-19 Table 2

Depreciation Limitations for Trucks and Vans Placed in Service in Calendar Year 2015

Tax Year	Amount
1st tax year	$3,460**
2nd tax year	$5,600
3rd tax year	$3,350
Each succeeding year	$1,975

*Revised
**$11,460 with the additional first-year depreciation as per the PATH Act.
***$11,160 with the additional first-year depreciation as per the PATH Act.

THE 2016 LIMITS:

Rev. Proc. 2016-23 Table 1

Depreciation Limitations for Passenger Automobiles (that are not trucks or vans) Placed in Service in Calendar Year 2016 for which the §168(k) additional first-year depreciation deduction applies

Tax Year	Amount
1st tax year	$11,160
2nd tax year	$5,100
3rd tax year	$3,050
Each succeeding year	$1,875

Rev. Proc. 2016-23 Table 2

Depreciation Limitations for Trucks and Vans Placed in Service in Calendar Year 2016, for which the §168(k) additional first-year depreciation deduction applies

Tax Year	Amount
1st tax year	$11,560
2nd tax year	$5,700
3rd tax year	$3,350
Each succeeding year	$2,075

Rev. Proc. 2016-23 Table 3

Depreciation Limitations for Passenger Automobiles (that are not trucks or vans) Placed in Service in Calendar Year 2016 for which the §168(k) additional first-year depreciation deduction does not apply

Tax Year	Amount
1st tax year	$3,160
2nd tax year	$5,100
3rd tax year	$3,050
Each succeeding year	$1,875

Rev. Proc. 2016-23 Table 4

Depreciation Limitations for Trucks and Vans Placed in Service in Calendar Year 2016, for which the §168(k) additional first-year depreciation deduction does not apply

Tax Year	Amount
1st tax year	$3,560
2nd tax year	$5,700
3rd tax year	$3,350
Each succeeding year	$2,075

THE 2017 LIMITS:

Rev. Proc. 2017-29 Table 1

Depreciation Limitations for Passenger Automobiles (that are not trucks or vans) Placed in Service in Calendar Year 2017 for which the §168(k) additional first-year depreciation deduction applies

Tax Year	Amount
1st tax year	$11,160
2nd tax year	$5,100
3rd tax year	$3,050
Each succeeding year	$1,875

Rev. Proc. 2017-29 Table 2

Depreciation Limitations for Trucks and Vans Placed in Service in Calendar Year 2017, for which the §168(k) additional first-year depreciation deduction applies

Tax Year	Amount
1st tax year	$11,560
2nd tax year	$5,700
3rd tax year	$3,450
Each succeeding year	$2,075

Rev. Proc. 2017-29 Table 3

Depreciation Limitations for Passenger Automobiles (that are not trucks or vans) Placed in Service in Calendar Year 2017 for which the §168(k) additional first-year depreciation deduction does not apply

Tax Year	Amount
1st tax year	$3,160
2nd tax year	$5,100
3rd tax year	$3,050
Each succeeding year	$1,875

Rev. Proc. 2017-29 Table 4

Depreciation Limitations for Trucks and Vans Placed in Service in Calendar Year 2017, for which the §168(k) additional first-year depreciation deduction does not apply

Tax Year	Amount
1st tax year	$3,560
2nd tax year	$5,700
3rd tax year	$3,450
Each succeeding year	$2,075

THE 2018 LIMITS:

Rev. Proc. 2018 Table 1

Depreciation Limitations for Passenger Automobiles Acquired *before* September 28, 2017, and Placed in Service during Calendar Year 2018 for which the §168(k) additional first-year depreciation deduction applies

Tax Year	Amount
1st tax year	$16,400
2nd tax year	$16,000
3rd tax year	$9,600
Each succeeding year	$5,760

Rev. Proc. 2018 Table 2

Depreciation Limitations for Passenger Automobiles Acquired *after* September 27, 2017, and Placed in Service during Calendar Year 2018 for which the §168(k) additional first-year depreciation deduction applies

Tax Year	Amount
1st tax year	$18,000
2nd tax year	$16,000
3rd tax year	$9,600
Each succeeding year	$5,760

Rev. Proc. 2018 Table 3

Depreciation Limitations for Passenger Automobiles Placed in Service during Calendar Year 2018 for which No §168(k) additional first-year depreciation deduction applies

Tax Year	Amount
1st tax year	$10,000
2nd tax year	$16,000
3rd tax year	$9,600
Each succeeding year	$5,760

A van or light truck is not subject to the annual limit on the depreciation deduction for passenger autos if it is a qualified nonpersonal use vehicle (T.D. 9133, July 2004).

SUVs are listed property, so they are subject to limits. An SUV built on a truck chassis is considered a truck for these purposes.

Businesses can currently expense up to $1 million (for 2018) of the cost of pickup trucks that have a loaded gross vehicle rate weighing in excess of 14,000 pounds. Though post-2006 expensing has been cut to $25,000 for SUVs with loaded weight between 6,000 and 14,000 pounds, heavy pickups are exempt from that limit. For 2010, you deducted $25,000 plus 50 percent of the remainder as bonus business depreciation. So on a $50,000 purchase, $25,000 plus $12,500 plus the 20 percent first-year normal allowance on the remaining $12,500 was deducted. That was a total $40,000 first-year deduction! In 2012, 2013, 2014, 2015, 2016, and 2017 the bonus depreciation was 50 percent. If you bought a *new* $60,000 SUV with a loaded gross weight over 6,000 pounds, you could expense the first $25,000. Half the remaining $35,000 cost ($17,500) qualified as bonus depreciation. You also got 20 percent of the leftover basis ($17,500) or $3,500 as regular depreciation. Use the car 100 percent for business and you got a $46,000 first-year deduction. *Used*, heavy SUVs did not get the bonus depreciation.

To qualify, the vehicle must have a cargo area at least 6 feet in length separate from the passenger compartment. The cargo hold can be capped. Heavy vans and small buses also get the higher expensing limit. An eligible van cannot have seating behind the driver seat, and no part of the body can protrude more than 30 inches in front of the windshield. Small buses must have at least nine seats behind the driver's seat. For 2011, the 100 percent bonus depreciation allowed the cost of 100 percent business-use heavy SUVs to be expensed. The bonus depreciation for 2012, 2013, 2014, 2015, 2016, and 2017 was 50 percent.

Temporary 100 Percent Expensing for Certain Business Assets (First year Bonus Depreciation)

The Tax Cuts and Jobs Act of 2017 increased the bonus depreciation percentage from 50 percent to 100 percent for qualified property acquired and placed in service after Sept. 27, 2017, and before Jan. 1, 2023. The bonus depreciation percentage for qualified property that a taxpayer acquired before Sept. 28, 2017, and placed in service before Jan. 1, 2018, remains at 50 percent. Special rules apply for longer production period property and certain aircraft.

The definition of property eligible for 100 percent bonus depreciation was expanded to include used qualified property acquired and placed in service after Sept. 27, 2017, if all the following factors apply:

- The taxpayer didn't use the property at any time before acquiring it.
- The taxpayer didn't acquire the property from a related party.
- The taxpayer didn't acquire the property from a component member of a controlled group of corporations.
- The taxpayer's basis of the used property is not figured in whole or in part by reference to the adjusted basis of the property in the hands of the seller or transferor.
- The taxpayer's basis of the used property is not figured under the provision for deciding basis of property acquired from a decedent.

Also, the cost of the used qualified property eligible for bonus depreciation doesn't include any carryover basis of the property, for example in a like-kind exchange or involuntary conversion.

The 2017 changes added qualified film, television and live theatrical productions as types of qualified property that are eligible for 100 percent bonus depreciation. This provision applies to property acquired and placed in service after Sept. 27, 2017.

Under the 2017 law, certain types of property are not eligible for bonus depreciation. One such exclusion from qualified property is for property primarily used in the trade or business of the furnishing or sale of:

- Electrical energy, water or sewage disposal services,
- Gas or steam through a local distribution system or
- Transportation of gas or steam by pipeline.

This exclusion applies if the rates for the furnishing or sale have to be approved by a federal, state or local government agency, a public service or public utility commission, or an electric cooperative.

The 2017 law also added an exclusion for any property used in a trade or business that has floor-plan financing. Floor-plan financing is secured by motor vehicle inventory that a business sells or leases to retail customers.

Note that the 1986 law put automobiles in the 5-year class. However, if the amount limitation prevents full use of the percentage depreciation in any year, the recovery period will be extended. Any unrecovered cost will be treated as an automobile expense subject to the annual limitation in taxable years after the end of the ordinary recovery period. The annual depreciation deduction,

assuming the 200 percent declining-balance method, therefore, will be the lesser of the expense deduction or the percentage depreciation.

If qualified business use in the year the automobile is placed in service does not exceed 50 percent, then the basis must be recovered over 5 years using the straight-line method and the half-year convention. If qualified business use falls to 50 percent or less of total use during any part of the recovery period, part of the depreciation claimed in prior years must be included in the taxpayer's income, and a switch must be made to straight-line depreciation.

Appropriate limitations with respect to comparable dollar caps will be applicable to leased automobiles. Lessees of luxury automobiles used in business will be required to have income included to reflect the reduction in their deduction for lease payments. This income inclusion will be based on special tables provided by the Treasury after netting out the repeal of the investment tax credit. See Appendix C for inclusions required.

Appendix C

Auto Leases

Lessors of automobiles having a cost of more than $11,250 had to include in their 1986 income an amount based on tables in Announcement 85-127 that was equal to the value of the limitations imposed by the 1985 law change. For example, a lessee(s) (including an employer or self-employed individual) who leased a car worth $14,300 that was first used on September 1, 1985, and was used 90 percent for business, included approximately $61 in income ($204 times 122/365 of a year times 90 percent business use).

For any passenger automobile leased after April 2, 1985, the inclusion amount is based on the fair market value of the automobile, the lessee's amount of business use, and the quarter of the taxable year during which the automobile was first used under the lease.

The inclusion amount is based upon the following tables and is computed as follows:

1. For the appropriate range of fair market values, find the dollar amount from the column for the quarter of the taxable year in which the automobile is first used under the lease.

2. Prorate the dollar amount for the number of days of the lease term included in the taxable year.

3. Multiply the prorated dollar amount by the percentage of business use for the taxable year.

 Here are the tables for the last decade:

REV. PROC. 2008-22 TABLE 5
Dollar Amounts for Passenger Automobiles (That Are Not Trucks or Vans) with a Lease Term Beginning In Calendar Year 2008

Fair Market Value of Passenger Automobile		Tax Year During Lease				
Over	Not Over	1st	2nd	3rd	4th	5th and Later
$18,500	$19,000	$ 20	$ 42	$ 62	$ 73	$ 84
19,000	19,500	22	47	71	83	94
19,500	20,000	25	53	78	93	106
20,000	20,500	27	58	87	102	117
20,500	21,000	30	63	95	112	128
21,000	21,500	32	69	103	122	139
21,500	22,000	34	75	111	131	151
22,000	23,000	38	83	123	146	167
23,000	24,000	43	94	139	165	190
24,000	25,000	48	105	155	185	212
25,000	26,000	53	115	172	204	235
26,000	27,000	58	126	188	223	257
27,000	28,000	63	137	204	243	279
28,000	29,000	68	148	220	262	302
29,000	30,000	73	159	236	282	324
30,000	31,000	78	170	252	301	347
31,000	32,000	83	181	268	321	368
32,000	33,000	88	192	284	340	391
33,000	34,000	93	202	301	359	414
34,000	35,000	98	213	317	379	436
35,000	36,000	103	224	333	398	459
36,000	37,000	108	235	349	418	481
37,000	38,000	113	246	365	437	503
38,000	39,000	118	257	381	457	525
39,000	40,000	123	268	397	476	548
40,000	41,000	128	279	413	495	571
41,000	42,000	133	289	430	515	593
42,000	43,000	137	301	446	534	615
43,000	44,000	142	312	462	553	638
44,000	45,000	147	323	478	573	659
45,000	46,000	152	333	495	592	682

REV. PROC. 2008-22 TABLE 5
Dollar Amounts for Passenger Automobiles (That Are Not Trucks or Vans)
with a Lease Term Beginning In Calendar Year 2008 *(continued)*

Fair Market Value of Passenger Automobile		Tax Year During Lease				
Over	Not Over	1st	2nd	3rd	4th	5th and Later
$ 46,000	$ 47,000	$157	$ 344	$ 511	$ 611	$ 705
47,000	48,000	162	355	527	631	727
48,000	49,000	167	366	543	650	750
49,000	50,000	172	377	559	670	772
50,000	51,000	177	388	575	689	794
51,000	52,000	182	399	591	709	816
52,000	53,000	187	410	607	728	839
53,000	54,000	192	420	624	747	862
54,000	55,000	197	431	640	767	884
55,000	56,000	202	442	657	785	906
56,000	57,000	207	453	673	805	928
57,000	58,000	212	464	689	824	951
58,000	59,000	217	475	705	844	973
59,000	60,000	222	486	721	863	996
60,000	62,000	229	502	746	892	1,029
62,000	64,000	239	524	778	931	1,074
64,000	66,000	249	546	810	970	1,118
66,000	68,000	259	567	843	1,008	1,164
68,000	70,000	269	589	875	1,047	1,209
70,000	72,000	279	611	907	1,086	1,253
72,000	74,000	289	633	939	1,125	1,298
74,000	76,000	299	654	972	1,164	1,342
76,000	78,000	309	676	1,004	1,203	1,387
78,000	80,000	319	698	1,036	1,242	1,432
80,000	85,000	336	736	1,093	1,309	1,511
85,000	90,000	361	791	1,173	1,406	1,623
90,000	95,000	386	845	1,255	1,503	1,734
95,000	100,000	410	900	1,335	1,600	1,846
100,000	110,000	448	981	1,457	1,745	2,014
110,000	120,000	497	1,090	1,619	1,939	2,238
120,000	130,000	547	1,199	1,780	2,133	2,462

(continues)

REV. PROC. 2008-22 TABLE 5
Dollar Amounts for Passenger Automobiles (That Are Not Trucks or Vans)
with a Lease Term Beginning In Calendar Year 2008 *(continued)*

Fair Market Value of Passenger Automobile		Tax Year During Lease				
Over	Not Over	1st	2nd	3rd	4th	5th and Later
$130,000	$140,000	$ 597	$1,308	$1,942	$2,327	$2,685
140,000	150,000	646	1,417	2,103	2,521	2,910
150,000	160,000	696	1,526	2,265	2,715	3,133
160,000	170,000	745	1,635	2,427	2,908	3,357
170,000	180,000	795	1,744	2,588	3,103	3,581
180,000	190,000	845	1,853	2,750	3,296	3,805
190,000	200,000	894	1,962	2,912	3,490	4,028
200,000	210,000	944	2,071	3,073	3,684	4,252
210,000	220,000	994	2,179	3,235	3,878	4,476
220,000	230,000	1,043	2,289	3,396	4,072	4,700
230,000	240,000	1,093	2,397	3,559	4,265	4,924
240,000	and up	1,142	2,507	3,720	4,459	5,148

REV. PROC. 2008-22 TABLE 6
Dollar Amounts for Trucks and Vans with a Lease
Term Beginning in Calendar Year 2008

Fair Market Value of Truck or Van		Tax Year During Lease				
Over	Not Over	1st	2nd	3rd	4th	5th and Later
$19,000	$19,500	$ 17	$ 37	$ 54	$ 65	$ 73
19,500	20,000	20	42	63	73	85
20,000	20,500	22	48	70	84	96
20,500	21,000	25	53	79	93	107
21,000	21,500	27	59	86	103	118
21,500	22,000	30	64	95	112	130
22,000	23,000	33	72	107	128	146
23,000	24,000	38	83	123	147	168
24,000	25,000	43	94	139	166	191
25,000	26,000	48	105	155	186	213
26,000	27,000	53	116	171	205	236
27,000	28,000	58	127	187	225	258
28,000	29,000	63	138	204	243	280
29,000	30,000	68	148	221	263	302
30,000	31,000	73	159	237	282	325
31,000	32,000	78	170	253	301	348
32,000	33,000	83	181	269	321	370
33,000	34,000	88	192	285	340	393
34,000	35,000	93	203	301	360	414
35,000	36,000	98	214	317	379	437
36,000	37,000	103	225	333	399	459
37,000	38,000	108	235	350	418	482
38,000	39,000	113	246	366	437	505
39,000	40,000	118	257	382	457	526
40,000	41,000	123	268	398	476	549
41,000	42,000	128	279	414	496	571
42,000	43,000	133	290	430	515	594
43,000	44,000	137	301	447	534	616
44,000	45,000	142	312	463	553	639
45,000	46,000	147	323	479	573	661

(continues)

REV. PROC. 2008-22 TABLE 6
Dollar Amounts for Trucks and Vans with a Lease
Term Beginning in Calendar Year 2008 *(continued)*

Fair Market Value of Truck or Van		Tax Year During Lease				
Over	Not Over	1st	2nd	3rd	4th	5th and Later
$ 46,000	$ 47,000	$152	$ 334	$ 495	$ 592	$ 684
47,000	48,000	157	345	511	612	705
48,000	49,000	162	356	527	631	728
49,000	50,000	167	366	544	651	750
50,000	51,000	172	377	560	670	773
51,000	52,000	177	388	576	689	796
52,000	53,000	182	399	592	709	817
53,000	54,000	187	410	608	728	840
54,000	55,000	192	421	624	748	862
55,000	56,000	197	432	640	767	885
56,000	57,000	202	443	656	787	907
57,000	58,000	207	453	673	806	929
58,000	59,000	212	464	689	825	952
59,000	60,000	217	475	705	845	974
60,000	62,000	224	492	729	874	1,008
62,000	64,000	234	513	762	913	1,052
64,000	66,000	244	535	794	951	1,098
66,000	68,000	254	557	826	990	1,142
68,000	70,000	264	579	858	1,029	1,187
70,000	72,000	274	600	892	1,067	1,232
72,000	74,000	284	622	924	1,106	1,276
74,000	76,000	294	644	956	1,145	1,321
76,000	78,000	304	666	988	1,184	1,366
78,000	80,000	314	687	1,021	1,222	1,411
80,000	85,000	331	726	1,077	1,290	1,489
85,000	90,000	356	780	1,158	1,387	1,601
90,000	95,000	381	835	1,238	1,484	1,713
95,000	100,000	405	889	1,320	1,581	1,825
100,000	110,000	443	971	1,440	1,727	1,993
110,000	120,000	492	1,080	1,602	1,921	2,216
120,000	130,000	542	1,189	1,764	2,114	2,440

REV. PROC. 2008-22 TABLE 6
Dollar Amounts for Trucks and Vans with a Lease
Term Beginning in Calendar Year 2008 *(continued)*

Fair Market Value of Truck or Van		Tax Year During Lease				
Over	Not Over	1st	2nd	3rd	4th	5th and Later
$130,000	$140,000	$ 592	$1,297	$1,926	$2,308	$2,665
140,000	150,000	641	1,407	2,087	2,502	2,888
150,000	160,000	691	1,515	2,249	2,696	3,112
160,000	170,000	740	1,625	2,410	2,890	3,336
170,000	180,000	790	1,733	2,573	3,083	3,560
180,000	190,000	840	1,842	2,734	3,278	3,783
190,000	200,000	889	1,951	2,896	3,472	4,007
200,000	210,000	939	2,060	3,058	3,665	4,231
210,000	220,000	989	2,169	3,219	3,859	4,455
220,000	230,000	1,038	2,278	3,381	4,053	4,678
230,000	240,000	1,088	2,387	3,542	4,247	4,903
240,000	and up	1,137	2,496	3,704	4,441	5,126

REV. PROC. 2009-24 TABLE 5
Dollar Amounts for Passenger Automobiles (That Are Not Trucks or Vans)
with a Lease Term Beginning in Calendar Year 2009

Fair Market Value of Passenger Automobile		Tax Year During Lease				
Over	Not Over	1st	2nd	3rd	4th	5th and Later
$18,500	$19,000	$ 9	$ 19	$ 28	$ 34	$ 38
19,000	19,500	10	21	32	38	43
19,500	20,000	11	24	36	42	48
20,000	20,500	12	27	39	46	54
20,500	21,000	13	29	43	51	58
21,000	21,500	15	31	47	55	64
21,500	22,000	16	34	50	60	68
22,000	23,000	17	38	56	66	76
23,000	24,000	20	42	64	75	86
24,000	25,000	22	47	71	84	96
25,000	26,000	24	52	78	93	107
26,000	27,000	26	58	85	101	117
27,000	28,000	29	62	93	110	127
28,000	29,000	31	67	100	119	138
29,000	30,000	33	72	108	128	147
30,000	31,000	35	77	115	137	157
31,000	32,000	38	82	122	146	167
32,000	33,000	40	87	129	155	178
33,000	34,000	42	92	137	163	188
34,000	35,000	44	97	144	172	199
35,000	36,000	47	102	151	181	208
36,000	37,000	49	107	159	189	219
37,000	38,000	51	112	166	199	228
38,000	39,000	53	117	173	208	239
39,000	40,000	56	122	180	216	250
40,000	41,000	58	127	188	225	259
41,000	42,000	60	132	195	234	269
42,000	43,000	62	137	203	242	280
43,000	44,000	65	141	210	252	290
44,000	45,000	67	146	218	260	300
45,000	46,000	69	151	225	269	311

REV. PROC. 2009-24 TABLE 5
Dollar Amounts for Passenger Automobiles (That Are Not Trucks or Vans)
with a Lease Term Beginning in Calendar Year 2009 *(continued)*

Fair Market Value of Passenger Automobile		Tax Year During Lease				
Over	Not Over	1st	2nd	3rd	4th	5th and Later
$ 46,000	$ 47,000	$ 71	$157	$232	$278	$ 320
47,000	48,000	74	161	240	286	331
48,000	49,000	76	166	247	296	340
49,000	50,000	78	171	255	304	351
50,000	51,000	80	176	262	313	361
51,000	52,000	83	181	269	322	371
52,000	53,000	85	186	276	331	381
53,000	54,000	87	191	284	339	392
54,000	55,000	89	196	291	349	401
55,000	56,000	92	201	298	357	412
56,000	57,000	94	206	306	365	423
57,000	58,000	96	211	313	375	432
58,000	59,000	98	216	320	384	442
59,000	60,000	101	221	327	393	452
60,000	62,000	104	228	339	406	467
62,000	64,000	109	238	353	424	488
64,000	66,000	113	248	368	441	509
66,000	68,000	118	258	382	459	529
68,000	70,000	122	268	397	476	550
70,000	72,000	127	277	413	493	570
72,000	74,000	131	288	427	511	590
74,000	76,000	136	297	442	529	610
76,000	78,000	140	307	457	546	631
78,000	80,000	145	317	471	564	651
80,000	85,000	152	335	497	595	686
85,000	90,000	164	359	534	639	737
90,000	95,000	175	384	570	683	789
95,000	100,000	186	409	607	727	839
100,000	110,000	203	446	662	793	916
110,000	120,000	226	495	736	881	1,018
120,000	130,000	248	545	809	970	1,119

(continues)

REV. PROC. 2009-24 TABLE 5
Dollar Amounts for Passenger Automobiles (That Are Not Trucks or Vans)
with a Lease Term Beginning in Calendar Year 2009 *(continued)*

Fair Market Value of Passenger Automobile		Tax Year During Lease				
Over	Not Over	1st	2nd	3rd	4th	5th and Later
$130,000	$140,000	$271	$ 594	$ 883	$1,058	$1,220
140,000	150,000	293	644	956	1,146	1,322
150,000	160,000	316	693	1,030	1,234	1,424
160,000	170,000	338	743	1,103	1,322	1,526
170,000	180,000	361	792	1,177	1,410	1,628
180,000	190,000	383	842	1,250	1,498	1,730
190,000	200,000	406	891	1,324	1,586	1,831
200,000	210,000	428	941	1,397	1,675	1,932
210,000	220,000	451	990	1,471	1,762	2,035
220,000	230,000	473	1,040	1,544	1,851	2,136
230,000	240,000	496	1,089	1,618	1,939	2,238
240,000	And up	518	1,139	1,691	2,027	2,340

REV. PROC. 2009-24 TABLE 6
Dollar Amounts for Trucks and Vans with a Lease
Term Beginning in Calendar Year 2009

Fair Market Value of Truck or Van		Tax Year During Lease				
Over	Not Over	1st	2nd	3rd	4th	5th and Later
$18,500	$19,000	$ 8	$ 17	$ 25	$ 30	$ 35
19,000	19,500	9	19	29	35	40
19,500	20,000	10	22	33	38	45
20,000	20,500	11	25	36	43	50
20,500	21,000	12	27	40	48	55
21,000	21,500	13	30	43	52	60
21,500	22,000	15	32	47	56	66
22,000	23,000	16	36	52	64	72
23,000	24,000	18	41	60	72	83
24,000	25,000	21	45	68	81	93
25,000	26,000	23	50	75	90	103
26,000	27,000	25	56	82	98	114
27,000	28,000	27	61	89	107	124
28,000	29,000	30	65	97	116	134
29,000	30,000	32	70	104	125	144
30,000	31,000	34	75	112	134	154
31,000	32,000	36	80	119	143	164
32,000	33,000	39	85	126	151	175
33,000	34,000	41	90	134	160	184
34,000	35,000	43	95	141	169	195
35,000	36,000	45	100	148	178	205
36,000	37,000	48	105	155	187	215
37,000	38,000	50	110	163	195	226
38,000	39,000	52	115	170	204	236
39,000	40,000	55	120	177	213	246
40,000	41,000	57	125	185	221	256
41,000	42,000	59	130	192	231	266
42,000	43,000	61	135	199	240	276
43,000	44,000	64	139	207	249	286
44,000	45,000	66	144	215	257	296
45,000	46,000	68	149	222	266	307

(continues)

REV. PROC. 2009-24 TABLE 6
Dollar Amounts for Trucks and Vans with a Lease
Term Beginning in Calendar Year 2009 (continued)

Fair Market Value of Truck or Van		Tax Year During Lease				
Over	Not Over	1st	2nd	3rd	4th	5th and Later
$ 46,000	$ 47,000	$ 70	$155	$229	$274	$ 317
47,000	48,000	73	159	237	283	327
48,000	49,000	75	164	244	292	338
49,000	50,000	77	169	251	301	348
50,000	51,000	79	174	259	310	357
51,000	52,000	82	179	266	318	368
52,000	53,000	84	184	273	328	378
53,000	54,000	86	189	281	336	388
54,000	55,000	88	194	288	345	399
55,000	56,000	91	199	295	354	408
56,000	57,000	93	204	302	363	419
57,000	58,000	95	209	310	371	429
58,000	59,000	97	214	317	381	439
59,000	60,000	100	219	324	389	450
60,000	62,000	103	226	336	402	465
62,000	64,000	107	236	351	420	485
64,000	66,000	112	246	365	438	505
66,000	68,000	116	256	380	455	526
68,000	70,000	121	266	394	473	546
70,000	72,000	125	276	409	491	566
72,000	74,000	130	286	423	509	586
74,000	76,000	134	296	438	526	607
76,000	78,000	139	305	454	543	627
78,000	80,000	143	316	467	561	648
80,000	85,000	151	333	493	592	684
85,000	90,000	163	357	531	635	735
90,000	95,000	174	382	567	680	785
95,000	100,000	185	407	604	724	836
100,000	110,000	202	444	659	790	912
110,000	120,000	225	493	733	878	1,014
120,000	130,000	247	543	806	966	1,116

REV. PROC. 2009-24 TABLE 6
Dollar Amounts for Trucks and Vans with a Lease
Term Beginning in Calendar Year 2009 *(continued)*

Fair Market Value of Truck or Van		Tax Year During Lease				
Over	Not Over	1st	2nd	3rd	4th	5th and Later
$130,000	$140,000	$270	$ 592	$ 880	$1,054	$1,218
140,000	150,000	292	642	953	1,143	1,319
150,000	160,000	315	691	1,027	1,230	1,421
160,000	170,000	337	741	1,100	1,319	1,522
170,000	180,000	360	790	1,174	1,407	1,624
180,000	190,000	382	840	1,247	1,495	1,726
190,000	200,000	405	889	1,321	1,583	1,828
200,000	210,000	427	939	1,394	1,671	1,930
210,000	220,000	450	988	1,468	1,759	2,031
220,000	230,000	472	1,038	1,541	1,847	2,134
230,000	240,000	495	1,087	1,615	1,935	2,235
240,000	and up	517	1,137	1,688	2,024	2,336

REV. PROC. 2010-18 TABLE 3
Dollar Amounts for Passenger Automobiles
(That Are Not Trucks or Vans) with a Lease
Term Beginning in Calendar Year 2010

Fair Market Value of Passenger Automobile		Tax Year During Lease				
Over	Not Over	1st	2nd	3rd	4th	5th and Later
$16,700	$17,000	$ 3	$ 7	$ 10	$ 11	$ 14
17,000	17,500	4	8	13	15	16
17,500	18,000	5	10	16	19	21
18,000	18,500	6	13	18	23	26
18,500	19,000	7	15	22	26	31
19,000	19,500	8	17	25	30	35
19,500	20,000	9	19	29	34	39
20,000	20,500	10	21	32	38	44
20,500	21,000	11	23	35	42	48
21,000	21,500	12	26	38	45	53
21,500	22,000	13	28	41	50	57
22,000	23,000	14	31	46	56	63
23,000	24,000	16	36	52	63	73
24,000	25,000	18	40	59	71	81
25,000	26,000	20	44	66	78	90
26,000	27,000	22	49	71	86	100
27,000	28,000	24	53	78	94	108
28,000	29,000	26	57	85	101	118
29,000	30,000	28	61	92	109	126
30,000	31,000	30	66	97	117	135
31,000	32,000	32	70	104	125	144
32,000	33,000	34	74	111	132	153
33,000	34,000	36	79	117	140	161
34,000	35,000	38	83	123	148	171
35,000	36,000	40	87	130	156	179
36,000	37,000	42	92	136	163	188
37,000	38,000	44	96	143	170	198
38,000	39,000	46	100	149	179	206
39,000	40,000	48	105	155	186	215
40,000	41,000	50	109	162	194	224

REV. PROC. 2010-18 TABLE 3
Dollar Amounts for Passenger Automobiles
(That Are Not Trucks or Vans) with a Lease
Term Beginning in Calendar Year 2010 *(continued)*

Fair Market Value of Passenger Automobile		Tax Year During Lease				
Over	Not Over	1st	2nd	3rd	4th	5th and Later
$41,000	$42,000	$ 52	$113	$169	$201	$233
42,000	43,000	54	118	174	210	241
43,000	44,000	56	122	181	217	251
44,000	45,000	58	126	188	225	259
45,000	46,000	60	131	194	232	269
46,000	47,000	61	135	201	240	277
47,000	48,000	63	140	207	248	286
48,000	49,000	65	144	213	256	295
49,000	50,000	67	148	220	263	304
50,000	51,000	69	153	226	271	313
51,000	52,000	71	157	232	279	322
52,000	53,000	73	161	239	287	331
53,000	54,000	75	166	245	294	340
54,000	55,000	77	170	252	302	348
55,000	56,000	79	174	258	310	358
56,000	57,000	81	178	265	318	366
57,000	58,000	83	183	271	325	375
58,000	59,000	85	187	278	333	384
59,000	60,000	87	191	284	341	393
60,000	62,000	90	198	294	352	406
62,000	64,000	94	207	306	368	424
64,000	66,000	98	215	320	382	443
66,000	68,000	102	224	332	398	460
68,000	70,000	106	232	346	413	478
70,000	72,000	110	241	358	429	496
72,000	74,000	114	250	371	444	513
74,000	76,000	118	258	384	460	531
76,000	78,000	122	267	396	476	549
78,000	80,000	126	276	409	491	566
80,000	85,000	132	291	432	518	598

(continues)

REV. PROC. 2010-18 TABLE 3
Dollar Amounts for Passenger Automobiles
(That Are Not Trucks or Vans) with a Lease
Term Beginning in Calendar Year 2010 *(continued)*

Fair Market Value of Passenger Automobile		Tax Year During Lease				
Over	Not Over	1st	2nd	3rd	4th	5th and Later
$ 85,000	$ 90,000	$142	$313	$ 464	$ 556	$ 643
90,000	95,000	152	334	497	594	687
95,000	100,000	162	356	528	634	731
100,000	110,000	177	388	577	691	798
110,000	120,000	196	432	641	768	887
120,000	130,000	216	475	705	846	976
130,000	140,000	236	518	770	922	1,065
140,000	150,000	256	561	834	1,000	1,154
150,000	160,000	275	605	898	1,077	1,243
160,000	170,000	295	648	963	1,153	1,333
170,000	180,000	315	691	1,027	1,231	1,421
180,000	190,000	334	735	1,091	1,308	1,510
190,000	200,000	354	778	1,155	1,386	1,599
200,000	210,000	374	821	1,220	1,462	1,688
210,000	220,000	393	865	1,284	1,539	1,777
220,000	230,000	413	908	1,348	1,617	1,866
230,000	240,000	433	951	1,413	1,693	1,956
240,000	and up	453	995	1,476	1,771	2,044

REV. PROC. 2010-18 TABLE 4
Dollar Amounts for Trucks and Vans with a Lease
Term Beginning in Calendar Year 2010

Fair Market Value of Truck or Van		Tax Year During Lease				
Over	Not Over	1st	2nd	3rd	4th	5th and Later
$ 17,000	$ 17,500	$ 3	$ 6	$ 9	$ 10	$ 11
17,500	18,000	4	8	12	14	16
18,000	18,500	5	10	15	18	21
18,500	19,000	6	12	19	22	24
19,000	19,500	7	15	21	26	29
19,500	20,000	8	17	25	29	34
20,000	20,500	9	19	28	33	38
20,500	21,000	10	21	31	37	43
21,000	21,500	11	23	35	41	47
21,500	22,000	12	25	38	45	51
22,000	23,000	13	29	42	51	58
23,000	24,000	15	33	49	58	67
24,000	25,000	17	37	56	66	76
25,000	26,000	19	42	62	73	85
26,000	27,000	21	46	68	82	93
27,000	28,000	23	50	75	89	103
28,000	29,000	25	55	81	97	111
29,000	30,000	27	59	88	104	121
30,000	31,000	29	63	94	113	129
31,000	32,000	31	68	100	120	138
32,000	33,000	33	72	107	127	148
33,000	34,000	35	76	114	135	156
34,000	35,000	37	81	119	143	165
35,000	36,000	39	85	126	151	174
36,000	37,000	41	89	133	158	183
37,000	38,000	43	94	139	166	191
38,000	39,000	45	98	145	174	201
39,000	40,000	47	102	152	182	209
40,000	41,000	49	106	159	189	218
41,000	42,000	51	111	164	198	227
42,000	43,000	53	115	171	205	236
43,000	44,000	55	119	178	213	245
44,000	45,000	57	124	184	220	254
45,000	46,000	59	128	190	228	263

(continues)

REV. PROC. 2010-18 TABLE 4
Dollar Amounts for Trucks and Vans with a Lease
Term Beginning in Calendar Year 2010 *(continued)*

Fair Market Value of Truck or Van		Tax Year During Lease				
Over	Not Over	1st	2nd	3rd	4th	5th and Later
$ 46,000	$ 47,000	$60	$133	$197	$235	$272
47,000	48,000	62	137	203	244	280
48,000	49,000	64	142	209	251	290
49,000	50,000	66	146	216	259	298
50,000	51,000	68	150	223	266	308
51,000	52,000	70	154	229	275	316
52,000	53,000	72	159	235	282	325
53,000	54,000	74	163	242	290	334
54,000	55,000	76	167	249	297	343
55,000	56,000	78	172	254	305	352
56,000	57,000	80	176	261	313	361
57,000	58,000	82	180	268	320	370
58,000	59,000	84	185	274	328	378
59,000	60,000	86	189	280	336	388
60,000	62,000	89	195	291	347	401
62,000	64,000	93	204	303	363	418
64,000	66,000	97	213	315	379	436
66,000	68,000	101	221	329	394	454
68,000	70,000	105	230	341	410	472
70,000	72,000	109	239	354	424	490
72,000	74,000	113	247	367	440	508
74,000	76,000	117	256	380	455	526
76,000	78,000	121	264	393	471	543
78,000	80,000	125	273	406	486	561
80,000	85,000	131	289	428	513	592
85,000	90,000	141	310	461	552	636
90,000	95,000	151	332	492	591	681
95,000	100,000	161	353	525	629	726
100,000	110,000	176	386	573	686	793
110,000	120,000	195	430	637	763	882
120,000	130,000	215	473	701	841	971

REV. PROC. 2010-18 TABLE 4
Dollar Amounts for Trucks and Vans with a Lease
Term Beginning in Calendar Year 2010 *(continued)*

Fair Market Value of Truck or Van		Tax Year During Lease				
Over	Not Over	1st	2nd	3rd	4th	5th and Later
$130,000	$140,000	$235	$516	$ 766	$ 918	$1,059
140,000	150,000	255	559	830	995	1,149
150,000	160,000	274	603	894	1,072	1,238
160,000	170,000	294	646	958	1,150	1,326
170,000	180,000	314	689	1,023	1,226	1,416
180,000	190,000	333	733	1,087	1,303	1,505
190,000	200,000	353	776	1,151	1,381	1,594
200,000	210,000	373	819	1,216	1,457	1,683
210,000	220,000	392	863	1,280	1,534	1,772
220,000	230,000	412	906	1,344	1,612	1,861
230,000	240,000	432	949	1,409	1,689	1,949
240,000	250,000	452	992	1,473	1,766	2,039

REV. PROC. 2011-21 TABLE 5
Dollar Amounts for Passenger Automobiles (That are not Trucks or Vans) with a Lease Term Beginning in Calendar Year 2011

Fair Market Value of Passenger Automobile		Tax Year During Lease				
Over	Not Over	1st	2nd	3rd	4th	5th and Later
$18,500	$19,000	$ 3	$ 8	$11	$ 13	$ 16
19,000	19,500	4	9	13	15	18
19,500	20,000	4	10	15	17	20
20,000	20,500	5	11	16	19	23
20,500	21,000	5	12	18	21	25
21,000	21,500	6	13	19	24	26
21,500	22,000	6	14	21	26	29
22,000	23,000	7	16	23	29	32
23,000	24,000	8	18	27	32	37
24,000	25,000	9	20	30	36	42
25,000	26,000	10	23	33	40	46
26,000	27,000	11	25	36	44	51
27,000	28,000	12	27	40	48	55
28,000	29,000	13	29	43	52	60
29,000	30,000	14	31	47	55	65
30,000	31,000	15	34	49	60	69
31,000	32,000	16	36	53	63	73
32,000	33,000	17	38	56	68	77
33,000	34,000	18	40	60	71	82
34,000	35,000	19	42	63	75	87
35,000	36,000	20	45	66	79	91
36,000	37,000	21	47	69	83	96
37,000	38,000	22	49	73	87	100
38,000	39,000	23	51	76	91	105
39,000	40,000	24	53	80	94	110
40,000	41,000	25	56	82	99	114
41,000	42,000	26	58	86	102	119
42,000	43,000	27	60	89	107	123
43,000	44,000	28	62	93	110	128
44,000	45,000	29	64	96	114	133

REV. PROC. 2011-21 TABLE 5
**Dollar Amounts for Passenger Automobiles (That are not Trucks or Vans)
with a Lease Term Beginning in Calendar Year 2011** *(continued)*

Fair Market Value of Passenger Automobile		Tax Year During Lease				
Over	Not Over	1st	2nd	3rd	4th	5th and Later
$ 45,000	$ 46,000	$ 30	$ 67	$ 98	$119	$137
46,000	47,000	31	69	102	122	141
47,000	48,000	32	71	105	127	145
48,000	49,000	33	73	109	130	150
49,000	50,000	34	76	111	134	155
50,000	51,000	35	78	115	138	159
51,000	52,000	36	80	118	142	164
52,000	53,000	37	82	122	146	168
53,000	54,000	38	84	125	150	173
54,000	55,000	39	87	128	153	178
55,000	56,000	40	89	131	158	182
56,000	57,000	41	91	135	161	187
57,000	58,000	42	93	138	166	191
58,000	59,000	43	95	142	169	196
59,000	60,000	44	98	144	174	200
60,000	62,000	46	101	149	179	207
62,000	64,000	48	105	156	187	216
64,000	66,000	50	109	163	195	225
66,000	68,000	52	114	169	203	234
68,000	70,000	54	118	176	211	243
70,000	72,000	56	123	182	218	253
72,000	74,000	58	127	189	226	262
74,000	76,000	60	132	195	234	270
76,000	78,000	62	136	202	242	279
78,000	80,000	64	140	209	250	288
80,000	85,000	67	148	220	264	304
85,000	90,000	72	159	237	283	327
90,000	95,000	77	170	253	303	350
95,000	100,000	82	181	269	323	372
100,000	110,000	90	198	293	352	406
110,000	120,000	100	220	326	391	452

(continues)

REV. PROC. 2011-21 TABLE 5
Dollar Amounts for Passenger Automobiles (That are not Trucks or Vans)
with a Lease Term Beginning in Calendar Year 2011 *(continued)*

Fair Market Value of Passenger Automobile		Tax Year During Lease				
Over	Not Over	1st	2nd	3rd	4th	5th and Later
$120,000	$130,000	$110	$242	$359	$430	$ 497
130,000	140,000	120	264	392	469	543
140,000	150,000	130	286	424	509	588
150,000	160,000	140	308	457	548	633
160,000	170,000	150	330	490	587	679
170,000	180,000	160	352	523	626	724
180,000	190,000	170	374	555	666	769
190,000	200,000	180	396	588	705	815
200,000	210,000	190	418	621	744	860
210,000	220,000	200	440	654	784	904
220,000	230,000	210	462	687	823	950
230,000	240,000	220	484	719	863	995
240,000	and up	230	506	752	902	1,040

REV. PROC. 2011-21 TABLE 6
Dollar Amounts for Trucks and Vans with a
Lease Term Beginning in Calendar Year 2011

Fair Market Value of Truck or Van		Tax Year During Lease				
Over	Not Over	1st	2nd	3rd	4th	5th and Later
$19,000	$19,500	$ 3	$ 7	$ 9	$ 12	$ 13
19,500	20,000	3	8	11	14	15
20,000	20,500	4	9	13	15	18
20,500	21,000	4	10	15	17	20
21,000	21,500	5	11	16	20	22
21,500	22,000	5	12	18	22	24
22,000	23,000	6	14	20	24	29
23,000	24,000	7	16	24	28	32
24,000	25,000	8	18	27	32	37
25,000	26,000	9	20	31	36	41
26,000	27,000	10	23	33	40	46
27,000	28,000	11	25	37	43	51
28,000	29,000	12	27	40	48	55
29,000	30,000	13	29	43	52	60
30,000	31,000	14	31	47	56	64
31,000	32,000	15	34	49	60	69
32,000	33,000	16	36	53	63	74
33,000	34,000	17	38	56	68	78
34,000	35,000	18	40	60	71	83
35,000	36,000	19	43	62	76	87
36,000	37,000	20	45	66	79	92
37,000	38,000	21	47	69	83	97
38,000	39,000	22	49	73	87	101
39,000	40,000	23	51	76	91	105
40,000	41,000	24	54	79	95	109
41,000	42,000	25	56	82	99	114
42,000	43,000	26	58	86	103	118
43,000	44,000	27	60	89	107	123
44,000	45,000	28	62	93	110	128
45,000	46,000	29	65	95	115	132
46,000	47,000	30	67	99	118	137
47,000	48,000	31	69	102	123	141
48,000	49,000	32	71	106	126	146
49,000	50,000	33	73	109	130	151
50,000	51,000	34	76	112	134	155

(continues)

REV. PROC. 2011-21 TABLE 6
Dollar Amounts for Trucks and Vans with a
Lease Term Beginning in Calendar Year 2011 *(continued)*

Fair Market Value of Truck or Van		Tax Year During Lease				
Over	Not Over	1st	2nd	3rd	4th	5th and Later
$51,000	$52,000	$ 35	$ 78	$115	$138	$160
52,000	53,000	36	80	118	143	164
53,000	54,000	37	82	122	146	169
54,000	55,000	38	84	125	150	173
55,000	56,000	39	87	128	154	177
56,000	57,000	40	89	131	158	182
57,000	58,000	41	91	135	162	186
58,000	59,000	42	93	138	166	191
59,000	60,000	43	95	142	169	196
60,000	62,000	45	99	146	175	203
62,000	64,000	47	103	153	183	212
64,000	66,000	49	107	160	191	221
66,000	68,000	51	112	166	199	229
68,000	70,000	53	116	173	206	239
70,000	72,000	55	121	179	214	248
72,000	74,000	57	125	186	222	257
74,000	76,000	59	129	192	231	266
76,000	78,000	61	134	198	239	275
78,000	80,000	63	138	205	246	285
80,000	85,000	66	146	217	260	300
85,000	90,000	71	157	233	280	322
90,000	95,000	76	168	250	299	345
95,000	100,000	81	179	266	319	368
100,000	110,000	89	196	290	348	402
110,000	120,000	99	218	323	387	447
120,000	130,000	109	240	355	427	493
130,000	140,000	119	262	388	466	538
140,000	150,000	129	284	421	505	583
150,000	160,000	139	306	454	544	629
160,000	170,000	149	328	487	583	674
170,000	180,000	159	350	519	623	719

REV. PROC. 2011-21 TABLE 6
Dollar Amounts for Trucks and Vans with a
Lease Term Beginning in Calendar Year 2011 *(continued)*

Fair Market Value of Truck or Van		Tax Year During Lease				
Over	Not Over	1st	2nd	3rd	4th	5th and Later
$180,000	$190,000	$169	$372	$552	$662	$ 765
190,000	200,000	179	394	585	701	810
200,000	210,000	189	416	618	740	856
210,000	220,000	199	438	651	779	901
220,000	230,000	209	460	683	819	946
230,000	240,000	219	482	716	858	992
240,000	and up	229	504	749	897	1,037

REV. PROC. 2012–23 TABLE 5
**Dollar Amounts for Passenger Automobiles (that are not trucks or vans)
with a Lease Term Beginning in Calendar Year 2012**

Fair Market Value of Passenger Automobile		Tax Year During Lease				
Over	Not Over	1st	2nd	3rd	4th	5th and later
$18,500	$19,000	$ 2	$ 4	$ 5	$ 6	$ 8
19,000	19,500	2	4	7	7	9
19,500	20,000	2	5	8	8	10
20,000	20,500	3	5	9	10	11
20,500	21,000	3	6	9	12	12
21,000	21,500	3	7	10	12	14
21,500	22,000	3	8	11	13	16
22,000	23,000	4	8	13	15	17
23,000	24,000	4	10	15	17	20
24,000	25,000	5	11	17	19	23
25,000	26,000	6	12	19	21	26
26,000	27,000	6	14	20	24	28
27,000	28,000	7	15	22	26	31
28,000	29,000	7	16	25	28	33
29,000	30,000	8	18	25	32	35
30,000	31,000	9	19	27	34	38
31,000	32,000	9	20	30	36	41
32,000	33,000	10	21	32	38	43
33,000	34,000	10	23	33	41	46
34,000	35,000	11	24	35	43	49
35,000	36,000	12	25	37	45	52
36,000	37,000	12	27	39	47	54
37,000	38,000	13	28	41	49	57
38,000	39,000	13	29	43	52	59
39,000	40,000	14	30	45	54	62
40,000	41,000	14	32	47	56	65
41,000	42,000	15	33	49	58	68
42,000	43,000	16	34	51	61	70
43,000	44,000	16	36	52	63	73
44,000	45,000	17	37	54	66	75
45,000	46,000	17	38	57	67	78

REV. PROC. 2012–23 TABLE 5
Dollar Amounts for Passenger Automobiles (that are not trucks or vans) with a Lease Term Beginning in Calendar Year 2012 *(continued)*

Fair Market Value of Passenger Automobile		Tax Year During Lease				
Over	Not Over	1st	2nd	3rd	4th	5th and later
$ 46,000	$ 47,000	$18	$ 39	$ 59	$ 70	$ 80
47,000	48,000	19	40	61	72	83
48,000	49,000	19	42	62	75	86
49,000	50,000	20	43	64	77	89
50,000	51,000	20	45	66	79	91
51,000	52,000	21	46	68	81	94
52,000	53,000	21	47	70	84	96
53,000	54,000	22	48	72	86	99
54,000	55,000	23	49	74	88	102
55,000	56,000	23	51	76	90	104
56,000	57,000	24	52	78	92	107
57,000	58,000	24	54	79	95	110
58,000	59,000	25	55	81	97	113
59,000	60,000	26	56	83	100	115
60,000	62,000	26	58	86	103	119
62,000	64,000	28	60	90	108	124
64,000	66,000	29	63	94	112	129
66,000	68,000	30	66	97	117	135
68,000	70,000	31	68	102	121	140
70,000	72,000	32	71	105	126	145
72,000	74,000	33	74	109	130	151
74,000	76,000	35	76	113	135	156
76,000	78,000	36	78	117	140	161
78,000	80,000	37	81	120	145	166
80,000	85,000	39	86	127	152	176
85,000	90,000	42	92	137	163	189
90,000	95,000	45	98	147	175	202
95,000	100,000	48	105	155	187	215
100,000	110,000	52	115	170	203	235
110,000	120,000	58	127	189	227	262
120,000	130,000	64	140	208	250	288

(continues)

REV. PROC. 2012–23 TABLE 5
Dollar Amounts for Passenger Automobiles (that are not trucks or vans)
with a Lease Term Beginning in Calendar Year 2012 *(continued)*

Fair Market Value of Passenger Automobile		Tax Year During Lease				
Over	Not Over	1st	2nd	3rd	4th	5th and later
$130,000	$140,000	$ 70	$153	$227	$272	$315
140,000	150,000	75	166	246	296	340
150,000	160,000	81	179	265	318	368
160,000	170,000	87	192	284	341	394
170,000	180,000	93	204	304	364	420
180,000	190,000	99	217	323	387	446
190,000	200,000	105	230	342	409	473
200,000	210,000	111	243	361	432	499
210,000	220,000	116	256	380	455	526
220,000	230,000	122	269	399	478	552
230,000	240,000	128	282	418	501	578
240,000	And up	134	294	437	524	605

REV. PROC. 2012–23 TABLE 6
Dollar Amounts for Trucks and Vans with a Lease
Term Beginning in Calendar Year 2012

Fair Market Value of Truck or Van		Tax Year During Lease				
Over	Not Over	1st	2nd	3rd	4th	5th and later
$19,000	$19,500	$ 1	$ 4	$ 5	$ 6	$ 7
19,500	20,000	2	4	6	7	9
20,000	20,500	2	5	7	8	10
20,500	21,000	2	5	8	10	11
21,000	21,500	3	6	9	10	13
21,500	22,000	3	6	10	12	14
22,000	23,000	3	8	11	14	15
23,000	24,000	4	9	13	16	18
24,000	25,000	4	10	15	19	21
25,000	26,000	5	11	17	21	24
26,000	27,000	6	12	19	23	26
27,000	28,000	6	14	21	25	29
28,000	29,000	7	15	23	27	32
29,000	30,000	7	17	24	30	34
30,000	31,000	8	18	26	32	37
31,000	32,000	9	19	28	34	40
32,000	33,000	9	20	31	36	42
33,000	34,000	10	21	33	39	44
34,000	35,000	10	23	34	41	48
35,000	36,000	11	24	36	44	50
36,000	37,000	12	25	38	46	53
37,000	38,000	12	27	40	48	55
38,000	39,000	13	28	42	50	58
39,000	40,000	13	29	44	53	60
40,000	41,000	14	31	45	55	63
41,000	42,000	14	32	48	57	66
42,000	43,000	15	33	50	59	69
43,000	44,000	16	34	52	61	72
44,000	45,000	16	36	53	64	74
45,000	46,000	17	37	55	66	77
46,000	47,000	17	38	58	68	79

(continues)

REV. PROC. 2012–23 TABLE 6
Dollar Amounts for Trucks and Vans with a Lease
Term Beginning in Calendar Year 2012 *(continued)*

Fair Market Value of Truck or Van		Tax Year During Lease				
Over	Not Over	1st	2nd	3rd	4th	5th and later
$ 47,000	$ 48,000	$18	$ 40	$ 59	$ 70	$ 82
48,000	49,000	19	41	61	73	84
49,000	50,000	19	42	63	75	87
50,000	51,000	20	43	65	78	89
51,000	52,000	20	45	66	80	93
52,000	53,000	21	46	68	83	95
53,000	54,000	21	48	70	84	98
54,000	55,000	22	49	72	87	100
55,000	56,000	23	50	74	89	103
56,000	57,000	23	51	76	92	105
57,000	58,000	24	52	78	94	108
58,000	59,000	24	54	80	96	111
59,000	60,000	25	55	82	98	114
60,000	62,000	26	57	85	101	118
62,000	64,000	27	60	88	106	123
64,000	66,000	28	62	93	110	128
66,000	68,000	29	65	96	115	134
68,000	70,000	30	67	100	120	139
70,000	72,000	32	70	103	125	144
72,000	74,000	33	72	108	129	149
74,000	76,000	34	75	111	134	155
76,000	78,000	35	78	115	138	160
78,000	80,000	36	80	119	143	165
80,000	85,000	38	85	125	151	175
85,000	90,000	41	91	135	163	187
90,000	95,000	44	98	144	174	201
95,000	100,000	47	104	154	185	214
100,000	110,000	52	113	169	202	234
110,000	120,000	57	127	187	225	261
120,000	130,000	63	139	207	248	287
130,000	140,000	69	152	226	271	313
140,000	150,000	75	165	245	294	339

REV. PROC. 2012–23 TABLE 6
Dollar Amounts for Trucks and Vans with a Lease
Term Beginning in Calendar Year 2012 *(continued)*

Fair Market Value of Truck or Van		Tax Year During Lease				
Over	Not Over	1st	2nd	3rd	4th	5th and later
$150,000	$160,000	$ 81	$178	$264	$316	$366
160,000	170,000	87	190	283	340	392
170,000	180,000	92	204	302	362	419
180,000	190,000	98	216	322	385	445
190,000	200,000	104	229	340	409	471
200,000	210,000	110	242	359	431	498
210,000	220,000	116	255	378	454	524
220,000	230,000	122	267	398	477	551
230,000	240,000	127	281	416	500	577
240,000	And up	133	294	435	523	603

REV. PROC. 2013–21 TABLE 5
Dollar Amounts for Passenger Automobiles
(that are not trucks or vans) with a Lease
Term Beginning in Calendar Year 2013

Fair Market Value of Passenger Automobile		Tax Year During Lease				
Over	Not Over	1st	2nd	3rd	4th	5th and later
$19,000	$19,500	$ 2	$ 4	$ 6	$ 7	$ 8
19,500	20,000	2	5	6	9	9
20,000	20,500	2	5	8	9	11
20,500	21,000	3	6	8	10	12
21,000	21,500	3	6	10	11	13
21,500	22,000	3	7	10	13	14
22,000	23,000	4	8	11	14	16
23,000	24,000	4	9	14	16	18
24,000	25,000	5	10	15	18	21
25,000	26,000	5	12	16	21	23
26,000	27,000	6	12	19	23	25
27,000	28,000	6	14	20	25	28
28,000	29,000	7	15	22	27	30
29,000	30,000	7	16	24	29	33
30,000	31,000	8	17	26	31	35
31,000	32,000	8	19	27	33	38
32,000	33,000	9	20	29	35	40
33,000	34,000	10	21	31	37	43
34,000	35,000	10	22	33	39	45
35,000	36,000	11	23	35	41	48
36,000	37,000	11	25	36	43	50
37,000	38,000	12	26	38	45	53
38,000	39,000	12	27	40	47	55
39,000	40,000	13	28	42	49	58
40,000	41,000	13	29	44	52	59
41,000	42,000	14	30	45	54	63
42,000	43,000	14	32	47	56	64
43,000	44,000	15	33	48	59	67
44,000	45,000	15	34	51	60	69
45,000	46,000	16	35	52	63	72

REV. PROC. 2013–21 TABLE 5
Dollar Amounts for Passenger Automobiles
(that are not trucks or vans) with a Lease
Term Beginning in Calendar Year 2013 *(continued)*

Fair Market Value of Passenger Automobile		Tax Year During Lease				
Over	Not Over	1st	2nd	3rd	4th	5th and later
$ 46,000	$ 47,000	$17	$ 36	$ 54	$ 65	$ 74
47,000	48,000	17	38	55	67	77
48,000	49,000	18	39	57	69	79
49,000	50,000	18	40	59	71	82
50,000	51,000	19	41	61	73	84
51,000	52,000	19	42	63	75	87
52,000	53,000	20	43	65	77	89
53,000	54,000	20	45	66	79	92
54,000	55,000	21	46	68	81	94
55,000	56,000	21	47	70	84	96
56,000	57,000	22	48	72	85	99
57,000	58,000	22	50	73	88	101
58,000	59,000	23	51	75	90	103
59,000	60,000	24	52	76	92	106
60,000	62,000	24	54	79	95	110
62,000	64,000	25	56	83	99	115
64,000	66,000	27	58	87	103	120
66,000	68,000	28	60	90	108	125
68,000	70,000	29	63	93	112	130
70,000	72,000	30	65	97	117	134
72,000	74,000	31	68	100	121	139
74,000	76,000	32	70	104	125	144
76,000	78,000	33	73	107	129	149
78,000	80,000	34	75	111	133	154
80,000	85,000	36	79	117	141	162
85,000	90,000	39	85	126	151	174
90,000	95,000	41	91	135	162	186
95,000	100,000	44	97	144	172	199
100,000	110,000	48	106	157	188	217
110,000	120,000	53	118	174	210	241

(continues)

REV. PROC. 2013–21 TABLE 5
Dollar Amounts for Passenger Automobiles
(that are not trucks or vans) with a Lease
Term Beginning in Calendar Year 2013 *(continued)*

Fair Market Value of Passenger Automobile		Tax Year During Lease				
Over	Not Over	1st	2nd	3rd	4th	5th and later
$120,000	$130,000	$ 59	$129	$193	$230	$266
130,000	140,000	64	141	210	252	290
140,000	150,000	70	153	227	273	315
150,000	160,000	75	165	245	294	339
160,000	170,000	80	177	263	315	363
170,000	180,000	86	189	280	336	388
180,000	190,000	91	201	298	357	412
190,000	200,000	97	212	316	378	436
200,000	210,000	102	224	333	400	461
210,000	220,000	107	236	351	420	486
220,000	230,000	113	248	368	442	509
230,000	240,000	118	260	386	463	534
240,000	And up	124	272	403	484	558

REV. PROC. 2013–21 TABLE 6
Dollar Amounts for Trucks and Vans with a
Lease Term Beginning in Calendar
Year 2013

Fair Market Value of Truck or Van		Tax Year During Lease				
Over	Not Over	1st	2nd	3rd	4th	5th and later
$19,000	$19,500	$ 1	$ 3	$4	$ 5	$ 6
19,500	20,000	2	3	5	6	7
20,000	20,500	2	4	6	7	8
20,500	21,000	2	5	7	8	9
21,000	21,500	2	5	8	9	11
21,500	22,000	3	6	8	10	12
22,000	23,000	3	7	10	11	14
23,000	24,000	4	8	11	14	16
24,000	25,000	4	9	14	16	18
25,000	26,000	5	10	15	18	21
26,000	27,000	5	12	17	20	23
27,000	28,000	6	13	18	23	25
28,000	29,000	6	14	20	25	28
29,000	30,000	7	15	22	27	30
30,000	31,000	7	16	24	29	33
31,000	32,000	8	17	26	31	35
32,000	33,000	8	19	27	33	38
33,000	34,000	9	20	29	35	41
34,000	35,000	10	21	31	37	43
35,000	36,000	10	22	33	39	46
36,000	37,000	11	23	35	41	48
37,000	38,000	11	25	36	43	51
38,000	39,000	12	26	38	45	53
39,000	40,000	12	27	40	48	55
40,000	41,000	13	28	42	49	58
41,000	42,000	13	29	44	52	60
42,000	43,000	14	30	46	54	62
43,000	44,000	14	32	47	56	65
44,000	45,000	15	33	48	59	67
45,000	46,000	15	34	51	60	70

(continues)

REV. PROC. 2013–21 TABLE 6
Dollar Amounts for Trucks and Vans with a
Lease Term Beginning in Calendar
Year 2013 *(continued)*

Fair Market Value of Truck or Van		Tax Year During Lease				
Over	Not Over	1st	2nd	3rd	4th	5th and later
$ 46,000	$ 47,000	$16	$ 35	$ 52	$ 63	$ 72
47,000	48,000	17	36	54	65	74
48,000	49,000	17	38	55	67	77
49,000	50,000	18	39	57	69	79
50,000	51,000	18	40	59	71	82
51,000	52,000	19	41	61	73	84
52,000	53,000	19	42	63	75	87
53,000	54,000	20	43	65	77	89
54,000	55,000	20	45	66	80	91
55,000	56,000	21	46	68	81	94
56,000	57,000	21	47	70	84	96
57,000	58,000	22	48	72	86	98
58,000	59,000	22	50	73	88	101
59,000	60,000	23	51	75	90	103
60,000	62,000	24	52	78	93	108
62,000	64,000	25	55	81	97	113
64,000	66,000	26	57	85	101	118
66,000	68,000	27	60	88	106	122
68,000	70,000	28	62	92	110	127
70,000	72,000	29	64	96	114	132
72,000	74,000	30	67	99	118	137
74,000	76,000	31	69	103	122	142
76,000	78,000	32	72	105	127	147
78,000	80,000	34	73	110	131	151
80,000	85,000	35	78	116	138	160
85,000	90,000	38	84	124	149	172
90,000	95,000	41	90	133	160	184
95,000	100,000	44	95	142	171	196
100,000	110,000	48	104	156	186	214
110,000	120,000	53	116	173	207	240

REV. PROC. 2013–21 TABLE 6
Dollar Amounts for Trucks and Vans with a
Lease Term Beginning in Calendar
Year 2013 *(continued)*

Fair Market Value of Truck or Van		Tax Year During Lease				
Over	Not Over	1st	2nd	3rd	4th	5th and later
$120,000	$130,000	$ 58	$128	$191	$228	$264
130,000	140,000	64	140	208	249	288
140,000	150,000	69	152	226	270	313
150,000	160,000	75	164	243	292	336
160,000	170,000	80	176	261	312	361
170,000	180,000	85	188	278	334	386
180,000	190,000	91	199	296	355	410
190,000	200,000	96	211	314	376	434
200,000	210,000	101	223	332	397	459
210,000	220,000	107	235	349	418	483
220,000	230,000	112	247	367	439	507
230,000	240,000	118	259	384	460	532
240,000	And up	123	271	401	482	556

REV. PROC. 2014–21 TABLE 3
Dollar Amounts for Passenger Automobiles
(that are not trucks or vans) with a Lease
Term Beginning in Calendar Year 2014

Fair Market Value of Passenger Automobile		Tax Year During Lease				
Over	Not Over	1st	2nd	3rd	4th	5th and later
$18,500	$19,000	3	5	8	10	11
19,000	19,500	3	6	10	11	13
19,500	20,000	3	8	11	13	14
20,000	20,500	4	8	13	14	17
20,500	21,000	4	9	14	17	18
21,000	21,500	5	10	15	18	21
21,500	22,000	5	11	17	20	22
22,000	23,000	6	13	18	23	25
23,000	24,000	7	14	22	26	29
24,000	25,000	8	16	25	29	33
25,000	26,000	8	19	27	32	38
26,000	27,000	9	20	31	35	42
27,000	28,000	10	22	33	40	45
28,000	29,000	11	24	36	43	49
29,000	30,000	12	26	39	46	53
30,000	31,000	13	28	41	50	57
31,000	32,000	14	30	44	53	61
32,000	33,000	14	32	47	56	65
33,000	34,000	15	34	50	59	69
34,000	35,000	16	36	52	64	72
35,000	36,000	17	38	55	67	76
36,000	37,000	18	39	59	70	80
37,000	38,000	19	41	61	74	84
38,000	39,000	20	43	64	77	88
39,000	40,000	21	45	67	80	92
40,000	41,000	21	47	70	84	96
41,000	42,000	22	49	73	87	100
42,000	43,000	23	51	75	91	104
43,000	44,000	24	53	78	94	108
44,000	45,000	25	55	81	97	112

REV. PROC. 2014–21 TABLE 3
Dollar Amounts for Passenger Automobiles
(that are not trucks or vans) with a Lease
Term Beginning in Calendar Year 2014 *(continued)*

Fair Market Value of Passenger Automobile		Tax Year During Lease				
Over	Not Over	1st	2nd	3rd	4th	5th and later
$45,000	$46,000	26	56	84	101	116
46,000	47,000	27	58	87	104	120
47,000	48,000	28	60	90	107	124
48,000	49,000	28	62	93	111	127
49,000	50,000	29	64	96	114	131
50,000	51,000	30	66	98	118	135
51,000	52,000	31	68	101	121	139
52,000	53,000	32	70	104	124	143
53,000	54,000	33	72	106	128	147
54,000	55,000	34	74	109	131	151
55,000	56,000	34	76	112	135	155
56,000	57,000	35	78	115	138	159
57,000	58,000	36	80	118	141	163
58,000	59,000	37	81	121	145	167
59,000	60,000	38	83	124	148	171
60,000	62,000	39	86	128	153	177
62,000	64,000	41	90	134	159	185
64,000	66,000	43	94	139	167	192
66,000	68,000	44	98	145	173	201
68,000	70,000	46	102	150	180	209
70,000	72,000	48	105	156	188	216
72,000	74,000	50	109	162	194	224
74,000	76,000	51	113	168	200	232
76,000	78,000	53	117	173	208	239
78,000	80,000	55	120	179	215	247
80,000	85,000	58	127	189	226	261
85,000	90,000	62	137	203	243	281
90,000	95,000	67	146	217	260	301
95,000	100,000	71	156	231	277	320
100,000	110,000	77	170	253	303	349

(continues)

REV. PROC. 2014–21 TABLE 3
Dollar Amounts for Passenger Automobiles
(that are not trucks or vans) with a Lease
Term Beginning in Calendar Year 2014 *(continued)*

Fair Market Value of Passenger Automobile		Tax Year During Lease				
Over	Not Over	1st	2nd	3rd	4th	5th and later
$110,000	$120,000	86	189	281	337	389
120,000	130,000	95	208	310	370	428
130,000	140,000	103	228	337	405	467
140,000	150,000	112	247	366	438	507
150,000	160,000	121	266	394	473	545
160,000	170,000	130	284	423	507	585
170,000	180,000	138	304	451	541	624
180,000	190,000	147	323	479	575	663
190,000	200,000	156	342	507	609	703
200,000	210,000	164	361	536	643	742
210,000	220,000	173	380	565	676	781
220,000	230,000	182	399	593	710	821
230,000	240,000	190	418	622	744	860
240,000	And up	199	437	650	778	899

REV. PROC. 2014–21 TABLE 4
Dollar Amounts for Trucks and Vans with a
Lease Term Beginning in Calendar
Year 2014

Fair Market Value of Truck or Van		Tax Year During Lease				
Over	Not Over	1st	2nd	3rd	4th	5th and later
$19,000	$19,500	2	4	5	7	8
19,500	20,000	2	5	7	8	10
20,000	20,500	3	6	8	10	12
20,500	21,000	3	7	10	11	14
21,000	21,500	3	8	11	14	15
21,500	22,000	4	9	12	15	18
22,000	23,000	5	10	15	17	21
23,000	24,000	5	12	18	21	24
24,000	25,000	6	14	20	25	28
25,000	26,000	7	16	23	28	32
26,000	27,000	8	18	26	31	36
27,000	28,000	9	20	28	35	40
28,000	29,000	10	21	32	38	44
29,000	30,000	11	23	35	41	48
30,000	31,000	11	26	37	45	52
31,000	32,000	12	27	41	48	56
32,000	33,000	13	29	43	52	60
33,000	34,000	14	31	46	55	64
34,000	35,000	15	33	49	58	68
35,000	36,000	16	35	51	62	72
36,000	37,000	17	37	54	65	76
37,000	38,000	18	38	58	69	79
38,000	39,000	18	41	60	72	83
39,000	40,000	19	43	63	75	87
40,000	41,000	20	44	66	79	91
41,000	42,000	21	46	69	82	95
42,000	43,000	22	48	72	85	99
43,000	44,000	23	50	74	89	103
44,000	45,000	24	52	77	93	106
45,000	46,000	24	54	80	96	111

(continues)

<div align="center">

REV. PROC. 2014–21 TABLE 4
Dollar Amounts for Trucks and Vans with a
Lease Term Beginning in Calendar
Year 2014 *(continued)*

</div>

Fair Market Value of Truck or Van		Tax Year During Lease				
Over	Not Over	1st	2nd	3rd	4th	5th and later
$46,000	$47,000	25	56	83	99	115
47,000	48,000	26	58	86	102	119
48,000	49,000	27	60	88	106	123
49,000	50,000	28	62	91	109	127
50,000	51,000	29	63	95	113	130
51,000	52,000	30	65	97	117	134
52,000	53,000	31	67	100	120	138
53,000	54,000	31	69	103	123	142
54,000	55,000	32	71	106	126	146
55,000	56,000	33	73	108	130	150
56,000	57,000	34	75	111	133	154
57,000	58,000	35	77	114	137	157
58,000	59,000	36	79	116	141	161
59,000	60,000	37	80	120	144	165
60,000	62,000	38	84	123	149	172
62,000	64,000	40	87	130	155	180
64,000	66,000	41	91	136	162	187
66,000	68,000	43	95	141	169	195
68,000	70,000	45	99	146	176	203
70,000	72,000	47	102	153	182	211
72,000	74,000	48	107	158	189	219
74,000	76,000	50	110	164	196	227
76,000	78,000	52	114	169	203	235
78,000	80,000	54	118	175	209	243
80,000	85,000	57	124	185	222	256
85,000	90,000	61	134	199	239	276
90,000	95,000	65	144	213	256	295
95,000	100,000	70	153	227	273	315
100,000	110,000	76	168	248	298	345
110,000	120,000	85	187	277	332	383

REV. PROC. 2014–21 TABLE 4
Dollar Amounts for Trucks and Vans with a
Lease Term Beginning in Calendar
Year 2014 *(continued)*

Fair Market Value of Truck or Van		Tax Year During Lease				
Over	Not Over	1st	2nd	3rd	4th	5th and later
$120,000	$130,000	93	206	305	366	423
130,000	140,000	102	225	334	400	462
140,000	150,000	111	244	362	434	501
150,000	160,000	120	263	390	468	541
160,000	170,000	128	282	419	502	580
170,000	180,000	137	301	447	536	619
180,000	190,000	146	320	475	571	658
190,000	200,000	154	339	504	604	698
200,000	210,000	163	358	532	639	736
210,000	220,000	172	377	561	672	776
220,000	230,000	180	397	589	706	815
230,000	240,000	189	416	617	740	854
240,000	And up	198	435	645	774	894

REV. PROC. 2015–19 TABLE 3
Dollar Amounts for Passenger Automobiles (that are not trucks or vans) with a Lease Term Beginning in Calendar Year 2015

Fair Market Value of Passenger Automobile		Tax Year During Lease				
Over	Not Over	1st	2nd	3rd	4th	5th and later
$17,500	$18,000	3	6	9	10	11
18,000	18,500	4	7	11	13	15
18,500	19,000	4	9	14	15	18
19,000	19,500	5	11	15	19	21
19,500	20,000	6	12	18	22	24
20,000	20,500	6	14	20	25	27
20,500	21,000	7	15	23	27	31
21,000	21,500	8	17	25	30	34
21,500	22,000	9	18	28	32	38
22,000	23,000	10	21	31	37	42
23,000	24,000	11	24	36	42	49
24,000	25,000	12	27	41	48	55
25,000	26,000	14	30	45	54	62
26,000	27,000	15	34	49	60	68
27,000	28,000	17	37	54	65	75
28,000	29,000	18	40	59	71	81
29,000	30,000	20	43	64	76	87
30,000	31,000	21	46	69	81	95
31,000	32,000	23	49	73	88	100
32,000	33,000	24	52	78	93	107
33,000	34,000	25	56	82	99	114
34,000	35,000	27	59	87	104	120
35,000	36,000	28	62	92	110	126
36,000	37,000	30	65	96	116	133
37,000	38,000	31	68	102	121	139
38,000	39,000	33	71	106	127	146
39,000	40,000	34	75	110	132	153
40,000	41,000	35	78	115	138	159
41,000	42,000	37	81	120	143	166
42,000	43,000	38	84	125	149	172

REV. PROC. 2015–19 TABLE 3
Dollar Amounts for Passenger Automobiles
(that are not trucks or vans) with a Lease
Term Beginning in Calendar Year 2015 *(continued)*

Fair Market Value of Passenger Automobile		Tax Year During Lease				
Over	Not Over	1st	2nd	3rd	4th	5th and later
43,000	44,000	40	87	129	155	179
44,000	45,000	41	90	134	161	185
45,000	46,000	43	93	139	166	191
46,000	47,000	44	97	143	172	198
47,000	48,000	45	100	148	177	205
48,000	49,000	47	103	153	183	210
49,000	50,000	48	106	158	188	218
50,000	51,000	50	109	162	194	224
51,000	52,000	51	112	167	200	230
52,000	53,000	53	115	172	205	237
53,000	54,000	54	119	176	211	243
54,000	55,000	56	122	180	217	250
55,000	56,000	57	125	186	222	256
56,000	57,000	58	128	191	227	263
57,000	58,000	60	131	195	234	269
58,000	59,000	61	135	199	239	276
59,000	60,000	63	137	205	244	283
60,000	62,000	65	142	212	253	292
62,000	64,000	68	149	220	265	304
64,000	66,000	71	155	230	275	318
66,000	68,000	73	162	239	287	331
68,000	70,000	76	168	249	298	343
70,000	72,000	79	174	258	309	357
72,000	74,000	82	180	268	320	370
74,000	76,000	85	186	277	332	383
76,000	78,000	88	193	286	343	396
78,000	80,000	91	199	296	354	408
80,000	85,000	96	210	312	374	431
85,000	90,000	103	226	335	402	464
90,000	95,000	110	242	359	430	496
95,000	100,000	117	258	382	458	529

(continues)

REV. PROC. 2015–19 TABLE 3
Dollar Amounts for Passenger Automobiles
(that are not trucks or vans) with a Lease
Term Beginning in Calendar Year 2015 *(continued)*

Fair Market Value of Passenger Automobile		Tax Year During Lease				
Over	Not Over	1st	2nd	3rd	4th	5th and later
100,000	110,000	128	281	418	500	577
110,000	120,000	142	313	464	556	643
120,000	130,000	157	344	511	613	707
130,000	140,000	171	376	558	668	772
140,000	150,000	185	408	604	725	837
150,000	160,000	200	439	651	781	902
160,000	170,000	214	470	699	837	966
170,000	180,000	228	502	745	894	1,031
180,000	190,000	243	533	792	950	1,096
190,000	200,000	257	565	839	1,006	1,161
200,000	210,000	271	597	886	1,061	1,226
210,000	220,000	286	628	933	1,118	1,290
220,000	230,000	300	660	979	1,174	1,356
230,000	240,000	315	691	1,026	1,231	1,420
240,000	and over	329	723	1,073	1,286	1,485

REV. PROC. 2015–19 TABLE 4
Dollar Amounts for Trucks and Vans with a
Lease Term Beginning in Calendar
Year 2015

Fair Market Value of Truck or Van		Tax Year During Lease				
Over	Not Over	1st	2nd	3rd	4th	5th and later
$18,500	$19,000	2	4	6	8	9
19,000	19,500	3	6	8	11	12
19,500	20,000	4	7	11	13	16
20,000	20,500	4	9	13	16	19
20,500	21,000	5	11	15	19	22
21,000	21,500	6	12	18	22	25
21,500	22,000	6	14	20	25	28
22,000	23,000	7	16	24	29	33
23,000	24,000	9	19	29	34	40
24,000	25,000	10	23	33	40	46
25,000	26,000	12	25	38	46	53
26,000	27,000	13	29	42	51	60
27,000	28,000	15	32	47	57	65
28,000	29,000	16	35	52	62	73
29,000	30,000	18	38	56	68	79
30,000	31,000	19	41	61	74	85
31,000	32,000	20	45	66	79	91
32,000	33,000	22	48	70	85	98
33,000	34,000	23	51	75	91	104
34,000	35,000	25	54	80	96	111
35,000	36,000	26	57	85	101	118
36,000	37,000	28	60	89	108	124
37,000	38,000	29	63	94	113	131
38,000	39,000	30	67	98	119	137
39,000	40,000	32	70	103	124	144
40,000	41,000	33	73	108	130	150
41,000	42,000	35	76	113	135	157
42,000	43,000	36	79	118	141	163
43,000	44,000	38	82	122	147	169
44,000	45,000	39	85	127	153	176
45,000	46,000	40	89	131	158	183
46,000	47,000	42	92	136	163	189

(continues)

REV. PROC. 2015–19 TABLE 4
Dollar Amounts for Trucks and Vans with a
Lease Term Beginning in Calendar
Year 2015 *(continued)*

Fair Market Value of Truck or Van		Tax Year During Lease				
Over	Not Over	1st	2nd	3rd	4th	5th and later
47,000	48,000	43	95	141	169	195
48,000	49,000	45	98	145	175	202
49,000	50,000	46	101	151	180	208
50,000	51,000	48	104	155	186	215
51,000	52,000	49	108	159	192	221
52,000	53,000	51	110	165	197	228
53,000	54,000	52	114	169	203	234
54,000	55,000	53	117	174	208	241
55,000	56,000	55	120	178	214	248
56,000	57,000	56	123	183	220	254
57,000	58,000	58	126	188	225	261
58,000	59,000	59	130	192	231	267
59,000	60,000	61	133	197	236	273
60,000	62,000	63	137	204	245	283
62,000	64,000	66	144	213	256	296
64,000	66,000	68	150	223	268	308
66,000	68,000	71	157	232	278	322
68,000	70,000	74	163	241	290	335
70,000	72,000	77	169	251	301	348
72,000	74,000	80	175	261	312	361
74,000	76,000	83	182	269	324	374
76,000	78,000	86	188	279	335	386
78,000	80,000	89	194	288	346	400
80,000	85,000	94	205	305	366	422
85,000	90,000	101	221	328	394	455
90,000	95,000	108	237	351	422	488
95,000	100,000	115	253	375	450	519
100,000	110,000	126	276	410	492	569
110,000	120,000	140	308	457	548	633
120,000	130,000	155	339	504	604	698

REV. PROC. 2015–19 TABLE 4
Dollar Amounts for Trucks and Vans with a
Lease Term Beginning in Calendar
Year 2015 *(continued)*

Fair Market Value of Truck or Van		Tax Year During Lease				
Over	Not Over	1st	2nd	3rd	4th	5th and later
130,000	140,000	169	371	551	660	763
140,000	150,000	183	403	597	717	827
150,000	160,000	198	434	644	773	893
160,000	170,000	212	466	691	829	957
170,000	180,000	226	497	738	885	1,023
180,000	190,000	241	528	785	942	1,087
190,000	200,000	255	560	832	997	1,152
200,000	210,000	269	592	878	1,054	1,217
210,000	220,000	284	623	925	1,110	1,282
220,000	230,000	298	655	972	1,166	1,346
230,000	240,000	312	687	1,019	1,222	1,411
240,000	and over	327	718	1,066	1,278	1,476

REV. PROC. 2016–23 TABLE 5
Dollar Amounts for Passenger Automobiles
(that are not trucks or vans) with a Lease
Term Beginning in Calendar Year 2016

Fair Market Value of Passenger Automobile		Tax Year During Lease				
Over	Not Over	1st	2nd	3rd	4th	5th and later
$19,000	$19,500	6	13	20	23	27
19,500	20,000	7	15	23	27	30
20,000	20,500	8	17	26	30	35
20,500	21,000	9	19	29	33	39
21,000	21,500	10	21	31	38	42
21,500	22,000	11	23	34	41	47
22,000	23,000	12	26	39	46	53
23,000	24,000	14	30	44	54	60
24,000	25,000	16	34	50	60	69
25,000	26,000	17	38	56	67	78
26,000	27,000	19	42	62	74	85
27,000	28,000	21	46	68	81	93
28,000	29,000	23	50	73	89	101
29,000	30,000	25	53	80	95	110
30,000	31,000	26	58	85	102	118
31,000	32,000	28	62	91	109	126
32,000	33,000	30	65	98	116	134
33,000	34,000	32	69	103	123	142
34,000	35,000	34	73	109	130	150
35,000	36,000	35	77	115	137	158
36,000	37,000	37	81	121	144	166
37,000	38,000	39	85	127	151	174
38,000	39,000	41	89	132	158	183
39,000	40,000	42	93	138	166	190
40,000	41,000	44	97	144	172	199
41,000	42,000	46	101	150	179	207
42,000	43,000	48	105	155	187	215
43,000	44,000	50	109	161	193	223
44,000	45,000	51	113	167	201	231
45,000	46,000	53	117	173	207	239

REV. PROC. 2016–23 TABLE 5
Dollar Amounts for Passenger Automobiles
(that are not trucks or vans) with a Lease
Term Beginning in Calendar Year 2016 *(continued)*

Fair Market Value of Passenger Automobile		Tax Year During Lease				
Over	Not Over	1st	2nd	3rd	4th	5th and later
46,000	47,000	55	121	179	214	247
47,000	48,000	57	124	185	222	255
48,000	49,000	59	128	191	228	264
49,000	50,000	60	133	196	236	271
50,000	51,000	62	136	203	242	280
51,000	52,000	64	140	209	249	288
52,000	53,000	66	144	214	257	295
53,000	54,000	68	148	220	263	304
54,000	55,000	69	152	226	271	312
55,000	56,000	71	156	232	277	320
56,000	57,000	73	160	238	284	328
57,000	58,000	75	164	243	292	336
58,000	59,000	77	168	249	298	345
59,000	60,000	78	172	255	306	352
60,000	62,000	81	178	264	316	364
62,000	64,000	85	185	276	330	381
64,000	66,000	88	194	287	344	397
66,000	68,000	92	201	299	358	413
68,000	70,000	95	209	311	372	430
70,000	72,000	99	217	322	387	445
72,000	74,000	102	225	334	400	462
74,000	76,000	106	233	346	414	478
76,000	78,000	110	241	357	428	494
78,000	80,000	113	249	369	442	510
80,000	85,000	120	262	390	467	538
85,000	90,000	128	282	419	502	579
90,000	95,000	137	302	448	537	620
95,000	100,000	146	322	477	572	660
100,000	110,000	160	351	521	625	721

(continues)

REV. PROC. 2016–23 TABLE 5
Dollar Amounts for Passenger Automobiles
(that are not trucks or vans) with a Lease
Term Beginning in Calendar Year 2016 *(continued)*

Fair Market Value of Passenger Automobile		Tax Year During Lease				
Over	Not Over	1st	2nd	3rd	4th	5th and later
110,000	120,000	178	390	580	695	801
120,000	130,000	196	430	638	765	882
130,000	140,000	214	469	697	835	963
140,000	150,000	232	508	755	906	1,044
150,000	160,000	249	548	814	975	1,126
160,000	170,000	267	588	872	1,045	1,207
170,000	180,000	285	627	930	1,116	1,288
180,000	190,000	303	666	989	1,186	1,368
190,000	200,000	321	706	1,047	1,256	1,449
200,000	210,000	339	745	1,106	1,326	1,530
210,000	220,000	357	784	1,165	1,396	1,611
220,000	230,000	375	824	1,223	1,466	1,692
230,000	240,000	393	863	1,281	1,537	1,773
240,000	and over	411	902	1,340	1,607	1,854

REV. PROC. 2016–23 TABLE 6
Dollar Amounts for Trucks and Vans with a
Lease Term Beginning in Calendar
Year 2016

Fair Market Value of Truck or Van		Tax Year During Lease				
Over	Not Over	1st	2nd	3rd	4th	5th and later
$19,500	$20,000	3	8	12	14	16
20,000	20,500	4	10	15	17	20
20,500	21,000	5	12	17	21	25
21,000	21,500	6	14	20	25	28
21,500	22,000	7	16	23	28	32
22,000	23,000	8	19	28	33	38
23,000	24,000	10	23	33	41	46
24,000	25,000	12	26	40	47	55
25,000	26,000	14	30	46	54	63
26,000	27,000	16	34	51	62	70
27,000	28,000	17	38	58	68	79
28,000	29,000	19	42	63	76	86
29,000	30,000	21	46	69	82	95
30,000	31,000	23	50	75	89	103
31,000	32,000	25	54	80	97	111
32,000	33,000	26	58	86	104	119
33,000	34,000	28	62	92	111	127
34,000	35,000	30	66	98	117	136
35,000	36,000	32	70	104	124	143
36,000	37,000	34	73	110	132	151
37,000	38,000	35	78	115	139	160
38,000	39,000	37	82	121	146	167
39,000	40,000	39	85	128	152	176
40,000	41,000	41	89	133	160	184
41,000	42,000	42	94	139	166	192
42,000	43,000	44	97	145	174	200
43,000	44,000	46	101	151	181	208
44,000	45,000	48	105	157	187	217
45,000	46,000	50	109	162	195	224
46,000	47,000	51	113	169	201	233

(continues)

REV. PROC. 2016–23 TABLE 6
Dollar Amounts for Trucks and Vans with a
Lease Term Beginning in Calendar
Year 2016 *(continued)*

Fair Market Value of Truck or Van		Tax Year During Lease				
Over	Not Over	1st	2nd	3rd	4th	5th and later
47,000	48,000	53	117	174	209	240
48,000	49,000	55	121	180	216	248
49,000	50,000	57	125	186	222	257
50,000	51,000	59	129	191	230	265
51,000	52,000	60	133	197	237	273
52,000	53,000	62	137	203	244	281
53,000	54,000	64	141	209	250	290
54,000	55,000	66	144	216	257	298
55,000	56,000	68	148	221	265	305
56,000	57,000	69	153	226	272	314
57,000	58,000	71	156	233	279	321
58,000	59,000	73	160	239	285	330
59,000	60,000	75	164	244	293	338
60,000	62,000	77	170	253	304	350
62,000	64,000	81	178	265	317	366
64,000	66,000	85	186	276	331	383
66,000	68,000	88	194	288	345	399
68,000	70,000	92	202	299	360	414
70,000	72,000	95	210	311	374	431
72,000	74,000	99	217	324	387	447
74,000	76,000	102	226	335	401	463
76,000	78,000	106	233	347	415	480
78,000	80,000	110	241	358	430	495
80,000	85,000	116	255	379	454	524
85,000	90,000	125	274	409	489	564
90,000	95,000	134	294	437	525	605
95,000	100,000	143	314	466	560	645
100,000	110,000	156	344	510	612	706
110,000	120,000	174	383	569	682	787
120,000	130,000	192	422	628	752	868

REV. PROC. 2016–23 TABLE 6
Dollar Amounts for Trucks and Vans with a
Lease Term Beginning in Calendar
Year 2016 *(continued)*

Fair Market Value of Truck or Van		Tax Year During Lease				
Over	Not Over	1st	2nd	3rd	4th	5th and later
130,000	140,000	210	462	685	823	949
140,000	150,000	228	501	744	893	1,030
150,000	160,000	246	540	803	963	1,111
160,000	170,000	264	580	861	1,033	1,192
170,000	180,000	282	619	920	1,102	1,274
180,000	190,000	300	658	979	1,172	1,354
190,000	200,000	318	698	1,036	1,243	1,435
200,000	210,000	335	738	1,095	1,313	1,516
210,000	220,000	353	777	1,154	1,383	1,597
220,000	230,000	371	816	1,212	1,454	1,678
230,000	240,000	389	856	1,270	1,524	1,759
240,000	and over	407	895	1,329	1,594	1,839

REV. PROC. 2017–29 TABLE 5
Dollar Amounts for Passenger Automobiles
(that are not trucks or vans) with a Lease
Term Beginning in Calendar Year 2017

Fair Market Value of Passenger Automobile		Tax Year During Lease				
Over	Not Over	1st	2nd	3rd	4th	5th and later
$19,000	$19,500	6	14	20	23	27
19,500	20,000	7	16	23	27	31
20,000	20,500	8	18	26	30	35
20,500	21,000	9	20	28	35	39
21,000	21,500	10	21	32	38	44
21,500	22,000	11	23	35	42	47
22,000	23,000	12	27	39	47	53
23,000	24,000	14	31	45	54	62
24,000	25,000	16	34	52	61	70
25,000	26,000	18	38	58	68	78
26,000	27,000	19	43	63	75	87
27,000	28,000	21	47	69	82	95
28,000	29,000	23	51	75	89	103
29,000	30,000	25	55	80	97	112
30,000	31,000	27	58	87	104	120
31,000	32,000	29	62	93	111	128
32,000	33,000	30	67	99	118	136
33,000	34,000	32	71	104	126	144
34,000	35,000	34	75	110	133	152
35,000	36,000	36	79	116	140	160
36,000	37,000	38	82	123	147	169
37,000	38,000	40	86	129	154	177
38,000	39,000	41	91	134	161	186
39,000	40,000	43	95	140	168	194
40,000	41,000	45	99	146	175	202
41,000	42,000	47	103	152	182	210
42,000	43,000	49	106	159	189	218
43,000	44,000	50	111	164	197	226
44,000	45,000	52	115	170	204	234
45,000	46,000	54	119	176	211	243

REV. PROC. 2017–29 TABLE 5
Dollar Amounts for Passenger Automobiles
(that are not trucks or vans) with a Lease
Term Beginning in Calendar Year 2017 *(continued)*

Fair Market Value of Passenger Automobile		Tax Year During Lease				
Over	Not Over	1st	2nd	3rd	4th	5th and later
46,000	47,000	56	123	182	218	251
47,000	48,000	58	127	187	225	260
48,000	49,000	60	130	194	232	268
49,000	50,000	61	135	200	239	276
50,000	51,000	63	139	206	246	284
51,000	52,000	65	143	211	254	292
52,000	53,000	67	147	217	261	301
53,000	54,000	69	151	223	268	309
54,000	55,000	70	155	229	275	318
55,000	56,000	72	159	235	282	326
56,000	57,000	74	163	241	289	334
57,000	58,000	76	167	247	296	342
58,000	59,000	78	171	253	303	350
59,000	60,000	80	174	260	310	359
60,000	62,000	82	181	268	321	371
62,000	64,000	86	189	280	335	387
64,000	66,000	90	197	292	349	404
66,000	68,000	93	205	304	364	420
68,000	70,000	97	213	315	379	436
70,000	72,000	101	221	327	393	453
72,000	74,000	104	229	339	407	470
74,000	76,000	108	237	351	421	486
76,000	78,000	111	245	363	436	502
78,000	80,000	115	253	375	450	518
80,000	85,000	122	267	396	474	548
85,000	90,000	131	287	425	511	588
90,000	95,000	140	307	455	546	630
95,000	100,000	149	327	485	581	671
100,000	110,000	162	357	530	635	733
110,000	120,000	181	397	589	706	815

(continues)

REV. PROC. 2017–29 TABLE 5
Dollar Amounts for Passenger Automobiles
(that are not trucks or vans) with a Lease
Term Beginning in Calendar Year 2017 *(continued)*

Fair Market Value of Passenger Automobile		Tax Year During Lease				
Over	Not Over	1st	2nd	3rd	4th	5th and later
120,000	130,000	199	437	649	777	898
130,000	140,000	217	477	708	849	980
140,000	150,000	235	517	768	920	1,062
150,000	160,000	254	557	827	991	1,145
160,000	170,000	272	597	887	1,062	1,227
170,000	180,000	290	637	946	1,134	1,309
180,000	190,000	308	677	1,006	1,205	1,391
190,000	200,000	326	718	1,064	1,277	1,473
200,000	210,000	345	757	1,124	1,348	1,556
210,000	220,000	363	797	1,184	1,419	1,638
220,000	230,000	381	837	1,244	1,490	1,721
230,000	240,000	399	878	1,302	1,562	1,803
240,000	and over	418	917	1,362	1,633	1,885

REV. PROC. 2017–29 TABLE 6
Dollar Amounts for Trucks and Vans with a
Lease Term Beginning in Calendar
Year 2017

Fair Market Value of Truck or Van		Tax Year During Lease				
Over	Not Over	1st	2nd	3rd	4th	5th and later
$19,500	$20,000	4	8	11	13	16
20,000	20,500	4	10	14	17	20
20,500	21,000	5	12	17	21	23
21,000	21,500	6	14	20	24	28
21,500	22,000	7	16	23	28	32
22,000	23,000	9	19	27	33	38
23,000	24,000	10	23	34	40	46
24,000	25,000	12	27	39	48	54
25,000	26,000	14	31	45	55	62
26,000	27,000	16	35	51	62	71
27,000	28,000	18	39	57	69	79
28,000	29,000	19	43	63	76	88
29,000	30,000	21	47	69	83	96
30,000	31,000	23	51	75	90	104
31,000	32,000	25	55	81	97	112
32,000	33,000	27	59	87	104	120
33,000	34,000	29	63	93	111	129
34,000	35,000	30	67	99	119	136
35,000	36,000	32	71	105	126	145
36,000	37,000	34	75	111	133	153
37,000	38,000	36	79	117	140	161
38,000	39,000	38	83	122	148	169
39,000	40,000	40	87	128	155	177
40,000	41,000	41	91	135	161	186
41,000	42,000	43	95	141	168	194
42,000	43,000	45	99	146	176	203
43,000	44,000	47	103	152	183	211
44,000	45,000	49	107	158	190	219
45,000	46,000	50	111	165	196	228
46,000	47,000	52	115	170	204	236

(continues)

REV. PROC. 2017–29 TABLE 6
Dollar Amounts for Trucks and Vans with a
Lease Term Beginning in Calendar
Year 2017 *(continued)*

Fair Market Value of Truck or Van		Tax Year During Lease				
Over	Not Over	1st	2nd	3rd	4th	5th and later
47,000	48,000	54	119	176	211	244
48,000	49,000	56	123	182	218	252
49,000	50,000	58	127	188	225	261
50,000	51,000	60	131	194	232	269
51,000	52,000	61	135	200	240	277
52,000	53,000	63	139	206	247	285
53,000	54,000	65	143	212	254	293
54,000	55,000	67	147	218	261	301
55,000	56,000	69	151	224	268	309
56,000	57,000	70	155	230	275	318
57,000	58,000	72	159	236	282	326
58,000	59,000	74	163	242	289	335
59,000	60,000	76	167	248	296	343
60,000	62,000	79	173	256	308	355
62,000	64,000	82	181	269	321	372
64,000	66,000	86	189	280	336	388
66,000	68,000	90	197	292	350	404
68,000	70,000	93	205	304	365	420
70,000	72,000	97	213	316	379	437
72,000	74,000	101	221	328	393	453
74,000	76,000	104	229	340	407	470
76,000	78,000	108	237	352	421	487
78,000	80,000	111	245	364	436	503
80,000	85,000	118	259	384	461	532
85,000	90,000	127	279	414	497	573
90,000	95,000	136	299	444	532	614
95,000	100,000	145	319	474	567	656
100,000	110,000	159	349	518	621	717
110,000	120,000	177	389	578	692	800
120,000	130,000	195	429	637	764	882

REV. PROC. 2017–29 TABLE 6
Dollar Amounts for Trucks and Vans with a
Lease Term Beginning in Calendar
Year 2017 *(continued)*

Fair Market Value of Truck or Van		Tax Year During Lease				
Over	Not Over	1st	2nd	3rd	4th	5th and later
130,000	140,000	213	470	696	835	964
140,000	150,000	232	509	756	906	1,047
150,000	160,000	250	549	816	977	1,129
160,000	170,000	268	589	875	1,049	1,211
170,000	180,000	286	630	934	1,120	1,293
180,000	190,000	305	669	994	1,191	1,376
190,000	200,000	323	709	1,054	1,262	1,458
200,000	210,000	341	750	1,112	1,334	1,540
210,000	220,000	359	790	1,172	1,405	1,623
220,000	230,000	377	830	1,231	1,477	1,705
230,000	240,000	396	870	1,290	1,548	1,787
240,000	and over	414	910	1,350	1,619	1,870

REV. PROC. 2018–** TABLE 4
Dollar Amounts for Passenger Automobiles
with a Lease Term Beginning in
Calendar Year 2018

Fair Market Value of Passenger Automobiles		Tax Year During Lease				
Over	Not Over	1st	2nd	3rd	4th	5th and later
$50,000	51,000	1	3	5	5	6
51,000	52,000	4	9	13	16	19
52,000	53,000	7	15	22	27	31
53,000	54,000	10	21	31	37	44
54,000	55,000	12	27	40	48	56
55,000	56,000	15	33	49	59	68
56,000	57,000	18	39	58	69	81
57,000	58,000	20	45	67	80	93
58,000	59,000	23	51	76	91	105
59,000	60,000	26	57	85	101	117
60,000	62,000	30	66	98	118	135
62,000	64,000	36	78	116	139	160
64,000	66,000	41	90	134	160	185
66,000	68,000	46	102	152	181	210
68,000	70,000	52	114	169	203	235
70,000	72,000	57	126	187	225	259
72,000	74,000	63	138	205	246	284
74,000	76,000	68	150	223	267	309
76,000	78,000	74	162	241	288	333
78,000	80,000	79	174	259	310	357
80,000	85,000	89	195	290	347	401
85,000	90,000	102	225	335	400	463
90,000	95,000	116	255	379	454	525
95,000	100,000	130	285	423	508	586
100,000	110,000	150	330	491	587	679
110,000	120,000	178	390	579	695	802
120,000	130,000	205	450	669	801	926
130,000	140,000	232	510	758	908	1,049
140,000	150,000	260	570	847	1,015	1,172
150,000	160,000	287	630	936	1,122	1,296

REV. PROC. 2018– TABLE 4**
Dollar Amounts for Passenger Automobiles
with a Lease Term Beginning in
Calendar Year 2018 *(continued)*

Fair Market Value of Passenger Automobiles		Tax Year During Lease				
Over	Not Over	1st	2nd	3rd	4th	5th and later
160,000	170,000	314	691	1,024	1,230	1,419
170,000	180,000	342	750	1,114	1,336	1,543
180,000	190,000	369	810	1,204	1,442	1,666
190,000	200,000	396	871	1,292	1,550	1,789
200,000	210,000	424	930	1,382	1,656	1,913
210,000	220,000	451	991	1,470	1,764	2,036
220,000	230,000	478	1,051	1,559	1,871	2,159
230,000	240,000	505	1,111	1,649	1,977	2,283
240,000	and over	533	1,171	1,738	2,084	2,406

Index

About the Author

Jeff A. Schnepper, Esq., is the author of multiple books on finance and taxation, including all 35 previous editions of *How to Pay Zero Taxes.* He is a financial, tax, and legal advisor for Estate Planning of Delaware Valley and operates a tax, accounting, and legal practice in Cherry Hill, New Jersey. Schnepper formerly was Microsoft's MSN MONEY tax expert and a Professor of Accounting, Finance, and Taxation at the American College in Bryn Mawr, Pennsylvania. He currently is an economics editor for *USA Today* and tax counsel for Haran, Watson & Company.

macOS Mojave

THE MISSING CD

There's no
CD with this book—
you just saved $5.00!

Instead, every single web address, practice
file, and piece of downloadable software
mentioned in this book is available at
missingmanuals.com (click the Missing
CD icon). There you'll find a tidy
list of links, organized
by chapter.

Colophon

This book was written on a 13-inch MacBook Pro that remained attached to David Pogue like an appendage. It was updated from the High Sierra edition of the same book directly in Adobe InDesign, with substantial assistance from the typing-shortcut program TextExpander *(smileonmymac.com)*.

The book's screen illustrations were captured with macOS Mojave's new screenshot toolbar, edited in Adobe Photoshop *(adobe.com)*, and overlaid with labels, lines, and circles in Adobe Illustrator.

The book was designed and laid out in Adobe InDesign CC. The fonts include Formata (as the sans-serif family) and Minion (as the serif body face). To provide the symbols (, ⌘, ⏏, and so on), Phil Simpson and Julie Van Keuren designed several custom fonts using FontLab Fontographer and TypeTool 3.

The book was then exported as Adobe Acrobat PDF files for final transmission to the printing plant.

Index

Index

Dialog boxes

⌘-comma	Opens Preferences dialog box (any Apple program)
Esc	"Clicks" the Cancel button in a dialog box
Return	"Clicks" the OK button (or other blue, highlighted button) in a dialog box
Option-⌘-F	Moves the insertion point to the search box in most Apple programs
⌘-D, ⌘-R	"Clicks" the Don't Save or Replace button

Trackpad gestures

You can change many of these gestures, or turn them on and off, in the Trackpad pane of System Preferences. But here are the factory settings:

Two-finger click	Right-click
Two-finger drag up/down	Scroll up/down
Two-finger swipe left-/right	Move among open web or document pages
Two-finger swipe from right edge	Open Notification Center
Two-finger pinch or spread	Zoom in or out of a picture, PDF, or web page
Two-finger rotate	Rotate photo or PDF
Two-finger double-tap (not click)	"Smart zoom" into Safari or Preview page
Three-finger swipe up	Mission Control
Three-finger swipe down	Show all windows in this app (Exposé)
Three-finger swipe left/right	Previous/next Spaces screen or full-screen app
Three-finger drag	Move window
Three-finger tap (not click)	Look up this word in Dictionary
Four-finger pinch	Open Launchpad
Four-finger spread	Reveal desktop (Exposé)

Magic Mouse gestures

A few important gestures also work on the top surface of the Magic Mouse:

One-finger double-tap (not click)	"Smart zoom" into Safari or Preview page
Two-finger double-tap (not click)	Mission Control
One-finger swipe left-/right	Move between pages
Two-finger swipe left/right	Previous/next Spaces screen or full-screen app

Managing programs

Shift-Option-click a Dock icon	Switches to new program and hides the previous one
Option-click in a window	Switches to new program and hides the previous one
⌘-H	Hide this program's windows (works in most apps)
Option-⌘-H	Hide all *other* programs' windows (most apps)
Control-◀, ▶	Previous/next Spaces screen
F9	Exposé: Shrinks and tiles all windows in all programs
Shift-F9	Exposé: Shrinks and tiles all windows in slow motion
F10	Exposé: Shrinks and tiles all windows in frontmost program
F11	Exposé: Flings all windows in all programs to edges of screen, revealing desktop
F12	Dashboard widgets
⌘-Tab	Press and release: Switches back and forth between current and previous open programs
⌘-Tab	Hold down ⌘: Displays floating icons of open programs. Press Tab repeatedly to cycle through them. (Add Shift to cycle *backward* through open programs.)
⌘-`	Switches to next open window in this program. (Add Shift to cycle in the opposite direction.)
Option-⌘-Esc	Opens the Force Quit dialog box (to close a stuck program)
Shift-⌘-3	Captures the screen image as a PNG file on your desktop
Shift-⌘-4	Produces a crosshairs; drag to capture a selected portion of the screen as a PNG graphics file. (Press space to get the "camera" cursor that snips out just a menu, icon, or window.)
Shift-⌘-5	Opens a sophisticated set of options for screen captures
Control-space	Switches keyboard layout (if more than one is installed)

Shift-⌘-L	Library window
Shift-⌘-C	Computer window
Shift-⌘-R	AirDrop window
Shift-⌘-K	Network window
Shift-⌘-A	Applications window
Shift-⌘-G	Go to Folder
Shift-⌘-I	iCloud Drive window
Shift-⌘-U	Utilities
Option	Makes Library Command Appear
Option-⌘-L	Downloads window

Window menu

⌘-M	Minimize
Option-⌘-M	Minimize All
⌘-`	Cycle through windows

Help menu

| Shift-⌘-? | Opens help search box |

Power keys

Control-⏏	Brings up dialog box for Shut Down, Sleep, or Restart
Option-⌘-⏏	Sleep
Control-Option-⌘-⏏	Shut Down
Control-⌘-⏏	Restart

The Dock

Shift-Option-click a Dock icon	Switches to new program and hides previous one
Option-⌘-D	Hides/shows the Dock
⌘-click a Dock or Stacks icon	Reveals its actual Finder icon
Option-⌘-click a Dock icon	Switches to this program and hides all others
Control-click a Dock icon	Opens a shortcut menu
⌘-drag an icon onto a Dock icon	Prevents Dock icons from moving, so you can drop your icon onto one of them
⌘-drag a Dock icon	Drags the actual item
Option-⌘-drag an icon onto the Dock	Forces a Dock program to open the icon you're dropping on it

⌘-Delete Move to Trash

⌘-E Eject

⌘-F Find

Shift-Control-⌘-F Find by Name

Edit menu

⌘-Z Undo

Shift-⌘-Z Redo

⌘-C, ⌘-X, ⌘-V Copy, Cut, Paste

Option-⌘-V Move item here

⌘-A Select All

Option-⌘-A Deselect All

Control-⌘-space bar Open Emoji & Symbols panel

View menu

⌘-1, -2, -3, -4 Icon, list, column, gallery views

Control-⌘-1, -2, -3, -4, -5, -6, -7 Sort by Name, Kind, Date Last Opened, Date Added, Date Modified, Size, Tags

Option-⌘-1, -2, -5, -6, -7 Clean up by Name, Kind, Date Modified, Size, Tags

Shift-⌘-T Show/hide Tabs bar

Shift-⌘-P Show/hide preview pane

Option-⌘-P Show/hide Path bar

Option-⌘-S Show/hide Sidebar

⌘-/ Show/hide status bar

⌘-J Show/hide View Options palette

Control-⌘-F Full Screen mode

Go menu

⌘-[, ⌘-] Back, Forward

⌘-▲ Enclosing folder

⌘-K Connect to Server

Control-⌘-▲ Enclosing folder in new window

Shift-⌘-F Recents window

Shift-⌘-O Documents window

Shift-⌘-D Desktop window

Shift-⌘-H Home window

ᴥ Menu

Option	Changes "About This Mac" to "System Information"
Shift-⌘-Q	Logs out
Shift-Option-⌘-Q	Logs out without confirmation box

Finder menu

Option	Eliminates the confirmation box from Empty Trash
Shift-⌘-Delete	Empties the Trash
⌘-Delete	Puts back a highlighted icon now in the Trash
Shift-Option-⌘-Delete	Empties the Trash without confirmation box
Option-Empty Trash	Empties the Trash without confirmation box
⌘-comma	Opens Preferences (also works in most programs)
⌘-H	Hide this program
Option-⌘-H	Hide other programs

File menu

⌘-N	New Finder window
⌘-T	New Finder tab
Shift-⌘-N	New folder
Control-⌘-N	New folder with selection
⌘-O or ⌘-▼	Open
Control-⌘-O	Open in new window
Option-click File menu	Changes "Open With" to "Always Open With"
⌘-W	Close window
Option-⌘-W	Close All
⌘-I	Get Info
Option-⌘-I	Show Inspector
Control-⌘-I	Summary Info (of selected icons)
⌘-D	Duplicate
Control-⌘-A	Make Alias
⌘-Y	Quick Look
Option-⌘-Y	Slideshow (of selected icons)
Option-Control-⌘-A	Show Original (of alias)
Control-⌘-T	Add to Sidebar
Shift-Control-⌘-T	Add to Dock

F12, mouse down, or trackpad button down	Ejects a stuck CD or DVD
Shift	Just after you hear the startup tone: Starts up in Safe Mode (page 799)
Shift	Just after logging in: Prevents Finder windows and startup items from opening (they'll return the next time you start up)

Speech recognition

Tap fn twice	Begin "speak to type"
Hold down ⌘-space	Summon Siri

In the Finder

⌘-space	Opens Spotlight search box
▶, ◀	Expands or collapses a selected folder in list view
Option-▶	Expands a folder in a list view *and* all folders inside it
Option-◀	Collapses a folder *and* all folders inside it
⌘-▲	Opens parent folder
⌘-▼ (or ⌘-O)	Opens the selected icon
Option-click the flippy triangle	Expands or collapses all folders within that window
Tab	Selects next icon alphabetically
Shift-Tab	Selects previous icon alphabetically
space bar	Opens Quick Look preview of highlighted icon(s)
space bar	During a spring-loaded folder drag, opens the disk or folder under the mouse immediately
Option-click Zoom button	Enlarges the window (but not into Full Screen mode)
Option-click Close button	Closes all Finder windows
Option-click Minimize button	Minimizes all windows (works in most apps)
Option	Changes Quick Look button to Slideshow button
⌘-drag	Rearranges or removes menulets or toolbar icons
⌘-click window title	Opens a pop-up menu showing the folder path

The Master Secret Keystroke List

Here it is, by popular, frustrated demand: the master list of every secret (or not-so-secret) keystroke in macOS, including all the keys you can press during startup. Clip and post to your monitor (unless, of course, you got this book from the library).

Note: For the most part, the following list doesn't include the keystrokes already listed in your menus, like ⌘-P for Print, ⌘-S for Save, and so on.

Keys to hold down at startup

N	Starts up from a NetBoot server
T	Puts the Mac into Target Disk mode
D	Starts up to diagnostic or hardware test mode
Option-D	Starts up to diagnostic or hardware test mode over the internet
⌘-R	Starts Recovery Mode
Option-⌘-R	Starts up from Recovery Mode over the internet
Option	Starts up to Startup Manager, which allows you to choose a startup disk
Option-⌘-P-R	Zaps the parameter RAM (PRAM) (hold down until you hear the second chime)
⌘-V	Shows Unix console messages during startup, logout, and shutdown

Windows Messenger

MacOS's instant-messaging, audioconferencing, and videoconferencing software is called Messages, and it's described in Chapter 19.

WordPad

The TextEdit program (in the Applications folder) is a word processor along the lines of WordPad. It can even open and save Word files, as WordPad can. See page 484.

Zip files

Zip files exist on the Mac, too, and you create them almost the same way: Right-click or two-finger click a file or folder and choose Compress from the shortcut menu.

you hold down your cursor on one of these icons (or right-click it, or two-finger click it), you get a pop-up list of the open windows in that program, exactly as in Windows.

On the other hand, some conventions never die. Much as in Windows, you cycle through the various open Mac programs by holding down the ⌘ key and pressing Tab repeatedly.

This PC or (My) Computer

The Mac's Computer window (choose Go→Computer) is very similar, in that it shows the icons of all disks (hard drive, CD, and so on). On the other hand, it shows *only* the disks that are actually inserted or connected. (See "Disks.")

"Three-fingered salute"

Instead of pressing Control-Alt-Delete to jettison a stuck program, on the Mac you press Option-⌘-Esc. A Force Quit dialog box appears. Click the program you want to toss, click Force Quit, confirm your choice, and then relaunch the program to get on with your day.

Tooltips

Small, yellow identifying balloons pop up on the Mac almost as often as they do in Windows. Just point to a toolbar icon or truncated file name without clicking. (There's no way to turn these labels off.)

User Accounts control panel

Like every Windows operating system since Windows 2000, macOS was designed from Square One to be a multiuser operating system, keeping each person's files, mail, and settings separate. You set up and manage these accounts in System Preferences→Users & Groups (Chapter 12).

Windows (or WINNT) folder

MacOS's operating system resides in a folder simply called System, which sits in your main hard drive window. Exactly as in recent Windows versions, you're forbidden to add, remove, or change anything inside. Also as in Windows, most of it is invisible anyway.

Windows logo key

The Mac has no equivalent for the ⊞ key on most PC keyboards.

Windows Media Player

The Mac comes with individual programs for playing multimedia files:

- **QuickTime Player** (page 631) to play back and record movies and sounds.

- **iTunes** (page 427) to play CDs, internet radio, MP3 files, and other audio files.

Shortcuts

On the Mac, they're known as *aliases*. See page 89.

Start menu

There's no Start menu in macOS. Instead, you stash the icons of the programs, documents, and folders you use frequently onto the Dock at the edge of the screen, or into the Places section of the Sidebar at the left edge of every Finder window.

Exactly as with the Start menu, you can rearrange these icons (drag them horizontally) or remove the ones you don't use often (drag them away from the Dock and then release). To add new icons of your own, just drag them into place (applications go to the left of the Dock's divider line, documents and folders to the right).

Startup folder

To make programs launch automatically at startup, include them in the list of Login Items in the System Preferences→Accounts pane.

System control panel

The Mac has no central equivalent of the System window on a Windows PC. But its functions have analogs here:

- **Version number.** To find out your macOS version number and the amount of memory on your Mac, choose →About This Mac.

- **Computer name.** Open System Preferences, click Sharing, and edit your computer's network name here.

- **Hardware.** The closest thing the Mac has to the Device Manager is System Profiler (in your Applications→Utilities folder).

- **Advanced.** In macOS, you can't easily adjust your virtual memory, processor scheduling, or user profile information.

- **System Restore.** MacOS's Time Machine feature is like System Restore on steroids; see page 266.

- **Updates.** Open App Store→Updates.

- **Remote control.** MacOS's remote control is Screen Sharing, described starting on page 595.

Notification area

The macOS equivalent of the system tray (also called the notification area) is the row of *menulets* at the upper-right corner of your screen.

Taskbar

MacOS doesn't have a taskbar, but it does have something very close: the Dock (Chapter 4). Open programs are indicated by a small dot beneath their icons in the Dock. If

Regional and Language Options control panel

The equivalent is the Language & Region panel of System Preferences.

Registry

There is no registry. Let the celebration begin!

Run command

The Mac's command line is Terminal (page 515).

Safe Mode

You can press the Shift key during startup to suppress the loading of certain software libraries, but macOS's "safe mode" isn't quite as massively stripped down as Windows' Safe Mode.

ScanDisk

Just like Windows, the Mac automatically scans and, if necessary, repairs its hard drive every time your machine starts up. To run such a check on command, open Disk Utility (located in the Applications→Utilities folder), click the name of your hard drive, and then click the First Aid tab.

Scheduled Tasks

To schedule a task to take place unattended, use the *launchd* Unix command in Terminal (page 515), or one of the scheduling programs listed at *downloads.com*.

Scrap files

On the Mac, they're called *clipping files,* and they're even more widely compatible. You create them the same way: Drag some highlighted text, or a graphic, out of a program's window and onto the desktop. There it becomes an independent clipping file that you can drag back in—to the same window or a different one.

Screen Saver Gallery

The Mac's screen savers are impressive. Open System Preferences and click the Desktop & Screen Saver icon.

Search

In macOS, you have the ultimate file-searching tool: Spotlight (Chapter 3). Get psyched!

To find websites, use the Google search box at the top of the Safari browser.

Shortcut menus

They work exactly the same as they do in Windows. You produce a shortcut menu by right-clicking—or two-finger clicking, or Control-clicking—things like icons, list items, and so on.

Power Options

To control when your Mac goes to sleep and (if it's a laptop) how much power it uses, use the Energy Saver pane of System Preferences (page 353).

Printer Sharing

To share a USB inkjet printer with other Macs on the network, open the Sharing pane of System Preferences on the Mac with the printer. Turn on Printer Sharing.

To use the shared printer from across the network, open the document you want to print, choose File→Print, and choose the name of the shared printer from the first pop-up menu.

Printers and Faxes

For a list of your printers, open the Print & Scan pane of System Preferences. Faxing is no longer built into macOS.

PrntScrn key

You capture pictures of your Mac screen by pressing Shift-⌘-3 (for a full-screen grab) or Shift-⌘-4 (to grab a selected portion of the screen). There are many options available; see page 626.

Program Files folder

The Applications folder (Go→Applications) is like the Program Files folder in Windows—except that you're not discouraged from opening it and double-clicking things. On the Mac, every program bears its true name; Microsoft Word, for example, is called Microsoft Word, not WINWORD.EXE.

Properties dialog box

You can call up something very similar for any *icon* (file, folder, program, disk, printer) by highlighting its icon and then choosing File→Get Info. But objects in Mac *programs* generally don't contain Properties dialog boxes.

Recycle Bin

MacOS has a Trash icon at the end of the Dock. In general, it works exactly like the Windows Recycle Bin—and why not, since the Mac Trash was Microsoft's inspiration?—but there are a couple of differences. By default, the Mac never automatically empties it, for example (see page 97). That job is up to you: The simplest way is to right-click or two-finger click it, and then choose Empty Trash from the shortcut menu.

The Mac never bothers you with an "Are you sure?" message when you throw something into the Trash, either. It asks you for permission only when you choose File→Empty Trash. And you can even turn that confirmation off, if you like (in Finder→Preferences).

To put icons into the Trash, drag them there, or highlight them and then press ⌘-Delete.

Mail control panel

MacOS comes with its own email program (described in Chapter 17); all of its settings are contained within the program.

Maximize button

On the Mac, clicking the Zoom button (the green ⊗ in the upper-left corner of a window) does something like the Maximize button in Windows: It shoots that program into *Full Screen mode,* where every last pixel of screen space is put to work displaying your document (page 25).

Menus

On the Mac, there's only one menu bar, always at the very top of the screen. The menus change depending on the program and the window you're using, but the point is that the menu bar is no longer inside each window you open.

Tip: Just because you don't see the little underlines in the menus doesn't mean you can't operate all the menus from the keyboard, as in Windows. See page 206 for details.

Minimize button

You can minimize a macOS window to the Dock, just the way you would minimize a Windows window to the taskbar. You do so by double-clicking its title bar, pressing ⌘-M, choosing Window→Minimize, or clicking the yellow Minimize button at the top left of a window. (Restore the window by clicking its icon in the Dock.)

Mouse control panel

The equivalent settings can be found in the Mouse panel of System Preferences.

Network Places

On the Mac, the "network neighborhood" is almost always on the screen: It's the Sidebar, the panel at the left side of every Finder window. All the Macs and PCs on your network are always listed here, in the Shared category (unless you turned this feature off in Finder→Preferences).

Notepad

Page 446 documents the Notes app, which is far more powerful than the Notepad of old.

Personal Web Server

To find out how to turn your Mac into a state-of-the-art web server, see page 778.

Phone and Modem Options control panel

To find the modem settings for your Mac, see the free appendix to this book, "Setting Up a Dial-Up Connection," available on its "Missing CD" page at *missingmanuals.com.*

- **File Types tab.** Just as in Windows, you can reassign certain document types so that double-clicking opens them in the program of your choice. But on the Mac, you can reassign either a whole class of files at once, as in Windows, *or* one file at a time. To do it, use the Get Info window, as described on page 100.

- **Offline files.** There's no equivalent feature on the Mac.

Fonts

The Mac and Windows PCs both use TrueType, PostScript, and OpenType fonts. (In fact, your Mac can even use the exact font files you had in Windows.) On the Mac, however, there are actually three different folders that can contain them. A complete discussion starts on page 615.

Help and Support

At the desktop, choose Help→Mac Help. In other programs, the Help command is generally at the right end of your menus, exactly as in Windows.

Hibernation

On a PC, hibernation cuts all power but remembers what programs and documents you had open for a faster restart later. The Mac's Sleep mode does that automatically when it loses power or runs out of battery; see "Standby mode."

Internet Explorer

Microsoft's most famous web browser doesn't exist on the Mac—or even in Windows 10! Apple would prefer, of course, that you try Safari, its own web browser, but many a power user prefers Firefox or Chrome, which are nearly identical to the Windows versions.

Internet Options

On the Mac, you find the options for your web browser by choosing Safari→ Preferences.

Java

This interpreter of tiny web page programs is alive and well in macOS. Java programs run fine in all Mac web browsers.

Keyboard control panel

You can make exactly the same kinds of settings—and more—on the Keyboard pane of System Preferences.

Logging in

The multiple-accounts feature of macOS is extremely similar to that of Windows. In each case, you can, if you wish, create a requirement to log in with a name and password before using the computer. This arrangement keeps separate the documents, email, and settings of each person who uses the computer. Chapter 12 tells all.

DOS prompt

There's a command line in macOS, but it's Unix, not DOS. For details, see page 515.

Drivers

See "Add or Remove Programs control panel."

End Task dialog box

If some Mac program is hung up or frozen, you escape it pretty much the same way you would in Windows: by forcing it to quit. To bring up the Force Quit dialog box, press Option-⌘-Esc or choose → Force Quit.

Exiting programs

You can quit a program either by choosing Quit from the menu bearing its name (next to the menu), or by right-clicking or two-finger clicking its Dock icon and then choosing Quit from the pop-up menu.

Explorer

The Mac has its own "tree" view of the files and folders on your hard drive: list view. By expanding the "flippy triangles" of your folders, you build a hierarchy that shows you as much or as little detail as you like.

If you prefer the Explorer effect of clicking a folder in *one* pane to see its contents in the next, try column view instead. Both views are described in Chapter 1.

Favorites

In macOS, there isn't one single Favorites menu that lists both favorite websites and favorite icons. The Bookmarks menu of Safari lists only websites, and the Sidebar at the desktop (page 17) lists only favorite files, folders, disks, and other icons.

File Sharing

See Chapter 13 for an in-depth look at the Mac's networking and file-sharing system.

Folder Options

The Folder Options control panel in Windows is a collection of unrelated settings that boil down to this:

- **General tab.** Exactly as in Windows, it's up to you whether or not double-clicking a folder opens up a second window—or just changes what's in the first one. On the Mac, you make these changes using the Finder→Preferences command. There you'll find the option called "Always open folders in a new window."

- **View tab.** Most of the options here don't exist on the Mac. For example, system files are *always* hidden on the Mac; you can't opt to make them visible (at least not with the built-in controls). You can, however, choose whether you want to see the file name extensions in your desktop windows (like .doc and .html). Choose Finder→Preferences→Advanced, and turn "Show all file extensions" on or off.

Defragment and Optimize Drives

There's no such utility included with macOS; the system auto-defragments in the background. (A *defragmenting* program moves around the pieces of files on your hard drive to optimize their placement and speed of opening.)

Delete key (Forward Delete)

Most desktop Mac keyboards have a forward-delete key (labeled ⌦ or *Del*) exactly like the ones on PCs. On Mac laptops, and on Apple's aluminum keyboards, you trigger the forward-delete function by pressing the Delete key while simultaneously pressing the fn key.

Desktop

The Mac desktop is pretty much the same idea as the Windows desktop, with a few key differences:

- **You change the desktop picture** using the Desktop & Screen Saver panel of System Preferences. (Or just right-click or two-finger click the desktop.)

- **The Trash is an icon in the Dock,** not on the desktop.

Directories

Most people call them *folders* on the Mac.

Disks

Working with disks is very different on the Mac. Every disk inside, or attached to, a Mac can be represented on the screen by an icon. MacOS does have something like the This PC or My Computer window (choose Go→Computer), but the icons there reflect only the disks currently inserted in your Mac. You'll never see an icon for an empty drive, as you do in Windows, and there's no such thing as drive letters (because the Mac refers to *disks,* not to *drives*—and calls them by name).

Mojave doesn't display icons for disks on the desktop, as earlier Mac versions did—but you can bring them back by choosing Finder→Preferences→General and turning on the checkboxes for different kinds of disks.

Display control panel

The functions of the Windows Display control panel lurk in the macOS System Preferences program—just not all in one place. You set up your desktop picture and screen saver using the Desktop & Screen Saver pane and adjust your monitor settings using the Displays pane. (MacOS offers no equivalent to the Appearance tab in Windows, for changing the system-wide look of your computer.)

(My) Documents, (My) Music, (My) Pictures

The equivalent buckets for your everyday documents, music files, and pictures are the Documents, Music, and Pictures folders in your Home folder.

right-clicking or two-finger clicking its desktop icon and then choosing Eject from the shortcut menu.

Character Map

This Windows program helps you find out what keys you need to press to trigger trademark symbols, copyright symbols, and other special characters. The equivalent on the Mac is called the Character Viewer (page 250).

Clean Install

The macOS installer can give you a fresh copy of the operating system, just as the Windows installer can. Instructions are in Appendix A.

Clipboard

The Mac's Clipboard works much like the one in Windows. In the Finder, you can choose Edit→Show Clipboard to see whatever you most recently copied or cut.

Command line

In macOS, the command line is alive and well—but it speaks Unix, not DOS. You get to it by opening Terminal; see page 515.

Control Panel

The Control Panel in macOS is called System Preferences, and you open it from your menu. As in Windows, you can view these icons either by category or in a simple alphabetical list: Just choose either Organize by Categories or Organize Alphabetically from the View menu.

Copy, Cut, Paste

When you're editing in a word processor or graphics program, the macOS Cut, Copy, and Paste commands work exactly as they do in Windows.

At the desktop, however, there are a few differences. You can indeed copy icons and paste them into a new window using the Copy and Paste commands—but *cutting* them out of a window, as you can in Windows, works differently: After you've copied the icons from the first window, open the destination window. Then press the Option key, open the Edit menu, and choose Move Items Here.

Ctrl key

On the Mac, you generally substitute the ⌘ key in keystrokes that would involve the Ctrl key in Windows. In other words, the Save command is now ⌘-S instead of Ctrl+S, Open is ⌘-O instead of Ctrl+O, and so on.

Date and Time

To set your Mac's calendar and clock, open Date & Time in System Preferences.

Add or Remove Programs control panel

Here's another one you just don't need on the Mac. Installing a program onto the Mac is described starting on page 165. Removing a program simply involves dragging its icon to the Trash. (For a clean sweep, inspect your Home→Library→Preferences and Library→Application Support folders to see if any preference files got left behind.)

All Programs

There's no Programs menu built into macOS, like the one on the Windows Start menu. If you'd like one, drag your Applications folder onto the end of the Dock. Now its icon is a tidy pop-up menu of every program on your machine.

Alt key

On the Mac, it's the Option key, although the key usually says "Alt" on it, too. (In some countries, it says *only* "Alt.") You can substitute Option for Alt in any keystroke in most popular programs. The Option key has a number of secondary features on the Mac, too: It hides the windows of one program when you click into another, and so on.

Automatic Update

The App Store's automatic updates feature does exactly the same thing (page 165).

Backspace key

It's in the same place on the Mac keyboard, but it's called Delete.

BIOS

You'll never have to update or even think about the ROM of your Mac (the approximate equivalent of the BIOS on the PC). It's permanent and unchanging. The very similar *firmware* of your Mac does occasionally have to be updated in order to work with a new version of the Mac operating system or some dramatic new feature—once every four years, perhaps. You'll be notified on the screen when the time comes.

Calculator

The Calculator program in macOS is almost identical to the one in Windows, except that it can also perform conversions (temperature, distance, currency, and so on) and features an editable "paper tape." It sits in your Applications folder and is described starting on page 394. (And don't forget that you can type quick math equations into the ⌕ Spotlight box.)

Camera and Scanner Wizard

When you connect a digital camera or scanner to your Mac, Photos opens and prepares to download the pictures automatically.

CDs and DVDs

In the unlikely event that you've outfitted your Mac with an external disc drive, you spit out the disc that's in it by holding down the ⏏ key on your Mac keyboard, or by

The Windows-to-Mac Dictionary

Maybe you were convinced by the old Apple "Switch" ad campaign. Maybe you like the looks of today's Macs. Or maybe you've just endured one virus, spyware download, or service pack too many. In any case, if you're switching to macOS from Windows, this appendix is for you. It's an alphabetical listing of every common Windows function and where to find it in macOS. After all, an operating system is an operating system. The actual functions are pretty much the same—they're just in different places.

About [this program]

To find out the version number of the program you're using, don't look in the Help menu. Instead, look in the *application* menu next to the menu—the one that bears the name of the program you're in. That's where you find the About command for Mac programs.

Accessibility Options control panel

The special features that let you operate the computer even with impaired vision, hearing, or motor control are called "Accessibility" in macOS. They're in System Preferences (see Chapter 9).

Add Hardware control panel

The Mac requires no program for installing the driver for a new external gadget. The drivers for most printers, mice, keyboards, cameras, camcorders, and other accessories are preinstalled. If you plug something into the Mac and find that it doesn't work immediately, just install the driver from the manufacturer's website.

another to be patched in the next pass. Type *fsck -y* a second time, a third time, and so on, until you finally arrive at a "volume appears to be OK" message.

Type *exit* at the prompt and press Return to get back to the familiar world of icons and windows.

Where to Get Troubleshooting Help

If the basic steps described in this appendix haven't helped, the universe is crawling with additional help sources. Apple's Support website is a great one. But the truth is, you'll find more answers faster using Google than you ever will using individual help sites. That's because Google *includes* all those help sites in its search!

Suppose, for example, that you've just installed the 10.14.2 software update, and it's mysteriously turned all your accounts into Standard ones. You could go to one website after another, hunting for a fix, repeating your search—or you could just type *Mojave 10.14.2 standard accounts* into Google. You'll get your answers after just a few seconds of clicking and exploring the results.

Help Online

These websites contain nothing but troubleshooting discussions, tools, and help:

- **Apple Discussion Groups** (*discussions.apple.com*). The volume and quality of question-and-answer activity here dwarfs any other free source. If you're polite and concise, you can post questions to the multitudes and get more replies from them than you'll know what to do with.

- **Apple's help site** (*apple.com/support*). Apple's site includes downloadable manuals, software updates, frequently asked questions, and many other resources.

 Its search box is your ticket to the Knowledge Base, a collection of 100,000 technical articles that Apple technicians themselves consult when answering calls for help.

Help by Telephone

Finally, consider contacting whoever sold you the component that's making your life miserable: the printer company, scanner company, software company, or whatever.

If it's a macOS problem, you can call Apple at 800-275-2273 (that's 800-APL-CARE). For the first 90 days after your installation of macOS, the technicians will answer your questions for free.

After that, unless you've paid for AppleCare for your Mac (a three-year extended-warranty program), Apple will charge you to answer questions. Fortunately, if the problem turns out to be Apple's fault, they won't charge you.

same thing. And because it's contained in a macOS-style window, Terminal is not as disorienting as the three methods you're about to read about.

All these techniques take you into *console mode,* shown in Figure B-4. In console mode, Unix takes over your screen completely, showing white type against black, no windows or icons in sight. Abandon the mouse, all ye who enter here; in console mode, you can't do anything but type commands.

Figure B-4:
In console mode, your entire screen is a command line interface. Unix jockeys can go to town here. Everyone else can timidly type fsck -y after the local-host# prompt—see this prompt on the very last line?—and hope for the best.

```
Found old device 0x0cdea00
IOFireWireDevice,  ROM unchanged 0x0xcdea00
IOFireWireDevice, 0x0xcdea00,  ROM generation zero
Got boot device =
IOService:/Core99PE/pc@f20000000/AppleMacRiscPCI/mac-
io@17/KeyLargo/ata-4@1f000/KeyLargoATA/ATADeviceNub@0/IOA
TABlockStorageDriver/IOATABlockStorageDevice/IOBlockStorageDr
iver/QUANTUM FIREBALL CX13.6A
Media/IOApplePartitionScheme/Untitled
@9
BSD root: disk0s9, major  14,  minor  9
Rereading ROM up to 25 quads
devfs on /dev
USB:    4.947: AppleUSBKeyboard[0xDOE80014::start    USB  Generic
Keyboard @ 3 (0x18110000)
Mon Nov 19 23:18:53 EST 2001
Singleuser boot -- fsck not done
Root device is mounted read-only
If you want to make modifications  to files,
run '/sbin/fsck  -y' first and then '/sbin/mount  -uw/'
localhost#
```

To get there in times of startup troubleshooting, press ⌘-S while the Mac is starting up. (If you're stuck at the frozen remnants of a previous startup attempt, you may first have to force-restart your Mac; hold down the ⏻ button for five seconds.)

Instead of arriving at the usual desktop, you see technical-looking text scrolling up a black screen as the Mac runs its various startup routines. When it finally stops at the *localhost#* prompt, you're ready to type commands. You're now in what's called *single-user mode,* meaning that the Unix multiple-accounts software has yet to load. You won't be asked to log in.

At the *root#* prompt, type *fsck -y* (note the space before the hyphen) and press Return. (The *y* means "yes," as in "Yes, I want you to fix any problems automatically.")

Now the file-system check program takes over, running through five sets of tests. When it's complete, you'll see one of two messages:

- **The volume Macintosh HD appears to be OK.** All is well. Type *exit* and press Return to proceed to the usual Login screen and desktop.

- **File system was modified.** A good sign, but just a beginning. You need to run the program again. One *fsck* pass often repairs only one layer of problems, leaving

Method 1: Disk Utility

The easiest way to check your disk is to use the Disk Utility program. Use this method if your Mac can, indeed, start up. (See Method 2 if you can't get even that far.)

For best results, restart the Mac into Recovery Mode and run Disk Utility from there. The process goes like this:

1. **Start up the Mac from the Recovery HD or a recovery flash drive.**

 They're both described earlier in this appendix. You wind up, after some time, at the Utilities screen.

2. **Click "Disk Utility: Repair or erase a disk using Disk Utility."**

 After a moment, the Disk Utility screen appears.

3. **Click the disk or disk partition you want to fix, click the First Aid button, and then click Run.**

 The Mac whirls into action, checking a list of very technical disk-formatting parameters.

If you see the message "The volume 'Macintosh HD' appears to be OK," that's meant to be *good* news. Believe it or not, that cautious statement is as definitive an affirmation as Disk Utility is capable of making about the health of your disk.

Disk Utility may also tell you that the disk is damaged but that it can't help you. In that case, you need a more heavy-duty disk-repair program like DiskWarrior (*alsoft.com*).

Method 2: *fsck* at the Console

Techier folk can boot into the Mac's raw Unix underlayer to perform some diagnostic (and healing) commands.

Specifically, you can run the Unix program *fsck*, for which Disk Utility is little more than a pretty faceplate.

Note: Even so, Apple recommends you use Disk Utility if at all possible. Use *fsck* only if all else fails.

Like any Unix program, *fsck* runs at the command line. You launch it from the all-text, black Unix screen by typing *fsck* and pressing Return. (You can also use *fsck -f.*)

You can't, however, just run *fsck* in Terminal. You have to run it when the usual arsenal of graphic-interface programs—like the Finder and its invisible suite of accessory programs—isn't running.

Single-user mode (⌘-S at startup)

The Terminal program is the best-known form of macOS's command line, but it's not the only one. In fact, there are several other ways to get there.

In general, you don't hear them mentioned except in the context of troubleshooting, because the Terminal program offers many more convenient features for doing the

- **Your Mac creates these snapshots** only if there's enough disk space.

- **The Mac deletes every snapshot** after 24 hours.

OK? Then here's how you perform the rewind:

1. **Start up the Mac in Recovery mode.**

 That is, press ⌘-R as it's starting up, so that you see the dialog box shown in Figure B-3 at bottom.

2. **Click Restore From Time Machine Backup. Hit Continue, and then Continue.**

 "But wait!" you protest. "I don't have a Time Machine backup! I don't have a backup drive! I never turned it on!"

 Never you mind. You're going to restore from one of those *local* snapshots.

3. **On the Select a Restore Source screen, click your startup drive; click Continue.**

 Now you see a list of the automatic snapshots your Mac has created. There's probably only one.

4. **Click the most recent snapshot; click Continue. In the "Are you sure?" box, click Continue again.**

 The restoring process takes a few minutes. When it's over, the Mac restarts—and you're back in business.

Fixing the Disk

The beauty of macOS's design is that the operating system itself is frozen in its perfect, pristine state, impervious to conflicting system extensions, clueless Mac newbies, and other sources of disaster.

That's the theory, anyway. But what happens if something goes wrong with the complex software that operates the hard drive itself?

Fortunately, macOS comes with its own disk-repair program. In the familiar Mac universe of icons and menus, it takes the form of a program in Applications→ Utilities called Disk Utility. In the barren world of Terminal and the command line interface, there's a utility that works just as well but bears a different name: *fsck* (for file system check).

In any case, running Disk Utility or its alter ego *fsck* is a powerful and useful troubleshooting tool that can cure all kinds of strange ills, including these problems:

- **Your Mac freezes during startup,** either before or after the Login screen.

- **The startup process interrupts itself** with the appearance of the text-only command line.

- **You get the "applications showing up as folders" problem.**

Now your Mac downloads a disk image containing just enough software to get you to the Utilities screen described in the previous section.

Note: Once you're up and running, you can re-download the copies of Photos, iMovie, and GarageBand that came with your Mac. Just open the App Store program, log in with your Apple ID, click Purchases, and click Accept to download those iLife programs. You won't be charged for them.

Physical Recovery Disks

But what if the hard drive is so sick that you can't start up from the Recovery HD—*and* your Mac isn't new enough to offer the Internet Recovery feature? (Or what if it *does* offer that feature, but you'd rather repair your Mac a quicker way?)

The solution is to build yourself a bootable macOS flash drive or hard drive, as described on page 793. Not only is it capable of starting up or reinstalling macOS, but it also has a complete set of recovery tools on board.

To use this emergency disk, hold down the Option key as the Mac starts up. You wind up at the Startup Manager screen shown in Figure B-3, top. From the pop-up menu, choose your Wi-Fi hotspot.

Now click the up-arrow button below the Recovery HD icon. (You may even see *two* Recovery HD icons—one of them is the USB flash drive, and the other is the invisible partition on your hard drive. Either one works.) Your Mac is starting up from the flash drive! After a moment, you wind up at the Utilities screen described previously.

Note: The recovery flash drive you made will work only on the Mac model you used to make it.

Use a Local Snapshot to Rewind Your OS

If you have a laptop, you have a secret safety net: MacOS has been quietly creating an hourly backup snapshot *of* the startup drive, *on* the startup drive (page 270). In case of disaster, you can open Time Machine and recover any file you've deleted or destroyed, even if you're on the road and far from any external backup drive.

But macOS Mojave offers a safety net: It also creates a snapshot of your drive's contents every time you install a macOS update—from 10.14.1 to 10.14.2, for example. If it turns out that the new version does something bad to your Mac, you can rewind the whole thing to its previous (10.14.1) condition.

Tip: You can also force the Mac to create a local snapshot, on command. Open Terminal (page 515), type *sudo tmutil snapshot*, and press Return.

Here's the fine print:

- **Mojave creates these snapshots** only of APFS-formatted drives (that is, solid-state, or SSD, drives—like the one in every Mac laptop).

Tip: Remember how all of this started? You pressed ⌘-R to open the Recovery screen?

At this point, the "Reinstall macOS" routine will reinstall whatever macOS version you already had. But if you press *Option-*⌘-R to begin this process instead, you'll upgrade to the latest macOS version that your Mac can handle. And if you press *Shift*-Option-⌘-R, you'll install whatever OS came on your Mac originally. Those Apple engineers think of everything, don't they?

- **Get Help Online.** This option opens your Safari web browser, which presents you with some helpful information about using the Recovery Mode that you've fired up. You're actually online at this point, so you can also visit any other website you might find helpful.

 Quit Safari when you're finished browsing; you return to the main macOS Utilities window.

- **Disk Utility.** Use this option to open Disk Utility, the Mac's hard drive diagnostics-and-repair program. You can use it to check, fix, erase, or partition any of your hard drives. For example, you can repair the main startup disk, which is often the most useful option.

Those are the big-ticket items, but don't miss the menu bar. The commands here let you open the Firmware Password Utility (page 542), Network Utility (page 516), and Terminal (page 515).

Internet Recovery

OK, the Recovery HD concept is clever. And most of the time, it's all you need.

But what if your hard drive is *completely* hosed? What then, smart guy? You can't very well boot up from the Recovery HD if it's sitting on the same dead hard drive.

Or what if you've just installed a brand-new, bigger, or faster hard drive? It doesn't have macOS on it. It doesn't have Recovery HD on it. How are you supposed to install Mojave?

In those situations, recent Mac models—those released in 2011 and later—offer an even cleverer option: Internet Recovery. This mode offers the same exact options that the Utilities screen of Recovery HD would have—but you're connecting to that software *online,* over a high-speed internet connection. You're literally starting up from *Apple's* hard drives, perhaps thousands of miles away.

So even if your hard drive is dead as a doornail, you can still repair it, reinstall macOS, and get on with your life.

To fire up Internet Recovery, make sure your computer is in a Wi-Fi hotspot or connected to an Ethernet network. Then hold down ⌘-R as the computer is starting up. You can let go when you see the screen that asks you to choose a Wi-Fi network. Do that, and then enter the password for the network, if necessary.

macOS itself—from the Time Machine backup you carefully set up as you read Chapter 6.

This option *completely erases* your existing hard drive, so—you know. Be sure.

Once you choose this option, click Continue. You're now asked to choose the Time Machine drive, then the time-stamped backup you want to restore from and, finally, the drive or partition you want to wipe out. You get one more warning that you're about to wipe out the destination drive. When you click Continue, the restoration begins. When it's all over—usually a couple of hours later—the Mac restarts as though nothing ever happened.

Figure B-3:
Top: This simple display of disk icons is known as the Startup Manager. It's an easy way to specify which disk you want to start up from.

Bottom: Here's the point of the Recovery HD partition: a screen full of emergency utilities that can fix your Mac's regularly scheduled hard drive. If there's a pop-up menu at the bottom, it's for choosing a Wi-Fi hotspot so you can access the rest of your network. That might be useful when, for example, you want to access your Time Machine backups.

- **Reinstall macOS.** You can use this option to install a copy of macOS onto any hard drive—for example, you could reinstall it on your main internal drive. This option will download the actual copy of Mojave from the internet—all 5 gigabytes of it. In other words, it requires an internet connection and patience.

Gray Screen During Startup

Confirm that your Mac has the latest firmware, as described earlier. Detach and test all your non-Apple add-ons. Finally, perform a disk check (read on).

Forgotten Password

If you or one of the other people who use your Mac have forgotten the corresponding account password, no worries: Just read the box on page 545.

Recovery Mode: Three Emergency Disks

When your Mac won't even start up, there's no DVD to insert as a backup startup disk. That's a scary place to be; if your hard drive is sick, then everything on it may be inaccessible to you. What you need is an emergency drive that can repair the hard drive and get you back in operation.

Apple is way ahead of you on this one. It offers *three* simulated repair disks: three ways to repair disks and system software in times of crisis.

The Recovery HD

Here's the sneaky surprise: When you install Mojave, it automatically creates an invisible hidden "hard drive" (a partition of your main drive that has its own icon) called Recovery HD. It's a 650-megabyte "drive" that's generally invisible to you. It's also invisible to Disk Utility, so even if you erase your hard drive, the Recovery HD is still there to help you.

But if you can't seem to start up your Mac properly, or if your hard drive is acting a little flaky, you'll be glad you have this "separate" startup disk. On it, Apple has provided some emergency tools for fixing drive or software glitches, restoring files, browsing the web, and even reinstalling macOS.

Note: The macOS installer creates the Recovery HD partition only if your startup drive is an internal drive. In certain other situations, it won't create the partition—for example, if you're installing macOS onto a RAID volume or one with a non-standard Boot Camp partition setup.

You can power up your Mac from the Recovery HD in either of two ways:

- **Hold down ⌘-R as the Mac is starting up.** You can let go when the Apple logo appears.

- **Hold down the Option key as the Mac is starting up.** When you see the Startup Manager (Figure B-3, top), let go. Click the up-arrow button below the Recovery HD icon.

Either way, you wind up at the Utilities screen shown in Figure B-3, bottom.

Here Apple has supplied you with four important tools:

- **Restore From Time Machine Backup.** If your Mac is really hosed, then this is the option you want. It restores your *entire* software world—programs, data, settings,

- **Brought up the Login screen.** When you do a safe boot, you must click your name and enter your password, even if you normally have Automatic Login turned on.

- **Turned off noncritical kernel extensions (drivers).** All kinds of software nuggets load during the startup process. Some of them you choose yourself, like icons you add to the Login Items list in the System Preferences→Accounts pane. Others are normally hidden, including a large mass of *kernel extensions*, which are chunks of software that add various features to the basic operating system. (Kernel extensions live in your System→Library→Extensions folder.)

 If you're experiencing startup crashes, some non-Apple installer may have given you a kernel extension that doesn't care for macOS 10.14—so in Safe Mode, they're all turned off.

- **Turned off your fonts.** Corrupted fonts are a chronic source of trouble—and because you can't tell by looking, they're darned difficult to diagnose. So just to make sure you can at least get into your computer, Safe Mode turns them all off (except the authorized, Apple-sanctioned ones that macOS needs to run, which are in your System→Library→Fonts folder).

- **Trashed your font cache.** The font cache is a speed trick. MacOS stores the visual information for each of your fonts on the hard drive so the system won't have to read every single typeface off your hard drive when you open your Font menus or the Fonts panel.

 When these files get scrambled, startup crashes can result. That's why a Safe Boot moves all these files into the Trash. (You'll even see them sitting there in the Trash after the startup process is complete, although there's not much you can do with them except hold your nose and point.)

- **Turned off your login items.** Safe Mode also prevents any Finder windows from opening *and* prevents your own handpicked startup items from opening—that is, whatever you've asked your Mac to auto-open by adding them to the System Preferences→Accounts→Login Items list.

 This, too, is a troubleshooting tactic. If some login item crashes your Mac every time it opens, you can squelch it just long enough to remove it from your Login Items list.

Tip: If you don't hold down the Shift key until you click the Log In button (after entering your name and password at the Login screen), then you disable your login items but *not* the fonts and extensions.

Once you reach the desktop, some standard features may be inoperable. (The next time you restart, all this goodness will be restored, assuming you're no longer clutching the Shift key in a sweaty panic.)

In any case, the beauty of Safe Mode is that it lets you get your Mac going. You have access to your files, so at least the emergency of crashing-on-startup is over. And you can start picking through your fonts and login items to see if you can spot the problem.

Tip: This advice goes for your Mac itself. Apple periodically updates the Mac's *own* "drivers" in the form of a *firmware update*. You download these updates from the Support area of Apple's website (if indeed macOS's own Software Update mechanism doesn't alert you to their existence).

Figure B-2:
A kernel panic is almost always related to some piece of add-on hardware. And look at the bright side: At least you get this handsome dialog box. That's a lot better than the OS X 10.0 and 10.1 effect: random text gibberish superimposing itself on your screen.

> You need to restart your computer. Hold down the Power button for several seconds or press the Restart button.
>
> Veuillez redémarrer votre ordinateur. Maintenez la touche de démarrage enfoncée pendant plusieurs secondes ou bien appuyez sur le bouton de réinitialisation.
>
> Sie müssen Ihren Computer neu starten. Halten Sie dazu die Einschalttaste einige Sekunden gedrückt oder drücken Sie die Neustart-Taste.
>
> コンピュータを再起動する必要があります。パワーボタンを数秒間押し続けるか、リセットボタンを押してください。

There's one other cause for kernel panics, by the way, and that's moving, renaming, or changing the access permissions for macOS's essential system files and folders—the Applications or System folder, for example. (See page 578 for more on permissions.) This cause isn't even worth mentioning, though, because nobody would be that foolish.

Safe Mode (Safe Boot)

In times of troubleshooting, Windows fans press an F-key to start up in Safe Mode. That's how you turn off all nonessential system-software nubbins in an effort to get a sick machine at least powered up.

Although not one person in a hundred knows it, macOS offers the same kind of emergency keystroke. It can come in handy when you've just installed some new piece of software and find that you can't even start up the machine, or when one of your fonts is corrupted, or when something you've designated as a login item turns out to be gumming up the works. With this trick, you can at least turn on the computer so you can uninstall the cranky program.

The trick is to *press the Shift key* as the machine is starting up. Hold it down from the startup chime until you see the words "Safe Boot," in red lettering, on the Login screen.

Welcome to Safe Mode.

What have you accomplished?

- **Checked your hard drive.** The Shift-key business makes the startup process seem to take a very long time; as the progress bar suggests, macOS is actually scanning your entire hard drive for problems.

Here are the different ways you can go about *force-quitting* a stuck program (the equivalent of pressing Ctrl+Alt+Delete in Windows), in increasing order of desperation:

- **Force-quit the usual way.** Choose → Force Quit to terminate the stuck program, or use one of the other force-quit methods described on page 177.

- **Force-quit the sneaky way.** Some programs, including the Dock, don't show up at all in the usual Force Quit dialog box. Your next attempt, therefore, should be to open the Activity Monitor program (in Applications→Utilities), which shows *everything* that's running. Double-click a program and then, in the resulting dialog box, click Quit to force-quit it. (Unix hounds: You can also use the *kill* command in Terminal.)

- **Force-quit remotely.** If the Finder itself has locked up, you can't very well get to Activity Monitor (unless it occurred to you *beforehand* to stash its icon in your Dock—not a bad idea). At this point, you may have to abort the locked program from another computer across the network, if you're on one, by using the *SSH* (secure shell) command. Page 776 offers a blow-by-blow description of how you might terminate a program by remote control in this way, either from elsewhere on the office network or even from across the internet.

Tip: If all of this seems like a lot to remember, you can always force-restart the Mac. On most Macs, you do that by holding down the power button for five seconds. If that doesn't work, press Control-⌘-power button.

Startup Problems

Not every problem you encounter is related to running applications. Sometimes trouble strikes before you even get that far. The following are examples.

Kernel Panic

When you see the cheerful, multilingual dialog box shown in Figure B-2, you've got yourself a *kernel panic*—a Unix nervous breakdown.

(In such situations, *user panic* might be the more applicable term, but that's programmers for you.)

If you experience a kernel panic, it's almost always the result of a *hardware* glitch— most often a bad memory (RAM) board, but possibly an accelerator card, graphics card, or USB hub that macOS doesn't like. A bad USB or FireWire cable can bring on a kernel panic, too.

If simply restarting the machine doesn't help, then detach every shred of gear that didn't come from Apple. Restore these components to the Mac one at a time until you find out which one was causing macOS's bad hair day. If you're able to pinpoint the culprit, then visit its manufacturer (or its website) on a quest for updated drivers, or at least try to find out for sure whether the add-on is compatible with macOS.

problem program. Is the problem gone? If so, then the glitch exists only when *you* are logged in—which means it's a problem with *your* copy of the program's preferences.

Return to your account. Open your Home→Library→Preferences folder, where you'll find neatly labeled preference files for all the programs you use. (To open the hidden Library folder, press the Option key as you open the Go menu; choose Library.)

Each preference file ends with the file name suffix .plist. For example, *com.apple.finder.plist* is the Finder's preference file, *com.apple.dock.plist* is the Dock's, and so on.

Put the suspect preference file into the Trash, but don't empty the Trash. The next time you run the recalcitrant program, it will build itself a brand-new preference file that, if you're lucky, lacks whatever corruption was causing your problems.

If not, quit the program. You can reinstate its original .plist file from the Trash, if you find that helpful as you pursue your troubleshooting agenda.

Remember, however, that you actually have *two* Preferences folders. In addition to your own Home folder's stash, there's a second one in the Library folder in the main hard drive window (which administrators are allowed to trash; this one contains system-wide preferences, like your network·configuration).

In any case, the next time you open the sick program or log in, the Mac creates fresh, virginal preference files.

Fourth Resort: Restart

Sometimes you can give macOS or its programs a swift kick by restarting the Mac. It's an inconvenient step, but not nearly as time-consuming as what comes next. And it can fix problems that cropped up when you started the computer.

Last Resort: Trash and Reinstall the Program

Sometimes reinstalling the problem program clears up whatever the glitch was.

First, however, throw away all traces of it. Open the Applications folder and drag the program's icon (or its folder) to the Trash. In most cases, the only remaining pieces to discard are its .plist file (or files) in your Home→Library→Preferences folder, and any scraps bearing the program's name in your Library→Application Support folder. (You can do a quick search to round up any other pieces.)

Then reinstall the program from its original disk or installer—after first checking the company's website to see if there's an updated version, of course.

Frozen Programs (Force-Quitting)

The occasional unresponsive application has become such a part of macOS life that, among the Mac cognoscenti online, the dreaded, endless "please wait" cursor has been given its own acronym: SBOD (spinning beachball of death). When the SBOD strikes, no amount of mouse clicking and keyboard pounding will get you out of the insubordinate program.

Minor Eccentric Behavior

All kinds of glitches may befall you, occasionally, in macOS. A menu doesn't open when you click it. A program doesn't open—it just bounces in the Dock a couple of times and then stops. A program freezes.

When a single program is acting up like this, but quitting and restarting it does no good, try the following steps, in the following sequence.

First Resort: Repair the Disk

An amazing number of mysterious glitches arise because of tiny file corruptions on your hard drive.

When something doesn't seem to be working right, therefore, open your Applications→Utilities folder and open Disk Utility. Proceed as shown in Figure B-1.

This is a really, *really* great trick to know.

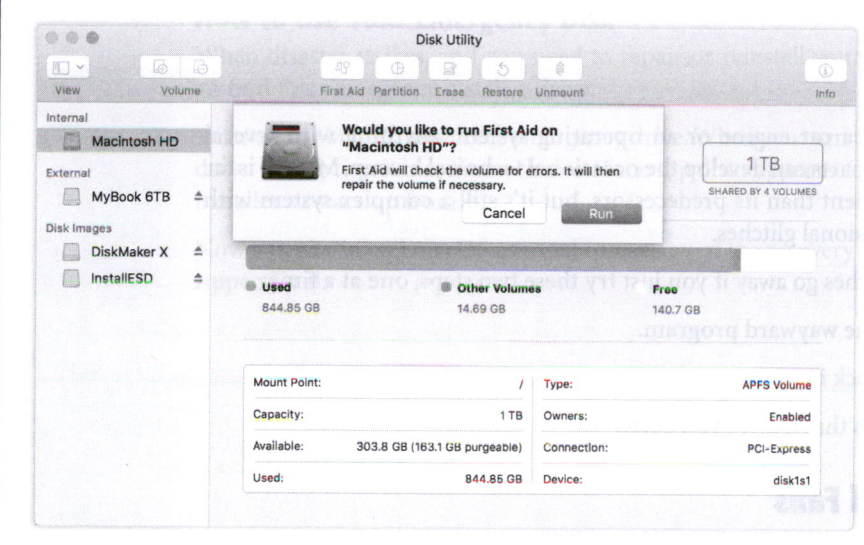

Figure B-1:
Click your hard drive's name in the left-side list, click the First Aid button, click Run, and then read an article while the Mac checks out your disk.

Second Resort: Look for an Update

If a program starts acting up immediately after you've installed macOS 10.14, chances are good that it has some minor incompatibility. Chances are also good that you'll find an updated version on the company's website.

Third Resort: Toss the Prefs File

A corrupted preference file can bewilder the program that depends on it.

Before you go on a dumpfest, however, try this simple test: Log in using a *different account* (perhaps a dummy account that you create just for testing purposes). Run the

- **Sign In with Your Apple ID.** Here you're offered the chance to type in an Apple ID (an email address and password for all your Apple dealings), which is more essential in Mojave than ever before. If you don't have one, just click Continue; you can get one and fill it in later.

Note: You'll be asked to enter a six-digit code sent to your phone. That's part of Apple's two-factor authentication process described on page 551.

- **Terms and Conditions.** Hello, Apple lawyers!

- **Create a Computer Account.** You're about to create your *account*—your Administrator account, in fact, as described on page 524.

 This is also where you can choose an account picture for yourself. Click the round starter icon, and then choose Defaults (an assortment of Apple-supplied images) or Camera (take a photo of yourself to use as your account icon).

- **iCloud Keychain.** Want Apple to memorize all your passwords (for the web and for networking), so that you don't have to reenter them on multiple gadgets (Mac, iPhone, iPad, and so on)? Then turn on iCloud Keychain and hit Continue. Your other Apple gadgets will suddenly sprout a confirmation box to prove that you're the owner of them all.

- **Express Setup.** Turn on Siri, let Apple know your location (for use by Maps and other features), and share crash data with Apple. If you're opposed, then click Customize Settings to deny or approve these one at a time.

- **All your files in iCloud.** Do you want to keep your Desktop and Documents folders online? It's a complicated question; see page 224.

- **FileVault Disk Encryption.** See page 554.

- **Touch ID.** If your laptop has a fingerprint sensor, here's where you train it to recognize yours.

- **Choose your look.** Do you want Dark Mode? (See page 158.)

At last you wind up at the macOS desktop, just as described in Chapter 1.

The Homemade Installer Disk

MacOS's download-only shtick is incredibly convenient. But sometimes you'll miss having a physical disk with the installer on it. You might wish you had one if, for example, you want to install Mojave on a huge array of Macs, like the ones at a school or in a business; downloading that 5-gig installer over and over again would drive you crazy.

You might also wish you had an installation disk for when your Mac starts acting up and the tricks described in Appendix B don't seem to work.

• **Transfer Information to This Mac.** The Setup Assistant can suck all your old programs, files, folders, and settings from the old Mac to the new one—or even from an old *Windows PC* to your new Mac. Meet the Migration Assistant.

Your choices here are From another Mac (connect your old Mac to this one over a network, even a wireless one); From a Windows PC (ditto); From Time Machine or other disk (connect your new Mac to your backup drive); and Don't Transfer now.

Tip: You can always perform this sluggish task later. Just open the Migration Assistant program, in your Applications→Utilities folder, when it's a better time. See the box below for more on migrating from Windows.

If you choose one of the first options and then click Transfer, the data-copying process begins. It can take a *wicked* long time.

GEM IN THE ROUGH

Windows Migration

If, on the Transfer Information screen of the Setup Assistant, you choose From a Windows PC, then you're treated to an unsung hero in macOS: the Windows Migration tool. It's an automatic tool that copies all your important data from a Windows PC (running Windows XP SP3 or later) to your Mac.

When all is said and done, it transfers your email into Mail from Outlook or Windows Live Mail accounts (POP or IMAP); your address book into Contacts from Outlook contacts and Windows Contacts from the Contacts home folder on your PC; your calendar into Calendar from Outlook's calendar; your iTunes collection from iTunes on Windows into iTunes for the Mac; everything in your Windows Home folder into the corresponding Mac folders (Music, Pictures, Desktop, Documents, and Downloads); your browser bookmarks and home page into Safari from Explorer, Firefox, and Safari for Windows; and your account settings like language and even your desktop wallpaper.

All of this winds up in a *new* account on your Mac. The migration program doesn't make any attempt to *merge* your Windows world into your existing account on the Mac.

For this to work, your Windows PC and Mac have to be on the same network; see Chapter 13. To begin, you'll need the free Windows Migration Assistant program. It's waiting at *apple.com/migrate-to-mac.* On your PC, download, install, and then open this program. Click Continue.

The steps now depend on how you arrived at the Transfer Your Information screen on the Mac.

If you're in the process of installing Mojave: Click From a Windows PC and then click OK. Click your PC's name and then click OK.

If you're doing this later, using the Migration Assistant program in your Mac's Applications→Utilities folder: On the Mac, quit all programs. Click "From another Mac, PC, Time Machine backup, or other disk" and then click Continue. Authenticate yourself, and then click "From another Mac or PC." Click Continue; click the PC's name.

No matter how you got here: When the six-digit passcode appears on the Mac and PC screens, click Continue again.

After a while, the Mac shows you a list of all the stuff it can bring over from the PC. Turn on the ones you care about, and then click Continue.

The transfer may take a *long* time. When you finally start up your Mac again, you're asked to provide a name and password for the new account that the Migration Assistant created for your Windows-world-on-the-Mac. (If you didn't *want* your Windows stuff to wind up in a different account, you can always copy it back into your main account using the Users→Shared folder as a tunnel between the two accounts.)

4. **Click Install. Enter an administrator's account name and password (page 524) when you're asked for it.**

 Now you're in for a 15- to 20-minute wait as the installer copies software onto your hard drive. (That's why, if you're using a laptop, the Mac will encourage you to plug it in.) At one point, the installer restarts the Mac and carries right on.

MacOS 10.14 is now installed on your Mac. That, if you hadn't noticed, was a far less harrowing experience than it was in some previous operating system installations. You were never asked what kind of installation you wanted, which language translations or printer drivers you wanted installed, which optional components you wanted, and so on.

Still, you're not quite ready to dive in yet. Read on.

The Setup Assistant

What you see depends on whether you installed Mojave onto an older macOS drive or an empty drive. Either way, it's called the Setup Assistant, and it's meant to interview you about which features you'd like turned on.

TROUBLESHOOTING MOMENT

Journaling

If your Mac has a solid-state drive (SSD), it gets automatically formatted with the new Apple File System (page 505).

If you have a traditional hard drive, though, or if you're setting up an external drive, you're offered a choice of several formats for it. But you should stick with the factory setting, "Mac OS Extended (Journaled)." It turns on a special background feature of macOS known as *file journaling*.

When file journaling is turned on, your Mac keeps a personal diary of everything you do on your hard drive—opening, saving, deleting files, and so on. Journaling offers two benefits: a shorter startup time and safety in the event of a crash.

Here's how it works: When you press the power button, macOS checks to see whether your computer was shut down properly (by choosing →Shut Down, for example, instead of just pulling the plug).

If you didn't shut down properly, macOS examines your hard drive the next time you start up to see if it needs repair. It has to scan the whole drive—which can take quite a while. Thanks to file journaling, however, macOS can tell what was

happening when your computer shut down—and therefore spend a lot less time checking your hard drive.

There are some downsides to the journaled format, however. First, this procedure doesn't actually recover what you were working on when your Mac shut down; it can only try to keep files you already saved from getting corrupted. Second, file journaling can make it take slightly longer for your programs to save files.

MacOS doesn't prevent you from having different hard drives with different formats. You can use the journaled format on your main hard drive but not on your external FireWire drive—or vice versa. (If you ever want to change the format of one of your disks, use Disk Utility, although you'll have to erase all the information on the disk first.)

If you leave your Mac on all the time (if you run it as a web server, for example), it's a good idea to use the journaled hard drive format. Keep in mind, too, that blackouts affect your hard drive just as much as pulling the plug. So if you live in Iraq, a solar-powered house, or anywhere else where power can be inconsistent, journaling might be a lifesaver.

3. **Choose the disk or partition where you want to install macOS.**

The installer proposes the obvious hard drive: the main one inside your Mac.

If you have other drives, you can click Show All Disks to see their icons and choose one. Yellow exclamation-mark icons mean "You can't install here," for one technical reason or another. You can install Mojave only onto a blank hard drive, formatted as a Mac drive, or onto a drive that has Snow Leopard or later on it.

Note: As noted on page 505, installing macOS Mojave onto an SSD (solid state drive) automatically formats it with the Apple File System (APFS); installing onto a traditional spinning drive gives you Mac OS Extended (Journaled) format, described in the box on the facing page.

Figure A-2:
You've never experienced such a simple operating-system installation. You don't even have to restart the computer before you get to work. You have far fewer options and decisions to make.

Reinstalling: Tricks of the Trade

You can install macOS on as many Macs as you own. To install it on a second Mac, for example, open the App Store, find Mojave, and download it again.

That's what most people will do, anyway. Unfortunately, downloading the 5-gigabyte installer again and again takes a lot of time and eats up a lot of your monthly data allotment.

There is, fortunately, a trick that saves you the trouble of re-downloading Mojave over and over again: Copy the

Install MacOS Mojave installer program from the *first* Mac to all your other Macs (over the network or on a flash drive, for example).

There's a tricky part to this trick: Ordinarily, installing Mojave on the first Mac *deletes* that installer program once it's finished, to save you the disk space. The trick to this trick, then, is to copy the installer to another Mac or drive (or at least to take it out of your Applications folder) *before* you install Mojave on the first Mac.

You'll know when the downloading is over, because the installer opens up automatically.

The procedure from here:

1. **Click Continue.**

 The installer begins its work (see Figure A-2). It follows a pattern: Read the instructions, make a couple of choices, and then click Continue to advance to the next screen. As you go, the list on the left side of the screen reveals where you are in the overall procedure.

2. **Click Agree to pass the Software License Agreement screen, and then click Agree again.**

 The license agreement requires you to agree with whatever Apple's lawyers say.

Figure A-1:
Enter your Apple ID and password when you're asked for it, and enjoy a mug of your favorite hot beverage as the download begins. If you have a typical broadband internet connection, expect to wait nearly half an hour.

POWER USERS' CLINIC

The Partitioning Question

Before you install Mojave, you might want to confront the issue of *partitioning* your Mac's hard drive—dividing its space so that it shows up on your desktop with two different icons and two different names. You can keep Mojave on one and El Capitan on the other, for example.

Now you can live like a king, enjoying all the advantages of having two hard drives. The Mac even comes with a partitioning program: Disk Utility (page 504). And it no longer requires first erasing the drive completely; you can repartition on the fly, without disturbing whatever is already on the drive.

Hardware Requirements

For starters, you need to make sure you and your Mac have what it takes to handle Mojave—specifically:

- **A Mac that's not a geezer.** Mojave can run on any Mac laptop made since mid-2012; any iMac or Mac Mini made since late 2012; and any Mac Pro made since mid-2013 (plus a few older, especially beefy Mac Pros).

- **Free storage space.** You need at least 12.5 GB free on your Mac if you're upgrading from El Capitan, Sierra, or High Sierra; you need 18.5 GB or more if you have something older. More space, of course, is better.

- **A lot of memory.** Apple recommends at least 2 GB of memory, but macOS absolutely *loves* memory. For the greatest speed, install 4 gigabytes—more if you can afford it. (And these days, you probably can.)

- **A full backup.** It's a really, *really* good idea to back up your entire Mac before you begin this, or any, upgrade. Even if things go wrong for only, say, 0.01 percent of Mac owners, that's still thousands of people. If you don't have a second hard drive, this is your excuse to buy one; they're dirt cheap these days. You can use Time Machine in your current version of macOS to make a complete, automatic backup of your Mac as it is now.

Tip: Not all programs run well on Mojave—old ones, in particular, sometimes have problems. Before you take the upgrade plunge, therefore, you should visit *roaringapps.com*, a massive, crowdsourced compatibility table of every known Mac program—and its compatibility with macOS Mojave.

The Standard Installation

To do the actual installation, open the App Store program on your Mac. If you don't see "macOS Mojave" advertised right there on the home page, you can find it by searching for *Mojave*. Click the Free Upgrade button, and then click again when it changes to say Download (see Figure A-1).

Tip: If you don't have a fast internet connection, or if your internet provider imposes monthly data limits, you might not be thrilled about the prospect of waiting for a 5-gigabyte download.

Your best bet is to take your Mac to an Apple Store and use *its* free, fast Wi-Fi to download Mojave. (Or go to a friend's house, a library, a coffee shop…)

When the download begins, behind the scenes, the App Store puts a program called *Install macOS Mojave* into your Applications folder and onto your Launchpad, if you have it.

Tip: At this moment, you can duck out of the installer to make a safety copy of it, so you won't have to download it again the next time. See the box on page 788.

Installing macOS Mojave

I f your computer came with macOS Mojave already installed on it, you can skip this appendix—at least for now. But if you're running an earlier version of the Mac operating system and want to really savor the Mojave experience, this appendix is for you. It describes how to install the new OS on your Mac.

If you're new in these parts, you may be in for a shock: You can't buy macOS in a box, or on a DVD. You download it from the Mac App Store.

There are some attractive elements to that system. For example, there's no copy protection and no serial numbers to type in. There's no cost to Apple for manufacturing or shipping, which may explain why Mojave isn't even $20 or $30, like some of its predecessors—it's free.

There's no disc to hunt down when you want to install macOS again (onto a new Mac, for example).

And when you do need a copy again, you'll download the latest version—10.14.3 or whatever it is—instead of having to install whatever updates have come out since you got your DVD.

(And what if you don't have a fast internet connection for downloading macOS? The world won't come to an end; read on.)

Part Six: Appendixes

6

manufacturer for more information. For example, the first-generation (silver) AirPort base stations can't handle VPNs at all.

- **If the corporate network** doesn't seem to like your name and password, you might need to add your NT domain name and a backslash to the beginning of your account name (like this: *dom01\msmith*) before trying again.

- **If you're able to make the connection** but experience trouble reaching services by their DNS names (for example, *big-blue-server.com*), then your Mac could be having difficulty finding the right DNS server. Working with your network administrator, open the Network pane of System Preferences. Click VPN, then Advanced, and then DNS; enter the desired DNS server addresses in the DNS Servers box. Click OK, then Apply, and then try the VPN connection again.

- **If you're still having problems using the VPN,** look at the *logs* (automatically kept technical records) for clues to share with your network administrator. To view these records, open the Console program (in Applications→Utilities). Click Show Log List, expand the */var/log* section, and click *ppp.log.*

Tip: If you always connect to the same VPN, you can turn on VPN on Demand. It autoconnects you to your corporate VPN every time you direct your web browser to a website, file server, or resource that requires the VPN connection, saving you some steps.

To set this up, click Advanced. (You can see this button in Figure 20-3.) Click VPN on Demand; click +. Enter the corporate VPN domain. You're good to go—as long as you've got your network geek's permission. (Some of them get understandably nervous about you storing your network password in your Keychain. It's convenient, yes, but it could open up your company's entire network to the evil intentions of whoever walks up to your laptop while you're away from your desk.)

Close System Preferences. You're ready to connect.

Connecting to a VPN

Connect the way you normally do—via cable modem, DSL, office network, modem, AirPort, or whatever. Once you're online, choose your VPN's name from the 🔲 menulet. You'll be asked for your credentials: your password, for example, or the code displayed on your SecurID card.

If all goes well, several status messages go by. The last one says "Connected To" and gives the IP address of the network equipment you've reached out and touched.

At this point, you're connected to the corporate network. You can perform the same network-related tasks you could if you were actually in that office: check your email, view internal corporate web pages, access internal FTP servers, make printouts on laser printers thousands of miles away, and so on.

Depending on your network, you might even be able to use your Sidebar to view a list of the other computers on the office network or see a list of networked printers.

If not, to access these services, you must know their IP addresses. For example, to connect to a shared folder on another computer, choose Go→Connect to Server, type its network address, and press Return.

Tip: To connect to a shared folder on a Windows machine, the address looks like this: *smb://111.222.33.4/sales-docs*. Of course, you'd substitute the correct IP address for the dummy one shown here and insert the actual name of the shared folder. (You can also use its *DNS name* instead of the IP address, if you know it, like this: *smb://big-blue-server.ferret-lan.com/sales-docs.*)

When you're finished accessing the remote network, choose Disconnect from the VPN menulet. (Accessing other websites can be slow while you're on a VPN.)

The Fine Points of VPN

For all the wonders of VPN, here are some possible complications:

- **If you're using a *router* at home** (a little box that shares one cable modem or DSL box with several computers), it might not be able to handle the tunneling protocols, or it might not have that feature turned on. Check the router's manual, or ask its

3. **After you choose the type of VPN from the VPN Type pop-up menu, type a name for this connection (it can be anything you want). Click Create.**

You return to the main Network pane, where the settings boxes for your VPN are waiting (Figure 20-3).

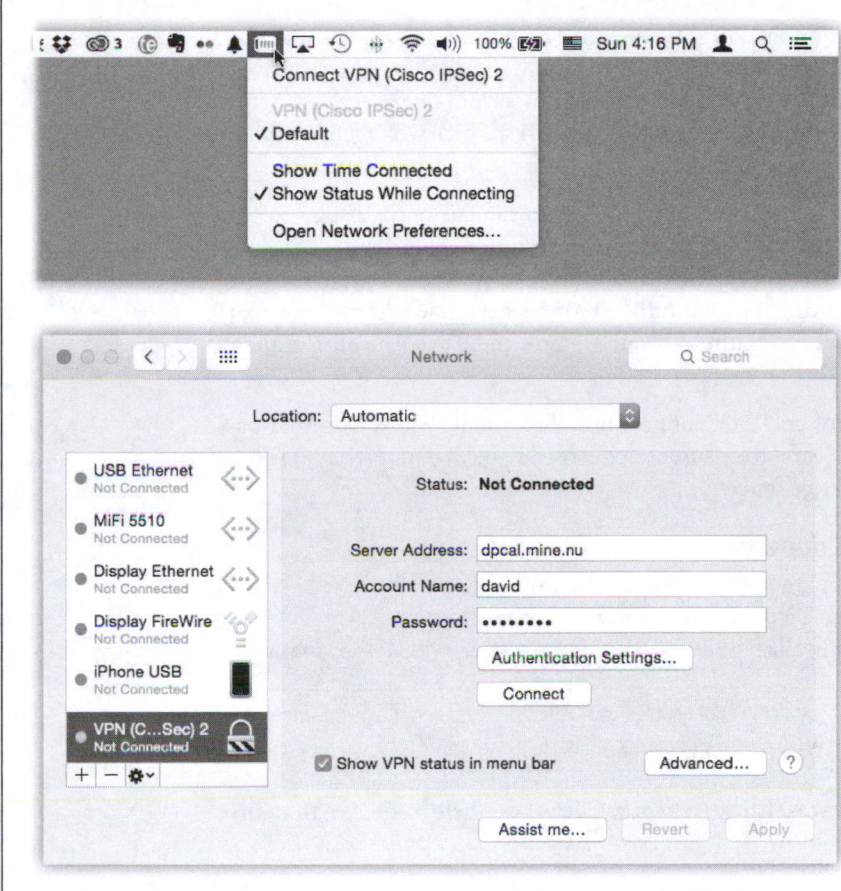

Figure 20-3:
You're on your way to joining the corporate network— from thousands of miles away. Virtual private network- ing is ideal for the paranoid (because it's very secure) and the cheap (because you're using the internet as a giant wire connecting you to your office).

4. **Fill in the server address and account name. Click Authentication Settings to specify your password and other security settings.**

Here, for example, is where you indicate that you have one of those SecurID cards.

5. **Click Connect. Turn on "Show VPN status in menu bar."**

That checkbox makes the VPN menulet () appear; it's your ticket to getting connected (Figure 20-3, top).

You'll also need to know the internet address of your VPN server (for example, *vpn.ferrets-r-us.com*).

- **An account on the remote network that allows VPN access.** Your remote network can be set up in many different ways, but in every case, you'll still need to confirm with your network administrator that your account on it allows VPN access.

- **All necessary account information.** Make sure you have all the scraps of connection information you'll need to dial in. That would include your user (account) name, at the very least. You may also need a Windows Domain name; VPN servers are often part of Microsoft Windows Server networks, which won't let you in until you know this domain name.

Some networks also may require that you type in the currently displayed password on an RSA SecurID card, which your administrator will provide. This James Bondish, credit card–like or flash drive–like thing displays a password that changes every few seconds, making it rather difficult for hackers to learn "the" password. (If your network doesn't require a SecurID card, then you'll need a standard password instead.)

Finally, if your office offers L2TP connections, then you'll need yet another password called a Shared Secret to ensure that the server you're connecting to is really the server you intend to connect to.

Setting Up the VPN Connection

If you're lucky, your company's network geek has provided you with a VPN settings file, a little double-clickable icon that automatically opens the Network pane of System Preferences and fills in the blanks for you. If not, you can do all that manually:

Note: OpenVPN is a free, very popular VPN program. If your VPN uses OpenVPN, then you'll need to get some connection software from your company's network geeks.

1. **Open System Preferences. Click Network. Click the + below the list of connections at the left side.**

 The "Select the interface" sheet appears.

2. **From the pop-up menu, choose VPN.**

 Now a new pop-up menu appears, called VPN Type; you're supposed to choose either L2TP over IPSec (Layer 2 Tunneling Protocol over IP Security), PPTP (Point-to-Point Tunneling Protocol), or Cisco IPSec (IP Security). Find out which system your company's network uses.

Note: MacOS can't connect to all Cisco setups; in some cases, you'll still have to use Cisco's own connection software to dial in.

• **A VPN server.** If your tech department tells you it doesn't have one, then that's that—no tunneling for you.

If they do have one, then you'll need to know what type of server it is. MacOS's VPN software can connect to VPN servers that speak *PPTP* (Point-to-Point Tunneling Protocol), *L2TP/IPSec* (Layer 2 Tunneling Protocol over IP Security), or Cisco IPSec. Most corporate VPN servers work with at least one of these protocols.

POWER USERS' CLINIC

Web Sharing—and macOS Server

For many years, you could turn your Mac into a website (or server), accessible from the web browsers of people on your office network, the internet at large, or both. All you had to do was visit the Sharing pane of System Preferences and turn on "Web Sharing."

After you provided your friends and co-workers with your Mac's website address, they could view your web pages, graphics, and documents in their own web browsers. And whenever your Mac was online, your website was also available to anyone on the internet—but you didn't have to pay a penny to a web-hosting company.

Web sharing was also an easy and efficient way to share your Mac files with Windows PCs, either those on your office network or those on the internet. No special software or translation required.

MacOS's Web Sharing feature wasn't some feeble junior version, either. Inside was Apache, one of the strongest and most popular Unix web server programs—precisely the same one that drives over 60 percent of the internet's commercial websites.

The bottom line: If you built it, they didn't necessarily come. But you had the capacity to handle them if they did.

Why the past tense? Because the Web Sharing button disappeared back in Mountain Lion. Weirdly, though, the Apache server is still there. It just lacks a front end so you can set it up.

Apple cheerfully points out that macOS Server, a $20 add-on, offers all the controls you need for hosting websites on that Apache software.

So what is macOS Server? Many of its features are of interest only to people who run servers in a small business or a school: calendar server, mail server, file server. For normal, nontechnical people, iCloud offers these same features for free—so why would you want a server running in your home?

Well, macOS Server's built-in file-sharing feature lets you share files over your Wi-Fi network on your iPad (a feature called File Sharing for iPad). So you can put files on the server in your home, and you can access them directly from your iPad.

But perhaps the most interesting tool included with macOS Server is Profile Manager. With Profile Manager, you can set up Macs, iPhones, iPads, and iPod Touches—centrally, directly from the Mac that's running Server. What's more, you can send these configuration changes to those machines wirelessly, by remote control.

These configurations can include almost any setting you can think of: Set restrictions on all sorts of things (great for families with young kids), restrict multiplayer gaming, and turn on restrictions on TV and movies. You can even remotely configure email accounts or lock or erase a device.

MacOS Server gets even more interesting when you combine its features. Want to share an address book with the whole family? Set up the Contacts Server feature, and use Profile Manager to configure all your Macs and iOS devices to use that address book. You can do the same with calendars, too.

MacOS Server is aimed at small businesses—and techier ones, at that. But if you want that web server back, then macOS Server is one good way to get it.

Either way, the Finder promptly quits (and relaunches in a healthier incarnation, you hope). You could also, at this point, type *sudo shutdown -h now* to make your Mac, elsewhere on the network, shut down. (Terminal doesn't type any kind of response.)

If you ended your SSH session by shutting down the other Mac, you can just close the Terminal window now. Otherwise, type *exit* to complete your SSH session.

Tip: Want a quicker, dirtier method of doing SSH that doesn't even require knowing the other machine's IP address? OK: Open Terminal. Choose Shell→New Remote Connection. In the list of connection types, choose ssh/ftp/telnet. Every Bonjour-enabled Mac on your network shows up; click one and then click Connect to connect!

Virtual Private Networking

After reading the previous pages, you might assume it's a piece of cake for business-people to connect to their corporate networks across the internet from wherever they happen to be: their homes, hotel rooms, or their local Starbucks. But even though the steps on the preceding pages work fine if you're dialing into your *home* machine, they'll probably fail miserably when you want to connect to a corporate network. There's one enormous obstacle in your way: internet security.

The typical corporate network is guarded by a team of steely-eyed administrators, for whom Job One is preventing access by unauthorized visitors. They perform this job primarily with the aid of a super-secure firewall that seals off the company's network from the internet.

So how can you tap into the network from the road? One solution is to create a hole in the firewall for each authorized person—software that permits incoming internet traffic only from specified IP addresses like your Mac's. Unfortunately, this setup isn't bulletproof, security-wise. It's also a pain for administrators to manage.

Back in the dial-up modem days, you could dial directly into the corporate network, modem-to-modem. That was plenty secure, but it bypassed the internet and there-fore wound up being expensive. (Want proof? Make a call from the Tokyo Hilton to the Poughkeepsie Sheet Metal home office. Have a look at your hotel bill when you check out.)

Fortunately, there's a third solution that's both secure and cheap: a *virtual private network,* or *VPN.* Running a VPN allows you to create a super-secure "tunnel" from your Mac, across the internet, and straight into your corporate network. All data passing through this tunnel is heavily encrypted; to the internet eavesdropper, it looks like so much undecipherable gobbledygook.

And it's free—whether you're accessing the internet via your home DSL, a local ISP number from a hotel, or wirelessly from your stool at Starbucks.

Remember, though, that VPN is a corporate tool, run by corporate nerds. You can't use this feature without these pieces in place:

Remote Control Program Killing

One of the most common uses of SSH is quitting a stuck program. Maybe it's a program that doesn't respond to the usual Force Quit commands—maybe even the Finder or Terminal. Or maybe, having just arrived in Accounting on the fifth floor, you realize that you accidentally left your web browser, open to *Dilbert.com*, up on your screen in clear view of passersby.

In any case, you'd fire up Terminal and proceed like this (what you type is shown in bold; the Mac's responses are in normal type):

```
home-mac:~ chris$ ssh 172.24.30.182
The authenticity of host '111.222.3.44
(111.222.3.44)' can't be established.
RSA key fingerprint is d9:f4:11:b0:27:
1a:f1:14:c3:cd:25:85:2b:78:4d:e7.
Are you sure you want to continue
connecting (yes/no)? yes
Warning: Permanently added
'172.24.30.182' (RSA) to the list of
known hosts.
chris@111.222.3.44's password: fisheggs
Last login: Thu Apr 22 17:23:38 2010
Welcome to Darwin!
office-mac:~ chris$ top -u
```

The *top -u* command displays a list of running programs. After a block of memory statistics, you might see a list like this:

```
1156 top          6.6 00:00.27 1/1 0 28   29   1344K+ 216K 2052K+17M
139  Terminal     2.4 00:34.24 5   1 130-192- 11M-   28M 26M-  51M
788  bash         0.0 00:00.02 1   0 20   24   656K   840K 1436K 17M
787  login        0.0 00:00.04 2   1 34   62   880K   260K 2144K 49M
283  Finder       0.0 00:23.02 9   3 247  666  33M    96M 81M   0M
426  SystemUIServ 0.0 00:14.24 3   1 290  410  30M    47M 47M   112M
151  Dock         0.0 00:05.95 4   2 201  851  22M    36M 59M   73M
```

As you can see, the Finder is process number 283. If that's the stuck program, then you could quit it like so:

```
office-mac:~ chris$ kill 283
```

Or if you're sure of the program's exact name, just use the *killall* command with the program's name instead of its process ID. To handle a stuck Finder, you would type this:

```
office-mac:~ chris$ killall Finder
```

control of it, copying files, running commands, rearranging folders, or even shutting it down, all by remote control.

Getting In

Here's how you go about using SSH:

1. **Set up your Mac by opening the Sharing panel of System Preferences and then turning on the Remote Login checkbox.**

 You've just told the Mac it's OK for you (or other people with accounts on your machine) to connect from the road. Quit System Preferences.

2. **Go away.**

 You can move to another machine on the network or another computer on the internet (if you've dealt with the port-forwarding issue described in the box on the facing page). Once you're online with that other machine, you can contact your home-base machine from within a program like Terminal.

Tip: It doesn't have to be Terminal, and it doesn't have to be a Mac. You can get *SSH client* programs for almost any kind of computer.

For pre–OS X Macs, for example, you can try MacSSH or NiftyTelnet SSH, both of which you can download from this book's "Missing CD" page at *missingmanuals.com.* For Windows, try Putty (*puttyssh.org*).

3. **At the prompt, type *ssh -l chris 111.222.3.44*. Press Return.**

 Instead of *chris,* substitute your short account name (as you're known on the Mac you're tapping into), and replace the phony IP address shown here with your real public address. (If your Mac back home has a domain name unto itself, such as *macmania.com,* you can type that instead of the IP address. And if you've turned on port forwarding, use your cable modem/DSL box's IP address.)

 If all goes well, the *ssh* command acknowledges your first successful connection by displaying a message like this: "The authenticity of host '111.222.3.44 (111.222.3.44)' can't be established. RSA key fingerprint is d9:f4:11:b0:27:1a:f1:14:c3:cd:25:85:2b:78:4d:e7. Are you sure you want to continue connecting (yes/no)?" This message won't appear on subsequent connections. You're seeing SSH's security features at work.

4. **Type *yes* and press Return.**

 Now you see one more note: "Warning: Permanently added '111.222.3.44' (RSA) to the list of known hosts." You're then asked for your account password.

5. **Type your account password and press Return.**

 You're in. Issue whatever commands you want. You can now conduct a full Unix Terminal session—but by remote control.

If you answered "What's SSH?" or "I'm *already* being quiet," then the following discussion of Unix remote control may not interest you. To be sure, SSH is not a program with a graphic user interface (icons and menus). You operate it from within a program like Terminal by typing commands. (For details on Terminal, see the free downloadable appendix called "Terminal Crash Course" on this book's "Missing CD" page at *missingmanuals.com*.)

If you're willing to overlook that little peccadillo, though, SSH (Secure Shell) is an extremely powerful tool. It lets you connect to your Mac from anywhere—from across the network or across the internet. And once you're connected, you can take complete

The IP Address Mess: Port Forwarding

There are so many ways to connect to your Mac from another computer. You can use SSH, file sharing, screen sharing, and so on. They're easy to use—when you want to connect across your home or office network.

When you want to connect from across the *internet*, though, things get complicated fast.

In that case, you need to know your home Mac's *IP address*. (IP stands for Internet Protocol.) An IP address is always made up of four numbers separated by periods, like 192.168.1.104. Every computer on earth that's directly connected to the internet has its own unique IP address.

Now, if you have only one Mac, and it's connected directly to your broadband modem, no big deal. You can find out its IP address by opening System Preferences, clicking Sharing, and turning on File Sharing.

Unfortunately, your Mac at home probably *isn't* connected directly to the internet. If you're like most people, it's connected to a router, or maybe an AirPort base station, so that several computers in your house can share the same internet connection. In this setup, the *router* (or base station) has a unique IP address—not the Macs connected to it.

(The router doles out private IP addresses to each computer in your house or office, usually beginning with 192 or 10. If you check your Mac's IP address in System Preferences, you'll find out only its *private* address—not the public one that's accessible from the internet. To find out that information, you have to check your router or base station's configuration screen; check the router's manual for instructions.)

All right: How are you supposed to connect to one particular Mac if it's connected to a router and doesn't have a true, "public" IP address? Your best bet is to turn on a router feature called *port forwarding*. It makes the router pass signals intended for a specific port to one particular computer on the network. For example, you could direct all port-80 communications to the Mac doing web serving and all port-548 traffic to the Mac doing file sharing.

The point is that, even with port forwarding, you still can't access two different machines using the same port. (For some services, including SSH and Timbuktu, you can work around this limitation by logging into the machine specified for port forwarding, and then from that machine, log into the others on the rest of the network.)

Turning on port forwarding doesn't require a programming degree, but it's not simple by any means. For starters, the steps are different for every router model.

Fortunately, you can find guided tutorials on the web. You can use Google to search for your particular router model, or check *portforward.com*, which offers free step-by-steps for hundreds of router models, including Apple's AirPort base stations. Even so, try to arrange the assistance of someone who knows networking.

In this chapter, the term "your IP address" means your *public* IP address. If you have only one Mac, that's its IP address. If you have a router or wireless network, use *that* device's IP address—as passed along by port forwarding.

ftp.apple.com icon appear on your desktop, looking just like your other disks. Open it up and drag out whatever you want to download.

Connecting from the Road

You can also connect to your Mac's regular File Sharing feature (page 571) from over the internet. This feature is a blessing to anyone who travels, whether with a laptop or to a branch office, because you'll never be up a creek without a paddle if you discover that you left an important file at home.

You can also set up a remote file-sharing system on your own. Start by setting up the home-base Mac for file sharing, as directed in Chapter 13; then figure out your Mac's public IP address, as described in the box on the next page.

Finally, once you're on the road, go online and proceed like this:

1. **Choose Go→Connect to Server.**

 The Connect to Server dialog box appears, as shown in Figure 20-2.

Figure 20-2:
The Connect to Server dialog box lets you type in the IP address for the shared Mac you want to access. (Ensuring that the shared Mac is turned on and connected to the internet is the network administrator's problem.)

2. **Type in the public IP address of the Mac to which you want to connect, and then click Connect (or press Return).**

 See the box on the next page for a discussion of public vs. private IP addresses.

3. **Enter your name and password, and then click Connect.**

 From here, it's just as though you were connecting to another computer on your office network (Chapter 13), although it's a good bit slower. But when you're in Hong Kong and need a document from your Mac in Minneapolis, you may not care.

Remote Access with SSH

Are you a geek? Take this simple test at home: Do you get excited about macOS's ability to permit SSH access?

Using these programs, web designers, for example, can view a list of all the text and graphics documents, sitting there on an internet-connected computer somewhere, that make up their web pages. The effect is shown in Figure 20-1.

When they want to update one of those pages, they add it to this list; to delete a web page, they remove it from this list.

Figure 20-1:
Top: To access your macOS machine from across the internet, fire up a program like RBrowser and use the address ftp://111.222.33.4 (or whatever your public IP address is).

Bottom: Once you're looking at an FTP server's contents, you can drag files from your desktop into the list, copy them to your Mac by dragging them out of the list onto your desktop, or open them by double-clicking.

Just Downloading from FTP Sites

If you're just going to *look at* and *download* files (but not upload or delete any), you don't even need a special FTP program. You can get to the files much more directly using one of these two methods:

- **Any old web browser will work.** Open Safari, for example, and type *ftp://ftp.apple. com* (or whatever the address is) into the address/search bar. A dialog box asks for an account name and password, if they're required. Once you're in, you switch to the Finder and see the contents of the FTP site as a window full of file icons. (In other browsers, you may see the list of the FTP site right in the browser window.)

- **Using the Finder's Go→Connect to Server command,** you can mount read-only FTP volumes right on your desktop. In other words, they appear just like any other disk icons.

In the Connect to Server dialog box, just enter the address of the file server you would like to mount—*ftp://ftp.apple.com,* for example. You'll soon see the

FTP, SSH, VPN & Web Sharing

Email and web surfing may be the most popular internet activities, but the world's most gigantic network has many other uses. The general idea is always the same, though: letting one computer reach out and touch another.

MacOS offers a few features that embrace the more literal aspects of that notion. For example, this chapter explores various advanced methods of manipulating your own Mac from the road, including *remote access* technologies like long-distance file sharing, FTP, SSH, and virtual private networking (VPN).

FTP

FTP (file transfer protocol) sites store pieces of software that can be accessed from the internet. If you've heard of FTP at all, it was probably under one of two circumstances—either you've downloaded software from an internet FTP site, or you've created and maintained your own website.

Uploading and Downloading from FTP Sites

Hooking into an FTP site generally requires an FTP *client program* that runs on the kind of computer you use (Mac, Windows, or whatever). On macOS, popular FTP client programs include the shareware programs Transmit, CyberDuck, Fetch, Interarchy, and Captain FTP, and the free RBrowser (which is available from the "Missing CD" page at *missingmanuals.com*).

Once a typed chat is underway, click Details (top right), and then click ⊡ (see Figure 19-7, top). If that icon is dimmed gray instead of blue, it's because the other person isn't using a Yosemite-or-later Mac.

The icon sprouts two choices: Invite to Share My Screen (meaning the other guy sees *your* screen) and Ask to Share Screen (you're going to see *his* screen). Click the one you want.

He receives an invitation. When he clicks Accept, the sharing is underway. He sees your screen on his Mac, or vice versa, as though some freaky cosmic wormhole has opened up.

Once the screen sharing is going, a new ⊡ menu appears at the top of your screen. It offers options like these:

- **Allow [other guy] to control my screen.** He can operate your mouse and keyboard—from his Mac, thousands of miles away.

- **Mute Audio.** During a screen share, Messages automatically turns on audio chatting, so you can explain stuff to each other. Mute Audio mutes the audio.

- **Pause Screen Sharing** is like drawing a privacy curtain when you want to duck into your email program to read something. The other guy sees only a "Paused" screen until you unpause.

- **End Screen Sharing.** You guessed it.

document, without her having to attempt to *explain* it to you over the phone. ("And then the little thingy disappeared and the doohickey got scrambled…")

Tip: Once you're controlling someone else's screen remotely, your keyboard shortcuts operate his Mac instead of yours. Press ⌘-Tab to bring up the application switcher, hit ⌘-Q to quit a program, use all the Mission Control and Spotlight shortcuts, and so on.

To make Messages' screen sharing work, you and your buddy must both be using an iCloud account, or be on the same Wi-Fi network (the Mac's Bonjour feature will make your Macs show up on each other's screens).

iCloud Screen Sharing

From within an iMessages conversation (that is, a chat between two iCloud members), you can share your whole Mac screen, right there in Messages. Both people have to be using Macs running Yosemite or later (not an iPhone, and not an older Mac).

There are other ways to share screens, of course (page 595)—but this is by far the easiest to set up.

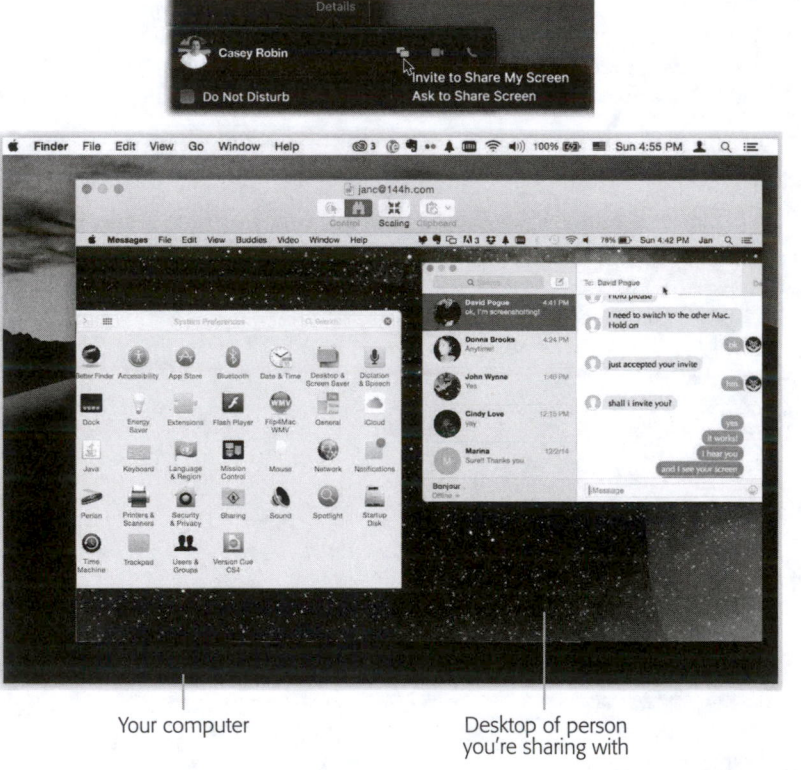

Figure 19-7:
Top: You either send or receive an invitation to start sharing your screen, but make sure you know with whom you're dealing before accepting the offer and starting the sharing process.

Bottom: When you're sharing someone else's screen, you have the option to click back and forth between the two Mac screens.

You can move the cursor, click things, and even highlight text on the other guy's screen. That's great for explaining to someone, via remote control, how to perform some task.

Your computer

Desktop of person you're sharing with

Audio and Video Chats

Messages no longer has audio-chat and video-chat features; that's the FaceTime app's job! Messages does, however, make it simple to jump from a typed chat directly into an audio or video call in FaceTime—involving as many as 32 people (see page 417).

If you're in a text chat, you can jump into audio or video in either of these ways:

- **Choose Buddies**→**FaceTime Audio** (or FaceTime Video).

- **Click Details;** on the panel, click either ☎ or ▢◁. (If you're making a voice call, a pop-up menu offers you either a FaceTime Audio call [page 419] or a regular speakerphone call through your iPhone [page 308].)

The call begins, courtesy of the FaceTime app, which opens automatically. (Unless you're making a cellular voice call, as noted above.)

Sharing Your Screen

As you've seen already, Messages lets you share your thoughts, your voice, and your image. And now, for its next trick, it lets you share…your computer.

Messages' screen-sharing feature is a close relative of the *network* screen-sharing feature described on page 595. It lets you not only *see* what's on a faraway buddy's screen, but also control it, taking command of the distant mouse and keyboard. (You can share your screen with the other guy, too.)

You can open folders, create and edit documents, and copy files on the shared Mac screen. Sharing a screen makes collaborating as easy as working side by side around the same Mac, except now you can be sitting in San Francisco while your buddy is banging it out in Boston.

And if you're the family tech-support specialist—but the family lives all over the country—screen sharing makes troubleshooting infinitely easier. You can now jump on your mom's shared Mac and figure out why the formatting went wacky in her Word

UP TO SPEED

The Chat Transcript

When you close a chat by clicking the ✕ in its tab, the conversation is gone forever. *Unless*, that is, you've opened Messages→Preferences→General and turned on "Save history when conversations are closed."

In that case, Messages autosaves the text of your conversations. Even if you close one, you can retrieve its contents by starting another chat with the same person; the history reappears.

Behind the scenes, your transcripts are saved in your Library→Messages→Archives folder. (To get to your Library folder, press Option as you choose Go→Library in the Finder.)

If you do have "Save history" turned on, and you wind up having a particularly incriminating chat, you can tell Messages *not* to save its transcript by pressing ⌘-Delete. Messages asks if you're sure. If so, that prose is hosed.

emotional reactions: what Apple calls tapbacks. Figure 19-3 shows you the ropes. Tapbacks take the form of six reaction icons: Heart, Thumbs Up, Thumbs Down, Ha Ha, Exclamation Points, and Question Mark. When you choose one, it appears instantly on your screen and your buddy's.

Tip: What's cool is that you can change your tapback icon later, if new information affects your reaction; just right-click or two-finger click again, and choose Tapback again, to bring up the same palette.

- **Incoming fanciness.** Messages on the Mac doesn't let you express yourself in all the ways Messages on an iPhone does in iOS 10 and later. But it can *receive* some of the cool effects that your iOS friends send you, like handwriting, invisible ink, and stickers; see Figure 19-4.

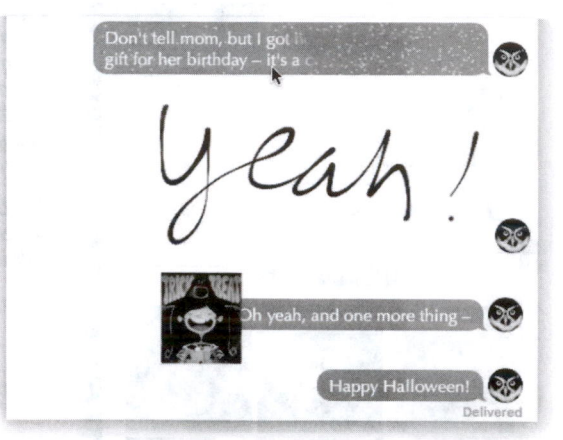

Figure 19-4:
Among the cool Messages effects (from top): invisible ink (text that doesn't appear until you move your mouse across it—useful when the sender doesn't want to embarrass you), handwriting, and stickers (still or animated images your pal has dragged onto a message). You can't create these effects on the Mac, but you can receive them when they're sent by iPhones and iPads.

- **Big, plentiful emoji.** You can use the emoji pop-up menu (at the right end of the typing box) to insert emoticons and smileys.

 If you know the correct codes to produce the emoji you want—typing :) produces a yellow happy face, for example, and <3 produces a red heart—you can save time by typing them instead of using the pop-up menu. Messages converts them into smiley or heart icons on the fly, as soon as you send your reply.

 The emoji you transmit appear enormous—at three times their usual size—if you've typed three of them or fewer on a single line. (If, that is, your recipient is using an Apple device running iOS 10 or Sierra or later versions.)

Tip: If you have a Touch Bar (page 233), you'll find it much easier to enter emoji by tapping. Touch the ☺ button to see a row of frequently used emoji, any of which you can insert by tapping. Or you can tap the ☺ button to see a row of icons representing the other *categories* of emoji available to your fingertip.

- **Real-time feedback.** The tiny word "Delivered" appears beneath any message you send to let you know that your recipient's gadget has received it. If the recipient has

- **Built-in suspense.** Whenever the other guy is typing, you see "..." in his balloon, so you know he's working on a response and not just ignoring you.

Tip: The ellipsis dots appear as soon as the other guy starts typing—and remain on your screen for 60 seconds, even if he *stopped* typing a long time ago. Conversely, they *disappear* from your screen after 60 seconds, even if he's still typing! Often you'll see the dots disappear shortly before you get a huge, long paragraph—because the other guy took longer than 60 seconds to write it.

- **Insta-file sending.** You can drag photos, movies, or other files (up to 100 megabytes!) into the typing box. They'll show up on the other guy's Mac, phone, or tablet just fine.

- **Easy switching to phone or video.** If you find that typing is losing too much emotional nuance, and you are signed into FaceTime on your Mac, you can jump into a voice call or video call at any point. For voice calls, you can choose either a FaceTime Audio call or a phone call; for video, the FaceTime app opens, and you can proceed as described on page 415.

To jump into a voice call, click Details (top right); on the panel, click ☎; click FaceTime Audio. (Or, if you have an iPhone, you can click the person's phone number and make an actual phone call.) Once your invitation is accepted, you can begin speaking to each other. The bars of the sound-level meter let you know that the microphone is working.

To switch to a video call, click Details at the upper right of the Messages window, and then click ☐◁. A FaceTime call begins right away.

- **Tapbacks.** How many trillions of times a day do people respond to texts with repetitive reactions like "LOL" and "Awww" and "!!!!!"? Many. It's how you demonstrate to your chat partner that you appreciate the import of her text.

But if you and your buddy are both using iOS 10 or macOS Sierra or later, you've now got a quicker, less cluttery, more visual way to indicate those sorts of standard

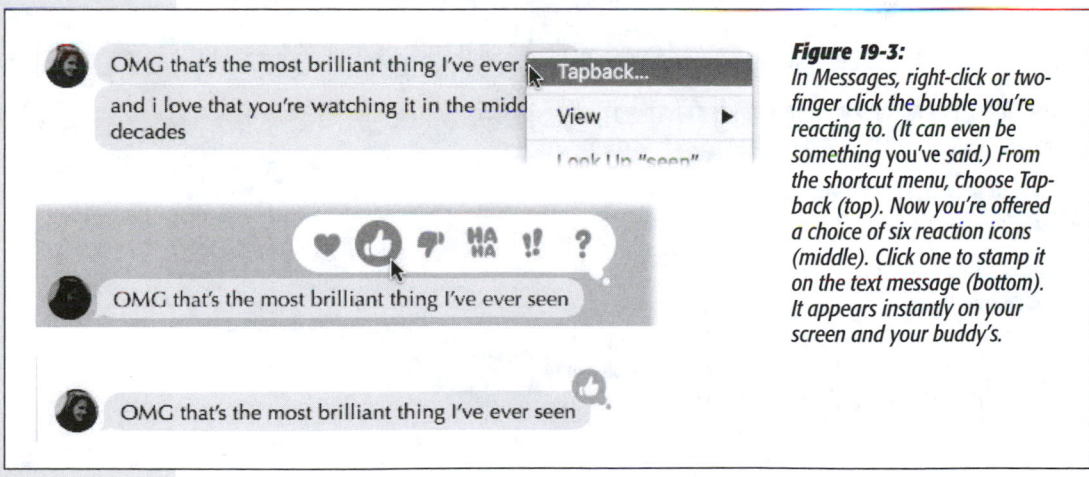

Figure 19-3:
In Messages, right-click or two-finger click the bubble you're reacting to. (It can even be something you've said.) From the shortcut menu, choose Tapback (top). Now you're offered a choice of six reaction icons (middle). Click one to stamp it on the text message (bottom). It appears instantly on your screen and your buddy's.

That's extremely useful, because it means you can (for example) start texting on your phone when you're out and about and pick up seamlessly on your Mac when you get home, enjoying the real keyboard and big screen.

- **Link previews.** When you send a web address in an iMessage, it appears on the recipient's screen as a little preview of the actual web page, for convenient identification. And if you send a video link, your buddy can play it right there in Messages, without having to lurch off to a web browser! (Click once to make the tiny video start playing; click a second time to make it stop. There's no scroll bar.)

Tip: And what if you *want* to lurch off to a web browser—for example, because you want to see that YouTube video bigger than a Wheat Thin? In that case, click the label *beneath* the video thumbnail.

GEM IN THE ROUGH

Messages in iCloud

For years, it was a real hassle of Messages: You'd pick up one Apple gadget after doing a lot of texting on another—for example, switching to your iPhone after doing a lot of texting on your Mac during a flight. Then you'd have to wait a very long time for your phone's copy of Messages to catch up—to download all the conversations you had on your Mac.

In 2017, Apple introduced an optional feature that neatly solves that problem: Your message history would be saved online, in iCloud.

If you choose to turn on this feature, here's what you get:

Your text messages and iMessages (and all associated photos, videos, and attachments) are now stored online instead of on your iPhone, iPad, and Mac. Which means you save several gigabytes, or *many* gigabytes, of storage on every single device. That's storage that was duplicated on every machine—the same database stored in multiple places.

Your Mac, iPhone, and iPad backups are much smaller, because they no longer include your Messages database.

All your messages are synced. Delete a message or a conversation, and it's also deleted on all your other machines.

No more waiting for one device to "catch up." That should sound like a pleasant development to anyone who, for example, uses Messages on the MacBook on a plane ride—and then upon landing can't use Messages on the phone for 10 minutes because it's still syncing.

If you get a new Apple device, your entire history of text messages and attachments appears on it. (Without Messages in iCloud, your current and future messages appear, but you can't scroll to see past ones—at least not without restoring from a backup.)

There's one big downside of Messages in iCloud: Moving your database into your iCloud account online eats up space there. You're saving tons of space on all your Apple machines, but losing space on your iCloud account online—and that may cost you money (page 221).

If you decide it's worth doing, here's how to set it up.

First, you have to have two-factor authentication turned on, for security (page 551). Second, on each device, turn on Messages in iCloud:

On an iPhone or iPad, open Settings. Tap your name at the top, tap iCloud, and then turn on Messages.

On the Mac, open Messages→Preferences→iMessage, and turn on Enable Messages in iCloud.

It takes a few minutes for your devices to offload your entire Messages history; the phone/tablet must be plugged into power and on Wi-Fi before the process can begin.

Once that's done, you'll be treated to a technical but handy upgrade to your texting world.

If someone invites *you* to chat, a notification appears in the top-right corner of your screen. If you point to it in time, you get a Reply button; see Figure 19-2.

If you click the notification instead, Messages opens automatically; click in the message box at the bottom and type your witty reply.

Figure 19-2:
When someone messages you, a bubble like this appears in the top-right corner of your screen. If you point to it before it vanishes, the Reply button appears, as shown here.

If you click it, you can type a quick response right there in the notification window (bottom), without having to fire up Messages at all.

iMessages

If the box where you type says "iMessage" in faint lettering, then you're about to chat with a fellow iCloud member—and you'll be sending iMessages. (Another clue: Your speech bubbles appear in blue, rather than green.) And you'll enjoy a long list of extra benefits as you chat (as compared with, for example, standard cellphone text messages).

For example:

- **Fancier, longer posts.** You can type outrageously long messages (unlike standard text messages, which are limited to 160 characters). And iMessages are unlimited and free.

- **Dressier chats.** You can use fonts and colors in your conversation.

- **Multigadget simulcasting.** If you have multiple Apple gadgets, and you've set up your iMessages email address or phone number identically in the Settings or System Preferences of each one, then your conversation appears simultaneously on all the gadgets. ("Simultaneously," however, is relative. If one of your devices has been offline for some time while you've been chatting on the other, it may take a few minutes to catch up. You'll see all the iMessages it missed pouring in.)

a *lot* of conversations listed there, you can use the search box above the list to find that person.) Click the name and then start typing into the message box. The "conversation" with that person continues, even if the last exchange was months or years ago.

To start chatting with someone you've never corresponded with before, click the Compose button (⧉) next to the search box. The To field appears. As you type your buddy's name into it, Messages sprouts a list of matching names from your Contacts.

Some of them probably feature a blue speech bubble (⬤). Those are people with iCloud accounts—with whom you can exchange iMessages, described next.

Note: An iMessage address can be either an email address or a phone number. Most people register both of those data bits as part of their iMessage setup, so that any message you send arrives on all your correspondent's Apple gadgets at once.

You can also click the ⊕ button to get a pop-up version of your Contacts, complete with a search bar at the top.

Once you've selected your lucky conversation partner(s), just type what you want to say into the message box at the bottom of the window. As you correspond, the conversation appears in speech bubbles, scrolling up like a screenplay, making it easy to identify who said what—and to scroll back up to see what someone said earlier. (See Figure 19-1.)

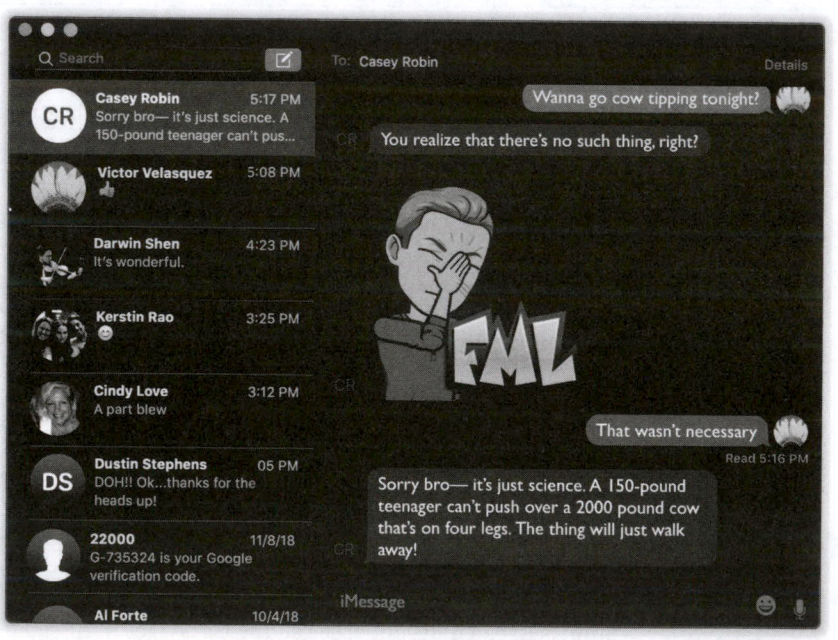

Figure 19-1:
Messages keeps tabs on your various simultaneous conversations—literally. Click the different tabs to switch chats. Double-click one to open it into its own window, without the tabs taking up space.

- **Unified chat/text messages with phones (iMessages).** This is huge. If you and your conversation partner both have iCloud accounts, then you both can move freely from phone to tablet to Mac. Your conversation appears in real time on all your gadgets simultaneously. If you started texting someone on the train home, you can sit down at your Mac and open Messages—and pick up right where you left off.

 The messages, which Apple calls iMessages, are a lot more flexible than regular text messages. They can be much longer than 160 characters. They can include photos, movies, or other kinds of files. They give you feedback that lets you know when a message has arrived on the recipient's gadget.

 And they don't count as text messages. They're routed through the internet rather than the cellphone voice network. As far as your cellphone company is concerned, you're not texting at all, and therefore you don't have to pay for a texting plan.

- **Send text messages.** If you have an iPhone, you can also exchange text messages with *any* cellphone—from Messages, while seated at your *Mac*. That's a mind-bending violation of the usual rules that confine text messages to cellphones only.

- **Send audio clips.** Instead of just typing a line or two to somebody, you can speak it. That short recording winds up on the other person's Mac, iPhone, or iPad. It's like leaving a voicemail.

- **Free videoconferencing.** Messages can auto-open FaceTime, for those situations when having a face-to-face video chat (or a high-quality voice call) is more efficient than typing.

- **File transfers.** Got an album of high-quality photos or a giant presentation file that's too big to send by email? Forget about using some online file-transfer service or networked server; you can drag that monster file directly to your buddy's Mac, through Messages, for a direct machine-to-machine transfer. (It lands in the other Mac's Downloads folder.)

- **Screen sharing.** Next time your parents or neighbors are throwing themselves upon your mercy for tech support, remember this: Messages lets you see their screen, and even control it, from across the internet. Or you can volunteer your own screen for sharing, so you can demonstrate things to them.

When you open Messages for the first time, you're invited to sign into (or sign up for) your iCloud or Apple account. Take the opportunity to set this up; you'll be glad you did. (You may have to *authenticate* your account—prove it's really you—by entering a six-digit code that Apple sends to all the other gadgets on your Apple account, like your iPhone.)

Let the Chat Begin

If you've ever corresponded with someone in Messages before, you see that person's name in the left-side list of conversations, as shown in Figure 19-1. (Or, if you've got

Messages

Somewhere between email and the telephone lies the joyous communication tool called instant messaging. Plenty of IM programs run on the Mac, but macOS comes with its very own instant messenger program called Messages. (It used to be called iChat.) It's built right into the system and ready to connect to your friends on Apple's iCloud network.

Note: At one time, the Messages app could handle chats on a bunch of different chat networks: AIM, Yahoo, Facebook, Jabber, Gtalk, and so on. In macOS Mojave, though, Messages is primarily a gateway to Apple's own chat network, called iMessages. It requires that both you and your chat partner have iCloud accounts (Chapter 16). (The one exception: It can also show you regular text messages from your iPhone.)

This chapter covers how to use Messages to communicate by video, audio, and text with your online pals.

Welcome to Messages

Messages does seven things very well:

- **Instant messaging.** Instant messaging combines the privacy of email and the immediacy of the phone. You type messages in a chat window, and your friends type back to you in real time.

 You can *keep* your text messages, too. They're not locked onto your phone, like regular text messages, and they don't scroll away forever, like regular text messages. You can archive them, search them, copy and paste them, print them, forward them, and so on.

Stifle Pop-Ups and Pop-Unders

The world's smarmiest advertisers inundate us with *pop-up* and *pop-under* ads—nasty little windows that appear in front of the browser window or, worse, behind it, waiting to jump out the moment you close your current window.

If this kind of thing is driving you crazy, choose Safari→Preferences→Security→Block Pop-Up Windows. It's a war out there—but at least you now have some ammunition.

Tip: This feature doesn't block windows that appear when you *click a link*—only those that appear unbidden.

Most cookies are perfectly innocuous—and, in fact, helpful, because they let websites remember your tastes, your name, and so on. But fear is widespread, and the media fan the flames with tales of sinister cookies that track your movements on the web.

To take some control, choose Safari→Preferences→Privacy tab (Figure 18-23), where your cookie preference settings await. "Block all cookies" means no cookies can come in, and no cookie information can go out. You'll have to reenter your information upon every visit to every web page.

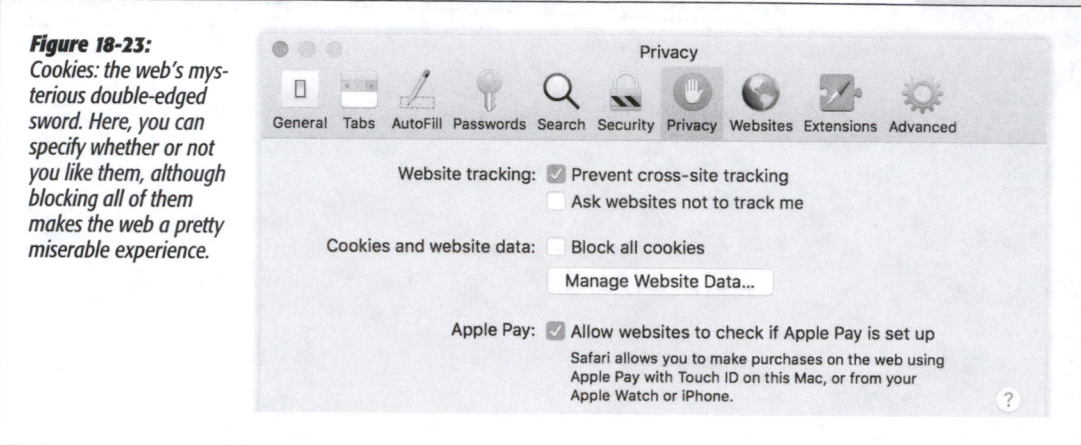

Figure 18-23:
Cookies: the web's mysterious double-edged sword. Here, you can specify whether or not you like them, although blocking all of them makes the web a pretty miserable experience.

If you don't use that checkbox, then Safari works as though you had the old "Only from websites I visit" option turned on. That is, you get cookies from sites you want to open, but not cookies deposited on your hard drive by sites you're *not* actually visiting—cookies that an especially evil banner ad gives you, for example.

The Manage Website Data button here reveals the complete list of all your cookies, and you can delete any scary ones. While you're in there, notice that there's other stuff websites have dumped onto your Mac. There are things like cache files and local storage files (data that web applications leave behind on your hard drive—a bit like cookies, except that websites can't retrieve this information later). All of it is available for your removal with a click on the Remove All button.

Also while you're in this box: "Prevent cross-site tracking" doesn't affect how many ads you see—but it does prevent advertisers from delivering ads *based on your interests* (as exhibited by your other web surfing). You'll just get generic ads.

"Ask websites not to track me" signs you up for an online "Do not track" program. The problem is that this program is voluntary—so the sleazy operators just ignore it.

Finally, "Allow websites to check if Apple Pay is set up" appears only if your Mac has a Touch ID fingerprint reader, or if you have an iPhone or Apple Watch that works with Apple Pay. It permits shopping sites to show the Pay with Apple Pay button on product detail pages only if you do, in fact, have Apple Pay set up.

world's innocent web audiences. In macOS, Apple strikes back with some very clever privacy and security features indeed.

Erasing Your History

Some people find it creepy that Safari maintains a complete list of every website they've seen recently, right there in plain view of any co-worker who wanders by.

To delete just one particularly incriminating History listing, choose History→Show All History. In the resulting organizer window, highlight the offending address, and then press your Delete key. Choose History→Hide History to return to normal browsing. You've just rewritten History!

Or, to erase the entire History menu, choose History→Clear History. In the resulting box, you can specify that you want to erase only the *last hour's* worth of history, only *today's* history, the last *two days'* worth—or your *entire* history.

Of course, the History list isn't the only set of footprints you leave as you surf. But the Clear History command erases all other shreds of your activities: any cookies (web page preference files) you've accumulated, your list of past downloads, the cache files (bits of the web pages that a browser stores on your hard drive to save time when you return to the page they came from), and so on. This is good information to know; you might be nominated to the Supreme Court someday.

Private Browsing

Of course, that's a lot of work just to cover your tracks; it also erases a lot of valuable cookies, passwords, and History entries you'd probably like to keep. Is all that really necessary just so you can duck in for an occasional look at the Hot Bods of the Midwestern Tax Preparers' Association website?

No, it's not. *Private browsing* lets you surf without adding any pages to your History list, searches to your Google search suggestions, passwords to Safari's saved password list, or autofill entries to Safari's memory. (Apple says this feature is intended for use at public Macs, where you don't want to reveal anything personal to subsequent visitors. Ha!)

The trick is to choose File→New Private Window *before* you open the naughty site. (Your other Safari windows can stay open, in non-private mode.) A banner across the top of your new private window explains what's happening: Within this window, Safari records nothing while you surf. When you're ready to browse "publicly" again, just close the window.

In other words, what happens in Private Browsing stays in Private Browsing.

Cookie Control—and Privacy Control

Cookies are something like web page preference files. Certain websites—particularly commercial ones like Amazon.com—deposit them on your hard drive like little bookmarks so they'll remember you the next time you visit.

Tip: See Safari's Help menu? It features a search box that lets you search all the menu commands in Safari—including Safari's History menu. That's just a *crazy* powerful feature. It means you can re-find a site without having to hunt through all the History submenus manually; just search for any word you remember from the title.

PDF Pages Online

PDF files are all over the web as, among other things, forms to download, online brochures, and scanned book pages. But they aren't always especially readable in a browser window.

Unless, that is, you're using Safari. The next time you're squinting at a PDF in a window, point to the bottom edge of the document; you'll see a toolbar like the one in Figure 18-20 appear. With these four icons, you can zoom out, zoom in, open the file in Preview, or save the PDF file to your Downloads folder.

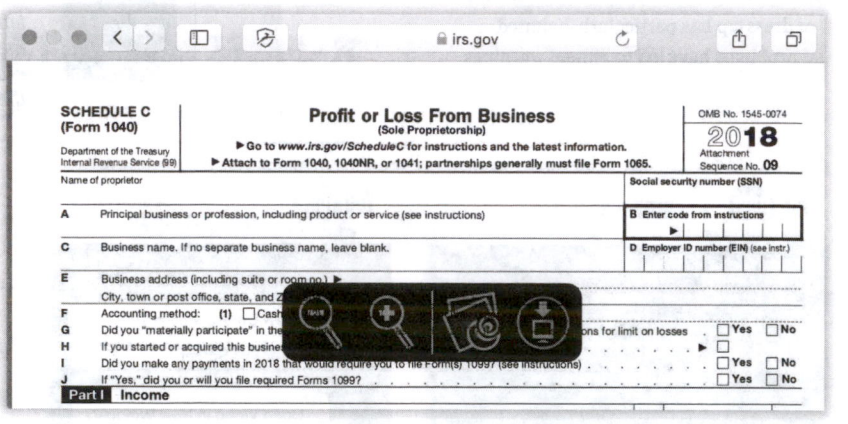

Figure 18-20:
If you're having trouble reading the tiny type in a PDF, point your mouse to the bottom of it to invoke Safari's PDF toolbar. You can zoom out, zoom in, open the file in the Mac's Preview program, or even download it from the website with a well-placed click.

Picture-in-Picture Video

Apple recently added a feature to Safari: picture-in-picture video (Figure 18-21).

When you're watching a video, you can click a PIP icon (⊡) to detach it into a small, floating, movable window, so that you can keep watching as you do other work. That floating mini-video window even hangs around when you switch Spaces (page 187).

Once it's on the screen, you can resize it (drag by the lower-right corner), move it to a different corner of the screen (drag the picture), pause it, or pop it full-screen (those buttons appear when you point to the video without clicking).

This feature works in Safari and iTunes—but not, alas, on any video you come across. It works only on videos that use HTML5, like those on Vimeo and ESPN.

Note: A nearly identical pop-up menu is available for "New tabs open with." That is, you can specify one starter-page preference for new *tabs* and another for new *windows.*

Finding Text on Web Pages

The address/search bar can help you find websites that match your keywords. But some pages are so long, dense, or poorly designed that finding the words *on* the page takes a whole 'nother search engine. Fortunately, Safari's search-within-the-page function shines a light on the word or phrase you're seeking.

To use it, press ⌘-F and then type your search word into the Find box (Figure 18-19). As Safari locates the word or words, it displays them within a bright-yellow box and dims the background of the rest of the page. The Find bar also tells you how many times the word or phrase occurs on the page; you can jump to each instance. Click the ⊗ to start over with new search terms, or click Done to close the Find box and return to your normal browsing activity.

Tip: When you use the Find command, are you looking for words on the page that *begin* with your search term, or that contain it *anywhere?* You can specify. Click the very tiny 🔍 in the search box and choose either Contains or Starts With from the very tiny pop-up menu.

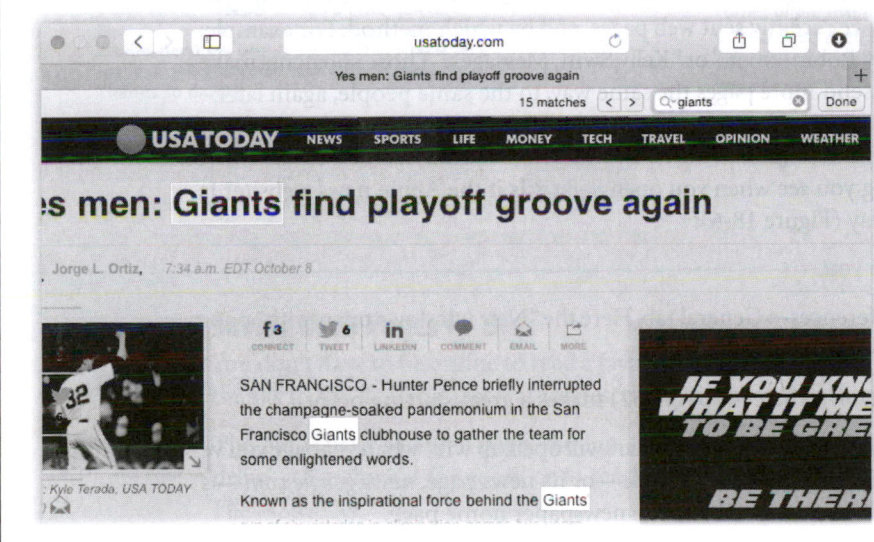

Figure 18-19:
Once you enter your search word ("giants," in this case), the browser dims the page and highlights every instance of that word—making it much easier to find what you're looking for across a crowded web page.

The History Menu

The History menu lists the websites you've visited in the past week or so, neatly organized into subfolders like Earlier Today and Yesterday. (A similar menu appears when you click *and hold* the ‹ or › button.) These are great features if you can't recall the URL for a website you remember having visited recently.

The Reader button (≡) in the address/search bar is amazing. With one click (or press of Shift-⌘-R), it eliminates *everything* from the web page you're reading except the text and photos. No ads, blinking, links, banners, promos, or anything else.

The text is also changed to a clean, clear font and size, and the background is made plain white. Basically, it makes any web page look like a printed book page or a Kindle page, and it's glorious (Figure 18-17).

To exit Reader, press the same keyboard shortcut, or click ≡ again. Best. Feature. Ever.

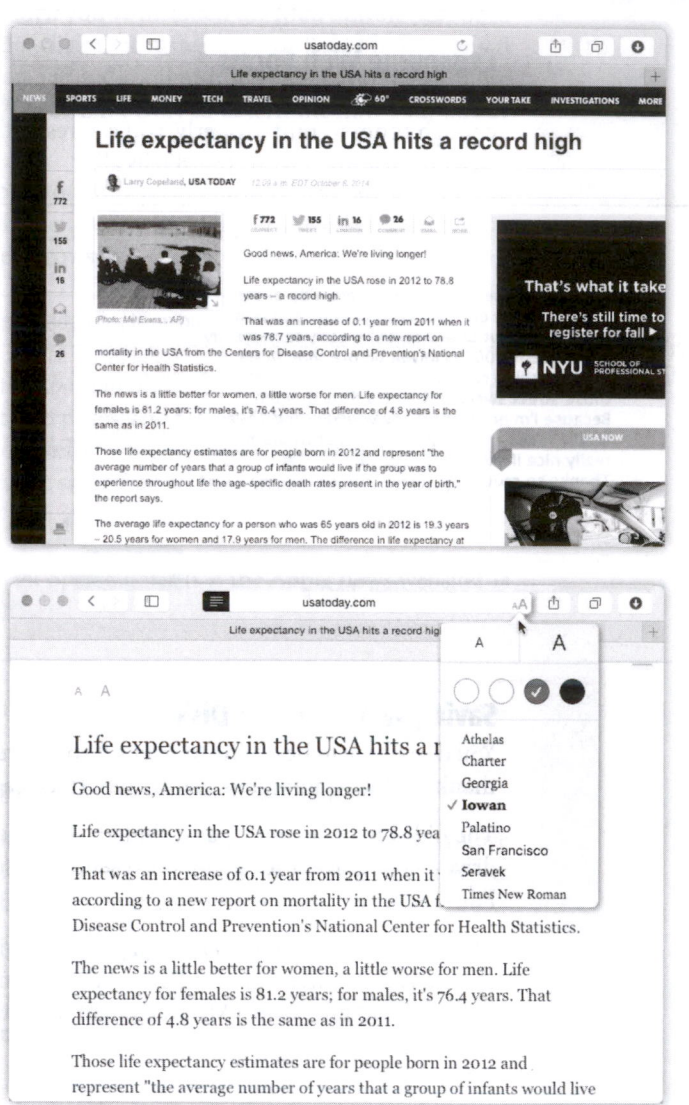

Figure 18-17:
Seriously, which way would you rather read an article? Like this (top)? Or in the calm peace of this (bottom)? Not only does Reader get rid of all the ads and clutter and blinking, it even knits multipage articles together into one seamless, scrolling page. Use the space bar or two fingers to scroll, as usual.

Using the ₐA button as a pop-up menu, you can change the typeface for your Reader view—or click one of the four circles to change the back-ground color. Some people find that light text against a dark background is especially soothing.

When you click a link to download something from a web page, it *visibly* flies to the upper-right corner of the Safari window, where the Downloads button (⊕) appears. You can then monitor the progress of the download at a glance—because the Downloads button *fills up* with blue as the download completes.

As Figure 18-16 shows, you can also view and manipulate a list of everything you've downloaded recently, all without leaving the comfort of whatever page you're on.

To pause downloading, click the ✕ button next to the download's name. Later, you can generally pick up from where you left off by clicking the Resume (⏻) button.

Tip: In Safari→Preferences→General, you can opt to have your download listings removed from the Downloads window as soon as they've been successfully downloaded, maybe for privacy reasons.

Figure 18-16:
Click the Downloads (⊕) button to view this list of recent downloads. Double-click an icon to open the download. Drag it out of the list onto your desktop, or onto a folder on the desktop. You can even drag it onto a Dock icon to open that file with a particular program.

Click the ⚲ button to jump to the file wherever it's sitting in the Finder. To remove an item from the list, click it and then press Delete. (The Clear button erases the whole list.)

Status Bar

The status bar at the bottom of the window tells you what Safari is doing (such as "Opening page…" or "Done"). When you point to a link without clicking, the status bar also tells you which URL will open if you click it.

For those two reasons, it's a useful strip, but it doesn't appear when you first run Safari. You have to summon it by choosing View→Show Status Bar.

Reader

How can people read web articles when there's Times Square blinking going on all around them? Fortunately, you'll never have to put up with that again.

- **Click the ⊕ button.** This button appears only when you move your cursor to the left end of the address box.

- **Use the menu.** Choose Bookmarks→Add to Reading List, or press Shift-⌘-D.

- **Use the Share button.** You can also click ⬆ on the toolbar and choose Add to Reading List.

To view your saved pages, open the Sidebar (click ▯); then click the Reading List (◯◯) tab. Or just choose View→Show Reading List Sidebar (Control-⌘-2).

To read the pages in the Reading List, you can press Option-⌘-▼ or Option-⌘-▲ to move up and down your list.

Tip: If you're reading one article in your Reading List using the Reader feature (described in a moment), and then select another article, then it, too, will appear in Reader.

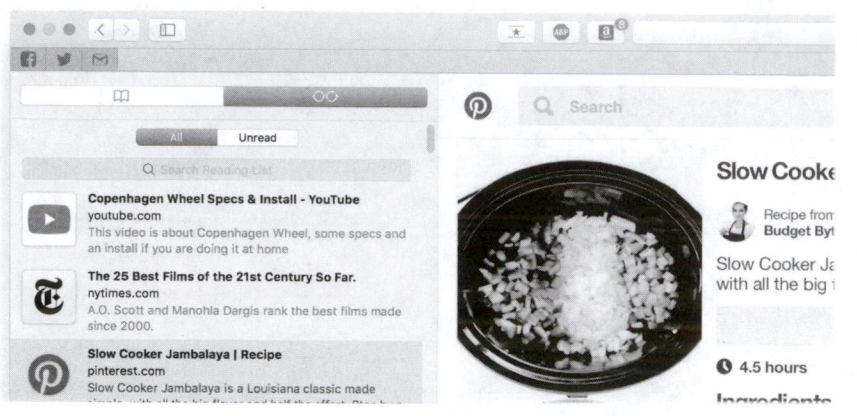

Figure 18-15:
To revisit a page in the Reading List, just click it. Screen out the pages you've already read by clicking the Unread tab at the top. Delete an entry by right-clicking or two-finger clicking it and choosing Remove Item from the shortcut menu.

Keyboard Control

Efficiency freaks generally prefer keyboard shortcuts to using the mouse, so Safari is filled with them.

Press Tab to jump from one text box or pop-up menu to the next on your web page. Add the Option key to jump from one *link* to another (and when you highlight a link, press Return to "click" it).

Tip: For a shockingly complete list of Safari's keyboard shortcuts, open the Help menu. In the search box, type *safari shortcuts*. Wait a moment. Click "Safari keyboard and other shortcuts" in the list of Help topics.

The Download Manager

No browser has ever made tracking downloads simpler.

As a bonus, clicking a link on a pinned page opens up in a new tab, so the original page is waiting for you when you're done. When you're reading your Twitter feed, for example, you can click a link in someone's tweet to open the page he wanted you to see...you read it...you hit ⌘-W to close the tab...and you're right back in your Twitter feed, ready to click another link.

See Figure 18-14 for details on creating (and removing) pinned tabs.

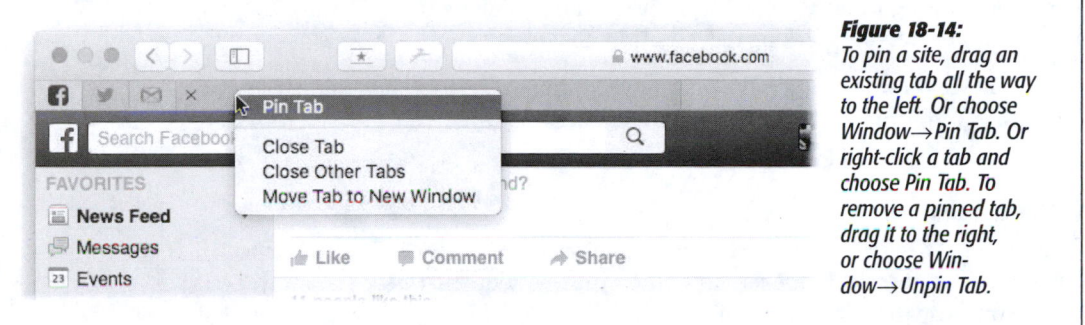

Figure 18-14:
To pin a site, drag an existing tab all the way to the left. Or choose Window→Pin Tab. Or right-click a tab and choose Pin Tab. To remove a pinned tab, drag it to the right, or choose Window→Unpin Tab.

Tips for Better Surfing

Safari is filled with shortcuts and tricks for better speed and more pleasant surfing. For example:

The Reading List

The Reading List (◯◯) stores entire web pages that you want to read later (Figure 18-15). These aren't just bookmarks (links); the Reading List downloads and stores the full contents of each page you've requested so you can read them when you don't have an internet connection. Better than that, actually: It stores that page *and* any other pages necessary to continue reading an article you've flagged.

The Reading List also makes it faster to flag a web page you like—you don't have to make up a name or a location for it, as with a bookmark. Also, the Reading List keeps track of what you've read; you can use the All/Unread buttons at the top of the list to view everything or just what you haven't yet read.

You might treat the Reading List as a list of pages you'll want to read *once* later, and use bookmarks for pages you like to revisit *frequently*.

To make matters even sweeter, iCloud synchronizes your Reading List among your Mac, iPhone, iPad, and so on (if you've turned on Safari syncing in System Preferences→ iCloud). It's as though the web keeps your place as you move from gadget to gadget.

To add a page to the Reading List, use one of these techniques:

- **Shift-click a link.** That simple trick adds the linked page to the Reading List. You don't have to *visit* the page itself (only the link to it), or even to open the Reading List first.

iPhones or iPads. Thanks to the miracle of iCloud syncing, the last windows and tabs you had open on that other gadget (even if the gadget is turned off) show up here.

The concept is to unify your Macs and i-gadgets into one glorious, seamless web-browsing experience. You're reading three browser windows and tabs on your phone—why not resume on the big screen when you get home and sit down in front of your Mac?

Amazingly enough, you can even *close* the tabs and windows on your other gadgets, by remote control—by clicking the ✕ button next to each one.

You won't see these tabs unless the Macs have Mountain Lion or later. And, of course, Safari has to be turned on in System Preferences→iCloud (on the Mac), or Settings→iCloud (on the phone or tablet).

Pinned Tabs

This feature is hard to describe but handy to have: *pinned* tabs. These are special, square, icon-only tabs at the far left end of your window that never go away, even when you close the window or quit Safari. (You can see three of them at the left end in Figure 18-14.)

That might sound like the same thing as a bookmark, but there's a difference: When you click a bookmark, Safari takes a couple of seconds to fetch that web page and then display it. A pinned tab, on the other hand, is *already* loaded; Safari keeps its underlying page constantly updated.

That effect is especially useful for sites you check often throughout the day—sites like Facebook and Twitter, or mail sites like Gmail. Every time you click that pinned tab, the corresponding page appears, already loaded and up to date.

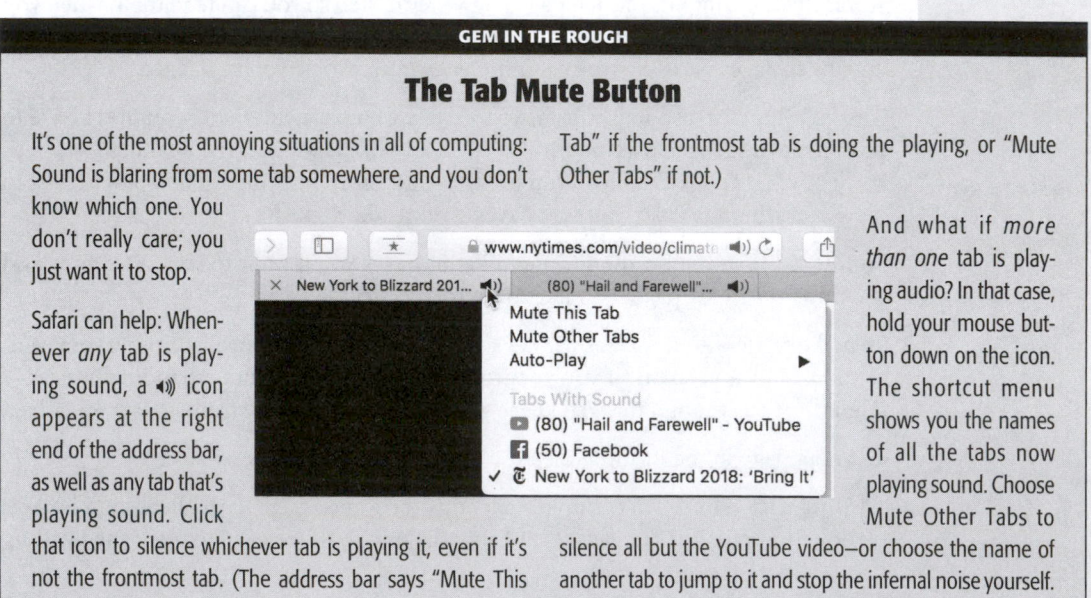

GEM IN THE ROUGH

The Tab Mute Button

It's one of the most annoying situations in all of computing: Sound is blaring from some tab somewhere, and you don't know which one. You don't really care; you just want it to stop.

Safari can help: Whenever *any* tab is playing sound, a 🔊 icon appears at the right end of the address bar, as well as any tab that's playing sound. Click that icon to silence whichever tab is playing it, even if it's not the frontmost tab. (The address bar says "Mute This Tab" if the frontmost tab is doing the playing, or "Mute Other Tabs" if not.)

And what if *more than one* tab is playing audio? In that case, hold your mouse button down on the icon. The shortcut menu shows you the names of all the tabs now playing sound. Choose Mute Other Tabs to silence all but the YouTube video—or choose the name of another tab to jump to it and stop the infernal noise yourself.

Tab View

When you've opened a few tabs, their names, in titles across the top of your Safari window, get pretty cramped. Fortunately, there's also Tab view: Miniatures of all your open tabs. To see it, click the Show All Tabs button on the toolbar (⬚)—or how about this? Just pinch two fingers on your trackpad. Figure 18-13 explains all.

Tip: Once you've opened Tab view, you can perform a cool trick: You can search all the open tabs at once (either for words in the web page's names, or text in their addresses). You don't have to click into any search box first; just type. As you type, Safari hides all but the matching tabs.

iCloud tabs

At the bottom of Show All Tabs view (Figure 18-13), a special treat awaits: A list of whatever browser windows and tabs you had open on your *other* Apple gadgets, like

Figure 18-13:
Tab view gives you a horizontally scrolling parade of miniatures so you can easily spot what's in your open tabs.

To get here, pinch with two fingers on your trackpad, or click the Show All Tabs button (shown by the cursor here).

In Tab view, you can scroll among the tabs in the usual way (drag two fingers on your trackpad, for example). Sites with multiple pages open appear as stacked thumbnails. When you find the tab you want, click or press Return.

You can also back out of Tab view without switching tabs at all, just by spreading two fingers on the trackpad.

Autofill: Credit Cards

When you buy something online, Safari can enter your credit-card information with one click, making shopping infinitely easier. It's as easy as 1, 2. Figure 18-10 shows you how to store your credit cards in Safari and how to use them to buy things online.

This feature is a lot like the popular password/credit card keeper programs 1Password and Dashlane—better, really, because it's free, and because iCloud Keychain autosyncs your credit card information to your iPhones, iPads, and iPod Touches, too.

But in one way, it's worse: As yet another security layer, Safari doesn't memorize the security code, also known as the CVV or CV2 code, that you need to complete a credit card transaction. You have to fill that in yourself every time you buy something.

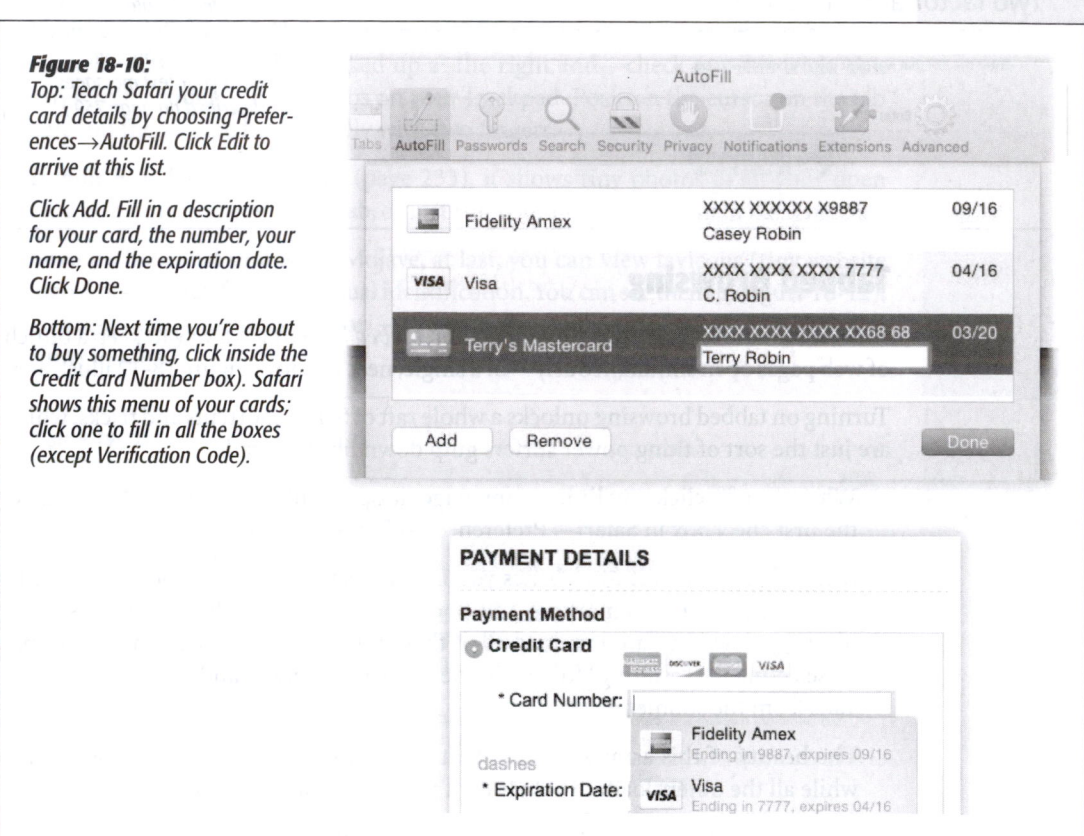

Figure 18-10:

Top: Teach Safari your credit card details by choosing Preferences→AutoFill. Click Edit to arrive at this list.

Click Add. Fill in a description for your card, the number, your name, and the expiration date. Click Done.

Bottom: Next time you're about to buy something, click inside the Credit Card Number box). Safari shows this menu of your cards; click one to fill in all the boxes (except Verification Code).

Autofill: Text-Message Authentication Codes

You know how, when you try to log onto certain websites, they first send your phone a text message to prove that you're you? (It's called two-factor authentication. Security experts love it. People hate it.)

When you're signing up for an account on some website, and you tap in the box where you're supposed to enter a password, Safari offers to make up a password for you. It's a doozy, too, along the lines of *23k2k4-29cs8-58384-ckk3322* (Figure 18-8, bottom left).

You're not expected to remember that. Safari saves this password, so that it can enter it automatically on your next visit (Figure 18-8, lower right).

And if System Preferences→iCloud→Keychain is turned on, then your memorized passwords will be available on your other Apple machines (phones, tablets, Macs), too.

Note: If you have several accounts for the same site, you'll see a button for each one.

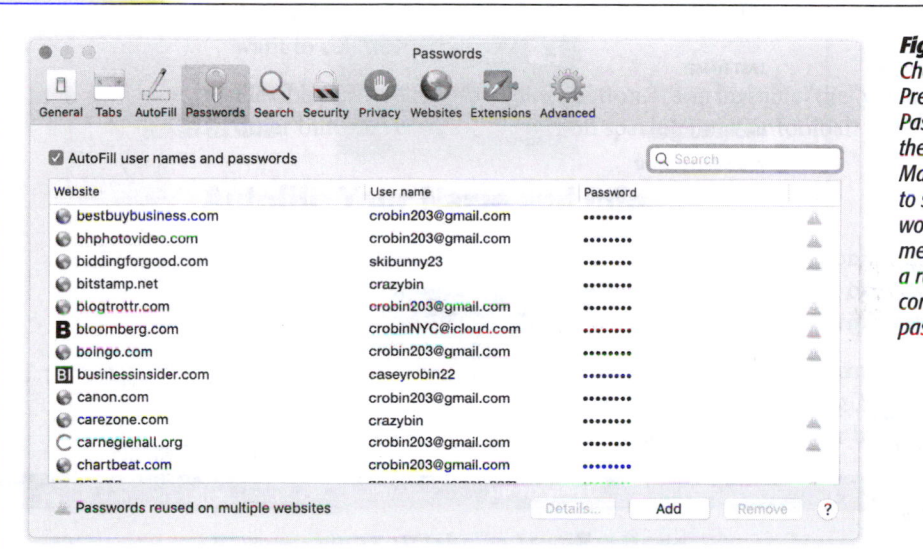

Figure 18-9: Choose Safari→Preferences→Passwords (and then enter your Mac password) to see the passwords Safari has memorized. Click a row to view the corresponding password.

The master password list

You can view a master list of the actual memorized names and passwords. It waits for you at Safari→Preferences→Passwords. You have to prove your identity with your Mac password or Touch ID before you're allowed to see them.

On this screen, you can view a password by clicking its row (Figure 18-9). You can change any saved password, too; double-click it. To add a password manually, click Add. Or, if a login no longer pleases you, click it and hit Remove.

This list, by the way, might display the occasional ⚠ symbol. That's flagging passwords you've used more than once, for different sites. Almost everyone does that, because who's really going to memorize 300 different passwords? But security experts frown on the practice, because it means once a hacker gets the password for one of your accounts (from some corporate data breach, for example), then he's got access to your other accounts, too. Since macOS can remember and fill in your passwords all by itself, you might as well avoid that fate.

- **Share.** Here's the standard macOS Share menu, for sending a web page to another person, or to your Notes app, for example.

- **Show All Tabs.** See page 744.

- **Top Sites** opens, of course, the Top Sites window (page 733).

- **Home.** Click to bring up the web page you've designated as your home page (in the Safari→Preferences→General tab).

- **History.** Click to open the list of websites you've visited recently in a window—a much easier-to-navigate display than the History *menu*.

- **Sidebar** shows or hides the Sidebar, the left-side column of bookmarks, saved articles, or RSS feeds.

- **Favorites Bar.** Hides or shows the horizontal toolbar that lists your favorite bookmarks (the equivalent of choosing View→Favorites Bar).

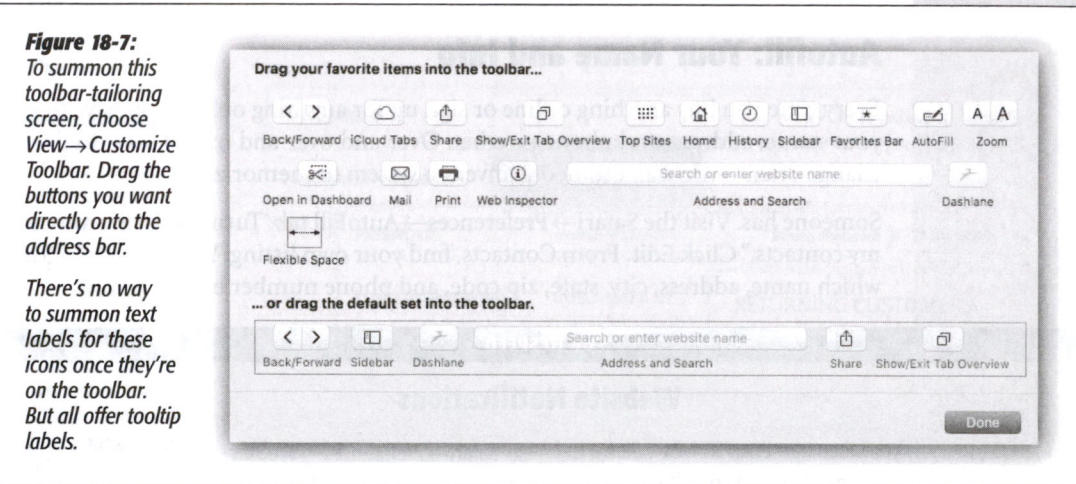

Figure 18-7:
To summon this toolbar-tailoring screen, choose View→Customize Toolbar. Drag the buttons you want directly onto the address bar.

There's no way to summon text labels for these icons once they're on the toolbar. But all offer tooltip labels.

- **AutoFill.** Click this button to make Safari fill in web order forms with your name, address, and other information. See the next section.

- **Zoom.** These handy buttons make the current page smaller or bigger each time you click. The keyboard shortcuts are ⌘-plus or ⌘-minus.

- **Open in Dashboard.** This icon is the key to creating a Dashboard *web clip,* which is a snippet of web content that you can keep available in your Dashboard. Click this button, and then select the part of the page you want to widgetize.

- **Mail.** Opens a new, outgoing message in your email program. The subject line contains the *name* of the site you were visiting; the body contains the actual web page. But in the Send Web Content As pull-down menu, you can choose from three other ways to send the page: in Reader view, as a PDF, or a link only. You can

today's screens, which work by packing their pixels together more tightly—and making everything look smaller.

Fortunately, Safari is well equipped to help you with this problem. In fact, it offers many solutions:

- **Enlarge the screen.** Press ⌘-plus or ⌘-minus to enlarge or reduce the entire web page. Or use the two-finger "spread" gesture on your laptop trackpad. Or use the Zoom button, if you've added it to your toolbar. The advantage of this method is that the whole web page's layout remains proportional.

- **Magnify a block.** Lightly double-tap (don't fully click) with *two fingers* on your trackpad to zoom in to one block of text or graphics on a page, as already described.

- **Blow up just the text.** If you add the Option key to ⌘-plus and ⌘-minus, the Zoom In and Zoom Out options become Make Text Bigger and Make Text Smaller, magnifying or shrinking *only the text* on your page. Graphics remain at their original size. You're now distorting the original layout, but you're maximizing the amount of reading you can do before you have to scroll.

- **Zoom in the usual way.** Remember the Control-key zooming technique described on page 327? It's not the same thing as the ⌘-plus or ⌘-minus tricks, which keep the window frame and menu at normal size. The Control-key zooming technique magnifies *everything*—the entire screen, menus and all. It also doesn't keep text as sharp as the ⌘-plus/⌘-minus trick.

- **Specify a minimum type size.** This may be the best option of all, because it saves you all that zooming. Open Safari→Preferences→Advanced and set the "Never use font sizes smaller than" option to, for example, 14 points. Now *every* web page shows up with legible text. (Except a few oddballs that use weird coding to prevent text-size changing.)

Customizing the Toolbar

There's no title bar in Safari. So the real estate on the bar that remains—the address/search bar, the one Apple calls the toolbar—is precious. Fortunately, you can summon or dismiss individual buttons on the toolbar, in effect customizing it (Figure 18-7).

Here's a catalog of your options:

- **Back/Forward.** Click the Back button (<) to revisit the page you were just on, or > to return to the page you were on *before* you clicked the Back button. See page 725 for more details.

- **iCloud Tabs** open whatever browser windows and tabs you had open on your other Apple gadget, like an iPhone or iPad or another Mac (running Mountain Lion or later). Thanks to the miracle of iCloud syncing, the last windows and tabs you had open on that other gadget (even if the gadget is turned off) show up here. (This is visible in Figure 18-13.)

The beauty of the Favorites page is that it has lots of room both horizontally and vertically. And it doesn't eat up any space—it's completely hidden until you click in the address bar.

You can edit the icons on the Favorites page, of course:

- **Rearrange them.** You can drag any icon to a new spot.

- **Remove them.** Drag an icon out of the main Favorites view window to make it disappear in a puff of cartoon smoke.

- **View them as folders.** If you put several bookmarks into a folder, it appears on the Favorites panel as a single icon filled with even tinier icons.

- **Add an icon.** When you find a page you'd like to add to the Favorites screen, choose Bookmarks→Add Bookmark (⌘-D); on the "Where" sheet that appears, choose Favorites. Click Add.

Top Sites

The Top Sites window (Figure 18-6) *used* to be the starting-out page in Safari. It's exactly the same idea as the Favorites view—it's a screen full of website icons—except that Safari chooses them, not you. It calculates which are your favorite websites according to *how often* and *how recently* you've visited them. The idea, again, is to save you time; the sites you're most likely to want to revisit are one click away.

POWER USERS' CLINIC

Quick Website Search

This crazy and obscure feature lets you search *within* a certain site (like Amazon, Reddit, or Wikipedia) right from within Safari's regular search bar.

For example, typing *wiki mollusk* can offer a one-click search of Wikipedia for its entry on mollusks. Typing *amazon ipad* can offer links to buy an iPad from Amazon. Typing *reddit sitcoms* can open *reddit.com* to its search results for sitcoms.

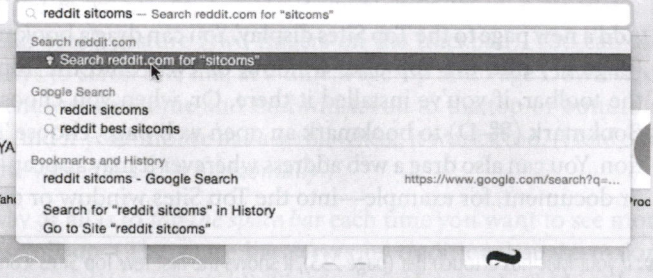

None of this works, however, until (a) the feature is turned on (Safari→Preferences→Search→Enable Quick Website Search), and (b) you've *manually* taught Safari how to search those sites one time each. To do that, pull up the home page of

the site you'll want to search (let's say it's *reddit.com*) and use its regular search bar. Search for anything. Close the window.

That site's name now appears in the list in Safari→Preferences→Search→Enable Quick Website Search→Manage Websites. (Usually. Many sites don't work with Quick Website Search.)

From now on, you can search that site by typing, for example, *reddit sitcoms* into the address bar. But before you press Return, look closely at the suggestions: The first one is a ready-to-click search for that item on that site, as shown here.

Click it to jump directly to that site's search results. You've saved yourself a few clicks and page-loads.

Tip: You can also drag a *link* from a web page (not just the tiny website logo) onto your Favorites bar. In fact, you can also drag a link directly to the desktop, where it turns into an internet location file. Thereafter, to open Safari and visit the associated web page whenever you like, just double-click this icon.

Better yet, stash a few of these icons in your Dock or Sidebar for even easier access.

- **Remove a button** from the Favorites bar by dragging it down and away.

- **Rearrange the buttons** by dragging them horizontally.

- **Edit a button** by right-clicking or two-finger clicking its name. From the shortcut menu, choose Rename or Edit Address.

Tip: Actually, you can rename a bookmark on the Favorites bar just by click-and-holding on its name. You'll see it highlighted; you can just retype. No right-clicking necessary!

Favorites View

Apple figures that, many times, you'll want to *begin* your surfing session with one of your Favorites. So whenever you open a new window, create a new tab, or click in the address bar (and don't type anything), you're shown the Favorites page (Figure 18-5). Or just click the ::::: icon at the far left of the Favorites bar. (If that's not what you see when you open a new window or tab, you must have changed the settings in Safari→Preferences→General→ "New pages open with" or "New tabs open with.")

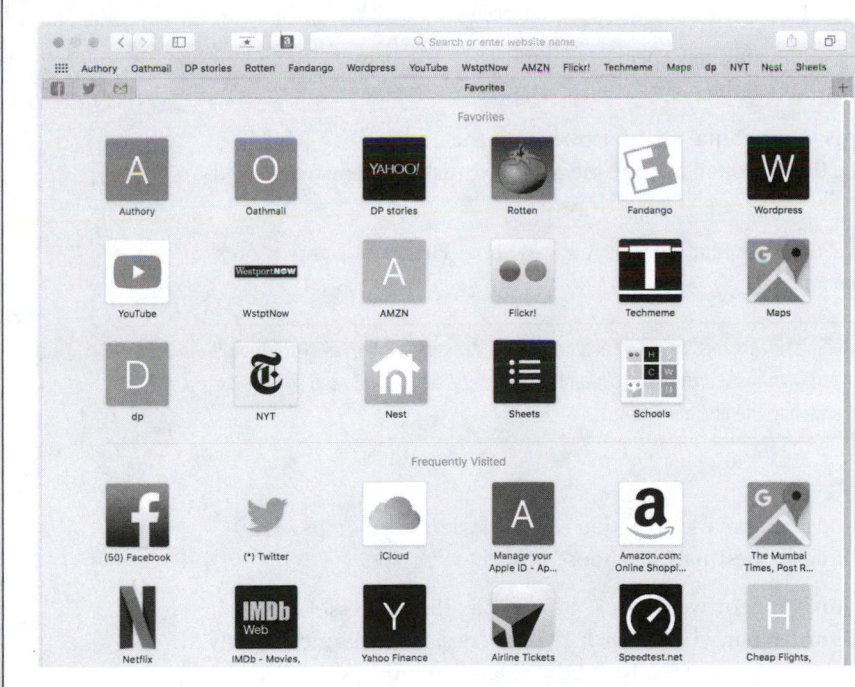

Figure 18-5:
Here's Favorites View. It's a good starting point—a page of icons for your favorite bookmarks.

If you turn on Bookmarks→ Show Frequently Visited in Favorites, you get a second section that lists the websites you visit often.

organize those same items. The Bookmarks Menu folder performs that same function for the Bookmarks menu; it gives you an easy way to organize what's listed there.

Organizing Bookmarks in the Editor

Before the slick new Sidebar came along, there was an earlier way to organize bookmarks: the bookmarks *editor*. You can open this special, spreadsheety window by choosing Bookmarks→Edit Bookmarks or by pressing Option-⌘-B.

In the bookmarks editor window, drag the bookmarks up and down to rearrange them. You can edit a bookmark's name or underlying address by clicking it. Delete one by clicking it and then pressing Delete. There's a New Folder button at top right, too.

Tip: Safari is equipped to help you move out of other web browsers. If you've been using Chrome or Firefox, for example, then the first time you use Safari, your bookmarks and browsing history get imported from the other browser automatically. (You'll see a note to that effect at the bottom of the Favorites or Top Sites view; you can click either Keep or Don't Keep. You can always import them later, using the File→Import From→ Google Chrome or File→Import From→Firefox commands.)

If you have some other weirdo browser, like Internet Explorer or OmniWeb, then importing your bookmarks is only a little more complicated. Use that browser's Export feature to save them to a file, and then use Safari's File→Import Bookmarks command to save you the time of reentering the bookmarks by hand.

Favorites Bar

Some people amass dozens or hundreds of bookmarks—so many that, in day-to-day surfing, it's an unwieldy list.

Fortunately, Safari lets you elevate a few special bookmarks to Favorites status. These are the sites you figure you'll open the most. And Safari gives you two ways to see them.

First, the Favorites bar is a horizontal strip just beneath the address bar (visible in Figure 18-4). If you leave this bar open all the time, you have instantaneous, one-click access to a few very special sites.

To make this bar appear or disappear, choose View→Show Favorites Bar. Or press Shift-⌘-B.

Tip: You can jump to the first nine bookmarks on your Favorites bar by pressing Option-⌘-1 through 9. That's one key more complicated than it used to be (in Yosemite, it was just ⌘-1, ⌘-2, and so on)—but those simpler keystrokes now switch to the first nine *tabs*.

Then:

- **Add a favorite.** You add a bookmark to this bar exactly as described on page 729— but for the new bookmark's destination, choose Favorites.

 You can also drag your current web page's *name* from the address/search bar directly onto the Favorites bar. (Don't click first—just start dragging directly downward on the address bar.) You're offered the chance to type a shorter name for your new Favorite.

this bookmark stored. This is a quick method, but it doesn't offer you the chance to rename the bookmark.

Organizing Bookmarks in the Sidebar

See the ▯ button on the toolbar? It opens the Sidebar, the left-side panel shown at left in Figure 18-4. (You can also choose Bookmarks→Show Bookmarks, or choose View→Show Bookmarks Sidebar, or press Control-⌘-1.)

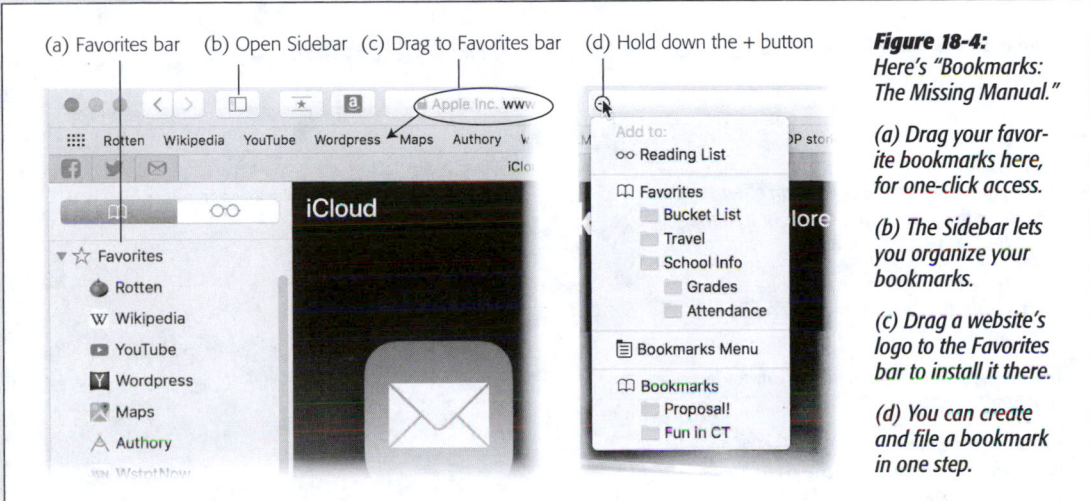

(a) Favorites bar (b) Open Sidebar (c) Drag to Favorites bar (d) Hold down the + button

Figure 18-4:
Here's "Bookmarks: The Missing Manual."

(a) Drag your favorite bookmarks here, for one-click access.

(b) The Sidebar lets you organize your bookmarks.

(c) Drag a website's logo to the Favorites bar to install it there.

(d) You can create and file a bookmark in one step.

At the top of this panel, two tabs await. On the first one, the ▥ tab, you can really go to town with bookmark management. For example:

- **Rearrange bookmarks or folders** by dragging them up or down.

- **Create a folder** by choosing Bookmarks→Add Bookmark Folder. Or right-click or two-finger click anywhere in the list; from the shortcut menu, choose New Folder.

 Type a name for the folder, press Return, and then start filling it up by dragging existing bookmark names onto it.

- **To delete a bookmark or a folder,** right-click or two-finger click its name. From the shortcut menu, choose Delete.

- **To edit a bookmark's name,** right-click or two-finger click it, or hold your cursor down in it. From the shortcut menu, choose Rename.

- **To edit the web address a bookmark opens,** right-click or two-finger click its name. From the shortcut menu, choose Edit Address.

While you're poking around, you might notice a special folder that was here before you arrived. The Favorites folder lists the bookmarks you've installed on the Favorites screen described on the following pages; it's just another way to see, choose, and

one from a list, you save yourself the trouble of searching the web or typing out an address.

Safari happens to be overrun with systems of adding and choosing bookmarks; you can't move your cursor without bumping into one. Read on.

Adding a Bookmark

When you find a web page you might like to visit again, do yourself a favor: Bookmark it. Here's how:

- **Press ⌘-D, or choose Bookmarks→ Add Bookmark.** Proceed as shown in Figure 18-3.

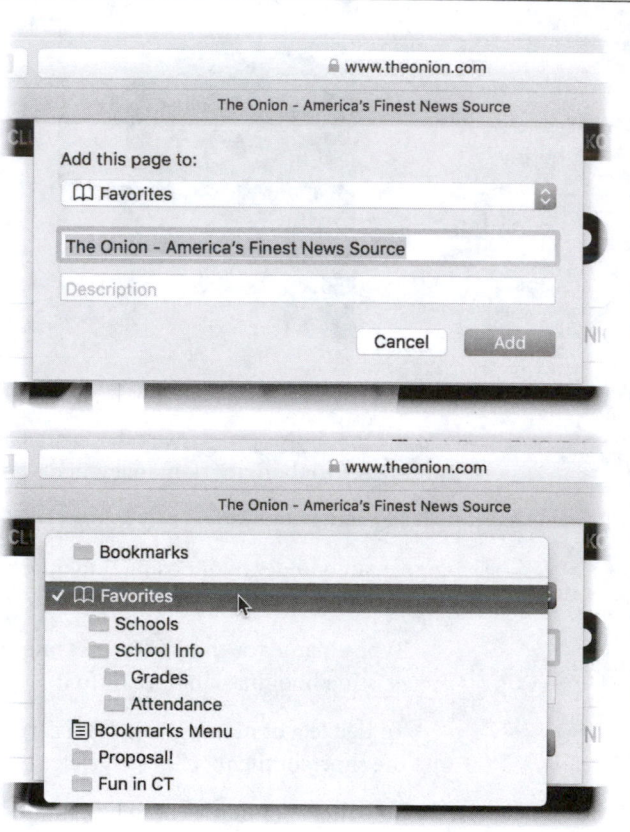

Figure 18-3:
When you add a bookmark, Safari offers to memorize this web page's name, or a shorter name that you specify for it.

You also have to specify where you want to save your new bookmark; Safari offers several options.

There's the Bookmarks menu, or any folders you've set up inside it.

There are the Favorites, a special set of bookmarks that you think you'll use a lot. They get their own special screen and their own special bar, as you'll read in a moment.

There are the Top Sites (page 733).

Finally, there's the master list, the Bookmarks list in the Sidebar; as you can see by (a) in Figure 18-4, this list lets you further categorize your bookmarks by putting them into folders.

- **Press Shift-⌘-D to add the page to the Reading List.**

- **Point to the far-left edge of the address bar; hold your cursor down on the ⊕ button that appears.** This time, you get a pop-up menu of the standard locations (Reading List, Favorites, Bookmarks Menu, and so on); choose where you want

Tip: You can turn off the Google suggestions in Safari→Preferences→Search. Turn off "Include search engine suggestions."

Address/Search Bar Tips

Because typing internet addresses and searching for things are so central to the internet experience and such a typo-prone hassle, the address/search bar is rich with features that minimize keystrokes. For example:

- **You don't have to click there before typing;** just press ⌘-L.

- **You can highlight the entire address** (so it's ready to be typed over with a new one) by clicking anywhere inside the bar. Or press ⌘-L.

- **You don't have to type out the whole internet address.** You can omit the *http://* and *www* portions; Safari fills in those standard address bits for you. To visit *http://www.nytimes.com,* for example, a speed freak might press ⌘-L to highlight the address bar, type *nytimes.com,* and then press Return.

- **You don't have to use Google.** If you prefer to use Bing, Yahoo, or DuckDuckGo for searching instead of Google, then open Safari→Preferences→Search and use the "Search engine" pop-up menu. (DuckDuckGo is more limited than Google and its rivals. But it has gained a following among privacy fans because it doesn't store any information about its visitors or the searches they conduct.)

- **You can look up a word on a page.** If you right-click or two-finger click a highlighted word or phrase on a web page, you can choose Search with Google (or whatever your chosen search site is) from the shortcut menu to search for that text. And, even cooler, this trick works in *all* Cocoa programs—not just Safari.

Bookmarks, Favorites, and Top Sites

Another way to begin your web session is to click a bookmark. In any web browser, bookmarks are essential. They represent sites you want to visit again later. By picking

Extensions

An extension is what, in another time, might have been called a plug-in. It's software from another company that plugs into Safari to add new features.

Maybe you've decided to install ClickToFlash, for example, a Safari extension that prevents animated ads from playing unless you click them. Or maybe you've installed a password-memorizing program like Dashlane. The Pin It button (a key to the popularity of *Pinterest.com*) is an extension, too.

To look over a catalog of available extensions, visit *extensions.apple.com.* Or open Safari→Preferences→Extensions and click More Extensions. The ones you find on Apple's extensions site are safe and solid. But they are intended to modify Safari, and it's possible that some extension, or some combination of them, will make Safari unstable.

So it's handy that on that same Preferences screen, you can find the list of all the extensions you've installed so far, complete with on/off switches and Uninstall buttons.

- **Stop/Reload.** Click the ✕ (or press Esc, or ⌘-period) to interrupt the downloading of a web page you've just requested—if you've made a mistake, for instance.

 Once a page has finished loading, the Stop button turns into a Refresh button (↻). Click it (or press ⌘-R) if a page doesn't look or work quite right, or if you want to see the updated version of it (like for a breaking-news site that changes constantly). Safari re-downloads the web page and reinterprets its text and graphics.

- **Share** (⎙) lets you send the current web page to the Reading List, install it as a bookmark, send it by email or text message, or post it to Twitter or Facebook. See page 263 for details.

- **Show All Tabs** (⎚) displays all your open tabs at once, attractively arrayed as miniatures; see page 744.

- **Downloads** (⬇). Here's Safari's awesome Downloads button (page 747). Click to see everything you've downloaded, or *are* downloading.

Searching the Web

Press ⌘-L to deposit your insertion point inside the unified toolbar, type something you're looking for—*phony baloney,* say—and then press Return. Safari takes you directly to the results page of Google or whatever search site you've selected.

As Figure 18-2 makes clear, Safari offers plenty of assistance as you type, in the form of Google suggestions, matching listings from your Bookmarks and History list, and suggestions from Maps, Wikipedia, iTunes, and other sources.

For example, if you type *empire state building* into the address bar, the first suggestion may not be from the web—but instead from Maps. Click it to open the Empire State Building's page in the Maps program. And if you type *small mouthed salamander*, the first hit is likely to be a link to that critter's Wikipedia page, complete with a tiny photo and the first lines of text.

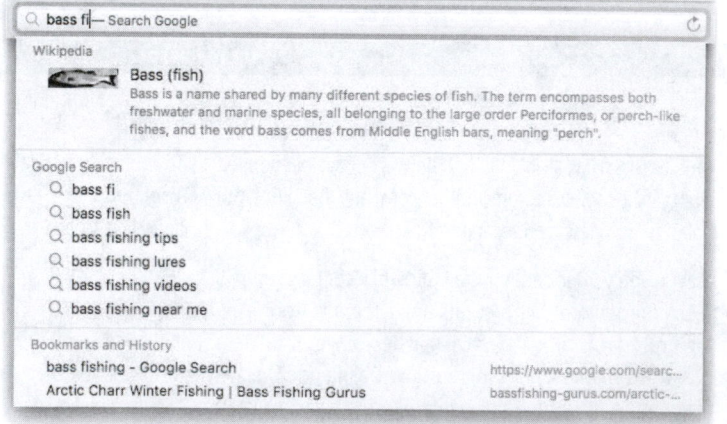

Figure 18-2:
As you type, Safari offers autocomplete suggestions from Wikipedia; Google's own Suggest feature; and matching pages that you've either bookmarked or visited recently.

To save typing, click the correct complete address with your mouse, or use the ▼ key to reach the desired listing and then press Return.

Once you've clicked ‹, you can then click › (or press ⌘-▶, or ⌘-], or use a two-finger swipe to the *right*) to return to the page you were on before you clicked the Back button. Click and hold the ‹ or › button for a pop-up menu of *all* the web pages you've visited during this online session.

That pop-up menu lists the sites by name, as in "*The New York Times*—Breaking News, World News & Multimedia." To view the actual *addresses* instead, Option-click (and hold the mouse down on) the ‹ or › button.

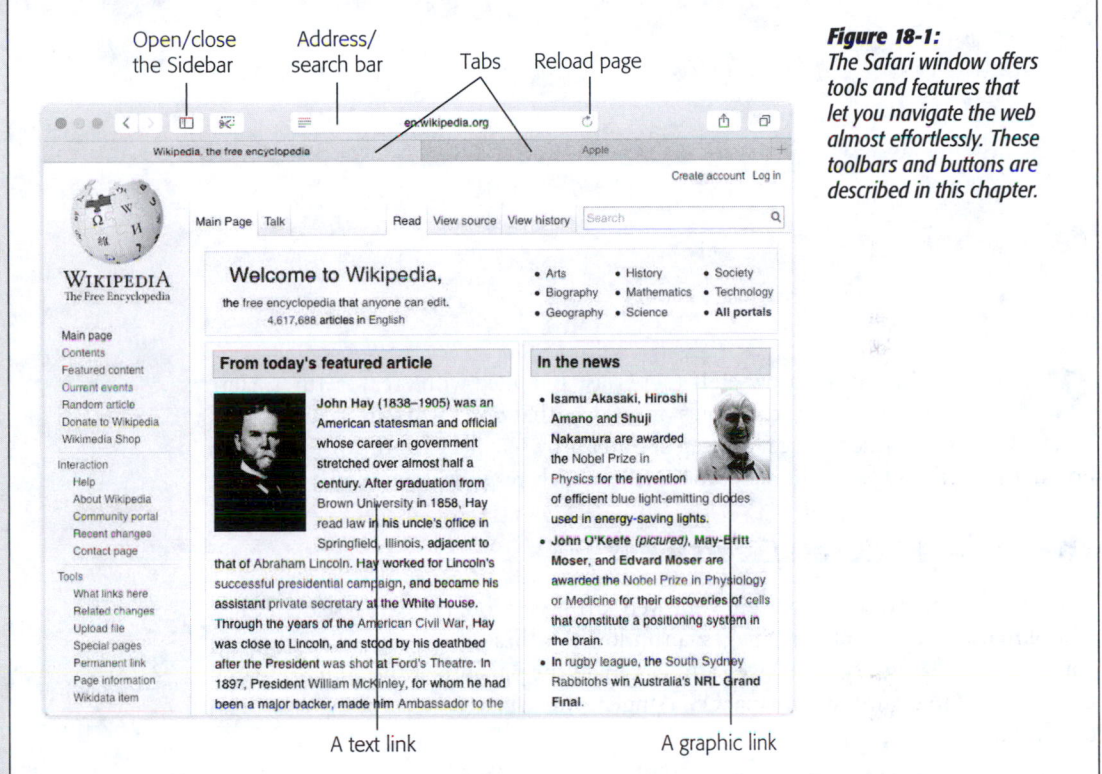

Figure 18-1:
The Safari window offers tools and features that let you navigate the web almost effortlessly. These toolbars and buttons are described in this chapter.

- **Sidebar** (⊟). Click to show or hide the Sidebar, which offers lists of your bookmarks, Reading List, and RSS feeds. (All of this is described on the following pages.)

- **Reader View** (≡). This button appears at the left end of the address/search box, only when you're reading a web page article—a decent-sized block of text. See page 748 for more.

- **Add to Reading List** (⊕). This button appears only when you move your cursor to the far-left end of the address/search box. With one click, you add the current page to your Reading List (page 746). Or, if you hold down the mouse, you can add this page as a bookmark.

Safari

Safari is the Mac's web browser. It's superfast and filled with great features. Here and there, you'll find certain sites or services that don't work in Safari (grrrr), which is why many Mac fans keep another browser, like Chrome or Firefox, on board just in case. Overall, though, Safari makes a slick, responsive window to the web.

The Unified Address/Search Bar

There are all kinds of ways to begin your web surfing session. Perform a search. Click a bookmark. On the following pages: a rundown of these starting points. Often, of course, you'll want to type in a web address; that's the purpose of the address/search bar identified in Figure 18-1. In macOS, a single, unified box serves as both the address bar and the search bar.

If you type a web address there, like *amazon.com,* then pressing Return takes you to that website; if you type anything else, like *cashmere sweaters* or just *amazon,* then pressing Return gives you the Google search results for that phrase, as described next.

Note: The address/search bar doesn't show the full address of the page you're on. You may be reading *http://www.nytimes.com/2019/2/28/us/politics/house-vote-moves-budget-deal-closer-to-approval.html,* but the address bar shows only *nytimes.com.* If you'd rather see the full address, then choose Safari→Preferences→Advanced and turn on "Show full website address."

A few important buttons come installed on the toolbar:

- **Back, Forward.** Click the Back button (‹) to revisit the page you were just on. Keyboard shortcut: ⌘-◄ or ⌘-[, or a two-finger swipe left on the trackpad. (On an Apple Mouse or older Mighty Mouse, that's a *one*-finger swipe.)

Note: Both the Mailing Labels and Envelopes options print *only* the contacts for which you have, in fact, entered physical mailing addresses.

- **Lists.** If all you want is a paper backup of your Contacts entries, then use this setting. In the Attributes list, turn on the checkboxes of the fields you want printed—just name and phone number, for example.

- **Pocket Contacts.** This feature prints a convenient *paper* address book from your virtual one. If you pick Indexed from the Flip Style pop-up menu, then each page's edge will even list the first letters of the last names listed on the page, making it a cinch to find the page with the address you want. (Here again, you can pick which fields you'd like to include—phone numbers, addresses, and so on.)

As you fiddle with the options presented here, you get to see a miniature preview, right in the dialog box, that shows what you're going to get.

No matter which mode you choose, the only cards that print are the ones that were selected when you chose File→Print. If you want to print *all* your cards, therefore, click All in the Group column before you print.

Tip: You can combine the smart-groups feature with the printing features in one clever way: to print yourself a portable phone book when you're heading off for a visit to a different city. That is, set up a smart group that rounds up everyone you know who lives in Chicago, and then print that as a pocket address book.

Contacts Backups

Your Contacts may represent *years* of typing and compiling effort. Losing all that information to a corrupted database or a hard drive crash could be devastating. Here are three ways to protect your Contacts data:

- **Back up your entire Contacts database.** Choose File→Export→Contacts Archive. Store the resulting backup file on another drive, if you like. Later, you can use the File→Import command to find that data and slurp it back in.

- **Turn on iCloud syncing.** An iCloud account has its privileges—and one of them is automatic synchronizing with the iCloud mother ship online.

- **Back up your whole Mac with Time Machine.** Page 266 tells you how.

Once you've found the card you're looking for, you can perform some interesting stunts. If you click the label of a phone number (see Figure 17-24), you see the Show in Large Type option: Contacts displays the number in a gigantic font, making it possible to read the number from across the room. Or also click the label of an email address to create a preaddressed email message, or click a home page to launch your browser and go to somebody's site. You can also copy and paste (or drag) address card info into another program or convert it into a Sticky Note.

Tip: Once you find a street address in your Contacts, you can find those coordinates on a map by clicking the label (such as Home or Work) and, from the shortcut menu, choosing Show in Maps. The Maps app obediently leaps open to display the address.

Changing the Contacts Display

You can't do much to customize Contacts' appearance, but the Preferences pane (Contacts→Preferences) gives you at least a couple of options in the General pane that are worth checking out:

- **Show first name.** Choose to have names displayed with the first name followed by the last name, or vice versa.

- **Sort By.** Sort the entries in Contacts by either first or last name.

Printing Options

When you choose File→Print and click Show Details, the Style pop-up menu offers four ways to print whatever addresses are selected at the moment:

- **Mailing Labels.** This option prints addresses on standard sheets of sticky mailing labels—Avery, for example—that you buy at office-supply stores.

Tip: As you manipulate settings, you can see your changes in the preview pane on the left. If the preview is too small for you to see, use the Zoom slider. (It doesn't affect your printout.)

- **Envelopes.** This feature is great if you have bad handwriting; rather than hand addressing your envelopes, you can have Contacts print them out for you. Use the Layout pop-up menu to pick the size of your envelopes—it's usually listed on the outside of the envelope box.

POWER USERS' CLINIC

Secrets of the Mailbox Files

Mail keeps your messages in a series of mailbox folders in your Home→Library→Mail folder, inside folders (Outbox, Deleted Messages, and so on) named for each account.

Knowing this permits you to perform a number of interesting tricks. First of all, now you know what files to back up for safekeeping. (To see the invisible Library folder, press Option as you choose Go→Library in the Finder.)

Second, if you have messages on an old Mac that you'd like to copy to your new one, now you know where they're stored.

massive research mission. Using your contacts' names and phone numbers as matching criteria, it ventures off to Facebook, finds the profile photos of everyone in your Contacts, and installs them into Contacts automatically.

Crazier still, it even grabs the headshots of people in your Contacts who *aren't your Facebook friends!*

If you already have a photo for somebody, don't worry; it doesn't get replaced. Of course, you can switch to the new Facebook profile picture if you prefer. Use the Linked heading in the photo picker as described already.

Tip: You can use the Get Profile Photos button even if you don't want your Facebook friends loaded into your copy of Contacts (by turning off Contacts in System Preferences→Internet Accounts→Facebook).

Finding an Address

You can search for a Contacts entry inside the currently selected group by typing a few letters of a name (or address, or any other snippet of contact information) in the search box. To search *all* your contacts instead of just the current group, click All Contacts in the Group list.

Tip: You can press ⌘-F to jump directly to the search field and start typing. Your savings: one mouse click.

With each letter you type, Contacts filters your social circle and displays the number of matches at the bottom. The matching records themselves appear in the Name column, the first of the matching card entries appears in the far-right pane, and the matching text itself appears highlighted in the matching card.

If Contacts finds more than one matching card, use the ▼ and ▲ keys, or Return and Shift-Return, to navigate through them.

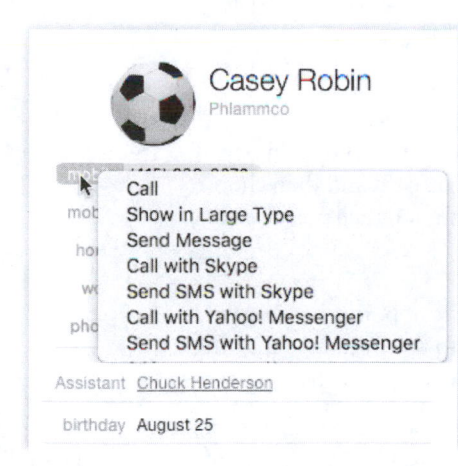

Figure 17-24:
The options that become available when you click the field labels on an address card vary according to field type. Pop-up menus let you send email, open a web page, or view a map, depending on the type of field you've clicked.

If you have an iPhone, and it's on the same Wi-Fi network, you even see this Call option. It lets you use your Mac as a speakerphone, as described on page 308.

The Send Message command sends an iMessage to the phone number or email address whose label you've clicked—if, in fact, it's an iMessages-registered number or address.

And the Show Map button appears when you point to an address. It opens the Maps program and shows you this address on a map.

Removing someone from a group

To take someone out of a group, first click the group name, and then click the person's name in the Name column and press the Delete key. If you want to remove the person from Contacts *itself,* click Delete in the resulting dialog box. Otherwise, just click Remove from Group or press Return. Contacts keeps the card but removes it from the currently selected group.

Note: If you selected All Contacts in the Group column, rather than a specific group, then you don't get a Remove from Group option. Instead, the Mac just asks you to confirm that you do, in fact, want to permanently remove the card.

Adding Pictures

You can dress up each Contacts entry with a photo. Whenever you're editing somebody's address book card, drag a digital photo—preferably 64 pixels square, or a multiple of that—onto the empty headshot square. Or double-click the picture well. You can choose from categories like Defaults (canned symbolic photos like animals and bugs); Recents (photos you've used recently); Camera (handy if this person is *with* you—take a new photo); and Linked (photos from online services like Facebook). Don't miss the swirly button, which lets you apply nutty Photo Boothish effects. At that point, you can enlarge, reposition, or crop the photo. Click Done when you're done.

You don't necessarily have to use a photo, of course. You could add any graphic you want to represent someone, even if it's a Bart Simpson face or a skull and crossbones. You can use any standard image file format in an address card—JPEG, GIF, PNG, TIFF, or even PDF. You can drag any of these directly into one of the squares here.

From now on, if you receive an email from that person, the photo shows up right in the email message—even on your phone or iPad.

Tip: If you've got snapshots in Photos, it's particularly easy to add a picture to any address card. Just drag a picture directly from the main Photos window to the picture frame on the address card to insert it.

Replacing and removing a picture

To replace a photo on an address card, just drag a new image on top of the old one. If you want to get rid of a picture without replacing it, select the card and then choose Card→Clear Custom Image (or, in Edit mode, select the picture and then press Delete).

Free headshots from Facebook

Yes, there's a little photo well on each card of your Contacts app. But here's a wild guess: Most of yours are empty. After all, who's going to go to the trouble of hunting down headshots of 500 acquaintances, just to fully illustrate his Contacts?

Fortunately, macOS stands ready to help. With one click, it can harvest headshots from the world's largest database of names and faces: Facebook.

Visit System Preferences→Internet Accounts. Click your Facebook account to see the magical button: Get Profile Photos. When you click it, macOS goes online for a

Now you have to fill up the group with the appropriate subset of names. There are three ways to do that:

- **To turn a set of address cards into a group quickly** when you're in regular address-book mode (not Groups), select multiple entries from the Names column. You can do that either by Shift-clicking the names (to make contiguous selections) or by ⌘-clicking (for noncontiguous selections)—and then choose File→New Group From Selection. You end up with a new group containing all the selected names.

- **While you're on the Groups page,** click All Contacts at the top of the screen. Now your full names list appears on the right page; drag names directly onto the group names to put them there.

- **If you're not on the Groups page,** drag contacts up onto the Groups bookmark at the top of the page—leave the mouse button down as Contacts shows you the Groups page—and continue dragging onto the group's name.

> **Note:** You're not *moving* those names; in essence, you're creating *aliases* of them, just as you might put songs in different playlists in iTunes. The only exception is Exchange accounts; those names can exist in only one group or folder at a time.

Once you've created some groups, you can even add groups to *other* groups, as though you were nesting folders. You might find it useful to keep a Nieces group and a Nephews group, for example, but to keep both groups inside a master Family group. To do this, create the two groups. Then drag each onto the Family group. Now, whenever you select Family, you'll see both Nieces and Nephews listed among the rest of the cards; double-click either group to see its members.

> **Tip:** If, while viewing the list of groups, you Option-click someone's name in the main list, Contacts shows you all the groups and folders that person belongs to.

Smart groups

The Finder has smart folders, Mail has smart mailboxes, and iTunes has smart playlists; inevitably, Contacts has smart *groups.*

Smart address groups, like smart folders in the Finder, automatically populate themselves with items that match criteria you specify. For example, you might create a smart group called "Apple Employees" that lists all your contacts with "apple.com" in their email addresses.

To create a smart group, choose File→New Smart Group (Option-⌘-N). Then use the resulting dialog box (which looks a lot like Mail's smart mailbox dialog box) to specify how you'd like the smart group to fill itself.

Once you're done, you can use your new smart group much like you'd use a regular group. You can't add contacts to a smart group yourself, but you can still send an email to all the members of a smart group, for example, or drag one to the Finder to create a composite vCard.

Tip: If you enter some people's birthdays in Contacts, they can show up automatically in Calendar. To make that happen, open Calendar, and then choose Calendar→Preferences→General. Turn on "Show Birthdays calendar."

Groups

A *group* is a collection of related address cards, saved under a single descriptive name (see Figure 17-23).

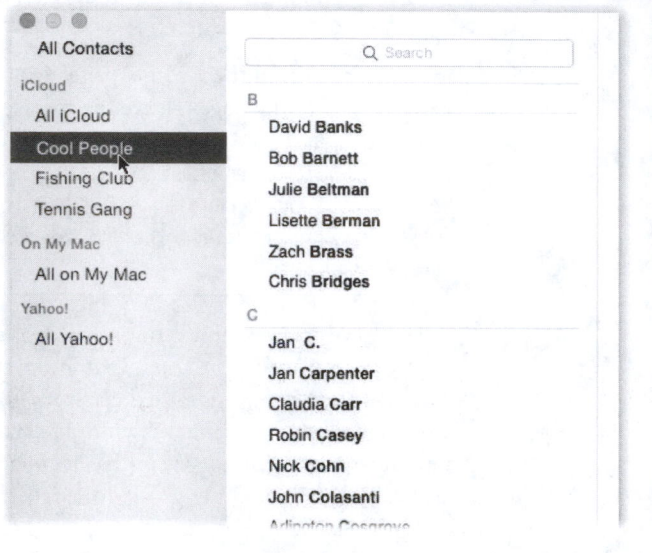

Figure 17-23:
Groups are handy. If, for example, you regularly send out a family newsletter to 35 relatives, you might gather the address cards of all your assorted siblings, cousins, nieces, nephews, uncles, and aunts into a single group called Family. When addressing an outgoing message using Mail, you can type this group name to reach all your kin at once.

Organizing your contacts into groups can make them much easier to find and use—especially when your database of addresses climbs into the hundreds.

Tip: When you send an email message to a group en masse, how does Mail know *which* email address to use for each person?

Because you've *told* it. In Contacts, choose Edit→Edit Distribution List. A special dialog box appears, listing everyone in each group, along with each person's complete list of email addresses. (Use the tiny pop-up menu above the list to choose Phone or Address; that way, you can also indicate the preferred phone number and mailing address.) Just click the preferred email address to make it bold.

To see your groups, choose View→Groups, press ⌘-3, or click the red bookmark at the top of the page that shows individuals' names.

To create a group, click the + button at the bottom of the Group column in the Contacts window, or choose File→New Group (Shift-⌘-N). Type a name for the newly spawned group icon in the Group column.

Tip: If you find yourself constantly adding the same fields to new cards, check out the Template pane of Contacts' Preferences (Contacts→Preferences). There you can customize exactly which fields appear for new cards.

Each card also contains a free-form Note field at the bottom, where you can type any other random crumbs of information you'd like to store about the person (pet's name, embarrassing nicknames, favorite Chinese restaurant, whatever).

Editing an address

When you create a new address card, you're automatically in Edit mode, which means you can add and remove fields and change the information on the card. To switch into Browse mode (where you can view and copy contact information but not change it), click the Edit button or choose Edit→Edit Card (⌘-L). You can switch *out* of Browse Mode in the same ways.

Adding addresses from Mail

You can make new contacts right in Mail, saving you the trouble of having to type names and email addresses manually. Select a message in Mail, and then choose Message→Add Sender to Contacts (Shift-⌘-Y). Presto: MacOS adds a new card to the Contacts, with the name and email address fields already filled in. Later, you can edit the card in Contacts to add phone numbers, street addresses, and so on.

TROUBLESHOOTING MOMENT

Resolving Conflicts and Duplicates

Suppose you tell Contacts to sync its information with one of your online accounts. And suppose that someone is listed in both places—with a different phone number in each place. Which address-book information "wins"? What's the Mac supposed to do?

Ask you, of course. And that's exactly what it does.

The first warning you may see lets you know that the other address book is very different from the one on your Mac—more than, say, 25 percent different. If you know what you're doing, go ahead and click Sync Contacts. If you'd like to inspect the differences name by name, click Show Details instead. You'll see a summary box that indicates how many people need to be added to one list or the other, and how many people's information is different.

That "these two address books are radically different" warning isn't quite the same thing as the warning you may get about sync conflicts. That's when you've entered the same person into each address book source, but with different information. Maybe one has a different phone number, for example. If you click Review Now, you're shown one conflict after another—the complete address cards—so that you can make a ruling on which version "wins."

One other problem may crop up when you're combining accounts: You may wind up with duplicates.

Fortunately, Contacts is ready for you here. On the Groups page (press ⌘-3), click the account with the problem (or All Contacts). Choose Card→Look for Duplicates.

The program lets you know about any duplicates it finds, even if only the name is the same and everything else is different. It even flags cards that have duplicate bits of information, like the same phone number twice. All you have to do is click Merge; Contacts merges the multiple cards into a single one, preserving all the details that are unique to each. (If there were duplicate photos, whichever one was on the first card becomes the new photo.)

Tip: In addition to letting you create vCards of individual entries, Contacts makes it easy to create vCards that contain several entries. To do so, ⌘-click the entries in the Name column that you want included, and drag them to the desktop. There they'll appear all together as a single vCard. You can even drag an item from the Group page to the desktop to make a vCard that contains all the group's entries.

Keep this trick in mind if you ever want to copy all your contacts from an old PC to a new Mac. By creating a single vCard containing all your contacts, you've made it trivial to import them into the copy of Contacts running on your new Mac.

Creating Address Cards

Each entry in Contacts is called a *card*—like a paper Rolodex card, with predefined spaces to hold all the standard contact information.

To add a new person, choose File→New Card, press ⌘-N, or click the + button beneath the Name column. Then type in the contact information, pressing the Tab key to move from field to field, as shown in Figure 17-22.

Figure 17-22 shows some unusual fields that you can plug into your address cards. The phonetic first/last name fields (shown at top) let you store phonetic spellings of hard-to-pronounce names. There's a "birthday" field and a place to store the Twitter name, too. To add fields like these, choose from the Card→Add Field menu.

Figure 17-22:
If one of your contacts happens to have three office phone extensions, a pager number, two home phone lines, a cellphone, and a couple of fax machines, no problem—you can add as many fields as you need. Each time you fill up a phone, email, chat name, or address box, a new, empty one magically sprouts up. Click a field's name to change its label; you can select one of the standard labels from the pop-up menu ("home," "work," and so on) or make up your own labels by choosing Custom.

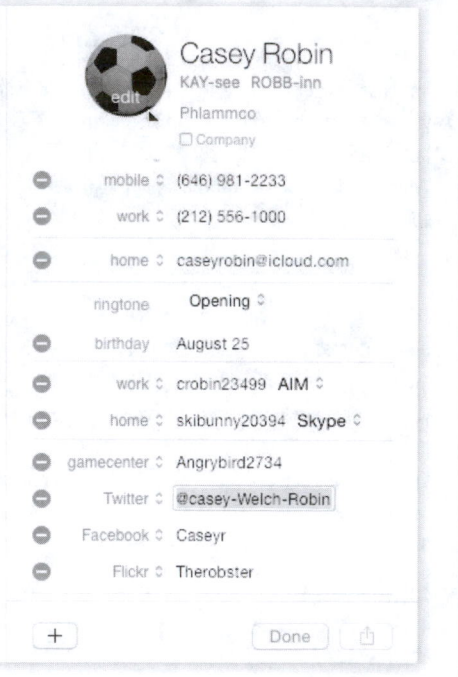

If some other online service maintains your address book, Contacts can sync with it, too, as long as it uses one of the standard sharing formats (Exchange, CardDAV, or Lightweight Directory Access Protocol, known to the pros as LDAP). To teach Contacts about those, choose Contacts→Preferences→Accounts. Click the + button in the lower left, enter your account information on the resulting screen, click Create, and away you go.

Note: Contacts may display an advanced Account Settings screen, where you have to enter more detailed information. If you're a hands-on sort of nerd, you can also force this screen to open on your command. To do that, press Option and point to the Create button, which now says Continue. Click it.

Once you've set up a Contacts account, you can also change its settings, right there in the same Preferences dialog box. Specify how often you want your Mac to sync changes with the online account, for example.

Importing from another address-book program

Contacts can also slurp in contact info from other address-book or list programs, like Microsoft Outlook, Palm Desktop, Excel, and others. Not directly, of course; that would be too easy. But most of those programs can *export* their information as an intermediary file in one of four popular formats: vCard, LDAP Interchange Format (LDIF), tab-delimited, or comma-separated value (CSV).

For example, Microsoft's programs can export addresses as vCards; Thunderbird can export in LDIF format; Excel can export tab-delimited or CSV files.

It's a fine art, this importing business; all kinds of things can go wrong. The fields (like Name, Street, Phone) may not be in the right order. Tab-separated export files may not have the right number of empty fields. And so on.

For best results, choose Contacts→Help and search for "Importing contacts from other applications." The resulting page gives special tips for each kind of export/import file format. (Fortunately, if the fields are out of order, Contacts will offer you the chance to straighten them out.)

About vCards

Contacts exchanges contact information with other programs primarily through *vCards*. "vCard" is short for *virtual business card*. More and more email programs send and receive these electronic business cards, which you can identify by their .vcf file name extensions (if, that is, you've set your Mac to display these extensions).

If you ever receive an email with a vCard file attached, drag the .vcf file into your Contacts window to create an instant entry with a complete set of information. You can create vCards of your own, too. Just drag a name out of your Contacts and onto the desktop (or into a piece of outgoing mail).

VIPs

In the real world, VIPs are people who get backstage passes to concerts or special treatment at business functions (it stands for "very important person"). In macOS, it means "somebody whose mail is important enough that I want it brought to my attention immediately when it arrives."

So who should your VIPs be? That's up to you. Your spouse, your boss, and your doctor come to mind.

To designate someone as a VIP, follow the steps shown in Figure 17-19. From now on, lots of interesting things happen:

- **A new mailbox, called VIPs, appears in your mailboxes list.** Click it to see all the mail from all your VIPs (even messages you've deleted). Or click the flippy triangle to see your VIPs' names, each representing messages from that person.

- **A new menu button called VIPs appears on your Favorites toolbar.** Click to see all VIP messages, or click the ▾ to see a pop-up menu of all the VIPs' names. Here again, the point is that you can jump to the messages from just that person.

- **If you use iCloud, the same person is now a VIP on all your other Macs** (running Mountain Lion or later), plus iPhones and iPads (running iOS 6 or later).

- **Best of all, you can set up your Mac so that when a new message from a VIP comes in, an alert bubble appears in the top-right corner of your screen** (Figure 17-19, bottom). That feature, of course, is part of the Notification Center, and it's described in Chapter 10. See the box on the next page for instructions on setting this up.

Figure 17-19:
Top: To designate a VIP, open a message she's sent you. Point to her name. A hollow star appears; click there. The star darkens. (Or choose Add to VIPs from the pop-up menu that appears when you point to her name.) Note: If that person one day insults you, fires you, or dumps you, then you can remove her VIP status by clicking that same star again.

Bottom: MacOS can alert you when VIP messages arrive—and you can reply right on the spot.

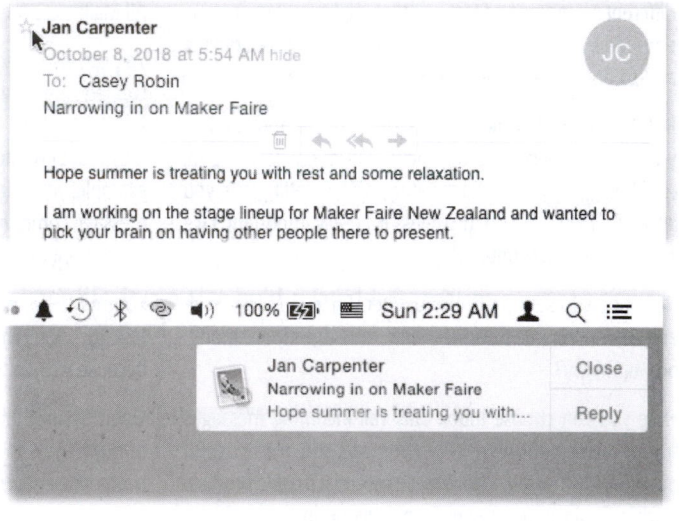

3. **Use the criteria options (at the top) to specify how Mail should select messages to process.**

 For example, if you'd like the program to watch out for messages from a particular person, you would set up the first two pop-up menus to say "From" and "Contains," respectively.

 To flag messages containing *$$$$, XXX, !!!!*, and so on, set the pop-up menus to say "Subject" and "Contains."

 You can set up *multiple* criteria here to flag messages whose subjects contain any one of those common spam triggers. (If you change the "any" pop-up menu to say "all," then *all* the criteria must be true for the rule to kick in.)

4. **Specify which words or people you want the message rule to watch for.**

 In the text box to the right of the two pop-up menus, type the word, address, name, or phrase you want Mail to watch for—a person's name, or *$$$$*, in the previous examples.

5. **In the lower half of the box, specify what you want to happen to messages that match the criteria.**

 If, in steps 1 through 4, you've told your rule to watch for junk mail containing *$$$$* in the subject line, here's where you can tell Mail to delete it or move it into, say, a Junk folder.

 With a little imagination, you'll see how the options in this pop-up menu can do absolutely amazing things with your incoming email. Mail can colorize, delete, move, redirect, or forward messages—or even play a sound when you get a certain message.

 By setting up the controls as shown in Figure 17-18, for example, you'll have specified that whenever your mother sends something to you that mentions a visit, you'll hear a specific alert noise—and the email will be highlighted in red, so it will jump out at you in the Inbox.

6. **In the very top box, name your mail rule. Click OK.**

 At this point, Mail offers to apply your freshly minted rule to all the messages in the mailboxes that are currently selected. It's your one chance to go back in time—because from now on, the rule will apply only to *new* messages. Click either Apply or Don't Apply.

 Now you're back to the Rules pane (Figure 17-18, top). Here you can choose a sequence for your rules by dragging them up and down. Here, too, you can turn off the ones you won't be needing at the moment but may use again one day.

Tip: Mail applies rules as they appear, from top to bottom, in the list. If a rule doesn't seem to be working properly, it may be that an earlier rule is intercepting and processing some messages before the "broken" rule even sees them. To fix this, try dragging the rule (or the interfering rule) up or down in the list.

- **Choose Mailbox→Erase Deleted Items (Shift-⌘-Delete).** (If you have multiple accounts, choose Erase Deleted Items→In All Accounts.)

- **Right-click or two-finger click the Trash mailbox icon,** and then choose Erase Deleted Items from the shortcut menu. Or choose the same command from the ✿ pop-up menu at the bottom of the window.

- **Wait.** Mail will permanently delete these messages automatically after a week.

 If a week is too long (or not long enough), you can change this interval. Choose Mail→Preferences, click Accounts, and select the account name from the list at left. Then click Mailbox Behaviors and change the "Erase deleted messages" pop-up menu. If you choose "When quitting Mail" from the pop-up menu, then Mail will take out the trash every time you quit the program.

Turning deleted mail invisible

Mail offers another—and very unusual—method of deleting messages that doesn't involve the Trash folder at all. Using this method, pressing the Delete key (or clicking the 🗑 toolbar button) simply hides the selected message in the list. Hidden messages remain hidden, but they don't go away for good until you use the rebuild mailbox command described in the box below.

If this arrangement sounds useful, choose Mail→Preferences; click Accounts and select the account from the list on the left; click Mailbox Behaviors; from the Trash Mailbox pop-up menu, choose None.

From now on, messages you delete vanish from the list. They're not really gone, however. You can bring them back, at least in gray, dimmed, ghostly form, by choosing View→Show Deleted Messages (or pressing Ctrl-⌘-L). Using this system, in other words, you never truly delete messages; you just hide them.

TROUBLESHOOTING MOMENT

Rebuilding Your Mail Databases

Mail keeps your messages in your Home→Library→Mail folder. (Your Library folder is usually invisible, but you can jump to it by pressing Option as you choose Go→Library in the Finder.)

Over time, as you add and delete hundreds of messages from these database files, some digital sawdust gets left behind, resulting in general Mail sluggishness. You also wind up with *massive* message files hidden on your hard drive, which can consume hundreds of megabytes of disk space. That's a particular bummer if you like to copy your message databases to your laptop when you go on a trip.

Fortunately, it's easy enough to *rebuild the message databases*. Doing so cleanses, repairs, and purges your message files. As a result, you wind up with a much more compact and healthy database.

To rebuild a mailbox, highlight it in the mailboxes column in Mail. (Highlight several by ⌘-clicking, if you like.) Then choose Mailbox→Rebuild. MacOS takes several minutes (or hours, depending on the size of your mailboxes) to repair your database—but if you're experiencing Mail weirdness or slowness, it's well worth the sacrifice.

A few last notes on searching:

- **Mail searching is almost exactly like Finder searching,** right down to the saved-search mechanism. See Chapter 3 for details.

- **You can also search for certain text** *within* **an open message.** Choose Edit→Find→Find (or press ⌘-F) to bring up the Find dialog box (Figure 17-17).

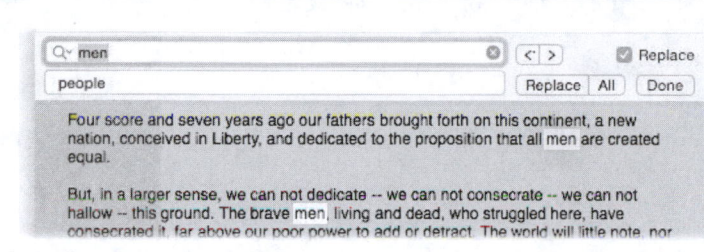

Figure 17-17:
The Find box works just as it does in a word processor, except that the Replace function works only on messages you're writing—Mail doesn't let you change the words of received mail. Lawyers would have a field day with that one.

- **As with regular Spotlight, Mail matches your search term** by looking only at the *beginnings* of words. Searching for *flag* will find messages that contain the words *flagstone* and *flagellum,* but not *Redflag Incorporated.*

- **In Mail→Preferences→General, you can specify** whether you want Mail to include the Trash folder, Junk folder, and encrypted messages when you search all mailboxes.

Deleting Messages

Sometimes it's junk mail. Sometimes you're just done with it. Either way, it's a snap to delete a selected message, several selected messages, or a message that's currently before you on the screen. You can press the Delete key, click the Delete (🗑) button on the toolbar, choose Edit→Delete, or drag messages out of the list window and into your Trash mailbox—or even onto the Dock's Trash icon.

Actually, even that's not the end of the list of ways: You can also swipe/drag leftward all the way across a message (with two fingers on your trackpad, or using a mouse) to delete it; a red Trash button appears briefly during your drag to let you know what's about to happen. It's the same way you'd do it on an iPhone.

Tip: If you delete a message by accident, the Undo command (Edit→Undo or ⌘-Z) restores it.

All these commands move the messages to the Trash folder. If you like, you can then click that Trash icon to view a list of the messages you've deleted. You can even rescue messages by dragging them back into a mailbox (back to the Inbox, for example).

Emptying the Trash folder

Mail doesn't vaporize messages in the Trash folder until you "empty the trash," just like in the Finder. You can empty the Trash folder in any of several ways:

- **Click a message (or several) within the Trash folder list,** and then click the 🗑 icon on the toolbar (or press the Delete key). Now those messages are *really* gone.

But this initial search is a pretty broad one. Mail is rounding up messages that match your search term *in any way*. If you type *veg*, you see messages from Murray Vegelstein, messages from vegan@militanteaters.org, and messages with the subject line "HOT DEALS IN VEGAS." All of them in one big stew.

To help you sort through it, Mail produces a Suggestions list, which sprouts from the search box. As in the Finder, it's Mail's way of asking what sort of *thing* your search term is. Is it a person? A subject? The status of a message? A date? Figure 17-16 shows the idea.

3. **Click the suggestion you want.**

Mail filters the list. For example, if you click Murray Vegelstein, you'll see *only* the messages to or from Murray.

4. **Edit the search token.**

The *search token* is the little bubble that appears in the search box after you've clicked one of the suggestions. You can click the little ▾ in the search token to change it. For example, if you've clicked somebody's name, that pop-up menu says To, From, or Entire Message (including the header and the body).

You can also type more into the search box to add *another* search token. For example, the first token might limit the search to messages from one person; you could then create another one that limits the search to a certain date.

Tip: Once you've built up a complicated search like this, save yourself the effort next time by *saving* that search. Click the Save button just below the search box. You get the Smart Mailbox dialog box, shown in Figure 17-15, already filled out with the search setup you've specified. All you have to do is give it a name and click OK to transform your search into a smart mailbox that you can open anytime.

You've done a lot of refining of this search. But you still haven't limited your results by *account* or *folder*. Mail is showing you results from either *all* mailboxes, or from only the most recent mailbox you've searched. Fortunately, your Favorites bar has now sprouted two new buttons: one called All, and one that names the folder you most recently clicked.

5. **Click a button on the Favorites bar to change which mailbox is being searched.**

The results list updates itself.

Tip: If you ⌘-click *several* mail folders before you search, you can limit the search to that particular *set of* mailboxes. (In that case, you see a button on the Favorites bar called Selected Mailboxes.)

When you're finished hunting around, you can empty out the search box, and get back to your regularly scheduled lists of email, by clicking any other mailbox, or by clicking the ✖ button at the right end of the search box.

This search box incorporates the same pop-up suggestions lists and "search tokens" as regular file searching in the Finder. In fact, it understands plain-English search requests like "messages from Charlene about Halloween."

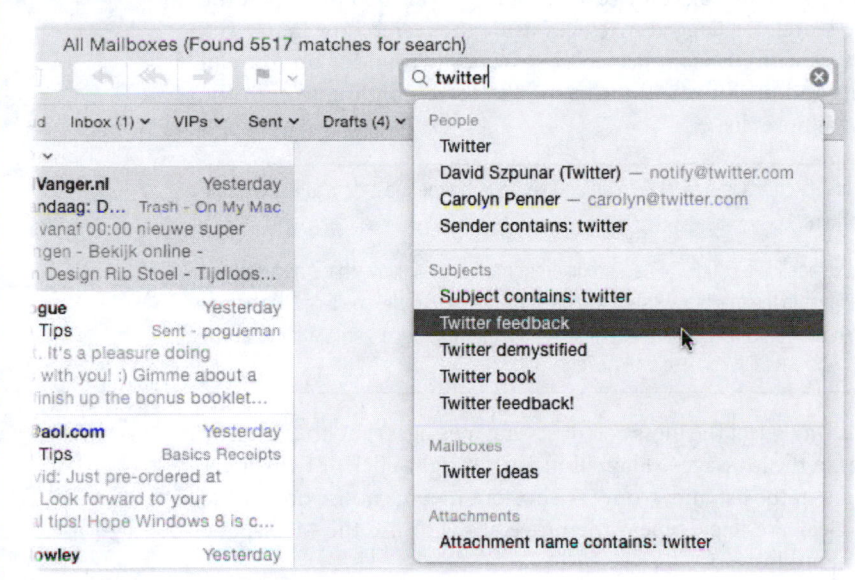

Figure 17-16:
You can jump to the search box by clicking or by pressing Option-⌘-F. As you type, Mail shrinks the list of messages—and simultaneously displays a list of suggestions. You can fine-tune your results using the mailbox buttons you've installed on the Favorites bar. To return to the full messages list, click the tiny ⊗ at the right side of the search box.

Here's how it works:

1. **Press Option-⌘-F (or click in the search box).**

 The cursor jumps up there.

2. **Start typing what you're looking for.**

 As you type, the messages list changes to show only the matching messages from all your mail folders.

 New in macOS Mojave, in fact, is a first section of list results called Top Hits. These are the results Mail thinks are most likely to be what you're looking for, based on factors like the age of the messages, whether you've read or replied to them, whether the correspondent is one of your VIP contacts, and so on.

 You can also type "natural-language" phrases that mention any combination of a person, time period, or subject. For example, you can type "mail from Casey last week," "mail to Alex last year," "messages about Italy yesterday," and so on.

 Tip: *The word "mail" or "messages" in these phrases might feel more English-like, but it's optional. Typing "from Casey last week" or "about Italy yesterday" finds exactly the same messages.*

 If you see the message you're looking for, great. Click it and off you go.

Once you've applied some flags, you can use their power in all kinds of ways. For example, you can view all of them in one place—in the Flagged folder that appears near the top of the mailboxes list.

You can also sort your mail list by flag color (choose Sort by→Flags at the top of the messages list). You can search for flagged messages using the search box. Better yet, you can view all messages with a certain flag color—magically rounded up from all your different accounts and mailboxes—by clicking the corresponding icon in the Flagged folder of the mailboxes list.

Tip: Just in case you don't find "Red," "Orange," "Yellow," and so on to be the most descriptive possible flag names, you can change them.

First, though, make sure you've applied a couple of flags to different messages already. That's necessary to make the Flagged mailbox appear in the mailboxes list. If you open the flippy triangle, you'll see the names of the flags you've applied so far. You can change a flag's name just the way you'd name a file–start by double-clicking it.

To flag a message in this way, select the message (or several messages) and then choose one of the colored flags in the Message→Flag submenu. Or right-click or two-finger click the message's name in the list and, from the shortcut menu, choose one of the seven flag colors. (To clear the flags, repeat the procedure, but use the Message→Flag→Clear Flag command instead.)

If you're using only one flag to simply mean "flag this," and you don't need all the colors, you can also press Shift-⌘-L.

Mark as Read/Unread

Once you've looked at a message, Mail removes the blue dot from its name—the dot that tells you it's a new message. But what if you had only glanced at it, and you don't really consider it fully processed?

In that situation, you can use the Mark As Unread command, which basically means "Put the blue dot back." That turns into a Mark As Read command, too.

You'll find these commands in the Message menu, as well as in the shortcut menu that appears when you right-click or two-finger click a message or group of selected messages.

In fact, there's a swipey way to do the same job: On a trackpad or Magic Mouse surface, drag two fingers to the right across a message to mark it as read (or unread).

Finding Messages

The box in the upper-right corner of the main mail window is Mail's own private Spotlight—a fast, powerful search command. That's essential when you have to deal with masses of email (see Figure 17-16).

When you click OK, a new icon appears in the mailboxes column, ready for use.

You can move a selected message (or a group of messages) into a mailbox folder in any of three ways:

• **Drag it out of the messages list** onto a mailbox icon.

• **Click the new Move button on the toolbar.** Most of the time it says "Move to" and lists all your mailboxes.

 Sometimes, though, the button shows the name of a certain mailbox. The idea here is that Mail has noticed where you filed a message from this person, or on this topic, in the past—and is trying to save you some time by proposing that folder as a one-click destination.

• **Choose from the Message→Move To submenu,** which lists all your mailboxes.

• **Right-click or two-finger click a message,** or one of several you've highlighted. From the resulting shortcut menu, choose Move To, and then, from the submenu, choose the mailbox you want.

Of course, the only way to change the contents of a *smart* mailbox is to change the criteria it uses to populate itself. To do so, double-click the smart mailbox icon and use the dialog box that appears (Figure 17-15).

Figure 17-15:
Mail lets you create self-populating folders. In this example, a smart mailbox will automatically display all messages from Momma Smith that you've received in the past week.

Flagging Messages

Sometimes you'll receive email that prompts you to some sort of action, but you may not have the time (or the fortitude) to face the task at the moment. ("Hi there… it's me, your accountant. Would you mind rounding up your expenses for 2004 through 2014 and sending me a list by email?")

That's why Mail lets you *flag* a message, summoning a little flag icon in a new column next to the message's name. In fact, you can use seven differently *colored* flags.

These indicators can mean anything you like—they simply call attention to certain messages.

Redirecting Messages

A *redirected* message is similar to a forwarded message, with one useful difference: When you forward a message, your recipient sees that it came from you. When you redirect it, your recipient sees the *original* writer's name as the sender. In other words, a redirected message uses you as a low-profile relay station between two other people.

Treasure this feature. Plenty of email programs don't offer a Redirect command at all. You can use it to transfer messages from one of your own accounts to another, or to pass along a message that came to you by mistake.

To redirect a message, choose Message→Redirect, or press Shift-⌘-E. You get an outgoing copy of the message—this time without any quoting marks. (You can edit redirected messages before you send them, too, which is perfect for April Fools' Day pranks.)

Printing Messages

Sometimes there's no substitute for a printout. Choose File→Print, or press ⌘-P to summon the Print dialog box.

Filing Messages

Mail lets you create new mailboxes (mail folders) in the mailboxes list. You might create one for important messages, another for order confirmations from web shopping, still another for friends and family, and so on. You can even create mailboxes *inside* these mailboxes, a feature beloved by the hopelessly organized.

Tip: You can drag mailbox folders up and down in the list to rearrange them. Sweet.

Mail even offers *smart mailboxes*—self-updating folders that show you all your mail from your boss, for example, or every message with "mortgage" in its subject. It's the same idea as smart folders in the Finder or smart playlists in iTunes: folders whose contents are based around criteria you specify (Figure 17-15).

The commands you need are all in the Mailbox menu. For example, to create a new mailbox folder, choose Mailbox→New Mailbox. To create a smart mailbox, choose Mailbox→New Smart Mailbox.

Mail asks you to name the new mailbox. If you have more than one email account, you can specify which one will contain the new folder. (Smart mailboxes, however, always sit outside your other mailboxes.)

Tip: If you want to create a folder inside a folder, then use slashes in the name of your new mailbox. (If you use the name *Cephalopods/Squid,* for example, then Mail creates a folder called Cephalopods, with a subfolder called Squid.) You can also drag the mailbox icons up and down in the drawer to place one inside another.

That trick doesn't work for smart mailboxes, however. The only way to organize smart mailboxes is to put them inside a smart mailbox *folder,* which you create using Mailbox→New Smart Mailbox Folder. You might do that if you have several smart mailboxes for mail from your co-workers ("From Jim," "From Anne," and so on) and want to put them together in one collapsible group to save screen space.

Tip: Use the Return key to create blank lines in the original message. Using this method, you can splice your own comments into the paragraphs of the original message, replying point by point. The brackets preceding each line of the original message help your correspondent keep straight what's yours and what's hers.

When you're finished, click Send ().

Figure 17-14:
In Mail messages formatted with Rich Text (not to be confused with the Rich Text Format word-processing format, which is very different), a reply includes the original message, marked in a special color (which you can change in Mail→Preferences→Fonts & Colors) and with a vertical bar to differentiate it from the text of your reply.

(In plain-text messages, each line of the reply is >denoted >with >brackets, although only your recipient will see them.)

Forwarding Messages

Instead of replying to the person who sent you a message, you may sometimes want to pass the note on to a third person.

To do so, click the Forward (➡) toolbar button (or choose Message→Forward, or press Shift-⌘-F). A new message opens, looking a lot like the one that appears when you reply. You may wish to precede the original message with a comment of your own, along the lines of: "Frank: I thought you'd be interested in this joke about your mom."

Finally, address it as you would any outgoing piece of mail.

Tip: If the attachments are pictures, then clicking Quick Look gives you a full-screen slideshow of every attached image. If you jiggle the mouse a little during the slideshow, you get a useful row of slideshow-control buttons along the bottom of the screen, too.

- **Click the Save button** in the message header to save it to your Downloads folder, nestled within easy reach in the Dock. (It's a pop-up menu, which is handy if there's more than one attachment. You can either save *all* attachments at once or choose from the pop-up menu to save them individually.)

Tip: If you don't want to use the Downloads folder, you can choose a new autosave location for attachments by choosing Mail→Preferences→General→Downloads folder.

- **Drag the attachment icon** (it appears at the bottom of the message) out of the message window and onto any visible portion of your desktop or any visible folder window.

- **Double-click the attachment's icon,** or single-click the blue link underneath the icon. If you were sent a document (a photo, Word file, or Excel file, for example), it now opens in the corresponding program.

Note: After the attachment is open, use the File→Save As command to save the file into a folder of your choice. Otherwise, any changes you make to the document will be lost.

- **Right-click or two-finger click** the attachment's icon at the bottom of the message. From the shortcut menu, you can open it, save it, Quick Look it, and so on.

Replying to a Message

To answer a message, click the Reply (←) button on the message toolbar (or choose Message→Reply, or press ⌘-R). If the message was originally addressed to multiple recipients, you can send your reply to everyone simultaneously by clicking Reply All (←←) instead (Shift-⌘-R).

A new message window opens, already addressed. As a courtesy to your correspondent, Mail places the original message at the bottom of the window, set off by a vertical bar, as shown in Figure 17-14.

Tip: If you highlight some text before clicking Reply, then Mail pastes only that portion of the original message into your reply. That's a great convenience to your correspondent, who now knows exactly which part of the message you're responding to.

The original sender's name is automatically placed in the To field. The subject is the same as the original subject with the addition of "Re:" (shorthand for "regarding"). You're now ready to type your response.

At this point, you can add or delete recipients, edit the subject line or the original message, attach a file, and so on.

Data detectors are especially useful—*primarily* useful, in fact—in Mail. Watch for the dotted rectangle that appears when you point to a name, address, date, time, or flight number.

Here's what's neat: If a Data Detector detects that there's discussion of an appointment in the body of a message, or if it finds somebody's contact information, it displays a banner strip at the top, as shown in Figure 17-13. With one click of the Add button, you can add that appointment to your Calendar, or that phone number to Contacts. (You see a similar banner if the person is *already* in Contacts but this message contains an additional or updated address or phone number.)

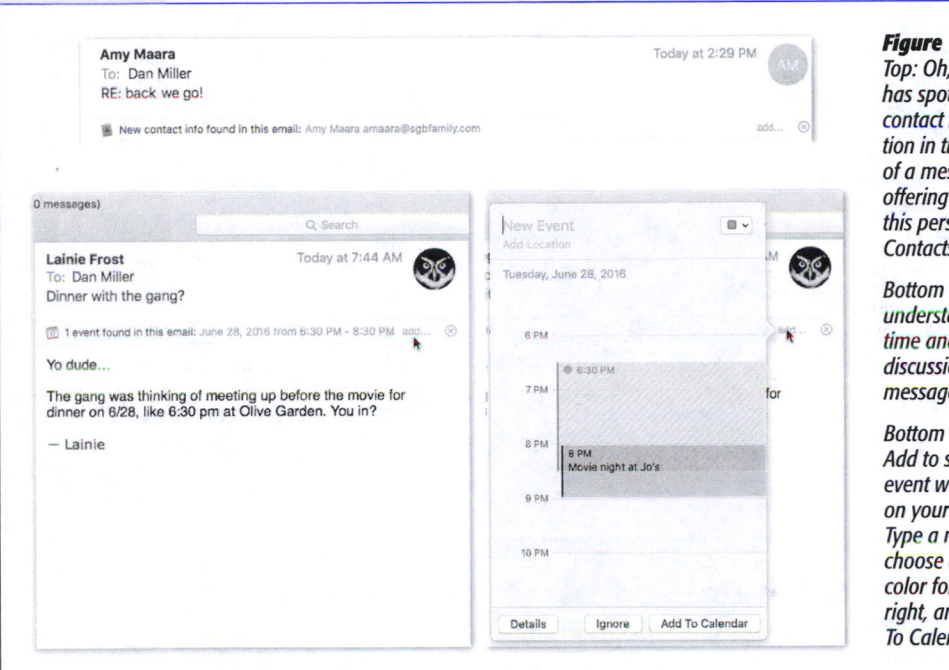

Figure 17-13:
Top: Oh, look! Mail has spotted some contact information in the body of a message. It's offering to add this person to your Contacts.

Bottom left: Mail understands the time and date discussion in the message.

Bottom right: Click Add to see how this event would look on your calendar. Type a name for it, choose a category color for it at top right, and click Add To Calendar.

Opening File Attachments

Just as you can attach files to a message, so can people send files to you. Sometimes they don't even bother to type a note; you wind up receiving an empty email message with a file or two attached. Only the presence of the file's icon in the message body (or the paper clip icon in the header) tells you there's something attached.

Mail stores downloaded files in a hidden folder on your hard drive. To bring them out into the open, you must proceed in one of these ways:

- **Click the Quick Look button** in the message header. You're treated to a nearly full-size preview of the file's contents. Yes, Quick Look has come to email. It works exactly as described on page 58.

You might have to hunt for the ⊜ button, but it's there, atop the list of messages. When you click it, you automatically turn on the first filter: Unread. All the messages in the list that you have read are hidden—until you click the ⊜ button again to turn off the filter.

When the filter is on, you can click the word "Unread" to see a list of other ways to filter the list, as shown in Figure 17-12.

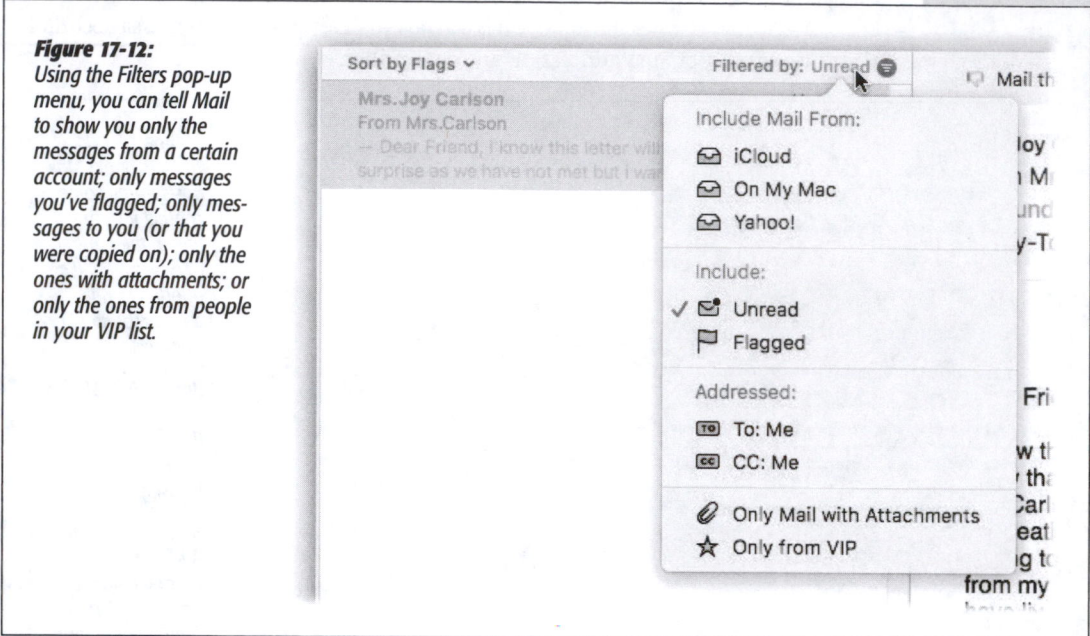

Figure 17-12:
Using the Filters pop-up menu, you can tell Mail to show you only the messages from a certain account; only messages you've flagged; only messages to you (or that you were copied on); only the ones with attachments; or only the ones from people in your VIP list.

Adding the Sender to Contacts

When you choose the Message→Add Sender to Contacts command, Mail memorizes the email address of the person whose message is on the screen. In fact, you can highlight a huge number of messages and add *all* the senders simultaneously using this technique.

Thereafter, you'll be able to address a new message to somebody just by typing the first few letters of her name or email address.

Data Detectors

Data detectors are described on page 252. They're what you see when macOS recognizes commonly used bits of written information: a physical address, a phone number, a date and time, a flight number, and so on. With one quick click, you can send that information into the appropriate macOS program, like Calendar, Contacts, the Flight Tracker widget in Dashboard, or your web browser (for looking up an address on a map).

Note: When "Include related messages" is turned on, the related messages do *not* display the big gray numbers in the corner; only the ones in the current mailbox sprout numbers.

- **Move all the messages in a conversation to a new mailbox** by dragging the main message. You might find this useful, for example, when you've just finished a project and want to file away all the email related to it quickly. You can even delete all the messages in a thread at once by deleting its main entry.

Note: If you drag a message to a different folder, it still appears in the conversation thread.

- **Send someone all the messages in a thread** by selecting the main message and then clicking Forward as usual. Mail automatically copies all the messages of the thread into a new message, putting the oldest at the top. You might find this useful, for instance, when you want to send your boss all the correspondence you've had with someone about a certain project.

- **Manipulate an individual message in a conversation** by first clicking it in the message-reading pane. For example, if you have five messages in a conversation, and you want to forward only the juicy one, which happens to be message #2, then click #2 and then use the Forward command—or Reply, Delete, or whatever. (You can also click one of the four light-gray buttons that appear when you point to the message header—Delete, Reply, Reply All, Forward.)

Tip: In Mail→Preferences→Viewing, you'll find a bunch of fine-tuning tweaks that apply to conversations. For example, you can ask that messages that are part of the same conversation show up highlighted in a color you choose—even when conversation grouping is turned *off*.

Filters

Mail offers one-click filters that hide or show all messages in the list of a certain kind—like ones you haven't yet read.

GEM IN THE ROUGH

The Email Answering Machine

If you're going on vacation, you can turn Mail into an email answering machine that sends a canned "I'm away until the 15th" message to everyone who writes you.

To do so, set the first set of pop-up menus in the Rules dialog box so that they say Account and the name of your account. In the bottom half of the dialog box, select Reply to Message from the pop-up menu. Click "Reply message text," and then type your outgoing message in the resulting box.

Keep in mind, though, that mail rules work only when Mail is open and connected to the internet. If your computer is set to turn off after a certain period of time, therefore, make sure to disable that feature before you go on vacation.

Also: If you subscribe to mailing lists, set up another mail rule that intercepts and files them *before* your answering-machine rule kicks in. Otherwise, you'll incur the wrath of other internet citizens by littering their email discussion groups with copies of your autoreply message.

Tip: To make things more interesting for your recipients, pick At Random; Mail selects a different signature each time you send a message. Or, if you're not *that* much of a risk-taker, choose In Sequential Order; Mail picks the next signature in order for each new message you write.

Remember that you can always change your signature on a message-by-message basis, using the Signature pop-up menu in any new email message.

- **To use the signature feature as a prefix in replies:** Turn on "Place signature above quoted text." If you turn on this setting, your signature gets inserted *above* any text that you're replying to, rather than below. You'd use this setting if your "signature" said something like, "Hi there! You wrote this to me!"

Tip: If you're into consistent typographical styling, also turn on "Always match my default font." That setting makes sure that any messages you send contain the signature in the same font as the rest of the message, lending it an air of professionalism.

Reading Email

Mail puts all incoming email into your Inbox; the statistic after the word *Inbox* lets you know how many messages you haven't yet read. New messages are also marked with light-blue dots in the main list.

Tip: The Mail icon in the Dock also shows how many new messages you have waiting; it's the number in the red circle. In Mail→Preferences→General, you can specify *which* mailbox it's tallying up—or have it tally up all of them.

Click the Inbox folder to see a list of received messages. If it's a long list, press Control-Page Up and Control-Page Down to scroll. (Page Up and Page Down without the Control key scroll the message pane instead.)

Tip: If you ⌘-click more than one mailbox folder, you can combine them (and their total-message counts) into one unified messages list.

Click the name of a message once to read it in the message window, or double-click a message to open it into a separate window. (If a message is already selected, then pressing Return also opens its separate window.)

When you click the name of a message in the messages list (or press the ▲ and ▼ keys to highlight successive messages in that list), you see the message itself, along with any attachments, in the message pane.

Tip: Instead of reading your email yourself, you might prefer to have Mojave read it *to* you, as you sit back in your chair sipping a strawberry daiquiri. Highlight the text you want to hear (or choose Edit→Select All), and then choose Edit→Speech→Start Speaking. To stop the insanity, choose Edit→Speech→Stop Speaking.

You can customize your signatures by choosing Mail→Preferences→Signatures. Here's what you should know:

- **To build up a library of signatures that you can use in any of your accounts:** Select All Signatures in the leftmost pane, and then click the + button to add each new signature (Figure 17-9). Give each new signature a name in the middle pane, and then customize the signatures' text in the rightmost pane.

Tip: If you ever get tired of a signature, you can delete it forever by selecting All Signatures→ [your signature's name], clicking the — button, and then clicking OK.

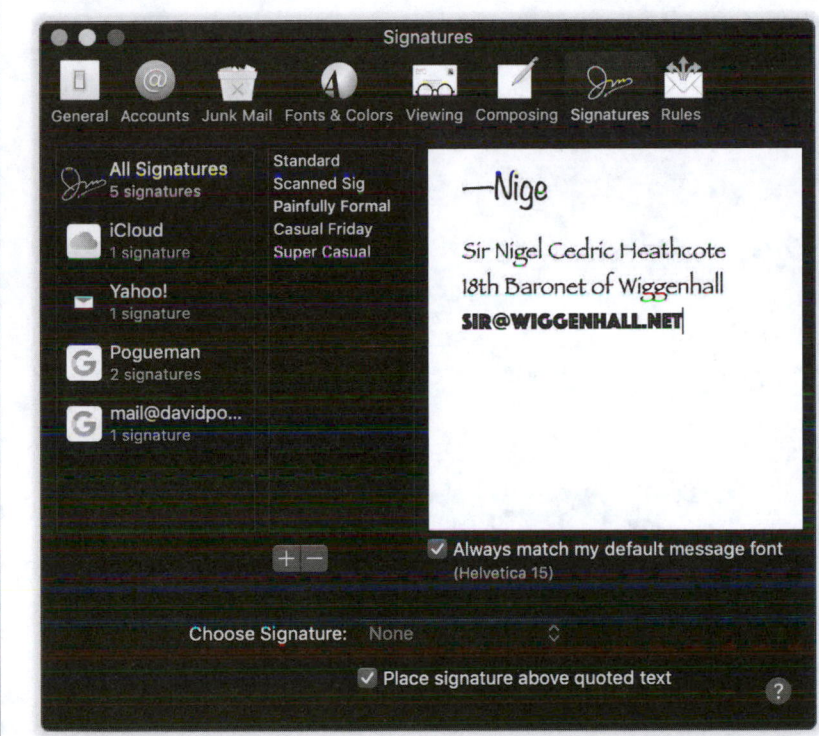

Figure 17-9:
After naming your signature in the middle pane and typing the text on the right, don't miss the Format menu, which you can use to dress up your signature with colors and formatting. You can even paste a graphic (like a scan of your handwritten signature) into the box. Click OK. (You can use formatted signatures only when sending Rich Text messages.)

- **To make a signature available in one of your email accounts:** Drag the signature's name from the middle pane onto the name of the account in the leftmost pane. In other words, you can make certain signatures available to only your work (or personal) account, so you never accidentally end up appending your secret FBI contact signature to the bottom of a birthday invitation.

- **To assign a particular signature to one account:** In the left pane, click an account; pick from the Choose Signature pop-up menu. Each time you compose a message from that account, Mail inserts the signature you selected.

Marking Up, Signing, and Drawing on Attachments

You can mark up PDF and graphics attachments at the moment of sending them, too. You can add your signature to a contract, circle a typo on a document, draw arrows on a diagram, and so on.

All this magic awaits in the Markup toolbar—but finding it is a bit tricky. First, you have to attach a graphic—a photo, PDF file, or other kind of image—using any of the tricks described on page 687.

Once the image appears in your outgoing message, click to select it. At that point, the tiny ⌄ icon appears in its upper-right corner; from it, choose Markup (Figure 17-8).

What you'll quickly discover is that this entire markup feature is shared, pixel for pixel, with the markup feature in your Preview program. And it's described in detail on page 472.

Figure 17-8:
Top: This button doesn't appear until you attach a graphic and then select it.

Bottom: The buttons on this toolbar let you draw and type on your image. Don't miss the ⤾ tool, upper right, which auto-perfects your attempts to draw lines, circles, and angles.

Signatures

Signatures are bits of text that get stamped at the bottom of your outgoing email messages. A signature might contain a name, a postal address, a pithy quote, or even a scan of your *real* signature, as shown in Figure 17-9.

The first time you attach a big file to an outgoing message and then click Send, Mail offers the message shown in Figure 17-7.

Note: Mail Drop is an iCloud feature. It works only if your Mac is currently signed into your iCloud account. (The files you send don't count toward your iCloud storage limit, though.)

Behind the scenes, Mail Drop uploads your file to iCloud's computers, where it sits for up to 30 days, waiting for your recipient to get a clue and download it.

If the recipient also has Yosemite or later Mail, the attachment is quietly auto-downloaded in the background, so that it's on his Mac already when he opens the message. He'll click, it'll open, and he'll probably never even consider the miracle of what just happened.

If you're sending to any other computer or mail program, your message contains an indication of the file's 30-day expiration date, and a "Click to download" link. (Clicking it opens the recipient's web browser, where the file begins to download immediately.) It's one extra step, and a little waiting—but that's what people get for not drinking the Apple Kool-Aid.

And now Apple's entirely reasonable fine print:

- **Mail Drop allows you to send** a maximum of 200 messages a day, or messages to more than 1,000 recipients a day from your iCloud account. A single message sent via iCloud can have a maximum of 100 recipients.

- **iCloud's online holding tank** for Mail Drop attachments doesn't hold more than 1 terabyte of files. In other words, once you've Mail Dropped that many attachments, you won't be able to send any more until those files have been downloaded (or 30 days have elapsed on some of them).

Mail Drop is fantastic.

UP TO SPEED

All the Little Symbols

The left edge of the messages list shows little symbols that let you know at a glance how you've processed certain messages. The most common one is, of course, the blue dot, which means "new message." (After reading a message, you can mark it once again as an *unread* message by choosing Message→Mark As Unread [Shift-⌘-U]—or by right-clicking or two-finger clicking the message's name and then choosing Mark As Unread from the shortcut menu.)

You might also see these symbols, which represent messages you've replied to (◀), forwarded (➡), redirected (➡ ᴵ), or flagged (🚩).

A well-guarded secret, however, is that the "replied to" and "forwarded" symbols aren't just indicators—they're also *buttons*. When you see one of these symbols next to your original message, click it to jump straight to your reply (or forwarded message). You're spared the trouble of having to search through all your mailboxes.

To remove an attachment, drag across its icon to highlight it, and then press the Delete key. (You can also choose Message→Remove Attachments.)

Mail Drop: Sending Huge Attachments

You're about to discover what may be one of the best features in the history of email.

Since the dawn of email, we, the downtrodden masses, have been told over and over again: Don't attach big files! Anything over about 5 megabytes is too much for most email systems. Best case, your entire message will bounce back to you; worst case, you'll clog the recipients' inboxes so that they can't receive any more mail.

So the world has slogged along with workarounds—sites like SendThisFile.com, or services like Dropbox that require signup.

Today, that era is over.

If you use Mail in macOS, you'll probably never have to think about the file sizes of your attachments again. Go ahead—attach a whole video. Attach a gigantic Photoshop document, or several, or dozens. Attach a gigantic Keynote or PowerPoint file. Your file-size limit is now 5 *gigabytes*—about 1,000 times what it used to be.

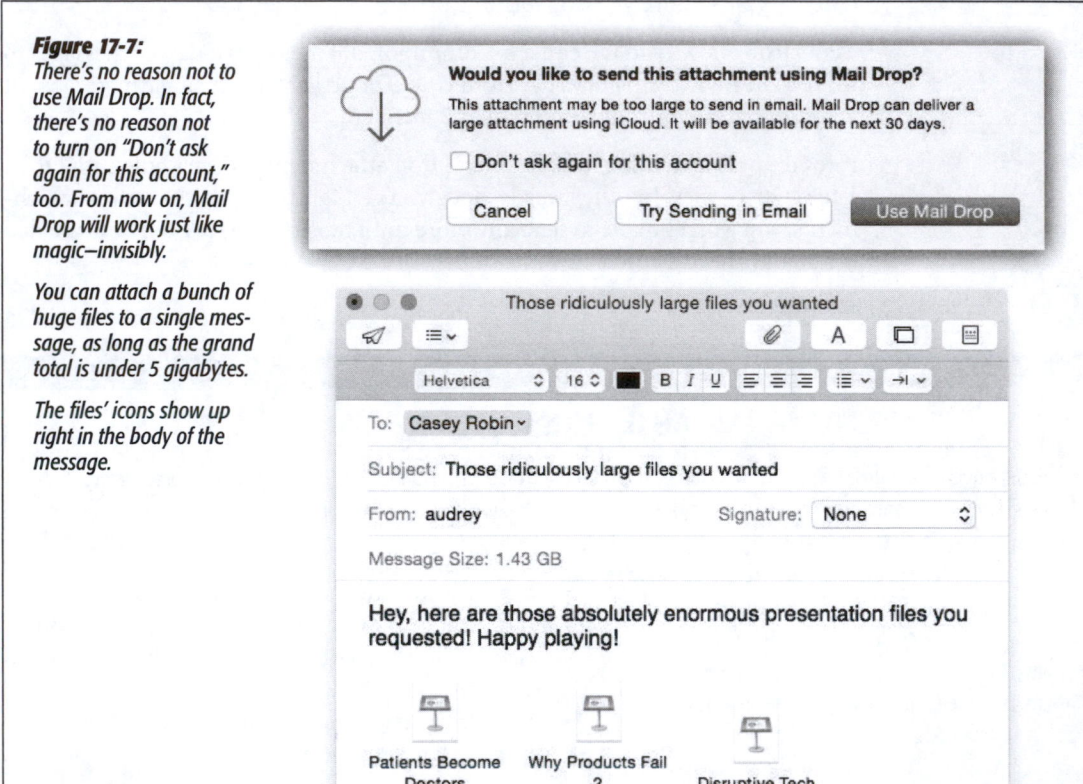

Figure 17-7:
There's no reason not to use Mail Drop. In fact, there's no reason not to turn on "Don't ask again for this account," too. From now on, Mail Drop will work just like magic—invisibly.

You can attach a bunch of huge files to a single message, as long as the grand total is under 5 gigabytes.

The files' icons show up right in the body of the message.

To attach a file to a message you've written, use one of these methods:

- **Drag the icons you want to attach directly off the desktop** (or out of a folder) into the New Message window. There your attachments appear with their own hyperlinked icons (visible in Figure 17-6), meaning that your recipient can simply click to open them.

Tip: Exposé was *born* for this moment. Hit ⌘-F3 to make all open windows flee to the edges of the screen, revealing the desktop. Root around until you find the file you want to send. Begin dragging it; without releasing the mouse, press ⌘-F3 again to bring your message window back into view. Complete your drag into the message window.

Mail makes it look as though you can park the attached file's icon (or the full image of a graphics file) inside the text of the message, mingled with your typing. On the receiving end, however, all the attachments might end up clumped together at the end of the message (depending on which email system your correspondent uses).

- **Drag the icons you want to attach from the desktop onto Mail's *Dock icon*.** Mail dutifully creates a new outgoing message, with the files already attached.

- **Click 📎 on the New Message toolbar,** choose File→Attach Files, or press Shift-⌘-A. The Open File sheet appears so you can find the files you want to include. (You can choose multiple files simultaneously in this dialog box. Just ⌘-click or Shift-click them as though you were selecting them in a Finder window.)

Once you've selected them, click Choose File (or press Return). You return to the New Message window, where the attachments' icons appear, ready to ride along when you send the message.

POWER USERS' CLINIC

A Windows Attachment Trick

What's attached to an email message is often more important than the message itself. You might send a PowerPoint file to a co-worker or send your aunt a picture of your new dog, for example, without bothering to write anything more than "See attached" in the body of the message.

That's why it's such a pain when email attachments don't go through. Luckily, macOS provides a tool for making attachments more compatible with Windows, so you'll never get another frustrated "I *can't* see attached!" reply again.

You can pick from two formats for your attachments: normal or Windows-friendly. Normal attachments open correctly on both Macs and PCs. Trouble is, a normal attachment may show up on a PC accompanied by a useless second attachment whose name starts with "._" (which often frustrates

your recipients). Windows-friendly attachments, on the other hand, always work correctly on PCs—but when sent to Macs, they lose minor details like color labels and originating website information.

Bottom line: Unless you work in an all-Mac company, stick with the Windows-friendly setting.

To use the Windows-friendly setting for an open message, choose Edit→Attachments→Send Windows-Friendly Attachments. (If no message is open, then the command says *Always* Send Windows-Friendly Attachments instead.) You can also adjust the setting on a per-email basis using the Send Windows-Friendly Attachments checkbox at the bottom of the attachment dialog box.

Tweaking the Classic Layout

Out of the box, Mail assumes a three-column layout (Figure 17-2, top): mailboxes list at left, messages list in the middle, and the message itself at right.

There are two advantages to this layout. First, your Mac's screen is wider than it is tall, so *columns* of information make more sense than *horizontal* strips. Second, by devoting only about half the screen to the message itself, the column of text is kept to a comfortable reading width; too wide, and your eyeballs have to scan across the whole screen, which is supposedly tiring.

But if you hate that layout, you can always go back to the older layout, shown at bottom in Figure 17-2, by choosing Mail→Preferences→Viewing and turning on "Show Classic layout." Here again, you can adjust the sizes of the panes and columns by dragging the divider lines. You can also control *which* columns appear using the commands in the View→Columns menu.

Tweaking the Full-Screen Layout

Mail, of all programs, benefits from Full Screen mode (page 178), because there are a lot of panels to keep open. In macOS Mojave, you can opt to see the new-message (or Reply) pane off to the right, rather than superimposed (see Figure 17-5).

To set that up, open Mail→Preferences→General→"Prefer opening messages in split view when in full screen mode."

Note: Weirdly enough, this feature works only if the "Displays have separate spaces" checkbox is turned on in System Preferences→Mission Control. Log out and then back in again to make the change take effect.

Figure 17-5:
In Full Screen mode, a new outgoing message or reply usually floats in a window on top of the rest of the Mail program (top). That can be frustrating, because you can't refer to any other messages while writing.

In macOS Mojave, though, the composition window can sit in a third pane off to the right (bottom).

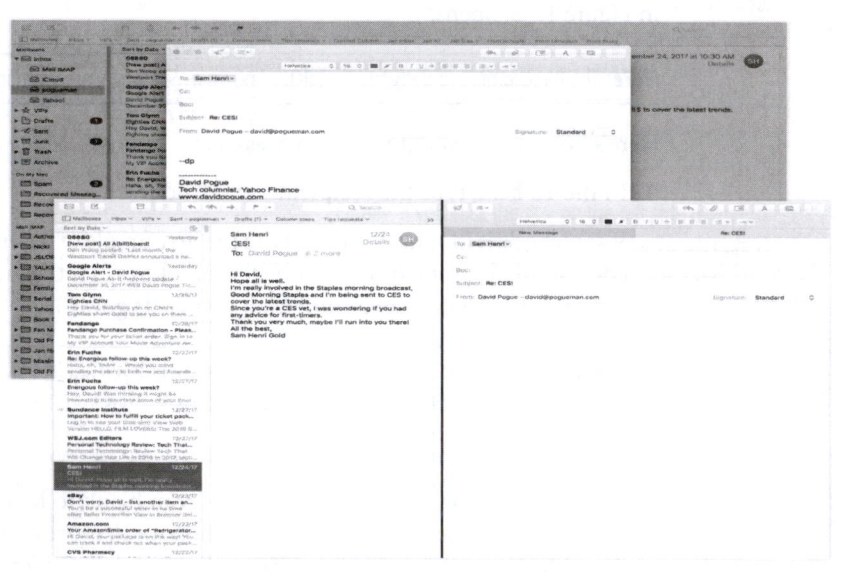

- **Adjust the message window width.** Drag the very right edge of the window inward or outward to adjust the width of the message itself. Double-click the edge of the messages list to make it snap to what Mail thinks is its proper width.

- **Adjust the width of the mailboxes or messages list.** Similarly, you can drag the right edges of the first two columns to adjust their width. Or double-click the right edge to make the column exactly as wide as Mail thinks it should be.

- **Change what morsels show up in the messages list.** The messages list (center column) usually shows the sender's name, subject line, and the first few lines of the message itself (an iPhone/iPad feature brought to the Mac). But you can add additional info displays to the list—message size, mailbox, date sent, and so on—by choosing from the View→Message Attributes submenu.

- **Change what details show up in the header.** The *header* is the top part of a message, where you see the details of how the message reached you. Ordinarily, Mail shields you from the geekiest details of the header; if you really want to see it all, choose View→Message→All Headers.

 But if you'd rather, you can tailor the standard header so that Mail always shows you exactly the information you want. In Mail→Preferences→Viewing, use the "Show message headers" pop-up menu to choose Custom. Now you can add just the details you always want to see: Attachments, Bcc, Cc, Flag, From, Reply-To, Resent-Cc, and so on.

- **Control how many lines of preview text appear.** In Mail→Preferences→Viewing, you can use the List Preview pop-up menu to control how many lines of each message you want to appear, in light gray, as a preview of what's in the message itself. You can choose up to five lines, or choose None to hide the preview completely.

- **Sort the messages.** Use the "Sort by" pop-up menu ("by Date," "by Attachment," "by Unread," and so on). Use the bottom two commands—Ascending or Descending—to control *which way* the sorting goes (A to Z, Z to A, or whatever).

Tip: If you click the "Sort by" bar above the messages list, you jump directly to the top—just like you do on the iPhone or iPad. Some ideas you just can't keep down.

GEM IN THE ROUGH

Favorites Bar Keyboard Shortcuts

One of the best parts of the Favorites bar is that you have complete keyboard control over the buttons there. The keystrokes ⌘-1 through ⌘-9 "click" the first nine buttons on the Favorites bar. Press ⌘-1, for example, to see what's in the first mailbox you've installed on the Favorites bar.

Even cooler yet, if you add the Control key, you now know the keyboard shortcuts for moving selected messages to those

corresponding folders. For example, you can highlight a message and then press Control-⌘-3, confident that you've just filed that message away into your third Favorites-bar folder.

In other words, you can file messages using only the keyboard—and when you're in the thick of things, the less time you spend using the mouse, the better.

- **Drafts** holds messages you've started but don't want to send just yet.

- **Sent,** unsurprisingly, holds copies of messages you've sent.

- **Trash** works a lot like the Trash on your desktop, in that messages you put there don't actually disappear. They remain in the Trash folder until you permanently delete them—or until Mail's automatic trash-cleaning service deletes them for you.

- **Junk** appears when you use Mail's spam filter, as described starting on page 712.

Tailoring the Look of Mail

Apple put a lot of energy into exploiting the size and shape of your screen. In a program made for managing lists and reading messages, you need all the room you can get.

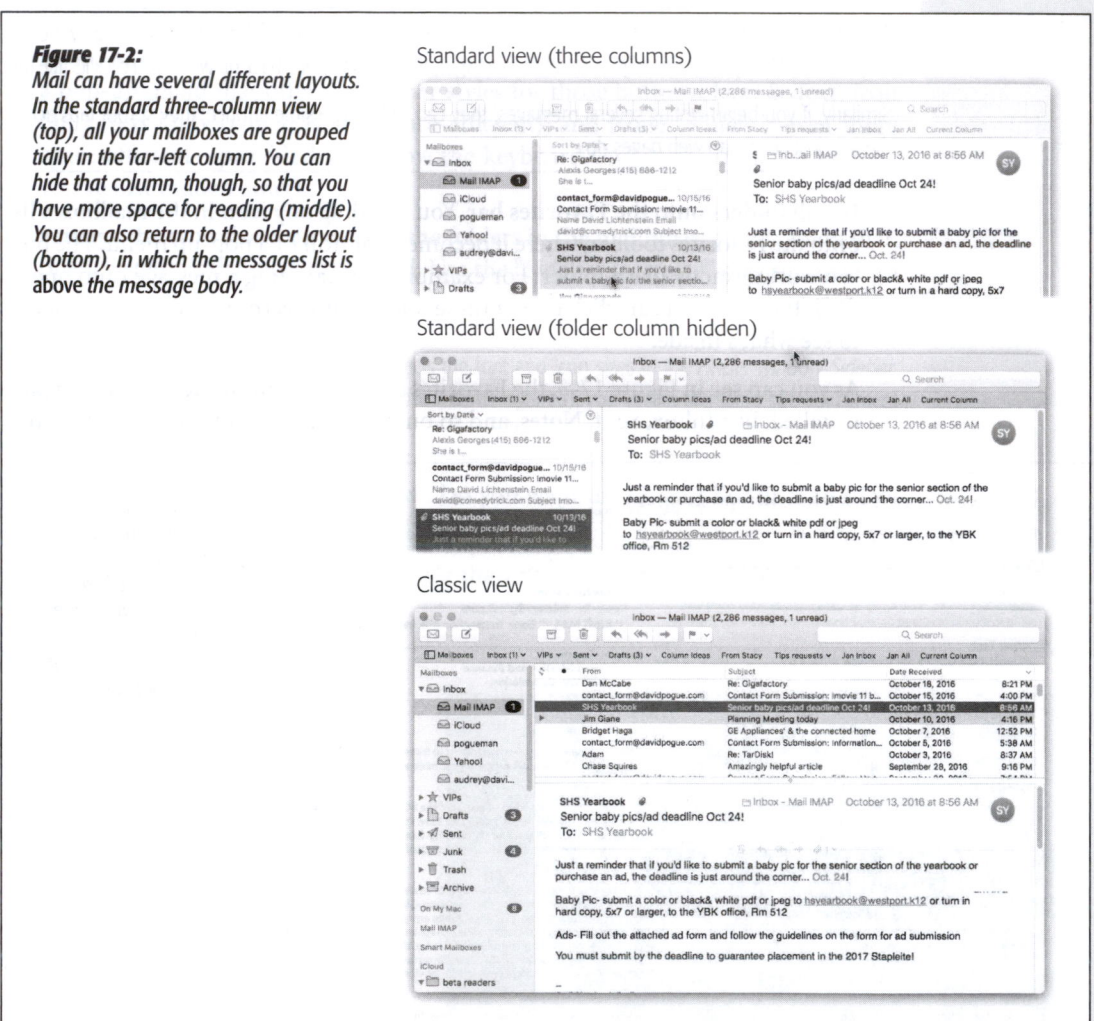

Figure 17-2:
Mail can have several different layouts. In the standard three-column view (top), all your mailboxes are grouped tidily in the far-left column. You can hide that column, though, so that you have more space for reading (middle). You can also return to the older layout (bottom), in which the messages list is above the message body.

Standard view (three columns)

Standard view (folder column hidden)

Classic view

- **VIPs** displays messages from the most important people in your life—those you've designated as VIPs (page 711). This folder doesn't appear if you haven't identified any VIPs.

- **Flagged.** If you've flagged any messages, the flag headings appear here, too. (Flags are described starting on page 702.)

- **Outbox** holds mail you've written but haven't yet sent (because you were on an airplane when you wrote it, for example). If you have no mail waiting to be sent, then the Outbox disappears.

UP TO SPEED

POP, IMAP, Exchange, and Web-Based Mail

When it comes to email, there are four primary flavors of *servers* (internet computers that process email): *POP* (also known as POP3), *IMAP* (also known as IMAP4), *Exchange,* and *web-based.* Each has its own distinct taste, with different strengths and weaknesses.

POP accounts (Post Office Protocol) are still pretty common. Your Mac downloads your incoming mail from a POP server to your hard drive before you read it, which works fine as long as you're using only one computer for email.

The problem with POP, of course, is that things get complicated when you have more than one machine—a phone and a Mac, for example, or a laptop and a desktop. For example, if you usually use a desktop Mac, but you want to take your email along on the road on your laptop, you have to copy the Mail folder from your Home→Library folder into the corresponding location on your laptop's hard drive. That's the only way you'll see your messages and attachments in place when you open Mail on the laptop.

IMAP servers (Internet Message Access Protocol), a newer type, solve that problem. IMAP servers keep all your mail online, rather than making you store it on your hard drive; as a result, you can access the same mail regardless of the computer or phone you use. IMAP servers remember which messages you've read and sent, to boot. (With these accounts, you're not so much *downloading* mail as *synchronizing* your computer with what's online.) It's a great setup if, for example, you check your email on an iPhone, because the deletions and replies you process on the phone will be there on your Mac when you get home. (You can opt for a Gmail or AOL account to be an IMAP account, too.)

Exchange servers are popular in corporations and some schools. Most of the time, employees tap into these servers using a Windows program like Outlook. Corporate geeks like Exchange servers because they're easy to set up and maintain, and because they offer many of the same features as IMAP servers. Luckily, Mail can read and send email through Exchange servers as though your Mac were just another beige PC.

Free, **web-based services** like Hotmail, Yahoo, and Gmail also store your mail on the internet, but you can use a web browser on any computer to read and send messages. They're slower and more cumbersome to use than "regular" email accounts, but they're usually free.

Unfortunately, Mail can't check accounts that are entirely web-based. Fortunately, the big-name web-based email services also offer POP or IMAP servers. If you have a Gmail account, for example, you'll find that you can read your email using either a web browser or Mail (see Gmail's help pages for details on making that work).

Conversely, more and more POP and IMAP accounts are also offering a *web-based* component. For example, whoever provides your internet service—EarthLink, Verizon, or MegaPath, for instance—probably provides both POP service and a web-based way of accessing your email, so you can access your mail either from home or from an internet café in Bangladesh.

All Mail cares about, though, is whether your email account allows POP, IMAP, or Exchange access; what you do on the web is, as far as Mail is concerned, your own business.

Note: If you have multiple email accounts, you can also use the Mailbox→Get New Mail submenu to pick just *one* account to check for new mail.

- **Right-click or two-finger click Mail's Dock icon and choose Get New Mail from the shortcut menu.** You can use this method from within any program, as long as Mail is already open.

- **Wait.** Mail comes set to check your email automatically every few minutes. To adjust its timing or to turn this feature off, choose Mail→Preferences, click General, and then choose a time interval from the "Check for new messages" pop-up menu.

Tip: If you choose Automatically, you'll get incoming messages the instant they arrive—at least in any accounts that offer "push" email.

Now Mail contacts the mail servers listed in the Accounts pane of Mail's preferences, retrieving new messages and downloading any files attached to those messages. It also *sends* any outgoing messages that couldn't be sent when you wrote them.

Tip: If you'd like to monitor your mail progress in a separate window, choose Window→Activity or press ⌘-0. The Activity window gives you a Stop button, progress bars, and other useful information.

Also, if you're having trouble connecting to some (or all) of your email accounts, choose Window→Connection Doctor. There you can see detailed information about accounts that aren't responding. If your computer's internet connection is at fault, you can click Network Diagnostics to try to get back online.

The Mailboxes List

The mailboxes panel, the leftmost list on the screen, lists all your email accounts' folders (and subfolders, and sub-subfolders) for easy access.

Tip: You can also collapse or expand the various sections of the mailboxes list (On My Mac and Reminders, for example) by clicking the Hide or Show button next to each one. That button doesn't appear, however, until you *point* to the capitalized section title (like MAILBOXES or ON MY MAC).

Under the Mailboxes heading, you may find these folders:

- **Inbox** holds mail you've received. If you have more than one email account, you can expand the triangles to see separate folders for each of your accounts. You'll see this pattern repeated with the Sent, Junk, and other mailboxes, too—separate accounts have separate subheadings.

Tip: If Mail has something to tell you about your Inbox (like, for instance, that Mail can't connect to it), a tiny warning triangle (⚠) appears on the right side of the Mailboxes heading. Click it to see what Mail is griping about.

If you see a wavy ⊗ icon, that's Mail's way of announcing that you're offline. Click the icon to try to connect to the internet.

If that happens to you, you'll have to enter details like your name, password, mail-server addresses (incoming and outgoing), and security settings.

When you've made it through the setup screens, turn on Take Account Online to make your new account "live." If you entered everything correctly, Mail checks for new mail right away.

Choose a Mail account provider...

○ **iCloud**

○ **E⊠ Exchange**

○ **Google⁻**

○ **YAHOO!**

○ **Aol.**

○ Other Mail Account...

? Cancel Continue

Figure 17-1:
This dialog box lets you plug in the email settings provided by your internet service. If you want to add another email account later, choose Mail→Add Account and then enter your information in the resulting dialog box. (Or, if you like doing things the hard way, choose Mail→Preferences→Accounts tab, click the + in the lower-left corner of the window, and then enter your account information in the fields on the right.)

Importing Old Mail

Mail also can import your email collection from an email program you've used before—Thunderbird, Netscape/Mozilla, Eudora, or even a version of Mail that's stored somewhere else (say, on an old Mac's hard drive). Importing is a big help in making a smooth transition between your old email world and your new one.

To bring over your old mail and mailboxes, choose File→Import Mailboxes. Mail offers to import your old email collection from just about any other Mac email program.

Later in the process, you can even specify which email folders you want to import. When the importing process is finished—and it can take a very long time—you'll find precisely the same folders set up in Mail.

Checking Your Mail

You get new mail and send mail you've already written using the Get Mail command. You can trigger it in any of several ways:

• Click the ⊠ button on the toolbar.

• Choose Mailbox→Get All New Mail (or press Shift-⌘-N).

Mail & Contacts

If you have an email address or two, you'll be happy to discover that macOS includes Mail, a program that lets you get and send email without having to wade through a lot of spam (junk mail). Mail is a surprisingly complete program, filled with shortcuts and great features around every turn.

Setting Up Mail

Mail can't get your mail unless it knows the details of your email account. The first time you open Mail, then, it asks you for your account information. It's kind of hoping you use a common email service like Gmail, Yahoo, AOL, or Microsoft Exchange (Figure 17-1), or a common internet provider like Verizon or Comcast. In those situations, all you have to do is type your email name and password. If Mail recognizes the suffix (for example, *@gmail.com*), then it does the heavy lifting for you. Mail is ready to go online.

Note: You can perform exactly the same account setup in the Internet Accounts pane in System Preferences. There's no advantage of one method or the other, except that the System Preferences pane lets you enter your account information for online calendars and address books, too.

Now, if you use a service provider that Mail doesn't recognize when you type in your email name and password—you weirdo—then you have to set up your mail account the long way. Mail prompts you along, and you confront dialog boxes, where you're supposed to type in various settings to specify your email account. Some of this information may require a call to your internet service provider (ISP).

Automatic Backup

If you have an iPhone, iPad, or iPod Touch, iCloud can back it up, automatically and wirelessly (over Wi-Fi, not over cellular connections). It's a quick backup, since iCloud backs up only the changed data.

Continuity

The set of features Apple calls Continuity turn the iPhone into a part of the Mac. They let you make calls from your Mac as though it were a speakerphone. They let you send and receive text messages from your Mac—to any cellphone on earth. They let you AirDrop files between computer and phone, wirelessly. And more.

Continuity gets its own chapter (Chapter 8).

Books, Music, Apps, Movies: The Locker in the Sky

Apple, if you hadn't noticed, has become a big seller of multimedia files. It has the biggest music store in the world. It has the biggest app store, for both i-gadgets and Macs. It sells an awful lot of TV shows and movies. Its ebook store, Books, is no Amazon.com, but it's chugging along.

When you buy a song, movie, app, or book, you've always been allowed to copy it to all your other Apple equipment—no extra charge. But iCloud automates, or at least formalizes, that process. Once you buy something, it's added to a tidy list of items that you can download to all your *other* machines.

Here's how to grab them:

- **iPhone, iPad, iPod Touch.** Open the App Store icon (for apps), the Books app (for books), or the iTunes Store app (for songs, movies, or TV shows; tap the category you want). Tap More. Tap Purchased. Tap Not on This iPhone.

 There they are: all the items you've bought on your *other* machines using the same Apple ID. To download anything listed here onto *this* machine, tap the ☁ button. Or tap an album name to see the list of songs on it so you can download just *some* of those songs.

 You can save yourself all that tapping by opening Settings→iTunes & App Store and turning the Automatic Downloads switches to On (for Music, Apps, and Books & Audiobooks). From now on, whenever you're on Wi-Fi, stuff you've bought on other Apple machines gets downloaded to this one *automatically*, in the background.

- **Mac.** Open the App Store program (for apps) or the iTunes app (for songs, TV shows, books, and movies). Click Purchased (on the right), and there they are: all the digital goodies you've bought using this Apple ID, ready to open or re-download if necessary.

Tip: To make this automatic, open iTunes. Choose iTunes→Preferences→Downloads. Under Automatic Downloads, turn on Music, Movies, and TV Shows, as you see fit. Click OK.

The Shopping

Next time you're shopping at an Apple Pay–friendly website, and you're on the payment screen where the "Buy with Apple Pay" logo appears, click it.

A sheet appears where you can choose a different credit card (if you've registered more than one)—and where you must authenticate. If you're using a Mac with a fingerprint reader, just touch your finger to it, and the whole thing is complete.

If you're shopping on a Mac that *doesn't* have its own fingerprint reader, a "Confirm on iPhone" or "Confirm on Apple Watch" message lets you know you can authenticate with your iPhone's fingerprint reader or Face ID, or with a double-press of the Watch's side button. The "OK, all clear" signal gets sent to your Mac automatically.

Figure 16-16:
Top: Here's the iCloud home screen, showing the major online features of this service. All of this stuff, of course, is an online mirror of what's on your Mac.

Bottom: Once you're in one of the modules—Mail, Calendar, Notes, or whatever—you can switch among iCloud features using the ⌄ that always appears in the upper-left corner.

More iCloud Features

Not all of iCloud's goodies are represented as checkboxes in System Preferences→iCloud. Don't forget that iCloud's online hub is waiting for you—available from any computer, tablet, or phone—at *iCloud.com* (Figure 16-16).

And even that's not all there is to iCloud. Read on.

have to wake the phone up; just hold your finger on the Home button (it reads your fingerprint to make sure it's you) or look at the Face ID camera (on iPhones and iPads with that feature). You've just paid.

You can't pay for things everywhere; the merchant has to have a wireless terminal attached to the register. You'll usually know, because you'll see the Apple Pay logo or a wireless-transmission logo displayed. Even so, Apple says over a million stores and restaurants accept Apple Pay, including chains like McDonald's, Walgreens, Macy's, Subway, Panera Bread, Duane Reade, Bloomingdale's, Staples, Chevron, and Whole Foods. More are coming. (The list is here: *apple.com/apple-pay/where-to-use*.)

You can't do that with your Mac, although it sure would be fun to see someone hold an iMac up to the Starbucks cash register.

What you *can* do on the Mac is buy stuff in the Safari browser, on websites that accept Apple Pay. (About 200,000 do, including Apple, Seamless, StubHub, Airbnb, Fandango, Groupon, Ticketmaster, and so on.)

If you have a laptop with a fingerprint reader, you can complete those purchases with a single tap on your Touch ID sensor. If not, you can use an Apple Watch or an iPhone as the identification authenticator; read on.

The Setup

To set up Apple Pay, you have to teach your Mac about your credit card (if you haven't already on your phone).

- **If your Mac has a fingerprint (Touch ID) sensor.** Open System Preferences→Wallet & Apple Pay. Click Add Card.

 If you've already set up a credit card with Apple (through the App Store or iTunes, for example), then all you have to do is supply the security code and then tap Next, Accept, and Done.

 If not, on the Add Card screen, you're asked to hold your Visa, Mastercard, or American Express card up to the Mac's camera. Hold steady until the digits of your card, your name, and the expiration date blink onto the screen, autorecognized. Cool! You can manually edit any of those four fields before clicking Next, Accept, and Done. (You can also choose Enter Card Details Manually and type in the numbers yourself.)

 Next, your bank has to verify that all systems are go for Apple Pay; it's generally instantaneous. (Most banks work with Apple Pay, but not all of them.) You'll see a notification when it's all ready.

- **If your Mac doesn't have a fingerprint sensor.** You can't set up Apple Pay without an iPhone or iPad. (Open Settings→Wallet & Apple Pay and turn on "Allow Payments on Mac.")

As a final step, open Safari→Preferences→Privacy. Turn on "Allow websites to check if Apple Pay is set up."

Tip: Anything you buy, your kids will see. Keep that in mind when you download a book like *Tough Love: Sending the Unruly Child to Military School.*

However, you have two lines of defense. First, you can hide your purchases so nobody sees them. On the Mac, in iTunes, click Store and then Purchased (right side). Point to the thing you want to hide, click the ⊗, and click Hide. Second, remember that you can set up parental control on each kid's Mac or phone, shielding their impressionable eyes from R-rated movies and stuff. See page 531.

- **Where are you?** Go to *iCloud.com* and click Find iPhone (see page 664) to see where their phones or gadgets are right now, which may or may not be with their owners. Or, on an iPhone or iPad, use the Find My Friends app to see where in town (or in the world) your posse is right now.

Note: If one of you needs secrecy for the afternoon (Apple sweetly gives, as an example, shopping for a gift for your spouse), open System Preferences→iCloud. Click Manage Family. Click the person you want to hide from. Turn off "Allow [this person] to see your location." Now you're untrackable until you turn the switch on again.

- **Photos, appointments, and reminders.** In Photos, Calendar, and Reminders, each of you will find a new category, called Family, that's auto-shared among you all. You're all free to make and edit appointments in this calendar, to set up reminders in Reminders ("Flu shots after school!"), or to add photos or videos (or comments) to this album; everyone else will see the changes instantly.

Apple Pay on the Web

Apple Pay (Figure 16-15) is a feature of recent iPhones. It lets you pay for things without cash, without cards, without signing anything, without your wallet: Just hold the phone. You don't have to open an app, don't have to enter a code, don't even

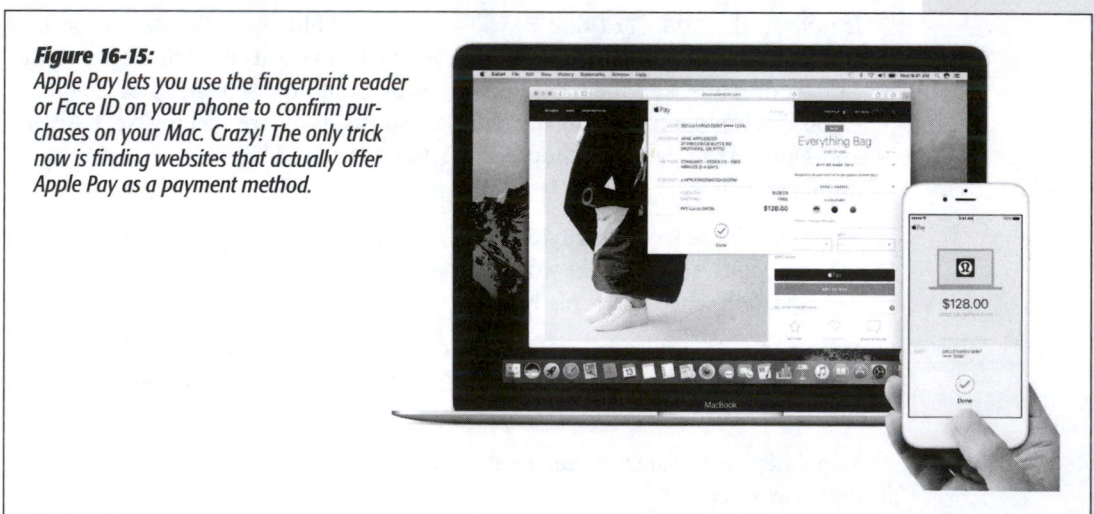

Figure 16-15:
Apple Pay lets you use the fingerprint reader or Face ID on your phone to confirm purchases on your Mac. Crazy! The only trick now is finding websites that actually offer Apple Pay as a payment method.

- **Turn Ask To Buy on or off.** This option appears when you've selected a child's name. If you decide that your kid is responsible enough not to need your permission for each purchase, you can turn this option off.

Note: If you turn off Ask To Buy for someone after she turns 18, you can't turn it on again.

- **Turn Parent/Guardian on or off.** This option appears when you've selected an adult's name. It gives Ask To Buy approval privileges to someone else besides you—your spouse, for example.

- **Turn "Allow [this person] to see your location" on or off.** Do you want this person to be able to see where you are (by using Messages, Find My Mac, or Find My Friends)?

Once kids turn 13, by the way, Apple automatically gives them more control over their own lives. They can, for example, turn off Ask To Buy *themselves*, on their own Macs or phones. They can even express their disgust for you by leaving the Family Sharing group. (On her own phone, for example, your daughter can visit Settings→iCloud→ Family, tap her name, and then tap Leave Family. Harsh!)

Life in Family Sharing

Once everything's set up, here's how you and your nutty kids will get along:

- **Purchases.** Whenever one of your kids (for whom you've turned on Ask To Buy) tries to buy music, videos, apps, or books from Apple—even free items—he has to ask you (Figure 16-14).

Furthermore, each of you can see and download everything everyone else has bought. To do that, open the appropriate program: App Store, iTunes, or Books. Click Purchased, and then tap the family member's name to see what he's got; tap the ☁ to download any of it for yourself.

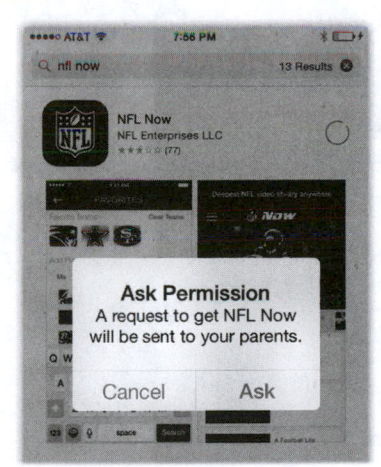

Figure 16-14:
Your kid can't download anything from one of Apple's stores without your OK.

You're notified about the purchase on your phone or Mac, and you can decline it or click Review to read about it on its Store page. If it seems OK, you can tap Approve. You also have to enter your iCloud password to prevent your kid from sneaking over to your Mac or phone and approving his own request.

(If you don't respond within 24 hours, the request expires. Your kid has to ask again.)

Choose "Create an Apple ID for a child who doesn't have an account." Click Continue. On the screen that follows, you'll enter the kid's name and birth date (Figure 16-13, top).

Make up a name and password for the new iCloud account, too. Decide whether you want the family to be able to see where the kid is at all times. Click Continue.

On the Parent Privacy Disclosure screen, enter the security code for your credit card yet again (to prove that you're you, and not, for example, your naughty kid).

On the next screen, you choose and answer three security questions for this new iCloud account. Click Continue. Then more legalese on two screens (click "I agree," and then Agree).

Figure 16-13:
Top: You'll notice that the dialog box requires a birth year that confirms that your kid's age is under 13. If your kid is over 13, you should set up an iCloud account in the usual way—at iCloud.com, for example, or in System Preferences→iCloud.

Bottom: A newly added family member has some decisions to make. First, the Purchases pop-up menu lets her specify her iCloud address—the one whose purchases she'll be pooling with the family. (It's usually the same address you just specified, but not always.)

Second, here she can turn on location sharing. In other words: The rest of the family will be able to see where she is, using Messages, Find My Mac, and the Find My Friends app on the iPhone or iPad.

You can, of course, repeat this cycle to add additional family members, up to a maximum of six. Their names and ages appear on the Family screen.

From here, you can click someone's name to perform stunts like these:

- **Delete a family member.** Man, you guys really don't get along, do you? Anyway, click the — button.

You're asked to confirm that you're actually present with her by entering the security code for your credit card. When you click Continue, she can now enter her iCloud password on your Mac to complete her setup.

On the next screen, she has a couple of decisions to make.

Figure 16-12:
The iCloud pane of System Preferences is the central hub of Family Sharing planning. The setup process involves a bunch of dialog boxes, but at least you have to walk through them only once.

- **If the kid has an iCloud account but isn't with you at the moment:** Type in her email address. Click Send an Invitation.

 Your little darling gets an email at that address. She must open it on her Apple gadget—in the Mail app on her iPhone or Mac, for example.

 When she hits View Invitation, she can either enter her iCloud name and password (if she has an iCloud account), or get an Apple ID (if she doesn't).

 Once she accepts the invitation, she can choose a picture to represent herself; tap Confirm to agree to be in your family; enter her iCloud password to share the stuff she's bought from Apple; agree to Apple's lawyers' demands; and, finally, opt in to sharing her location with the rest of the family.

- **If the kid is under 13:** Your kid doesn't have an iCloud account, because until Family Sharing came along, you had to be over 13 to get an iCloud account. No longer!

Family Sharing solves those problems. Once you've turned on Family Sharing and invited your family members, here's how your life will be different:

- **One credit card to rule them all.** Up to six of you can buy books, movies, apps, and music on your master credit card.

- **Ask before buying.** When your kids try to buy stuff, your device pops up a permission request. You have to approve each purchase.

- **Younger Appleheads.** Within Family Sharing, you can now create Apple accounts for tiny tots; 13 is no longer the age minimum.

- **Shared everything.** All of you get instant access to one another's music, video, ebooks, and app purchases—again, without having to know one another's Apple passwords.

- **Find one another.** You can use your phone to see where your kids are, and vice versa (with permission, of course).

- **Find one another's phones.** The miraculous Find My Mac feature (page 664) now works for every device in the family. If your daughter can't find her phone, you can find it for her with your Mac.

- **Mutual photo album, mutual calendar, and mutual reminders.** When you turn on Family Sharing, your Photos, Calendar, and Reminders apps each sprout a new category that's preconfigured to permit access by everyone in your family.

Setting Up Family Sharing

You can turn on Family Sharing either on the Mac (in System Preferences→iCloud) or on the phone. Since this book is about the Mac, here are the steps to do it there (Figure 16-12).

In System Preferences→iCloud, click Set Up Family. Read about the juicy features, and then click Continue. The next screen asks you to confirm that you are the sage adult, the Organizer—the one with the power, the wisdom, and the credit card. Click Continue (unless it's listing the wrong iCloud account, in which case you can fix it now).

On successive screens, you read about the idea of shared Apple Store purchases; you're shown the credit card that Apple believes you want to use; you're offered the chance to share your location with the others. Each time, read and click Continue or Confirm.

Finally, you're ready to introduce the software to your family.

Click the + button at lower left. Then:

- **If the kid has an iCloud account and is standing right there with you in person:** Type in her name or email address. (Your child's name must already be in your Contacts; if not, go add her first. By the way, you're a terrible parent.)

Note: If they're not online, or if they're turned all the way off, the map shows you the last known location (if that was within the past 24 hours). If it's been longer than 24 hours, you don't see their current locations. If they're just asleep—even if your laptop's lid is closed—you do.

If just knowing where the thing *is* isn't enough to satisfy you, click the little pushpin that represents your Mac (or choose its name from the menu at top center), and try one of these three buttons:

- **Play Sound.** When you click this button, a very loud sonar-like pinging sound instantly chimes on your Mac, wherever it is, no matter what its volume setting. Even if your laptop is closed and asleep, it will ring. The idea is to help you find it in whatever room of the house you left it in.

 When it's all over, Apple sends an email confirmation to your @me.com address.

- **Lock.** What if you worry about the security of your Mac's info, but you don't want to erase it completely and just want to throw a low-level veil of casual protection over the thing? Easy: Lock it by remote control.

 The Lock button lets you make up a four-digit passcode (which overrides the one you already had, if any). Without it, the sleazy crook can't erase your Mac, and can't even get into it.

 You're also offered the opportunity to type a message; it will appear on the Unlock screen, below the four boxes where you're supposed to type in the four-digit code. You might type something like "Thank you for finding my lost laptop! Please call me at 212-555-1003 for a delicious frosty reward."

- **Erase Mac.** This is the last-ditch security option, for when your immediate concern isn't so much the Mac as all the private stuff that's on it. Click this button, confirm the dire warning box, and click Erase All Data. By remote control, you've just erased everything from your Mac, wherever it may be. (If the Mac is ever returned, you can restore it from your Time Machine backup.)

 Once you've wiped the Mac, you can no longer find it or send messages to it using Find My Mac.

Family Sharing

It took years, but Apple has finally acknowledged a fundamental fact of life: Many of us have *families*.

It used to be a hassle to manage your Apple life with kids. What if they wanted to buy a book, movie, or app? They had to use your credit card—and you had to reveal your iCloud password to them. Or what if they wanted to see a movie that you bought? Should they really have to buy it again?

(That's *if* it's online, and *if* you turned on Find My Mac in the iCloud panel of System Preferences.)

If an ethical person finds your Mac, you might get it back. If it's a person who says, "Hey, cool! A free MacBook!" then maybe you can bombard him with so many of these messages that he gives it back in exasperation.

If not, you can either lock the gadget with a password (yes, by remote control) or even avail yourself of one more amazing last-ditch feature: Erase Mac (or iPhone or iPad).

That means *deleting your data by remote control,* from wherever you happen to be. The greedy thief can do nothing but stare in amazement as the Mac, phone, or tablet suddenly erases itself, winding up completely empty.

Note: And by the way: That thief can't erase your stolen phone or tablet himself, thanks to Apple's ingenious Activation Lock feature. It prevents the phone or tablet from being erased without your Apple ID and password. Good luck with that, bad guy!

Figure 16-11:
The location process takes a minute. You can zoom in to or out of the map, click Satellite to see an overhead photo of the area, or click Hybrid to see the photo with street names superimposed.

The big green dot indicates that one of your Apple gadgets isn't as lost as you thought.

To set up your Mac so you can find it remotely, open System Preferences→iCloud. Make sure Find My Mac is turned on. That's all there is to it.

Later, if the worst should come to pass and you can't find your Mac, go to any computer and call up *iCloud.com*. Log in with your Apple name and password.

Click Find iPhone. If you're asked for your password again, type it; Apple wants to make sure it's really, *really* you who's messing around with your account settings.

The website updates to show you, on a map, the current location of your Macs (and iPhones, iPod Touches, and iPads); see Figure 16-11.

synchronized. Delete a phone number on your computer at home, and you'll find it gone from your phone. Enter an appointment on your iPhone, and you'll find the calendar updated everywhere else.

- **Reminders.** This option refers to the to-do items you create in the phone's Reminders app; very shortly, those reminders will show up on your Mac (in Reminders, Calendar, or BusyCal) or PC (in Outlook). How great to make a reminder for yourself in one place and have it reminding you later in another one!

- **Safari.** If a website is important enough to merit bookmarking while you're using your phone, why shouldn't it also show up in the Bookmarks menu on your desktop PC at home, your Mac laptop, or your iPad? This option syncs your Safari Reading List, too.

- **Notes.** This option syncs the notes from your phone's Notes app into the Notes app on the Mac, the email program on your PC, your other i-gadgets, and, of course, the iCloud website.

- **Keychain.** The iCloud Keychain keeps all your online name/password combinations synchronized across all your Apple machines, so you don't have to memorize them or even type them as you log into various sites. Credit card numbers, too. See page 562.

- **Voice Memos.** New in macOS Mojave (and iOS 12): The audio recordings you make on your phone can be synced to the new Voice Memos app on your Mac, and vice versa. But finding the On switch for this feature isn't easy. In System Preferences→ iCloud, click Options next to iCloud Drive. *Here* is the Voice Memos switch.

To set up syncing, turn on the checkboxes for the items you want synced. That's it. There is no step 2.

Note: You may notice that there are no switches here for syncing stuff you buy from Apple, like books, movies, apps, and music. They're not so much synced as they are stored for you online. You can download them at any time to any of your machines.

Find My Mac, Find My iPhone

Did you leave your iPhone somewhere? Did your laptop get stolen? Has that mischievous 5-year-old hidden your iPad again?

You can check into *iCloud.com* to see the exact location of your Mac, iPhone, iPad, Apple Watch, or AirPods (out of their case and near your phone); see Figure 16-11. You can even make it beep loudly for 2 minutes, so you can figure out which room of the house you left it in. If the missing item is an iPad or an iPhone, you can make it beep even if the ringer switch is off, and even if the device is asleep. You can also make a message pop up on the screen; if you actually left the thing in a taxi or on some restaurant table, you can use this feature to plead for its return. The bottom line: If you ever lose your Apple gear, you have a fighting chance at getting it back.

mail sent to *YourName@Me.com* comes to exactly the same place. These addresses are aliases of each other.)

Second, me.com addresses are integrated into macOS's Mail program, as you'll see in Chapter 17. You can also read your me.com email from any computer anywhere in the world, via the *iCloud.com* website, or on your iPhone/iPod Touch/iPad.

Besides, it's always great to have a backup account, one you never enter on websites so that it never gets overrun with spam. Or vice versa: Let this be your junk account, the address you use for online forms. Either way, it's great to have a second account.

To make things even sweeter, your me.com or *iCloud.com* mail is completely synced. Delete a message on one gadget, and you'll find it in the Deleted Mail folder on another. Send a message from your iPhone, and you'll find it in the Sent Mail folder on your Mac. And so on.

Data Synchronization

iCloud began life as a *synchronization* service. It can keep your calendar, address book, reminders, notes, bookmarks, and documents updated and identical on all your gadgets: Mac, PC, iPhone, iPad, iPod Touch. Also your web passwords and credit card numbers. And all your photos, too, rounded up from all your Apple gadgets.

It's a huge convenience—almost magical. It's one of the great payoffs of living within Apple's ecosystem of gadgets. It offers both the convenience factor—all your stuff is always on all your gadgets—and a safety/backup factor, since you have duplicates everywhere.

It works by storing the master copies of your stuff—email, notes, reminders, contacts, calendars, web bookmarks, and documents—on the web. (Or "in the cloud," as the product managers would say.)

Whenever your Macs, PCs, or i-gadgets are online—over Wi-Fi or cellular—they connect to the mother ship and update themselves. Edit an address on your iPhone, and shortly thereafter you'll find the same change in Contacts (on your Mac) and Outlook (on your PC). Send an email reply from your PC at the office, and you'll find it in your Sent Mail folder on the Mac at home. Add a web bookmark anywhere and find it everywhere else. Edit a spreadsheet in Numbers on your iPad and find the same numbers updated on your Mac.

Actually, there's even another place where you can work with your data: on the web. Using your computer, you can log into *iCloud.com* to find web-based clones of Calendar, Contacts, and Mail.

Figure 16-8 shows the on/off switches for these sync features. They include these:

- **Contacts, Calendars.** There's nothing as exasperating as realizing that the address book you're consulting on your home Mac is missing somebody you're sure you entered—on your phone. This option keeps all your address books and calendars

After a party or some other get-together, you can send your best shots to everyone who attended; after a trip, you can post your photographic memories for anyone who might care.

The lucky recipients can post comments about your pix, click a "like" button to indicate their enthusiasm, or even submit their pictures and videos. It's like having a tiny Instagram network of your very own, consisting solely of people you invite.

The steps for creating Shared Albums vary by program. Figure 16-10, for example, shows how it works in the Photos app.

iCloud Drive

The iCloud Drive is Apple's version of Dropbox. It's a folder, present on every Mac, iPhone, iPad, and iPod Touch, that lists whatever you've put into it—an online "disk" that holds 5 gigabytes (more, if you're willing to pay).

The iCloud Drive is a perfect place to put stuff you want to be able to access from any Apple gadget, wherever you go. It's a great backup, too.

If you click Options next to iCloud Drive in the iCloud pane of System Preferences (shown in Figure 16-8), you find two tabs. The first, Documents, lists all the Mac apps that have stored files or preference settings on your Drive. Look Me Up By Email is a list of apps that permit other iCloud members to find you by looking up your address.

You can read more about iCloud Drive—and its offshoot, iCloud Desktop & Documents—starting on page 221.

Email Address

Apple offers an email address as part of each iCloud account. Of course, you already *have* an email account. So why bother? The first advantage is the simple address: *YourName@Me.com*. (It may look like what you've got is *YourName@icloud.com*, but

And once a photo arrives, you can save it to your Camera Roll, where it's permanently saved. See Figure 16-9.

Note: Photo Stream is the one iCloud feature that doesn't sync over the cellular airwaves. It sends photos around only when you're in a Wi-Fi hotspot or connected to a wired network.

To find your Photo Stream, open the Photos app on your phone, tablet, Apple TV, or Mac. There it is, in the Albums list: An "album" called My Photo Stream. (On a Windows PC, you'd get a Photo Stream folder in your Pictures folder.)

Note: If you've turned this feature on in System Preferences, but you don't see the My Photo Stream album in Photos, it's because you've *also* turned on iCloud Photos. When that's on, you're *already* getting all your pictures and videos stored everywhere, so there's no point in having a folder containing only your last 1,000 pictures.

This, in its way, is one of the best features in all of iCloudland, because it means you don't have to sync your iPhone over a USB cable to get your photos onto your computer. It all happens automatically, wirelessly over Wi-Fi.

Shared Albums

Shared Albums lets you send photos or videos to other people's Apple gadgets (Macs, iPhones, iPads, Apple TVs)—and, in a more limited way, even to non-Apple people.

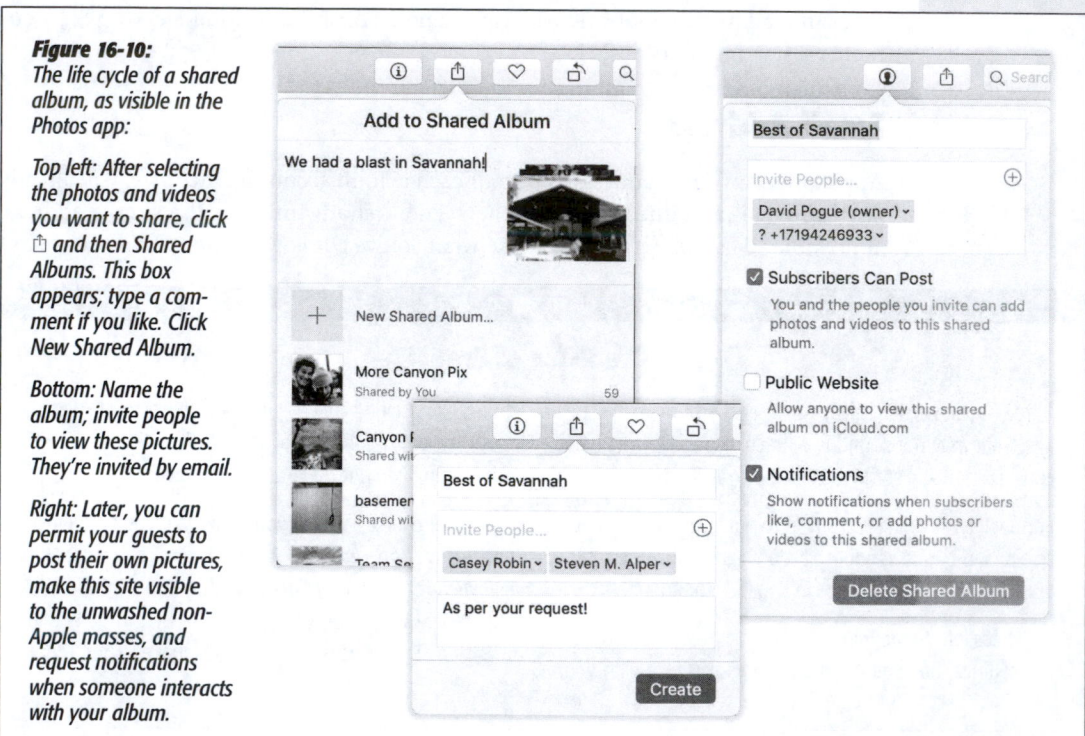

Figure 16-10:
The life cycle of a shared album, as visible in the Photos app:

Top left: After selecting the photos and videos you want to share, click ⬆ and then Shared Albums. This box appears; type a comment if you like. Click New Shared Album.

Bottom: Name the album; invite people to view these pictures. They're invited by email.

Right: Later, you can permit your guests to post their own pictures, make this site visible to the unwashed non-Apple masses, and request notifications when someone interacts with your album.

In System Preferences→iCloud, click the Options button next to Photos to see three on/off checkboxes: iCloud Photos (formerly iCloud Photo Library), My Photo Stream, and Shared Albums (formerly iCloud Photo Sharing). Read on.

iCloud Photos

This feature keeps your photos and videos backed up online and synced. *All* your photos and videos are always backed up, and always accessible from any of your gadgets. That's all there is to it. Every photo that winds up on your Mac, every picture you take with your iPhone, all wind up on both. You can even see all of this at *iCloud.com* (click Photos), complete with tabs for Moments, Albums, and the other Photos categories.

There is, of course, a catch. Your entire iCloud account comes with only 5 gigabytes of free storage. If you start backing up your photo library to it, too, you'll have to pay to expand that storage.

My Photo Stream

Every time a new photo enters your life—when you take a picture with an i-gadget, for example, or import one onto your Mac—it gets added to your Photo Stream. In other words, it appears automatically on all your *other* iCloud machines.

Unlike iCloud Photos, this feature is free. On the other hand, it maintains only the most recent 1,000 photos you've taken (Figure 16-9). There's another limitation, too: The iCloud servers store your photos for only 30 days. But as long as your gadgets go online at least once a month, they'll remain current with the Photo Stream.

Figure 16-9:
Left: Why, look! It's photos you imported onto your Mac at home. How'd they get here on the iPhone? iCloud!

To rescue one of these photos from the 1,000-photo rule, open it. Then tap the ⬆ button.

Right: Finally, tap Save Image (bottom row, right). Now, even after that photo disappears from the Photo Stream, having been displaced by the 1,001st incoming photo, you'll still have your permanent copy.

created a *software* base station. The Mac itself is now the transmitter for internet signals to and from any other Wi-Fi computers within range.

> **Tip:** You can let a wired Mac share a *wireless* connection, too. Suppose, for example, that you and a buddy both have laptops in a hotel lobby. You're online, having paid $13 to use the hotel's Wi-Fi network. If you set up Internet Sharing appropriately, your buddy can connect to your Mac via an Ethernet cable and surf along with you—no extra charge.

Meet iCloud

If you have a Mac, you'll see frequent references to Apple's free iCloud service. It's a huge array of features that are designed to make you glad you belong in the Apple ecosystem. iCloud synchronizes information across all your Macs, iPhones, iPads, iPod Touches, across family members, across the world, wirelessly and automatically. It keeps track of every song, book, movie, app, and TV show you've bought from Apple, so that you can download them onto any other gadget with an Apple logo on the back. It lets you find a lost Apple gadget. It gives you an email account. And a lot more.

The rest of this chapter details each of iCloud's goodies, one at a time. They're described in the order they appear in System Preferences→iCloud (Figure 16-8).

Figure 16-8:
The headquarters of iCloud's features. You'll find a nearly identical panel on your iPhone, iPad, or iPod Touch (in Settings→iCloud).

Photos

For most people, pictures are extremely important data. iCloud takes the worry out of maintaining your collection by making sure they're backed up and available online.

cellular modem, or Bluetooth DUN (dial-up networking—that is, tethering to your cellphone or iPad).

- **To computers using.** Using these checkboxes, specify how you want your Mac to rebroadcast the internet signal to the others. (It has to be a *different* network channel. You can't get your signal via Wi-Fi and then pass it on via Wi-Fi.)

> **Note:** Which checkboxes appear here depends on which kinds of internet connections are turned on in the Network pane of System Preferences. If the gateway Mac doesn't have Wi-Fi circuitry, for example, or if Wi-Fi is turned off in the current configuration, then the Wi-Fi option doesn't appear.

Now visit each of the other Macs on the same network. Open the Network pane of System Preferences. Select the network method you chose in the second step above: Wi-Fi, Built-in Ethernet, or FireWire. Click Apply.

If the gateway Mac is rebroadcasting using Wi-Fi—by far the most common use of this feature—then you have one more step. In your 🛜 menulet, you'll see a strange new "hotspot" that wasn't there before, bearing the name of the gateway Mac. (It might say, for example, "Casey's MacBook Air.") Choose its name to begin your borrowed internet connection.

As long as the gateway Mac remains on and online, both it and your other computers, even Windows PCs, can get onto the internet simultaneously, all at high speed. You've

POWER USERS' CLINIC

Internet Sharing as a Bridge

Ordinarily, only one Mac has Internet Sharing turned on: the one that's connected directly to the internet.

But sometimes, you might want another Mac "downstream" to have it on, too. That's when you want to *bridge* two networks.

Consider the setup shown here. There are really two networks: one that uses Wi-Fi, and another connected to an Ethernet hub.

Gateway Mac: Internet Sharing ON

To cable modem, DSL, or Bluetooth phone

Hub

Bridge Mac (with AirPort): Internet Sharing ON

AirPort Macs

If you play your cards right, all these Macs can get online simultaneously, using a single internet connection.

Set up the gateway Mac so that it's a Wi-Fi base station, exactly as described on these pages.

Start setting up the *bridge* Mac the way you'd set up the other Wi-Fi Macs—with Wi-Fi selected as the primary connection method, and Using DHCP turned on in the Network panel.

Then visit the bridge Mac's Sharing panel. Turn on Internet Sharing here, too, but this time select "To computers using: Built-in Ethernet."

The bridge Mac is now on both networks. It uses the Wi-Fi connection as a bridge to the gateway Mac and the internet—and its Ethernet connection to share that happiness with the wired Macs in its own neighborhood.

- **Use Internet Sharing.** MacOS's Internet Sharing feature is the software version of a router: It distributes a single internet signal to every computer on the network. But unlike a router, it's free. You just fire it up on the one Mac that's connected directly to the internet—the *gateway* computer.

 But there's a downside: If the gateway Mac is turned off or asleep, then the other machines can't get online.

Most people use Internet Sharing to share a broadband connection like a cable modem or DSL. But there are other times when it comes in handy. If you have a cellular modem, for example, you might want to share its signal via Wi-Fi so the kids in the back seat can get online with their iPod Touches.

The only requirement: The internet-connected Mac must have some *other* kind of connection (Ethernet, Wi-Fi, Bluetooth, FireWire) to the Macs that will share the connection.

Turning On Internet Sharing

To turn on Internet Sharing on the gateway Mac, open the Sharing panel of System Preferences. Click Internet Sharing, as shown in Figure 16-7, but don't turn on the checkbox yet.

Before you do that, you have to specify (a) how the gateway Mac is connected to the internet, and (b) how it's connected to the other Macs on your network:

- **Share your connection from.** Using this pop-up menu, identify how *this Mac* (the gateway machine) connects to the internet—via built-in Ethernet, Wi-Fi,

Figure 16-7:
Ka-ching! You and your buddy are about to save money. In this example, an Ethernet wire is getting this Mac online. But it's sharing that internet connection with other Macs via Wi-Fi. They can get online, too.

Creating a New Location

To create a *location,* which is nothing more than a set of memorized settings, open System Preferences, click Network, and then choose Edit Locations from the Location pop-up menu. Continue as shown in Figure 16-6 at bottom.

Tip: You can use the commands in the ⚙ menu to rename or duplicate a location.

When you click Done, you return to the Network panel. Take this opportunity to set up the kind of internet connection you use at the corresponding location, just as described on the first pages of this chapter. If you travel regularly, you can build a *list* of locations, each of which "knows" the way you like to get online in each city you visit.

A key part of making a new location is putting the various internet connection types (Ethernet, Wi-Fi, Modem, Bluetooth) into the correct order. Your connections will be slightly quicker if you give the modem connection priority in your Hotel setup, the Wi-Fi connection priority in your Starbucks setup, and so on.

You can even turn off some connections entirely. For example, if you use nothing but a cable modem when you're at home, you might want to create a location in which *only* the Ethernet connection is active. Use the Make Service Inactive command in the ⚙ menu.

Conversely, if your laptop uses nothing but Wi-Fi when you're on the road, then your location could include *nothing* but the Wi-Fi connection. You'll save a few seconds each time you try to go online, because your Mac won't bother hunting for an internet connection that doesn't exist.

Making the Switch

Once you've set up your various locations, you can switch among them using the →Location submenu, as shown in Figure 16-6. As soon as you do so, your Mac is automatically set to get online the way you like.

Internet Sharing

If you have cable modem or DSL service, you're a very lucky individual. You get terrific internet speed and an always-on connection. Too bad only one computer in your household or office can enjoy these luxuries.

It doesn't have to be that way. You can spread the joy of high-speed internet to every Mac (and PC) on your network in either of two ways:

- **Buy a router.** A *router* is a little box, costing about $50, that connects directly to the cable modem or DSL box. In most cases, it has multiple internet jacks so you can plug in several Macs, PCs, and/or wireless base stations. As a bonus, a router provides excellent security, serving as a firewall to keep out unsolicited visits from hackers on the internet.

Still, millions of people never got the memo. If you're among them, then you need to sign up for internet service. Once you've selected a service provider, you plug its settings into the Network pane of System Preferences. You get the necessary information directly from your ISP by consulting either its web page, the instruction sheets that came with your account, or a help-desk agent on the phone.

Further details on macOS's dial-up modem setup are in the free appendix to this chapter, "Setting Up a Dial-Up Connection." It's available on this book's "Missing CD" page at *missingmanuals.com*.

Switching Locations

If you travel with a laptop, you may find yourself frequently opening up System Preferences→Network so you can switch between internet settings: Ethernet at the office, Wi-Fi at home.

The simple solution is the →Location submenu, which appears once you've set up more than one location. As Figure 16-6 illustrates, all you have to do is tell it where you are. MacOS handles the details of switching internet connections.

Figure 16-6:
Top: The Location feature lets you switch from one "location" to another by choosing its name—either from the menu or from an identical pop-up menu that appears in the Network pane of System Preferences.

Automatic means "the standard, default one you originally set up." (Don't be fooled: Despite its name, Automatic isn't the only location that offers multihoming, described earlier in this chapter.)

Bottom: When you choose Edit Locations, your locations appear; click the + button. A new entry appears at the bottom of the list. Type a name for your new location, such as Chicago Office or Dining Room Floor.

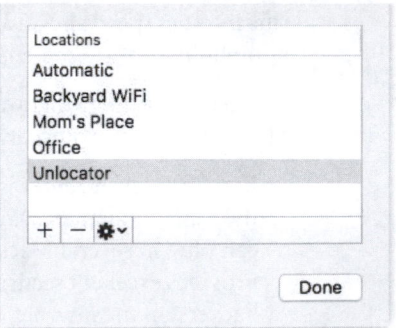

The nice part is that you can get online almost anywhere there's cellphone coverage. The less-nice part is that the connection isn't always blazing fast, and you usually have to pay your cellphone company extra for the privilege.

Here's a typical example: Suppose you have an iPhone. You open Settings→ Personal Hotspot. You turn Personal Hotspot on. You use the password your phone has supplied or assign one to your private little hotspot.

Now, on your laptop, you choose your iPhone's name from the 🛜 menulet. (The menulet shows the iPhone's name even if it's asleep and Personal Hotspot is turned off, as described on page 311.)

You enter your hotspot password (just this time—later, your laptop will remember), and presto: Your laptop is online. A bright blue "Personal Hotspot: 1 Connection" banner appears on your iPhone to remind you, and your 🛜 menulet changes to the International Symbol for Apple Tethering: ꩜.

Tethering eats up your phone's battery like crazy; you'll be lucky to get 3 hours out of it. So you probably shouldn't count on watching Netflix on your laptop via your phone.

But for email, emergency web checks, and other mobile crises, tethering is a convenient, useful feature. And when you're on the road for a couple of weeks, it's a heck of a lot cheaper than paying your hotel $13 a night for Wi-Fi.

Cellular Modems

No wonder laptop luggers across America are getting into *cellular* internet services. All the big cellphone companies offer USB sticks or wireless MiFi pucks that let your laptop get online at high speed *anywhere* in major cities. No hunting for a coffee shop; with a cellular internet service, you can check your email while zooming down the road in a taxi. (Outside metropolitan areas, you can still get online wirelessly, though slowly.) It's the same idea as tethering, except you're not draining your phone's battery.

Verizon, Sprint, and AT&T all offer cellular internet networks with speeds approaching a cable modem's. So why isn't the world beating a path to this delicious technology's door? Because it's expensive—maybe $50 a month on top of your phone bill.

To get online, insert the USB stick or turn on the MiFi; it may take about 15 seconds for the thing to latch onto the cellular signal. Now you're supposed to make the internet connection using the special "dialing" software provided by the cellphone company. Technically, though, you may not need it. You can start and stop the internet connection using a menulet—no phone-company software required.

Dial-Up Modem Connections

Macs haven't come with built-in modems for years. You can get a non-Apple USB modem for $50, but clearly Apple is trying to shove the trusty dial-up technology into the recycling bin.

Unfortunately, joining a *commercial* Wi-Fi hotspot—one that requires a credit card number (in a hotel room or an airport, for example)—requires more than just connecting to it. You also have to *sign into* it before you can send so much as a single email message.

To do that, open your web browser—if, in fact, macOS doesn't auto-open the sign-up screen (see Figure 16-4). You'll see the "Enter your payment information" screen either immediately or as soon as you try to open a web page of your choice. (Even at free hotspots, you might have to click OK on a welcome page to initiate the connection.)

Supply your credit card information or (if you have a membership to this Wi-Fi chain, like Boingo or T-Mobile) your name and password. Click Submit or Proceed, try *not* to contemplate how this $8 per hour is pure profit for somebody, and enjoy your surfing.

Tethering (Personal Hotspot)

Wi-Fi hotspots are fast and usually cheap—but they're *spots*. Beyond 150 feet away, you're offline.

Fortunately, if you have an iPhone, Android phone, or another smartphone, you've got a cellular modem in your pocket. Most smartphones nowadays offer *tethering*, where the cellphone passes the internet along to your laptop (or even your desktop computer). The phone connects to your laptop either with a USB cable or wirelessly (Bluetooth or Wi-Fi).

POWER USERS' CLINIC

The Secret Wi-Fi Menulet—and a Word About MAC Addresses

Here's something not one Mac fan in a thousand knows about: a secret diagnostic mode in the 🛜 menulet.

Turns out that if you press the Option key as you open the 🛜 menulet, you get a special treat: a faint gray *interior* menu that identifies some diagnostic details of your current wireless network. You get to see the hotspot's channel, your current data rate, and the BSSID (address of the base station you're using).

This secret menu also offers direct access to a hidden app called Wireless Diagnostics. It's for troubleshooting: It can capture network traffic, create a diagnostic report, or log all events for debugging purposes.

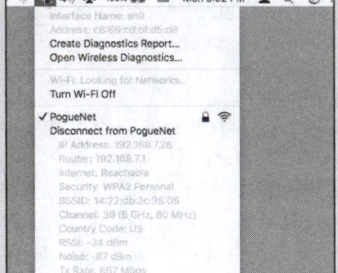

By the way: Some Wi-Fi networks aren't password-protected (there's no 🔒 next to their names), and yet they won't get you online. Why not? Because some hotspots are so restrictive that the network administrator has to register *each MAC address* that's allowed to use it.

A MAC address has nothing to do with Macintosh computers. It stands for media access control, although the equivalent term, Ethernet Hardware Address, is much more descriptive. It's a unique identifier for your networking card, whether it's your Ethernet card or your Wi-Fi circuitry.

MAC-address filtering is another, even more exclusive, way to keep the unwashed masses from using a hotspot.

- **You haven't logged in yet.** Commercial hotspots (the ones you have to pay for) don't connect you to the internet until you've supplied your payment details on a special web page that appears automatically when you open your browser, as described in the next section.

- **The router's on, but the internet's not connected.** Sometimes a wireless router is broadcasting but its internet connection is down. It'd be like a cordless phone that has a good connection back to the base station in the kitchen—but the phone cord isn't plugged into the base station.

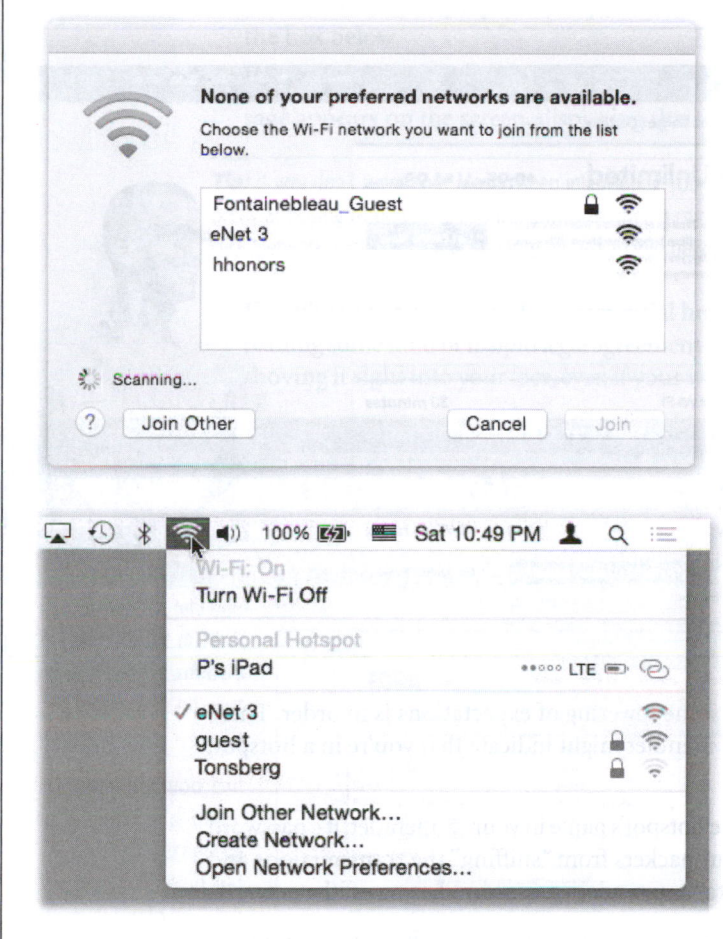

Figure 16-5:

Top: Congratulations—your Mac has discovered new Wi-Fi hotspots all around you! You even get to see the signal strength right in the menu. Double-click one to join it. But if you see a 🔒 icon next to the hotspot's name, beware: It's been protected by a password. If you don't know it, then you won't be able to connect.

Bottom: Later, you can always switch networks using the Wi-Fi menulet.

Or, if you have an iPhone or cellular iPad with Instant Hotspot turned on (page 311), you can hop right onto your own private network.

Commercial Hotspots

Choosing the name of the hotspot you want to join is generally all you have to do—if it's a *home* Wi-Fi network.

On the Network pane, click your internet connection (Wi-Fi, built-in Ethernet, cellular modem, whatever). Click Advanced; click TCP/IP. Now you see something like Figure 16-3. Don't be alarmed by the morass of numbers and periods—it's all in good fun. (If you find TCP/IP fun, that is.)

Note: There's a bright side to having a *static IP address,* an internet address that's all your own and won't change: Because your Mac has this one reliable address, several cool macOS features are available to you. For example, it's easier to access your files from anywhere in the world, as described in Chapter 20.

Figure 16-3:
Here's the setup for a cable-modem account with a static IP address, which means you have to type in all these numbers yourself.

Ethernet Connections

The beauty of Ethernet connections is that they're super-fast and super-secure. No bad guys sitting across the coffee shop, armed with shareware "sniffing" software, can intercept your email and chat messages, as they theoretically can when you're on wireless.

And 99 percent of the time, connecting to an Ethernet network is as simple as connecting the cable to the Mac. That's it. You're online, quickly and securely, and you never have to worry about connecting or disconnecting.

Wi-Fi Connections

Your Mac can communicate with a wireless base station up to 300 feet away. Doing so lets you surf the web from your laptop in a hotel room, for example, or share files with someone across the building from you.

Chapter 13 has much more information about *setting up* a Wi-Fi network. The real fun begins, however, when it comes time to *join* one.

4. **Click OK.**

You return to the Network pane of System Preferences, where the master list of connections magically re-sorts itself to match your efforts.

Your Mac will now be able to switch connections even in real time, during a single internet session. If lightning takes out your Ethernet hub in the middle of your web surfing, your Mac will seamlessly switch to your Wi-Fi network, for example, to keep your session alive.

All right, then: Your paperwork is complete. The following pages guide you through the process of setting up these various connections.

Broadband Connections

If your Mac is connected wirelessly or, um, *wirefully* to a cable modem, DSL, or office network, you're one of the lucky ones. You have a high-speed broadband connection to the internet that's always available, always on. You never have to wait to dial.

Automatic Configuration

Most broadband connections require no setup whatsoever. Take a new Mac out of the box, plug in the Ethernet cable to your cable modem—or choose a wireless network from the 🛜 menulet—and you can begin surfing the web instantly.

That's because most cable modems, DSL boxes, and wireless base stations use *DHCP.* It stands for *Dynamic Host Configuration Protocol,* but what it means is "We'll fill in your Network pane of System Preferences automatically." (Including techie specs like IP address and DNS server addresses.)

Manual Configuration

If, for some reason, you're not able to surf the web or check email the first time you try, it's remotely possible that your broadband modem or your office network *doesn't* offer DHCP. In that case, you may have to fiddle with the Network pane of System Preferences, preferably with a customer-support rep from your broadband company on the phone.

POWER USERS' CLINIC

PPPoE and DSL

If you have DSL service, you may be directed to create a *PPPoE service.* (You do that on the Network pane of System Preferences; click the + button, choose PPPoE, select the connection you're using to PPPoE, and then click Create.)

It stands for PPP over Ethernet, meaning that although your DSL "modem" is connected to your Ethernet port, you still have to make and break your internet connections manually, as though you had a dial-up modem.

Fill in the PPPoE dialog box as directed by your ISP (usually just your account name and password). From here on in, you start and end your internet connections exactly as though you had a dial-up modem.

or an office network—Ethernet, Wi-Fi, Bluetooth, cellular modem card, VPN (Chapter 20), and so on.

Multihoming

The *order* of the network connections listed in the Network pane is important. That's the sequence the Mac uses as it tries to get online. If one of your programs needs internet access and the first method isn't hooked up, then the Mac switches to the next available connection automatically.

In fact, macOS can maintain multiple simultaneous network connections—Ethernet, Wi-Fi, dial-up, even FireWire—with a feature known as *multihoming*.

This feature is especially relevant for laptops. When you open your web browser, your laptop might first check to see if it's plugged into an Ethernet cable, which is the fastest, most secure type of connection. If there's no Ethernet, then it looks for a Wi-Fi network.

Here's how to go about setting up the connection-attempt sequence you want:

1. **Open System Preferences→Network.**

 The Network status screen (Figure 16-1) brings home the point of multihoming: You can have more than one network connection operating at once.

2. **From the ✿ pop-up menu, choose Set Service Order.**

 Now you see the display shown in Figure 16-2. It lists all the ways your Mac knows how to get online, or onto an office network.

3. **Drag the items up and down the list into priority order.**

 If you have a wired broadband connection, for example, you might want to drag your Ethernet connection to the top of the list, since that's almost always the fastest way to get online.

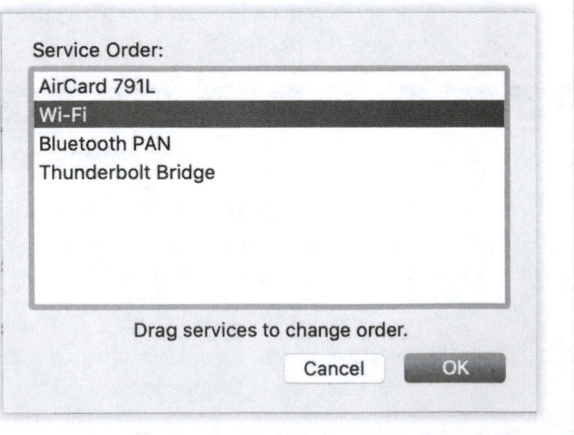

Figure 16-2:
The key to multihoming is sliding the network connection methods' names up or down. Note that you can choose a different connection sequence for each location. (Locations are described later in this chapter.)

• **Dial-up modems.** Their numbers are shrinking, but some people still connect to the internet using a modem that dials out over ordinary phone lines. The service is cheap, but the connection is slow.

This chapter explains how to set up each one of these. It also describes some of macOS's offbeat internet featurettes. It tackles Family Sharing, which lets several computers in the same household share a single broadband connection; the popular virtual wallet feature Apple Pay; and iCloud, Apple's suite of free online syncing tools.

The Best News You've Heard All Day

If you upgraded to macOS Mojave from an earlier version of the Mac operating system, breathe easy: You're already online, since the installer picked up your networking and internet settings from that earlier installation. The moment you see the macOS desktop, you're ready to use the internet (and skip the next dozen pages).

Read on, however, if you need to plug in the internet settings manually. If you're setting up a new Mac, or if you simply want to create a new internet account, you definitely have some typing to look forward to.

Network Central and Multihoming

In this chapter, you'll be spending a lot of time in System Preferences→Network (Figure 16-1). This list summarizes the ways your Mac can connect to the internet

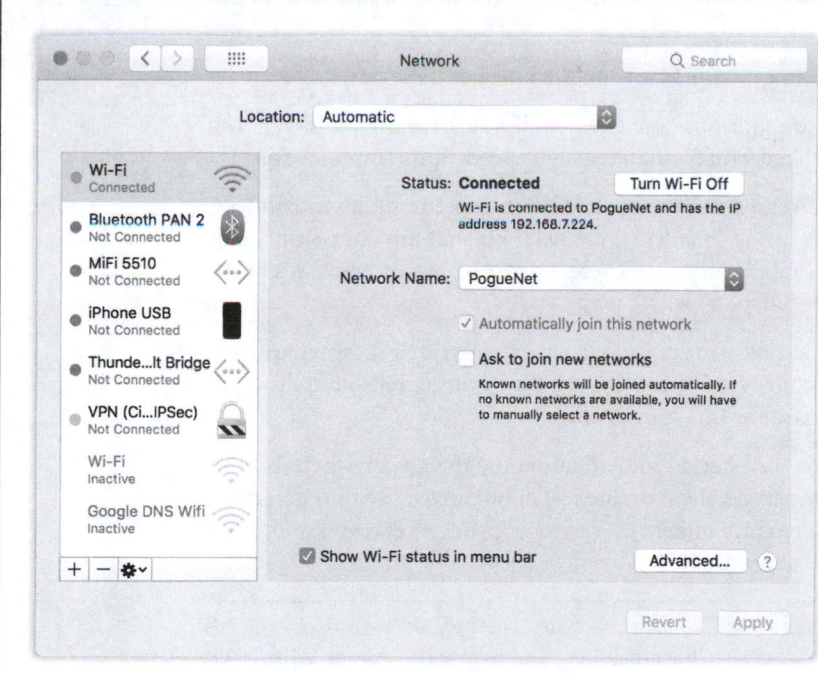

Figure 16-1:
You set up your network connections here, and you can connect to and disconnect from them here. The listed network connections are tagged with color-coded dots. A green dot means turned on and connected to a network; yellow means the connection is working but some other setting is wrong (for example, your Mac can't get an IP address); and red means there's no connection or you haven't yet set up a connection.

CHAPTER
16

Internet Setup & iCloud

A s Apple's programmers slogged away for months to create the Mac operating system, there were areas where they must have felt like they were happily gliding on ice: networking and the internet. For the most part, the internet already runs on Unix, and hundreds of extremely polished tools and software chunks were already available.

There are all kinds of ways to get your Mac onto the internet these days:

- **Wi-Fi.** Wi-Fi hotspots are glorious conveniences if you have a laptop. Without stirring from your hotel bed, you're online at high speed. Sometimes for free.

- **Cable modems, DSL.** Over 80 percent of the U.S. internet population connects over higher-speed wires, using *broadband* connections that are always on: cable modems, DSL, or corporate networks. (These, of course, are often what's at the other end of an internet hotspot.)

- **Tethering.** *Tethering* is letting your cellphone act as a glorified internet antenna for your Mac, whether connected by a cable or a Bluetooth wireless link. You pay your phone company extra for this convenience.

- **Cellular modems.** A few well-heeled individuals enjoy the go-anywhere bliss of *USB cellular modems,* which get them online just about anywhere they can make a phone call. These modems are offered by Verizon, Sprint, AT&T, and so on, and usually cost around $50 a month.

Note: A MiFi is sort of a cellular modem, too. It's a pocketable, battery-operated, portable hotspot. It converts the cellular signal into a Wi-Fi signal, so up to five people can be online at once, while the MiFi itself sits happily in your pocket or laptop bag.

645

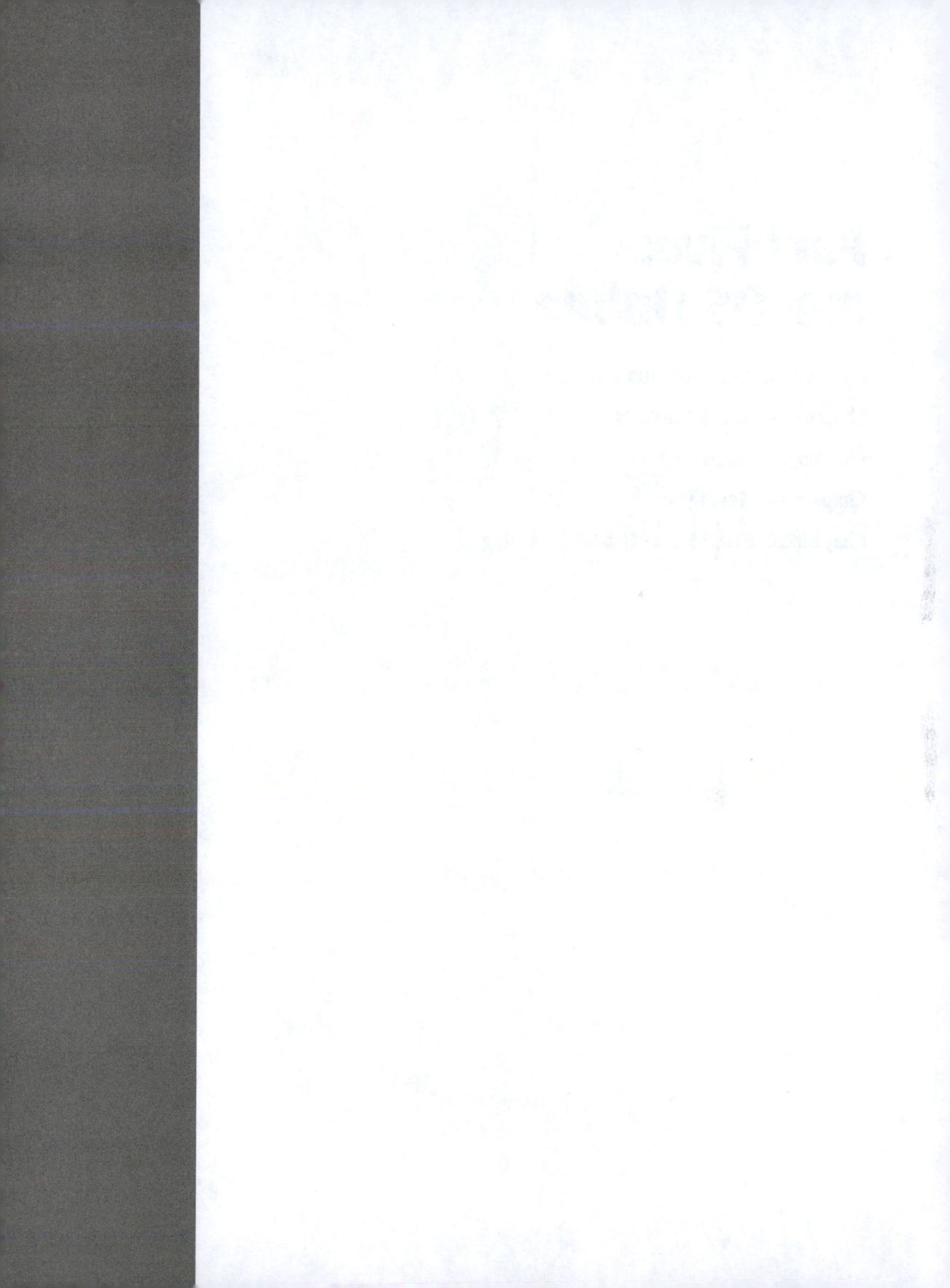

5

Part Five: macOS Online

Making the Recording

Get some sound-recording software—like QuickTime Player, which is in your Applications folder. (GarageBand works, too, although it's a much beefier app.)

Choose File→New Audio Recording. Use the pop-up menu to specify the audio quality and sound source (Figure 15-8). Click the round, red Record button and begin to speak; click the square Stop button to finish up. Now you can use the volume slider and the ▶ button to listen to your masterpiece.

Tip: Don't adjust the tiny volume slider in the Audio Recording window unless you're wearing headphones. This slider lets you monitor the sound—and turning it up while the Mac's speakers are live risks producing the hideous shriek known as feedback.

Figure 15-8:
There's a lot going on in this tiny window. The pop-up menu lets you choose audio quality and audio input. As you record, you see a VU meter (audio level) and an indication of the recording's length and file size.

Alert Beeps and You

Alert beeps are the quacks, beeps, or trumpet blasts that say, "You can't click here." (Try typing letters into a dialog box where a program expects numbers, for example.)

Choosing an alert beep

Open System Preferences→Sound→Sound Effects. Press the ▲ and ▼ keys to walk through the 14 sound snippets you can use as error beeps. The "Alert volume" slider adjusts the error-beep volume relative to your Mac's overall speaker setting.

Adding new alert beeps

MacOS's error beeps are AIFF sound files, a standard Mac/Windows/internet sound format—also the standard sound-file format for music CDs. (The abbreviation stands for *audio interchange file format,* if you're scoring at home.)

As with fonts, macOS builds the list of error beeps you see in the Sound pane of System Preferences from several folder sources:

- **System→Library→Sounds folder.** This folder contains the basic macOS set. Because it's in the System folder, it's off-limits to manipulation by you. You can't easily delete one of the original macOS error beeps or add to this collection.

- **Home→Library→Sounds folder.** It's easy enough to add sounds for your own use—just put them in this folder. (Your Home→Library folder is usually invisible; to open it, press Option as you choose Go→Library in the Finder.)

- **Library→Sounds folder.** If you, an administrator, want to make a sound file available to all account holders on your Mac, create a new Sounds folder in the main hard drive window's Library folder. Any sound files you put there now appear in every account holder's list of alert sounds.

The sound files you put into these folders must be in AIFF format, and their names must end with .aiff or .aif. Changes you make to these Sounds folders don't show up in the Sound pane until the next time you open it.

Recording Sounds

Your microphone situation depends on the kind of Mac you have:

- **Laptop, iMac.** You have a built-in microphone, usually a tiny hole near the screen.

- **Mac Pro, Mac mini.** You can plug in an external USB microphone or use an adapter that accommodates a standard microphone.

The System Preferences→Sound→Input pane lets you choose which mike to use.

Tip: Actually, there's a quicker way to change audio inputs—if you know the secret. Option-click the ◀» menulet, if you've installed it. The resulting menu lists all your audio inputs and outputs, making it simple to switch.

When you choose File→Export As, the Format pop-up menu offers these choices:

- **4K.** Ultra-high definition in H.264 format, with resolution up to 3840×2160 pixels.

- **1080p.** High-def video in H.264 format, resolution up to 1920×1080 pixels.

- **720p.** High-def video in H.264 format, resolution up to 1280×720 pixels.

- **480p.** Standard-definition video in H.264 format.

- **Audio Only.** Just the *audio* from a movie. That's handy if you want to listen on your phone, post an interview online, or use the audio track in another movie.

Playing Sounds

You can have a lot of fun with digital sounds—if you know where to find them, where to put them, and how to edit them. You can play almost any kind of digitized sound files, even MP3 files, right in the Finder—if you put their windows into column view or gallery view (or use Quick Look). But that's just the beginning.

Controlling the Volume

Adjusting the volume of your Mac's speakers couldn't be easier: Tap the ◁ and ◁) keys on your keyboard. (The ◁ key next to them is the Mute button, which instantaneously cuts off all the Mac's sound—a wonderful feature when you find yourself trying to use the Mac surreptitiously in a library or a church.)

Alternatively, you can use the ◁) menulet on your menu bar (Figure 15-7).

Figure 15-7:
The tiny speaker silhouette in the upper-right corner of your screen turns into a volume slider when you click it. To make this sound menulet appear or disappear, open the Sound pane of System Preferences and use "Show volume in menu bar."

The Output tab of the System Preferences→Sound pane, by the way, is designed to let you adjust the left-to-right balance of your stereo speakers, if you have them. The stereo speakers on most Macs that have them (iMacs, laptops) are already perfectly centered, so there's little need to adjust this slider unless you generally list to one side in your chair. (You might find additional controls here if you have extra audio gear—an old iSub subwoofer system, for example.)

Tip: In the Audio MIDI Setup program (in Applications→Utilities), you can configure much fancier speaker setups, including 5.1 and 6.1 surround-sound systems.

Finally, click Sign In. On the next screen (Figure 15-6), type a title and description for the movie. Enter keywords (search categories like "funny" or "sports") so people on that service will find your video when they search.

Work through the remaining upload screens; click Share. In a few minutes, your video will be live for the whole world to see—no charge.

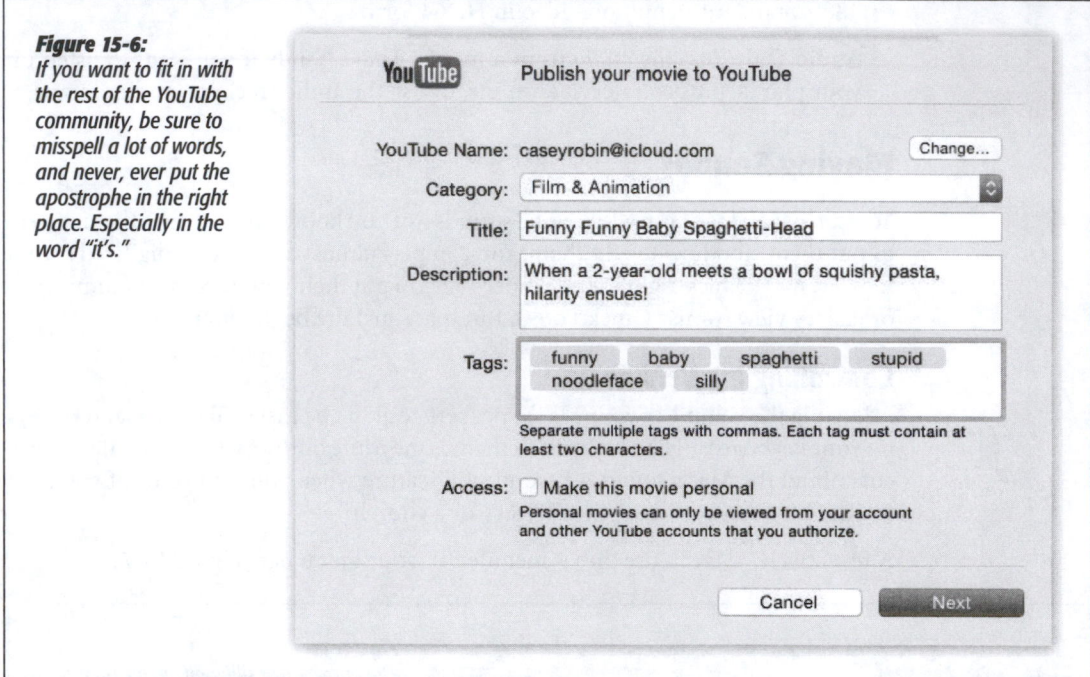

Figure 15-6:
If you want to fit in with the rest of the YouTube community, be sure to misspell a lot of words, and never, ever put the apostrophe in the right place. Especially in the word "it's."

Send to email, Messages, AirDrop

To email your video, choose Mail from the ⬆ menu. QuickTime Player hands the movie file off to your email program, attaches it to an outgoing message, and sits there awaiting the email address and maybe a comment. Of course, many email systems have file-size limits, and movies are big; the recipient's email system may reject it on those grounds. You'll get a "bounce-back" message in that case.

The ⬆ menu also offers commands like Messages (which sends the movie to someone's Mac, phone, or tablet via Messages, described in Chapter 19) and AirDrop (which sends the movie to someone's Mac wirelessly, provided that it's within 30 feet of you; see page 313).

Saving the finished movie

After you've edited a movie (or not), you can use the Export command to specify a new name for your masterpiece—and, if you wish, to convert it to a different format, depending on what kind of machine will be playing it.

To record the Mac's screen, choose File→New Screen Recording. Use the pop-up menu on the resulting Screen Recording panel to turn the microphone on or off.

Tip: This pop-up menu also contains an option called Show Mouse Clicks in Recording. It helps your viewers understand when and where you actually clicked the mouse during the tutorial—by briefly displaying a little circle around the cursor each time you click. (It appears only in playback—not while you're recording.)

Finally, click the red Record button (or press Return).

Press Return, or click Start Recording, to begin the capture. When you finally click the Stop button in the menu bar, your finished movie appears in a regular playback window, ready to trim or to send away to your fans.

Recording Movies from an iPhone or iPad Screen

You can also use QuickTime Player to view and record your *iPhone's* screen (or your iPad's, or your iPod Touch's). Yes, it's incredibly useful to be able to capture videos of the iPhone/iPad screen activity. But this trick is equally handy when you want to project your iPhone/iPad demonstration for a large crowd, using the Mac as a go-between.

To begin, connect the i-gadget to the Mac with its white USB cable. Open QuickTime Player. Choose File→New Movie Recording.

In the recording palette shown in Figure 15-4, click ∨ to open the pop-up menu; choose the iPhone's name (or the iPad's). In just a moment, the live image of the i-gadget now appears on your Mac. You can use this arrangement to show your phone activity to a crowd on the Mac's screen, or even click Record to record it as a movie.

Ways to Export Your Video

One of QuickTime Player's most important talents is *sharing* a video: posting it directly to Facebook, YouTube, Vimeo, Flickr, or your own website; converting it to the right format for an iPod, iPhone, or other cellphone; stashing it in iTunes for easy transfer to your iPod/iPhone; handing it off to iMovie for further editing; saving it to the hard drive as a double-clickable movie; and so on.

Let us count the ways.

Post to YouTube, Vimeo, Flickr, Facebook

The Share button (⬆) offers one-click commands for posting to YouTube (the world's most popular and famous website for short videos), Vimeo (a less well-known, but classier, more high-def video-sharing site), Flickr (mainly a photo-sharing site, but it handles videos, too), or Facebook (the most visited website on earth).

All of these services require that you first sign up for a free account. You do that online, not in QuickTime Player.

Then, with your movie open in QuickTime Player, choose from the ⬆ menu. You're asked for your name and password for the service. If you turn on "Remember this password in my keychain," then you won't have to enter it the next time.

Laptops and iMacs, of course, have a video camera built right in, above the screen. If you have another model, you can attach a webcam, an old iSight camera, or even a FireWire camcorder.

Then open QuickTime Player and choose File→New Movie Recording. The preview window appears. Use the pop-up menu shown in Figure 15-4 to specify what mike and camera you want to use (in the unlikely event that you have more than one) and what video quality you want.

Then, to record, click the red Record button (or press the space bar). Do your schtick. Press the space bar again to stop recording.

Your new video appears in its own playback window. Check it out, trim it if necessary, and then shoot it off to iTunes, Vimeo, YouTube, or whatever.

Recording Screen Movies from the Mac

You can also record movies *of the screen*—either the Mac's screen or an iPhone's or iPad's.

Why is it useful to capture screen activity as a video? Because you can make mini-tutorials for techno-clueless relatives. You can make video podcasts that show how to do things in software programs. You can preserve web animations that you used to think you had no way to capture.

There are limitations. Your movies don't include the Mac's own sounds (game soundtracks and so on), so forget about capturing videos playing on YouTube. (You can record from the *mike,* though, so you can narrate what you're doing.)

But who cares? It's fantastically handy. And you can capture only a *portion* of the screen—one particular window, for example—instead of being stuck with the entire monitor's worth (see Figure 15-5).

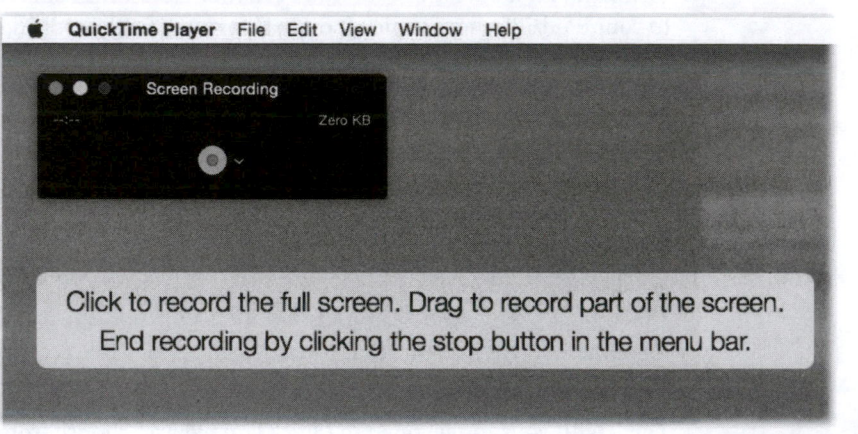

Figure 15-5:
This message appears when you tap the Record button. If you just click to start recording, you'll capture the entire monitor. But if you drag first, defining a rectangle, you'll capture only that area.

Click to record the full screen. Drag to record part of the screen.
End recording by clicking the stop button in the menu bar.

The Open dialog box now appears. Find and double-click the clip you want to tack on. Repeat as necessary.

You can also drag movie clips' icons from the desktop right into a movie window. QuickTime Player adds them to the end of the existing movie.

If you want the second movie to appear somewhere in the middle of the first movie, then open up the clip map (View→Show Clips). Click the clip that appears right *before* the spot where the new movie will go. Choose Edit→Insert Clip After Selection; in the resulting dialog box, find and double-click the movie file you want to bring in.

Or drag a movie file from the Finder directly into the gap between two subclips.

Tip: QuickTime Player automatically shrinks or crops the incoming movies so that they fit the same "screen size" as the original. If they're *not* exactly the same size or proportions, you can then use the Edit→Clip Alignment submenu (Top, Left, Center, and so on) to specify which edge of the movie frame the imported video should hug.

Recording Movies with QuickTime Player

QuickTime Player does more than *play* movies; it can also *record* them. Yes, your Mac is now a camcorder, and a darned handy one; you can pop out quick video greetings, gross out your roommates, impress your co-workers with a dress rehearsal of your pitch, and so on.

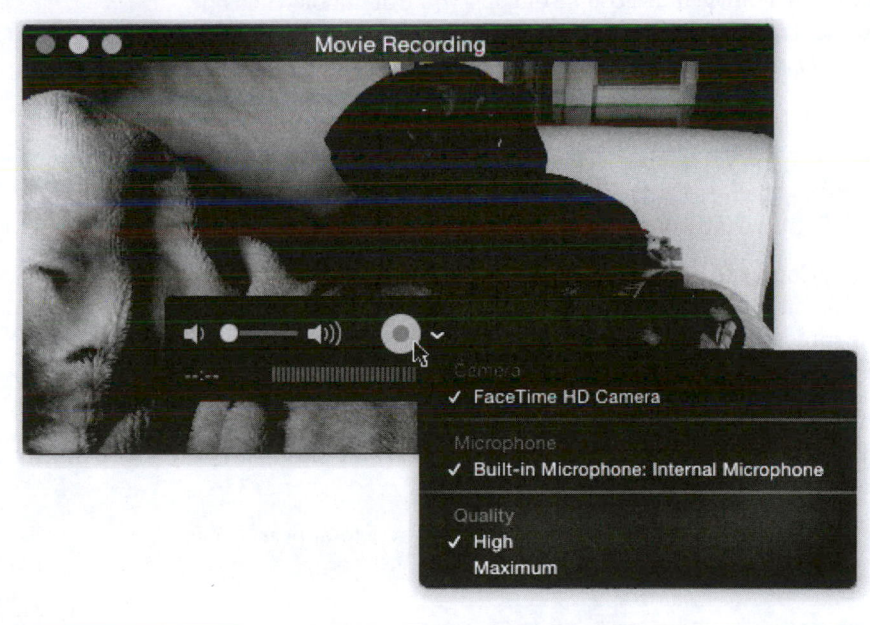

Figure 15-4:
Use the pop-up menu to set up your flick; check the audio level (reflected by the dancing "VU-meter" bars at the bottom of the control bar); and choose a camera and mike.

- **Splitting a clip.** *Clips* are subsections of a movie. To chop a movie in two, move the playhead to the spot where you want the movie to split, and then choose Edit→Split Clip. As shown in Figure 15-3, a clips map appears at the bottom of the window, showing the two resulting clips.

Figure 15-3:
The Split Clip command chops the video into two clips—and produces the map shown at bottom. If you click a clip and then press the space bar to play the video, you'll see the red vertical line that represents the playhead. To chop one of your clips up into further subclips, move that red line into position and then use the Split Clip command again.

- **Chopping video out of the middle.** If you want to trim some video from the *middle* of a movie, first open up the clips map. Then split the movie as described above. Once you've split a movie into a couple of clips, you can double-click one of the clips to produce trim handles just for it. In this way, you can cut unwanted sections from the *middle* of a video.

Or just split the clip into three chunks—and delete the middle one.

- **Rearranging clips.** Once you've chopped a video into subclips using the Split Clip command, you can drag them around within the map. (If you don't see the map, shown in Figure 15-3, then choose View→Show Clips.)

You can use the Cut, Copy, and Paste commands in the Edit menu, too, to move chunks around—even among different movies. (Just remember to first split the target movie at the spot where you want to paste the new clip. The pasted material appears just *after* whatever clip is currently highlighted.)

- **Combining movies.** Combining clips, as already described, is one way to merge videos together. But you can also merge entire movie files that are sitting in the Finder.

Start by opening the first movie. If you want the second movie to appear at the *end* of it, just choose Edit→Add Clip to End.

Tip: If you press Option, the command says Add Clip to Beginning. Sneaky!

Tip: You can make the movie window bigger or smaller by pressing ⌘-plus (+) or ⌘-minus (-).

- **Play more than one movie.** You can open several movies at once and run them simultaneously. (Of course, the more movies you try to play at once, the jerkier the playback gets.)

- **Loop the movie.** When you choose View→Loop and then click Play, the movie repeats endlessly until you make it stop.

- **Navigate chapters.** A few movies, like the ones you buy or rent from Apple, come with built-in chapter markers, just like a DVD. They let you jump around in the film at your whim.

Editing Movies

QuickTime Player is also QuickTime Editor. The program doesn't offer selection handles, so you might think there's no way to select a portion of the middle of a movie (to chop it out, for example). But in fact, commands for trimming, splitting, and merging video clips let you perform just about any editing trick you can imagine:

- **Trimming video from the ends.** You can very easily trim dead space off the ends of a video. Figure 15-2 shows how.

 You don't have to worry about damaging the original video when trimming—you couldn't modify the original if you tried. The instant you use the Trim command, QuickTime Player peels off the shortened version as a new, untitled movie, which you'll have to name and save separately (choose File→Export As).

Figure 15-2:
Top: To trim a video, choose Edit→Trim or press ⌘-T. Drag the yellow handles inward to isolate the chunk you want to preserve. (You can click ▶ or tap the space bar to check your work.) When everything looks good, click Trim or press Return.

Bottom: If you choose View→Show Audio Track, then you can use the sound waves as a guide to your precision editing.

- **Share button** (⬆). Click for a pop-up menu of choices for passing on this video to your adoring fans: via Email, Messages, AirDrop, Facebook, YouTube, Vimeo, or Flickr. All of these options are described later in this chapter.

- **Full Screen** (⊘). Click to make the video fill your entire monitor, just as though you'd chosen View→Enter Full Screen. And what if the proportions of the movie don't quite match your screen? If you make the menu bar return by pointing to the top of your screen, you can handle this problem using one of the choices in the View menu, described next.

Note: When you enter Full Screen mode, the movie doesn't begin playing automatically (unless it was already playing, of course). You have to tap the space bar to get the show underway.

Fancy Playback Tricks

Playing one movie, start to finish, is kid stuff. Here's what else QuickTime Player can do:

- **Rotate or flip.** The Edit menu contains commands for Rotate Right, Rotate Left, Flip Horizontal, and Flip Vertical. Those commands can be handy when a movie turns out to be flipped or rotated—or when *you* want to flip or rotate it for creative purposes.

- **Change the screen size.** As noted already, you can drag the window to any size using the edges as handles. But the View menu commands are handy, too:

 Actual size represents the movie on your screen at its real size—no larger. (If it's truly huge, larger than your screen, then it may be scaled *smaller* to fit. But that's a rarity.)

 Fit to Screen fills your screen without cropping or distorting; the menu bar and other windows remain visible.

 Fill Screen is especially satisfying, because it turns your entire monitor into a movie playback area.

 Panoramic squishes the outer edges of the video, distorting them slightly, so that nothing gets chopped off *and* the movie fills the screen. (These last two options are available only in Full Screen mode.)

Tip: These same options are available via keyboard shortcuts: ⌘-1, ⌘-3, ⌘-4, and ⌘-5. There's even a little button on the control bar, second from right, that switches back and forth between Fit to Screen and Fill Screen. (This button appears only when you're already in Full Screen mode.)

Making the window larger may also make the movie coarser, because QuickTime Player simply enlarges every dot that was present in the original. Still, when you want to show a movie to a group of people more than a few feet back from the screen, these larger sizes are perfectly effective.

Tip: To mute the sound, click the ◀ icon or press Option-▼. Press Option-▲ to make the volume slider jump to full-blast position.

- **Rewind, Fast-Forward (◀◀, ▶▶).** By clicking one of these buttons, you get to speed through your movie at double speed, backward or forward, complete with sound. Click again for 5x speed, again for 10x.

Tip: You don't have to keep your mouse button pressed on these. Just click once and let QuickTime Player do the work. Click ▶ or tap the space bar to stop scanning.

Figure 15-1:
QuickTime Player displays this control bar only when you move your mouse into its window, or whenever playback is stopped.

- **Play/Pause (▶/❚❚).** Click ▶ to start playback, ❚❚ to pause/stop. Or just tap the space bar for both functions.

- **Scroll bar.** Drag the little vertical bar, or just click inside its track, to jump to a different spot in the movie. The counters at the beginning and end of the scroll bar tell you, in "hours:minutes:seconds" format, how far your playhead cursor has moved into the movie and how far you are from the end. (Click the right-hand readout to see the total movie duration.)

Tip: You can also press the ◀ and ▶ keys to step through the movie one frame at a time. If you press Option-◀ or Option-▶, you jump to the beginning or the end of the movie. That's important to know, since there are no longer dedicated Jump to Start/Jump to End buttons on the control bar.

- **Window edges.** Drag any edge, or the lower-right corner, to make the window bigger or smaller. QuickTime Player always maintains the same *aspect ratio* (relative dimensions) of the original movie, so you won't accidentally squish it.

Movies & Sound

Macs have been capable of handling sound and graphics from Day One, years before the word *multimedia* was even coined. MacOS's QuickTime technology, for example, plays digital movies and live "streaming" broadcasts from the internet. This chapter covers it all: how to record video and sound, edit it, and play it back.

QuickTime Player

A QuickTime movie is a playable video file, on your Mac or online. Like any movie, it creates the illusion of motion by flashing many individual frames (photos) per second before your eyes, while also playing a synchronized soundtrack.

The cornerstone of macOS's movie software is QuickTime Player, which sits in your Applications folder. Despite its name, QuickTime Player also lets you edit movies and even record new ones, either using your Mac's built-in camera or by recording screen activity. Finally, when everything looks good, you can post your masterpiece to YouTube, Facebook, Vimeo, or another online site.

You open a movie file by double-clicking it. When QuickTime Player opens, you get a borderless playback window. Just hit the space bar to play the movie.

There's a control toolbar at the bottom of the window (Figure 15-1), but it fades away after a few seconds—or immediately, if you move the cursor out of the frame. The toolbar reappears anytime your mouse moves back into the movie frame. These are the controls:

- **Volume slider** (◂…◂»). Click in the slider, or drag the dot, to adjust the volume—although it's actually easier to just tap the ▲ or ▼ keys.

Now drag diagonally to capture a rectangular chunk of screen. When you release the mouse, you hear the camera-click sound, and the screenshot file appears in the lower-right corner of your screen—containing only the rectangle you enclosed.

But that's just the beginning. Once you've begun dragging diagonally, while the mouse is still down, you can press any of these keys for special manipulation effects:

- **Space bar.** While you hold down the space bar with one hand, your selection rectangle is frozen in size and shape. With your mouse, you can move the cursor with the selection rectangle attached, the better to fine-tune your positioning relative to your target.

- **Shift key.** When you hit Shift, you confine the dragging action of your mouse to a single dimension: horizontal or vertical. Which dimension depends on how you move your mouse after you hit Shift. For example, suppose you drag out a 2-inch square and then pause. With the mouse button still down, you press Shift. If you now continue to drag downward, the selected area maintains a fixed width; you're increasing only the rectangle's height.

- **Option key.** If you hold down Option after beginning to drag, you create a rectangular selection that grows from the center point outward. That is, it treats your initial click as the rectangle's center point, rather than as a diagonal corner.

- **Control key.** If you're pressing the Control key as you release the mouse, you copy the screenshot to your Clipboard, ready for pasting, rather than saving it as a new graphics file on your desktop. (In this case, you don't get the lower-right floating thumbnail.)

- **Esc.** If you change your mind about taking a screenshot, tap Esc. The darkened selection area disappears, and you've exited screenshot mode.

A Dialog Box, Menu, Window, or Icon

Why fuss with cleaning up a screenshot after you've taken it? Using this trick, you can neatly snip *one screen element* out from its background.

Make sure the dialog box, menu, window, or icon is visible. Then press Shift-⌘-4. But *instead of* dragging diagonally, tap the space bar.

Your cursor turns into a tiny camera. Move it so the misty-blue highlighting fills the window or menu you want to capture—and then click. The resulting picture file snips the window or menu neatly from its background.

Pressing Shift-⌘-4 and then the space bar also captures the Dock in one quick snip. Once you've got the camera cursor, click any *blank* spot in the Dock (between icons).

Tip: Here again, if you hold down the Control key as you click or drag, you copy the screenshot to your *Clipboard.*

on the desktop; 🗑 to delete the whole thing; or ⬆ to send your screenshot masterpiece to someone else.

For a video, the only buttons are Trim (makes the yellow trim handles appear, exactly as described on page 634), 🗑, and ⬆.

Figure 14-12:
The screenshot editor lets you annotate, crop, share, or delete your newly hatched screen-capture image.

Here you can see that the editor has corrected your freehand circle, making it perfectly round—but the tiny shape menu at far left lets you choose your original sketch, if you prefer.

The Old Whole-Screen Keystroke

The new screenshot toolbar offers tremendous flexibility—but the old ways of doing things are still around. You can still press Shift-⌘-3 to create a picture file, in PNG format, that depicts the entire screen image. A satisfying camera-shutter sound tells you that you were successful.

Tip: It doesn't *have* to be Shift-⌘-3. You can change any of these screenshot keystrokes to anything you like. Open System Preferences→Keyboard→Shortcuts→Screenshots. Click the keystroke you want to change, press Return to highlight the current keyboard combo, and then press the new keystroke you prefer.

In Mojave, the thumbnail appears at the lower-right corner of your screen for editing, as described.

One Section of the Screen

Another long-standing combo still around: You can capture a rectangular region of the screen by pressing Shift-⌘-4. Your cursor turns into a crosshairs with two tiny digital readouts—the horizontal and vertical coordinates of your cursor on the screen at this moment. (The numbers are in pixels, as measured from the upper-left corner of the screen, which has coordinates 0, 0.)

you like it: a menu open, for example, or certain text highlighted, or the cursor in the right place.

Microphone. When you're recording video of the screen activity, do you want to narrate? If so, which microphone should the Mac use?

Show Floating Thumbnail is the on/off switch for the whole "thumbnail in the lower-right corner of the screen" business described already. If you turn it off, then screenshots go straight to your desktop (or wherever you assigned them to go) as file icons, without the option to edit them. Basically you're back in 2017.

Remember Last Selection is useful for the "Selected Portion" option described previously. When it's turned on, then each time you select Selected Portion, the Mac will start out highlighting the same region you used last time. That's especially useful when you're trying to document something changing on the screen, step by step, screenshot by screenshot.

Show Mouse Clicks is for video recordings of the screen. It produces a little circle around the cursor each time you click, making it easier for future generations to understand when and where you were clicking. (Otherwise it would be hard to tell—there's no sound.)

In each case, after you snap the snap or record the video, a thumbnail image of your new screenshot appears in the lower-right corner of your screen. If you just smile and nod and go on working, then that thumbnail vanishes after about seven seconds, and the Mac creates a PNG-format graphics file. These files are named after the current time and date. They're called "Screenshot 2019-01-19 at 5.18.13 PM," "Screenshot 2019-01-19 at 5.18.32 PM," and so on.

Or, if you made a video, you get a QuickTime movie named, for example, "Screen Recording 2019-1-19 at 3.35.34 PM.mov."

If you click the thumbnail before it's gone, though, you open the screenshot into the new screenshot-editing mode, described next.

The Screenshot Editor

If, after snapping a screenshot, you click the thumbnail that appears at the lower-right corner of your screen, you open the new screenshot-editing window (Figure 14-12).

In this window, you can use any of the tools across the top. These are the standard macOS markup tools, as described on page 472: the Sketch pen, Shapes menu, Text tool, Highlight Selection, Sign pop-up menu, and controls for line thickness, line color, fill color, and font. (You can press ⌘-Z to Undo your last step, as you'd hope.)

Then come three buttons for rotating and cropping the image.

At the right end of that toolbar, you choose a fate for your edited screenshot. Click Revert to undo all the edits you've made; Done to preserve your work as a file saved

- **Record Entire Screen, Record Selected Portion.** This time, you're creating a *video* of all the action on the screen (or within the rectangle that you specify). Alas, these videos don't include sound. (For that, you'll have to buy a program like Screenflow.)

Begin the recording by selecting which video option you want and then clicking Record (far-right button on the toolbar); end it by clicking the ⊙ in your menu bar. (You can also press Shift-⌘-5 again to bring the toolbar back, and click the ⊙ button on *it*.) A thumbnail appears at the lower-right corner of your screen. If you click the thumbnail, you get the editing window described in the next section.

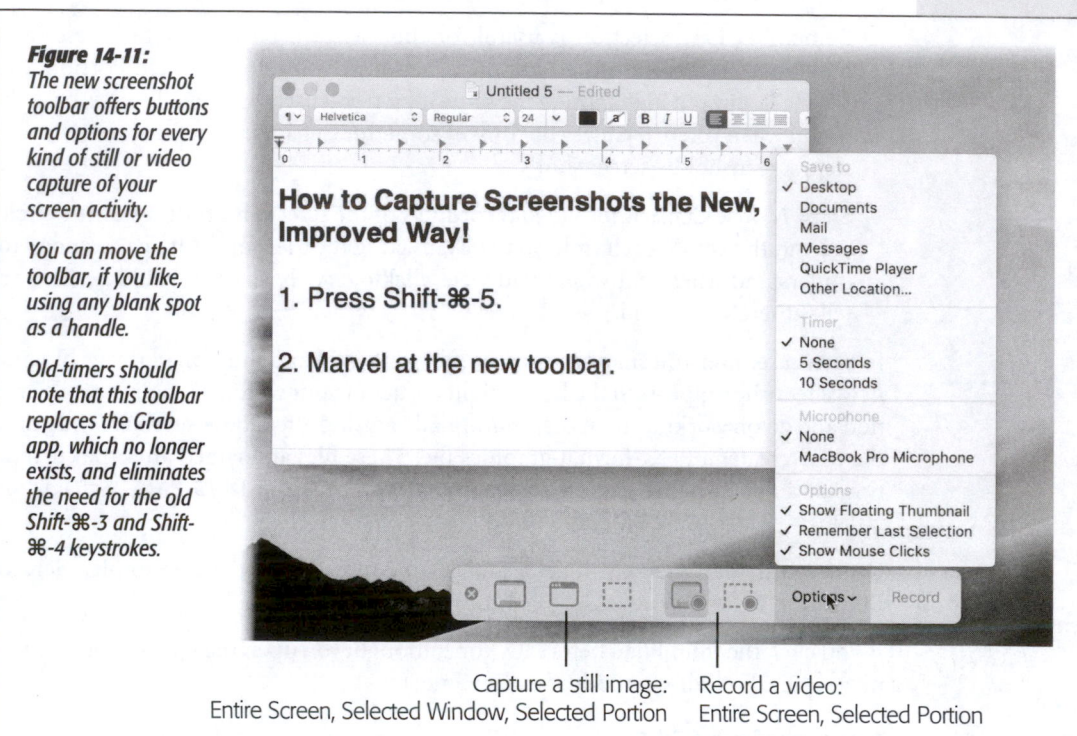

Figure 14-11:
The new screenshot toolbar offers buttons and options for every kind of still or video capture of your screen activity.

You can move the toolbar, if you like, using any blank spot as a handle.

Old-timers should note that this toolbar replaces the Grab app, which no longer exists, and eliminates the need for the old Shift-⌘-3 and Shift-⌘-4 keystrokes.

Capture a still image: Record a video:
Entire Screen, Selected Window, Selected Portion Entire Screen, Selected Portion

- **Options menu.** This icon offers powerful options for your screenshotting pleasure:

The **"Save to"** options specify where you want macOS to put the finished image file. Some of the options are folder locations, like Desktop and Documents. But don't miss the *apps* listed here, like Mail and Messages. They pre-attach your finished shot to an outgoing email or message, which can save you a few steps. The Other Location command lets you choose a folder (or app!) you prefer.

Timer gives you a five- or ten-second countdown before the Mac captures the screen. That's usually long enough for you to get everything positioned the way

new format called HEIF (high efficiency image file format) for photos, and HEVC (high efficiency video coding) format for video. MacOS apps like Photos, Preview, and Quick Look can recognize and open these files, too.

- **Photoshop files.** If you're a graphic designer or webmeister, this one is kind of neat: MacOS can open (and Preview can even export) actual Photoshop files (except for so-called *16-bit RGB* files). In practical terms, the fact that macOS can open and display these files means you could use a Photoshop masterpiece, complete with layers and transparency, as, for example, a macOS desktop background.

- **BMP files.** You can think of this graphics format as the PICT of the Windows world. It's nice that macOS can open (and Preview can export) them, especially because you may occasionally find .bmp files on the web or attached to email messages.

- **Silicon Graphics, MacPaint, Targ.** You could go your whole life without ever seeing a graphic in one of these formats. Silicon Graphics is, unsurprisingly, the format created by Silicon Graphics computers. MacPaint is a black-and-white, 8×10–inch maximum, ancient Macintosh graphics format that disappeared from the scene in about 1988. And Targ (Targa) is the format once used by products from Truevision.

Screen-Capture Keystrokes

If you're reading a chapter about printing and graphics, you may be interested in creating *screenshots*—captured images of the Mac screen. Screenshots are a staple of articles, tutorials, and books about the Mac (including this one). The Mac has a secret built-in feature that lets you make them—and in macOS Mojave, it's been beefed up to an astonishing degree. Here's how it goes.

The Screenshot Toolbar

For decades, the Mac has offered special keystrokes for taking digital pictures of the screen: Shift-⌘-3 to capture the entire screen, or Shift-⌘-4 to capture a rectangular piece of it. And those keystrokes still work.

But in macOS Mojave, there's something new, which should become your first thought when it's "I need to capture this" time: Shift-⌘-5.

That combo opens the new screenshot toolbar, which teems with options for capturing the screen (Figure 14-11).

Here's what you'll find on the screenshot toolbar, from left to right:

- **Entire Screen, Selected Window, Selected Portion.** These buttons specify what you want in your screenshot: the entire screen; only one open window (whichever you click); or a rectangular portion you choose by dragging the corners of the dotted-line rectangle and then pressing Return (or clicking Capture).

Graphics Formats on the Mac

MacOS understands dozens of Mac and Windows graphics file formats. Better yet, its Preview program can open such graphics and export them in a different format, making it an excellent file-conversion program. You can confidently double-click graphics files—from a digital camera, scanner, or web download, for example—in any of these formats:

- **PICT files.** For almost 20 years, the PICT file was the graphics format Mac fans were most familiar with. It was the graphics format used by the Mac Clipboard. Unfortunately, no other kinds of computers could open these files, and so PICT is pretty much dead.

- **TIFF files** are high-quality, uncompressed *bitmaps*—that is, the Mac has memorized the color of each pixel in the file. Trying to enlarge one is like enlarging a fax: Make it too big, and the image breaks down into visible dots.

 Nonetheless, TIFF files are popular in the printing industry—the graphics in this book, for example, were stored as TIFF files. They print beautifully, work nicely in page-layout programs, and are understood by both Macs and Windows PCs.

- **JPEG files** are popular on the web, particularly for photos and other full-color artwork. What makes JPEG files ideal for online use is that they've been compressed (using a program like Photoshop). Just enough of the color data has been thrown out from the original file to make the image a quick download without noticeably affecting its quality.

- **GIF** stands for *graphics interchange format.* Today, GIF files are used almost exclusively on the web, usually for solid-colored graphics like cartoons, headlines, and logos. (A GIF file can have a maximum of 256 colors, which is not even close to the photorealism of, say, JPEG. That's what makes the GIF format inappropriate for photographs.) Crude, soundless *animated* GIFs have made a bit of a comeback lately, too.

- **PNG files.** As it turns out, one of the algorithms used by GIF files is, technically speaking, the property of a company called Unisys, which threatened to sue everybody who was creating GIF files. "No problem," said the World Wide Web Consortium. "We'll just come up with our own replacement—a file format that has no legal strings attached." What they created was PNG (Portable Network Graphics). You can save Photoshop and Preview documents in PNG format, and every web browser understands it. Screenshots you take in macOS are in PNG, too.

 PNG files don't lose quality when compressed, as JPEG files do. On the other hand, PNG files don't accommodate animation, as GIF files do. And when it comes to photos, they don't offer as impressive a size/quality balance as JPEG.

- **HEIF.** In iOS 11 (for iPhones and iPads), photos and videos occupy only half the space they used to—and look exactly the same. That's because Apple has adopted a

the knowledge contained in the profiles, the ColorSync software can compensate for the quirks of the different devices and even the different kinds of paper they print on.

Most of the people who lose sleep over color fidelity are those who do commercial color scanning and printing, where "off" colors are a big deal. After all, a customer might return a product after discovering that the actual product color doesn't match the photo on a company's website.

Getting ColorSync Profiles

ColorSync profiles for many color printers, scanners, and monitors come built into macOS. When you buy equipment or software from, say, Kodak, Agfa, or Pantone, you may get additional profiles. If your equipment didn't come with a ColorSync profile, let Google be your friend; it shouldn't be hard to find. Put new profiles into the Library→ColorSync→Profiles folder.

Default Profiles

In professional graphics work, a ColorSync profile is often embedded right in a photo, making all this color management automatic. Using the ColorSync Utility program (in Applications→Utilities), you can specify which ColorSync profile each of your gadgets should use. Click the Devices button, open the category for your device (scanner, camera, display, printer, or proofer), click the model you have, and then use the Current Profile pop-up menu to assign a profile to it.

Tip: In the Displays pane of System Preferences, you'll find a Color tab. Its Calibrate button is designed to create a profile for your particular monitor in your particular office lighting—all you have to do is answer a few fun questions onscreen and drag a few sliders.

More on ColorSync

If you ache to learn more about ColorSync, you won't find much in macOS's Help system. Instead, search the web. You'll find Googling *ColorSync* to be a fruitful exercise.

Graphics in macOS

Everywhere you look in macOS, you'll find visual effects that would make any other operating system think about early retirement.

For example: Menus are transparent. You can set Excel 3D graphs to be slightly transparent so they don't block other bars in a 3D graph. When you paste files into windows in icon view, their icons fade into view. When you open an especially long message in Mail, its text fades in from white. When you use Launchpad, it fades in and out. And when you switch accounts using fast user switching, your work environment slides off the screen as though it's pasted on the side of an animated cube.

All these visual goodies owe their existence to Quartz or its enhanced successor, Quartz Extreme (which is not available on older Macs).

- **Edit Sizes.** The point sizes listed in the Fonts panel are just suggestions. You can actually type in any point size you want. By choosing this command, in fact, you can edit this list so that the sizes you use most often are only a click away.

- **Manage Fonts.** Opens Font Book, described starting on page 616.

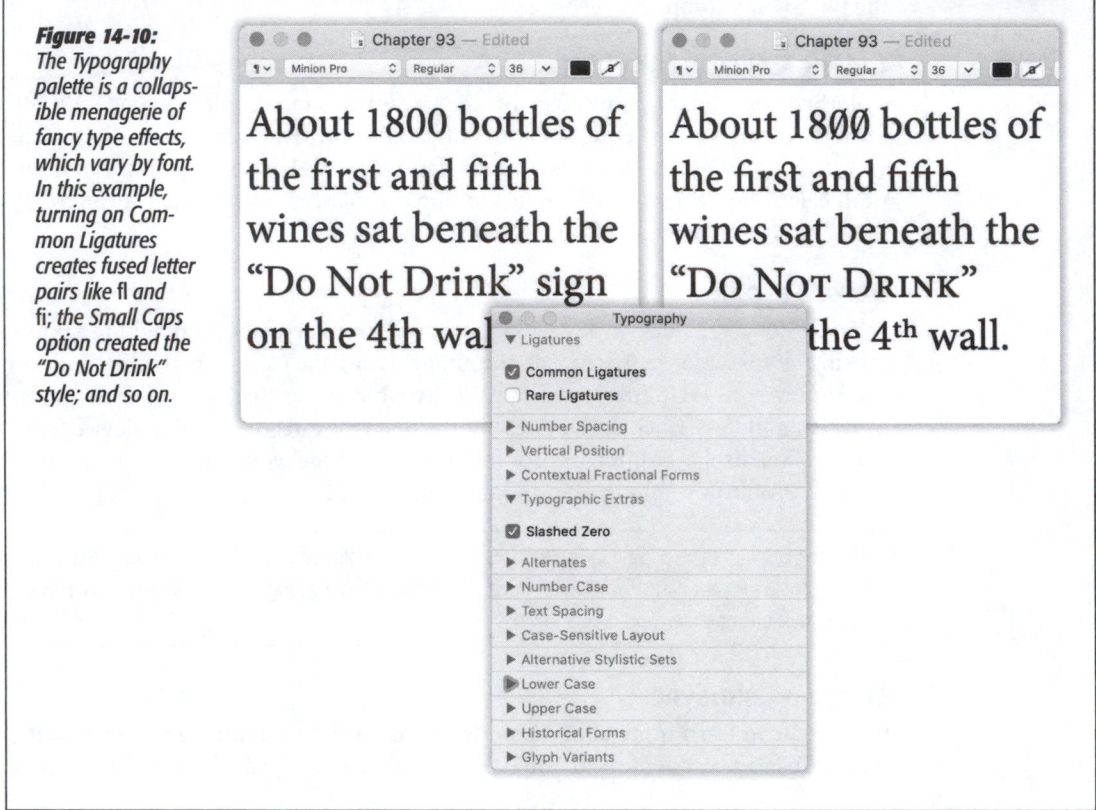

Figure 14-10:
The Typography palette is a collapsible menagerie of fancy type effects, which vary by font. In this example, turning on Common Ligatures creates fused letter pairs like fl and fi; the Small Caps option created the "Do Not Drink" style; and so on.

ColorSync

As you may have discovered through painful experience, computers aren't great with color. Each device you use to create and print digital images "sees" color a little bit differently, which explains why the deep amber captured by your scanner may be rendered as chalky brown on your monitor yet come out as a fiery orange on your Epson inkjet printer. Since every gadget defines and renders color in its own way, colors are often inconsistent as a print job moves from design to proof to press.

ColorSync attempts to sort out this mess, serving as a translator for all the different pieces of hardware in your workflow. For this to work, each device (scanner, monitor, printer, digital camera, copier, proofer, and so on) has to be calibrated with a unique *ColorSync profile*—a file that tells your Mac exactly how it defines colors. Armed with

Designing collections and favorites

At the top of the Fonts panel, the ✿ menu offers a few useful customization tools:

- **Add to Favorites.** To designate a font as a favorite, specify a font, style, and size by clicking in the appropriate columns of the Fonts panel. Then use this command. From now on, whenever you click Favorites in the Collection column, you'll see a list of the typefaces you've specified.

- **Show Preview.** The Fonts panel is great and all that, but you may have noticed that, until you choose this option, it doesn't actually *show* you the fonts you're working with—something of an oversight in a window designed to help you find your fonts. See Figure 14-9 for details. (Choose this command again—now called Hide Preview—to get rid of the preview.)

Tip: Once you've opened the preview pane, feel free to click the different sizes, typeface names, and family names to see the various effects.

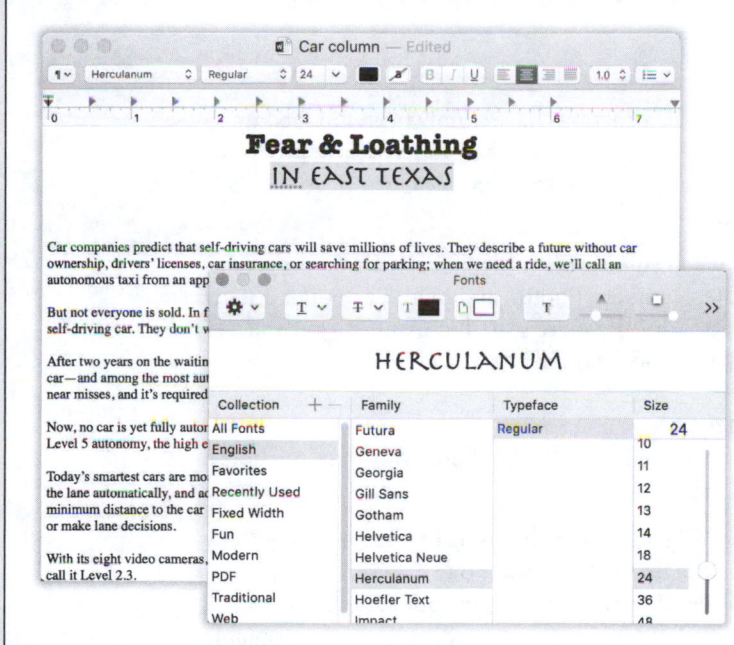

Figure 14-9:
The Fonts panel, generally available only in modern Cocoa programs, offers elaborate controls over text color, shadow, and underline styles.

See the handy font sample shown here above the font lists? To get it, choose Show Preview from the ✿ pop-up menu. Or use the mousy way: Place your cursor just below the title bar (where it says Fonts) and drag downward.

- **Color.** Opens the Color Picker, so you can specify a color for the highlighted text.

- **Characters.** Opens the Character Viewer, so you can choose a symbol or emoji without having to remember the crazy keyboard combo that types it.

- **Typography.** Opens the Typography palette (see Figure 14-10).

Once you've added some fonts to a library, you can even set up collections *within* that library.

To create a library, choose File→New Library; the library appears at the top of the left side of Font Book under User. Now you can drag fonts into it right from the Finder.

Exporting fonts

Next time you submit a design project to a print shop or a graphics bureau, you won't have to worry that it won't have the right fonts. It's easy to collect all the fonts you used in a document and export them to a folder, ready to submit along with your file.

Use the Services→Font Book→Create Collection From Text command. Font Book opens and shows you the new collection it's created, containing all the fonts used in your document. Click the collection and then choose File→Export Collection. The software prompts you to name and choose a location for the exported fonts folder.

Note: The Create Collection From Text command doesn't work in all programs, but you can always build and export a collection manually.

The Fonts Panel

As noted on page 227, some existing Mac programs have simply been touched up— *Carbonized*, in the lingo—to be macOS-compatible. Choosing fonts in these programs works exactly as it always has on the Mac: You choose a typeface name from the Font menu or from a formatting palette.

Things get much more interesting when you use the more modern *Cocoa* programs, like TextEdit, iMovie, Pages, Keynote, Numbers, Photos, and Mail. They offer a standard macOS feature called the Fonts panel. If you're seated in front of your macOS machine now, fire up TextEdit or Pages and follow along.

Choosing fonts from the Fonts panel

Suppose you've just highlighted a headline in TextEdit and now you want to choose an appropriate typeface for it.

In TextEdit, you open the Fonts panel (Figure 14-9) by choosing Format→Font→Show Fonts (⌘-T). Just as in Font Book, the first column lists your Collections. The second column, Family, shows the names of the actual fonts in your system. The third, Typeface, shows the style variations—Bold, Italic, Condensed, and so on—available in that type family. (Oblique and Italic are roughly the same thing; Bold, Black, and Ultra are varying degrees of boldface.)

The last column lists a sampling of point sizes. You can use the Size slider, choose from the point-size pop-up menu, or type any number into the box at the top of the Size list.

But you can create collections called, for example, Headline or Sans Serif, organized by font type. Or you can create collections like Brochure or Movie Poster, organized by project. Later, you can switch these groups of fonts on or off at will, or jump right to them in programs that use the standard Fonts panel, which saves you time wading through hundreds of fonts.

To create a new collection, click the leftmost + button to create a new entry in the Collection column, whose name you can edit. Then click one of the font storage locations—User or Computer—and drag fonts or font families onto your newly created collection icon. (Recognize this process from playlists in iTunes, or albums in Photos?) Each font can be in as many collections as you want.

To remove a font from the collection, click its name and then press Delete. You're not actually removing the font from your Mac—only from the collection.

Note: Each time you create a new font collection, macOS records its name and contents in a little file in your Home folder→Library→FontCollections folder.

By copying these files into the Users→Shared folder on your hard drive, you can make them available to anyone who uses the Mac. If your sister, for example, copies a file from the Shared folder into her own Home folder→Library→FontCollections folder, then she'll see the name of your collection in her own Fonts panel. This way, she can reap the benefits of the effort and care you put into its creation.

Smart collections

Font Book can create a collection *for* you, too. If you choose File→New Smart Collection, a new dialog box lets you specify criteria for this always-updated collection. For example, you might use the + buttons to specify "Kind is TrueType" and "Design style is Sans-serif." The effect is exactly like smart folders in the Finder (page 138) or smart playlists in iTunes (page 430): Once you set up the smartness, the set stays up to date as your font collection changes.

Font libraries

Don't get confused; a font *library* is not the same as a font *collection.*

A font library is a set of fonts *outside* Font Book that you can install or uninstall on the fly. They don't have to be in any of your Fonts folders; Font Book can install them from wherever they happen to be sitting on your hard drive (or even on the network). Font Book never copies or moves these font files as you install or remove them from libraries; it simply adds them to your Font menus by referencing them right where they sit.

Tip: That can be a handy arrangement if you periodically work on different projects for different clients. Why burden your day-to-day Font menu with the 37 fonts used by *Beekeepers Quarterly* magazine when you need to work with those fonts only four times a year?

Looking over your fonts

Right off the bat, Font Book is great for looking at samples of each typeface. For example, click Computer, click the first font name, and then press the ▼ key. As you walk down the list, the rightmost panel shows you a sample of each font (Figure 14-7).

Figure 14-7:
Each account holder can have a separate set of fonts; your set is represented by the User icon. You can drag fonts and font families among the various Fonts folders represented here—from your User account folder to the Computer icon, for example, making them available to all account holders.

You can also click any font family's flippy triangle (or highlight its name and then press ▶) to see the font *variations* it includes: Italic, Bold, and so on.

Tip: You can customize the type you see in the right panel. To see a full display of every character, choose Repertoire by clicking ⠿ in the toolbar or pressing ⌘-2. To type your own text, choose Custom by clicking AaI or pressing ⌘-3.

Printing a reference sheet

You can print a handy, whole-font sampler of any font. Click its name and then choose File→Print. In the Print dialog box, click the Show Details button to expand the dialog box, if necessary.

As shown in Figure 14-8, you can use the Report Type pop-up menu to choose from three reference-sheet styles:

- **Catalog** prints the alphabet twice (uppercase and lowercase) and the numbers in each selected font; use the Sample Size slider to control the size. This style is the most compact, because more than one print sample fits on each sheet of paper.

- **Repertoire** prints a grid that contains every single character in the font. This report may take more than one page per font.

MacOS also comes with a program that's *just* for installing, removing, inspecting, and organizing fonts. It's called Font Book (Figure 14-7), and it's in your Applications folder.

Where Fonts Live

Brace yourself. In macOS, there are *three* Fonts folders. The fonts you actually see listed in the Font menus and Fonts panels of your programs are combinations of these Fonts folders' contents.

Here's a rundown:

- **Your private fonts (your Home folder→Library→Fonts).** This Fonts folder sits right inside your own Home folder. You're free to add your own custom fonts to it. Go wild—it's your font collection and yours alone. Nobody else who uses the Mac can use these fonts; they'll never even know you have them.

Note: Your Home→Library folder is ordinarily hidden. The quickest way to see it is to press Option as you choose Go→Library in the Finder.

- **Main font collection (Library→Fonts).** Any fonts in this folder are available to everyone to use in every program. (As with most features that affect everybody who shares your Mac, however, only the administrator can change the contents of this folder.)

- **Essential system fonts (System→Library→Fonts).** This folder contains the few dozen fonts the Mac itself needs: the typefaces you see in your menus, dialog boxes, icons, and so on. You can open this folder to *see* these font suitcases, but you can't do anything with them, such as opening, moving, or adding to them. Remember that, for stability reasons, the System folder is sealed under glass. Only the Unix entity known as the *superuser* can touch these files—and even that person would be foolish to do so.

 With the exception of the essential system fonts, you'll find an icon representing each of these locations in your Font Book program, described next.

Note: And just to make life even more exciting, Adobe's software installers may donate even *more* fonts to your cause, in yet *another,* deeply hidden folder.

Font Book: Installing and Managing Fonts

One of the biggest perks of macOS is its preinstalled collection of over 50 great-looking fonts—"over $1,000 worth," according to Apple, which licensed many of them from type companies. In short, fewer Mac fans than ever will wind up buying and installing new fonts.

But when you do buy or download new fonts, you're in luck. There's no limit to the number of fonts you can install.

Creating PDF Files

Opening, schmopening—what's really exciting is the ability to create your *own* PDF files. The easiest way is to click the PDF pop-up button in the standard Print dialog box (Figure 14-6). When you click it, you're offered a world of interesting PDF-creation possibilities. Several of them convert whatever document you're on the verge of printing into a frozen PDF file that opens into Preview, sends in Mail as an attachment, adds itself to the Books app for reading, saves to your iCloud Drive, or sends via Messages. A few merit further explanation:

- **Save as PDF** saves your document to the disk as a PDF instead of printing it.

- **Save as PostScript** gives you a PostScript file instead of a PDF. (PostScript is a format preferred by some designers and print shops. It consists of highly precise "what to draw" instructions for PostScript laser printers.)

Figure 14-6:
The PDF button is crawling with neat ways to process a document while it's still open—and you can add to this pop-up button's list, too, by choosing Edit Menu.

For example, you can create even more elaborate pathways for documents you want to print or convert to PDF using an Automator workflow you've built yourself—if you're that kind of technical.

- **Save to Web Receipts** is one of the simplest and sweetest features in all of macOS.

 You use it when you've just ordered something on a website, and the "Print this receipt" screen is staring you in the face. Don't waste paper and ink—and, later, time trying to find it! Instead, use this command. You get a perfectly usable PDF version, stored in your Home→Documents→Web Receipts folder, where you can use Spotlight to find it later, when you need to consult or print it because your gray-market goods never arrived.

Note: You may see other commands here, too, as you install other companies' software programs.

Fonts—and Font Book

MacOS type is all smooth, all the time. Fonts in macOS's formats—called TrueType, PostScript Type 1, and OpenType—always look smooth onscreen and in printouts, no matter what the point size.

PDF Files

Sooner or later, almost everyone with a personal computer encounters PDF (portable document format) files. Many a software manual, ReadMe file, and downloadable "white paper" come in this format. Until recently, you needed the free program called Adobe Reader if you hoped to open or print these files. Many Windows devotees still do.

PDF files, however, are one of macOS's common forms of currency. In fact, you can turn *any document* (in any program with a Print command) into a PDF file—a trick that once required a $250 program called Adobe Acrobat Distiller.

But why would you want to create PDFs? What's the big deal about them? Consider these advantages:

- **Other people see your layout.** When you distribute PDF files to other people, they see precisely the same fonts, colors, page design, and other elements you put in your original document. And here's the kicker: They get to see all of this even if they don't *have* the fonts or the software you used to create the document. (Contrast with the alternative: Say you're sending somebody a Microsoft Word document. If your correspondent doesn't have precisely the same fonts you have, he'll see a screwy layout. And if he doesn't have Word or another program that can open Word files, he'll see nothing at all.)

- **It's universal.** PDF files are very common in the Mac, Windows, Unix/Linux, and even smartphone worlds. When you create a PDF file, you can distribute it (by email, for example) without worrying about what kinds of computers your correspondents are using.

- **It has very high resolution.** Professionally produced PDF files print at the maximum quality of any printer. A PDF file prints great both on cheapo inkjets and on high-quality image-setting gear at professional print shops. (Right now you're looking at a PDF file that was printed at a publishing plant.)

Note: MacOS creates *screen-optimized* PDF files: compact, easy-to-email files that look good onscreen but don't have high enough resolution for professional printing. For high-end purposes and more optimization for specific uses (web, fancy press machines, and so on), you still need a program like Adobe Acrobat, Illustrator, or InDesign.

- **You can search it.** A PDF file may look like a captured graphic, but behind the scenes, its text is still text; Spotlight can find a word in a PDF haystack in a matter of seconds. That's an especially handy feature when you work with electronic software manuals in PDF format.

Opening PDF Files

There's nothing to opening a PDF file: Just double-click it. Preview takes over from there and opens the PDF file on your screen. (You can also highlight its icon in the Finder and tap the space bar for a Quick Look at it.)

If your PC-wielding friends install Bonjour for Windows (a free download from this book's "Missing CD" page at *missingmanuals.com*), then they can print to your Mac's shared printer, too.

Note: Of course, your Mac (the one actually attached to the printer) must be turned on in order for the other computers to print. In part, that's because the documents-in-waiting from other people pile up on *your* hard drive.

Figure 14-5:
Top: On the Mac with the printer, open the Sharing panel of System Preferences. Turn on Printer Sharing, and then turn on the checkboxes for the printers you want to share. Switch to the Printers & Scanners pane, and turn on "Share this printer on the network" for the printers you want to share.

Bottom: To use a shared printer elsewhere on the network, open the document you want to print, and then choose File→Print. In the Print dialog box, the shared printer is identified under the Nearby Printers heading.

Faxing

Apple giveth, and Apple taketh away. And Apple hath taken away faxing.

Apple has never been afraid to abandon technologies that strike it as obsolete, and faxing is one of them. Heck, macOS can't fax even if you have one of Apple's own USB fax modems.

If you still need to fax, you have a couple of options. First, you can sign up for a service like eFax or Faxaway, which lets you send and receive faxes online. Second, you're welcome to buy a non-Apple fax modem, some of which work fine. Whatever you buy comes with its own software and instructions.

need time to check or refill the printer, or when you're just about to print your letter of resignation as your boss drops by (maybe to offer you a promotion).

- **Halt them all.** You can stop all printouts from a printer by clicking Pause. (They resume when you click the button again, which now says Resume Printer.)

Tip: As you now know, the icon for a printer's queue window appears automatically in the Dock when you print. But it also *stays* in the Dock for the rest of the day; it doesn't disappear when the printing is complete. If you wish it would, right-click or two-finger click the printer's Dock icon; from the shortcut menu, choose Quit.

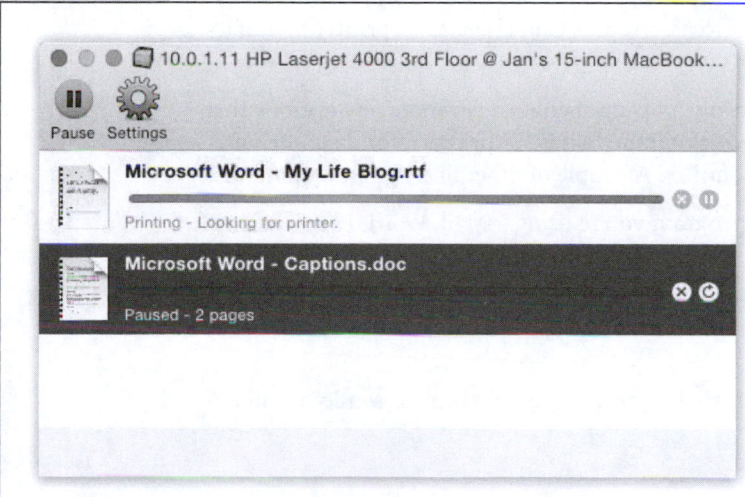

Figure 14-4:
Waiting printouts appear in this window.

If you click Settings, you'll find a place to rename this printer— and a Supply Levels tab, which includes a graph showing how much ink each cartridge has remaining (certain printer models only).

Printer Sharing

Printer sharing is for people (or offices) with more than one Mac, connected to a network, who'd rather not buy a separate printer for each machine. Instead, you connect the printer to one Mac, flip a couple of software switches, and then boom: The other Macs on the network can send their printouts to the printer—even wirelessly, if they're on a Wi-Fi network.

Note: Of course, this feature is most useful when you're sharing printers that can hook up to only one Mac at a time, like USB inkjet photo printers. Office laser printers are often designed to be networked from Day One.

Setting up printer sharing is easy; see Figure 14-5, top. To make a printout from across the network, see the instructions in Figure 14-5, bottom.

Tip: You can control *which* account holders on your network are allowed to use the printer you've shared. You know that idiot in Accounting who's always using up your cartridges by printing 200-page documents? Cut that sucker off! Just add the lucky guests' names to the Users column in System Preferences→Sharing→ Printer Sharing, as shown in Figure 14-5, top.

- **Cover Page.** Yes, that throwaway info page has made its way from the fax world into the hard-copy world.

- **Scheduler.** This option lets you specify *when* you want your document to print. If you're a freelancer, sitting at home with an inkjet on your desk, you might not immediately grasp why anyone wouldn't want the printouts *right now.* But try printing a 400-page catalog in a big office where other people on the network might conceivably resent you for tying up the printer all afternoon, and you'll get the idea.

- **ColorSync.** Most color printers offer this panel, where you can adjust the color settings—to add a little more red, perhaps. This is also where you indicate whose *color-matching system* you want to use: Apple's ColorSync, your printer manufacturer's, or none at all.

Then, below the light-gray line in this pop-up menu, you'll find a few options that are unique to the chosen printer or program. Some HP printers, for example, offer Cover Page, Finishing, and other choices. A couple of other likely guest commands:

- **[program name].** Whichever program you're using—Mail, Word, Pages, or anything else—may offer its own special printing options on this screen.

- **Summary.** This command summons a text summary of all your settings so far.

Printing

When all your settings look good, click Print (or press Return) to send your document to the printer.

Managing Printouts

After you've used the Print command, you can either sit there until the paper emerges from the printer, or you can *manage* the printouts-in-waiting. That option is attractive primarily to people who do a lot of printing, have connections to a lot of printers, or share printers with many other people.

Start by opening the printer's window. If you're already in the process of printing, just click the printer's Dock icon. If not, open System Preferences→Printers & Scanners, click the printer's name, and then click Open Print Queue.

At this point, you see something like Figure 14-4. The printouts that will soon be sliding out of your printer appear in a tidy list.

Here are some of the ways in which you can control these waiting printouts, which Apple collectively calls the *print queue:*

- **Delete them.** By clicking the tiny ✖ icon to the right of the document you want to delete, you remove that item from the list of waiting printouts. Now it won't print.

- **Pause them.** By clicking the tiny ❙❙ icon to the right of the document, you pause that printout. It doesn't print until you click the ↻ button. (Other documents continue to print.) This pausing business could be useful when, for example, you

- **Paper Size, Orientation.** Somebody at Apple finally realized how frustrating it was to have to open the Page Setup dialog box to change the paper-size and orientation settings and then open the Print dialog box for other settings. Now, in most programs, these controls are duplicated right in the Print dialog box for your convenience.

- **PDF.** A PDF file, of course, is an Adobe Reader (Acrobat) document—a file that any Mac, Windows, Linux, or Unix owner can view, read, and print using either Preview or the free Adobe Reader (included with every PC and Mac operating system).

 You can easily save any document as a PDF file instead of printing it—a truly beautiful feature that saves paper, ink, and time. The document remains on your hard drive, and the text inside is even searchable using Spotlight.

 And that's just the beginning. Apple has added a long list of additional PDF options (like password-protected PDFs, emailed ones, and so on). But Apple faced a design quandary: How could it offer a new list of PDF-related options without junking up the Print dialog box?

 Its solution was a strange little item called a pop-up *button,* shown in Figure 14-3, left. Use it like a pop-up menu. The command you'll use most often is probably Save as PDF, which turns the printout into a PDF file instead of sending it to the printer. For details on the other PDF-related options here, see page 615.

If you examine the unnamed pop-up menu just below the Orientation buttons, you'll find dozens of additional options. They depend on your printer model and the program you're using at the moment, but here are some typical choices:

- **Layout.** You can save paper and ink or toner cartridges by printing several miniature "pages" on a single sheet of paper.

- **Paper Handling.** You can opt to print your pages in reverse order so they stack correctly, or you can print just odd or just even pages so you can run them through again for double-sided printing.

- **Quality & Media** (inkjet printers only). Here's where you specify the print quality you want, the kind of paper you're printing on, and so on. (The name of this panel varies by manufacturer.)

- **Paper Feed.** If you chose the correct printer model when setting up your printer, then this screen knows about your printer's various paper trays. Here's where you specify which pages you want to come from which paper tray. (By far the most popular use for this feature is printing the first page of a letter on company letterhead and the following pages on blank paper from a second tray.)

- **Collation.** This controls the printing order for the pages. For example, if you print two copies of a three-page document, the Mac generally prints the pages in this order: 1, 2, 3, 1, 2, 3. If you turn off Collated, on the other hand, it prints in this order: 1, 1, 2, 2, 3, 3.

After you expand the box, the options you find vary by printer. But here are the common ones:

- **Printer.** If you have more than one printer connected to your Mac, then you can indicate which one you want to use for a particular printout by choosing its name from this pop-up menu.

- **Presets.** Here's a way to preserve your favorite print settings: Once you've proceeded through this dialog box, specifying the number of copies, which printer trays you want the paper taken from, and so on, you can choose Save Current Settings as Preset from the pop-up menu and then assign your settings set a name (like "Borderless, 2 copies"). Thereafter, you'll be able to recreate that elaborate suite of settings simply by choosing its name from this pop-up menu.

- **Copies.** Type the number of copies you want printed.

- **Pages.** You don't have to print an entire document—you can print, say, only pages 2 through 15.

Tip: You don't have to type numbers into both the From and To boxes. If you leave the first box blank, the Mac assumes you mean "From page 1." If you leave the second box blank, the Mac understands that you mean "To the end." To print only the first three pages, in other words, leave the first box blank and type 3 into the second box. (These page numbers refer to the physical pages you're printing, not any fancy numbering you've set up in your word processor. As far as the Print dialog box is concerned, the first printed page is page 1, even if you've told your word processor to label it "page 455.")

Figure 14-3:
Left: Most of the time, all you want is one darned copy of what's on your screen. So the standard Print dialog box is basic: a preview, page controls, and a Print button.

Right: But when you click Show Details, you get a new world of options: orientation, magnification, and so on.

Still, you can choose one particular printer from this pop-up menu to set it as the default printer—the one the Mac uses unless you intervene by choosing from the Printer pop-up menu in the Print dialog box.

- **Create desktop printer icons.** *This* handy, little-known feature gives you drag-and-drop access to your printers.

 From the Printers & Scanners pane of System Preferences, just drag a printer's icon out of the window and onto the desktop (or wherever you like). Repeat for your other printers. From now on, you can print a document on a certain printer just by dragging the document's icon onto the appropriate printer icon.

- **Check the ink level.** Click a printer, and then click Options & Supplies, to see how your inkjet ink or laser-printer toner level is. That way you won't be caught short when you're on an urgent deadline and your printer is out of ink. You also get a bright-yellow "low ink" warning in the dialog box that actually appears when you print.

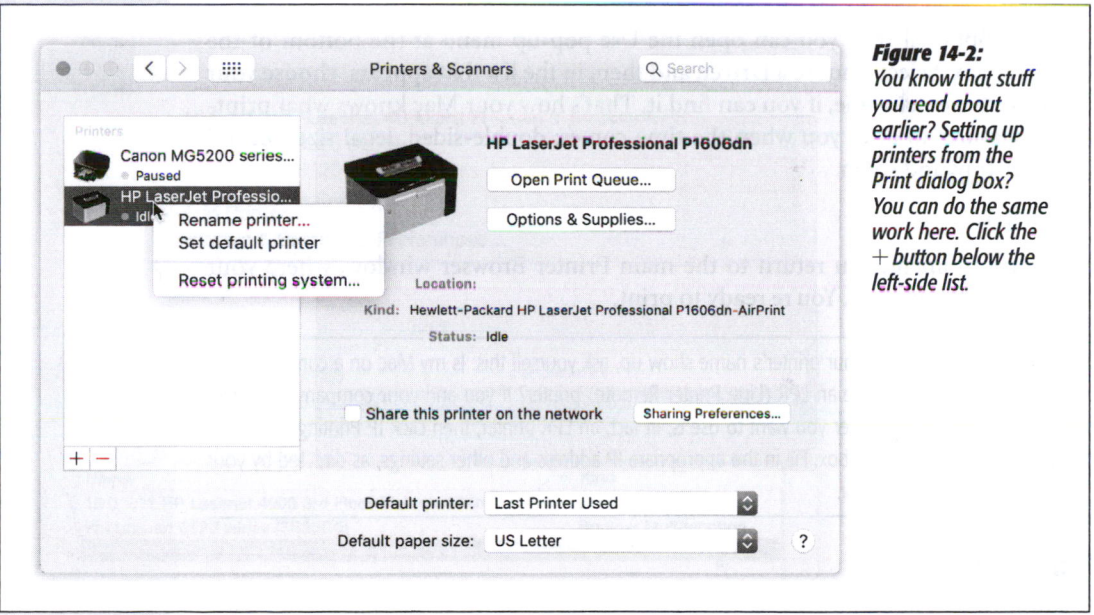

Figure 14-2:
You know that stuff you read about earlier? Setting up printers from the Print dialog box? You can do the same work here. Click the + button below the left-side list.

Making the Printout

You can't miss the Print dialog box. It appears, like it or not, whenever you choose File→Print in one of your programs.

The options you encounter depend on the printer you're using. They also depend on whether or not you *expand* the dialog box by clicking the Show Details button. That reveals a *lot* of useful options, including a handy preview; see Figure 14-3.

Printing, Fonts & Graphics

The Mac may be only the 10 percent solution in the mainstream business world, but in the graphics and printing industries, it's the 800-pound gorilla. You'd better believe that when Apple designed macOS, it worked very hard to keep its graphics and printing fans happy.

This chapter tackles printing, fonts, graphics, ColorSync, and PDF, which macOS uses as an everyday exchange format—one of the biggest perks of using a Mac.

Mac Meets Printer

MacOS used to come preloaded with the printing software for every conceivable printer model from every conceivable printer company—Epson, HP, Lexmark, Canon, and others—several gigabytes' worth. Clearly, most people wound up with wads of printing software they'd never use.

When you install macOS these days, though, you get *only* the printer drivers for the printers you actually have, or are nearby on the network. If you ever encounter a different printer model later, macOS offers to download it for you on the spot.

Setting Up a Printer

Setting up a printer is incredibly easy. The first time you want to print something, follow this guide:

1. **Connect the printer to the Mac, and then turn the printer on.**

 Inkjet printers and laser printers hook up either to your USB jack or to your network (Ethernet or wireless).

Tip: In theory, you can also connect from across the internet, assuming you left your Mac at home turned on and connected to a broadband modem, and assuming you've worked through the port-forwarding issue described on page 774.

In this case, though, you'd begin by choosing Go→Connect to Server in the Finder; in the Connect to Server box, type in *vnc://123.456.78.90* (or whatever your home Mac's public IP address is). The rest of the steps are the same.

3. **If you have a user account on the Other Mac, then click "Registered user" and log in. If not, but your Apple ID has been preapproved, click Using an Apple ID and supply your sharing password.**

 Your Mac, of course, *knows* your Apple ID already (because you've entered it in your account screen in System Preferences→Users & Groups). It shows up here in the dialog box; all you have to do is enter your password.

Figure 13-18:
Top: Start by clicking Share Screen in the strip at the top of Your Mac's window.

Middle: If you've been pre-added to the VIP list of authorized screen sharers, then you can sign in with either your account name and password or your Apple ID. If not, then you can request permission to share Other Mac's screen (provided the Mac owner has turned on that option in System Preferences→ Sharing→Screen Sharing→Computer Settings). You'll be granted permission only if Other Mac's owner is present and OKs you.

Bottom: If you request permission, the other person (sitting at the Other Mac) sees your request like this.

you'll have to grant it (by clicking OK on the screen), in real time, while you're there to watch what they're doing.

Your Mac: Take Control

All right, Other Mac has been prepared for invasion. Now suppose you're the person on the other end. You're the guru, or the parent, or whoever wants to take control.

Sit at Your Mac elsewhere on your home or office network, and proceed like this:

1. **Open a Finder window. Expand the Shared list in the Sidebar, if necessary, so you see the icon of Other Mac. Click it.**

 The strip at the top of the main window displays a button that wasn't there before: Share Screen (Figure 13-18, top).

2. **Click Share Screen.**

 Now you see the box shown at middle in Figure 13-18. It offers as many as three different ways for you to prove that you're not some German teenage hacker.

 "By requesting permission" sends the other Mac's current operator a message asking if it's OK for you to take over. If that person grants permission, that's it; the Other Mac's screen image appears on *your* screen, and you can skip the rest of these steps.

 But what if nobody's seated at the other Mac to grant permission? If you sometimes use the Other Mac yourself, and you have an account on it, then you can choose "Registered user."

 And what if nobody's at the other Mac to grant you permission *and* you don't have a user account on that machine? In that case, you may be able to use the Using an Apple ID option. If Other Mac's owner wants you to have access and has set you up that way (following the steps in the box on page 598), then you can connect just by entering your Apple ID and password.

GEM IN THE ROUGH

Screen Sharing with Windows and Other Oddball Machines

The beauty of Apple's screen-sharing technology is that it *isn't* Apple's screen-sharing technology. It's a popular open standard called VNC (Virtual Network Computing).

Once you've turned on Screen Sharing, any computer on earth with a free VNC client program—sort of a viewer program—can pop onto your Mac for a screen share. VNC clients are available for Windows, Linux, older Macs, and even some cellphones. (Not all VNC programs work with the Mojave version of screen sharing, alas; some require updates.)

To prepare your Mac for invasion, open the Sharing pane of System Preferences. Click Screen Sharing, and then click Computer Settings. Turn on "VNC viewers may control screen with password," and then make up a password. (VNC doesn't know anything about macOS account passwords, so you're making up one password for sharing your whole Mac.)

Give that password to the lucky few who have your trust. Let them plug your Mac's public IP address into their VNC clients—or let them connect over your office network, using the address displayed on the Screen Sharing pane (*vnc:// MacBook-Pro*, for example)—and let the sharing begin.

If "anyone" means "you and your spouse" or "you and the two other fourth-grade teachers," then that's probably perfectly fine.

- **Securer.** For greater security, though, you can limit who's allowed to stop in. Click "Only these users" and then click the +. A small panel appears, listing everyone with an account on your Mac. Choose the ones you trust not to mess things up while you're away from your Mac (Figure 13-17).

Tip: You can permit people to see your Mac's screen remotely by entering their Apple ID and passwords. That's a lot simpler and uses less disk space than before, when each person had to have a full-blown *account* on your Mac, complete with Pictures folder, Movies folder, and so on. To set this up, see the box on page 598.

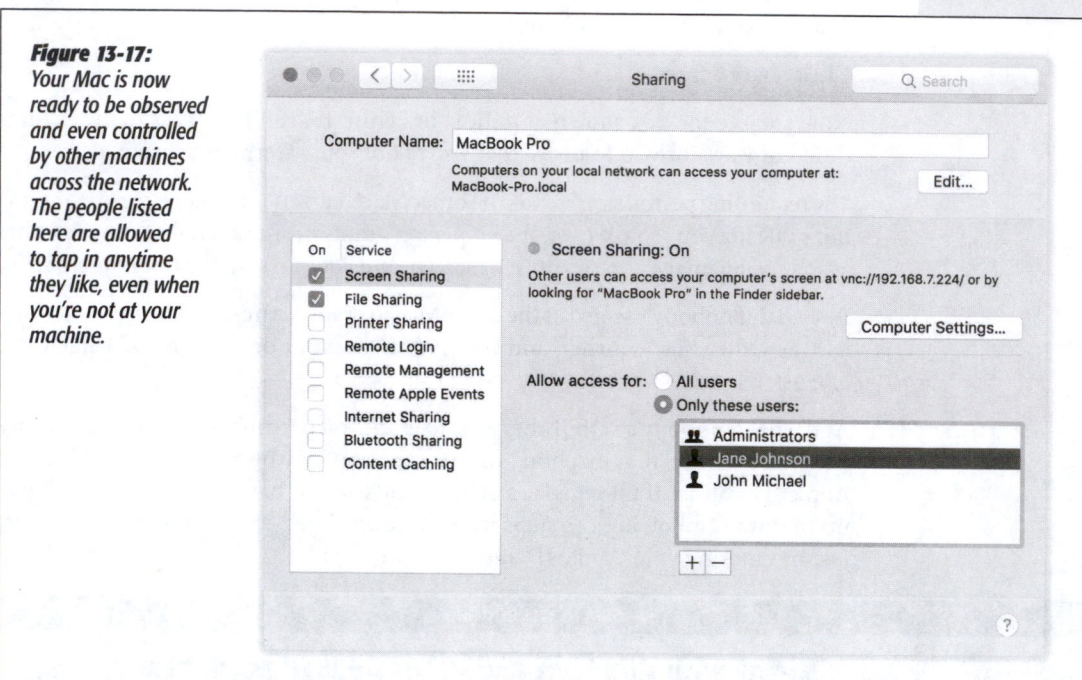

Figure 13-17:
Your Mac is now ready to be observed and even controlled by other machines across the network. The people listed here are allowed to tap in anytime they like, even when you're not at your machine.

- **Securest.** If you click "Only these users" and then don't add *anyone* to the list, then only people who have Administrator accounts on your Mac (page 524) can tap into your screen.

Alternatively, if you're only a *little* bit of a Scrooge, you can set things up so they can request permission to share your screen—as long as you're sitting in front of your Mac at the time and feeling generous.

To set this up, click Computer Settings and then turn on "Anyone may request permission to share screen." Now your fans will have to request permission to enter, and

approval, or just freaking people out. It can also be handy when *you* are the owner of both Macs (a laptop and a desktop, for example), and you want to run a program you don't have on the Mac in front of you. For example, you might want to adjust the playlist selection on the upstairs Mac that's connected to your sound system.

Or maybe you just want to keep an eye on what your kids are doing on the Macs upstairs in their rooms.

The controlling person can do *everything* on the controlled Mac, including running programs, messing around with the folders and files, and even shutting it down. You can even press keystrokes on *your* Mac—⌘-Tab, ⌘-space, ⌘-Option-Escape, and so on—to trigger the corresponding functions on the *other* Mac.

MacOS is crawling with ways to use screen sharing. You can do it over a network, over the internet, and even during a Messages chat.

Truth is, the Messages method, described in Chapter 19, is much simpler and better than the small-network method described here. It doesn't require names or passwords, it doesn't require the same macOS version on both Macs, it's easy to flip back between seeing the other guy's screen and your own, and you can transfer files by dragging them from your screen to the other guy's (or vice versa). Then again, the small-network method described here is built right into the Finder and doesn't require logging into Messages.

In modern macOS screen sharing, you can log into a distant Mac and control it as though you were logged into your own account—*while somebody else is using it* and seeing a totally different screen! Read on.

Other Mac: Give Permission in Advance

Trying to understand meta concepts like seeing one Mac's screen on the monitor of another can get confusing fast. So in this example, suppose that you're seated at Your Mac, and you want to control the Other Mac.

Now, it would be a chaotic world if any Mac could suddenly take control of any other Mac (although it could be fun). Fortunately, though, nobody can share your screen or take control of your Mac without your explicit permission. To give such permission, sit down at Other Mac. Choose System Preferences→Sharing, and then turn on Screen Sharing.

At this point, there are three levels of security to protect Other Mac against unauthorized remote-control mischief:

- **Secure.** If you select All Users, then *anyone with an account on your Mac* will be able to tap in and take control anytime they like, even when you're not around. They'll just have to enter the same name and password they'd use if they were sitting in front of your machine.

Screen Sharing

MacOS has answered the prayers of baffled beginners and exasperated experts everywhere. Now, when a novice needs help from a guru, the guru doesn't have to run all the way downstairs or fly to Omaha to assist. Thanks to macOS's screen-sharing feature, you can see exactly what's on the screen of another Mac, from across the network—and even seize control of the other Mac's mouse and keyboard (with the newbie's permission, of course).

(Anyone who's ever tried to help someone troubleshoot over the phone knows *exactly* how helpful this is. If you haven't, this small example may suffice: "OK, open the Apple menu and choose About This Mac." Pause. "What's the Apple menu?")

Nor is playing Bail-Out-the-Newbie the only situation when screen sharing is useful. It's also great for collaborating on a document, showing something to someone for

TROUBLESHOOTING MOMENT

When the Mac Doesn't See the PC

Are you having trouble getting your PC's icon to show up in your Finder's Sidebar?

Now, you can probably connect to the PC using the Mac's Go→Connect to Server command, but the Sidebar would be a lot more convenient.

And the problem is probably that the Mac doesn't know anything about Windows *workgroups*.

Even a lowly home PC is part of a workgroup (a corporate cluster), whether it knows it or not. And until your Mac is part of that very tiny club, it won't be able to see your PCs, and they won't be able to see it.

So if you're having no luck with this whole Mac-PC thing, try this. First, find out what your PC thinks its workgroup is. (It's usually either WORKGROUP or MSHOME.) Windows 8 and later: Right-click the Start-menu icon (▦); from the shortcut menu, choose System. Scroll down if necessary to see the workgroup's name.

Older Windows versions: Click Start, and then right-click Computer. From the shortcut menu, choose Properties. In the resulting info screen, you'll see the workgroup's name.

To find out the Mac's idea of its workgroup, open System Preferences→Network. Click the connection you're using (like Wi-Fi or Ethernet)→Advanced→WINS.

Now you see the peculiar controls shown here. Make sure that the Workgroup box shows the same name as the one on the PC. Click OK, and then click Apply.

Now your Windows PCs should show up in the Sidebar, like magic.

If they're *still* not showing up, then your PC's firewall software is probably turned on. Make sure it's turned off—and turn off your Mac's firewall, too (page 558). You can't do much connecting if there's a virtual wall between the computers.

Double-click the Mac's icon. Public-folder stuff is available immediately. Otherwise, you have to sign in with your Mac account name and password; Figure 13-16, middle, has the details.

In the final window, you see your actual Home folder—on the Windows PC! You're ready to open its files, copy them back and forth, or whatever (see Figure 13-16, bottom).

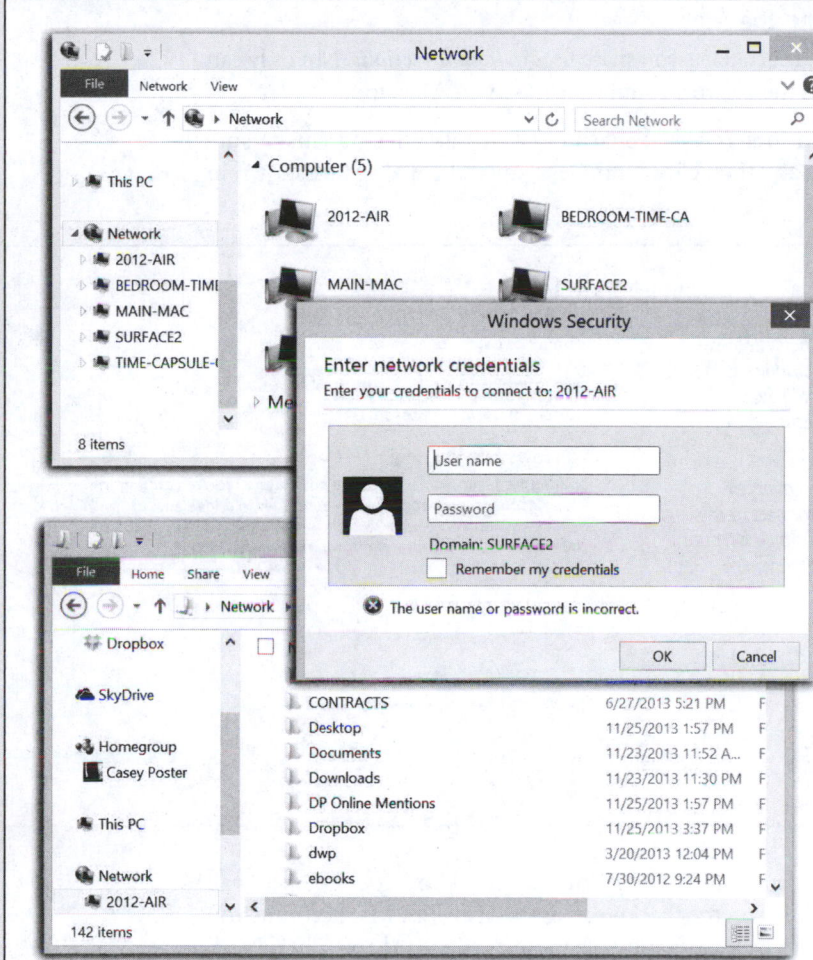

Figure 13-16:
Top: Double-click the Mac you want to visit from your PC (Windows 8.1 is shown here).

Middle: Type your Mac's name and password.

(If you're using Vista or earlier, it's more complicated. Enter your Mac's NetBIOS name in all capitals, or its IP address, and then a backslash, and then your Mac account short name. You can find out your Mac's NetBIOS name—what Windows calls it—on the Network pane of System Preferences. Click Advanced, and then WINS.)

Turn on "Remember my credentials" if you plan to do this again someday. Click OK.

Bottom: Here's your Mac Home folder—in Windows! Open it up to find all your stuff.

More Mac-Windows Connections

The direct Mac-to-Windows file-sharing feature of macOS is by far the easiest way to access one another's files. But it's not the only way. Chapter 6 offers a long list of other options, from flash drives to the third-party service Dropbox.

From here, it's a simple matter to drag files between the machines, open Word documents on the PC using Word for the Mac, and so on—exactly like you're hooked into another Mac.

Tip: Finally, for heaven's sake, make an alias of the Windows folder you've finally opened. That way, you can just double-click to open it the next time!

Seated at the PC, Seeing the Mac

Cross-platformers, rejoice: MacOS lets you share files in *both directions*. Not only can your Mac see other PCs on the network, but they can see the Mac, too.

On the Mac, open System Preferences→Sharing. Click File Sharing (make sure File Sharing is turned on), and then click Options to open the dialog box shown in Figure 13-15.

Figure 13-15:
Prepare your Mac for visitation by the Windows PC. It won't hurt a bit. The system-wide On switch for invasion from Windows is the first checkbox shown here, in the System Preferences→Sharing→File Sharing→Options box.

Next, turn on the individual accounts of people you want to allow to connect from the PC. You'll be asked to enter their account passwords, too. Click Done when you're done.

> ☑ Share files and folders using SMB
>
> Number of users connected: 0
>
> ☑ Share files and folders using AFP
>
> Number of users connected: 0
>
> **Windows File Sharing:**
> Sharing files with some Windows computers requires storing the user's account password on this computer in a less secure manner. When you enable Windows sharing for a user account, you must enter the password for that account.
>
On	Account
> | ☐ | Casey Robin |
> | ☑ | David Pogue |
> | ☐ | Jan Paulson |
>
> ? Done

Turn on "Share files and folders using SMB." Below that checkbox, you see a list of all the accounts on your Mac. Turn on the checkboxes to specify *which* Mac accounts you want to be able to access. You'll have to type in each person's password, too. Click Done.

Now you're ready to open your Mac files on the PC.

If your PC has Windows Vista, then choose Start→Network; if it's Windows 7 or later, then expand the Network heading in the Sidebar of any desktop (File Explorer) window. If you've sacrificed the proper animals to the networking gods, your Mac's icon should appear in the network window, as shown in Figure 13-16, top.

folder now appear on your Mac's screen. You can work with them just as you would your own files.

If you're using one of the "shared folder" methods, read on.

4. **Click Connect As.**

This button appears in the top-right corner of the Finder window. Now you're asked for your name and password (Figure 13-14, top).

Note: In Windows 8 and later, there are two ways to log into a computer—two kinds of user accounts. You can sign in with a *Microsoft ID* (which is just like an Apple ID) or with a regular *local* account. (Microsoft pushes you very hard to use a Microsoft ID; many features of Windows won't work without it.)

If you're trying to connect to a Windows account with a Microsoft ID, be sure to use *that* as the account name in this step (it looks like an email address), along with the corresponding password. If you enter the account's human name, you won't be able to connect.

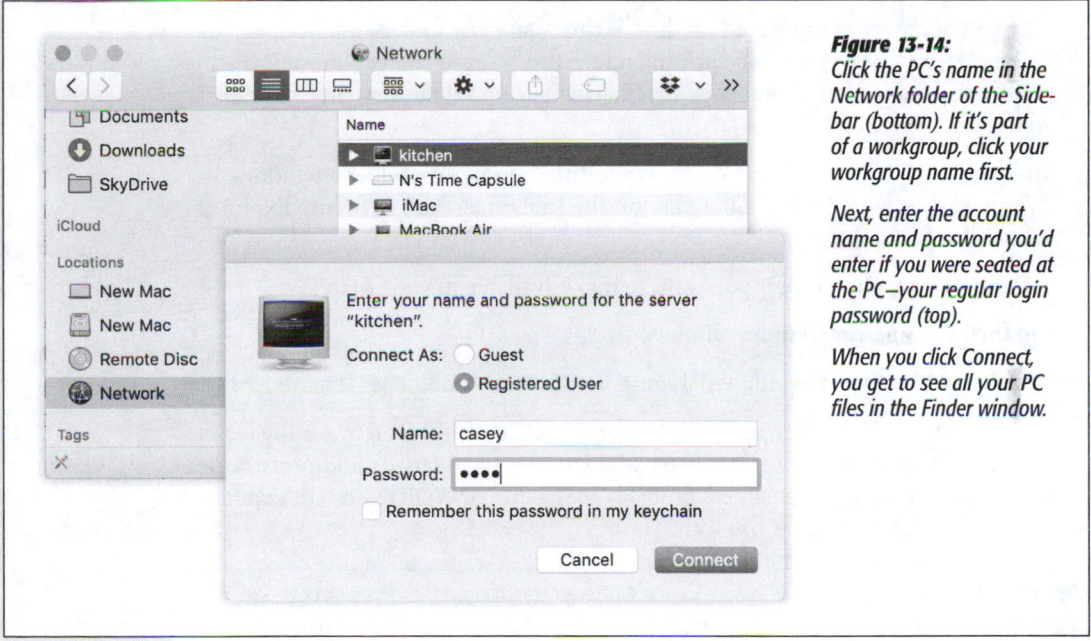

Figure 13-14:
Click the PC's name in the Network folder of the Sidebar (bottom). If it's part of a workgroup, click your workgroup name first.

Next, enter the account name and password you'd enter if you were seated at the PC—your regular login password (top).

When you click Connect, you get to see all your PC files in the Finder window.

5. **Enter the name and password for your account on the PC, and then click OK.**

The contents of the shared folder on the Windows machine appear in your Finder window, just as though you'd tapped into another Mac (Figure 13-14, bottom). The icon of the shared folder appears on your desktop, too, and an Eject button (⏏) appears next to the PC's name in your Sidebar.

If step 2 doesn't seem to work, then maybe your PC files aren't already shared, and you have some reading ahead of you:

Just as on the Mac, there are two ways to share files in Windows. One of them is super-simple: You just copy the files you want to share into a central, fully accessible folder. As long as nobody has turned off the Guest access feature, no passwords, accounts, or other steps are required.

In Windows Vista, that's the Public folder, which appears in the Navigation pane of every Explorer window. (In Vista, there's one Public folder for the whole *computer*, not one per account holder.)

In Windows 7, there's a Public folder in each library. That is, there's a Public Documents, Public Pictures, Public Music, and so on.

Note: There is no system of Public folders in Windows 8 and later—but if you upgraded your PC from an earlier Windows version, then the Public folders are still there and work the same way.

The second, more complicated method is the "share any folder" method, just as in macOS. In Vista, you right-click the folder you want to share, choose Properties from the shortcut menu, click the Sharing tab, and then turn on "Share this folder on the network."

In Windows 7, use the Share With menu at the top of any folder's window; in Windows 8 or later, use the Share tab on the Ribbon at the top of any Explorer window at the desktop.

Repeat for any other folders you want to make available to your Mac.

2. **On the Mac, open any Finder window.**

The shared PCs appear as individual computer names in the Sidebar (Figure 13-14).

(If you work in a big company, you may have to click the All icon to see the icons of their *workgroups*—network clusters. Unless you or a network administrator changed it, the workgroup name is probably MSHOME or WORKGROUP. Double-click the workgroup name you want.)

Tip: You can also access the shared PC via the Connect to Server command, as described on page 586. You could type into it *smb://192.168.1.103* (or whatever the PC's IP address is) or *smb://SuperDell* (or whatever its name is) and hit Return—and then skip to step 5. In fact, using the Connect to Server method often works when the Sidebar method doesn't.

3. **Click the name of the computer you want.**

If you're using one of the simple file-sharing methods on the PC, as already described, that's all there is to it. The contents of the Shared Documents or Public

Disconnecting Others

In macOS, you really have to work if you want to know whether other people on the network are accessing *your* Mac. You have to choose System Preferences→Sharing→File Sharing→Options. There you'll see something like "Number of users connected: 1."

Maybe that's because there's nothing to worry about. You certainly have nothing to fear from a security standpoint, since you control what others can see on your Mac. Nor will you experience much computer slowdown as you work, thanks to macOS's prodigious multitasking features.

Still, if you're feeling particularly antisocial, you can slam shut the door to your Mac. Just open System Preferences→Sharing and turn off File Sharing. If anybody is, in fact, connected to your Mac at the time (*from* a Mac), you, the door-slammer, get to see the dialog box in Figure 13-13, which sends a little warning message to whomever's connected to your Mac.

If nobody is connected right now, your Mac instantly becomes an island once again.

Figure 13-13:
This dialog box asks you how much notice you want to give your co-workers that they're about to be disconnected.

Networking with Windows

Macs and Windows PCs can see one another on the network, with no special software (or talent) required. In fact, you can go in either direction. Your Mac can see shared folders on a Windows PC, and a Windows PC can see shared folders on your Mac.

It goes like this.

Seated at the Mac, Seeing the PC

Suppose you have a Windows PC and a Mac on the same wired or wireless network. Here's how you get the Mac and PC chatting:

1. **On your Windows PC, share some files.**

 This isn't really a book about Windows networking (thank heaven), but here are the basics.

 On a PC with Windows 8 or Windows 10, there may be nothing to it. All your personal files probably come preshared. You can skip to step 2.

Once you type it and press Return, the FTP server's icon appears in the Sidebar. Its contents appear, too, ready to open or copy.

- **WebDAV server.** This special web-based shared disk requires a special address format, something like this: *http://Computer-Name/pathname.*

In each case, once you click OK, you may be asked for your name and password.

And now, some timesaving features in the Connect to Server box:

- **Once you've typed a disk's address,** you can click + to add it to the list of server favorites. The next time you want to connect, you can just double-click its name.

- **The clock-icon pop-up menu lists Recent Servers**—computers you've accessed recently over the network. If you choose one of them from this pop-up menu, you can skip having to type in an address.

Note: Like the Sidebar network-browsing method, the Connect to Server command displays each connected computer as an icon in your Sidebar, even within the Open or Save dialog boxes of your programs. You don't have to burrow through the Sidebar's Network icon to open files from them, or to save files onto them.

Disconnecting Yourself

When you're finished using a shared disk or folder, you can disconnect from it as shown in Figure 13-12.

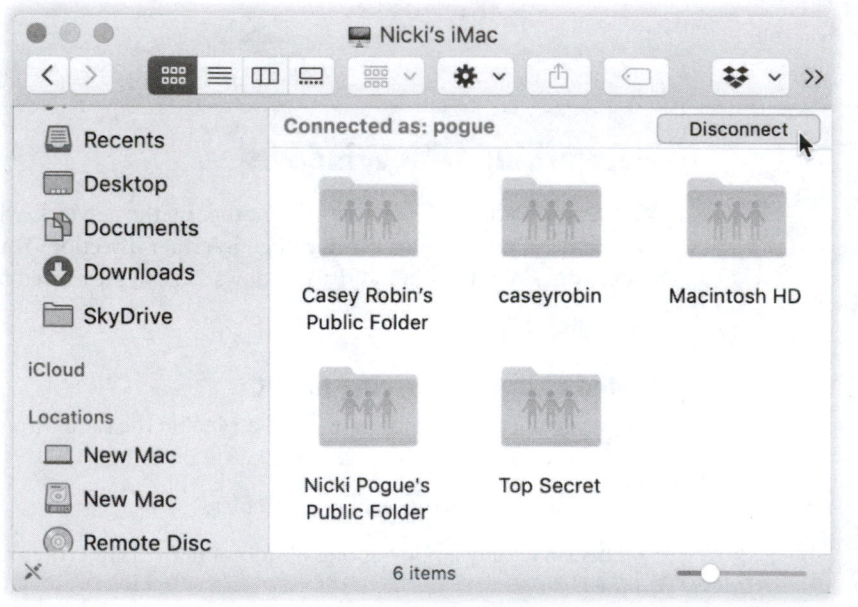

Figure 13-12:
To disconnect from a shared network disk or folder, click Disconnect at the top-right corner of the window.

- **Windows machines.** Find out the PC's IP address or computer name, and then use this format for the address: *smb://192.168.1.34* or *smb://Cheapo-Dell.*

 After a moment, you're asked to enter your Windows account name and password, and then to choose the name of the shared folder you want. When you click OK, the shared folder's contents appear in the window, ready to use, and the computer's icon appears in your Sidebar. (More on sharing with Windows PCs later in this chapter.)

Tip: If you know the name of the shared folder, you can add that after a slash, like this: *smb://192.168.4.23/ sharedstuff.* You save yourself one dialog box.

- **NFS servers.** If you're on a network with Unix machines, you can tap into one of their shared directories using this address format: *nfs://Machine-Name/pathname*, where *Machine-Name* is the computer's name or IP address, and *pathname* is the folder path to the shared item you want.

- **FTP servers.** MacOS makes it simple to bring *FTP servers* onto your screen, too. (These are the drives, out there on the internet, that store the files used by websites.)

 In the Connect to Server dialog box, type the FTP address of the server you want, like this: *ftp://www.apple.com*. If the site's administrators have permitted *anonymous* access—the equivalent of a Guest account—that's all there is to it. A Finder window pops open, revealing the FTP site's contents.

 If you need a password for the FTP site, however, you're now asked for your name and password.

Tip: You can eliminate that password-dialog-box step by using this address format: *ftp://yourname:your-password@www.apple.com.*

Hello, Bonjour

Throughout this chapter, and throughout this book, you'll encounter rituals in which you're supposed to connect to another Mac, server, or printer by typing in its IP address (its unique network address).

But first of all, IP addresses are insanely difficult to memorize (192.179.248.3, anyone?). Second, networks shouldn't require you to deal with them anyway. If a piece of equipment is on the network, it should announce its presence, rather than making you specifically call for it by name.

So you can appreciate the beauty of Bonjour, an underlying macOS networking technology that lets networked gadgets

detect one another on the network automatically and recognize one another's capabilities.

It's Bonjour at work, for example, that makes other Macs' names show up in your iTunes program so you can listen to their music from across the network. Bonjour is also responsible for filling up your Bonjour buddies list in Messages automatically, listing everyone who's on the same office network; for making shared Macs' names show up in the Sidebar's Shared list; and for making the names of modern laser printers from HP, Epson, or Lexmark appear like magic in the list of printers in the Print dialog box.

But the Sidebar method has its drawbacks. For example, the Sidebar doesn't let you type in a disk's network address. As a result, you can't access any shared disk *on the internet* (an FTP site, for example), or indeed anywhere beyond your local subnet (your own small network).

Fortunately, there's another way. When you choose Go→Connect to Server, you get the dialog box shown in Figure 13-11. You're supposed to type in the address of the shared disk you want.

Figure 13-11:
The Sidebar method of connecting to shared disks and folders is quick and easy, but it doesn't let you connect to certain kinds of disks. The Connect to Server method entails plodding through several dialog boxes, but it can find just about every kind of networked disk.

For example, from here you can connect to the following:

- **Everyday Macs on your network.** If you know the IP address of the Mac you're trying to access (you geek!), you can type nothing but its IP address into the box and then hit Connect. Or you can just type its Bonjour name, something like this: *afp://upstairs-PowerMac.local/.*

Tip: To find out your Mac's IP address, open the Network pane of System Preferences. There, near the top, you'll see a message like this: "Wi-Fi is connected to Tim's Hotspot and has the IP address 192.168.1.113." That's your IP address.

To see your Bonjour address, open the Sharing pane of System Preferences. Click File Sharing. Near the top, you'll see the computer name with ".local" tacked onto its name—and hyphens instead of spaces—like this: Little-MacBook.local.

After you enter your account password and choose the shared disk or folder you want, you're connected exactly as though you had clicked "Connect as" (Figure 13-10).

The next time you open the Connect to Server dialog box, macOS remembers that address, as a courtesy to you, and shows it pre-entered in the Address field.

- **Macs across the internet.** If your Mac has a permanent (static) IP address, then the computer itself can be a server, to which you can connect from anywhere in the world via the internet. Details on this procedure are in Chapter 20.

also show up on the desktop, if you've turned on the "Connected Servers" option in Finder→Preferences→Sidebar.)

Note: Once you've connected to a Mac using your account, the other Mac has a lock on your identity. You'll be able to connect to the other Mac over and over again during this same computing session, without ever having to retype your password.

Figure 13-10:
You can sign into your account on another Mac on the network (even while somebody else is using that Mac in person). Click "Connect as" and then enter your name and password. Turn on "Remember this password in my keychain" to speed up the process for next time. The Change Password button lets you change your account password on the other machine. No matter which method you use to connect to a shared folder or disk, its icon shows up in the Sidebar.

In the meantime, you can double-click icons to open them, make copies of them, and otherwise manipulate them exactly as though they were icons on your own hard drive. Depending on what permissions you've been given, you can even edit or trash those files.

Tip: There's one significant difference between working with "local" icons and working with those that sit elsewhere on the network. When you delete a file from another Mac on the network, either by pressing the Delete key or by dragging it to the Trash, a message appears to let you know that you're about to delete that item instantly and permanently. It won't simply land in the Trash "folder," awaiting the Empty Trash command.

You can even use Spotlight to find files on that networked disk. If the Mac across the network is running Leopard or a later Mac version, in fact, you can search for words *inside* its files, just as though you were sitting in front of it. If not, you can still search for text in files' names.

Connection Method B: Connect to Server

The Sidebar method of connecting to networked folders and disks is practically effortless. It involves nothing more than clicking your way through folders—a skill that, in theory, you already know.

If you see anything else at all in the Public folder you've opened, it's stuff the account holder has copied there for the enjoyment of you and your networkmates. You're not allowed to delete anything from the other person's Public folder or make changes to anything in it.

You can, however, open those icons, read them, or even copy them to *your* Mac—and then edit *your* copies.

Tip: Every now and then, you'll click the name of a Mac in the Finder Sidebar, hoping to see its contents—and instead of seeing a list of the shared Public folders, you'll get a Not Connected or Connection Failed message at the top of your window.

In that case, go to the shared Mac and do this: Open System Preferences→Sharing. Click File Sharing and then Options. Turn off "Share files and folders using SMB." Close System Preferences. Often, that's all it takes to make your Mac visible and connectable from other Macs on the network. (If not, then try restarting the shared Mac to make the SMB change stick.)

3b. To access your own Home folder on the other Mac, click the Connect As button (Figure 13-10). Sign in as usual.

When the "Connect to the file server" box appears, you're supposed to specify your account name and password (from the Mac you're tapping into). This is the same name and password you'd use to log in if you were actually sitting at that machine.

Type your account name (long or short version) and password. And if you didn't set up a password for your account, leave the password box empty.

Tip: The dialog box shown in Figure 13-10 includes the delightful and timesaving "Remember this password in my keychain" option, which makes the Mac memorize your password for a certain disk so you don't have to type it—or even see this dialog box—every darned time you connect. (If you have no password, though, then "Remember this password" doesn't work. You'll have to confront—and press Return to dismiss—the "Connect to the file server" box every time.)

When you click Connect (or press Return), the other Mac's icon shows up in your Sidebar, and its contents appear in the main window. (The other Mac's icon may

GEM IN THE ROUGH

Faster Ways to Connect Next Time

If you expect that you might want to access a shared disk or folder again later, take a moment to make an alias of it. The easiest way is to press Option-⌘ as you drag it out of the window where it first appears. Next time, you can bring it back to your screen just by double-clicking the alias. And if you turned on "Remember this password in my keychain," you won't even be asked for your name and password again.

Similarly, if you put an alias like this onto the Dock, you can bring it back to your screen later just by clicking its icon.

You can even drag the alias into the Login Items window described on page 530. Now the disk appears on your desktop automatically each time you log in—the most effortless arrangement of all.

tree). For example, you may see the names of network zones (clusters of machines, as found in big companies and universities).

Or, if you're trying to tap into a Windows machine, open the icon representing the *workgroup* (computer cluster) that contains the machine you want. In small office networks, it's usually called MSHOME or WORKGROUP. In big corporations, these workgroups can be called almost anything—as long as the name is no more than 15 letters long with no punctuation. (Thanks, Microsoft.)

If you *do* see icons for workgroups or other network "zones," double-click until you're seeing the icons for individual computers.

Note: If you're a network nerd, you may be interested to note that macOS can "see" servers that use the SMB/CIFS, NFS, FTP, and WebDAV protocols running on macOS Server, Unix, Linux, Novell NetWare, and Windows servers (NT, 2000, XP, Vista, and Windows 7, 8, or 10). But the Sidebar reveals *only* the shared computers on your *subnet* (your local, internal office network).

2. **Double-click the computer whose files you want to open.**

In the main window, you now see the Public Folder icons for each account holder on that computer: Mom, Dad, Sissy, whatever, as shown in Figure 13-9. (They *may* have shared other folders with you as well.) If you have an account on the other computer, you'll see a folder representing *your* stuff, too. At this point, you're considered a guest.

Note: This amount of access depends on a setting in System Preferences→Users & Groups. Click the Guest account to see it: "Allow guests to connect to shared folders." That checkbox is usually turned on—but it's something to check if you can't seem to connect.

From here, the remaining instructions diverge, depending on whether you want to access *other* people's stuff or *your* stuff. That's why there are two alternative versions of step 3 here:

3a. **If you want to access the stuff that somebody else has left for you, then double-click that person's Public folder.**

Instantly, that folder's contents appear in the Finder window.

In this situation, you're only a guest. You don't have to bother with a password. On the other hand, the only thing you can generally see inside the other person's account folder is his Public folder.

Tip: Actually, you *might* see other folders here—if the account holder has specifically shared them *and* decided that you're important enough to have access to them.

One thing you'll find inside the Public folder is the Drop Box folder. This folder exists so you can *give* files and folders to the other person. You can drop any of your own icons onto the Drop Box folder—but you can't open the Drop Box folder to see what *other* people have put there.

But you can add more icons to this list. Either drag them into the list directly from the desktop or a Finder window, or click the +, navigate to the item you want to share, select it, and then click Add. Either way, that item now appears in the Shared Folders list.

- **Users.** When you click a shared item, the second column sprouts a list of *who* gets to work with it from across the network. You're listed here, of course, since it's your stuff. There's also a listing here for Everyone, which really means "everyone *else*"—that is, everyone who's not specifically listed here.

 You can add to this list, too. Click + to open the person-selection box shown in Figure 13-7. It lists the other account holders on your Mac, and some predefined groups, as well as the contents of your Contacts.

Note: Most of the Contacts people don't actually have accounts on this Mac, of course. If you choose somebody from this list, you're asked to make up an account password. When you click Create Account, you've actually created a *Sharing Only* account on your Mac for that person, as described in the box below. When you return to the Accounts pane of System Preferences, you'll see that new person listed.

Double-click a person's name to add her to the list of people who can access this item from over the network, and then set up the appropriate privileges (described next).

To *remove* someone from this list, just click the name and then click the − button.

- **Users.** This *third* column lets you specify how much access each person in the *second* column has to this folder. Your choices, once again, are Read & Write (full access to change or delete this item's contents); Read Only (open or copy, but can't edit

GEM IN THE ROUGH

Sharing Only Accounts

In the bad old days, you couldn't share your files with other people unless you first created full-blown accounts for them on your Mac. You know: a Home folder, Music and Movies folders, and so on. That was an awful lot of disk space sacrificed, just so other people could visit your Mac over the network.

Nowadays, you can create a Sharing Only account for them. They can now share your files without actually having a presence on your hard drive.

This way, you don't even have to set up a name and password for them on your Mac, and they don't have to learn another name and password. They don't have an account on your Mac at all—just a Contacts card.

To set this up, open Contacts. Make sure there's a card in there for the person who will be visiting your Mac over the network.

Now visit System Preferences→Sharing. Click Screen Sharing. As shown in Figure 13-17, click the +. In the panel that appears, click Contacts, and then double-click the name of the prospective visitor. You're asked to enter a screen-sharing password for this person (twice) and then click Create Account.

That's it—the setup is ready. When attempting to connect to your Mac, your guest can log in—no account on your Mac necessary!

- **No access** is an option only for Everyone. It means other people can see this file or folder's icon but can't do a thing with it.

Tip: Usually, you'll want the privileges for the folder to also apply to everything *inside* it; it would be a real drag to have to change the sharing privileges of the contents one icon at a time. That's why the ⚙ menu at the bottom of the Get Info box has a command called "Apply to enclosed items."

5. **Close the Get Info window.**

Now the folder is ready for invasion from across the network.

The System Preferences Method

It's very convenient to turn on sharing one folder at a time, using the Get Info window. But there's another way in, too, one that displays *all* your shared stuff in a handy master list.

To see it, choose System Preferences→Sharing→File Sharing (and make sure it's turned on). Now you're looking at a slightly different kind of permissions table, shown in Figure 13-8. It has *three* columns:

- **Shared folders.** The first column lists the files, folders, and disks you've shared. You'll probably see that every account's *Public* folder is already listed here, since they're all shared automatically. (You can turn *off* sharing for a Public folder, too, just by clicking it and then clicking the — button.)

Figure 13-8:
Hiding in System Preferences is a list of every disk and folder you've shared. To stop sharing something, click it and then click the — button. To share a new disk or folder, drag its icon off the desktop, or out of its window, directly into the Shared Folders list.

Your job is to work through this list of people, specifying *how much* control each person has over the file or folder you're sharing.

To add the name of a person or group, click the + button below the list. The list shown in Figure 13-7 appears.

Figure 13-7:
This list includes every account holder on your Mac, plus groups you've set up, plus the contents of your address book. One by one, you can add them to the list of lucky sharers of your files or folders—give each a password, if they don't already have accounts on this Mac—and then change the degree of access they have to the stuff you're sharing.

Now click a name in the list. Then, from the Privilege pop-up menu, choose a permissions setting:

- **Read & Write** has the most access of all. This person, like you, can add, change, or delete any file in the shared folder, or make any changes she likes to a document. Give Read & Write permission to people you trust not to mess things up.

- **Read only** means "Look, but don't touch." This person can see what's in the folder (or file) and can copy it, but he can't delete or change the original. It's a good setting for distributing company documents or making source files available to your minions.

- **Write only (Drop Box)** means other people can't even open the folder. They can drop things *into* it, but it's like a mail slot: The letter disappears into the slot, and then it's too late for them to change their minds. As the folder's owner, you can do what you like with the deposited goodies. This drop-box effect is great when you want students, co-workers, or family members to be able to *turn things in* to you—homework, reports, scandalous diaries—without running the risk that someone else might see those files. (This option doesn't appear for documents— only disks and folders.)

3. **Expand the Sharing & Permissions panel, if it's not already visible. Click the 🔒 icon and enter your administrator's password.**

The controls in the Sharing & Permissions area spring to life and become editable. At the bottom of the Info panel is a little table. The first column can display the names of individual account holders, like Casey or Chris, or *groups* of account holders, like Everyone or Accounting Dept.

The second column lists the *privileges* each person or group has for this folder.

Now, the average person has no clue what "privileges" means, and this is why things get a little hairy when you're setting up folder-by-folder permissions. But read on; it's not as bad as it seems.

4. **Edit the table by adding people's names. Then set their access permissions.**

At the moment, your name appears in the Name column, and it probably says Read & Write in the Privilege column. In other words, you're currently the master of this folder. You can put things in, and you can take things out.

If you just want to share files with *yourself,* so you can transfer them from one computer to another, you can stop here.

If you want to share files with *other* people—well, at the moment, the privileges for Everyone are probably set to "Read only." Other people can see this folder, but they can't do anything with it.

Figure 13-6:
The file-sharing permissions controls are here, in the Get Info box for any file, folder, or disk.

So now that you've set up Public folder sharing, how are other people supposed to access your Public folder? See page 582.

Sharing Any Folder

If the Public-folder method seems too simple and restrictive, you can graduate to the "share any folder" method. In this scheme, you can make *any* file, folder, or disk available to other people on the network.

The advantage here is that you don't have to move your files into the Public folder; they can sit right where you have them. And this time you can set up elaborate *sharing privileges* (also known as *permissions*) that grant individuals different levels of access to your files.

This method is more complicated to set up than that Public-folder business. In fact, just to underline its complexity, Apple has created two different setup procedures. You can share one icon at a time by opening its Get Info window; or you can work in a master list of shared items in System Preferences. The following pages cover both methods.

The Get Info Method

Here's how to share a Mac file, disk, or folder disk using its Get Info window. The following steps assume you've turned on System Preferences→Sharing→File Sharing, as shown in Figure 13-5.

1. **Select the folder or disk you want to share. Choose File→Get Info.**

 The Get Info dialog box appears (Figure 13-6). Expand the General panel if it's not already visible.

Note: Sharing an entire disk means every folder and file on it is available to anyone you give access to. On the other hand, by sharing only a folder or two, you can keep *most* of the stuff on your hard drive private, out of view of curious network comrades. Sharing only a folder or two does *them* a favor, too, by making it easier for them to find the files they're supposed to have. This way, they don't have to root through your entire drive looking for the stuff they actually need.

2. **Turn on "Shared folder."**

 If file sharing isn't turned on, you're asked to confirm; click Enable. Enter your administrator password, if necessary.

Tip: To help you remember what you've made available to other people on the network, a banner labeled "Shared Folder" appears across the top of any Finder window you've shared. It even appears at the top of the Open and Save dialog boxes.

OK, this disk or folder is now shared. But with whom?

Sharing Your Public Folder

All right. If AirDrop is so great, why doesn't it wipe out all other forms of file transfer and save this book a bunch of pages? Because (a) it works only on Macs and Apple devices, (b) it works only wirelessly, and (c) it's a one-way street. Other people can't take files from your Mac—you have to shove the files to them.

This next method eliminates those limitations. It's the Public-folder method.

Inside your Home folder, there's a folder called Public. (Inside *everybody's* Home folder is a folder called Public.) Anything you put into this folder is automatically available to everyone else on the network. They don't need a password, they don't need an account on your Mac—they just have to be on the same network, wireless or wired. They can put files here *or* copy things out.

To make your Public folder available to your networkmates, you have to turn on the File Sharing master switch. Choose System Preferences→Sharing, and then turn on File Sharing (as shown in Figure 13-5).

Now round up the files and folders you want to share with all comers on the network and drag them into your Home→Public folder. That's all there is to it.

> **Note:** You may notice that there's already something in your Public folder: a subfolder called Drop Box. It's there so that other people can give *you* files from across the network, as described on page 579.

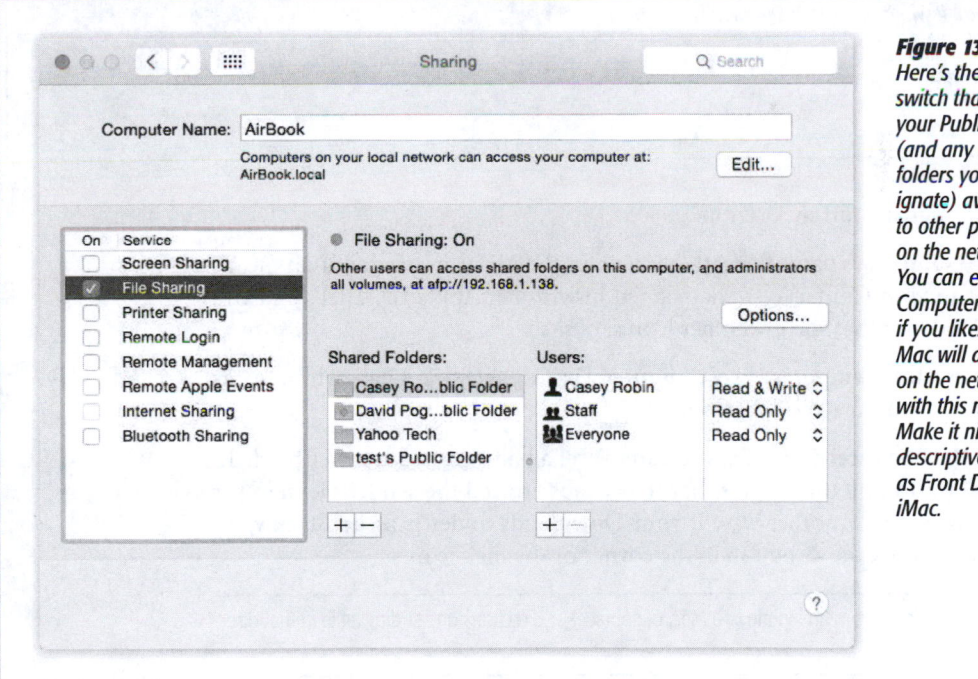

Figure 13-5:
Here's the master switch that makes your Public folder (and any other folders you designate) available to other people on the network. You can edit the Computer Name, if you like. Your Mac will appear on the network with this name. Make it nice and descriptive, such as Front Desk iMac.

The file winds up in your Downloads folder. This folder generally sits on the Dock, so it's easy to find. But you can also choose Go→Downloads, or press Option-⌘-L, to jump there.

- **Receiving on an iPhone/iPad/iPod Touch.** A message says "[Other guy's name] would like to share [the file's name]." Tap Decline or Accept.

If your iOS device knows what to do with the file, it opens automatically in the appropriate app (a photo in Photos, a web page in Safari, and so on). If it's not sure what to do with it, then it offers a list of apps that can open it. For example, suppose someone's just sent you a Word document. You're offered a choice of apps that can handle Word files (either to open them or to store them), like Evernote and Dropbox. Tap the one you want.

If you don't have any app that can open the file, iOS sometimes offers you the chance to download one that *can*. And if even that trick comes up empty-handed, your i-device rejects the incoming file altogether.

Figure 13-4:
A file arriving on your Mac via AirDrop announces itself with a notification. You can click either Decline (you don't want the file) or Accept. If you click Accept, the file transfer proceeds automatically. The transfer is encrypted, so evildoers nearby have no clue what you're transferring (or even that you're transferring). It winds up in your Downloads folder.

There's a lot of great stuff in AirDrop:

- **If you see someone's name beneath her icon in the AirDrop window,** that means that she's in your Contacts *and* has signed in with her Apple ID. That's an extra bit of confidence that she is who her icon says she is.

- **AirDrop creates a temporary two-computer wireless network.** That's why it works even if you're not in a Wi-Fi hotspot.

- **If *you're* the one receiving a file,** you can cancel a half-finished transfer by clicking the ⊗ button on the progress bar that wraps around the sender's icon in the AirDrop window. (Another way: If your Downloads folder is set to Stack view, then you can click the ⊗ button in the corner of the file's icon.)

Note: *AirDrop also works from an iPhone* to *a Mac, of course. For directions on sending a file in that direction, see page 313.*

- **On the Mac, AirDrop requires macOS Lion or later.** On an iPhone, iPad, or iPod Touch, it requires iOS 7 or later.

- **If your Mac can't seem to "see" other nearby, older Macs (pre-2012 models)**— either when sending or receiving an AirDrop file—the process may require an extra step. If you've right-clicked or two-finger clicked an icon or used the ⎋ button in a program, click "Don't see who you're looking for?" at top right (see Figure 13-2) and then click Search for an Older Mac.

 The "Don't see who you're looking for?" link also appears in the AirDrop *window* in the Finder (you can see it in Figure 13-3). Here again, only by clicking Search for an Older Mac will you see the icons for pre-2012 Mac models show up.

 And, by the way: When your Mac is seeing those *older* Macs, it can't see *newer* ones—and vice versa.

- **If you don't see the AirDrop icon in your Finder's Sidebar,** it's because somebody turned off its checkbox in Finder→Preferences→Sidebar. (You can still use Air-Drop, though.)

- **If your lucky recipient's icon still isn't showing up on your Mac,** he may have AirDrop turned off or restricted.

 Ask him to swipe up from the bottom of his screen and tap AirDrop (iOS device) or open the AirDrop window (Mac). Here you can control who can see you: Off (nobody), Contacts Only (people in your address book), or Everyone. It's supposed to be a security precaution, but you may as well leave it set to Everyone; after all, you have to approve every file individually, so it's not as though some passing hacker can shove evil files down your throat.

 And if one of you has turned on Contacts Only, you still won't be able to participate in AirDrop transactions unless you're also logged into your iCloud account.

- **AirDrop doesn't work if you've turned on "Block all connections"** in your firewall (page 558).

- **AirDrop requires both sending and receiving devices** to be on (awake).

Receiving a File by AirDrop

If someone's sending *you* a file by AirDrop, the steps depend on whether you're using a Mac or an i-gadget:

- **Receiving on the Mac.** You get a notification (see Figure 13-4).

Tip: Actually, if you're sending something to *yourself*—from your phone to your Mac, for example—this confirmation doesn't appear. Apple notices that both devices are signed into the same iCloud account and figures you don't need protection from *yourself*. So it just dumps the incoming file directly into your Down-loads folder without making you accept it first. (You still get a notification that the transaction has happened.)

on every page in Safari, map in Maps, photo in Photos, contact in Contacts, and note in Notes. Lots of non-Apple apps offer that ⬆ button, too. (See page 263 for more on the Share button.)

In each case, you should now proceed as shown in Figure 13-2.

Figure 13-3:
If there are other recent Macs within about 30 feet, you see their logged-in owners' icons here. Usually, the icons display the Mac owners' account pictures; but if they have facial photos in your Contacts, then you see those instead.

A message appears on the other gadget's screen, asking if the owner wants to accept your file. If she chooses Accept, then the transaction is complete. Quick, effortless, wireless, delightful.

Note: At one time, you and your recipient's Mac both had to have their AirDrop windows open. That's no longer true; AirDrop works whether that window is open or not.

Eight Reasons AirDrop Might Seem Not to Work

Miraculous though AirDrop may seem when it's working, certain stars do have to be in alignment. If AirDrop isn't working as advertised, here are some things to check:

- **Both sender and receiver must have Bluetooth and Wi-Fi turned on.** They also have to be within about 30 feet of each other.

- **AirDrop doesn't work with really old Apple models.** It does work with the MacBook Pro (made since late 2008), MacBook Air (since late 2010), MacBook (late 2008), iMac (early 2009), Mac mini (mid-2010), and Mac Pro (mid-2010).

 And among i-devices, it requires an iPhone 5 or later, iPad mini (any generation), iPad (4th generation or later), or iPod Touch (5th generation or later).

Of course, setting up all those levels of control means more work and more complexity.

The following pages tackle these three methods one at a time.

AirDrop

AirDrop is one of macOS's star attractions. It's a breakthrough in speed, simplicity, and efficiency. There's no setup, no passwords involved. It lets you copy files to someone else's Mac, iPhone, iPad, or iPod Touch up to 30 feet away, instantly and wirelessly; you don't need an internet connection or even a Wi-Fi network. It works on a flight, a beach, or a sailboat in the middle of the Atlantic. It also works if you're on a Wi-Fi network, doing other things online.

You can exchange files with any Mac running macOS Lion or later, and any i-gadget running iOS 7 or later.

Sending by AirDrop

Usually, you begin the sending process in one of two ways:

- **From the Finder.** Right-click or two-finger click the file's icon. From the shortcut menu, choose Share→AirDrop. The box shown in Figure 13-2 appears.

Note: Here's a second way to send something in the Finder: Open the AirDrop *window*. (It's listed in the Sidebar at the left side of every Finder window. Or choose Go→AirDrop, or press Shift-⌘-R.) Drag the icon(s) you want to send onto the icon of the receiving device (Figure 13-3).

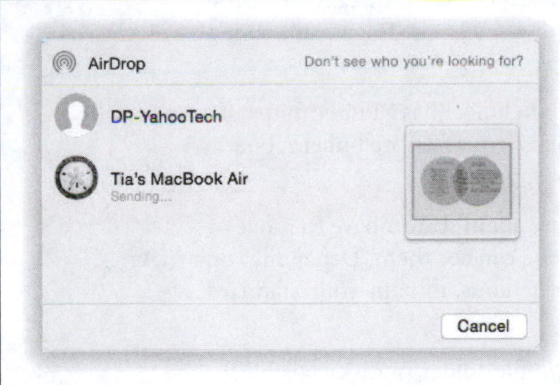

Figure 13-2:
The icons of nearby AirDrop-friendly Apple gadgets and Macs show up in this fun-sized window. You've already said what you want to send; now you just have to specify who gets it. Click the destination device's icon and then click Send.

- **From an app.** When you're looking at whatever you want to send, click the ⬆ button. From the shortcut menu, choose AirDrop.

 And where is that ⬆ button? Everywhere. It's at the top of every Finder window and at the top of every Quick Look window. It's in Open and Save boxes. It's available

them with nothing more than a FireWire cable. Details are in the free downloadable appendix to this chapter called "FireWire Networking." It's available on this book's "Missing CD" page at *missingmanuals.com*.

File Sharing: Three Ways

When you're done wiring (or not wiring, as the case may be), your network is ready. Your Mac should "see" any Ethernet or shared USB printers, in readiness to print (Chapter 14). You can now play network games or use a network calendar. And you can now turn on *file sharing,* one of the most useful features of all.

In file sharing, you can drag files back and forth between different Macs (or even Windows PCs) on the network, exactly as though the other computer's folder or disk were a hard drive connected to your own machine.

The thing is, it's not easy being Apple. You have to write *one* operating system that's supposed to please *everyone,* from the self-employed first-time newbie to the network administrator for NASA. You have to design a networking system simple enough for the laptop owner who just wants to copy things to a desktop Mac when returning from a trip, yet secure and flexible enough for the network designer at a large corporation.

Clearly, different people have different attitudes about the need for security and flexibility.

That's why macOS offers *three ways* to share files, striking three different positions along the simplicity-to-flexibility spectrum:

- **The easiest way: AirDrop.** This feature is dreamy—if there are other people in your house or office who have wireless Macs running Lion or later. Imagine this: You open the AirDrop folder, where you see everybody else's icons. To give someone a file, you drop its icon on that person's face. Done.

- **Slightly harder way: the Public folder.** Every account holder has a Public folder. It's free for anyone else on the network to access. Like a grocery store bulletin board, there's no password required. Super-convenient, super-easy.

 There's only one downside, and you may not care about it: You have to move or copy files *into* the Public folder before anyone else can see them. Depending on how many files you want to share, this can get tedious, disrupt your standard organizational structure, and eat up disk space.

- **The flexible way: any folder.** You can also make *any* file, folder, or disk available for inspection by other people on the network. This method means you don't have to move files into the Public folder, for starters. It also gives you elaborate control over who is allowed to do what to your files. You might want to permit your company's executives to see *and* edit your documents, but allow the peons in Accounting just to see them. And Andy, that unreliable goofball in Sales? You don't want him even *seeing* what's in your shared folder.

- **A modem.** A few, proud people still get online by dialing via modem, which is built into some old AirPort base station models. The base station is plugged into a phone jack. Wireless Macs in the house can get online by triggering the base station to dial by remote control.

Tip: If you connect through a modern router or AirPort base station, you already have a great firewall protecting you. You don't have to turn on macOS's firewall.

You use the AirPort Utility (in your Applications→Utilities folder) to set up your base station; if you have a typical cable modem or DSL, the setup practically takes care of itself.

Whether you've set up your own wireless network or want to hop onto somebody else's, Chapter 16 has the full scoop on *joining* Wi-Fi networks.

Cell Networks

If you have an iPhone or a similar cellphone, you may be able to get your Mac online even when you're hundreds of miles from the nearest Ethernet jack or Wi-Fi hotspot. Thanks to *tethering,* your phone can act as an internet antenna for your laptop, relying on the slow, expensive, but almost ubiquitous *cellular* network for its connection. Details are on page 653.

FireWire Networks

Apple is busily phasing out the convenient, fast *FireWire* jacks on its Macs. But if you have two FireWire-equipped Macs, you can create a blazing-fast connection between

UP TO SPEED

802 Dot Whatever: Better Every Year

Over the years, networking gear has come in several flavors, each offering different degrees of speed, distance, and compatibility. They have such appetizing-sounding names as 802.11a, 802.11g, 802.11n, and 802.11ac.

In general, each generation of Wi-Fi gear improves the speed and range of your hotspot. (Note that you never get the "up to" speed printed on the box; in fact, you'll usually get around half that speed, since a wireless network uses a lot of the bandwidth for such network housekeeping chores as correcting transmission errors.)

The current standard is 802.11ac, which offers better speed *and* better range than its predecessors (thanks to multiple antennas). Remember, though, you won't get the better speed unless both your base station *and* your networking cards "speak" ac.

Meanwhile, keep in mind that faster equipment doesn't speed up your email and web activity. A cable modem or a DSL box delivers internet information at a fraction of the speed of your home or office network. The bottleneck is the internet connection, not your network.

Instead, the speed boost you get with newer Wi-Fi gear is useful only for transferring files *among computers on your network,* streaming video or audio *between computers* (or PCs and your TV), and playing networked games.

Finally, the great thing about wireless networking is that it all works together, no matter what kind of computer you have. There's no such thing as an "Apple" wireless network or a "Windows" wireless network. All computers work with any kind of access point.

When you're in a Wi-Fi hotspot, your Mac has a very fast connection to the internet, as though it were connected to a cable modem or DSL.

Every Mac has Wi-Fi circuitry. It lets you connect to your network and the internet wirelessly, as long as you're within about 150 feet of a *base station* or (as Windows people call it) an *access point*. That box must in turn be physically connected to a network and internet connection.

The base station can take any of these forms:

- **AirPort base station.** Apple's sleek, white, squarish base stations ($100 to $200) come in two flavors, Express and Extreme, and permit as many as 50 computers to connect simultaneously. All of them have USB ports to connect printers, and you can also hook up an external hard drive to the AirPort Extreme.

- **A Time Capsule.** This Apple gizmo is exactly the same as the AirPort base station, except that it also contains a huge hard drive so that it can back up your Macs automatically over the wired or wireless network.

- **A wireless broadband router.** Linksys, Belkin, and lots of other companies make less expensive Wi-Fi base stations. You can plug the base station into an Ethernet router or hub, thus permitting 10 or 20 wireless-equipped computers, including Macs, to join an existing Ethernet network without wiring. (With all due non-fanboyism, however, Apple's base stations and software are more polished and satisfying to use.)

Tip: It's perfectly possible to plug a Wi-Fi base station into a regular router, too, to accommodate both wired and wireless computers.

- **Another Mac.** Your Mac can also *impersonate* an AirPort base station. In effect, the Mac becomes a software-based base station, and you save yourself the cost of a separate physical base station.

GEM IN THE ROUGH

Networking Without the Network

In a pinch, you can connect two Macs without any real network at all. You can create an Ethernet connection without a hub or a router—or an AirPort connection without a Wi-Fi base station.

To set up the wired connection, just run a standard Ethernet cable between the Ethernet jacks of the two Macs. (You don't need to use an Ethernet crossover cable, as you did in days of old.) To set up a wireless connection, from your 🛜 menulet, choose Create Network. Make up a name and

password for your little private network, and then click OK. On the second Mac, choose 🛜→Join Network, enter the same private network name, and then click Join.

At this point, your two Macs belong to the same ad hoc micronetwork. If you've shared some folders on the first Mac, its name (like "Casey's iMac") now appears in the Sidebar of the second Mac. Click it to see what's on it.

From here, proceed exactly as described on page 582.

Note: Until recently, Apple had its own name for Wi-Fi: AirPort. That's what it said in System Preferences→ Network, for example, and that's what the 🔗 menulet was called. *AirPort* was a lot cleverer, wordplay-wise, than the meaningless "Wi-Fi." Unfortunately, not many people realized that AirPort was the same thing as what the rest of the world called Wi-Fi. So at least in its onscreen references, these days, Apple gives AirPort a new name: Wi-Fi.

Ethernet Networks

Every desktop Mac has an Ethernet jack (Figure 13-1). Apple laptops don't have Ethernet jacks built in, but you can add one in the form of an adapter that plugs into one of your USB jacks.

Ethernet jack Ethernet hub

Figure 13-1:
Every desktop Mac has a built-in Ethernet jack (left). It looks like an overweight telephone jack. It connects to an Ethernet router or hub (right) via an Ethernet cable (also known as Cat 5 or Cat 6), which ends in what looks like an overweight telephone-wire plug (also known as an RJ-45 connector).

If you connect all the Macs and Ethernet printers in your small office to a central Ethernet hub, switch, or *router*—a compact, inexpensive box with jacks for five, 10, or even more computers and printers—you've got yourself a very fast, very reliable network. (Most people wind up hiding the hub in a closet and running the wiring either along the edges of the room or inside the walls.) You can buy Ethernet cables, plus the hub, at any computer store or, less expensively, from an internet-based mail-order house; none of this stuff is Mac-specific.

Tip: If you want to connect only two Macs—say, your laptop and your desktop machine—you don't need an Ethernet hub. Instead, you just need a standard Ethernet cable. Run it directly between the Ethernet jacks of the two computers. Then connect the Macs as described in the box on the facing page.

Or don't use Ethernet at all; just use a person-to-person Wi-Fi network.

Ethernet is the best networking system for many offices. It's fast, easy, and cheap.

Wi-Fi Networks

Wi-Fi, known to the geeks as 802.11, means wireless networking. It's the technology that lets laptops get online at high speed in any Wi-Fi "hotspot." Hotspots are every-where these days: in homes, offices, coffee shops, hotels, airports, and thousands of other places.

Tip: The primary purpose of the Keychain is, of course, to type in passwords for you automatically. However, it's also an excellent place to record all kinds of private information just for your own reference: credit card numbers, ATM numbers, and so on. Simply choose File→New Password Item (if it's a name and password) or File→New Secure Note Item (if you want to type a blob of very, very private text).

No, the Mac won't type them in for you automatically anywhere, but it will maintain them in one central location that is, itself, password-protected.

Multiple Keychains

By choosing File→New Keychain, you can create more than one Keychain, each with its own master password. On one hand, this might defeat the simplicity goal of the Keychain. On the other hand, it's conceivable that you might want to encrypt all your business documents with one master password and all your personal stuff with another, for example.

If you do have more than one Keychain, you can view all of them by clicking the little Show Keychains button at the lower-left corner of the Keychain Access window; now you see a list of all your Keychains (including some maintained by macOS itself). Click their names to switch among them.

Keychain files

Keychains are represented by separate files in your Home→Library→Keychains folder. Knowing that can be handy when you want to delete a Keychain or to copy it to another Mac—your laptop, for example. (Then again, the File→Export command may be even more convenient.)

Twelve Privacy Shields

In Apple's mind, there's a difference between *security* (protecting your Mac) and *privacy* (protecting your information from distribution).

The Privacy tab in the Security & Privacy pane of System Preferences harbors a list of privacy-related options. Each represents one hunk of your Mac's hardware or software—and lets you allow or disallow your apps' access to its treasures.

- **Location Services** means "knowing where I am." It lets your laptop figure out its own time zone automatically, for example, or lets a weather website show your *local* weather the first time you visit.

 Every time a program wants to use your current location for its own features, you'll be asked about it. (The Mac figures out your location based on its proximity to known Wi-Fi networks.) Each time you say OK, the program that did the asking installs its own name into the list here.

 You can turn off the checkboxes of the programs you'd rather didn't know where you are, or you can turn off location tracking altogether by turning off the "Enable location services" box (after unlocking this panel by clicking the lower-left padlock, of course).

the Mac sleeps. When you return, you're asked to reenter your account password in order to unlock the Keychain, restoring your auto-password feature.

Whenever the Keychain is locked, macOS no longer fills in your passwords.

Note: As noted, you unlock your Keychain using the same password you use to log into macOS, but that's just a convenience. If you're really worried about security, you can choose Edit→Change Password for Keychain [your name], thereby establishing a *different* password for your Keychain, so that it no longer matches your login password.

Of course, doing so also turns off the automatic-Keychain-unlocking-when-you-log-in feature.

Managing Keychain

To take a look at your Keychain, open the Keychain Access program in Applications→ Utilities. By clicking one of the password rows, you get to see its attributes—name, kind, account, and so on (Figure 12-18, bottom).

Figure 12-18:
In the main Keychain list, you can double-click a listing for more details about a certain password—including the actual password being stored. To see the password, turn on "Show password." The first time you try this, you're asked to prove your worthiness by entering your Keychain password (usually your account password). If you then click Always Allow, you won't be bothered for a password-to-see-this-password again.

Note: This offer is valid only if, in Safari→Preferences→AutoFill tab, "User names and passwords" is turned on. If not, the "Would you like to save this password?" message never appears.

Note, too, that some websites use a nonstandard login system that doesn't produce the "Would you?" message. Unless the website provides its own "Remember me" or "Store my password" option, you're out of luck; you'll have to type in this information with every visit.

- **When you connect to a shared folder or disk** on the network, the opportunity to save the password in your Keychain is equally obvious (Figure 12-17, bottom).

- **You also see a "Remember password (add to Keychain)"** option when you create an encrypted disk image using Disk Utility.

- **Mac email programs, like Mail and Outlook,** store your email account passwords in your Keychain. So do FTP programs; check their Preferences dialog boxes.

- **Your iCloud account information** is stored in the Keychain, too (as you entered it on the iCloud pane of System Preferences).

- **A "Remember password" option appears** when you type in the password for a wireless network or an AirPort base station.

- **The iTunes program memorizes** your iTunes Store password, too.

Locking and unlocking the Keychain

If you work alone, the Keychain is automatic, invisible, and generally wonderful. Login is the only time you have to type a password. After that, the Mac figures, "Hey, I know it's you; your password proved it. I'll fill in all your other passwords automatically." In Apple parlance, you've *unlocked* your Keychain by logging in.

But there may be times when you want the Keychain to *stop* filling in all your passwords, perhaps only temporarily. Maybe you work in an office where someone else might sit down at your Mac while you're getting a candy bar.

Of course, you can have macOS lock your Mac—Keychain and all—after a specified period of inactivity (page 547). But if you want to lock the Keychain *manually,* so that no passwords are autofilled until you unlock it again, you can use any of these methods. Each requires the Keychain Access program (in your Applications→Utilities folder):

- **Lock the Keychain manually.** In the Keychain Access program, choose File→Lock Keychain "login" (⌘-L), or just click the big lock icon in the toolbar (seen in Figure 12-18).

- **Choose Lock Keychain "login" from the Keychain menulet.** To put the Keychain menulet on your menu bar, open Keychain Access, choose Keychain Access→Preferences→General. Turn on "Show keychain status in menu bar."

- **Lock the Keychain automatically.** In the Keychain Access app, choose Edit→Change Settings for Keychain [your name]. The resulting box lets you set up the Keychain to lock itself, say, five minutes after the last time you used your Mac, or whenever

The Keychain

The information explosion of the computer age may translate into bargains, power, and efficiency, but it carries with it a colossal annoyance: the proliferation of *passwords* we have to memorize. Shared folders on the network, websites, FTP sites—each requires another password.

Apple has done the world a mighty favor with its *Keychain* feature. (It's an earlier, not-internet-based version of the iCloud Keychain described on page 739.) Whenever you log into macOS and type in your password, you've typed the master code that tells the computer, "It's really me. I'm at my computer now." From that moment on, the Mac *automatically* fills in every password blank you encounter, whether it's a website in Safari, a shared disk on your network, a wireless network, an encrypted disk image, or an FTP (File Transfer Protocol) program like Transmit or Cyberduck. With only a few exceptions, you can safely forget *all* your passwords except your login password.

All kinds of programs and services know about the Keychain and offer to store your passwords there. For example:

- **In Safari, whenever you type your name and password** for a certain web page and then click OK, a dialog box asks: "Would you like to save this password?" (See Figure 12-17, top.)

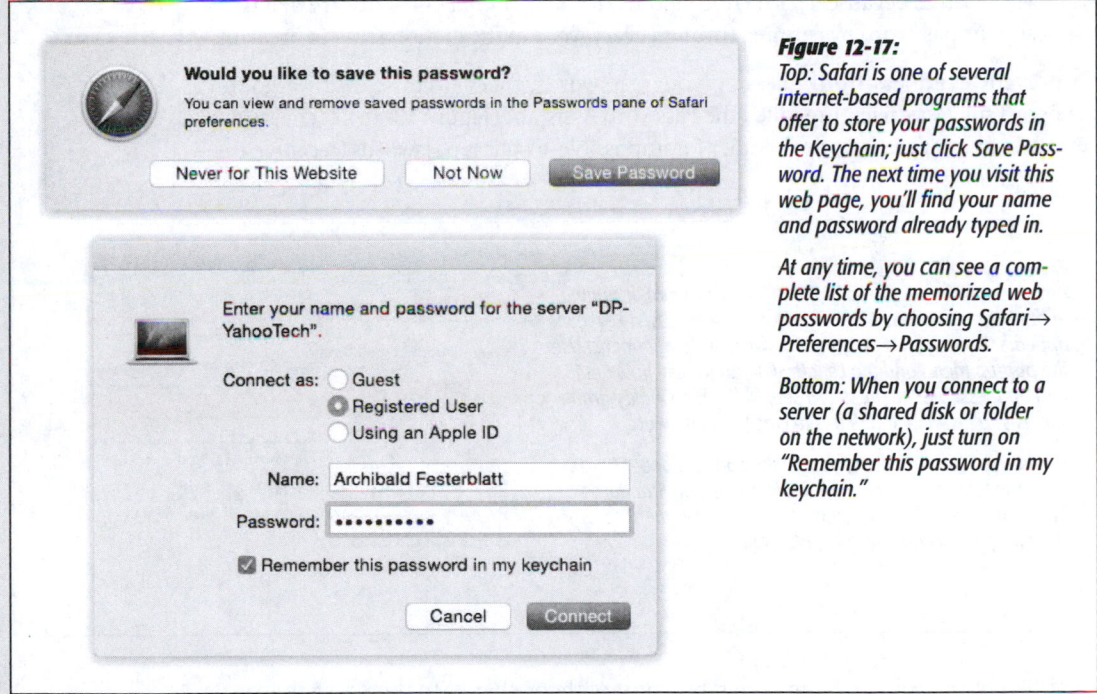

Would you like to save this password?

You can view and remove saved passwords in the Passwords pane of Safari preferences.

Never for This Website Not Now Save Password

Enter your name and password for the server "DP-YahooTech".

Connect as: ○ Guest
 ● Registered User
 ○ Using an Apple ID

Name: Archibald Festerblatt

Password: ••••••••••

☑ Remember this password in my keychain

Cancel Connect

Figure 12-17:
Top: Safari is one of several internet-based programs that offer to store your passwords in the Keychain; just click Save Password. The next time you visit this web page, you'll find your name and password already typed in.

At any time, you can see a complete list of the memorized web passwords by choosing Safari→ Preferences→Passwords.

Bottom: When you connect to a server (a shared disk or folder on the network), just turn on "Remember this password in my keychain."

messages. They're hoping to find computers that are turned on and connected full time to the internet. If your machine responds, and they can figure out how to get into it, they'll use it, without your knowledge, as a relay station for pumping out spam or masking their hacking footsteps.

"Enable stealth mode," then, makes your Mac even more invisible on the network; it means your Mac won't respond to the electronic signal called a *ping*. (On the other hand, *you* won't be able to ping your machine, either, when you're on the road and want to know if it's turned on and online.)

Note: You might have noticed that there doesn't seem to be any option to turn on *firewall logging*, which creates a little text file where macOS records every attempt that anyone from the outside makes to infiltrate your Mac. Logging is available, though—in fact, it's turned on all the time. To view the log, open the Applications→ Utilities→Console program. In the left-side list, expand the */private/var/log* heading, and click *appfirewall.log*.

The Password Assistant

Plenty of software features require you to make up a password: websites, accounts, networked disks, and so on. No wonder most people wind up trying to use the same password in as many situations as possible. Worse, they use something easily guessable like their names, kids' names, spouse's names, and so on. Even regular English words aren't very secure, because hackers routinely use *dictionary attacks*—software that tries to guess your password by running through every word in the dictionary—to break in.

To prevent evildoers from guessing your passwords, macOS comes with a good-password suggestion feature called the Password Assistant (Figure 12-16). It cheerfully generates one suggestion after another for impossible-to-guess passwords (*recharges8@ exchangeability,* anyone?).

Figure 12-16:
Anyplace you're supposed to make up a password, including in the Users & Groups pane of System Preferences, a key icon appears. When you click it, the Password Assistant opens. Use the pop-up menu and the Length slider to specify how long and unguessable the password should be. The Quality graph shows you just how tough it is to crack this password.

(In the Type pop-up menu, you might wonder about FIPS-181. It stands for the Federal Information Processing Standards Publication 181, which sets forth the U.S. government's standard for password-generating algorithms.)

Fortunately, *you* won't have to remember most of them, thanks to the Keychain password-memorizing feature described next. The only password you have to memorize is your account password.

Tip: As you can tell from the wording of this item, macOS's firewall blocks only *incoming* connections, which covers most of the dangerous stuff. But if you'd also like your Mac to block *outgoing* internet connections, you can install a shareware firewall program like Little Snitch. It's available on this book's "Missing CD" page at *missingmanuals.com.*

- [**List of individual programs**]. If the firewall is on but you haven't turned on "Block all," then the Mac uses this list of individual programs and features to determine what's allowed to accept network connections.

 In this window (Figure 12-15, bottom), features of macOS itself are listed. They get added to this list automatically when you turn them on in System Preferences: File Sharing, Printer Sharing, and so on.

 Non-Apple programs can gain passage through your firewall, too. You can add one to the list manually by clicking the + below the list and choosing it by hand; or you can simply respond to the request box that pops up whenever a new program wants to accept incoming internet connections.

 Click Allow for each such request (unless, of course, you see a request for an app called SneakyPoisonVirus or something). As you do so, their names get added to the list of programs in this dialog box.

 For each program, you can use the pop-up menu beside its name to specify either "Allow incoming connections" or "Block incoming connections," depending on your level of paranoia.

Note: From time to time, some program will ask for permission to accept incoming messages from its mother ship online. If it's a program you trust, then click Allow.

- **Automatically allow signed software to receive incoming connections.** *Signed* software means programs Apple recognizes as coming from legitimate companies.

Note: OK, technically, a signed program is one whose authenticity is confirmed by a third party—a "certificate authority" company like Verisign or GoDaddy. A system of invisible *keys* (security numbers) confirms that the software did indeed come from the creators it claims it came from, no matter how many detours it took to reach you.

One more point: When you explicitly grant permission to a program, as described below, *you're* signing that program.

 If this checkbox is *not* turned on, then each time you run a new program for the first time, you'll be interrupted so that the Mac can ask if it's OK to permit internet connections. The "signed software" box cuts down on the interruptions, since well-known apps are assumed not to be viruses or spyware.

- **Enable stealth mode.** This is designed to slam shut the Mac's back door to the internet. See, hackers often use automated tools that send out "Are you there?"

Either way, a list of account holders now appears (Figure 12-14, top). The button next to each one, Enable User, might sound like you're about to lead someone into drug addiction, but it's actually your chance to specify who else can unlock the disk by logging in.

Note: If an account has *no* password, you have to add one first. Click the Set Password button that appears.

3. **For each person you want to be able to log into this Mac with her own password, click Enable User. Type in that person's password and click OK. When you're finished, click Continue.**

(Anyone to whom you *don't* give access can still use the Mac—but only after persuading an administrator to come over and type in his name and password.)

4. **Click Restart.**

When you log in again, the Mac begins the process of encrypting your entire hard drive. This process takes a long time (the FileVault pane in System Preferences

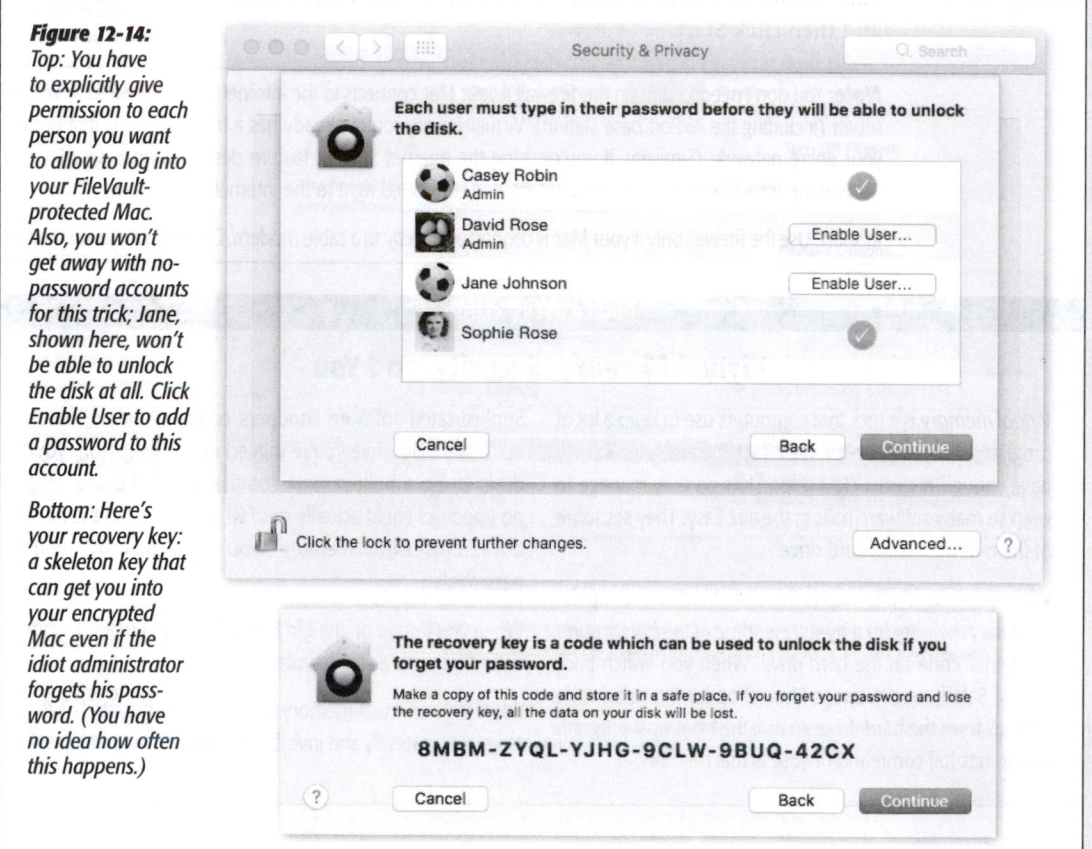

Figure 12-14:
Top: You have to explicitly give permission to each person you want to allow to log into your FileVault-protected Mac. Also, you won't get away with no-password accounts for this trick; Jane, shown here, won't be able to unlock the disk at all. Click Enable User to add a password to this account.

Bottom: Here's your recovery key: a skeleton key that can get you into your encrypted Mac even if the idiot administrator forgets his password. (You have no idea how often this happens.)

Each user must type in their password before they will be able to unlock the disk.

Casey Robin
Admin

David Rose
Admin
Enable User...

Jane Johnson
Enable User...

Sophie Rose

Cancel Back Continue

Click the lock to prevent further changes. Advanced... ?

The recovery key is a code which can be used to unlock the disk if you forget your password.
Make a copy of this code and store it in a safe place. If you forget your password and lose the recovery key, all the data on your disk will be lost.

8MBM-ZYQL-YJHG-9CLW-9BUQ-42CX

? Cancel Back Continue

Extended (Journaled, Encrypted) format. (And, yes, you have to *erase* the drive before you can encrypt it.)

- **You can turn FileVault off at any time.** Just revisit the FileVault pane in System Preferences. (It takes time to decrypt your drive, but you can keep right on working.)

To turn FileVault on, proceed like this:

1. **In System Preferences, click Security & Privacy, and then click FileVault. Click the 🔒, authenticate yourself, and then click Turn On FileVault.**

 Now, remember, FileVault encrypts all your files. If you forget your Mac account password—well, that would be bad.

 Yeah, yeah, the peons with Standard accounts forget *their* account passwords all the time. But with FileVault, a forgotten password would mean *the entire hard drive is locked forever.* So Apple gives you, the technically savvy administrator, a back door, for use in that situation.

 It offers to let you use your iCloud password (your Apple ID) as the back door. That's a much more reasonable one than the alternative, the *recovery key*.

 The recovery key is a long, complicated override password like UK84-LVT5-YFX9-XN3K-LT53-PL9N. It gives you another way to unlock the encrypted drive, even without knowing the account holder's password.

2. **Choose the backdoor method you prefer: "my iCloud account" or "recovery key." Click Continue.**

 If you chose the recovery key, the Mac now shows it to you: a long, complicated string of numbers and letters and hyphens. Write it down and store it in a place you'll never lose it! Then click Continue.

UP TO SPEED

Password Hell

In macOS, you have quite a few different passwords to keep straight. Each one, however, has a specific purpose:

Account password. You type this password in at the normal Login screen. You can't get into anyone else's account with it—only yours. Entering this password unlocks FileVault, too.

Administrator password. You're asked to enter this password whenever you try to install new software or modify certain system settings. If you're the only one who uses your computer (or you're the one who controls it), your administrator password *is* your account password. Otherwise, you're supposed to go find an administrator (the parent, teacher,

or guru who set up your account to begin with) and ask that person to type in his name and password once he's assessed what you're trying to do.

Recovery key. Think of this password as a master key. If anyone with FileVault forgets her account password, the administrator who knows the master password can unlock the account. This master password also lets an administrator change an account's password right at the Login screen, whether FileVault is turned on or not.

Root password. This password is rarely useful for anything other than Unix hackery; you know who you are.

As you know, the accounts system is designed to keep people out of one another's stuff. Ordinarily, for example, Chris isn't allowed to go rooting through Robin's email and files.

Until FileVault came along, though, there were ways to circumvent this protection system. A sneak or a show-off could start up the Mac in FireWire disk mode, for example, or even remove the hard drive and hook it up to a Linux machine or another Mac.

In each case, he'd then be able to run rampant through everybody's files, changing or trashing them with abandon. For people with sensitive or private files, the result was a security hole bigger than Kim Kardashian's bank account.

FileVault is an extra line of defense. When you turn on this feature, your Mac automatically *encrypts* (scrambles) *everything* on your startup hard drive—not just what's in your Home folder. Every time you create or save a new file, it, too, is insta-encrypted.

Note: FileVault uses something called XTS-AES 128 encryption. How secure is that? It would take a password-guessing computer *149 trillion years* before hitting pay dirt. Or, put another way, slightly longer than two *Transformers* movies.

This means unless someone knows (or can figure out) your password, FileVault renders your files unreadable for anyone but you and your computer's administrator—no matter what sneaky tricks they try to pull. (You can, if you like, authorize other account holders to get in, too.)

You won't notice much difference when FileVault is turned on. You log in as usual, clicking your name and typing your password. Only a slight pause as you log out indicates that macOS is doing some housekeeping on the encrypted files: freeing up some space and/or backing up your home directory with Time Machine.

Here are some things you should know about FileVault's protection:

- **It's useful only if you've logged out.** Once you're logged in, the entire drive is unlocked and accessible. If you want the protection, be sure to log out before you wander away from the Mac.

- **An administrator can access your files, too.** According to macOS's caste system, anyone with an Administrator account can theoretically have unhindered access to his peasants' files—even with FileVault on—if that administrator has the master password (the recovery key) described in the box on the next page.

- **FileVault relies on the Recovery HD partition.** You can read about this secret chunk of your hard drive on page 801. For now, the point is that if you've deliberately reformatted your hard drive in some nonstandard way, you may not be able to use FileVault.

- **FileVault can encrypt external drives, too—even flash drives.** The controls to do this, though, are in a different place—not in System Preferences at all. Instead, open Disk Utility (in your Utilities folder). Erase the external drive using Mac OS

Tip: As you may have noticed, a third option that used to be here—Anywhere—is gone; see the box below. But if there's one particular non-kosher app you want to run, you can override Gatekeeper just for that one app. To do so, right-click or two-finger click the program's icon; from the shortcut menu, choose Open. In the "Are you sure?" box, click Open.

Weird and roundabout? Yes. But that's the point: Apple doesn't want people easily overriding Gatekeeper—because then the Mac could lose its reputation for being virus-free.

Gatekeeper is a pretty powerful disincentive for the world's bad eggs; if millions of people leave Gatekeeper turned on, the bad guys might as well not even bother. Their apps will never be downloaded and can therefore never spread.

There are, however, some important limitations to note:

- **Gatekeeper doesn't uninstall programs you've already installed.** (Once you've run any program once, Gatekeeper never checks it again.)

- **Gatekeeper is intended to stop malware that you get by *downloading*.** It doesn't do anything about programs you've installed from, for example, a DVD or USB drive.

- **It doesn't stop Flash and Java programs.**

Overall, Gatekeeper is a pretty convincing barrier to a Windows-like nightmare scenario, where some virus breaks out into the wild and takes down hundreds of thousands of computers. If most people leave the factory setting selected—and they will—that outcome is virtually impossible.

FileVault

FileVault is one of macOS's most powerful security features. Understanding what it does, however, may take a little slogging.

POWER USERS' CLINIC

Bringing Back Gatekeeper's "Anywhere" Option

Before macOS Sierra came along in 2016, the Gatekeeper screen (Figure 12-13) offered a third option: Anywhere. It turned Gatekeeper off. You were free to download and install any programs you want, with no checking for their hygiene.

That's gone now. Too many people were turning on "Anywhere," thereby defeating the whole purpose of Gatekeeper, and winding up with viruses.

But if you're a confident Mac power user, then you can use Terminal (page 515) to restore the Anywhere option to the control panel.

Quit System Preferences. Open Terminal. Type this:

```
sudo spctl --master-disable
```

Press Enter, and then enter your account password.

Now, when you return to System Preferences, you'll see that the Anywhere option is back. Be careful out there.

If you ever want to get rid of it again, repeat the process, but use this Terminal command:

```
sudo spctl --master-enable
```

things, it's both *sandboxed* (blocked from accessing parts of the Mac that it doesn't need) and *digitally signed* (set up to notify that Mac if it's been altered in any way since it left the software company).

So what happens if you try to download a program that didn't come from the App Store? The Mac won't let you install it, period.

- **App Store and identified developers.** This option, the factory setting, lets you download and install both App Store programs and those from "identified developers." That means software companies that have registered with Apple and received, in turn, an encrypted code (a "certificate") that's embedded in their programs.

This certificate lets Apple track who created the app, and also digitally signs it, as described. Now, Apple may not know this software company, and Apple doesn't inspect its software. But if anybody reports that some program is actually a virus in disguise, Apple can instantly add that program to its blacklist—and prevent millions of other people from installing it. (MacOS updates its blacklist once a day.)

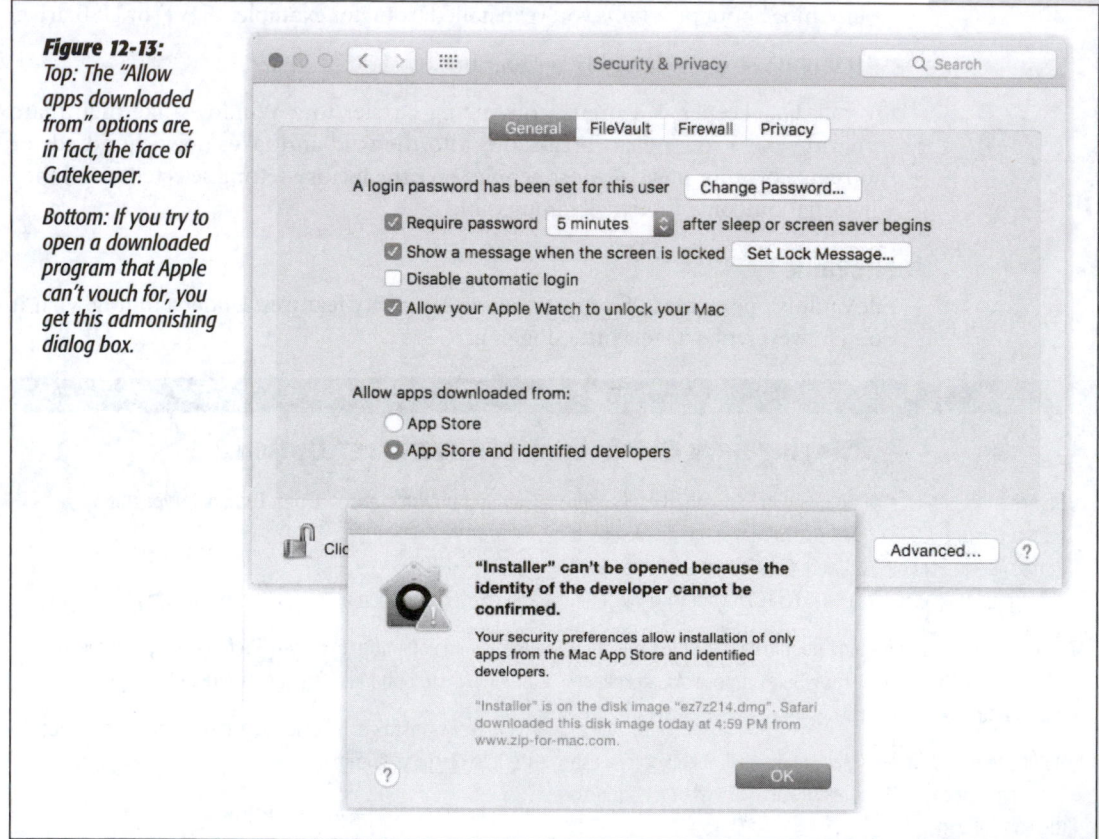

Figure 12-13:
Top: The "Allow apps downloaded from" options are, in fact, the face of Gatekeeper.

Bottom: If you try to open a downloaded program that Apple can't vouch for, you get this admonishing dialog box.

Note: Just in case you thought you understood this much, note that Apple's two-factor authentication system is not the same thing as its earlier system, which was called *two-step verification*. Not kidding. That earlier system was very similar but worked by sending the code as a text message.

2FA is better, because it can send the code not just as a text message, but also with an automated voice phone call or as a dialog box in your phone or Mac's operating system. 2FA also shows you a map that indicates *where* the login request is coming from.

Finally, instead of giving you a 14-character "Recovery Key" password to use as a last resort (in case you forget your password and lose your phone), Apple will call you on the phone number you've registered in advance to establish your identity and give you back your account. (It takes time, though—on purpose. Apple wants to frustrate the process if the perp is a hacker.)

To turn on this feature on your Mac, open System Preferences→iCloud. Click Account Details and then Security. At this point, you're offered the chance to set up 2FA. You're asked for your phone number, and you're sent one of the verification codes to type in.

Each time you use a new Apple device, or a new web browser, for the first time, you'll go through this setup process (just once). Each time, you're adding to your list of trusted devices. At any time, you can look over a list of them in System Preferences→iCloud→Account Details.

Note: All of this works pretty smoothly on gadgets and programs made by Apple. But other companies' programs—like non-Apple calendar and email programs—aren't part of it. They're locked out of your iCloud account just as though they were hackers.

Fortunately, you can go to *appleid.apple.com/account/manage* to generate an *app-specific* password. If you enter this 16-character password as your iCloud account password in your third-party calendar or email program, it will now be able to access your iCloud account as it did before.

Gatekeeper

This security feature sends Eastern European teenage hackers into therapy.

Nasty programs aren't very common on the Mac to begin with. But unless you turn Gatekeeper off, downloading a program that's secretly designed to damage your Mac is virtually impossible. Gatekeeper won't even let you *install* programs that haven't been proved to be safe (Figure 12-13).

To find Gatekeeper, you open System Preferences→Security & Privacy→General. At the bottom of this screen (Figure 12-13, top), you see two options. These two humble buttons are Gatekeeper.

Click the 🔒 and enter your password to unlock this panel. Here are your choices, under "Allow apps downloaded from":

- **App Store.** This is the safest option. *Every* program that Apple allows into its Mac App Store is safe. Each has been tested by Apple to make sure that, among other

the Mac until you hunt down the account holders whose stuff is still open in the background so they can log out.

Tip: You can avoid this awkward situation in either of two ways: (1) Trust one another completely, or (2) Save all your documents before you let anyone else cut in and send your account to the background.

- **Remember the Shared folder** (in the Users folder on the hard drive)? It's still the wormhole connecting all accounts. If you want to share a file with another account holder, put it there.

- **Your account isn't anesthetized completely** when it's switched into the background. In fact, it keeps on doing whatever you set it to doing. If you were downloading some big file, for example, it keeps right on downloading when the next guy logs in.

macOS and Security

The Mac has a spectacular reputation for stability and security. You hardly ever hear of a Mac virus. There's also no Windows-esque plague of spyware (downloaded programs that do something sneaky behind your back).

Here are a few of macOS's big-ticket defenses.

Two-Factor Authentication

These days, having a complicated password isn't enough to protect you from the bad guys. Even if your password is é$*@çg45e$+!!!>?!+r6ü, someone can still steal it. (There are all kinds of ways. An inside job. An FBI demand. Poor security on a company's servers. Social engineering, where someone calls up pretending to be you and saying, "I forgot my password.")

Impressively enough, security experts have come up with a way to keep baddies out of your account even if they've *got* your password.

Here's how it works: The first time you try to access your account using a new gadget (a new laptop or phone, for example) or a new web browser, the company instantly sends a special, one-time code to a phone, tablet, or computer it knows you own. You need that code to get into your account.

If some Russian hacker does get your password, you won't care! He still can't get into your account, because the code will be sent to *your* machine, not his.

This ingenious system has earned the awful name *two-factor authentication.* (Let's call it 2FA to save paper.)

Now, 2FA is available for your iCloud account. If you turn it on, the odds of someone else being able to access your account (email, calendar, messages, movies, music, backups, photos) drop close to zero. They'd have to have your password *and* steal your phone or laptop *and* know your account password on that device.

and turn on the "Show fast user switching menu as" checkbox. And while you're at it: You can change what this menu looks like by using the "Show fast user switching menu as" pop-up menu.)

Next time you need a fellow account holder to relinquish control so you can duck in to do a little work, just choose your name from the Accounts menu. Type your password, if one is required, and feel guiltless about the interruption.

Tip: If your Mac has a Touch Bar (page 233), and Person B has registered a fingerprint, then using fast user switching is even easier. All Person B has to do is click the Touch ID sensor (power button) at the right end of the Touch Bar. Boom: Accounts switched!

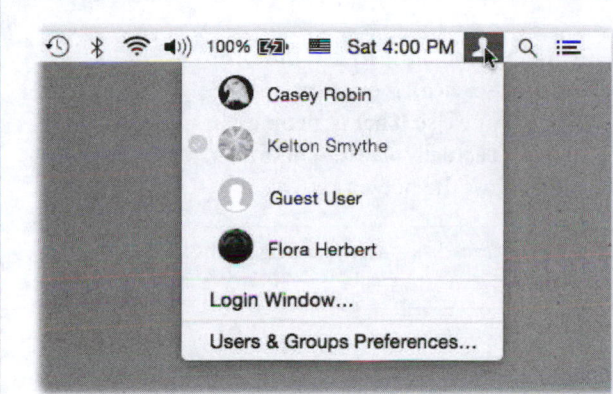

Figure 12-12:
In the Fast User Switching menu, the ● and dimmed name show who's logged in right now.

And now, the finer points of fast user switching:

- **To exit an open account,** choose →Log Out as usual. Or just choose Login Window from the Accounts menu. It ensures that you can get to your own account no matter whose is running at the moment.

- **Weirdly enough, a bunch of account holders** can be using the same program simultaneously in their own parallel universes.

- **You can't make changes to accounts** (in System Preferences) that are still logged in. You can't turn off fast user switching or turn on FileVault while other people are logged in, either.

- **If you try to shut the Mac down or restart it** while other people are logged in, a dialog box tells you "There are currently logged in users who may lose unsaved changes if you shut down this computer." And you're asked to type in an administrator's name and password to establish that you know what you're doing.

 Here's a moral dilemma for the modern age: If you proceed by typing the password and clicking Shut Down, you shut down all accounts that were open in the background *and* any open documents. If you click Cancel, you can't shut down

you try to open anybody else's Home folder, you'll see a tiny red ⊖ icon superimposed on almost every folder inside, telling you "Look, but don't touch."

Fortunately, there are a couple of wormholes between accounts (Figure 12-11):

• **The Shared folder.** Sitting in the Users folder is one folder that doesn't correspond to any particular person: Shared. Everybody can freely access this folder, inserting and extracting files without restriction. It's Central Park, the farmers market, and the grocery-store bulletin board.

• **The Public folder.** In your Home folder, there's a folder called Public. Anything you copy into it becomes available for inspection or copying (but not changing or deleting) by any other account holder, whether she logs into your Mac or signs in from across the network.

• **The Drop Box.** And *inside* your Public folder is another cool little folder: the Drop Box (not to be confused with the free online Dropbox service). It exists to let *other* people give files to *you*, discreetly and invisibly to anyone else. That is, people can drop files and folders into your Drop Box, but they can't actually *open* it. This folder, too, is available both locally (in person) and from across the network.

Note: You can also share files in similar ways with people on *different* machines; start your journey on page 571.

Fast User Switching

The account system described so far in this chapter has its charms. It keeps everyone's stuff separate, it keeps your files safe, and it lets you have the desktop picture of your choice.

Unfortunately, it can go from handy to hassle in one split second. That's when you're logged in, and somebody else wants to duck in just for a second—to check email or a calendar, for example. What are you supposed to do—log out completely, closing all your documents and quitting all your programs, just so the interloper can look something up? Then afterward, you'd have to log back in and fire up all your stuff again, praying that your inspirational muse hadn't fled in the meantime.

Fortunately, fast user switching lets Person B log in and use the Mac for a little while. All *your* stuff, Person A, simply slides into the background, still open the way you had it; see Figure 12-12.

When Person B is finished working, you can bring your whole work environment back to the screen without having to reopen anything. All your windows and programs are still open, just as you left them.

Do you see your own account name, or a human silhouette, in the upper-right corner of the screen (Figure 12-12)? That's a button that lists all account holders.

(If you don't see this Fast User Switching menu, open the Users & Groups panel of System Preferences; click the 🔒, if necessary, to unlock the panel. Click Login Options

Sharing Across Accounts

It's all fine to say that every account is segregated from all *other* accounts. It's nice to know your stuff is safe from the prying eyes of your co-workers or family. But what about collaboration? What if you *want* to give some files or folders to another account holder?

You can't just open up someone else's Home folder and drop it in there. Yes, every account holder has a Home folder (all in the Users folder on your hard drive). But if

Figure 12-11:

Top: In other people's Home folders, the Public folder is available for your inspection. It contains stuff other people have "published" for the benefit of their co-workers.

Middle: In the Public folder is the Drop Box, which serves the opposite purpose. It lets anyone else who uses this Mac hand in files to you; they, however, can't see what's in the box.

Bottom: Inside the Users folder (to get there from a Home folder, press ⌘-▲) is the Shared folder, a wormhole connecting all accounts. Everybody has full access to everything inside.

If you click the Advanced button (at the bottom of the Security & Privacy pane of System Preferences), you get these bonus tweaks:

- **Log out after [60] minutes of inactivity.** You can make the Mac sign out of your account completely if it figures out that you've wandered off (and it's been, say, 15 minutes since the last time you touched the mouse or keyboard). Anyone who shows up at your Mac will find only the standard Login screen.

- **Require an administrator password to access system-wide preferences.** Ordinarily, certain System Preferences changes require an administrator's approval—namely, the ones that affect the entire computer and everyone who uses it, like Date & Time, Users & Groups, Network, Time Machine, and Security & Privacy. If you're *not* an administrator, you can't make changes to these panels until an administrator has typed in her name and password to approve your change.

 However, once Mr. Teacher or Ms. Parent has unlocked *one* of those secure preference settings, they're *all* unlocked. Once the administrator leaves your desk, you can go right on making changes to the *other* important panels (Network *and* Time Machine *and* Security & Privacy) without the administrator's knowledge.

 Unless this "Require an administrator password" box is turned on, that is. In that case, an Administrative account holder has to enter her name and password to approve *each* of those System Preferences panes individually.

GEM IN THE ROUGH

Automatic Login with the Apple Watch

If you're one of the few, the proud, who own an Apple Watch, you are in for a spectacular treat. You never have to type in a password to unlock your Mac again!

The watch on your wrist can act as a wireless master key. (For security, it has a very short range—about 5 feet.)

The requirements: The watch must be running watchOS 3 or later. The Mac has to be a 2013 or later model, running macOS Sierra or later. Watch and Mac must be associated with the same iCloud account. Watch and Mac must both be passcode-protected.

And—here's the eyebrow-raising part—you must have *two-factor authentication* turned on. That's Apple's new security

system for logging into things, and it's described in detail starting on page 551.

All that set? OK. On the Mac, open System Preferences→Security & Privacy→General. Turn on "Allow your Apple Watch to unlock your Mac." Enter your account password to prove that you're you.

And that is it! From now on, just waking your Mac—raising the laptop lid, for example—logs you in, instantly and securely. In place of the usual password box on your Mac's screen, it says "Unlocking with Apple Watch." And your watch says "Mac Unlocked." And you're in.

Maybe the Apple Watch has a killer feature at long last.

Logout Options

When you choose →Log Out and confirm your intention to log out, the Login screen appears, ready for its next victim.

But sometimes people forget. You might wander off to the bathroom for a minute, but run into a colleague there who breathlessly begins describing last night's date and proposes finishing the conversation over pizza. The next thing you know, you've left your Mac unattended but logged in, with all your life's secrets accessible to anyone who walks by your desk.

You can tighten up that security hole, and many others, using the options in the Security & Privacy→General panel of System Preferences:

- **Require password [immediately] after sleep or screen saver begins.** This option gives you a password-protected screen saver that locks your Mac when you wander away. Now, whenever somebody tries to wake your Mac after the screen saver has appeared (or when the Mac has simply gone to sleep according to your settings in the Energy Saver panel of System Preferences), the "Enter your password" dialog box appears. No password? No access.

 The pop-up menu here (which starts out saying "immediately") is a handy feature. Without it, the person most inconvenienced by the password requirement would be *you*, not the snitch from Accounting; even if you just stepped away to the bathroom or the coffee machine, you'd have to unlock the screen saver with your password. It would get old fast.

 Instead, the password requirement can kick in after you've been away for a more serious amount of time—5 minutes, 15 minutes, an hour, whatever. You can still put the Mac to sleep, or you can still set up your screen saver to kick in sooner than that. But until that time period has passed, you'll be able to wake the machine without having to log in.

- **Show a message when the screen is locked.** Whatever you type into this box will appear on the Login screen (where you click your name in the list) or the screen saver. It could be, "Getting coffee…" or your name and cellphone number, or anything you like.

- **Disable automatic login.** This is just a duplicate of the "Automatic login" on/off switch described on page 541. Apple figured that this feature really deserved *some* presence on a control panel called Security & Privacy.

- **Allow your Apple Watch to unlock your Mac.** You don't need a password to unlock your Mac anymore—if you're wearing an Apple Watch. It acts as a wireless master key that logs you in automatically, as described in the box on the facing page. This master switch for that glorious feature appears only if you've turned on two-factor authentication (page 551).

Once you're in, the world of the Mac looks just the way you left it (or the way an administrator set it up for you). Everything in your Home folder, all your email and bookmarks, your desktop picture and Dock settings—all of it unique to you.

Unless you're an administrator, you're not allowed to install any new programs (or, indeed, to put anything at all) into the Applications folder. That folder, after all, is a central software repository for *everybody* who uses the Mac, and the Mac forbids everyday account holders from moving or changing all such universally shared folders.

Logging Out

When you're finished using the Mac, choose →Log Out (or press Shift-⌘-Q). A confirmation message appears; if you click Cancel or press Esc, you return to whatever you were doing. If you click Log Out or press Return, you return to the screen shown in Figure 12-1, and the sign-in cycle begins again.

Tip: If you press Option as you choose →Log Out (or as you press Shift-⌘-Q), then the confirmation box doesn't appear.

FREQUENTLY ASKED QUESTION

The Forgotten-Password Survival Guide

Help—I forgot my password! And I never told it to anybody!

No problem. Your administrator can simply open up System Preferences, click Users & Groups, click your account name, and then click Reset Password to reestablish the password.

But you don't understand. I am the administrator! And I'm the only account!

Lucky for you, Apple has provided not one, not two, but three safety nets. None of them work, however, unless you, the administrator, turned them on in advance.

First: On your third attempt to type your password, the Mac shows you your password hint (if you have one, and if the administrator left the Hint option turned on).

Second: If the administrator has turned on the "Allow user to reset password using Apple ID" in System Preferences→ Users & Groups, then you can click the ? button right there in the Password box when you're logging in. A tiny message appears, letting you know that "If you forgot your password, you can reset it using your Apple ID."

To proceed, click the ⊙ button to bring up the Reset Password dialog box. Enter your Apple ID and password, and then click Reset Password. A message appears to let you know changing your account password will also create a new Keychain (page 562). (The old one is still around, ready to be unlocked if you remember the old password at some point.) Click OK. Now enter a new password (twice) and a password hint, and then click Reset Password.

You've just reset your account password. Click Continue Log In to finish logging in with your new, improved, not-forgotten password.

Third: If the administrator has turned on FileVault, described starting on page 554, then you can use its recovery key to log in, in a pinch. It's the master password: a last-ditch, emergency-backup password.

If you have your recovery key, read on. (If not, and you opted to store it with Apple, call Apple tech support; they'll give it to you. If not, and you didn't store it with Apple, you're completely out of luck. Your hard drive is encrypted, and you can't do anything but erase it and kiss your files goodbye.)

Anyway, restart the Mac. On the Login screen, click your name; then click the ? button. If the hint appears and it helps you out, great. If not, click "Reset it using your Recovery Key," type in your recovery key, and then praise the Apple gods that this final safety net actually worked.

Identifying Yourself

When you first turn on the Mac—or when the person who last used this computer chooses →Log Out—the Login screen shown in Figure 12-1 appears. At this point, you can proceed in any of several ways:

- **Restart.** Click if you need to restart the Mac for some reason. (The Restart and Shut Down buttons don't appear here if the administrator has chosen to hide them as a security precaution.)

- **Shut Down.** Click if you're done for the day, or if sudden panic about the complexity of accounts makes you want to run away. The computer turns off.

- **Log In.** To sign in, click your account name in the list. If you're a keyboard speed freak, you can just type the first letter or two—or press the up or down arrow keys—until your name is highlighted. Then press Return.

Either way, the password box appears now, if a password is required. (Of course, if you're lucky enough to have a Touch ID sensor on your laptop, and you've taught it to recognize your fingerprint [page 369], then no password box appears. You can just touch your finger to the power button to log in, as shown in Figure 12-10.)

Figure 12-10:
Touch ID—the fingerprint reader on Macs with Touch Bars—really is the ultimate. You can wake your Mac and prove your authenticity simultaneously, with a single touch of the power button.

If you accidentally clicked the wrong person's name on the first screen, you can click Back. Otherwise, type your password, and then press Return (or click Log In).

You can try as many times as you want to type the password. With each incorrect guess, the entire password box shudders violently from side to side, as though shaking its head no. (If you see a ⇧ icon in the password box, guess what? You've got your Caps Lock key on, and the Mac thinks you're typing an all-capitals password.)

If you try unsuccessfully three times, your hint appears—if you've set one up. And if even that safety net fails, you can use your Apple ID as the key to resetting your password. See the box on the facing page.

Open System Preferences, click Users & Groups, click the 🔒, enter an admin password to prove your worthiness, and then click the Login Options button (Figure 12-9). Here are some of the ways you can shape the login experience for greater security (or greater convenience):

- **Automatic login.** This option eliminates the need to sign in at all. It's a time-saving, hassle-free arrangement if only one person uses the Mac, or uses it most of the time.

 When you choose an account holder's name from this pop-up menu, you're prompted for his password. Type it and click OK.

 From now on, the screen shown in Figure 12-1 won't appear *at all* at startup time. After turning on the machine, you, the specified account holder, zoom straight to your desktop.

 Of course, everybody else must still enter their names and passwords. (But how can they, since the Mac rushes right into the Automatic person's account at startup time? Answer: The Automatic thing happens only at startup. The usual Login screen appears whenever the current account holder logs out—by choosing 🍎→Log Out, for example.)

- **Display login window as.** Under normal circumstances, the Login screen presents a list of account holders when you power up the Mac, as shown in Figure 12-1. That's the "List of users" option in action.

 If you're especially worried about security, however, you might not want even that list to appear. If you turn on "Name and password" (Figure 12-9), then each

Figure 12-9:
These options make it easier or harder for people to sign in, offering various degrees of security. By the way: Turning on "Name and password" also lets you sign in as >console, an advanced geeky troubleshooting technique. It's also one way to sign in with the root account, if you're Unixy enough to know what that is.

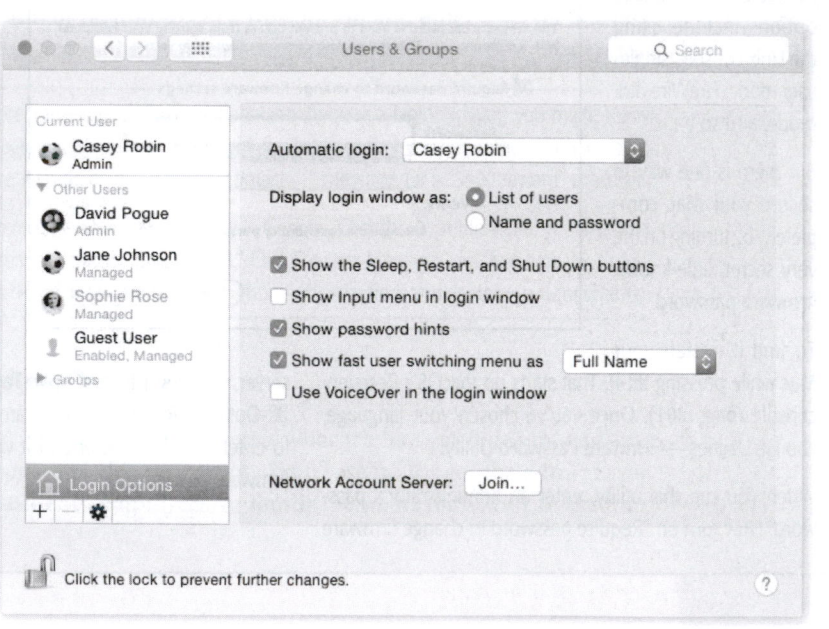

Preferences—but it leaves the *Home folder* right where it is. Use this option if you don't intend to dispose of the dearly departed's belongings right here and now.

- **Delete the home folder.** This button offers the "Hasta la vista, baby" approach. The account and all its files and settings are vaporized forever, on the spot. (And the "Erase home folder securely" option even records gibberish over the spot where that Home folder was, such that its contents couldn't be recovered even by the NSA.)

Note: If you delete a Sharing Only account, you're not offered the chance to preserve the Home folder contents—because a Sharing Only account doesn't *have* a Home folder.

Setting Up the Login Process

Once you've set up more than one account, the screen shown in Figure 12-1 appears whenever you turn on the Mac, whenever you choose →Log Out, or whenever the Mac logs you out automatically. But a few extra controls let you, an administrator, set up either more or less security at the Login screen—or, put another way, build in less or more convenience.

POWER USERS' CLINIC

The Secret Account Options

Anyone who knows macOS very well might object to one sentence in this section: "If you're an administrator, you can change your own account in any way you like."

Because there's one aspect of an account that even an admin can't change: the account's *short name* (the account name, as opposed to the Full Name). Once that's created, it's yours forever, or at least until you delete the account.

Or at least that's what Apple *wants* you to think. There is, however, a secret way to pick a different short name. You can't easily *change* the one you created originally, but you can create *another* one—shorter, more memorable—that *also* works when you're logging in or authenticating yourself.

To find it, right-click or two-finger click the account's name in the list at the left side of the Users & Groups panel in System Preferences. From the shortcut menu, choose Advanced Options. The strange and wonderful Advanced Options panel appears. Right there in the middle is an "Account name" box, but don't bother editing that; it won't work.

Instead, click the + button below the Aliases list. You're offered the chance to type in an *alternative* account name. Do it and then click OK. You can create as many of these aliases as you like.

When it's all over, click OK. The next time you log into your Mac, you'll be able to use your new, improved short name instead of the old one.

And rejoice that you lived to see the day.

When that time comes, click the account name in the Users & Groups pane of System Preferences and then click the minus-sign button beneath the list. MacOS asks what to do with all the dearly departed's files and settings (Figure 12-8):

- **Save the home folder in a disk image.** This option represents the "I'll be back" approach. MacOS preserves the deleted account holder's folders on the Mac, in a tidy digital envelope that won't clutter your hard drive and can be reopened in case of emergency.

 In the Users→Deleted Users folder, you find a disk image file (.dmg). If you double-click it, a new, virtual disk icon named for the deleted account appears on your desktop. You can open folders and root through the stuff in this "disk," just as if it were a living, working Home folder.

 If fate ever brings that person back into your life, you can use this disk image to reinstate the deleted account. Start by creating a brand-new account. Then copy the contents of the folders in the mounted disk image (Documents, Pictures, Desktop, and so on) into the corresponding folders of the new Home folder.

- **Don't change the home folder.** This time, macOS removes the *account*, in that it no longer appears in the Login list or in the Users & Groups panel of System

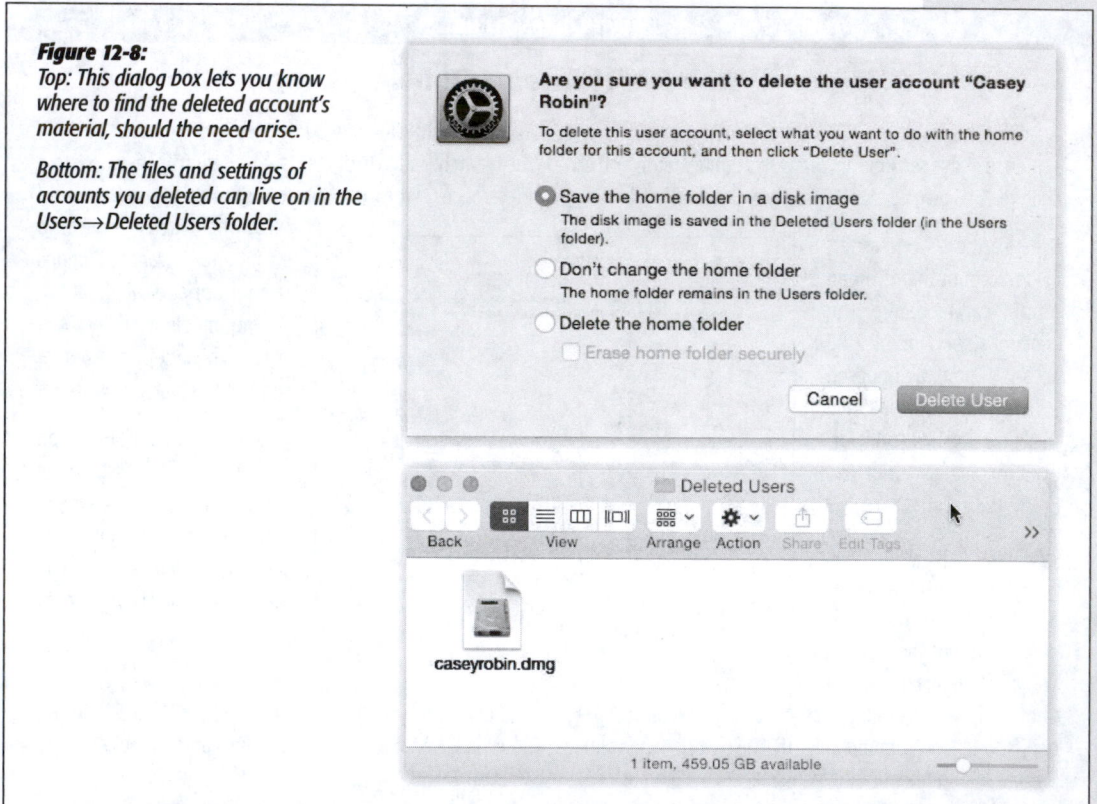

Figure 12-8:
Top: This dialog box lets you know where to find the deleted account's material, should the need arise.

Bottom: The files and settings of accounts you deleted can live on in the Users→Deleted Users folder.

- **Shared.** This is the same Shared folder described on page 549. It's provided so you and other account holders can exchange material. However, you can't open any of the folders here, only the documents.

- **Trash.** The Trash is here, but selecting or dragging any icon is against the rules, so you're left with no obvious means of putting anything into it.

The only program with its own icon on the Dock is the Finder.

To keep things extra simple, macOS permits only one window at a time to be open. It's easy to open icons, too, because *one* click opens them, not two.

The File menu is stunted, offering only a Close Window command. The Finder menu gives you only two options: About Finder and Run Full Finder. (The latter command prompts you for an administrator's name and password, and then turns back into the regular Finder—a handy escape hatch. To return to Simple Finder, just choose Finder→Return to Simple Finder.)

The menu is *really* bare-bones: You can Log Out, Force Quit, or go to Sleep. That's it. And there's no trace of Spotlight.

Otherwise, you can essentially forget everything else you've read in this book. You can't create folders, move icons, or do much of anything beyond clicking the icons your benevolent administrator has provided. It's as though macOS moved away and left you the empty house.

Although the Simple *Finder* is simple, any program (at least, any the administrator has permitted) can run from Simple Finder. A program running inside the Simple Finder still has all its features and complexities—only the Finder itself has been whittled down to its essence.

In other words, Simple Finder is great for streamlining the Finder, but novices won't get far in combating their techno-fear until the world presents us with Simple iMovie, Simple Mail, and Simple Microsoft Word. Still, it's better than nothing.

Editing Accounts

If you're an administrator, you can change your own account in any way you like.

If you have any other kind of account, though, you can't change anything but your picture, password, Apple ID, and login items. If you want to make any other changes, you have to ask an admin to log in, make the changes you want made to your account, and then turn the computer back over to you.

Deleting Accounts

Hey, it happens: Somebody graduates, somebody gets fired, somebody dumps you. Sooner or later, you may need to delete an account from your Mac.

- **Prevent the Dock from being modified.** Just what it says.

- **Use Simple Finder.** Use this option only if you're *really* concerned about somebody's ability to survive the Mac—or the Mac's ability to survive that somebody. Read on.

Simple Finder

Suppose you've been given a Simple Finder account. When you log in, you discover the barren world shown in Figure 12-7. There are only three menus (, Finder, and File), a single onscreen window, no hard drive icon, and a bare-bones Dock. The only folders you can see are in the Dock. They include these:

- **My Applications.** This folder holds aliases of the applications that the administrator approved on the Apps tab shown in Figure 12-5. They appear on a strange, fixed icon view called "pages." List and column views don't exist. As a Simple person, you can't move, rename, delete, sort, or change the display of these icons—you can merely click them. If you have too many to fit on one screen, you get numbered page buttons beneath them, which you can click to move from one set to another.

- **Documents.** Behind the scenes, this is your Home→Documents folder. Of course, as a Simple Finder kind of soul, you don't *have* a visible Home folder. All your stuff goes in here.

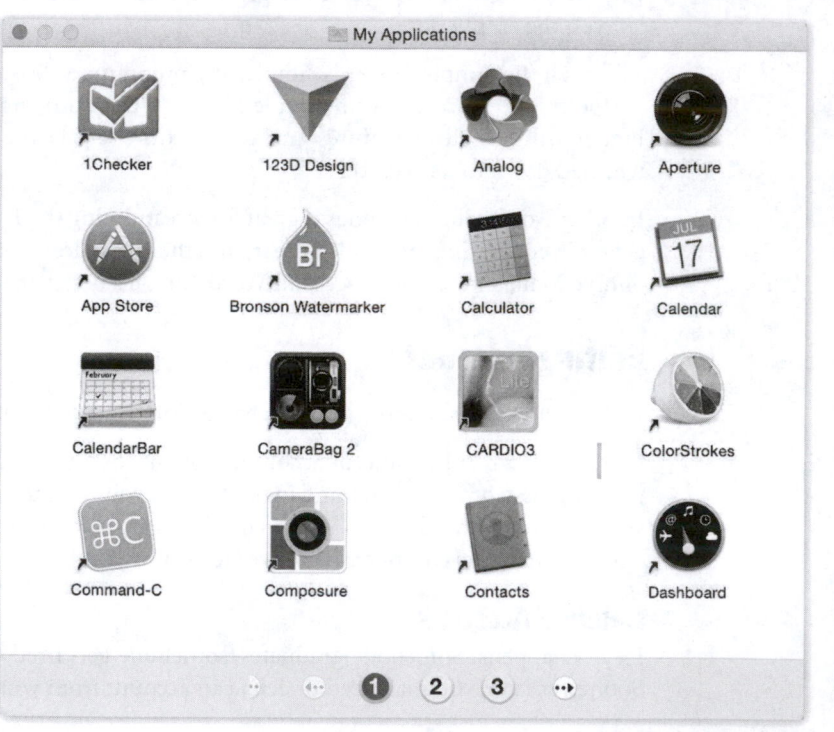

Figure 12-7:
The Simple Finder doesn't feel like home–unless you've got one of those spartan, space-age, Dr. Evil–style pads. But it can be just the ticket for Mac novices, with few options and a basic one-click interface. Every program in the My Applications folder is actually an alias to the real program, which is safely ensconced in the off-limits Applications folder.

Privacy Tab

The Manage Privacy button takes you directly to the System Preferences panel described on page 565. It's where your kid has control over which apps access Contacts, Calendar, and so on.

Below that, the "Allow changes to" checkboxes exist to protect *your* privacy. Turning off a checkbox means that no app your kid uses can make any changes to the apps listed here.

Other Tab

This tab offers a few miscellaneous options, including the following:

- **Turn Off Dictation.** Those kids can't turn on the Dictation feature. They can talk only to you and other humans.

- **Disable editing of printers and scanners.** When this checkbox is on, your underlings aren't allowed to change your Mac's printer or scanner settings. You wouldn't want them deleting or installing printers, would you?

- **Block CD and DVD burning in the Finder.** In a school lab, for example, you might want to turn off the ability to burn discs (to block software piracy).

- **Restrict explicit language in Dictionary.** MacOS comes with a complete electronic copy of the *New Oxford American Dictionary.* And "complete," in this case, means "It even has swear words."

Turning on this option is like having an Insta-Censor™. It hides the naughty words from the dictionary whenever your young account holder is logged in.

POWER USERS' CLINIC

Parental Remote Controls

It occurred to somebody at Apple that the Parental Controls feature might be especially useful in a classroom. That person further realized that it'd be very cool if you could adjust the settings for Macs A, B, C, and D while *seated* at Mac E. That is, the teacher might prefer not to have to scurry from desk to desk to make changes.

And that's why you can operate Parental Controls from another Mac on the same network.

Phase 1: While seated at the first kid's Mac, open System Preferences, open Parental Controls, click the 🔒, and then enter your password.

Now click the name of the account you want to manage remotely. Then, from the ✲ menu below the list of accounts, choose Allow Remote Setup. Close System Preferences.

Repeat for each account on each Mac that you'll want to manage from afar.

Phase 2: Go back to your teacher's desk. On your own Mac, choose Go→Connect to Server. In the resulting dialog box, click Browse. Now you get a list of the other Macs on the network. Click one and enter an administrator's name and password for that Mac.

Now open System Preferences, click Parental Controls, click the 🔒, and then enter your password again. This time, you'll see a section in the Users & Groups list called Other Computers. Click the account name on the kid's Mac whose settings you want to change. Enter the administrator name and password of the remote computer one more time, and off you go!

Time Tab

Clever folks, those Apple programmers. They must have kids of their own.

They realize that some parents care about *how many* hours their kids spend in front of the Mac, and that some also care about *which* hours (Figure 12-6):

- **How much time.** In the "Weekday time limits" and "Weekend time limits" sections, turn on "Limit weekday use to" or "Limit weekend use to" and then adjust the sliders.

- **Which hours.** In the "Bedtime" section, turn on the checkbox for either "School nights" or "Weekend," and then set the hours of the day (or, rather, night) when the Mac is unavailable to your young account holder.

In other words, this feature may have the smallest pages-to-significance ratio in this entire book. Doesn't take long to explain, but it could bring the parents of Mac addicts a lot of peace.

Tip: When time limits have been applied, your little rug rats can now check to see how much time they have left to goof off on the Mac before your digital iron fist slams down. When they click the menu-bar clock (where it now says the current time), a menu appears, complete with a readout that says, for example, "Parental Controls: Time Remaining 1:29." Good parenting comes in many forms.

Figure 12-6:
If this account holder tries to log in outside the time limits you specify here, she'll encounter only a box that says "Computer time limits expired." She'll be offered a pop-up menu that grants her additional time, from 15 minutes to "Rest of the day"—but it requires your parental consent (actually, your parental password) to activate.

Similarly, as her time on the Mac winds down, she'll get a "Your computer time is almost up" message. Once again, you, the all-knowing administrator, can grant her more time.

When your child fires up Messages or Mail, she'll discover that her buddies list is empty except for the people you've identified.

Handling the teenage hissy fit is your problem.

- **Limit Applications on this Mac.** When you turn this on, the list shown at bottom in Figure 12-5 springs to life. It's all your programs (Other Apps) and all the apps in your Utilities folder. Only checked items will show up in the account holder's Applications folder. (If you don't see a program listed, then use the search box, or drag its icon from the Finder into the window.)

Web Tab

This feature is designed to limit which websites your kid is allowed to visit.

Frankly, trying to block the racy stuff from the web is something of a hopeless task; if your kid doesn't manage to get around the blockade by simply using a different browser, then he'll just see the dirty pictures at another kid's house. But at least you can enjoy the illusion of taking a stand, using approaches with three degrees of severity:

- **Allow unrestricted access to websites.** No filtering. Anything goes.

- **Try to limit access to adult websites automatically.** The words "try to" are Apple's way of admitting that no filter is foolproof.

 In any case, macOS analyzes what's on a web page your child tries to call up and filters out websites with naughty material. These sites won't appear in Safari while this account holder is logged in. By clicking Customize and then editing the "Always allow" and "Never allow" lists, you can override its decisions on a site-at-a-time basis.

- **Allow access to only these websites.** This is the most restrictive approach of all: It's a *whitelist,* a list of the *only* websites your youngster is allowed to visit. It's filled with kid-friendly sites like Disney and Discovery Kids, but of course you can edit the list by clicking the + and − buttons below the list.

Stores Tab

Concerned that your little angel might run up bank-busting bills buying stuff from Apple's online music, movie, app, and book stores? You wouldn't be the first one.

That's why Apple gives you checkboxes that let you block access to the iTunes Store (music, movies, TV shows, apps) and the Apple Books Store. (There's a separate checkbox for iTunes U, a category of free educational videos. Apple reasons that *that* corner of the iTunes Store might be OK.)

Here, too, are options that shield your youngster's eyes and ears from music, movies, books, and apps that contain sexy stuff or bad words. You can limit movie watching to those with, for example, a PG rating at worst. The "Apps to" pop-up menu even lets you specify an appropriate age group for permitted apps. If you choose "up to 9+," for example, your well-parented offspring will be allowed to use all App Store programs that have been rated for use by anyone who's 9 or older.

Turn the checkbox on and then click Manage. In the next dialog box, you can build a list of email addresses corresponding to the people you feel comfortable letting your kid exchange emails with. Click the + button below the list, type a few letters of the person's name, click the correct result (drawn from your Contacts app). Lather, rinse, repeat.

The best part is at the top—the "Send requests to" option. Turn it on and fill in your own email address.

Now, when your young ward tries to send a message to someone who's *not* on the approved list, she gets a message: "You do not have permission to send messages to this email address." If she clicks Ask Permission, then *your* email address receives a permission-request message.

If you're convinced that the would-be correspondent is not, in fact, a stalker, you can grant permission by clicking Always Allow. Your youngster gets the good news the next time she visits her Drafts folder, where the message has been awaiting word from you, the Good Parent.

Note: This feature works only in Mail. It doesn't involve *other* email programs, like Microsoft Outlook. If you're worried about your efforts being bypassed, block access to those programs using the Limit Applications feature described on the next page.

GEM IN THE ROUGH

Logs

At the bottom of the Parental Controls panel, you'll find a button called Logs. That, my friends, is Big Brother Central.

It gives you a complete rundown of what your kids have been up to. Its two tabs—denoting Applications used and websites visited—are extremely detailed.

For example, in Apps, you can see exactly which programs your kids tried to use when, and how much time they spent in each one.

Also on the Applications tab, if you see an app that you really think should be off-limits, click its name and then click Restrict. You've just nipped that one in the bud.

On the Web tab, you can see how many times the little squirt has visited each site. You can have some good sleuthing fun by clicking the pie wedges in turn to find out which website corresponds to each one—a handy way of figuring out which sites are consuming most of your child's time.

Expand one of the flippy triangles to see which pages within a site the little tyke has visited.

And if you're wondering what a certain web page *is,* just click it and then click Open.

It's spying, sure, but it's for the good of the child. (Right?)

the System category—are equally useful for people of *any* age who feel overwhelmed by the Mac, are inclined to mess it up by not knowing what they're doing, or may be tempted to mess it up deliberately.

Note: If you apply any of these options to a Standard account, then the account type listed on the Users & Groups panel changes from "Standard" to "Managed."

To begin, click Open Parental Controls at the bottom of the Users & Groups pane. Click Enable Parental Controls, if necessary. After you enter your administrator-account password, you see the screen shown in Figure 12-5.

Figure 12-5:
In the Parental Controls window, you can control the capabilities of any account holder on your Mac. If you turn on "Limit Applications on this Mac," then the lower half of the window lets you choose applications (from the Mac App Store and others), and even Dashboard widgets, by turning on the boxes next to their names. (Expand the flippy triangles if necessary.) Those are the only programs the account holder will be allowed to use. The search box helps you find programs without knowing their categories.

Apps Tab

On this tab (Figure 12-5), you can limit what your Managed-account flock is allowed to do on the Mac—including which programs they can use. (Limiting what people can do to your Mac is a handy feature under any shared-computer circumstance. But if there's one word tattooed on its forehead, it would be "Classrooms!")

For example, here are some of the options on the Parental Controls screen:

- **Allow use of camera.** With this control, you can prevent your kids from filling up your hard drive with photos of their body parts.

- **Limit Mail to allowed contacts.** Here you can control your kid's access to correspondents by email.

items, so their windows will be open and waiting when you arrive at the computer each morning.

Tip: Here's a much quicker way to add something to the Login Items list: Right-click or two-finger click its Dock icon and choose Open at Login from the shortcut menu.

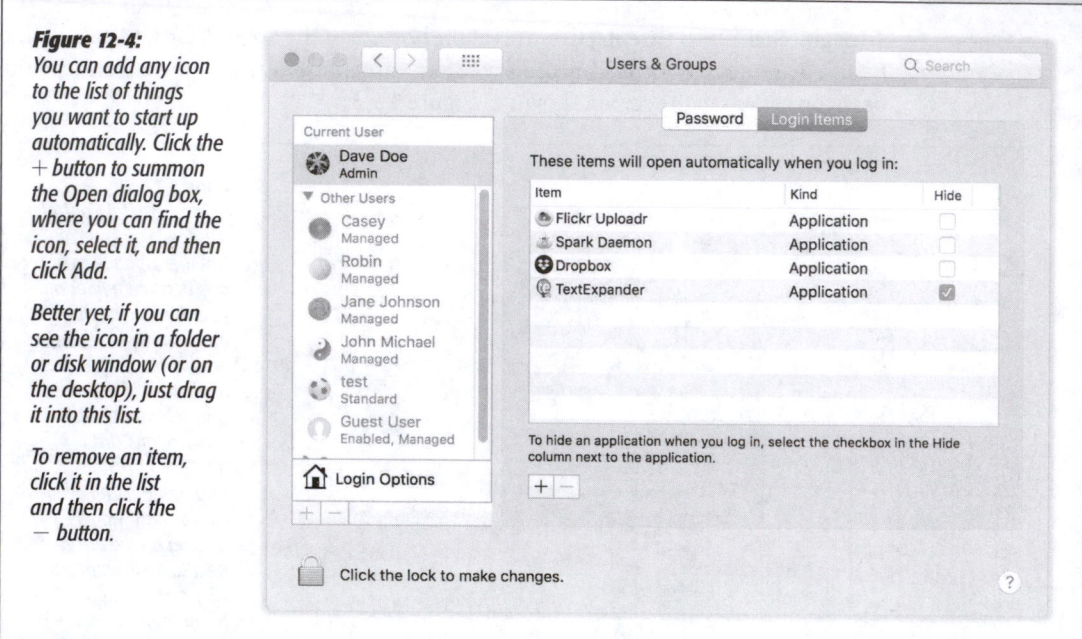

Figure 12-4:
You can add any icon to the list of things you want to start up automatically. Click the + button to summon the Open dialog box, where you can find the icon, select it, and then click Add.

Better yet, if you can see the icon in a folder or disk window (or on the desktop), just drag it into this list.

To remove an item, click it in the list and then click the − button.

Parental Controls

If you're setting up a Standard/Managed account, the Parental Controls feature affords you the opportunity to shield your Mac—or its very young, very fearful, or very mischievous operator—from confusion and harm. This set of options is helpful to remember when you're setting up accounts for students, young children, or easily intimidated adults. (This checkbox is available for Administrator accounts, too, but turning it on produces a "Silly rabbit—this is for kids!" sort of message.)

You can specify how many hours a day each person is allowed to use the Mac, and declare certain hours (like sleeping hours) off-limits. You can specify exactly whom your kids are allowed to communicate with via email (if they use Mail) and instant messaging (if they use Messages), what websites they can visit (if they use Safari), what programs they're allowed to use, and even what words they can look up in the Mac Dictionary.

Here are all the ways you can keep your little Managed account holders shielded from the internet—and themselves. For sanity's sake, the following discussion refers to the Managed account holder as "your child." But some of these controls—notably those in

If you'd rather supply your *own* graphic—a photo of your head, for example—use one of these options:

- **Defaults.** Apple starts you off with a selection of account photos, intended to represent various personalities: eagles, flowers, chalkboard math, basketball, and so on.

- **Camera.** Click Take Photo. The Mac takes the picture, while flashing the screen to add brightness. You can enlarge or shrink it, or drag to move it within the circular frame.

- **Photos.** Here you get access to your entire Mac photo collection, grouped just as it is in the Photos program (page 456).

- **Photo Booth.** And here are whatever zany funhouse photos you've taken with the Photo Booth app (page 453).

In each case, click Save to enshrine your account photo forever (or until you feel like picking a different one).

Figure 12-3:
The account-photo box offers you access to every photo on your Mac—and even to your Mac's camera (for taking a new shot). Once you've selected a photo to represent yourself, you can adjust its position relative to the round "frame," or adjust its size by dragging the slider. Finally, when the picture looks correctly framed, click Save.

Phase 4: Login Items (Startup Items)

There's one additional setting that your account holders can set up for themselves: which programs or documents open automatically upon login. (This is one decision an administrator *can't* make for other people. It's available only to the person logged in at the moment.)

To choose your own crew of self-starters, open System Preferences and click Users & Groups. Choose your account. Click the Login Items tab. As shown in Figure 12-4, you can now build a list of programs, documents, disks, and other goodies that automatically launch each time you log in. You can even turn on the Hide checkbox for each one so that the program is running in the background at login time, waiting to be called into service with a quick click.

Don't feel obligated to limit this list to just programs and documents, by the way. Disks, folders, servers on the network, and other fun icons can also serve as startup

Tip: Actually, having *some* password comes in handy if you share files on the network, because Mac A can *store* your name and password from Mac B—and therefore you can access Mac B without entering your name and password *at all.* So consider making your password something very short and easy, like the apostrophe/quote mark—the ' key. It's a real password, so it's enough for Mac A to memorize. Yet when you *are* asked to enter your password—for example, when you're installing a new program—it's incredibly fast and easy to enter, because it's right next to the Return key.

- **Password Hint.** If your password is the middle name of the first person who ever kissed you, for example, your hint might be "Middle name of the first person who ever kissed me."

 Later, if you forget your password, the Mac will show you this cue to jog your memory.

When you finish setting up these essential items, click Create User.

You then return to the Users & Groups pane, where you see the new account name in the list at the left side.

Three final decisions await your wisdom:

- **Allow user to reset password using Apple ID.** If this person ever forgets his password, he'll be offered, on the Login screen, a chance to recover it by entering his Apple ID. Nice little safety net. (Available only for accounts for which you've entered an Apple ID, of course.)

- **Allow user to administer this computer.** This checkbox lets you turn ordinary, unsuspecting Standard or Managed accounts into Administrator accounts. You know—when your kid turns 18.

- **Enable Parental Controls.** "Parental Controls" refers to the feature that limits what your offspring are allowed to do on this computer—and how much time a day they're allowed to spend glued to its screen. Details are on page 531.

Actually, if your Mac has a Touch Bar (page 233), a fourth option awaits, the most delicious of all: You can now log into the new account, open System Preferences→ Touch ID, and let its owner register a fingerprint. One touch on the Touch ID sensor built into the laptop's power button will now act as that person's security authentication, wherever fine passwords are requested. Page 235 has the details.

Phase 3: Choose a Picture

The usual sign-in screen (Figure 12-1) displays each account holder's name, accompanied by a little picture.

When you click the sample photo, you get the dialog box shown in Figure 12-3, where you choose a picture to represent you. It becomes not only your icon on the sign-in screen, but also your "card" photo in the Contacts program and your icon in Messages.

Phase 2: Name, Password, and Status

All right. So you clicked the + button. And from the New Account pop-up menu, you chose the type of account you wanted to create. (If you chose a Managed with Parental Controls account, you've also specified the age of this person.)

Now, on the same starter sheet, it's time to fill in the most critical information about the new account holder:

- **Full Name.** If it's just the family, this could be "Chris" or "Robin." If it's a corporation or school, you probably want to use both first and last names.

- **Account Name.** You'll quickly discover the value of this Account Name, particularly if your name is, say, Alexandra Stephanopoulos. It's meant to be an abbreviation of your actual name.

 When you sign into your Mac in person, you can use either your full name or account (short) name. But when you access this Mac by dialing into it or connecting from across the network (as described in the next chapter), the short version is more convenient.

 As soon as you tab into this field, the Mac proposes a short name for you. You can replace the suggestion with whatever you like. Technically, it doesn't even have to be shorter than the "long" name, but spaces and most punctuation marks are forbidden.

- **Password.** You're supposed to type this password twice, to make sure you didn't introduce a typo the first time. (The Mac displays only dots as you type, to guard against the possibility that somebody is watching over your shoulder.)

 The usual computer book takes this opportunity to stress the importance of a long, complex password—a phrase that isn't in the dictionary, something that's made up of mixed letters and numbers. This is excellent advice if you create sensitive documents or work in a big corporation.

 But if you share the Mac only with a spouse, or trusted colleagues in a small office, you may have nothing to hide. You may see the accounts feature more as a convenience (keeping your settings and files separate) than a protector of secrecy and security. In these situations, there's no particular urgency to the mission of thwarting the world's hackers with a convoluted password.

 In that case, you may want to consider setting up *no* password—leaving both password blanks empty. Later, whenever you're asked for your password, just leave the Password box blank. You'll be able to log in that much faster each day.

 (The first box says "Required," but it lies; no password is actually required. After setting up this new account and clicking Create User, the Mac asks if you're *sure* you don't want to make up a password; just click Continue and get on with your life.)

you're normally the only person who uses this Mac, you don't need to have it staring you in the face every day.

So to use the Guest account, bring it to life by choosing Guest User and then turning on "Allow guests to log into this computer." You can even turn on the parental controls described on page 531 by clicking Open Parental Controls, or permit the guest to exchange files with your Mac from across the network (Chapter 13) by turning on "Allow guests to connect to shared folders."

Just remember to warn your vagabond friend that once he logs out (and acknowledges the warning), all traces of his visit are wiped out forever.

At least from your *Mac*.

Group

A *group* is just a virtual container that holds the names of other account holders. You might create one for your most trusted colleagues, another for those rambunctious kids, and so on—all in the name of streamlining the *file-sharing privileges* feature described on page 577. The box below covers groups in more detail.

POWER USERS' CLINIC

Creating Groups

Changing permissions settings on a networked Mac, or one with a lot of account holders, is a lot easier if you sweep all your minions into subsets called groups.

This process used to require a complicated series of Unixy steps that, if not performed carefully, could seriously foul up your Mac.

But in macOS, you can create a group as easily as you'd create an account. And in the same place: the Users & Groups pane of System Preferences.

Click the tiny 🔒 in the lower-left corner. When prompted, type in your administrator's name and password, and then click OK. The Mac is just making sure that somebody with a clue is at the helm.

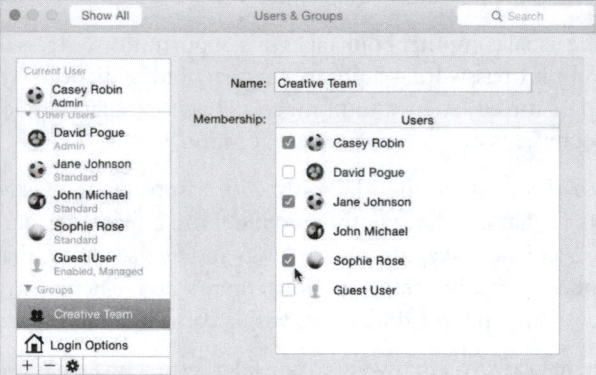

Now click the + button as though you were about to create a new account. But from the New Account pop-up menu (shown at bottom in Figure 12-2), choose Group. Type a name for the new group (Accounting, Kids, or whatever), and then click Create Group.

Now you see something like the list shown here: checkboxes for all of this Mac's account holders. Turn on the checkboxes for the ones you consider worthy of being a part of this group.

You can create as many groups as you like. Later, when it comes time to share a folder or file, you'll save time by choosing a group name instead of setting these permissions one person at a time.

See, ordinarily, you can log in and access the files on your Mac in either of two ways:

- **In person, seated in front of it.**

- **From across the network.**

This arrangement was designed with families and schools in mind: lots of people sharing a *single* Mac.

This setup gets a little silly, though, when the people on a home or office network each have their *own* computers. If you wanted your spouse or your sales director to be able to grab some files from you, you'd have to create full-blown accounts for them on *your* Mac, complete with utterly unnecessary Home folders they'd never use.

That's why the *Sharing Only* account is such a great idea. It's available *only* from across the network. You can't get into it by sitting down at the Mac itself—it has no Home folder!

Finally, of course, a Sharing Only account holder can't make any changes to the Mac's settings or programs. (And since they don't have Home folders, you also can't turn on FileVault for these accounts.)

In other words, a Sharing Only account exists *solely* for the purpose of file sharing on the network, and people can enter their names and passwords *only* from other Macs.

Once you've set up this kind of account, all the file-sharing and screen-sharing goodies described in Chapter 13 become available.

Guest account

For years, macOS has offered a special account called the *Guest* account. It's great for accommodating visitors, buddies, or anyone else who's just passing through and wants to borrow your Mac for a while. If you let such people use the Guest account, your own account remains private and un-messed-with.

Note: The Guest account isn't listed among the account *types* in the New Account pop-up menu (Figure 12-2). That's because there's only *one* Guest account; you can't actually create additional ones.

But it's still an account type with specific characteristics. It's sitting right there in the list of accounts.

In the early days of the Guest account, there was a problem: Any changes your friend made—downloading mail, making web bookmarks, putting up a raunchy desktop picture—would still be there for the *next* guest, unless you painstakingly restored everything back to neutral. The Guest account was like a hotel room shared by successive guests. And *you* were the housekeeping staff.

Today, though, any changes your guest makes while using your Mac are automatically erased when she logs out. Files are deleted, email is nuked, setting changes are forgotten. It's like a hotel that gets demolished and rebuilt after each guest departs.

As noted, the Guest account is permanently listed in the Users & Groups panel of System Preferences. Ordinarily, though, you don't see it in the Login screen list; if

- **Decide who gets to have accounts on the Mac.**

- **Open, change, or delete anyone else's files.**

- **Bypass FileVault using a recovery key** (page 545).

The administrator concept may be new to you, but it's an important pill to swallow. For one thing, you'll find certain settings all over macOS that you can change *only* if you're an administrator—including many in the Users & Groups pane itself. For another thing, administrator status plays a huge role when you want to network your Mac to other kinds of computers, as described in the next chapter. And, finally, in the bigger picture, the fact that the Mac has an industrial-strength accounts system, just like traditional Unix and recent Windows operating systems, gives it a fighting chance in the corporations of America.

As you create accounts for other people who'll use this Mac, you're offered the opportunity to make each one an administrator just like you. Needless to say, use discretion. Bestow these powers only upon people who are as responsible and technically masterful as yourself.

Standard accounts

Most people, on most Macs, are ordinary *Standard* account holders. These people have everyday access to their own Home folders and to the harmless panes of System Preferences, but most other areas of the Mac are off-limits. MacOS won't even let them create new folders on the main hard drive, except inside their own Home folders (or in the Shared folder described starting on page 548).

A few of the System Preferences panels display a padlock icon (🔒). If you're a Standard account holder, you can't make changes to these settings without the assistance of an administrator. Fortunately, you aren't required to log out so that an administrator can log in and make changes. You can just call the administrator over, click the padlock icon, and let him type in his name and password (if, indeed, he feels comfortable with you making the changes you're about to make).

Managed accounts with Parental Controls

A *Managed* account is the same as a Standard account—except that you've turned on Parental Controls. (These controls are described starting on page 531.) You can turn a Managed account into a Standard account just by turning off Parental Controls, and vice versa.

That is, this account usually has even fewer freedoms—because you've limited the programs this person is allowed to use, for example. Use a Managed account for a child or anyone else who needs a Mac with padded walls.

Sharing Only accounts

This kind of account is extremely useful—*if* your Mac is on a network (Chapter 13).

Administrator accounts

If this is your own personal Mac, then just beneath your name on the Users & Groups pane of System Preferences, it probably says *Admin*. This, as you could probably guess, stands for Administrator.

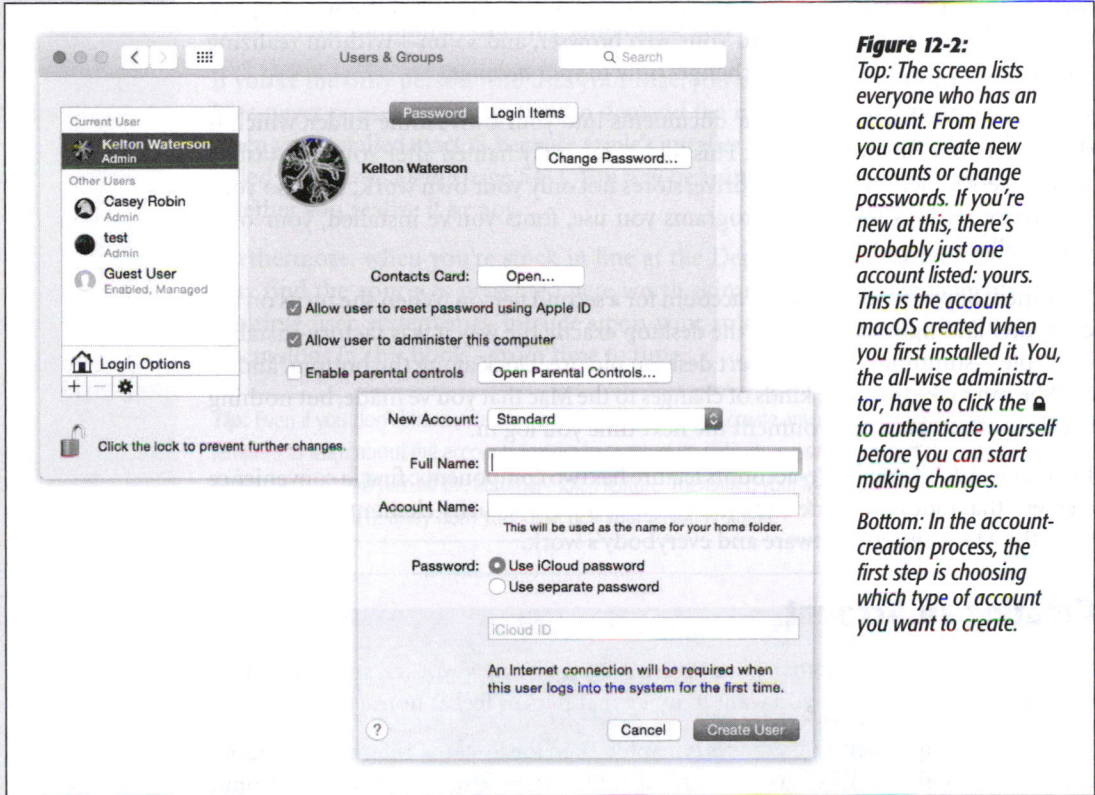

Figure 12-2:
Top: The screen lists everyone who has an account. From here you can create new accounts or change passwords. If you're new at this, there's probably just one account listed: yours. This is the account macOS created when you first installed it. You, the all-wise administrator, have to click the 🔒 to authenticate yourself before you can start making changes.

Bottom: In the account-creation process, the first step is choosing which type of account you want to create.

Because you're the person who originally installed macOS, the Mac assumes that you are its *administrator*—the technical wizard in charge of it. You're the teacher, the parent, the resident guru. You're the one who will maintain this Mac. Only an administrator is allowed to do the following:

- **Install new programs into the Applications folder.**

- **Add fonts that everybody can use.**

- **Make changes to certain System Preferences panes** (including Network, Date & Time, Energy Saver, and Startup Disk).

- **Use some features of the Disk Utility program.**

- **Create, move, or delete folders outside of your Home folder.**

Accounts, Security & Gatekeeper

I n an era when *security* is the hottest high-tech buzzword, Apple was smart to make it a focal point for macOS. It was already virus-free and better protected from internet attacks than Windows. But macOS Mojave is the most impenetrable Mac system yet, filled with defenses against the dark arts. This chapter covers the whole range of them.

On the premise that the biggest security threat of all comes from other people in your home or office, though, the most important security feature in macOS is the *accounts* system.

Introducing Accounts

The concept of *user accounts* is central to macOS's security approach. Like the Unix under its skin (and also like recent versions of Windows), macOS is designed from the ground up to be a *multiple-user* operating system. That is, you can set up your macOS so that everyone must log in—click his name and type his password—when the computer turns on (Figure 12-1).

Upon doing so, you discover the Macintosh universe just as you left it, including these elements:

• **Your documents, files, and folders.**

• **Your preference settings** in every program you use: web browser bookmarks and preferred home page; desktop picture, screen saver, and language; icons on the desktop and in the Dock—and the size and position of the Dock itself; and so on.

• **Email account(s)**, including personal information and mailboxes.

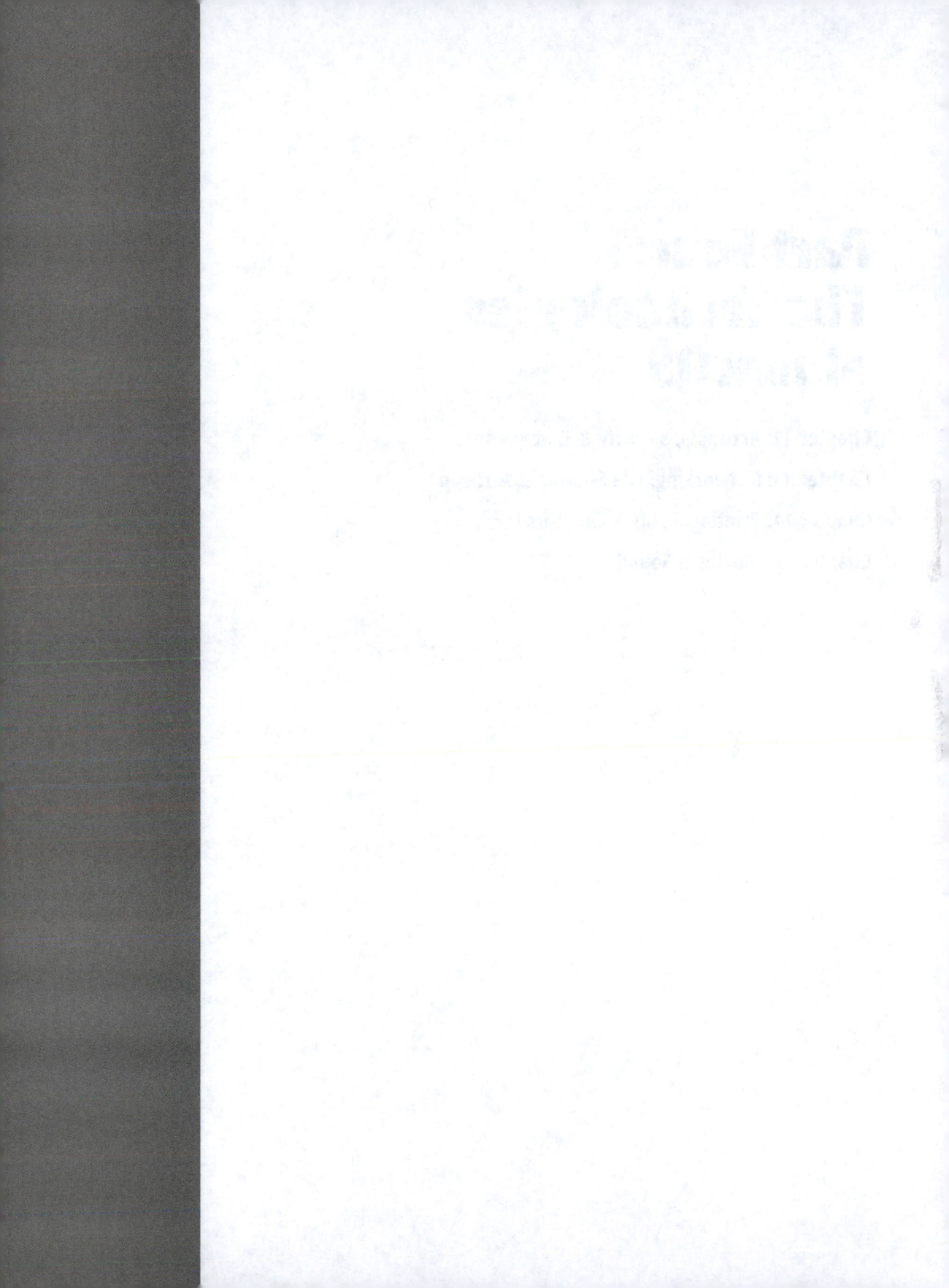

Part Four:
The Technologies
of macOS

4

Storage Management

The "how to free up more space on your hard drive" feature described on page 105 is actually this little app at work.

System Image Utility

Here's another obscure app intended exclusively for professional corporate network administrators. It's for creating "disks" on the network that all Macs can access. Details at *support.apple.com/guide/system-image-utility/welcome/mac.*

Wireless Diagnostics

If you're having Wi-Fi problems, here's a handy troubleshooting trick: While pressing the Option key, open the 🛜 menu and choose Open Wireless Diagnostics. This app opens. It walks you through some Wi-Fi troubleshooting steps.

A full guide is online at *support.apple.com/en-us/HT202663.*

response time in milliseconds—a useful test when you're trying to see if a remote server (a website, for example) is up and running. (The time it takes for the ping to report back to you also tells you how good your connection to it is.)

- **Traceroute lets you track how many "hops"** are required for your Mac to communicate with a certain server (an IP address or web address). You'll see that your request actually jumps from one *trunk* of the internet to another, from router to router, as it makes its way to its destination. You'll learn that a message sometimes crisscrosses the entire country before it arrives. You can also see how long each leg of the journey took, in milliseconds.

- **Whois ("who is") can gather an amazing amount of information** about the owners of any particular domain (such as *apple.com*)—including name and address info, telephone numbers, and administrative contacts. It uses the technique shown in Figure 11-56.

Figure 11-56:
The whois tool is a powerful part of Network Utility. First enter a domain that you want information about, and then choose a whois server (you might try whois.internic.net). When you click the Whois button, you get a surprisingly revealing report about the owner of the domain, including phone numbers and contact names.

RAID Utility

If you're a hard-core Mac nerd, you know what a RAID drive is. It's a hard drive that, behind the scenes, is made up of multiple spinning disks. Depending on the choices you make in RAID Utility, you can set them up so they all appear to the Mac as one giant disk—or you can set things up so that it's one half-sized hard drive, and the other half is a real-time mirror, a backup.

Apple's techie details for techie people are here: *images.apple.com/xserve/pdf/RAID_Utility_User_Guide.pdf*.

Screen Sharing

This app does the heavy lifting for the Screen Sharing feature described on page 595.

drives. If you are that highly paid network administrator, you should read Apple's guide without delay: *support.apple.com/guide/directory-utility/*.

DVD Player

For the six people whose Macs still have physical DVD drives, Apple offers this ancient relic of a playback program.

Feedback Assistant

Apple tests out new versions of its operating systems on willing volunteers. Anyone who's interested can sign up for Apple's public beta-testing program at *beta.apple.com*. If you join, you'll get to try out upcoming versions of macOS before they're released to the teeming masses. Along the way, you'll probably encounter bugs, crashes, and other unfinished business.

When that happens, Apple hopes you'll use this app to submit reports of the problems you find. On its end, Apple's programmers collect all these bug reports, organize them, and set about fixing as many as they can in time for the public release of the software.

Folder Actions Setup

This app opens up when you right-click or two-finger click a desktop folder and, from the shortcut menu, choose Folder Actions Setup. You're offered a list of folder actions—canned processes that run automatically every time you drop a file into this folder.

For example, maybe you want every graphics file in this folder automatically converted into PNG format. Or maybe you want every PDF document rotated 90 degrees. Or maybe you want the Mac to alert you every time someone puts a file into this folder.

All of this is part of Apple's ancient, technical, but (in some circles) beloved Apple-Script programming system. You can read more about it on this book's "Missing CD" at *missingmanuals.com*, in a document called "AppleScript & Automator."

Network Utility

You can find and open Network Utility with a Spotlight search, or from within System Information, described on page 512 (choose Window→Network Utility).

In any case, it gathers information about websites and network citizens. It offers a suite of standard internet tools like netstat, ping, traceroute, DNS lookup, and whois—advanced tools, to be sure, but ones that even Mac novices may be asked to fire up when calling a technician for internet help.

Otherwise, you probably won't need to use Network Utility to get your work done. However, Network Utility can be useful when you're doing internet detective work:

- **Use ping to enter an address** (either a web address like *google.com* or an IP address like 192.168.1.110), and then "ping" (send out a "sonar" signal to) the server to see how long it takes for it to respond to your request. Network Utility reports the

Tip: If any of these screens is showing you more technical information than you'd like, then use the File→Show Less Information command to pare down the overload to just the human-recognizable items.

Terminal

Underneath its shiny skin, macOS is actually Unix, one of the oldest and most respected operating systems in use today. But you'd never know it by looking; Unix is a world without icons, menus, or dialog boxes. You operate it by typing out memorized commands at a special prompt, called the command line. The mouse is almost useless here.

Wait a minute—Apple's ultramodern operating system, with a command line? What's going on? Actually, the command line never went away. At universities and corporations worldwide, professional computer nerds still value the efficiency of pounding away at the little *C:* or *$* prompts.

You never *have* to use macOS's command line. In fact, Apple has swept it pretty far under the rug. There are, however, some tasks you can perform *only* at the command line.

Terminal is your keyhole into macOS's Unix innards. There's a whole chapter on it waiting for you on this book's "Missing CD" page at *missingmanuals.com*.

VoiceOver Utility

For details on this screen-reader software, see page 325.

Core Services: The Island of Misfit Apps

You thought the apps in Utilities were geeky? Wait till you meet the ones Apple has hidden away in the System→Library→Core Services→Applications folder. (That's the Library folder in your main hard drive window, not the hidden one in your own User folder.)

These are *very* specialized gizmos; most are primarily of interest to network administrators or Unix geeks obsessed with knowing what kind of computer-code gibberish is going on behind the scenes. In any case, here's what you'll find there.

About This Mac

Turns out that the information screen shown in Figure 11-54, which opens when you choose →About This Mac, is actually a standalone app. It's in your the Library→Core Services→Applications folder.

Archive Utility

Here is the actual app that performs the zipping and unzipping functions described on page 105.

Directory Utility

On a corporate network, a highly paid network administrator may use this little app to access and manage the corporate directory servers—centralized databases and

When System Information opens, it reports information about your Mac in a list down the left side (Figure 11-55). The details fall into these categories:

- **Hardware.** Click this word to see precisely which model Mac you have, what kind of chip is inside (and how many), how much memory it has, and its serial number.

 If you expand the flippy triangle, you get to see details about which Memory slots are filled and the size of the memory module in each slot; what kind of Disc Burning your Mac can do (DVD-R, DVD+R, and so on); what PCI cards are installed in your expansion slots; what Graphics/Displays circuitry you have (graphics card and monitor); what's attached to your SATA bus (internal drives, like your hard drive); what's connected to your Thunderbolt, USB, and FireWire chains, if anything; and much more.

Figure 11-55:
Does your MacBook's chip run at 2 GHz or 2.6? What percentage of your external hard drive is filled up? What are the version numbers of every program installed on your Mac? Can your DVD burner burn dual-layer discs? Does your laptop have any open slots for extra RAM?

- **Network** details what Wi-Fi components you have, what internet connection Locations you've established, and so on.

- **Software** shows which version of macOS you have and what your computer's name is, as far as the network is concerned ("Pat's Computer," for example).

 The Applications list documents every program on your system, with version information. It's useful for spotting duplicate copies of programs.

 Similar information shows up in the Extensions panel. Extensions are the drivers for the Mac's various components, which sit in the System→Library→Extensions folder. Whatever is in that folder is what you see listed in this panel. Other categories include self-explanatory lists like Fonts, Preference Panes, and Startup Items.

 Finally, the Logs panel reveals your Mac's secret diary: a record of the traumatic events it experiences from day to day. (Many of these are the same as those revealed by the Console utility; see page 503.)

There are actually two versions of System Information: a quick, easy snapshot and a ridiculously detailed version:

- **Snapshot.** Choose →About This Mac. You get a concise, attractive summary info screen that reveals your macOS version, your Mac's memory amount, its serial number, what processor it has inside, and so on (Figure 11-54, top).

Tip: If you click your macOS version number in the Overview box, you get to see its *build number*—something primarily of interest to programmers and people who beta-test macOS.

Figure 11-54:
This dialog box gives you a plain-English display of the Mac details you probably care the most about: memory, screen, storage, serial number, macOS version, and so on. (Click the tabs across the top for more details.) To proceed from here to the full System Information program, click System Report.

The tabs across the top reveal similarly precise details about your Displays and Storage. The Support tab offers links to various sources of online help, and the Service tab reveals your options for getting the Mac fixed.

- **Ridiculously detailed.** Open Applications→Utilities; double-click System Information. (You can also open the System Information program from inside the About This Mac dialog box shown in Figure 11-54 at top; just click System Report.)

When it's all over, you can preserve your masterpiece using any of these techniques:

- **Export a graphic** by choosing File→Export.

- **Copy an equation to the Clipboard** by right-clicking or two-finger clicking it and choosing Copy As→TIFF (or EPS, or text, or whatever) from the shortcut menu. Now you can paste it into another program.

- **Export an animated graph** by choosing Equation→Create Animation. The dialog box lets you specify how long you want the movie to last (and a lot of other things).

Tip: If you click the Orientation tab, you can Shift-drag the starting or ending images at the bottom to change their size.

Finally, click Create Animation. After a moment, the finished movie appears. If you like it, choose File→Save As to preserve it on your hard drive for future generations.

Keychain Access

Keychain Access memorizes and stores all your secret information—passwords for network access, file servers, FTP sites, web pages, and other secure items. For instructions on using Keychain Access, see page 562.

Migration Assistant

This little cutie automates the transfer of all your stuff from another Mac, or even a Windows PC, to your current Mac: your Home folder, network settings, programs, and more. This comes in extremely handy when you buy a newer, better Mac—or when you need Time Machine to recover an entire dead Mac's worth of data. (It can also copy everything over from a secondary hard drive or partition.) The instructions on the screen guide you through the process (see Appendix A).

Screenshot

You know the fancy new screen-capture feature Apple added to macOS Mojave? (If not, you can read up on page 626.) Well, behind the scenes, it's just this application at work. It opens when you press that Shift-⌘-5 keystroke.

Script Editor

This little program, formerly called AppleScript Editor, is where you can type up your own *AppleScripts*. You can read about these programmery software robots in the free online appendix to this chapter, "Automator & AppleScript." It's available on this book's "Missing CD" page at *missingmanuals.com*.

System Information

System Information (formerly called System Profiler) is a great tool for learning exactly what's installed on your Mac and what's not—in terms of both hardware and software. The people who answer the phones on Apple's tech-support line are particularly fond of System Information, since the detailed information it reports can be very useful for troubleshooting nasty problems.

blocks that appear when you choose Equation→New Equation from Template or Window→Show Equation Palette (a floating window containing a huge selection of math symbols and constants).

Tip: If you don't know the keystroke that produces a mathematical symbol like π or θ, you can just type *pi* or *theta.* Grapher replaces it with the correct symbol automatically.

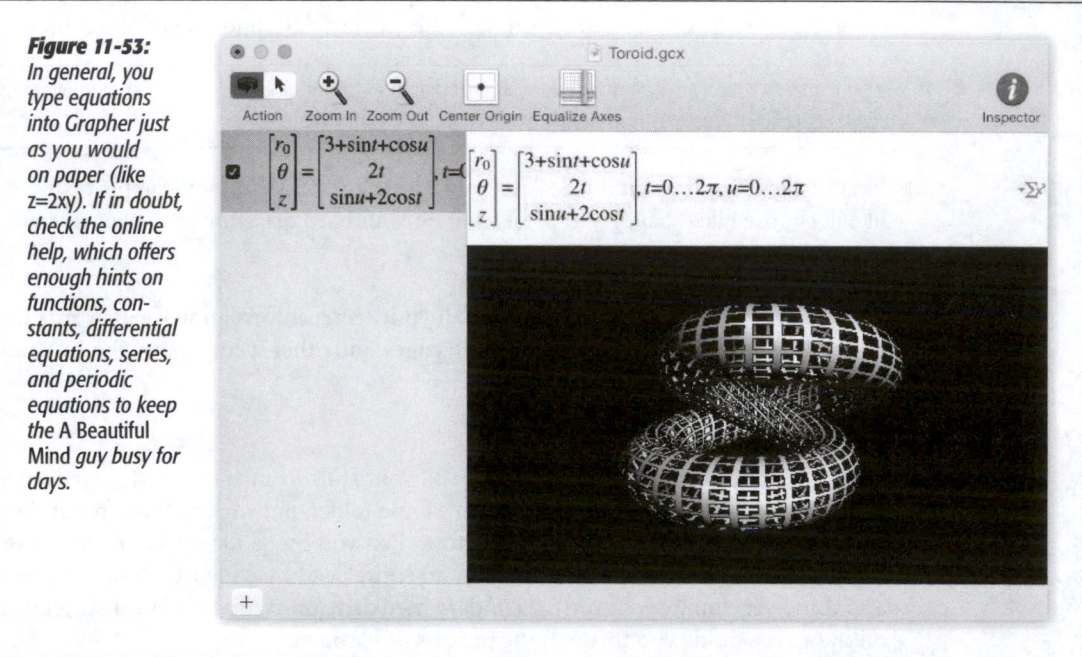

Figure 11-53:
In general, you type equations into Grapher just as you would on paper (like z=2xy). If in doubt, check the online help, which offers enough hints on functions, constants, differential equations, series, and periodic equations to keep the A Beautiful Mind *guy busy for days.*

Once the graph is up on the screen, you can tailor it like this:

- **To move a 2D graph** in the window, choose View→Move Tool and then drag; to move a 3D graph, ⌘-drag it.

- **To rotate a 3D graph,** drag in any direction. If you add the Option key, you flip the graph around on one axis.

- **To change the colors, line thicknesses, 3D "walls," and other graphic elements,** click the ❶ button (or choose Window→Show Inspector) to open the formatting palette. The controls you find here vary by graph type, but rest assured that Grapher can accommodate your every visual whim.

- **To change the fonts and sizes,** choose Grapher→Preferences. On the Equations panel, the four sliders let you specify the relative sizes of the text elements. If you click the sample equation, the Fonts panel appears, so you can go to town fiddling with the type.

Choose "DVD/CD master" if you're copying a CD or a DVD. The resulting file is a perfect mirror of the original disc, ready for copying onto a blank CD or DVD when the time comes. Finally, "hybrid image" is a combo format that can be used with file system standards such as HFS+, ISO, and UDF.

- **Save As.** Choose a name and location for your new image file. The name you choose here doesn't need to match the original disk or folder name.

When you click Save (or press Return), if you opted to create an encrypted image, you're asked to make up a password at this point.

Otherwise, Disk Utility now creates the image and then *mounts* it—that is, turns the image file into a simulated, yet fully functional, disk icon on your desktop.

When you're finished working with the disk, eject it as you would any disk (right-click or two-finger click it and choose Eject, for example). Hang on to the .dmg disk-image file itself, however. This is the file you'll need to double-click if you ever want to recreate your "simulated disk."

Grapher

This little unsung app is an amazing piece of work. It lets you create 2D or 3D graphs of staggering beauty and complexity.

When you first open Grapher, you're asked to choose what kind of virtual "graph paper" you want: two-dimensional (standard, polar, logarithmic, and so on) or three-dimensional (cubic, spherical, cylindrical, and so on). Click a name to see a preview; when you're happy with the selection, click Open.

Now the main Grapher window appears (Figure 11-53). Do yourself a favor. Spend a few wow-inducing minutes choosing canned equations from the Examples menu and watching how Grapher whips up gorgeous, colorful, sometimes animated graphs on the fly.

When you're ready to plug in an equation of your own, type it into the text box at the top of the window. If you're not such a math hotshot, or you're not sure of the equation format, work from the canned equations and mathematical building

POWER USERS' CLINIC

For Mathematicians (and Physicists, Scientists, and Students) Only

If you're into math, science, or studying math or science, Grapher is a tremendous addition to macOS. There's a whole lot to it—but if you're just getting started, here are a few features not to miss.

You can calculate values, intercepts, derivatives, and integrals (even indefinite integrals) by using the Equation→Evaluation and Equation→Integration commands.

Some useful ready-made equation components await in the pop-up button at the right side of the equation text box. Using the Sum and Product symbols, for example, you can quickly calculate summations and products.

That same pop-up menu can help you generate piecewise, parametric, and other specialized kinds of graphs (this means you, math students).

- **Encryption.** Here's an easy way to lock private files away into a vault that nobody else can open. If you choose one of these two AES encryption options (choose AES-128, if you value your time), you'll be asked to assign a password to your new image file. Nobody can open it without the password—not even you. On the other hand, if you save it into your Keychain (page 562), then it's not such a disaster if you forget the password.

- **Image Format.** If you choose "read/write," your disk image file, when double-clicked, turns into a superb imitation of a hard drive. You can drag files and folders onto it, drag them off of it, change icons' names on it, and so on.

If you choose "read-only," however, then the result behaves more like a CD. You can copy things off of it but not make any changes to it.

The "compressed" option is best if you intend to send the resulting file by email, post it for web download, or preserve the disk image on some backup disk for a rainy day. It takes a little longer to create a simulated disk when you double-click the disk image file, but it takes up a lot less disk space than an uncompressed version.

GEM IN THE ROUGH

The Sparse Image

One of the coolest Disk Utility features is also one of the most buried. Turns out you can make a nice, hermetically sealed, password-protected disk image that starts out small but magically increases as you stuff more files into it. If the usual disk image is like a steel bucket—a fixed size forever—a sparse image is like an accordion file folder.

Just choose File→ New Image→ Blank Image. In the resulting box, name the file you're creating (which you'll double-click to make the virtual disk appear), as well as the virtual disk itself. In the Size box, type the maximum size this disk image will ever be. The beautiful part is that it will probably never occupy that much disk space; it starts out small and slowly expands only as necessary. But you're setting the maximum here. From the Encryption pop-up menu, choose one of the two scrambling methods

that will password-protect your disk image. Finally, from the Image Format pop-up menu—this is the key step—choose "sparse bundle disk image."

Click Save. Make up a password (type it twice); store in your Keychain, if you like (meaning that you won't need to enter the password whenever you're logged into your Mac). Then click Create.

Now, on your desktop, there's a disk-image file with the suffix ".sparseimage." It occupies only 26 MB on your hard drive to start with.

Double-click it and enter your password to bring the actual virtual disk icon to your desktop. You can now start filling the disk image up with private stuff. The .sparseimage file will grow automatically to accommodate it—but only as necessary.

Tip: *After you double-click a disk image, click Skip in the verification box that appears. If something truly got scrambled during the download, you'll know about it right away–your file won't decompress correctly, or it'll display the wrong icon, for example.*

You can create disk images, too. Doing so can be very handy in situations like these:

- **You want to create a backup of a CD.** By turning it into a disk-image file, you'll always have a safety copy, ready to burn onto a *new* CD. (This is a good practice for educational CDs that kids will be handling soon after eating peanut butter and jelly.)

- **You want to replicate your entire hard drive**—complete with all its files, programs, folder setups, and so on—onto a new, bigger hard drive (or a new, better Mac), using the Restore feature already described.

- **You want to back up your entire hard drive,** or maybe just a certain chunk of it, onto an iPod or another disk. (Again, you can later use the Restore function.)

- **You want to send somebody else a copy of a disk via the internet.** You simply create a disk image, and then send *that*—preferably in compressed form.

Here's how to make a disk image:

- **To image-ize a disk or partition.** Click the name of the disk in the list, where you see your currently available disks. (The topmost item is the name of your *drive*, like "484.0 MB MATSHITA DVD-R" for a DVD drive or "74.5 GB Hitachi" for a hard drive. Beneath that entry, you generally see the name of the actual partition, like "Macintosh HD," or the CD's name as it appears on the screen.)

 Then choose File→New Image→Disk Image from [the disk or partition's name].

- **To image-ize a folder.** Choose File→New Image→Image from Folder. In the Open dialog box, click the folder you want, and then click Choose. Either way, the next dialog box (Figure 11-52) offers some fascinating options.

Figure 11-52:
*These two pop-up menus let you specify
(a) whether you want your disk image
password-protected, and (b) what kind
of disk image you want. The latter option
is great when you want to password-
protect one folder without bothering with
your entire Home folder.*

then click Restore. Choose the volume you want to replicate, click Restore again, and then Done.

- **Unmount.** This button ejects whatever disk you've selected in the left-side list.

- **Info.** Click to view a little table of super-technical details about the selected drive.

Disk Utility, the disk-image program

Disk images are very cool. Each is a single icon that behaves precisely like an actual disk—a flash drive or hard drive, for example—but can be distributed electronically. For example, a lot of macOS apps arrive from your web download in disk-image form.

Disk images are popular for software distribution for a simple reason: Each image file precisely duplicates the original master disk, complete with all the necessary files in all the right places. When a software company sends you a disk image, it ensures that you'll install the software from a disk that *exactly* matches the master disk.

As a handy bonus, you can password-protect a disk image, which is the closest macOS comes to offering the ability to password-protect an individual folder.

It's important to understand the difference between a *disk-image file* and the *mounted disk* (the one that appears when you double-click the disk image). If you flip back to page 168 and consult Figure 5-2, this distinction should be clear.

POWER USERS' CLINIC

Partition Adjustments on the Fly

You can expand, shrink, or create partitions without having to erase the whole hard drive. If you're into partitioning at all, this is a *huge* convenience.

Expanding a partition. Suppose, for example, that your hard drive has two partitions: a main one (200 gigs) and a secondary one (50 gigs) that used to hold all your photos and movies. But you've outgrown the second partition and have moved all those photos and movies to their own external hard drive. Wouldn't it be nice to add the newly unoccupied 50 gigs to your main partition?

You can do that without having to erase the whole hard drive. (This process, however, nukes everything on the *second* partition, so make sure you're prepared to lose it all.)

Open Disk Utility. Click the name of the hard drive (for example, "Hitachi HTS541616J9SA00"–*not* "Macintosh HD"). Click Partition. You see a display like the one in Figure 11-51.

Click the second partition (or third, or whatever partition is *just after* the one you want to expand) and then click the — button below the list. Poof! It's gone.

Now you can drag the main partition's pie wedge larger (or type a new size into the Size box), expanding it into the free area. Take a deep breath, and then click Apply.

Shrinking a partition. In Figure 11-51, you can see that a portion of the first partition is colored. That section represents data; you can't shrink a partition so much that it crowds out your files. You can, however, shrink the partition to eliminate empty space. Just drag the lower edge of its map chunk upward.

Creating new partitions. Anytime there's leftover space on the hard drive, you can create *new* partitions from it. To do that, click the + button and proceed as described in Figure 11-51.

navigation when you want to open a particular file, and offers no speed or safety benefits. And if you're using APFS (see the box on the previous page), of course, creating new *volumes* is a much more modern, flexible way of subdividing your drive.

On the other hand, there's one very good reason *to* do it: Partitioning is the only way to use Boot Camp, described starting on page 498. When you're using Boot Camp, your Mac is a Mac when running off of one partition, and a Windows PC when starting up from another one. (But you don't use Disk Utility in that case; you use Boot Camp Assistant.)

Note: Partitioning is not the same thing as creating APFS volumes, described in the box on the previous page.

Figure 11-51:
To add each new partition, click +.

Now drag the tiny, round handles to adjust the dividers in the pie chart; that's how you specify the relative sizes of the partitions you want. Assign a name and a format for each partition in the Partition Information area, and then click Apply.

- **Erase.** Select a disk, choose a format—*always* APFS or macOS Extended (Journaled), unless you're formatting a disk for use on a Windows PC—give it a name, and then click Erase to wipe a disk clean. See the box on the previous page for more on APFS.

Tip: Click Security Options to view a slider. It can strike four spots on the spectrum from the *speed* of the disk erasing to the *security* of it. At the far-left position, macOS erases the drive quickly, but a recovery app could recover the files. At the more secure settings, macOS performs various additional time-consuming scrubbing tasks, writing over your old files with randomized gibberish, making file recovery impossible. Something to remember if you sell your Mac!

- **Restore.** You can create an exact replica of a volume. From the Sidebar, choose the target volume—the one that will become a replica of some other one—and

- **First Aid.** This is the disk-repair part of Disk Utility, and it does a terrific job at fixing many disk problems. When you're troubleshooting, Disk Utility should be your first resort.

 To use it, click the icon of a disk and then click First Aid. After asking for confirmation (click Run), this function scours every single file on your drive, checking for corruption, flakiness, or trouble spots on the disk.

 If Disk First Aid reports that it's unable to fix the problem, *then* it's time to invest in a program like DiskWarrior (*alsoft.com*).

- **Partition.** With the Partition tools, you can erase a hard drive in such a way that you subdivide its surface. Each chunk will be represented on your screen by another hard drive icon (Figure 11-51).

There are some very good reasons *not* to partition a drive these days: A partitioned hard drive is more difficult to resurrect after a serious crash, requires more

GEM IN THE ROUGH

The Quiet Power of APFS

The *file system* is the underlying software that organizes all your documents, photos, mail, and so on—and by 2016, the file system driving the Mac was 19 years old. (It's called HFS+, if you're keeping score at home.)

So one of the biggest-ticket items in macOS is the Apple File System (APFS), developed for the new era of solid-state drives and increased security threats. It's standard across all of Apple's gadgets: macOS, iOS, tvOS, and watchOS.

All of this is very satisfying to programmers. But you, the average person, will probably notice only a couple of changes.

First, when you duplicate a file or folder on an APFS drive, it happens instantly. There's no progress bar, no waiting—and the copy takes up almost no space, at least until you make changes to it. Second, getting the size of a folder (page 50) is also instantaneous.

In macOS Mojave, APFS now works on spinning hard drives or even Apple Fusion drives (which combine solid-state [SSD] technology with spinning drives for greater speed). It used to work only on SSDs.

There are a few things to note as you enter the exciting new world of APFS, though. First, macOS and APFS require each

other. If you install macOS onto a solid-state drive (SSD), like the one on an Apple laptop, it gets converted to APFS automatically. Conversely, if you move an external APFS drive to a pre–High Sierra Mac, it doesn't show up on the desktop.

APFS is theoretically capable of great features like **snapshots**, where the current state of your entire drive is memorized in space-efficient format; if disaster befalls, you can "rewind" to that condition. Someday, Time Machine (page 266) will use this feature to save space; but at the moment, your Mac uses snapshots only when storing *local* snapshots (page 270), and, as always, only on SSDs.

APFS offers **space sharing**, too, where you can create sub-disks (APFS *volumes*) that all share space on the main disk, and flexibly grow or shrink as necessary. (To create one, click the $+$ button in Disk Utility. Name it, click Size Options to specify a minimum and maximum size for its growth [Reserve and Quota] if you like, and then click Save.)

Overall, APFS is supposed to reduce wear on drives, make them faster, and make them more secure. Only some of it benefits you today, but Apple promises that APFS is the first step to a glorious disk-formatting future.

Disk Utility

This important program has two key functions:

- **It serves as macOS's own disk-repair program:** a powerful administration tool that lets you repair, erase, format, and partition disks. You'll probably use Disk Utility most often for its First Aid feature, which solves a number of weird little Mac glitches. But it's also worth keeping in mind in case you ever find yourself facing a serious disk problem.

- **Disk Utility also creates and manages** *disk images,* electronic versions of disks or folders that you can exchange electronically with other people.

Note: In 2015, Apple put Disk Utility on a bit of a diet. A few features are no longer part of the program, including burning a CD from a disk image and formatting RAID drives. Most shocking of all, there's no longer a Repair Permissions button, a powerful troubleshooting tool that used to be one of Disk Utility's most important functions; it could fix all kinds of weird Mac glitches. Apple says macOS now checks and repairs disk permissions automatically every time you install a system update.

The following discussion tackles the program's two personalities one at a time.

Disk Utility, the hard drive repair program

When you first open Disk Utility, you see, at a glance, what kinds of files are eating up your disk space (see Figure 11-50).

Figure 11-50:
The left Disk Utility panel lists your hard drive and any other disks in or attached to your Mac at the moment.

The main welcome screen shows where all your disk space is going, color coded by category.

When you click the name of your hard drive's mechanism, like "500 GB Hitachi iC25N0…" (not the "Macintosh HD" volume label below it), you see a cluster of buttons, one for each of the main Disk Utility functions:

• **Profiles.** This tab lets you review all the ColorSync profiles installed on your system. The area on the right side of the window displays information about each ColorSync profile you select from the list on the left.

For more information on ColorSync, see page 623.

Console

Console is a viewer for all of macOS's logs—the behind-the-scenes, internal Unix record of your Mac's activities.

Opening the Console log is a bit like stepping into an operating room during a complex surgery: You're exposed to stuff the average person just isn't supposed to see. (Typical Console entries: "kCGErrorCannotComplete" or "doGetDisplayTransferBy-Table.") You can adjust the font and word wrapping using Console's Font menu, but the truth is that the phrase "CGXGetWindowType: Invalid window -1" looks ugly in just about *any* font!

Console isn't useless, however. These messages can be of significant value to programmers who are debugging software or troubleshooting a messy problem, or, occasionally, to someone you've called for tech support.

For example, your *crash logs* are detailed technical descriptions of what went wrong when various programs crashed, and what was stored in memory at the time.

Unfortunately, there's not much plain English here to help you understand the crash, or how to avoid it in the future. Most of it runs along the lines of "Exception: EXC_BAD_ACCESS (0x0001); Codes: KERN_INVALID_ADDRESS (0x0001) at 0x2f6b657d."

DigitalColor Meter

DigitalColor Meter can grab the exact color value of any pixel on your screen, which can be helpful when matching colors in web page construction or other design work. After launching the DigitalColor Meter, just point anywhere on your screen. A magnified view appears in the meter window, and the RGB (red-green-blue) color value of the pixels appears in the meter window.

Here are some tips for using the DigitalColor Meter to capture color information from your screen:

• **To home in on the exact pixel** (and color) you want to measure, drag the Aperture Size slider to the smallest size: 1 pixel.

• **Press ⌘-X** (View→Lock X) to freeze your cursor at its current horizontal position; you can now move it only horizontally. Or press ⌘-Y (View→Lock Y) to freeze your cursor at its current vertical position. You can also lock the cursor in both directions by pressing ⌘-L (View→Lock Position). (Press the keystroke again to unlock.) The idea is to make it easier for you to snap to exactly the pixel you want.

• **When the Aperture Size slider** is set to view more than one pixel, DigitalColor Meter measures the *average* value of the pixels being examined.

Tip: You know that awesome two-finger scrolling trick on Mac laptops? It works when you're running Windows, too.

If you really want to understand how your Mac keyboard corresponds to a PC keyboard, don't miss Apple's thrilling document on the subject at *support.apple.com/ kb/HT1167*.

Accessing Mac files from the Dark Side—and vice versa

When you've started up in one operating system, it's easy to access documents that "belong" to the other one. For example:

- **When you're running macOS,** you can get to the documents you created while you were running Windows, which is a huge convenience. Just double-click the Windows disk icon (called NO NAME or Untitled), and then navigate to the Documents and Settings→[your account name]→My Documents (or Desktop).

 You can only copy files *to* the Mac side, or open them without the ability to edit them.

Tip: You can rename the Windows disk, if you want, so it doesn't say NO NAME the rest of its life—as long as you do it while you're running Windows.

- **When you're running Windows,** you can get to your Mac documents, too. Click Start→Computer. In the resulting window, you'll see an icon representing your Mac's hard drive partition. Open it up.

 You can see and open these files. But if you want to edit them, you have to copy them to your Windows world first—onto the desktop, for example, or into a folder. (The Mac partition is "read-only" in this way, Apple says, to avoid the possibility that your Mac stuff could get contaminated by Windows viruses.)

Tip: If you did want to edit Mac files from within Windows, one solution is to use a disk that both macOS and Windows "see," and keep your shared files on *that.* A flash drive works beautifully for this. So does a shared drive on the network, or an internet-based disk like Dropbox, Microsoft's OneDrive, or even Apple's iCloud Drive (page 221). You can make each of these show up in both Mac and Windows.

ColorSync Utility

If you use ColorSync, then you probably know already that this utility is for people in the high-end color printing business. Its tabs include these two:

- **Profile First Aid.** This tab performs a fairly esoteric task: repairing ColorSync profiles that may be "broken" because they don't strictly conform to the *ICC profile* specifications. (International Color Consortium profiles are part of Apple's ColorSync color management system.) If a profile for your specific monitor or printer doesn't appear in the Profiles tab of this program when it should, then Profile First Aid is the tool you need to fix it.

Note: Once you're running Windows, you might wonder: How am I supposed to right-click? I don't have a two-button mouse or two-button trackpad!

Yes, you do. See page 239 for a panoply of options.

Forth and back, Windows/Mac

From now on, your main interaction with Boot Camp will be telling it what kind of computer you want your Mac to be today: a Windows machine or a Mac.

Presumably, though, you'll prefer one operating system *most* of the time. Figure 11-49 (top and middle) shows how you specify your favorite.

Tip: If you're running Windows and you just want to get back to macOS right now, you don't have to bother with all the steps shown in Figure 11-49. Instead, click the Boot Camp system-tray icon and, from the shortcut menu, choose Restart in macOS.

From now on, each time you turn on the Mac, it starts up in the operating system you've selected.

If you ever need to switch—when you need Windows just for one quick job, for example—press the Option key as the Mac is starting up. You'll see something like the icons shown in Figure 11-49 (bottom).

Keyboard translation guide

Now, if you really want to learn about Windows, you need a book like *Windows 10: The Missing Manual.*

But suggesting that you go buy *another* huge book would be tacky. So here's just enough to get by.

First of all, a Mac keyboard and a Windows keyboard aren't the same. Each has keys that would strike the other as extremely goofy. Still, you can trigger almost any keystroke that Windows is expecting by substituting special Apple keystrokes, like this:

Windows keystroke	Apple keystroke
Ctrl+Alt+Delete	Control-Option-Delete
Alt	Option
Ctrl key	⌘
Backspace	Delete
Delete (forward delete)	⌦ (on laptops, fn-Delete)
Enter	Return
Num Lock	Clear (laptops: fn-F6)
Print Screen (PrtScn)	F14 (laptops: fn-F11)
Print Active Window (Alt+PrtScn)	Option-F14 (laptops: Option-fn-F11)

The keyboard shortcuts in your programs are *mostly* the same as on the Mac, but you have to substitute the ⌘ key for the Ctrl key. So in Windows programs on the Mac, Copy, Save, and Print are now ⌘-C, ⌘-S, and ⌘-P.

When it's all over, a crazy, disorienting sight presents itself: your Mac, running Windows. There's no trace of the desktop, Dock, or menu; it's Windows now, baby.

Walk through the Windows setup screens, creating an account, setting the time, and so on.

Using Boot Camp

At this point, your Mac is actually a true Windows PC. You can install and run Windows programs, utilities, and even games; you'll discover that they run *really* fast and well.

Most of your Mac's features work in Windows: Ethernet and Wi-Fi networking, audio input and output, built-in camera, brightness and volume keys, ⏏ key, multitouch trackpad gestures, Bluetooth, and so on. You'll also discover a new Control Panel icon and system-tray pop-up menu, as described later in this section.

Figure 11-49:

Top: To choose your preferred operating system—the one that always starts up unless you intervene—choose → System Preferences. Click Startup Disk, and then click the icon for either macOS or Windows. Next, either click Restart (if you want to switch right now) or close the panel. The same controls are available when you're running Windows.

Middle: To open the Boot Camp Control Panel, choose its name from its icon in the Windows system tray.

Bottom: This display, known as the Startup Manager, appears when you press Option during startup. It displays all the disk icons or partitions that contain bootable operating systems. Click the one you want, and then click the up-arrow button.

- **Open Parallels or Fusion.** The problem with Boot Camp is that every time you switch to or from Windows, you have to close down everything you were working on and restart the computer. You lose two or three minutes each way.

There is another way: an $80 utility called Parallels Desktop for Mac (*parallels.com*), or its rival, VMware Fusion (*vmware.com*). These two programs let you run Windows and macOS simultaneously; Windows hangs out in a window of its own, while the Mac is running macOS. You're getting about 90 percent of Boot Camp's Windows speed—which is plenty fast for everything but 3D games.

Having virtualization software on your Mac is a beautiful thing. You can be working on a design in iWork, duck into a Microsoft Access database (Windows only), look up an address, copy it, and paste it back into the Mac program.

You can even install Boot Camp *and* Parallels/Fusion. They coexist beautifully on a single Mac and can even use the same copy of Windows.

Both techniques require you to provide your own copy of Windows. Since Boot Camp comes with the Mac, here's a quick rundown.

Installing Boot Camp

To set up Boot Camp, you need the proper ingredients:

- **A copy of Windows 8 or later.** It has to be the *64-bit version* of Windows, and it has to be a full installation copy—not an upgrade version. And you need the ISO (disk image) of the Windows installer. (If you got Windows on a flash drive instead, then download the ISO from Microsoft and use the serial number that came with the flash drive.)

- **At least 55 gigs of free hard drive space** on your built-in hard drive, or a second internal drive. Windows is not svelte, and you can't install Windows on an external drive using Boot Camp.

- **The keyboard and mouse that came with your Mac.** You can also use a generic USB keyboard and mouse; what you *can't* use is a non-Apple cordless keyboard and mouse.

- **A USB flash drive, 16 GB or bigger.** The Boot Camp installer may require this, depending on your Mac model.

Before you install, Apple strongly recommends that you back up your Mac, make sure it's running the latest version of macOS, and acquire the latest version of Boot Camp (visit *apple.com/support/bootcamp*). If you're using a laptop, plug it in for the surgery.

The step-by-steps for installation are long, and they vary according to your Mac model and whether you're doing a fresh installation of Windows or upgrading to a newer version.

Fortunately, Apple has written out detailed instructions for you here: *support.apple. com/en-us/HT201468.*

Tip: Using the ⚙ menu at the bottom of the window, you can turn your various audio inputs (that is, microphones, line inputs, and so on) on or off. You can even direct your Mac's system beeps to pour forth from one set of speakers (like the one built into your Mac), and all other sound, like music, through a different set.

- **MIDI.** MIDI stands for Musical Instrument Digital Interface, a standard "language" for inter-synthesizer communication. It's available to music software companies who have written their wares to capitalize on these tools.

 When you choose Window→Show MIDI Window, you get a window that represents your recording-studio configuration. By clicking Add Device, you create a new icon that represents one of your pieces of gear. Double-click the icon to specify its make and model. Finally, by dragging lines from the "in" and "out" arrows, you teach your Mac and its MIDI software how the various components are wired together.

Bluetooth File Exchange

One of the luxuries of using a Mac that has Bluetooth is the ability to shoot files (to colleagues who own similarly clever gadgets) through the air, up to 30 feet away. Bluetooth File Exchange makes it possible, as described on page 260.

Boot Camp Assistant

Since 2006, Macs have come with Intel chips inside, meaning that Macs and PCs use exactly the same memory, hard drives, monitors, mice, keyboards, networking protocols, and processors. With just a little bit of setup, therefore, your Mac can run Windows and Windows programs!

Think of all the potential switchers who are tempted by the Mac's sleek looks, yet worry about leaving Windows behind entirely. Or the people who love Apple's productivity programs but have jobs that rely on Microsoft Access, Outlook, or some other piece of Windows corporateware. Even true-blue Mac fans occasionally look longingly at some of the Windows-only games, websites, or movie download services they thought they'd never be able to use.

Today, there are two ways to run Windows on a Mac:

- **Restart it in Boot Camp.** Boot Camp Assistant lets you *restart* your Mac into Windows.

 At that point, it's a full-blown Windows PC, with no trace of the Mac on the screen. It runs at 100 percent of the speed of a real PC, because it is one. Compatibility with Windows software is excellent. The only downsides: Your laptop battery life isn't as good, and you have to restart the Mac to return to the familiar world of macOS.

Tip: What's cool, though, is that even when you're running Windows, you can still access your Mac files and folders, as described next.

Tip: You may also want to watch this graph right in your Dock (choose View→Dock Icon→Show CPU Usage) or in a bar at the edge of your screen (choose Window→CPU Usage).

Finally, there's the Window→CPU History command. It makes a resizable, real-time monitor window float on top of all your other programs, so you can't miss it.

- **Memory.** Here's a glorious revelation of the state of your Mac's RAM at the moment.

 The graph shows "memory pressure"—how much your programs are straining the Mac's memory. If, when your Mac is running a typical complement of programs, this graph is nearly filled up, then it's time to consider buying more memory. You're suffocating your Mac.

- **Energy.** How much battery power is each of your programs responsible for sucking away? This fascinating tab tells all.

- **Disk.** Even when you're not opening or saving a file, your Mac's hard drive or flash storage is frequently hard at work, shuffling chunks of program code into and out of memory, for example. Here's where the savvy technician can see exactly how frantic the disk is at the moment.

- **Network.** Keep an eye on how much data is shooting across your office network with this handy tsunami of real-time data.

AirPort Utility

You use the AirPort Utility to set up and manage AirPort base stations (Apple's wireless Wi-Fi networking routers).

If you click Continue, it presents a series of screens, posing one question at a time: what you want to name the network, what password you want for it, and so on. Once you've followed the steps and answered the questions, your AirPort hardware will be properly configured and ready to use.

Audio MIDI Setup

This program has a split personality; its name is a description of its two halves:

- **Audio.** When you first open Audio MIDI Setup, you see a complete summary of the audio inputs and outputs available on your Mac right now. It's a like the Sound pane of System Preferences, but with a lot more geeky detail. Here, for example, you can specify the recording level for your Mac's microphone, or even change the audio quality it records.

 For most people, this is all meaningless, because most Macs have only one input (the microphone) and one output (the speakers). But if you're sitting in your darkened music studio, humming with high-tech audio gear whose software has been designed to work with this little program, you'll smile when you see this tab.

 There's even a Configure Speakers button, for those audiophilic Mac fans who've attached stereo or even surround-sound speaker systems to their Macs.

• **Windowed Processes.** Now, *this* is probably what you were expecting: a list of actual programs with actual English names, like Activity Monitor, Finder, Safari, and Mail. These are the only ones running in actual windows, the only ones that are *visible*.

The System Monitor tabs

At the top of Activity Monitor, you're offered five tabs that reveal intimate details about your Mac and its behind-the-scenes efforts (Figure 11-48):

• **CPU.** As you go about your usual Mac business, opening a few programs, playing QuickTime movies, playing a game, and so on, you can see the CPU graphs rise and fall, depending on how busy you're keeping the central processing unit. You see a different graph color for each of your Mac's cores (independent subchips on your processor), so you can see how efficiently macOS is distributing the work among them.

Figure 11-48:
The many faces of Activity Monitor.

Top: It can be a graph of your processor (CPU) activity, your RAM usage at the moment, your disk capacity, and so on. Usually, only the processes listed here with tiny icons beside their names are actual windowed programs—those with icons in the Finder, the ones you actually interact with.

The top-left Quit Process button (⊗) is a convenient way to jettison a locked-up program when all else fails.

Bottom: If you double-click a process's name, you get a dialog box that offers reams of data (mostly of interest only to programmers) about what that program is up to. (The Open Files and Ports tab, for example, shows you how many files that program has opened, often invisibly.)

Tip: There's a menu command and a keystroke that can take you there. In the Finder, choose Go→Utilities (Shift-⌘-U).

Activity Monitor

Activity Monitor is designed to let the technologically savvy Mac fan see how much of the Mac's available power is being tapped at any given moment.

The list of processes

Even when you're running only a program or two on your Mac, dozens of computational tasks (*processes*) are going on in the background. The top part of the window, which looks like a table, shows you all the different processes—visible and invisible— that your Mac is handling at the moment.

Check out how many items appear in the Process list, even when you're just staring at the desktop. It's awesome to see how busy your Mac is! Some are easily recognizable programs (such as Finder), while others are background system-level operations you don't normally see. For each item, you can see the percentage of the CPU being used, who's using it (either your account name, someone else's, or *root*, meaning the Mac itself), and how much memory it's using.

Or use the View menu to see views like these:

- **All Processes.** This is the complete list of running processes; you'll notice that the vast majority are little Unix applications you never even knew you had.

- **All Processes, Hierarchically.** In Unix, one process launches another, creating a tree-like hierarchy. The big daddy of them all is the process called *launchd*. Here and there, you'll see some other interesting relationships: For example, the Dock launches DashboardClient.

- **My Processes.** This list shows only the programs that pertain to *your* world, your login. There are still plenty of unfamiliar items, but they're all running to serve *your* account.

- **System Processes.** These are the processes run by *root*—that is, opened by macOS itself.

- **Other User Processes.** Here's a list of all *other* processes—"owned" by neither root nor you. Here you might see the processes being run by another account holder, for example (using fast user switching), or people who have connected to this Mac from across a network or the internet.

- **Active Processes, Inactive Processes.** Active processes are the ones that are actually doing something right now; inactive are the ones that are sitting there, waiting for a signal (like a keypress or a mouse click).

Editing Your Recording

You might not guess that such a tiny, self-effacing app actually offers some basic editing functions, but it does. Click a recording, then Edit to open its Edit screen (Figure 11-47, right).

Here you have four options:

- **Record over it.** When the blue playhead line is parked at the beginning or middle of the audio, the big red button says Replace. Click it to record over part (or all) of your original recording. This is kind of handy. If you recorded a brilliant speech, but stumbled on the opening line (or any line, actually), you can replace it without having to redo the whole thing. Hit **II** to stop.

- **Add onto it.** You can also add on more audio to your existing recording. Just park the blue playhead line at the end of the current sound waves, and then hit Resume. Hit **II** to stop.

- **Trim it.** You can trim off the beginning or end of your audio clip—which is great, since that's where you'll usually find "dead air" or microphone fumbling before the good stuff starts playing.

 To do that, click the Crop button (⬚). At this point, the "map" of the entire sound recording (at the middle of the screen) sprouts yellow crop handles. Drag them inward to isolate the part you want to keep. When you're close, use the magnified area at top to fine-tune the trip points, using the vertical yellow lines. Play the sound as necessary to guide you (▶).

 Click Trim to shave away everything outside your selected area. If you like the result, click Save. If you'd rather try again, choose Edit→Undo. Or hit Cancel to forget the whole thing.

- **Cut out a chunk.** To cut something out of the middle, isolate the undesired audio using the crop and trim handles as described above. This time, though, hit the Delete button. You've just chopped the selection out of the middle.

 Here again, you can hit Save (to preserve the edit), or Cancel to back out of the entire operation.

The beauty of all of this, by the way, is that your audio recordings can now magically and wirelessly appear on all your other Apple machinery, just as though they're calendar appointments or Safari bookmarks. The on/off switch for this syncing is hiding away in System Preferences→iCloud→iCloud Drive→Options→Voice Memos.

Utilities: Your macOS Toolbox

The Utilities folder (inside your Applications folder) is home to another batch of freebies: a couple of dozen tools for monitoring, tuning, tweaking, and troubleshooting your Mac.

- **Rewind, Fast Forward.** Drag the scrubber bar to skip backward or forward in the recording. It's a great way to skip over the boring pleasantries. Or click the ⏱ or⏱ buttons to jump forward or back by 15 seconds. Or just click a spot to jump there.

- ⬆. Click to open the standard Share menu. It gives you the chance to send your recording to someone else by AirDrop, email, or Messages—or to drop the audio file into a Notes page.

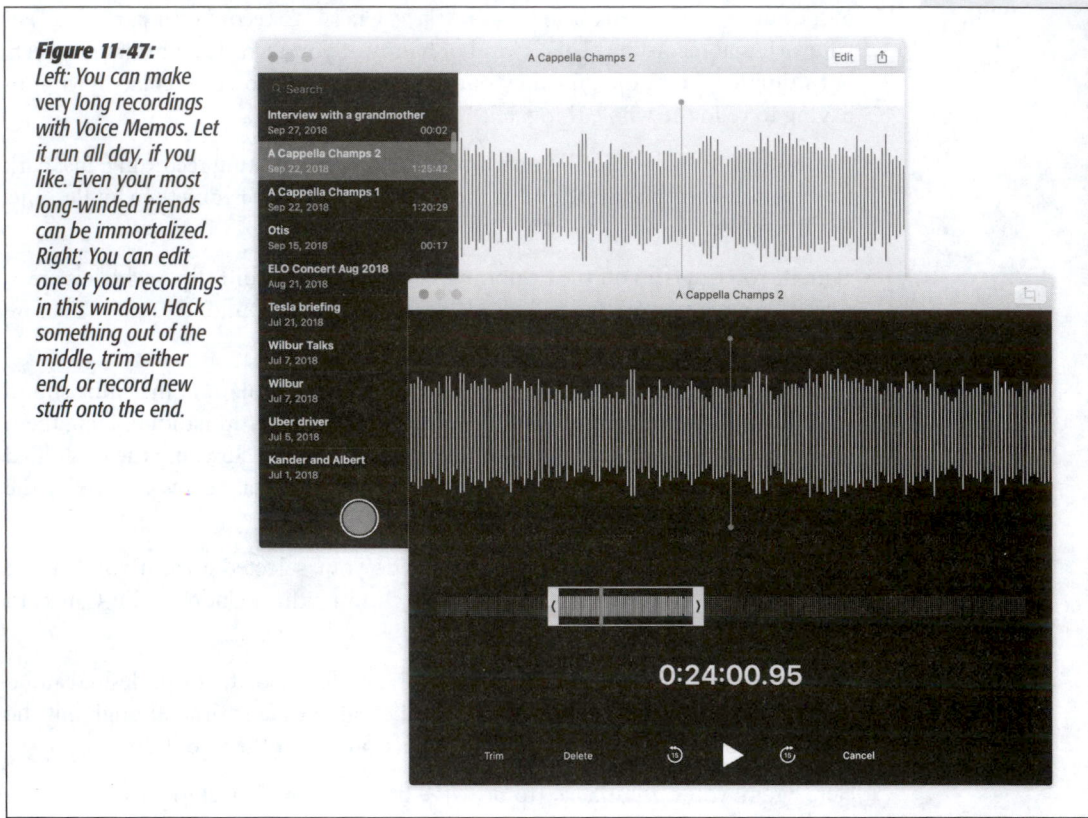

Figure 11-47:
Left: You can make very long recordings with Voice Memos. Let it run all day, if you like. Even your most long-winded friends can be immortalized. Right: You can edit one of your recordings in this window. Hack something out of the middle, trim either end, or record new stuff onto the end.

To delete a recording, click its name in the list and then press Delete. You're not asked for confirmation, but you do have a safety net: The deleted recording will sit in the Recently Deleted folder at the very bottom of the list for 30 days.

To see these recordings on death row, click Recently Deleted. Your options here are Recover All (rescue them from deletion), Erase All, or erase just one recording (select it, press the Delete key, and then click Erase to confirm).

Tip: In Voice Memos→Preferences→Clear Deleted, you can specify how quickly these deleted recordings disappear. Your choices are Immediately, After 1 Day, After 7 Days, After 30 Days, or Never.

TextEdit's Other Writing Tools

TextEdit includes a few other very useful document-editing tools:

- **Allow Hyphenation.** When you select this command from the Format menu, TextEdit breaks up words by syllable and inserts hyphens when necessary in order to create more visually pleasing line breaks.

Tip: It's especially important to turn this feature on if your paragraph alignment is set to Justify, or if you create narrow columns of text. If hyphenation is turned off, then TextEdit won't break up long words at the end of a line—even if it leaves big, ugly gaps between words.

- **Prevent Editing.** When you turn this option on (in the Format menu), you're locked out. You can select and copy text to your heart's content, but you can't change anything. Prevent Editing mode can be useful if you want to prevent yourself from making accidental changes to a file, but it's not much of a security feature. (All anyone has to do is choose Format→Allow Editing to regain full editing privileges.)

- **Spelling and Grammar.** These aren't TextEdit features; they're system-wide macOS features, and they're described starting on page 241.

Time Machine

This marquee feature of macOS is described on page 266.

Voice Memos

This audio app, the fourth of the new macOS apps that Apple adapted from iOS, is ideal for recording lectures, musical performances, notes to self, and cute child utterances (Figure 11-47). It can even sync your recordings with your iPhone and other Apple gizmos automatically, courtesy of iCloud.

Click ◎ to start recording from your Mac's built-in microphone (or whatever source you've chosen in System Preferences→Sound). You get to watch the actual sound waves as the recording proceeds (Figure 11-47, left).

You can pause the recording (**II**) at any time, and then click Resume to continue; hit Done when the recording session is over.

The recording shows up with a name based on your current location, like 200 Madison St. (You can turn off this place-naming convention in Voice Memos→Preferences. In that case, every new recording is called, for example, New Recording 35.) You can rename it easily enough: Double-click the temporary name and then type something better ("Baby's First Words," "Orch Concert," whatever).

When you click a recording in the list (Figure 11-47, left), a convenient set of controls appears. Here's what you can do here:

- ▶. Click to play the recording. You can pause with the **II** button. (The space bar plays and pauses, too.)

- **To save a brand-new document as an HTML** (web page) file, choose File→Save; from the File Format pop-up menu, choose Web Page. (To save an existing TextEdit document as an HTML file, choose File→Duplicate and then File→Save; choose Web Archive Document from the pop-up menu.)

- **Don't miss the HTML options** in TextEdit→Preferences. On the Open and Save tab, you can specify what kind of HTML document you want to produce, what Cascading Style Sheets (CSS) setting you want, and whether or not you want TextEdit to include code to preserve blank areas (white space) in your layout.

Tip: When you open a web page document—that is, an HTML document—TextEdit is faced with a quandary. Should it open up the page as though it's a web page, interpreting the HTML code as though it's a browser? Or should it reveal the underlying HTML code itself?

Actually, that's up to you. When you choose File→Open, turn on "Ignore rich text commands" to make the document open up as HTML code. (To make this change permanent, turn on the same checkbox on the Open and Save pane of the TextEdit→Preferences dialog box.)

TextEdit Preferences

Most of the settings in the TextEdit Preferences→New Document pane have no effect on documents that are *already* open—only on documents you open or create from now on. Most of the settings are self-explanatory; nonetheless, handy explanatory balloons appear if you point to an option without clicking. Here are a few settings that may not be immediately clear:

- **Font.** If Helvetica 12 doesn't float your boat, you can change TextEdit's starting font. In fact, you can set *two* default fonts—one for Rich Text documents and another one for plain text files.

Note: By definition, plain text files don't have any formatting. So whatever font you choose here for plain text files is for your viewing pleasure only. If you plan to send the file to anyone else, remember that the font choice won't be saved with the document.

- **Window Size.** These settings have no effect unless you're in Wrap to Window mode, in which the text rewraps to fit the window width, as opposed to Wrap to Page mode. (You choose these options from TextEdit's Format menu.) If you *are* in Wrap to Window mode, then these dimensions determine the size of the window that appears each time you create a new TextEdit document.

- **Properties.** These boxes—Author, Company, and Copyright—are some of the tags that Spotlight inspects when it searches your Mac. If you'd like to be able to round up your documents by these characteristics, fill them in here to specify the information you want to use for *most* documents. (To fill them in differently for individual documents, choose File→Show Properties instead.)

- **Options.** These are the on/off switches for the various typing aids described in Chapter 6: smart quotes, data detectors, text replacement, and so on.

- **Nest a table inside a cell of another** by clicking in the cell and then clicking Nest Table. Change the numbers in the Row and Columns boxes to set up its dimensions (Figure 11-46).

Figure 11-46:
Note to web designers: TextEdit may not be Dreamweaver, but it's great for spinning out quick web pages, thanks to the table features. Here you can see that a big table forms the underlying structure for this web page, along with a couple of nested ones and color selections.

TextEdit as Web Designer

The Table palette isn't the only clue that Apple intends TextEdit to be a quick-and-dirty web page design program. Consider these other tools:

- **You can easily add graphics to the page** by dragging or pasting them into a document. The program understands many common image formats, including TIFF, PICT, JPEG and PNG.

- **You can add web-style hyperlinks** by highlighting "Click here" (or whatever the link says), choosing Edit→Add Link (⌘-K), and then entering the web address in the resulting dialog box. Or just drag a link in from Safari, Mail, or another program. (To edit the link later, right-click or two-finger click it, and then choose Edit Link.)

Tip: Of course, you can also have TextEdit convert typed links into clickable ones *automatically* as you type them. That's the purpose of the Smart Links option in TextEdit→Preferences.

To make this work, choose Show Styles from the ¶ pop-up menu. Choose the style you want to work on. (If Document Styles is selected, then click the ▶ button to page through the styles; if Favorite Styles is selected, then choose from the pop-up menu.) Then click Select.

In the little details sheet that appears, click the options you want, and then click Select. TextEdit highlights every occurrence of that style in the entire document (or selection). At this point, you can use any of the usual text-formatting controls to modify them all simultaneously.

- **Formatting by example.** In TextEdit, you can also use Option-⌘-C and Option-⌘-V (Format→Font→Copy Style and Format→Font→Paste Style) to grab formatting from one place in your document and reuse it elsewhere. (Of course, you can't apply styles in text-only documents.)

Tables

Tables can make life a lot easier when you want to create a resumé, agenda, program booklet, list, multiple-choice test, web page, or another document where numbers, words, and phrases must be aligned across the page. In the bad old days, people did it by pressing the Tab key to line up columns—a technique that turned into a nightmare as soon as you tried to add or delete text. But using a word processor's *table* feature is light-years easier and more flexible, because each row of a table expands to contain whatever you put into it. Everything else in its row remains aligned.

Tip: Tables are sometimes used for designing web pages. Even though you can't see the table outlines, many a web page is filled with columns of text that are aligned invisibly by tables. Because TextEdit can save your work as an HTML document, it's a viable candidate for designing basic web pages.

- **Create a table** by choosing Format→Table. The floating Table palette appears (Figure 11-46). Use it to specify how many rows and columns you want. The placeholder table in your document adjusts itself in real time.

- **Format the table** using the other controls in the Table palette. The Alignment controls let you specify how the text in the table cells hugs its border. Cell controls the thickness of the line around the selected cells' borders (or, if you enter *0*, makes the table walls invisible). The color swatch next to Cell specifies the color of the solid lines. The Cell Background controls let you color in the table cells with colors of your choice. (Choose Color Fill from the pop-up menu, and then click the color swatch.) This is an especially valuable option for web designers.

- **Adjust the rows and columns** by dragging the cell borders.

- **Merge two selected cells** by clicking Merge Cells in the Table palette. Once you've done that, you can use the Split Cells button to split them apart again. (Split Cells doesn't work except in cells you've previously merged.)

Tip: If you simply click inside a paragraph, applying a style affects only paragraph attributes, like line spacing, tab stops, and alignment. If you highlight a random chunk of text instead, applying a style affects only character attributes, like the font and type size. If you highlight an entire paragraph, however, both text and paragraph formatting appear.

- **Deleting a style.** To delete a superfluous style, choose Show Styles from the ¶ pop-up menu on the toolbar. Click the Favorite Styles button, choose the unwanted style's name from the pop-up menu, and then click Remove From Favorites. (Deleting a style doesn't affect any formatting that's already in your document; it just removes the name from the Styles menu.)

- **Replacing all occurrences.** You can highlight every occurrence of a certain style at once—and then change, copy, or delete them all at once.

POWER USERS' CLINIC

Advanced Typography in TextEdit

If you just spewed your coffee upon reading the heading of this sidebar, you're forgiven. Advanced typography in TextEdit? Isn't that a little bit like saying "advanced page layout in Notepad"?

Not at all. TextEdit is a gleaming showcase for macOS's typographical smarts.

Most of the commands in the Format→Font submenu should be familiar to you: Bold, Italic, Underline, and so on. But a few were once found only in expensive page-layout programs like InDesign and QuarkXPress. For example:

Kern. Use these commands, such as Tighten and Loosen, to nudge the letters of the selected text closer together or farther apart—an especially useful feature when you're fiddling with headlines and headings.

There are no controls to set how much you want to kern the text, but you can apply these commands repeatedly to the same text selection to intensify them. If you want your text to be very tight, for example, just keep choosing the Tighten command. The characters creep closer and closer together until they crash into one another.

Ligatures. Ligatures are letter pairs, such as fl and ff, that, in fancy typesetting, are conjoined into special combination

characters, as shown here. If you choose Format→Font→Ligatures→Use Default (or Use All), then TextEdit displays these letter pairs with the appropriate ligatures.

fluffy fluffy

(This works only if the font you're using has those ligatures built into it. New York, Charcoal, Apple Chancery, and all Adobe Expert fonts do, for example, but many other fonts don't.)

Baseline. The baseline is the imaginary "floor" for text characters in a line of type. You can push text above this line or sink it below the baseline using the Raise and Lower commands in the Baseline submenu. The Superscript and Subscript commands, meanwhile, shift characters far above or below the baseline, so you can write stuff like "H_2O."

Character Shape. In a few fonts, such as Adobe Expert fonts, this submenu offers a choice between Traditional Form and specialized type treatments like Small Caps.

Copy Style/Paste Style. If mastering the Styles pop-up menu is too much effort, then you should know that these commands offer another way to copy and paste just the font formatting to other text—the font, color, style, and size, but none of the actual text or paragraph attributes, such as alignment.

for instance). You can create as many styles as you need: chapter headings, sidebar styles, and so on. You end up with a collection of custom-tailored styles for each of the repeating elements of your document.

Once you've created your styles, you can apply them as you need them, confident in the knowledge that they'll be consistent throughout the document. During the editing process, if you notice that you accidentally styled a *headline* using the *Subhead* style, you can fix the problem by simply reapplying the correct style.

Note: TextEdit doesn't let you *change* a style's formatting and thereby update every occurrence of it. Fortunately, you *can* search for all occurrences of a style and change them all simultaneously (see page 488).

- **Creating a named style.** To create a style, format some text so it looks the way you like it, complete with font, color, line spacing, tab settings, and so on.

 Then, from the ¶ pop-up menu at the left end of the toolbar, choose Show Styles (Figure 11-45). Click Add To Favorites, type a name for the style, turn on both checkboxes, and then click Add.

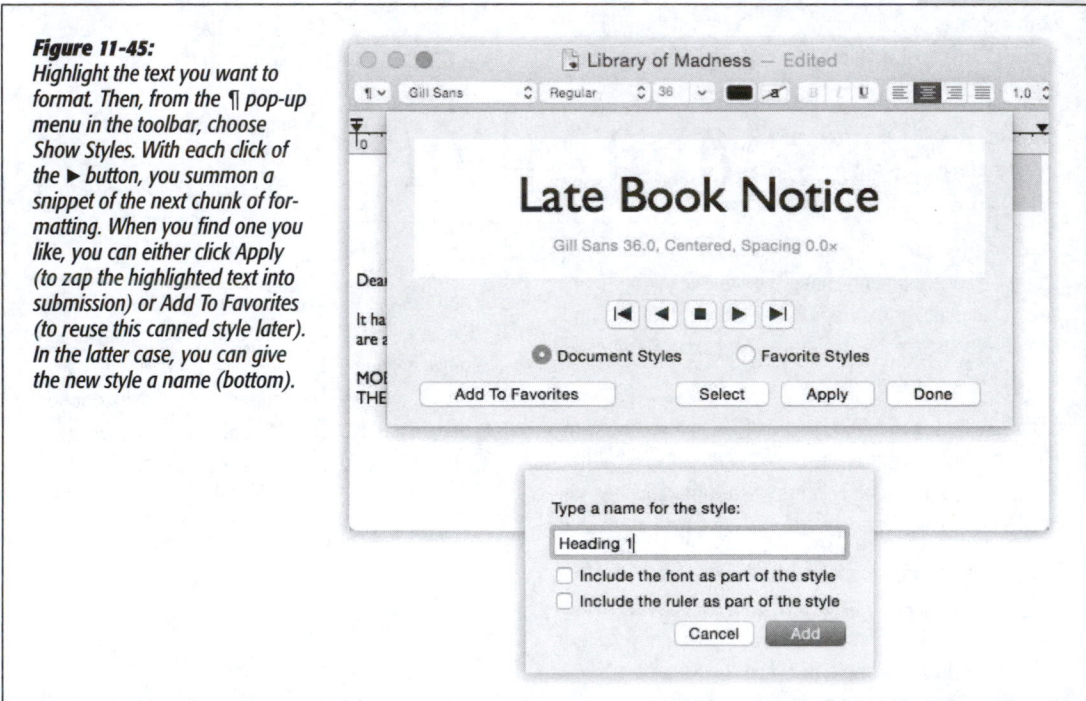

Figure 11-45:
Highlight the text you want to format. Then, from the ¶ pop-up menu in the toolbar, choose Show Styles. With each click of the ▶ button, you summon a snippet of the next chunk of formatting. When you find one you like, you can either click Apply (to zap the highlighted text into submission) or Add To Favorites (to reuse this canned style later). In the latter case, you can give the new style a name (bottom).

- **Applying a style.** Later, when you want to reuse the formatting you set up, highlight some text and then choose the appropriate name from the ¶ pop-up menu. TextEdit applies the formatting.

Working in TextEdit

As you begin typing, all the usual word-processing rules apply, with a few twists:

- **Choose bold, italic, and font sizes** using the formatting toolbar. (You can still use the commands in the Format menu.) You can even create subscripts or superscripts, change the color of the text (Format→Font→Show Colors), and so on.

- **Common paragraph-alignment options**—Align Left, Align Right, Center, Justify— are all available as toolbar buttons and also reside in the Format→Text submenu. Adjust the line spacing (single, double, or any fraction or multiple) using the Spacing pop-up menu in the toolbar.

- **The toolbar also offers automatic bulleting** and numbering of paragraphs. Just choose the numbering style you prefer from the pop-up menu at the right end of the toolbar.

Tip: If your Mac has a Touch Bar (page 233), all of these formatting controls appear as glowing buttons—the better to apply styles without lifting your hands from the keyboard.

- **You can select several nonadjacent bits** of text *simultaneously*. To pull this off, highlight your first piece of text by dragging, and then press ⌘ as you use the mouse to select more text. Bingo: You've highlighted two separate chunks of text.

When you're done selecting bits of text here and there, you can operate on them en masse. For example, you can make them all bold or italic in one fell swoop. You can even use the Cut, Copy, and Paste commands, as described in the next section. When you cut or copy, the command acts upon all your selections at once.

You can also drag any *one* of the highlighted portions to a new area, confident that the other chunks will come along for the ride. All the selected areas wind up consolidated in their new location.

Tip: If you *Option*-drag one of the highlighted bits, you *copy* all selected chunks, leaving the originals in place.

- **Similarly, you can use the Find command.** To do that, choose Edit→Find→Find (or just press ⌘-F). Fill in the search box; the sought-for term appears highlighted everywhere in your document at once. (You can also search and *replace,* using the other commands in the Edit→Find submenu.)

- **If you Option-drag vertically,** you can freely select an arbitrary column of text (not necessarily the entire page width). This technique is useful when you want to select only one column in a multicolumn layout, or when you want to select the numbers in a list and format them all at once.

Style Sheets

A *style* is a prepackaged collection of formatting attributes that you can apply and reapply with a click of the mouse (bold, 24-point Optima, double-spaced, centered,

Tip: You can magnify the type of a TextEdit document just the way you do on an iPhone or an iPad: by pinching or spreading. That is, spread two fingers on your trackpad to zoom in, or pinch on the trackpad to zoom out. Best. Tip. Ever.

TextEdit's Two Personalities

The one confusing aspect of TextEdit is that it's both a *plain text editor* (no formatting; globally compatible) and a true *word processor* (fonts, sizes, styles; compatible with other word processors). Here's the scheme:

- **You can change a plain text document** to a formatted one by choosing Format→ Make Rich Text or Shift-⌘-T. The ruler appears automatically to remind you that a new world of formatting has just become available.

- **Conversely, you can change a formatted document** (a Word file you've opened, for example) to a plain text document by choosing Format→Make Plain Text (or, again, Shift-⌘-T). An alert message appears to point out that you're about to lose all formatting.

- **If you know what kind of document you *always* want to open,** go to the TextEdit→ Preferences dialog box; on the New Document tab, select Rich Text or Plain Text. That's what you'll get each time you choose File→New.

Tip: Here's also where you can turn on smart links, smart quotes, smart dashes, and the other smart text-processing features described in Chapter 6.

UP TO SPEED

The Deal with Microsoft Word

Yes, it's true: Humble TextEdit can open and create Microsoft Word documents! Your savings: the $150 price of Microsoft Office!

Well, sort of.

When you open a Microsoft Word document in TextEdit, most of the formatting comes through alive: bold, italic, font choices, colors, line spacing, alignment, and so on. Even very basic tables make it into TextEdit, although with different column widths.

A lot of Word-specific formatting does not survive crossing the chasm, however: borders, style sheets, footnotes, and the like. Bullets and numbered lists don't make it, either, even though TextEdit can create its own versions of these. And TextEdit doesn't recognize the comments and tracked changes your collaborators might use to mark up your manuscript.

Saving a new TextEdit document as a Word document is a better bet, because Word understands the many kinds of formatting that TextEdit can produce—including bullets, numbering, and tables. (You can create a Word file the first time you save it from TextEdit, or you can convert a document into Word format later by choosing File→Duplicate, and then File→Save.)

The one disappointment is that Word doesn't recognize any style sheets you've set up in TextEdit. The formatting applied by those style names survives—just not the style names themselves.

Even so, a built-in Word-document editor is a huge, huge step for the Mac operating system. It means that, in many cases, you can be a first-class citizen on the playing field of American business. Nobody ever needs to know that you're (a) using a Mac, and (b) not using the real Microsoft Word.

System Preferences

This program opens the door to the nerve center of macOS's various preferences, settings, and options. Chapter 9 covers every option in detail.

TextEdit

TextEdit is a basic word processor—but it's not nearly as basic as people think it is. You can create real documents with real formatting, using style sheets, colors, automatic numbering and bullets, tables, and customized line spacing. You can even open, edit, and create Microsoft Word documents. If you had to, you could write a children's book in TextEdit, and it would look pretty decent.

Better yet, TextEdit (Figure 11-44) is now a showcase for macOS's iPaddish features, like Full Screen mode, Auto Save, and Versions (see Chapter 5). It can also save your files into your iCloud locker, as described on page 221.

And TextEdit works with macOS's long list of built-in text-editing features: smart links, smart quotes, smart dashes, smart copy/paste, abbreviation expansion, auto–typo correction, data detectors, and so on. (They're all described in Chapter 6.)

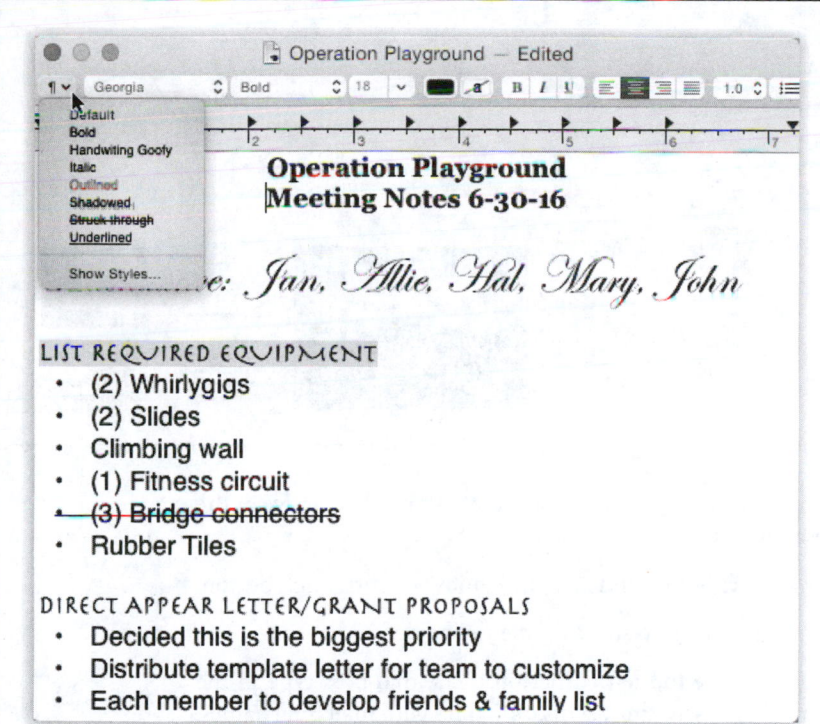

Figure 11-44:
The text ruler gives you control over tab stops, paragraph justification, and so on. Pressing ⌘-R makes it appear and disappear. On the toolbar, the Style pop-up menu (¶) lists canned sets of character and paragraph formatting, so you can apply them consistently throughout a document.

Customizing Your Portfolio

It's fairly unlikely that *your* stock portfolio contains just Apple, Google, and Facebook. Fortunately, you can customize the list of stocks to reflect the companies you *do* own (or want to track).

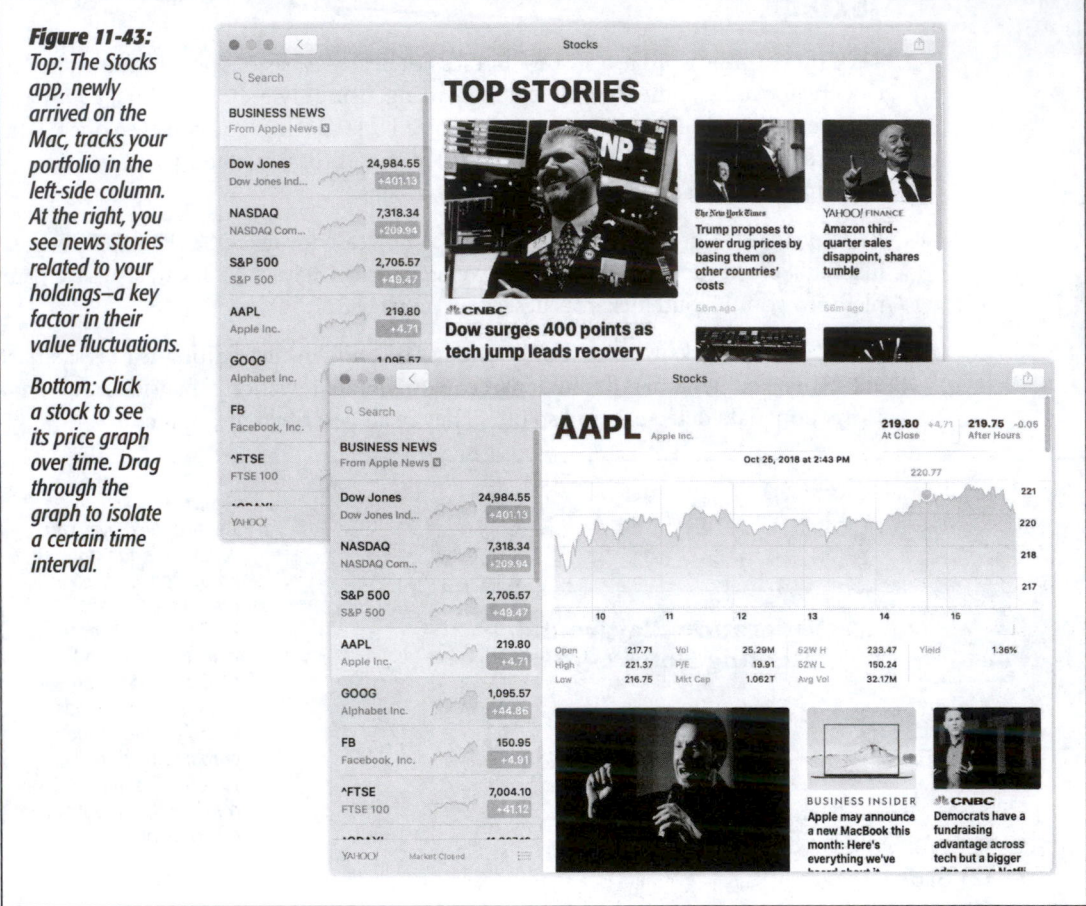

Figure 11-43:
Top: The Stocks app, newly arrived on the Mac, tracks your portfolio in the left-side column. At the right, you see news stories related to your holdings—a key factor in their value fluctuations.

Bottom: Click a stock to see its price graph over time. Drag through the graph to isolate a certain time interval.

To edit the list, click ≔ in the lower-right corner of the stocks list. You arrive at the editing screen, where these choices await:

- **Delete a stock** by clicking the ⊖ button and then the Remove confirmation button.

- **Rearrange the list** by dragging the grip strips on the right side.

- **Add a stock** by clicking + in the top-left corner; in the search box, type in the company's name or symbol for a scrolling list of companies with matching names. Click + for one you want to track. You return to the stocks-list editing screen.

When you're finished setting up your stock list, click Cancel and then Done.

but double-clicking the icon doesn't do anything. When you export the note as an RTFD file, the result is a TextEdit document that has embedded within it the *entire* program or document you dragged in. The program icon appears just as it did in the sticky note, but if you double-click the icon, the program actually opens.

You can also paste a graphic into your sticky note. When you export the note as an RTFD document, the resulting *package* file includes a graphics file of the format you pasted.

Stocks

This one's for you, big-time day trader. The Stocks app—another port-over from iOS, and therefore new in macOS Mojave—tracks the rise and fall of the stocks in your portfolio by downloading the very latest stock prices (see Figure 11-43).

(All right, maybe not the *very* latest. The price updates may be delayed as much as 20 minutes, which is typical of free stock-info services.)

When you first fire it up (and hit Continue to pass the welcome screen), Stocks shows you a handful of sample securities and indexes in the left-side column: the Dow Jones Industrial Average, the NASDAQ Composite Index, the S&P 500 Index, Apple, Google, and Facebook, for example.

Next to each, you see a spark graph (a miniature of today's price fluctuations), its current share price, and beneath *that*, how much that price has gone up or down today. As a handy visual gauge to how elated or depressed you should be, this final number appears on a *green* background if it's gone up, or a *red* one if it's gone down. Click this number to cycle the display from a percentage to a dollar amount to current market capitalization ("120.3B," meaning $120.3 billion in total corporate value).

When you click a stock, the top right part of the screen zooms in for the details on that company. Here's what it contains:

- **A table of statistics.** A capsule summary of today's price and volume statistics for this stock.

- **A graph of the stock's price.** It starts out showing you the graph of today's fluctuations. But by clicking the headings above the chart, you can zoom in or out, from one day (1D) to the entire history of the company (All), with many increments in between.

Tip: Move the cursor across the graph to see the readout for a certain day. Or drag to isolate a certain time period; pop-up labels show how much of a bath you took (or how much of a windfall you received) during the interval you highlighted. Cool!

- **An assortment of relevant headlines,** brought to you by the News app (page 444). Click a headline to read the article.

Have a favorite style for your sticky notes? First create a new note, choosing the color and text style you like and setting it to the size you prefer. Then choose Window→Use as Default. All new notes you create now appear in the size, font, and color you've chosen.

Growing and Shrinking Notes

Stickies includes a few built-in tricks for managing a deskful of notes:

- **Drag any corner of the note** to make it larger or smaller onscreen.

- **Use the small triangle in the upper-right corner** of each note to zoom and shrink note windows with a single click. The first click expands a note nearly to full-screen size. Another click pops the note back down to normal size.

- **The best option: Double-click anywhere** along the dark strip at the top of each note to collapse it into a compact one-line mini-note. You also can collapse a selected note by choosing Window→Collapse (⌘-M).

Tip: The most efficient way to use Stickies is to keep the notes in their collapsed state. When a note is collapsed, the first line of text shows up in tiny type in the collapsed title bar of the note, so you don't have to expand the note to remember what's in it. Plenty of notes can be summed up in a couple of words ("Pick up dry cleaning," "Call Mom"), so you may even be able to leave your notes this way.

Formatting Notes

Stickies has word processor–like commands for creating designer sticky notes, with any combination of fonts, colors, and styles (explore the Font menu). You can also choose from six background colors from the Color menu.

Saving Sticky Notes

The notes you create in Stickies last only as long as you keep them open. If you close a note to get it out of the way (and click Delete Note in the confirmation box), it vanishes permanently.

If you want to preserve the information you've stuffed into your notes in a more permanent form, you can do it in one of two ways: Close the note but hit the Save button, or use File→Export Text. Either way, you save the note as a standalone TextEdit document, with the following format options:

- **Plain Text.** This option saves your note as a plain text file, with neither formatting nor pictures.

- **RTF.** RTF stands for Rich Text Format, a special exchange format that preserves most formatting, including fonts, style, and color choices. You can open the resulting RTF file in just about any word processor with all your formatting still intact.

- **RTFD.** RTFD, a strange and powerful variant of RTF, is a Rich Text Format document *with attachments*. How do you "attach" items to an RTFD file? Drag the icon of an actual application (Preview, Calculator, or whatever) or a multipage PDF file, into a sticky note. The icon for the program or document appears in the note,

File→Close (⌘-W). Each time you close a note, a dialog box asks if you want to save it. If you click Delete Note, the note disappears permanently.

To create a new note, choose File→New Note (⌘-N). Then start typing or:

- **Drag text in from any other program.** Or drag text clippings from the desktop directly into your note. You can also drag a graphics file into a note to add a picture. You can even drag a sound or a movie in.

- **Drag the icon of a PDF file into a note.** (Stickies can accommodate multipage PDF files. At first, you see only the first page, but the scroll bar reveals the rest.)

- **Choose File→Import Text** and select any plain text file or RTF (Rich Text Format) document to bring it into a note.

- **Drag URLs** into a note directly from a web browser's address bar.

Tip: If one particular note contains your most important information—your to-do list, say—you can force it to remain in front of all other windows, even if Stickies itself gets shunted to the background. Just click the note, and then choose Note→Floating Window.

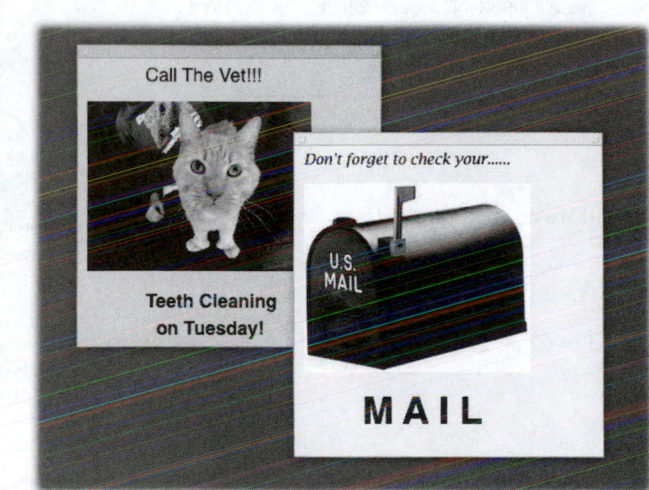

Figure 11-42:
In the old days of the Mac, the notes you created with Stickies were text-only, single-font deals. Today, however, you can use a mix of fonts, colors, and styles within each note. You can even paste in graphics, sounds, and movies (like PICT, GIF, JPEG, QuickTime, AIFF, whole PDF files, and so on), creating the world's most elaborate reminders and to-do lists.

After you paste in an image, you can even use the Markup tool to draw, scribble and highlight on it as you would in many other apps. Neat!

- **In many Apple programs, you can select a chunk of text** and then choose Make New Sticky Note from the program's Services menu, or press Shift-⌘-Y. This command launches Stickies, creates a new note, and fills it with your selected text—all in one step.

Note: All your notes are stored in a file called *StickiesDatabase*, located in your Home→Library folder. You're free to copy it, pass it along, and so on, just as you would any file.

You can assign a task to a different list by dragging it. Click any blank part of its line (not the text itself), and drag carefully onto the name of a different list in the List list at left.

Syncing Reminders

Once you've set up a few reminders in Reminders, you'll marvel as it gracefully integrates with the Notification Center when it wants your attention.

But it also auto-synchronizes your to-do lists across other gadgets, like iPhones, iPads, iPod Touches, other Macs, and even Windows PCs.

To give it permission for that kind of sharing, open System Preferences→iCloud and turn on the Reminders checkbox.

Note, however, that Reminders also can coordinate with the to-do list features of Exchange and so-called CalDAV services (Yahoo is one). To set them up, open System Preferences→Internet Accounts. Click the account you want (like Exchange or Yahoo); finally, turn the Reminders switch On.

That should do it. Now your to-do lists are synced, both ways.

Tip: You can also export your lists as .ics files, which you can then import into Google Calendar or another program. Just click the list and then choose File→Export. You can also *import* an existing .ics file (from another computer, for example) into a Reminders list you've selected: It's File→Import, of course.

QuickTime Player

There's a lot to say about QuickTime player, but it's all in Chapter 15.

Safari

The secrets of Apple's web browser are revealed in Chapter 18.

Stickies

Even in the age of the far more modern Notes program, the old Stickies app is still creaking along. It creates virtual Post-it notes that you can stick anywhere on your screen.

You can use Stickies for quick notes and to-do items, web addresses or phone numbers you need to remember, or any other little scraps and snippets of text you come across. They all show up whenever the Stickies program is running (Figure 11-42).

Creating Sticky Notes

The first time you launch Stickies, a couple of sample notes appear automatically, describing some of the program's features. You can quickly dispose of each sample by clicking the Close button in the upper-left corner of each note or by choosing

- **priority.** Click this pop-up menu to specify whether this item has High, Medium, or Low priority—or None. You'll see one, two, or three exclamation marks (!!!) next to each item in your Reminders list, indicating its urgency. In some of the calendar programs that sync with Reminders, you can sort your task list by priority.

- **note.** Here's a handy place where you can record freehand notes about this item: an address, a phone number, details of any kind.

Click Done to close the Details bubble and record your changes.

The Calendar of Deadline Hell

As you now know, Reminders can give you warnings of upcoming deadlines and to-do items. You don't have to wait until it gives you a reminder, though. Click Scheduled at the top of the list to review a list of all upcoming reminders.

Lists

Handily enough, you can create *more than one* to-do list, each with its own name: a Groceries list, Kids' Chores, a running tally of expenses, and so on. Here's a great way to log what you eat if you're on a diet, or to keep a list of movies people recommend.

If you share an iCloud account with another family member, you might create a different Reminder list for each person. (Of course, now you run the risk that your spouse might sneakily add items to *your* to-do list!)

If you have an Exchange account, one of your lists can be synced to your corporate Tasks list. It doesn't offer all the features of the other lists in Reminders, but at least it's kept tidy and separate. (Just set up your Exchange account in System Preferences→Internet Accounts.)

The list of lists is at the left side of Reminders; it's visible in Figure 11-41.

At the outset, the list of lists lists only one list: Reminders. But you can create others. Click the + button at the bottom-left corner, or choose File→New List, or hit ⌘-L, or just double-click any blank spot in the list of lists. (If you have more than one online account set up, like an iCloud account and a Yahoo account, you'll have to specify which account gets this list).

In any case, you've just made a new list called New List. Type to rename it to "Groceries list," "Movies list," whatever you like. (You can also get rid of a list by clicking it and then pressing the Delete key.)

Tip: You can view the contents of more than one list simultaneously. Just Shift-click the names of the lists you want in the left column; the right-side pane displays a unified, combined list of all their contents.

You can also open a list into a window of its own, just by double-clicking its name in the left column.

Once you've created some lists, you can switch among them by pressing the ▲ and ▼ keys to "walk" through the list.

Here are the options you'll find:

- **On a Day.** Reminders can remind you at a certain time on a certain date. In the Details bubble, next to "remind me," turn on On a Day. The proposed time is the next "o'clock"—if it's 12:15 now, the app suggests 1:00. But you can click the date to open a clickable mini-calendar (to change the date), or click the digits of the time to edit them.

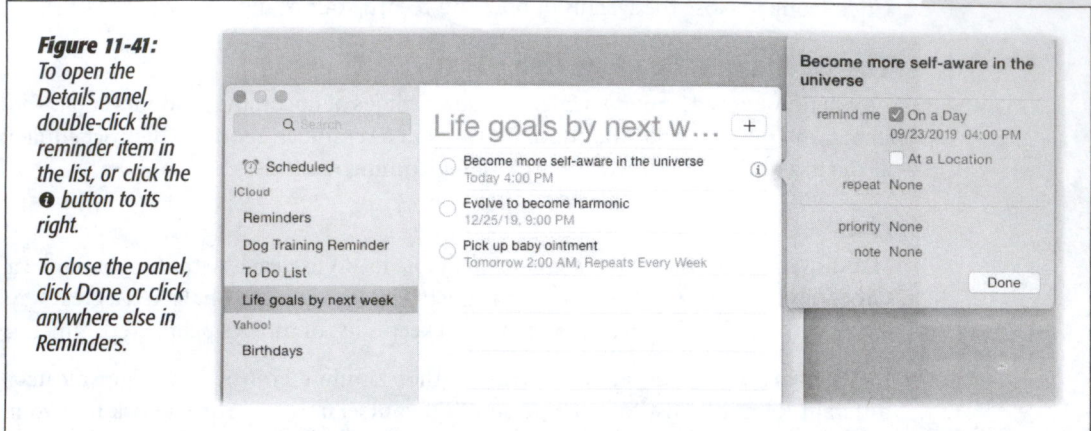

Figure 11-41:
To open the Details panel, double-click the reminder item in the list, or click the ⓘ *button to its right.*

To close the panel, click Done or click anywhere else in Reminders.

- **At a Location.** If you turn on this checkbox, your Mac or phone will use its location circuits to remind you of this item when you arrive at a certain place or leave a certain place. (Your laptop will remind you, if it's turned on and within a Wi-Fi hotspot. But more often, this option will be useful if you have an iPhone or iPad that's on the same iCloud account. Record the reminder on your Mac—receive the reminder on your phone.)

The little pop-up menu here proposes Current Location—wherever you are at the moment. That's handy if, for example, you're dropping off your dry cleaning and want to remember to pick it up the next time you're driving by.

But you can click that line to specify Home (your home address, as you've set it up in Contacts). You can also start typing any city name, or the name of any person in your Contacts whose address you've specified. You'll even see "Porky Pig Home" and "Porky Pig Work," if Porky has a couple of addresses on file.

The final step here is to click either Leaving or Arriving. Later, your gadgets will remind you at the appointed time, or as you approach (or leave) the appointed address. It's fairly mind-blowing the first few times it happens.

- **repeat.** Reminders can remind you about things that recur in your life, like quarterly tax payments, haircuts, and anniversaries. Click "repeat" if you want this reminder to appear every day, week, two weeks, month, or year. (This option appears only if you've turned on the On a Day option.)

Lots and lots of PDF documents are forms that you're supposed to fill out—from IRS tax forms to school permission slips. Preview is smart enough to recognize boxes to fill in, lines to type on, and checkboxes to click, meaning that you don't have to print, fill out, and then scan these things anymore. And it manages to find those lines, text boxes, and checkboxes on *any* PDF document, not just those that were originally designed to be filled in by PDF form-filling software. See Figure 11-40.

The Toolbar

There's a lot you can do with Preview's toolbar. You can customize it (by choosing View→Customize Toolbar), rearrange its icons (by ⌘-dragging them sideways), and remove icons (by ⌘-dragging them downward).

Reminders

Reminders is a to-do-list program. It not only records your life's little tasks, but it also reminds you about them when the time comes. On a laptop, Reminders can even remind you about something based on *where you are,* just as it does on the iPhone. For example, when you arrive home each day, it can remind you to feed your cats—or when you leave your vacation house, it can ask you if you've turned off the gas burners.

If you have an iCloud account, your reminders sync across all your gadgets. Create or check off a task on your iPhone, and you'll also find it created or checked off on your Mac, iPhone, iPad, iPod Touch, or PC. (Yes, PC. See *apple.com/icloud/setup/pc.html*).

The syncing business also explains why the location feature is useful even if you have a desktop Mac that doesn't move around a lot. You can program a reminder on your Mac—and your *phone or tablet* will alert you when you move into or away from a specified place.

Tip: Siri and Reminders are a match made in heaven. "Remind me to file the Jenkins report when I get to work." "Remind me to set the TiVo for tonight at 8." "Remind me about Timmy's soccer game a week from Saturday." "Add waffles to my Groceries list." Speech recognition rocks when it comes to leaving notes for yourself. And iCloud will take care of copying those reminders to your iPhone.

Once you've opened Reminders (Figure 11-41), you record a new task by clicking the + button in the upper right, or choose File→New Reminder (⌘-N). A new blank line appears in your list. Type your reminder.

Later, as you go through life completing tasks, click the checkbox next to each one. Doing that makes the item seem to disappear—but in fact, it whips into a separate list called Completed.

Tip: Reminders is another app that's greatly accelerated by the Touch Bar, if you have one (page 233). Here you get instant access to the +, ⓘ, and other useful buttons.

The Details Bubble

If you click an item's ⓘ button, you open the Details bubble. See Figure 11-41.

Once Preview has stored your signature, you can slap it into the PDF documents that will come through your life.

The first step is to teach Preview what your signature looks like. On the Markup toolbar, click the Sign pop-up menu, ⚭∨. In the resulting window, you're offered two tabs:

- **Trackpad.** If your Mac has a trackpad, this option lets you write out your signature with your finger! Click where it says "Click Here to Begin," and then draw away.

 Plan ahead; the width of the trackpad is all the space you've got. When you're done, press any key and then click Done. The result may not look exactly like your pen-and-paper signature, but it'll do for most purposes.

- **Camera.** Sign your name on a piece of white paper; hold it up to your Mac's camera, as shown in Figure 11-39. When the positioning looks good, click Done. You've just stored your signature. (You have to do this only once—per signature, anyway.)

Tip: As a handy bonus, whatever signatures you've saved this way also appear in Preview on all your *other* Macs. (At least those that are signed into the same iCloud account and are running Yosemite or later—and have iCloud Keychain turned on in Settings→iCloud.)

Now, then. When the time comes to sign a document, make the Markup toolbar visible. From the ⚭∨ pop-up menu, choose the signature's name (Figure 11-39, middle.)

The signature appears in its own graphics box. Drag it to a new position, or drag the blue handles to resize it (Figure 11-39, bottom).

Tip: To delete a signature, open the ⚭∨ pop-up menu, point to the signature, and click the ⊗ next to it in the menu.

Fill in PDF Forms

Here's a feature that could save a lot of trees: fill-inable PDF forms.

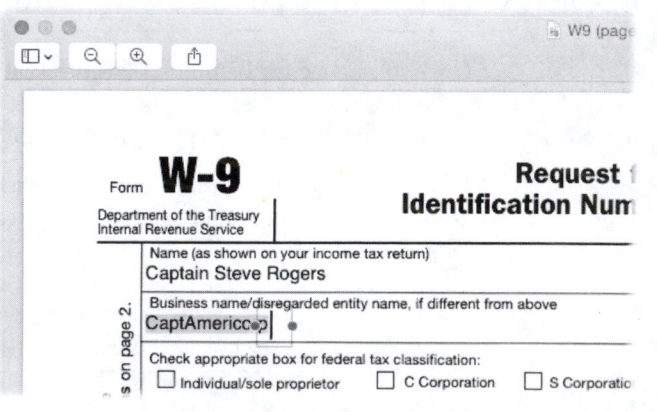

Figure 11-40:
When you fill in a form, the cursor changes automatically into an insertion point when it detects a box or a line you can fill in. And it turns into a pointing-finger icon when it's over a checkbox. Click to put a checkmark in that box; click again to remove the checkmark. It's hours of fun for the whole family!

When you're finished, save the document as you would any other. Amazingly, you'll be able to edit your responses when you open the PDF document again later.

Tip: Later you can view a tidy list of all your notes and highlighted passages by choosing View→Highlighting and Notes. On the resulting panel, Preview ordinarily displays each text note with your name and the date. If you'd rather not have that info added, then choose Preview→Preferences, click PDF, and then turn off "Add name to annotations."

- ≡ˇ **Shape Style.** This palette governs the thickness and style of whatever line or shape you're drawing (or you've selected). There are some cool options here, including dashed lines, shadowed ones, chalky-looking ones—and ones with arrowheads.

- ▢ˇ **Border Color,** ▱ˇ **Fill Color.** These palettes affect the border color (line color) and interior background color of whatever shape you're drawing (or have selected).

- *A*ˇ **Text Style.** Here are your font, size, and style commands for whatever text you're about to type (or have selected).

Once you've made an annotation, you can drag it around, drag its blue control dots to change its shape, edit the text inside it, and so on.

Signing PDF Documents with Your Real Signature

Of macOS's 47,000 features, few are quite as slick or useful as the PDF signature option (Figure 11-39). It lets your Mac memorize your signature, either by taking a picture of it—or by letting you sign with your finger on your laptop's trackpad.

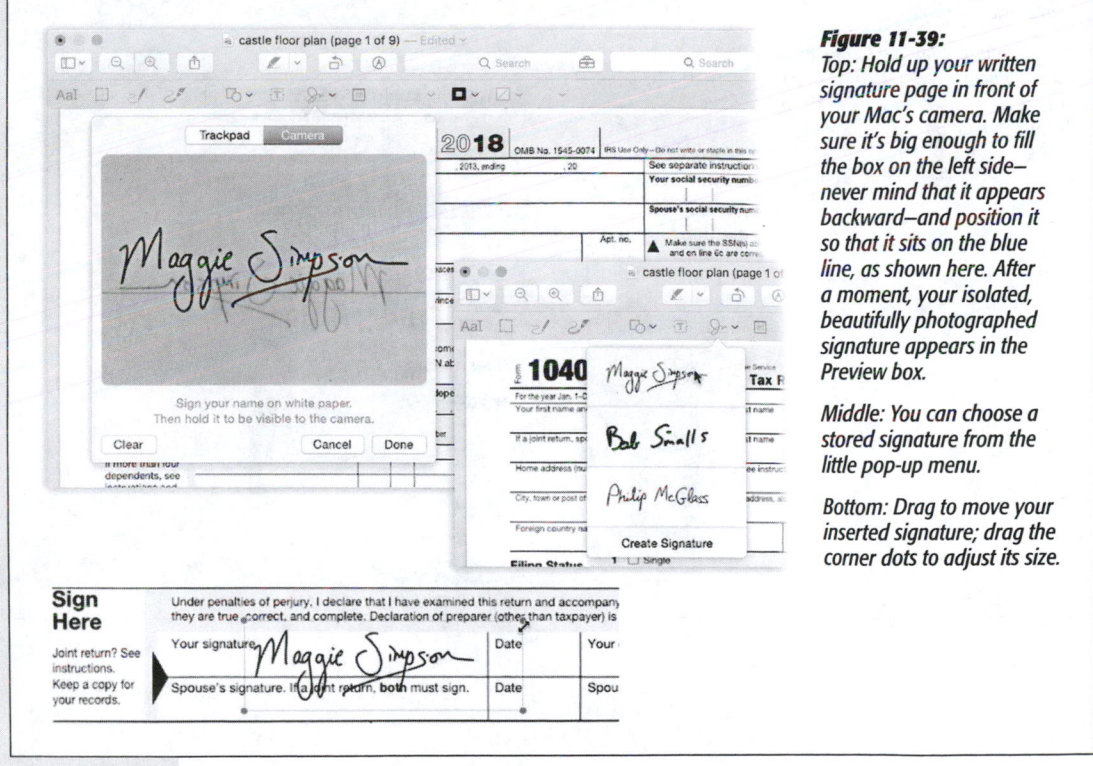

Figure 11-39:

Top: Hold up your written signature page in front of your Mac's camera. Make sure it's big enough to fill the box on the left side—never mind that it appears backward—and position it so that it sits on the blue line, as shown here. After a moment, your isolated, beautifully photographed signature appears in the Preview box.

Middle: You can choose a stored signature from the little pop-up menu.

Bottom: Drag to move your inserted signature; drag the corner dots to adjust its size.

- ⚲⌄ **Sign.** See the next section for details.

- ▣ **Note.** Click to place a virtual Post-it note onto the document. As you type or paste into it, the note expands; you can't otherwise control its size or shape. But when you click outside the note, it collapses down into a little square button. At this point, you can change the note's background color (right-click or two-finger click; choose a color from the shortcut menu); drag the little square to move the note; or open the note back up by double-clicking.

Figure 11-38:
As you draw a freehand shape (top), macOS helpfully straightens your straight lines and makes your curved ones perfect (middle).

If you actually prefer your imperfect original, then you can click the original (or any other variation) from the little floating palette (shown at left in the middle illustration).

The Shapes pop-up menu (⌖⌄) offers a range of fascinating drawing options. They include the classic Speech Bubble and the loupe, which produces a magnified view of one circular area (bottom).

While you're editing a loupe, you see a tiny green dot. Drag it to adjust the magnification inside the circle; drag the blue one to change the circle's size.

Annotations and Drawing Tools

Preview has become the Godzilla of PDF editing programs. It is, in fact, a full-blown drawing program now, with a choice of shapes, colors, lines, arrows, and text boxes to dress up a PDF document. These are identical to the drawing tools in Mail, so they're worth getting to know.

You can type notes (in a box or a bubble), add clickable links (to web addresses or other spots in the document), or use circles, arrows, rectangles, strikethroughs, underlining, or colored highlighting to draw your PDF readers' attention to certain sections. (You can dress up photos this way, too.) In fact, you can even use your laptop's trackpad to draw on a document—or to sign one.

To highlight text in a PDF document, click the ✍ button on the toolbar, and then drag across the text. Use the pop-up menu next to the ✍ to choose a different highlighter color, or to choose underlining or strikethrough styles.

For the more ambitious annotation styles, like signing a document or drawing on it, open the Markup toolbar, shown in Figure 11-38. To do that, click Ⓐ on the toolbar. At this point, the icons on the toolbar offer these features:

- **AaI Text Selection, ⬚ Rectangular Selection**. These toggles let you highlight text in a document (so you can copy it, for example) or select a chunk of a graphic.

- **✐ Sketch**. This remarkable tool lets you draw freehand in your document—and marvel as Preview cleans up your lines. For example, if you draw what's more or less a diagonal line, Preview straightens it and makes it a perfect 45 degrees. If you draw what seems to be a box or a circle, Preview zaps it into perfection. Use the ☰▾, ▣ ▾, and ⬚ ▾ buttons to specify the line thickness, add a colored border, or fill the interior with a background color. Figure 11-38 shows the process.

- **⌔▾ Shapes**. Use this pop-up menu to choose what kind of perfect shape you want to draw: line, arrow, circle, square, and so on. It will use whatever thickness and color you've chosen from the ☰▾ and ▣ ▾ pop-up menus. Once you've selected a tool, drag diagonally on your document to place the shape.

 The two icons at the bottom of this palette are unusual for a drawing program, but handy when you want to draw attention to some part of a document or photo.

 At lower left in the Shapes pop-up menu, the Mask dims out the entire document except the rectangular portion you enclose. The one at lower right, the loupe, magnifies a circular area to draw the viewer's eye to it (Figure 11-38, bottom). Whatever attention-flagging markings you enclose using these tools become part of the finished, exported PDF or graphic.

- **⊤ Text**. Click to place a text box on the image. You can drag it or reshape it—and, of course, you can replace the word "Text" inside it with much superior words of your own. Use the *A* ▾ pop-up menu to choose a font, color, size, and style; use the ▣ ▾ and ⬚ ▾ buttons to add a colored border or fill the interior with a background color.

Tip: Ordinarily, dragging across text selects the text from one edge of the page to the other, even if the PDF document is laid out in columns. But Preview is a bit smarter. It can tell if you're trying to get the text in only one column and highlights just that part automatically.

- **To find a word or phrase** somewhere in a PDF document, press ⌘-F (or choose Edit→Find→Find) to open the Find box—or just type into the ⚲ box on the right of the toolbar, if it's open. Proceed as shown in Figure 11-37.

 The search results show a snippet of the actual text surrounding each "find," along with the number of matches per page, and even a thumbnail of the page itself. It's all about context, baby.

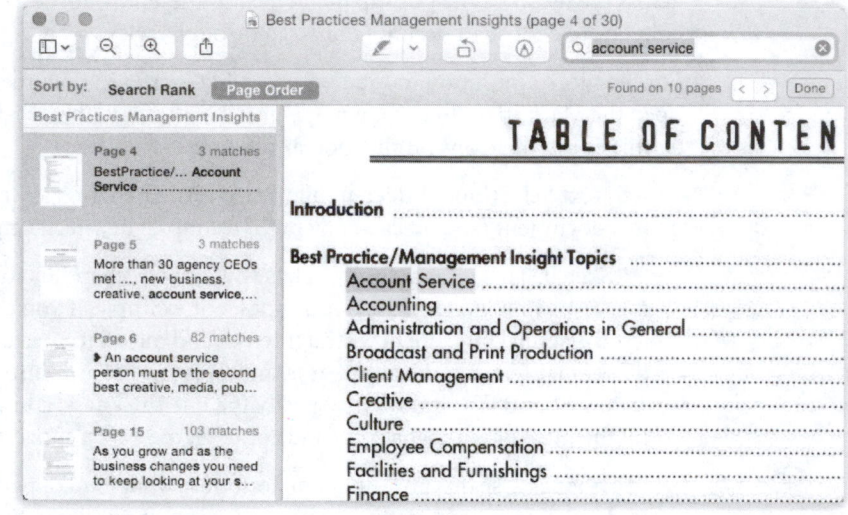

Figure 11-37:
Type into the search box. Matches appear in the Sidebar, with page numbers; click one to go there. You can sort the found list either by rank (how likely Preview thinks it is to be what you're looking for) or in page order; click the appropriate button to sort.

- **You can save a single page from a PDF** as a TIFF file to use it in other graphics, word-processing, or page-layout programs that might not directly recognize PDF.

 To extract a page, use the usual File→Export command, making sure to choose the new file format from the pop-up menu. (If you choose a format like Photoshop or JPEG, Preview converts only the currently selected page of your PDF document. That's because there's no such thing as a multipage Photoshop or JPEG document. But you already knew that.)

Tip: You can also scan a new page directly into an open PDF document, or use a page you shot on your i-gadget. Choose File→Import from [your device].

- **Add keywords to a graphic or PDF** (choose Tools→Show Inspector; click the ⚲ tab; click the + button to fill them in). Later, you'll be able to call up these documents with a quick Spotlight search for those details.

All you have to do is open the file you want to convert and choose File→Export. In the dialog box that appears, choose the new format for the image using the Format pop-up menu (JPEG, TIFF, or PNG, for example); if you press the Option key, you're offered even more file types. Finally, click Save to export the file.

Preview as PDF Reader

Preview is a nearly full-blown equivalent of Adobe Reader, the free program used by millions to read PDF documents. It lets you search PDF documents, copy text out of them, add comments, fill in forms, click live hyperlinks, add highlighting, circle certain passages, type in notes—features that used to be available only in Adobe's Acrobat Reader. You can even fill out *PDF forms*, typing into boxes on the electronic document.

Tip: Don't forget that Preview is one of macOS's certified full-screen apps, as described on page 178. You can also flip through the pages of a PDF using the "next page" gesture: a two-finger swipe on the trackpad.

Here are the basics:

- **Zoom in and out** using ⌘-plus and ⌘-minus.

Tip: Another way to get a closer look: Press the ` key (upper left of your keyboard), or choose Tools→Show Magnifier. Now a big magnifying glass follows your cursor; you can even press + or − to zoom in or out within it. Dismiss the magnifier by pressing ` again.

- **Use the View menu commands** to control how the PDF document appears: as two-page spreads; as single scrolling sheets of "paper towel"; with borders that indicate ends of pages; and so on.

- **Press the space bar to page through a document** (add Shift to page *upward*). The Page Up and Page Down keys do the same thing.

Tip: Some PDF documents include a table of contents, which you'll see in Preview's Sidebar, complete with flippy triangles that denote chapter headings. Use the ▲ and ▼ keys to walk through these chapter headings, and then expand one that looks good by pressing the ▶ key. Collapse it again with the ◀ key. In other words, you expand and collapse flippy triangles in Preview just as you do in a Finder list view.

- **Bookmark your place** by choosing Bookmarks→Add Bookmark (⌘-D). You'll be able to return to that spot by choosing its name—the page number and the first several words on the page—from the Bookmarks menu.

 These remain living, editable entities even after the document is saved and reopened. These are full-blown Acrobat annotations; they'll show up when your PDF document is opened by Acrobat Reader or even on Windows PCs.

- **If you want to copy material out of a PDF document**—for pasting into a word processor, for example, where you can edit it—click the Text tool (the AaI on the toolbar) or choose Tools→Text Selection. Now you can drag through some text (and even graphics) and then choose Edit→Copy, just as though the PDF document were a web page. You can even drag across page boundaries.

There's not much to it. Type in the new print dimensions you want for the photo, in inches or whatever units you choose from the pop-up menu. If you like, you can also change the resolution (the number of pixels per inch) by editing the Resolution box.

Tip: Here's a Photoshoppy feature you would never, ever expect to find in a simple viewer like Preview: You can extract a person (or anything, really) from the background. That's handy when you want to clip yourself out of a group shot to use as your Messages portrait, when you want to paste somebody into a new background, or when you break up with someone and want him out of your photos. See the free PDF appendix to this chapter, "Cutting People from Photos with Preview." It's on this book's "Missing CD" page at *missingmanuals.com*.

Converting file formats

Preview doesn't just open all these file formats—it can also convert among most of them. You can pop open some old Mac PICT files and turn them into BMP files for a Windows person, pry open a TIFF file from a scanner and turn it into a JPEG for use on your website, and so on.

Tip: What's even cooler is that you can open raw PostScript files right into Preview, which converts them into PDF files on the spot. You no longer need a PostScript laser printer to print out high-end diagrams and page layouts that come to you as PostScript files. Thanks to Preview, even an inkjet printer can handle them.

POWER USERS' CLINIC

Scaling and Resampling

When you're fooling around with a picture's size and resolution in the Adjust Size dialog box, you might find that a couple of the options take a little explaining.

If "Scale proportionally" is turned on, then Preview changes the Height number when you change the Width number, and vice versa. In other words, it won't let you change the *shape* of the photo; that's why a little padlock icon appears to bracket the Height and Width boxes.

If "Resample image" is turned off, then Preview adjusts the image's size by making the

existing dots bigger or smaller—but never changes the *number* of dots. (That's why a padlock bracket links all three boxes together. For example, you can make the image larger—but you'll lower the number of dots per inch.)

If "Resample image" is turned *on,* then you're giving Preview permission to add or subtract pixels as necessary to scale the photo up or down. Of course, it can't create detail that wasn't there in the original, but if you are scaling the picture *up*, it does a decent job of generating new pixels by averaging the colors of the neighboring ones.

Fixing up photos

Preview is no Photoshop, but it's getting closer every year:

- **Choose Tools→Show Inspector.** A floating palette appears. The tabs here depend on whether you've opened a PDF document or a photo, but they may include General Info (the photo's name, its pixel dimensions, and so on); More Info (camera settings like the lens type, ISO setting, focus mode, whether the flash was on, and so on); Keywords (add keywords so you'll be able to search for this image later using Spotlight); Crop (dimensions and selection size); and Annotations (markings that have been made to an image—maybe by you—using the Tools→Annotate function).

- **Choose Tools→Adjust Color.** A translucent, floating color-adjustment palette appears, teeming with sliders for brightness, contrast, exposure, saturation (color intensity), temperature and tint (color cast), sharpness, and more. See Figure 11-36.

Figure 11-36:
Humble little Preview has grown up into a big, strong mini-Photoshop. You can really fix up a photo if you know what you're doing, using these sliders. Or you can just click the Auto Levels button. It sets all the sliders for you, which generally does an amazing job of making almost any photo look better.

- **Choose Tools→Adjust Size.** This command lets you adjust a photo's resolution, which comes in handy a lot. For example, you can scale an unwieldy 10-megapixel, gazillion-by-gazillion-pixel shot down to a nice 640×480 JPEG that's small enough to send by email. Or you can shrink a photo down so it fits within a desktop window, for use as a window background.

- **Table of Contents.** If you're looking over photos, this option turns the Sidebar into a scrolling list of their names. If you've opened a group of PDFs all at once, you see a list of them. Or, if you have a PDF that contains chapter headings, you see them listed in the Sidebar as, yes, a table of contents.

- **Highlights & Notes.** Preview is a better PDF editor than ever. If you add comments and highlighting to a PDF document, as described later in this section, you can view all of them in this tidy list—and click one to jump to it.

- **Bookmarks.** Here you can see any bookmarks you've added to a PDF, as described later in this section.

- **Contact Sheet.** When you choose this view, the *main* window scrolls away, leaving you with a full screen of thumbnail miniatures. It's like a light table where you can look over all your photos or PDF pages at once. Make them bigger or smaller using the magnifying glass buttons at top left.

Tip: You can also change among these views by pressing Option-⌘-1, -2, -3, -4, -5, and -6.

Preview as Graphics Viewer

Preview is surprisingly versatile. It can display and manipulate pictures saved in a wide variety of formats, including common graphics formats like JPEG, TIFF, PICT, and GIF; less commonly used formats like BMP, PNG, SGI, and TGA; and even Photoshop, EPS, and PDF graphics.

Tip: Don't miss the Tools→Show Magnifier command. It gives you a loupe: a magnifying circle (or, in a PDF document, a magnifying rectangle) that lets you inspect part of your graphic or PDF file more closely.

Bunches o' graphics

If you highlight a group of image files in the Finder and open them all at once (for example, by pressing ⌘-O), Preview opens the first one but lists the thumbnails of the whole group in the Sidebar. You can walk through them with the ▲ and ▼ keys, or you can choose View→Slideshow (Shift-⌘-F) to open a full-screen slideshow.

Tip: You can change the order of the photos just by dragging them around in the Sidebar, in any of its views.

Cropping graphics

To crop graphics in Preview, drag across the part of the graphic that you want to keep. To redraw, drag the round handles on the dotted rectangle; or, to proceed with the crop, choose Tools→Crop. (The keyboard shortcut is ⌘-K.) Since Preview is an Auto Save program, you can always return to the original if you change your mind someday.

Tip: You can also rotate an image—even a PDF document—in 90-degree increments and then flip it vertically or horizontally, using the commands in the Tools menu. In fact, if you select several thumbnails in the Sidebar first, you can rotate or flip them all simultaneously.

Operating Your Scanner

Preview can also operate a scanner, auto-straighten the scanned images, and export them as PDF files, JPEG graphics, and so on.

This, too, is *exactly* like using Image Capture to operate your scanner. Only the first step is different. Open Preview, choose File→Import from Scanner→ [your scanner's name], and proceed as described on page 425. Clearly Apple saved some time by reusing some code.

Multiple Pages, Multiple Views

One hallmark of Preview is its effortless handling of *multiples:* multiple fax pages, multiple PDF files, batches of photos, and so on. The key to understanding the possibilities is mastering the Sidebar, shown in Figure 11-35. The idea is that these thumbnails let you navigate pages or graphics without having to open a rat's nest of individual windows.

Tip: You can drag these thumbnails from one Preview window's Sidebar into another. That's a great way to mix and match pages from different PDF documents into a single new one, for example.

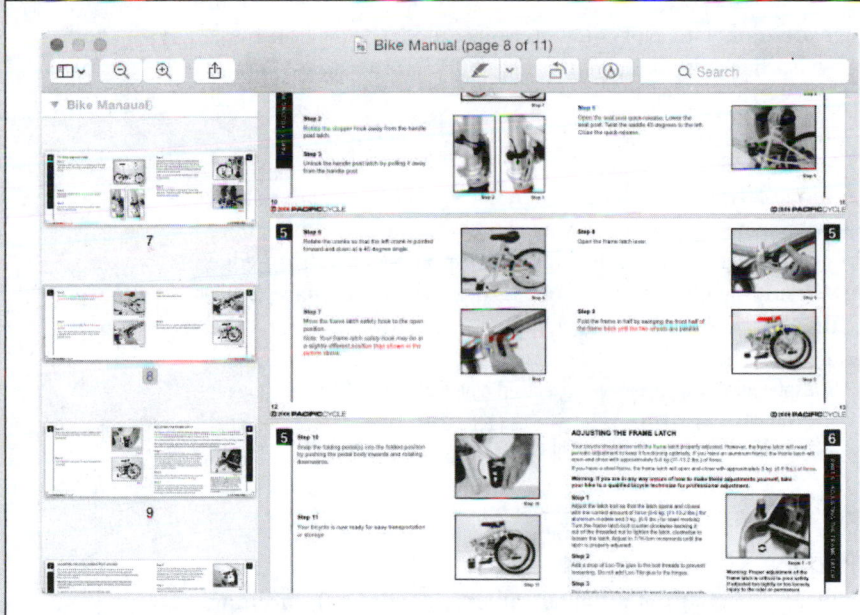

Figure 11-35:
The Sidebar can display thumbnails, a table of contents, or annotations, or it can appear as a full-screen array of thumbnail images. Drag the central scroll bar to make the Sidebar bigger; drag the lower-right corner of the Sidebar to make the whole Preview window bigger.

To control the Sidebar, choose one of these commands from the View menu:

- **Hide Sidebar.** Gets the Sidebar out of your way.

- **Thumbnails.** This standard view (Figure 11-35, left) offers a scrolling vertical list of miniature pages or photos. Click one to see it at full size in the main window. Make the thumbnails larger or smaller by dragging the window/Sidebar dividing line.

(individual histograms—graphs—showing the distribution of red, green, and blue pixel densities in the photo, with handles that let you shift that distribution); Curves (lets you draw your own pixel-distribution graphs); Definition (adds clarity by adjusting the contrast of the photo's midtones); Selective Color (adjusts the intensity and shade of individual colors, like yellow or red); Noise Reduction (attempts to minimize "grain," or speckles); Sharpen (slightly de-blurs the entire image); and Vignette (darkens the corners of the image, focusing the attention on the center).

Most of these controls come with sliders, pop-up menus, and other tweaks that let you specify the effect. Most also offer an Auto button, which spares you from having to know what you're doing.

Tip: The Extensions button, in Edit mode, gives you access to plug-ins from Apple and other companies that let you do even more with your photo retouching. The one called Markup comes with macOS; it lets you draw or type right onto your photos, exactly as described on page 472.

The Rest of Photos

Photos also offers keywords, searching, sharing via iCloud (see page 221), slideshows, video trimming, photo books and calendars, and more.

Honestly, Photos is a huge program with a lot going on; you could write a whole book about it. In fact, someone has; check out *Photos for Mac and iOS: The Missing Manual.*

Preview

Preview is macOS's scanning software, graphics viewer, fax viewer, and PDF reader. It's always been teeming with features that most Mac owners never even knew were there—but it's a flagship macOS program, offering all of Apple's pet cutting-edge features like Auto Save, Versions, Full Screen mode, saving to iCloud (page 221), and a Share button (⬆) that lets you send a document to somebody else (page 263).

Tip: Preview can even open Microsoft Office documents (Word, PowerPoint, Excel) and iWork documents (Pages, Numbers, Keynote). You can't edit them in Preview, but you can read them, search them, and print them. No longer must you pay homage to Microsoft's bottom line just to have a look at the documents people send you.

Importing Camera Photos

Preview can import pictures directly from a digital camera (or iPhone), meaning that there are now *three* macOS apps that can perform that duty. (Photos and Image Capture are the other two.) It's sometimes handy to use Preview for this purpose, though, because it has some great tools for photos: color-correction controls, size/resolution options, format conversion, and so on.

The actual importing process, though, is *exactly* like using Image Capture. Connect your camera, choose File→Import from [your camera's name], and carry on as described on page 422.

- **Retouch.** This very special brush can instantly and seamlessly paint out a minor flaw—a zit, a stray hair, or a dust speck or scratch on an old photo. All you have to do is dab away at the blemish with the mouse. Use the slider (or press the [and] keys) to resize your cursor until it's slightly bigger than the thing you want to remove.

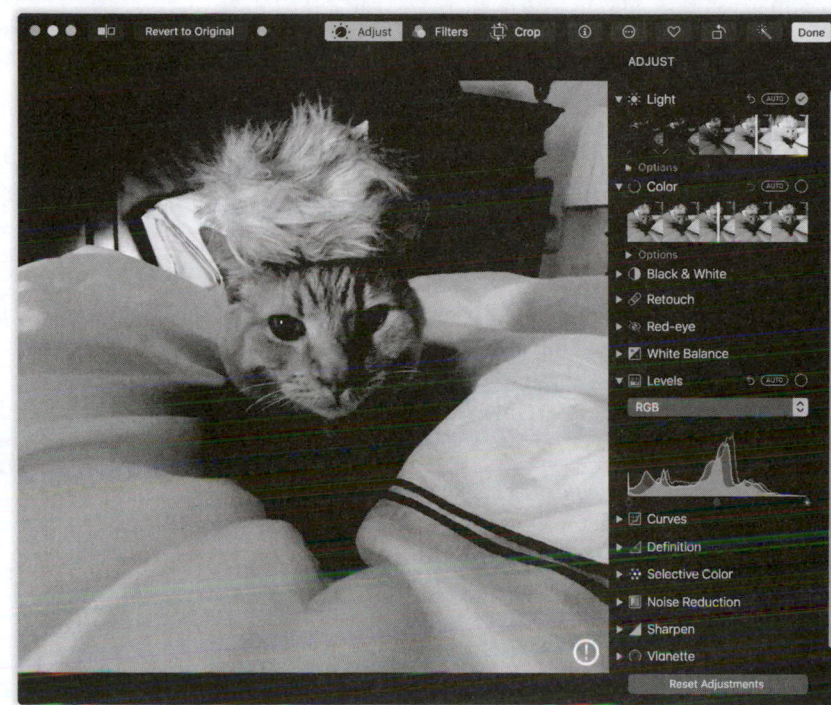

Figure 11-34:
The Edit window offers a zillion expandable control tiles, each with its own sliders and menus. It can get pretty technical— fortunately, each also has an Auto button.

- **Red-eye.** Devilish, glowing-red pupils in your subjects' eyes has ruined many an otherwise great photo. It's a reflection of the camera's flash off the blood-red retinal tissue at the back of the eyes.

 When you click this button, a message says, "Click each red-eye to correct." Do what it says: Click inside each eye that has the problem. The app turns the red in each eye to black.

Tip: It helps to zoom in first. Use the slider at top left, or press ⌘-plus.

At any point, you can compare your edited photo with the original by holding down the M key.

More control sliders

There's another book's worth of editing power in Photos. The other sliders include White Balance (the color of light in the shot—warmer, cooler, and so on); Levels

To make more fine-tuned corrections to a photo (either an open one or its thumbnail), press ⌘-Return key. The Edit mode appears, where three tabs greet you at the top, listed here from right to left:

Crop

When you click this tab, you get a crazy editing screen where you can adjust the size, shape, and angle of the photo.

First, Photos automatically analyzes whatever horizontal lines it finds in the photo—the horizon, for example—and uses them as a guide to straightening the photo automatically. You can reject the proposal (click Reset), or tilt the photo more or less (drag across the round scale).

If you want to rotate the photo more than 90 degrees—for example, if the camera took it sideways—click ⬏ as many times as necessary to turn the picture upright.

The other work you can do in this mode is cropping. Cropping means shaving off unnecessary portions of a photo. Usually, you crop a photo to improve its composition—adjusting where the subject appears within the frame of the picture. Cropping is also very useful if your photo needs to have a certain *aspect ratio* (length-to-width proportion), like 8 × 10 or 5 × 7.

To crop a photo you've opened, drag any edge or corner of the white border; press Return when the proposed crop looks good. Or use the canned proportions at the right—Square, 3 × 2, 3 × 5, 4 × 3, and so on—to limit the cropping frame to preset proportions.

Filters

Filters are effects that make a photo black and white, oversaturated, or washed out. Click each to see what it looks like on your photo; finish up by clicking Done.

Adjust

On this tab, the right-side panel contains a huge list of Photoshop-style adjustment sliders. For your learning-curve pleasure, they correspond exactly to the ones on the iPhone and iPad (Figure 11-34). For example:

- **Light, Color, Black & White.** When you click one of these categories, you see a "filmstrip" below or beside your photo. You can drag your finger across it, watching the effect on your photo.

 As it turns out, each of these sliders controls a handful of variables, all of which it's changing simultaneously, and each of which you can adjust manually. For example, the Light category includes Brilliance (a slider that, Apple says, "brightens dark areas and pulls in highlights to reveal hidden detail"), Exposure (adjusts the brightness of all pixels), Highlights (pulls lost details out of very bright areas), Shadows (pulls lost details out of very dark areas), Brightness (like Exposure, but doesn't brighten parts that are already bright), Contrast (heightens the difference between the brightest and darkest areas), and Black Point (determines what is "black," shifting the entire dark/light range upward or downward).

My Projects

This Sidebar item houses the photo books, cards, calendars, prints, and slideshows you've created. To create one, select the photos you want to include, and then choose from the File→Create submenu.

Opening Photos

To open any selected thumbnail so you can see it at full size, press the Return key. (Press it again to close the photo.)

While the photo is open, you can zoom in or out—either drag the top-left slider, or use two fingers on your trackpad (pinch or spread them). If your Mac has a Touch Bar (page 233), you can click or drag your finger through it to scroll through the photos in this set.

Tip: You can pop back and forth between actual size and a zoomed-in view by tapping the Z key.

You can open a video this way, too. Play it by clicking ▶ or hitting the space bar, or trim off the dead ends using the ✿→Trim command. For slo-mo videos from the iPhone, you can even adjust the start and stop points for the slow effect.

Editing Photos

Before reading a word about editing in Photos, first absorb this: All the changes described on these pages are *nondestructive*. That is, Photos never forgets the original photo. At any time, hours or years later, you can select a photo and then choose Image→Revert to Original, thus undoing any changes you've ever made. In other words, your changes are never really permanent.

Tip: If you want to do your editing in Photoshop (or any other external program), Apple has restored the "edit in another photo, see the changes back in Photos" feature, which was so useful in the old iPhoto program. Just right-click or two-finger click a photo and, from the shortcut menu, choose, Edit With→Photoshop (or whatever). Or use the Image→Edit With command.

The changes you make in the external app are nondestructive—you can undo *them* at any time, too. In other words, you can use Photos for its superior organizational and sharing tools, but Photoshop for editing.

Auto Enhance

The quickest way to fix the color and contrast for a photo is to click the ✎ button. It's so important that it appears at the top of the window when you're viewing any photo, even before you've entered Edit mode. When you click this magical button, Photos analyzes the relative brightness of all the pixels in your photo and attempts to "balance" it. After a moment, the app adjusts the brightness and contrast and intensifies dull or grayish-looking areas. Usually, the pictures look richer and more vivid as a result.

You may find that Auto Enhance has little effect on some photos, only minimally improves others, and totally rescues a few. In any case, if you don't care for the result, you can click ✎ again to turn Auto Enhance off.

took in each place. Double-click repeatedly to "drill down" until you're looking at the individual photos taken in a certain spot.

Imports

Any old photos-management program can show you the most recent batch of photos you've imported (from a camera card or the desktop, for example). But what's great about Photos is that this is a *scrolling* display. It shows *older* batches of imported photos, stretching back in time. Sometimes, that feature makes it super easy to find a photo or video you're looking for.

Recently Deleted

Even after you think you've deleted a photo or video from your phone, you have 30 days to change your mind. Deleted pictures and videos sit in this folder, quietly counting down to their own doomsdays.

If you wind up changing your mind, you can open Recently Deleted, click the photo you'd condemned, and click Recover. The photo pops back into its rightful place in the Photos app, saved from termination.

On the other hand, you can also zap a selected photo into oblivion immediately using the Delete Item button. If nothing is selected, you can hit Delete All.

Media Types

Here are specialized buttons for the kinds of photos the iPhone and iPad can take, like Videos, Selfies, Live Photos (three-second photo/video hybrids), Panoramas, Time-lapse, Slo-mo, and so on. Super handy when you're trying to show someone your latest time-lapse masterpiece, for example; now you know where to look for it.

My Albums

You can easily create photo "folders" called albums, for your organizing pleasure. A single photo can appear in as many albums as you like, without using any more disk space. If you delete a photo from an album, you're not removing it from Photos—only from this virtual grouping. You can drag thumbnails around in an album to rearrange them.

Tip: If you drag a photo into several albums, then editing it changes that photo everywhere. But if you copy and paste a photo into a different album, you can edit the two independently. And yet, amazingly enough, you're still not using any more disk space.

You can't move very far without finding another way to make an album: Choose File→New Album and then drag thumbnails into it. Or select some thumbnails and then choose File→New Album with Selection. Or click the ● that appears when you point to the My Albums in the Sidebar, and then fill it with photos.

If your photo collection came from iPhoto or Aperture, you also see an album (in a folder called, for example, iPhoto Events) for each iPhoto Event or Aperture Project you had in the older program. (Yes, you can also create folders to hold your albums.)

soundtracks—and then, when you click Play Slideshow, the show begins. It's usually fantastic.

When you come back to your senses, note that you can wiggle the mouse for playback controls—pause, skip, adjust volume, exit, and so on.

> **Note:** On the Mac, you can't edit which photos and videos appear in a Memory, as you can on the iPhone or iPad.

You can create a Memory using your own choice of photos, too. Open any album and click Show as Memory in the header. Or click the name of any Collection, Moment, or Year to open those photos as a Memory.

Favorites

Any time you spot a photo you might want to return to later, click the ♡ that appears on its thumbnail. Then click this folder in the Sidebar, and boom—there they all are. Handy even for temporary "set-asides"—for example, when you're choosing photos to include in a photo book, slideshow, or calendar.

People

Photos can auto-group the people in your photos, using facial recognition. For example, all pictures of your mom appear in a clump. This feature is fantastic to remember the next time someone—a potential date, the kindergarten teacher, the Passport Bureau—requests a photo of you or someone in your circle.

To see it at work, click People in the Sidebar. Here are thumbnails representing the faces Photos has found and grouped. Click beneath a thumbnail to edit that person's name. Double-click the thumbnail to see all the photos of this person, laid out exactly like a Memory, described earlier.

> **Tip:** The two buttons at top right, Photos and Faces, control what the thumbnails show—the *entire* photos containing this person, or a zoom-in of just that person's face.

At the bottom, you get options like Remove from People Album (great when this person dumps you) and Confirm Additional Faces (refines the training to recognize this person better, using a new set of photos).

> **Note:** This feature doesn't work until the Mac has *analyzed* your photos, which can take at least a day. Apple proudly points out that all this analysis is done on your Mac. (That's in contrast to services like Google Photos, which offers similar features but requires Google to access your photo library.)

You can even drag your favorites into the top of the screen for quick access later.

Places

Every photo you take with a smartphone (and a few very fancy cameras) gets *geo-tagged*—stamped, behind the scenes, with its geographical coordinates. When you click Places in the Sidebar, you see a map, dotted with clusters of photos that you

auto-recognize and auto-build slideshows of your pets, babies, outdoor activities, performances, weddings, birthdays, and games.

Double-click to open a Memory; at this point, you can scroll down to see more about what's in it. You'll see the photos that will be in it, as well as who's in it (People), and where the photos came from (Places).

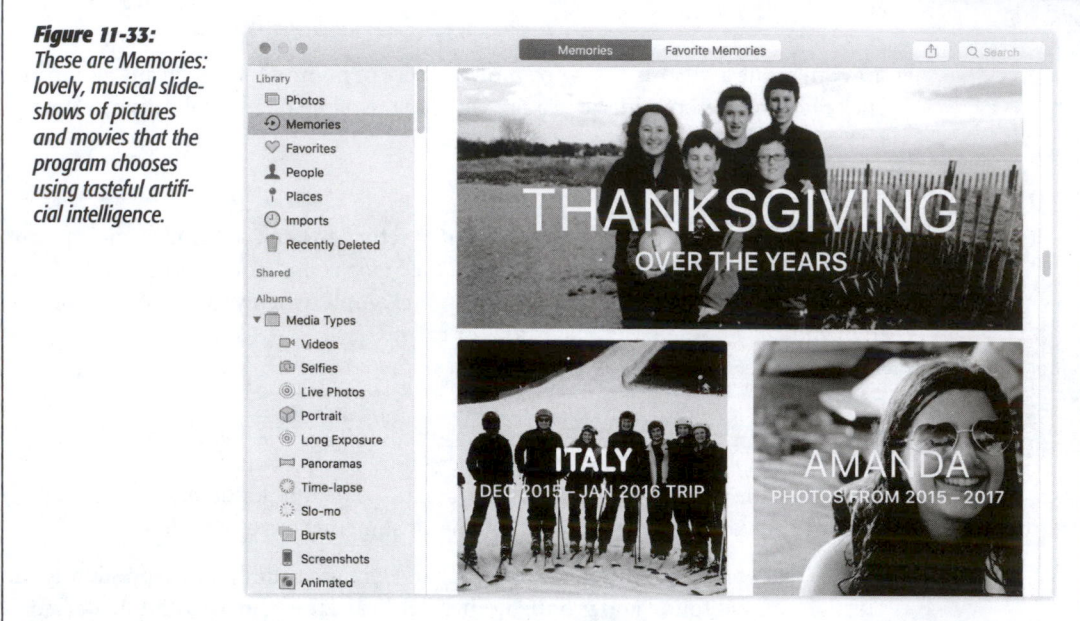

Figure 11-33:
These are Memories: lovely, musical slide-shows of pictures and movies that the program chooses using tasteful artificial intelligence.

At the very bottom, you'll see these options:

- **Delete Memory.** Vaporizes this computer-generated collection (does not touch the originals).

- **Add to Favorite Memories.** Adds this slideshow to a new folder on the Albums tab called Favorite Memories, for quick access later.

- **Block Memory.** This command sounds like a parody of a psychological technique, but it actually does what it says: It prevents Photos from ever reminding you again, in Memories, of this day, place, or person. (When you click Block Memory, a shortcut menu identifies the factors that Photos used to create this Memory— Person, Place, or Day—so that you can tell it which of those three is causing you the psychic pain.)

Tip: If, after years of therapy, you can face those painful memories again, click Photos→Preferences→ General→Reset Blocked Memories.

Anyway, the real fun begins when you click ▶ to start an instant slideshow. A panel offers a choice of transition styles (Sliding Panels, Reflections, and so on) and musical

The time groupings

Here they are, from smallest to largest (you'll see each view identified in the title bar):

- **Moments.** A moment is a group of photos you took in one place at one time—for example, all the shots at the picnic by the lake. If you take most of your pictures with an iPhone, you'll see that it uses its own GPS to give each moment a name: "San Francisco, California (Union Square)," for example. Otherwise, or if you have location sharing turned off, moments are simply grouped by date.

- **Collections.** Put a bunch of moments together, and what do you get? A collection. Here again, Photos tries to study the times and places of your photo taking—but this time, it puts them into groups that might span a few days and several locations. You might discover that your entire spring vacation is a single collection, for example.

- **Years.** If you "zoom out" of your photos far enough, you wind up viewing them by year: 2018, 2019, and so on.

Tip: Handily enough, the keystrokes ⌘-1, ⌘-2, ⌘-3, and ⌘-4 correspond to the Photos, Moments, Collections, and Years tabs.

You backtrack from a moment or collection by "pinching" on your trackpad, or by clicking the < button at top left.

Note: If the Photos window isn't wide enough to show tabs for all these groupings, you get a pop-up menu listing them instead.

The Sidebar

The Sidebar list, which lists your albums and other useful categories, is no longer hideable in macOS Mojave (at least until you enter Full Screen view). Its buttons correspond precisely to the ones you'd see on the iPhone or iPad in the Photos app.

The following pages describe each Sidebar entity in turn.

Photos

Here's where you'll do most of your hunting. This is Moments, Collections, and Years.

Memories

Memories (Figure 11-33) are automatically selected groups of pix and videos from certain time periods or trips, which, with a click, become gorgeous, musical slideshows. Photos creates three new ones a day, which often dredges up delightful photos of events you'd nearly forgotten about. Most people are pleasantly surprised at how coherent and well-created these are, even though they're totally automatic. Photos, short pieces of your videos, and even scrolling panoramas are all first-class citizens in these slideshows.

Right off the bat, you see a few of Photos' suggestions, represented as clearly labeled billboards ("Cape Cod Summer," "Best of Last Week"...). Memories can

Apple has done it again. It has replaced the beloved but aging iPhoto with a new Mac app called Photos. Apple says that times have changed in the 16 years since iPhoto first came along. We capture a lot more with our phones now, and that involves much more than plain old stills: square photos, panoramas, slow-motion videos, time-lapse videos, burst-mode sets, and so on.

And here's the biggest, baddest, best part of Photos: iCloud Photo Library. That's automatic, real-time syncing of your entire photo library, including edits and organization, across all your Apple gadgets.

The Layout

Photos is meant to look, feel, and work exactly like Photos on the iPhone/iPad. For example, when you click Photos in the source list at left, Photos automatically groups your photos into sets that are easy to navigate (Figure 11-32).

Tip: The slider at top left controls the size of the thumbnails.

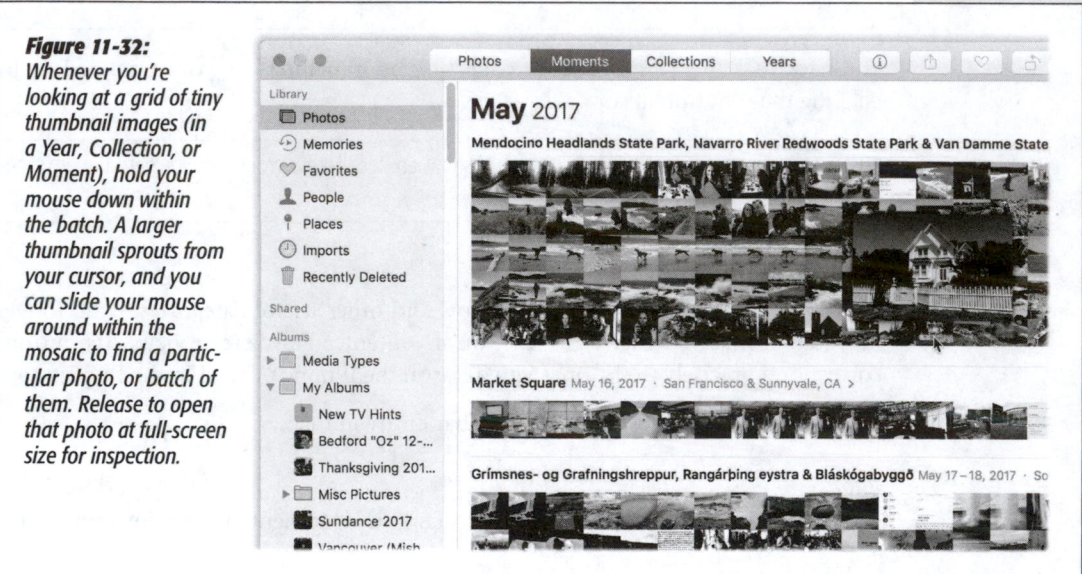

Figure 11-32:
Whenever you're looking at a grid of tiny thumbnail images (in a Year, Collection, or Moment), hold your mouse down within the batch. A larger thumbnail sprouts from your cursor, and you can slide your mouse around within the mosaic to find a particular photo, or batch of them. Release to open that photo at full-screen size for inspection.

Photos boasts a lot of recent improvements. For example, the Auto-Enhance button (✳) is now right on the main toolbar in Viewer mode. It does a very good job at fixing the color, exposure, and contrast values for a photo—and now you don't have to heave into Editing mode to apply it to a photo, or a whole batch of them.

The new Imports view shows not just the latest batch of imported photos, but the batch before that, and the batch before *that*, and so on.

Using the Showing pop-up menu at top right, you can now filter your view by Favorites, photos you've edited, only movies, only stills, and so on.

Exporting Shots and Movies

To look at a photo or movie you've captured, click its thumbnail in the scrolling row at the bottom of the screen. (To return to camera mode, click the ◉.)

Fortunately, these masterpieces of goofiness and distortion aren't locked in Photo Booth forever. You can share them with your adoring public in any of these ways:

- **Click the ⬆ button.** The pop-up menu offers the usual offerings of the Share menu (page 263): Mail, Messages, AirDrop, Twitter, Facebook, and Flickr, plus Add to Photos and Add to Aperture, if you use those programs.

 There's also a "Change profile picture" command (to make this photo represent you on the Login screen), and a More button that opens the System Preferences→ Extensions screen described on page 357.

 And speaking of interesting headshots: If you export a 4-Up image and choose it as your Buddy Picture, you'll get an *animated* buddy icon. That is, your tiny icon cycles among the four images, creating a crude sort of animation. It's sort of annoying, actually, but all the kids are doing it.

- **Click the photo or movie, and then choose File→Export.** (Or just right-click or two-finger click the photo or movie itself; choose Export from the shortcut menu.) You're asked to name and save the exported image or video.

Tip: If you choose File→Export Original instead, then the exported photo or video lacks any of the effects you've applied. You get the original, undistorted, underlying photo.

- **Drag a thumbnail out of the window to your desktop.**

Note: These files are stored in a single icon, a package file, that sits in your Home→Pictures folder. Ordinarily, you should never have to mess with it. But if you right-click or two-finger click this icon and choose Show Package Contents→Pictures, you'll find one JPEG apiece for single shots, four JPEG files for every 4-Up, and MOV files for videos.

As you set off on your Photo Booth adventures, a note of caution: Keep it away from children. They won't move from Photo Booth for the next 12 years.

Tip: Photo Booth is one of the certified full-screen apps. Click the green ⊙ button at upper left to make the app fill your screen, for added graphic juiciness.

Photos

Apple loves introducing or standardizing some new technology, persuading us to use it—and then abandoning it the minute a better tech comes along. (The floppy drive, CD burner, 30-pin iPhone connector, the headphone jack…)

The first page contains eight effects, some of which use sophisticated face-recognition smarts to track your face as it moves around the frame. That's how Dizzy and Love-struck are able to keep the animated birds or hearts circling your head, and how Chipmunk, Nose Twirl, and Bug Out are able to distort your cheeks, nose, and eyeballs even as you move around.

Some of the effects have sliders that govern their intensity; you'll see them appear when you click the preview.

Still Photos

When you find an effect that looks appealing (or unappealing, depending on your goals), click the camera button, or press ⌘-Return key. You see and hear a three-second countdown, and then *snap!*—your screen flashes white to add illumination, and the resulting photo appears on your screen. Its thumbnail joins the collection at the bottom.

Tip: Option-click the camera button to eliminate the countdown. You can get rid of the screen flash, too, by *Shift*-clicking. Needless to say, if you press Option *and* Shift, you get neither the countdown nor the flash.

4-Up Photos

If you click the 4-Up button identified at the bottom left of Figure 11-31, then when you click the Camera icon (or press ⌘-Return key), the 3-2-1 countdown begins, and then Photo Booth snaps *four* consecutive photos in two seconds. You can exploit the timing just the way you would in a real photo booth—make four different expressions, horse around, whatever.

The result is a single graphic with four panes, kind of like what you get at a shopping mall photo booth. (In Photo Booth, they appear rakishly assembled at an angle; but when you export the image, they appear straight, like panes of a window.) Its icon plops into the row of thumbnails at the bottom of the window, just like the single still photos.

Movies

Photo Booth can also record *videos,* complete with those wacky distortion effects. Click the third icon below the screen, the Movie icon (Figure 11-31), and then click the camera button (or press ⌘-T). You get the 3-2-1 countdown—but this time, Photo Booth records a video, with sound, until you click the Stop button. (The little digital counter at left reminds you that you're still filming.) When it's over, the movie's icon appears in the row of thumbnails, ready to play or export.

Tip: Want to edit your video? Click its thumbnail and then choose Edit→Trim Movie, or hit ⌘-T. When you do, yellow trim handles appear at both ends of the scroll bar (the same ones you'd see when trimming a video on the iPhone or iPad, or in Photos). Drag them inward to trim off any dead air at the beginning or end of your video clip. Hit the space bar to check your work. If the trim is OK, click the Trim button to confirm.

But then click the Effects button (Figure 11-31). You enter a world of special visual effects—and we're talking *very* special. Some make you look like a pinhead, or bulbous, or like a conjoined twin; others simulate Andy Warhol paintings, fisheye lenses, and charcoal sketches. In fact, there are five whole pages of effects, nine previews on a page. (The last two pages hold *backdrop* effects, as already described.)

To page through them, click the left or right arrow buttons, or press ◀ or ▶, or swipe with two fingers on your trackpad (one finger on the Magic Mouse).

Click an effect

4-Up | Movie
Still

Finished shots Effects pages

Figure 11-31:
Some of the Photo Booth effects are simple color filters; others must have been dreamed up one night in the midst of a serious beer party at Apple. They're disturbingly creative. If you decide that you really look best without any help from Apple's warped imagery, click the Normal icon in the center.

GEM IN THE ROUGH

De-Mirrorizing Your Photos

Technically, Photo Booth acts like a mirror, not a camera. That is, every picture you take is actually flipped, left-to-right. If there's ever text in the picture—something written on your T-shirt, for example—or if you ever examine the way your hair is parted, you'll realize that every image is backward.

That's why you can click a thumbnail at the bottom of the window and then choose Edit→Flip Photo (⌘-F). You've just made the photo match what a camera would have seen.

Or choose Edit→Auto Flip New Items if you want Photo Booth to do the flipping for you from now on.

Numbers, Pages

Numbers and Pages are Apple's spreadsheet and word-processing programs, something like Apple-flavored versions of Microsoft Excel and Microsoft Word. They're part of Apple's iWork suite, which comes preinstalled on every new Mac. And they're complicated enough that there's a whole book about them: *iWork: The Missing Manual*.

Photo Booth

It may be goofy, it may be pointless, but the Photo Booth program is a bigger time drain than Solitaire, the web, and *Dancing with the Stars* put together.

It's a match made in heaven for any Mac with a camera above the screen. (Photo Booth doesn't even open if your Mac doesn't have *some* kind of camera.)

Open this program and then peer into the camera. Photo Booth acts like a digital mirror, showing whatever the camera sees—that is, you.

GEM IN THE ROUGH

Still and Video Backdrops

Photo Booth and Messages are cousins, and they're closer than ever. One particular feature, in fact, is identical in each: custom backdrops. You can replace the actual, mundane background of your office or den with something far more exciting: a rushing waterfall, for example, or a rider's-eye view of a roller coaster. In fact, you can use any photo or video you want as the background.

It's just like the bluescreen or greenscreen technology that Hollywood uses to put actors someplace they're not—but without the bluescreen or greenscreen.

To replace your background in Photo Booth, click Effects. The fourth page of effects offers eight *canned* backgrounds, prepared by Apple for your enjoyment: various spectacular stills (cloudscape, pop art, the moon) and videos (Eiffel Tower, aquarium, roller coaster, Yosemite).

The final page offers eight empty preview squares. You're supposed to drag a still or a video from your desktop (or Photos) into these empty squares, making them not so empty.

In any case, prepare the backdrop by clicking one of the preview squares. Photo Booth says, "Please step out of the frame." Do it. Photo Booth is going to memorize what its field of view looks like without you in it, so that when you reappear, it can tell *you* apart from your boring office background.

Now, when you record the movie or take the photo, you'll be amazed to discover that Photo Booth has just transplanted you to the far more exotic locale you selected. (Alas, blotches may result if the real-life background includes movement or highly contrasting elements.)

(Cut, Copy, Paste) are now at your disposal. So are the Format-menu commands for bold, italic, underline, and so on.

- **Convert text into a table.** Select the text, and then click the table button (⊞). The selected text winds up in the first column—one cell per paragraph.

- **Convert table into text.** Click inside a cell, and then click ⊞. Choose Convert to Text.

Figure 11-30:
Top: Tables give Notes new information-storing capabilities.

Bottom: The key to adjusting and editing tables? The weird little ⌐⌐ and ⋮ handles on the cells.

Notes Accounts

Notes also can show you the contents of the Notes modules on Google, Yahoo, AOL, or another IMAP email account. You'll see each account's notes in the Folder list, as you can see in Figure 11-27—and from there, you can drag notes hither and yon, among accounts, with abandon. (If the Folder list is hidden, click the ⊞ button or choose View→Show Folders.)

To set this up, open System Preferences→Internet Accounts. Click the account you want (Exchange, Gmail, Yahoo, AOL, or whatever); finally, turn the Notes switch On.

That should do it. Now each account's notes appear under their own heading in the Folders list. And your notes are synced, both ways.

All of this makes life a little more complex, of course. For example, when you create a note, you have to worry about which account it's about to go into. To do that, be sure to specify an account name (and a folder within it, if necessary) *before* you create the new note.

or by clicking the ⊟ icon on the toolbar. Then you can adjust the Folder list's width by dragging the vertical line at its right edge.

To make a new folder, choose File→New Folder, or click New Folder below the list; name the folder and then press Return. You can then drag existing notes into its name in the Folders list. (The usual rules apply: You can select a swath of notes in a list by clicking the first and then Shift-clicking the last. Or you can click individual, nonconsecutive notes by clicking with the ⌘ key pressed.)

Tip: If you press Option as you drag a note, then you make a copy of it in the new folder instead of moving the original.

Click a folder's name to see the notes inside it. (Click "All [account name]" to see all the notes in that account. Note accounts are covered on the next page.)

To create a new note within a folder, click the folder's name first. If you don't click any folder's name before you create the note, then it goes into the general Notes category.

You can also rename a folder (right-click or two-finger click its name; choose Rename Folder), delete one (right-click or two-finger click its name; choose Delete Folder), put one inside another (drag its name), and move a folder to a different account—for example, from your iCloud account to your Google one—by dragging it.

Tip: If you're using the Folders feature, here's how to see them on your phone or tablet: Click the Accounts button in the upper-left corner of the Notes window. The list of accounts and folders appears, much as it does on your Mac.

Tables

When you click ▦, you get a table with two columns and two rows. Click in a cell and then start typing. To move to the next cell, press Tab on the keyboard (or click the cell).

Poke around long enough, and you can find controls for just about every formatting tool you'd ever need in a table (except the ability to manually adjust column widths and the ability to format the cell borders).

The keys to most of it are the tiny handles (⋯ and ⋮) that appear when you click inside a cell (Figure 11-30, top):

- **Add or delete columns.** Click inside a cell to make the ⋯ and ⋮ buttons appear. Click ⋯ to make the command menu (∨) appear (Figure 11-27, bottom). It offers commands like Add Column (Before or After the current one), and Delete Column. Click ⋮ and then ∨ to see equivalent commands for Rows.

 If you're typing in the lower-right cell, pressing Return also makes a new row.

- **Move a row or column.** Click ⋯ or ⋮ to highlight the corresponding row or column; now you can drag it to a new spot.

- **Select cells.** Drag across a couple of cells to make the selection handles appear; you can drag them to expand the highlighting. The usual Edit-menu commands

As long as your locked notes are all unlocked, you can still see and edit them. But when there's any risk of somebody else coming along and seeing them (on your Mac, iPhone, iPad, or any other synced gadget), click the 🔒 again—and this time choose Close All Locked Notes.

Now all you see of the locked notes are their titles. Everything on them is replaced by a "This note is locked" message (and a password box).

If you correctly enter the password, then all your hidden notes are suddenly viewable and editable.

Use your power wisely.

The Attachments Browser

The Attachments Browser in Notes is a single screen showing all attachments from all notes, all rounded up on one scrolling screen (see Figure 11-29). Just as in Messages, it's often incredibly convenient to scan the visual attachments as a way to find a particular note.

Figure 11-29:
The Notes Attachments Browser lists every photo, video, sketch, scan (from your iPhone), map, website, audio file, and other document that appears in any note in your Notes, all in one place. Click one to jump to the note that contains it—a great way to find something you're looking for without having to know when you wrote it or what it said.

Shown here: The Photos & Videos tab (top) and the Scans tab (bottom), which displays scans you've made on your iPhone or iPad (a feature introduced in iOS 11). You can't create a scan directly in Notes from your Mac.

Notes Folders

You can organize your notes into folders, for ease of wading through them. Any folders you create on the Mac also show up on your iPhone/iPad.

The key to understanding this feature is the slide-out Folders list, which you can see at left in Figure 11-27. You can make it appear by choosing View→Show Folders List,

Figure 11-28 shows the procedure.

Once you've shared a note, the person icon at the top turns dark, and a matching icon appears next to the note's name in the master list (Figure 11-28, bottom). At any time, you can stop sharing the note—or add more people to its collaboration—by clicking that person icon again and editing the sharing panel that appears.

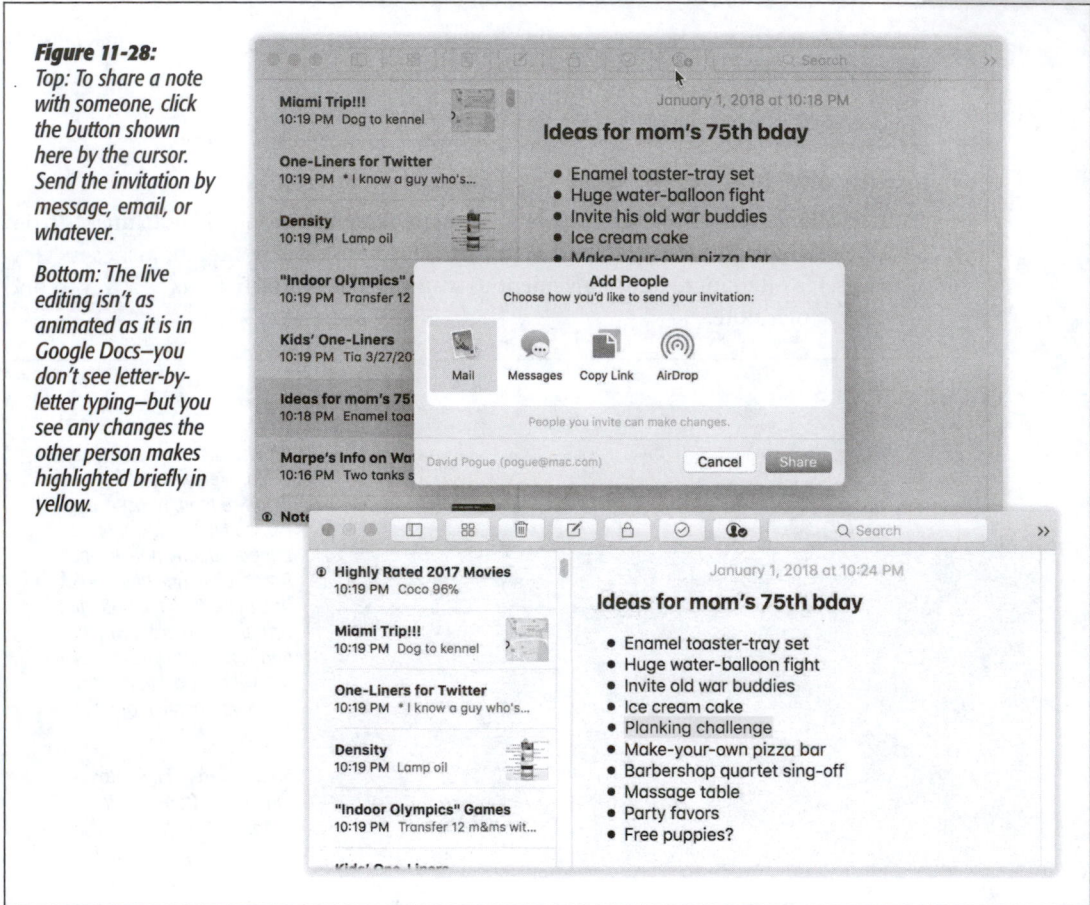

Figure 11-28:

Top: To share a note with someone, click the button shown here by the cursor. Send the invitation by message, email, or whatever.

Bottom: The live editing isn't as animated as it is in Google Docs—you don't see letter-by-letter typing—but you see any changes the other person makes highlighted briefly in yellow.

Locking Notes

Locked, hidden, password-protected Notes pages are here at last, suitable for listing birthday presents you intend to get for your nosy kid, the formula for your top-secret invisibility potion, or your illicit lovers' names.

Note that you hide and show all your locked notes with a single password. You can't (that is, don't have to) make up a different password for every note.

To lock a note, click the 🔒 button in the toolbar; from the shortcut menu, choose Lock This Note. Enter a password for locking/unlocking all your notes (or, if you've done this before, enter *the* password).

You can click 🗑 to delete the current note. Or you can click ⬆ to send the note to someone, by email, AirDrop, Messages, or whatever (page 263).

Conversely, the ⬆ button in lots of other programs now lists Notes, meaning that you can send material (map, photo, link, text, address, phone number…) directly *to* either a new note page or an existing one.

Tip: You can also print a note; choose File→Print. Just pointing that out.

The Notes List

As you create more pages, the list of pages (at center in Figure 11-27) becomes more useful. It's your table of contents for the Notes pad. It's a quick way to jump from one note to another.

Here's what this list displays:

- **The first lines of your notes,** along with the time or date you last edited them. If there's a photo or sketch on a note—an unlocked one, anyway—you see its thumbnail, too.

 To open a note, click its name. To delete a note, click it and then press the Delete key.

- **Pinned notes.** Ordinarily, your notes appear chronologically, most recent at the top. In Notes→Preferences, you can specify that they be sorted by Date Changed or Title instead.

 But you may have a couple of notes—things you refer to a lot—that you want to appear at the top all the time. Passwords, credit card numbers, or frequent-flyer numbers, for example.

 That's why you can *pin* an individual note to the top of the list, where it won't move. To do that, click a note and then choose File→Pin Note. Or right-click or two-finger click the note and, from the shortcut menu, choose Pin Note.

 You *un*pin a note using the same techniques (but choose Unpin Note instead).

There's a search box, too. You can search all your notes instantly.

Tip: If you double-click a note's name, it opens into a new window, floating on your screen. You can open multiple notes this way, drag them around the screen, and leave them floating there permanently, as though held by magnets on the great refrigerator door of life.

Collaborative Notes

You and your buddies can edit a page in Notes simultaneously, over the internet. It's great when you and your spouse are planning a dinner party and brainstorming about guests and the menu, for example. Also great for adding items to the grocery or to-do list even after your spouse has left the house to get them taken care of.

If you open the News app and see a bunch of news headlines right off the bat, well, sweet; you're the beneficiary of iCloud syncing (page 663). News has inherited your taste in news from some other Apple gadget.

If this is the very first time you've ever opened News, though, click Continue on the welcome screen. You're no longer directed to choose the topics or publications you want to follow. Instead, you're hit right between the eyes with today's headlines, beautifully laid out. It's like a specialized newspaper that's been lovingly cobbled together from all sorts of websites, magazines, and *real* newspapers.

This is the Today tab. (Tabs, in this case, are the headings in the left-side source list.) Scroll down far enough, and you'll discover that your "front page" is broken up into sections like Top Stories (chosen by human editors), Trending Stories (chosen by algorithm based on popularity), For You (stories that match your interests—read on), Top Videos, and so on (Figure 11-26). Eventually, you scroll down into topic areas like Politics, Sports, and Movies, plus super-specialized topics that you choose yourself.

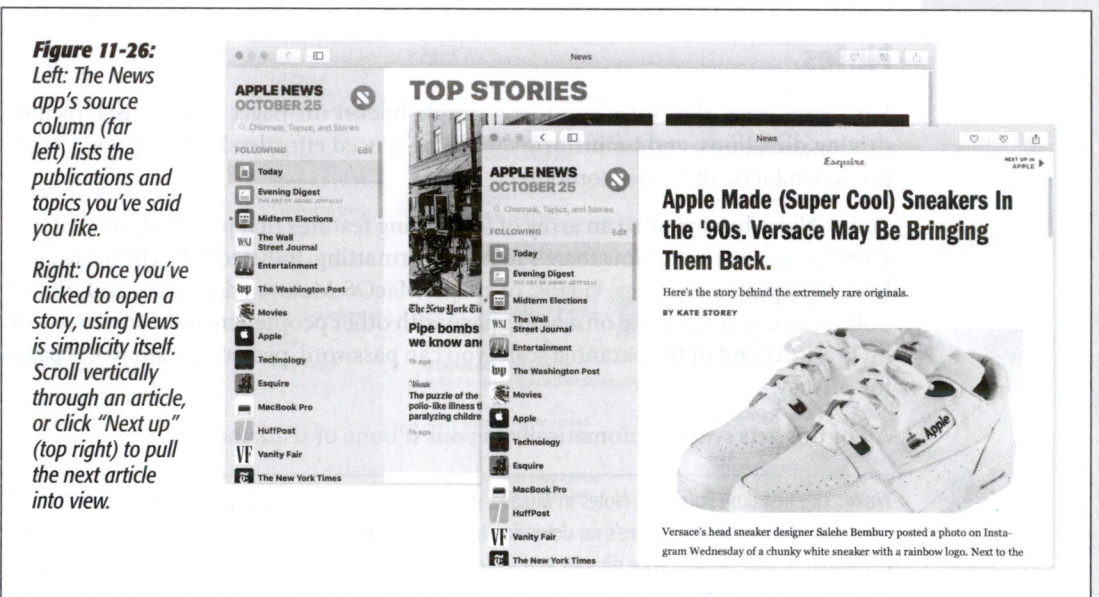

Figure 11-26:
Left: The News app's source column (far left) lists the publications and topics you've said you like.

Right: Once you've clicked to open a story, using News is simplicity itself. Scroll vertically through an article, or click "Next up" (top right) to pull the next article into view.

On the second tab (called, for example, Evening Digest), you'll find "a roundup of the day's best reads." These are editor-chosen; everybody sees the same stories here. On weekdays, it changes three times a day (morning, afternoon, evening); on weekends, it's called Weekend Pursuits and lets Apple's editors have some work/life balance.

The remaining tabs are the publications, websites, and topics (tech, business, politics, fashion, and so on) that you want to follow in your News app.

The Suggested list offers a few starter categories, based on your Mac's observations about the kinds of news you like to read; click ♡ if you do indeed like that kind of thing, or ♥ if you don't.

To engage Flyover, enter a city you'd like to tour, and then switch into Satellite view. Click the 3D logo in the lower-right corner.

Now you can go nuts, conducting your own virtual chopper tour of the city using the zooming and rotating tricks described earlier. Only a couple of things are different:

- **To move around the map,** drag it—or use two fingers on the trackpad.

- **To change your camera angle** relative to the ground, press Option as you use two fingers on the trackpad—or drag up or down on the compass at lower right.

- **To zoom in,** spread two fingers on the trackpad—or click the + and − buttons.

It's immersing, completely amazing, and very unlikely to make you airsick.

Flyover Tours

Apple wasn't satisfied with letting you pan around virtual 3D city models using your finger. It's also prepared to give you city *tours* in 3D.

Use the search box to enter the name of a big city or major landmark. (Some examples: San Francisco, New York, Tokyo, London, Paris, Rome, Madrid, Vancouver, San Jose, Cape Town, Stockholm. Or places like Yosemite National Park, the Sydney Opera House, Stonehenge, St. Peter's Basilica, or the Brooklyn Bridge.)

When you hit Search, a new button appears on the map: "3D Flyover Tour." (You can also find the button in the ⓘ Info panel for a city or place.) When you hit Start, you're in for a crazy treat: a fully automated video tour of that city or place. The San Francisco tour shows you the baseball park, the famous Transamerica Pyramid, the Alcatraz prison island, and so on. It's slow, soothing, cool, and definitely something that paper maps never did.

Messages

See Chapter 19 for details on Messages, the Mac's instant-messaging/audio-chat/video-chat/text-messaging program.

Mission Control

Chapter 5 covers macOS's window-management tool.

News

The News app, new in Mojave (and one of the four apps Apple brought over from iOS), does just what Apple promises: It "collects all the stories you want to read, from top news sources, based on topics you're most interested in."

Apple employs human editors to choose the stories in the Top Stories and Top Videos sections—rather than software robots. You see the same stories as everyone else here, no matter what your political leanings; in theory, this approach minimizes the triumph of propaganda and clickbait.

Note: The Transit feature of Maps is now available in dozens of locations worldwide. At this writing, they include, in the U.S., Alabama, Atlanta, Austin, Baltimore, Boston, Chicago, Cincinnati, Cleveland, Columbus, Dallas, Denver, Detroit, Honolulu, Houston, Kansas City, Los Angeles, Miami, Minneapolis, Nevada, New Orleans, New York, Philadelphia, Phoenix, Pittsburgh, Portland (Oregon), Sacramento, Salt Lake City, San Antonio, San Diego, San Francisco, Seattle, Tampa, and Washington, D.C.

Traffic

How's this for a cool feature? Free, real-time traffic reporting. From the Show pop-up menu (bottom of the screen), choose Show Traffic. Now traffic jams appear on the relevant roads, for your stressing pleasure; orange dotted lines for slow traffic, and red ones for true stop-and-go nightmares.

If you don't see any dotted lines, it's either because traffic is moving fine or because Apple doesn't have any information for those roads. Usually, you get traffic info only for highways, and only in metropolitan areas.

Tiny icons also appear, representing accidents, construction sites, closed roads, and general alerts. Click the icon to make a quick description tag appear (like "Accident, Park Ave at State St"); click that tag to read a full-screen account of what's going on.

Flyover

You don't need to be headed somewhere to use Flyover, the Maps app's most dazzling feature; it has nothing to do with navigation, really. You can operate it even while you're lying on your couch like a slug; see Figure 11-25.

Figure 11-25:
Flyover is a dynamic, interactive, photographic 3D model of 240 major cities. It looks something like an aerial video, except that you control the virtual camera. You can pan around these scenes, looking over and around buildings to see what's behind them. To create this feature, Apple says, it spent two years filming cities from helicopters.

When everything looks good, Maps displays an overview of the route you're about to follow. In fact, it may propose several routes on the map, labeled with tags that show how long they'll take: "1 hr 9 min," "1 hr 15 min," and "1 hr 28 min," for example.

If you click one of these routes or tags, the top of the Directions panel lets you know the distance and estimated time for that option and identifies the main roads you'll be on.

Now, nobody expects you to use your Mac as a portable GPS device. You're not going to park it on your dashboard and have it tell you when to turn.

What you can do, though, is send your selected directions to an iPhone or an iPad and use *that* as your GPS. See Figure 11-23.

Or, if you're just planning your trip, click any of the steps in the Directions panel; the map zooms in to that particular turn. Your route looks like it's been drawn in with a highlighter.

Public Transportation

Once you've called up some directions, you can click Transit (just below the Start/End box) to see Maps' suggestion of public-transportation methods to get there. Figure 11-24 shows the result.

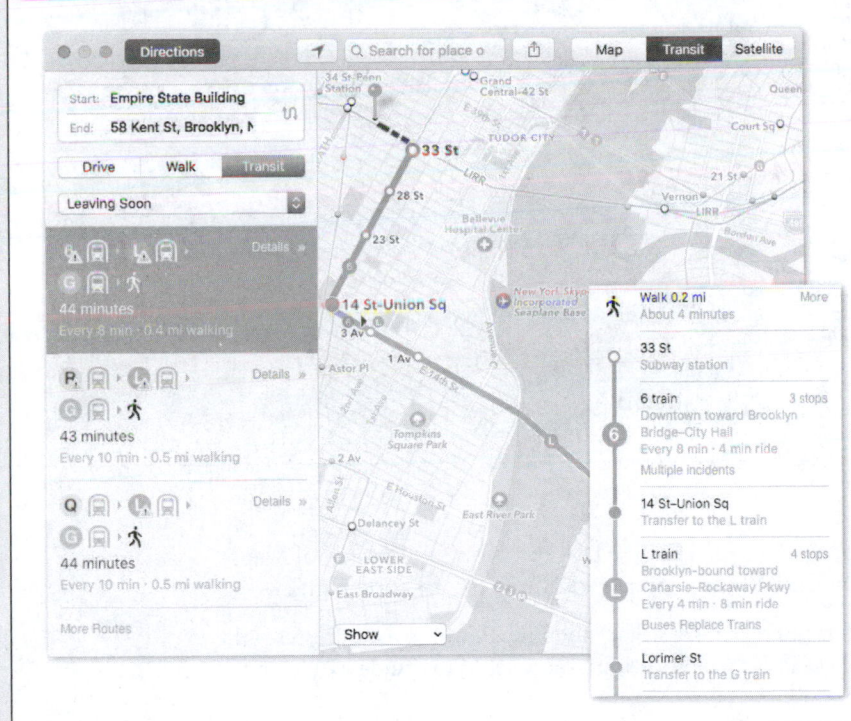

Figure 11-24:
Maps knows the complete bus, train, and subway schedules for an ever-growing number of cities. In those cities, click Transit to see your options.

Left: Here Maps is suggesting three different ways to get there using public transit. (Use the Leaving Soon pop-up menu to specify when you plan to travel.)

If you click Details, you're shown the specifics of each rail, bus, or walking segment (inset, right).

Finding Friends and Businesses

That pushpin business also comes into play when you use Maps as a glorified national Yellow Pages. If you type, for example, *pharmacy 60609*, then those red pushpins show you all the drugstores in that Chicago zip code. It's a great way to find a gas station, a cash machine, or a hospital in a pinch. Click a pushpin to see the name of the corresponding business.

As usual, you can click the pin's ⓘ bubble to open a details screen. If you've searched for a friend, then you see the corresponding Contacts card. If you've searched for a business, then you get a screen containing its phone number, address, website, and so on; often, you get a beautiful page of Yelp information (photos, reviews, ratings).

Remember that you can click a web address to open it or send the phone number to your phone to dial it. ("Hello, what time do you close today?")

Figure 11-23:
On the details screen that sprouts when you click a red pushpin, buttons let you bookmark the spot, get directions, or add the information to Contacts.

If the location is a restaurant or a business, you might get screens full of useful information: customer reviews, photos, hours of operation, delivery and reservation information, and so on.

Best of all, the ⬆ button lets you share this location with other people—via AirDrop, email, text message, and so on—or with your other Apple gadgets.

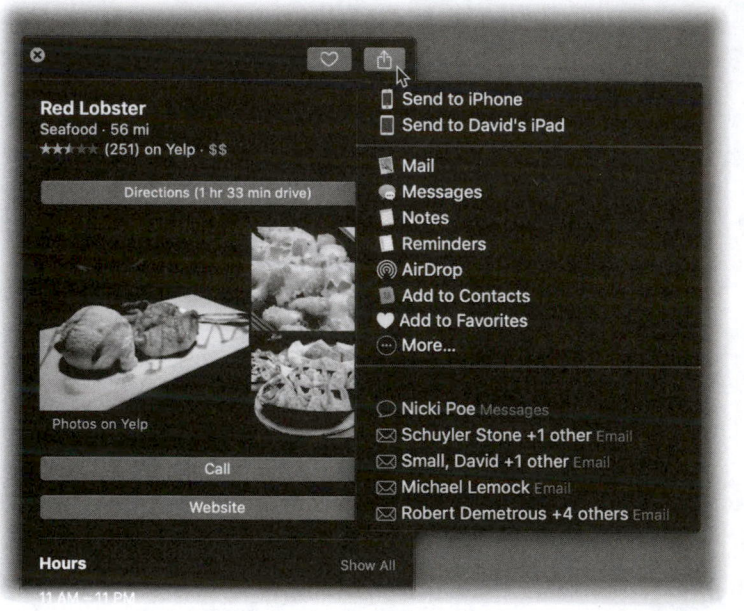

Directions

The Directions panel opens when you click the Directions button (top left of Maps), or when you click the Directions button on any location's information panel.

The Directions panel offers *two* search bars: Start and End. Plug in two addresses—the Start address may already say "Current Location"—and let Maps guide you from the first to the second.

Tip: The ⇅ button swaps the Start and End points. That's a great way to find your way back after a trip.

- **A city.** Type *chicago* to see that city. You can zoom in from there.

- **A zip code or a neighborhood.** Type *10012* or *greenwich village*.

- **A point of interest.** Type *washington monument* or *niagara falls*.

- **A business type.** Type *drugstores in albany ny* or *hospitals in roanoke va*. (Figure 11-22 shows this idea.)

Tip: Maps is far more useful now that Siri has come to the Mac. You can say things like, "Find pizza near me," "What's the quickest way to JFK Airport?" "Get transit directions to Brooklyn," "Mail these directions to Casey," or "Zoom in on the map."

And if your Mac has a Touch Bar (page 233), then you get one-click buttons for Food, Coffee, Banks, Hotels, Gas, and so on, glowing right at you.

When Maps finds a specific address, an animated, red-topped pushpin comes flying down onto its precise spot on the map. A bubble identifies the location by name. Click outside the bubble to hide it. Click the map pin to bring the bubble back. Click Directions for instant driving directions.

Tip: Or walking directions. Click Walk at the top of the Directions panel.

Click the ⓘ bubble to open the Location page; read on.

The Details Screen

Once you've found something on the map—your current position, say, or something you've searched for—you can drop a pin there for future reference. Choose Edit→Drop Pin. A purple pushpin appears. (You can drag the pin to move it, if your aim wasn't exact.)

Red pushpins represent addresses you've looked up. And the tiny icons represent restaurants, stores, and other establishments in Apple's (actually Yelp's) database.

All of these pushpins and nano-icons are clickable. You get little labels that identify them. And, if you click the label, you open a details screen (Figure 11-23).

Bookmarks, Recents, Contacts

Maps is also plugged into your Contacts list, which makes it especially easy to find a friend's house (or just to see how ritzy his neighborhood is).

When you click into the empty search bar at the top of the screen, the Bookmarks/Recents/Contacts menu appears; it can save you a lot of typing.

The list displays Recents (locations you've looked up recently—on your Mac or your iOS gadgets); Favorites (locations you've bookmarked); and Contacts (people whose addresses you've looked up).

When you click an entry in any of these lists, Maps drops a red, animated pushpin onto the map to identify that address.

At any time, you can click Satellite (top right) for stunning aerial photos. Using the Show pop-up menu at lower left, you can choose Show Labels to add street names to the aerial views. There's no guarantee that the Satellite view provides a very *recent* photo—the Maps database incorporates photography taken at different times—but it's still very cool.

Finding Yourself

Don't worry if you scroll away and can't find yourself on the map again. Click the ◄ at the top left. A blue dot shows your current location.

Searching the Maps

You're not always interested in finding out where you are; often, you know that much perfectly well. Instead, you want to see where something *else* is. Click in the search box and type what you're seeking—or, if you spot what you want in the list of recently sought addresses, click it there. (If there's already something in the box, then click ⊗ to clear it out.) Here's what Maps can find for you:

- **An address.** You can skip the periods (and usually the commas, too). And you can use abbreviations. Typing *710 w end ave ny ny* will find 710 West End Avenue, New York, New York. (In any of these examples, you can type a zip code instead of a city and state.)

- **An intersection.** Type *57th and lexington, ny ny*. Maps will find the spot where East 57th Street crosses Lexington Avenue in New York City.

UP TO SPEED

How the Mac Does GPS

When you first open Maps, your current location appears as a blue dot on the map. Now, the Mac doesn't have GPS; how does it do that?

It uses a sneaky trick. Metropolitan areas today are blanketed by overlapping Wi-Fi signals. At a typical Manhattan intersection, you might be in range of 20 base stations. Each one broadcasts its name and unique network address (its MAC address—nothing to do with Mac computers) once every second. Although you'd need to be within 150 feet or so to actually get onto the internet, a laptop or phone can detect this beacon signal from up to 1,500 feet away.

Imagine if you could correlate all those beacon signals with their physical locations. Why, you'd be able to simulate GPS—without the GPS!

So, for years, millions of laptops and iPhones have been quietly logging all those Wi-Fi signals, noting their network addresses and locations. (The Macs and iPhones never have to connect to these base stations. They're just reading the one-way beacon signals.)

At this point, Apple's database knows about millions of hotspots—and the precise longitude and latitude of each.

So your Mac sniffs for Wi-Fi base stations. If it finds any, it transmits their IDs back to Apple—which looks up those network addresses and sends coordinates back to Maps.

That accuracy is good to within only 100 feet, and of course the system fails completely once you're out of populated areas. On the other hand, it works indoors, which GPS definitely doesn't.

By the way: If you'd rather not have your Mac consulting Apple about its location, open System Preferences→Security & Privacy→Privacy and turn off Location Services.

showed bridges and roads melting into the sea. In a remarkable apology letter, Apple CEO Tim Cook recommended using one of Maps' rivals.

But some of Maps' features are pretty great—and now that Maps is a Mac app, too (Figure 11-22), there's some handy synergy with the iPhone and iPad. You can look up an address on the Mac and then wirelessly shoot it over to the phone for navigation in the car, for example. Or simply walk over to your Mac; thanks to Handoff (page 312), whatever map was on your phone is now on your Mac. And Maps' smarts are wired into other macOS programs, like Calendar, Contacts, and Safari.

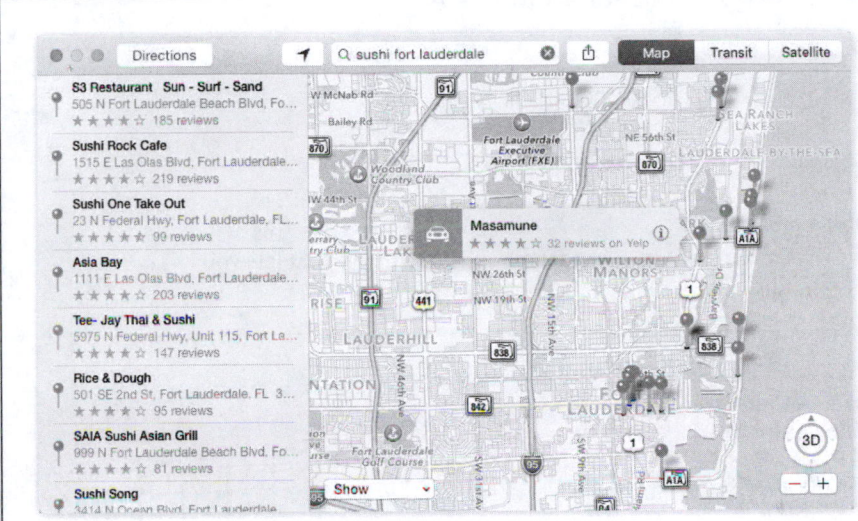

Figure 11-22:
Maps lets you type in any address or point of interest and see it on a map, with turn-by-turn directions. It also gives you a national Yellow Pages and real-time traffic alerts. You have a choice of a street-map diagram or actual aerial photos, taken by satellite.

Meet Maps

When you open Maps, you see a blue dot that represents your current location. You can manipulate the map in all the usual ways:

- **Zoom in or out** using the keyboard (press ⌘-plus or ⌘-minus), the mouse (double-click to zoom in, add the Option key to zoom out—or just click the + or − buttons), or the trackpad (pinch two fingers to zoom out; spread them to zoom in).

- **Scroll around the map** using the keyboard (press the arrow keys), the mouse (drag), or the trackpad (swipe two fingers in any direction).

- **Rotate the map** using the mouse (drag the small compass at lower right) or the trackpad (rotate two fingers). You can return the map to "north is up" by pressing ⌘-▲, by clicking the compass, or by double-tapping two fingers on the trackpad.

- **You can tilt into a 3D view,** which makes it look more like you're surveying the map at an angle instead of straight down. You can do that with the mouse (click the 3D button), keyboard (press ⌘-0), or the trackpad (press Option and drag with two fingers).

Keyboard control

You can control iTunes' music playback using its menus, of course, but the keyboard can be far more efficient.

Here are a few of the control keystrokes worth noting:

Function	Keystroke
Play, Pause	space bar
Next song/previous song	▼, ▲ or ▶, ◀
Louder, quieter	⌘-▲, ⌘-▼
Rewind, fast-forward	Option-⌘-◀, Option-⌘-▶
Eject the CD	⌘-E
Turn Visualizer on	⌘-T
Turn Visualizer off	⌘-T or mouse click
Full Screen mode	Control-⌘-F
Exit full-screen Visualizer	⌘-T, Esc, or mouse click

Playing with the graphic equalizer

If you choose Window→Equalizer, you get a handsome control console that lets you adjust the strength of each musical frequency independently (Figure 11-21).

Figure 11-21:
Drag the sliders (bass on the left, treble on the right) to accommodate the strengths and weaknesses of your speakers or headphones (and listening tastes). Or save yourself the trouble—use the pop-up menu above the sliders to choose a canned set of slider positions for Classical, Dance, Jazz, Latin, and so on. These settings even transfer to your i-gadgets.

Launchpad

See page 170 for the full story about the program-opening home screen.

Mail

See Chapter 17 for the missing Mail manual.

Maps

When Apple brought its Maps app to the iPhone in 2012, the underlying databases had a lot of problems. They didn't include nearly as many points of interest (buildings, stores, landmarks) as Google's. Addresses were sometimes wrong. Satellite view

within iTunes—just click the Sync button. It says "Sync" only if, in fact, anything has changed since your last sync.)

Once your iPhone is connected to the computer and you've clicked its icon at the upper-left corner of iTunes, the left column of the iTunes window reveals two sets of word buttons.

- **The top set includes** Summary, Music, Movies, TV Shows, Podcasts, Books, Photos, and Info. For the most part, these represent the categories of stuff you can sync to your device. They let you specify exactly what you want copied to it—which songs, which TV shows, which apps, and so on.

 For example, on the Music tab, you can turn on either "Entire music library" or "Selected playlists, artists, albums, and genres" for copying to your phone.

 Once you've made your selections, click the Summary tab and then click Apply. (The Apply button says Sync instead if you haven't actually changed any settings.)

- **The bottom set** is called On My Device. These buttons let you see what music, movies, and so on are already on your phone.

Playing with Playback

To play a song or video in iTunes, double-click it. Or click iTunes' Play button (▶) or press the space bar. The Mac immediately begins to play the selected files or playlists.

Tip: The central display at the top of the window shows not only the name of the song and the album, but also where you are in the song, as represented by the horizontal strip. Drag the handle, or click elsewhere in the strip, to jump around in the song.

As music plays, you can manipulate the music and the visuals of your Mac in all kinds of interesting ways. There are even playback controls on your Touch Bar, if you have one (page 233). Some people don't move from their Macs for months at a time.

Turning on the Visualizer

The Visualizer is an onscreen light show that pulses, beats, and dances in sync to the music. (For real party fun, invite some people who grew up in the '60s to your house to watch.)

To summon this psychedelic display, choose View→Visualizer→Show Visualizer, or just press ⌘-T.

iTunes now offers two options in this submenu, the iTunes Visualizer and iTunes Classic Visualizer. Check out the latter for that special early-aughts-style trippiness. The show begins immediately—although it's much more fun if you choose View→Enter Full Screen (Control-⌘-F) so the show takes over your whole monitor. True, you won't get a lot of work done, but when it comes to stress relief, Visualizer is a lot cheaper than a hot tub.

the white USB cable that came with it. (To save precious swaths of forest trees, the rest of this chapter refers to "iPhone" when it means "iPhone, iPad, or iPod Touch.")

Once the phone is connected, click the ☐ near the top-left corner of the iTunes screen. Now you can look over the iPhone's contents or sync it (read on).

Note: If you have more than one i-device, and they're all connected, this button is a pop-up menu. Choose the name of the one you want to manipulate.

Connecting the phone with a cable

Pretty simple: Plug one end of the white cable (supplied with your iPhone) into your computer's USB jack. Connect the other end to the phone. If the phone is turned on and awake, then it's officially connected.

Connecting over Wi-Fi

The familiar white USB cable is all well and good—but the iPhone is a wireless device, for Pete's sake. Why not sync it to your computer wirelessly?

The phone can be charging in its bedside alarm clock dock, happily and automatically syncing with your laptop somewhere else in the house. It transfers all the same stuff to and from your computer—apps, music, books, contacts, calendars, movies, photos, ringtones—but through the air instead of via your USB cable.

Your computer has to be turned on and running iTunes. The phone and the computer have to be on the same Wi-Fi network.

To set up wireless sync, connect the phone using the white USB cable, one last time. Ironic, but true. Now open iTunes and click ☐ at top left. On the Summary tab, scroll down; turn on "Sync with this iPhone over Wi-Fi." Click Apply. You can now detach the phone.

From now on, whenever the phone is on the Wi-Fi network, it's automatically connected to your computer, wirelessly. You don't even have to think about it. (Well, OK—you have to think about leaving the computer turned on with iTunes open, which is something of a buzzkill.)

Just *connecting* it doesn't necessarily mean *syncing* it, though; that's a more data-intensive, battery-drainy process. Syncing happens in either of two ways:

- **Automatically.** If the iPhone is plugged into power (like a speaker dock, an alarm-clock dock, or a wall outlet), and it's on the same Wi-Fi network, then it syncs with the Mac all by itself.

- **Manually.** You can also trigger a sync manually—and this time, the iPhone doesn't have to be plugged into power. To do that, on the phone, open Settings→General→iTunes Wi-Fi Sync and click Sync Now. (You can also trigger a Wi-Fi sync from

Note: The Podcasts category now includes iTunes U recordings: hundreds of thousands of downloadable college courses, all of them free and many of them amazing, for your personal-growth pleasure. Watch the videos of the professors, follow along with the reading materials. You won't actually earn a college degree this way, but you *will* attain a degree of enlightenment.

Audiobooks

Some people like to curl up with—or listen to—a good book, and Apple has plenty to offer, both as ebooks (which you buy and read in the Books app) and as audiobooks (which you listen to as you work in the garden or commute to work).

If iTunes doesn't offer the audiobook you're interested in, you can find a larger collection (over 50,000 of them) at Audible.com. This web store sells all kinds of audiobooks, plus recorded periodicals like *The New York Times* and radio shows. To purchase Audible's wares, you have to have either an Audible account or an Amazon account.

The files land in iTunes automatically when you buy them.

Internet Radio

When Apple says "radio," it could mean a couple of things.

It could mean the live, hosted Beats 1 radio station that debuted as part of Apple Music but is free to all. (To listen, open the Music Store and click Beats 1 Radio in the panel at right.)

Note: Until early 2016, it could also have meant the free feature called iTunes Radio: custom radio stations, based on songs or singers you like, delivered to you with full pause/skip capabilities and the occasional ad. Sadly, this feature has been discontinued.

Authorizing Computers

All movies and TV shows, and some old music files, are still copy protected. When you create an account in iTunes, you automatically *authorize* that computer to play copy-protected songs from the iTunes Store.

You can copy those songs and videos onto a maximum of four other computers. To authorize each one to play music from your account, choose Account→Authorizations→Authorize This Computer. (Don't worry—you have to do this just once per machine.) It's Apple's way of making sure you don't go playing those music tracks on more than five computers, which would greatly displease the music studios.

When you've maxed out your limit and can't authorize any more computers, you may need to *deauthorize* one. On the computer you wish to demote, choose Account→Authorizations→Deauthorize This Computer.

Syncing an iPad or iPhone

Another function of iTunes is to load up, and back up, your iPhone, iPad, or iPod Touch. You can connect it to your computer either wirelessly—over Wi-Fi—or with

iTunes Store

The iTunes software's third purpose is to be the face of Apple's original online music store, the iTunes Store. It's not like Apple Music, where you're only renting your music. Here you pay per song (or per movie or TV show), and you can play it as many times as you like, for as long as Apple is in business.

To shop, click Store (the final button in the top-of-screen row of buttons). Now you can buy and download whatever file type you choose from the top-left pop-up menu: Music, Movies, TV Shows, Podcasts, Audiobooks, and so on. This material goes straight into your iTunes library, just a sync away from your i-devices.

Tip: iTunes doesn't have a monopoly on music sales. Amazon, Google, Napster, and other services sell songs in MP3 format, meaning no copy protection (and Apple compatibility). eMusic.com has great MP3 prices, but the music comes from lesser-known bands. And Amazon's MP3 Downloader software can whip your purchases right into iTunes.

Music

Here it is, the store that made Apple a powerhouse in the music industry: the Music store. Here are millions of songs, individually downloadable, all without copy protection, for 79 cents, $1, or $1.29, depending on popularity.

There are all kinds of ways to slice, dice, and search this catalog. On the right side of the screen, there's a Genres pop-up menu that sorts the offerings by music type. Use the search box (top right) to find a song by name, album name, band, composer, and so on.

The various buttons on the front page of the Music store represent music Apple thinks you might like: new releases, big hits, and so on.

Learning these tools for finding songs is handy, because the same tools are available for finding TV shows, movies, podcasts, audiobooks, and so on.

TV, movies, and movie rentals

The iTunes store also offers a vast selection of downloadable TV episodes ($2 apiece, no ads) and movies (buy for $10 to $20, or rent for $3 to $5).

Once you rent a movie, you have 30 days to start watching—and once you start, you have 48 hours to finish before it turns back into a pumpkin (it deletes itself from your computer or phone).

If you download a rental movie to your iPhone, you can't move it to any other gadget. But if you download it to iTunes, you can move it from Mac to iPad, or whatever, although it can exist on only one machine at a time.

Podcasts

Not everything in the iTunes Store costs money. There are plenty of free audio and video podcasts in the Podcasts area of the store.

- **Beats 1 Radio**. Apple has a "global, 24-hour internet radio station" called Beats 1. (It actually broadcasts live for only 12 hours a day and then repeats.) Listening is free, even to nonpayers.

 Live DJs introduce songs and comment on the singers, just as on FM radio stations. Of course, you have no input on the style of music you hear on Beats 1, and you can't pause, rewind, fast-forward, or save anything you hear for later listening. It's old-style radio, offering the magic of serendipity.

- **iTunes Match**. iTunes Match, which dates back to 2011, is a cloud-based version of your iTunes library, available to any of your Apple devices. You can stream Apple's copies of any song files you actually own—ripped from CDs or even acquired illegally. The advantages: First, you save a lot of space on your phone. Second, you can play them on any Apple gadget you own. Third, the versions Apple plays are often of higher quality than your originals.

 iTunes Match continues as a separate service for non–Apple Music subscribers (the song limit is now 100,000 songs), for $25 a year. But if you do subscribe to Apple Music, in effect you get iTunes Match automatically.

Now: Two of iTunes' top-of-window buttons are useful only to Apple Music subscribers: For You (Apple's automated recommendations for new music you might like) and Browse (meander through Apple's 30 million tracks, playing them at will).

If you're not a subscriber, those two buttons are just taking up space. Fortunately, you can hide them: Choose iTunes→Preferences→General, and turn off Show Apple Music Features.

At this point, iTunes' top-of-window buttons change to say Library, Connect, Radio (page 434), and Store. You're no longer compelled to look at the two tabs reserved for paying customers.

GEM IN THE ROUGH

AirPlay Audio

On page 350, you can read about the miracle of AirPlay—a wireless technology that sends audio and video from your Mac to your Apple TV.

But even before there was AirPlay video, there was AirPlay audio. Your Mac can easily send audio to your Apple TV (or to your AirPort Express base station), and from there to what's presumably a better sound system than your Mac's puny built-in speakers. The official way to do that: Open System Preferences→Sound→Output. Click the name of the Apple TV or AirPort Express in the list of speakers.

But there are two faster ways:

Press Option as you open the ◀» menulet. The items in this menu magically sprout previously invisible choices—like Apple TV and your other AirPlay gear.

If you just want to play music that's in iTunes, you can choose your Apple TV's name (or AirPort Express's name) from the ▨ pop-up menu in the top-left corner of the window.

- **Add new songs to the playlist.** Tiptoe through your Music list and drag more songs or albums into the playlist list.

- **Delete songs from the playlist.** If your playlist needs pruning, or that banjo tune just doesn't fit in with the brass-band tracks, you can ditch it quickly: Click the song in the playlist window and then hit Delete or Backspace to get rid of it.

 Deleting a song like this doesn't delete it from your Mac—just from this playlist.

- **Delete the whole playlist.** To delete an entire playlist, click its name in the list of playlists (far left) and then press Delete. Again, this zaps only the playlist itself, not all the songs you had in it. (Those are still in your Mac's iTunes folder.)

Click ⊗ to close the playlist window.

Apple Music

The Apple Music service, which debuted in 2015, is a rich stew of components. For $10 a month (or $15 for a family of six), you get all of the following:

- **Unlimited streaming music.** You can listen to any band, album, or song in the Apple Music library of 30 million songs—on demand, no ads. It's not like listening to a radio station, where someone else is programming the music; *you* program the music.

 On the other hand, this is not like Apple's traditional music store, where you pay $1 per download and you own the song. If you ever stop paying Apple the $10 a month, the music stops. You're left with nothing.

 If you do subscribe, you can tell Siri things like, "Play the top songs of 2005" or "Play some good running music" or "Play some Taylor Swift."

 Nor are you obligated to do all your music programming manually. Apple Music comes equipped with ready-made playlists, prepared by human editors, in all kinds of categories. There are sets of starter songs by various singers ("Intro to Sarah McLachlan"), playlists by genre and era, and playlists for specific activities like Waking Up, Running, Getting It On, and even Breaking Up.

 You can freely mix the songs you're renting with the music you actually own. You can even download songs you don't own for playback when you have no internet connection (as long as you're still paying your $10 a month).

UP TO SPEED

The Apple (iCloud) ID

Once you become a member of the Apple cult, the key that unlocks all Apple doors is your Apple ID. The same email address and password get you into iCloud, the iTunes Store, Apple Music, the App Store, Messages, FaceTime, and almost any other Apple service that requires you to log in. In the unlikely event that you don't yet have an Apple ID, you can get one by opening System Preferences→iCloud and clicking "Create new Apple ID."

iTunes even starts you out with some playlists of its own devising, like "Top 25 Most Played" and "Purchased" (a convenient place to find all your iTunes Store goodies listed in one place).

Smart playlists

Smart playlists constantly rebuild themselves according to criteria you specify. You might tell one to assemble 45 minutes' worth of songs you've rated higher than four stars but rarely listen to, and another to list your most-often-played songs from the '80s.

Tip: To rate a song, click the Songs heading at left; make the window wide enough that you can see the Rating column. (If you don't see this column, right-click or two-finger click any column heading and choose Rating from the list of options.) Then just click the Rating column for a selected song. The appropriate number of stars appears—one, two, three, four, or five—depending on the position of your click. You can change a song's rating as many times as you like—a good thing, considering the short shelf life of a pop hit these days.

To make a smart playlist, choose File→New Smart Playlist (Option-⌘-N). The dialog box shown in Figure 11-20 appears. The controls here are designed to set up a search of your music database. Figure 11-20, for example, illustrates how you'd find up to 74 minutes of Beatles tunes released between 1965 and 1968—that you've rated three stars or higher and that you've listened to no more than twice.

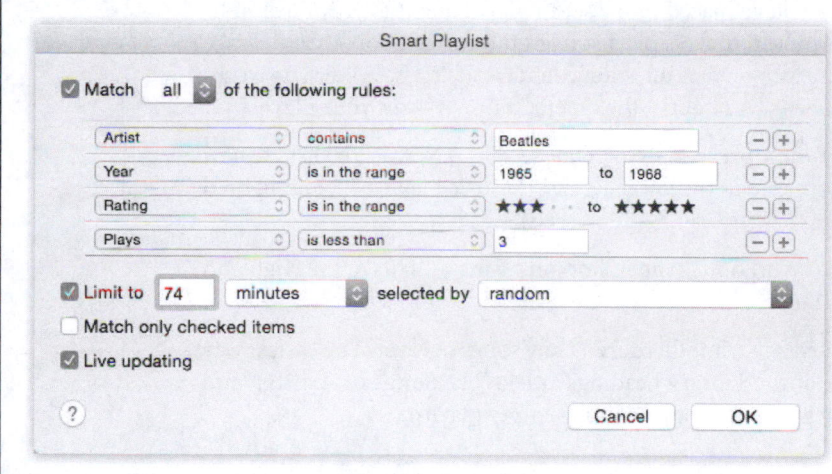

Figure 11-20:
A smart playlist is a powerful search command for your iTunes database. You can set up certain criteria, like the hunt for particular Beatles tunes illustrated here. The "Live updating" checkbox makes iTunes keep this playlist updated as your collection changes, as you change your ratings, as your play count changes, and so on.

Editing and deleting playlists

A playlist is easy to change with just a little light mousework. Click the playlist's name. If you click Open in New Window, a new playlist master window appears.

Now you can:

- **Change the order of songs in the playlist.** Drag song titles up or down within the playlist window to reorder them.

Four Ways to Fill Your Library

iTunes gives you at least four ways to get music and video onto your computer—ready for transferring to your devices, if you want:

- **Let iTunes find your files.** The first time you open iTunes, it offers to search your Mac for music files and add them to its library.

- **Pay for Apple Music.** For $10 a month, you can listen to, and download, all the music you want from Apple's multimillion-song catalog.

- **Visit the iTunes Store.** Another way to feed your library is to shop at the iTunes Store, buying songs to own them, as described starting on page 433.

- **Import music from a CD.** iTunes can also convert tracks from audio CDs into digital music files. Just start up iTunes and then stick a CD into your Mac's CD drive, if you have one. The program asks if you want to convert the songs to audio files for iTunes. (If it doesn't ask, then click the CD icon at the top of the window.)

 The program downloads song titles and artist information from the CD and begins to add the songs to the iTunes library. (For more control over this process, choose iTunes→Preferences→General. Click "Import Settings" to see your options.)

Playlists

A *playlist* is a list of songs you've placed into a set to play sequentially. For example, if you're having a party, you can make a playlist from the current Top 40 and dance music in your library. Some people may question your taste if you, say, alternate tracks from *La Bohème* with Queen's "A Night at the Opera," but hey—it's your playlist.

To create a playlist in iTunes, press ⌘-N or choose File→New→Playlist. A new playlist, called "Playlist," appears in the lower-left list ("Music Playlists"), highlighted so you can rename it.

Type a name for it: "Cardio Workout," "Shoe-Shopping Tunes," "Hits of the Highland Lute," or whatever. Press Enter.

At this point, you've created a list, but there aren't any songs in it yet. The easiest way to fix that is to click one of the Library headings at left (like Songs or Artists), and *drag* song or album names onto the name of your empty playlist.

Tip: Instead of making an empty playlist and then dragging songs into it, you can work the other way. You can scroll through a big list of songs, selecting tracks as you go by ⌘-clicking—and then, when you're finished, choose File→New→Playlist from Selection. All the songs you selected immediately appear on a brand-new playlist.

When you drag a song title onto a playlist, you're not actually moving or copying the song. In essence, you're creating an *alias* or *shortcut* of the original, which means you can have the same song on several different playlists.

The playback and volume controls are at the top-left corner of iTunes. At the upper-right corner is a search box that lets you pluck one track out of a haystack.

The following pages take you through the many faces of iTunes, one by one.

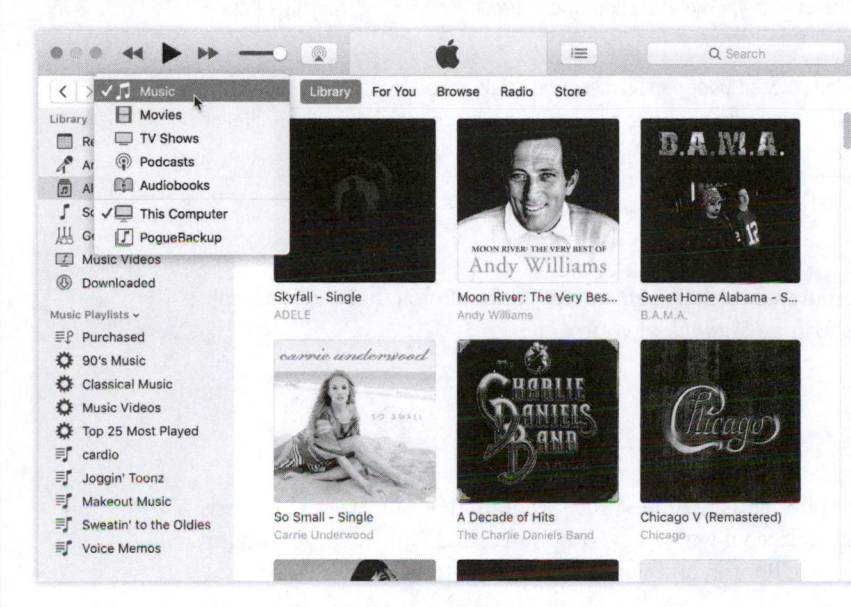

Figure 11-19:
iTunes can play music CDs; tune in to internet radio stations; load up your iPod, iPhone, or iPad; and play music files.

Your Stuff

The key to understanding iTunes' layout is the pop-up menu at top left. It lists the kinds of files iTunes can manage: Music, Movies, TV Shows, Podcasts, and Audiobooks.

To see what files are on your Mac, choose one of these file types, and then click Library at top center.

Tip: You can also choose a file type using the View→Media Kind submenu—or just by pressing ⌘-1 for Music, ⌘-2 for Movies, ⌘-3 for TV Shows, and so on.

The list at left lets you view your files grouped in different ways. For example, if you're viewing Music, you can see them sorted by Recently Added, Artists, Albums, Songs, Genres, or Videos.

You may see wildly different things in the main window, depending on which of those groupings you've chosen. For example, if you click Songs, you see a huge alphabetical list; if you click Albums, you see a square grid of album covers.

Finally, when you think you've got the selection rectangle(s) correctly positioned, click Scan to trigger the actual scan.

Note: These instructions apply to the most common kind of scanner—the *flatbed* scanner. If you have a scanner with a document feeder—a tray or slot that sucks in one paper document after another from a stack—the instructions are only slightly different.

You may, for example, see a Mode or Scan Mode pop-up menu; if so, choose Document Feeder. You'll want to use the Show Details option. You may also be offered a Duplex command (meaning "Scan both sides of the paper"—not all scanners can do this).

iMovie

Apple's video-editing program is big enough and complex enough that it gets a book all its own: *iMovie: The Missing Manual*, of course.

iPhoto

Well, *this* is awkward.

For years, iPhoto was the photo organizing/editing program that came free with every Mac. But in 2015, Apple replaced it with a new program called Photos. So you might have iPhoto, you might have Photos, and you might have both.

Since iPhoto is going away, Photos is the app described in this book (page 456).

iTunes

iTunes is the ultimate software jukebox (Figure 11-19).

The first thing to understand is that iTunes is four apps in one. It's designed to organize all the music, videos, podcasts, and audiobooks in four places: (1) on your Mac, (2) on your i-gadget, (3) in your $10-a-month Apple Music subscription, if you have one, and (4) in Apple's traditional $1-a-song music store.

Apple loves to play with the design of this program; every couple of years, it gets another overhaul. The following pages describe version 12.9.

Note: In iTunes 12.7 and later, you can't use iTunes anymore for syncing apps and ringtones with your iPhone or iPad. After years of listening to consumer complaints that iTunes has become too overloaded with functions, Apple felt this was one task it didn't need to handle. Today you have to buy and organize apps and ringtones directly from your phone.

The icons at top left (♫, ▤, ▭, and so on) affect what *kind* of file you're viewing; the buttons at top center affect whether you're looking on your computer or online.

Here are some of the most useful options:

- **Resolution.** This is the number of tiny scanned dots per inch. 300 is about right for something you plan to print out; 75 is standard for graphics that will be viewed on the screen, like images on a web page.

- **Name.** Here you can specify how you want each image file named when it lands on your hard drive. If it says *Scan,* then the files will be called *Scan 1, Scan 2,* and so on.

- **Format.** Usually, the file format for scanned graphics is TIFF. That's a very high-res format that's ideal if you're scanning precious photos for posterity. But if these images are bound for the web, you might want to choose JPEG instead; that's the standard web format.

- **Image Correction.** If you choose Manual from this pop-up menu, then, incredibly, you'll be treated to a whole expando-panel of color-correction tools: brightness, tint, saturation, a histogram, and so on.

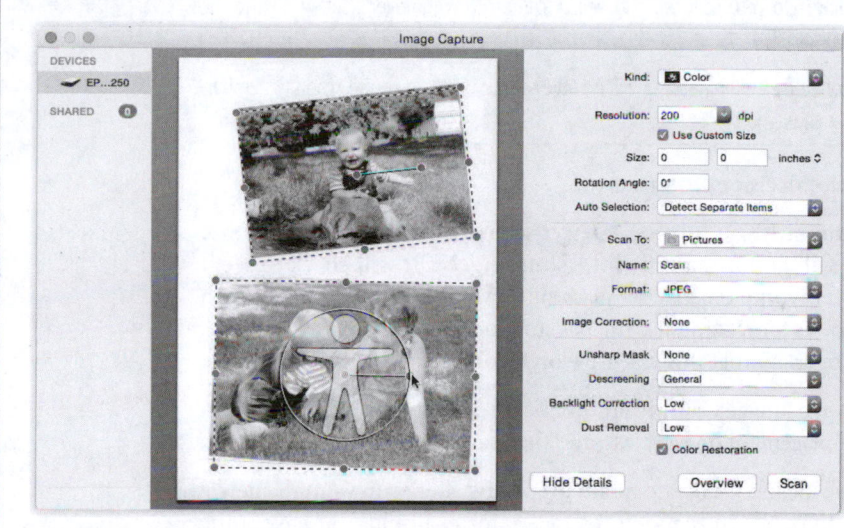

Figure 11-18:
When you use the Show Details button, you get a new panel on the right, where you can specify all the tweaky details for the scan you're about to make: resolution, size, and so on. See how the photos have dotted lines around them? That's because Detect Separate Items is turned on. These will be scanned into two separate files.

Opening the Details panel has another handy benefit, too: It lets you scan only a *portion* of what's on the scanner glass. Once you've put the document or photo into the scanner, click Overview. Image Capture does a quick pass and displays on the screen whatever is on the glass. You'll see a dotted-line rectangle around the entire scanned image—unless you've turned on "Detect separate images," in which case you see a dotted-line rectangle around *each* item on the glass.

You can adjust these dotted-line rectangles until you've enclosed precisely the portion of the image you want scanned. For example, drag the rectangles' corner handles to resize them; drag inside the rectangles to move them; drag the right end of the line inside the rectangle to rotate it; preview the rotation by pressing Control and Option.

If you prefer to import only *some* photos, then select them first. (In list view, you click and Shift-click to select a bunch of *consecutive* photos, and ⌘-click to add *individual* photos to the selection. In icon view, you can both ⌘-click *and* Shift-click to select individual photos.) Then click Import.

Scanning

If you own a scanner, chances are good that you won't be needing whatever special scanning software came with it. Instead, macOS gives you *two* programs that can operate any standard scanner: Image Capture and Preview. In fact, the controls are identical in both programs.

To scan in Image Capture, turn on your scanner and click its name in the left-side list. Put your photos or documents into the scanner.

Note: You can share a scanner on the network, if you like, by turning on Scanner Sharing in System Preferences→Sharing. That's sort of a weird option, though, for two reasons. First, what do you gain by sitting somewhere else in the building? Do you really want to yell or call up to whomever's sitting next to the scanner, "OK! Put in the next photo!"?

Second, don't forget that anyone else on the network will be able to see whatever you're scanning. Embarrassment may result. You've been warned.

Now you have a couple of decisions to make:

- **Separate and straighten?** If you turn on "Detect separate items" in the Scan Size menu, then macOS will perform a nifty little stunt indeed: It will check to see if you've put *multiple* items onto the scanner glass, like several small photos, as shown in Figure 11-18. (It looks for rectangular images surrounded by empty white space, so if the photos are overlapping, this feature won't work.)

 If it finds multiple items, Image Capture automatically straightens them, compensating for haphazard placement on the glass, and then saves them as individual files.

- **Where to file?** Use the "Scan to" pop-up menu to specify where you want the newly scanned image files to land—in the Pictures folder, for example. You have some other cool options beyond sticking the scans in a folder; for example, you can send the resulting images to Photos, Preview, or Mail.

Once you've put a document onto or into the scanner, click Scan. The scanner heaves to life. After a moment, you see on the screen what's on the glass. It's simultaneously been sent to the folder (or post-processing task) you requested using the "Scan to" pop-up menu.

More power to you

As you can see, Apple has tried to make *basic* scanning as simple as possible: one click. That idiotproof method gives you very few options.

If you click Show Details before you scan, though, you get a special panel on the right side of the window that's filled with useful scanning controls (Figure 11-18).

- **Build web page** creates an actual web page of your downloaded shots. Against a dark-gray background, you get thumbnail images of the pictures in a web page document called *index.html*. Just click one of the small images to view it at full size, exactly as your website visitors will be able to do once this page is actually on the web. (Getting it online is up to you.)

Note: Image Capture puts the web page files in a Home folder→Pictures→Webpage on [today's date and time] folder. It contains the graphics files incorporated into this HTML document; you can post the whole thing on your website, if you like.

Image Capture automatically opens up this page in your web browser, proud of its work.

- **Make PDF.** When you choose this option, you wind up with what looks like a Preview window, showing thumbnails of your photos. If you choose Save right now, you'll get a beautiful, full-color PDF of the selected photos, ready to print out and then, presumably, cut apart with scissors or a paper cutter. But if you use the Layout menu, you can choose different layouts for your photos: 3×5, 4×6, 8×10, and so on.

And what if a photo doesn't precisely fit the proportions you've selected? The Crop commands in the Layout menu (for example, "Crop to 4×6") center each photo within the specified shape and then trim the outer borders if necessary. The Fit commands, on the other hand, *shrink* the photo as necessary to fit into the specified dimensions, sometimes leaving white margins.

Note: The "crop" commands never touch the actual downloaded photos. The downloaded image files themselves retain their full sizes and resolutions.

- **Other.** The beauty of the Image Capture system is that people can, in theory, write additional processing scripts. Once you've written or downloaded them, drop them into your System→Library→Image Capture→Automatic Tasks folder. Then enjoy their presence in the Import To pop-up menu.

Tip: You can set up Image Capture to download everything on the camera *automatically* when you connect it. No muss, no fuss, no options.

To do that, connect the camera. Click its name in the Devices list. Then, from the "Connecting this camera opens" pop-up menu, choose AutoImporter. From now on, Image Capture downloads all pictures on the camera each time it's connected. When the downloading process is complete, a little green checkmark appears on the thumbnail of each imported photo.

Import Some, Import All

Clicking Import All, of course, begins the process of downloading the photos to the folder you've selected. A progress dialog box appears, showing you thumbnail images of each picture that flies down the wire.

Tip: Image Capture remembers your setting here separately for each camera. For example, you can set it up so that when you connect your fancy SLR camera, Aperture opens; when you connect your spouse's pocket camera, Photos opens; and when you connect your iPhone, Image Capture opens, so you can quickly grab the best shots and email them directly.

Once Image Capture is open, it looks like Figure 11-17. When you connect your camera, cellphone, or scanner, its name appears in the left-side list. To begin, click it. After a moment, Image Capture displays all the photos on the camera's card, in either list view or icon view (your choice).

Figure 11-17:
In many ways, Image Capture is like a mini Photos app; use the slider in the lower right to change the thumbnail sizes. You can choose the individual pictures you want to download, rotate selected shots (using the lower-left curved-arrow button), or delete shots from the camera.

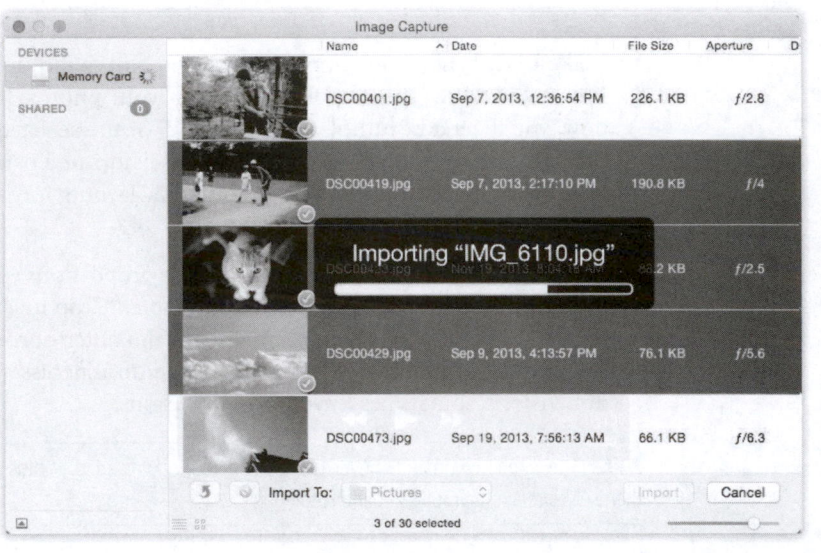

Import To:

Use this pop-up menu to specify what happens to the imported pictures. Image Capture proposes putting photos, sounds, and movies from the camera into your Home folder's Pictures folder. But you can specify any folder (choose Other from the pop-up menu).

Furthermore, there are some other very cool options here:

- **Photos.** Neat that you can direct photos from your camera to Photos via Image Capture. Might come in handy when you didn't *expect* to want to load photos into your permanent collection, but you change your mind when you actually look them over in Image Capture.

- **Preview** opens the fresh pictures in Preview so you can get a better (and bigger) look at them.

- **Mail** sends the pix directly into the Mac's email program, which can be handy when the whole point of getting the photos off the camera is to send them to friends.

Tip: You can take this concept one step further by putting your rooms into *zones*, which are usually "upstairs" or "downstairs." To get started: On the Rooms tab, choose Edit→Edit Room. At top left, click Rooms to see the complete list of rooms you've got so far. Click one, and then click Zone; choose a zone or hit Create New to make a new one. And voilà: Now you can say "Turn off the lights upstairs!"

- **Automate your gadgets.** On the Automation tab, you can automate those actions based on the time or when you, or other people, arrive or depart.

- **Create a scene.** A "scene" is a bunch of accessories that you switch on and off simultaneously. You might have one called "Goodnight" that turns off all the lights and locks the doors with a single Siri command. To create one, click +, and then Add Scene, and then Custom, and then Add Accessories. Once the scene is set up, click its icon on the Home tab to trigger it.

- **Control your home by remote control.** It's possible to set things up so that you can operate your gadgets from across the internet, when you're not even there. This does, however, require that you also own an Apple home hub, which can take the form of a recent Apple TV, a HomePod speaker, or an iPad.

- **Automate the whole works.** If you do, in fact, have a home hub, you can really smartify your home. You can set things up so that all the lights turn off when you leave the house, or that a certain scene happens at a certain time, or that the temperature goes up when your teenager gets home.

Yes, it can get really complicated. But imagine the magic once you get it all figured out!

Image Capture

This unsung little program was originally designed to download pictures from a camera and then process them automatically (turning them into a web page, scaling them to emailable size, and so on). Of course, after Image Capture's birth, iPhoto (now called Photos) came along, generally blowing its predecessor out of the water.

Even so, Apple includes Image Capture with macOS for these reasons:

- **Image Capture is a smaller, faster app** for downloading all or only some pictures from your camera (Figure 11-17). The Photos app can do that nowadays, but sometimes that's like using a bulldozer to get out a splinter.

- **Image Capture can grab images from scanners** (Figure 11-18), not just cameras.

- **Image Capture can download your *sounds*** (like voice notes) from a digital still camera; Photos can't.

You can open Image Capture in either of two ways: You can simply double-click its icon in your Applications folder, or you can set it up to open automatically whenever you connect a digital camera and turn it on. To set up that arrangement, open Image Capture manually. Using the "Connecting this camera opens:" pop-up menu, choose Image Capture.

Tip: You can do that either in the Home app or by using Siri voice commands ("Lock the front door," "Turn on the downstairs lights," and so on).

Figure 11-16:
If your Home app looks like this, then you've invested a lot of money into HomeKit-compatible smart-home gadgets, you control freak.

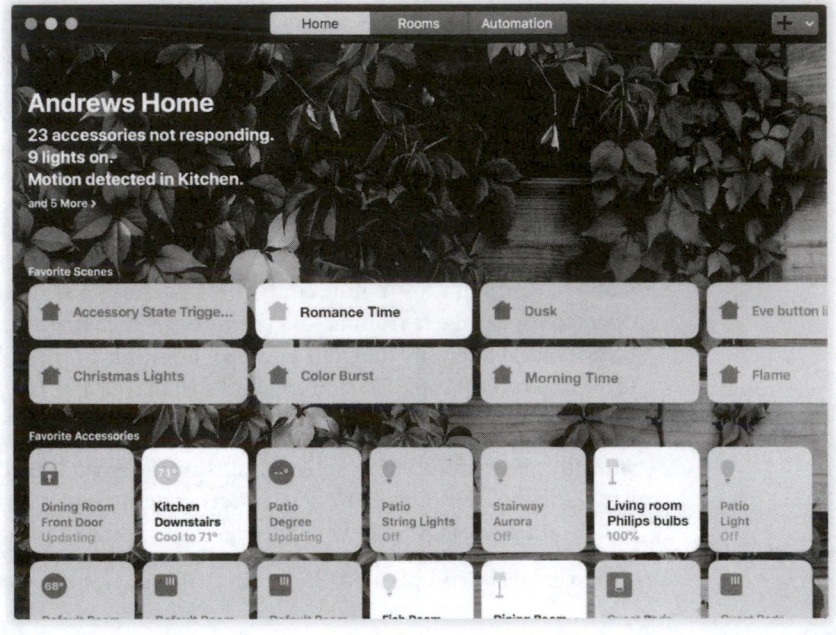

- **Adjust its home-control settings,** like the temperature for a thermostat. Double-click the gadget's icon, or right-click it and choose Controls.

- **Adjust its gadget settings,** like its name or which room it's on. Right-click its icon and choose Settings.

This isn't really a book about smart-home accessories, but here's some of the fun you can have once you've bought a few (and then read the instructions at *support.apple. com/en-us/HT204893*):

- **Set up rooms.** If you've got a lot of HomeKit accessories—you lucky duck—you may find it easier to keep track of them all by putting their icons on different screens, named for different rooms of your house. You'll also be able to tell Siri, "Turn off the lights in the living room."

 To create or assign a room, double-click the gadget's icon, click Settings at top right, click Room, and either choose a room from the list or hit Create New to establish a new one.

Receiving Calls

Life is even simpler when somebody calls *you*. A notification bubble appears on your screen, and you hear an incoming-call sound. (Which ringtone? That's up to you; in the FaceTime app, choose FaceTime→Preferences→Settings. Use the Ringtone pop-up menu.) If iTunes is playing music, it pauses automatically. Sweet.

If the Mac is asleep, it wakes; you can even answer the call on the Lock screen, without having to enter your password.

Click Accept to start the call, or Decline if now is not the time. (In that case, the caller will be told you're not available.)

FaceTime doesn't have to be running for you to receive a call. That's generally a cool feature—but if you really don't want to be interrupted, you can hang up a digital "Do Not Disturb" sign in any of these ways:

- **In FaceTime,** choose FaceTime→Turn FaceTime Off.

- **Use the Do Not Disturb feature** (page 378).

- **Sign out of FaceTime.** (Choose FaceTime→Preferences→Settings, and then click Sign Out.)

Font Book

For details on this font-management program, see Chapter 14.

GarageBand

GarageBand, Apple's do-it-yourself music construction kit, isn't actually part of macOS. If you have a copy, that's because it's part of the iLife suite that comes on every new Mac (along with iMovie and Photos).

Home

HomeKit is Apple's home-automation standard. The Home app lets you control any product whose box says "Works with HomeKit"—all those "smart" or "connected" door locks, security cameras, power outlets, thermostats, doorbells, lightbulbs, leak/freeze/temperature/humidity/air-quality sensors, and so on.

This app, new in macOS Mojave, is one of several that Apple has adapted from iOS to macOS. Among other limitations, this means you can't actually *set up* any HomeKit gadgets in the Mac app. You still need an iPhone or iPad for that. The miracle of iCloud syncing brings the information onto the Mac (assuming that System Preferences→iCloud→Home is turned on).

Once you've installed a gadget, you can use this app (Figure 11-16) to:

- **Turn it on and off** by clicking its icon on the Favorites tab. Handy for light bulbs and locks.

But even if someone's not speaking, you can bring him to the front on demand, with either of two degrees of prominence:

- **Click his box once.** It comes to the front, gets slightly larger, and reveals his name or iCloud ID.

- **Double-click his box.** Now it gets *much* bigger, shamelessly covering up everyone else's boxes. This is for when you really want to focus on this one person. (Click again to enshrink the box again.)

Tip: If you've clicked once, you can click the little ↗ icon to zoom that slightly enlarged box into the fully enlarged version.

The Roster

The FaceTime app can't display big rectangles for more than four people at once. Starting with the fifth joiner, a horizontally scrolling row of faces joins yours at the bottom of the screen—Apple calls it the Roster. But the idea is the same: If one of them speaks, her box jumps into one of the larger four spots on the screen. And even if she's not speaking, you can click or double-click her square to give it one of the two zoom treatments described already.

Coming and going

If someone's inviting you to a group call, a notification lets you know. You'll see an option called Join or ◼◀, depending on what you're doing on the Mac. Or, if you're in Messages in a group chat, you'll see a Join button.

If you'd like to add someone to a call that's underway, click the screen, click ···, and click Add Person.

If someone drops off the call (by clicking ⊗), everyone else stays on the call, just as with a traditional conference phone call.

FaceTime Audio Calls

Video calling is neat and all, but be honest: Don't you find yourself making regular phone calls more often? Video calling forces us to be "on," neatly dressed and well behaved, because we're on camera. Most of the time, we're perfectly happy (in fact, happier) with audio only.

To place an audio call, you start out exactly as you would when making a video call, as described earlier: in the FaceTime app, Contacts, or Messages. Click ☎, and then click FaceTime Audio (as opposed to whatever phone numbers are listed there).

When you place an audio FaceTime call, the other person's phone, tablet, or Mac rings. If she accepts your call, it's better than being on a phone call in two ways. First, you don't have the usual lag time that throws off your comic timing. And, second, the audio quality is amazing—more like FM radio than cellular. It sounds like the other person is right next to your head; you hear every breath, sniff, and sweater rustle.

Begin the call

Often, you'll want to dive into a group video call from within Messages, where a group chat is already underway. To do that, click Details at the top of the screen. Click ◼️◀. (Or, for a straight-up audio conference call, hit Audio.)

Each participant gets a special Group FaceTime message, complete with a Join button. Once you click it, that special button in Messages changes to show how long the call has been going.

Tip: If you're in a group Messages session, that Join button remains yours to click for as long as the group FaceTime call is still going. In other words, you don't have to hop on instantly.

Or you can start in the FaceTime app. Click the + at top right; in the To box, specify the names of the participants. Then click Audio or Video. The other peoples' phones start ringing, and when they click Accept, the audio or video conference begins!

During the call

In regular FaceTime calls, the other guy's image fills the screen. How are you supposed to conduct a call with dozens of people?

Each face occupies its own rectangle; the more people who join, the smaller the rectangles get (Figure 11-15).

Figure 11-15:
On a group FaceTime call, your icon always appears at lower right. The small icons at left, from left to right, mean: Hide/show call list; Mute microphone; Hang up; "Mute" camera; and Full screen.

When someone is talking, FaceTime brings that person's rectangle front and center (and makes it bigger) automatically. In a lively conversation, therefore, the four main boxes seem to be constantly inflating and deflating to reflect who's talking.

- **Press ⊙.** Yes, the Dictionary is one of the widgets in the Dashboard (page 192).

- **Right-click or two-finger click a highlighted word in a Cocoa program.** From the shortcut menu, choose Look Up [word]. You get a panel that pops out of the highlighted word, showing the Dictionary page for that word.

- **Use the *dict://* prefix in Safari.** This might sound a little odd, but it's actually ultra-convenient, because it puts the dictionary right where you're most likely to need it: on the web.

 Turns out that you can look up a word (for example, *preposterous)* by typing *dict://preposterous* into the address bar. When you hit Return, Dictionary opens automatically and presents the search results from all its resources (dictionary, thesaurus, Apple terms, and Wikipedia).

- **Point to a word in a basic Mac program, and then press Control-⌘-D.** That keystroke makes the definition panel sprout right from the word you were pointing to. (The advantage here, of course, is that you don't have to highlight the word first.) "Basic Mac program," in this case, means one of the Apple standards: Mail, Stickies, Safari, TextEdit, Messages, and so on.

The *front matter* of the *Oxford American Dictionary* (the reference section at the beginning) is here, too. It includes some delicious writers' tools, including guides to spelling, grammar, capitalization, punctuation, chemical elements, and clichés, along with the full text of the Declaration of Independence and the U.S. Constitution. Just choose Go→Front/Back Matter—and marvel that your Mac comes with a built-in college English course.

Tip: Got a big screen or poor eyesight? Then bump up the type size. Dictionary's toolbar has bigger/smaller buttons, and there's a Font Size pop-up menu in the Preferences window.

DVD Player

If you're one of the few, the proud, who own a DVD drive, you can play back DVD movies using macOS's aging but perfectly functional DVD Player app.

FaceTime

If you have a Mac laptop or an iMac, then it's got a built-in microphone and camera. And that means it's equipped to make free, very high-quality audio and video calls to other Apple computers, phones, and tablets (Figure 11-14). In macOS Mojave 10.14.1 and later, in fact, it can make *group* video calls, with as many as 32 people on the screen at once.

There's very little delay, and it works the first time and every time. Now Grandma can see the baby, or you can help someone shop from afar, or you can supervise brain surgery from thousands of miles away (medical training recommended).

Here's what you get:

- **The entire** *New Oxford American Dictionary.* The third edition, actually. You'll note that its entries give you more examples, background, and tables that help to differentiate fine shades of meaning (look up *weak* for an example).

- **The complete** *Oxford American Writer's Thesaurus.*

- **Two venerable guides to British English:** the *Oxford Dictionary of English* and *Oxford Thesaurus of English.*

- **A dictionary of Apple terms,** from "access control lists" to "Yosemite."

- **Wikipedia.** This famous citizen-created encyclopedia isn't actually on your Mac. Dictionary just gives you an easy way to search the *online* version, and display the results right in the comfy Dictionary window.

- **Foreign language dictionaries:** You also get Japanese, French, Spanish, German, Dutch, Korean, Italian, Chinese, Hindi, Norwegian, Swedish, Portuguese, Russian, Turkish, Thai, Hebrew, and Danish—plus English translation dictionaries for Arabic, Hindi, French, German, Dutch, Italian, Portuguese, Spanish, Russian, Japanese, Korean, and Chinese.

Note: You don't ordinarily see these reference books. You have to turn them on in Dictionary→Preferences.

MacOS also comes with about a million ways to look up a word:

- **Search it in Spotlight.** Press ⌘-space, type the word you want into the Spotlight search box, and marvel as the dictionary entry appears at the bottom of the results list. To read the definition, click it once.

- **If you have a trackpad, point to a word in a basic Mac program, and then double-touch the trackpad (don't actually click) with three fingers.** That's the gesture for the same dictionary panel already described. (It doesn't work unless you've turned it on in System Preferences→Trackpad.)

- **Double-click the Dictionary icon.** You get the window shown at bottom in Figure 11-13. As you type into the Spotlight-y search box, you home in on matching words; click a word, or highlight it and press Return, to view a full, typographically elegant definition, complete with sample sentence and pronunciation guide.

Tip: And if you don't recognize a word in the definition, click *that word* to look up *its* definition. (Each word turns blue and underlined when you point to it, as a reminder.) You can then click again in *that* definition—and on and on and on.

(You can use the ‹ and › buttons on the toolbar, or the ⌘-[and ⌘-] keystrokes to go back and forward in your chain of lookups. Hold down the ‹ for a pop-up menu of recent lookups.)

It's worth exploring the Dictionary→Preferences dialog box, by the way. There you can choose U.S. or British pronunciations and adjust the font size.

Tip: If you open this window before you begin a new game, you can see the game log fill in the moves as they happen.

Contacts

Here's the old Address Book program, now renamed so that it matches the iPhone and iPad versions. See page 713 for details.

Dashboard

Dashboard, described in Chapter 5, is a true-blue, double-clickable application. As a result, you can remove its icon from your Dock, if you like.

Dictionary

For word nerds everywhere, the Dictionary is a blessing—a handy way to look up word definitions, pronunciations, and synonyms (Figure 11-13). To be precise, macOS comes with electronic versions of multiple reference works in one.

Figure 11-13:
When you open the Dictionary, it generally assumes you want a word's definition (lower left). If you prefer to see the Wikipedia entry (top right) at startup time instead, for example, choose Dictionary→ Preferences—and drag Wikipedia upward so that it precedes New Oxford American Dictionary. *That's all there is to it!*

If you choose Game→New, however, you're offered a pop-up menu with choices like Human vs. Computer, Human vs. Human, and so on. If you switch the pop-up menu to Computer vs. Human, then you and your Mac trade places; the Mac takes the white side of the board and opens the game with the first move, and you play the black side.

Tip: The same New Game dialog box also has a pop-up menu called Variant, which offers three other chess-like games: Crazyhouse, Suicide, and Losers.

On some night when the bowling alley is closed and you're desperate for entertainment, you might also want to try the Computer vs. Computer option, which pits your Mac against itself. Pour yourself a beer, open a bag of chips, and settle in to watch until someone—either the Mac or the Mac—gains victory.

Chess Prefs

Choose Chess→Preferences to find some useful controls like these:

- **Style.** Apple has gone nuts with the computer-generated materials options in this program. You can choose all kinds of wacky materials for the look of your game board (Wood, Metal, Marble, or *Grass*) and for your playing pieces (Wood, Metal, Marble, or *Fur*).

- **Computer Plays.** Use this slider to determine how frustrated you want to get when trying to win at Chess. The farther you drag the slider toward the Stronger side, the more calculations the computer runs before making its next move—and, thus, the harder it gets for you to outthink it. At the Faster setting, Chess won't spend more than five seconds ruminating over possible moves. Drag the slider all the way to the right, however, and the program may analyze *each move* for as long as 10 fun-filled hours. This hardest setting, of course, makes it all but impossible to win a game (which may stretch on for a week or more anyway).

- **Speech.** The two checkboxes here let you play Chess using the Mac's built-in voice-recognition features, *telling* your chess pieces where to go instead of dragging them, and listening to the Mac tell you which moves it's making. See page 331.

Tip: If your Chess-playing skills are less than optimal, the Moves menu will become your fast friend. The three commands there undo your last move (great for recovering from a blunder), suggest a move when you're stuck, and display a previous move (in case you failed to notice what the computer just did).

Studying Your Games

You can choose Game→Save to save any game in progress, so you can resume it later.

To analyze the moves making up a game, use the Moves→Game Log command, which displays the history of your game, move by move. A typical move would be recorded as "Nb8 – c6," meaning the knight on the b8 square moved to the c6 square. With a Chess list document, you could recreate an entire game, move by move.

Syncing Calendar with Your iPhone, iPad, and Other Computers

Here's the real magic of Calendar, iCloud, and the rest of Apple's software archipelago: Your calendar can be autosynced among all your machines, like your iPhone, iPad, and Macs. Add an appointment on your phone, change an appointment on your iPad, whatever—all your other gadgets are wirelessly and automatically synced to match. See page 659 for details on this amazing setup.

Note: Wondering where the To Do list feature went? It was in iCal, but it's gone in Calendar. That's because macOS has its own full-blown Reminders app now, described later in this chapter.

Chess

MacOS comes with only one game, but it's a beauty (Figure 11-12). It's a traditional chess game played on a gorgeously rendered board with a set of realistic 3D pieces.

Note: The program is actually a sophisticated Unix-based chess program, Sjeng, that Apple packaged up in a new wrapper.

Figure 11-12:
You don't have to be terribly exact about grabbing the chess pieces when it's time to make your move. Just click anywhere within a piece's current square to drag it into a new position on the board (shown here in its Wood incarnation). And why is this chessboard rotated like this? Because you can grab a corner of the board and rotate it in 3D space. Cool!

Playing a Game of Chess

When you launch Chess, you're presented with a fresh, new game that's set up in Human vs. Computer mode—meaning that you, the Human (light-colored pieces) get to play against the Computer (your Mac, on the dark side). Drag the chess piece of your choice into position on the board, and the game is afoot.

A dialog box appears. This is where you specify your web address, its password (if necessary), and how your saved calendar is going to look and work. If you turn on "Publish changes automatically," then whenever you edit the calendar, Calendar connects to the internet and updates the copy there. (Otherwise, you can right-click or two-finger click the calendar's name and choose Refresh whenever you want to update the web copy.)

When you click Publish, your Mac connects to the web and then shows you the web address (the URL) of the finished page, complete with a Send Mail button that lets you fire the URL off to your colleagues.

Tip: Whenever you want to send someone the subscription information, click the calendar category you've published and choose Edit→Send Publication Email. Calendar will prepare an outgoing email message containing details on subscribing to your calendar.

To stop publishing that calendar, click its name in the Calendars pop-up list and then choose Edit→Stop Publishing.

Subscribing

Often, websites publish calendars that you can bring into Calendar. Maybe you use TripIt.com to manage your flights and hotel reservations. Maybe you've found a calendar you like at *icalshare.com*—a schedule of rocket launches, trade shows, National Hockey League games, NASCAR races, soccer matches, the *Survivor* TV show, holidays, or whatever.

Each of these web calendars has its own address. To subscribe, choose File→New Calendar Subscription. In the Subscribe to Calendar dialog box, paste the address of the published calendar.

You can also provide your own name for this category, specify how often you want your own copy to be updated (assuming you have a full-time internet connection), and indicate whether or not you want to be bothered with the publisher's alarms and notes.

When it's all over, you see a new "calendar" category in your left-side list, representing the published appointments.

Google, Yahoo, and Facebook Calendars

If you maintain a calendar online—at Google, Yahoo, or Facebook, for example—you may take particular pleasure in discovering how easy it is to bring those appointments into Calendar. It's one handy way to keep, for example, a husband's and wife's appointments visible on each other's calendars.

Setting this up is ridiculously easy. Choose Calendar→Preferences→Accounts. Click + below the list. Enter your Google, Yahoo, or Facebook address (for example, *psmithers@gmail.com*) and password. Click Create.

In a minute or so, you'll see all your Google, Yahoo, or Facebook events show up in Calendar. (Each web calendar has its own heading in the left-side list.) Better yet: It's a two-way sync; changes you make to these events in Calendar show up on the web, too.

Behind the scenes, Calendar sends an invitation to the recipient. If she has a Mac, iPhone, or iPad, she'll see a notification right in Calendar (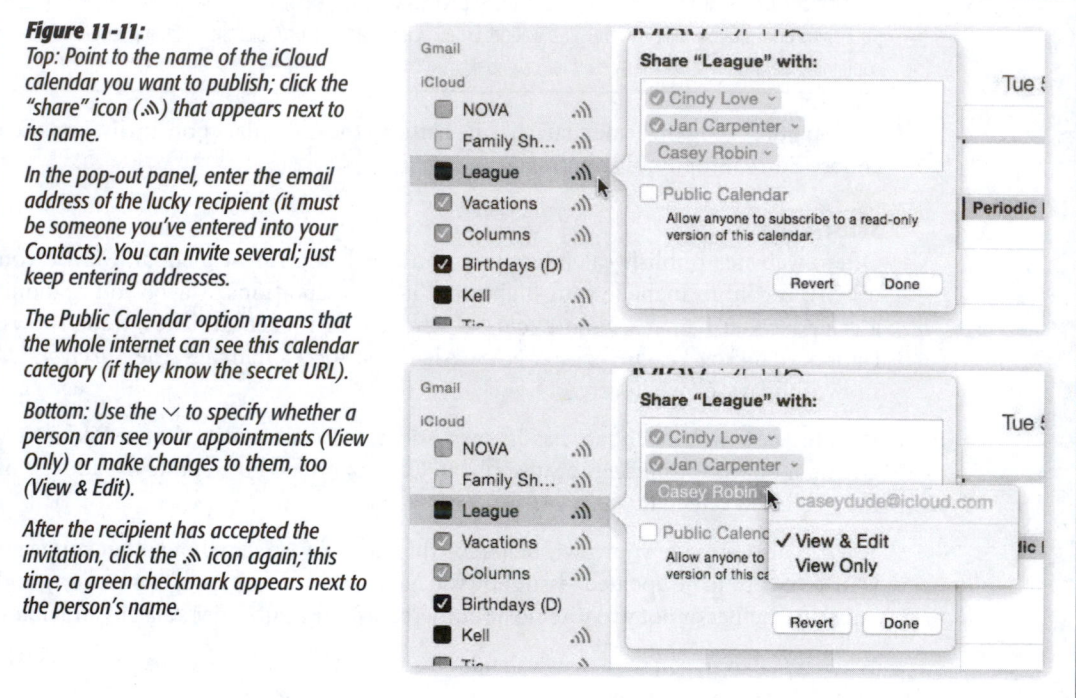); otherwise, she'll get the invitation by email. Once she clicks the invitation and clicks Accept, your shared calendar shows up on her machine.

Later you can modify the settings (Figure 11-11, bottom). Or you can stop sharing with someone by clicking the ⟋ next to a calendar name, clicking a person's name, and then pressing the Delete key.

Tip: You can also share an iCloud calendar at *icloud.com.* Just click the ⟋ icon beside a calendar's name.

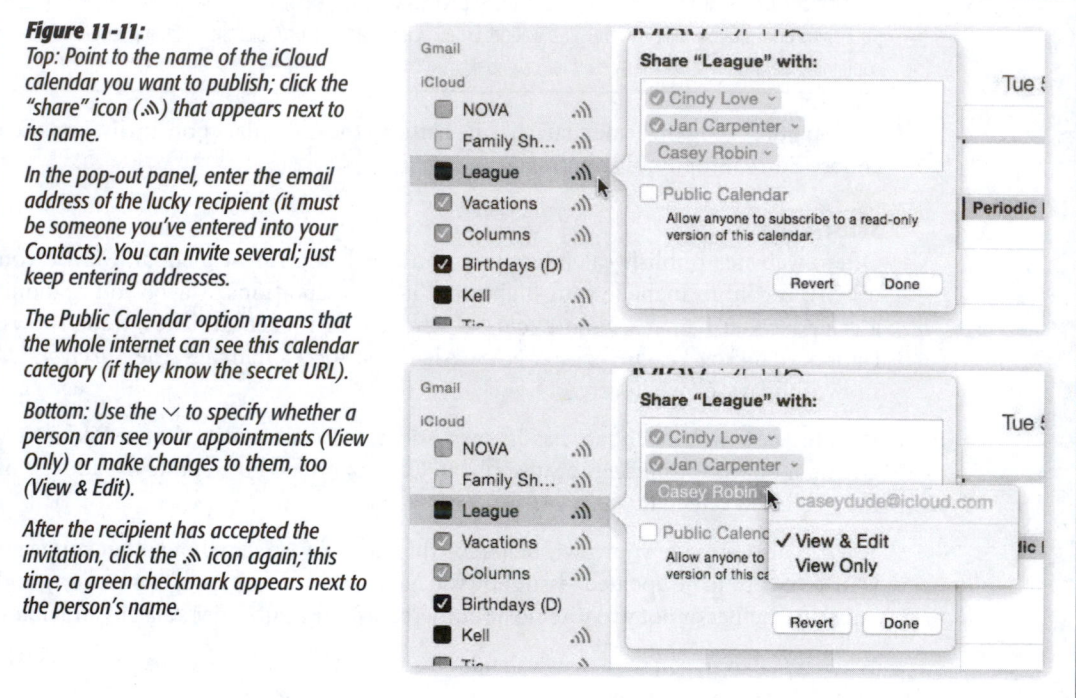

Figure 11-11:
Top: Point to the name of the iCloud calendar you want to publish; click the "share" icon (⟋) that appears next to its name.

In the pop-out panel, enter the email address of the lucky recipient (it must be someone you've entered into your Contacts). You can invite several; just keep entering addresses.

The Public Calendar option means that the whole internet can see this calendar category (if they know the secret URL).

Bottom: Use the ⌄ to specify whether a person can see your appointments (View Only) or make changes to them, too (View & Edit).

After the recipient has accepted the invitation, click the ⟋ icon again; this time, a green checkmark appears next to the person's name.

If you don't have an iCloud account: If you don't have iCloud, then you'll need a website of your own, where your online calendar can be hung. And it has to be a WebDAV-compatible server (ask your web-hosting company). You know what? It might just be easier to sign up for a free iCloud account and do it that way.

In any case, begin by making sure that the Calendars list is open. Click the calendar you want to share. Choose Edit→Publish Calendar. (This command doesn't appear if you have an iCloud account, since the sharing mechanism is so much simpler with iCloud.)

Tip: You have to perform this step individually for each calendar category. If you want to publish more than one calendar simultaneously, then create a calendar *group,* and publish *that.*

- **To see your list of categories,** click the Calendars button (upper left of the window). A Sidebar list appears, if it wasn't already open.

- **Hide or show an entire category of appointments at once** by turning on or off the appropriate checkbox in the Calendars Sidebar.

- **To change the color of a category,** right-click or two-finger click its name in the Sidebar list. In the pop-up bubble, you choose a new color.

- **To specify your *default* calendar,** choose Calendar→Preferences→General. Choose from the Default Calendar pop-up menu. (The Default calendar is the category that every new appointment falls into unless you change it. It's also the category that *other* apps, like Mail, propose putting new appointments into.)

- **To assign a new appointment to a calendar,** click the color swatch in the corner of its Info balloon.

- **To change an appointment's calendar category,** right-click or two-finger click the appointment's name and choose a calendar name from the shortcut menu.

- **You may be able to make calendar *groups*, too.** Those are containers that consolidate the appointments from several *other* calendars. For example, you could have a calendar group called Kids, containing the individual calendars for each of your offspring. Super-calendars like this make it easier to manage, hide, show, print, and search subsets of your appointments. (Sadly, this feature is available only for On My Mac categories, as described previously—not for online accounts.)

 To create a calendar group, choose File→New Calendar Group. Name the resulting item in the Calendar list; for the most part, it behaves like any other calendar. Drag other calendar names onto it to include them. Click the flippy triangle to hide or show the component calendars.

"Publishing" Calendars to the Web

One of Calendar's best features is its ability to post your calendar on the web, so that other people can subscribe to it, which adds *your* appointments to *their* calendars. Anyone with a web browser—or only people you designate—can also *view* your calendar, right online.

For example, you might use this feature to post the meeting schedule for a club that you manage, or to share the agenda for a series of upcoming financial meetings that all your co-workers will need to consult.

Publishing

The steps for sharing a calendar depend on whether or not you have an iCloud account. Observe:

If you have an iCloud account: Proceed as shown in Figure 11-11. Note that you can specify whether each person can just *see* the appointments or be able to edit them, too. That's a delightful, two-way collaboration—a terrific way for a couple or a family to coordinate everyone's calendars, for example.

Searching for events

When you type into the search box at the top right of the Calendar screen, you're offered some "search tokens" that indicate where you want to search for that phrase (in the name of an event, in its notes, location, and so on). The right-hand column offers a clickable list of search results. Figure 11-10 has the details.

Figure 11-10:
Left: Type into the search box; Calendar sprouts a list of suggestions ("Event contains 'school,' " "Notes contain 'school,' " and so on).

Right: Click one to create a search token exactly like the ones that Spotlight and Mail use. They let you build up complex searches, bubble by bubble. Double-click any row of the list to jump to the corresponding event on the calendar and open up its summary balloon.

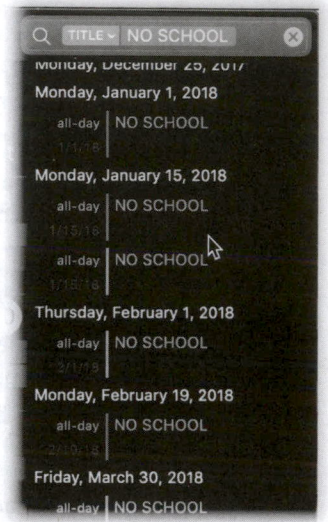

Deleting events

To delete an appointment, click it and then press the Delete key. If you delete a recurring event (like a weekly meeting), Calendar asks whether you want to delete only that particular instance of the event, or the whole series from that point forward.

The "Calendar" Category Concept

Calendar has *calendars* that let you organize appointments into subsets. One person might have calendars called Me, Spouse 'n' Me, and Whole Family. A small business could have categories called Deductible Travel, R&D, and R&R.

And now, the Calendar Tip-O-Rama:

- **To create a calendar,** choose File→New Calendar. You now have to specify *where* you want this category to live: On My Mac (meaning on your Mac), or on one of your online accounts, like iCloud, Google, Yahoo, or Exchange. Type a name that defines the category in your mind.

Note: When you set up an iCloud account either in System Preferences or when you first run macOS, Calendar automatically transfers your On My Mac categories to iCloud. You can no longer create categories that live only on your Mac. (There's one exception: If you created your iCloud account in Calendar Preferences, then you *can* have an On My Mac category.)

And if you want to change only an appointment's "calendar" category, right-click or two-finger click anywhere on the appointment and choose from the resulting Calendar shortcut menu. That way, you bypass the need to open the Info balloon.

Rescheduling events

If an event in your life gets rescheduled, you can drag an appointment block vertically in a Day- or Week-view column to make it later or earlier the same day, or horizontally to another date in any view. (If you reschedule a recurring event, Calendar asks if you want to change only *this* occurrence, or this *and* all future ones.)

If something is postponed for, say, a month or two, you can grab it in the Month view and drag it down as the months very slowly scroll by. Or you can open the Info balloon and edit the starting and ending dates or times—or just cut and paste the event to a different date.

Lengthening or shortening events

If a scheduled meeting becomes shorter or your lunch hour becomes a lunch hour-and-a-half (in your dreams), changing the length of the representative calendar event is as easy as dragging the bottom border of its block in any column view (see Figure 11-9).

Tip: In Week view, if you've grabbed the *bottom* edge of an appointment's block so that the cursor changes, you can drag *horizontally* to make an appointment cross the midnight line and extend into a second day.

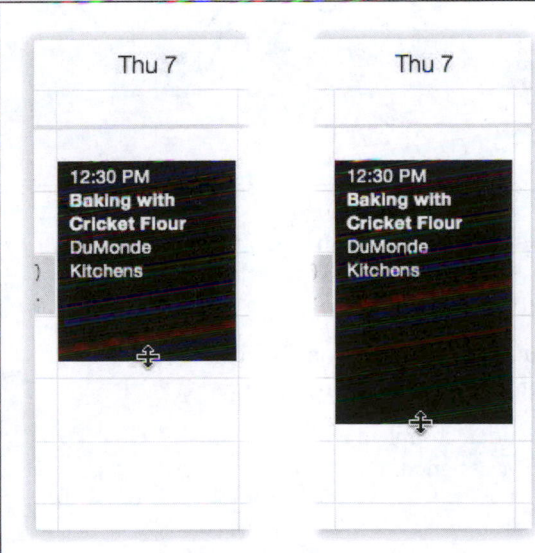

Figure 11-9:
You can resize any Calendar event just by dragging its bottom border. As your cursor touches the bottom edge of an event, it turns into a double-headed arrow. You can now drag the event's edge to make it take up more or less time on your calendar.

Printing events

To commit your calendar to paper, choose File→Print, or press ⌘-P. The resulting Print dialog box lets you include only a certain range of dates, only events on certain calendars, with or without To Do lists or mini-month calendars, and so on.

You might think: "Well, *duh*—if I've got something on the calendar, then I'm obviously busy!" But not necessarily. Some Calendar entries might just be placeholders, reminders to self, TV shows you wanted to watch, appointments you'd be willing to change—not things that would necessarily render you unavailable if a better invitation should come along.

- **Add Invitees.** If the appointment is a meeting or some other gathering, you can type the participants' names here. If a name is already in your Contacts program, then Calendar proposes autocompleting the name for you.

 If you separate several names with commas, Calendar automatically turns each into a shaded button. You can click it for a pop-up menu of commands like Remove Attendee and Send Email. (That last option appears only if the person in Contacts has an email address, or if you typed a name *with* an email address in brackets, like this: *Chris Smith <chris@yahoo.com>.*)

Tip: If you and your invitees are on the same CalDAV or Exchange calendar service—usually, co-workers at the same company—Calendar can show a "time map" of the invitees' days, all in a handy scrolling window, so you can find a time when everybody's free. To see this map, click the Available Meeting Times link beneath the addresses of the invitees you've specified, or choose Window→Availability Panel (see Figure 11-8).

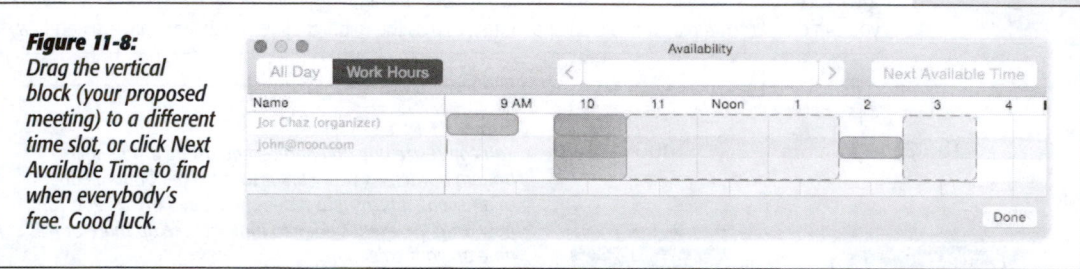

Figure 11-8:
Drag the vertical block (your proposed meeting) to a different time slot, or click Next Available Time to find when everybody's free. Good luck.

Once you've specified some attendees, a Send button appears in the Info box. If you click it, Calendar fires up Mail and prepares ready-to-send messages, each with an *.ics* attachment: a calendar-program invitation file. See the box on the facing page.

- **Add Notes, URL or Attachments.** You can type, paste, or drag any text you like in the note area—driving directions, contact phone numbers, a call history, or whatever.

Your newly scheduled event now shows up on the calendar, complete with the color coding that corresponds to the calendar category you've assigned.

What to Do with an Appointment

Once you've entrusted your agenda to Calendar, you can start putting it to work. Calendar is only too pleased to remind you (via pop-up messages) of your events, reschedule them, print them out, and so on. Here are a few of the possibilities.

Editing events

To edit a calendar event's details, click to open its Info balloon (Figure 11-6).

Actually, you can get a lot more particular than that. If you choose Custom, you can specify any advance-warning interval at all: "16 minutes before," or "15 days after," or whatever. (Yes, you can even set up an alarm to ring after the event—great if you want to follow up with something or check the oven.)

Here in Customland, you can also set any of three *kinds* of flags to get your attention. Calendar can display a message (with a sound, if you like), send you an email, or open a file on your hard drive. (You could use this unusual option to ensure that you don't forget a work deadline by having Calendar fling the relevant document open in front of your face at the eleventh hour.)

And if you've used the travel-time feature already described, Calendar offers choices related to the travel time, such as "at start of travel time" or 5, 15, or 30 minutes before, which may be helpful if you need to plot time for showering. (Figure 11-7, lower right).

Tip: You can set up more than one alarm for the same appointment, each with its own advance-warning interval. Just click the + button to add a new one.

- **show as (busy/free/tentative/out of office).** This little item shows up only if you've subscribed to a calendar server, like an internet-based calendar (in geek-speak, a CalDAV server) or your company's Exchange calendar. It communicates to your colleagues when you might be available for meetings.

Note: If your calendar comes from a CalDAV server, then your only options are "busy" and "free." The factory setting for most appointments is "busy," but for all-day events it's "free." Which is logical; just because it's International Gecko Appreciation Day doesn't mean you're not available for meetings (rats!).

Inviting Guests

When you click Send at the bottom of the info balloon, your guests receive your invitation. If they use Calendar, then the invitation appears in their Notifications panels. (To open the Notifications panel, click the tiny Inbox icon in the top-left corner of the window.) They can click Accept, Decline, or Maybe.

In your Notifications window, you then see the status of each invitee's name: a green checkmark for Accepted, red X for Declined, orange question mark for Maybe, and gray question mark for Not Yet Responded. (Your guests, meanwhile, will be delighted to find that the appointment automatically appears on their calendars once they commit.)

Now, suppose you send an invitation to your sister, who doesn't have a Mac. She just gets an email message that says, "Chris Smith has invited you to the event: Company Hoedown, scheduled for February 04, 2017 at 3:00 PM. To accept or decline this invitation, click the link below." (Unfortunately, there generally *is* no link. She just has to know to open the .ics attachment.)

If she uses a calendar program that understands this attachment, then the appointment appears on her calendar, and her RSVP shows up in your Calendar Notification panel.

- **repeat.** The pop-up menu here contains common options for recurring events: every day, every week, and so on. It starts out saying None.

Once you've made a selection, you get an *end* pop-up menu that lets you specify when this event should *stop* repeating. If you choose "Never," then you're stuck seeing this event repeating on your calendar until the end of time (a good choice for recording, say, your anniversary, especially if your spouse might be consulting the same calendar). You can also turn on "After [a certain number of times]," which is a useful option for car and mortgage payments. And if you choose "On date," you can specify the date when the repetitions come to an end; use this option to indicate the last day of school, for example.

"Custom" lets you specify repeat schedules like "First Monday of the month" or "Every two weeks."

Tip: If you don't see the following items in the editing bubble, then click the gray lettering that says "Add Alert, Repeat, or Travel Time" to make them appear.

- **travel time.** This item represents a breakthrough in common sense: It automatically builds travel time into Calendar's understanding of any appointment. After all, it's not very useful to get a reminder like "Lunch with Jenkins at 1 p.m." 10 minutes beforehand if it takes half an hour to get there.

Now, then: If Calendar is to calculate travel time, it has to know where you're starting out and where you're going.

To figure out your starting point, the Mac consults your "me" card in the Contacts app (page 713), and uses either your home address or your work address, depending on the time of day. (How does Calendar know when you're at work? It cleverly uses the "Day starts at" and "Day ends at" settings in Calendar→Preferences→General.)

If you haven't specified home and work addresses on your "me" card, then Calendar uses the current location of your Mac as the starting point. (And *that* works only if you've allowed the Mac to track your location; see page 439.)

For the arrival location, the travel-time feature requires that you've accepted one of the Mac's address suggestions, as described in Figure 11-7, top left.

Once all that's done, the travel-time pop-up menu shows you both the driving and walking times to your appointment. You can override these suggestions if you like; you can choose any time interval from five minutes to two hours, or choose Custom to plug in something not listed here.

The real payoff, of course, comes when you set a reminder for yourself; read on.

- **alert.** This pop-up menu tells Calendar to notify you when a certain appointment is about to begin. Choose how much notice you want: "At time of event," "5 minutes before," all the way up to "2 days before." If it's a TV show, a reminder five minutes before airtime is fine. If it's a birthday, you might set up a two-day warning, so there's time to buy a present.

under no obligation to choose one of these; you can ignore the suggestions and type "Casey's treehouse," for all Apple cares. But if you *do* choose from Apple's list of proposals, some cool things happen.

For example, you get a little map (which you can click to open the Maps app for a bigger view), as shown in Figure 11-7 (top right). You get to see the current weather, so you know how much to bundle up. And you get to use the travel-time feature described on the facing page.

Note: The next few controls appear only when you expand the Info bubble to see the time and date information. To do that, click whatever time is listed now—or, if you've just tabbed your way to the times, press Return.

- **all-day.** An "all-day" event, of course, refers to something that has no specific time of day associated with it: a holiday, a birthday. When you turn on this box, you see the name of the appointment jump to the top of the Calendar screen, in the area reserved for this kind of thing.

- **starts, ends.** You can adjust the times shown here by typing, clicking buttons, or both. Press Tab to jump from one setting to another, and from there to the hours and minutes of the starting time.

Note: The little calendar that pops up when you click the date is handier than typing a date manually.

For example, start by clicking the hour, and then increase or decrease this number either by pressing ▲ and ▼ or by typing a number. Press Tab to highlight the minutes and repeat the arrow-buttons-or-keys business. Finally, press Tab to highlight the AM/PM indicator, and type either *A* or *P*—or press ▲ or ▼—to change it, if necessary.

Tip: If you specify a different ending date, then a *banner* appears across the top of the calendar.

- **time zone.** This option appears only after you choose Calendar→Preferences→ Advanced and then turn on "Turn on time zone support." And you would do *that* only if you plan to be traveling on the day this appointment comes to pass.

Once you've done that, a time zone pop-up menu appears. It starts out with "America/New York" (or whatever your Mac's usual time zone is); if you choose Other, then a tiny world map appears. Click the time zone that represents where you'll be when this appointment comes due. From the shortcut menu, choose the major city that's in the same time zone you'll be in.

Tip: The time zone pop-up menu remembers each new city you select. The next time you travel to a city you've visited before, you won't have to do that clicking-the-world-map business.

Now, when you arrive in the distant city, use the time zone pop-up menu at the top-right corner of the Calendar window to tell Calendar where you are. You'll see all of Calendar's appointments jump, like magic, to their correct new time slots.

- **calendar.** A *calendar,* in Calendar's terminology, is a subset—a category—into which you can place appointments. You can create one for you, one for family-only events, one for book-club appointments, and so on. You can hide and show these categories at will. Details begin on page 407; for now, note that the tiny colored square in the top-right corner of the Info bubble is a pop-up menu of your calendars.

> **Tip:** Use this same pop-up menu to *change* an appointment's category. If you filed something in "Company Memos" that should have been in "Sweet Nothings for Honey-Poo," then open the event's information balloon and reassign it. Quick.

- **location.** This field makes a lot of sense; almost everyone needs to record *where* a meeting is to take place. You might type a reminder for yourself like *My place,* a specific address like *212 East 23rd,* or some other helpful information, like a contact phone number or flight number.

As you type, Calendar busily consults Apple's worldwide database of street addresses—and proposes a few matches, as shown in Figure 11-7 (top left). You're

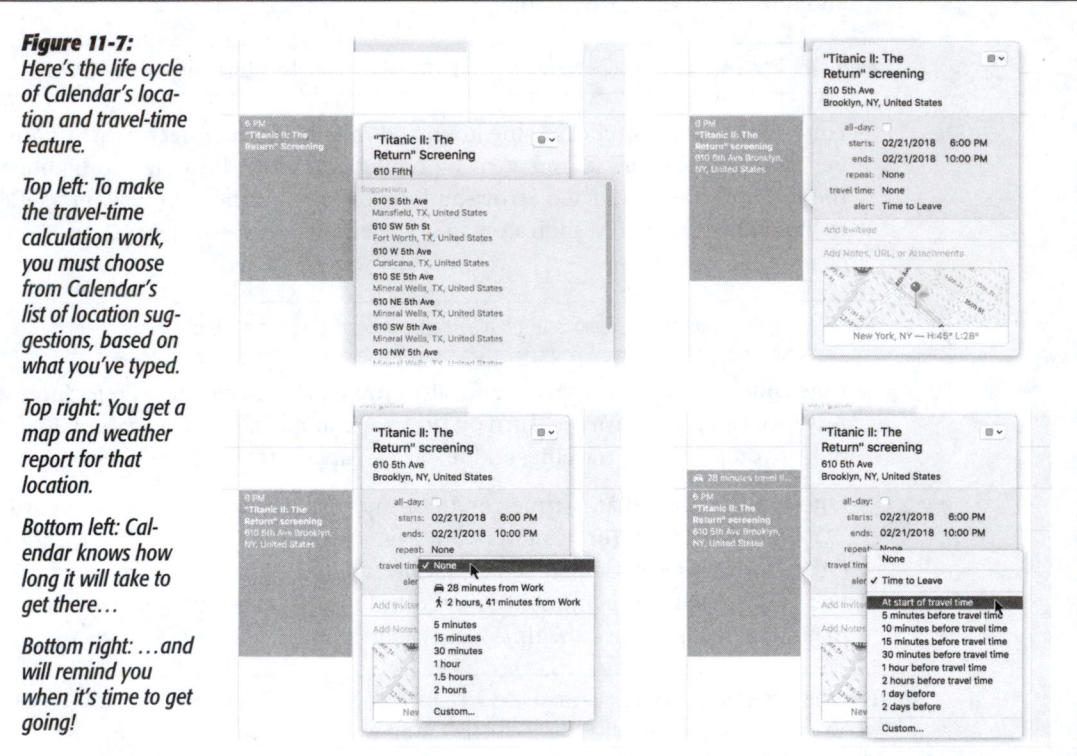

Figure 11-7:
Here's the life cycle of Calendar's location and travel-time feature.

Top left: To make the travel-time calculation work, you must choose from Calendar's list of location suggestions, based on what you've typed.

Top right: You get a map and weather report for that location.

Bottom left: Calendar knows how long it will take to get there...

Bottom right: ...and will remind you when it's time to get going!

Note: Calendar proposes adding the new appointment to your *default calendar*—that is, the category you use most often (read on for details on these calendar categories). Supposedly, you've already told it which category is your preferred one by using the Calendar→Preferences→General→Default Calendar pop-up menu.

But as you add a new appointment this way, you can override that setting by *holding down* the + button. You get a pop-up menu of your calendar categories; only after you click one do you see the Quick Event box shown in Figure 11-6.

Into the Quick Event box, type the name of your appointment and its date and time. For example, you could type *Report deadline Aug 12,* or *"Titanic 2: The Return" Sat 7 pm,* or *Cara date 11-11:15am.* When you press Return, Calendar interprets what you typed, using these rules:

- **If you didn't specify an ending time,** Calendar sets the appointment to one hour.

- **If you didn't enter** *any* **time information,** Calendar just schedules your event for all day.

- **If you typed** *breakfast* **or** *morning,* Calendar sets the appointment to start at 9 a.m.; *lunch* or *noon,* it starts at 12 p.m.; *dinner* or *night,* it starts at 7 p.m.

- **If you enter a weekday** (for example, *Chicago Monday*), Calendar assumes you mean the very next occurrence of that day. (If that's not what you want, enter the date, like *Chicago Jul 3.*)

- **If you enter a time but not a date or day** (for example, *Fishing 3:30 pm*), Calendar assumes you mean today.

The Quick Event system has a feature that saves you time and typos: As you type, Calendar displays a menu of similar appointments you've entered in the past (Figure 11-6, left). If you click one, Calendar fills in all the details of the new appointment in one fell swoop, copying them from the earlier event.

As soon as Calendar interprets your shorthand and turns it into a real appointment, its details balloon opens automatically (Figure 11-6, right), so you can clean up any errors and add more details.

Location, alarms, travel time, and other details

No matter which method you use to create the basic event (the mouse way or the Quick Event way), you're now presented with the information balloon shown at right in Figure 11-6. Here's where you go to town filling in the details. (This same balloon will appear when you double-click any existing appointment later.)

Tip: You can also open the Info balloon by clicking an appointment and then pressing ⌘-E (which is short for Edit→Edit Event).

For each appointment, you can tab your way to the following information areas:

- **subject.** That's the large, bold type at the top—the name of your appointment. For example, you might type *Fly to Phoenix.*

Even so, there are two ways to record a new appointment: using the mouse, or using the Quick Event box.

The mousy way

You can quickly record an appointment using any of several techniques, listed here in order of decreasing efficiency:

- **In Month view,** double-click a blank spot on the date you want. Type the name of the event and a time slot—for example, *Sales meeting 9am-4:30.* (See "The Quick Event way" below for details on how Calendar interprets these time notations.)

- **In Day or Week view,** double-click the starting time to create a one-hour appointment. Or drag vertically through the time slots that represent the appointment's duration. Either way, type the event's name inside the newly created colored box.

- **In Day, Week, or Month view,** right-click or two-finger click a date and choose New Event from the shortcut menu. Type the event's name.

Unless you use the drag-over-hours method, a new event believes itself to be one hour long. But in Day or Week view, you can adjust its duration by dragging the bottom edge vertically. Drag the dark top bar up or down to adjust the start time.

In many cases, that's all there is to it. You've just specified the day, time, and title of the appointment. Now you can get on with your life.

Tip: If the Edit balloon is blocking a part of the calendar you need to see, no biggie: Just drag the balloon out of the way, using any blank spot as a handle. It "tears off" and becomes independent.

The Quick Event way

In the *Quick Event* method, the program spares you the trouble of manually selecting dates, start times, and end times. Instead, the program understands notations like "7 pm Friday," and puts your new appointment into the right time slot automatically.

To use this feature, press ⌘-N. Or click + (top left of the window) or choose File→New Event. The Quick Event box appears. Proceed as shown in Figure 11-6.

Figure 11-6:
Left: Type a plain-English shorthand appointment. Press Return. Marvel as Calendar interprets the times you typed and inserts your meeting into the right time slot.

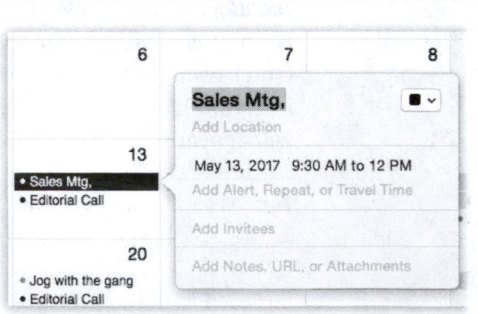

Tip: Month view scrolls endlessly vertically—and not necessarily a month at a time, either. You can park any week of the month at the top of the screen—not just the first week. That's a refreshing change from paper calendars.

• **Year** view displays the date numbers for the entire year (Figure 11-5).

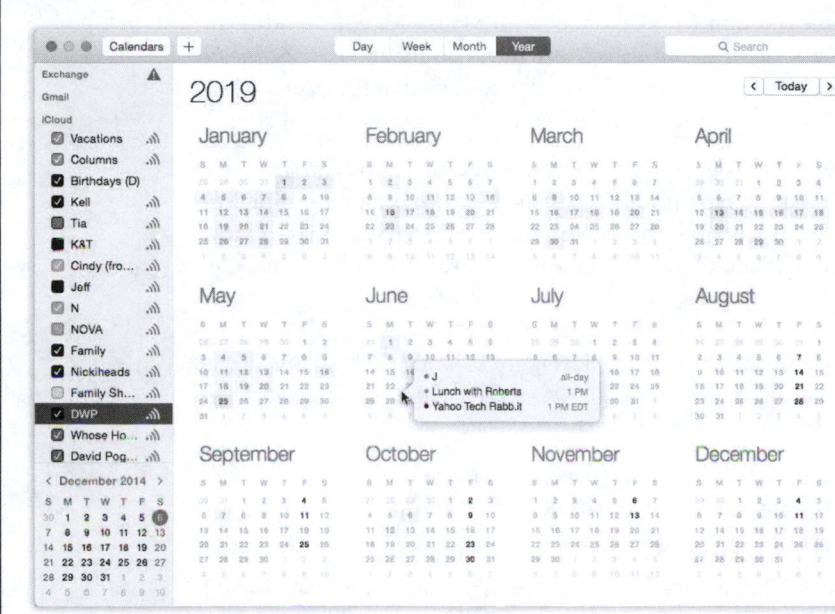

Figure 11-5:
Year view shows the entire year. In Calendar→Preferences→Advanced, you can turn on "Show events in year view," which actually means "Show me a 'heat map' to indicate how hectic my schedule is."

You can single-click a date number to see a pop-out list of the appointments scheduled for that date.

In Week or Month view, *double-click* an appointment to see more about it, or even make changes to it.

Tip: In Week or Day view, Calendar sprouts a handy horizontal line that shows where you are in time right now. (Look in the hours-of-the-day "ruler" down the left side of the window to see this line's little red bulb.) A nice touch, and a handy visual aid that can tell you at a glance when you're already late for something.

Also, in any view, you can switch into Full Screen mode by clicking the green ⊙ button (top left). See page 178 for more on Full Screen mode.

Tip: Each Calendar view scrolls smoothly and endlessly into the past or future. Day and Week views scroll horizontally; Month and Year views scroll vertically.

Making an Appointment

The basic Calendar is easy to figure out. After all, with the exception of one unfortunate Gregorian incident, we've been using calendars successfully for centuries.

But Calendar offers several advantages over paper calendars:

- **It can automate the process** of entering repeating events, such as weekly staff meetings or gym workouts.

- **Calendar can give you a gentle nudge** (with a sound, a dialog box, or even an email) when an important appointment is approaching.

- **Calendar can share information** with Contacts, with Mail, with your iPod/iPad/iPhone, with other Macs, or with "published" calendars on the internet. Some of these features require one of those iCloud accounts described in Chapter 16. But Calendar also works fine on a single Mac, even without an internet connection.

- **Calendar can subscribe to other people's calendars.** For example, you can subscribe to your spouse's calendar, thereby finding out when you've been committed to after-dinner drinks on the night of the big game. You can also tell Calendar to show your calendars from Google and Yahoo, or even your company's Exchange calendar.

Working with Views

When you open Calendar, you see something like Figure 11-4. By clicking one of the View buttons above the calendar, or by pressing ⌘-1, ⌘-2, ⌘-3, or ⌘-4, you can switch among these views:

- **Day** looks exactly like a day-at-a-time desk calendar. On the left side, you see today's schedule on an hour-by-hour chart. On the right, you see the details of whichever appointment is selected.

 If you choose Calendar→Preferences, you can specify what hours constitute a workday. This is ideal both for those annoying power-life people who get up at 5 a.m. for two hours of calisthenics and for the more reasonable people who sleep until 11.

Tip: Calendar provides four quick ways to get to the current day's date. Click Today (upper-right corner, between the ‹ and ›), choose View→Go to Today, or press ⌘-T. Or tap Today on the Touch Bar, if your Mac has one.

- **Week** fills the main display area with seven columns, reflecting the current week. (You can establish a five-day workweek instead in Calendar→Preferences.)

Tip: If you double-click the date above the calendar, you open the Day view for that day.

- **Month** shows the entire current month. The time of each appointment is listed in gray off to the right of each square.

 If a Month-view square is too small to show everything you've got scheduled that day, you'll see a notation at the bottom of the square, like "3 more…" Sometimes, making the window bigger (or full screen) helps make more room, or you can just double-click the date's number to switch to Day view and see everything at once.

But if you've already got Calculator open, here's the drill: Type in the starting measurement. Then, from the Convert menu, choose the kind of conversion you want (Area, Currency, Temperature, or whatever).

In the dialog box, use the pop-up menus to specify which units you want to convert to and from, and then click OK. There's your answer!

The next time you want to make this kind of conversion, you can skip steps 2, 3, and 4. Instead, just choose your desired conversion from the Convert→Recent Conversions submenu.

Calculator is especially amazing when it comes to *currency* conversions—from pesos to American dollars, for example—because it actually goes online to download up-to-the-minute currency rates.

> **Tip:** If you're working with big numbers, don't forget to turn on View→Show Thousands Separators. Calculator will add commas (like 1,242,939) to help you read your big numbers more easily.

Calendar

The calendar program that was called iCal for many years is now called Calendar, so that it matches its name on the iPhone and iPad.

Calendar is not so different from those "Hunks of the Midwest Police Stations" paper calendars that people leave hanging on the walls for months past their natural life span.

> **Tip:** Calendar's Dock icon displays today's date—even when Calendar isn't running.

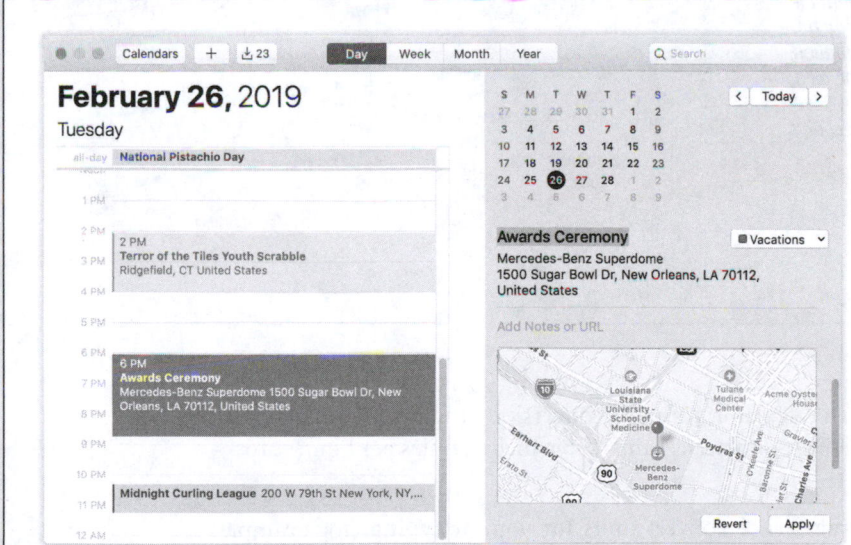

Figure 11-4:
In Calendar, the ‹ and › buttons at top right take you to the previous or next day, week, month, or year (depending on your current view). In the Day view, shown here, you can click the tiny numbers on the mini-calendar to change days.

- **Press the C key** to clear the calculator display.

- **As you go, you can make Calculator speak** each key you press. The Mac's voice ensures that you don't mistype as you keep your eyes on the receipts in front of you, typing by touch.

 Just choose Speech→Speak Button Pressed to turn this feature on or off. (You choose *which* voice does the talking in the Accessibility panel of System Preferences.)

- **Once you've calculated a result,** you can copy it (using Edit→Copy, or ⌘-C) and paste it directly into another program.

- **Calculator even offers reverse Polish notation (RPN),** a system of entering numbers that's popular with mathematicians, programmers, and engineers, because it lets them omit parentheses. Choose View→RPN Mode, or ⌘-R, to turn it on and off.

Tip: *If your Mac has a Touch Bar (page 233), you can add to it buttons for a few really advanced Calculator functions—Sine, Cosine, Tangent, Random Number, Pi, Hyperbolic Tangent, and many others. Choose View→Customize Touch Bar to get started.*

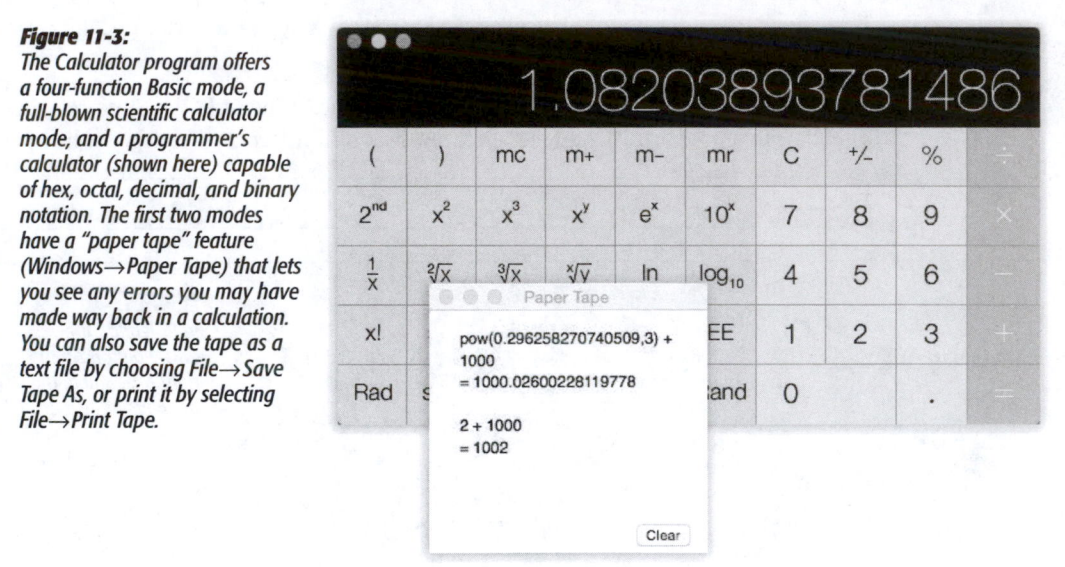

Figure 11-3:
The Calculator program offers a four-function Basic mode, a full-blown scientific calculator mode, and a programmer's calculator (shown here) capable of hex, octal, decimal, and binary notation. The first two modes have a "paper tape" feature (Windows→Paper Tape) that lets you see any errors you may have made way back in a calculation. You can also save the tape as a text file by choosing File→Save Tape As, or print it by selecting File→Print Tape.

Conversions

Calculator is more than a calculator; it's also a conversion program. No matter what units you're trying to convert—meters, grams, cubic inches, miles per hour, euros—Calculator is ready.

Now, the truth is, asking Siri to convert units for you, or typing (for example) *35 degrees in centigrade* into Spotlight is simpler and quicker to open than this older Calculator feature.

Parental tab

If you're a parent, you might wish to shield your impressionable offspring from dirty reading material—or to shield your credit card from wild teenage book-buying sprees (we should all have that problem!).

Click the 🔒 and enter your administrator's password; now you can turn on "Disable the Book Store" to prevent purchases, or "Restrict books with explicit content" to block the downloading of raunchy material.

Advanced tab

This tab offers exactly one control: A checkbox called "Enable Advanced menu in menu bar." It creates an Advanced menu that itself contains exactly one command: "Add EPUB to Library as Proof."

This is designed to help one very small group: People who create their *own* Apple-format ebooks, and wish to look them over on various other Apple gadgets to make sure they look right.

Once you've exported your book as an ePub file (from Pages, Adobe InDesign, or some other app), use this command to add it to Books as a finished book. When you open it, use the Devices button at top right to choose an iPhone or iPad you've connected to your Mac. (The Books app has to be open on that device.) Presto: Your book gets copied to the other gadget, for your proofreading pleasure. The best part: Each time you make a fix in the ePub document, that change is automatically carried through to the Book versions on the Mac and on iOS.

Calculator

For quick calculations, you don't need any calculator at all. Just ask Siri: "What's 17 percent of 300?" or "What's the square root of 77?" or "What's 35 times 22?"

Tip: The Spotlight menu is a calculator, too. Type or paste an equation into the Spotlight search box; instantly, the answer appears in the results menu.

If you really need to see the numbers, though, you can use this app, which is much more than a simple four-function memory calculator. It can also act as a scientific calculator for students and scientists, a conversion calculator for metric and U.S. measures, and even a currency calculator for world travelers.

The little Calculator widget in the Today pane of the Notification Center is quicker to open, but the stand-alone Calculator program is far more powerful. For example:

- **Calculator has three modes:** Basic, Scientific, and Programmer (Figure 11-3). Switch among them by choosing from the View menu (or pressing ⌘-1 for Basic, ⌘-2 for Scientific, or ⌘-3 for Programmer).

- **You can operate Calculator** by clicking the onscreen buttons, but it's much easier to press the corresponding number and symbol keys on your keyboard.

In the More menu, a few additional options lurk:

- **Search Book** opens the same search box you'd get by clicking the Q icon—except that this time the highlighted word is already filled in, saving you a bit of typing.

- **Search Web, Search Wikipedia** hand off the highlighted text to Safari, which searches Google or Wikipedia.

- **Mail, Messages, Notes** opens the share sheet (page 263) so you can send the highlighted material to somebody else by message or email, or add it to a Notes page.

- **Speak** reads the highlighted passage aloud.

Tip: The Mac's speaking feature isn't limited to a blob of text you've highlighted. You can use the Edit→ Speech→Start Speaking command to have the *entire book* read to you—in a voice that's only a *little* robotic. Yes, this is exactly the feature that debuted in the Amazon Kindle and was then removed when publishers screamed bloody murder—but somehow, so far, Apple has gotten away with it.

Once you've added bookmarks, notes, and highlighting to your book, they're magically and wirelessly synced to any other copies of that book—on other gadgets, like the iPad or iPod Touch, other iPhones, or other Mavericks-or-later Macs. Very handy indeed.

Furthermore, if you click the ▣ button, you'll see the Notes pane. It presents a tidy list of all your bookmarked pages, notes, and highlighted passages. You can click one of the listings to jump to the relevant page.

Books Settings

If you've embraced the simple joy of reading electronic books, then you deserve to know where to make settings changes: in Books→Preferences. Here are the options waiting there.

General tab

- **Let lines break naturally.** Ordinarily, Books presents text with ragged-right margins. Select "Justify text" if you like the text to stretch from edge to edge of the screen.

- **Auto-hyphenate words.** Sometimes, typesetting looks better if hyphens allow partial words to appear at the right edge of each line. Especially if you've also turned on "Justify text."

- **Display Sleep.** If you've set your screen to go dark after a period of inactivity (to save power—see page 353), this checkbox adds a 10-minute grace period to your definition of "inactivity." The idea is to prevent the screen from going dark just because you're a slow reader.

- **Sync.** Turn this on if you'd like your bookmarks, highlighting, and book collections to be synced with your other Apple gadgets.

Store tab

See the Note on page 388.

The same pop-out panel offers a Fonts menu, where you can choose from eight typefaces for your book.

- **Adjust the background color.** The AA button also offers a choice of four page-background colors: white, sepia (off-white), brown (with white text), or black (for nighttime reading).

While you're reading, Books makes all the onscreen controls fade away so you can read in peace. But if you move your mouse to the top of the window, a row of additional controls appears (Figure 11-2):

- 📕 **takes you back to the bookshelf (Library view).**

- ☰ **opens the Table of Contents panel.** The chapter or page names are "live"— you can click one to jump there.

- 🗐 **opens the Notes panel,** described next.

- 🔍 **opens the search box.** It lets you search for text within the book you're reading, which can be extremely useful.

- 🔖 **adds a bookmark to the current page.** This isn't like a physical bookmark, where there's only one in the whole book; you can use them to flag as many pages, for as many reasons, as you like. (The same button appears on your Touch Bar, if you have one.)

 Once you've accumulated a bookmark or two, use the ⌄ next to the 🔖 menu to see a list of them—and to jump back to one.

Tip: A Books book can include pictures and even videos. Double-click a picture in a book to zoom in on it.

Notes, Highlighting, and Other Options

Here are some more stunts that you'd have trouble pulling off in a printed book. If you *double-click* a word, you get a graceful, elegant page from Books' built-in dictionary. You know—in the unlikely event that you encounter a word you don't know.

If you drag across some text to highlight it, you get a few surprise options (Figure 11-2):

- **Highlight.** Click one of the colored dots to add tinted, transparent highlighting, or underlining, to the word you clicked. (To remove highlighting, click inside a highlighted area and click Remove Highlighting.)

- **Note.** When you click Add Note, Books creates highlighting on the selected passage *and* opens an empty, colored sticky note so you can type in your own annotations. When you click outside the note, it collapses down to a tiny Post-it square in the margin. Click to reopen it.

 To delete a note, click the highlighted text. Click Remove Note or Remove Highlight & Note.

- **Copy** copies the highlighted text, ready for pasting in some other program.

In general, reading is simple: Just read. Turn pages like this:

- **Press the space bar.** (Add Shift to turn back a page.)

- **Tap the ▶ key.** (Press ◀ to turn back.)

- **Point to the right margin;** click the > button that appears. (Left margin to go back.)

- **Swipe two fingers across the trackpad**—to the right (to go forward) or left (to go back a page).

Tip: The Touch Bar, if you have one (page 233), displays a handy "map" of the entire book. By clicking it or dragging your finger through it, you can jump directly to a different spot in the book. As you drag, your main screen shows the page number you're about to open.

What's super cool is that, after having jumped to that distant spot to check something, the Touch Bar then offers you a ↺ button, which teleports you right back to where you were.

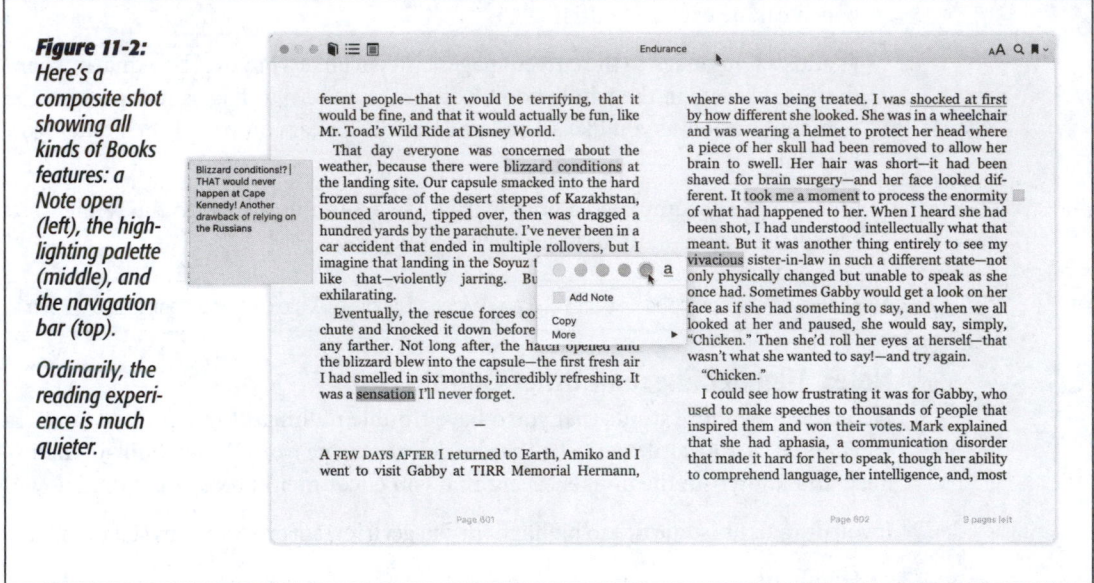

Figure 11-2:
Here's a composite shot showing all kinds of Books features: a Note open (left), the high-lighting palette (middle), and the navigation bar (top).

Ordinarily, the reading experience is much quieter.

You should also take a moment to adjust your reading environment. For example:

- **Enter Full Screen mode** for the biggest, least distracting view of your book (see page 178).

- **Specify either a one-page or a two-page spread** (use the Single Page or Two Pages commands in the View menu). In Full Screen mode, Single Page isn't available.

- **Adjust the type size** using the A**A** button. That's a huge feature for people with tired or over-40 eyes. And it's something paper books definitely can't do.

- **To delete a book,** click it and then press the Delete key; confirm in the warning box. Of course, deleting a book from the Mac doesn't delete your safety copy on your other gadgets or online.

- **Organize your books into folders.** In Books, the "folders" are called collections, but it's the same idea. You might have one for school, one for work, and a third for somebody who shares your Mac, for example.

To see your collections, click Collections; the Collections list opens at the left side. Make a new collection by clicking the + button (or choose Use File→New Collection); type to name it.

Now, to file your books away, select them (you can press ⌘ as you click to select multiple books); then choose File→Add to Collection and choose the name of the collection you want them in.

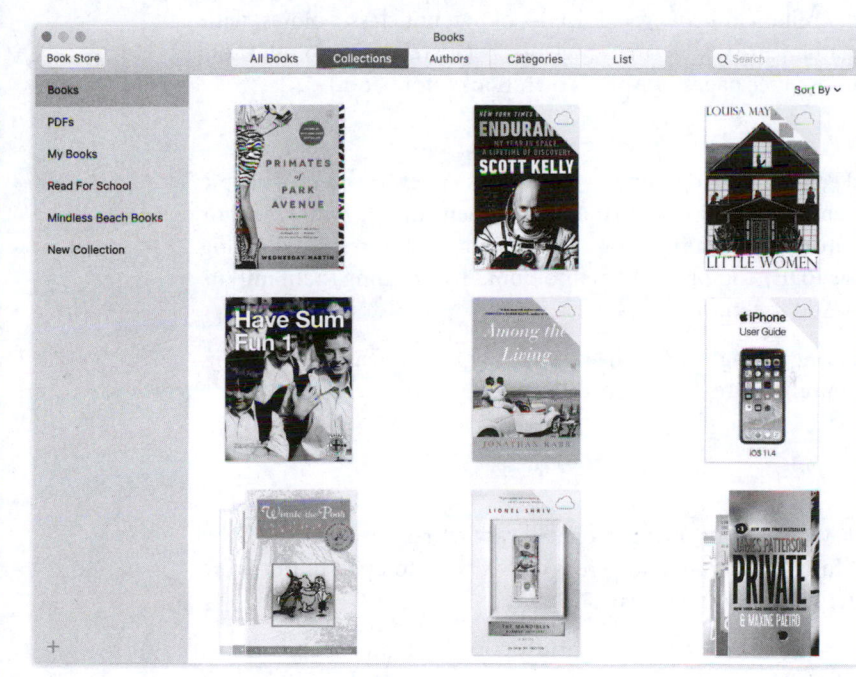

Figure 11-1:
Your Books library is more than just book covers. Stamps at the top-right corner indicate which are new, which are free samples, and which are actually online, waiting to be downloaded (☁).

In the Sort By pop-up menu (upper right), you can choose Show Title & Author to add that information beneath the book covers.

Reading

But come on—you're a reader, not a librarian. Here's how you read an ebook.

Open the book by double-clicking the book cover. Now the book opens, ready for you to read. Looks great, doesn't it (Figure 11-2)? If you're returning to a book you've been reading, Books remembers your place.

Tip: You can open several books at once, you multitasking maniac.

If you see a book cover bearing the ☁ icon, that's a book you own—it's available in your online locker—but you haven't downloaded it to this Mac yet. Click to download.

ePub Files

Apple's bookstore isn't the only way to get books. You can also load up your ebook reader from your computer, feeding it with ePub files.

Actually, ePub is the normal Books format. It's a very popular standard for ebook readers, Apple's and otherwise. The only difference between ePub documents you create and the ones Apple sells is that Apple's are copy protected.

To add your own ePub documents to your Books library, just drag their icons off the desktop and into the Books window. Or choose File→Add to Library.

And where are you supposed to get all these files? Free (and not free) ebooks in ePub format are everywhere. There are 53,000 free downloadable books at *gutenberg.org*, for example, and over a million at *books.google.com*—oldies, but classic oldies, with lots of Mark Twain, Agatha Christie, Herman Melville, H.G. Wells, and so on. (Lots of these are available in the Free pages of Apple's own Books store, too.)

PDF Files

Books can display and catalog PDF documents, too. PDFs are everywhere—people send them as attachments, and you can turn any document into a PDF file. (For example, on the Mac, in any program, choose File→Print; in the resulting dialog box, click PDF→Save as PDF.) You bring them into Books by dragging them into its window, or with File→Add to Library.

When you double-click one, though, it doesn't open in Books; it opens into *Preview*. Which is, after all, a program expressly designed for reading PDF documents.

You've been warned.

Your Library

When you open Books, you see your own personal library represented as little book covers (Figure 11-1). Mostly what you'll do here is click a book to open it. But there are all kinds of other activities waiting for you:

- **You can reorganize your bookshelf.** Use the Sort By pop-up menu to choose Most Recent or Title—or Sort Manually, which means you can drag books around into any order you like.

- **You can view your library as a compact list.** Click List at the top to switch the book-cover view to a much more boring (but more compact) list view. The column headings let you sort the list by author, title, category, and so on. And there's a search box, too, which lets you search your books' titles—helpful if you have an enormous library.

Automator

This software-robot program is described in a free downloadable PDF appendix to this chapter, "Automator & AppleScript." You can download it from this book's "Missing CD" page at *missingmanuals.com*.

Books

Books (formerly called iBooks) is Apple's ebook reading program. It lets you carry around dozens or hundreds of books, which, in the pre-ebook days, would have drawn some funny looks in public.

The beauty of all this is iCloud syncing. If you're reading a book on your iPhone in line for the DMV, you'll find that your iPad opens up to exactly the same page when you're on the train home. And when you open your MacBook at home, the book will be on the same page as where you left the iPad. Your books, documents, notes, highlighting, and other details are synced among your Apple gadgets, too. (You can turn that syncing feature off in Books→Preferences→General if it spooks you.)

Most people think of Books as a reader for books that Apple sells on its iTunes bookstore—best-sellers and current fiction, for example—and it does that very well. But you can also load it up with your own PDF documents, as well as thousands of free, older, out-of-copyright books.

Tip: In the interest of fairness, it's worth noting that Amazon's free Kindle app, and Barnes & Noble's free B&N eReader app, are much the same thing—but offer much bigger book libraries at lower prices than Apple's.

Downloading Books

To shop the Books bookstore, open the Books app. Click Book Store in the upper-left corner; the app becomes the literary equivalent of the App Store, complete with the icons across the top. The links here offer everything you'd need in your bibliographic quest: Bestsellers, Read It Before You Watch It (movie tie-ins), and so on. You can also search by name or click Purchased to see what you've bought.

Note: Once you've bought a book from Apple, you can download it again on other Macs, iPhones, iPod Touches, and iPads. Buy once, read many times. That's the purpose of the Not in My Library tab, which appears when you click Purchased.

But unless you have some kind of privacy concern, you may as well tell Books to download your books *automatically* as you buy them on your other Apple gadgets. Open Books→Preferences→Store and turn on "Download new purchases automatically." That way you'll never forget what you bought on your iPad as you sit down at your Mac.

Once you find a book that looks good, you can click Get Sample to download a free chapter, read ratings and reviews, or click the price itself to buy the book and download it straight to the Mac.

The Free Programs of macOS

R ight out of the box, macOS comes with a healthy assortment of about 50 freebies: programs for sending email, writing documents, doing math, even playing games. Some have been around for years. Others, like Maps and Books, are newer. They're designed not only to show off some of macOS's most dramatic technologies, but also to let you get real work done without having to invest in additional software.

Your Free Programs

A broad assortment of programs sits in the Applications folder in the main hard drive window, and another couple dozen less frequently used apps await in the Applications→Utilities folder.

This chapter guides you through every item in your new software library, one program at a time. (Of course, your Applications list may vary. Apple might have blessed your particular Mac model with some bonus programs, or you may have downloaded or installed some on your own.)

Tip: A reminder: You can jump straight to the Applications folder in the Finder by pressing Shift-⌘-A (the shortcut for Go→Applications), or by clicking the Applications folder icon in the Sidebar. You might consider adding the Application folder's icon to the Dock, too, so you can access it no matter what program you're in. Shift-⌘-U (or Go→Utilities) takes you, of course, to the Utilities folder.

App Store

See page 165 for full details on the Mac App Store.

You have two choices here: **always** (always show the message in the notification banner) or **when unlocked** (show it only if you're actually *using* the Mac).

- **Show in Notification Center.** Do you want this app's notifications to appear in the Notification Center? If you turn this off for an app, you'll still get its alert messages, but you won't see them listed in the Notification Center panel.

- **Badge app icon.** If you turn this option on, then each app's actual icon (in your Launchpad and on your Dock) sprouts a red, circled number. This number lets you know how many times it's tried to flag you about something.

- **Play sound for notifications.** Some apps play a sound when a new notification arrives. For example, Calendar dings to remind you of an upcoming event. It's a little extra insurance that you won't miss a nudge, but here's where you can turn these sounds off.

- **FaceTime** tells you when you've missed an incoming call.

- **Mail** lets you know when you've received a new message. You can also specify whether or not the notification displays the beginning of the message itself when you're not seated at your Mac, which you may consider to be either useful or a scary privacy violation. (Mercifully, Mail's Preferences→General tab lets you limit these alerts, so you won't be buried in a barrage of meaningless heads-up bubbles. You can tell Mail to alert you only when somebody in your Contacts list has written to you, only when a message lands in a smart mailbox folder, only when you get email from someone you've designated as a VIP—or whenever any message lands in any mailbox.)

- **Messages** lets you know when somebody has sent you an instant message.

- **Safari** allows certain websites, if they're open on your Mac, to send you notifications (known as HTML web notifications).

Other companies' apps may appear in this list, too: BusyCal, Evernote, Skype, and so on.

Now it's time to change the settings for one app at a time. Click an app's name to see its individual Notifications settings (Figure 10-5—the Calendar app, in this case). For example, as hinted above, different apps can get your attention in different ways:

- **None.** If certain apps seem to bug you with news you really don't care about, you can make them shut up forever. They won't bother you with pop-up messages, although they can still insert items into the Notification Center panel.

- **Banners.** This option makes incoming notifications slide quietly and briefly onto the top right of your screen. Each message holds still long enough for you to read it, but it goes away automatically after a few seconds. Banners are a good option for things like Facebook and Twitter updates and incoming email messages.

- **Alerts.** These notifications don't go away until you click a button to dismiss them. Good for important messages, like alarms and flight updates.

At the bottom of the Notifications window, you get more settings for each app:

- **Show notifications on lock screen.** Do you want summaries of all your missed notifications to appear on your Lock screen ("5 email notifications") when you wake the Mac? It's a great feature, as long as you don't mind passing busybodies knowing how popular you are.

- **Show notification preview.** This is a privacy thing. Suppose you've wandered away from your desk. When someone sends you a text, do you want the notification banner to include the message itself, on the Lock screen where anyone can read it? (That's the Preview.) Or do you want the banner to indicate only that a person has sent *some* message, which you can read only after unlocking the Mac?

And it's not just texts. Do you want Uber information to appear in the banner? How about Facebook updates? The name of your alarm or reminder?

notifications by Recents, the ⊗ button deletes a *day* of notifications; if you've chosen Recents by App, it deletes all the notifications from a particular *app*.

Customizing the Notification Center

You can (and should) specify *which* apps are allowed to junk up your Notification Center. Open System Preferences→Notifications to see the list of apps that might want to get your attention in the master Notifications list (Figure 10-5).

This is also the place where you can specify the *order* of the various apps' notifications in the center. Use the "Notification Center sort order" pop-up menu at the bottom of the window.

Figure 10-5:
Here in System Preferences, you can specify which apps are permitted to intrude on the precious billboard that is your Notification Center—and how they're permitted to intrude.

Some individual apps, including Mail and Calendar, offer additional controls in their Preferences boxes. For example, in Calendar, you can turn off notifications from shared calendars and from meeting invitations.

If you choose Recents, the apps with the newest alerts appear at the top. If you choose Recents by App, the notifications are grouped under headings that correspond to the app generating them. And if you tap Manually by App, you can simply drag the app names up or down in the list to specify their top-to-bottom order on the Notification Center list.

Out of the box, a lot of macOS apps are listed in the Notification Center (along with Do Not Disturb, already described). Here are some of the most significant:

• **Calendar** lets you know about imminent appointments.

• **Facebook** governs the appearance of updates from your Facebook friends.

report, news headlines) that you've installed there. (More on this in a moment.) You also see the answers to any Siri queries that you decided to pin here, as described on page 301.

- **Notifications.** This tab lists all your apps' notifications, as well as all your Mac's messages, reminders, upcoming appointments, and so on.

Each produces a scrolling panel; read on.

Today Tab

The Today panel presents an executive summary of everything you need to know today, in plain English: your upcoming appointments (" 'Personnel meeting' is next up on your calendar, at 2 PM"); reminders coming due; weather and stock information; and a preview of your schedule tomorrow. It's identical to the Today panel on the iPhone or iPad, if you're scoring at home.

Each of these little info-panels is called a widget, and there are tons of them available. For example, the Mac comes with ones called Calculator, which puts a calculator at your fingertips, and Find My Friends, which lets you see on a map where your loved ones are (this presumes they have iPhones and have permitted you to track them).

To add, remove, or rearrange widgets, click Edit at the bottom of the panel; proceed as described in Figure 10-4.

Intriguingly, Apple also allows apps to add their *own* sections to the Today list. For example, Dropbox can show a list of files that have been added to your Dropbox folder; Evernote can add buttons for creating new notes or reminders; The New York Times, Yahoo Digest, and Huffington Post apps can add headlines; the Kindle app offers links to the books you're reading right now; and so on.

Tip: If you're feeling widget-deprived, click App Store. It opens a special section of the Mac App Store dedicated to apps that install widgets on your Today panel.

Notifications Tab

On the Notifications tab (Figure 10-3, right), you can have two kinds of fun:

- **Click an item to open the relevant app for more details.** For example, click an appointment listed there to open its information panel in Calendar. Click the name of a software update to open the Mac App Store program, where you can read about it and download it. Click a message's name to open Mail, where you can read the entire message.

- **Click the little ⊗ to dismiss one day's entire list of notifications**—or one app's worth—once you've seen them. (The ⊗ appears when you point to a notification.)

So which is it—all the notifications from one app? Or from one day? That's up to you. It depends on how you've set things up in System Preferences→Notifications, as described in the next section. For example, if you've chosen to sort your

it's an iMac, for example. (You can also set up a keystroke or a "hot corner" to open the Notification Center, if you like. See pages 210 and 186.)

Either way, the Notification Center slides onto the screen like a classy gray window shade, showing every recent item of interest.

Tip: To close the Notification Center, swipe the opposite way (left to right) with two fingers. Or click any other part of the screen. Or click the ☰ again. Or just blink really hard.

The Notification Center has two tabs at the top:

- **Today.** On the Today tab (Figure 10-4), you see today's weather, all your upcoming appointments and reminders, and an assortment of widgets (calculator, stock

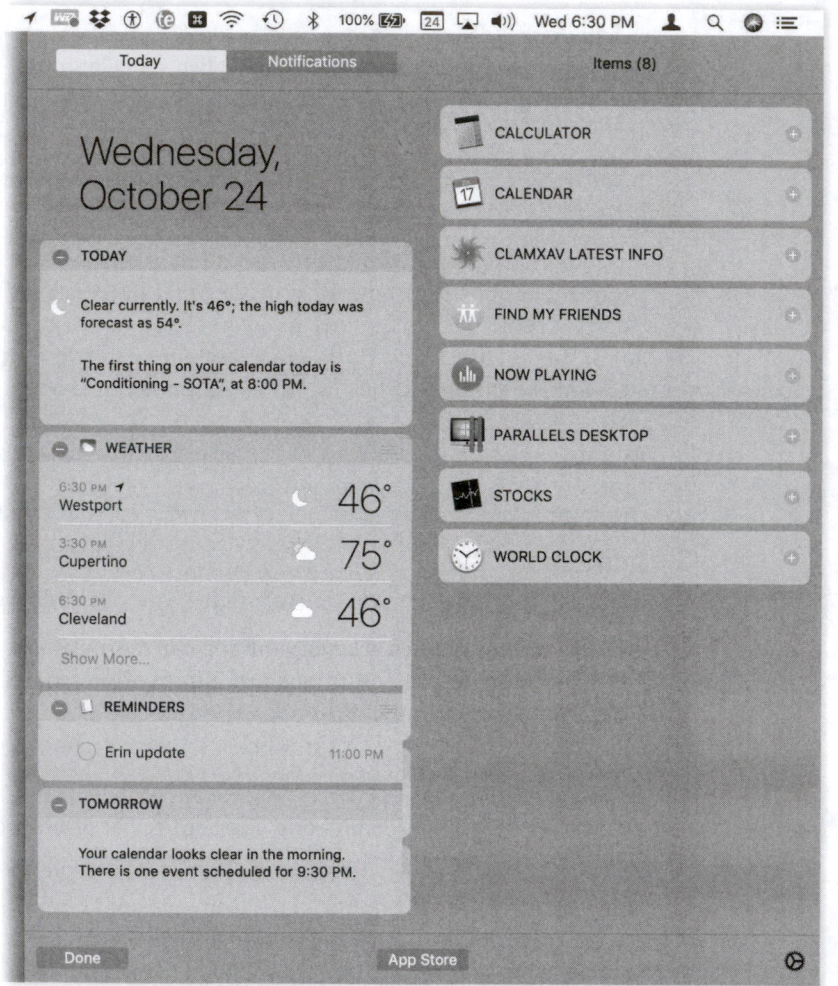

Figure 10-4:
Editing the widgets of the Today list is simple enough. The left column represents what's in the Today list now; the right column lists widgets that aren't installed at the moment. Click ⊖ to remove a widget from the Today list, or tap ⊕ to add a module.

Drag the ≡ up or down to move it higher or lower in the list. Then tap Done.

All other notifications are still silenced when Do Not Disturb is engaged—just not phone calls and FaceTime calls.

- **Allow repeated calls.** If you turn this on, and somebody tries to call you more than once within three minutes, it will ring through. The idea here is that nobody *would* call you multiple times unless it was urgent. You certainly wouldn't want Do Not Disturb to block somebody trying to tell you that there's been an accident, that you've overslept, or that you've just won the lottery.

The Notification Center

All right, now you know how to dismiss, stifle, or respond to notification bubbles. But what if you miss one? Or you decide to act on it later?

Thought you'd never ask.

All those "Hey you!" messages collect on a single screen called the Notification Center (Figure 10-3).

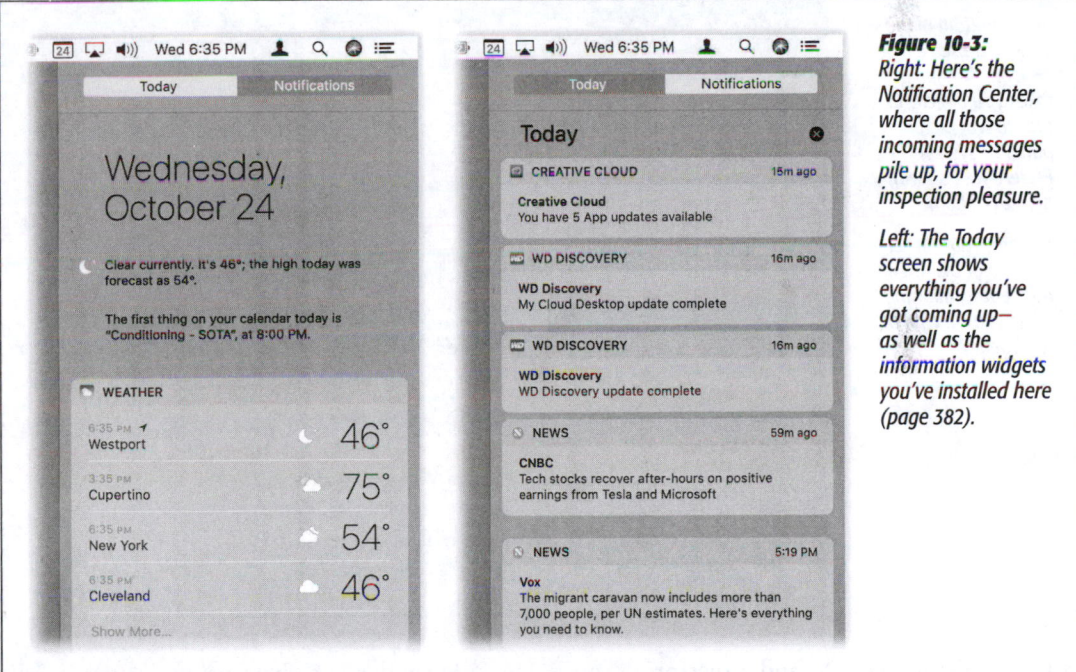

Figure 10-3:
Right: Here's the Notification Center, where all those incoming messages pile up, for your inspection pleasure.

Left: The Today screen shows everything you've got coming up— as well as the information widgets you've installed here (page 382).

To make it appear on a laptop, swipe two fingers *onto* the trackpad from the right. (Start the swipe off to the right of the trackpad. It's the first time you've ever crossed the edge of the trackpad with a Mac gesture. Weird.)

You can also open the Notification Center by clicking the ☰ in the upper-right corner of your screen. That's a handy trick if your Mac doesn't have a trackpad—if

To see it, open System Preferences→Notifications (Figure 10-2, bottom). You'll find that this version of Do Not Disturb offers all kinds of useful options:

- **On a schedule.** Here you can specify starting and ending hours for Do Not Disturb to kick in automatically. It's handy if you'd like the Mac to go dark during the same hours you do every night. (There's no separate setting for weekends; Do Not Disturb will turn on and off for the same hours every day of the week.)

- **When the display is sleeping.** When the screen is dark, it means you're not at your Mac. You probably don't need passersby seeing your incoming love notes; besides, you're not there to witness them arriving anyway.

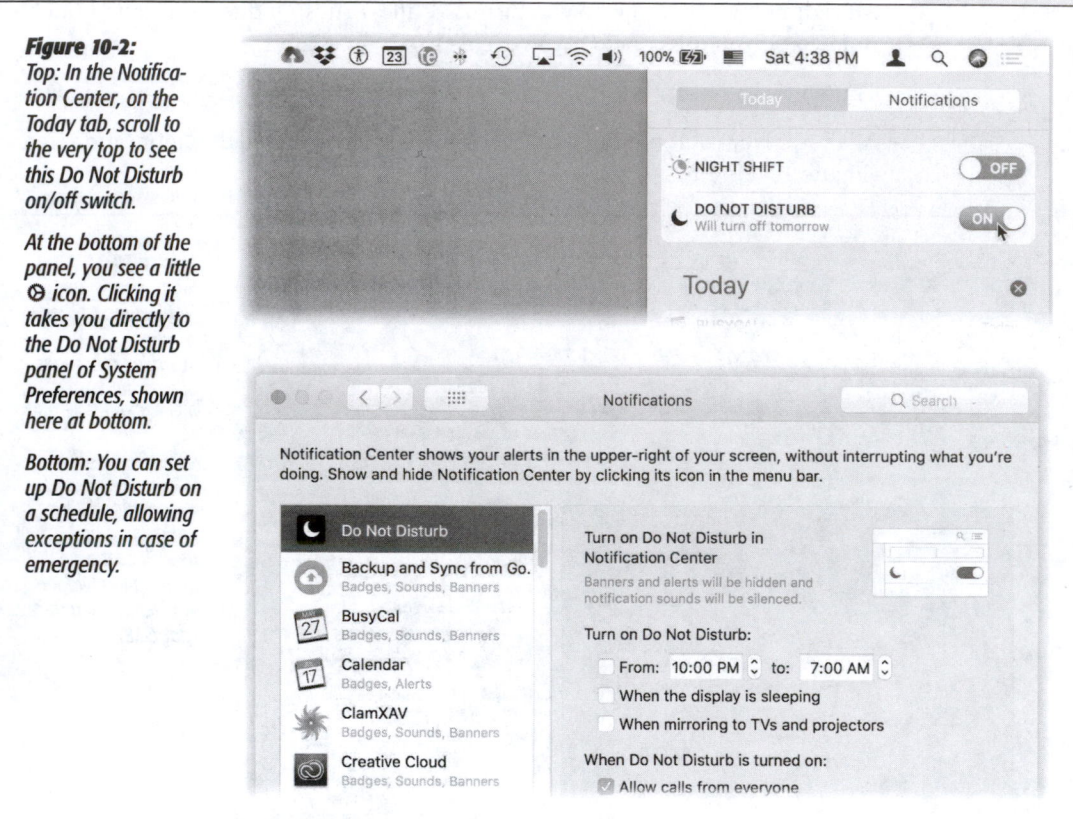

Figure 10-2:
Top: In the Notification Center, on the Today tab, scroll to the very top to see this Do Not Disturb on/off switch.

At the bottom of the panel, you see a little ⚙ icon. Clicking it takes you directly to the Do Not Disturb panel of System Preferences, shown here at bottom.

Bottom: You can set up Do Not Disturb on a schedule, allowing exceptions in case of emergency.

- **When mirroring to TVs and projectors.** If you're showing an audience something from your Mac, chances are pretty good that you don't want little notice bubbles to interrupt the show. There's nothing worse than an audience of 500 witnessing the embarrassing subject lines of your incoming email.

- **Allow calls from everyone.** If you use your Mac as a speakerphone (page 308), you might still want it to ring for incoming calls. In that case, turn on this option.

Insta-Respond to Bubbles

Some of those notification bubbles aren't just the Mac's way of speaking to you; they're interactive. That's particularly handy when the bubble represents an incoming iMessage, FaceTime call, or email—because you can reply to them. See Figure 10-1.

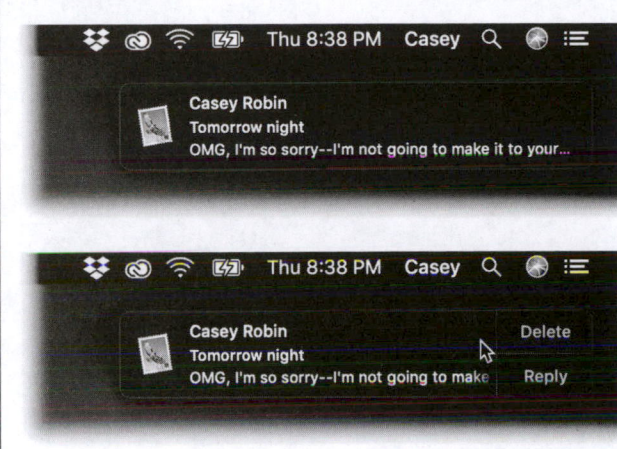

Figure 10-1:

Top: MacOS tries to get your attention using notification bubbles.

Bottom: If you point to a bubble before it disappears, it may offer buttons that let you take action. For example, if it's an incoming instant message, you can hit Reply and then type your response right in the bubble. If it's a FaceTime call, you can answer it or decline it.

And if it's email, you can click either Delete or Reply. If you hit Reply, an outgoing, floating message window opens, already addressed, already set up as a response. Just type your reply and hit Send.

Shutting Up the Bubbles

Of course, little bubbles sliding into the top-right corner of your screen may not always be what you want, especially if you're trying to beat a deadline.

Dismiss One Bubble

If you're in a hurry, you can get rid of one of these bubbles with a right-swipe on it (two fingers on a trackpad, one on a Magic Mouse, or just drag it off to the right with your mouse).

Do Not Disturb (Manual)

But to truly shut up all notifications, turn on Do Not Disturb (Figure 10-2, top).

Tip: The efficiency nut may prefer to simply Option-click the ☰ button at the right end of the menu bar. It turns gray, indicating that you've stifled all bubbles until midnight (or until you Option-click it again).

When Do Not Disturb is on, your messages quietly pile up in the Notification Center (described in a moment); they don't pop up on your screen individually as they happen, and they certainly don't make any noises.

Do Not Disturb (Automatic)

The Mac can also shut up the bubbles automatically, either according to a daily schedule (like when you're asleep) or when you're giving a presentation.

Notifications

A notification is an important status message or warning. On a smartphone, you get one every time a text message comes in, an alarm goes off, a calendar appointment is imminent, or your battery is running low.

It's no different on your Mac. Mail and Messages might want to let you know that a new message has arrived. The Calendar app might want to remind you that an important meeting is about to start.

In macOS, you know when some app is trying to get your attention: A message bubble slides into view at the top right of your screen (Figure 10-1, top). Some of these alerts slide away again after five seconds; others require you to click a button, like Close, Snooze, or Show (which opens the program that's waving its little hand in your face).

Note: Only apps you got from the Mac App Store can tap into the Notification Center. Other programs use whatever alert mechanisms they always have—pop-up dialog boxes, for example.

You're also notified this way when one of your App Store apps has been automatically updated, or when that update requires you to quit the app or restart the Mac (and you're offered a Later button).

All kinds of warnings—dying battery, failed Time Machine backups, disks ejected improperly—appear in these subtle notification bubbles, rather than bleating their news in showstopping dialog boxes.

- **Drop a pin in Maps** by force-clicking that spot.

- **GarageBand.** You can force-click all kinds of things in GarageBand: a region (to rename it), a note (to delete it), an empty Software Instrument track (to create an empty MIDI region), a region while dragging (to zoom in), and so on.

Variable pressure

A Force Touch trackpad can actually tell *how hard* you're pressing. How is that useful?

- **QuickTime, iMovie.** Your finger pressure controls how fast you rewind or fast-forward (on the corresponding buttons).

- **Maps.** Pressing harder zooms in faster.

- **Photos.** When you're moving through photos in an Album or a Moment by pressing the arrow buttons, pressing harder makes you go faster.

"Notch" clicks

Finally, the Force Touch trackpad can make that artificial click sound, complete with a little "click" vibration, to signal certain notch points in onscreen activity. For example, you'll feel that "notch" click when you've dragged a video clip to the maximum length in iMovie, or in Maps when you rotate the compass to north, or in Photos when you're rotating a photo (inside the Crop tool) and it reaches 0 degrees rotation.

Over time, in theory, you'll get used to these little shortcuts—and you'll come to be more productive with them.

On the other hand, they may just annoy you. In that case, open System Preferences→ Trackpad and turn the whole thing off. (The "Force Click and haptic feedback" checkbox is the one you want—or, rather, don't want.)

Tip: Also on the System Preferences→Trackpad screen: a slider that lets you adjust how hard you have to press to generate a simulated click: Light, Medium, or Firm (see Figure 9-23).

Users & Groups

This is the master list of people who are allowed to log into your Mac. (In previous Mac versions it was called Accounts.) It's where you can adjust their passwords, startup pictures, self-opening startup items, permissions to use various features of the Mac, and other security tools. All of this is described in Chapter 12.

Wallet & Apple Pay

This panel is where you can set up Apple Pay, the step-saving feature that lets you complete web purchases without having to type in a credit card number. See page 671 for details.

information, or something else the data detectors feature recognizes (page 252), then you get a bubble that proposes opening that item in the corresponding program. (Neither feature works in all programs.)

- **Secondary click.** This means "right-click." As you know, right-clicking is a huge deal on the Mac; it unleashes useful features just about everywhere.

 This pop-up menu offers you three options. You can click with two fingers; click once in the lower-right corner of the trackpad; or click once in the lower-left corner. You can also trigger a right-click by clicking with your thumb while resting your index and middle fingers on the trackpad. Weird, but wonderful.

- **Tap to click.** Usually, you touch your laptop's trackpad only to move the cursor. For clicking and dragging, you're supposed to push down on the clicker (the lower half of the actual trackpad surface). Many people find, however, that it's more direct to tap and drag directly on the trackpad, using the same finger that's been moving the cursor. That's the purpose of this checkbox. When it's on, you can tap the trackpad surface to register a mouse click at the location of the cursor. (Also handy when your trackpad is broken, sticky, or balky.) Double-tap to double-click.

- **Click.** This option appears if you have one of the Force Touch trackpads described on page 375. It lets you adjust *how hard* you have to press to produce a click: Light, Medium, or Firm.

- **Tracking speed.** This is a duplicate of the Tracking Speed slider described on page 364—but it lets you establish an independent tracking speed for the *trackpad*.

- **Silent clicking.** This option appears on older (pre-2016) laptops with Force Touch trackpads. It lets you trigger clicks without actually producing a click sound. Perfect for mousing in bed next to a light sleeper.

- **Force Click and haptic feedback.** This is the on/off switch for the force-clicking features described on page 375.

Scroll & Zoom

- **Scroll direction: natural.** Here's the heart of macOS's once-controversial feature: scrolling *up* when you drag your fingers (or the scroll wheel, or the scroll bar) *up*.

 If you can't stand this arrangement, turn it off here. But first read the discussion on page 29.

- **Zoom in or out.** If you've used an iPhone or iPad, this one will seem familiar. What it means is, "Put two fingers on the trackpad and spread them apart to *enlarge* what's on the screen. Slide two fingers *together* to shrink it down again." It doesn't work in every program—it affects pictures and PDFs in Preview, photos in Photos, text in Safari, text in a TextEdit window—but it's great when it does.

- **Smart zoom.** You can double-tap a block of text or a graphic on a web page to enlarge just that block to full-screen size. The "smart" element of this is the way the software senses that block's borders and zooms in exactly right. Double-tap your trackpad (touch, don't click) with *two* fingers to do it.

All of this is great news. Most of us would be happy if we never, ever had to type in another password.

Trackpad

You may love your Mac laptop now, but these special features make your laptop *crazy* better. Turns out you can point, click, scroll, right-click, rotate things, enlarge things, hide windows, and switch programs, all on the trackpad itself, without ever having to lift your fingers. (You can do most of this on a desktop Mac, too, if it has an Apple Magic Mouse, or an external trackpad like Apple's Magic Trackpad.)

The options here depend on your Mac model, but usually you see something like Figure 9-23: three tabs. Each governs how you do pointing, clicking, scrolling, and other mouselike maneuvers. Each time you click one, the right half of the dialog box plays a looping movie that shows you that technique clearly and visibly.

Figure 9-23:
The Trackpad pane of System Preferences offers hours of entertainment— because each setting triggers a little movie that shows what Apple means.

This is what the pane looks like if you have a Force Touch trackpad (which comes on the latest laptop models).

Here's what's on the three main tabs.

Point & Click

- **Look up & data detectors.** This gesture lets you tap the trackpad with three fingers simultaneously (*don't* click—just touch the surface) to bring up two kinds of supplementary information. If you're tapping a single word, you get a handy dictionary definition. If you're tapping a web address, map address, block of contact

and over, maybe six times. Each time, the gray lines of the onscreen fingerprint darken a little more (Figure 9-22).

Once the registration is complete, the screen says "Touch ID is ready."

3. Click Done.

You return to the Touch ID panel, where your fingerprint is now represented by an icon named something like "Finger 1." Feel free to click those words and type a better name ("Right-hand pointer" or whatever). To delete one, point to its icon and then click the ⊗ that appears; click Delete to confirm.

Tip: It's perfectly legal to register the same finger several times. That technique makes Touch ID more reliable if it seems to be having trouble recognizing that finger.

You can register your toes instead of fingers, if that's helpful. Or even patches of your wrist or arm, if you're patient (and weird).

Anyway, you are now ready to start using the fingerprint. Try it: Put the Mac to sleep. Then press the power button with your very special finger. The Mac reads your fingerprint and instantly unlocks itself.

And now, a few notes about using your fingerprint as a password:

- **Apple says the image of your fingerprint is encrypted** and stored in the Touch Bar's dedicated processor chip. It's never transmitted anywhere, it never goes online, and it's never collected by Apple.

- **The Touch ID scanner may have trouble** if your finger is wet, greasy, or scarred.

- **The fingerprint reader isn't just a camera;** it doesn't just look for the image of your fingerprint. It's actually measuring the tiny differences in electrical conductivity between the raised parts of your fingerprint (which aren't conductive) and the skin just beneath the surface (which is). That's why a plastic finger won't work—and even your own finger won't work if it's been chopped off (or if you've passed away).

- **If you've registered fingerprints belonging to several account holders,** then fast user switching (page 549) is *really* fast. All Person B has to do is click the power button with the registered finger, and boom: Person A's account world slides away, and Person B's heaves into view.

Fingerprints for Apps, Websites, and Apple Pay

At the bottom of the System Preferences→Touch ID screen, you see the on/off switches for the three things your fingerprint can do: It can unlock the computer (Unlocking your Mac), pay for things (Apple Pay—see page 671), and serve as your password when you buy books, music, apps, and videos from Apple's online stores (iTunes & App Store). That last feature is handy: At the moment when you're usually asked to type your iCloud password, you're asked to touch the fingerprint sensor to authorize the purchase instead.

This sensor is built right into the power button (clever!). It reads your finger at any angle. It can't be faked out by a plastic finger or even a chopped-off human one. You can teach it to recognize up to five different fingerprints. They can be a few of your fingers or, for example, you could teach it one finger each for five family members.

Before you can use your fingertip as a password, though, you have to teach the Mac to recognize it, and here's where you do it:

1. **Create a password.**

 That's right: You can't use a fingerprint *instead* of a password; you can only use a fingerprint in addition to one. You'll still need a password from time to time to keep the Mac's security tight. For example, you need to enter your password if you can't make your fingerprint work (maybe it got encased in acrylic in a hideous crafts accident).

 So open System Preferences→Accounts and create a password (page 528), if you haven't already.

2. **Teach a fingerprint.**

 Click the "Add a fingerprint" button.

 Start by entering your account password, to prove you're not a sinister spy. Click OK.

 Now place the finger you want to train onto the power button—your index finger is the most logical candidate. You're asked to touch it to the power button over

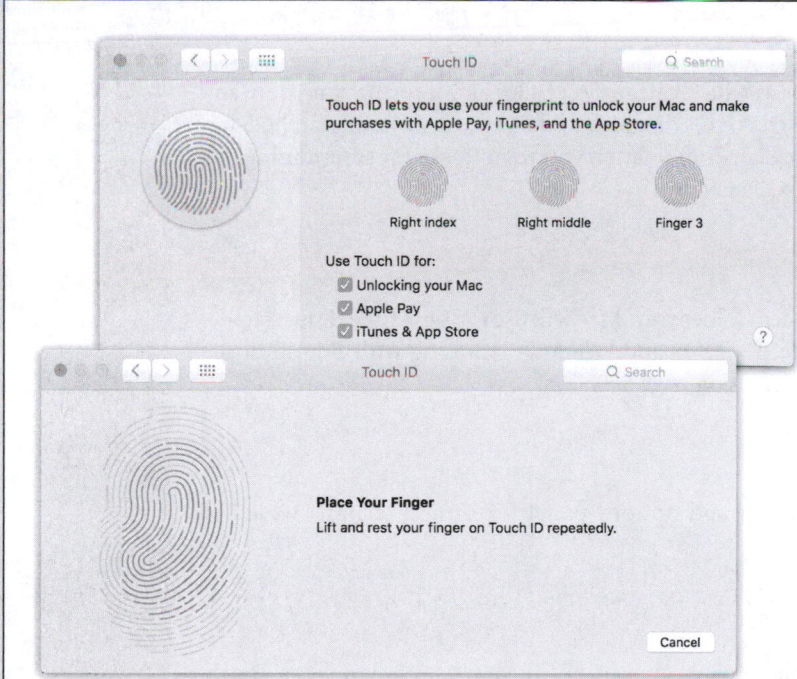

Figure 9-22:
Each time you touch your finger to the power button, a little more of the fingerprint map gets filled in. Once you've filled in the fingerprint, the dialog box advises you to keep going, this time tipping the finger a little each time so the sensor gets a better view of your finger's edges.

The Advanced checkboxes govern the process:

- **Check for updates.** You grant permission to your Mac to ping the mother ship periodically to see if there are updates available. Turn it off and you're stuck with today's software versions forever.

- **Download new updates when available.** If you leave this option turned on, you'll still be notified before anything gets installed, but you won't have to wait for the downloading—the deed will already be done.

- **Install macOS updates.** If you turn this off, you won't automatically get macOS updates as they come along.

- **Install app updates from the App Store.** If you turn this off, you won't get updates to your apps. It's hard to think of a reason why you wouldn't want the latest, most refined versions of apps. But maybe you want to read about some update online before installing it.

- **Install system data files and security updates.** These files are part of macOS's automatic, ongoing virus protection. If you turn this option off, your Mac won't know how to recognize and fight the latest viruses. Also, you're nuts.

Tip: In case this automatic-update thing feels a little *too* automatic, you can always see a list of what updates were installed while you weren't looking. Open the App Store app and click the Updates tab to see everything that's been installed in the past 30 days.

Spotlight

Here's how you tell the Mac (a) which categories of files and information you want the Spotlight search feature to search, (b) which folders you *don't* want searched, for privacy reasons, and (c) which key combination you want to use for summoning the Spotlight menu or dialog box. Details are in Chapter 3.

Startup Disk

Use this panel to pick the System folder your Mac will use the next time it starts up—when you're swapping between macOS and Windows (running with Boot Camp), for example. Check out the details on page 500.

Time Machine

Here's the master on/off switch and options panel for Time Machine, which is described on page 266.

Touch ID

As you could probably guess, this panel appears only if your Mac laptop has a Touch ID fingerprint sensor—for example, it's a Touch Bar laptop or a 2018 MacBook Air.

If you turn off this checkbox, then the Mac won't make any sound at all as you adjust its volume. Instead, you'll see only a visual representation of the steadily decreasing (or increasing) volume level.

Tip: The Shift key reverses the logic. So if you have "Play feedback" turned *on,* holding down Shift as you tap the volume keys makes them silent. If it's turned *off,* you can force the volume-gauging beeps to play by pressing Shift as you tap the volume keys.

Output Tab

"Output" means speakers or headphones. For most people, this pane lists only Internal Speakers (and a Balance slider for left-to-right stereo balancing).

This panel is more useful when you've connected external speakers, a Bluetooth or USB phone headset, or an AirPlay receiver like an Apple TV—and then clicked its name. All Mac audio now flows to that device. MacOS will even remember your volume setting for each gadget independently.

Tip: Here's a much quicker way to change your audio input or output: Press Option as you click the ◀)) menulet. You get a secret pop-up menu that lists your various microphones, speakers, and headphones, so you can switch things without a visit to System Preferences.

Input Tab

This panel lets you specify which sound source you want the Mac to "listen to," if you have more than one connected: external microphone, internal microphone, line input, USB headset, or whatever. It also lets you adjust the sensitivity of that microphone—its *input volume*—by dragging the slider and watching the real-time Input level meter above it change as you speak. Put another way, it's a quick way to see if your microphone is working.

If you'd prefer even more control over your Mac's sound inputs and outputs, don't miss the Audio MIDI Setup program in your Applications→Utilities folder.

Software Update

Whenever Apple improves some piece of macOS or an Apple-branded program, the Mac can notify you, download the update, and install it automatically. These updates may include new versions of programs like Photos and Maps; drivers for newly released printers, scanners, cameras, and such; bug fixes and security patches; and so on.

This System Preferences panel (formerly called App Store) governs when and how your Mac auto-downloads new versions of macOS and apps you've acquired from the App Store (Chapter 5). The panel also lets you know the last time updates were automatically installed.

"Automatically keep my Mac up to date" means your Mac won't automatically install new macOS versions and new versions of your App Store apps. (In other words, it turns off the third and fourth checkboxes described in this section.)

Just click the sound of your choice to make it your default system beep. Most of the canned choices here are funny and clever, yet subdued enough to be practical as alert sounds (Figure 9-21).

Figure 9-21:
You can adjust your overall speaker volume independently from the alert-beep volume, thank goodness.

The other controls on the Sound Effects panel include these:

- **Play sound effects through.** Intriguingly enough, you can specify one sound source (a speaker or headset) for most sound playback—and a different one just for your error beeps. That's the one you specify with this pop-up menu.

- **Alert volume.** The *main* volume slider for your Mac is the "Output volume" slider at the bottom of the Sound pane. The "Alert volume" slider is *just* for error beeps; Apple was kind enough to let you adjust the volume of these error beeps independently.

- **Play user interface sound effects.** This option produces a few subtle sound effects during certain Finder operations: when you drag something off the Dock, into the Trash, or into a folder, or when the Finder finishes a file-copying job.

- **Play feedback when volume is changed.** Each time you press one of the volume keys (◀, ◁, ◀))), the Mac beeps (or, rather, pops) to help you gauge the current volume.

 That's all fine when you're working at home. But more than one person has been humiliated in an important meeting when the Mac made a sudden, inappropriately loud sonic outburst—and then amplified that embarrassment by furiously and repeatedly pressing the volume-down key, beeping all the way.

- **Remote Management.** Lets someone else control your Mac using Apple Remote Desktop, a popular add-on program for teachers and system administrators.

- **Remote Apple Events.** Lets AppleScript gurus send commands to Macs across the network.

- **Bluetooth Sharing.** This pane lets you set up Bluetooth file sharing, a way for other people near you to shoot files over to (or receive files from) your laptop—without hassle, or passwords. Page 260 has the details.

- **Content Caching.** Technical, but cool: If you turn on this checkbox, then your Mac keeps a copy of all the Apple software that *all* Macs on your network download. That includes macOS updates, App Store apps and their updates, and iCloud photos and documents.

 Why? Because the next time one of the *other* Macs needs that app or update, it grabs it from your Mac. That's much faster than re-downloading it from the internet. Note, however, that Apple recommends turning this feature on only if your Mac gets online over a wired Ethernet connection—not Wi-Fi.

Tip: As you can imagine, Content Caching eats up a lot of disk space. If you turn it on and then click Options, you can set a limit to how much software is allowed to pile up on your Mac. Then again, don't worry; if your disk runs out of space, your Mac will auto-delete the cache as needed. (It's part of the purgeable storage described on page 105.)

And if you Option-click that button, it opens Advanced Options: some dizzyingly technical additional settings. Here, for example, you have some control over which other Macs are allowed to access your Mac's cache.

Siri

This pane houses the settings for Siri, as described on page 303.

Sound

At the bottom of this panel, there's an "Output volume" slider—the master volume control for your Mac. (It's a duplicate of the one in the menu bar, and useful only when you've forgotten about the volume keys on your keyboard.)

Using the panes of the Sound panel, you can configure the sound system of your Mac in any of several ways.

Tip: Here's a quick way to jump directly to the Sound panel of System Preferences—from the keyboard, without ever having to open System Preferences or click Sound. Just press Option as you tap the ◀, ◀), or ◀)) key on the top row of your Apple keyboard.

Sound Effects Tab

"Sound effects" means *error beeps*—the sound you hear when the Mac wants your attention, or when you click someplace you shouldn't.

Dictation

This pane used to be part of its own System Preferences panel, but now it's a tab here in Keyboard, even though the entire purpose of the Dictation feature is to *avoid* using the keyboard. Anyway, it's described on page 277.

Language & Region

The primary job of this pane is to set up your Mac to work in other languages. If you bought your Mac already set up in your own language—you're already using the only language, number format, and keyboard layout you'll ever need—then you can ignore most of this panel. But when it comes to showing off macOS to your friends and loved ones, the "wow" factor on the Mac's polyglot features is huge.

Details appear on page 246.

Mission Control

Mission Control, the joint venture of the Exposé, Spaces, and Dashboard window-management features, is described in detail in Chapter 5—and so is this joint-venture control panel.

Mouse

This pane (Figure 9-20) looks different depending on what kind of mouse (if any) is attached to your Mac.

You might have the wireless, Bluetooth Magic Mouse (version 1 or 2), whose flat, broad top surface is also a trackpad. You might have the wired or wireless Apple Mouse, formerly called the *Mighty* Mouse, which has a domed top surface. And, of course, you can connect any old USB or Bluetooth mouse, from a Windows PC or whatever.

Note: On a laptop without any mouse attached, the Mouse pane still appears in System Preferences—but its sole function is to help you "pair" your Mac with a wireless Bluetooth mouse. At that point, the Mouse pane looks just as it does on a desktop Mac.

Scroll Direction

You can make your mouse's scroll wheel make your window scroll what Apple considers the right way ("Natural"), even though that feels *unnatural* to people who've been using mice for a long time. See page 29.

Secondary Click

Just by looking, you'd never know an Apple mouse has both a right button and a left button. Once you turn on the "Secondary click" feature in System Preferences (Figure 9-20), though, each side clicks independently.

how quickly the keyboard backlight fades to black once you've stopped typing or mousing.

- **"Touch Bar shows," "Press Fn key to."** These pop-up menus govern what appears in the Touch Bar, so they appear only if you have one. Details are on page 233.

- **Show keyboard and emoji viewers in menu bar.** You can read all about these special symbol-generating windows on page 250. Here's the on/off switch for the menulet that makes them appear.

- **Use all F1, F2, etc. keys as standard function keys.** This option appears *only* on laptops and aluminum-keyboard Macs. It's complicated, so read page 198 slowly.

- **Change Keyboard Type.** The Mac is supposed to detect what kind of keyboard you're using (U.S., European, or Japanese layout) automatically, so this option is essentially a troubleshooting tool. Use it when Mac doesn't seem to type the right character when you press some keys.

- **Customize Control Strip.** This control, too, appears only if your laptop has a Touch Bar. It lets you edit the buttons on the Control Strip, the rightmost, ever-present chunk of system controls. See page 237.

- **Modifier Keys.** This button lets you turn off, or remap, the functions of the Option, Caps Lock, Control, and ⌘ keys. It's for Unix programmers whose pinkies can't adjust to the Mac's modifier-key layout; for anyone using a PC keyboard on which the Option (Alt) and ⊞ (Windows) keys are in the "wrong" positions relative to each other; and for anyone who keeps hitting Caps Lock by accident during everyday typing.

- **Set Up Bluetooth Keyboard.** Yes, you're absolutely right: This button lets you set up a Bluetooth (wireless) keyboard. See page 339.

Text Tab

Here's where you set up the Mac's automatic abbreviation-expansion feature, described on page 243. This is also where you choose a language for spell-checking and autocorrect.

Shortcuts Tab

This pane lets you make up new keystrokes for just about any function on the Mac, like capturing a screenshot, operating the Dock, triggering one of the Services, or operating a menu in *any program* from the keyboard. You can come up with keyboard combinations that, for example, are easier to remember, harder to trigger by accident, or easier to hit with one hand.

Step-by-step instructions for using this pane appear on page 210.

Input Sources

These are the keyboard layouts for various languages. See page 249.

iCloud

This pane is, of course, the master setup page for Apple's free iCloud synchronization service. For complete details on setting up iCloud and using it, see Chapter 16.

Internet Accounts

For years, this System Preferences pane was called Mail, Contacts & Calendars. It's a single, handy, central place to tell macOS your user names and passwords for all kinds of internet services: Gmail, Yahoo, Exchange, Twitter, Vimeo, Flickr, LinkedIn, and so on.

To get started entering your account names and passwords, click one of the big-name logos (Gmail, Yahoo, whatever) or click the + button below the list. The Mac is smart enough to feed the account information here into the right programs (Mail, Calendar, Contacts, and the Share button described on page 263).

Keyboard

The changes you make on this panel are tiny but can have a cumulatively big impact on your daily typing routine. The options have been organized into five panes: Keyboard, Text, Shortcuts, Input Sources, and Dictation. If your Mac has a Touch Bar, its settings appear here, too.

Keyboard Tab

On this pane, you have these choices:

- **Key Repeat, Delay Until Repeat.** In macOS, holding down letter and number keys doesn't make them repeat, much to the disappointment of people who like to type, for example, "AAAAAARRRRRRGGGGHHH!" Instead, holding down a key produces a palette of alternative accented versions of that letter, like é, è, ê, ë, and so on.

 Only the punctuation keys still repeat, so you can still type ****** or ????? or !!!!!!!.

 There are sneaky ways to make your regular keys repeat, as they did in days gone by; see page 248. In the meantime, these two sliders govern the repeating behavior of the punctuation keys. On the right: a slider that determines how long you must hold down a key before it starts repeating (to prevent triggering repetitions accidentally). On the left: a slider that governs how fast each key spits out characters once the spitting has begun.

- **Adjust keyboard brightness in low light.** Recent Mac laptops' keys light up when you're working in the dark—a showy but useful feature. Here's the on/off switch. (Even if you've turned off the feature here, you can always turn on the keyboard backlighting by tapping the ☼ and ☼ keys.)

- **Turn keyboard backlight off after __ seconds of inactivity.** If you're watching a video, those glowing keys can be a distraction. You can use this control to specify

- **Click in the scroll bar to.** For details on "Jump to the next page" and "Jump to the spot that's clicked," see the box on page 29.

- **Default web browser.** When you click a link in, for example, an email message—or on Twitter or Facebook—which web browser should open? Safari? Chrome? Firefox? Here's where you decide.

- **Ask to keep changes when closing documents.** This option is for people who liked the old "Save changes before closing?" message that appears when you close a document—instead of the Auto Save feature (page 216). If you turn this item on, Auto Save will still be there in case your program crashes, for example. But when you close that document or its program, you'll be *asked* whether or not you want to preserve the changes you've made since your last manual Save. Auto Save programs like Pages and TextEdit, in other words, will work just like they used to—and the way all other programs do.

- **Close windows when quitting an app.** Here it is: the master on/off switch for the macOS feature responsible for reopening your last-used documents and windows each time you open an app.

 Usually, the auto-reopening feature saves you time and helps you resume your mental flow. But if you find it disturbing (or if you're worried about someone else discovering what you're up to), then turn on this checkbox.

- **Number of recent items.** Just how many of your recently opened documents, networked servers, and programs do you want the Mac to show using the Recent Items command in the menu? Pick a number from the pop-up menus.

- **Allow Handoff between this Mac and your iCloud devices.** You know that fantastic synergy you gain if you own both an iPhone and a Mac—the features described starting on page 312? This is the master on/off switch.

- **Use font smoothing when available.** The Mac's built-in text-smoothing (*antialiasing*) feature is supposed to produce smoother, more commercial-looking text anywhere it appears on your Mac: in word-processing documents, email messages, web pages, and so on (Figure 9-19).

Smoothing is turned off.

Smoothing is turned on.

Figure 9-19:
Experiment with Font Smoothing to see how you like the effect; it's fairly subtle. Furthermore, it has no effect until the next time you open the program in question. In the Finder, for example, you won't see a difference until you log out and in again. (These settings don't affect your printouts, only the onscreen display.)

- **Finder.** Here are the document-editing options known as Quick Actions; Apple starts you off with Rotate, Markup, Create PDF, and Trim. They appear on the preview pane (page 56), the Quick Look window (page 58), and the contextual shortcut menu (page 102) for a selected document. Most people see them only when examining a photo, PDF, audio, or movie file, as described on page 56.

- **Touch Bar.** In theory, software companies can add new buttons to the MacBook Pro's Touch Bar (page 233); they'll appear here if you have them.

Each of these extension categories works in the same way, as shown in Figure 9-18.

General

This panel is mostly about how things look on the screen: windows, menus, buttons, scroll bars, and fonts:

- **Appearance** and **Accent color** make a huge difference to the visual character of your Mac's screen elements. They're described on page 158.

- **Highlight color.** When you drag your cursor across text, its background changes color to indicate that you've selected it. *Which* color the background becomes is up to you; choose a shade from the pop-up menu. The Highlight color also affects such subtleties as the lines on the inside of a window as you drag an icon into it.

 If you choose Other, the Color Picker palette appears, from which you can choose any color your Mac is capable of displaying.

- **Sidebar icon size.** This pop-up menu controls the size of the icons in the Sidebar (page 17), as you'd expect. But you might not guess that it also controls the *type size* of those icons. And you'd *definitely* not guess that it simultaneously adjusts the size and type of the mailbox icons in the Mail program.

- **Automatically hide and show the menu bar.** This checkbox has nothing to do with colors, of course. But it can make a big difference on a small screen (this means you, laptoppers). When it's turned on, your menu bar disappears (including the menu-bar clock and other menulets). It reappears only as needed—when you move your cursor to the top of the screen.

- **Show scroll bars.** If you choose "Automatically based on mouse or trackpad," then whether the scroll bars appear or not depends on what you have plugged in.

 If you have a trackpad or a Magic Mouse, for example, Apple assumes you'll scroll by dragging your fingers—so you won't be needing the scroll bars at the edges of the windows. Therefore, the scroll bars appear only when you're actually scrolling (and then only to show you where you are in the window). But if you have no way of using touch gestures—for example, if you have a regular mouse or the Apple Mouse—then scroll bars are always visible, so you don't freak out.

 "When scrolling" means that the scroll bars pop into view during the actual scroll, when your mouse or fingers-on-trackpad are actually in motion. And Always, of course, means the scroll bars never disappear.

Extensions (Figure 9-18) can modify seven parts of the Mac:

- **Actions, Photos Editing.** You probably have only one item in each of these items, called Markup. That's Apple's own extension, and it lets you mark up attachments in Mail, TextEdit, Photos, and some other programs; page 472 describes these annotation tools. In theory, these extensions do *something* to whatever text or graphics you've selected.

- **Finder Extensions.** These features operate on files at the desktop level. The most common example is Dropbox; its extension adds Dropbox commands (like Share Dropbox Link) to the shortcut menu when you right-click or two-finger click an icon in your Dropbox folder, and adds a green checkmark icon to each file that's been synced with Dropbox online. (Google Drive and Microsoft's OneDrive work similarly.)

- **Share Menu.** You know the Share button that appears all across macOS (page 263)? It produces a list of different ways (Mail, Messages, Facebook) you can share whatever you've got selected (a map, a web page, a photo). Well, that list is extensible. Your programs can insert their own sharing options into it.

- **Today.** The Today pane of the Notification Center is described on page 382—but what's fascinating is that you can now install new information chunks (widgets, as Apple calls them) to that display. Everybody can choose from the starter widgets like Calculator, Calendar, and Weather—but other programs can install additional info-bits here.

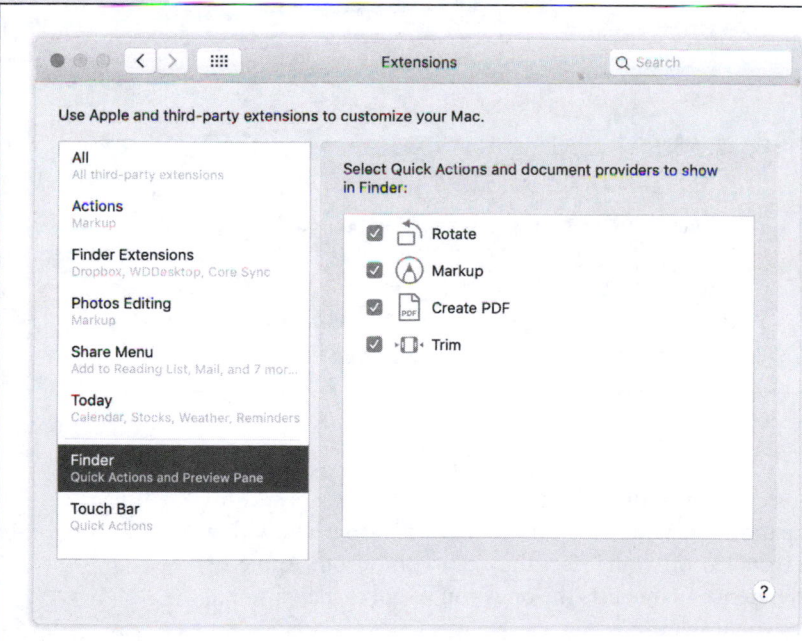

Figure 9-18:
Once you click the category name, you can operate on the individual extensions listed within. You can hide or show them by turning their checkboxes off or on, and you can change the order in which they appear in your menus by dragging them up or down.

Scheduled Startup and Shutdown

By clicking Schedule, you can set up the Mac to shut itself down and turn itself back on automatically (Figure 9-17, bottom).

If you work from 9 to 5, for example, you can set the office Mac to turn itself on at 8:45 a.m. and shut itself down at 5:30 p.m.—an arrangement that conserves electricity, saves money, and reduces pollution but doesn't inconvenience you in the least. In fact, you may come to forget that you've set up the Mac this way, since you'll never actually see it turn itself off.

Note: The Mac doesn't shut down automatically if you've left unsaved documents open onscreen. It will go to sleep, though.

Figure 9-17:
Top: Here's what Energy Saver looks like on a laptop. In the "Turn display off after" option, you can specify an independent sleep time for the screen.

Bottom: Here are the Schedule controls—the key to the Mac's self-scheduling abilities.

Extensions

One of macOS's unsung features is the ability to install *extensions*. These are add-on features—plug-ins—that expand what your Mac can do. Each is associated with a full-blown program you've installed on your Mac; they can come from Apple or anybody else. This System Preferences panel lists the ones you've got installed so far, and lets you turn off the ones you don't use.

the Battery tab, it says "Enable Power Nap while on battery power"; on the Power Adapter tab, it says "Enable Power Nap while plugged into a power adapter."

Most of those network functions take place even when the laptop is on battery power. But when it's plugged in, Power Nap also performs two more time-consuming functions: Time Machine backups and App Store software updates.

Of course, Power Nap means your laptop isn't quite as somnolent as it used to be while the lid was closed—it's using a little power.

- **Start up automatically after a power failure.** This checkbox appears only on desktop Macs. It's handy if you leave your Mac unattended and access it remotely, or if you use it as a network file server or web server. It ensures that, if your lonely Mac seizes up or crashes, it will start itself right back up again.

Tip: If you've also turned off (or left off) "Ask to keep changes when closing documents" and "Close windows when quitting an app" in System Preferences→General, then your Mac will both restart *and* restore everything you were doing. You may, in fact, never even realize that a crash or freeze occurred while you were away! (The telltale sign: Any web pages you had logged into, like banking websites, will have logged you out.)

- **Show battery status in menu bar.** This on/off switch (laptops only) controls the battery menulet described in the box below.

GEM IN THE ROUGH

Mysteries of the Battery Menulet

If you've got a laptop, don't miss the checkbox in Energy Saver called "Show battery status in the menu bar." It puts a handy status indicator (⬚) in the menu bar.

Without clicking the menulet, all you see is an icon that represents the battery charge. If you turn on Show Percentage from the menulet's actual menu, then the menulet can also show how much charge remains, in percentage form.

Here's what the menulet icon may show:

Lightning bolt in the battery. The laptop is plugged in and the battery is charging or charged.

Superimposed X. The laptop is plugged in, but the battery isn't in right, is missing, or isn't getting a charge.

Emptying black battery. The laptop is on battery power and has at least 25 percent power left. (The width of the bar reveals how much charge remains.)

Emptying red battery. The laptop is running off of battery power but has less than 25 percent charge remaining.

A nearly invisible red bar means you have less than nine minutes left. Save those documents, buddy.

If you click the menulet, you see an estimate of actual time remaining on your battery charge, in hours:minutes form. (If the battery is *charging*, then you see how much time remains until the battery is fully recharged, like this: "0:24 Until Full.") Either way, the readout is counting down (or up) to that joyous moment.

The menu also offers a terrific list: Using Significant Energy. When your battery is running low, it's a great way to see which apps are guzzling down your juice.

Finally, if you Option-click the menulet, you get a health report for your battery. It might say, for example, "Condition: Normal." When the battery needs your attention—when it says "Service Battery," "Replace Soon," "Replace Now," or "Check Battery"—you don't have to press Option. You'll see that message every time you open the menulet.

Note: The wording of this option reflects how your Mac can connect to a network. If it can connect either over an Ethernet cable or a wireless hotspot, it says "Wake for network access." If it's not a wireless Mac, you'll see "Wake for Ethernet network access." If it's a MacBook without an Ethernet adapter, it says "Wake for Wi-Fi network access." On a laptop, the "wake" feature is available only when the machine's lid is left open and you're plugged into a power outlet.

- **Enable Power Nap.** Power Nap is an ingenious and extremely useful feature for laptops—specifically, flash-storage laptop models introduced in 2012 or later. (On older laptops, it doesn't appear at all.)

 Anyway, when you turn on Enable Power Nap, the Mac keeps updating internet data even while it's closed and asleep. About once every hour, it wakes itself—without activating any fans or lights—long enough to check for mail, calendar updates, Photo Stream updates, software updates, and so on. When you wake the laptop later, you'll be delighted to find it's completely up to date, with new email waiting and all your iCloud programs (Notes, Messages, Reminders, and so on) updated. And the lid was closed the whole time!

 Power Nap comes set to work only when your laptop is plugged into a power outlet, but you can make it work on battery power, too (Apple says the battery hit is very slight). You'll find separate on/off switches on each of the Energy Saver tabs. On

GEM IN THE ROUGH

Auto-Wake for Network Access

You should put your Mac to sleep as much as possible; you'll save power, money, and pollution. Unfortunately, a sleeping Mac is useless on your network. For example, you can't access files on it from another machine.

But Wake on Demand gives you the best of both worlds. It keeps a sleeping Mac available on the network, so you can wake it up remotely when you need it.

How can you do that? Is the Mac sleeping or isn't it?

Yes, it's sleeping. But before it dozes off, it hands over its list of available network services—file sharing, screen sharing, printer sharing, and so on—to your Apple wireless base station. The base station becomes your sleeping Mac's agent, continuing to broadcast the available features of the sleeping Mac (via Apple's Bonjour networking technology) to the rest of the network.

To make this work, you need an AirPort wireless base station or a Time Capsule, running the latest Apple firmware. If

you're using a WPA or WPA2 password on your base station or Time Capsule, it can't be in "bridge mode" (you'd know if you'd turned that on). Only Macs made since late 2008 can be awakened over a wireless network (all Macs can be awakened over an Ethernet wired network). To find out if yours is eligible, open System Information (page 512); under the Network heading, click Wi-Fi and look to see if Wake on Wireless is listed as Supported.

(Longtime Mac nuts may observe that "Wake for network access" has been available in Energy Saver for years. That older method, however, worked only on wired networks, not wireless ones.)

Once you've turned on Wake on Demand, by the way, you might hear brief sounds from the DVD drive, hard drive, or fans, even when the Mac is asleep. That's normal; it means the Mac is checking in with the Bonjour sleep switchboard.

That's right: Even your Mac sometimes stirs in its sleep.

and pollution. On a laptop, it extends the length of the battery charge by controlling the activity of the hard drive and screen.

Best of all, this pane offers the option to have your computer turn off each night automatically—and turn on again at a specified time in anticipation of your arrival at the desk (Figure 9-17).

Sleep Sliders

The Energy Saver controls are different on a laptop Mac and a desktop Mac. In fact, they differ depending on which laptop or desktop model you have.

- **Turn off display after (or Display sleep).** This slider controls when the screen goes black to save power.

- **Computer sleep.** This slider exists only on pre-2013 Macs. (The processors in newer models sleep automatically.) It controls when the *Mac* will automatically go to sleep—anywhere from one minute after your last activity to Never. (Activity can be mouse movement, keyboard action, or internet data transfer; Energy Saver won't put your Mac to sleep in the middle of a download.)

At that time, the screen goes dark, the hard drive stops spinning, and your processor chip slows to a crawl. Your Mac is now in *sleep* mode, using only a fraction of its usual electricity consumption. To wake it up when you return to your desk, press any key. Everything you were working on, including open programs and documents, is still onscreen, exactly as it was.

Checkbox Options

Below the sliders, you see a selection of additional power-related options. On a laptop, the two tabs at the top of the dialog box let you create different settings for the two states of life for a laptop: when it's plugged in (Power Adapter) and when it's running on battery power (Battery). That's important, because on a laptop, every drop of battery power counts. Here's what you may see:

- **Put hard disks to sleep when possible.** This saves even more juice—and noise—by letting your drives stop spinning when not in use. This option appears on both the Battery and Power Adapter tabs, so you can control it independently for each power source.

- **Slightly dim the display while on battery power.** You see this checkbox only on the Battery tab for a laptop. It means "Don't use full brightness, so I can save power."

Tip: And when your laptop is plugged in, the sudden dimming of the screen becomes a handy signal that you've lost power. Maybe your power cord needs replugging, the power strip went out, or there's a massive blackout in your half of the country.

- **Wake for Wi-Fi network access.** This option (on the Power Adapter tab) lets you access a sleeping Mac from across the network. How is that possible? See the box on the facing page.

Tip: If the Apple TV is the third generation or later, the two machines don't even have to be on the same wireless network. This feature, called peer-to-peer AirPlay, is terrific. It makes life so much simpler when you want to give a presentation at some company or school whose Wi-Fi network is complicated and secure; now your Mac doesn't have to be on it at all. (It does, however, have to have Bluetooth turned on.)

Using AirPlay is so simple, it would confuse only an AirHead. The ⌹ menulet (Figure 9-16) offers controls like these:

- **AirPlay to: Apple TV.** Here's how you start projecting to your TV. (It says Turn AirPlay Off once you're connected.)

- **Mirror Built-in Retina Display, Mirror Apple TV, Use As Separate Display.** Your Mac and TV are two screens with two different resolutions (numbers of pixels).

Figure 9-16:
Make sure the Apple TV is on the same Wi-Fi network as your Mac. At that point, the ⌹ menulet appears.

Choose the name of your Apple TV, and presto: Whatever is on your Mac simultaneously plays on your big screen, both stereo audio and high-def video.

Top: Use the ⌹ to control whether the TV displays a mirror image of your Mac or an extension of it.

Bottom: Whenever two monitors are going, the Arrangement tab lets you specify which one gets the menu bar and where the monitors are relative to each other.

If you're confused about which screen is which, click and hold one of the miniatures; a matching red border appears on the corresponding actual monitor.

Arrangement Tab (Multiple Monitors)

From the dawn of the color-monitor era, Macs have had a terrific feature: the ability to exploit multiple monitors all plugged into the computer at the same time. Sometimes you want the Mac to project the same thing on both screens (*mirror mode*); that's useful in a classroom when the "external monitor" is a projector. Other times, you want to make one monitor act as an *extension* of the other. For example, you might have your Photoshop image window on your big monitor but keep all the Photoshop controls and tool palettes on a smaller screen. Your cursor passes from one screen to the other as it crosses the boundary.

To connect a second monitor or projector, you have a couple of options.

The wired way

Connect the appropriate cable or adapter to your Mac's video-output jack. This jack may be any of several types. Older Mac laptops and iMacs use a weird, tiny connector called a *Mini DisplayPort*; you'll need an adapter cord to connect it to the VGA, DVI, or HDMI input that most monitors or projectors expect.

More recent Macs also have something called Thunderbolt jacks. You can connect them to a few Thunderbolt-equipped external monitors, notably Apple's.

Current MacBook Pro laptops use USB-C jacks, which Apple calls Thunderbolt 3; you'll need an adapter for these jacks, too, to connect to monitors and projectors.

Finally, there's the black, cylindrical Mac Pro. It also has an HDMI jack, which is the easiest of all to connect to screens and projectors.

To set this up, hook up the monitor or projector. Your Mac should discover (and start projecting to) the external screen automatically; if it doesn't, close and then reopen the lid (if you're using a laptop), or choose Detect Displays from the Displays *menulet*.

The wireless way

If you'd shown this feature to the masses in 2005 or so, they'd have fallen down and worshiped it as a god. With one click, you can send whatever is on your Mac's screen to your TV's screen, in high-def. No wires. You can make the TV either a mirror of your Mac's screen or an extension of it. You can present photo slideshows on the TV from your laptop. Or play movies you've found online. Or give presentations from PowerPoint or Keynote. Or present software lessons to a class.

This trick requires both a Mac made since mid-2011 and an Apple TV. That's a tiny black box that connects to a high-def TV and lets you watch videos from services like YouTube, Netflix, MLB.TV, NBA, NHL, and Vimeo. It can also play videos, music, and photos from Macs or PCs on the network.

But with AirPlay, the Apple TV (and therefore your TV) can now play anything you can see on your Mac. You can play your iTunes music while watching those cool screen-savery visualizers on your HDTV. And you can carry your Apple TV around with you to corporate boardrooms to project your pitches, rather than a $1,500 projector.

The specific controls depend on the kind of monitor you're using, but here are the ones you'll most likely see.

Display Tab

This tab is the main headquarters for your screen controls. It governs these settings:

- **Resolution.** All Mac screens today can make the screen picture larger or smaller, thus accommodating different kinds of work. You perform this magnification or reduction by switching among different *resolutions* (measurements of the number of dots that compose the screen).

 When you use a low-resolution setting, such as 800×600, the dots of your screen image get larger, enlarging (zooming in on) the picture—but showing a smaller slice of the page. Use this setting when playing a small web movie, for example, so that it fills more of the screen. (Lower resolutions usually look blurry on flat-panel screens, though.) At higher resolutions, such as 1280×800, the screen dots get smaller, making your windows and icons smaller, but showing more overall area. You could use this kind of setting when working on two-page spreads in your page-layout program, for example.

 If you select "Default for display," then the Mac uses the highest resolution possible for your screen—the one that makes it look sharpest. If you click Scaled, you see a choice of other resolution settings for your built-in monitor—not by number ("1280×800" or whatever), but as little representative thumbnails showing the effect you're about to have on text size.

Tip: If you've connected an external monitor or projector, you can *Option-click* the Scaled button to see a scrolling list of additional, less-common display resolutions for that monitor. That's an important trick to remember when you're trying to make some external projector work right.

- **Brightness.** This slider lets you make the screen look good in the prevailing lighting conditions. Of course, most Apple keyboards have brightness-adjustment *keys,* so this software control is included just for the sake of completeness.

- **Automatically adjust brightness.** Your laptop's light sensor dims the screen automatically in dark rooms—*if* this checkbox is turned on.

- **True Tone.** This on/off switch, new in Mojave, goes beyond the old Auto-Brightness setting. Now it's Auto-Brightness and Auto-*Tint.* That is, the screen colors actually shift, based on the current lighting color of the room you're in. The idea is to make colors on the screen seem consistent from one lighting condition to another.

 If you find the result off-putting, you can always turn True Tone off. Now the tint never shifts.

- **AirPlay Display.** Read on for details on AirPlay.

- **Show mirroring options in menu bar when available.** Turn on this box if you'd like the Displays menulet to appear automatically whenever you've connected a second monitor or a projector. (Mirroring is described on the following pages.)

to read more, or click Options to specify which dictionary you want: the standard New Oxford American or the Japanese dictionary.

No matter which screen-saver mode you choose, you can also turn on either of these two options:

- **Show with clock.** This option superimposes the current time on whatever screen saver you've selected. You'd be surprised at how handy it can be to use your Mac as a giant digital clock when you're getting coffee across the room.

- **Use random screen saver.** The Mac chooses a different screen saver each time. Surrender to the power of chance!

Activating the screen saver

You can control when your screen saver takes over your monitor in a couple of ways:

- **After a period of inactivity.** Using the "Start after" pop-up menu, you can set the time that has to pass without keyboard or mouse activity before the screen saver starts. The duration can be as short as one minute or as long as one hour, or you can choose Never to prevent the screen saver from ever turning on by itself.

- **When you park your cursor in the corner of the screen.** If you click the Hot Corners button, you can turn each corner of your monitor into a *hot corner* (Figure 9-15).

If you work in a business, or in a nosy family, it might be worth noting that you can set things up so that your password is required to exit the screen saver. Visit System Preferences→Security & Privacy, and turn on "Require password immediately after sleep or screen saver begins."

Figure 9-15:
This "sheet" lets you set certain corners of your screen as instant-activation spots, or never-come-on spots. Sliding the mouse to the Start Screen Saver corner, for example, turns on your screen saver.

Displays

This is the center of operations for all your monitor settings. Here you set your monitor's resolution, calibrate color balance and brightness, and turn AirPlay on and off—a cool feature that duplicates whatever is on your Mac screen on a TV set. Wirelessly.

Tip: You can open this panel with a quick keystroke from any program on the Mac. Just press Option as you tap one of the screen-brightness keys (☀) on the top row of your keyboard.

When you click a module's name in the Screen Saver list, you see a mini version of it playing back in the preview screen. Click the preview to give the module a dry run on your full screen. When you've had enough of the preview, just move the mouse or press any key.

The screen-saver modules offer two categories of screen savers.

Slideshows

At the top of the scrolling list of icons at left, Apple has installed 12 "slideshows"— attractive animations that gracefully fling photos around in different show-offy ways—that began life in programs like Photos.

At right, use the Source pop-up menu to specify which photos you want included in the slideshow. You can use any of the photo sets Apple provides (Flowers, Landscapes, Colors, Sierras). You can also select Choose Folder to specify some photos of your own from a folder on your Mac, Recent Photos Events to use some photos you've recently imported, or Photo Library to see a list of your Photos albums. Each creates an amazingly dramatic, almost cinematic experience, worthy of setting up to "play" during dinner parties like the lava lamps of the '70s.

"Shuffle slide order," of course, scrambles the photo sequence so that it's different every time. Wouldn't want you to get bored staring at your screen, now.

Tip: Once a slideshow screen saver kicks in, you can control it as you would a real slideshow. Press the ◄ and ► keys to visit previous or subsequent photos. That's great for those times when someone passing your Mac says, "Hey, what was that?"

Nonphotographic displays

Beneath the list of slideshows, you'll find the icons for six more-traditional, nonphoto-graphic slideshow displays (Flurry, Arabesque, and so on). Each has options worth exploring. For example, Flurry offers flaming, colorful, undulating arms of fire, which resemble a cross between an octopus and somebody arc welding in the dark. If you click Screen Saver Options, you can control how many streams of fire appear at once, the thickness of the arms, the speed of movement, and the colors.

Similarly, Word of the Day offers a parade of interesting words drawn from the Dictionary program. You're invited to tap the D key to open the dictionary to that entry

GEM IN THE ROUGH

Secrets of the Screen-Saver Modules

The canned screen-saver modules are stored in your Macintosh HD→Library→Screen Savers→Default Collections folder. Each folder within that folder contains individual images for the slideshow-ish modules (the outer-space photos, for example).

Why bother looking in there?

Because some of these spectacular photos make really good desktop pictures. You're free to copy them and use them for that purpose.

Fortunately, macOS offers a number of solutions to this problem. Using the pop-up menu just to the right of the desktop preview well, you can choose any of these options:

- **Fill Screen.** Enlarges or reduces the image so it fills every inch of the desktop. Parts may get chopped off, but this option never distorts the picture.

- **Fit to Screen.** Your photo appears as large as possible without distortion *or* cropping. If the photo doesn't precisely match the proportions of your screen, you get "letterbox bars" on the sides or at top and bottom. Apple provides a color-swatch button next to the pop-up menu shown in Figure 9-14. When you click it, the Color Picker appears so you can specify a color for those letterbox bars.

- **Stretch to Fill Screen.** Makes your picture fit the screen exactly, come hell or high water. Larger pictures are squished vertically or horizontally as necessary, and small pictures are drastically blown up *and* squished, usually with grisly results.

- **Center.** Centers the photo neatly on the screen. The edges may be chopped off. If the picture is smaller than the screen, then it sits smack in the center of the monitor at actual size, leaving a swath of empty space all the way around. (Use the swatch button just to the right of the pop-up menu to specify a color for that background.)

- **Tile.** This option makes your picture repeat over and over until the multiple images fill the entire monitor. (If your picture is larger than the screen, no such tiling takes place. You see only the top-center chunk of the image.)

Auto picture changing

The novelty of any desktop picture, no matter how interesting, is likely to fade after several months of all-day viewing. That's why the randomizing function is so delightful.

Turn on "Change picture" at the bottom of the dialog box (Figure 9-14, bottom). From the pop-up menu, specify when you want your background picture to change: "every day," "every 15 minutes," or, if you're *really* having trouble staying awake at your Mac, "every 5 seconds." (The option called "when waking from sleep" refers to the *Mac* waking from sleep, not you.)

Finally, turn on "Random order," if you like. If you leave it off, then your desktop pictures change in alphabetical order by file name.

Now, at the interval you specified, your desktop picture changes automatically, smoothly cross-fading between the pictures like a slideshow. You may never want to open a window, because you'll hate to block your view.

Screen Saver

On the Screen Saver panel, you can create your own screen-saver slideshows—an absolute must if you have a huge screen and a cool Manhattan loft apartment.

Note: Of course, a screen saver doesn't really save your screen. Flat-panel screens, the only kind Apple sells, are incapable of "burning in" a stationary image of the sort that originally inspired the creation of screen savers years ago. No, these screen savers serve two unrelated functions. First, they mask what's on your screen from passersby whenever you leave your desk. Second, they're kind of fun.

Using your own pictures

Of course, you may feel that decorating your Mac desktop is much more fun if you use one of your *own* pictures. You can use almost any graphics file: JPEG, GIF, TIFF, Photoshop, and even PDF. (Guess you could use the PDF option to teach yourself your camera's user guide by staring at your desktop every morning.)

That's why icons for your own Pictures folder and Photos albums also appear here, along with a + button that lets you choose *any* folder of pictures. When you click one of these icons, you see thumbnail versions of its contents in the main screen to its right. Just click the thumbnail of any picture to apply it immediately to the desktop. (There's no need to remove the previously installed picture first.)

Tip: If there's a certain picture you like, but it's not in any of the listed sources, you can drag its image file onto the *well* (the miniature desktop displayed in the Desktop panel). A thumbnail instantly appears in the well, and a moment later the picture is plastered across your monitor.

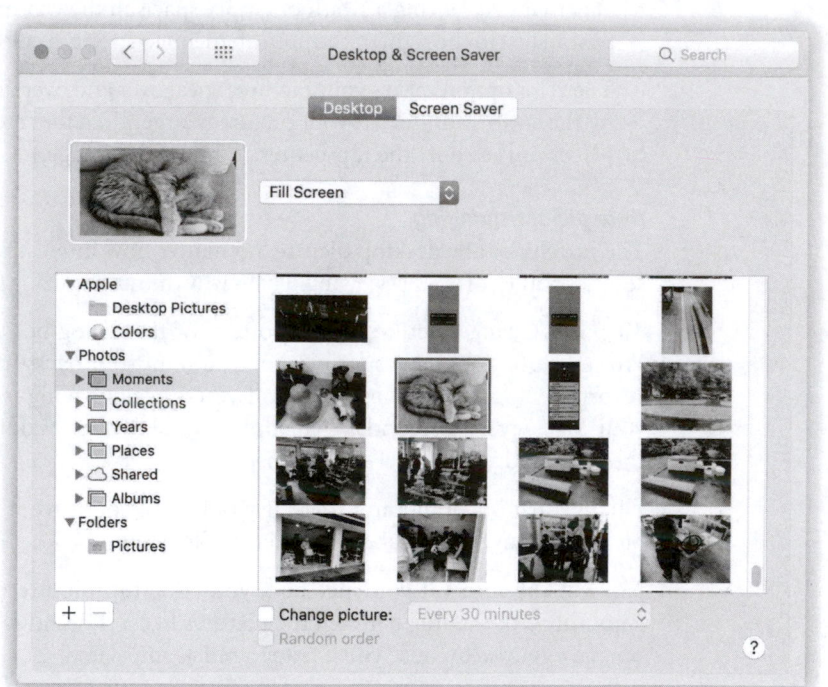

Figure 9-14:
Using the list of picture sources at left, you can preview an entire folder of your own images before installing one as your new desktop picture. Use the + button to select a folder of assorted graphics—or, if you're a Photos veteran, click a Photos album name, as shown here. Clicking one of the thumbnails installs the corresponding picture on the desktop.

Making the picture fit

Unless you've gone to the trouble of editing your chosen photo so that it matches the precise dimensions of your screen (1920 × 1080 pixels, for example), it probably isn't exactly the right size.

Tip: At the bottom of the dialog box, you'll find a feature called "Announce the time." At the intervals you specify, the Mac can speak, out loud, the current time: "It's 10 o'clock." If you tend to get so immersed in "working" that you lose track of time, macOS just removed your last excuse.

The menu-bar clock can show not just the time and day of the week, but also today's *date*. Turn on the "Show the day of the week" and "Show date" checkboxes if you want to see, for example, "Wed May 8 7:32 PM" on your menu bar.

If you decide you don't need all that information—if your menu bar is crowded enough as it is—you can always look up today's day and date just by *clicking* the time on your menu bar. A menu drops down revealing the complete date. The menu also lets you switch between digital and analog clock types and provides a shortcut to the Date & Time Preferences pane.

Tip: This one's for Unix geeks only. Use *sudo*, type *date mmddhhmmyyyy.ss*, and press Return. (Of course, replace that code with the actual date and time you want, such as *040517552019*.00 for April 5, 2019, 5:55 p.m.) You might find this method faster than the System Preferences route.

Desktop & Screen Saver

This panel offers two ways to show off macOS's glamorous graphics features: *desktop pictures* and *screen savers*.

Desktop Pictures

MacOS comes with a mountain of desktop pictures, ranging from plain solid colors to *National Geographic*–style nature photos. To install a new background first choose one of the image categories in the list at the left side of the window, as shown in Figure 9-14.

Your choices include Desktop Pictures (muted, soft-focus swishes and swirls and lovely nature shots) and Solid Colors (simple grays, blues, and greens).

Tip: You can choose *any* solid color—not just one of the preselected shades Apple gives you. Click Custom Color and go nuts.

In the Desktop Pictures category, don't miss the two new Dynamic Desktop pictures—images whose lighting changes through the day, according to the way the sun would hit it in the real world. One shows a Mojave Desert scene. The other is a much less busy color gradient that suggests the sky: a lighter blue during the day, fading to a deep midnight blue at night. It's rather stunning.

Tip: The Mojave Desert photo doesn't have to be dynamic. When you select it, a new pop-up menu appears, offering you a choice of Dynamic (changes through the day), Light (Still), and Dark (Still). The latter two are just handsome still photos whose lighting doesn't change.

Time Zone Tab

You'd be surprised how important it is to set the time zone for your Mac. If you don't do so, the email and documents you send out—and the Mac's conception of what documents are older and newer—could be hopelessly skewed.

MacOS can set its own time zone *automatically* by consulting the locations of nearby Wi-Fi hotspots. That's a useful feature if you're a laptop warrior who travels a lot.

If you turn on "Set time zone automatically using current location" (Figure 9-13), the Mac will think for a moment. Then, if the Wi-Fi gods are smiling, it will, before your eyes, drop a pin onto the world map to represent your location—and set the time zone automatically. (The world map dims to show that you can no longer set your location manually.)

Often, though, you'll be told that the Mac is "Unable to determine current location at this time." In that case, specify your location manually, as shown in Figure 9-13.

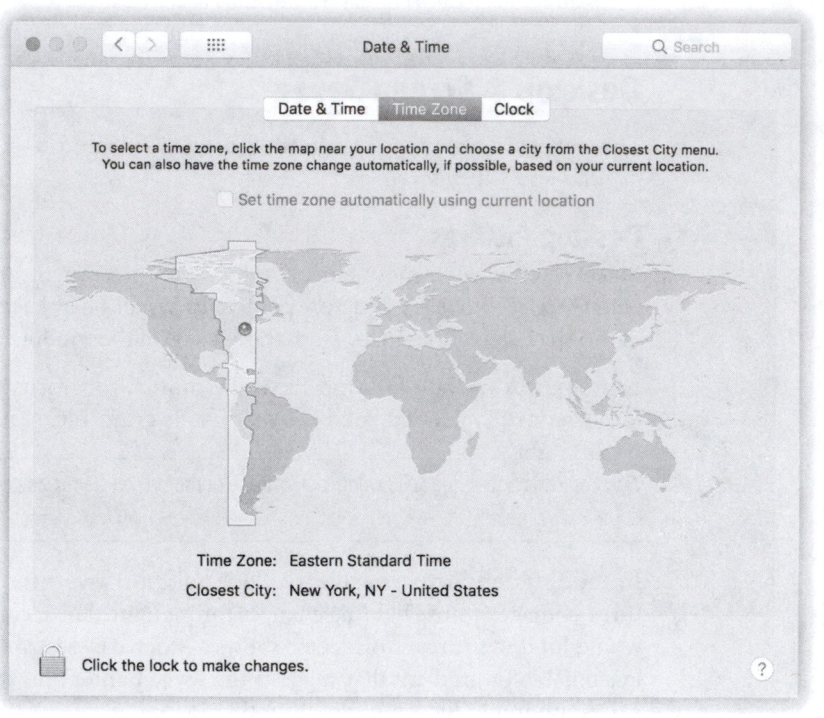

Figure 9-13:
To set your time zone the quick and dirty way, click a section of the map to indicate your general region of the world. To teach the Mac more precisely where you are in that time zone, use the Closest City pop-up menu. (Or, instead of using the pop-up menu with the mouse, you can also highlight the text in the Closest City box. Then start typing your city name until the Mac gets it.)

Clock Tab

In the Clock pane, you can turn the menu-bar clock on or off. You can choose between two clock styles: digital (3:53 p.m.) or analog (a round clock face). You also get several options for the digital clock display: whether to show seconds, designations for a.m. and p.m., the day of the week, a blinking colon, and a 24-hour clock.

CDs & DVDs

This pane appears only if your Mac does, in fact, have a DVD drive. It lets you tell the Mac what it should do when it detects that you've inserted a CD or DVD. For example, when you insert a music CD, you probably want iTunes to open automatically so you can listen to the songs or convert them to MP3 or AAC files on your hard drive.

Date & Time

Your Mac's conception of what time it is can be very important. Every file you create, save, or even open is stamped with this time, and every email you send or receive is marked with it. As you might expect, setting your Mac's clock is what the Date & Time pane is all about.

Date & Time Tab

Click the Date & Time tab. If "Set date and time automatically" is turned on, then your Mac sets its own clock by consulting a highly accurate online scientific clock. (There's no need to worry about daylight savings time, either; the time servers take that into account.)

Note: You have to authenticate yourself before making any Date & Time adjustments. Click the little 🔒 and enter your administrator's account password.

If you're not online and have no prospect of getting there, you can also set the date and time manually. To change the month, day, or year, click the digit that needs changing and then either (a) type a new number, (b) press the ▲ or ▼ keys on the keyboard, or (c) click the little arrow buttons. Press the Tab key to highlight the next number. (You can also specify the day of the month by clicking a date on the minicalendar.)

To set the time of day, use the same technique—or, for more geeky fun, you can set the time by dragging the hour, minute, or second hands on the analog clock.

Finally, click Save. (If you get carried away with dragging the clock hands around and lose track of the *real* time, click the Revert button to restore the panel settings.)

Tip: If you prefer seeing 24-hour "military time" notation on your menu bar (that is, *17:30* instead of *5:30 p.m.*)—then click the Clock tab and turn on "Use a 24-hour clock."

Note, however, that this affects only the menu-bar clock. If you'd like to reformat the menu-bar clock *and* all other dates and times (like the ones that show when your files were modified in list views), click the Open Language & Region button at the bottom of the Date & Time pane. Once there, you'll see an Advanced button; its Times tab leads you to a whole new world of time-format customization. You can drag elements of the current time (Hour, Minute, Second, Millisecond, and so on) into any order, and separate them with any desired punctuation. In the Dates tab, you can also set up your date displays in (for example) the European format, expressing April 13 as 13/4 instead of 4/13.

When it's all over, the new gadget is listed in the panel, in the list of Bluetooth stuff that you've previously introduced to this Mac. (You can click it and then click ⊗ to get rid of the pairing, when that day comes.)

A few footnotes:

- **If you're pairing a mobile phone** or something else that has a keypad or a keyboard, the Mac may display a large, multiple-digit *passcode*. It's like a password, except that you'll have to input it only this once, to confirm that *you* are the true owner of both the Mac and the gadget. (If it weren't for this passcode business, some guy next to you at the airport could enjoy free laptop internet access through the cellphone in *your* pocket.)

 At this point, the phone, computer, or tablet displays a message to the effect that you have 30 seconds to type that passcode. Do it. When the gadget asks if you want to pair with the Mac and connect to it, say yes. (If you're pairing one Mac with another, just click Continue on both machines; you *see* the same passcode on both but don't have to type it.)

- **If you intend to send a file to another Mac,** set up that other machine by visiting System Preferences→Sharing; turn on Bluetooth Sharing.

Advanced Options

If you click Advanced, you arrive at a few more tweaky Bluetoothisms:

- **Open Bluetooth Setup Assistant at startup if no keyboard is detected.** Here's where you can tell the Bluetooth Setup Assistant to open up automatically when the Mac thinks no keyboard is attached (because it assumes you have a wireless Bluetooth keyboard that has yet to be set up).

- **Open Bluetooth Setup Assistant at startup if no mouse or trackpad is detected.** Same deal, this time suggesting that the assistant will open if the Mac can't find a trackpad or mouse. Once again, the Mac is assuming you'll be wanting to connect a *wireless* one.

- **Allow Bluetooth devices to wake this computer.** Turn this on if you want to be able to wake a sleeping Mac when you press a key, just like a wired keyboard does.

The Bluetooth Menulet

The Bluetooth menulet (Figure 9-12, top) gives you an easy way to turn Bluetooth on and off, to connect to Bluetooth gadgets, to disconnect from them, and to send files to them (page 260). If you don't see this menulet, then turn on "Show Bluetooth in menu bar" (Figure 9-12, bottom).

Tip: If you Option-click the Bluetooth menulet (✳), you get a couple of lines of secret Bluetooth details. The menu reveals the name of your Mac, as it will appear to other Bluetooth wireless gadgets, and the version of Bluetooth you're running.

Pairing

Now, you wouldn't want the guy in the next cubicle to be able to operate *your* Mac using *his* Bluetooth keyboard. So the first step in any Bluetooth relationship is *pairing,* or formally introducing the two gadgets that will be communicating. Figure 9-12 shows how that goes.

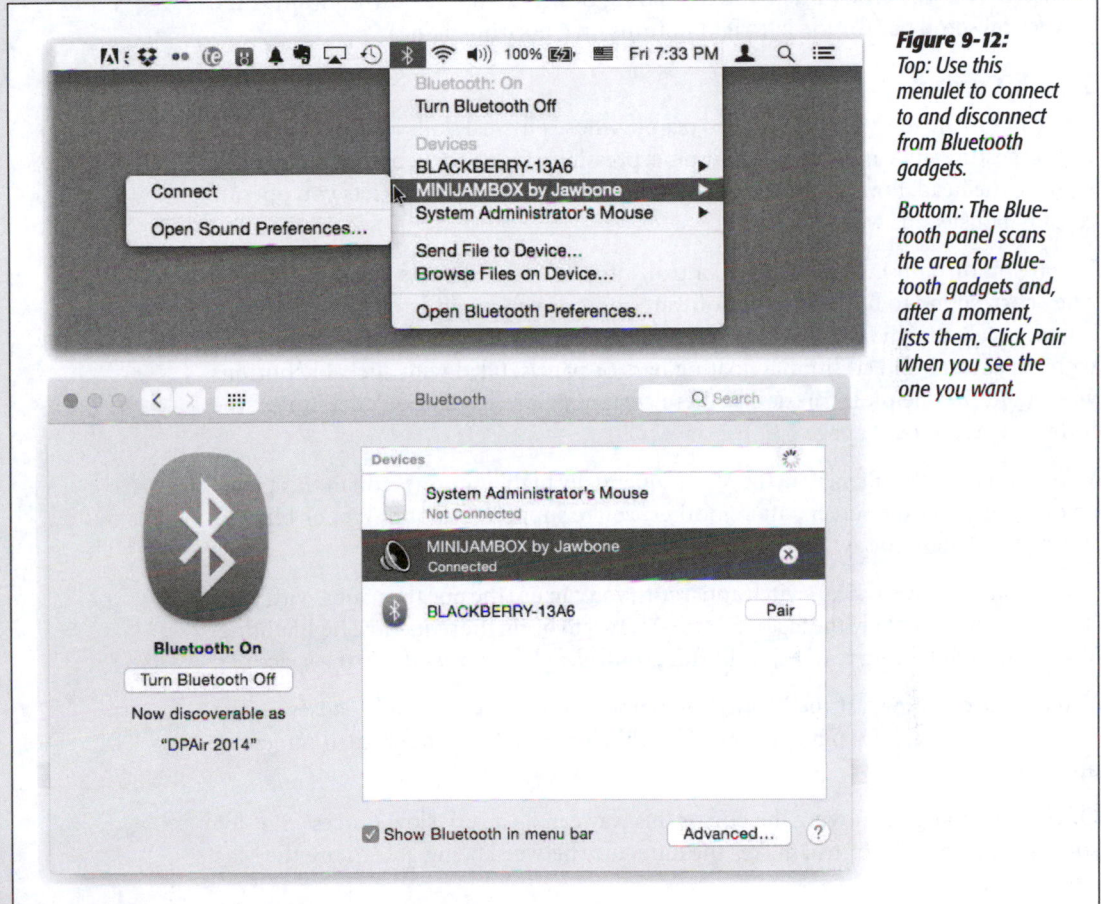

Figure 9-12:
Top: Use this menulet to connect to and disconnect from Bluetooth gadgets.

Bottom: The Bluetooth panel scans the area for Bluetooth gadgets and, after a moment, lists them. Click Pair when you see the one you want.

To do that, open System Preferences→Bluetooth. Make sure Bluetooth is On. (The only reason to turn it off is to save laptop battery power.)

You don't have to turn on a Discoverable switch to make the Mac "visible" to other Bluetooth gadgets in range; whenever the Bluetooth pane of System Preferences is open, it's discoverable.

In fact, you don't have to click some Add New Device button, either. When the Bluetooth pane is open, the Mac automatically starts searching for nearby Bluetooth gadgets within range (see Figure 9-12, bottom)—nearby headsets, laptops, cellphones, and so on. Usually, it finds the one you're trying to pair. Just click it, and then click Pair.

"with Drag Lock" is turned on, then the "mouse button" remains down until you repeat the double-tap business. In "without Drag Lock" mode, *one* tap ends the dragging. And "three-finger dragging," of course, means you have to swipe with three fingers to do the moving.)

- **Mouse Options.** This one should really be called *scroll bar* options. It affects how fast a window scrolls when you're holding down the up or down buttons on a vertical scroll bar (or the left/right buttons on a horizontal one).

Switch Control

Apple has made the Mac accessible to people whose physical skills are limited to very simple gestures, like puffing on an air pipe, pressing a foot switch, blinking an eye, or turning the head, for example. A hardware accessory called a *switch* lets you operate certain gadgets this way.

When you turn on Enable Switch Control, a row of icons appears on a floating bar. They correspond to hardware and software controls you might have trouble operating physically: Keyboard, Pointer, Dock, and so on. (Among them: a Custom item, which lets you build additional floating bars or panels, filled with clickable buttons you might find helpful. You design these custom panels using the Panel Editor, the little app described on page 336.)

When you trigger your switch, the Mac sequentially highlights one icon in this panel, or one object on the screen, after another; you're supposed to puff, tap, or blink at the right moment to say, "Yes, *this* one."

If you don't have a physical switch apparatus, you can use the one that came with your keyboard: the space bar (the factory setting). Tap it to begin the sequential highlighting. When the highlighting reaches the button, control, or key you want, tap the space bar.

You can specify how fast the highlighting proceeds, whether or not it pauses on the screen's first item, how many times the highlighting cycles through each screenful, and so on.

Of course, typing or moving the cursor this way can be a very slow process. But for some people, switch control makes the difference between being able to use the Mac slowly or not at all.

For details on adding your own switch and customizing how it works, read *support. apple.com/kb/PH25778?viewlocale=en_US&locale=en_US*.

Bluetooth

Bluetooth is a short-range, low-power, wireless *cable-elimination* technology. It's designed to connect gadgets in pairings that make sense, like cellphone+earpiece, Mac+wireless keyboard, phone+portable speaker, or Mac+cellphone. Bluetooth is also the key to the Continuity features described in Chapter 8; it's the wireless link between your Mac and your iPhone.

Tip: You may prefer to turn one of your custom panels *into* the main keyboard. In the Panel Editor, choose Show→As Home Panel.

Mouse & Trackpad

On this pane, several motley options await:

- **Mouse Keys** is designed to help people who can't use the mouse—or who want more precision when they do. It lets you click, drag, and otherwise manipulate the cursor by pressing the keys on your numeric keypad. (It's not very useful on keyboards that don't *have* separate numeric keypads, like laptops.)

 When Mouse Keys is turned on, the 5 key acts as the clicker—hold it down for a moment to "click the mouse," do that twice to double-click, and so on. Hold down the 0 key to lock down the mouse button, and the period key to unlock it. (The amount of time you have to hold them down depends on how you've set the Initial Delay slider.)

 Move the cursor around the screen by pressing the eight keys that surround the 5 key. (For example, hold down the 9 key to move the cursor diagonally up and to the right.) If you hold one of these keys down continuously, the cursor, after a pause, begins to move smoothly in that direction—according to the way you've adjusted the sliders called Initial Delay and Maximum Speed.

Tip: The checkbox, in Options, called "Press the Option key five times to toggle Mouse Keys" saves you the trouble of opening System Preferences.

- **Double-click speed.** This setting specifies how much time you have to complete a double-click. If you click too slowly—beyond the time you've allotted yourself with this slider—the Mac "hears" two *single* clicks instead.

- **Spring-loading delay.** This option has to do with *spring-loaded folders,* the feature described on page 87. This slider controls how long a folder waits before springing open (when your cursor, in mid-drag, is poised on top of it).

- **Ignore built-in trackpad when mouse or wireless trackpad is present.** If you've plugged in a mouse or external trackpad, then your laptop's built-in trackpad really isn't doing you much good. And it could even mess you up (for example, if your thumb hits it while you're typing). If this option is turned on, then the built-in trackpad no longer responds to touches.

- **Trackpad Options.** Here you can adjust your Mac's response when you scroll by dragging across the trackpad—do things keep scrolling a little after you lift your finger ("inertia")?

 You can also enable *trackpad dragging,* which means moving things across the screen without having to keep the trackpad button down. To drag, tap *twice* (don't fully click); leave your finger touching the trackpad on the second tap. At this point, your "mouse button" is down. Swipe across the trackpad to move the object. (If

or Typing Suggestions. That's a row of autocomplete suggestions, exactly like you'd find on a smartphone; if you type *pi*, you get buttons for *pick*, *picked*, *picture*, and so on, which can really save you time if you have trouble typing (or spelling).

Tip: With one command, you can create a panel full of buttons, each of which insta-types a paragraph of boilerplate, canned text. Start by using a program like TextEdit to create a plain-text document full of the words, phrases, or sentences you use a lot; each line or paragraph will become a button. Save this document, and then, in Panel Editor, choose File→Import Phrase List.

2. **Specify the program in which you want this onscreen keyboard to appear.**

 That's right—you can create different panels that open automatically in every app you use. Use the Show For Applications pop-up menu. (It lists all open programs, but you can choose Find App to select one that's not currently open.)

3. **Once the starter layout appears, add a new "key" by clicking Add Button.**

 Dress up the button that appears by editing its name, font and font color, symbol (Image), and color. Then specify what this button does, using the Action pop-up menu. It can Go Back (to the previous panel); Open Panel (another panel that you specify); Dwell (turn on/off); run an AppleScript; Enter Text (insta-type some text that you specify); Press Keys (for example a key combination); Open App (any program you choose); trigger a System Event (adjust the Mac's volume or brightness, play/pause/rewind the music, or hide or show an onscreen version of the MacBook Pro's Touch Bar [page 233]); or display the Typing Suggestions bar.

 All of this can be incredibly useful. You could, for example, create a panel that does nothing but present a floating set of buttons for the apps you open most often. Or you could create a keyboard whose onscreen keys fill in for sticky buttons on your actual keyboard.

 As you build your panel, note that you can group and ungroup sets of selected buttons, for ease in moving them around as a unit (use the Group and Ungroup buttons in the toolbar). The Edit menu contains commands for aligning buttons, or making them all the same height or width. And the File menu offers commands for duplicating, exporting, or importing your keyboard masterpieces for use on other Macs by other people.

4. **Save your work and close the window.**

 You return to the Accessibility pane of System Preferences. If Enable Accessibility Keyboard is turned on, you're ready to go.

Using the Accessibility Keyboard

Once the Accessibility Keyboard is on the screen, of course, you can click the mouse (or point and wait out the dwell time) to type that key or press that button.

The upper-right button (▤) hides the main keyboard and shows, instead, any custom panels you've built, as described above. Click ⌂ to return to the main keyboard.

Note: The dwell feature lets you operate the mouse even if you have very limited motor control. You can move the mouse using hardware accessories like reflective-dot headbands or eye-trackers, and you click the mouse by waiting (as the cursor sits in one position) until a timer counts down.

Once the dwell period is over, the hot-corner action kicks in. Your choices for each of your four corners are Hide/Show Home Panel (meaning the onscreen keyboard); Toggle Dwell Pause (shuts off the waiting period); Left Click or Right Click the mouse; Drag and Drop (hold your mouse where you want to start the drag, wait for the Dwell circle to fill in, move the mouse to a new spot, and "release" the mouse by holding still while the Dwell circle fills in); Scroll Menu (opens the next menu you point to); or open the Options Menu (a palette of six round buttons that replicate the actions described in this paragraph).

Now, ordinarily, the Accessibility Keyboard looks just like the Mac's physical keyboard. But if you click the Panel Editor, you open a complete customization app. Here you can design additional keyboards (see Figure 9-11). You can put any of the "keys" in any order, and group them into clumps you drag around.

Figure 9-11:
The Panel Editor lets you build your own onscreen keyboards and panels. The buttons *you put here, what they look like, and what they do are all up to you.*

Better yet, you can add, to any of these onscreen keyboards, buttons that perform tricks like typing out blobs of canned text, pressing certain key combinations, opening favorite programs, or running AppleScripts.

Here's how it goes:

1. **To create a new onscreen keyboard, click Add Panel; from the pop-up menu, choose a ready-made layout.**

 Your choices are Empty (you'll have to add all the "keys" yourself); ANSI (the usual key layout); Alphabetical (all the keys in an A-to-Z row); ISO or JIS (international and Japanese standard layouts); Numeric (only the number and punctuation keys);

The original idea was to create an onscreen keyboard (Figure 9-10). If you have trouble typing on a physical keyboard, or if your Mac doesn't *have* a keyboard, you can still enter text and trigger keyboard shortcuts.

This keyboard is infinitely customizable. You can build all kinds of alternate keyboards—floating palettes of your own design, whose buttons can type blobs of text, open apps, run scripts, adjust the brightness or volume, and so on.

Figure 9-10:
The Accessibility Keyboard offers both an onscreen version of the main keyboard, as well as the option to build your own keyboard "panels," like the one here at left. Its buttons spit out paragraphs of canned text, to save you time and typing.

To see this keyboard, turn on Enable Accessibility Keyboard. The floating keyboard appears, ready to use, and to customize with these options:

- **Fade panel.** After a specified time of inactivity, the keyboard becomes transparent to get out of your way.

- **Play key sounds.** Do you want to hear little taps when you click the onscreen keys with your mouse?

- **Keys should be entered on.** When do you want a letter to be typed: When you click *down* on the mouse button or trackpad? Or when you *release* the mouse button or trackpad (which might be easier if you have motor-control difficulties)?

- **Hot Corners.** These options can help you if you can't click the mouse or use the keyboard. You can trigger any of the actions described next when you move your cursor into one of the screen's four corners and pause for three seconds. That's what Apple calls the *dwell* time, and it's represented by a triangular progress bar; it's to prevent you from triggering a hot corner *accidentally*. You can adjust the dwell period and other settings in Dwell Options.

If you press a modifier key *twice*, you lock it down. (Its onscreen symbol gets brighter to let you know.) When a key is locked, you can use it for several commands in a row. For example, if a folder icon is highlighted, you could double-press ⌘ to lock it down—and then type O (to open the folder), look around, and then press W (to close the window). Press the ⌘ key a third time to "unpress" it.

Tip: The checkbox called "Press the Shift key five times to toggle Sticky Keys" (click Options to see it) gives you the flexibility of turning Sticky Keys on and off at will, without making a trip to System Preferences. Whenever you want to turn on Sticky Keys, press the Shift key five times in succession. You'll hear a special clacking sound effect alerting you that you just turned on Sticky Keys. (Repeat the five presses to turn Sticky Keys off again.)

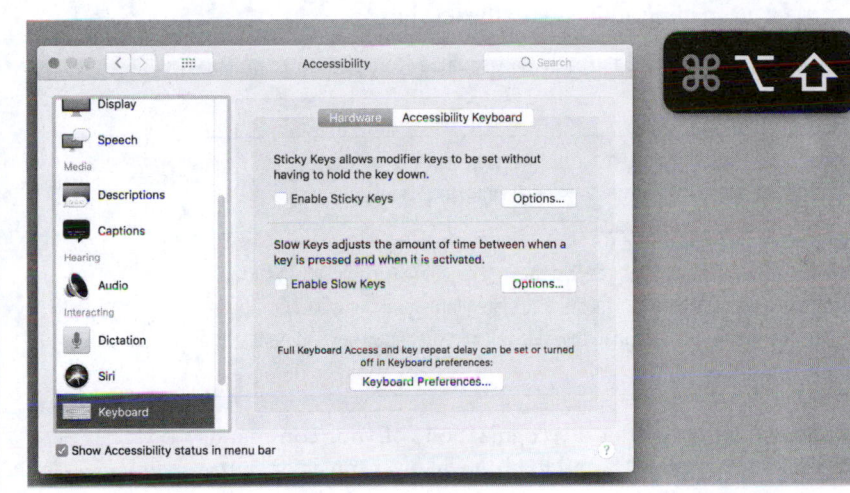

Figure 9-9:
To press a multikey keystroke like Option-Shift-⌘-D, press them one at a time. You see ghost images of the keys on your screen, as though to show you which keystrokes you've added to your temporary collection. To "unpress" a key, press it again twice.

- **Slow Keys,** on the other hand, doesn't register a key press at all until you've held down the key for more than a second or so—a feature designed to screen out accidental key presses.

If you click Options and then turn on "Use click key sounds," you'll hear a little typing sound each time you press a key—but none of these key presses registers unless you hold the key down for a moment. (Use the Acceptance Delay slider to govern this threshold.)

You hear a different sound when the Mac actually accepts the key press—and, of course, you see the letter you typed appear onscreen.

Accessibility Keyboard

This feature is a classic example of a tool that seems on the surface to appeal to people with disabilities—but turns out to be a powerful utility for almost anyone.

you want typed out. Don't use proper names or words that the Mac might confuse with similar-sounding ones.

- **While using.** Specify which program you want this command to work in (or leave it set to Any Application).

- **Perform.** From this pop-up menu, specify what you want the Mac to do. It can open a file, open an app, run an Automator workflow, paste a certain blob of text, or "press" a certain keystroke.

For example, suppose you want to create a command that types out your mailing address when you're composing email. In the "When I say" box, type "Paste my address." In the "While using" box, choose Mail. From the Perform pop-up menu, choose Paste Text; then type your mailing address into the text box.

When you click Done, your new command is ready to use, and it appears at the top of the command list at left.

Tip: Of course, pressing the fn key twice is *also* how you make the Mac start listening for text you want *typed out*. So what happens if you're dictating text and you want to issue a command? How do you stop the Mac from typing out "Go to end" (or whatever your command is)?

The solution is "Enable the dictation keyword phrase" on the System Preferences→Accessibility→Dictation panel. Turn it on and enter the phrase you'll want to say to get the Mac's attention—something like "Computer" or "Listen up" or "Hey, Macbrain." Each time you say that, the Mac will interpret your next utterance as a command—and it won't do any typing on its own.

If you like, you can ask the Mac to beep after it recognizes one of your commands ("Play sound when command is recognized") and to hush whatever music or sound is playing when you're trying to speak ("Mute audio output while dictating").

The Mac doesn't quite have the flexibility or accuracy of, say, the computer in *Star Trek*. Then again, the spoken-command feature can save you time, is easy to set up and use, and has the distinct advantage of not being fictional.

Siri

This panel has only one purpose: to let you turn on Type to Siri (page 288).

Keyboard

This panel offers clever features for people who have trouble using the keyboard—or who want a little productivity boost. There are now two panes of this screen.

Hardware

You have two options here:

- **Sticky Keys** lets you press multiple-key shortcuts (involving keys like Shift, Option, Control, and ⌘) one at a time instead of all together.

 To make Sticky Keys work, first turn on Enable Sticky Keys. Then go to work on the Mac, triggering keyboard commands as shown in Figure 9-9.

Note: On the other hand, the controls here are dimmed until you turn on the main Dictation feature (page 277) *and* Enhanced Dictation. Weird, right?

This is an older speak-to-trigger-commands feature, one that doesn't overlap Siri—much. This one lets the Mac understand dozens of commands for selecting and formatting text, navigating and editing documents, and operating the Mac itself (quitting apps, searching with Spotlight, opening documents, and so on). To look over the list of commands the Mac recognizes, click the Dictation Commands button.

Tip: If you turn on "Enable advanced commands" (there's no reason not to), you open up another batch of possibilities. Now you can control programs and documents, too, with commands like these: "Switch to Safari." "Quit Calendar." "Click File menu." "Save document." "Close window."

You'll discover you can create your own commands, too.

To make the Mac start listening, tap the fn key twice. (You can change that keystroke if you like; see page 210.)

The "listening" button appears, as shown at left in Figure 9-8. Say, "Show commands" to open a list of commands you can say (Figure 9-8, right).

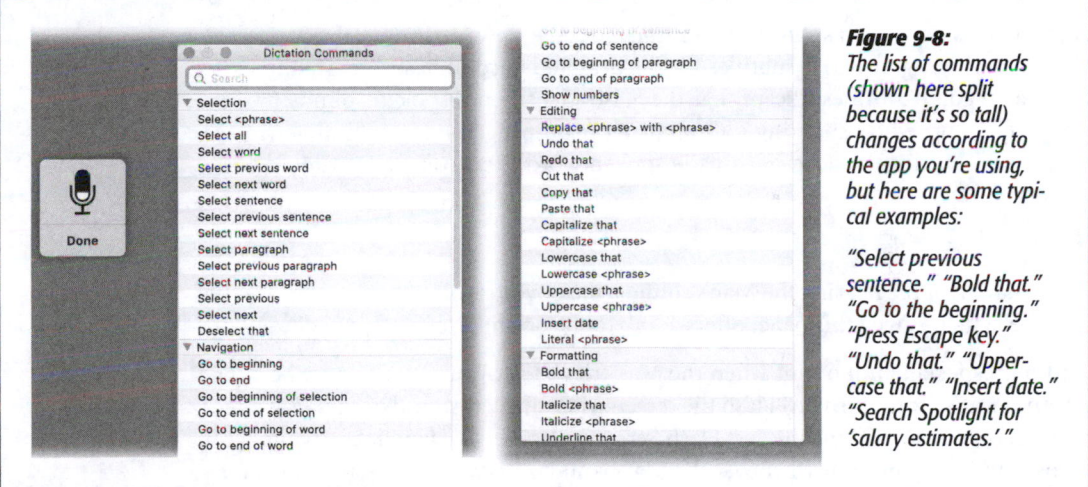

Figure 9-8:
The list of commands (shown here split because it's so tall) changes according to the app you're using, but here are some typical examples:

"Select previous sentence." "Bold that." "Go to the beginning." "Press Escape key." "Undo that." "Uppercase that." "Insert date." "Search Spotlight for 'salary estimates.' "

You may discover that you're triggering some commands accidentally. In that case, you can turn off a command in the list (in System Preferences→Accessibility→Dictation→Dictation Commands). Click the command, and then click the − button below it.

The + button is there so you can *add* to the list of commands the Mac recognizes. When you click +, you're offered three boxes to fill in:

- **When I say.** Type what you're going to say to trigger this command. It has to include at least two words; otherwise, the Mac might think you're speaking text

Speech

This panel lets you choose a voice (male, female, British, fast, whatever) for the Mac—when it reads error messages aloud to you. Details are on page 305.

Descriptions

This option, "Play audio descriptions when available," is for internet movies that come, or may someday come, with a narration track that describes the action for the blind.

Captions

This option controls the look of subtitles in movies, TV shows, videos, and podcasts you've bought, rented, or streamed from Apple. (Subtitles are an option in iTunes, QuickTime, and DVD Player.)

Tip: In the iTunes Store, videos equipped with subtitles bear a small CC icon.

When you first click Captions, you can see that Apple has supplied you with four different caption styles: Transparent Background, Classic, Large Text, and Outline Text; each has its own font, color, and background color. If you click the + button, though, you can whip up a new subtitle style to your own taste; you get an insane number of font, size, opacity, and color options.

A few videos have been subtitled specifically for deaf people. Those subtitles, called closed captioning or SDH (subtitles for the deaf and hard of hearing), are the same thing as regular subtitles, except that they also identify nonspoken sounds ("Glass breaking") and who's speaking ("Captain Picard: Engage!"). If you'd prefer to see these SDH captions instead of just the spoken words, turn on Prefer Closed Captions and SDH.

Audio

If you have trouble hearing the Mac's sounds, the obvious solution is to increase the volume, which is why this panel offers a link to the Sound Preferences pane.

Audio is especially important when the Mac tries to get your attention by beeping. For those situations, turn on "Flash the screen when an alert sound occurs" (an effect you can try out by clicking the Test Flash Screen button). Now you'll see a white flash across the entire monitor whenever the Mac would otherwise beep—not a bad idea on laptops, actually, so you don't miss beeps when you've got the speakers muted.

The "Play stereo audio as mono" option is intended for people with hearing loss in one ear. This way, you won't miss any of the musical mix just because you're listening through only one headphone.

Dictation

This Dictation feature is not the Dictation feature described on page 277, where you can speak what you want the Mac to type.

- **Differentiate without color** is intended for color-blind people, but it's fairly pointless. The only thing it affects is the "unavailable" status indicators (like "Away" and "Out to lunch") in Messages. They're denoted by red *squares* instead of circles.

- **If all of macOS's animations** are making you seasick, you can turn on "Reduce motion." This option also gives you a bit of a speed boost, especially in programs like Mission Control.

- **Increase contrast** darkens the lines that form buttons, sliders, and checkboxes on the screen, making them easier to distinguish.

- **Display contrast.** As you drag this slider toward Maximum, macOS's gray shades gradually bleach out, becoming closer and closer to pure black and white, which may be easier to see if you have limited vision.

- **The "Cursor size" slider** is a godsend not only to people with failing vision, but also to anyone using one of Apple's large, super-high-resolution screens; as the pixel density increases, the cursor gets smaller and smaller. This slider lets you make the arrow cursor larger—much larger, if you like—making it easier to find.

- **Shake mouse pointer to locate.** Year by year, computer screens get bigger, and the resolution (number of dots per inch) gets smaller. But in general the arrow pointer stays the same size: tiny.

That's why millions of people have gotten into the habit, upon waking up a Mac, of wiggling the mouse or making circles on the trackpad—so they can spot the cursor's movement and thereby see where it is.

And that's why Apple offers this feature: Anytime you wiggle the cursor or make tight little circles with it, the arrow cursor gets big. Really big. So big you can't miss it (Figure 9-7).

Figure 9-7:
Apple figures: Why would you ever wiggle the mouse for any other reason? You've got to be hunting for the cursor—and macOS is happy to help you find it.

- **Cursor style.** Within the magnification lens, your cursor can look like it always does, or it can take on the look of a big crosshairs (+) for more precision.

- **Invert colors** turns your screen into a color negative: Black is white, blue is yellow, and so on—within the magnification "lens," for greater clarity.

- **Temporarily toggle zoom and temporarily detach zoom.** These work exactly as they do in the "Full screen" options.

Display

If you have trouble seeing the screen, then, boy, does macOS have features for you:

- **Invert colors** swaps the colors of the screen, so that text appears white on black—an effect that some people find easier to read. (This option also freaks out many Mac fans who turn it on by *mistake*. They think the Mac's expensive monitor has just gone loco. Now you know better.)

- **Use grayscale** banishes all color from your screen. This is another feature designed to improve text clarity, but it's also a dandy way to see how a color document will look when printed on a monochrome laser printer.

- **Reduce transparency** eliminates all of macOS's translucency; see Figure 9-6.

Figure 9-6:
When you turn on "Reduce transparency," those semi-transparent menu bars, window edges, and panels (top) become opaque (bottom). The translucence is a trademark feature of macOS, but it doesn't actually help you use the computer; plenty of people find opaque menus and windows less visually confusing.

magnification keystrokes: a large zoom that you'll get when you press Option-⌘-plus, and a smaller degree of zoom when you press Option-⌘-minus. (At either point, you can adjust the zoom in either direction by pressing Option-⌘-plus or Option-⌘-minus *again*.)

- **Show preview rectangle when zoomed out.** If you turn this option on, then a black rectangle appears on the screen at all times when you *haven't* magnified the screen. It shows you what part of the screen image will fill your monitor when you press the "zoom-in" keystroke, Option-⌘-8.

- **Temporarily toggle zoom.** This one's great. It means that at any time, in any program, you can summon the magnified lens at your cursor location by holding down your Control and Option keys together. (It works only if Zoom is turned on.) It's a great way to dip into a magnified view of something on your screen, briefly.

 Or, if you're zoomed in, you can press those two keys to *unzoom* temporarily.

- **Temporarily detach zoom from pointer.** Sometimes, you may want to scroll your zoomed-in screen without moving your cursor. Since moving the mouse usually moves the zoom window, how can you do that? By turning on this option. When you press ⌘ and Control together, you can move the mouse to scroll the screen, but your cursor remains wherever it was.

- **Flash screen when notification banner appears outside zoom view** lets you work without worrying about missing a notification in the top-right corner.

- **When zoomed in…** specifies how you want to scroll around within your zoomed-in screen image. The first setting, "Continuously with pointer," is actually pretty frustrating; the whole screen shifts around whenever you move the cursor. ("So the pointer is at or near the center of the screen" is very similar.) "Only when the pointer reaches an edge" is a lot less annoying and lets you *use* the cursor (to click buttons, for example) without sending the entire screen image darting away from you.

When "Picture-in-picture" is turned on, the options are different. You have these choices:

- **Window position.** If you choose Stationary, the lens remains parked on the screen. You can't move or resize it—at least not once you've left the Options dialog box.

Tip: You *can* change its size and position for good, though, by clicking Adjust Size and Location in the corner of the Options dialog box. You'll be offered the chance to drag the little inset window (Figure 9-5, bottom) to move it, or drag its edges to change its shape. When you like the result, click OK.

"Follow mouse cursor" makes the inset window follow your cursor around, as though you're moving a high-tech magnifying glass over a map. And if you choose "Tiled along edge," then the lens becomes much bigger—in fact, it becomes an enormous rectangular swath at the left side of your screen. The image scrolls as you move your cursor around.

- **With the trackpad or mouse wheel.** To prepare, turn on "Use scroll gesture with modifier keys to zoom."

All right; you're ready to zoom. Next time you need to magnify things, do this:

- **From the keyboard.** Press Option-⌘-8. You've either opened up the magnifying lens or magnified the entire screen. The magnification is 200 percent of original size. At this point, you can increase or decrease the amount of zooming by pressing Option-⌘-plus or Option-⌘-minus (the - key). With each press, the entire screen image (or the image in the magnifying lens, depending on which you've chosen as your zoom style) gets larger or smaller, creating a virtual monitor that follows your cursor around the screen.

- **Using the trackpad or mouse wheel.** While pressing the Control key, drag two fingers up your trackpad, or turn your mouse wheel upward. The amount of dragging or turning controls the degree of magnification.

Once you're zoomed in, you can pan around inside the lens (or pan the entire virtual giant screen) by dragging with two fingers on your trackpad. The lens moves to follow your cursor; in Picture-in-picture mode, the whole screen scrolls when your cursor hits the edge of the magnified area.

Customizing your zoom

You can tweak the zooming feature to within an inch of its life on this panel:

- **Use scroll gesture with modifier keys to zoom.** You can substitute the Option or ⌘ key, if Control isn't working out for you.

- **Smooth images** adds a pixel-smoothing feature, a certain blurriness, to the zoomed-in image.

- **Zoom follows the keyboard focus.** The area of magnification will jump when you press the Tab key to highlight different areas of whatever program you're using.

- **Enable Touch Bar zoom.** This option appears only on MacBook Pro laptops—those with a Touch Bar (page 233). When you touch the Touch Bar, you see a magnified version of it at the bottom of your screen, so you can see better what you're doing.

- **Speak items under the pointer.** Just what it says. Use the slider to adjust the pause before the Mac speaks aloud whatever text your mouse rests on.

- **Zoom Style.** If you choose "Full screen," then zooming magnifies the entire screen. (And that, as many Apple Genius Bar employees can tell you, freaks out a lot of people who don't know what's happened.) If it's set to "Picture-in-picture," then zooming will produce a movable rectangular magnifying lens (Figure 9-5, bottom).

If you click Options, you find yet another raft of choices. What you see here depends on whether you've chosen "Full screen" or "Picture-in-picture" zoom mode. In "Full screen," you get choices like these:

- **Maximum Zoom, Minimum Zoom.** Turns out pressing Option-⌘-8 isn't the only way to turn on zooming. These sliders establish starting points for two other

Zoom Tab

This feature, shown in Figure 9-5, lets you enlarge the area surrounding your cursor in any increment. It's incredibly useful incredibly often, especially if you have over-40 eyes.

You can start enlarging things in either of two ways:

• **From the keyboard.** To set this up, turn on "Use keyboard shortcuts to zoom."

Figure 9-5:
Top: You'll be amazed at how much you can zoom using this Accessibility pane. In fact, there's nothing to stop you from zooming in so far that a single pixel nearly fills the entire monitor. (That may not be especially useful for people with limited vision, but it can be handy for graphic designers learning how to reproduce a certain icon, dot by dot.)

Bottom: This inset window makes it easier for you to keep your bearings. It zooms into the screen only within this window.

The purpose of *this* dashboard (the General tab) is to choose which checkboxes you want to appear on *that* dashboard. Any checkboxes you turn off here won't appear in the panel shown in Figure 9-4.

Figure 9-4:
With a quick tap of Option-⌘-F5 (or a triple-click on the Touch ID button on MacBook Pro laptops), you can summon this panel of on/off switches for Accessibility features.

VoiceOver Tab

The Mac has always been able to read stuff on the screen out loud. But Apple has taken this feature light-years further, turning it into a full-blown *screen reader* for the benefit of people who can't see. VoiceOver doesn't just read every scrap of text it finds on the screen—it also lets you control everything on the screen (menus, buttons, and so on) without ever needing the mouse.

On a laptop, you can interact with what's visible on the screen by using the trackpad itself as a map of the current window or screen area; in Trackpad Commander mode, VoiceOver speaks whatever is under your finger (represented by a blue ring on the screen). You can flick in any direction to move to the next thing on the screen. It's all in the name of helping you "feel" where everything is.

MacOS can also read entire web pages, navigate tables, hop from link to link, and so on. You can navigate by pressing the arrow keys, by using the mouse, or by using the trackpad.

Learning VoiceOver is a *huge* task that can take days or weeks; there's an entire app (VoiceOver Utility) with *10 pages* of preference settings. But if it's your ticket to being able to use a computer at all, you'll probably be happy to have such a full-fledged monster of a program. Apple offers a complete user's guide here: *apple.com/voiceover/info/guide/.*

- **Faster:** Click the Show All (::::) icon in the upper-left corner of the window (or press ⌘-L, a shortcut worth learning). Then click the icon of the new panel you want.

- **Fastest:** You can choose a panel's name from any of three menus. There's the View menu, the Show All button (::::), or the System Preferences Dock icon pop-up menu described already.

Hiding the Icons You Never Use

Let's face it: Especially for a beginner, System Preferences can be daunting. You just want to change your screen saver, and suddenly you're face-to-face with the space shuttle dashboard.

Fortunately, you can hide the System Preferences icons you don't use often. Figure 9-3 shows the way.

All right. What follows, then, is your grand tour of the built-in System Preferences panes. (You may have more if you've installed any non-Apple panes.)

Figure 9-3:
Super-top-secret trick: If you choose Customize (from the View menu or, believe it or not, the Show All button ::::), the icons sprout checkboxes. You can turn off—and hide—the icons you never use. (You can still choose their names from the View menu, even if you've hidden them.)

Accessibility

The Accessibility panel is designed for people who, for example, type with one hand, find it difficult to use a mouse, or have trouble seeing or hearing.

Accessibility is a huge focus for Apple. In fact, there's a whole Apple website dedicated to explaining these controls: *apple.com/accessibility*. Here, though, is an overview of the noteworthiest features, broken down according to the tabs at the left side.

General Tab

Apple assumes that many of the Accessibility features are things you'll want to turn on and off on the fly, as you need them. So in macOS, there's a keyboard shortcut that pulls up a dashboard of Accessibility features and their on/off checkboxes (Figure 9-4): Option-⌘-F5. (If you have a Touch Bar laptop, fast–triple-click the Touch ID fingerprint reader instead. Those should be audible click-downs, not just touches.)

press ⌘-F.) Type a few letters of *volume, resolution, wallpaper, wireless,* or whatever feature you want to adjust. In a literal illustration of Spotlight's name, the System Preferences window darkens *except* for the icons where you'll find relevant controls (Figure 9-2). Click the name or icon of the one that looks the most promising.

Figure 9-2:
Even if you don't know which System Preferences panel contains the settings you want to change, Spotlight can help. Type into the box at the top, and watch as the "spotlight" shines on the relevant icons.

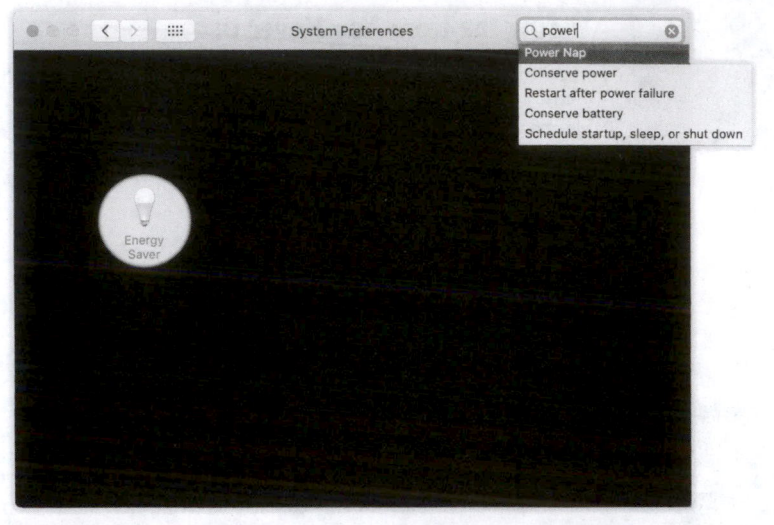

UP TO SPEED

System Preferences: Under the Hood

The entire System Preferences program is nothing more than a series of graphical front ends for underlying Unix settings. (If you know Unix you can, in fact, use the *defaults* command in macOS's Terminal program to make any of the changes described in this chapter—and many others.)

The individual preferences panes are represented by package icons in your Library folders. For example, the icons Apple supplies are in System→Library→PreferencePanes. MacOS also looks for preferences modules in the Network→Library→PreferencePanes folder, if there is one.

Suppose you've downloaded some new preferences module and you want to install it. Just double-clicking a downloaded System Preferences pane does the trick.

If you prefer manual control, you can put a downloaded module into your Home→Library→PreferencePanes folder. (To get to your Library folder, which is usually invisible, press the Option key; choose Go→Library in the Finder.)

The beauty of this arrangement is that everyone who shares the Mac now can see a different assortment of customized preference panes. If you're an administrator, you can use the PreferencePanes folder in the Mac's main Library folder; it lets everyone with an account on the Mac (Chapter 12) access your newly added panes.

When you install some new System Preferences pane, like TiVo Desktop, it takes the form of a new icon in one of those four PreferencePanes folders. That's good to know if you ever want to remove an add-on pane. Usually, you remove these non-Apple preference panes by right-clicking or two-finger clicking them and choosing Remove Preference Pane from the shortcut menu—but in a pinch, you could also delete one by removing it from one of these special folders.

Within the System Preferences program, any new panes you add this way appear in a new row of icons labeled Other (when you're viewing System Preferences in Category view).

- **If you know the name of the System Preferences panel** you want, it's often quicker to use Spotlight. To open the Parental Controls panel, for example, hit ⌘-space, type *pare*, and then press Return. See Chapter 3 for more on operating Spotlight from the keyboard.

- **If you put the System Preferences icon in your *Dock*** (Chapter 4), you can open it *and* jump to a particular panel in one smooth move: Click-and-hold the System Preferences icon. You get a pop-up menu of every System Preferences panel.

Suppose, then, that by hook or by crook, you've figured out how to open System Preferences. At first, the rows of icons are grouped according to function, as shown in Figure 9-1, bottom. But you can also view them in tidy alphabetical order, as shown in Figure 9-1 at top. That can spare you the tedious ritual of hunting around to find a panel icon whose name you already know. (Quick, without looking: Which row is Date & Time in?) This chapter describes the various panels following this alphabetical arrangement.

Either way, when you click one of the icons, the corresponding controls appear.

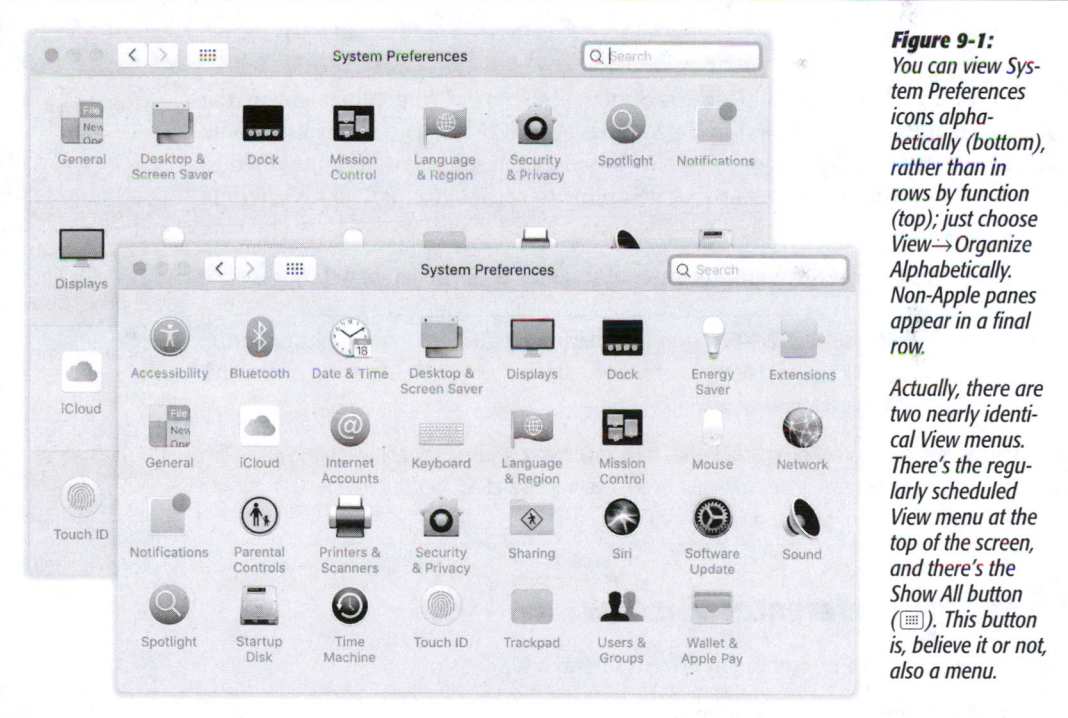

Figure 9-1:
You can view System Preferences icons alphabetically (bottom), rather than in rows by function (top); just choose View→Organize Alphabetically. Non-Apple panes appear in a final row.

Actually, there are two nearly identical View menus. There's the regularly scheduled View menu at the top of the screen, and there's the Show All button (⊞). This button is, believe it or not, also a menu.

Choosing a Preferences Pane

To access a different preferences pane, you have a number of options:

- **Fast:** When System Preferences first opens, the insertion point is blinking in the System Preferences search box. (If the insertion point is *not* blinking there, then

System Preferences

The hub of Mac customization is System Preferences, the equivalent of the Control Panel (Windows) or the Settings app (iPhone, iPad, Android). Some of its panels are extremely important, because their settings determine whether or not you can connect to a network or go online to exchange email. Others handle the more cosmetic aspects of macOS.

This chapter guides you through the System Preferences program, panel by panel.

Note: Only a system administrator (page 524) can change settings that affect everyone who shares a certain machine: most of its Network settings, Energy Saver settings, and so on. If you see a bunch of controls that are dimmed and unavailable, now you know why.

A tiny 🔒 in the lower-left corner of a panel is the other telltale sign. If you, a nonadministrator, would like to edit some settings, then call an administrator over to your Mac and ask her to click the 🔒, input her password, and supervise your tweaks.

The System Preferences Window

You can open System Preferences in dozens of ways:

- **Choose its name from the menu.**

- **Jump directly to a System Preferences pane** by pressing Option as you tap keys on the top row of your keyboard: Option-▦ for Mission Control preferences, Option-volume key (◀, ◀), or ◀))) for Sound prefs, Option-brightness keys (☼ or ☀) or Option-keyboard-brightness key (✲ or ✲) for the Displays prefs. At that point, you can click ⦂⦂⦂⦂ or press ⌘-L to see the full spread.

Part Three:
The Components
of macOS

3

Apple Watch Login

If you have an Apple Watch running watchOS 3 or later, you don't need a password to unlock your Mac anymore. The watch on your wrist acts as a wireless master key.

All you have to do is come within 10 feet of your Mac and wake it up. The logging-in takes place instantly and automatically. It may be the lowest-effort security system ever invented.

Note: You still have to enter your Mac's password after shutting it down or restarting it. The watch method works only if the Mac has been sleeping.

Here's the fine print:

- **The watch must be running watchOS 3 or later.** The Sierra or later Mac must have been made since mid-2013. Both devices must have Wi-Fi and Bluetooth turned on.

- **You must have a passcode set up on the watch.** (Open the Apple Watch app on the iPhone; tap General→Apple ID.)

- **You have to set up the feature on the Mac.** In System Preferences→Security & Privacy→General, turn on "Allow your Apple Watch to unlock your Mac."

- **You have to turn on two-factor authentication for your iCloud account.** See page 551.

From now on, everything is automatic. You wake your Mac (open the laptop lid, for example). You see "Unlocked with Apple Watch" flash on the lock screen, you see "[Your Mac] unlocked by this Apple Watch" on the watch's screen—and you're in!

You'll never have to enter your password on the Mac again (at least until you shut it down or restart it).

These features could be brilliant time-savers for researchers and students. If you use Messages on your Mac to do your texting, it's life-changing: Now you can pop a photo into the conversation without any file-transferring nonsense.

The Universal Clipboard

Now, this is magic—and useful magic, at that. You can copy some text, a picture, or a video on your iPhone, iPad, or iPod Touch—and then, without any further steps, turn to your Mac and paste it. Or go the other way. Somehow, the contents of the Clipboard transfer themselves wirelessly between the two machines.

There's no on/off switch, no extra steps, no visible sign of this feature in Settings or System Preferences. It just works. (Provided, of course, that you've obeyed the Three Laws of Continuity Setup: The Mac and phone have to be on the same Wi-Fi network, both have to have Bluetooth turned on, and both have to be signed into the same iCloud account.)

If you don't paste within two minutes of copying, then macOS restores whatever was already on the Mac's Clipboard, so you don't get confused later. Figure 8-9 shows all.

Figure 8-9:
Top: On your iPad, you copy some text (or a picture, or a video clip).

Bottom: If, on your Mac, you use the Paste command within two minutes—in any program—then the material you copied on the phone appears!

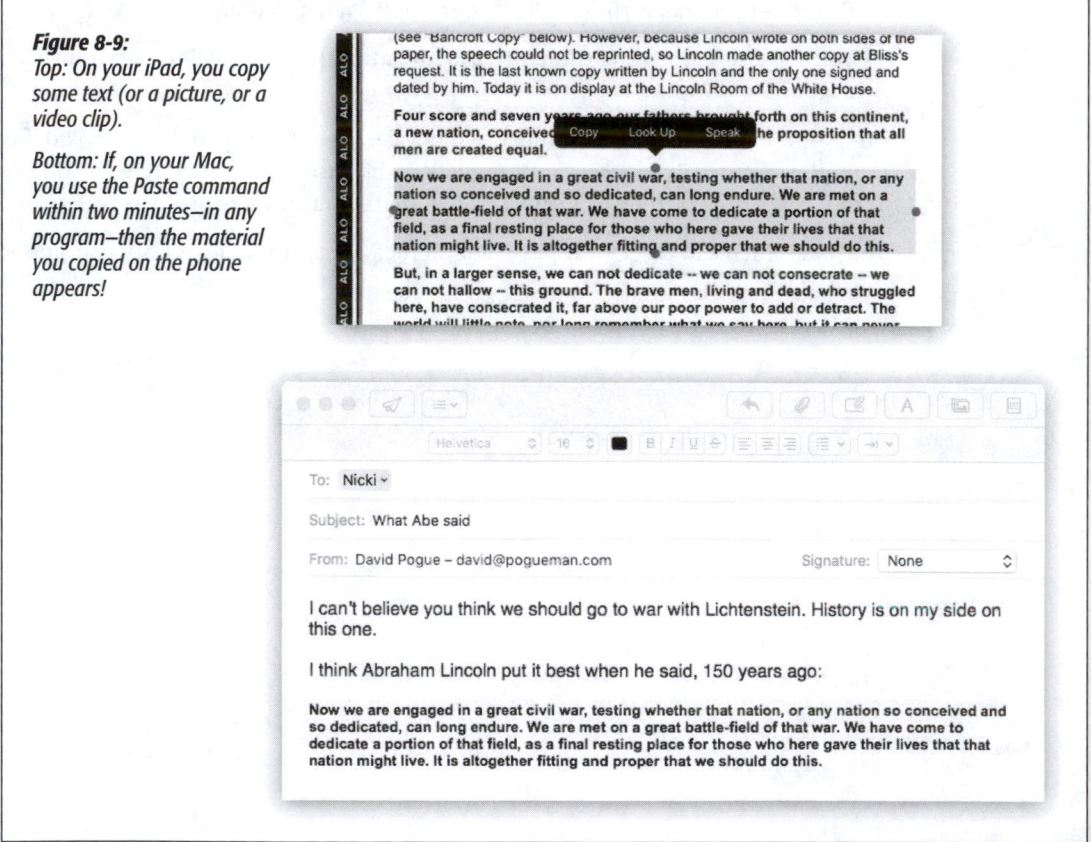

3. **On the phone or tablet, frame and take the shot (Figure 8-8, right). If it looks good, tap Use Photo on the iPhone screen.**

Instantly, that picture appears on your Mac, pasted right into the document (Figure 8-8, bottom).

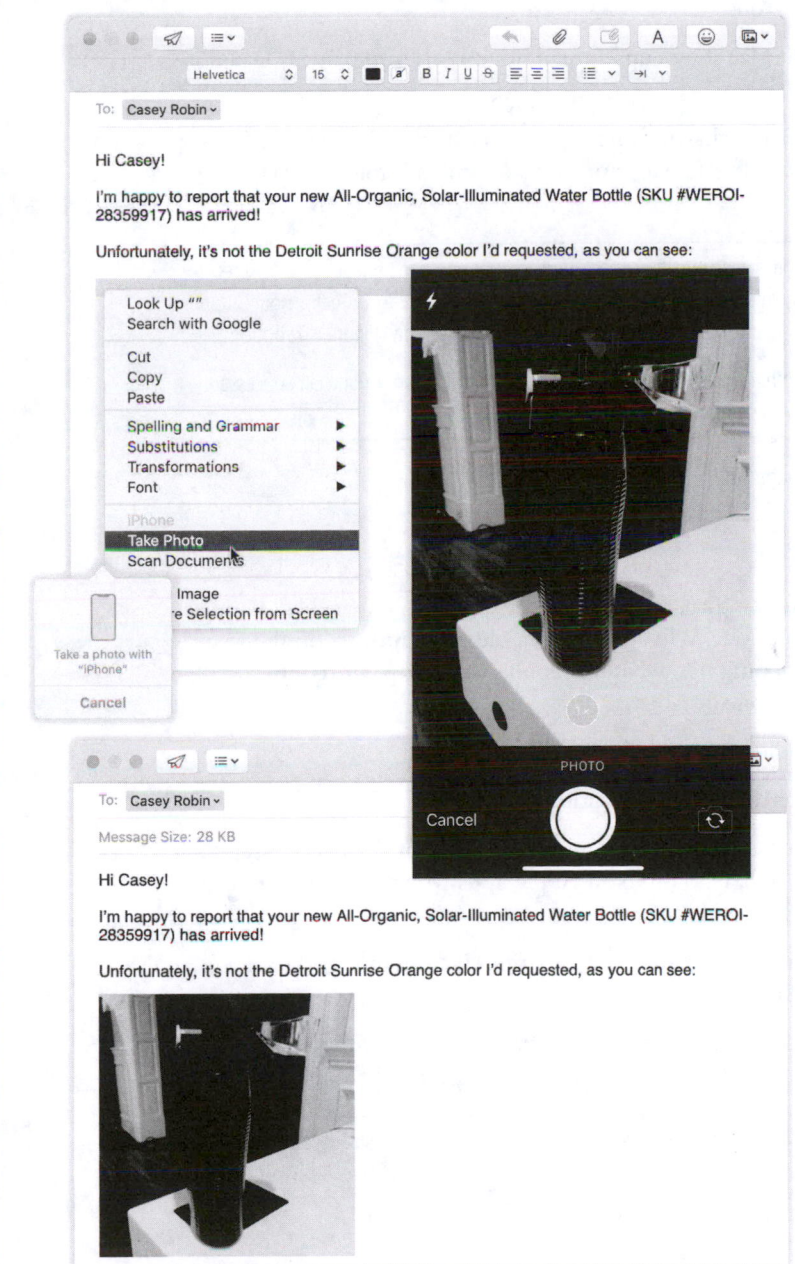

Figure 8-8:

Top left: You're working on some email, note, presentation, or document when you need a quick photo. You choose Take Photo.

Middle right: Your phone awakens. Use it to take a picture.

(If you change your mind, tap Cancel on the phone, or click Cancel on the little "Take a photo" tab on the Mac, shown here at middle left.)

Bottom: Once you tap Use Photo on the phone, it appears by magic on the Mac.

If the Mac's icon *doesn't* show up, it's probably because its owner hasn't made the Mac discoverable by AirDrop.

Instruct him to open the AirDrop *window* on his Mac. (Click AirDrop in the Sidebar of any Finder window.) See the small blue control at the bottom? It governs who can "see" this Mac for AirDrop purposes: No One, Contacts Only (that is, people in the Mac's address book), or Everyone.

Once that's set up right, that Mac shows up in the iPhone's AirDrop panel ("David" in Figure 8-7). Send away.

The receiving Mac displays a note like the one shown at bottom in Figure 8-7. Click Accept (to download the incoming item to your Mac's Downloads folder) or Decline (to reject it).

Tip: If the phone and the Mac are both signed into the same iCloud account, you don't encounter that Accept/Decline thing. The file goes directly into your Downloads folder without asking. You do get a notification on the Mac that lets you know how many files arrived, and it offers an Open button (Figure 8-7, bottom).

Apple figures that, since you own both the phone and the Mac, the usual permission routine isn't necessary. You're probably not trying to send yourself some evil virus of death.

For more on AirDrop, see page 572.

Continuity Camera

This cool new feature in Mojave turns your iPhone or iPad into a detached, hand-held, wireless camera for your Mac. When you snap a photo, it appears on the Mac a moment later, for incorporating into whatever app you're using. (It requires that iOS 12 be running on your phone or tablet.)

The feature is fairly buried, though. Follow along in Figure 8-8:

1. **Open one of the programs that offer this feature.**

 At the moment, they're mostly the built-in Apple apps like Notes, Mail, Messages, Preview, Pages, Keynote, and TextEdit. Non-Apple apps won't offer this feature unless their makers decide to add it.

2. **Right-click or two-finger click a blank spot in your Mac document. From the shortcut menu, choose Take Photo (Figure 8-8, top left).**

 On your iPhone or iPad, you'll see that the camera app opens, magically and automatically (Figure 8-8, right).

Tip: If you choose Scan Document, the iPhone's document-scanning module opens instead, complete with auto-straightening and -clarifying magic for whatever piece of paper you're scanning (page 425). Insta-PDF!

another. Wirelessly. Without having to set up names, passwords, or permissions. Without even having an internet connection.

Now, the process of using AirDrop from your *Mac* is described on page 572. Below are the instructions for using AirDrop from your *phone*.

To get started, open whatever it is you want to send: a photo, map, website, contact… anything with a ⬆ button.

When you tap ⬆, you see the AirDrop panel—and, after a moment, the icons of any nearby Yosemite or later Macs, iPhones, and iPads show up, too. Including yours (Figure 8-7, top).

Figure 8-7:
AirDrop goes both ways: from iPhone to Mac (shown here), or Mac to iPhone. Actually, it goes many more ways than that, because the iPad and iPod Touch can do it, too.

A typical transaction works like this: You choose some photos on the phone and then tap the icon representing the nearby Mac/iPhone/iPad/iPod Touch you're sending it to (top).

Bottom: On the receiving device (in this case, a Mac), a notification pops up to let you know files are incoming.

Tip: There's another way to find the Handoff icon that nobody ever mentions: It's in the app switcher on both devices (see Figure 8-6, bottom).

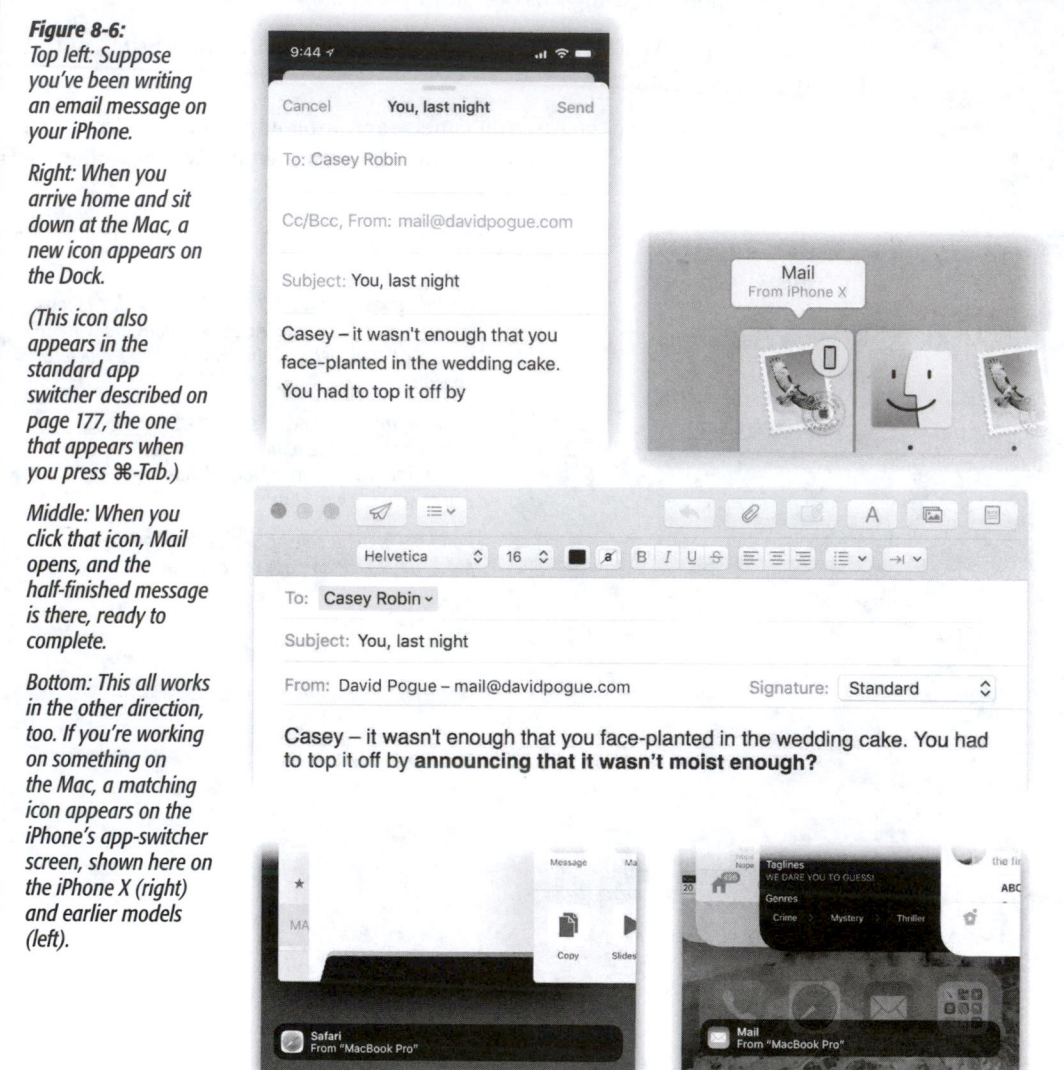

Figure 8-6:

Top left: Suppose you've been writing an email message on your iPhone.

Right: When you arrive home and sit down at the Mac, a new icon appears on the Dock.

(This icon also appears in the standard app switcher described on page 177, the one that appears when you press ⌘-Tab.)

Middle: When you click that icon, Mail opens, and the half-finished message is there, ready to complete.

Bottom: This all works in the other direction, too. If you're working on something on the Mac, a matching icon appears on the iPhone's app-switcher screen, shown here on the iPhone X (right) and earlier models (left).

AirDrop

AirDrop is pretty great. It lets you shoot photos, videos, maps, Contacts cards, PDF files, Word documents—and all kinds of other stuff—from one Apple product to

Hotspot is turned off! Handily enough, the 🛜 menu also shows the phone's battery and signal status (Figure 8-5).

As usual, this works only if the iPhone and Mac both have Bluetooth turned on and are signed into the same iCloud account.

Figure 8-5:
Once your Mac is online through your iPhone's cellular connection, it tries to save you money by suspending data-intensive jobs like full backups and software updates. And it closes down the connection when you no longer need it, to save your iPhone's battery.

Handoff

Handoff is a feature that passes half-finished documents between the phone and the Mac, wirelessly and automatically. Figure 8-6 shows how it works.

It doesn't have to be an email message, either. If you were reading a web page or a map on your phone, then that icon on the Mac opens the same web page or map. If you were working on an entry in Calendar, Contacts, Maps, Mail, Reminders, Safari, Pages, Numbers, or Keynote, you can open the same in-progress item on the Mac. (Some non-Apple apps do the Handoff thing now, too, including Pocket, Wunderlist, and NYTimes.)

Here's the setup: Once again, both gadgets must be signed into your iCloud account. Both must have Bluetooth turned on, and the Mac and phone have to be sitting within Bluetooth range of each other (about 30 feet).

On the Mac, open System Preferences→General; turn on "Allow Handoff between this Mac and your iCloud devices."

On the iPhone, the on/off switch is in Settings→General→Handoff & Suggested Apps.

Now try it out. Start an email message on your iPhone. Have a look at the Dock on your Mac: There, at the left end, pops up the little icon of whatever program can finish the job.

Watch for the little lower-left icon on your screens to make it work.

And all of it works in the other direction, too. If you're working on something on the Mac, but you're called away, an icon appears on the lower-left corner of your iPhone's Lock screen that opens the same item (Figure 8-6, bottom).

it appears—in Contacts, in a Spotlight search result, in Safari, in Mail—and choose Send Message from there. And when a text message comes in, a standard Mac notification bubble appears at top right (Figure 8-4).

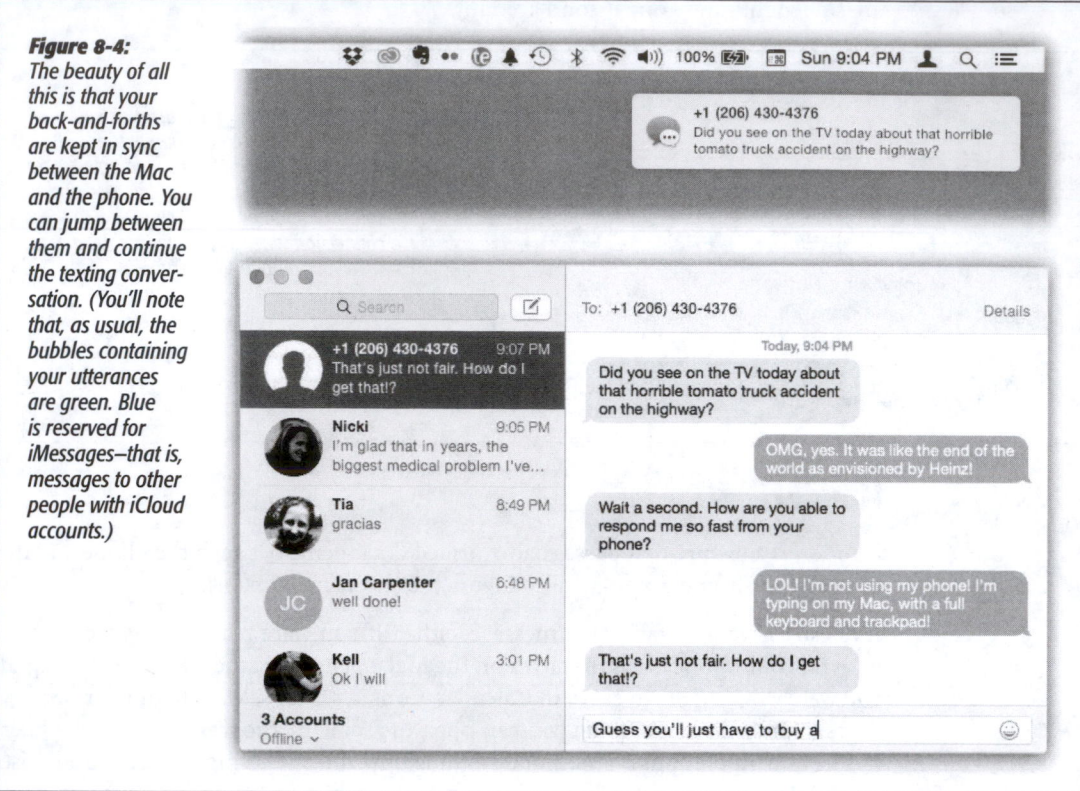

Figure 8-4:
The beauty of all this is that your back-and-forths are kept in sync between the Mac and the phone. You can jump between them and continue the texting conversation. (You'll note that, as usual, the bubbles containing your utterances are green. Blue is reserved for iMessages—that is, messages to other people with iCloud accounts.)

Instant Hotspot

Paying your cell carrier another few bucks every month entitles you to use the iPhone's Personal Hotspot feature. That's where the phone itself acts as a portable Wi-Fi hotspot, so that your laptop (or any other gadgets) can get online almost anywhere.

It used to be kind of a pain to get going. Each time you wanted your laptop to get online, you had to wake your iPhone, unlock it, open Settings, and turn on Personal Hotspot. Then you had to wait about 20 seconds, until the phone's name showed up in your 🛜 menu.

Not anymore.

Now the phone can stay in your pocket. Its name appears in your 🛜 menu, ready for choosing at any time—even if the phone is asleep and locked, and even if Personal

Tip: If you own a bunch of Apple machines, it might drive you crazy that they all now ring at once when a call comes in. Fortunately, you can turn off the ringing on each device that you'd rather be peaceful.

To make one of your iPhones, iPads, or iPod Touches stop ringing, turn off Settings→FaceTime→iPhone Cellular Calls. To make a Mac stop ringing, open the FaceTime program; choose FaceTime→Preferences→Settings, and turn off iPhone Cellular Calls.

Texting from the Mac

You can send and receive text messages (and picture, audio, and video messages) on your Mac, too. We're not talking about sending texts to other *Apple* people (with iCloud accounts). Those are called iMessages, and they're a special, Apple-only kind of message. We're talking about something much better: You can type *any* cellphone number and send a regular SMS text message to *anyone*. Or receive them when they're sent to your iPhone number.

Or you can initiate the text conversation by clicking a phone number in Contacts, Calendar, or Safari to send an SMS message. Once again, your iPhone acts as a relay station between the cellular world and your Mac. Here's how to set it up.

1. **On the iPhone, open Settings→Messages. Tap Text Message Forwarding.**

 Your Mac's name appears. Turn on the switch.

2. **Now, on the Mac, open Messages.**

 (If all is going well, its icon is probably popping out of your Dock at this moment, trying to get your attention.) When you open Messages, a code appears. You're supposed to type into the corresponding box on your phone (Figure 8-3).

Figure 8-3:
The purpose of having to enter this setup code is to prove, really and truly, that you're the owner of both devices. You wouldn't want some bad guy reading your text messages, would you?

To send and receive your iPhone text messages from "+1 (408) 797-7897" on this Mac, enter the code below on your iPhone now.

227724

Waiting for verification... Cancel

This same code appears right now on any iPad or iPod Touch you own. They, too, will be able to send and receive texts, with your iPhone doing the relaying.

That's it—your gadgets are paired. You can now use Messages to send standard text messages to *any* cellphone. You can also click and hold on a phone number wherever

And if It's Not Working

"It just works" is fantastic—when it just works.

If your Mac isn't able to send and receive calls and texts through your phone, here's the checklist. One of these things, you'll discover, isn't set correctly.

- **The iPhone and Mac have to be on the same network** (for example, the same Wi-Fi network).

Note: Actually, iOS 9 introduced a radical enhancement to the Continuity feature—called Continuity over Cellular. It lets you take calls on your Mac or iPad over the *cellular* network, even if your iPhone is somewhere else in the world! Yes, you can now make calls or send texts from your Mac, even if you left your phone at the office or at your buddy's house. So far, though, only T-Mobile offers this feature.

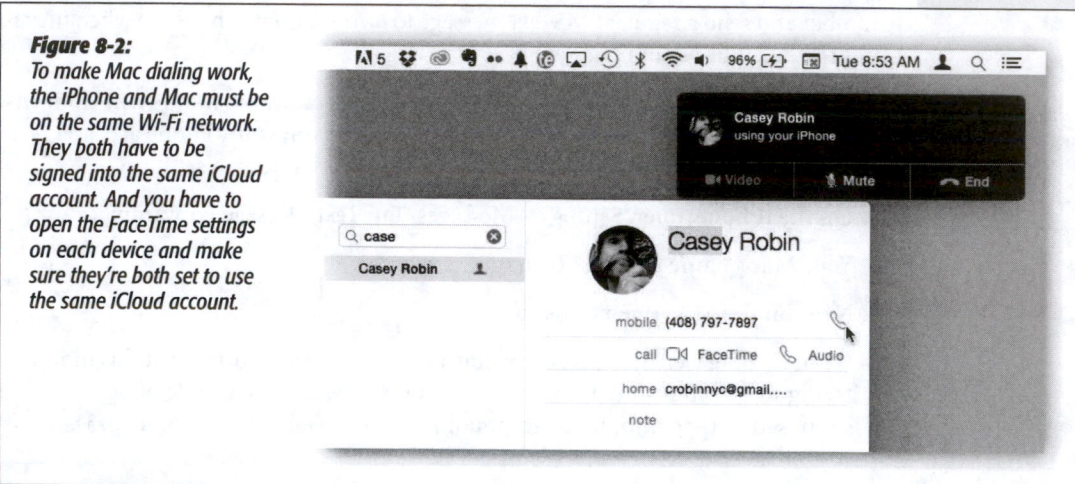

Figure 8-2:
To make Mac dialing work, the iPhone and Mac must be on the same Wi-Fi network. They both have to be signed into the same iCloud account. And you have to open the FaceTime settings on each device and make sure they're both set to use the same iCloud account.

- **On the phone, open Settings→FaceTime.** Make sure FaceTime, too, is signed into that same iCloud account. Turn on iPhone Cellular Calls.

- **On the phone, open Settings→General→Handoff & Suggested Apps.** Make sure Handoff is turned on.

- **On the Mac, open System Preferences→General.** Confirm that "Allow Handoff between this Mac and your iCloud devices" is turned on.

- **On the Mac, open the FaceTime program.** Choose FaceTime→Preferences. Confirm that, once again, you're signed in with the same iCloud account, that your phone number's checkbox is turned on, and that "iPhone Cellular Calls" is turned on.

did, so it's fine to leave it on. But older Macs don't have Bluetooth LE, so most Continuity features work only on 2012 and later Macs.

All right. Setup ready? Time to experience some integration!

Mac as Speakerphone

You can now make and take phone calls on your Mac. The iPhone, sitting anywhere in your house, can be the cellular module for your Mac—even if that iPhone is asleep and locked.

When a call comes in to your iPhone's number, your *Mac* plays whatever ringtone your phone is playing. And a notice appears on your Mac's screen (Figure 8-1).

Tip: If your Mac has a Touch Bar (page 233), you get buttons on it that let you Accept or Decline the call.

Figure 8-1:
When a call comes in to your iPhone, a notification appears on your Mac (top). You can click to answer it (or decline it); your Mac's microphone and speaker become your speakerphone (bottom).

You can *place* a call the same way: Just click any phone number you find on the Mac: in Contacts, in Safari, in an email message, and so on (Figure 8-2).

After that—it just works. Even call-waiting works—if a second call comes in, your Mac notifies you and offers you the chance to put the first one on hold. And on the Mac, the Contacts app now offers Ringtone and Texttone menus, so you can assign custom sounds that play when your *Mac* rings. Crazy.

Tip: You may soon discover that there's no dialing pad on the Mac, so there's no easy way to dial a number that's not already in Contacts. The workaround: Create a temporary fake person in Contacts!

Continuity: Mac+iPhone

Apple products have always been designed to work together. Macs, phones, tablets, watches: similar software, design, wording, philosophy. That's nice for you, of course, because you have less to learn and less to troubleshoot. But it's also nice for Apple, because it keeps you in velvet handcuffs; pretty soon, you've got too much invested in its product "ecosystem" to consider wandering over to a rival.

Now, Apple has taken this gadget symbiosis to an astonishing extreme. Your iPhone can be an *accessory* to your Mac. Suddenly the Mac can be a speakerphone, using the iPhone as a wireless antenna. Suddenly the Mac can send and receive regular text messages. Suddenly AirDrop lets you drag files back and forth, wirelessly, from phone to computer. Suddenly a Mac laptop can get onto the internet with one click, even miles from home. And you can even copy and paste between your phone and Mac, or take a picture with the iPhone that appears instantly on your Mac.

Apple's name for this suite of symbiosis is "Continuity." These are the primary rules:

- **You need a Mac running Yosemite or later and an iPhone running iOS 8.1 or later.** (The copy/paste thing requires Sierra or later and iOS 10 or later on the phone. The "take a picture with the iPhone" thing requires macOS Mojave and iOS 12.)

- **The Mac and the phone have to be signed into the same iCloud account.** That's a security thing—it proves you're the owner of both machines, and therefore unlikely to pose a risk to yourself. On the Mac, you do that in System Preferences→iCloud. On the phone, you do that in Settings→iCloud, but also make sure you've entered the same iCloud address in Settings→Messages and Settings→FaceTime.

- **Both gadgets must have Wi-Fi and Bluetooth turned on.** The modern Bluetooth—called Bluetooth LE, or low energy—doesn't drain your battery the way it once

Here are all the different occasions when the Mac can talk to you.

Announce when alerts are displayed or applications need your attention

This checkbox makes the Mac read aloud error messages and alert messages that may appear on your screen. If you then click Options, you'll find these useful controls:

- **Voice.** Use this pop-up menu to specify the voice you want reading your error messages. (It doesn't have to be the same as the standard Mac voice that's used for other purposes.)

- **Phrase.** Use this pop-up menu to specify which utterance the Mac speaks before the actual error message—for example, "*Excuse me!* The Trash could not be emptied," or "*Attention!* The document could not be printed." ("Application name" just speaks the name of the program that needs your help.)

 If you choose "Next in the phrase list" or "Random from the phrase list," you'll never hear the same expletive twice. Better yet, choose Edit Phrase List to specify your own words of frustration. (Apple Inc. is not liable for any trouble you may get into with people in neighboring cubicles.)

- **Delay.** The ostensible purpose of the Talking Alerts feature is to get your attention if you've wandered away from your Mac—mentally or physically. If you're still sitting there, you may not need the Mac to speak to get your attention; you could simply read the onscreen message. That's why you can set this slider to make the Mac wait, after the error message appears, for up to a minute before trying to flag you with its voice. That way it won't harangue you unnecessarily.

Speak selected text when the key is pressed

As promised, this is the feature that makes the Mac read you any web page, any email message, any sticky note—a welcome break for sore eyes. Furthermore, if you do any kind of writing at all, you'll discover the value of having your material read back to you out loud; it's a proofreading technique that reveals all kinds of typos and wordos that you wouldn't catch just by reading, even if you read it 50 times.

The very first time you turn on this checkbox, the Mac prompts you to specify a keystroke. (Later, you can always change the keystroke by clicking Change Key.) Choose a keystroke that doesn't conflict with the program you're using, like Control-T.

Now go to the program where you'd like the reading to happen. Highlight some text (or press ⌘-A to select all of it). Then press the keystroke you specified. The Mac begins reading it aloud immediately. To interrupt the playback, press the same keystroke again.

And be glad you were alive to see the day.

Setting Up the Mac's Voice

Open System Preferences→Accessibility→Speech tab. Here, you can control which of the Mac's voices you want your computer to use, as well as how fast it should speak. As shown in Figure 7-11, though, the Mac comes with a huge range of additional voices that you can add to the pop-up menu here.

Tip: Don't ignore the "international" voices just because you're an American English speaker. There are also voices that speak English with British, South African, Irish, and Australian accents—always fun.

All those voices have to be downloaded, so you can't grab them without an internet connection. They're huge files, so don't be impatient. (They're stored in your System→Library→Speech→Voices folder.)

Figure 7-11:
Top: At the outset, you see only six voices.

Bottom: Choose Customize to see the complete list of voices (including dozens of international voices); turn on the ones you want the Mac to download. Then, for 15 minutes of hilarity, try clicking the voices in turn to hear sample sentences. Drag the slider to affect how fast each one speaks. (Clearly, Apple's programmers had some fun with this assignment.)

Voices to Sing About

The Mac's built-in speaking voices are no end to fun, as noted in Figure 7-11.

Five of the voices, in fact, *sing* rather than speak. Good News sings to the tune of "Pomp and Circumstance," otherwise known as the Graduation March. Bad News sings to the tune of Chopin's *Prelude in C minor,* better known as the Funeral March. Cellos sings to the tune of Grieg's *Peer Gynt* suite. Pipe Organ sings to the tune of the Alfred Hitchcock TV theme. Bells sings the typical church-bell carillon melody.

In other words, these voices sing whatever words you type to those melodies. (To hear the melody in its entirety, don't use any punctuation.)

- **Siri Voice.** That's right, kids: Siri can have either a man's voice or a woman's voice—and she can speak in a selection of accents. Even if you're American, it's fun to give Siri a cute Australian, South African, Irish, or British accent.

- **Voice Feedback.** Siri generally replies to your queries with both text and a synthesized voice. Here you can tell Siri not to bother speaking when you're looking at the screen and can read the responses for yourself.

- **Show Siri in menu bar.** Ordinarily, Siri's little blue round icon is at the top right of your screen—a handy clickable way to make her listen. But if you've mastered a keystroke, there's no reason to have that icon cluttering up your menu bar.

- **Siri Suggestions & Privacy.** In Apple's mind, Siri isn't just a voice assistant. "Siri" refers to all kinds of artificial-intelligence features scattered across the Mac. In Mail, for example, when you start typing an address, you may see some suggested addresses under the heading, "Siri Found in Apps." On somebody's card in Contacts, you might see a few phone numbers or email addresses that Siri found in *other* apps that she thinks might belong to this person. You might even see a gray proposed appointment in Calendar that you didn't put there. Siri found it in a Mail message (a flight confirmation, for example), and thinks she's helping you save steps.

 You can make those suggestions stop appearing. There's a clearly labeled checkbox in the Preferences for each of those apps (Mail, Contacts, Calendar, and so on).

 On this screen, though, you can choose which apps supply those suggestions *to* Mail, Contacts, Calendar, and so on.

The Mac Reads to You

As you know from this chapter so far, the Mac can type out what you say and obey spoken *commands*. But there's a third talent: The Mac can *talk*.

Most Apple programs have a Start Speaking command built right in: Safari, Mail, TextEdit, Stickies, Pages, and so on. Just right-click or two-finger click inside a window full of text and, from the pop-up menu, choose Speech→Start Speaking. How cool is that? Your Mac can read your email or a web article to you—in any of 41 languages—while you're getting dressed.

But that's kid stuff. Truth is, the Mac can read almost anything you like: text you pass your cursor over, alert messages, menus, and *any text document in any program*. It can speak in your choice of dozens of voices, ages 8 to 50. Some of the newest voices (like Alex, Jill, Samantha, and Tom) sound scarily like professional human voice-over artists.

Note: This text-reading business is not the same thing as the Mac's VoiceOver feature. VoiceOver is designed to read everything on the screen, including pop-up menus, buttons, and other controls, to visually impaired Mac fans (and to permit complete control, mouse-free, of everything). Details are on page 325.

In each case, with tremendous courtesy, Siri walks you through the process of teaching her the correct pronunciation. She offers you three ▶ buttons; each triggers a different pronunciation. Tap Select next to the correct one (or tap Tell Siri again if none of the three is correct).

By the end of the process, Siri knows two things: how to speak that person's name aloud, and how to recognize that name when *you* say it aloud.

Siri Settings

In System Preferences→Siri, you can fiddle with several Siri settings (Figure 7-10):

- **Listen for "Hey Siri."** This option, available only on the most powerful and recent Macs, is described on page 287.

- **Allow Siri when locked.** If your Mac works with "Hey Siri," you can even ask questions at the password screen, as though it were some kind of Apple-branded Amazon Alexa machine. ("Hey Siri" does not work when the Mac is asleep, though. If the screen is totally dark, you'll first have to slap the space bar to wake it to the Lock screen.)

- **Enable Ask Siri.** If you turn this off, you can no longer command your Mac using the Siri commands described in this chapter.

- **Keyboard Shortcut.** How would you like to make Siri start listening? This pop-up menu starts you off with a key combo to *hold down* (⌘-space) and one to *tap* (fn-space)—but you can also choose Customize and enter any key combination you like. Of course, it has to be one that's not already "taken" by the Mac, which can be tricky.

- **Language.** What language do you want Siri to speak and recognize? The options here include 41 languages and dialects. For example, Siri can speak English in seven flavors—Australian, American, British, Canadian, Indian, New Zealand, and Singaporean.

Figure 7-10:
Why would anyone turn off Siri? One reason: Siri involves transmitting data to Apple, which gives some people the privacy willies. Apple's collect everything you say to Siri, the names of your songs and playlists, and the names in your Contacts (so that Siri can recognize them when you refer to them).

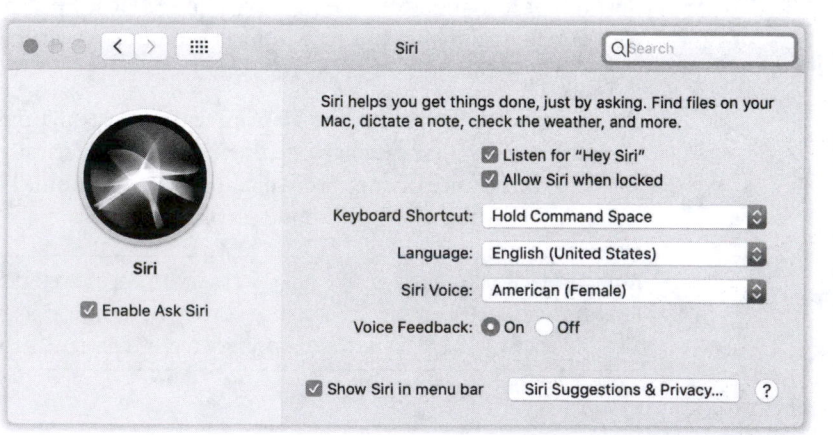

Note: You see the ⊕ button only when you've asked questions with concrete answers—about, for example, time, weather, stocks, or sports, or when Siri has fetched an answer from Wikipedia, Twitter, or the web. When you've asked Siri to *do* something (like dim the screen or open an app), on the other hand, no ⊕ appears.

Advanced Siri

With a little setup, you can extend Siri's powers in some intriguing ways.

Teach Siri About Your Relationships

When you say, "Text my mother" or "Call my manager," how does Siri know whom you're talking about? Sure, Siri is powerful artificial intelligence, but she's not actually *magic.* Turns out you teach her by referring to somebody in your Contacts list. Say to her something like, "My assistant is Jan Carpenter" or "Tad Cooper is my boyfriend." When Siri asks for confirmation, say "Yes" or tap Confirm.

Or wait for Siri to ask you herself. If you say, "Email my dad," Siri asks, "Who is your dad?" Just say his name; Siri remembers that relationship from now on. (You can add relationships like mother, father, parent, brother, sister, son, daughter, child, friend, spouse, partner, assistant, manager, wife, husband, fiancé, and boss.)

Behind the scenes, Siri lists these relationships on your card in Contacts.

Now that you know that, you can figure out how to edit or delete these relationships. Which is handy—not all relationships, as we know, last forever.

Fix Siri's Name Comprehension

Siri easily understands common names—but if someone in your family, work, or social circle has an unusual name, you may quickly become frustrated. After all, you can't text, call, email, or get directions to someone's house unless Siri understands the person's name when you say it.

One workaround is to use a relationship, as described earlier. That way, you can say, "Call my brother" instead of "Call Ilyich" (or whatever his offbeat name is).

Another is to use Siri's pronunciation-learning feature. It kicks in in several different situations:

- **When you're texting.** If Siri offers the wrong person's name when you try to text someone by voice, say, "Someone else." After you've sent the message, Siri apologetically says, "By the way, sorry I didn't recognize that name. Can you teach me how to say it?"

- **After Siri botches a pronunciation.** Tell her, "That's not how to pronounce his name."

- **Whenever it occurs to you.** You can start the process by saying, "Learn to pronounce Reagann Tsuki's name" or "Learn to pronounce my mom's name."

What do you dream about?	Winter is coming.
I am your father.	Which came first, the chicken or the egg?
What is zero divided by zero?	
Are you human?	Merry Christmas!

Tip: You may notice that Siri addresses you by name in her *typed* answers, but she doesn't always speak it when she reads those answers out loud.

Ordinarily, she calls you whatever you're called in Contacts. But you can make her call you whatever you like. Say, "Call me Master" or "Call me Frank" or "Call me Ishmael." If you confirm when she asks, then from now on that's what Siri will call you in her typed responses.

What to Do with Siri's Results

On the phone, your interaction with Siri is over once she produces her response. On the Mac, though, you can *interact* with the results.

When you've asked a question that produces an answer from the web, for example, a ⊕ button appears at the top right of the Siri results panel. If you click it, then the Siri result gets pinned to the top of your Notifications pane (page 380), so that you can look at it again later without having to repeat the whole Siri query. Figure 7-9 shows the idea.

Figure 7-9:
When Siri has fetched an answer online (left), you can "pin" it to the Notification Center (right). To do so, click the ⊕ button, as shown by the cursor at left.

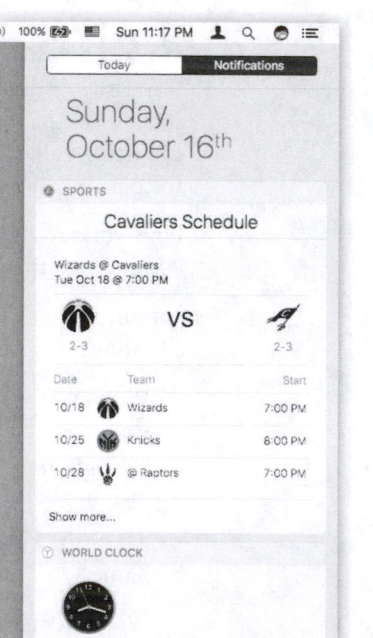

You: "Why did the chicken cross the road?" Siri: "I am not perspicacious about the peregrinations of poultry."

You: "Klaatu barada nikto." Siri: "OK, I'll pass the message on to Gort." (You kind of have to know *The Day the Earth Stood Still* to get it.)

You: "Do you have a boyfriend?" Siri: "Why? So we can get ice cream together, and listen to music, and travel across galaxies, only to have it end in slammed doors, heartbreak and loneliness? Sure, where do I sign up?"

Here are a few other things to say to Siri when you get bored:

What does "Siri" mean?

Am I your best friend?

Do you believe in love?

What should I wear for Halloween?

Testing 1, 2, 3.

I'm tired.

What's your secret?

What's your sign?

What do you think of Android?

What do you think of Windows?

You don't understand love.

You don't understand me.

I'm sorry.

Do blondes have more fun?

Supercalifragilisticexpialidocious.

Who's on first?

Why are you so awesome?

What's your favorite color?

Where are you?

When is the world going to end?

What's the best computer?

How much do you cost?

What are you doing later?

Make me a sandwich.

This statement is false.

Do you believe in Santa Claus?

I don't like your voice.

Are you serious?

Are you kidding me?

Blah blah blah.

LOL.

You are good to me.

Give me a kiss.

What are the three laws of robotics?

Read me a haiku.

Take me to your leader.

Can I borrow some money?

I love you, Siri.

Will you marry me?

When is your birthday?

What's the best phone?

You're boring.

Can you sing?

You're cute.

You make me so mad!

What do you want?

Tell me a joke.

Tell me a story.

I'm cold.

Do you love me?

What are you doing?

Do you like Pokémon Go?

Beatbox.

Guess what?

You're an idiot.

Have a nice day.

If she's working properly but misrecognizes your instructions, you'll know it, because you can see her interpretation of what you said. You can click Siri's interpretation to make corrections by typing.

Tip: You can also correct a misheard command just by speaking the correct version, like this, "I meant Chicago." Siri gets what you mean.

If Siri recognizes what you said but it isn't within her world of comprehension, she offers you a "Search the web" button as a last resort.

Siri's Personality

Siri's understanding of casual spoken commands is so impressive that you might sometimes think she's almost human. And that, of course, is exactly what Apple wants you to think.

You can say all kinds of off-kilter things to Siri. Whoever programmed her had a sassy sense of humor.

For example, if you ask her, "What is the meaning of life?" she responds with one of more than a dozen different answers. She might say, "I can't answer that now, but give me some time to write a very long play in which nothing happens." Or: "It's nothing Nietzsche couldn't teach ya." Or: "All evidence to date suggests it's chocolate."

Siri is full of such comebacks, and there are whole websites dedicated to her snark. Here are a few examples. (This list won't ruin the fun, because Siri actually has several different comebacks to most of these questions.)

You: "Who's your daddy?" Siri: "You are. Can we get back to work now?"

You: "Open the pod bay doors, Hal." Siri: "I'm sorry, I'm afraid I can't do that." (Then: "Are you happy now?")

You: "Knock knock." Siri: "Knock knock. Who's there? Joshua. Joshua who? Joshua, I don't do knock-knock jokes."

You: "What are you wearing?" Siri: "You have the wrong personal assistant, David."

You: "Who's the boss?" (Siri presents the vital statistics of Bruce Springsteen.)

You: "Beam me up, Siri!" Siri: "Please remove your belt, shoes, and jacket, and empty your pockets."

You: "Show me the money." Siri: "I've found 23 ATMs that are fairly close to you…"

You: "How much wood would a woodchuck chuck if a woodchuck could chuck wood?" Siri: "42 cords of wood, to be exact. Everyone knows that."

You: "Guess what." Siri: "You won the lottery?"

You: "Talk dirty to me." Siri: "Humus. Compost. Pumice. Silt. Gravel."

Result: Siri displays the results of your search right on her own screen. Tap one of the results to open the corresponding web page in Safari.

• **Facts and figures.** This is a huge category. It represents Siri's partnership with the Wolfram Alpha factual search engine (*wolframalpha.com*). The possibilities here could fill an entire chapter—or an entire encyclopedia.

You can say things like, "How many days until Valentine's Day?" "When was Abraham Lincoln born?" "How many teaspoons are in a gallon?" "What's the exchange rate between dollars and euros?" "What's the capital of Belgium?" "How many calories are in a Hershey bar?" "What's a 17 percent tip on 62 dollars for three people?" "What movie won the Oscar for Best Picture in 1985?" "When is the next solar eclipse?" "What's the tallest mountain in the world?" "What's the definition of 'schadenfreude'?" "How much is 23 dollars in pesos?" "Generate a random number." "Graph x equals 3y plus 12." "What flights are overhead?"

In Mojave, Siri offers better answers about celebrities ("Where was Jennifer Lawrence born?") and food and nutrition ("How much caffeine is in a cup of coffee?" or "How many calories in a hot dog?")

Result: For simple math and conversions, Siri just shows you the answer. For more complex questions, you get a specially formatted table, ripped right out of Wolfram Alpha's knowledge base.

Tip: Siri can also harness the entire wisdom of Wikipedia. You can say, for example, "Search Wikipedia for Harold Edgerton," or "Tell me about Thomas Jefferson," or "Show me the Wikipedia page about Richard Branson."

• **Search Twitter.** If you say something like, "What are people saying?" or "What's going on?" or "What's happening on Twitter?" you see a list of tweets on the current trending topics on Twitter. (Tap a tweet in the list to open it into a new window that contains more information and a View in Twitter button.)

Or ask, "What are people saying about the Chicago Bears?" to read tweets on that subject. Or "Search Twitter for the hashtag 'FirstWorldProblems.'" (A *hashtag* is a searchable phrase like #toofunny or #macOS, which makes finding relevant tweets on Twitter much easier.)

Result: Siri displays 10 tweets that match your query.

You may never find the end of the things Siri understands, or the ways that she can help you. If her repertoire seems intimidating at first, start simple—use her to open apps, find files, send text messages, and take notes. You can build up your bag of tricks as your confidence builds.

When Things Go Wrong

If Siri doesn't have a good enough internet connection to do her thing, she'll tell you so.

In Mojave, Apple has, somewhat mystifyingly, put extra work into making motorsport answers better: Current standings, schedules, and stats.

Result: Neat little box scores or factoids, complete with team logos.

 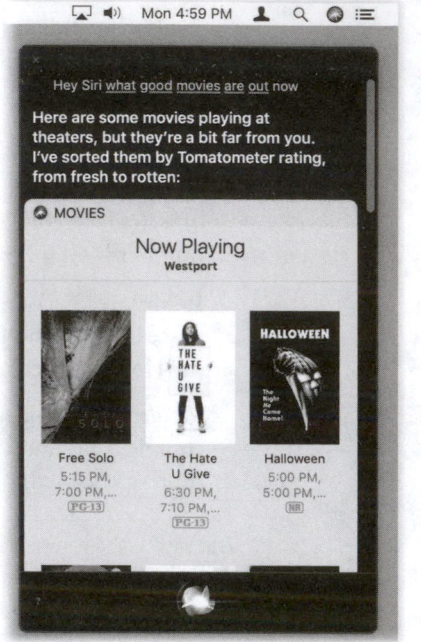

Figure 7-8:
Everything you always wanted to know about sports and movies but thought it'd be too much trouble to ask.

- **Movies.** Siri is also the virtual equivalent of an insufferable film buff. She knows *everything.* "Who was the star of *Groundhog Day*?" "Who directed *Chinatown*?" "What is *Waterworld* rated?" "What movie won Best Picture in 1952?"

 It's not just about old movies, either. Siri knows everything about current showtimes in theaters (Figure 7-8, right). "What movies are opening this week?" "What's playing at the Watton Cineplex?" "Give me the reviews for *Titanic 2: The Return*." "What are today's showtimes for *The Next Jedi*?"

 Result: Tidy tables of movie theaters or movie showtimes. (Click one for details.) Sometimes you get a movie poster filled with facts—and, of course, a link to rent or buy it on iTunes.

- **Search the web.** "Search the web for a 2016 Ford Mustang." "Search for healthy smoothie recipes." "Search for news about the Netflix-Amazon merger." "Search the web for pictures of cows."

Tip: Siri uses Google to perform its web searches. If you prefer Bing, just say so. Say, "Bing Benjamin Franklin." (For that matter, you can also ask Siri to "Yahoo" something—for example, "Yahoo low-cal dessert recipes.")

While music is playing, Siri's happy to tell you what you're listening to. ("What song is this?" "Who's the singer?" "What album is this from?") You can also tell her, "Like this song" or "Rate this song five stars." She'll note that and offer you more songs like it on the For You screen of the Apple Music app.

You can ask her to play the top hits of any year or decade. ("Play the top song from 1990." "Play the top 35 songs of the 1960s.")

Result: Just what you asked for!

- **Identifying music.** Whenever the Mac is playing music, you can say things like, "What's that song?" or "What song is this?"

Result: Siri identifies whatever song the Mac is playing—song name, singer, album, and so on. At this point, you can (shocker!) say, "Buy this song" or "Add this song to my wish list."

- **Weather.** "What's the weather going to be today?" "What's the forecast for tomorrow?" "Show me the weather this week." "Will it snow in Dallas this weekend?" "Check the forecast for Memphis on Friday." "What's the forecast for tonight?" "Can you give me the wind speed in Kansas City?" "Tell me the windchill in Anchorage." "What's the humidity right now?" "How's the weather in Paris?" "What's the high for Washington on Friday?" "When will Jupiter rise tomorrow?" "When's the moonrise?" "How cold will it be in Houston tomorrow?" "What's the temperature outside?" "Is it windy out there?" "When does the sun rise in London?" "When will the sun set today?" "Should I wear a jacket?"

Result: A convenient miniature Weather display for the date and place you specified.

- **Stocks.** "What's Google's stock price?" "What did Ford close at today?" "How's the Dow doing?" "What's Microsoft's P/E ratio?" "What's Amazon's average volume?" "How are the markets doing?"

Result: A tidy little stock graph, bearing a wealth of up-to-date statistics.

- Books. "Find *Little Women* in Books." "Buy *The Corrections* in Books." "Find books by Martha Stewart."

Result: The Books app opens and does your bidding.

- **Sports.** At last you have a buddy who's just as obsessed with sports trivia as you are (Figure 7-8, left). You can say things like, "How did the Indians do last night?" "What was the score of the last Yankees game?" "When's the next Cowboys game?" "What baseball games are on today?"

You can also ask questions about individual players, like, "Who has the best batting average?" "Who has scored the most runs against the Red Sox?" "Who has scored the most goals in British soccer?"

Team stats are fair game, too, like, "Show me the roster for the Giants," "Who is pitching for Tampa this season?" and "Is anyone on the Marlins injured right now?"

- **Businesses.** Siri is a walking (well, all right, non-walking) Yellow Pages. Go ahead, try it: "Find coffee near me." "Where's the closest Walmart?" "Find some pizza places in Cincinnati." "Search for gas stations." "French restaurants nearby." "I'm in the mood for Chinese food." "Find me a hospital."

Result: Siri displays a handsome list of businesses nearby that match your request.

Tip: She's a sly dog, that Siri. She'll help you out even if your requests are, ahem, somewhat off the straight and narrow. If you say, "I think I'm drunk," she'll offer a "Call me a taxi" button, which produces a list of cab companies. If you indicate that you're craving relief from your drug addiction, she'll provide you with a list of rehab centers.

- **Passwords.** In macOS Mojave, Siri can look up passwords for you. That's a godsend when you're trying to log into a website in a new Mac or on a different computer. "What's my Hulu password?" "Look up my Netflix password." "I need my Citibank password."

Result: The iPhone requests proof that you're you—your Mac password, or Touch ID—and then displays the Passwords screen in Safari. Super cool. (If you have several passwords for the same item, click the one you mean.)

- **Playing music.** Instead of fumbling around in iTunes, save yourself steps and time by speaking the name of the album, song, or band: "Play some Beatles." "Play 'I'm a Barbie Girl.'" "Play some jazz." "Play my jogging playlist." "Play the party mix." "Shuffle my 'Dave's Faves' playlist." "Play." "Skip."

And, of course, podcasts work the same way. "Play podcasts." "Jump back 15 seconds." "Skip ahead two minutes." "Find the 'Serial' podcast in the iTunes Store."

Result: Siri plays (or skips, or shuffles) the music you asked for—without ever leaving whatever app you were using.

- **Apple Music.** If you subscribe to Apple's $10-a-month Apple Music service, Siri offers a huge range of even more useful voice controls. For example, you can call for any music in Apple's 30 million–song catalog by song name, album, or performer: "Play 'Mr. Blue Sky.'" "Show me some Elton John albums." "Play 'Yesterday' next" (or "…after this song"). Or ask to have a singer or album played in random order: "Shuffle Taylor Swift."

When you hear a song you like, you can say, "Play more like this." Or "Add this song [or album] to my library." (Or, if you don't like it, "Skip this song.")

If more than one person performed a song, be specific: "Play 'Smooth Criminal' by Glee." You can even ask for a song according to the movie it was in. "Play that song from *Frozen*."

Or start one of your playlists by name ("Play 'Jogging'"). Or re-listen to a song: "Play previous." Or ask for one of Apple Music's radio stations: "Play Beats 1" or "Play Charting Now."

me the reviews for Olive Garden in Youngstown." (See Figure 7-7, right.) On the Mac, Siri can't book reservations through OpenTable, as she can on the iPhone.

Result: Siri displays a list of matching restaurants—with ratings, distance, prices, and so on. Click a name for more information.

- **Notes.** You create a new note (in the Notes app) by saying things like, "Make a note that my shirt size is 15 and a half" or "Note: Dad will not be coming to the reunion after all." You can even name the note in your request: "Create a 'Movies to Download' note."

But you can also call up a certain note to the screen, like this: "Find my frequent-flyer note." You can even summon a table-of-contents view of all your notes by saying, "Show all my notes."

Result: A miniature Notes page appears, showing your newly dictated text (or the existing note that you've requested).

Tip: You can keep dictating into the note you've just added. Say, "Add 'Return books to library' " (or just say, "Add," and Siri will ask you what to add). She'll keep adding to the same note until you say, "Note that…" or "Start a note" or "Take a note" to begin a fresh note page.

You can add text to an earlier note: "Add *Titanic II: The Voyage Home* to my 'Movies to Download' note." (The first line of any note is also its title—in this case "Movies to Download.")

- **Directions.** Siri can set up the Maps app to answer requests like these: "How do I get to the airport?" "Show me 1500 Broadway, New York City." "Directions to my assistant's house." "Take me home." You just have to make sure Siri can access Location Services; you can do that in the System Preferences→Security & Privacy→ Privacy. But, if you don't, Siri will just direct you there the first time you ask for directions. You can ask for directions to the home or work address of anyone in your Contacts list—provided those addresses are *in* your Contacts cards.

Result: Siri fires up the Maps app, with the start and end points of your driving directions already filled in.

- **Reminders.** Siri is a natural match for the Reminders app. She can add items to that list at your spoken command. For example: "Remind me to file my IRS tax extension." "Remind me to bring the science supplies to school." "Remind me to take my antibiotic tomorrow at 7 a.m."

If you also have an iPhone, the *location-based* reminders are especially amazing. They rely on the phone's GPS to know where you are. So, on the Mac, you can say, "Remind me to visit the drugstore when I leave the office," or "Remind me to water the lawn when I get home," or "Remind me to check in with Nancy when I leave here." Since iCloud magically syncs all of your reminders across devices, the *phone* will pop up a reminder when you reach, or leave, the specified locations.

Result: A miniature entry from the Reminders app, showing you that Siri has understood.

September 23?" "When's my next appointment?" "When is my meeting with Charlize?" "Where is my next meeting?" "What's my day tomorrow?"

Result: Siri reads you your agenda and displays a tidy Day view of the specified date.

- **Text messages.** "Send a text to Alex Rybeck." "Send a message to Peter saying, 'I no longer require your services.'" "Tell Cindy I'm running late." "Send a message to Jane's mobile asking her to pick me up at the train." "Send a text message to 212-561-2282." "Text Frank and Ralph: Did you pick up the pizza?"

Result: Siri prompts you for the body of the message, if you haven't specified it. Then you see a miniature outgoing text message. Siri asks if you want to send it; say "Yes," "Send," or "Confirm" to proceed. (See Figure 7-7, left.)

Figure 7-7:
Left: Siri is your little text-message secretary. She's happy to send and read text messages for you, right from your Mac.

Right: Hey, look—it's restaurant info, right in Siri's window!

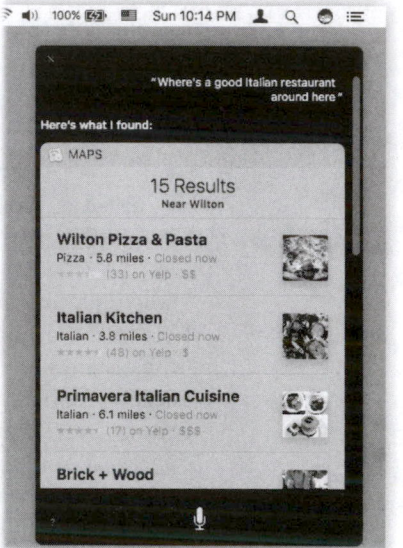

If you need to edit the message before sending it, you can say, "Change it to" to re-dictate the message; "Add" to add more to the message; "No, send it to Frank" to change the recipient; "No" to leave the message on the screen without sending it; or "Cancel" to forget the whole thing.

You can also ask Siri to read incoming text messages to you. For example, you can say, "Read my new messages," "Read that again," or "Read my last message from Tia."

You can even have Siri reply to messages she's just read to you. "Reply, 'Congratulations (period). Can't wait to see your trophy (exclamation point)!'" Or: "Tell him I have a flat tire and I'm going to be late."

- **Restaurants.** Siri is also happy to serve as your personal concierge. Try "Good Italian restaurants around here," "Find a good pizza joint in Cleveland," or "Show

Or you can use the summary-listing commands. When you say, "Read my email," Siri starts walking backward through your Inbox, telling you the subject of each, plus who sent it and when.

After a few listings, Siri asks, "Shall I read the rest?" That's your opportunity to shut down what could be a very long recitation. If you say, "Yes," she goes on to read the entire list of subject lines, dates, and senders.

Tip: You can also use commands like "Any new mail from Chris today?" "Show new mail about the world premiere." "Show yesterday's email from Jan." All of those commands produce a list of the messages, but Siri doesn't read them.

Result: Siri reads aloud.

You can also compose a new message by voice; anytime you use the phrase "about," that becomes the subject line for your new message. "Email Mom about the reunion." "Email my boyfriend about the dance on Friday." "New email to Freddie Gershon." "Mail Mom about Saturday's flight." "Email Frank and Cindy Vosshall and Peter Love about the picnic." "Email my assistant and say, 'Thanks for arranging the taxi!'" "Email Gertie and Eugene about their work on the surprise party, and say I really value your friendship."

(If you've indicated only the subject or addressee, Siri prompts you for the rest.)

You can reply to a message Siri has just described, too. "Reply, 'Dear Robin (comma), I'm so sorry about your dog (period). I'll be more careful next time (period).'" Or "Send him a text message saying, 'I got your note.'"

Result: A miniature Mail message, showing you Siri's handiwork before you send it.

- **Calendar.** Siri can make appointments for you. Considering how many tedious clicks it usually takes to schedule an appointment in the Calendar app, this is an enormous improvement. "Make an appointment with Patrick for Thursday at 3 p.m." "Set up a haircut at 9." "Set up a meeting with Charlize this Friday at noon." "Meet Danny Cooper at six." "New appointment with Steve, next Sunday at 7." "Schedule a conference call at 5:30 tonight in my office."

Result: A slice of that day's calendar appears, filled in the way you requested.

Tip: Siri may also alert you to a conflict, something like this: "Note that you already have an all-day appointment about 'Boston Trip' for this Thursday. Shall I schedule this anyway?" Amazing.

You can also move previously scheduled meetings by voice. For example, "Move my 2:00 meeting to 2:30." "Reschedule my meeting with Charlize to a week from Monday at noon." "Add Frank to my meeting with Harry." "Cancel the conference call on Sunday."

You can even *consult* your calendar by voice. You can say, "What's on my calendar today?" "What does the rest of my day look like?" "What's on my calendar for

In Mojave, in fact, Apple has beefed up the Mac's knowledge of what's *in* your photos. "Show me photos with dogs," you might say. Or, "Show me pictures of Max from last year in San Francisco." Can you imagine how much time that might save you?

Result: The Photos app opens, with the requested photos already isolated and presented to you.

- **Navigating your Mac.** "Open the Downloads folder." "Open Documents." "Open the Trash."

Result: The Finder folder pops open. If you ask for a folder you've made, the Mac shows it to you in a list instead of opening it directly; you have to double-click the folder to open it.

- **Wrap up for the day.** "Put the Mac to sleep." "Shut Down the Mac."

Result: Your Mac blinks off. Creepy.

- **FaceTime calls.** Siri can place FaceTime calls for you. "Call Nicole." "Call the office." "Start a FaceTime call with Sheila Withins." "FaceTime Alex."

Result: Siri hands you off to the FaceTime app and places the call. At this point, it's just as though you'd initiated the call yourself. Strangely, Siri can't place *phone* calls for you, even though the Mac can (see page 308).

- **Clock.** "What time is it?" "What time is it in San Francisco?" "What's today's date?" "What's the date a week from Friday?" Or just "Time."

Result: When you ask about the time, you see the clock identifying the time in question. (For dates, Siri just talks to you and writes out the date.)

- **Contacts.** You can ask Siri to look up information in your address book (the Contacts app)—and not just addresses. For example, you can say, "What's Gary's work number?" "Give me Sheila Jenkins' office phone." "Show Tia's home email address." "What's Casey's home address?" "When is my husband's birthday?" "Show Larry Murgatroid." "Who is P.J. Frankenberg?"

Result: A half "page" from your Contacts list. You can tap it to jump into that person's full card in Contacts. (If Siri finds multiple listings for the person you named—"Bob," for example—she lists all the matches and asks you to specify which one you meant.)

Tip: In many of the examples on these pages, you'll see that you can identify people by their relationship to you. You can say, "Show my mom's work number," for example, or "Give me directions to my boss's house" or "Call my girlfriend." For details on teaching Siri about these relationships, see "Advanced Siri" on page 302.

- **Email.** Siri can read your email to you. For example, if you say, "Read my latest email" or "Read my new email," Siri reads aloud your most recent email message. (She then offers you the chance to dictate a response.)

my Mac?" "Is Bluetooth on?" "How much memory does this Mac have?" "How much iCloud storage do I have left?"

Result: Siri displays the answer.

- **Round up files.** This is a big one—and a Mac Special (not on the iPhone): You can use Siri to manage files. "Find the documents I worked on last week." "Show me the PDFs in my Downloads folder." "What was I working on yesterday?" "Show me the Microsoft Word documents I worked on two days ago." "Show me the files I shared with Casey yesterday." "Round up all my Photoshop files." "Where are the files tagged In Progress?" "List all the files with the word 'Asparagus.'" "Let's see the files on my desktop." "Get my Vacation folder." "Show me the file I sent Casey."

Siri remembers context, too, so you can then add, "Just the presentations that Bill sent me."

Result: Siri shows you a tidy list of matching files (Figure 7-6). Double-click one to open it, or drag one into any other window or folder. Or right-click a listing and, from the shortcut menu, choose Quick Look or Reveal in Finder.

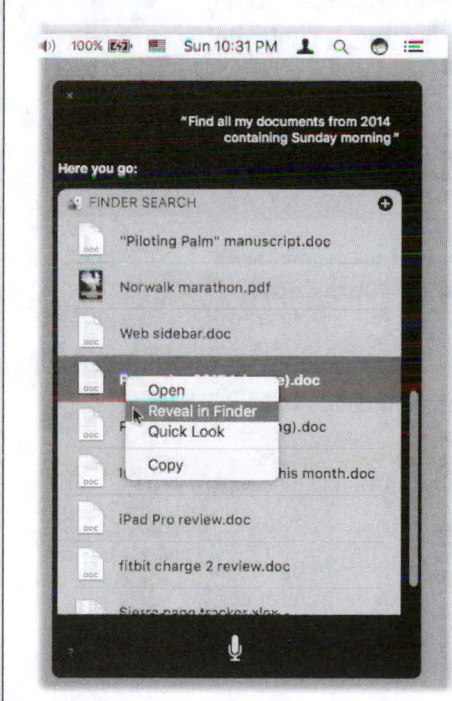

Figure 7-6:
Siri is now the fastest way to get a list of files on your Mac that meet certain criteria—in this example, documents containing the words "Sunday morning" that were written in 2014. Right-click or two-finger click for the shortcut menu shown here.

- **Find photos fast.** Siri is especially handy with files you keep in the Photos app. "Show me the videos from Halloween last year." "Get me the videos from Utah." "Show me the Disney World album." "Open the Panoramas presentation." "Show me the slow-mo videos from Oberlin College." "Give me the pictures from last summer."

From now on, when you click the Siri button in your menu bar or press the Siri keystroke, you get a Type to Siri box and a keyboard. Tap out your query and then hit Return; Siri shows and speaks her response, exactly as though you had spoken.

What to Say to Siri

Siri comes with a cheat sheet to help you learn her capabilities. To see it, open Siri. After five seconds of silence, Siri begins displaying screen after screen of example commands, under the heading "Some things you can ask me."

Or just open Siri and then say, "What can I say?" or "What can you do?" or "Help me!" The same cheat sheet appears.

Here are the general categories of things you can say to Siri:

- **Opening apps.** Even if you don't learn to use Siri for anything else, for the love of Mike, learn this one.

 You can say, "Open Calendar" or "Play Angry Birds" or "Launch Calculator."

 Result: The corresponding app opens instantly. It's exactly the same as clicking around to navigate to the app you're looking for and clicking it to open it—but without clicking around to navigate to the app you're looking for and then clicking it to open it.

Tip: You can also get apps by voice, with commands like "Search the App Store for time tracking" or "Download the Scrabble app."

- **Change your settings.** You can make changes to certain basic settings just by speaking your request. You can say, for example, "Turn on Bluetooth," "Turn off Wi-Fi," "Turn on Do Not Disturb."

 You can also make screen and speaker adjustments: "Make the screen brighter." "Dim the screen." "Turn on the screen saver." Or volume adjustments: "Make the volume louder." "Mute the sound." "Make the speaker softer."

 Result: Siri makes the requested adjustment, tells you so, and displays the corresponding switch in case she misunderstood your intention.

- **Open System Preferences panels.** When you need to make tweakier changes, you can open the most important panels by voice. "Open Wi-Fi System Preferences," "Open Notification settings," "Open Sounds settings," "Open wallpaper settings," and so on.

 Result: Siri silently opens the corresponding page of System Preferences.

- **Questions about your Mac.** "How much free space do I have on my Mac?" "What version of macOS is running?" "What's this Mac's serial number?" "How fast is

6. **Click Done.**

Close System Preferences, if you like.

From now on, saying "Hey, Alfred" (or whatever name you chose in step 5) opens the Siri palette, exactly as though you'd pressed the Siri keystroke or opened the Siri app.

Thanks to "Hey Siri," you now have a front-seat conversationalist, a little software friend who's always happy to listen to what you have to say—and whose knowledge of the world, news, sports, and history can help make those Monday mornings a little less dull.

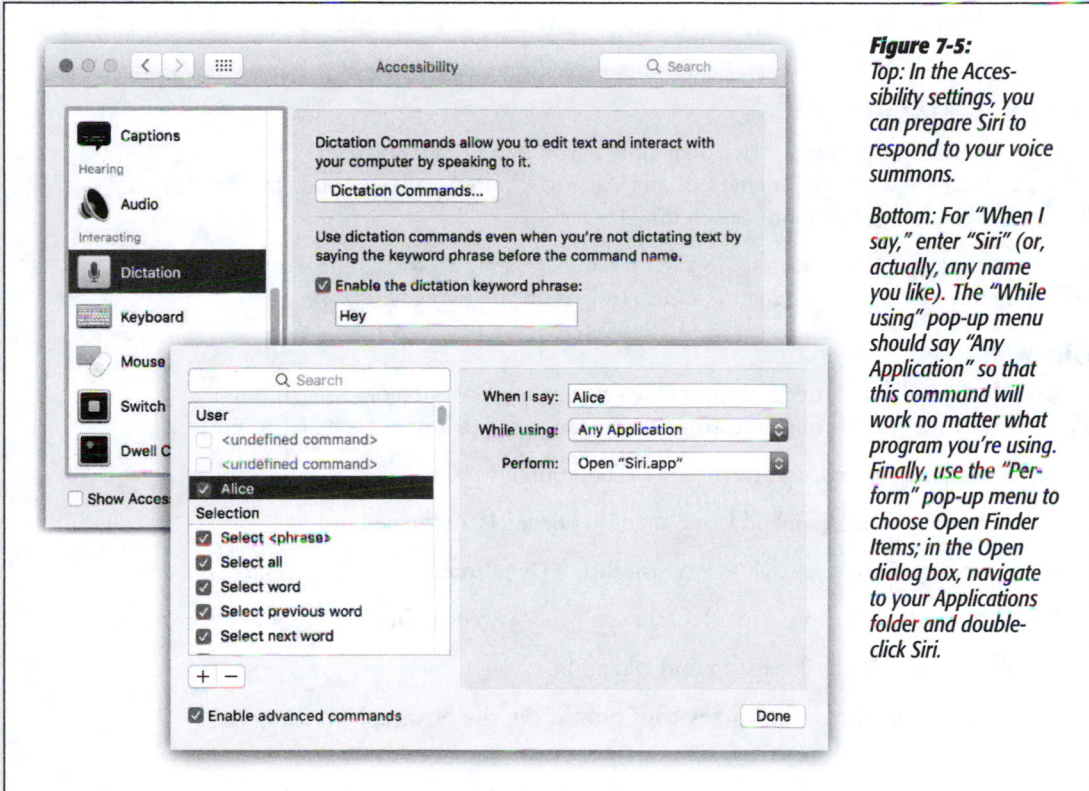

Figure 7-5:
Top: In the Accessibility settings, you can prepare Siri to respond to your voice summons.

Bottom: For "When I say," enter "Siri" (or, actually, any name you like). The "While using" pop-up menu should say "Any Application" so that this command will work no matter what program you're using. Finally, use the "Perform" pop-up menu to choose Open Finder Items; in the Open dialog box, navigate to your Applications folder and double-click Siri.

Type to Siri

You can also *type* your questions and commands to Siri instead of speaking them. Every now and then, that silent method could be preferable to the talk-aloud method—when you've got your laptop in a library, for example, or when your query is of a delicate nature.

To set this up, open System Preferences→Accessibility→Siri. Turn on "Enable Type to Siri."

And when you're completely finished talking to Siri, you can make her panel slide away off your screen in any of the following ways:

- **Press the Esc key** (or ⌘-period).

- **Click the** ✖ **in the upper-left corner.**

- **Trigger Siri again** and say something like "Goodbye," "See you later," or "Adios."

How to Use "Hey Siri"

On the phone, of course, Siri can also accept spoken commands without your clicking anything. That's an ideal feature for use in the car, when your hands and eyes should be focused on driving.

The Latest Models

On the Mac, Siri responds to "Hey Siri" only if you have a MacBook Pro (2018 or later), a MacBook Air (2018 or later), or an iMac Pro. On those models, open System Preferences→Siri, and turn on "Listen for 'Hey Siri.' "

The screen asks you to speak a few Siri commands ("Hey Siri, what's the weather?" and "Hey Siri, open my downloads," and so on)—and you're ready to go.

Older Models

It's possible to use hands-free Siri commands even if you have an older Mac, though. These steps guide you through creating a voice command that opens the Siri app:

1. **Open System Preferences→Keyboard→Dictation tab.**

 Make sure both Dictation and Use Enhanced Dictation are turned on.

2. **In System Preferences, switch to Accessibility→Dictation.**

 For example, from the previous step, choose View→Accessibility.

 Scroll down in the left-side list to find Dictation.

3. **Turn on "Enable the dictation keyword phrase"; in the box, replace** *Computer* **with** *Hey*.

 Actually, this can be any attention-getting word you like.

4. **Click Dictation Commands.**

 In the resulting box, make sure "Enable advanced commands" is turned on.

5. **Click the + button. Fill in the resulting box as shown in Figure 7-5.**

 If you want "Hey Siri" to be the listening trigger, then type *Siri* into the first box. But you should also feel free to substitute any name you like here: Jeeves, Alfred, Birdbrain—anything you like. For one thing, that idea would prevent Siri on your *phone* from responding every time you say "Hey Siri" within its earshot.

- **Click the Siri icon on the Dock,** or open the Siri app (in your Applications folder) in any of the ways people open apps.

- **Touch the Siri button** on the Touch Bar, if your Mac has one (page 233).

- **Say, "Hey Siri."** You have to set up this feature in advance, as described on the next page.

Once you hear the double-beep, and see the little Siri palette (Figure 7-4), Siri is listening. Ask your question or say your command. You don't have to lean up against your Mac; Siri works perfectly well at arm's length.

Note: Apple insists that Siri is neither male nor female. In fact, if you ask Siri her gender, she'll say something noncommittal, like, "Is this relevant?" But that's just political correctness. Any baby-name website—or Norwegian dictionary—will tell you that Siri is a girl's name. In any case, you can change what her gender *sounds* like in System Preferences→Siri.

Figure 7-4:
Top left: Siri's listening! Bottom left: Siri's answering!

Right: If you didn't ask the right thing, or if you want to ask it again differently, you can actually edit the text of your original query. (Here you're about to edit the percentage number.)

When you're finished speaking, be quiet for a moment. About a second after you stop speaking, Siri connects with her master brain online and processes your request. After a moment, she presents (and speaks) an attractively formatted response.

Tip: You generally see only the most recent question and response on the Siri screen. But you can scroll up to see all the previous exchanges you've had with Siri during this session.

To cancel your request—maybe because you've decided to rephrase your question—press the Esc key (or press ⌘-period), or click the Siri panel to interrupt Siri's work. Click the microphone icon to trigger your new attempt.

you a password you've forgotten; and answer questions about food, celebrities, and motorsports. You can operate her hands-free, too. With a couple of tweaks in System Preferences, you can teach Siri to respond anytime you say, "Hey Siri."

Most of the voice commands, in fact, that work on the iPhone work on the Mac, too.

It's not *Star Trek*. You can't ask Siri to clean your gutters or to teach you French. (Well, you can *ask*.)

But, as you'll soon discover, the number of things Siri *can* do for you is rather impressive. Furthermore, Apple continues adding to Siri's intelligence through software updates.

How to Use Siri

To use Siri, you have to turn on the master Siri switch. You were offered that chance the first time you started up Mojave (page 13); you can also turn Siri on at any time in System Preferences→Siri→Enable Siri.

Anytime thereafter—well, anytime you have an internet connection—you can put her to work for you.

To get Siri's attention, you have four choices:

- **Hold down ⌘+space bar** until you hear a quick double-beep. The beep comes in about a second. (You can change this keystroke, if you like, in System Preferences→Siri.)

- **Click the Siri icon** on the menu bar (Figure 7-3).

Figure 7-3:
Here are some of the ways you can make Siri start listening. You can open the Siri app in your Applications folder (left); click the Siri icon on your menu bar (second icon from right); or click the Siri icon on your Dock (second icon from top).

- **About Dictation and Privacy.** Here you can read more about that business of your utterances and address-book names being transmitted to Apple.

Note: You can also issue spoken commands to your Mac with an older dictation feature—you can say, "Open Safari," for example, or "Select the last paragraph" or "Bold that." This one is hiding in System Preferences→Accessibility. For details, see page 331.

Siri on the Mac

Siri is a crisply accurate, astonishingly understanding, uncomplaining, voice-commanded servant. For years, she's made using the iPhone much easier—and now she's on the Mac. In macOS Mojave, her voice sounds clearer and younger.

Older speech-recognition systems work only if you issue certain limited commands with predictable syntax, like "Call 445-2340" or "Open Microsoft Word." But Siri is different. She's been programmed to respond to casual speech, normal speech. It doesn't matter if you say, "What's the weather going to be like in Tucson this weekend?" or "Give me the Tucson weather for this weekend" or "Will I need an umbrella in Tucson?" Siri understands almost any variation.

And she understands regular, everyday speaking. You don't have to separate your words, talk weirdly, or train her. You just speak normally. In fact, she understands dozens of languages.

You can say, "What's Janet's work number?" or "How do I get to the airport?" or "What's the weather going to be like in San Francisco this weekend?" Siri can also round up files for you: "Show me the presentation I worked on yesterday" or "Show me all the emails about the company picnic." She can round up photos or videos according to their date, location taken, or album name ("Show me all the pictures I took in SeaWorld last year").

You can also ask questions about movies, sports, and restaurants. Siri displays a beautifully formatted response and speaks in a calm voice. In macOS Mojave, Siri can now control HomeKit gadgets in your home ("Siri, turn off the lights downstairs"); show

UP TO SPEED

A Brief History of Siri

In 2010, Apple bought Siri, a company that made a voice-control app (no longer available) for the iPhone. Apple cleaned it up, beefed it up, integrated it with the iPhone's software, and wound up with Siri, your virtual servant. Believe it or not, Siri is a spin-off from a Department of Defense research project called CALO (Cognitive Assistant that Learns and Organizes), which at one time was the largest artificial-intelligence project ever launched. In a very real way, therefore, Siri represents your tax dollars at work.

The spin-off was run by the Stanford Research Institute (SRI). But that's not where Siri's name came from. Siri, it turns out, is a Norwegian name meaning "beautiful woman who leads you to victory." (Co-creator Dag Kittlaus named Siri. He's Norwegian.)

Note: You'll also discover that your words fly onto the screen as you speak them. But as you speak more of a sentence, and the Mac uses context clues to figure out what you intended, you'll see words flip around and revise themselves. That, too, is part of Enhanced, and it's all in the name of giving you the best possible transcription.

Speech Settings

In System Preferences→Keyboard →Dictation tab (Figure 7-2), you can fiddle with several settings:

- **On/Off.** If you turn Dictation off, you can no longer dictate to type; the little microphone button won't appear.

- **Use Enhanced Dictation.** As described already.

- **Language.** What language and accent do you have? If you choose Add Language, you'll see that your options include English in 13 dialects, plus nearly 50 other languages, including Arabic, Catalan, Chinese, Croatian, Czech, Danish, Dutch, Finnish, French, German, Greek, Hebrew, Hindi, Hungarian, Indonesian, Italian, Japanese, Korean, Malay, Norwegian, Polish, Portuguese, Romanian, Russian, Slovak, Spanish, Swedish, Thai, Turkish, Ukrainian, and Vietnamese.

- **Shortcut.** Here's where you specify what key you want to double-tap in order to dictate. From this pop-up menu, you can choose the fn key (on laptops) or the right or left ⌘ key—or you can choose Customize to make up any keystroke you want. The Shortcut box goes empty; press a key combination you prefer (Control-S, for example).

Figure 7-2:
In System Preferences, you specify what microphone, language, and trigger key you want to use for dictating.

Keyboard

Keyboard | Text | Shortcuts | Input Sources | Dictation

Use Dictation wherever you can type text. To start dictating, use the shortcut or select Start Dictation from the Edit menu.

Internal Microphone ⌄

Dictation: ● On ○ Off
☑ Use Enhanced Dictation
Allows offline use and continuous dictation with live feedback.

Language: English (United States)

Shortcut: Press Fn (Function) Key Twice

About Dictation and Privacy

Say this:	To get this:	For example, saying this:	Types this:
"all caps"	Types just the next word in all caps	"We (all caps) really don't belong here"	We REALLY don't belong here
"no caps"	Types the next word in lowercase	"see you in (no caps) Texas"	see you in texas
"no caps on," then "no caps off"	Prevents any capital letters	"I'll ask (no caps on) Santa Claus (no caps off)"	I'll ask santa claus
"no space"	Runs the next two words together	"Try new mega (no space) berry flavor"	Try new megaberry flavor
"no space on," then "no space off"	Eliminates all spaces	"(No space on) I can't believe you ate all that (no space off) (comma) she said excitedly"	Ican'tbelieveyou ateallthat, she said excitedly
[alphabet letters]	Types the letters out, though usually not very accurately	"The stock symbol is A P P L"	The stock symbol is APPL

You don't always have to dictate these formatting commands, by the way. The Mac automatically inserts hyphens into phone numbers (you say, "2125561000," and it types "212-556-1000"), formats two-line street addresses without your having to say "New line" before the city, and handles prices automatically ("six dollars and thirty-two cents" becomes "$6.32"). It formats dates and web addresses well, too; you can even use the nerdy shortcut "dub-dub-dub" when you want the "www" part of a web address.

The Mac recognizes email addresses, too, as long as you remember to say "at sign" at the right spot. You'd say, "harold (underscore) beanfield (at sign) gmail (dot) com" to get harold_beanfield@gmail.com.

Enhanced Dictation

In Enhanced Dictation mode, you can dictate without an internet connection. You're not limited to 30-second utterances, and the words appear on the screen as you speak them. The only downside: The accuracy isn't as good as non–Enhanced Dictation.

If, after you've searched your soul, you decide to try Enhanced, open System Preferences→Keyboard →Dictation tab. Turn on Use Enhanced Dictation. (Or accept the Mac's invitation to turn it on when you first attempt to dictate. If you say yes, you're treated to a 1.2-gigabyte download.)

When the downloading is over, everything about dictation works just as described on the previous pages, except you can dictate offline, you can dictate forever, and the accuracy—well, you know.

Say this:	To get this:	For example, saying this:	Types this:
"asterisk," "plus sign," "minus sign," "equals sign"	*, +, −, =	"numeral eight (asterisk) two (plus sign) one (minus sign) three (equals sign) fourteen"	8*2+1−3=14
"ampersand," "dash"	&, −	"Dexter (ampersand) Logan (dash) the best (exclamation point)"	Dexter & Logan—the best!
"hyphen"	- [without spaces]	"Don't give me that holier (hyphen) than (hyphen) thou attitude"	Don't give me that holier-than-thou attitude
"backquote"	'	"Back in (backquote) (numeral) fifty-two"	back in '52
"smiley," "frowny," "winky" (or "smiley face," "frowny face," "winky face")	:-) :-(;-)	"I think you know where I'm going with this (winky face)"	I think you know where I'm going with this ;-)

You can also say "percent sign" (%), "at sign" (@), "dollar sign" ($), "cent sign" (¢), "euro sign" (€), "yen sign" (¥), "pounds sterling sign" (£), "section sign" (§), "copyright sign" (©), "registered sign" (®), "trademark sign" (™), "greater-than sign" or "less-than sign" (> or <), "degree sign" (°), "caret" (^), "tilde" (~), "vertical bar" (|), and "pound sign" (#).

The software automatically capitalizes the first new word after a period, question mark, or exclamation point. But you can also force it to capitalize words you're dictating by saying "cap" right before the word, like this: "Dear (cap) Mom, I've run away to join (cap) The (cap) Circus (comma), a nonprofit cooperative for runaway jugglers."

Here's another table—this one shows the other commands for capitalization, plus spacing and commands.

Say this:	To get this:	For example, saying this:	Types this:
"cap" or "capital"	Capitalizes the next word	"Give me the (cap) works"	Give me the Works
"caps on," then "caps off"	Capitalizes the first letter of every word	"Next week (caps on) the new england chicken cooperative (caps off) will hire me"	Next week The New England Chicken Cooperative will hire me
"all caps on," then "all caps off"	Capitalizes everything	"So (all caps on) please please (all caps off) don't tell anyone"	So PLEASE PLEASE don't tell anyone

Punctuation

Here's a handy table that shows you what punctuation you can say to your Mac, and how to say it.

Say this:	To get this:	For example, saying this:	Types this:
"period" or "full stop"	. [space and capital letter afterward]	"Best (period) date (period) ever (period)"	Best. Date. Ever.
"dot" or "point"	. [no space afterward]	"My email is frank (dot) smith (at sign) gmail (dot) com"	My email is frank. smith@gmail.com
"comma," "semicolon," "colon"	, ; :	"Mom (comma) hear me (colon) I'm dizzy (semicolon) tired"	Mom, hear me: I'm dizzy; tired
"question mark," "exclamation point"	? ! [space and capital letter afterward]	"Ellen (question mark) Hi (exclamation point)"	Ellen? Hi!
"inverted question mark," "inverted exclamation point"	¿ ¡	"(inverted question mark) Que paso (question mark) "	¿Que paso?
"ellipsis" or "dot dot dot"	…	"Just one (ellipsis) more (ellipsis) step (ellipsis)"	Just one… more… step…
"space bar"	[a space, especially when a hyphen would normally appear]	"He rode the merry (space bar) go (space bar) round"	He rode the merry go round
"open paren" then "close paren" (or "open bracket/close bracket," or "open brace/close brace")	() or [] or { }	"Then she (open paren) the doctor (close paren) gasped"	Then she (the doctor) gasped
"new line"	[a press of the Return key]	"milk (new line) bread (new line) quinoa"	milk bread quinoa
"new paragraph"	[two presses of the Return key]	"autumn leaves (new paragraph) softly falling"	autumn leaves softly falling
"quote," then "unquote"	" "	Her perfume screamed (quote) available (unquote)	Her perfume screamed "available"
"numeral"	[writes the following number as a digit instead of spelling it out]	"Next week she turns (numeral) eight"	Next week she turns 8

The Mac plays another xylophone note—higher this time—and transmits the audio data to distant computers. They analyze your speech and transmit the resulting typed-out text back to your screen. (During this time, three blinking purple dots occupy the text area where you dictated. You can click Cancel if you're getting impatient.) The transcribed text appears all at once, in a big blob.

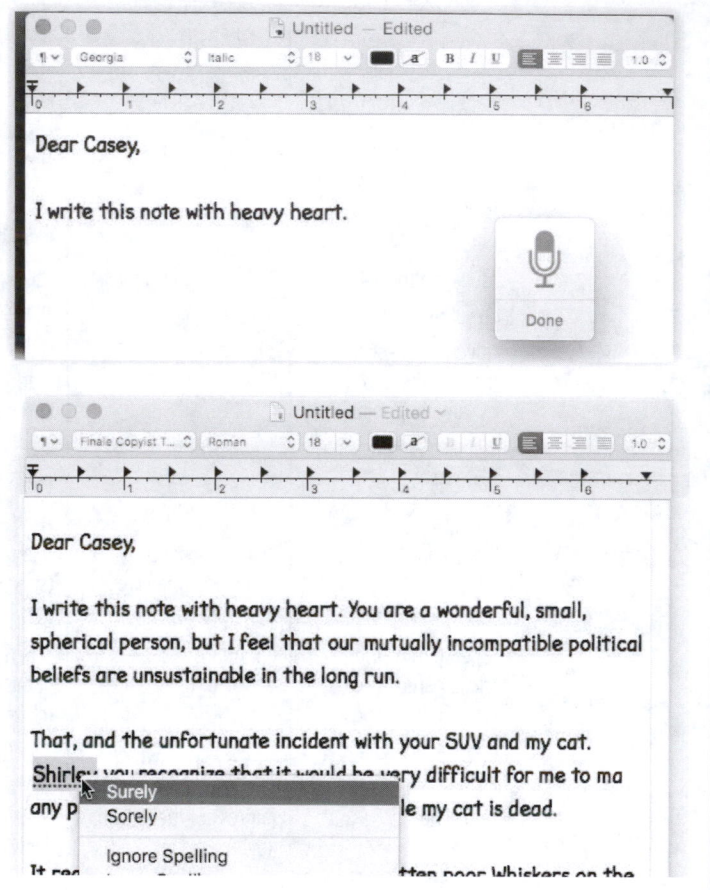

Figure 7-1:
The Mac has a built-in "speak to type" feature!

Top: When you double-press the fn key, the Mac goes into listening mode. The bouncing glow of the microphone icon is your level meter. It lets you know that the Mac hears you.

If you haven't released the fn key or clicked Done (or pressed Return) after 30 seconds, then the Mac stops listening on its own. Thirty seconds is the maximum talking time per blurt.

Bottom: If you see the dashed under-line, right-click or two-finger click it. You get a pop-up menu that includes alternative transcriptions.

If the transcription contains errors, you can click to edit them, exactly as you would fix an error in something you typed. Better yet, if the Mac *knows* it made errors, it underlines them, and you can often fix them with a quick click (Figure 7-1, bottom). Or, if the whole thing is a mess, you can press ⌘-Z, the universal keystroke for Undo.

Usually, you'll find the accuracy pretty darned good, considering that you didn't have to train the software to recognize your voice. You'll also find that the accuracy is better when you dictate complete sentences, and long words fare better than short ones.

- **Voice typing isn't always practical,** since everybody around you can hear what you're doing.

- **Voice typing isn't 100 percent accurate.** Very often, you'll have to correct an error or two. (Your accuracy is much, much better when you wear a headset.)

On the other hand, how's this for some good news? You don't need an internet connection to use voice typing; the Enhanced Dictation option downloads the conversion software right to your Mac. As a bonus, Enhanced Dictation means that you're no longer limited to 30 seconds of dictation per burst. You can keep on blabbing away until you've dictated your entire dissertation or letter to Congress. (As a *bonus* bonus, the words appear on the screen *as you speak*, instead of waiting until you stop talking.)

Unfortunately, Enhanced Dictation is not quite as accurate as non-Enhanced. So the following pages describe both the standard and the Enhanced features, in that order.

All right—expectations set? Then here's how to type by speaking.

Dictation Step by Step

First, fire up some program where you can type. TextEdit, Mail, Word, whatever. Dictation works in any program.

Now tap the fn key twice. (You can also choose the Start Dictation command, which magically appears in almost every program's Edit menu. Or you can choose a different keystroke, as described on the following pages.)

Note: The first time you trigger dictation, the Mac asks for confirmation that you do, indeed, want to turn on dictation. It offers to turn on Enhanced Dictation, too (page 282).

And it warns you that proceeding means that the Mac will send the names in your Contacts app to Apple, so that you'll be able to say things like "Dear Mr. Szvredyk" and get a correct transcription. If that prospect unnerves you—if you think that it means that some Apple or Nuance employee will wind up reading the list of names in your personal Rolodex—then you shouldn't proceed.

See the microphone button (Figure 7-1, top)? When it appears, you hear a single xylophone note. Say what you have to say. You don't have to speak slowly, loudly, or weirdly; speak normally.

You have to speak your own punctuation, like this: "Dear Dad (colon): Send money (dash)—as much as you can (comma), please (period)." The table at the end of this section describes all the punctuation symbols you can dictate.

After you finish speaking, click Done or press Return.

Tip: Here's a shortcut: You can also *hold down the fn key* on the second tap; do your speaking; and then release the key when you're done. In other words, you can use it like a push-to-talk button on a walkie-talkie. That saves you the final press of the Return key.

Dictation & Siri

I t was been a popular sci-fi fantasy for decades: That someday, we'd talk to our computers instead of typing into them. Blame Captain Kirk and the minds of the *Star Trek* writers who dreamed him up.

Dictation came to the Mac before it came to phones. But Siri—the virtual assistant who not only understands what you say, but also executes your commands and answers your questions—was an iPhone-only feature first. But now Siri has come to the desktop.

This chapter covers both of the Mac's speech-recognition features: Dictation (that is, *typing by speaking*) and Siri (giving your Mac *commands and questions* by voice).

Dictation

Dictation is built into the Mac, just as it is on the latest iPhones and iPads. You can speak to enter text anywhere, into any program, just by speaking. (Behind the scenes, it's using the same Nuance recognition technology that powers Dragon Dictate.) You can blather away into an email, fire off a text message, or draft a memo without ever looking at the screen.

Now, before you get all excited, here are the necessary footnotes:

- **Voice typing works best if there's not a lot of background noise.** If you're not wearing a headset microphone, this feature prefers Macs that have dual microphones, like MacBooks with Retina Displays; those two mikes create a "beam array"—a directional alignment that helps them differentiate your voice from the background noise.

MACOS MOJAVE: THE MISSING MANUAL

use the Recovery Disk Assistant that you wisely made long in advance of your horror-story dead-disk day.

Appendix B covers these recovery modes in more detail. The point is, however, that all three present "Restore from a Time Machine backup" as one of the options.

2. **Choose "Restore from a Time Machine backup." Click Continue.**

Now you're shown a list of Time Machine backup disks. You probably have only one.

3. **Click your Time Machine backup disk. In the list, click the most recent backup.**

The installer goes about copying *everything* from the backup disk onto your new, empty hard drive. When it's all over, you'll have a perfect working system, just the way it was before your series of unfortunate events.

Beware, however: Restoring your earlier version also *erases any files* you've created or changed. Back them up manually before you proceed! Then, when you're asked to choose a backup to restore, choose the most recent one. When it's all over, copy the files that you manually backed up back onto the hard drive.

Recovering to another Mac

Weirdly enough, you can also use Time Machine to bring over some or part of any Time Machine backup to a totally different Mac.

On the new machine, connect your backup disk. In the Applications→Utilities folder, open Migration Assistant. Click "From another Mac, PC, Time Machine backup, or other disk." The subsequent screens invite you to choose which backup, which Home folder, and which elements (applications, settings, files) you want to bring over.

Frequently Asked Questions

Time Machine is a very different kind of backup program, and a real departure for longtime Mac addicts. A few questions, therefore, are bound to come up—like these:

- **Can I back up more than one Mac onto the same disk?** Yes. Each Mac's backup is stored in a separate folder on that disk.

- **Can I use more than one backup disk—like one at the office and one at home?** Yes. Just use the Time Machine pane of System Preferences (or the Time Machine Dock icon's shortcut menu) to select the new backup drive each time you switch.

- **Can I delete something from all the backups at once?** Yes. Click the Time Machine icon on the Dock to enter the Restore mode. Find and select the file or folder you want to obliterate. From the ✿ menu, choose Delete All Backups of [the Thing's Name]. (Sneaky, huh? That command is never in the ✿ menu *except* when you're in Time Machine restoring mode.)

Note: Time Machine prides itself not just on recovering files and folders, but also on putting them back where they belong. If you recover a different version of something that's still there, macOS asks if you want to replace it with the recovered version—or to keep both versions.

And if you're recovering a document whose original folder no longer exists, Time Machine asks if you want to choose another place for the document or recreate the missing folder, perhaps so that the recovered item feels at home. Choose accordingly.

Recovering from Contacts and Mail

The Finder isn't the only program hooked into Time Machine's magic. Contacts and Mail work with Time Machine, too. Other software companies can also revise their own applications to work with it.

In other words, if you want to recover certain addresses or email messages that have been deleted, you don't start in the Finder; you start in Contacts or Mail.

Then click the Time Machine icon on the Dock. Once again, you enter the recovery mode—but this time, you're facing a strange, disembodied, stripped-down copy of Contacts or Mail.

You're ready to find your missing data. Click the Jump Back arrow to open the most recent version of your address book file or email stash that's different from what you've got now. (You can also use the timeline on the right if you remember the date when things went wrong.)

Tip: If you're looking for something particular, specify that before you start clicking. For example, type a name into the Contacts search box first.

At this point, you can select individual Contacts entries or email messages to restore; just click the Restore button. Contacts may discover a lot of duplicate name-and-address entries and invite you to step through them, deciding which ones "win" (the old or the new).

Note: When you finish restoring in Mail, you'll find the restored messages in the On My Mac→Time Machine→Recovered folder at the left side of the window.

Recovering the entire hard drive

Every hard drive will die at some point. You just hope it won't happen while *you* own the computer. But if it does, you, as a Time Machine aficionado, won't care. You'll just repair or replace the hard drive, and then proceed as follows.

1. **Connect the Time Machine backup disk to the Mac. Start the recovery mode.**

 There are actually three ways to recover a dead Mac or a dead hard drive. If the hard drive is fine but it just can't start up your Mac, hold down ⌘-R during startup. If the hard drive is empty, you can restart from the internet itself (if it's a Mac released since Mac OS X Lion came out). And, if all else fails, you can always

- **Click one of the two big, flat arrows.** The one pointing into the past means "Jump directly to the most recent window version that's *different* from the way it is right now." In other words, it's often a waste of time to go flipping through the windows one at a time, because your missing or changed file might have been missing or changed for the last 25 backups (or whatever). What you want to know is the last time the contents of this window *changed*. And that's what the big, flat arrows do. They jump from one *changed* version of this window to another. (Or, if you began with a search, the arrow takes you to the most recent backup with a matching result.)

- **Use the search box in the corner of the window.** You can search for whatever you're missing in the current backup.

As you go, the very bottom of the screen identifies where you are in time—that is, which backup you're examining.

Tip: You can let Time Machine take you on a guided tour of folders past, or you can go your own way to find your files. Just open the backup disk itself, whose icon appears on your desktop. Inside, you'll find nested folders, neatly representing every computer, every backup, every day, and every hour—which you can rummage through by hand.

In many ways, the recovery mode is just like the Finder. You can't actually open, edit, rename, or reorganize anything here. But you can use Quick Look to inspect the documents to make sure you've got the right version. And you can use icon, list, column, or gallery views to sort through the files you're seeing.

If you're trying to recover an older *version* of a file or folder, highlight it and then click the flat arrow button that's pointing away from you; Time Machine skips back to the most recent version that's *different* from the current one.

If you're trying to restore a deleted file or folder that you've now located, highlight it and then click Restore (lower right). Presto: The lost file or folder is back in the window where it belonged.

FREQUENTLY ASKED QUESTION

The End of Time

What happens when my backup drive gets full?

The whole idea of Time Machine is that it preserves multiple backups, so that you can rewind a window or a drive not just to *a* backup, but to *any* date in the past. The bigger the hard drive, the farther back those monthly backups are preserved.

Eventually, of course, your backup drive runs out of space. At that point, Time Machine notifies you and offers you a choice: "Your backup disk is now full. The oldest remaining backup disk is…" (and then the date). You can keep using that drive; Time Machine deletes the oldest backups to make room for newer ones. Or you can install a new Time Machine backup drive. New backups will go on that one; your older backups will still be available on the original drive.

If you ever need to retrieve files or folders from the older disk, right-click or two-finger click the Time Machine icon in the Dock; from the shortcut menu, choose Browse Other Time Machine Disks. Choose the older disk. Then click the Time Machine icon on the Dock to enter the Restore mode.

- **Type what you're looking for** into the search box at the top of any Finder window. Click the location button that makes the most sense: "This Mac" or the name of the window you're in.

In the case of deleted files or folders, the search will probably come up empty; that's totally OK.

Now click the Time Machine icon on the Dock, or choose Enter Time Machine from the menulet (Figure 6-19, top).

Everything else on your desktop fades away. Front and center is your Finder window—or, rather, dozens of them, stretching back in time (Figure 6-19, bottom). Each is a snapshot of that window at the time of a Time Machine backup.

Figure 6-19:
Top: Choose Enter Time Machine from the menulet. (If you don't see this menulet, then turn on "Show Time Machine in menu bar," shown in Figure 6-18.)

Bottom: The starry outer-space background of the old Time Machine is gone, but everything works the same way: You see dozens of copies of the Finder window, representing its condition at each backup, stretching back to the past.

You have four ways to peruse your backup universe:

- **Click individual windows to see what's in them.**

- **Drag your cursor through the timeline at the right side.** It's like a master dial that flies through the windows into the past.

Finally, there's its System Preferences pane, where you adjust its settings (Figure 6-18). To see it, choose System Preferences→Time Machine. Or choose Time Machine Preferences from Time Machine's Dock icon or menulet.

Recovering Lost or Changed Files

All right, you've got Time Machine on the job. You sleep easy at night, confident that your life is in order—and your stuff is backed up.

Then, one day, it happens: Your hard drive crashes. Or you can't find a file or folder you know you had. Or you save a document in some non–Auto Save program and then wish you could go back to an earlier draft. Some kind of disaster—sunspots, clueless spouse, overtired self—has befallen your files. This is Time Machine's big moment.

Start by pinpointing what you're looking for, in one of these two ways:

• **Open the disk or folder window** where the missing or changed item was.

POWER USERS' CLINIC

Declaring Stuff Off-Limits to Time Machine

The whole point of Time Machine is to have a backup of your entire hard drive. That's how most people use it.

It's conceivable, though, that you might want to exclude some files or folders from the Time Machine treatment. There are two reasons.

First, you might not want certain, ahem, private materials to be part of your incriminating data trail.

Second, you might want to save space on the backup drive, either because it's not

as big as your main drive or because you'd rather dedicate its space to more backups of the essential stuff. For example, you might decide not to back up your collection of downloaded TV shows, since video files are enormous. Or maybe you use an online photo-sharing website as a backup for all your photos, so you don't think it's necessary to include those in the Time Machine backup.

To eliminate certain icons from the backup, open the Time Machine pane of System Preferences. Click Options.

In the resulting list, click the + button; navigate to your hard drive, and then select the files or folders you don't want backed up. Or just find their actual icons in the Finder and drag them into the list here. (Use the − button to remove items from the list, thereby excluding them from the excluded list.)

If you're strapped for disk space, one logical candidate to exclude is the System folder on your main hard drive—that is, macOS itself. After all, if you lose your hard drive, you already have a copy of macOS: the original App Store installer.

When you add the System folder to the exclusion list, Time Machine makes another space-saving offer: "Would you like to also exclude other files installed with macOS, such as system applications and UNIX tools?"

Agreeing (by clicking Exclude All System Files) saves you another several gigabytes of backup space.

Local Snapshots

If you're among the 75 percent of Mac owners with a laptop, Time Machine used to be something of a bust in one regard: Whenever you were away from your backup disk (at home or the office, for example), you lost the benefits of Time Machine.

Today, crazy as this may sound, Time Machine keeps on working even on a laptop that's far from home. Thanks to a feature called local snapshots, Time Machine works as usual by making its backups right on the laptop's own hard drive.

Of course, this system won't help you if your hard drive dies; your backup is on the same drive, so you'll lose the originals and the backups simultaneously. But what local snapshots do provide is a safety net—a way to recover a file you deleted or changed during this time away. Better yet, once you're home again, when your laptop rejoins the network, the local snapshots intelligently merge with the master Time Machine backups, as though you'd never been away.

If Time Machine is turned on on your laptop, it makes local snapshots automatically—once an hour, as usual. As time goes on, Time Machine deletes snapshots more than 24 hours old to save disk space.

Note: If your laptop gets really low on disk space, Time Machine stops making new snapshots and may even delete old ones so you can keep using your Mac. When you make more space, snapshots resume automatically.

If you need to recover a file, enter Time Machine as usual. Your local snapshots show up on the same timeline as backups made on your external backup disk, but they're color-coded: pink tick marks for external backups, gray for local ones. If the pink bars are dimmed, it's because you're not hooked up to your Time Machine backup drive.

Tip: To see how much disk space your local snapshots are eating up, choose → About This Mac. Click the Storage tab. The color-coded graph clearly indicates the space being used for backups.

Changing Time Machine Settings

Time Machine has four faces. There's the application itself, which sits in your Applications folder; open it only when you want to enter Restore mode. There's its Dock icon, which also enters Restore mode, but which has a shortcut menu containing useful commands like Back Up Now (and Stop Backing Up).

There's the Time Machine menulet, which may be the handiest of all. It identifies the time and date of the most recent backup, offers Back Up Now/Skip This Backup commands, and has direct access to Time Machine's Restore mode and preferences pane.

Tip: If you Option-click the Time Machine menulet, you get two secret commands: Verify Backups (just in case you're nervous about your backups' integrity) and Browse Other Backup Disks. Yes, it's perfectly possible to back up onto multiple hard drives—to keep one offsite in case of fire, flood, or burglary, for example—and this is how. (Right-clicking or two-finger clicking Time Machine's Dock icon is another way to get this command.)

How the Backups Work

From now on, Time Machine quietly checks your Mac once an hour. If any file, folder, or setting has changed, it gets backed up at the end of the hour. These follow-up backups are quick; Time Machine backs up only what's changed. So, should disaster strike, the only files you can lose are those you've changed within the past 59 minutes.

Tip: You can force more frequent backups if you want to. Just choose Back Up Now from the Time Machine menulet. Or choose Back Up Now from the shortcut menu of the Dock's Time Machine icon.

You can pause the backup the same way—if you need to use the backup drive for another quick task, for example. Choose Skip This Backup from the Time Machine menulet, open System Preferences→Time Machine and click the ⊗ next to the backup progress bar, or choose Stop Backing Up from shortcut menu of the Dock's Time Machine icon.

By the end of the day, you'll have 24 hourly backups on that second disk, all taking up space. So at day's end, Time Machine replaces that huge stash with a single *daily* backup. You can no longer rewind your system to 3:00 p.m. last Monday, but you can rewind to the way it was at the *end* of that day.

Similarly, after a month, Time Machine replaces those 30 dailies (for example) with four weekly backups. Now you may not be able to rewind to October 12, but you can rewind to the end of that week. (Apple assumes it won't take you that long to notice that your hard drive has crashed.)

Tip: You can see these backups, if you want. Open your backup drive, open the *Backups.backupdb* folder, and then open the folder named for your computer. Inside, you'll find a huge list of backup folders, bearing names like 2016-07-22-155831. That's the backup from July 22, 2016, at 15:58 (that is, 3:58 p.m.) and 31 seconds.

The point is that Time Machine doesn't just keep *one* copy of your stuff. It keeps *multiple* backups. It remembers how things were in every folder—not just yesterday, but last week, last month, and so on. It keeps on making new snapshots of your hard drive until the backup drive is full.

At that point, the oldest ones get deleted to make room for new ones.

Tip: Ordinarily, Time Machine alerts you when it has to start deleting old backups. If you'd rather have it just do it without bothering you, open System Preferences, click Time Machine, click Options, and then turn off "Notify after old backups are deleted."

By the way, if a backup is interrupted—if you shut down the Mac, put it to sleep, or take your laptop on the road—no big deal. Time Machine can keep working on its own, as you'll see in the next section, and resumes backing up to the backup drive the next time you're connected.

Tip: You can create multiple backups on different disks—a great feature if you have a laptop you carry between work and home. You can have a backup drive at both places; Time Machine will seamlessly switch between them. To set this up, just choose another backup disk in System Preferences→Time Machine. Time Machine will automatically back up to that drive, too.

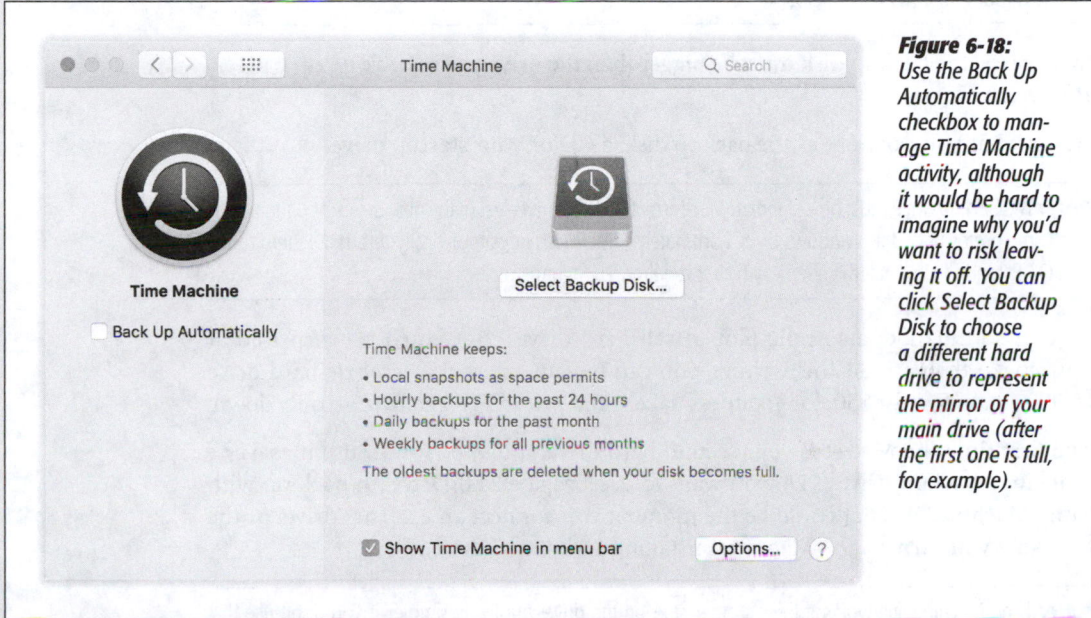

Figure 6-18:
Use the Back Up Automatically checkbox to manage Time Machine activity, although it would be hard to imagine why you'd want to risk leaving it off. You can click Select Backup Disk to choose a different hard drive to represent the mirror of your main drive (after the first one is full, for example).

POWER USERS' CLINIC

Encrypted Time Machine Backups

Time Machine can encrypt your backups.

Without encryption, an evildoer could theoretically bust into your house, steal your backup disk, and have full, unfettered access to all your backed-up files. It's never happened yet, but—you know. It could.

If you're interested in encrypting your backups, there are some prerequisites. The hard drive must use HFS (Journaled) formatting—a Mac hard drive, in other words. The drive has to be physically, directly connected to your Mac using USB, FireWire, or Thunderbolt—or else a wireless Apple Time Capsule.

To turn this feature on, open System Preferences→Time Machine. Click Select Disk. Turn on "Encrypt backup disk." You're asked for a password. Type it in and, whatever you

do, don't forget it! Without that password, you won't be able to recover your files if something goes wrong. Keep that password somewhere safe—on the bottom of the backup drive, for example. (Joke! That's a joke.)

Once you click OK, the encryption begins. It takes a long time. Go away for the weekend.

Once it's done, you won't notice any difference—until the day comes when you need to recover your files. At that point, you'll be asked for your password when you enter Time Machine.

If something serious ever happens to your Mac, you can connect the encrypted Time Machine drive to any other Mac that's running Lion or later. You'll be able to enter your password there and recover your files onto that different Mac.

- **The hard drive of another Mac on the network** (OS X 10.5 or later) that you've mounted on your screen.

Tip: It's perfectly OK to back up several Macs onto the same external hard drive, as long as it's got enough room. You can also back up onto a hard drive that has other stuff on it, although of course that means you'll have less room for Time Machine backups.

In all cases, the backup disk must be bigger than the drive you're backing up (preferably *much* bigger).

Here's what you *can't* use as the backup disk: a CD or your startup drive.

Note: The backup drive must be a standard Mac-formatted hard drive—yet many new drives bought by Mac fans come preformatted as Windows disks. Fortunately, Time Machine automatically reformats them to the Mac OS Extended (Journaled) scheme, which it requires. Thoughtful, really.

Sure, it sounds like an Apple plot to sell hard drives. But you'd be surprised at how cheap they are. At this writing, you can buy an external 2-*terabyte* hard drive (2,000 gigabytes) for $50, for goodness' sake—and prices-per-gigabyte go only down.

The first time the Mac sees your second hard drive, it invites you to use it as Time Machine's backup drive ("Do you want to use 'Seagate 2TB Drive' to back up with Time Machine?"). That could be the moment you connect an external drive, or the first time you turn on the Mac after installing an internal drive.

Note: Time Machine still works if there's other stuff on the drive, but life is simpler if you don't use that drive for anything but Time Machine.

If you click Use as Backup Disk, you're taken immediately to the Time Machine pane of System Preferences (Figure 6-18). Here's where you see that Time Machine is turned on and has a drive it can use for backups.

Soon enough, the Mac starts copying *everything* on your hard drive, including macOS itself, all your programs, and everyone's Home folders. You know that because you see the ↻ symbol in the Sidebar (next to the backup disk's name), and the menu-bar Time Machine icon looks like ↻.

And that, ladies and gentlemen, is the easiest setup for a backup program in history.

Note: Unless you turn on encryption (see the box on the next page), Time Machine doesn't use any compression or encoding; it's copying your files exactly as they sit on your hard drive, for maximum safety and recoverability. On the other hand, it does save some space on the backup drive, because it doesn't bother copying cache files, temporary files, and other files you'll never need to restore.

Now go away and let the Mac do its thing. The first backup can take hours, as the Mac duplicates your entire internal hard drive onto the second drive. The Mac may feel drugged during this time.

that the most useful ones appear at the top of the Share menu from now on. (You're not allowed to turn off the Big Three: Mail, Messages, and AirDrop.) For more on Extensions, see page 357.

Time Machine

There are two kinds of people in the world: those who have a regular backup system—and those who *will*.

You'll get that grisly joke immediately if you've ever known the pain that comes with deleting the wrong folder by accident, or making changes that you regret, or worst of all, having your hard drive die. All those photos, all that music you've ripped over the years, all your email—gone.

Yet the odds are overwhelming that at this moment, you do not have a complete, current, automated backup of your Mac. Despite about a thousand warnings, articles, and cautionary tales a year, guess how many do? About *4 percent*. Everybody else is flying without a net.

If you don't have much to back up—you don't have much in the way of photos, music, or movies—you can get by with using a free online backup system like iCloud Drive, Dropbox, or CrashPlan. But those methods leave most of your Mac unprotected: all your programs and settings.

What you really want, of course, is a backup that's rock-solid, complete, and *automatic*. You don't want to have to remember to do a backup, to insert a disc, and so on. You just want to know you're safe.

That's the idea behind Time Machine, a marquee feature of macOS. It's a silent, set-it-and-forget-it piece of peace of mind. You sleep easy, knowing there's a safety copy of your *entire* system: your system files, programs, settings, music, pictures, videos, document files—*everything*. If your luck runs out, you'll be *so* happy you set up Time Machine.

Setting Up Time Machine

Here's the bad news: Time Machine requires a second hard drive. That's the only way to create a completely safe, automatic backup of your *entire* main hard drive.

That second hard drive can take any of these forms:

- **An external USB, FireWire, or Thunderbolt hard drive.**

- **An AirPort Time Capsule.** That's an AirPort wireless base station/network backup hard drive in one; it's available in gigantic capacities.

- **Another internal hard drive.**

- **A *partition* of any one of those drives.**

Note: What you don't find here in Mojave anymore are links to Twitter, Facebook, Vimeo, YouTube, or Flickr. Apple removed those options from the Share sheet in hopes of making macOS even more secure.

Figure 6-17:
Top: Here's how you might save some text from Safari into a new Notes page. Right-click or two-finger click the selected text; from the shortcut menu, choose Share→Notes.

Bottom: The Choose Note pop-up menu offers to paste the text into a new note—or one of your pinned notes (page 448), or any existing note in your Notes app. (You may have hundreds of notes, which is why the search box can be especially handy at this point.)

Click Save to finish up.

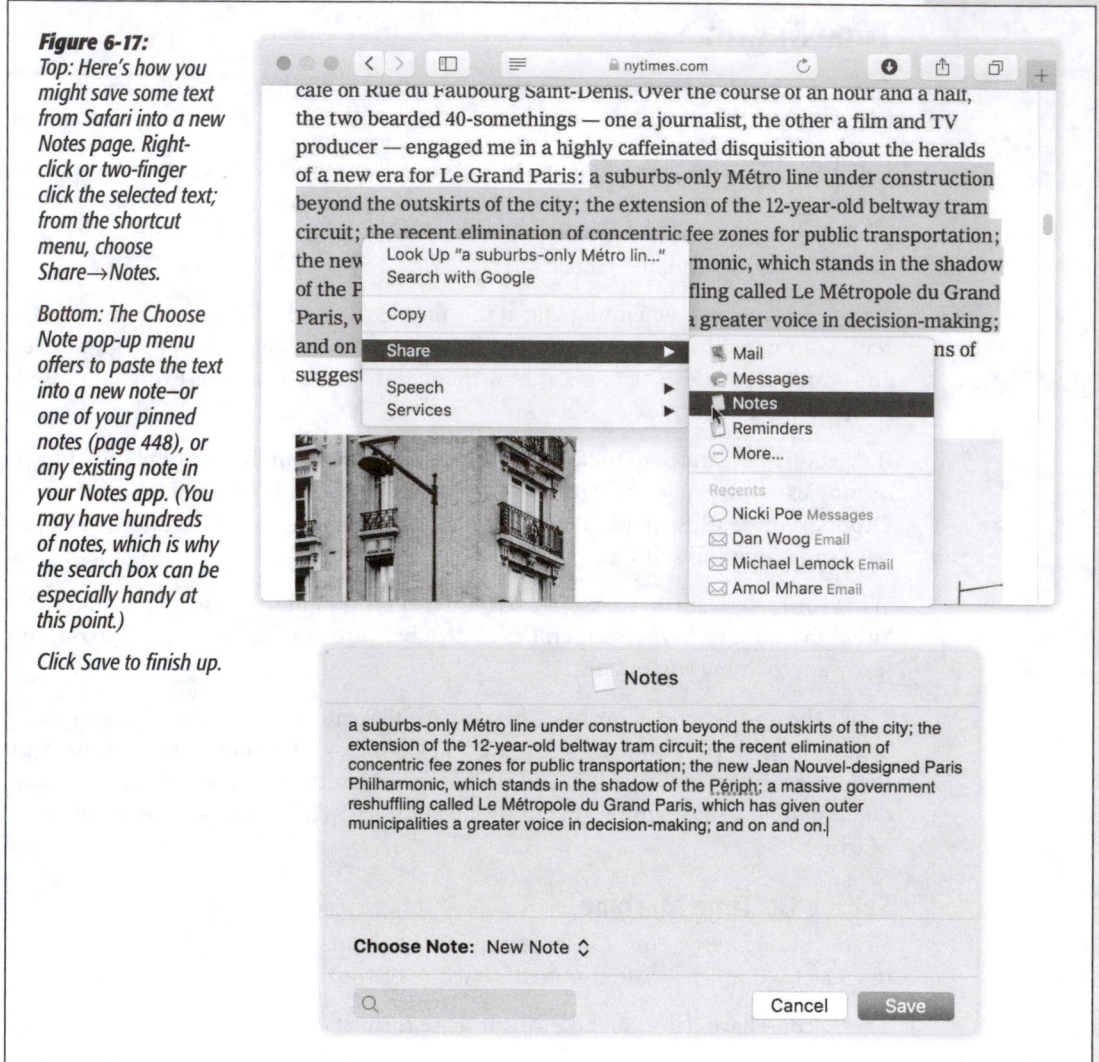

Editing the Share Menu

You can choose the options in your Share menu, and in which order they appear.

For that, you can thank the pane in System Preferences called Extensions. (One quick way to open it: From the Share menu itself, choose More.) If you click Share Menu in the left-side list, you're treated to a System Preferences box where you can turn off the Share-menu options you never use. You can also drag items' names up or down, so

If you've seen an iPhone or iPad, then you've probably seen this icon: ⬆. On the Mac, this button, or a command that just says Share, pops up in all kinds of programs: the Finder's shortcut menus. Quick Look panels. The Open File dialog box in Apple programs. Mac programs like Contacts, Notes, Preview, Safari, Photo Booth, TextEdit, Photos, and so on. Other companies can add it to their programs, too, or install new commands into the Share menu for transmitting stuff to new channels.

To use this feature, select or open some text, a photo, a video, a file icon, a web link, or something else that you want to send to friends. When you click this button or command, you're offered various ways to share the selected item. The choices vary according to the program you're using, but here are some examples:

- **Mail.** The Mac copies the selected material into a new, outgoing email message, or attaches the selected file to an outgoing message. Just add a few explanatory notes, address the message, and send.

- **Messages.** Puts the selected material into an outgoing message, ready to send as a text message or an iMessage (Chapter 19). Just address and send.

Tip: In the Finder, the Share command offers a brilliantly simple way to send a file to somebody. Just right-click or two-finger click a file icon, choose Share→Message, and then enter the person's phone number (to send to an iPhone) or Apple ID (to send by iMessage). Click Send—off it goes!

- **AirDrop.** As you can read on page 572, AirDrop lets you shoot Finder files to nearby Macs, iPhones, and iPads—wirelessly, without having to fuss with passwords, file sharing, mounting disks, and so on.

 In the Finder, right-click or two-finger click the file icon (or icons) you want to send to another Mac. From the shortcut menu, choose AirDrop. In a flash, you get the AirDrop share sheet (page 314). It lists every nearby Mac, iPhone, or iPad. Click the one you want, and then click Send; if the other guy clicks Accept, then the file is on its way to his Apple gadget.

- **Notes.** Anything you've highlighted—text, graphics, links, whatever—gets plopped onto a new page in the beefed-up Notes app (page 446). Figure 6-17 shows the sequence.

- **Reminders.** This option turns the highlighted text (in whatever app) into the entry for a Reminder (page 476)—either a new one or an existing one. The process works just as it does for Notes (Figure 6-17).

This list of options in the Share menu isn't complete; you may find other oddball options in the Share menus of certain programs. For example, in Photo Booth, you also get choices like Add to Photos, Set Buddy Picture, Set Account Picture, or Change Twitter Profile Picture—all handy things to do with a picture you've just taken with your Mac's built-in camera.

Does the file have the correct file name suffix?

Every document on your hard drive has some kind of tag to tell the computer what program is supposed to open it: either a pair of invisible four-letter codes or a file name suffix like .docx.

Microsoft Windows uses *only* the latter system for identifying documents. Here are some of the most common such codes:

Kind of document	Suffix	Example
Microsoft Word (old)	.doc	Letter to Mom.doc
Microsoft Word	.docx	Letter to Mom.docx
Excel	.xls or .xlsx	Profit Projection.xlsx
PowerPoint	.ppt or. pptx	Slideshow.pptx
JPEG photo	.jpg	Baby Portrait.jpg
GIF graphic	.gif	Logo.gif
Web page	.htm	index.htm

The beauty of macOS is that its programs add these file name suffixes automatically and invisibly, every time you save a new document. You and your Windows comrades can freely exchange documents without ever worrying about this former snag in the Macintosh/Windows relationship.

Notes on Disk Swapping

Once you've created a document destined for a Windows machine, your next challenge is to get it *onto* that machine. One way is to put the file on a disk—a CD you've burned, for example—which you then hand to the Windows owner.

Macs and PCs format *hard drives* differently. The Mac can read Windows disks and flash drives (which use unappetizingly named formatting schemes like FAT32 and NTFS), but Windows can't read Mac hard drives or flash drives. CDs and DVDs use the same format on both kinds of computers, though, so you should have very little problem moving these between machines.

Network Notes

MacOS can "see" shared disks and folders on Windows PCs that are on the same network. Complete instructions are in Chapter 13.

Via the Internet

Chapter 20 offers details on FTP and web sharing, two ways to make your Mac available to other computers—Windows PCs or not—on the internet. And, of course, you can always email files between Macs and PCs.

The Share Button

The Share button into many spots is a quick, one-click way to send something (text, link, photo, video) to somebody else (by email, Twitter, Facebook, text message, AirDrop).

To make a Mac invadable, the person to be invaded must open System Preferences→ Sharing and turn on Bluetooth Sharing. Here's also where he can specify what folder is available to you for examination (the Mac proposes his Home→Public folder), and what kind of security he wants to set up.

Then all you have to do is choose Browse Files on Device from your own menulet (you can see it in Figure 6-16)—and let the rummaging begin!

Exchanging Data with iPhones or iPads

Apple has dreamed up some clever wireless ways for you to shoot files and information between a Mac and an iOS phone or tablet. These features are part of Continuity, described in Chapter 8.

Exchanging Data with Windows PCs

Documents can take one of several roads between your Mac and a Windows machine: via disk (such as a CD), flash drive, Dropbox, network, email, Bluetooth, iPod, web page, FTP download, and so on.

Preparing the Document for Transfer

The Mac is more Windows-compatible than ever. Still, before sending a document to a colleague who uses Windows, you must be able to answer "yes" to both of the following questions.

Is the document in a file format Windows understands?

Most popular programs are sold in both Mac and Windows flavors, and the documents they create are freely interchangeable. For example, documents created by recent versions of Word, Excel, PowerPoint, FileMaker, Illustrator, Photoshop, Dreamweaver, and many other Mac programs don't need any conversion. The corresponding Windows versions of those programs open such documents with nary a hiccup.

Files in standard exchange formats don't need conversion, either. These formats include JPEG and PNG (digital photos), GIF (cartoon/logo graphics on web pages), HTML (raw web page documents), Rich Text Format (a word-processor exchange format that maintains bold, italic, and other formatting), plain text (no formatting at all), MP3 and AAC files (for audio), MIDI files (for music synthesizers), and so on.

But what about documents made by Mac programs that don't exist on the typical Windows PC hard drive, like Keynote or Pages? You certainly can't count on your recipient having the application.

Do your recipients the favor of first saving such documents into one of those exchange formats. In Pages, for example, choose File→Export To→Word; the resulting dialog box will confirm your choice. Click Next. Now name this special version of the document (complete with the .docx suffix), and then click Save.

Sending a file

To shoot a file or two across the airwaves to a fellow Bluetooth-equipped Mac fan, first *pair* your Mac with the other Bluetooth machine. In System Preferences→Bluetooth, make sure your Mac is Discoverable. *Discoverable* means "Other Bluetooth gadgets can see me." (Check the receiving gadget, too, to make sure *it's* in Discoverable mode.) Then you're ready to send:

1. **From the Bluetooth ✳ menulet, choose the device's name—and, from the submenu, "Send file to device" (Figure 6-16).**

 If you don't *have* the Bluetooth menulet on your menu bar, then open System Preferences. Click Bluetooth, and turn on "Show Bluetooth status in the menu bar."

 After a moment, the Select File to Send dialog box appears. (You've actually succeeded in opening a program called Bluetooth File Exchange, which sits in your Applications→Utilities folder.)

Figure 6-16:
Once your Mac is paired with the other gadget, it's easy to shoot a file to it wirelessly. In this example, you'll start by choosing "Send file to device."

2. **Navigate to, and select, the files you want to send.**

3. **Click Send.**

 What happens now depends on how the receiving machine has been set up. In most cases, a dialog box tells the receiver that files are arriving; if he clicks Accept, then the download proceeds. He's then offered the chance to either (a) open each transferred file or (b) reveal its highlighted icon in the Finder.

Tip: In System Preferences→Sharing→Bluetooth Sharing, you can control what happens when someone sends you files via Bluetooth. Usually, you'll want your Mac to ask whether to accept these files. (That's what "Ask What to Do" means.) You can also specify where you want received files to wind up.

Fetching a file

You can also perform this entire procedure in reverse. That is, you can go fishing through your buddy's files without him explicitly having to send anything.

2. **On the MacBook, choose** →**System Preferences. Click Startup Disk.**

The Startup Disk panel opens.

3. **Click Target Disk Mode. In the confirmation box, click Restart.**

The MacBook turns off and then on again. A giant gray FireWire icon (🙂) or Thunderbolt icon (𝄇) bounces around the laptop screen.

Now take a look at the iMac's screen: Sure enough, there's the MacBook's hard drive icon on the desktop. You're ready to copy files onto or off of it, at extremely high speeds, and go on with your life.

4. **When you're finished working with the MacBook, eject it from the iMac's screen as you would any disk. Then turn off the laptop by pressing the power button.**

The next time you turn on the MacBook, it'll start up from its own copy of macOS, even if the cable is still attached. (You can disconnect the cable whenever you please.)

Note: The steps here describe the modern method of setting up Target Disk Mode. But the old way still works, too. Leave the iMac turned on, but shut down the MacBook. (Make sure it's plugged in. You wouldn't want the battery to die in the middle of this process.) Now turn the MacBook on again, but hold down the T key immediately after the chime. After a moment, you see the big Y-shaped FireWire icon (🙂) on the laptop screen, and the laptop's hard drive shows up on the iMac's desktop. Finish with step 4 above.

This method is arguably quicker, because you don't have to open System Preferences. And this method works when the Mac is too sick even to start up.

Via Bluetooth

Bluetooth is a cable-elimination technology. It's designed to let Bluetooth-equipped gadgets communicate within about 30 feet, using radio signals.

Bluetooth comes built into most computers and cellphones, plus the occasional printer, pocket organizer, and even camera or camcorder.

Bluetooth is built into all recent Macs. It's ready, therefore, to connect with Apple's wireless keyboard and mouse, to get on the internet using a Bluetooth cellphone as a cordless modem, to listen to music through wireless headphones or speakers, and to transfer files through the air to similarly equipped gear.

Bluetooth is pretty slow. (You get transfer speeds of 30 to 150 K per second, depending on the distance.) But when you consider the time you'd have taken for wiring, passwords, and configuration using any other connection method, you may find that Bluetooth wins, at least in casual, spur-of-the-moment, airport-seat situations.

And Bluetooth works no matter what the gadget—Mac, Windows, smartphone—so it's great as a universal file-exchange translator, too.

Note: For more details on configuring your Mac for Bluetooth connections, see page 339.

Via iCloud Drive

In many ways, iCloud Drive (page 221) is identical to Dropbox. It, too, acts as a magic folder that reproduces itself on as many Macs as you own.

It's a fantastic way to transfer big files among your own computers. And now, thanks to iCloud file sharing, you can even make your big files available to other macOS fans with just a couple of clicks (see page 222).

Via Flash Drive

A flash drive, also called a thumb drive, is one of those keychain-like doodads that plug into your USB jack. Inside is a big chunk of memory that acts like a miniature hard drive. When the flash drive is plugged into your Mac, its icon shows up on the desktop as a disk. Use it as a tiny, 8-gigabyte hard drive (or whatever size you've bought).

The beauty of a flash drive is that it works instantly with any Mac *or* any Windows machine, without software installation or configuration. It's small and light enough to carry around on your keychain…and it's *so darned cool.* If you regularly transfer documents between Macs or between Macs and PCs, a flash drive will change your life.

FireWire Disk Mode/Thunderbolt Disk Mode (Target Disk Mode)

FireWire Disk Mode/Thunderbolt Disk Mode is a brilliant but little-known Macintosh-only feature that lets you turn one Mac into an external hard drive for another. This is by far the fastest method yet for transferring a lot of data—even faster than copying files over a network. It's extremely useful in any of these situations:

- **You're traveling with a laptop.** You want to copy your life onto it from your main Mac, including your entire 5 GB email folder and project files, before taking it on a trip, and then unload it when you return.

- **You have a new Mac.** You want to copy everything off the old one, without having to wait all night.

- **One Mac won't start up.** You want to repair it, using another Mac as a "front end."

Unfortunately, not all Macs have a FireWire or Thunderbolt jack. If you're among the lucky, though, you can use the following trick. (In these steps, suppose your main Mac is an iMac and you want to use a MacBook as an external hard drive for it.)

1. **Connect the FireWire (Thunderbolt) jacks of both computers with a cable.**

 If you have an older Mac with a FireWire 400 jack, you need a *6-pin* FireWire cable—*not* the one that connects a camcorder to a Mac. The one you need has the same large connector on both ends.

 Modern Macs have Apple's FireWire 800 jacks, which require a 9-pin FireWire cable (and give you much greater speed). If only one Mac has a FireWire 800 jack, then use that computer's traditional FireWire 400 connector instead. Otherwise, you need either a special FireWire 800–to–FireWire 400 cable, or the 400-to-800 adapter that came with your Mac.

Exchanging Data with Other Macs

Considering how many ways there are to move files back and forth between Macs, it seems almost comical that people complained when Apple discontinued built-in floppy disk drives. Here's a catalog of the different ways you can move your files from one computer to another, including some that might not have occurred to you.

By AirDrop or Network

You can shoot a file to another Mac with a single drag-and-drop operation, thanks to AirDrop or another file-sharing method. You can open files from the other drives, copy stuff back and forth—anything you would do with your own disk. (Step-by-step instructions for AirDrop start on page 572.)

Best for files of any size, when the computers are in the same building.

Tip: And for $0 you can create an *ad hoc* network, meaning a tiny wireless network between just two computers (or a handful). Great when you're in the car somewhere, or in the airport waiting lounge, or a hotel lobby, and someone says, "Hey, can I have a copy of that?" Details are on page 569.

By Email

High on convenience; computers can be in different countries. Of course, the traditional problem with email was that it couldn't handle file attachments larger than 5 or 10 megabytes. To get around that limitation, you had to use a free website like *sendthisfile.com*, which can handle enormous files by sending the recipient only a link to them by email.

The world has changed, though. Nowadays, the Mail program can cheerfully send huge file attachments to anyone, no matter what kind of computer she uses. See page 689 for details.

Using Dropbox

Dropbox is a free service, almost universally adored, that lets you create synchronized folders on multiple computers. Add a file to, say, your New Projects folder on your home Mac, and it appears instantly in the matching folder on your Windows folder at work.

You can use Dropbox to share files with other people, too. Just drag a file into a shared folder, and marvel as your associates get an auto-generated email message letting them know. They open the shared folder on their *own* desktops, and there is the file, waiting. (Details are at *dropbox.com/help/19.*)

The great thing about services like Dropbox is that you don't have to worry about the small file-size limits imposed by email. (There's a 2-gigabyte storage limit on Dropbox's free accounts, but you can upgrade to larger storage capacities for a fee; you also get more storage granted when you refer a friend to Dropbox.)

When you drag a clipping from your desktop *back* into an application window, the material in that clipping reappears. Drag-and-drop, in other words, lets you treat your desktop itself as a giant, computer-wide pasteboard—an area where you can temporarily stash pieces of text or graphics as you work.

Tip: When the material you drag to the desktop contains nothing but an internet address, such as an email address or a web page URL, it gets a special icon and a special function: an internet location file. You can stash it in a folder, double-click it for quick access, and so on.

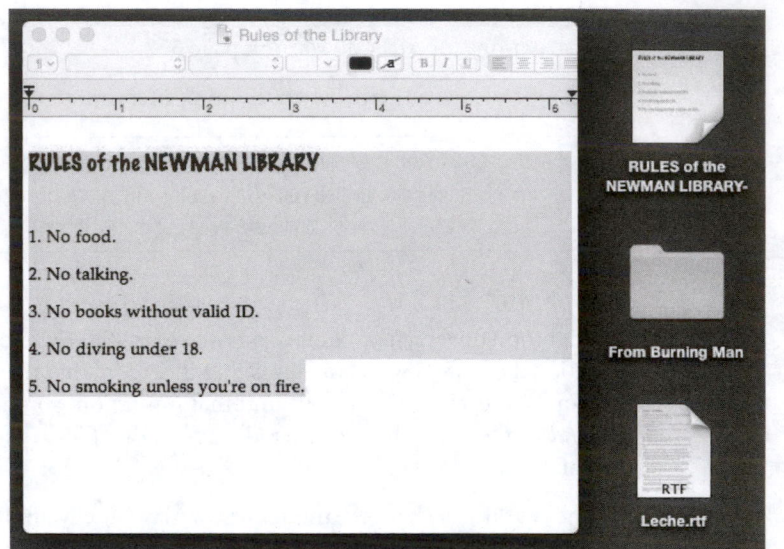

Figure 6-15:
When you drag material out of the document window and onto the desktop or into a folder, you get a clipping file. Its icon depends on the kind of material contained within, like a text clipping, picture clipping, or movie clipping. (For easy identification, macOS conveniently titles text clippings by the first line of the text contained inside.) You can view a clipping just by double-clicking it, so that it opens into its own window (left).

Export/Import

When it comes to transferring large chunks of information—especially address books, spreadsheet cells, and database records—from one program to another, none of the data-transfer methods described so far in this chapter does the trick. For these purposes, use the Export and Import commands found in the File menu of almost every database, spreadsheet, email, and address-book program. (In some programs, the Save As command serves this function.)

These Export/Import commands aren't part of macOS, so the manuals (if any) of the applications in question should be your source for instructions. For now, however, the power and convenience of this feature are worth noting—it means that your four years' worth of collected addresses in, say, some old email program can find their way into a newer program, like Contacts, in a matter of minutes.

Virtually every Apple program works with the drag-and-drop technique, including TextEdit, Stickies, Mail, QuickTime Player, Preview, iMovie, Photos, and System Information, not to mention other popular programs like Microsoft applications, web browsers, and so on.

When to use drag-and-drop

As shown in Figure 6-14, drag-and-drop is ideal for transferring material between windows or between programs—from a web page into Photoshop, for example. It's especially useful when you've already copied something valuable to your Clipboard, since drag-and-drop doesn't involve (and doesn't erase) the Clipboard.

Its most popular use, however, is rearranging text within a single document. In Word or Pages, for example, you can rearrange entire sections, paragraphs, sentences, or even individual letters, just by dragging them—a wonderfully efficient editing technique.

Tip: When you use drag-and-drop to move text within a document, the Mac moves the highlighted text, deleting the highlighted material from its original location. If you press Option as you drag, however, you make a copy of the highlighted text.

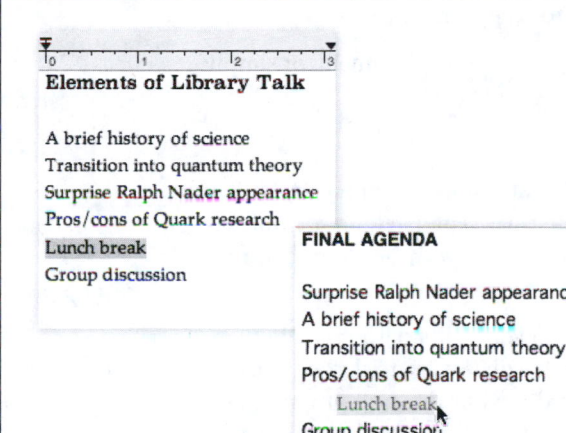

Figure 6-14:
To use drag-and-drop, highlight some material. Click anywhere in the highlighted area and press the mouse button for about half a second. Now, with the button still pressed, drag to another place in the document, into a different window, or into a different application. As your cursor enters the target window, a shaded outline appears inside the window's boundaries—the Mac's way of letting you know it understands your intention. When you release the mouse, the highlighted material appears instantly in its new location.

Drag-and-drop to the desktop

You can also use drag-and-drop in the Finder itself. As shown in Figure 6-15, you can drag text, graphics, sounds, and even movie clips out of your document windows and directly onto the desktop. Graphics and movies generally turn into ordinary graphic or movie files; text becomes an icon called a *clipping file*.

Later, you can examine a clipping's contents using Quick Look—just select its icon and then tap the space bar. Or you can double-click a clipping file and then select a portion of the text to copy.

the Cut, Copy, and Paste commands from the keyboard, quickly and without even thinking. Here's how the process works:

1. **Highlight some material in a document.**

 Drag through some text in a word processor, for example, or highlight graphic, music, movie, database, or spreadsheet information, depending on the program you're using.

2. **Use the Edit→Cut or Edit→Copy command.**

 Or press the keyboard shortcuts ⌘-X (for Cut—think of the X as a pair of scissors) or ⌘-C (for Copy). The Macintosh memorizes the highlighted material, socking it away on an invisible storage pad called the Clipboard. If you chose Copy, nothing visible happens. If you chose Cut, the highlighted material disappears from the original document.

 At this point, most Mac fans take it on faith that the Cut or Copy command actually worked. But if you're in doubt, switch to the Finder (by clicking its Dock icon, for example), and then choose Edit→Show Clipboard. The Clipboard window appears, showing whatever you've copied.

3. **Click to indicate where you want the material to reappear.**

 This may entail switching to a different program, a different document, or simply a different place in the same document.

4. **Choose the Edit→Paste command (⌘-V).**

 The copy of the material you had originally highlighted now appears at your insertion point—*if* you're pasting into a program that can accept that kind of information. (You won't have much luck pasting, say, a block of spreadsheet numbers into World of Warcraft.)

The most recently cut or copied material remains on your Clipboard even after you paste, making it possible to paste the same blob repeatedly. Such a trick can be useful when, for example, you've designed a business card in your drawing program and want to duplicate it enough times to fill a letter-sized printout. On the other hand, whenever you next copy or cut something, whatever was already on the Clipboard is lost forever.

Drag-and-Drop

As useful and popular as it is, the Copy/Paste routine doesn't win any awards for speed. After all, it requires four steps. In many cases, you can replace that routine with the far more direct (and enjoyable) drag-and-drop method. Figure 6-14 illustrates how this works.

Note: Most Cocoa programs (page 227) require you to press the mouse button for a split second before beginning to drag.

- **A phone number.** The shortcut menu here offers you things like Add to Contacts, FaceTime, and Message. The Large Type option is great when you want to call this person right now—it displays the phone number in huge type, filling your screen, so you can see it from across your mansion.

- **A flight number.** When you highlight flight information (for example, "AA 152"), the shortcut menu shows you the flight's departure time, arrival time, and other details. It works only if the airline is represented as a two-letter code.

- **A web address.** When you click the ▾ next to a URL, you get a pop-up balloon that contains the *actual web page!* You don't even have to leave your email message.

- **A package tracking number.** When you send a package using a service like FedEx, UPS, or the U.S. Postal Service, you usually get a confirmation email. A data detector can recognize such numbers and, when you click the ▾, show you a pop-up window right there at your cursor, showing the courier company's tracking page for that package, and thereby letting you know exactly where your package is right now.

Tip: In the unlikely event that you don't actually care for data detectors and would rather not see those dotted lines and ▾ buttons, you can shut down the whole feature. To do that, open Terminal (page 515). Carefully type this command, and then press Return:

```
defaults write com.apple.mail DisableDataDetectors YES
```

You can always turn them back on again by repeating that step—and substituting *NO* for the final word.

Moving Data Between Documents

You can't paste a picture into your web browser, and you can't paste MIDI music information into your word processor. But you can put graphics into TextEdit, paste movies into your database, insert text into Photoshop, and combine a surprising variety of seemingly dissimilar kinds of data.

Cut, Copy, and Paste

The original copy-and-paste procedure of 1984—putting a graphic into a word processor—has come a long way. Most experienced Mac fans have learned to trigger

GEM IN THE ROUGH

Styled Text

When you copy text from, for example, Microsoft Word, and then paste it into another program, such as Mail, you may be pleasantly surprised to note that the formatting of that text—bold, italic, font (size, color, and so on)—appears intact in Mail. You're witnessing one of the Mac's most useful but underpublicized features: its handling of styled text on the Clipboard.

Almost all Mac programs transfer the formatting along with the copied text. Every time you paste formatted text copied from one of these programs, the pasted material appears with the same typographical characteristics it had in the original program. Over time, this tiny time-saver spares us years' worth of cumulative reformatting effort—yet another favor the noble Macintosh does humanity.

date and time, and so on. With one quick click, you can send that information into the appropriate program, like Calendar, Contacts, or your web browser.

Here's how it works: When you spot a name, address, date, or time, point to it without clicking. A dotted rectangle appears around it (Figure 6-13). Right-click or two-finger click inside the rectangle, or click the ▾ at the right side.

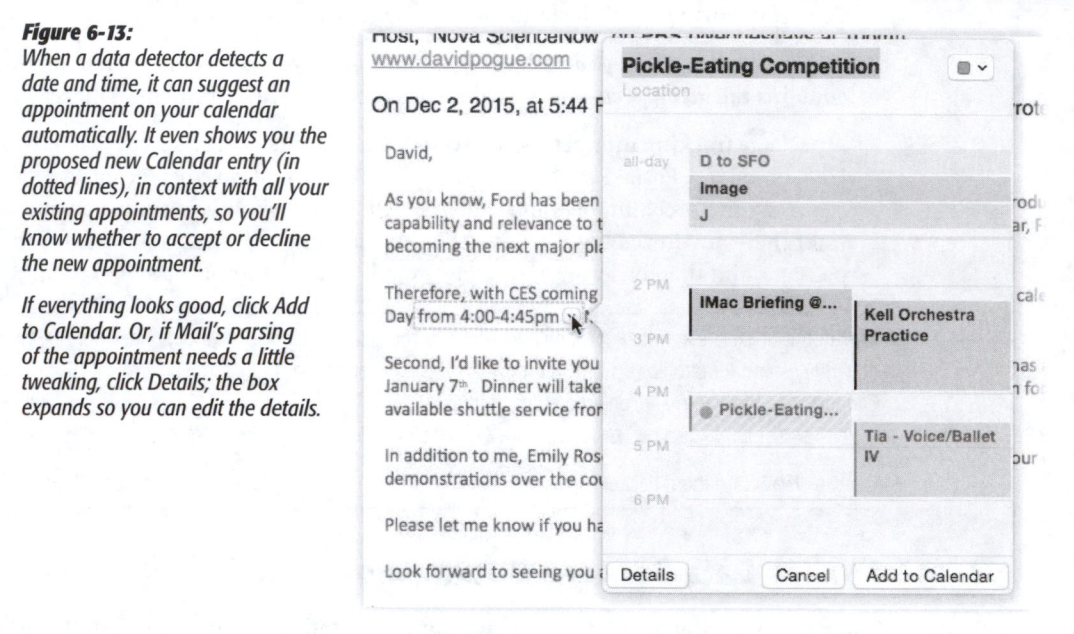

Figure 6-13:
When a data detector detects a date and time, it can suggest an appointment on your calendar automatically. It even shows you the proposed new Calendar entry (in dotted lines), in context with all your existing appointments, so you'll know whether to accept or decline the new appointment.

If everything looks good, click Add to Calendar. Or, if Mail's parsing of the appointment needs a little tweaking, click Details; the box expands so you can edit the details.

A shortcut menu appears. Its contents vary depending on what you're pointing to:

- **A date and time.** When you click the ▾, you get the amazing pop-up menu shown in Figure 6-13. It shows you the actual Calendar day view where macOS is proposing adding the appointment. The logic of this feature is overwhelming; after all, when someone emails you to ask if you're free for drinks next Thursday at 10, what's the first thing you usually want to do? Check your calendar, of course.

Tip: If, while working in Calendar, you ever forget where this event came from, double-click it. In the Info panel, you'll see a link that takes you back to the original Mail message that started it all.

- **A mailing address.** You can choose Open in Maps from the shortcut menu; the app opens automatically and shows you that address.

 Alternatively, you can choose Add to Contacts. Like magic, a little editing box sprouts out of the data-detected rectangle, prefilled with the information from the message, so you can create a new Contacts entry or add it to an existing entry.

you hold down any of the modifier keys on your keyboard (like ⌘, Option, Shift, or Control), you can see exactly which keys produce which characters. The point, of course, is to help you learn which keys to press when you need special symbols or non-English characters, such as © or ñ, in each keyboard layout.

Note: Keyboard Viewer shows only the symbols you can produce by typing keystrokes. A font may contain thousands of other characters that can't actually be typed; the Character Viewer, accessed by clicking Show Emoji & Symbols, is the only way to see these other symbols.

Keyboard Viewer is a great tool—if you can find it. The secret is to open System Preferences→Keyboard→Keyboard tab. Then turn on "Show keyboard and emoji viewers in menu bar." You open the Keyboard Viewer by choosing its name from the new menulet that appears.

To see the effect of pressing the modifier keys, either click the onscreen keys or press them on your actual keyboard. The corresponding keys on the onscreen keyboard light up as they're pressed.

Tip: You're not stuck viewing the characters in a 12-point font size—a good thing, because some of them are hard to read when displayed that small. You can make the Keyboard Viewer window bigger by dragging its lower-right corner. That will magnify the Keyboard Viewer window and its font size.

Ink: Handwriting Recognition

In the same way that your grandmother turned yesterday's dinner into today's sandwich (and tomorrow's soup), Apple recycled the handwriting technology of its failed Newton handheld and added it to macOS. It's now called Ink, and it does exactly what it used to: turn your handwriting into "typed" text in any program. Can Ink replace the keyboard? Not for anything more than quick notes, that's for sure. But it can be handy when you're web surfing, sketching, filling in database forms, and so on.

Ink appears in macOS only if you have a graphics tablet, one of those stylus-and-pad devices found generally only on the desks of graphic artists. (Wacom is the best-known tablet company, but there are a couple of others.) You could count on one hand the number of people with Wacom tablets who use them for handwriting input. And so, to avoid sacrificing any more old-growth trees than absolutely necessary, the how-to for Ink is available as a free downloadable PDF appendix to this chapter. You'll find it on this book's "Missing CD" page at *missingmanuals.com*.

Data Detectors

Here's a cool step-saver that no other computer operating system offers—a little something Apple likes to call *data detectors*.

In short, Mac programs like Mail and TextEdit can recognize commonly used bits of information that may appear in your text: a physical address, a phone number, a

Similarly, for Calendar purposes, you'll want to specify what you consider to be the first day of the week and which calendar style you observe. (Hint: If you're reading this book, it's probably Gregorian.)

Choose the French *keyboard layout* from the Input Sources tab, as explained next.

Note: MacOS and most Apple apps are only localized for 39 languages, but Calendar app can display the names of months and days in a huge number.

Input Sources

While the Mac can display many different languages, *typing* in those languages is another matter. The symbols you use when you're typing in Swedish aren't the same as when you're typing in English. Apple solved this problem by creating different keyboard layouts for different languages. (Apple calls them *input sources*, because not all of them technically use a keyboard.) Each rearranges the letters that appear

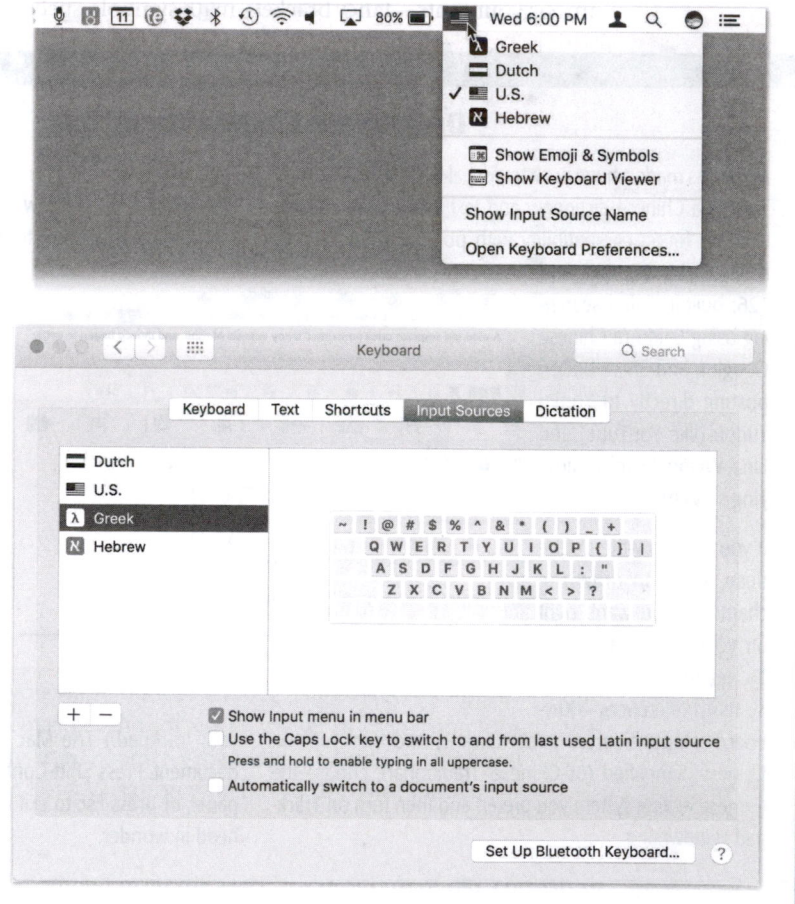

Figure 6-11:
Bottom: Click the + button to view a list of keyboard layouts; choose one to add to this list.

When you do so, "Show Input menu in menu bar" turns on. That option puts a tiny flag in your menu bar (top)—a keyboard menulet that lets you switch layouts just by choosing their names.

If you turn on "Automatically switch to a document's input source," then each document stays put with the keyboard you've been using in it, even if you've switched to a different input source in other documents.

The "Use the Caps Lock key to switch to and from last used Latin input source" option provides a quick way to switch among certain keyboard layouts. (This option appears only if you've turned on a non-Roman input source like Arabic, Hebrew, or Chinese.)

Now launch Safari, TextEdit, Mail, or Stickies. Every menu, button, and dialog box is now in the new language you selected! If you log out and back in (or restart) at this point, the entire Finder will be in the new language, too.

Formats

Of course, if you're *really* French (for example), you'll also want to make some formatting changes on the System Preferences→Language & Region panel. First, choose your French-speaking country from the Region pop-up menu, so that time and date formats, number punctuation, and currency symbols also conform to your local customs.

For example, the decimal and thousands separator characters for displaying large numbers differ from country to country. (The number 25,600.99, for example, would be written as "25 600,99" in France, and as "25.600,99" in Spain.) And what appears to an American to be July 4 (the notation "7/4"), to a European indicates April 7.

Instant Accented Characters, Courtesy of the iPhone

It's been a problem since the dawn of computing: How do you produce accented characters—líké thêsë—on a keyboard with only 26 letter keys?

For most of history, the answer has been: You bring up some special palette on the screen, or you memorize key combinations. And, yes, those options are still available in macOS.

But today there's a new option, which Apple stole from its own iPhone software: Hold down the letter you want accented—e, for example. After a moment, you get a

pop-up panel of possible accented versions. You can click the one you want, or, if you'd rather not lift your hands off the keyboard, you can type the corresponding number that appears in light gray beneath each letter.

This feature works in almost all programs, although there may be some where it doesn't…pop up.

Now, if you're the kind of person who needs accents from time to time, you're probably delighted with this new,

clever way to get them. But if holding down a key produces an accented character, that means holding down a key no longer *repeats* the key, right? It means you can no longer type, "You go, grrrrrrrrrl!" or "rated XXXXXXXX" or "I love you SOOOOOOOOOOO much!" Right?

Right. A few characters that people routinely type lines of, like ***** and ……. and ____, still repeat when you hold them down. But none of the 26 letter keys repeat anymore.

There is, fortunately, a quick and easy way to restore the old key-repeating behavior, if you're a "SOOOOOOO much" kind of person.

Open up Terminal (page 515). Type this one line, exactly as it appears here:

```
defaults write -g ApplePressAnd-
HoldEnabled -bool false
```

…and then press Return. Log out and back in.

You've just flipped off the switch for the accent picker. Now every key repeats, just as it always used to.

(including the ones you need for 10 Indian languages); offers "filtering by tones, ordering and filtering by radical or stroke count, and improved pinyin-han conversion accuracy" (you have to be a Chinese speaker to appreciate those tweaks); and much more.

First, tell your Mac which languages you'd like to have available. Open System Preferences→Language & Region. You see a listing of the languages the Mac can switch into, in the corresponding languages—Français, Español, and so on. (If you don't see the one you want, click the + and choose it from the list.) Just drag one of the languages to the top of the list to select it as your primary language, as shown in Figure 6-10.

Note: You can mix English with right-to-left languages like Hebrew and Arabic. There's even a split-cursor option that makes the pointer flip directions at the boundary between right-to-left and left-to-right text.

Figure 6-10:
Top: You can flip your copy of macOS into any of dozens of languages. Click +
to see them all— and add them to the list of Preferred Languages. You can also specify the default temperature unit.

Bottom: Here's what your Mac looks like running in Dutch. Actually understanding Dutch would be useful at a time like this—but even if you don't, it can't help but brighten up your workday to choose commands like Spraakfunctie or Knip.

Auto-Periods, Auto-Caps

On the iPhone, the software comes to your rescue every time you reach the end of a sentence. All you have to do is tap the space bar twice. The phone automatically gives you a period and a space and capitalizes the first letter of the next sentence.

Believe it or not, those features have now made their way into macOS. In System Preferences→Keyboard→Text, you can now turn on these options:

- **Capitalize words automatically**. You can give your Shift keys a break. From now on, the Mac can capitalize proper nouns (*Ohio, Texas, Pepsi, Bible, Empire State, American Express*) and the first words of sentences *for* you. Just type away, and marvel as those lowercase letters become capitals an instant after you've typed them.

- **Add period with double-space**. Truth is, there's not much point to this feature on the Mac. On an iPhone, it's a godsend because it saves you from having to swap onscreen keyboard layouts every time you want a period. On the Mac, the period key is always there! Still, for the sake of consistency, here it is: the "type two spaces to get a period" option.

Screamingly important note: Sadly, these features don't work in all programs. They have an effect in Apple's apps (Mail, TextEdit, Pages, Notes, and so on), but not in Microsoft or Adobe apps.

Case Swapping

The final feature in macOS's text-massaging tool chest is case swapping—that is, changing text you've already typed (or pasted) from ALL CAPS to lowercase or Just First Letters Capitalized.

This one's simple: Select the text you want to change, and then choose from the Edit→ Transformations submenu. Your options are Make Upper Case (all caps), Make Lower Case (no caps), and Capitalize (first letters, like a movie title).

Keep that in mind the next time some raving lunatic SENDS YOU AN EMAIL THAT WAS TYPED ENTIRELY WITH THE CAPS LOCK KEY DOWN.

Tip: Here's a sneaky one: You can tap a word with three fingers on your trackpad to get a pop-up dictionary and thesaurus definition. (That's a light three-finger *tap,* not a full *click.*) This trick doesn't work in all programs, and it requires you to turn it on in System Preferences→Trackpad→Point & Click. And it's a tad bit finicky.

But once you have it working, check it out: It also works in text documents you're examining in Quick Look!

The Many Languages of macOS Text

Apple has always taken pride in its language-friendliness. You can shift from language to language on the fly, as you type, even in midsentence—without reinstalling the operating system or even restarting the computer.

MacOS's facility with language, though, goes the extra overseas mile. It lets you type vertical Japanese and Chinese text; includes fonts for 23 more non-Roman alphabets

This feature has been in Microsoft Office forever (called AutoCorrect), and it's always been available as a shareware add-on (TypeIt4Me and TextExpander, for example). But now it's built right into most Apple programs, plus any others that use Apple's text-input plumbing.

You build your list of abbreviations in the System Preferences→Keyboard→Text tab, shown in Figure 6-9. See the list at left? Click the + to create a new row in the scrolling table of substitutions.

Click in the left column and type the abbreviation you want (for example, *addr*). Click in the right column and type, or paste, the text you want macOS to type instead.

Tip: Don't be shy—you're not limited to short snippets. The replacement text can be pages long, which is handy if you're a lawyer and you build your contracts out of boilerplate chunks of canned text.

You can even create multiple paragraphs—but not by hitting Return when you want a new line; no, hitting Return means "I'm finished entering this text" and closes up the box. Instead, press Option-Return when you want a paragraph break.

That's it! Now, whenever you type one of the abbreviations you've set up, the Mac instantly replaces it with your substituted text.

And not just the Mac, either; your abbreviations autosync to iPhones, iPads, iPod Touches, and other Macs. If, that is, you've turned on System Preferences→ iCloud→iCloud Drive. (Remember, you can *turn off* the text-replacement feature in individual programs, if you like—TextEdit, Mail, Stickies, and so on. To do that, choose Edit→Substitutions→Text Replacement, so that the checkmark disappears.)

GEM IN THE ROUGH

The Least-Known Typing Feature

This may come as a shock if you think you know your Mac pretty well, but here goes: MacOS actually offers system-wide autocomplete of big words, just like the iPhone.

We're not talking about the spelling checker, and we're not talking about text substitution. (And we're also not talking about the Touch Bar on newer MacBooks, which performs a similar trick with its QuickType feature.) We're talking, you start typing a word and the Mac finishes it for you. It's ideal when you're in a hurry, when you're not sure how to finish a word (is it "independance" or "independence"?), or

when you're trying to solve a crossword puzzle. It works in all the standard Mac programs (TextEdit, Mail, Safari, Pages, and so on).

Dear Harold,

It has come to our attention

> attention
> attentive
> attentions
> attentively
> attentiveness
> attention's
> attentional

Once you've begun typing a word, press either fn-F5 or Option-Esc to produce the list of possible word completions shown here. If the Mac correctly anticipates the rest of the word, great; press Tab, Return, or the space bar to accept the suggestion, and then keep right on typing. If it guesses wrong, you can either select a different word in the list (using the mouse or the arrow keys), or tap Esc to ignore the suggestions and continue typing.

manually, in each program. (These commands are available anywhere you do a *lot* of typing, like TextEdit, Mail, and Stickies. Look for the Edit→Substitutions submenu.)

- **Auto-quotes.** To make the quotes curlify themselves, choose Edit→Substitutions→ Smart Quotes, so that a checkmark appears.

> **Note:** In the System Preferences→Keyboard→Text tab, you can specify which kind of fancy quotation mark you prefer: «this kind,» „this kind," or whatever. You international thing, you!

- **Auto-dashes.** To turn double hyphens into these (—) long dashes, choose Edit→ Substitutions→Smart Dashes, so that a checkmark appears.

- **Smart links.** There's also an option to create smart links, where any web address you type turns into a blue, underlined, *clickable* link to a web page. Turn on Edit→ Substitutions→Smart Links.

> **Tip:** You can also choose Edit→Substitutions→Show Substitutions to make a floating panel appear, complete with on/off checkboxes for all these features.

Replace abbreviations with much longer phrases

You can program *addr* to type your entire return address. Create two-letter abbreviations for big legal or technical words you have to type a lot. Set up *goaway* to type out a polite rejection letter for use in email. And so on.

Figure 6-9:
This is where you can manage macOS's typographic substitutions. (They're in the Keyboard pane of System Preferences—not Language & Region anymore.)

You can add all kinds of auto-typo corrections and even boilerplate text paragraphs.

using—but specifying the language in System Preferences→Keyboard→Text→ Spelling is generally more reliable.

- **Fix spelling as you type.** Note the difference. *Checking* your spelling just means "finding the misspelled words." *Fixing* means autocorrecting the errors as they occur, as you type. You might not even notice that it's happening!

This most tantalizing option is found in Edit→Spelling and Grammar→Correct Spelling Automatically. And sure enough, when this option is turned on, common typos like *teh* and *frmo* and *dont* get fixed as you type.

Note: If you're typing slowly enough, you might see the suggestion bubble illustrated in Figure 6-8. That, of course, is a feature Apple brought to the Mac from the iPhone/iPad. It's saying, "Here's the word I *think* you meant—and if you just keep on typing, I'll go ahead and make the change I'm proposing. If you disagree, click on the ✖ in the word bubble to make me shut up and leave what you typed, just as you typed it."

It's not perfect. It doesn't correct all errors (or even most of them). It occasionally even corrects a word you didn't mean to have corrected. (When it makes a mistake, hit ⌘-Z, the Undo command, to restore what you typed.) And sometimes it doesn't make the change until you're halfway through the sentence.

Still, though. Kind of cool.

Text Substitution (Abbreviation Expansion)

This useful feature autoreplaces *one* thing you type with something else. Why? Because it can do any of these things.

Insert the proper typographical symbols

For example, the Mac can insert attractive "curly quotes" automatically as you type "straight ones," or em dashes—like this—when you type two hyphens (-- like that).

You can see the built-in sample substitution ("omw" for "On my way!")—and create your own—in the System Preferences→Keyboard→Text tab, as shown in Figure 6-9.

Apple doesn't want to drive you nuts, though, so it makes sure *you're* sure you really want these swappings to take place. So you have to turn on each of these features

FREQUENTLY ASKED QUESTION

Smart Copy and Paste

Hey, I saw one more autofix feature in the Edit→Substitutions submenu: "Smart Copy/Paste." What's that about?

It's about spaces.

Ordinarily, when you cut or copy a word out of a sentence and then paste it into a new one, you have some cleanup to do. You leave an extra space behind, and you have to add a space after the word when you paste.

Smart Copy/Paste cleans up these spaces for you. If you cut a word out of a sentence, only *one* space gets left between the words where it used to be. And when you paste text, a space is added on either side automatically—but only one.

- **Check spelling as you type.** Choose Edit→Spelling and Grammar→Check Spelling While Typing. (If Check Grammar With Spelling is turned on in the same submenu, you'll get a grammar check, too.)

Now, as you type, you'll see those red and green underlines on words the Mac thinks represent spelling or grammar mistakes. To fix one, right-click or two-finger click the underlined word, and proceed as shown in Figure 6-8.

Tip: In TextEdit, the factory setting for error-underlining is On. To turn it off for all new documents, choose TextEdit→Preferences, click New Document, and then turn off "Check spelling as you type."

Figure 6-8:
Top: You're never more than a right-click or two-finger click away from more accurate spelling. Once you right-click a questionable word, the suggestions of Apple's built-in dictionary appear right in the shortcut menu, along with the Ignore Spelling and Learn Spelling commands.

Bottom: If you've opted for autocorrected spelling, you get the little iPhoney suggestion bubble when you pause after typing a word. Ignore it to accept the suggestion; click the × in the bubble to keep what you typed.

- **Check spelling after the document is finished.** Choose Edit→Spelling and Grammar→Show Spelling and Grammar (or press ⌘-:). The Spelling dialog box appears. The first error it spots appears in the top box, with the proposed corrections in the bottom one.

If you like one of Apple's proposals, then click it and click Change. If the word was correct already (for example, the guy's last name really is Teh), then click Find Next ("Leave the word as I typed it"), Ignore ("It's OK everywhere in this document"), or Learn ("Never flag this word again").

Handily enough, you can also click Define to look up a highlighted word (one of the spelling suggestions, for example) in the Mac's built-in Dictionary app. Also handily enough, the spelling checker maintains dictionaries for 15 languages. It's often smart enough to recognize, within a single document, which language you're

- **Use the trackpad.** If you have a trackpad (on a laptop, for example), you can trigger a right-click in all kinds of ways.

 Out of the box, you do it by *clicking the trackpad with two fingers*. The shortcut menu pops right up.

 Or you can point to whatever you want to click. Rest two fingers on the trackpad—and then click with your thumb.

 But even those aren't the end of your options. In System Preferences→Trackpad, you can also turn on even more right-click methods (and watch little videos on how to do them; see Figure 6-7). For example, you can "right-click" by clicking either the lower-right or lower-left corner of the trackpad—one finger only.

When shortcut menus are mentioned throughout this book, rather than repeat this explanation for "101 ways to right-click" over and over, you'll find only the two best methods: Right-click (if you have a mouse) or two-finger click (if you have a trackpad).

Power Typing

Something strange has been quietly taking place at Apple: *Typing* has been getting a lot of attention.

It began when Apple created *system-wide* spelling and grammar checkers. For the first time in computer history, the *operating system* took over typos and grammos. You didn't have to maintain a separate spelling checker for each program you used. Now there's just one, and it works in most programs: TextEdit, Stickies, Messages, Mail, Calendar, Safari, Pages, Photos, iMovie, and so on. Add a word to the dictionary in one program, and it's available to all the others.

Today, there's much more. There's text substitution, where you type *addr* and the system types out "Irwina P. McGillicuddy, 1293 Eastport Lane, Harborvilletown, MA 02552." (The same system autocorrects common typos like *teh* instead of *the.*) There's also a case-flipping feature that can change selected text to ALL CAPS, all lowercase, or First Letter Capped. Both of these features are available in most Apple programs and in any other programs that tap into macOS's built-in text-processing circuitry (although not, alas, Microsoft programs).

The Spelling and Grammar Checker

Your Mac can give you live, interactive spelling and grammar checking, just as in Microsoft Word and other word processors. That is, misspelled words or badly written sentences or fragments get flagged with a dashed red underline (for grammar problems, a green underline) the moment you type them. Here's the crash course:

- **Check the spelling of one word:** Highlight the word. Choose Edit→Spelling and Grammar→Show Spelling and Grammar. The spell-check dialog box opens, with the proposed corrections visible.

- **Right-click.** Experienced computer fans have always preferred the one-handed method: right-clicking. That is, clicking something by pressing the *right* mouse button on a two-button mouse.

Every desktop Mac since late 2005 has come with a two-button mouse—but you might not realize it. Take a look: Is it a white, shiny, plastic capsule with a tiny, gray scrolling track-pea on the far end? Then you have an Apple Mouse. Is it a cordless, flattened capsule instead? Then it's a Magic Mouse. Each has a *secret* right mouse button. It doesn't work until you ask for it.

To do that, choose System Preferences. Click Mouse. There, in all its splendor, is a diagram of the Apple or Magic Mouse.

Your job is to choose Secondary Button from the pop-up menu that identifies the right side of the mouse. (The reason it's not called a "right button" is because left-handers might prefer to reverse the right and left functions.)

From now on, even though there aren't two visible mouse buttons, your Apple Mouse does, in fact, register a left-click or a right-click depending on which side of the mouse you push down. It works a lot more easily than it sounds like it would.

Tip: You can also attach any old $6 USB two-button mouse to the Mac, and it'll work flawlessly. Recycle the one from your old PC, if you like.

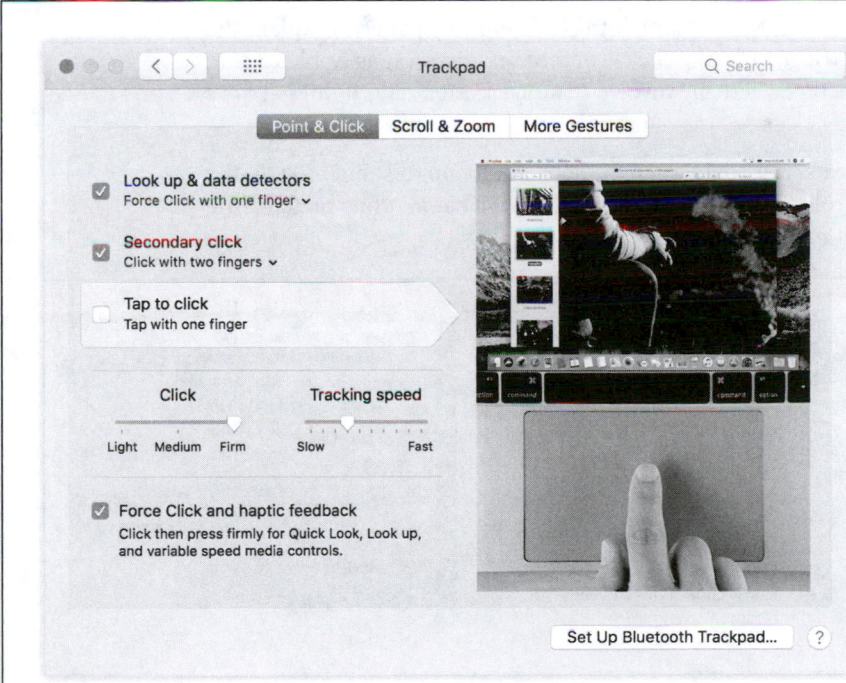

Figure 6-7:
The Trackpad pane of System Preferences looks different depending on your laptop model. But this one shows all the ways to get a "right-click."

Thanks to the Touch Bar, the QuickType suggestions are now on your Mac, too. They're available in any Touch Bar–enabled program where you can type, like Mail, Notes, and TextEdit. (If you don't see the suggestions, they may currently be collapsed. Tap the ⟨⌨ button to bring them up.)

Of course, on the Mac, you have a real keyboard; you're not trying to hit keys the size of Tic Tacs on a glass screen. And QuickType means you have to split your focus; you have to pay attention to both the words you're tapping and the text on the main screen.

You could argue, therefore, that QuickType is less important on the Mac than on the iPhone. It might be useful if you're unsure of a word's spelling, or if you're a very slow typist—but if you can type fairly quickly, it's usually faster to just use the keyboard.

In that case, you may want to turn off the QuickType feature entirely, or maybe only for one program.

The key is the "Show typing suggestions" checkbox on the Customize Touch Bar screen (Figure 6-4). If you turn it off (for the program whose Touch Bar you're editing), then the QuickType suggestions no longer appear. There's that much more space for your app-specific function buttons.

Notes on Right-Clicking

In macOS, *shortcut menus* are more important than ever (Figure 6-6).

They're so important, in fact, that it's worth this ink and this paper to explain the different ways you can trigger a "right-click" (or a *secondary click,* as Apple calls it, because not all these methods actually involve a mouse button, and it doesn't *have* to be the right one):

- **Control-click.** For years, you could open the shortcut menu of something on the Mac screen by Control-clicking it—and you still can. That is, while pressing the Control key (bottom row), click the mouse on your target.

Figure 6-6:
A shortcut menu pops out of something you're clicking—an icon, a button, a folder. The beauty of it is that its commands are contextual. They bring up commands in exactly the spots where they're most useful.

- **Rearrange existing buttons.** Once the Customize dialog box is open, you can use your finger to drag the existing Touch Bar buttons into a new order.

Tip: Truth is, you can use your mouse, too. No cursor appears on the Touch Bar, which is a little weird. But as you move your mouse, the existing buttons light up to show where the cursor *would* be. Once a button is lit up, you can drag it horizontally to move it.

- **Delete a button.** Once the Customize dialog box is open, use your finger to drag the unwanted button all the way to the left; release it on top of the Trash icon that appears there.

Tip: Here again, you can use your mouse to drag a button to the Touch Bar Trash, too. The buttons light up to show the invisible cursor's position.

In each case, hit Done (either at the far left of the Touch Bar, or on your main screen) to wrap it up.

QuickType on the Touch Bar

On a phone, what Apple calls its QuickType keyboard can save you a lot of time, tapping, and errors. As you type a sentence, the software predicts which word you might type next—the three most likely words—and displays them as three buttons above the keyboard. (See Figure 6-5.)

Figure 6-5:
QuickType is autocomplete on steroids. Frankly, it's a rush when it finishes a long word for you.

If you begin the sentence by typing, "I really," then the three suggestions might be *want, don't,* and *like.* But what if you intended to say, "I really hope…"? In that case, type the first letter of "hope." Instantly, the three suggestions change to *"h," hope,* and *hate.* (The first button always shows, in quotes, whatever non-word you've typed so far, just in case that's what you really intend. To place it into your text, you can tap that button or tap the space bar or some punctuation.)

When someone texts you a question that ends with a choice ("Coffee, tea, or me?"), the QuickType buttons cleverly offer those same choices. Before you've even typed a single letter, the choices say "coffee," "tea," and "you."

QuickType automatically adds a space after each word you select, so you don't have to mess with the space bar. And, sometimes, QuickType offers you several words on a single button, to save you even more time (for example, "up to" or "in the").

the collapsed Control Strip if there are other functions you use more often. In fact, you can even customize the *expanded* Control Strip (Figure 6-3, second from top).

The key to making these changes: Open System Preferences→Keyboard; click Customize Control Strip. Now you've opened the weird, wonderful world of Touch Bar customizing, as described in the next section. Note that, in this case, you can expand or collapse the Control Strip during this process, thereby editing either version. For example, you could get rid of the Siri button (there are, after all, other ways to trigger Siri), which makes more room for app-specific buttons. Or maybe you never use the Launcher button in the expanded Control Strip; this is your chance to replace it with, for example, the Screenshot button or the Show Desktop button.

Customizing the Touch Bar

The key to choosing which buttons you want on your Touch Bar is the View→Customize Touch Bar command. You'll find that command in the Finder, Mail, Photos, and a few other major programs. (If the program you're using doesn't let you customize its Touch Bar, then that command doesn't appear.)

The dialog box shown in Figure 6-4 shows what you'd see in the Finder.

Figure 6-4:
When the Customize dialog box is on the screen, you can move, delete, or add buttons on the Touch Bar. All the existing buttons begin gently wiggling to indicate that they're movable or deletable.

Editing your Touch Bar is a strange, delightful procedure. It goes like this:

- **Install a new button.** Inspect the palette of available Touch Bar buttons on your Mac's main screen. You can *drag* one of those buttons downward with your mouse, down off the screen, "through" the laptop's hinge, and onto the Touch Bar.

 If you drag onto a blank spot (anywhere marked by ---- dashes), you can drop it there to install it. If you drag it onto an existing button, then a dotted outline appears; that means that you'll replace the existing button when you let go.

back. Tap the thin ❮ button to the left of the ☀ button. The collapsed Control Strip now expands to stretch the full length of the keyboard, precisely replicating the function keys that used to be painted on the top row of physical keys (Figure 6-3, second from top).

Tip: You can also set things up so that tapping the physical fn key expands the Control Strip temporarily. Open System Preferences→Keyboard and from the "Press Fn key to" pop-up menu, choose Expand Control Strip.

Control Strip (collapsed)

Control Strip (expanded)

Hold down the Brightness button...

...and slide.

Figure 6-3:
Top: The Control Strip is always present on the right—and usually collapsed, to make room for your programs' buttons in the center of the Touch Bar. To expand the Control Strip to the full width of the keyboard, tap the skinny ❮ button.

Bottom: The Brightness and Volume buttons transform into sliders when you hold your finger down on them.

- **Bring back the function keys permanently.** If you prefer to have the standard function keys at all times, open System Preferences→Keyboard. From the "Touch Bar shows" pop-up menu, choose Expanded Control Strip. At this point, the Touch Bar never changes, never shows you app-specific buttons; it *always* shows the traditional function keys, pictured second from top in Figure 6-3.

- **Get rid of the Control Strip.** On the other hand, maybe you don't adjust your brightness or volume much, or you have another way to do it. And you'd rather have the entire width of the Touch Bar dedicated to app-specific buttons.

 In that case, open System Preferences→Keyboard. From the "Touch Bar shows" pop-up menu, choose App Controls. Now the Control Strip is always hidden; you've got a lot more space available for function buttons within each program.

- **Change the buttons on the Control Strip.** Apple's probably correct that the functions most people want most of the time are Brightness, Volume, and Mute. (Siri? Well, maybe in time.) But that doesn't mean you can't add or delete buttons from

The Fingerprint Sensor

On Touch Bar laptops, the power button sits at the right end of the Touch Bar—and it's also a Touch ID fingerprint reader, the same sensor that's on the iPhone and iPad. (The 2018 MacBook Air has this button, too, even though it doesn't have a Touch Bar.) Once you've taught the Mac to recognize your fingerprint in System Preferences→ Touch ID, then just resting your finger on this button is enough to unlock the Mac, bypassing the password screen.

In fact, if you've set up your Mac with different accounts, the next person can insta-switch to his account just by clicking the Touch ID sensor himself—no logging out, no menu commands, no other steps.

Finally, your fingerprint can approve App Store purchases, or buy stuff on the web without having to enter your name, address, and credit card info over and over again. That part's called Apple Pay on the Web, and it's described on page 671.

The Control Strip

Some Touch Bar buttons are always present. At the left end, for example, what Apple calls a System button is always available. Usually, it's the Esc key (page 232). Some-times the System button says Done or ⊗, but you get the idea.

At the right end, Apple offers something called the Control Strip. You're probably too young to remember the Control Strip (in System 7, which ran Macs from 1991 to 1998). But this is the same idea: a collapsible row of buttons that give you direct access to settings you're likely to want to change without burrowing into System Preferences.

Out of the box, the Control Strip seeks to restore the most essential functions of the F-keys that the Touch Bar replaces: screen brightness and speaker volume (plus a button for Siri), as shown at top in Figure 6-3.

When the Control Strip is collapsed, you have two ways to adjust the brightness and volume:

- **Tap the ☀ or ◀ button.** A slider springs out to the left of the button. Touch or drag your finger inside the slider to adjust the brightness or volume.

- **Slide from the ☀ or ◀ button.** In other words, you can adjust the brightness or volume with one continuous finger move instead of two—just keep your finger down after the initial tap, and drag within the slider (Figure 6-3, bottom).

Tip: Starting with the 2018 MacBook Pro models, making brightness or volume changes can be a little quicker: You can make little horizontal swipes directly on top of the ☀ or ◀ buttons. No slider ever appears, and you save a couple of seconds.

Now, not everybody likes change. And some people don't like the way Apple makes changes. Fortunately, the Control Strip is a change you can change.

- **Bring back the function keys temporarily.** If you need the standard full-row set of Mac function keys as described on pages 198 and 233, you can bring them

It's a half-inch–tall, high-resolution ("Retina"), 2170×60 pixel, multitouch, OLED screen. It can display whatever programmers want: buttons for functions you might need right now, or a rainbow of color selections, or a timeline of the video you're editing. The Touch Bar is designed to give you quick access to commands and features that are usually hidden in menus—but now you don't have to memorize keystrokes to trigger them.

The controls here *change* according to what you're doing at this moment—what program you're using, and what function within that program.

When you're typing, you might see QuickType (autocomplete buttons for the three words the Mac thinks you're most likely to want to type next). When you're in Safari, you see little buttons for your open page tabs. When you've selected text, you get formatting controls. When you're editing video or reading a Books book, you see a horizontal "map" of your movie or book, for quick navigation with a finger touch.

Note: The Touch Bar fades to black if you haven't used it in a while. Just tap to make the buttons light up again.

All the major programs that come with the Mac have been outfitted with Touch Bar controls: the Finder, Automator, Calculator, Contacts, GarageBand, Books, iMovie, iTunes, Keynote, Mail, Maps, Messages, Notes, Numbers, Pages, Photos, Preview, QuickTime Player, Reminders, Safari, Stickies, System Preferences, and TextEdit. (Apple has even blessed some of the utility programs with Touch Bar buttons, like Activity Monitor, Script Editor, Terminal, and Xcode.)

Other software companies, including Adobe and Microsoft, have added Touch Bar buttons to their programs, too.

In many programs, you can *customize* what's on the Touch Bar, so that the functions you use most often are always glowing there.

The Touch Bar is especially useful when you're in Full Screen mode (page 178), where the whole point is to maximize your document's area on the screen. Now the editing controls you might need are on the Touch Bar, out of the way of the big screen.

There's no feedback when you tap the Touch Bar—no little beep or vibration—so you do have to glance at it to see what you're doing. Fortunately, the Touch Bar image is actually angled, not flat, so it's looking right at you.

The Touch Bar may not revolutionize your work in every program. But you'll probably find some situations where it's a truly helpful work accelerator: navigating a video you're editing without having to fuss with the onscreen scroll bar, for example, or tapping out emoji symbols in Messages.

Oh—and being able to log in without entering a password 65 times a day (thanks to your fingerprint) is a joy; read on.

Tip: If you miss the old function keys (F1, F2, F3…), you can have them back on command. Just hold down the physical fn key on your keyboard; the Touch Bar buttons change to the old F-keys.

The Complicated Story of the Function Keys

As the previous section makes clear, the F-keys at the top of modern Mac keyboards come with predefined functions: brightness, volume, music playback, and so on.

But they didn't always. Before Apple gave F9, F10, and F11 to the fast-forward and speaker-volume functions, those keys controlled the Exposé window-management function described starting on page 196.

So the question is: What if you don't *want* to trigger the hardware features of these keys? What if you want pressing F1 to mean "F1" (which opens the Help window in some programs)? What if you want F9, F10, and F11 to control Exposé's three modes, as they once did?

For that purpose, you're supposed to press the fn key. The fn key (lower left on small keyboards, center block of keys on the big ones) switches the function of the function keys. In other words, pressing fn *and* F10 triggers an Exposé feature, even though the key has a Mute symbol (◂) painted on it.

But here's the thing: What if you use those F-keys for software features (like Cut, Copy, Paste, and Exposé) *more often* than the hardware features (like brightness and volume)?

In that case, you can reverse the logic, so that pressing the F-keys *alone* triggers software functions and governs brightness and audio only when you're pressing fn. To do that, choose System Preferences→Keyboard. Turn on the cryptically worded checkbox "Use F1, F2, etc. as standard function keys."

And that's it. From now on, you press the fn key to get the functions painted on the keys (◂◂, ▸❙❙, ▸▸, ◂, ◂⟩, ◂⟩)), ·̣·, ·̣·̣, and so on).

The Touch Bar + Fingerprint Reader

The 2016 MacBook Pro models introduced an eye-popping feature, a first on computers: Above the keyboard, where the function keys (F1, F2, F3…) once sat, there's a colorful strip of touchscreen. Apple calls it the Touch Bar (Figure 6-2).

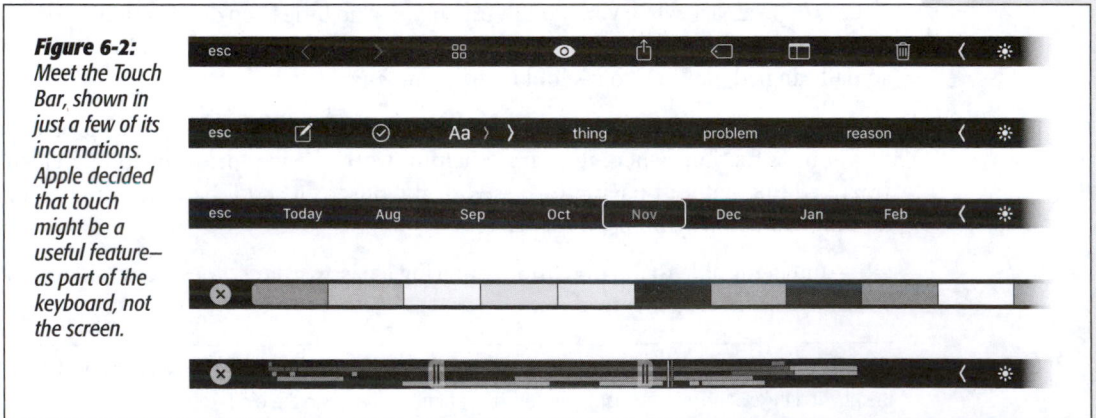

Figure 6-2:
Meet the Touch Bar, shown in just a few of its incarnations. Apple decided that touch might be a useful feature—as part of the keyboard, not the screen.

(In Word, they jump to the beginning or end of the line. But then again, Microsoft has always had its own ways of doing things.)

On keyboards without a dedicated block of number keys, you get these functions by holding down fn as you tap the ◄ and ► keys.

- **Page Up, Page Down.** These keys scroll up or down by one screenful. The idea is to let you scroll through word-processing documents, web pages, and lists without having to use the mouse.

On keyboards without a numeric keypad, you get these functions by pressing fn plus the ▲ and ▼ keys.

- **Clear.** Clear (on the old full-size keyboards only) gets rid of whatever you've high-lighted, but without putting a copy on the invisible Clipboard, as the Cut command would do.

- **Esc.** Esc stands for escape, and it means "cancel." It's fantastically useful. It closes dialog boxes, dismisses menus, and exits special modes like Quick Look, slideshows, screen savers, and so on. Get to know it.

- **Delete.** The backspace key.

- ⌦. Many a Mac fan goes for years without discovering the handiness of this delightful little key: the Forward Delete key. Whereas Delete backspaces over whatever letter is just to the *left* of the insertion point, this one (labeled "Del" on older keyboards) deletes whatever is just to the *right* of the insertion point. It comes in handy when, for example, you've clicked into some text to make an edit—but wound up planting your cursor in just the wrong place.

The old full-size Apple keyboard has a dedicated key for this. On all other keyboards, you get this function by holding down fn as you tap the regular Delete key.

- **Return/Enter.** Most Apple keyboards have a single Return/Enter key. On the old-style wide keyboards, there are separate Return and Enter keys (very few programs treat these keys as different, although Microsoft Excel is one of them). In any case, pressing Return wraps your typing to the next line. When a dialog box is on the screen, tapping the Return key is the same as clicking the confirmation button (like OK or Done).

- ⌘. This key triggers keyboard shortcuts for menu items.

- **Control.** The Control key (represented by ⌃ in software menus) triggers shortcut menus, described on the following pages.

- **Option.** The Option key (sometimes labeled Alt, and represented by ⌥ in menus) is sort of a "miscellaneous" key. It's the equivalent of the Alt key in Windows. It lets you access secret features—you'll find them described all through this book—and type special symbols. For example, you press Option-4 to get the ¢ symbol, and Option-Y to get the ¥ (yen) symbol.

- **Help.** In the Finder, Microsoft programs, and a few other places, this key opens up the electronic help screens. But you'd guessed that.

- ☼, ☀ (**F1, F2**). These keys control the brightness of your screen. Usually, you can tone it down a bit when you're in a dark room or when you want to save laptop battery power; you'll want to crank it up in the sun.

Tip: If you hold down the Shift and Option keys, tapping the brightness keys adjusts the brightness by just a little bit—a fraction of one of the larger brightness steps. Control freaks, rejoice.

- ▦ (**F3**). This one fires up Mission Control, the handy window-management feature described starting on page 183.
- ☉ or ⊞ (**F4**). Tap the ☉ key to open Dashboard, the archipelago of tiny, single-purpose widgets like Weather, Stocks, and Movies. See page 192 for more about Dashboard.

On recent Macs, the F4 key bears a ⊞ logo instead. Tapping it opens Launchpad, which is described starting on page 170.

- ☼, ☼ (**F5, F6**). Most recent Mac laptops have light-up *keys,* which is very handy indeed when you're typing in the dark. The key lights are supposed to come on automatically when it's dark, but you can also control the illumination yourself by tapping these keys. (On most other Macs, the F5 and F6 keys aren't assigned to anything. They're free for you to use as you see fit, as described on page 210.)
- ◄◄, ►ıı, and ►► (**F7, F8, F9**). These keys work in the programs you'd expect: iTunes, QuickTime Player, DVD Player, and other programs where it's handy to have Rewind, Play/Pause, and Fast Forward buttons.

Tip: Tap either ◄◄ or ►► to skip to the previous or next track or chapter. Hold one down to rewind or fast-forward.

- ◄, ◄), ◄)) (**F10, F11, F12**). These three keys control your speaker volume. The ◄ key means Mute; tap it once to cut off the sound completely and again to restore its previous level. Tap the ◄) repeatedly to make the sound level lower, the ◄)) key to make it louder.

With each tap, you see a big white version of each key's symbol on your screen, your Mac's little nod to let you know it understands your efforts.

Tip: If you hold down the Shift and Option keys, then tapping the volume keys adjusts the volume by smaller increments, just as with the brightness keys.

- ⏏. This is the Eject key. When there's a flash drive or a memory card in your Mac (or, less likely, a CD or a DVD), tap this key to make the computer spit it out. (If you don't have this key, then choose File→Eject, or press ⌘-E.)
- **Home, End.** The Home key jumps to the top of a window, the End key to the bottom. If you're looking at a list of files, the Home and End keys jump you to the top or bottom of the list. In Photos, they jump to the first or last photo in your collection. In iMovie, the Home key rewinds your movie to the very beginning. In Safari, it gets you to the top or bottom of the web page.

Here, then, is a guided tour of the non-typewriter keys on the modern Mac keyboard:

Tip: To see close-ups of Apple's current wired and wireless keyboards, visit *apple.com/keyboard*.

- **fn.** How are you supposed to pronounce fn? Not "function," certainly; after all, the F-keys on the top row are already known as function keys. And not "fun"; goodness knows, the fn key isn't particularly hilarious to press.

 What it *does,* though, is quite clear: It changes the purpose of certain keys. That's a big deal on laptops, which don't have nearly as many keys as desktop keyboards. So for some of the less commonly used functions, you're supposed to press fn and a regular key. (For example, fn turns the ▲ arrow key into a Page Up key, which scrolls upward by one screenful.)

Note: On most Mac keyboards, the fn key is in the lower-left corner. The exception is the full-size Apple desktop keyboard (the one with a numeric keypad); there the fn key is in the little block of keys between the letter keys and the number pad.

Figure 6-1:
On the top row of aluminum Mac keyboards, the F-keys have dual functions. Ordinarily, the F1 through F4 keys correspond to Screen Dimmer (☼), Screen Brighter (☀), Mission Control (▣), and either Dashboard (◉) or Launchpad (⊞). Pressing the fn key in the lower-left corner changes their personalities.

You'll find many more fn examples in the following paragraphs.

- **Numeric keypad.** The number-pad keys do exactly the same thing as the numbers at the top of the keyboard. But, with practice, typing things like phone numbers and prices is much faster with the number pad, since you don't have to look down at what you're doing.

 Apple has been quietly eliminating the numeric keypad from most of its keyboards, but you can still find it on some models. And on some old Mac laptops, the numbers 0 through 9 were painted onto a block of *letter* keys near the right side (1, 2, and 3 were J, K, and L, for example). You could turn those letter keys into their numeric alter egos by pressing the fn key with your left hand.

 Eventually, Apple eliminated this embedded-keyboard effect from its laptops, having discovered that almost nobody was using it.

Data: Typing, Sharing & Backing Up

The original 1984 Mac didn't make jaws drop because of its speed, price, or sleek looks. What amazed people was the simplicity and elegance of the user interface. At some point in every Apple demo, the presenter copied a graphic drawn in a painting program (MacPaint) and pasted it directly into a word processor (MacWrite), where it appeared neatly nestled between typed paragraphs of text.

Today, the Mac is even more adept at helping you enter, move, and share your hard-won data. MacOS offers several ways to move information within a single document, between documents, between programs, and even between Mac and Windows computers. This chapter leads you through this broad cycle of data: from entering it with the mouse and keyboard, to moving it around, to backing it up.

The Mac Keyboard

All through this book, you'll find references to certain keys on Apple's keyboards. "Hold down the ⏏ key," you might read, or "Press Control-F2." If you're coming from Mac OS 9, from Windows, or even from a typewriter, you might be a bit befuddled.

To make any attempt at an explanation even more complicated, Apple's keyboards keep changing. The one you're using right now is probably one of these models:

- **The current keyboards,** where the keys are flat little jobbers that poke up through square holes in the aluminum (Figure 6-1). That's what you get on current laptops, wired keyboards, and Bluetooth wireless keyboards.

- **The old, plastic desktop keyboards,** or the white or black plastic laptop ones.

- **Highlight several passages simultaneously** by ⌘-dragging. Each time you ⌘-drag, you highlight another block of text, even though the earlier blocks are still selected.

Tip: In most Cocoa programs, you can combine these two tricks. That is, you can select multiple, arbitrary (not full-page-width) blocks of text by pressing both Option and ⌘ as you drag.

Secret Keyboard Shortcuts

Most Cocoa apps respond to certain keystrokes left over from the NeXT operating system, which was macOS's ancestor. If you're a card-carrying member of KIAFTMA (the Keyboard Is Always Faster Than the Mouse Association), you'll love these strokes:

- **Control-A.** Moves your insertion point to the beginning of the paragraph. (*Mnemonic:* A = beginning of the Alphabet.)

- **Control-E.** Jumps to the end of the paragraph. (*Mnemonic:* E = End.)

- **Control-D.** Forward delete (deletes the letter to the *right* of the insertion point).

- **Control-K.** Instantly deletes all text from the insertion point to the right end of the line. (*Mnemonic:* K = Kills the rest of the line.)

- **Control-O.** Inserts a paragraph break, much like Return, but leaves the insertion point where it was, above the break. This is the ideal trick for breaking a paragraph in half when you've just thought of a better ending for the first part.

- **Control-T.** Moves the insertion point one letter to the right—and, along with it, drags whichever letter was to its left. (*Mnemonic:* T = Transpose letters.)

- **Option-Delete.** Deletes the entire word to the left of the insertion point. When you're typing along in a hurry and discover that you've just made a typo, this is the keystroke you want. It's much faster to nuke the previous word and retype it than to fiddle around with the mouse and the insertion point just to fix one letter.

Four additional keystrokes duplicate the functions of the arrow keys. Still, as long as you've got your pinky on the Control key…

- **Control-B, Control-F.** Move the insertion point one character to the left or right, just like the left and right arrow keys. (*Mnemonic:* Back, Forward.)

- **Control-N, Control-P.** Move the insertion point one row down or up, like the down and up arrow keys. (*Mnemonic:* Next, Previous.)

The Cocoa Advantage

MacOS can run two different kinds of programs, each with different characteristics: *Cocoa and Carbon.* These were the two kinds of apps that software companies could create for the Mac when OS X first appeared. Those companies could either update their existing programs, using a conversion kit called Carbon, or they could rewrite their programs from scratch, using Apple's Cocoa tools.

The two resulting kinds of programs look identical, but Cocoa apps offer a number of special features that Carbonized programs don't offer. (Almost all of Apple's own included apps are Cocoa apps, including the Finder, TextEdit, Mail, and so on.)

Here are some of the advantages that only Cocoa programs offer. May it clear up any confusion you have about why certain features seem to be present only occasionally.

The Fonts Panel

When you use a Carbon program, you usually access fonts the same way as always: using a Font menu. But when you use a Cocoa program, you get the Fonts *panel,* which makes it far easier to organize, search, and use your font collection. Chapter 14 describes fonts, and the Fonts panel, in more detail.

Title Bar Tricks

You may remember from Chapter 1 that the title bar of every Finder window harbors a secret pop-up menu. When you Control-click it (or right-click it, or two-finger click it, or ⌘-click it), you're shown a little ladder that delineates your current position in your folder hierarchy. The tiny icon just to the left of the window's name is actually a handle you can drag to move a folder into a different window.

In Cocoa programs, you get the same features in *document* windows, as shown back in Figure 2-7 (page 86). By dragging the tiny document icon next to the document's name, you can perform stunts—like dragging that little icon to the desktop or to the Dock icon of a different program for opening—right from your document's title bar.

Background Window Control

The ⌘ key unlocks a slick trick in Cocoa programs: It lets you operate the buttons and controls of an inactive background window without bringing it to the front. You can operate a background window's resize box, buttons, pop-up menus, and scroll bars, all while another window is in front of it. In fact, you can even *drag through text* in a background window—and then drag-and-drop it into the foreground window. (Freaky!) In every case, the secret is simply to keep ⌘ pressed as you click or drag.

Cool Text-Selection Tricks

By holding down certain keys while dragging through text in a Cocoa program, you gain some wild and wacky text-selection powers (especially useful in, for example, TextEdit and Pages):

- **Highlight only one column** out of several by Option-dragging. Instead of highlighting margin to margin, you get only the text within your selection rectangle.

from what's on the desktops of those *other* Macs. If you have two computers, then, you might see folders on your desktop called *Desktop - MacBook Air* and *Desktop - Kitchen iMac*. (Figure 5-28, middle right, shows this effect.)

Of course, if you primarily use only one Mac, the icons you once kept on your desktop are now in a desktop *folder* that seems to be *on* your desktop, which seems silly.

Fortunately, there's nothing to stop you from dragging the contents of "Desktop - MacBook Air" right back onto your actual desktop. The only caution here is that, if you do that on more than one Mac, you wind up with a commingled desktop. All the icons from your laptop desktop *and* all the icons from your iMac desktop are now on the desktops of both machines. You've just duplicated them. And any changes you make—any new icons you save to any desktop—get likewise duplicated to your other Macs.

That may be exactly what you want. Just watch out for disk space.

Note: What you see on your iPhone and at iCloud.com, meanwhile, is identical to what you see on your Mac.

- **Everything in your Documents folder disappears, too.** All *those* icons get shunted into a new folder in your Documents folder called "Documents - MacBook Air."

- **The real Desktop and Documents folders are no longer in your Home folder.** And in the Finder sidebar, they're no longer listed under the Favorites heading; now they're listed under iCloud Drive (Figure 5-28, middle left), to remind you that their new home is online, in the iCloud Drive.

- **You get a warning if you drag something out of Documents or off your desktop.** The warning is alarming (Figure 5-28, bottom), but it's perfectly logical: If you move an icon out of the Documents folder or from your desktop into another folder, you're removing it from the iCloud Drive. (The iCloud Drive's only responsibility is to mirror what's in your *Documents and Desktop* folders.)

- **If you turn off iCloud Desktop & Documents, you get an alarming message.** It says: "If you continue, documents on your Desktop and in your Documents folder will be visible in iCloud Drive only. No documents will be deleted from iCloud Drive."

What this means is that the icons on your desktop, and in your Documents folder, will disappear!

OK, be confused, but don't be hysterical; your files *are* on your Mac. The message makes it sound like you'll have to re-download them from iCloud, but that's not true. They're already on your Mac—in the iCloud Drive folder.

Turning off iCloud Desktop & Documents leaves only an empty Desktop folder on your desktop, and an empty Documents folder in your Documents folder. If you want to put your files back where they belong, you have to drag them there manually—out of the iCloud Drive folders.

If you don't have enough iCloud Drive space, you're cheerfully offered a list of price plans at this moment. The cheapest plan available that will fit your documents is highlighted.

Figure 5-28:

Top: Here's how you enter the rabbit hole known as iCloud Desktop & Documents.

Middle left: Desktop and Documents are now listed under iCloud Drive. The actual folders have moved, too.

Middle right: You see a separate Desktop folder for each Mac for which you've turned this feature on. (Documents, too.)

Bottom: If you move something from Desktop or Documents into any other folder, you get a warning that you're actually deleting it from your iCloud Drive (assuming that checkbox is turned on in Finder→Preferences→Advanced).

Once that's all set up, you'll discover a few alarming changes to your Mac universe:

- **Everything on your desktop has disappeared.** It's all been swept into a new folder on your desktop called "Desktop - MacBook Air" (or whatever your Mac's name is).

 So why does macOS create a new Desktop folder bearing your Mac's name? Because you might turn on this feature on a *second* Mac that you own, or even a third. The folder-naming system is designed to separate what's on the desktop of *this* Mac

at the box shown in Figure 5-27, so you can amend the settings or shut off sharing altogether (click Stop Sharing).

iCloud Drive on Other Devices

If the iCloud Drive behaves just like a folder on your Mac, how does it appear on iPhones, iPads, and Windows computers? Like this:

- **On the iPhone, iPad, or iPod Touch.** iCloud Drive is an app in iOS 9 and 10; in iOS 11 and later, it's called Files. Just open it to see a list of the folders and files on your iCloud Drive (including the Desktop and Documents folders from your Macs).

- **On another Mac.** Click the iCloud Drive icon in the sidebar of any Mac (to which you've logged in with your iCloud ID), and there's your stuff.

- **On the web.** You can pull up iCloud.com, log in, and click the iCloud Drive icon. Presto: a list of the files and folders on your Drive. (Including Desktop and Documents folders, if you've turned that on.)

- **On a Windows PC.** Your computer needs Windows 7 or later, and it requires the iCloud control panel. (You can download it from this book's "Missing CD" page at *missingmanuals.com*.) It does just what you'd expect: It creates an iCloud Drive icon in your File Explorer windows, exactly as on the Mac.

iCloud Desktop & Documents

An optional feature makes everything on your *desktop* and in your *Documents folder* accessible everywhere—on every Mac you own, every iOS device, every Windows PC, and even online, at iCloud.com.

If you think about it, those are the two places that most people, most of the time, leave their stuff: on the desktop or in the Documents folder. The point of this feature is that you no longer have to *remember* to copy some file or folder you'll need onto the iCloud Drive; if you left it on your desktop or in your Documents folder, it'll just be there. When you need a file you don't have with you, you'll be able to grab it from wherever you are.

Of course, you get only 5 gigabytes of iCloud Drive storage free, which is shared by all of iCloud's features. So to use this system, you'll almost certainly have to pay for additional storage, month after month.

If you didn't turn on iCloud Desktop & Documents when you installed macOS Mojave, you can also turn it on at any time:

- **In System Preferences→iCloud.** Next to the first checkbox, iCloud Drive, click Options; in the resulting dialog box, on the Documents tab, turn on Desktop & Documents Folders. (See Figure 5-28, top.)

- **In About This Mac→Storage→Manage→Store in iCloud (page 107).** Turn on "Store files from Desktop and Documents in iCloud Drive."

two-finger click the document and, from the shortcut menu, choose Share.) The box shown in Figure 5-27 appears. Here you have three decisions to make:

- **How to invite people.** You can welcome your collaborators to this document by Messages, Email, AirDrop (if they're nearby)—or using the Copy Link button. That command puts a web link on your Clipboard, so that you can share it in any other electronic way—in a Facebook post, in Slack, or whatever.

Figure 5-27:
Sharing a document from your iCloud Drive means that you can either publish a document to the entire web from the convenience of a desktop folder, or collaborate with co-workers on a single document.

- **Who can access.** Of course, if you post the invitation link online somewhere, you might wind up with hundreds of people descending on your document. If you're posting a flier advertising a garage sale, maybe that's just what you want. But if you're sharing the first draft of your screenplay, maybe you want to be more selective. That's why, in Share Options, you can specify either that "Only people you invite" have access, or "Anyone with the link."

- **What they can do.** If, from the Permission pop-up menu, you choose "Can make changes," then your document is editable on both ends, and both of you see the changes the other makes. Great for party planning, co-authoring papers, and editing novels. If you choose "View only," well, they can see your document but can't touch it.

Once you click Share, the ball is rolling. An email, text message, or AirDrop notification goes out to your lucky colleagues. Next to the document on your iCloud Drive, the legend "Shared by me" appears, for your reference. As long as you're all online, anyone can make changes to the shared document, and you all see the results almost immediately.

At any time, you can revisit the list of invitees or how much access they have. Right-click or two-finger click the document's icon; this time, choose Share→Show People (that command has nothing to do with Broadway performers). You're right back

Putting Files onto the iCloud Drive

On the Mac, you use the iCloud Drive just as you would a folder or a flash drive. Click its name in the Sidebar to see what's in there. Drag files into its window to copy them there. Make folders, add files, delete files, rename them—whatever. Any changes you make are reflected on your other Apple (and Windows) gadgets within seconds.

Inside a program, you can choose File→Save in the usual way. When the Save box appears, click iCloud Drive in the Sidebar. Or choose an iCloud Drive folder's name, if you've made one.

Tip: The window shown in Figure 5-26 shows your iCloud Drive documents and lets you open them, even when you're offline. How? Turns out your Mac stores a secret "local" copy. The changes you make won't update the online copy until you're online again, but at least you're never cut off from your own files.

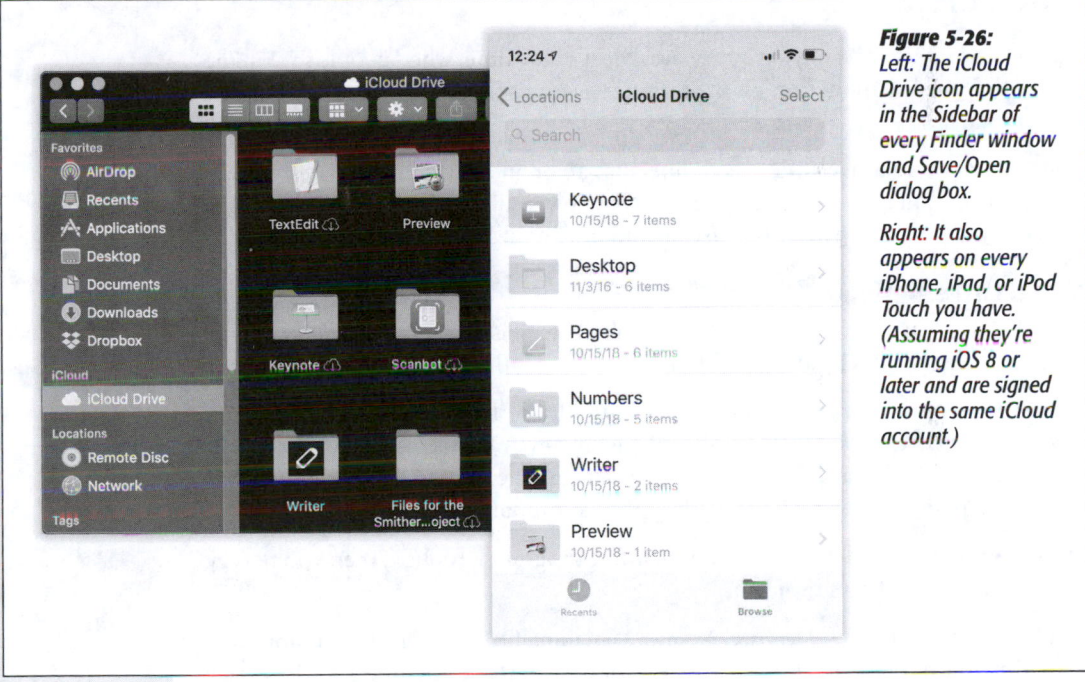

Figure 5-26:

Left: The iCloud Drive icon appears in the Sidebar of every Finder window and Save/Open dialog box.

Right: It also appears on every iPhone, iPad, or iPod Touch you have. (Assuming they're running iOS 8 or later and are signed into the same iCloud account.)

Sharing iCloud Drive Files

You can also share individual files in your iCloud Drive with other people electronically, so that you can collaborate across the internet. It's exactly like the same feature in popular services like Dropbox and Google drive, except that, inconveniently, it limits your collaborators to other people using Mojave (or iOS 11).

In the Finder, in the iCloud Drive, click the file (you can't, alas, share a *folder*); from the ⬆ menu, choose Add People. (That option also appears when you right-click or

- **Delete a version.** Once you've found a draft you never want to see again, move your cursor to the top of the screen; the menu bar appears. Choose File→Revert To→Delete This Version.

Tip: If you press Option, the command changes to Delete Old Versions; it gets rid of *all* old versions of the file.

Revert

Even though Auto Save is constantly backing up your document, it also remembers how the file looked the moment you opened it. And you want to know what's crazy? It can revert to that condition even if you've been manually saving your work all along! That's better than the old Revert command ever was. Just choose File→Revert to→Last Saved (or Last Opened).

iCloud Drive

Truth is, "cloud" is an annoying buzzword. Most of the time, when people say "in the cloud," they mean "online" or "on the internet"—terms that have served us perfectly well for years.

In any case, you can save your files online, into an online "hard drive" called iCloud Drive. The advantage here is that your files are now available for opening or editing from any computer or gadget you use, including iPhones, iPads, and iPod Touches.

iCloud Drive Defined

iCloud Drive, part of Apple's iCloud suite of services, is like a magic folder. In the Finder, it's represented by an iCloud Drive icon (△) in the Sidebar of every window.

Whatever you put into it appears, almost instantly, in the iCloud Drive folders on all your other machines: Macs, iPhones, iPads, and even Windows PCs. In fact, your files are even available at *iCloud.com*, so you can grab them when you're stranded on a desert island with nothing but somebody else's computer. (And internet access.)

(If this concept reminds you of the popular free program Dropbox, then you're very wise.) Figure 5-26 shows the idea.

This is an incredibly useful feature. No more emailing files to yourself. No more carrying things around on a flash drive. After working on some document at the office, you can go home and resume from right where you stopped; the same file is waiting for you, exactly as you left it.

iCloud Drive also makes a gloriously simple, effective backup disk. Anything you drag into this "folder" is instantly copied to all your devices and computers. And, as you know, the more copies that exist of something (and in the more locations), the better your backup. Even if your main Mac is stolen or burned to aluminum dust, your iCloud Drive files are safe.

Your drive holds 5 gigabytes of files for free. You can pay extra for more space: $1 a month for 50 gigs, $3 a month for 200 gigs, or $10 for 2 terabytes (2,000 gigs).

- **Restore an earlier version.** If you finally find the incarnation of the document you consider superior to your current one, click Restore. You leave Blurry Versionland and return to your document, which has now been rewound to its earlier condition.

 If you later decide you should not have gone back to that earlier version, no problem. Your later version—the one you started out with—is still in the version browser, too. So you can fast-forward back to it, if necessary.

Tip: If you press Option, the Restore button changes to say Restore a Copy. In other words, you'll create a previous-version duplicate of the document, without disturbing the current condition of the one you've just been working on.

- **Restore *part* of an earlier version.** Often, the current version of your work is *generally* good, but you really wish you could recover *one* magical sentence or paragraph or section—something you've since edited or deleted.

 You can do that in Blurry Versionland, too, because Copy and Paste work here!

 Use the time ruler to find the earlier edition of your document, the one containing the good stuff. Then drag through the desired text or graphics in the window on the right, as shown in Figure 5-25. Now copy the highlighted material (either press ⌘-C, or move your mouse to the top of the screen so that the menu bar appears, and choose Edit→Copy). Click in the *current* version of the document, the one at left, and now paste (⌘-V, or use the menu bar). Click Done to complete this astonishing act of salvation.

FREQUENTLY ASKED QUESTION

Report to Apple

What the—I was working along in Safari, and all of a sudden it just vanished! Poof! And all I got was this lousy dialog box about "reporting to Apple." What's going on?

Apple is trying to assimilate you.

Or, more accurately, it's trying to enlist your help in ferreting out all the little glitches that make modern computing so much fun. If you're willing to click the Report button and type a few comments ("I was running Word, minding my own business, and when I clicked the Print button, the whole thing just crashed"), then Apple will add your report to the thousands flowing in from everyone else.

The idea is that when its programmers get a moment, they'll study these reports, track down the patterns ("Hmm, we've received 50,000 reports about that Print button in Word"), and then chase down the software company responsible—and, presumably, get a fix underway.

The report you submit is full of technical info that helps the programmers figure out what was happening at the time of the crash, but no personal information goes along for the ride. So if you feel like doing some good for your fellow Mac fans, by all means submit the report (via the internet) whenever you're offered the chance.

The quick way is to choose File→Revert to→Last Saved (or Last Opened). That command restores the document to the last snapshot version (or to the way it was when you most recently opened it, if no new versions have been created).

You can revert your document to *any* snapshot, even an ancient one from weeks or months ago. To do that, choose File→Revert to→Browse All Versions.

After a moment, you see the stunning display shown in Figure 5-25. On the left, you see your document in its current condition. On the right, you see a stack of windows that represent all the different snapshots of your document, going back in time.

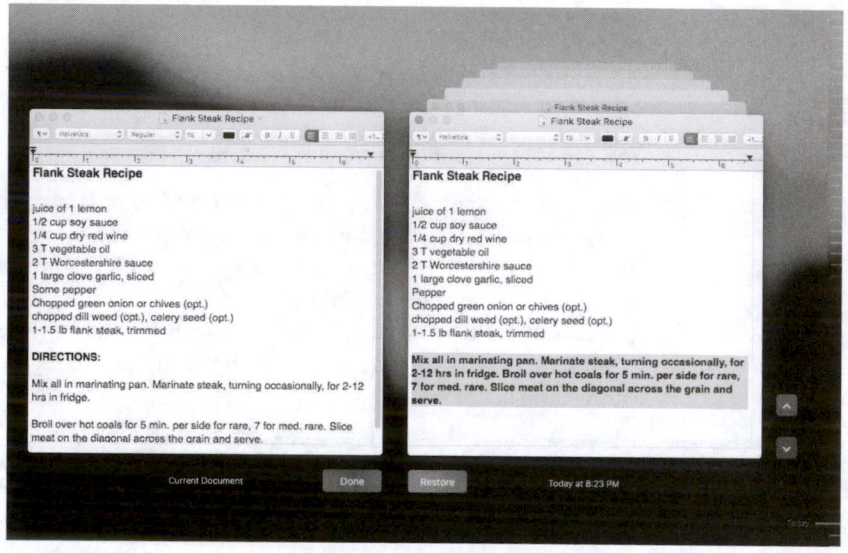

Figure 5-25:
If you've ever used macOS's Time Machine feature, this display should look familiar. It's your chance to go back in time to recover an earlier, better version of your document (or just a part of it).

You can have all kinds of productive fun in this version browser:

- **Compare the current version (on the left) with the next-most-recent one (on the right).** These are live documents, so you can scroll through them as necessary. If you decide to stick with the latest edition on the left, just click Done. You leave the version-history world and go back to editing.

- **Zoom back in time to inspect older versions (snapshots) of your document.** On the right side of the screen, you see earlier versions of the document—maybe even dozens of them, stretching back in time.

 You can click individual windows' title bars to see what's in them. You can also click or drag your cursor through the notches at the right side. It's like a time ruler that flies through the windows into the past. (As you go, the time/date stamp below the right-side window identifies where you are in time—that is, which version you're examining.)

These snapshots, or *versions,* represent rewind points that you can return to later, even months or years after you first created the document. Thoughtfully enough, the Mac records, invisibly, only what's *changed* between versions, so your files don't get all big and bloated.

Note: All right, you don't have *total* time-rewinding control. MacOS stores hourly versions for a day, daily versions for a month, and weekly versions for all previous months.

- **There's a secret menu in the title bar.** Point to the name of your document. In Auto Save–compatible files, a little ⌄ appears in the title bar (Figure 5-24).

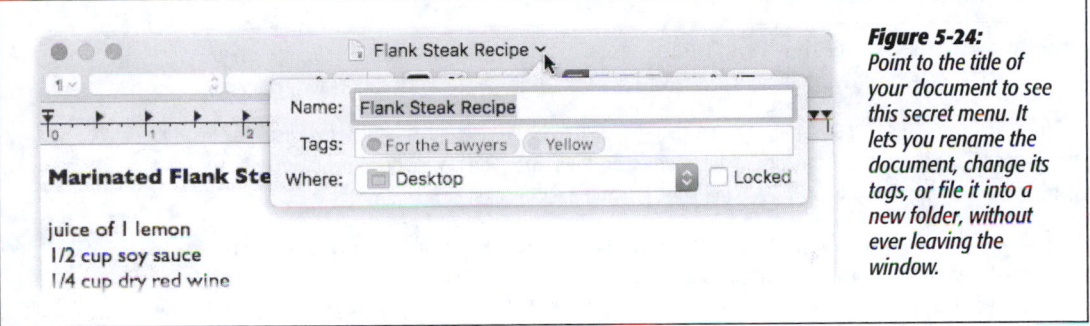

Figure 5-24:
Point to the title of your document to see this secret menu. It lets you rename the document, change its tags, or file it into a new folder, without ever leaving the window.

- **The Save As command is hidden in these programs.** It appears in the File menu only when you hold down the Option key.

Apple is hoping that you'll learn to use the new way. When you want to spin off a different version of a document—to experiment with taking it into a radical new direction, for example—choose File→Duplicate. Before your very eyes, a copy of the open window springs into existence. If the original was called "Kumquat Tarts," then the new one is called "Kumquat Tarts copy"—but that name is highlighted, selected, right in the title bar.

To leave your duplicated document in the same folder as the original, just type a new name and press Return. To file it in a different folder, choose File→Save. You get the standard Save dialog box, where you can choose a name and a folder for it.

Tip: You can also choose to move a document to a different folder later right there in the program. Just choose File→Move To and choose a new storage bin for it. (You can even store it in iCloud at this point; see page 221.) Or use the secret menu-bar menu shown in Figure 5-24.

Rewinding to an earlier version
The point of all this, of course, is to make it easy to go back in time—to undo the mediocre work you've done, or to resurrect some genius work that you later deleted.

even know it. Why shouldn't *all* programs save your work as you go, automatically and invisibly? As long as you also have the option to rewind and take your document in a different direction, what could possibly be the harm?

And so it is that, in macOS today, Auto Save is here. Unfortunately, it's available in only a few programs. You'll find it in Apple's showcase programs: Pages, Keynote, Numbers, Preview, and TextEdit.

In these programs, your document is saved every time there's even the tiniest pause in your typing or working—in the background. No progress bar, no interruption. If you quit or close the document without remembering to save, no problem: Your work will be there when you open the document again later.

Note: "But wait a minute," cry the masses, "I *like* being able to close a document without saving changes! Sometimes all I wanted to do was fool around, play 'what-if' games—and then close it without saving changes!"

Just for you, Apple offers a pair of sneaky little checkboxes in System Preferences→General. First, "Ask to keep changes when closing documents." If that's turned on, then when you close a document with unsaved changes, the Mac asks if you want to keep the edits, just as it does in all other programs.

But if you *quit* the program without saving, your changes *are* auto-preserved; Auto Save apps autosave your documents when you quit their programs, so you can pick up where you left off the next time. You can override that, too, if you like; turn on "Close windows when quitting an app," also in System Preferences→General. Now you'll get the "Save changes?" box when you quit the app with unsaved changes.

Versions

In those enlightened programs that work with Auto Save, there's a more complicated but more powerful feature at work: Versions. It's an invisible paper trail of every in-progress condition of your document—and you can return to any earlier version at any time. You can even return to an earlier version and copy just a *chunk* of it into the current version, which is great when one paragraph of your previous draft was gold but the rest was junk.

The Versions world of document management is quite a bit different from the old setup. Here's what you need to know:

- **All the version information is stored in the same original document file.** (It's not like there's a rat's nest of icons for each thing you're working on.) But when you send the document to somebody else (by email or network, for example), the Mac sends only the current version, stripping out all the history. Nobody will ever know how much you labored over your work (or how little).

Note: Behind the scenes, the various versions of each document are saved in an invisible folder on your hard drive called *.DocumentRevisions-V100*. But you probably guessed that.

- **MacOS creates a new snapshot of your document once an hour.** You can also create new snapshots manually at even shorter intervals—by using the File→Save command (⌘-S), as you always have.

navigation by seeing what's on the desktop (press ⌘-D) or in your Home folder (Shift-⌘-H).

Once again, you can find a folder or a disk by beginning your quest with the Sidebar and then navigate using icon, list, or column view. And, once again, you can drag a folder, disk, or file icon off your desktop and directly into the dialog box to specify where you want to look. (If you drag a *file* icon, then you're shown the folder that contains it.)

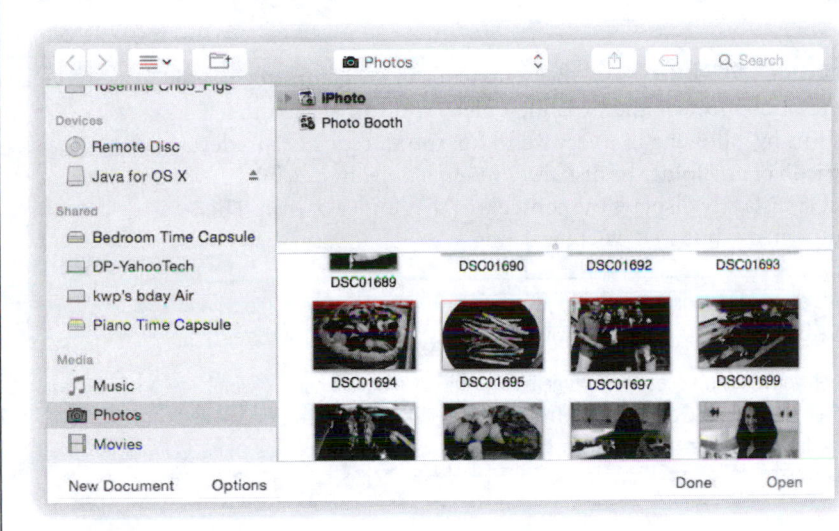

Figure 5-23:
The Media Browser is built right into the Open box. You get miniature listings of your iTunes, Photos, and movie files right in the Sidebar, for convenience in importing them into (for example) Keynote, PowerPoint, or a web design program.

When you've finally located the file you want to open, double-click it or highlight it (which you can do from the keyboard), and then press Return or ⌘-O.

In general, most people don't encounter the Open File dialog box nearly as often as the Save File dialog box. That's because the Mac offers many more convenient ways to *open* a file—double-clicking its icon in the Finder, choosing its name from →Recent Items, and so on—but only a single way to *save* a new file.

Auto Save and Versions

In the beginning, Jobs created the Save command—because computers were slow.

Every time you saved, your work was interrupted for a few seconds (or a lot of seconds) as the very slow program on your very slow computer saved your work onto a very slow floppy disk.

And *that*, ladies and gentlemen, is why most programs still don't autosave: because the interruptions were just too annoying.

Apple figured it was high time the world revisit that scenario. Computers now have plenty of horsepower. They could be saving your work *continuously*, and you'd never

The next time you save a new document, the Save sheet reappears in whatever condition you left it. That is, if you used column view the last time, it's still in column view. You can collapse it into simplified view, shown at top in Figure 5-22, by clicking the ∧ button to the right of the Save As pop-up menu.

Tip: For years, there's been a keyboard shortcut for the Don't Save button that appears when you close a new document without saving it: ⌘-D. But in some modern Apple programs, including TextEdit, Preview, Grab, Pages, and Keynote, the button says Delete instead of Don't Save. In those cases, press ⌘-Delete to "click" it instead of using the mouse.

Insta-Jumping to a Folder Location

Whether you're using the mini-sheet or the expanded view, you can save yourself some folder-burrowing time by following this very weird tip: You can specify a folder location by dragging the icon of any folder or disk *from your desktop* directly into the Save or Open sheet. MacOS instantly displays the contents of that folder or disk. This feature is totally undocumented—but well worth learning.

Tip: If, when the Save box is in its expanded condition, you click the name of an existing file, macOS thoughtfully copies the name of the clicked file into the Save As text box (which otherwise said "Untitled" or was blank).

This trick can save you time when you're saving a second document with a slightly modified name ("Oprah and Me: The Inside Story, Chapter 1" and then "Oprah and Me: The Inside Story, Chapter 2"). It's also useful if you want to replace the original file with the new one you're saving. Instead of having to type out the entire name of the file, you can just click it.

The File Format Pop-Up Menu

The Save dialog box in many programs offers a pop-up menu of file formats below the Save As box. Use this menu when preparing a document for use by somebody else—somebody whose computer doesn't have the same software. For example, if you've used a graphics program to prepare a photograph for use on the web, this menu is where you specify JPEG format (the standard web format for photos).

The Open Dialog Box

The dialog box that appears when you choose File→Open is almost identical to the expanded Save File sheet. Because you encounter it only when you're opening an existing file, this dialog box lacks a Save button, a Tags box, a file name field, and so on.

Note: Furthermore, the Open dialog box gives you access only to disks, folders, and documents that you can actually open at this moment. For example, when you're using GarageBand, picture files show up dimmed.

But the Open box adds a special Sidebar category called Media (see Figure 5-23), which gives you direct access to all your photos, music, and movies. Apple figures you might want to import these items *into* a document you're working on.

Most of the other Save File dialog box controls are equally useful here. That handy Spotlight search bar is still there, only a ⌘-F away. Once again, you can begin your

Tip: In column view, your first instinct should be to widen this window, making more columns available. Do so by carefully dragging either edge of the dialog box. The Mac remembers the size for this Save sheet independently in each program.

And in list view, how's this for a tip? If you right-click or two-finger click one of the column headings, like Name or Date Modified, you get a secret pop-up menu of column names: Last Opened, Size, Kind, Label, and so on. That's right: You can customize the list view within an Open or Save dialog box. You can sort, too, by clicking one of the column headings, just as at the desktop.

- **Search for files.** The search box at the top of the Open or Save dialog box is a clone of the Finder's search box (Chapter 3). Press ⌘-F to make your insertion point jump there. Type a few letters of the name of the file or folder you're looking for, and up it pops, regardless of its actual hard-disk location.

- **Delete a document or folder** right from this list. Just right-click or two-finger click it and choose Move to Trash.

- **Rename a document or folder.** Right-click or two-finger click it; from the shortcut menu, choose Rename.

- **Create a new folder.** Click the New Folder button (or press the usual New Folder keystroke, Shift-⌘-N) to create a new folder *inside* the folder you're looking at. You're asked to type the new name for the folder. After you've done so, click Create (or press Return). The new folder appears and opens before you, empty. You can now proceed with saving your new document into it, if you like.

- **Use Quick Look** (page 58). Select a file or folder in the list and tap the space bar to view it in a full-size window.

- **Add folders to the left-side Favorites list.** Drag them into the Sidebar here, either from the desktop, if it's visible, or right out of the dialog box in front of you. You can remove things from the Sidebar, too; just drag them away.

- **Navigate from the keyboard.** Most of the familiar Finder navigation shortcuts work here, too. Press the ◄ and ► keys to navigate the columns, or the ▲ and ▼ keys to highlight the disk and folder names *within* a column. Once you've highlighted a column, you can also type to select the first letters of disk or folder names.

- **Get Info.** Even in the Save or Open dialog box, you can highlight an icon (or several) and then press ⌘-I. You switch back to the Finder, where the Get Info box is waiting with the date, size, and other details about the selected icons.

When you're finished playing around, open the folder where you want to save your newly created document and then click Save to store it there.

Tip: Here's one of the weirdest tricks yet. When the Open or Save dialog box is open before you, you can press Shift-⌘-period to make all your Mac's *hidden* files appear. (As a Unix-based outfit, macOS is crawling with these invisible files, which are of interest primarily to technical types.) Press that keystroke again to re-hide the hidden files. Fun for geeks! If you use a non-American number-formatting system (where one thousand is 1.000, for example), use Shift-⌘-comma instead.

In most Mac programs, there's no mystery regarding which document you're saving, because a little Save dialog box called a *sheet* slides directly out of the document's title bar.

Better still, this little Save box is a sticky note attached *to the document*. It stays there, neatly attached and waiting, even if you switch to another program, another document, the desktop, or wherever. When you finally return to the document, the Save sheet is still there, waiting for you to type a file name and save the document.

The Mini-Finder

Of course *you*, O savvy reader, have probably never saved a document into some deeply nested folder by accident, never to see it again. But millions of novices (and even a few experts) have fallen into this trap.

When the Save sheet appears, a pop-up menu shows you precisely where the Mac proposes to put your newly created document: usually in the Documents folder of your own Home folder. For most people, this is an excellent suggestion. If you keep everything in your Documents folder, it will be extremely easy to find, and you'll be able to back up your work just by dragging that single folder to a backup disk.

As shown at top in Figure 5-22, the Where pop-up menu gives you direct access to some other places where you might want to save a newly created file. (The keystrokes for the most important folders work here, too—Shift-⌘-H for your Home folder, for example.)

In any case, when you save a file, the options in the Where pop-up menu have you covered 90 percent of the time. Most people work with a limited set of folders for active documents.

But when you want to save a new document into a new folder, or when you want to navigate to a folder that isn't listed in the Where pop-up menu, all is not lost. Click the ∨ button identified in Figure 5-22. The Save sheet expands into a very familiar sight: a miniature version of the Finder.

Tip: You can switch back and forth between the compact and expanded versions of this dialog box by pressing the undocumented shortcut ⌘-=.

You might be shocked to find out just how many Finder features are available, all within this little Save dialog box. The whole Save box is getting to be more Findery every year. For example:

- **Navigate with the Sidebar.** It's here, complete with access to the other computers on your network and your iCloud Drive.

- **Navigate with keystrokes.** All the usual keyboard shortcuts for navigating your Mac work within the Open and Save boxes. You can press ⌘-D to see what's on your desktop, Shift-⌘-H for your Home folder, Shift-⌘-A for your Applications folder, and so on.

- **Switch views** (icon, list, column), as shown in Figure 5-22 at bottom.

Sheets

In the days of operating systems gone by, the Save dialog box appeared dead center on the screen, where it commandeered your entire operation. Moreover, because it seemed stuck to your *screen* rather than to a particular *document*, you couldn't actually tell which document you were saving—a real problem when you quit out of a program that had three unsaved documents open.

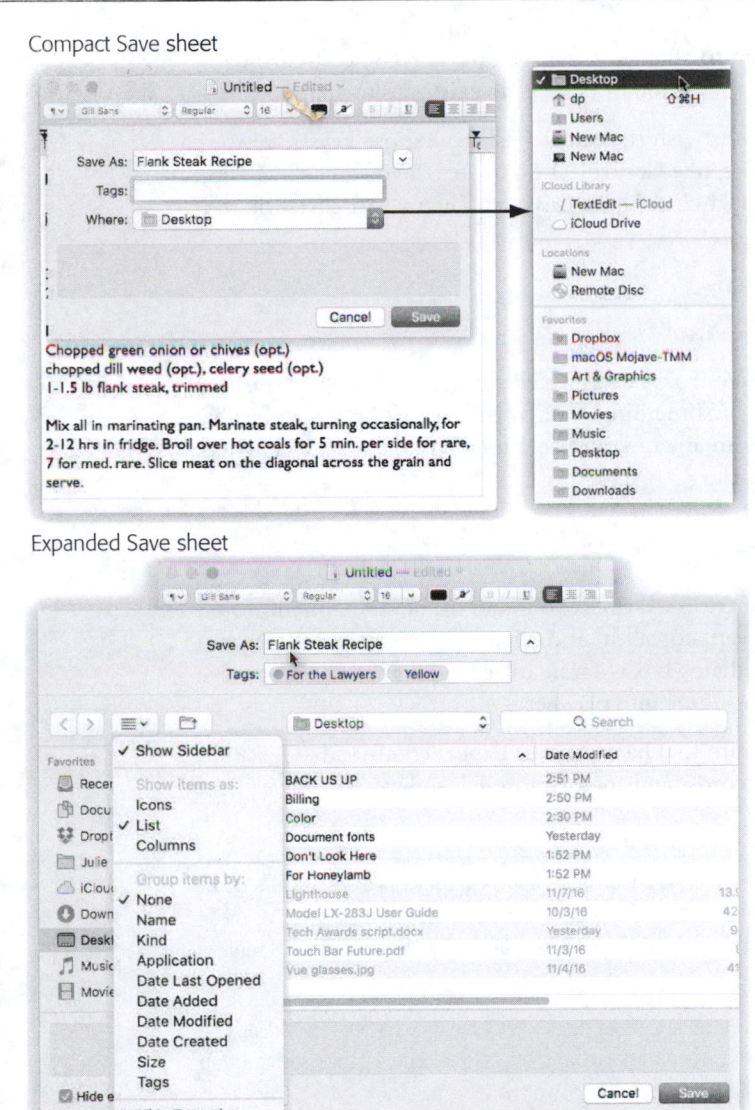

Compact Save sheet

Expanded Save sheet

Figure 5-22:
Top left: The Save dialog box, or sheet, often appears in its compact form.

Top right: If you open the Where pop-up menu, you'll find that macOS lists all the places it thinks you might want to save your new document: online (iCloud), on the hard drive, in a folder you've put into your Sidebar ("Favorites"), or into a folder you've recently opened.

Bottom: If you want to choose a different folder or to create a new folder, click the ⌄ button (next to the Save As box) to expand the dialog box.

Here you see the equivalent of the Finder. In the menu shown open here, you even get a choice of icon, list, or column view, the option to see the files in various groupings, and the option to hide the suffixes (like .jpg or .pdf). Even the Sidebar is here, complete with access to other disks on the network.

Tip: In most programs, you can enlarge the Save or Open dialog box by dragging one of its edges. You can also adjust the width of the Sidebar by dragging its right edge.

2. **In the left-side list, click the category or function you want.**

 Your choices include Launchpad & Dock, Mission Control, Keyboard, and so on. When you click a category name, you see the available shortcuts.

Tip: You don't have to be content with *changing* one of these keyboard shortcuts. You can also *turn it off* by clicking the corresponding checkbox. That's great if one of Apple's predefined keystrokes—for a function you don't even use—is interfering with one in a program you like.

3. **Click the command you want to change. Then click the current keyboard combination (or the "add shortcut" button, if there is no existing shortcut).**

 Suppose, for example, that you wish the Show Desktop Exposé keystroke were something easier to remember, like Control-D. So in step 2, you'd click Mission Control. In this example, you'd click Show Desktop. Then you'd click where it currently says "F11."

4. **Press a new key combination.**

 In this example, you'd press Control-D.

 Be careful, though. MacOS keystrokes take precedence over *all others*. So if you choose a keystroke like ⌘-P for something, well, by golly, you'll no longer be able to use ⌘-P to print anything in any of your programs. Think before you assign. Run a couple of tests afterward.

The Save and Open Dialog Boxes

When you choose File→Save, you're asked where you want the new document stored on your hard drive, what you want to call it, and what Finder tags (page 92) you want applied to it. The resulting dialog box is a miniature Finder. All the skills you've picked up working at the desktop come into play here.

To give it a try, launch any program that has a Save or Export command—TextEdit, for example. Type a couple of words, and then choose File→Save. The Save sheet appears (Figure 5-22).

Tip: In most programs, a quick glance at the Close button in the upper-left corner of a document window tells you whether it's been saved. When a small dot appears in the red button, it means you've made changes to the document that you haven't saved yet. (Time to press ⌘-S!) The dot disappears as soon as you save your work.

In programs that offer the Auto Save and Versions features described later in this chapter, like TextEdit, the red-dot convention has been retired. Instead, when you've made changes to a document since saving it, you see the light-gray word *Edited* in the title bar.

Tip: To delete or change one of your custom menu shortcuts, open System Preferences→Keyboard→Shortcuts. Click App Shortcuts in the list at left. Click the command you'd like to edit. Press Delete to get rid of it; or, to try a different key combo, click where the existing keyboard shortcut appears and then press a new one.

Redefining a Keystroke

As you've no doubt become painfully aware, there are *hundreds* of keyboard combinations for the various macOS functions and settings. That's good, because keyboard shortcuts are efficient and quicker than using the mouse. But that's also bad, because there's no *way* you'll be able to remember all of them—and some of the most useful shortcuts are ridiculous, multikey affairs that you'll never remember at all.

In the keyboard-shortcut center, shown in Figure 5-21, you can look over all the common macOS hidden keyboard functions—for Mission Control, Exposé, Spotlight, Dashboard, the Dock, and many others—and *change them*.

Here's how it goes:

1. **Choose →System Preferences. Click Keyboard. Click the Shortcuts tab.**

 You arrive at the dialog box shown in Figure 5-21.

Figure 5-21:
The keyboard-shortcut center lets you redefine the keystrokes that trigger many basic macOS features, menu commands in your programs, and software you've built yourself using Automator.

4. **Carefully type in the name of the menu command whose keyboard shortcut you want to change or add.**

 Type it *exactly* as it appears in the menu, complete with capitalization and the little ellipsis (…) that may follow it. (You make the ellipsis character by pressing Option-semicolon.)

5. **Click in the Keyboard Shortcut box. Press the new or revised key combo you want.**

 For example, press Control-R for Photos' Revert to Original command. You'll see the Mac's notation of your keystroke appear in the Keyboard Shortcut box—unless, of course, the combo you selected is already in use within that program. In that case, you hear only an error sound that means "Try again."

6. **Click Add.**

 The dialog box closes. By scrolling down in your Keyboard Shortcuts list, you see that the keystroke you selected has now been written down for posterity under the appropriate program's flippy triangle. (To get rid of it, click its name and then click the — button beneath the list.)

 The next time you open the program you edited, you'll see that the new keystroke is in place.

Figure 5-20:
If you choose All Applications from the top pop-up menu, you can change the keyboard combo for a certain command wherever it appears. You could, for example, change the keystroke for Page Setup in every program at once. (Beware the tiny yellow triangles; they let you know if a chosen keystroke conflicts with another macOS keystroke.)

buttons on the palette. You can see the effect when, for example, you're editing text in TextEdit and you've also opened the Font palette. Pressing Control-F6 highlights the Font palette, taking the "focus" off your document.

Control Menulets

Here's a gem you may not have heard about: You can operate *menulets*—those menu-bar status indicators for your speaker volume, wireless networks, and so on—from the keyboard, too.

This time, the trick is to hit Control-F8. That highlights the leftmost Apple menulet. Now you can use your ◄ and ► arrow keys to move around the menu bar; when you've highlighted the one you want, press Return or the space bar to "click" that menu and open it.

Control Dialog Boxes

You can also navigate and manipulate any *dialog box* from the keyboard.

See the dialog box shown in Figure 5-20? If you turn on "All controls" at the bottom, then pressing the Tab key highlights the next control of any type, whatever it may be—radio button, pop-up menu, and so on. Press the space bar to "click" a button or to open a pop-up menu. Once a menu is open, use the arrow keys (or type letter keys) to highlight commands on it, and use the space bar to "click" your choice.

Changing a Menu Keyboard Shortcut

Suppose you love Photos (and who doesn't?). But one thing drives you crazy: The Revert to Original command, which discards all the changes you've ever made since taking the photo, has no keyboard shortcut. You must trek up to the menu bar every time you need that command.

This is why macOS lets you add keyboard shortcuts to menu commands that lack them—or change the commands in programs whose key assignments break with tradition. (It works in any program that uses the standard macOS menu software, which rules out older versions of Microsoft Office.) Here's the routine:

1. **Choose System Preferences→Keyboard. Click the Shortcuts tab, and then click App Shortcuts in the left-side list.**

 You're shown a list of any keyboard assignments you've created so far.

2. **Click the + button just beneath the list.**

 The dialog box shown in Figure 5-20 appears.

3. **Indicate which program needs behavior modification.**

 In this example, you'd choose Photos from the Application pop-up menu. (If the program's name doesn't appear in the pop-up menu, then choose Other; navigate to, and double-click, the program you want.)

Here are some of the ways you can control your Mac mouselessly. In the following descriptions, you'll encounter the factory settings for the keystrokes that do the magic—but as you'll see in a moment, you can change these key combos to anything you like. (The System Preferences→Keyboard→Shortcuts tab contains the on/off switches for these features.)

Note: On modern-day aluminum keyboards, the keystrokes described below may not work unless you also press the fn key simultaneously.

If that seems clumsy, you can eliminate the fn-key requirement either by using the "Use all F1, F2, etc. keys as standard function keys" option described in the box on page 198–or by choosing a different keystroke altogether (page 210).

Control the Menus

When you press Control-F2, the menu is highlighted. At this point, you can "walk" to another menu by pressing the ◀ or ▶ keys (or Tab and Shift-Tab). When you reach the menu you want, open it by pressing ▼, space, or Return.

Walk down the commands in the menu by pressing ▲ or ▼, or jump directly to a command in the menu by typing the first couple of letters of its name. Finally, "click" a menu command by pressing Return or the space bar.

You can also close the menu without making a selection by pressing Esc or ⌘-period.

Control the Dock

Once you've pressed Control-F3, you can highlight *any* icon on the Dock by pressing the appropriate arrow keys (or, once again, Tab and Shift-Tab).

Then, once you've highlighted a Dock icon, you "click" it by pressing Return or the space bar. Again, if you change your mind, press Esc or ⌘-period.

Tip: Once you've highlighted a disk or folder icon, you can press the ▲ or ▼ keys to make its shortcut menu appear. (If you've positioned the Dock vertically, then use ◀ or ▶ instead.)

Cycle Through Your Windows

Every time you press Control-F4, you bring the next window forward, eventually cycling through *every window in every open program*. Add the Shift key to cycle through them in the opposite order.

You may remember that macOS offers a different keystroke for cycling through the different windows in your *current* program (it's ⌘-~, the tilde symbol at the upper left on your keyboard). Control-F4, on the other hand, tours all windows in *all* programs. Both keystrokes are useful in different situations.

Control Tool Palettes

In a few programs that feature floating tool palettes, you can highlight the frontmost palette by pressing Control-F6. At this point, use the arrow keys to highlight the various

Tip: You can use a similar trick to reassign the parenthood of a whole *flock* of selected icons at once. Once you've selected them, keep the Option key pressed as you choose File→Show Inspector. In the "Open with" section of this specialized Get Info window, choose a new program from the pop-up menu. The message at the top of the window—"22 items," for example—reminds you that you're changing the whole batch at once.

Reassigning all documents of one type

So much for reassigning one document (or a group of documents) at a time. What if you're writing, say, a book about macOS, and you've been taking a lot of screenshots? MacOS saves each captured screen illustration as a graphics file in something called PNG format. That's all fine, except that every time you double-click one of these, it opens into Preview, where you can't paint out unwanted details.

You could reassign all these files, one at a time, to a different program, but your grand-children would have grandchildren by the time you finished. In this case, you want to tell macOS, "For heaven's sake, make *all* PNG files open in Photoshop from now on!"

To make it happen, start by highlighting *any* PNG file. Choose File→Get Info. (The shortcut menus won't help you in this case.) Open the "Open with" panel.

From its pop-up menu, choose the program you want to open this kind of document from now on.

Tip: If the one you prefer isn't listed, use the Other option, which opens the "Choose an application" dialog box so you can navigate to the one you want, as shown in Figure 5-19. Find and double-click the program.

Or, instead of choosing Other, you can also choose App Store. It's Apple's way of saying, "Hey—if you don't have a program that can open this document, maybe you should just *go buy one right now!*"

This time, follow up by clicking Change All beneath the pop-up menu. (This button is dimmed until you've actually selected a different program from the pop-up menu.) Confirm by clicking Continue or pressing Return.

From now on, double-clicking any similar kind of document opens it in the newly selected program.

Keyboard Control

MacOS offers a fantastic feature for anyone who believes life is short: keyboard-controllable menus, dialog boxes, pop-up menus, and even Dock pop-up menus. You can operate every menu in every program without the mouse.

In fact, you can operate every control in every dialog box from the keyboard, including pop-up menus and checkboxes. And you can even redefine many of the built-in macOS keystrokes, like Shift-⌘-3 to capture the screen as a graphic.

In fact, you can add or change *any menu command in any program*. If you're a keyboard-shortcut lover, your cup runneth over.

- **Start out with one of the previously described techniques** (for example, File→Open With, or right-click the file's icon and choose Open With)—but after you see the menu, press the Option key, too. Before your very eyes, the Open With command changes to say *Always* Open With.

- **Highlight the icon, and then choose File→Get Info.** Open the "Open with" panel. Choose a new "parent" program's name from the pop-up menu. You'll see that the word "(default)" changes position, now tacking itself onto the name of the program you've chosen.

Figure 5-19:
Top: The shortcut menu offers a list of programs capable of opening an icon. If you were to press the Option key right now, the words "Open With" would suddenly change to say "Always Open With."

Bottom: If you choose Other, you're prompted to choose a different program. Turn on Always Open With if you'll always want this document to open in the new parent program. Otherwise, this is a one-time reassignment.

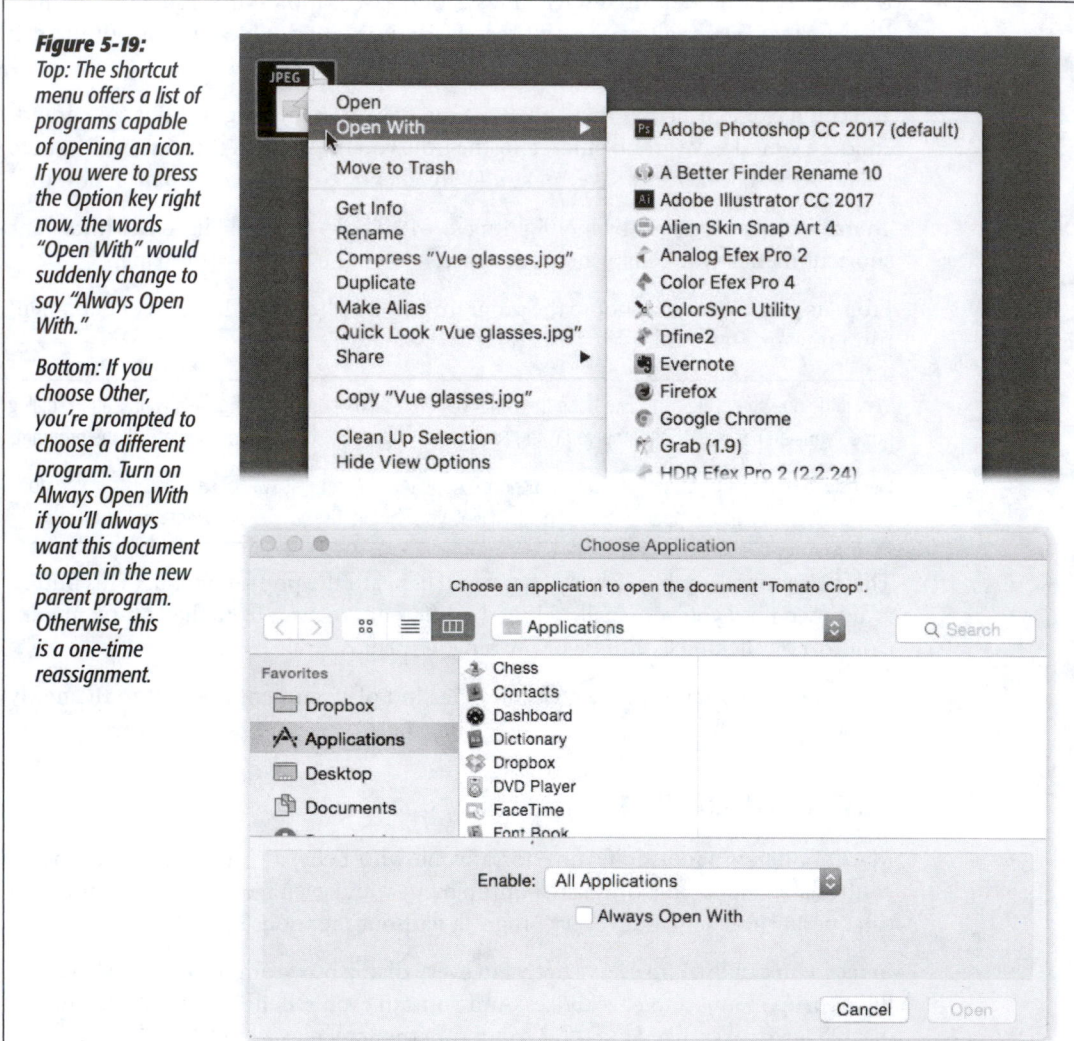

- **Your preferences.** If you've used the Always Open With command to *specify* which program opens your document, then that's the one that opens; this preference overrides the file name extension system. MacOS memorizes that new pairing.

It's possible to live a long and happy life without knowing anything about these suffixes and relationships. But if you're prepared for a little bit of technical bushwhacking, you may discover that understanding document-program relationships can be useful in troubleshooting, keeping your files private, and appreciating how macOS works.

Reassigning Documents to Programs

Unfortunately, file name extensions aren't always especially specific. Suppose you've downloaded a graphic called Sunset.jpg. Well, almost any program these days can open a JPEG graphic—Photoshop, Pages, Word, Preview, Safari, and so on. How does macOS know which of these programs to open when you double-click the file?

Fortunately, *you* can decide. You can *reassign* a document (or all documents of its kind) to a specific program. Here's the rundown.

Reassigning a certain document—just once

Double-clicking a graphics file generally opens it in Preview (page 465). Most of the time, that's a perfectly good arrangement. But Preview has limited editing powers. What if you decide to edit a graphics file more substantially? You'd want it to open, just this once, into a different program—Photoshop Elements, for example.

To do so, you must access the Open With command. You can find it in three places:

- **Highlight the icon and then choose** File→Open With (Figure 5-19).

- **Highlight the icon and then open** the ✿ menu. In the menu, choose Open With.

- **Right-click or two-finger click** the file's icon. From the shortcut menu, choose Open With.

Study the submenu for a moment (Figure 5-19, top). The program whose name says "(default)" indicates which program *usually* opens this kind of document. From this pop-up menu, choose the name of the program you'd *rather* open this particular file, right now, just this once.

Reassigning a certain document—permanently

After opening a TIFF file in, say, Photoshop Elements for editing, you haven't really made any changes in the fabric of your Mac universe. The next time you double-click that file, it opens once again in Preview.

If you wish this particular file would *always* open in Photoshop Elements, the steps are slightly different. In fact, there are three different ways:

- **In the Choose an Application dialog box** (the one that appears when you double-click a document whose "parent" program isn't clear), turn on Always Open With (shown at bottom in Figure 5-19).

How Documents Know Their Parents

Every operating system needs a mechanism to associate documents with the applications that created them. When you double-click a Microsoft Word document icon, for example, it's clear that you want Microsoft Word to launch and open the document.

So how does macOS know how to find a document's mommy?

It actually has two different mechanisms:

- **File name extensions.** A *file name extension* is a suffix following a period in the file's name, as in *Letter to Mom.doc.* (It's usually three letters long, but it doesn't have to be.) These play a role in determining which documents open into which programs.

 That's how Windows identifies its documents, too. If you double-click something called *memo.doc,* it opens in Microsoft Word. If you double-click *memo.wri,* it opens in Microsoft Write, and so on.

Note: MacOS comes set to hide most file name extensions, on the premise that they make the operating system look more technical and threatening. If you'd like to see them, however, then choose Finder→Preferences, click the Advanced button, and then turn on "Show all filename extensions." Now examine a few of your documents; you'll see that their names display the previously hidden suffixes.

You can hide or show these suffixes on an icon-at-a-time basis, too (or a clump-at-a-time basis). Just highlight the icon or icons you want to affect, and then choose File→Get Info. In the resulting Info window, proceed as shown in Figure 5-18.

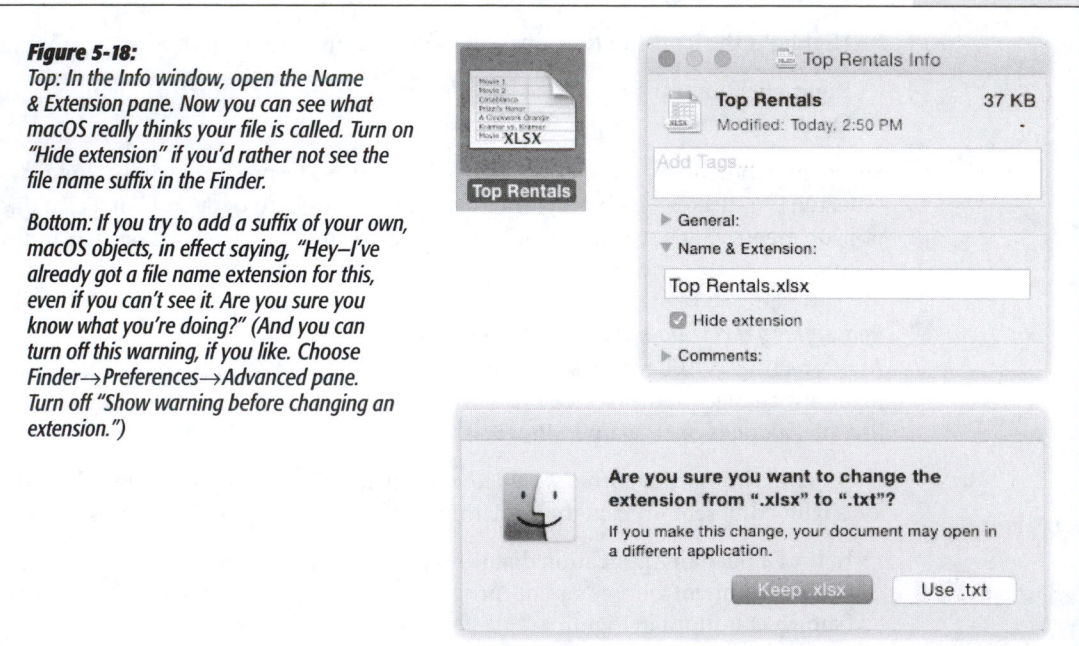

Figure 5-18:
Top: In the Info window, open the Name & Extension pane. Now you can see what macOS really thinks your file is called. Turn on "Hide extension" if you'd rather not see the file name suffix in the Finder.

Bottom: If you try to add a suffix of your own, macOS objects, in effect saying, "Hey—I've already got a file name extension for this, even if you can't see it. Are you sure you know what you're doing?" (And you can turn off this warning, if you like. Choose Finder→Preferences→Advanced pane. Turn off "Show warning before changing an extension.")

Tip: The Dock continues to display the icons of all running programs without any indication that you've hidden them. Fortunately, that's easy enough to fix. All you need is the free program TinkerTool, which is available on this book's "Missing CD" page at *missingmanuals.com.* It offers a simple checkbox that makes hidden programs appear with transparent Dock icons.

Hiding All Other Programs

Choosing Hide Others from your program's Application menu means, of course, "Hide the windows of every program but this one." It even hides your Finder (desktop) windows, although desktop icons remain visible.

Better yet, there's a keystroke for this command: Option-⌘-H. That's one small step for keystrokes, one giant leap for productivity geeks.

Tip: If you right-click or two-finger click a program's Dock icon, you get its shortcut menu, including a Hide command. If you press Option, it changes to say Hide Others. It's a lot more work than the methods described already, but…you know. One strives for thoroughness.

If this trick interests you, then you might also enjoy its corollary, described next.

The Bring-Forward, Hide-All-Others Trick

Here's a terrific technique that lets you bring one program to the front (along with all its open windows) and hide all other windows of all *other* open programs—with one click.

You might think of it as Hero mode, or Front-and-Center mode, or Clear My Calendar mode.

In any case, the trick is to Option-⌘-click the lucky program's icon on the Dock. As it jumps to the fore, all other windows on your Mac are instantly hidden. (You can bring them back, of course, by clicking the appropriate Dock icons.)

Hiding (Minimizing) Individual Windows

You can also hide or show *individual windows* of a single program. In fact, Apple must believe that hiding a window will become one of your favorite activities, because it offers at least three ways to do it:

- **Choose Window→Minimize Window,** if your program offers such a command, or press ⌘-M.

- **Click the Minimize button** on the window's title bar.

- **Double-click the window's title bar.** (If this doesn't work, choose System Preferences→Dock. Make sure "Double-click a window's title bar to minimize" is turned on.)

In any case, the affected window shrinks down until it becomes a new icon on the right side of the Dock. Click that icon to bring the window back.

your age," you'll tell your grandchildren, "we used to have to *hold down the Option key* to hide windows!"

But you know the drill at software companies: They giveth, but they never taketh away. All the old techniques are still around for the benefit of Mac fans who use them by force of habit.

Hiding the Program You're Using

For the purposes of this discussion, when a program is *hidden,* all its windows, tool palettes, and button bars disappear. You can bring them back only by bringing the program to the front again (by clicking its Dock icon, for example).

If your aim is to hide only the frontmost program, macOS offers a whole raft of approaches. Many of them involve the Option key, as listed here:

- **Option-click any visible portion of the desktop.** The program you were in vanishes, along with all its windows.

- **Option-click any other program's icon on the Dock.** You open that program (or bring its windows to the front) *and* hide all the windows of the one you were using.

- **Option-click any visible portion of another program's windows.** Once again, you switch programs, hiding the one you were using.

- **From the Application menu, choose Hide Photos (or whatever the program is).** The Application menu is the boldfaced menu that bears the program's name.

- **From the program's Dock icon shortcut menu, choose Hide.** You open the shortcut menu, of course, by right-clicking or two-finger clicking. You also get a Hide button if you click-and-hold on the Dock icon for half a second.

- **When you've highlighted a program's icon by pressing ⌘-Tab to rotate through the running programs, press the letter H key.** The program hides itself instantly. Leave the ⌘ key down the whole time and, after pressing the H, press Tab again to move on to the next program. If you release the keys while "stopped" on the program instead, you'll bring it forward rather than hiding it.

- **Press ⌘-H.** This may be the easiest and most useful trick of all (although it doesn't work in a few oddball programs). Doing so hides the program you're in; you then "fall down" into the next running program.

Tip: Consider this radical time-saving proposal: Never quit the programs you use frequently. Instead, simply hit ⌘-H whenever you're finished working in a program. That way, the next time you need it, the program launches with zero wait time.

In general, macOS's virtual-memory scheme is so good that there's almost no downside to leaving your programs open all the time.

To unhide a program and its windows, click its Dock icon again, choose the Show All command in the Application menu, or press ⌘-Tab to summon the heads-up application display.

- **Hold down instead of two presses.** Most of the time, you'll probably use Exposé in two steps. You'll tap the keystroke once to get the windows out of the way and again to bring them back (if, indeed, you haven't *clicked* a window to bring them back).

 In some cases, though, you may find it easier to *hold down* the relevant key. For example, hold down ⌘-F3 (Show Desktop) to see if a file is finished copying to the desktop, and then release the keys to bring back all the windows. (Actually, you can let go of the ⌘ key as soon as you've entered Exposé.) For quick window-clearing situations, that method saves you the step of having to press the keystroke a second time to turn off Exposé.

- **Use the spring-loaded Dock.** This trick is great when you want to drop a file from one program into a particular window belonging to another.

 The most common example: You want to add an attachment to an outgoing email message. In the Finder, locate the file's icon. Drag it directly onto your email program's Dock icon—and *pause* with your finger still on the button. After a half-second, Exposé happens, showing all your email program's open windows. Now continue your drag onto the miniaturized window of the outgoing message so it's highlighted, tap the space bar to open it, and then release. Presto! The file is attached.

 This trick also works great when you want to drop a photo into a newsletter, for example, or a text clipping into a word-processing document.

- **Dip into Quick Look.** Once you've got shrunken windows on the screen, tap your arrow keys to highlight a window (or point with your mouse at one without clicking). A bright-blue border moves from window to window.

 At any point, you can press the space bar to make that one window return to life size. You haven't really activated it—you can't edit it—but at least you can see it at full size.

 And here's the very cool part: Once you've triggered Quick Look like this, you can press the arrow keys to zap *other* miniwindows back to full size, without having to exit Quick Look. Or, again, point to other windows without clicking. Each zooms in to 100 percent size. (All of this is much easier to do than to imagine.)

 You can keep examining your windows at full size until you spot the one you're after; now tap Return (or click the mouse in the window) to exit Quick Look *and* Exposé. You've just opened that window, and you're ready to roll.

Tip: Keep in mind that you can change all of these Exposé triggers—keyboard shortcuts, hot corners, and so on. See page 185.

Hiding Programs the Old-Fashioned Way

When it comes to getting windows out of your way, nothing can touch Mission Control and Exposé for speed and entertainment value. Once you've mastered those features, the traditional rituals of hiding windows will seem charmingly quaint. "When I was

- **Press Control-F3 (⊞).** That's the keystroke on aluminum keyboards. (If you have a plastic keyboard, press F10.)

Tip: As noted in the box on the next page, you can also press fn-F10 or, with some tweaking, F10 alone. Or you can change the keystroke altogether, as described on page 210.

- **Enter Exposé from the heads-up display.** The heads-up display is the macOS application switcher—the row of "These are your open programs" icons—which appears when you press ⌘-Tab.

Figure 5-17:

Top: When you trigger one-app Exposé, you get a clear shot at any window in the current program (TextEdit, in this example). In the meantime, the rest of your screen attractively dims. In model Apple apps, like TextEdit and Preview, you even get a little row of icons at the bottom. They represent recently opened files, ready for clicking.

Bottom: Trigger desktop Exposé when you need to duck back to the desktop for a quick administrative chore. Here's your chance to find a file, throw something away, eject a disk, or whatever, without having to disturb your application windows.

Tap the same key again to turn off Exposé.

TV right now instead of working). There are also FedEx package trackers, joke-of-the-day widgets, comic-strip-of-the-day widgets, and many other varieties.

When you download a widget, macOS asks if you're sure you want to install it. If you confirm, macOS downloads it and then it proudly in the Widget Browser. Click it to open. (Behind the scenes, it's been copied into your Home→Library→Widgets folder. Only you will see that Dashboard widget, because it's been copied into the Widgets folder of *your account*. Anyone else who has an account on this Mac won't see it.)

Exposé

Before Mission Control, there was Exposé. It was flexible, it was novel, it was a little confusing. A few years ago, Apple incorporated the main functions of Exposé into Mission Control—but Apple didn't want to break all those Exposé fans' hearts. So Exposé is still there, for the benefit of old-timers who don't like change.

Well, it's *mostly* there. There used to be three different Exposé modes. One showed you miniatures of all windows in all programs, one showed you miniatures of all windows in just one program (Figure 5-17, top), and one hid all windows in all programs so you could see the desktop (Figure 5-17, bottom).

These days, only the second and third Exposé functions still exist. (The first one—showing *all* windows in *all* programs—is what Mission Control is for.)

You can trigger both of these modes using different combinations of the mouse and keyboard. The following pages cover all of them, but of course you're not expected to learn all that. Just find the *one* trigger that seems most convenient, and stick with it.

One-App Exposé

When you trigger Mission Control, you see the thumbnails of *all* windows in *all* apps.

But sometimes it's useful to see only the windows of *one* app arrayed before you—the app you're *using*.

That's great when you're web browsing or word processing. This Exposé function makes the program's windows spread out, and shrink if necessary, so you can click the one you want (Figure 5-17, top).

Here's how Apple intends for most people to trigger this option:

- **Swipe down on your trackpad with three fingers.** You're shown the miniatures of your current app's windows. If you point to an icon *on the Dock* before you swipe, you trigger Exposé for that app instead. (There's no equivalent on the Magic Mouse—although if you install the free BetterTouchTool, you can dream up a gesture of your own.)

Note: You have to turn this feature on in System Preferences→Trackpad→More Gestures. Once you've done that, you can change this gesture to four fingers on the trackpad using the pop-up menu—handy if you find yourself triggering the function by accident.

a sort of ice-cream swirl (you've got to see it to believe it) and then untwists to reveal the new data.

- **You can open more than one copy of the same widget.** Just click its icon more than once in the Widget Browser. You wind up with multiple copies of it on your screen: three World Clocks, two Stock Trackers, or whatever. That's a useful trick when, for example, you want to track the time in more than one city, or when you maintain two different stock portfolios.

- **If you keep the Shift key pressed when you click the big ✚ button,** the Widget Browser fades in, in gorgeous *slow motion.* Aren't you just glad to be alive?

Dashboard Preferences

To change the Dashboard keystroke to something other than F4 or F12, open System Preferences→Mission Control.

Here you'll discover that you can choose almost any other keyboard combination to summon and dismiss the Dashboard, or even choose a screen corner that, when your mouse lands there, acts as the Dashboard trigger. This works exactly as described on page 185.

Note: Yes, you can also change the Dashboard keystroke on the Keyboard→Shortcuts pane of System Preferences. But if you use the Mission Control pane instead, then you can set up a screen corner or a mouse button to trigger Dashboard—not just a keyboard combo.

Widget Catalog

Apple starts you off with 15 standard widgets: Calculator, Calendar, Contacts, Dictionary, ESPN, Flight Tracker, Movies, Stickies, Stocks, Tile Game, Translation, Unit Converter, Weather, Web Clip, and World Clock. They look awfully simple, but some of them harbor a few secrets.

For a detailed guide to each of these widgets, see the free downloadable appendix, "Dashboard Widgets," on this book's "Missing CD" page at *missingmanuals.com.*

More Widgets

Thousands of new widgets, written by other people, were once just a click away: games, chat and email notifiers, gas-price reporters, calculators and translators, news and sports updaters, finance and health trackers, and on and on. You could install them directly from Dashboard.

Not in Mojave, though. In preparing its fans for the imminent demise of Dashboard, Apple has killed off the More Widgets button, which once took you to the Widget Store online. At this writing, at least, that store is still available; you just have to call it up manually, at *apple.com/downloads/dashboard/.*

There you'll still find offerings like the Yahoo Local Traffic widget (gives you the traffic conditions in your area), Air Traffic Control (identifies wireless AirPort base stations within range of your laptop), and TV Tracker (shows what you could be watching on

The Widget Browser

The Widget Browser screen appears when you click the big ⊕ button at the bottom of the Dashboard. As shown in Figure 5-16, it's simply a master collection of every widget on your Mac, even the ones that you haven't dragged onto the main Dashboard screen. Its goal in life: managing all your *other* widgets.

For example, you can enter icon-deleting mode by holding your cursor down on any one of them; they all start wiggling—and displaying the ⊗ button at the top-left corner.

Note: Even in wiggling-icon mode, you're not allowed to delete Apple's widgets—only ones you've downloaded and installed yourself.

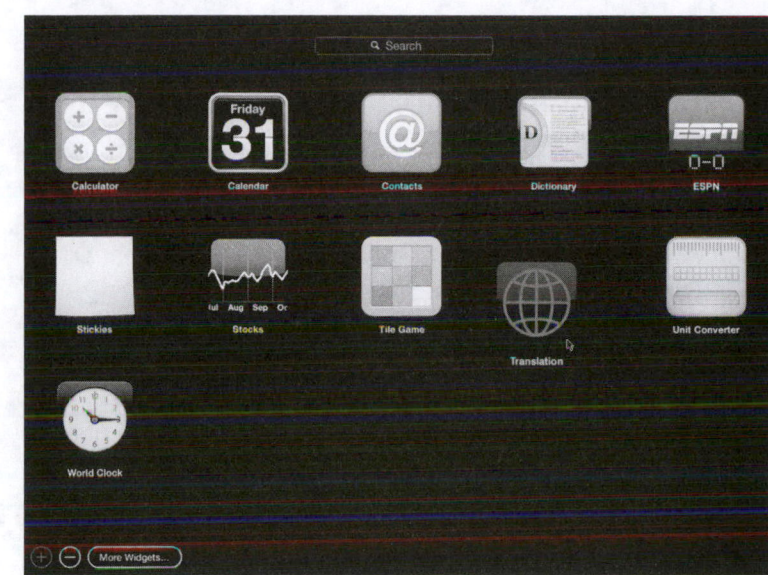

Figure 5-16:
The Widget Browser works exactly like the Launchpad. Move widget icons around by dragging. Drag one widget on top of another to create a folder. Search using the box at the top of the screen. Start them wiggling, for ease of mass deletion, by holding your cursor down on any icon, or by clicking the big ⊖ button. Read pages 170–174 again, taking care to mentally substitute the word "widget" for "app."

But what you'll do here most often is simply *click* a widget's icon to install it onto the main Dashboard screen.

(To close the browser without pulling a new icon out of it, click anywhere on the background.)

The Widget Browser also harbors the godlike power of the More Widgets button, described on the next page.

Dashboard Tips

Dashboard is crawling with cool tips and tricks. Here are a few of the biggies:

- **To refresh a certain widget**—for example, to update its information from the internet—click it and press ⌘-R. The widget instantly *twist-scrambles* itself into

Segment

But yes, incredibly, Dashboard limps on in Mojave; here's how it works.

Turn on the Dashboard Feature

Open System Preferences→Mission Control. From the Dashboard pop-up menu, choose either As Space (the Dashboard will appear on its own desktop) or As Overlay. That option makes the Dashboard widgets float *on top* of whatever you're doing.

Opening the Dashboard

Once you've brought the Dashboard back from the dead, here's how you open it:

- **If you've set up the Dashboard as a Space**, well, it's one of your virtual desktops. Swipe to the left with three fingers on your trackpad—repeatedly, if necessary—until you reach the far-left "desktop." (On a Magic Mouse, swipe with *two* fingers.)

 Or just open Mission Control, and then click the Dashboard thumbnail at the top left of the screen.

- **If you've set up the Dashboard as an overlay**, press the Dashboard keystroke.

 On older Macs, that would be F4, bearing the Dashboard logo (☉). On more recent Macs, where the F4 key bears a Launchpad icon (▦) instead, the keystroke is F12. (If F12 adjusts the volume when you press it, then you must hold down the fn key as you press F12.) In all of these cases, you can change the Dashboard keystroke to whatever you like, as described on page 195.

Tip: Dashboard is an actual program, with an icon of its own in your Applications folder. If you're desperate, you can always open it with a double-click or by using any of the usual program-opening tricks.

Using Dashboard

If you do, in fact, manage to open Dashboard, you now see the display shown in Figure 5-15. Welcome to the Dashboard.

These weird, hybrid entities are like little web pages. They're meant to display information, much of it from the internet, and they're written using web programming languages like HTML and JavaScript.

Mastering the basics of Dashboard won't take you long at all:

- **To move a widget,** drag it around the screen. (Click anywhere except on a button or a control.)

- **To close a widget,** press the Option key as you move the mouse across the widget's face. You'll see the ⊗ button appear at the widget's top-left corner; click it.

- **To open a closed widget,** click the big ⊕ button at the bottom of the screen. Now the Widget Browser appears (Figure 5-16), as described in the next section. Open the widget you want by clicking its icon.

- **To hide one of Apple's widgets,** or to delete one you've installed yourself, use the Widget Browser described next.

The point, of course, is to make it quick and easy to return to whatever you were doing most recently. But if you find it disorienting to have your desktops constantly changing their sequence, you can turn this option off.

• **When switching to an application, switch to a Space with open windows for the application.** There must be some clearer way to write this checkbox.

In any case, it means that when you click the Dock icon for a running program, you jump to the Space that contains that program's open windows already, instead of leaving you on the current Space.

For example, suppose you're working in your browser on Desktop #3. Then you click the Mail icon on the Dock. If this option is turned on, you jump to Desktop #2 (or wherever you've been already working in Mail). If it's not turned on, Mail jumps to the foreground, but you won't see any windows—they're stranded back on Desktop #2.

Dashboard

As you know, the essence of using a computer is running *programs*, which often produce *documents*. In macOS, however, there's a third category: a set of weird, hybrid entities that Apple calls *widgets*. They appear, all at once, on a virtual desktop called the Dashboard (Figure 5-15).

Truth is, the Dashboard's days are numbered. For one thing, this feature comes turned off in Mojave. For another, the information modules of your Today panel (page 382) are *also* called widgets—and they feel a lot newer and more immediate than the Dashboard's.

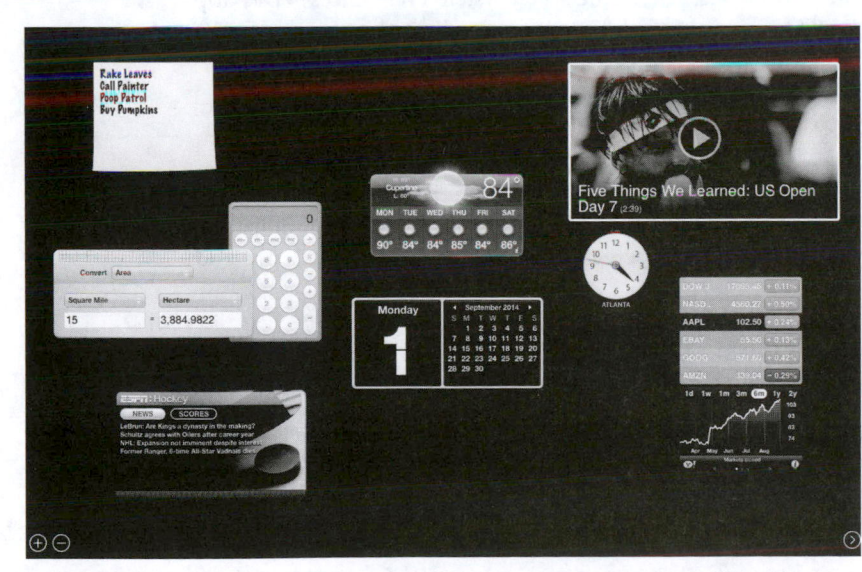

Figure 5-15:
The Dashboard is a fleet of mini-programs that convey or convert all kinds of useful information, on a Spaces screen all their own. You get rid of the Dashboard either by pressing the same key again (F4 or whatever), by swiping three fingers to the right on your trackpad, or by clicking anywhere except on a widget.

- **Move a window to a different Space.** Of course, you can always move a window to a different Space by dragging its tiny icon within Mission Control. But there are two faster ways.

First, you can drag a window (using its title bar as a handle) all the way to the edge of the screen. Stay there with the mouse button still down. After about a second, the adjacent screen slides into view; you've just moved the window.

Second, switch to the new Space. Hold your mouse down on the app's Dock icon; from the shortcut menu, choose Options→Assign To→This Desktop. The Mac whisks that app's windows from whatever *other* screen they're on to *this* screen.

- **Move a window to all Spaces.** Usually, you slap each app (or each window) onto only *one* Spaces desktop. Your web browser on Space 1. Email on Space 2. And so on.

Sometimes, though, you might want one app's windows on *all* your desktops—perhaps because you use it so often, you want it always with you. The Finder and System Preferences are great examples. Or maybe your calendar app, your browser, or your email program.

To do that, hold the mouse button down on the program's Dock icon until the shortcut menu appears. From this menu, choose Options→Assign To→All Desktops.

- **Wallpaper for every desktop.** Coolly enough, though, you can set a different wallpaper photo (desktop photo) to each Space. You might find it easier to get your bearings that way. When you restart the computer, the Mac will remember not just which Spaces you had open and what was on them, but also what pictures lay behind them.

You can go about assigning desktop pictures in two ways. First switch to the Space whose picture you want to change. Then either open System Preferences→Desktop & Screen Saver→Desktop, or right-click or two-finger click a blank spot on the existing desktop background, and choose Change Desktop Background.

Note: In both cases, you may have to move the System Preferences window onto your current Space. You can do that by popping into Mission Control.

Either way, you wind up in the Preferences panel for choosing desktop wallpaper. Click the backdrop you want for this screen. Then switch to the next Space and repeat.

Two Eccentric Spaces Settings

In System Preferences→Mission Control, two settings govern the way Spaces works:

- **Automatically rearrange Spaces based on most recent use.** If this option is turned on, then macOS will constantly rearrange your virtual desktops so that the most recently used ones are first. (The most recent one becomes Desktop #2, since Desktop #1 is always your main desktop.)

When you make a switch, you see a flash of animation as one screen flies away and another appears. Now that you're "on" the screen you want, open programs and arrange windows onto it as usual.

Tip: What if you're using Spaces, and you want to drag something from one screen (like a photo in Photos) into a window that's on a different screen (like an outgoing email message)?

There are two ways; take your pick. First, you can start dragging whatever it is—and then, in mid-drag, press the keystroke for Mission Control (usually fn-F9); complete the drag directly onto the other Space, and even into the relevant window *in* that Space.

Another approach: Start dragging. With the mouse button still down, press ⌘-Tab to open the application switcher. Continue the drag onto the *icon* of the receiving program, and still keep the mouse button down. MacOS switches to the appropriate virtual screen automatically.

Deleting a Desktop

To delete a desktop, enter Mission Control. Point to one of the screen thumbnails without clicking until a ⊗ appears in its corner; click it. The desktop disappears, and whatever windows were on it get shoved onto your main desktop.

Tip: If you don't have the 1 ½ seconds to wait for the ⊗ to appear, then press Option as you point. The Close button appears instantly.

In apps using Full Screen mode, the symbol is different; instead of ⊗, it looks like this: ⊘. When you click, the desktop flies off the Spaces bar into the main part of your screen. That app is now a plain-vanilla window thumbnail, just like all the others in Mission Control.

The Finer Points of Spaces

Yes, Spaces is an advanced feature. But there are actually advanced features *within* this advanced feature. For example:

• **Rearrange your Spaces.** Open Mission Control, and then drag the Space thumbnails around horizontally.

Note: If you've decided to turn on the Dashboard as a Space, as described later in this chapter, you can even drag the Dashboard out of its traditional left-side position. Put it off to the right of the other Spaces, for all Apple cares.

• **Multiple monitors.** If you have a second monitor connected to your Mac (or even several), each one can have its own set of Spaces.

If "Displays have separate Spaces" is turned on in the Mission Control panel of System Preferences (Figure 5-12), then each monitor has its own set of Spaces. When you use one of the gestures or keystrokes for switching Spaces, you affect the Spaces on only one monitor: the one that contains your cursor at the moment.

Switching Spaces

Once you've got Spaces set up and turned on, the fun begins. Start by moving to the virtual screen you want; it's like changing the channel. Here are some ways to do that:

- **Swipe horizontally on your trackpad with three fingers.** (On the Magic Mouse, it's two fingers.) If you have a trackpad or a Magic Mouse, this is definitely the method to learn; it's fast, fluid, and happy.

 You can change this gesture so that it requires an additional finger, if you like, in System Preferences→Trackpad (or Mouse)→More Gestures.

Tip: If you perform this swipe *slowly,* you can drag the next Space only *partway* onto the screen. That's sometimes handy when you want to get your bearings or to just *peek* into the next screen.

- **While pressing the Control key,** type the number of the desktop you want. For example, hit Control-3 to jump to your third screen. (You have to turn on this feature first, though. See Figure 5-14.)

- **Enter Mission Control,** and then click the desktop you want.

- **Press Control-◀ or Control-▶** to rotate to the previous or next desktop.

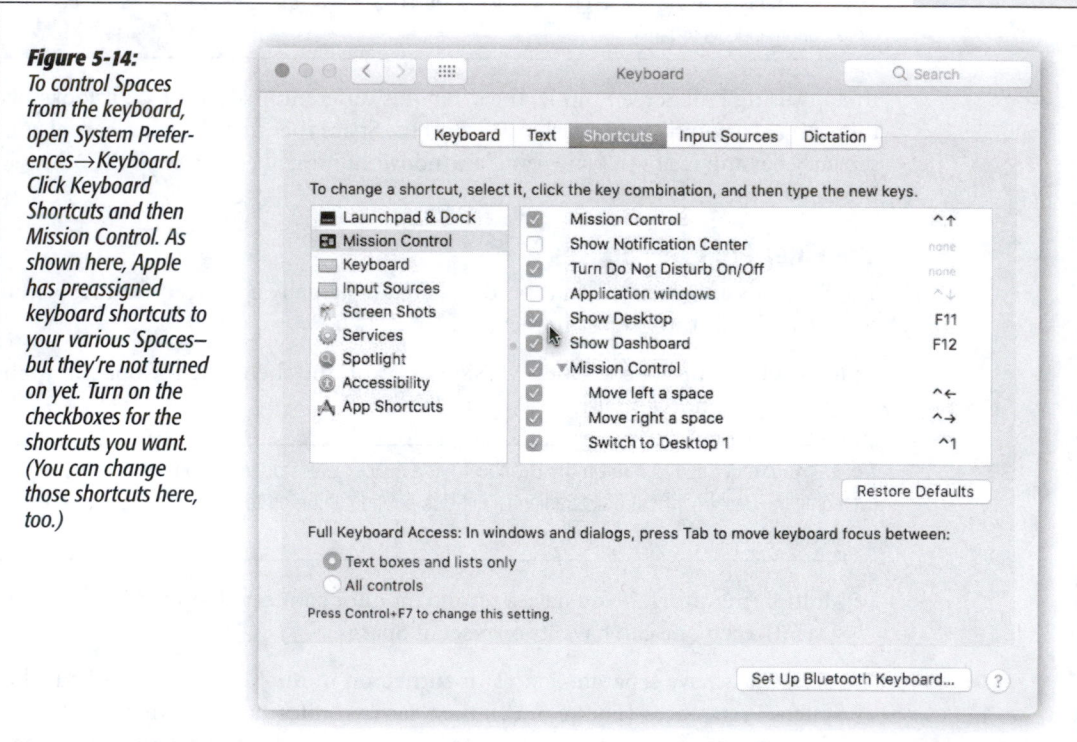

Figure 5-14:
To control Spaces from the keyboard, open System Preferences→Keyboard. Click Keyboard Shortcuts and then Mission Control. As shown here, Apple has preassigned keyboard shortcuts to your various Spaces—but they're not turned on yet. Turn on the checkboxes for the shortcuts you want. (You can change those shortcuts here, too.)

Note: To save space, the Spaces bar starts out as a very thin strip bearing only the names of your desktops (Figure 5-13, top). Move your cursor into this strip to expand it vertically, so you can now see the actual thumbnail images of your desktops (Figure 5-13, bottom).

Once you're in Mission Control, you can proceed in either of two ways:

• **The long way.** See Figure 5-13 for the step-by-steps of clicking the + button in the upper-right corner.

Note: If you've positioned your Dock against the right side of the screen, then the + button appears when you point to the upper-*left* corner. And to create a new screen by dragging a window's icon (see "The short way," next), drag to the upper-*left* corner of the screen.

• **The short way.** Drag one window thumbnail onto any blank spot on the Spaces bar. The Mac creates a new desktop to hold it.

Figure 5-13:
Top: When you enter Mission Control, the Spaces bar is thin and collapsed.

Middle: Click the ⊕ button to create a new blank desktop, numbered sequentially.

Bottom: Drag one of the window miniatures onto this new desktop. Or several.

The trouble with miniaturized windows is that, well, they're miniaturized. The more windows you have open, the smaller they are, and the harder it is to see what's in them.

If you need a little help identifying a window miniature, you have three options:

- **Point to a window thumbnail without clicking.** MacOS displays a label for that window.

- **If that's not enough information, press the space bar.** That, of course, is the Quick Look keystroke, and it works here, too. It magnifies the window you're pointing to, making it full size—big enough for you to read its contents and identify it.

- **Press ⌘-~.** That keystroke takes you into Exposé, described later in this chapter.

Spaces (Virtual Desktops)

Mission Control's other star feature, Spaces, gives you up to 16 *full-size monitors.* Ordinarily, of course, attaching so many screens to a single computer would be a massively expensive proposition, not to mention detrimental to your living space and personal relationships.

Fortunately, Spaces monitors are *virtual.* They exist only in the Mac's little head. You see only one at a time; you switch using Mission Control or a gesture.

But just because the Spaces screens are simulated doesn't mean they're not useful. You can dedicate each one to a different program or *kind* of program. Screen 1 might contain your email and chat windows, arranged just the way you like them. Screen 2 can hold Photoshop, with an open document and the palettes carefully arrayed. On Screen 3: your web browser in Full Screen mode.

You can also have the *same* program running on multiple screens—but with different documents or projects open on each one.

These desktops are also essential to macOS's *full-screen apps* feature, because each full-screen app gets its own Spaces desktop.

Now, virtual screens aren't a new idea—this sort of software has been available for years. But the Mac was the first to make it a standard feature of a consumer operating system.

It's still what most people would consider an advanced feature, and it's definitely confusing at first. But it'll be here when you're ready for it.

Creating a Desktop

Mission Control generally starts you off with just one Space (or "desktop," as it's labeled)—the one you've been using all along. If you've clicked the ⊙ button in an app to make it full screen, it fills an additional desktop unto itself.

To create another desktop, enter Mission Control. At the top edge of the screen, the gray strip—the Spaces bar—is the command center for creating, deleting, rearranging, and configuring your virtual desktops.

Note: This is only an example. Repeat: This is only an example. *Actually* using the Shift key to open Mission Control is a terrible, terrible idea, as you'll quickly discover the next time you try to type a capital letter. This feature is intended exclusively for hunt-and-peck typists who never use the Shift key on one side.

If you have a laptop, you'll also find out that you can tap the fn key alone for Mission Control—and this time, it's a great choice, because fn otherwise has very little direction in life.

If your mouse has more than one button, you'll see a second column of pop-up menus in System Preferences (Figure 5-12). Each pop-up menu offers choices like Right Mouse Button and Middle Mouse Button. Use these pop-up menus to assign Mission Control (or Exposé or Dashboard) to the various clickers on your mouse: Right-click to hide all windows, middle-click to reveal the desktop, and so on.

Note, by the way, that on a laptop, the wording isn't "right mouse button"—it's "secondary mouse button." Which means "right-click." Which means that on a laptop, you can set it up so that a "right-click" *trackpad gesture* triggers one of these functions. See page 239 for all the different ways you can trigger a right-click.

Screen corners

If you click Hot Corners, you see something like Figure 9-15 (page 348). The four corners here represent the corners of your screen. Using these menus, you can assign a window-management feature to each corner; for example, if you choose Mission Control from the first pop-up menu, then when your pointer hits the upper-left corner of the screen, you'll open Mission Control. (Launchpad and Notification Center are options here, too.)

Depending on the size of your screen, this option can feel awkward at first. But if you've run out of keystrokes that aren't assigned to other functions, be glad that Apple offers you this alternative.

Note: In previous versions of the operating system, whipping the pointer into a corner was one good way to turn on your *screen saver.* Apple hasn't forgotten about that, which is why you'll also find commands called Start Screen Saver and Disable Screen Saver in the pop-up menus. Apple wants to make sure you don't get confused and assign two different functions to the same corner.

Managing Windows in Mission Control

Once you open Mission Control, you can click any window's thumbnail to open it.

Tip: Try holding down the Shift key as you do it. You'll enjoy watching all your windows shift around with macOS's patented slow-motion animation, which can be quite a sight.

Or, if you decide to abandon ship and return to whatever you were doing, swipe *downward* with three fingers on the trackpad (two on the Magic Mouse), or press the Esc key.

Note: To *exit* Mission Control without clicking any of your windows or virtual screens, swipe *down* with three fingers. Or tap the Esc key. Or click a spot in the empty background.

Mission Control keystrokes

You can reassign the Mission Control functions to a huge range of other keys, with or without modifiers like Shift, Control, and Option. To view your options, choose ⌘→System Preferences and then click the Mission Control icon.

Here you'll find four pop-up menus (Figure 5-12). The first, Mission Control, lets you specify how you want to open Mission Control. The other three—Application windows, Show Desktop, and Show Dashboard—correspond to the three functions of the older Exposé and Dashboard features, described later in this chapter.

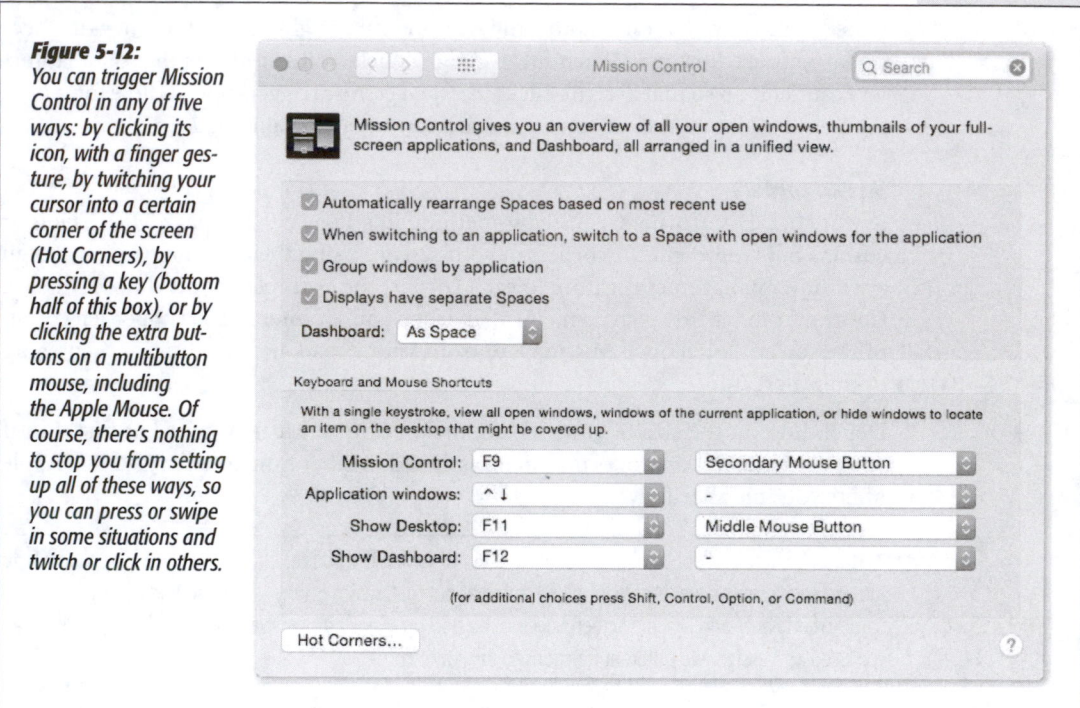

Figure 5-12:
You can trigger Mission Control in any of five ways: by clicking its icon, with a finger gesture, by twitching your cursor into a certain corner of the screen (Hot Corners), by pressing a key (bottom half of this box), or by clicking the extra buttons on a multibutton mouse, including the Apple Mouse. Of course, there's nothing to stop you from setting up all of these ways, so you can press or swipe in some situations and twitch or click in others.

Within each pop-up menu, for example, you'll discover that all your F-keys—F1, F2, F3, and so on—are available as triggers. If, while the pop-up menu is open, you press one or more of your modifier keys (Shift, Option, Control, or ⌘), then all these F-key choices *change* to reflect the key you're pressing; now the pop-up menu says Shift-F1, Shift-F2, Shift-F3, and so on. That's how you can make *Shift*-F1 trigger Mission Control, for example.

These pop-up menus also contain choices like Left Shift, which refers to the Shift key on the left side of your keyboard. That is, instead of pressing F9 to open Mission Control, you could simply tap the Shift key.

Note: You can change this gesture so that it requires *four* fingers, if you like, in System Preferences→Trackpad (or Mouse)→More Gestures→Mission Control. Use the pop-up menu.

Or you can press the dedicated ⌘ key (formerly the Exposé key), if you have one, on the top row of your keyboard.

Or you can press Control-▲.

And even that's just the beginning of the ways you can open Mission Control; read on.

Figure 5-11:
Top: Quick! Where's the Finder in all this mess?

Bottom: With a three- or four-finger upward swipe on the trackpad, you can open Mission Control and spot every window, shrunken but not overlapped. These aren't static snapshots of the windows at the moment you Mission Controlled them. They're live, still-updating windows, as you'll discover if one of them contains a QuickTime movie or a web page that's still loading.

That window becomes a normal floating window. (The *other* window remains in Full Screen mode, on its own desktop; you can switch to it as described on page 189.)

- **Mission Control method.** Enter Mission Control, as described next. (For example, press the ⌘ key on your keyboard.) Move your cursor to the top of the screen to make the Spaces bar expand. Point to the desktop icon that contains the split screen; click the ⊗ in the top left.

In this case, *both* windows exit Full Screen and become floating windows again.

Mission Control: Death to Window Clutter

These days, managing all the open windows in all the open programs can be like herding cats. Off you go, burrowing through the microscopic pop-up menus of your Dock, trying to find the window you want. And heaven help you if you need to duck back to the desktop—to find a newly downloaded file, for example, or to eject a disk. You have to fight your way through 50,000 other windows on the way to the bottom of the "deck."

Mission Control tackles this problem in a fresh way. The concept is delicious: With one mouse click, keystroke, or finger gesture, you shrink all windows in all programs to a size that fits on the screen (Figure 5-11), like index cards on a bulletin board. Now you feel like an air-traffic controller, with all your screens arrayed before you. You click the window you want, and you're there. It's efficient, animated, and a lot of fun.

Tip: If you use Mission Control a lot, the zooming animation might get a little tiresome. Fortunately, you can turn that off. Open System Preferences→Accessibility→Display, and turn on Reduce Motion. From now on, Mission Control simply *pops* to the screen instead of zooming.

The window miniatures are scattered all over your screen. The placement isn't entirely random; macOS tries to place the thumbnails on the screen relative to their full-size windows' positions, relative to the top, bottom, and sides of your monitor.

You can impose a little more order on all of this, though. Open System Preferences→Mission Control, and turn on "Group windows by application." The windows still don't overlap, but at least the windows of each program are laid out near one another in Mission Control.

Starting and Stopping Mission Control

Mission Control is a program, just like any other. So you can open it with a click on its Dock icon, from Launchpad, from the Applications folder, and so on.

But it's really meant to be opened quickly, fluidly, naturally, whenever the mood seizes you—with a *gesture*. On the trackpad, that's a swipe upward with three fingers. (On the Magic Mouse, it's a double-tap with *two* fingers—taps, not clicks.)

2. **Release the mouse or trackpad.**

And sure enough: Window #1 now fills exactly half the screen (Figure 5-9, third from top). Meanwhile, all other open windows shrink down into miniature cards. *That's* the Mac's way of telling you: "Please choose Window #2, the one you'd like to fill the *rest* of the screen."

3. **Click the miniature window you want to fill the remaining half of the screen.**

Now you've got two windows sharing your screen space 50-50 (Figure 5-9, bottom).

If you like, you can now grab the divider line and drag it, thereby adjusting the proportion of the screen occupied by each app.

Starting Split Screen Mode, Method 2

The second method makes sense only after you've read about Mission Control and Spaces, starting on the next page. Bookmark this spot, go read that, and then return here.

Back so soon? OK, great!

Now that you know what the Spaces bar is, here's the tip: You can drag a second window onto an existing full-screen app's thumbnail in the Spaces bar; see Figure 5-10 for details.

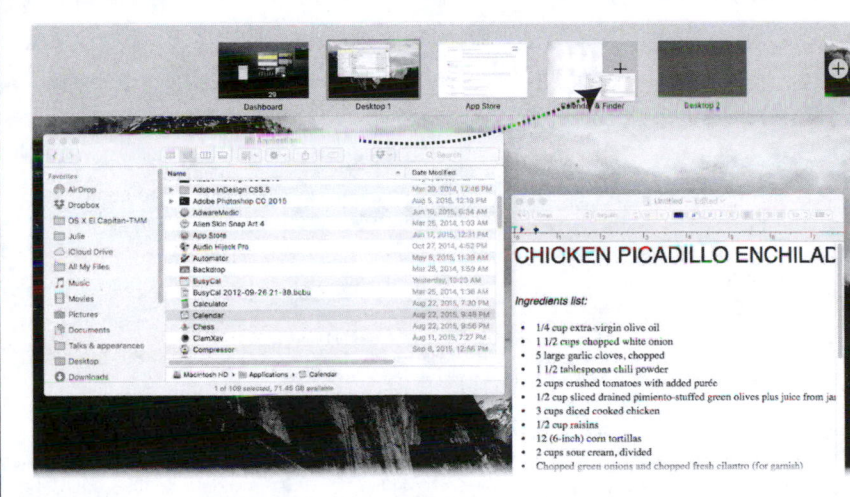

Figure 5-10:
Drag a window onto an existing Full Screen–mode window's thumbnail. The + shows you which side of the screen this new window will occupy in Split Screen mode. Release the mouse, and then click the split thumbnail to make it fill your screen.

Exiting Split Screen Mode

Just as there are two ways to enter Split Screen mode, there are also two ways to exit it.

- **The title-bar method.** Move your cursor to the top edge of either window and pause; its title bar appears. Now click the green ⊕ button.

This combination works very well when you want to keep a continuously updating app visible—Twitter, Mail, or FaceTime, for example—while continuing to do work in a second app. It's also handy when you're referring to one app (a recipe in your web browser) and making notes in another (an ingredients list in Notes).

Once again, though, Split Screen doesn't work in all apps—only the ones that work in Full Screen mode.

Starting Split Screen Mode, Method 1

There are two ways to get in and out of Split Screen mode, but this one is quickest:

1. **Click-and-hold the green ⊙ button at the top-left corner of Window #1. (See Figure 5-9, top.)**

 The weirdest thing now happens: Whichever half of your monitor contains this window (usually the left side) becomes shaded blue (Figure 5-9, second from top). That's the Mac's way of telling you: "When you release your mouse or trackpad, this window will snap to fill only this half of the screen."

Tip: At this point, you could, if you liked, drag the window to the opposite side of the screen—still holding down the mouse or trackpad—to make it fill *that* half.

NOSTALGIA CORNER

Window Layering

MacOS takes a layered approach to your programs' windows. They're not all in front or all in back; it's entirely possible to wind up with the windows of different programs sandwiched and layered, front to back.

Suppose, for example, you have Microsoft Excel in the foreground but Word in the background. If you click within a visible portion of a background window, you bring only that window of Word to the front.

The remedy for this situation, if it bothers you, is the Window→Bring All to Front command, which appears in the Finder and many other programs. It brings all of a program's windows to the front.

(You can do the same thing by simply clicking the program's Dock icon, or using the ⌘-Tab "heads-up" display.)

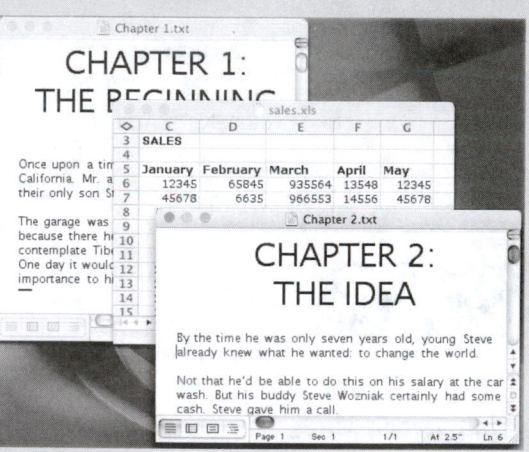

Layered windows shine when you're comparing two documents in two different programs, because they free you of the window clutter of other open documents. But the time will come when you're ready to bring all of a background program's windows to the front. Get into the habit of clicking its Dock icon, or pressing ⌘-Tab to select its icon, rather than clicking inside one window. When you do that, all open windows in that application come forward, from wherever they may be.

Split Screen Mode

Once Apple gave us Full Screen mode, the next step was obvious: *split* Full Screen mode. In this arrangement, two windows fill the screen, edge to edge and top to bottom (Figure 5-9). Just as in Full Screen mode, the menu bar, Dock, and all other cluttery extras are hidden to maximize screen space; the only difference is that two apps are now sharing that big monitor canvas.

Figure 5-9:
Here's the complete tutorial for turning on Split Screen mode.

Top: Hold down the green ⊗ button in the first app.

Second from top: That half of your screen gets a blue tint.

Third from top: Release the mouse; that window now fills half your entire screen. Meanwhile, all other open windows appear in miniature so that you can choose the one you want to fill the other half of your screen. (There may even be a little pile of additional window cards at the bottom corner. These are apps whose software companies have been too lazy to make them compatible with the Full Screen/Split Screen feature.)

Bottom: And voilà: Two apps, perfectly splitting your screen's full height and width. Feel free to drag the divider line sideways to adjust the proportions.

if your program even offers Full Screen mode? As your cursor approaches the green dot button, a tiny double-arrow logo appears inside: ⊗. If it's a ⊕ instead, then the app isn't eligible for Full Screening.)

When you click the green ⊗, the Mac hides the menu bar, scroll bars, Dock, status bars, and any other bars or palettes surrounding your work area. The window's edges expand all the way to the edges of the screen (Figure 5-8, bottom).

Tip: You may as well learn the keyboard shortcut to enter Full Screen mode: Control-⌘-F. The same keystroke *leaves* Full Screen mode, but you can also tap the Esc key for that purpose.

The menu bar is available—it's just hidden. Move the pointer to the top of the screen to make it reappear.

To *exit* Full Screen mode, make the menu bar appear, and then click that green dot in the upper-left corner of the window (which now looks like this: ⊗).

Figure 5-8:

Top: So much for the glorious web. You're seeing a web page segment, swimming in an ocean of toolbars, scroll bars, status bars, menu bars, and distracting desktop.

Bottom: In Full Screen mode, Safari stretches to the very edges of your screen, and everything else disappears. (Your address bar and tab bars are still available in this case.)

Each full-screen app becomes its own desktop in Mission Control. And you can put a full-screen app on each of your monitors, too.

To leave Full Screen mode, move your cursor to the top of the screen so that the menu bar reappears. Click the green dot once again (top left of your document window).

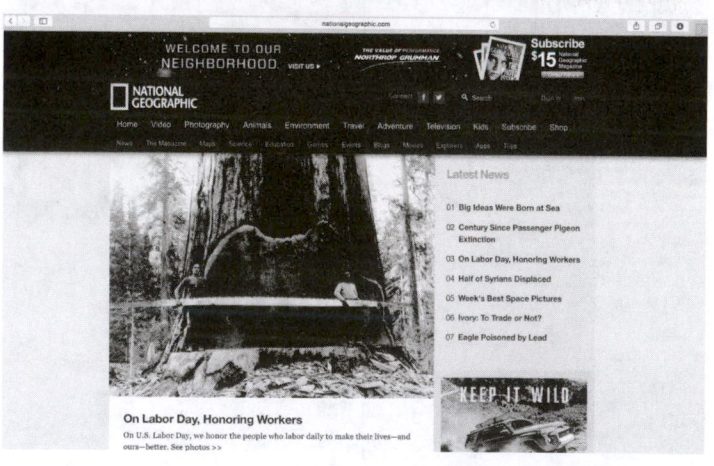

You can use this feature in three different ways, which are well worth learning:

- **If you keep the ⌘ key pressed,** then each press of the Tab key highlights the Dock icon of another program, in left-to-right Dock order. Release both keys when you reach the one you want. MacOS brings the corresponding program to the front. (To move *backward* through the open programs, press *Shift-*⌘-Tab.)

- **If you leave the ⌘ key pressed,** you can choose a program by clicking its icon with your mouse or by pressing the ◀ or ▶ keys.

- **A single press of** ⌘-Tab takes you to the program you used most recently, and another, separate ⌘-Tab bounces back to the program you started in.

Imagine, for example, that you're doing a lot of switching between two programs, like your web browser and your email program. If you have five other programs open, you don't want to waste your time ⌘-tabbing your way through all the open programs just to get back to your web browser.

Tip: Here's a related keystroke, equally awesome. If you press ⌘-~ (the tilde key next to the number 1), you switch to the next window in the *same* program.

Figure 5-7:
Apple once called this row of open program icons a "heads-up display," named after the projected data screen on a Navy jet wind-shield that lets pilots avoid having to look down at their instruments.

Preview

Full Screen Mode

Features are great and all. But the more of them your software accumulates, the more toolbars and icon panels fill the screen, and the bigger the clutter problem becomes. After a while, all that "chrome" (as software designers call it) winds up crowding out the document you're actually trying to work on.

That's why Apple invented Full Screen mode. It's not available in all programs, but it's showing up in more and more of them—including almost all Apple programs: App Store, Calendar, Chess, Final Cut Pro, Font Book, GarageBand, Books, iMovie, iTunes, Keynote, Mail, Maps, Messages, Notes, Photo Booth, Photos, Preview, Safari, and so on.

To take a program into Full Screen mode, click the Full Screen button: the round, green dot in the upper-left corner of the document window. (And how do you know

Force-Quitting Programs

MacOS is a rock-solid operating system, but that doesn't mean that *programs* never screw up. Individual programs are as likely as ever to freeze—or, rather, to *hang* (lock up and display the "spinning beachball of death" cursor). In such cases, you have no choice but to *force-quit* the program—the computer equivalent of terminating it with a blunt instrument.

Doing so doesn't destabilize your Mac; you don't have to restart it. In fact, you can usually reopen the very same program and get on with your life.

You can force-quit a stuck program in any of several ways:

- **Click-and-hold on the program's Dock icon,** or two-finger click it, or right-click it. A Quit button appears just above your cursor. Press the Option key to make the button say Force Quit. Click it. Bingo—that program is outta here.

- **Press Option-⌘-Esc,** the traditional Mac force-quit keystroke, or choose → Force Quit. Either way, proceed as shown in Figure 5-6.

The only downside to force-quitting a program is that you lose any unsaved changes to your open documents, along with any preference settings you may have changed while the program was open.

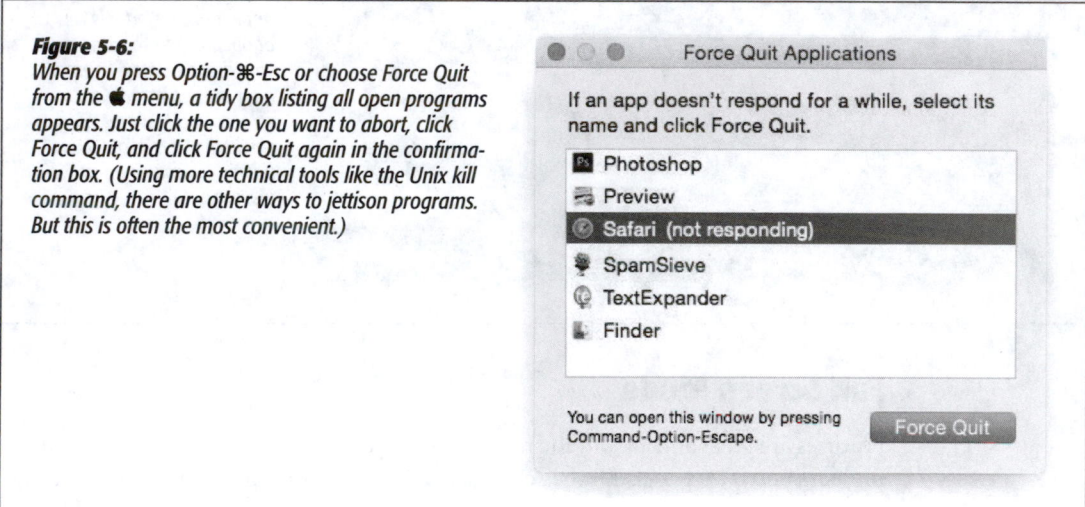

Figure 5-6:
When you press Option-⌘-Esc or choose Force Quit from the menu, a tidy box listing all open programs appears. Just click the one you want to abort, click Force Quit, and click Force Quit again in the confirmation box. (Using more technical tools like the Unix kill command, there are other ways to jettison programs. But this is often the most convenient.)

The App Switcher

Only one program can be in front, or active, at a time.

To switch to a different program, you could click or double-click its icon (in the Dock, the Applications folder, Launchpad, or wherever). But the fastest method is often to use the ⌘-Tab keystroke (Figure 5-7).

virginal state by pressing the Shift key as it opens. That forces the program to forget the previous window setup.

- **Turn off auto-open for one program.** Suppose you like the auto-window-reopening feature in *most* programs. But there's one particular program that you *never* want to memorize your window setup—maybe for security reasons, or maybe because you use that app for something different every day.

 Before long, some shareware program will crop up to make that easy. For now, though, you can do the job manually. It's a quick, one-time step, but it does involve mucking around with one of the Mac's invisible folders. See the box on the previous page.

The Application Menu

In every app, the very first menu (to the right of the menu) appears with bold lettering and identifies the program you're using. It might say iTunes, or Microsoft Word, or Stickies.

This Application menu (Figure 5-5) offers a number of commands pertaining to the entire program and its windows, including About, Quit, and Hide.

Figure 5-5:
The first menu in every program lets you know, at a glance, which program you're actually in. It also offers overall program commands like Quit and Hide.

Quitting Programs

You quit a program by pressing ⌘-Q, the keyboard equivalent of the Quit command. (The Quit command is always at the bottom of the Application menu.)

But macOS offers two much more fun ways to quit a program:

- **Right-click or two-finger click a program's Dock icon** to make its shortcut menu appear. Then choose Quit. (Or, if you do the *click-and-hold* thing on a program's Dock icon, a Quit button appears just above your cursor.)

- **When you've pressed ⌘-Tab** to summon the app switcher (read on), type the letter Q without releasing the ⌘ key. The highlighted program quits without further ado.

You can skip fussing with the Open command, remembering what you were doing, rearranging the windows the way you like them, and so on.

Then again, maybe you can't stand this feature.

Fortunately, it's easy to turn it off, either globally, on a per-program basis, or on a per-Quit basis:

- **Turn off auto-reopen for good.** Open System Preferences→General. Turn on "Close windows when quitting an app."

- **Prevent your current setup from being memorized.** You can also prevent just *one particular* program from reopening its documents the next time—at the time you're quitting it. To do that, press Option while you quit the program (for example, when you choose Safari→Quit or press ⌘-Q). The Quit command magically changes to Quit and Close All Windows. The next time you open the program, it will have forgotten all about your window setup.

 (On the other hand, if you've turned *off* the "Restore windows" feature in System Preferences, then pressing the Option key makes the Quit command say Quit and *Keep* Windows.)

- **Make a program forget its window setup as you reopen it.** If it's too late for the tip in the previous paragraph, you can force a program to start up in its empty,

POWER USERS' CLINIC

Shutting Down One Program's Window Memorizing

MacOS stashes information about your window setup in a "saved state" folder for each program. This data is in your Home→Library→Saved Application State folder.

The thing is, your Library folder is ordinarily invisible, which makes it a little tough to see the Saved Application State folder inside. Fortunately, you can jump directly to its contents by pressing Option as you choose Go→Library. Then open the Saved Application State folder within.

You get something like the window shown here: a folder for each program you use. You can delete one of these folders manually, but of course the Mac will recreate it the next time you run that program.

So if you want the Mac to stop memorizing a program's setup for good, find its Saved State folder. For Safari, for example, it's called *com.apple.Safari.savedState*.

Open the Saved State folder and empty it out; you've just made it forget the most recent settings. Now close the folder.

With the folder still highlighted, choose File→Get Info and, in the Get Info box, turn on the Locked checkbox. From now on, the Mac won't be able to record that program's window setup. (To undo your surgery later, you can just turn the Locked checkbox off again.)

CHAPTER 5: DOCUMENTS, PROGRAMS & MISSION CONTROL

figure out what category they both belong to—and names the new folder accordingly ("Music," "Photos," "Games," or whatever). This new name is only a proposal; an editing window also appears so that you can type a custom name you prefer.

A folder can hold several rows' worth of icons; if you add more apps than that, Launchpad adds additional "pages" that you scroll horizontally. (Little white dots indicate which page you're on.)

Take an app out of a folder by dragging its icon anywhere else on the screen. The other icons scoot aside to make room. If you remove all but one app from a folder, the folder disappears.

Move a folder around by dragging, as you would any other icon.

Deleting App Store Programs

If you've downloaded some apps from the App Store, you'll find a bonus feature here in Launchpad: They're especially fun to delete.

Start by holding the mouse down on any icon until, after about a second, all the icons begin to—what's the correct term?—*wiggle*. (If you have an iPhone, iPad, or iPod Touch, this should look familiar.)

Tip: You can also just press the Option key to trigger the wiggling. Sometimes, every second counts.

At this point, you may notice that some of them have sprouted little red ⊗'s. Those are the ones you downloaded from the App Store.

To delete an App Store program you don't need anymore, click that ⊗ to make it say bye-bye—instantly and for good. It doesn't even have a layover in the Trash.

Note: You can't delete non–App Store apps this way, so no ⊗ appears on those icons. Why not? Because this deletion method is so fast and permanent. It's not much of a risk for App Store apps, because you can always download them again—but that would not be true of other apps.

Windows That Auto-Reopen

For decades, opening a program on the Mac presented exactly the same thing every time: a blank screen, or maybe a welcome screen. It was up to you to specify what *document* you then wanted to work on.

Now, though, whatever documents were open when you last quit that program magically *reopen*, ready for you to get back to work. Everything is *exactly* as it was, including your window and palette positions. Incredibly, any text that was highlighted when you last quit the program is still highlighted, and the insertion point is just where you left it.

This is all handy if you tend to work on the same documents day after day; the auto-reopened document serves as a refresher on what you were in the middle of doing.

The little white dots are your map. Each represents one Launchpad screen. If the third one is "lit up," then you're on the third screen.

To move among the screens, press ⌘-arrow keys, or swipe horizontally with two fingers on the trackpad (Magic Mouse: one finger). Or tap directly on one of the little dots to jump to the corresponding screen.

Tip: To exit Launchpad without opening anything, click a blank spot, tap the Esc key, or—most fun of all—*spread* the same four fingers on the trackpad.

Redesigning the Launchpad Screens

If you use Launchpad a lot, it's worth taking a moment to arrange its icons into logical categories or a sensible sequence. As it turns out, you can freely drag them into new spots; the other icons scoot aside to make room.

Tip: You can even drag an icon directly to the Dock to install it there for quicker access.

You can create additional screens, too. To do that, drag an icon to the right edge of the screen; keep your mouse button down. The first screen slides off to the left, leaving you on a new, blank one where you can deposit the icon.

You can organize your icons on these Home pages by category, frequency of use, color, or whatever tickles your fancy.

Folders

The Launchpad just wouldn't be like the iPad if it didn't also let you organize your apps into *folders*. Folders let you organize your apps, de-emphasize the ones you don't use often, and restore order to that horribly flat, multipage display of icons.

To create a folder, drag one app's icon *on top of another*. MacOS puts both of them into a single new folder (Figure 5-4). If they're the same kind of app, it even tries to

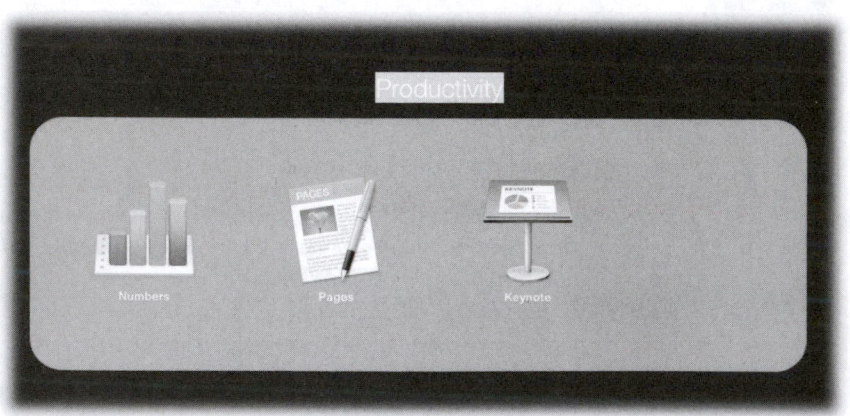

Figure 5-4:
Open a folder by clicking once, or by pressing ⌘-▼. A panel sprouts from the folder icon, revealing its contents; the rest of the screen goes away. Now you can drag the icons around inside it. You can also edit the folder's name (click it first).

Note: The only program icon that *doesn't* appear in Launchpad…is Launchpad's. That's a good thing. You wouldn't want to wind up in an infinite loop.

- **Search box.** This box at the top of the screen lets you pluck one needle from your haystack of apps, no matter what page it's on. You don't have to click there first—just start typing when Launchpad is before you. With each letter you type, Launchpad hides everything but the matching app icons.

- **Home-page dots.** As you install more and more programs, Launchpad makes room for them by creating additional screens. You can spread your new programs' icons across an unlimited number of launch screens.

UP TO SPEED

When Programs Are Actually Folders

MacOS programs don't seem to have 50,000 support files strewn across your hard drive. Most programs just sit there, naked and shivering, in your Applications folder—seemingly unaccompanied by libraries, dictionaries, foreign language components, and other support files and folders.

The question is: Where did all those support files go?

MacOS features *packages* or *bundles*, which are folders that behave like single files. Every properly written macOS program looks like a single, double-clickable application icon. Yet to the Mac, it's actually a folder that contains both the actual application icon and all its hidden support files. (Even documents can be packages, including iDVD project files, Keynote files, and some TextEdit documents.)

If you'd like to prove this to yourself, try this experiment: Choose Go→Applications. See the Calculator program? Right-click or two-finger click it. From the shortcut menu, choose Show Package Contents. You're asking macOS to show you what's inside the Calculator's "application icon" folder.

The Calculator package window opens, revealing a Contents folder you've never seen before. If you open this folder, you'll find a handful of strange-looking, Unix-named folders and files that are, behind the scenes, pieces of the Calculator program itself.

The application-as-folder trick is convenient for you, of course, because it means you're generally free to move the application to a different window—or to uninstall the program by dragging this single icon to the Trash—without worrying that you're leaving behind its entourage of support files. It's also convenient for programmers, because they can update certain aspects of their applications just by replacing one of these component files, without having to rewrite the entire program.

You can try out this programmery benefit for yourself. In the case of the Calculator and many other macOS programs, the Resources folder contains individual graphics files—PDF or TIFF files—that serve as the graphic elements you see when using the program. For example, the file lcd.tiff in the Calculator's Resources folder contains the image of the calculator's screen (where the numbers appear as you punch the calculator buttons).

Using a graphics program, you can change the background of this light-yellow calculator screen to, say, light blue. The next time you double-click Calculator—which you now realize is actually a folder behind the scenes—you'll see your modified calculator design.

(P.S. There are still hundreds or thousands of support files that aren't embedded within their programs' icons. They're sitting in your Library→Application Support folder, organized by software company.)

- **Press the Launchpad key.** Recent Macs have a special Launchpad icon painted right on the F4 key (⊞).

- **Click its icon on the Dock.** It's the one resembling a rocket (🚀).

- **Press a keyboard shortcut of your choice.** To set that up, choose System Preferences→Keyboard. Click the Shortcuts tab, and then click Launchpad & Dock in the left-side list. On the right, make sure Show Launchpad is turned on—and then double-click in the blank space to the right of it and press the key combination you want.

- **Move the cursor into one of the screen's four corners.** To set up these options, open System Preferences→Mission Control. Click Hot Corners to choose a corner of the screen for Launchpad.

- **Open it as you would any other program.** It's in your Applications folder.

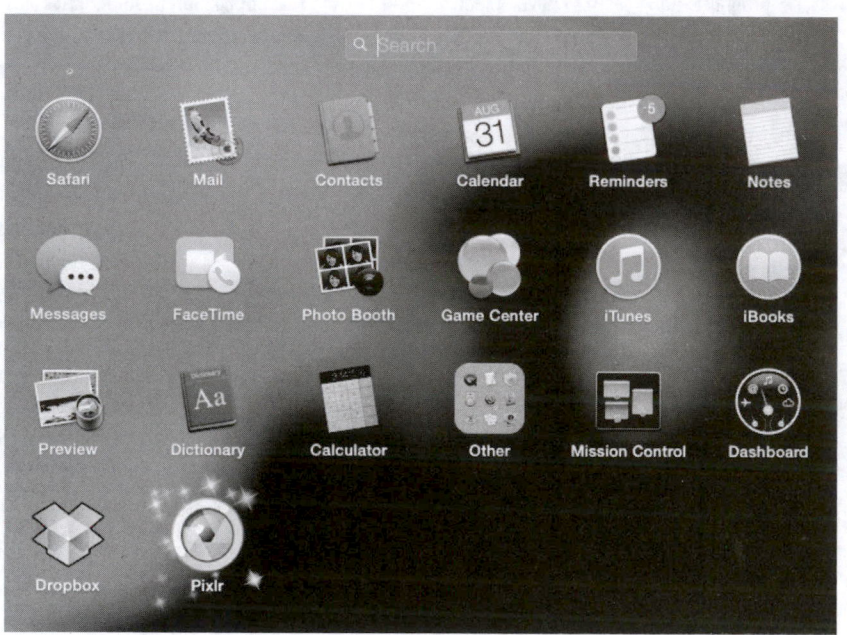

Figure 5-3:
You can open Launchpad by clicking its Dock icon or by using a four-finger pinching gesture on your trackpad. Launchpad covers your entire main monitor, hiding everything else.

Use the arrow keys to navigate a page; press ⌘-arrow to move between pages; press Option to make the icons start wiggling, ready for deletion.

One thing's for sure: Sooner or later, you'll wind up in Launchpad. Only three visual elements appear there:

- **Icons.** Each icon represents one of your programs. Apple's programs are listed first, in alphabetical order: App Store, Automator, Calculator, and so on. Then come all your other programs, again in A-to-Z order. Click one to open that program.

 Sparkly animated twinkles surround any new app you've installed. (You can see them at bottom in Figure 5-3.)

- Open a *document* icon in any of these ways, or drag a document onto the icon of a program that can open it (whether in the Dock, the Finder toolbar, the Sidebar, or a folder window).

Tip: If you press Option as you open an application (or anything else) in the Finder, you automatically close the window that contains its icon. Later, when you return to the Finder, you find a neat, clean desktop—no loitering windows.

Launchpad

The Launchpad app presents a dark background with evenly spaced icons that represent all your programs (Figure 5-3). You can open one with a single click.

Why did Apple feel the need to create yet *another* way to open programs?

First, because Launchpad fits right into a general Apple effort to make the Mac look and work more like the iPad. Launchpad is a dead ringer for the Home screens of an iPad, iPhone, or iPod Touch.

Second, it's a much less intimidating place for technophobes to learn to love than, say, the Applications folder.

And, third, it's a lot quicker to get to than the Applications folder. You can summon it instantly, using any of these methods:

- **Put four fingers on your trackpad and pinch them together.** The Launchpad appears instantly, no matter what program you were in; you don't have to duck back into the Finder, navigate to the Applications folder, and so on.

FREQUENTLY ASKED QUESTION

What's with the Big "Duh"?

So I double-click an Excel document, and the Mac asks me: "You are opening Microsoft Excel for the first time. Do you want to continue?" Well, HELLO! I double-clicked the icon, didn't I? Does Apple think I'm some kind of idiot?

It's not you Apple is worried about. It's the silent parade of evil hackers, lurking out there in Internet Land, waiting for the right moment to bring down the Mac.

See, spyware authors have to be sneaky about how they install their stuff on your computer. You wouldn't be so stupid as to double-click an application called Spyware Installer™, of course. So the spyware *tricks* you into running its installer. In the Windows world, it commandeers a

certain document type (like MP3 or JPEG), reassigning it to its installer. You innocently double-click some document, but an unanticipated program opens—and you've just opened Pandora's box.

In macOS, that can't happen. When you double-click some document that opens a program for the first time, this dialog box appears, just to let you know what's about to happen. If the program that's about to open isn't the one you were expecting, well, you've got a chance to back out of it.

And if it *is* the program you were expecting, click Continue. You won't be asked again about this version of this particular program.

The disk image icon, the one that contains the actual software or its installer (top right in Figure 5-2), is a phantom drive, held in memory, that will go away by itself when you log out. So after installing its software, feel free to drag it to the Trash (or select it and press ⌘-E to "eject" it).

Performing the installation

Once you've got a disk icon on your desktop—either a pseudo-disk from a disk image or a CD or DVD you've inserted—you're ready to install the software. You can install many macOS programs just by dragging their icons or folders to your hard drive (usually the Applications folder). Others offer a traditional installer program that requires you to double-click, read and accept a license agreement, and so on.

Uninstalling Software

If you got a program from the App Store, it's easy to delete from the Launchpad (page 170).

If you got it from some other source, well, there's generally no Uninstall program. To uninstall a program, you just drag it (or its folder) to the Trash.

Some programs leave harmless scraps of themselves behind; to check for them, look for preference files or folders bearing the dearly departed program's name in your Library folders (especially in Application Support) and in your Home→Library→Preferences folder.

Opening macOS Programs

You can launch (open) an application in any of several ways:

- **Single-click an icon on the Launchpad,** described on the following pages.

- **Single-click a program's icon on the Dock, the Sidebar, or the Finder toolbar.**

- **Use Spotlight.** Hit ⌘-space bar, type the first letters of the program's name, and then press Return.

- **Double-click an app's icon in the Finder.**

- **If you've added the Applications folder to your Dock,** then click the Dock icon to open the pop-up fan, grid, or list of icons. Then click the program you want (or even type the first few letters of its name and then press Return).

- **Select an application icon** and then press ⌘-O (short for File→Open) or ⌘-▼.

- **Use the submenus** of the menu's Recent Items→Applications command.

Tip: Once you've opened the Recent Items→Applications submenu, you can hold down the ⌘ key to witness a startling sight: All the program names (Preview, Photoshop, and so on) change to say "*Show* Preview in Finder," "*Show* Photoshop in Finder," and so on. The Recent Items command, in other words, now gives you a direct way to jump to the icon of a program you might want to open, huddling in Applications or whatever window it's in.

Disk images are common in macOS. All you have to do is double-click the .dmg icon. After a moment, it magically turns into a disk icon on your desktop, which you can work with just as though it were a real disk (top right in Figure 5-2). For example:

- **Double-click it to open it.** The software you downloaded is inside.

- **Remove it from your desktop** by dragging it to the Trash (whose icon turns into a big silver ⏏ key as you drag), selecting it and pressing ⌘-E (the shortcut for File→Eject), clicking its ⏏ button in the Sidebar, or right-clicking or two-finger clicking it and then choosing Eject from the shortcut menu.

You've still got the original .dmg file you downloaded, so you're not really saying goodbye to the disk image forever.

Figure 5-2:
A: This is the down-loaded compressed file. Double-click to get…

B: The .dmg (disk image) file. Double-click it to "mount" the disk image.

C: And now, the disk image itself. Double-click to open the installer window. (Dismiss the warning that the software came from the internet.) "Eject" it after the installation is complete.

D: Here's the actual installer.

After the installation, you can delete all this stuff (except maybe the .dmg file, if you think you might want to install the software again later).

When you've finished unzipping or unstuffing a downloaded file, you may have several icons on your desktop or in the Downloads folder. It's generally safe to throw them away—the .sit, .tar, .gz, or .tgz file you originally downloaded, for example, or the .dmg icon.

the ⌘→App Store command. The updates are small files, so they download quickly; the App Store delivers only the pieces that have actually changed.

Some details:

- **You can opt to have new versions of your programs** quietly and automatically downloaded and installed in the background, so you're never bugged about their arrival. (In App Store→Preferences, the Automatic Updates checkbox takes care of that.)

- **"Automatically download apps purchased on other Macs"** (also in Preferences) ensures that when you download an app on one Mac, it auto-downloads on all your other ones, too (assuming they're logged in with the same iCloud account). Handy, really.

One final advantage of the App Store concept: If you decide to use Launchpad, described starting on page 170, then anything you've bought from the App Store is easy to delete with a single click.

In general, the App Store works exactly like the iPhone/iPad App Store. Click a program's icon to open its details page. Here you'll find reviews and ratings from other people, a description, pictures (screenshots) of the program, and much more information to help you make a good buying decision. See Figure 5-1 for more details.

When you buy an app, Launchpad opens automatically, so you can see where it went.

Other Ways to Get Mac Software

In general, new programs arrive on your Mac via one of two avenues: as a download (whether from the App Store or not) or, rarely, on a CD or DVD.

Downloading Compressed Files

Programs you download from the web (not the App Store) generally arrive in a specially encoded, compressed form (Figure 5-2). And unless you've changed the settings, they arrive in the Downloads folder on your Dock.

The downloaded file's name usually has a file name extension like .zip (the standard compression file format for Windows and Mac files) or .dmg (a disk image file, described below).

Very rarely, you may run into .tar files (*tape archive*, an ancient Unix utility), .gz (*gzip*, a standard Unix compression format), or combo formats like .tar.gz or .tgz.

Fortunately, you generally don't have to worry about any of this; most web browsers, including Safari, automatically unzip and unstuff downloads of all types.

Disk images (.dmg files)
Once you've downloaded a program, it often takes the form of a disk image file, whose name ends with the letters .dmg (middle top in Figure 5-2).

warnings like "Please enter your password to install this software" or "This software appears to have been downloaded from the internet." Once you click Buy, the software downloads and installs itself *automatically*, without any interaction from you.

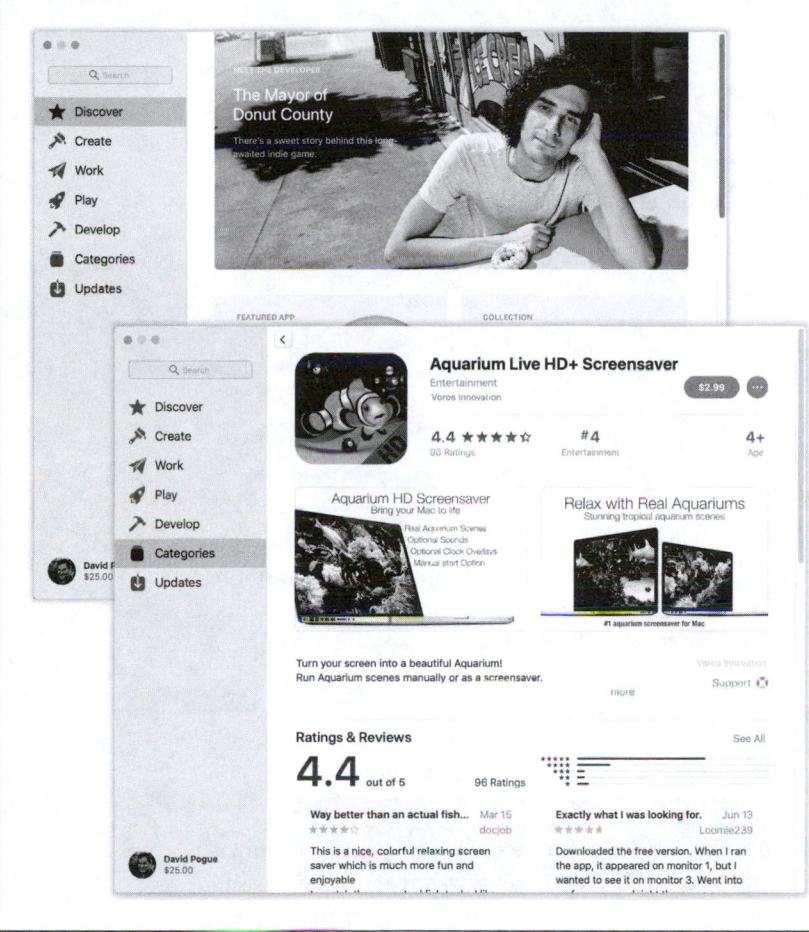

Figure 5-1:
Top: Mastering the App Store won't take you long; just about everything you need is in the sidebar, including a search box and buttons like Discover, Create, and Categories, which are meant to help you dive into the catalog of Mac software. Click the lower-left icon to see everything you've bought, for easy re-downloading. Updates is where you'll find new versions of your apps.

Bottom: You can read reviews of each piece of software, written by other people who've tried it.

And there are no discs to store and hunt down later. If you ever get a new Mac, or if you ever need to reinstall a program from the App Store, you just re-download it from the Purchases tab; the App Store remembers that you're a legitimate owner. Better yet, you'll be downloading the latest version of that program; you won't have to install all the ".01" patches that have come along since.

Tip: To hide an app you've bought so it no longer appears in Purchased, click ☺ and, from the menu, choose Hide Purchase. (To unhide it later, click "View Information" on the same page; under Hidden Items, click Manage.)

And speaking of updates: Since Apple knows what programs you have, it can let you know when new versions are available. And it does: A numbered badge appears next to

Documents, Programs & Mission Control

The whole point of owning a computer, of course, is to run *programs*—or, as Apple likes to call them, apps. This chapter covers Apple's Way of Running Programs, and all its Capitalized Elements: the Mac App Store, Launchpad, Mission Control, Full Screen, Auto Save, Versions, and more.

The Mac App Store

For years, people installed software onto their computers by buying disks: floppies, CDs, and, later, DVDs.

But starting with the iPhone, people installed software onto their phones by downloading it directly from the internet. Once everybody saw how convenient (and profitable) that system was, it didn't take Apple long to realize it could bring the same convenience to the Mac.

So now there's the Mac App Store, newly redesigned in Mojave—or, as the program is called in your Applications folder, just App Store (Figure 5-1). It's an online catalog of software from huge software companies, tiny one-person software companies, and everything in between. You can read about the programs, check out customer reviews, and download them directly to your Mac. (As you probably know, Mojave itself is an App Store download.)

There are some huge advantages to this system. Since there's no box, disc, registration card, shipping, or stocking, the software can cost a lot less; Apple's own programs certainly reflect this price advantage. Plenty of programs in the App Store are actually free.

Furthermore, Apple controls the transaction on both ends—it knows who you are—so there are no serial numbers to type in. The installation no longer interrupts you with

Here's what *doesn't* change in Dark Mode:

- **Your desktop picture.** Or any pictures at all, for that matter.

- **Web pages in Safari.**

- **Preexisting non-Apple apps.** Software companies have to update their programs if they want them to take on Dark Mode's dusky hues.

In general, you'd really have to stretch to say Dark Mode helps with your productivity. Mainly it's just cool-looking.

Note: If you're using one of the two dynamic wallpaper options (page 344), then turning on Dark Mode also jumps to the nighttime versions of those images.

Figure 4-10:
Some people argue that Dark Mode blasts less obnoxious light from the screen to your sleeping partner when you're working in bed. Others say Dark Mode makes photos stand out more, or that it's less fatiguing to your eyes.

Desktop Sounds

Desktop sounds are the tiny sound effects that accompany certain mouse drags. And we're talking tiny—they're so subdued that you might not have noticed them. You hear a little plink/crunch when you drop an icon onto the Trash, a boingy thud when you drag something into a folder, and so on. The little thud you hear at the end of a file-copying job is actually useful, because it alerts you that the task is complete.

If all that racket is keeping you awake, however, it's easy enough to turn it off. Open System Preferences, click the Sound icon, and then turn off "Play user interface sound effects."

And if you decide to leave them turned on, please—use discretion when working in a library, church, or neurosurgical operating room.

Designing Your Desktop

In some ways, just buying a Macintosh was already a renegade act of self-expression. But that's only the beginning. Now it's time to fashion the computer screen itself according to your personal sense of design and fashion.

Backgrounds and Screen Savers

Cosmetically speaking, macOS offers two dramatic full-screen features: desktop backgrounds and screen savers. For details, see page 344.

Accent Colors

For years, macOS has offered a choice of accent colors—used for scroll-bar handles, progress bars, OK buttons, highlighted menu names and commands, and so on.

Well, it wasn't a *huge* choice. You could choose either the standard blue or Graphite (gray). Graphite was intended to pacify Apple's core constituency: artists and graphic designers, some of whom complained that the lively, brightly colored look of the Mac threw off their color judgment.

In macOS Mojave, Graphite is only one of eight available accent colors. Choose System Preferences→General, and then choose from the "Accent color" dots.

While you're here, say hello to the "Highlight color" pop-up menu. This is an accent color, too—the background color of highlighted text, the colored oval that appears around highlighted icon names, and a window's "lining" as you drag an icon into it.

Dark Mode

The System Preferences panel just described (General) offers another option, too—one of the most arresting and radical design changes in Mac history. It's Dark Mode (Figure 4-10). You're also offered the chance to turn it on during the installation process.

Dark Mode is a dark-gray color scheme. Once you turn it on, most of Apple's built-in apps—Finder, Mail, Calendar, Photos, Messages, iTunes, Notes, Xcode, and so on—take on a stunning, white-on-black appearance.

FREQUENTLY ASKED QUESTION

Desktop Fonts

How do I change the fonts used by the macOS Finder?

In Mac versions gone by, you could choose any font you liked for your icon labels. You even had a choice of fonts for use in your menus.

Nowadays, that flexibility is gone. The font used by your menus and icon labels is a modified version of Helvetica

Neue called San Francisco—and you can love it or leave it.

For now, Apple intends to remain conservative with the look of macOS—both for "branding" reasons (to make macOS instantly recognizable) and for technical ones (to make sure it doesn't open a Pandora's box of interface hacks that wind up destabilizing the machine).

• **Quick Look.** Triggers a preview of the icon (page 58).

If the window ever gets too narrow to show all the icons you've added to the toolbar, the right end of the toolbar sprouts a **»** symbol. Click it for a pop-up menu that names whichever icons don't fit at the moment. (You'll find this toolbar behavior in many macOS programs, not just the Finder: Safari, Mail, and so on.)

Adding your own stuff

Millions of Mac fans never realize that they can drag *any icons at all* onto the toolbar—files, folders, disks, programs, or whatever—to turn them into one-click buttons.

In short, you can think of the Finder toolbar as yet another Dock or Sidebar (Figure 4-9).

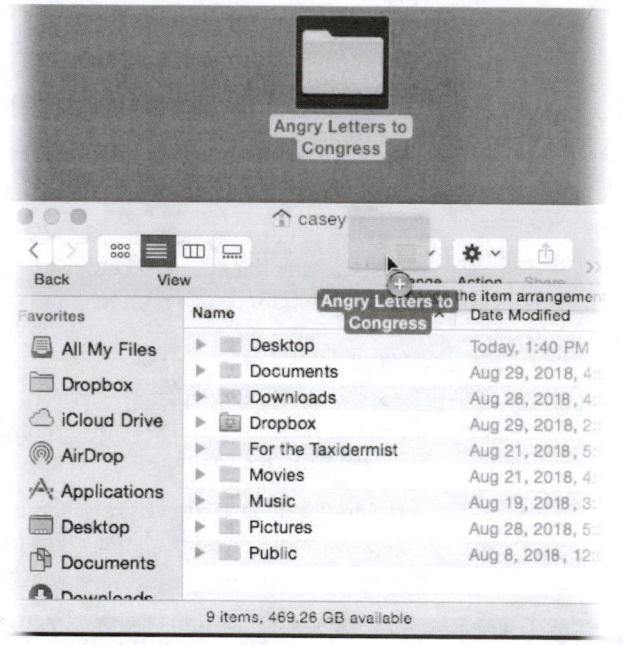

Figure 4-9:
You don't need to choose View→Customize Toolbar to add your own icons to the toolbar. Just hold down the ⌘ and Option keys, and then drag an icon from the desktop or any folder window directly onto the toolbar at any time.

To remove the icon later, press ⌘ as you drag it away from the toolbar.

Rearranging or Removing Toolbar Icons

You can drag toolbar icons around, rearranging them horizontally, by pressing ⌘ as you drag. Taking an icon off the toolbar is equally easy. While pressing the ⌘ key, just drag the icon clear away from the toolbar. (If the Customize Toolbar sheet is open, you can perform either step without the ⌘ key. You can also get rid of a toolbar icon by right-clicking or two-finger clicking it and choosing Remove Item from the shortcut menu.)

This is your chance to rearrange the existing toolbar icons or delete the ones you don't use. You can also add any of Apple's buttons to the toolbar by dragging them from the "gallery" onto the toolbar itself. The existing icons scoot out of your cursor's way, if necessary.

Most of the options in the gallery duplicate the functions of menu commands. Here are a few that don't appear on the standard toolbar:

- **Path.** Most of the gallery elements are buttons, but this one creates a pop-up menu on the toolbar. When clicked, it reveals (and lets you navigate) the hierarchy—the path—of folders you open to reach whichever window is open. (Equivalent: ⌘-clicking a window's title.)

- **Eject.** This button ejects whichever disk or disk image is currently highlighted. (Equivalent: the File→Eject command, or holding down the ⏏ key, if you have it on your keyboard.)

- **Burn.** This button burns a blank CD or DVD with the folders and files you've dragged onto it. (Equivalent: the File→Burn [Thing Name] to Disc command.)

- **Space.** By dragging this mysterious-looking item into the toolbar, you add a gap between it and whatever icon is to its left. The gap is about as wide as one icon. (The fine, dark, rectangular outline that appears when you drag it doesn't actually show up once you click Done.)

- **Flexible Space.** This icon, too, creates a gap between the toolbar buttons. But this one expands as you make the window wider. Now you know how Apple got the search box to appear off to the right of the standard toolbar, a long way from its clustered comrades to the left.

- **New Folder.** Clicking this button creates a new folder in whichever window you're viewing. (Equivalent: the File→New Folder command, or the Shift-⌘-N keystroke.)

- **Delete.** This option puts the highlighted file or folder icons into the Trash. (Equivalent: the File→Move to Trash command, or the ⌘-Delete keystroke.)

Tip: Weirdly enough, if you highlight an icon in the Trash and then press ⌘-Delete, you trigger the Put Back function—flinging the icon back into the folder it came from (and opening that folder to show you). That is, using the ⌘-Delete keystroke in this case actually *un*deletes.

- **Connect.** If you're on a home or office network, this opens the Connect to Server dialog box so you can tap into another computer. (Equivalent: the Go→Connect to Server command, or ⌘-K.)

- **Get Info.** This button opens the Get Info window for whatever's selected.

- **Drag the default set.** If you've made a mess of your toolbar, you can always reinstate its original Apple arrangement by dragging this rectangular strip directly upward onto your toolbar.

Hiding or Shrinking the Toolbar

With the toolbar, the Dock, the Sidebar, and the large icons of macOS, it almost seems like there's an Apple conspiracy to sell big screens.

Fortunately, the toolbar doesn't have to contribute to that impression. You can hide it by choosing View→Hide Toolbar or by pressing Option-⌘-T. (That will work only if you don't have multiple tabs in that Finder window.) That same keystroke, or choosing View→Show Toolbar, brings it back. You can also just make it smaller by hiding the labels (or the icons), as shown in Figure 4-7.

Customizing the Icons on the Toolbar

MacOS offers a collection of beautifully designed icons for alternate (or additional) toolbar buttons. But you can also add anything to the toolbar, turning it into a supplementary Dock or Sidebar. This is great news for people who've run out of space for stashing favorite icons in the Dock or the Sidebar. (Of course, if that's your problem, you need a bigger monitor.)

Apple's toolbar-icon collection

The first step in tweaking the toolbar is choosing View→Customize Toolbar. The window shown in Figure 4-8 appears.

Figure 4-8:
While this window is open, you can add icons to the toolbar by dragging them into place from the gallery before you. You can also remove icons from the toolbar by dragging them up or down off the toolbar. Rearrange the icons by dragging them horizontally.

The Back button (<) returns you to whichever folder you were just looking at. (Instead of clicking <, you can also press ⌘-[, or choose Go→Back—particularly handy if the toolbar is *hidden*, as described in the next section.)

The Forward button (>) springs to life only after you've used the Back button. Clicking it (or pressing ⌘-]) returns you to the window you just backed out of.

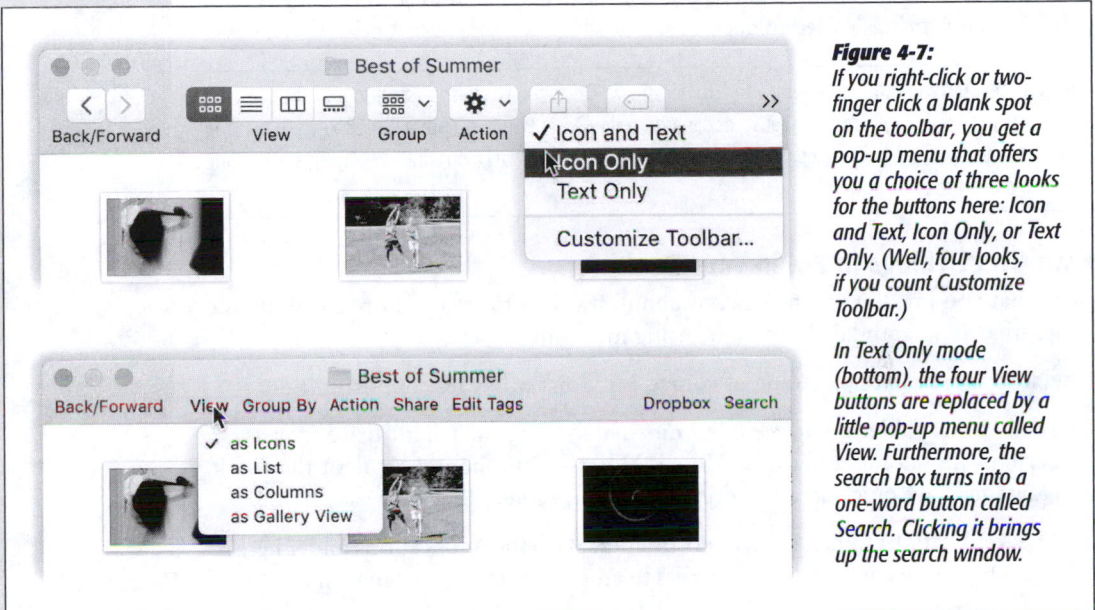

Figure 4-7:
If you right-click or two-finger click a blank spot on the toolbar, you get a pop-up menu that offers you a choice of three looks for the buttons here: Icon and Text, Icon Only, or Text Only. (Well, four looks, if you count Customize Toolbar.)

In Text Only mode (bottom), the four View buttons are replaced by a little pop-up menu called View. Furthermore, the search box turns into a one-word button called Search. Clicking it brings up the search window.

- **View controls.** The four tiny View buttons switch the current window into icon, list, column, or gallery view, respectively. And, remember, if the toolbar is hidden, you can get by with the equivalent commands in the View menu at the top of the screen—or by pressing ⌘-1 for icon view, ⌘-2 for list view, ⌘-3 for column view, or ⌘-4 for gallery view.

- **Group (▦).** This pop-up menu lets you group the files in a window by date, name, or other criteria; see page 41.

- **Action (✿).** You can read about this context-sensitive pop-up menu on page 103.

- **Share (⬆).** You can read about this context-sensitive pop-up menu on page 263.

- **Tags (◁).** Here's the Tags menu described on page 92.

- **Search box.** This little round-ended text box is yet another entry point for the Spotlight feature described in Chapter 3. It's a handy way to search your Mac for some file, folder, disk, or program.

Better yet, they're easily accessible for putting away files; you can drag files directly into the Dock's folder icons as though they were regular folders.

In fact, you can even drag a file into a subfolder in a Dock folder. That's because, again, Dock folders are spring-loaded. When you drag an icon onto a Dock folder and pause, the folder's window appears around your cursor, so you can continue the drag into an inner folder (and even an *inner* inner folder, and so on). Page 87 has the details on spring-loaded folders.

Tip: When you try to drag something into a folder on the Dock, the Dock icons scoot out of the way; the Dock assumes you're trying to put that something *onto* the Dock. But if you press the ⌘ key as you drag an icon to the Dock, the existing icons freeze in place. Without the ⌘ key, you wind up playing a frustrating game of chase-the-folder.

Find Great Things to Put in Your Dock

Now that you know what the Dock is about, it's time to set up shop, installing the programs, folders, and disks you'll be using most often.

They can be whatever you want, of course, but don't miss these opportunities:

- **Your Home folder.** Many people immediately drag their hard drive icons—or, perhaps more practically, their Home folders—onto the right side of the Dock. Now they have quick access to every file in every folder they ever use.

- **The Applications folder.** Here's a no-brainer: Stash the Applications folder here so you'll have quick pop-up-menu access to any program on your machine.

- *Your* **Applications folder.** As an even more efficient corollary, create a new folder of your own. Fill it with the aliases of just the programs you use most often and park it in the Dock. Now you've got an even more useful Applications folder that opens as a stack.

- **The Shared folder.** If you're using the Mac's accounts feature (Chapter 12), this is your wormhole to all the accounts—the one place you can put files where everybody can access them (page 549).

- **A tag.** You know those color-coded Finder tags (page 92)? You can drag one directly out of a Finder window's Sidebar and onto the right side of the Dock. When you click its Dock icon, you get a window that displays the icons of everything on your Mac you've tagged that way.

The Finder Toolbar

At the top of every Finder window is a small set of function icons, all in a gradient-gray row (Figure 4-7). The first time you run macOS, you'll find only these icons on the toolbar:

- **Back (<), Forward (>).** The Finder works something like a web browser. Only a single window remains open as you navigate the various folders on your hard drive.

System Preferences icon sprouts a complete list of the preference panes (Sound, Keyboard, Trackpad, and so on). You get the idea.

> **Tip:** If you Control-⌘-click a program's Dock icon, you get an abbreviated shortcut menu. It lists *only* the Options, Hide, and Quit commands and maybe some recent documents—not the full list of commands. If all you want to do is quit a program or something, this abbreviated menu is faster and easier to comprehend.

Conduct Speed Tests

When you click an application icon in the Dock, its icon jumps up and down a few times as the program launches, as though with excitement at having been selected. The longer a program takes to start up, the more bounces you see. This has given birth to a hilarious phenomenon: counting these bounces as a casual speed benchmark for application-launching times. "InDesign took twelve bouncemarks to open in Mac OS X 10.10," you might read online, "but only three bouncemarks in 10.12."

> **Tip:** If you find the icon-bouncing a bit over the top, try this: Choose System Preferences→Dock. Turn off "Animate opening applications." From now on, your icons won't actually bounce—instead, the little dot underneath it will simply *pulse* as the application opens.

Drag and Drop

Dock icons are spring-loaded. That is, if you drag any icon onto a Dock folder or disk icon and pause—or, if you're in a hurry, tap the space bar—the Dock icon opens to receive the dragged file.

> **Note:** It opens, that is, *if* the spring-loading delay feature is turned on in System Preferences→Accessibility→Mouse & Trackpad.

This technique is most useful in these situations:

- **Drag a document icon onto a Dock folder icon.** The folder's Finder window pops open so you can continue the drag into a subfolder.

- **Drag a document into an application.** The classic example is dragging a photo onto the Photos icon. When you tap the space bar, Photos opens automatically. Since your mouse button is still down, and you're technically still in mid-drag, you can now drop the photo directly into the appropriate Photos album or Event.

 You can drag an MP3 file into iTunes or an attachment into Mail or Outlook in the same way.

Do Your Filing

Once you've tried stashing a few important folders on the right side of your Dock, you'll never look back. You can mostly forget all the other navigation tricks you've learned in macOS. The folders you care about are always there, ready for opening with a single click.

Note: Once you've hidden a program's windows, this command changes to say Show, which is how you make them reappear.

- **Quit.** You can quit almost any program directly from its Dock shortcut menu. (Finder, Launchpad, and Mission Control are exceptions.) The beauty of this feature is that you don't have to switch into a program to get to its Quit command.

 (If you get nothing but a beep when you use this Quit command, it's because you've hidden the windows of that program, and one of them has unsaved changes. Click the program's icon, save your document, and then try to quit again.)

Tip: If you hold down the Option key—even after you've opened the pop-up menu—the Quit command changes to say Force Quit. That's your emergency hatch for jettisoning a locked-up program.

- **Miscellaneous.** You might find other commands in Dock shortcut menus; software companies are free to add specialty options to their own programs.

 For example, the Finder icon's shortcut menu offers direct access to commands like Find, Connect to Server, and New Finder Window. Microsoft Office programs (Word, Excel, and so on) come with an Open Recent command, with a list of documents you've opened recently. The Mail icon offers Get New Mail and Compose New Message commands. The Safari icon has a New Window command. The

GEM IN THE ROUGH

Using the Dock or Sidebar for Drag-and-Drop

The Mac is smart about the relationship between documents and applications. If you double-click a TextEdit document icon, for example, TextEdit opens automatically and shows you the document.

But it's occasionally useful to open a document using a program other than the one that created it. Perhaps, as is often the case with downloaded internet graphics, you don't *have* the program that created it, or you don't know which one was used. This technique is also useful if you want to open a ReadMe file into your word processor, such as Word, instead of the usual TextEdit program.

In such cases, the Dock is handy: Just drag the mystery document onto one of the Dock's tiles, as shown here. Doing so forces the program to open the document—if it

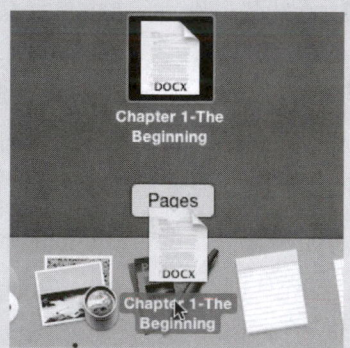

can. (Dragging onto a program's icon in the Sidebar or even the Finder toolbar works just as well.)

Incidentally, in general only the Dock icons of programs that can, in fact, open the file you're dragging become highlighted. The others just shrug indifferently or even scoot aside, thinking you're trying to drag the file into the Dock.

Pressing Option-⌘ as you drag forces Dock icons to be more tolerant. Now all of them "light up" as your document touches them, indicating that they'll *try* to open your file. Even so, a "could not be opened" error message may result.

As they say in Cupertino, sometimes what a can really needs is a can opener.

As soon as you quit the program, its icon disappears again from the Dock.

Tip: You can get rid of that "running program" indicator dot, if you like. Open System Preferences→Dock and turn off "Show indicators for open applications."

If you understand that much, then the Keep in Dock command makes a lot of sense. It means, "Hello, I'm this program's icon. I know you don't normally keep me in your Dock, but I *could* stay here even after you quit my program. Just say the word." If you find you've been using, for example, Terminal a lot more often than you thought you would, then this command may be the ticket.

Tip: Actually, there's a faster way to tell a running application to remain in the Dock from now on. Just drag its icon off the Dock and then right back onto it—yes, while the program is running. You have to try it to believe it.

If you don't want a program's icon to appear in the Dock when it's not running, then choose this command again so the checkmark disappears.

Note: If the program is already running, turning off Keep in Dock doesn't *immediately* remove its icon from the Dock. That's because a program always appears in the Dock when it's open. What you're doing here is saying, "Disappear from the Dock when you're *not* running"—and you'll see the proof as soon as you quit that program.

Options→Open at Login. This command lets you specify that you want this icon to open itself automatically each time you log into your account. It's a great way to make sure your email inbox, your calendar, or the Microsoft Word thesis you've been working on is fired up and waiting on the screen when you sit down to work.

To make this item *stop* auto-opening, choose this command again so the checkmark no longer appears.

Options→Show in Finder. This command highlights the actual icon (in whatever folder window it happens to sit) of the application, alias, folder, or document you've clicked. You might want to do this when, for example, you're using a program that you can't quite figure out, and you want to jump to its desktop folder in hopes of finding a ReadMe file there.

- **Hide/Show.** You can hide all traces of the program you're using by choosing Hide from its Dock icon. (You could accomplish the same thing in many other ways, of course; see page 23.)

What's cool here is that (a) you can even hide the Finder and all *its* windows, and (b) if you press Option, the command changes to say Hide Others. This, in its way, is a much more powerful command. It tells all the programs you're *not* using—the ones in the background—to get out of your face. They hide themselves instantly.

useful feature means you can jump directly not only to a certain program but also to a certain open window in that program.

For example, suppose you've been using Word to edit three different chapters. You can use Word's Dock icon as a Window menu to pull forward one particular chapter, or (if it's been minimized) to pull it up—even if a different program is in front of Word. (The checkmark indicates the *frontmost* window, even if the entire program is in the background. A diamond symbol means that the window is minimized and therefore not visible on the screen at the moment.)

In certain Apple showcase programs like TextEdit and the iWork programs, there are actually two lists of documents, separated by a horizontal line. (You can see the effect in Figure 4-6.) The top group lists files you've recently opened in that program; the next batch lists currently open documents.

Tip: The Finder tile that's always at the beginning of the Dock is, in effect, its own Window menu. Its shortcut menu lists all open desktop windows. The Window menu at the top of the Finder screen does the same thing, but the Dock is available no matter what program you're using.

Figure 4-6:
Left: Right-click or two-finger click a Dock icon to open the secret menu. In certain recent Apple programs, the top half of the menu lists recently opened documents, followed by currently open ones.

Right: Right-click or two-finger click the divider bar to open a different hidden menu. This one lists a bunch of useful Dock commands.

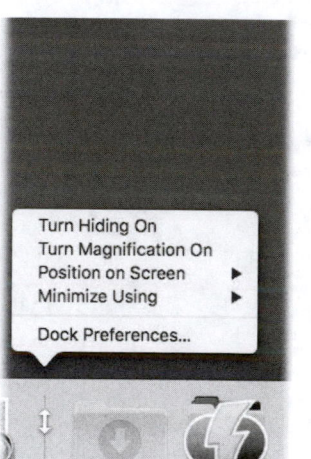

- **Show All Windows/Show Recents.** When a program on the Dock is open, this command says Show All Windows; when it's not running, it says Show Recents. Either way, it takes you to a screen where the icons of recently opened documents appear for easy clicking and reopening. (OK, they *may* appear. Only some apps, including TextEdit and Pages, show these recent icons.) To exit the screen, press Esc or click an empty spot on your desktop.

- **Options.** This submenu contains a bunch of miscellaneous commands:

 Options→Keep in Dock. Whenever you open a program, macOS puts its icon in the Dock—marked with a dot—even if you don't normally keep its icon there.

Using the Dock

Most of the time, you'll use the Dock as either a launcher (you click an icon once to open the corresponding program, file, folder, or disk) or as a status indicator (the tiny spots identified in Figure 4-1 indicate which programs are running).

But the Dock has more tricks than that up its sleeve. You can use it, for example, to pull off any of the following stunts.

Switch Applications

The Dock isn't just a launcher; it's also a switcher. Here are some of the tricks it lets you do:

- **Jump among your open programs** by clicking their icons.

- **Drag a document** (such as a text file) onto a Dock application (such as the Microsoft Word icon) to open the former with the latter. (If the program balks at opening the document, yet you're sure the program should be able to open it, then add the ⌘ and Option keys as you drag.)

- **Hide all windows of the program you're in** by Option-clicking another Dock icon.

- **Hide all other programs' windows** by Option-⌘-clicking the Dock icon of the program you do want (even if it's already in front).

- **Switch windows in one program** by pointing to that program's Dock icon without clicking and then doing a three-finger downward swipe on your trackpad. (This feature, called App Exposé, doesn't work until you turn it on in System Preferences→Trackpad→More Gestures.)

Tip: This trick—the three-finger downswipe—works even on the Dock icons of Apple programs that aren't running. In those situations, you get the effect shown on page 197. For some Apple programs, at least, it's a quick way to get to the icons of recently opened documents.

Operate the Dock by Keyboard Control

If you turn on keyboard navigation, you can operate the Dock entirely from the keyboard; see page 206.

Find Secret Menus

If you right-click, two-finger click, or click-and-hold on a Dock icon, you see its very useful shortcut menu (Figure 4-6).

If you've clicked a minimized window icon, this shortcut menu says only Open (and possibly also Close).

But if you've clicked any other kind of icon, you get some very useful hidden commands. For example:

- **[Window names].** The secret Dock menu of a running program usually lists one or more tiny, neatly labeled window icons, like those shown in Figure 4-6. This

There's a much faster way to resize the Dock, though: Just position your cursor carefully on the Dock's divider line so that it turns into a double-headed arrow (shown in Figure 4-5). Now drag up or down to enlarge or shrink the Dock.

Tip: If you press Option as you drag, the Dock snaps to certain canned icon sizes—those that the programmer actually drew. (You won't see the in-between sizes that macOS generally calculates on the fly.)

Figure 4-5:
Look closely—you can see the secret cursor that resizes the Dock. If you don't see any change in the Dock size as you drag upward, then you've reached the size limit.

You may not be able to enlarge the Dock if it's already at its size limit. But you can make it almost infinitely smaller. This may make you wonder: How can you distinguish among icons if they're the size of molecules?

The answer lies in the Magnification option (see Figure 4-4). Now your Dock icons balloon to a much larger size as your cursor passes over them.

Tip: You can get Dock magnification à la carte, too. If you press Shift-Control as your cursor approaches the Dock, you temporarily reverse the magnification setting. That is, if magnification is turned off, the icons now swell into magnification mode—and vice versa.

Moving the Dock to the sides of the screen

Yet another approach to getting the Dock out of your way is to rotate it, so that it sits vertically against a side of your screen. You can rotate it in either of two ways:

- **The long way.** Choose System Preferences→Dock, and choose Left, Bottom, or Right, as you see fit.

- **The mouse way.** While pressing Shift, drag the Dock's divider line, like a handle, to the side of the screen you want.

You'll probably find that the right side of your screen works better than the left. Most macOS programs put their document windows against the left edge of the screen, where the Dock and its labels might get in the way.

Note: When you position your Dock vertically, the "right" side of the Dock becomes the bottom of the Dock. In other words, the Trash now appears at the bottom of the vertical Dock. So, in this book, mentally substitute the phrase "bottom part of the Dock" when you read references to the "right side of the Dock."

Three Ways to Get the Dock Out of Your Hair

The bottom of the screen isn't necessarily the ideal location for the Dock. All Mac screens are wider than they are tall, so the Dock eats into your limited vertical screen space. You have three ways out: Hide the Dock, shrink it, or rotate it 90 degrees.

Auto-hiding the Dock

To turn on the Dock's auto-hiding feature, press Option-⌘-D. (Or, if it's a slow day at work, choose System Preferences→Dock→"Automatically hide and show the Dock.")

When the Dock is hidden, it appears only when you move your cursor to the Dock's edge of the screen. (Individual Dock icons may still occasionally shoot upward into desktop territory when an app needs attention—cute, very cute.)

In practice, you may prefer to hide and show the Dock at will by pressing the hide/show keystroke, Option-⌘-D. This method makes the Dock pop on and off the screen without requiring you to move the cursor.

Shrinking and enlarging the Dock

Depending on your screen's size, you may prefer smaller or larger Dock buttons. The official way to resize them is shown in Figure 4-4.

Figure 4-4:
To make your Dock icons bigger or smaller, choose System Preferences→Dock, and experiment with the Size slider.

Tip: Figure 4-3 shows you how to open a folder in a grid using the mouse—but you can do it all from the keyboard, too. Once a folder is selected, press Return, ⌘-O, or ⌘-▼ to see what's inside it; press ⌘-▲ to backtrack to the original display. When a folder is highlighted, you can press ⌘-Return to open it in a Finder window; add the Option key to open that Finder window without closing the grid or list.

Figure 4-3:
If you spot a folder inside a grid (left), click it once. You're now looking at a grid of its contents (right). You can go on burrowing like this as deeply as your folders go. You can also "back out" again by clicking the Back button (<) in the upper-left corner.

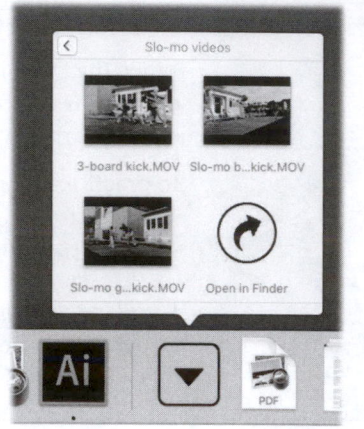

- **Type-selecting.** Once a list, fan, or grid is on the screen, you can highlight any icon in it by typing the first few letters of its name. For example, once you've popped open your Applications folder, you can highlight Safari by typing *sa*. (Press Return to open the highlighted icon.)

Tip: Alternatively, you can "walk" through the fan, grid, or list by pressing the arrow keys. A highlighting effect makes it crystal clear which icon you're selecting. Once an icon is selected, press Return to open it.

- **Two ways to bypass the pop-up.** If you just want to see what's in a folder, without all the graphic overkill of the fan or the grid, then right-click or two-finger click the Dock folder's icon and choose the first command—Open "Applications" (or whatever the folder's name is)—from the shortcut menu. You go straight to the corresponding window.

 Actually, if you *really* value your time, you'll learn the shortcut: Option-⌘-click the Dock folder's icon. That accomplishes the same thing.

Tip: Alternatively, you can ⌘-click a folder on the Dock—or, indeed, any icon on the Dock—to jump to the window that contains that folder's icon. (Bonus: This same ⌘-clicking trick also works in the list of Spotlight search results.)

Tip: The list view also displays a little ▶ to the right of each folder within the Dock folder. That is, it's a hierarchical list, meaning you can burrow into folders within folders, all from the original Dock icon, and all without opening a single new window. You can stick your entire Home folder, or even your whole hard drive icon, onto the Dock; now you have complete menu access to everything inside, right from the Dock.

- **Automatic.** There's a fourth option in the shortcut menu for a Dock folder, too: Automatic. If you turn this on, then macOS chooses either fan or grid view, depending on how many icons are in the folder.

So how do you choose which display you want? Right-click or two-finger click the Dock folder's icon, and make a selection from the shortcut menu. Each disk or folder icon remembers its own fan/grid/list setting.

The Finer Points of Pop-Up Dock Folders

Those were the basics of pop-up Dock folders. Here's the advanced course:

- **Ever-Changing Folder-Icon Syndrome (ECFIS).** When you add a folder or disk icon to the Dock, you might notice something disorienting: Its icon keeps changing to resemble whatever you most recently put into it. Your Downloads folder might look like an Excel spreadsheet icon today, a PDF icon tonight, and a photo icon tomorrow—but never a folder. You can't get to know a folder by its icon.

 Fortunately, this problem is easy to fix. Right-click or two-finger click the Dock folder. From the shortcut menu, in the "Display as" section, choose either Folder (which looks like a folder forever) or Stack (which changes to reflect its contents).

- **Ready-made pop-up folders.** When you install macOS, you get a couple of starter Dock folders, just to get you psyched. One is Downloads; the other is Documents. (Both of these folders are physically inside your Home folder. But you may well do most of your interacting with them on the Dock.)

 The Downloads folder collects all kinds of online arrivals: files you download from the web using Safari, files you receive in a Messages file-transfer session, file attachments you get via Mail, files sent to you using AirDrop (Chapter 13), and so on. Unless you intervene, they're sorted by the date you downloaded them.

 It's handy to know where to find your downloads—and nice not to have them all cluttering your desktop.

Tip: Once you've opened a stack's fan or grid, you can drag any of the icons right out of the fan or grid. Just drag your chosen icon onto the desktop or into any visible disk or folder. In other words, what lands in the Downloads folder doesn't have to stay there. (You can't drag out of a list, however.)

- **Hierarchical folders.** The lists and grids are hierarchical—that is, you can drill down from their folders into their folders. Figure 4-3 makes this concept clearer.

Fan vs. grid vs. list

When you click a disk or folder icon on the Dock, what happens? You see its contents, arrayed in your choice of four displays:

- **Fan.** The fan is a single, gently curved column of icons. It's ideal for folders that contain very few icons, because there's room for only a handful of items in a fan (the exact number depends on your screen size). After the first few, you see only a "31 More in Finder" button, which you can click to see everything in that folder—but now you've wasted time, not saved it.

Note: When your Dock is positioned on a side of the screen instead of the bottom, the fan option isn't available.

- **Grid.** If you've set a folder to open as a grid, you get to see all the icons in a big rectangular window. File names often get abbreviated because there's not enough horizontal room, but you get to see many more icons this way. Actually, thanks to the scroll bar, you get to see all the icons this way.

Tip: A cool highlighting effect is available that makes it easier to see which icon you're pointing to as you move your mouse around in a grid or a fan. To make it appear, click-and-hold a folder on the Dock—and then, without releasing the mouse, slide onto the grid or fan. The highlighting follows your cursor.

Alternatively, as soon as the grid or fan appears, press the arrow keys on your keyboard to move from icon to icon—complete with ghostly selection square.

- **List.** You can also opt for a simple list of the folder's contents, like a pop-up menu; you actually see little icons for the files and folders within. The list appears much faster than a fan or a grid does.

There's no scroll bar, but you can scroll the list nonetheless just by pointing to the top or bottom of it with your mouse.

GEM IN THE ROUGH

Living Icons

The Mac brought to life a terrific idea, later adopted by other mainstream operating systems: icons that *tell* you something. If the Dock is big enough, you can often tell documents apart just by looking at their icons.

Some program icons even change over time. The Mail icon, for example (Chapter 17), bears a live counter that indicates how many new email messages are waiting for you. (After all, why should you switch into the Mail program only to be disappointed?) The Messages icon lets you know how many chat responses are waiting. You can make your Activity Monitor graph show up right on its icon. Toast illustrates the progress of a disc you're burning.

Think of the possibilities. One day the Safari icon could change to let you know when interesting new web pages have appeared, the Quicken icon could display your current bank balance, and the Microsoft Word icon could change every time Microsoft posts a bug fix.

In principle, of course, pop-up folders are a great idea, because they save you time and clicking. Click a folder to see what's in it; click the icon you want inside; and you're off and running, without having had to open, manage, and close a window. (It's such a great idea, in fact, that it's now available on the desktop, too; see page 76.)

Anyway, here's how to operate pop-up Dock folders.

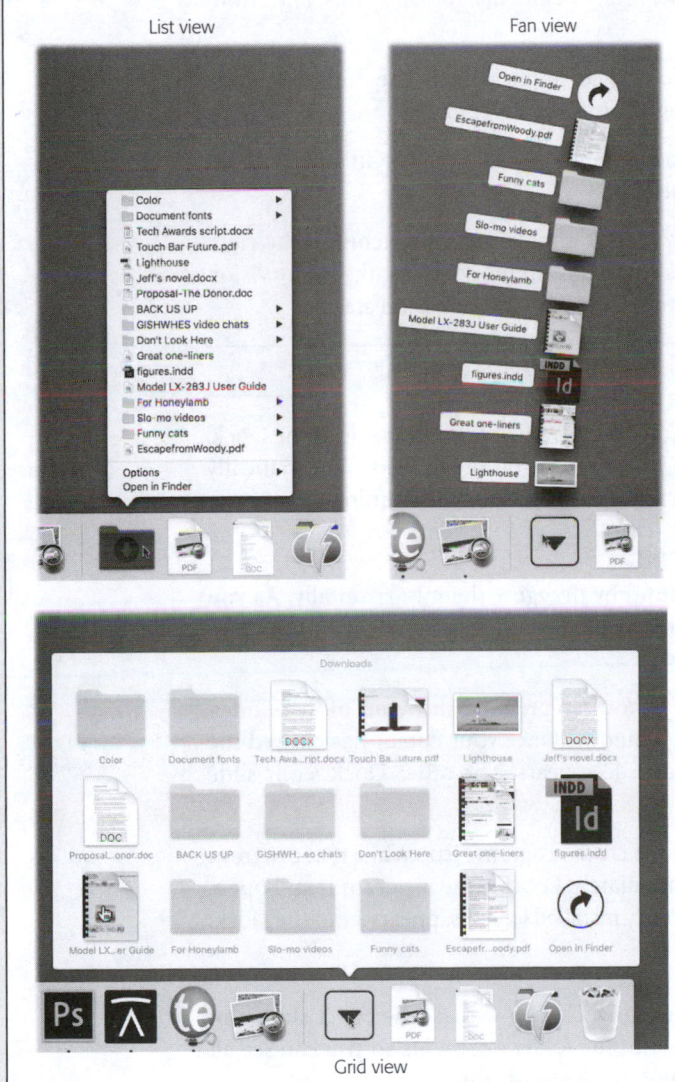

List view

Fan view

Grid view

Figure 4-2:
What happens when you click a folder in the Dock? You see its contents in one of three views. Here's how you choose the file you're looking for in each:

Top left: In list view, the folder contents appear as a pop-up menu; you can "drill down" into subfolders, and you can open something by choosing its name.

Top right: In fan view, click an icon to open it.

Bottom: In grid view, many more icons appear than can fit in fan view.

In any of the views, you can get a quick look at a document's contents by using Quick Look. That is, highlight the icon (point without clicking, or use the keyboard to select it), and then press the space bar. A window sprouts, showing the actual document contents.

apps you've most recently used. (If one of those apps is already represented on the Dock, it doesn't appear here.)

Note: In System Preferences→Dock, you can turn off "Show recent applications in Dock" (the middle section), making more room for other Dock icons.

Everything else goes on the right side: files, documents, folders, disks, and minimized windows.

Remember this division. If you try to drag an application to the middle or right sections, for example, the Mac teasingly refuses to accept it.

- **Its icon names are hidden.** To see the name of a Dock icon, point to it without clicking. The name appears above the icon.

- **Folders and disks sprout** *stacks.* If you click a folder or a disk icon on the right side of the Dock, a list of its contents sprouts from the icon. It's like X-ray vision without the awkward moral implications. Read on for details on stacks.

Tip: If you press Shift as you click, the stack opens in slow motion. Amaze your friends.

- **Programs appear there unsolicited.** You can put stuff on the *right* side of the Dock, but not the left or middle. Program icons appear on the left side automatically whenever you open one, and stay there for as long as they're running.

Organizing and Removing Dock Icons

You can move the tiles of the Dock around by dragging them horizontally. As you drag, the other icons scoot aside to make room. When you're satisfied with its new position, drop the icon you've just dragged.

To remove a Dock icon, just drag it away. (You can't remove the icons of the Finder, the Trash, or any minimized document window.) Once your cursor has cleared the Dock, release the mouse button. The icon disappears. The other Dock icons slide together to close the gap.

Something weird happens if you drag away a Dock program's icon while that program is running. You don't see any change immediately, because the program is still open. But when you quit the program, its previously installed icon disappears from the Dock.

Pop-Up Dock Folders ("Stacks")

When you click a disk or folder icon on the Dock, you witness the effect shown in Figure 4-2. In essence, macOS is fanning out the folder's contents so you can see all of them. If it could talk, it would be saying, "Pick a card, any card."

Tip: You can change how the icons in a particular stack are sorted: alphabetically, chronologically, or whatever. Use the "Sort by" section of the shortcut menu.

And that's why the Dock combines the launcher and status functions of a modern operating system. Only a tiny black dot beneath a program's icon tells you that it's open—and you can even hide that, if you want. (Choose System Preferences→Dock, and turn off "Show indicators for open applications.")

Apple has made it as easy as possible to like the Dock. You can customize the thing to within an inch of its life, use it to control and manipulate windows in elaborate ways, or even get rid of it completely. This section explains everything you need to know.

Setting Up the Dock

Apple starts the Dock off with a few icons it doesn't want you to miss: Finder, Siri, News, App Store, Mail, the Safari web browser, and so on. But using your Mac without putting your own favorite icons in the Dock is like buying an expensive suit and then turning down the free alteration service. At the first opportunity, you should make the Dock your own.

The concept of the Dock is simple: Any icon you drag onto it (Figure 4-1) is installed there as a button. You can even drag an open window onto the Dock—a Microsoft Word document you're editing, say—using its proxy icon (page 26) as a handle.

Tip: If you right-click or two-finger click a folder, or any other icon, in the *Sidebar* (page 17), you get an Add to Dock command for that icon. Bet you can't guess what it does.

Programs Recent apps Everything else

Open programs Minimized document

Figure 4-1:
To add an icon to the Dock, drag it there. You haven't moved the original file. You've just installed a pointer—like a Mac alias or a Windows shortcut.

A single click, not a double-click, opens the corresponding icon. In other words, the Dock is an ideal parking lot for the icons of disks, folders, documents, programs, and internet bookmarks that you access frequently.

You can even install batches of icons onto the Dock all at once—just drag them as a group. That's something you can't do with the other parking places for favorite icons, like the Sidebar and the Finder toolbar.

Here are a few aspects of the Dock that may throw you at first:

- **It has three sections.** See the divider lines (Figure 4-1)? Everything on the left side is an application—a program. Then, in the middle, you get the icons for the

Dock, Desktop & Toolbars

When you fire up a Mac, the first thing you see is the *desktop*—the great-great-grandchild of the original Mac's home-base screen that changed the world in 1984. There's the Dock, full of colorful icons on a see-through shelf. There are those Finder windows, slick and textureless with their solid-gray title bars. And then there's the shimmering backdrop of the desktop itself.

This chapter shows you how to use and control these most dramatic elements of macOS Mojave's home base.

The Dock

For years, most operating systems maintained two lists of programs. One listed unopened programs until you needed them, like the Start menu (Windows) or the Launcher (Mac OS 9). The other kept track of which programs were open at the moment for easy switching, like the taskbar (Windows) or the Application menu (Mac OS 9).

In macOS, Apple combined both functions into a single strip of icons called the Dock.

Apple's thinking goes like this: Why must you know whether or not a program is already running? That's the computer's problem, not yours. In an ideal world, this distinction should be irrelevant. A program should appear when you click its icon, whether it's open or not—just as on an iPhone or an iPad.

"Which programs are open" approaches unimportance in macOS, where sophisticated memory-management features make it hard to run out of memory. You can have dozens of programs open at once.

Smart Folders

A *smart folder* is a self-updating folder. It always contains exactly the items that match criteria you've specified in advance. (Smart folders are a lot like smart albums in iTunes, smart mailboxes in Mail, and so on.) The key to creating one, as it turns out, is the little Save button in the upper-right corner of the Searching window when you've built a search request.

Here's a common example. You choose File→Find. You set up the pop-up menus to say "last opened date" and "this week." You click Save. You name the smart folder something like Current Crises, and you turn on Add to Sidebar (Figure 3-13).

Note: Behind the scenes, smart folders are special files in your Home→Library→Saved Searches folder.

From now on, whenever you click that smart folder, it reveals all the files you've worked on in the past week or so. These items' *real* locations may be scattered around your Mac and your network. But through the magic of the smart folder, they appear as though they're all in one neat folder.

Tip: If your original search criteria need a little fine-tuning, click the smart folder. From the ✿ menu, choose Show Search Criteria. You're back on the original setting-up-the-search window. Use the pop-up menus and other controls to tweak your search setup, and then click the Save button once again. To delete a smart folder, just drag its icon out of the Sidebar. (Or if it's anywhere else, like on your desktop, then drag it to the Trash like any other folder.)

Figure 3-13:
MacOS can preserve your search as a smart folder listed in the Sidebar (left)—at least, it does as long as Add To Sidebar is turned on. You can stash a smart folder in your Dock, too, although it doesn't display a stack of its contents, as normal folders do.

On the other hand, if you choose a Spotlight keystroke that macOS uses for some other function, a little yellow alert icon appears in the Spotlight pane. This icon is actually a button; clicking it brings you to the Keyboard pane, where you can see exactly which keystroke is in dispute and change it.

Privacy Settings

You can hide certain folders from Spotlight searches. Maybe you have privacy concerns—for example, you don't want your spouse Spotlighting your stuff while you're away from your desk. Maybe you just want to create more focused Spotlight searches, removing a lot of old, extraneous junk from its database.

Either way, the steps are simple. Open the Spotlight panel of System Preferences, as described previously. Click the Privacy tab. Figure 3-12 explains the remaining steps.

Tip: When you mark a disk or folder as non-searchable, Spotlight actually deletes its entire *index* (its invisible card-catalog filing system) from that disk. If Spotlight ever seems to be acting wackily, you can use this function to make it rebuild its own index file on the problem disk. Just drag the disk into the Privacy list and then remove it again. Spotlight deletes, and then rebuilds, the index for that disk.

(Don't forget the part about "remove it again," though. If you add a disk to the Privacy list, Spotlight is no longer able to find *anything* on it, even if you can see it right in front of you.)

Once you've built up the list of private disks and folders, close System Preferences. Spotlight now pretends the private items don't even exist.

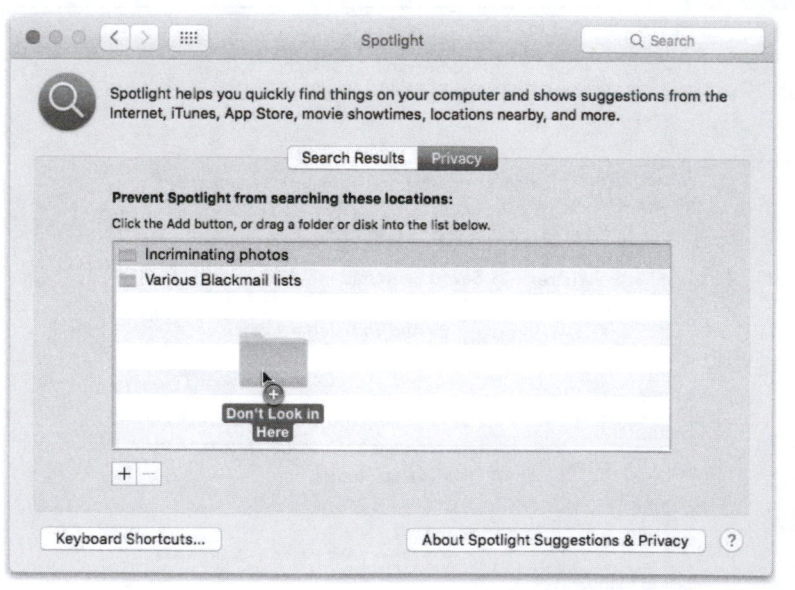

Figure 3-12:
You can add disks, partitions, or folders to the list of non-searchable items by dragging them into this window. Or, if the private items aren't visible at the moment, click +, navigate to your hard drive, select the item, and then click Choose. To remove something from this list, click it and then press the Delete key or click the − button.

In any case, you wind up face to face with the dialog box shown in Figure 3-11.

You can tweak Spotlight in two ways here, both very useful:

- **Turn off categories.** The list of checkboxes identifies what Spotlight tracks. If you find that Spotlight uses up menu space listing, say, web bookmarks or fonts—stuff you don't need to find very often—then turn off their checkboxes. Now the Spotlight menu's precious slots are allotted to icon types you care more about.

 This trick can be especially useful if you don't use Spotlight's internet-searching features. "I'm perfectly capable of looking up movies online," you might say. "I don't need to clutter my Spotlight results list with movie names." Fine—turn off Movies.

- **Change the keystroke.** Ordinarily, pressing ⌘-space bar highlights Spotlight in your menu bar, and Option-⌘-space bar opens the Searching window. If these keystrokes clash with some other key assignment in your software, though, you can reassign them to almost any other keystroke you like.

 To do that, click Keyboard Shortcuts; you jump directly to the System Preferences→Keyboard→Shortcuts tab. Here you can specify a new keystroke, as described on page 210. Apple assumes no responsibility for your choosing a keystroke that messes up some other function. ⌘-S, for example, would not be a good choice.

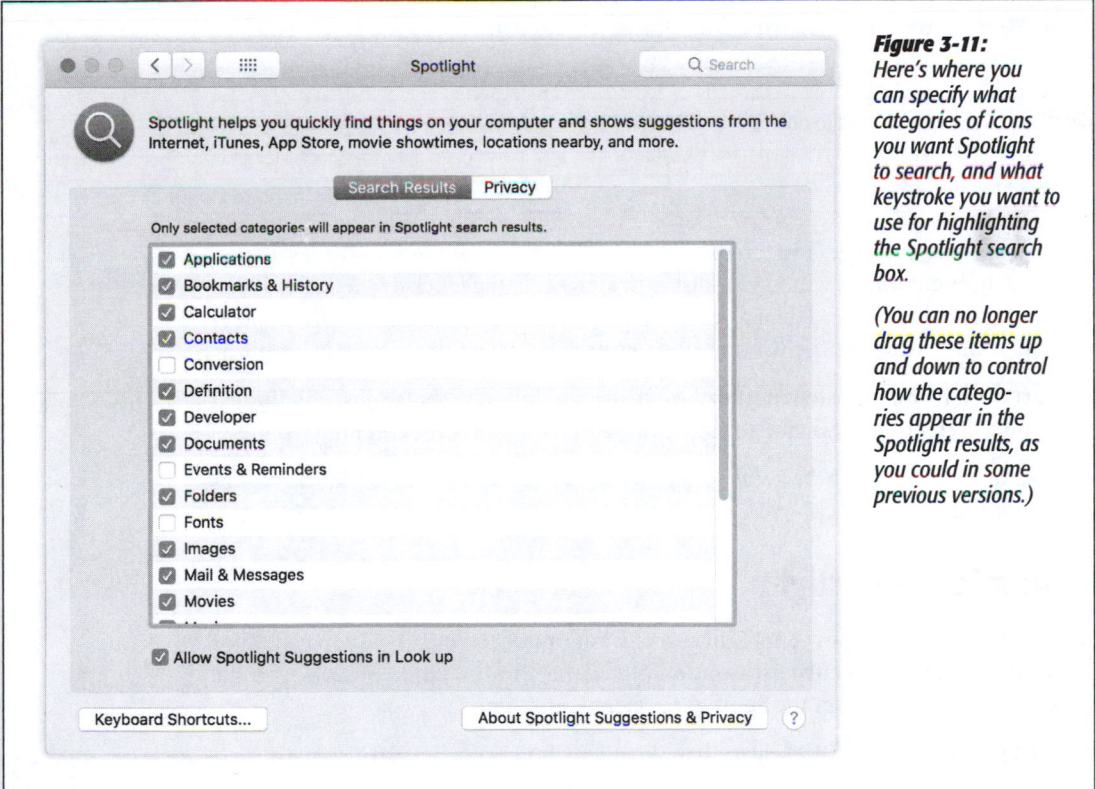

Figure 3-11:
Here's where you can specify what categories of icons you want Spotlight to search, and what keystroke you want to use for highlighting the Spotlight search box.

(You can no longer drag these items up and down to control how the categories appear in the Spotlight results, as you could in some previous versions.)

of additional columns (Date Modified, Date Created); change the icon size or text size; or turn on the "always" checkbox at the top, so that future results windows will have the look you've set up here.

- **Get more information** about a result by selecting it and then choosing File→Get Info (⌘-I). The normal Get Info window appears, complete with date, size, and location information.

- **Find out where it is.** It's nice to see all the search results in one list, but you're not actually seeing them in their native habitats: the Finder folder windows where they physically reside.

 If you click once on an icon in the results, the bottom edge of the window becomes a folder map that shows you where that item is. For example, in Figure 3-10, the notation in the Path strip means: "The 'Starry cliffs' icon you found is in the Sedona folder, which is in the Pictures folder, which is in dp's Home folder."

 To get your hands on the actual icon, choose File→Show in Enclosing Folder (⌘-R). MacOS highlights the icon in question, sitting there in its window wherever it happens to be on your hard drive.

- **Open the file (or one of the folders it's in).** If one of the found files is the one you were looking for, double-click it to open it (or highlight it and press either ⌘-O or ⌘-▼). In many cases, you don't know or care where the file was—you just want to get into it.

Tip: You can also double-click to open any of the folders in the folder map at the bottom of the window. For example, in Figure 3-10, you could double-click the "Starry cliffs" file to open it, or the Sedona folder to open *it*, and so on.

- **Move or delete the file.** You can drag an item directly out of the found-files list and into a different folder, window, or disk—or straight to the Dock or the Trash. If you click something else and then re-click the dragged item in the results list, the folder map at the bottom of the window updates itself to reflect the file's new location.

- **Start over.** If you'd like to repeat the search using a different phrase, just edit the text in the search box. (Press ⌘-F to empty the search box and the Searching window.)

- **Give up.** If none of these avenues suits your fancy, you can close the window as you would any other (⌘-W).

Customizing Spotlight

You've just read about how Spotlight works fresh out of the box. But you can tailor its behavior, both for security reasons and to adapt it to the kinds of work you do. Here are two ways to open the Spotlight preferences center:

- **Use Spotlight itself.** Hit ⌘-space bar, type *spotl*, and press Return.

- **Choose **→System Preferences. Click Spotlight.

The Raw Power of the Raw Query

You may have just slogged through 20 pages of Spotlight details—but, if you can believe it, there are another 40 or 60 someone could write. It turns out that the Spotlight most people see is only a subset of the true power awaiting in macOS.

For example, what if you wanted to see all the files you've opened in the past 24 hours *except* email messages and Contacts entries? Or what if you want to round up all PDF documents *and* PostScript files you've opened in the past week? Using the Spotlight tools that most people see, you wouldn't be able to set up searches or smart folders that are quite that smart.

Fortunately for the true geek, Spotlight also understands a *query language*—a programming-like syntax that lets you establish far more specific and nuanced searches.

To read about the basics of the query language, start at *j.mp/2092xHk;* it will lead you to a number of web pages that explain the full scope of Spotlight's internal lingo.

You may also get a kick out of studying how Spotlight uses the query language itself. To do that, create a smart folder, and then Get Info on it. On the General panel, inspect the string of query text that Spotlight generated behind the scenes (as shown above).

What you'll learn is that the basic search command always includes the command kMDItem. To search for something by its file type, your query should begin with *kMDItemContentType;* for when you last opened it, use *kMDItemLastUsedDate* and so on.

For example, here's how to type a query that rounds up all files that contain the word "kumquat": *kMDItemKeywords == "*kumquat*"*. (The double equals symbol just means "equals." You can also use <, >, <=, and so on. The asterisks are wildcards that mean "There may be other text here, or not.") To signify "and," use two ampersands, like this: &&. For "or," use two vertical bars, like this: ||.

Once you've read more about this query language, you can build much more complicated searches. This one, for example, finds all audio and video files whose author is either Kevin or Steve and were modified in the past week:

```
((kMDItemAuthors
== "Kevin"wc ||
kMDItemAuthors
== "Steve"wc) &&
(kMDItemContentType
== "audio"wc ||
kMDItemContentType
== "video"wc)) &&
```

```
(kMDItemFSContentChangeDate ==
$time.this_week)
```

And here's how you'd find all PDF documents and PostScript files with a single search:

```
((kMDItemContentTypeTree == 'com.
adobe.pdf') || (kMDItemKind ==
'PostScript document'))
```

(Most of this stuff actually stands for useful things: *MD* for metadata, *wc* for "word-based, case-insensitive," and so on.)

And where, you may ask, are you supposed to type all these queries? You have two options.

In the Finder, when you choose File→Find to produce the Spotlight window, choose Other from the Kind pop-up menu. In the list of 6 gazillion search parameters, choose Raw Query. You can type your elaborate search string into the text box that appears.

Second, you can open Terminal (page 515) and use Spotlight's Unix equivalent. The main command you want to learn about is *mdfind*. For example, at the Terminal prompt, you could type *mdfind "kMDItemAcquisitionModel == 'Canon PowerShot S95'"* (and then press Return) to see a list of all photos you took with that particular camera model.

Spotlight: The Missing Manual? Hmm. Has a nice ring to it.

What to Do with Search Results

The results window is a regular old Finder window, with all the familiar views and controls (Figure 3-10).

Figure 3-10:
Click a result to see where it sits on your Mac (shown at bottom). If the window is too narrow to reveal the full folder path, run your cursor over the folders without clicking. As your mouse moves, the Mac reveals each folder's name. (You can drag icons into these folders, too.)

You can work with anything in the results window exactly as though it were in a regular Finder window: Drag something to the Trash, rename something, press the space bar for a Quick Look at it, drag something to the desktop to move it there, drag something onto a Dock icon to open it with a certain program, Option-⌘-drag it to the desktop to create an alias, and so on.

You can move up or down the list by pressing the arrow keys, scroll a "page" at a time with the Page Up and Page Down keys, and so on. You can also highlight multiple icons simultaneously, the same way you would in a Finder list view: Highlight all of them by choosing Edit→Select All, highlight individual items by ⌘-clicking them, drag diagonally to enclose a cluster of found items, and so on.

Or you can proceed in any of these ways:

- **Change the view (list, column, and so on)** by clicking one of the View icons or choosing from the View menu (see Chapter 1). Actually, gallery view is a *great* one for search results; since this list is culled from folders all over the computer, you otherwise have very little sense of context as you examine the file names.

- **Sort the results** by clicking the column headings (in list and gallery views).

- **Arrange the results** by using the Group pop-up menu button (▦▾). That way, you group the results as described on page 41. It can be especially useful to clump them by Kind, so that similar file types are clustered together (Documents, Images, Messages, and so on), or to sort by Last Opened, so that the list is chronological.

- **Change the view options.** Press ⌘-J (or choose View→Show View Options) to open the View Options panel for the results window. Here you can add a couple

exposure program, exposure time, flash, f-number, focal length, ISO speed, max aperture, metering mode, orientation, pixel height, pixel width, red eye, resolution height, resolution width, and white balance.

- **Digital music files** have searchable metadata categories like album, audio bit rate, bits per sample, channel count, composer, duration, General MIDI sequence, key signature, lyricist, musical genre, recording date, sample rate, tempo, time signature, track number, and year recorded. There's even a special set of parameters for GarageBand and Soundtrack documents, including instrument category, instrument name, loop descriptors, loop file type, loop original key, and loop scale type.

- **Microsoft Office documents** can contain info bits like authors, contributors, fonts, languages, pages, publishers, and contact information (name, phone number, and so on).

This massive list also harbors a few criteria you may use more often, like File Size, File Label, and File Invisible (which lets you see all the invisible files on your hard drive).

Now, you could argue that in the time it takes you to set up a search for such a specific kind of data, you could have just rooted through your files and found what you wanted manually. But, hey—you never know. Someday you may remember *nothing* about a photo except that you used the flash and an f-stop of 1.8.

Tip: Don't miss the search box in this dialog box. It makes it super-easy to pluck one useful criterion needle– File Size, say–out of the haystack. Also don't forget about the In Menu checkbox in the right column. It lets you add one of these criteria to the main pop-up menu, so you don't have to go burrowing into Other again the next time.

Figure 3-9:
Here's the master list of search criteria. Turn on the In Menu checkboxes of the ones you'll want to reuse often. Once you've added some of these to the menu, you'll get an appropriate set of "find what?" controls ("Greater than" and "Less than" pop-up menus, for example).

- **Is.** This option finds only files named *precisely* what you type (except that capi-
talization still doesn't matter). Typing *then* won't find any of the file names in the
previous examples. It would unearth only a file called simply "Then." In fact, a file
with a file name suffix, like "Then.doc," doesn't even qualify.

Contents

You can think of this option as the opposite of Name. It finds *only* the text that's inside
your files and completely ignores their icon names. That's a handy function when, for
example, a document's name doesn't match its contents. Maybe a marauding toddler
whacking the keys renamed your doctoral thesis "xggrjpO#$5%////." Or maybe you
just can't remember what you called something.

Other

If this were a math equation, it might look like this: *options × options = overwhelming*.

Choosing Other from the first pop-up menu opens a special dialog box containing
more than 125 *other* criteria. Not just the big kahunas like Name, Size, and Kind, but
far more targeted (and obscure) criteria like "Bits per sample" (so you can round up
MP3 music files of a certain quality), "Device make" (so you can round up all digital
photos taken with, say, a Canon Rebel camera), "Key signature" (so you can find all
the GarageBand songs you wrote in the key of F-sharp), "Pages" (so you can find all
Word documents that are really long), and so on. As you can see in Figure 3-9, each
one comes with a short description.

You may think Spotlight is offering you a staggering array of file-type criteria. In fact,
though, big bunches of information categories (technically called *metadata*) are all
hooks for a relatively small number of document types. For example:

- **Digital photos and other graphics files** account for the metadata types alpha chan-
nel, aperture, color space, device make, device model, EXIF version, exposure mode,

Feeding the Barren Pop-Up Menus

The first little pop-up menu in the Searching
window lists these handy search starting
points: Kind, Last opened date, Name,
and so on.

But it's actually *less* fully stocked than it was
in days gone by. Apple has streamlined the
options a bit.

For example, you used to be able to search
by label (or *tag*, as it's now known). You
could therefore easily round up all files
pertaining to a certain project for backing up, deleting, or

burning to a CD en masse. That's off the
menu as you first see it.

Fortunately, you can restore these options
to the criterion pop-up menu easily enough.
The trick is to use the Other option, as
already described. In the dialog box shown
in Figure 3-9, search for *tag* (or whatever
the missing criterion is). When you find the
criterion you want, turn on the In Menu
checkbox and click OK.

Presto: You've got your menu back.

And what if the item you're looking for isn't among those 10 canned choices? What if it's an alias, or a Photoshop plug-in, or some other type? That's what the Other option is all about. Here you can type in almost anything that specifies a kind of file: *Word, Excel, TIFF, JPEG, AAC, final cut, alias,* or whatever.

Last opened date/Last modified date/Created date

When you choose one of these options, the second pop-up menu lets you isolate files, programs, and folders according to the last time you opened them, the last time you changed them, or when they were created.

- **Today, yesterday, this week, this month, this year.** This second pop-up menu offers quick, canned time-limiting options.

- **Within last, exactly, before, after.** If you choose "before," "after," or "exactly," then your criterion row sprouts a month/day/year control that lets you round up items that you last opened or changed before, after, or on a specific day, like 5/27/18. If you choose "within last," then you can limit the search to things you've opened or changed within a specified number of days, weeks, months, or years.

 These are awesomely useful controls, because they let you specify a chronological window for whatever you're looking for.

Tip: You're allowed to add two Date rows—a great trick that lets you round up files you created or edited between two dates. Set up the first Date row to say "is after" and the second one to say "is before."

Science!

Name

Spotlight likes to find text *anywhere* inside your files, no matter what their *names* are. But when you want to search for an icon by the text that's in only its *name,* this is your ticket. (Capitalization doesn't matter.)

Wouldn't it be faster just to click Filenames in the suggestions pop-up menu (Figure 3-6)? Yes—but using the Searching window gives you far more control, thanks to the second pop-up menu that offers these options:

- **Matches.** You'll see files whose names contain entire words you're looking for. If you search for *peas,* you'll find files called "Peas & Crackers" and "Snow Peas"—but not "Appeasement."

- **Contains.** The position of the letters you type doesn't matter. If you type *then,* you find files with names like "Then and Now," "Authentic Cajun Recipes" and "Lovable Heathen."

- **Starts with.** The Find program finds only files beginning with the letters you type. If you type *then,* you find "Then and Now," but not "Authentic Cajun Recipes" or "Lovable Heathen."

- **Ends with.** If you type *then,* you find "Lovable Heathen," but not "Then and Now" or "Authentic Cajun Recipes."

Tip: If you press Option, the ⊕ button changes into a "⊖" button. When you click it, you get sub-rows of parameters for a single criterion. A pop-up menu lets you choose Any, All, or None, so you can build what are called exclusionary searches.

The idea here is that you can set up a search for documents created between November 1 and 7 or between November 10 and 14. Or files named Complaint that are also either Word or InDesign files.

The mind boggles.

Figure 3-8:
By repeatedly clicking the ⊕ button, you can turn on as many criteria as you'd like; each additional row further narrows the search. To delete a row, click the ⊖ button at its right end.

Here's a rundown of the ways you can restrict your search, according to the options in the first pop-up menu of a row. Note that after you choose from that first pop-up menu (Last Opened, for example), you're supposed to use the additional pop-up menus to narrow the choice ("within last," "2," and "weeks," for example), as you'll read in a moment.

Note: It may surprise you that choosing something from the Kind pop-up menu triggers the search instantly. As soon as you choose Applications, for example, the window fills with a list of every program on your hard drive. Want a quick list of every folder on your entire machine? Choose Folders. (Want to see which folders you've opened in the past couple of days? Add another row.)

If you also type something into the search box at the very top of the window—before or after you've used one of these pop-up menus—the list pares itself down to items that match what you've typed.

Kind

When the first pop-up menu says Kind, you can use the second pop-up menu to indicate what kind of file you're looking for: Applications, Documents, Executables (programs and Dashboard widgets), Folders, Images, Movies, Music, PDF files, Presentations, Text files, or Other.

For example, when you're trying to free up some space on your drive, you could round up all your movie files, which tend to be huge.

4. Continue typing in the search box. This time, type *chris.*

The suggestions appear again, offering options for file names and, probably, a Sent By list that lists everyone named Chris who's ever sent you messages or files. What you want is images whose names contain the *word* "Chris."

5. Click *Filename.*

The list of files is much smaller now. It shows only image files with "Chris" in their names.

For your final stunt, you'll screen out all but the January images.

6. Continue typing in the search box. This time, type *january.*

The suggestions list offers dates like *January 2018.* You can see the result so far in Figure 3-7.

7. Click the month you want.

And voilà: The results list shows you only the January photos of Chris.

To delete a token, click it and then press the Delete key, or backspace over it. You can also edit one: Double-click the right side of the token bubble; now you can retype the search term.

Note: This same feature is also in Mail, where it's even more useful; you have search options like Subject, From, To, and so on.

Power Searching the Old Way

Search tokens are supposed to make multi-criteria searches easier than they used to be. But they're not as powerful as the Old Way, which is still around.

Using the Old Way of power searching, you can set up a search that finds a document whose name begins with the letters *Cro,* is over a megabyte in size, was created after 10/1/18 but before the end of the year, was changed within the past week, has the file name suffix *.doc,* and contains the phrase "attitude adjustment." (Of course, if you knew *that* much about a file, you'd probably know where it *was,* too. But you get the picture.)

In all, the Old Way lets you specify more than 125 different search criteria: date modified, file size, the "last opened" date, color label, copyright holder's name, shutter speed (of a digital photo), tempo (of a music file), and so on. Figure 3-8 illustrates how detailed this kind of search can be.

To set up a complex search like this, use the second row of controls at the top of the window. And the third, and the fourth, and the fifth. Each time you click one of the ⊕ buttons at the right end of the window, a new criterion row appears; use its pop-up menus to specify *what* date, *what* file size, and so on.

other hand, you just find them confusing, no big deal. Tap the Esc key to close the suggestions list and reveal the existing Searching window.

Power Searches with Tokens

The real beauty of the Searching window is that it can hunt down icons via more specific searches than you could using the main Spotlight feature. For example, a feature called *tokens* lets you combine criteria, so you can find only *music* files sent to you by *Casey*. (A token, in Apple's usage, means "a visual representation of a search criterion.")

Here, for example, is how you might search for pictures of Chris that were last opened in January.

Note: Before you get too invested in this tokens business, remember that you can do the same thing using Spotlight's plain-English searches. You can just type, for example, *photos of chris from january*.

1. **In the Finder, press ⌘-F.**

 The Searching window opens.

2. **In the search box, type *image*.**

 Sure enough: The window now shows everything on your Mac that *is* an image or *contains* the word "image" in its name, or even contains the word "image" within the file. But the list of suggestions (Figure 3-6) wants to know: Which do you really want? Files that are images? Or files with the word "image" in their names?

3. **In the suggestions menu, under Kinds, click *Image*.**

 You've just pared down the list of results. Now it shows only the files that *are* photos.

 Note, too, that the first *token* has appeared. Each time you click a refinement criterion, as you did in this step, macOS enshrines it in the search box as a shaded bubble. In this case, it created a token that says "Kind: Image." (You can see it in Figure 3-7.)

Note: See the tiny ▾ next to the search token's name? You can click it to see a very short pop-up menu of options: the criterion you selected (like "Kind:" or "Date:") and another command that says "Everything." Choosing it undoes the filtering effect of the suggestion, so that this token searches for *any* attribute of your file (like the words inside it).

Why do you need an "Everything" option here? If you'd wanted to search all attributes on your Mac, you could have just typed directly into the search box without even using the suggestions menu.

Three reasons. First, you might want to expand the scope (from "Kind" to "Everything," for example) without having to retype the search term. Second, because you might want to make this token part of a smart folder—a saved search—described at the end of this chapter. Finally, you might want to go on to add another search criterion—another search token—that builds on this search for "Everything."

Now you need to narrow the quest to files containing the word "Chris."

You may see any of these headings in the suggestions list:

- **Filenames.** The top option is always Filenames; click it to search by the files' names only. If you type *chris* into the box, you want files whose *names* contain that word.

- **Sent by.** If you type *chris,* the Mac wants to know if, by chance, you're looking for email messages and other documents from somebody *named* Chris (or Christina, or Christopher…).

- **Kinds.** If you type *image,* the Kinds option here offers you choices like "image" (any kind), "JPEG image," "Disk image," or "Portable Network Graphics Image." If you type *document,* you get options like "Word document" and "PDF document." If you search for *photo,* the menu lets you pinpoint files whose *file type* contains "photo"—like photo libraries or Adobe Photoshop files. And so on.

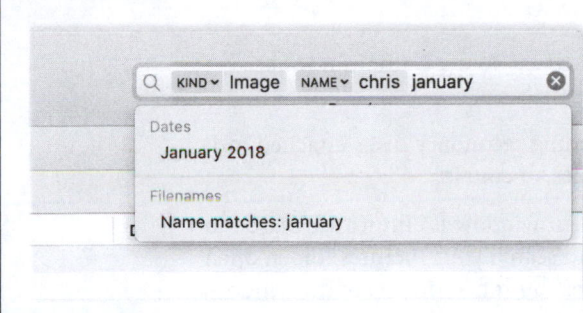

Figure 3-7:
Each time you add a criterion by clicking the drop-down list of suggestions, the Mac adds a new token (criterion bubble) to the search box.

Or you can just type what you're seeking instead of using the bubbles. For example, pictures of chris from january 2018.

- **Downloaded From.** You see this option when what you type is a web address. If you type *Macworld* into the search box, then "Downloaded From Macworld.com" appears in the results list—a handy way to round up all the files you've downloaded from a specific site.

- **Dates.** If you type a month (*august* or *august 2018)* or a year into the search box, the suggestions pop-up menu says "Dates: August 2018" (or whatever). Clicking it lets you do a quick roundup of all files you created, modified, last opened, or added during that period.

- **Tags.** Here's yet another way to use the file tags described on page 92. When you type a search term that matches one of your tags (for example, *green*), the suggestions menu includes "Tags: green."

In each case, the suggestions in this menu reflect only files that actually *exist* on your Mac. If you search for "green," but green isn't one of your Finder tags, then the Tags suggestion doesn't appear. If you haven't downloaded anything from *Macworld.com,* then that option doesn't appear. And so on.

Once you learn to actually start *using* these suggestions—once you get the hang of the kinds of things they offer—you can get a lot of mileage out of them. If, on the

- Open any desktop window, and type something into the search box at upper right. Presto—the mild-mannered folder window turns into the Searching window, complete with search results.

Tip: You can change the Find keystrokes to just about anything you like. See page 210.

The Basic Search

When the Searching window opens, you can start typing whatever you're looking for into the search box at the top.

As you type, the window fills with a list of the files and folders whose names contain what you typed. It's just like the Spotlight results, but without the item-count limit (Figure 3-6).

Where to look

The three phrases at the top of the window—This Mac, [Folder Name], and Shared—are buttons. Click one to tell the Mac where to search:

- **This Mac** means your *entire* computer, including secondary disks attached to it (or installed inside)—minus other people's files, of course.

- **"Letters to Congress"** (or whatever the current window is) limits the search to whatever window was open. So if you want to search your Pictures folder, open it first and *then* hit ⌘-F. You'll see the "Pictures" button at the top of the window, and you can click it to restrict the search to that folder.

- **Shared.** Click this button to expand the search to your *entire network* and all the computers on it. (This assumes, of course, that you've brought their icons to your screen as described in Chapter 13.)

 If the other computers are Macs running Leopard (OS X 10.5) or later, then the Searching window can search their files just the way it does on your own Mac—finding words inside the files, for example. If they're any other kind of computer, Spotlight can search for files only by name.

Tip: If the object of your quest doesn't show up, you can adjust the scope of the search with one quick click on another button at the top of the window, like This Mac or Shared. The Mac updates the results list.

The suggestions list

When you search, macOS tries to figure out whether you're looking for *file names* or *words inside files*. The Searching window may show you both in the same results list.

But more important, it offers a suggestions pop-up menu, shown in Figure 3-7. Its purpose is to help you narrow down the results list with one quick click. Whatever you click here is instantly immortalized as a search token, as described in the next section.

There is, however, a second, more powerful way into the Spotlight labyrinth. And that's to use the *Searching* window, shown in Figure 3-6.

You can open the Searching window in either of two ways.

From Spotlight

If the Spotlight results list—its Most Likely to Succeed list—doesn't include what you're looking for, click "Show all in Finder" at the bottom. You've just opened the Searching window.

Now you have access to the *complete* list of matches, neatly listed in what appears to be a standard Finder window.

From the Finder

When you're in the Finder, you can also open the Searching window *directly*, without using the Spotlight window as a trigger. Actually, there are three ways to get there:

- **⌘-F** (for *Find,* get it?). When you choose File→Find (⌘-F), you get an *empty* Searching window, ready to fill in for your search.

Tip: When the Find window opens, what folder does it intend to search?

That's up to you. Choose Finder→Preferences→Advanced. From the "When performing a search" pop-up menu, you can choose Search This Mac, Search the Current Folder (usually what you want), or Use the Previous Search Scope (that is, either "the whole Mac" or "the current folder," whichever you set up last time).

- **Option-⌘-space bar.** This keystroke opens the same window. But it always comes set to search the *currently open window*, rather than everything on your Mac, regardless of the setting you made in Preferences (as described in the previous Tip).

Figure 3-6:
When you type your search term, macOS presents a pop-up menu of suggestions. For example, when you type excel, *it's asking: "Would you like me to limit the search to Excel spreadsheets?" If you ignore the suggestions, the window shows you all matches— including files with the word "excel" inside them.*

Tip: Here again, you can string words together. To find all PDFs you opened today, use *date:today kind:PDF*. And if you're looking for a PDF document you created on July 4, 2018, containing the word "wombat," you can type *created:7/4/18 kind:pdf wombat*—although, at this point, you're not saving all that much time.

Now, those examples are just a few representative searches out of the dozens that macOS makes available. To see the complete list of searchable metadata options, choose Other in the Spotlight Searching window. You'll probably be stunned and amused by the tweakiness of the things you can search for. (Altitude? Tempo? Year recorded? Due date?)

Boolean searches

What comp sci professors call *Boolean* searches are terms that round up results containing *either* of two search terms, *both* search terms, or one term but *not* another.

To go Boolean, you're supposed to incorporate terms like *AND*, *OR*, or *NOT* into your search queries.

For example, you can round up a list of files that match *two* terms by typing, say, *vacation AND kids*. (That's also how you'd find documents co-authored by two people—you and a pal, for example. You'd search for *author:Casey AND author:Chris*. Yes, you have to type Boolean terms in all capitals.)

Tip: You can use parentheses instead of AND, if you like. That is, typing *(vacation kids)* finds documents that contain both words, not necessarily together. But the truth is, Spotlight runs an AND search whenever you type two terms, like *vacation kids*—neither parentheses nor *AND* is required.

If you use OR, you can find items that match *either* of two search criteria. Typing *kind:jpeg OR kind:pdf* turns up photos and PDF files in a single list.

The minus sign (hyphen) works, too. If you did a search for *dolphins*, hoping to turn up sea-mammal documents, but instead find your results contaminated by football-team listings, then by all means repeat the search with *dolphins -miami*. MacOS eliminates all documents containing "Miami."

Tip: The word *NOT* works the same way. You could type *dolphins NOT miami* to achieve the same effect. But the hyphen is faster to type.

The Searching Window

As you may have noticed, the Spotlight window doesn't list *every* match on your hard drive. Unless you own one of those extremely rare 60-inch Apple Skyscraper Displays, there just isn't room.

Instead, Spotlight uses some fancy behind-the-scenes analysis to display the *most likely* matches for what you typed. But at the bottom of the results list, you usually see that there are other matches; it says "Show all in Finder," meaning there are other candidates.

You can combine these codes with the text you're seeking, too. For example, if you're pretty sure you had a photo called "Naked Mole Rat," you could cut directly to it by typing *mole kind:images* or *kind:images mole* (the order doesn't matter).

Limit by recent date

You can use a similar code to restrict the search by chronology. If you type *date:yesterday*, then Spotlight limits its hunt to items you last opened yesterday.

Here's the complete list of date keywords you can use: *this year, this month, this week, yesterday, today, tomorrow, next week, next month, next year.* (The last four items are useful only for finding upcoming Calendar appointments. Even Spotlight can't show you files you haven't created yet.)

Limit by tag

Round up everything with a certain Finder tag (page 92) using "tag:" as the search prefix. For example, to find everything on your computer that you've tagged as Important, you'd search for *tag:important*.

Limit by metadata

If your brain is already on the verge of exploding, then you might want to take a short break before reading on.

These days, you can limit Spotlight searches by *any* of the 175 different info-morsels that may be stored as part of the files on your Mac: author, audio bit rate, city, composer, camera model, pixel width, and so on. Page 131 has a complete discussion of these so-called *metadata* types. (Metadata means "data about the data"—that is, descriptive info-bites about the files themselves.)

Here are a few examples:

- *author:casey.* Finds all documents with "casey" in the Author field. (This presumes that you've actually *entered* the name Casey into the document's Author box. Microsoft Word, for example, has a place to store this information.)

- *width:800.* Finds all graphics that are 800 pixels wide.

- *flash:1.* Finds all photos that were taken with the camera's flash on. (To find photos taken with the flash *off,* you'd type *flash:0.* A number of the yes/no criteria work this way: Use 1 for yes, 0 for no.)

- *modified:3/7/18-3/10/18.* Finds all documents modified between March 7 and 10, 2018. You can also type *created:6/1/18* to find all the files you created on June 1, 2018. Type *modified:<=3/9/18* to find all documents you edited *on or before* March 9, 2018.

 As you can see, three range-finding symbols are available for your queries: <, >, and - (hyphen). The < means "before" or "less than"; the > means "after" or "greater than"; and the hyphen indicates a range (of dates, sizes, or whatever).

Tip: Spotlight can even find words inside files on other computers on your network—as long as they're also Macs running Mac OS X Leopard (10.5) or later. If not, Spotlight can search only for the names of files on other networked computers.

Advanced Menu Searches

Most people just type the words they're looking for into the Spotlight box. But if that's all you type, you're missing a lot of the power of this feature.

Use quotes

If you type more than one word, Spotlight works just the way Google does. That is, it finds things that contain both words *somewhere* inside.

But if you're searching for a phrase where the words really belong together, put quotes around them. You'll save yourself from having to wade through hundreds of results where the words appear *separately*.

For example, searching for *military intelligence* rounds up documents that contain those two words, but not necessarily side by side. Searching for *"military intelligence"* finds documents that contain that exact phrase. (Insert your own joke here.)

Limit by kind

You can confine your search to certain categories using a simple code. For example, to find all photos, type *kind:image*. If you're looking for a presentation document but you're not sure whether you used Keynote, iWork, or PowerPoint to create it, type *kind:presentation* into the box. And so on.

Here's the complete list of kinds. Remember to precede each keyword type with *kind* and a colon.

To find this:	Use one of these keywords:
A program	app, application, applications
Someone in your address book	contact, contacts
A folder or disk	folder, folders
A message in Mail	email, emails, mail message, mail messages
A Calendar appointment	event, events
A Calendar task	to do, to dos, todo, todos
A graphic	image, images
A movie	movie, movies
A music file	music
An audio file	audio
A PDF file	pdf, pdfs
A System Preferences control	preferences, system preferences
A Safari bookmark	bookmark, bookmarks
A font	font, fonts
A presentation (PowerPoint, iWork)	presentation, presentations

that you're all ready to type in something different. Tap Esc a *second* time to close the Spotlight text box entirely, having given up on the whole idea of searching. (If you've managed to lose your Esc key, then ⌘-period does the same thing.)

- **You can drag things out of the results**—either to the desktop, where it becomes an icon, or onto an app's icon on the Dock to open it. For example, you might drag a JPEG graphic from the results list directly onto the Dock icon for Photoshop Elements to open it with that program (instead of whatever program would have opened when you double-clicked the result).

- **Think of Spotlight as your little black book.** When you need to look up a number in Contacts, don't bother opening Contacts; it's faster to use Spotlight. You can type somebody's name or even part of someone's phone number.

- **Among a million other things,** Spotlight tracks the keywords, descriptions, faces, and places you've applied to your pictures in Photos. As a result, you can find, open, or insert any photo at any time, no matter what program you're using, just by using the Spotlight box at the top of every Open File dialog box! This is a great way to insert a photo into an outgoing email message, a presentation, or a web page you're designing. The photo program doesn't even have to be running.

- **Spotlight is also a quick way to adjust** one of your Mac's preference settings. Instead of opening the System Preferences program, type the first few letters of, say, *volume* or *network* or *clock* into Spotlight. The Spotlight menu lists the appropriate System Preferences panel, so you can jump directly to it.

- **When something is selected in the results list,** you can press ⌘-B to summon a Google search of that term and ⌘-K to see the Wikipedia entry for it.

- **Spotlight's menu lists only a couple of dozen found items.** In the following pages, you'll learn about how to see the rest of the stuff. But, for now, note that you can eliminate some of the categories that show up here (like PDF files or bookmarks) to permit more of the *other* kinds of things to enjoy those limited seats of honor. Details are on page 136.

- **Spotlight shows you only the matches from** *your account* and the public areas of the Mac (like the System, Application, and Developer folders)—but not what's in anyone else's Home folder. If you were hoping to search your spouse's email for phrases like "meet you at midnight," forget it.

- **If Spotlight finds a different version** of something on each of two hard drives, it lets you know by displaying a faint gray hard drive name after each item in the menu.

- **Spotlight works by storing an** *index*—a private, multimegabyte Dewey Decimal System—on each hard drive, disk partition, or USB flash (memory) drive. If you have some oddball type of disk, like a hard drive that's been formatted for Windows, Spotlight doesn't ordinarily index it—but you can turn on indexing by using the File→Get Info command on that drive's icon.

and find it inside a file called "Frank's Favorite Fruits." The lettering tells you the document name.

The same sort of thing happens when you see a website's name in the results. The results list might show the ".com" name for the site (like *Amazon.com*), and the gray lettering might say "Top Sellers in Electronics."

- **If the very first item—labeled Top Hit—**is the icon you were looking for, then press Return to open it. This is a huge deal, because it means that in most cases you can perform the entire operation without ever taking your hands off the keyboard.

 To open Safari in a hurry, for example, press ⌘-space bar (to open the Spotlight search box), type *safa,* and hit Return, all in rapid-fire sequence, without even looking. Presto: Safari is before you.

 And what, exactly, is the Top Hit? MacOS chooses it based on its *relevance* (the importance of your search term inside that item) and timeliness (when you last opened it).

Tip: Spotlight makes a spectacular application launcher. That's because Job One for Spotlight is to display the names of matching *programs* in the results menu. Their names appear in the list nearly instantly—long before Spotlight has built the rest of the menu of search results.

If some program on your hard drive doesn't have a Dock icon, for example—or even if it does, actually—there's no faster way to open it than to use Spotlight.

- **To find out where something is on your hard drive**—that is, to see its folder path (page 133)—⌘-click its name. The folder path appears at the bottom of the preview pane (Figure 3-5).

- **To jump to (highlight) a search result's Finder icon** instead of opening it, ⌘-*double*-click its name. Or arrow-key your way to the result's name and then press ⌘-Return, or just ⌘-R. (If it's information from a program, like an email message, calendar appointment, or address-book entry, then it opens in Mail, Calendar, or Contacts instead.)

- **Spotlight's menu shows you, at most,** a couple dozen of the most likely suspects, evenly divided among the categories (Documents, Applications, and so on). To see the complete list, you have to open the Spotlight *searching window* (page 123). Scroll to the bottom of the list and double-click "Show all in Finder."

- **It's easy to open something in the results list** from the keyboard. Just press ⌘-▲ (or ⌘-▼) to jump from category to category. Once you've highlighted the first result in a category, you can walk through the remaining four by pressing the arrow key by itself. Then, once you've highlighted what you want, press Return to open it.

 In other words, you can get to anything in the Spotlight menu with only a few keystrokes.

- **The Esc key (top-left corner of your keyboard)** offers a two-stage "back out of this" method. Tap it once to close the Spotlight menu and erase what you've typed, so

If you click an application, it opens. If you select a System Preferences panel, System Preferences opens to that panel. If you choose an appointment, the Calendar program opens, already set to the appropriate day and time. Selecting an email message opens that message in Mail or Outlook. And so on.

Spotlight is so fast it eliminates a lot of the folders-in-folders business that's a side effect of modern computing. Why burrow around in folders when you can open any file or program with a couple of keystrokes?

Tip: You can drag icons right out of the results list. For example, you can drag one onto the desktop to park it there, into a window or a folder to move it, into the Trash to delete it, onto the AirDrop icon (in the Sidebar) to hand it over to a colleague, to another disk icon to back it up, and so on.

Spotlight Results Tips

It should be no surprise that a feature as important as Spotlight comes loaded with options, tips, and tricks. Here it is—the official, unexpurgated Spotlight Tip-O-Rama:

- **You may wonder why Spotlight bothers** to display, in big gray lettering, the name of each item you highlight in the results list. It's because sometimes the item's name doesn't match your search term. You might search for *kumquats*, for example,

UP TO SPEED

What Spotlight Knows About Your Files

The beauty of Spotlight is that it doesn't just find files whose names match what you've typed. That would be *so* 2004!

No, Spotlight actually looks *inside* the files. It can read and search the contents of text files, RTF and PDF documents, documents from iWork, Keynote, Pages, Photoshop, Microsoft Office (Word, Excel, Outlook, and PowerPoint), and so on.

Over time, software companies can release bits of add-on software—plug-ins—that will make their documents searchable by Spotlight, too. Check periodically by Googling, for example, *spotlight plug-in* and the kind of software you use. For example, free Spotlight plug-ins are available for OmniGraffle, OmniOutliner, MacDraft, REALbasic, Corel Painter, and many others.

But that's only the beginning. Spotlight searches files not only for the text inside them, but also for over 125 other bits of text—a staggering collection of information tidbits, including the names of the layers in a Photoshop document, the tempo of an MP3 file, the shutter speed of a digital-camera photo,

a movie's copyright holder, a document's page size, and on and on. Technically, this sort of secondary information is called *metadata*. It's usually invisible, although a lot of it shows up in the Get Info dialog box described on page 100.

You might think typing something into the Spotlight search box triggers a search. But to be technically correct, Spotlight has already done its searching. In the first 15 to 30 minutes after you install macOS—or in the minutes after you attach a new hard drive—Spotlight invisibly collects information about everything on your hard drive.

Like a kid cramming for an exam, it reads, takes notes on, and memorizes the contents of all your files. (During this time, if you click the 🔍 icon on the menu bar, you'll be told that Spotlight is indexing the drives.) Once it has indexed your hard drive in this way, Spotlight can produce search results in seconds.

After that initial indexing process, Spotlight continues to monitor what's on your hard drive, indexing new and changed files in the background, in the microseconds between your keystrokes and clicks in other programs.

Note: Spotlight doesn't offer to convert the lesser-known units, like furlongs, leagues, cubits, and spans. It leaves those conversions to the lucrative market already serving biblical scholars and sea captains.

The Preview Pane

Spotlight's window is divided in half. The left side is the list of results.

On the right, though, is a preview pane that shows what's *in* each result. When you click an item in the results list—or use the arrow keys to walk down that list—the preview pane bursts to life, presenting a visual display of that result (Figure 3-5).

Figure 3-5:
If you press ⌘ as you click one of the results, you get a line of text beneath the image that identifies the file's location.

Plenty of times, your quest for information *ends* with a glance at the preview pane. If you were hoping to find a dictionary definition, a phone number, an email address, a unit conversion, the address of a business from Maps, or the rating or plot summary of a current movie, for example, that information is now attractively arrayed before you. No need to open anything from here.

In the same way, you can grab yourself a Quick Look preview of what's inside a document. That is, you can see the actual photo when you highlight a JPEG file's name, or you can read the actual text when you highlight a Word document's name.

Tip: You can even copy material out of the preview pane. Just drag through it and then press ⌘-C.

Opening a Result

If you're using Spotlight to find and open an app or a document, double-click it to open it. Or use the arrow keys to walk down the menu, and then press Return to open the one you want.

You can copy the result to the Clipboard by pressing ⌘-C, so you can paste it into another program.

- **Conversions.** This handy feature (see Figure 3-4) converts units of measurement for you. It converts time, temperature, mass (weight), length, and even currency.

Usually, you don't have to type anything more than the amount you want to convert; Spotlight instantly converts it to the five most likely other units. For example, if you type *338 feet,* the preview pane shows you the same distance in meters, yards, kilometers, miles, and inches.

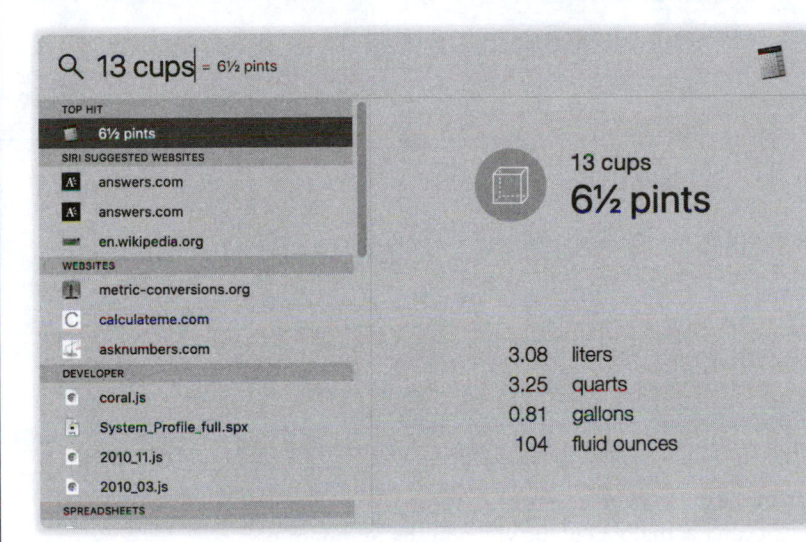

Figure 3-4:
Spotlight is a units-conversion mastermind. If you simply type a quantity (without even saying what you want it converted to), Spotlight displays five different conversions.

But what if what you really wanted was to know how many *miles* that is? Just keep typing. If you type *338 feet in miles,* you get the answer: 0.064 miles.

In the same way, you can convert **volume** (teaspoons, tablespoons, cups, pints, quarts, gallons, cubic feet, fluid ounces, centiliters, milliliters, liters, cubic feet, cubic inches, cubic meters); **weight and mass** (pounds, ounces, kilograms, grams, milligrams, short tons, metric tonnes, long tons); **area** (acres, hectares, square feet, square yards, square meters, square kilometers); **temperature** (Fahrenheit, Celsius, Kelvin—you can abbreviate F, C, or K); **force** (joules, calories, foot-pounds, newton meters, British thermal units); or **power** (watts, kilowatts, BTUs per minute). And those are just a few examples.

If you have an internet connection, you can even convert currencies. Type *134 euros,* for example, and you'll find out that that's $152.86 in U.S. dollars—a lot for a hamburger. The preview pane also offers the same figure in British pounds, Japanese yen, Canadian dollars, and Swiss francs. If you want a different unit, say so. Type *134 euros in yuan,* for example, to find out how much it's worth in China.

the iTunes program. (Only the biggest names show up in these searches; Spotlight doesn't search the entire music or movie store.)

- **Sports scores, standings, and info.** Spotlight is the world's most smug sports know-it-all; see Figure 3-3.

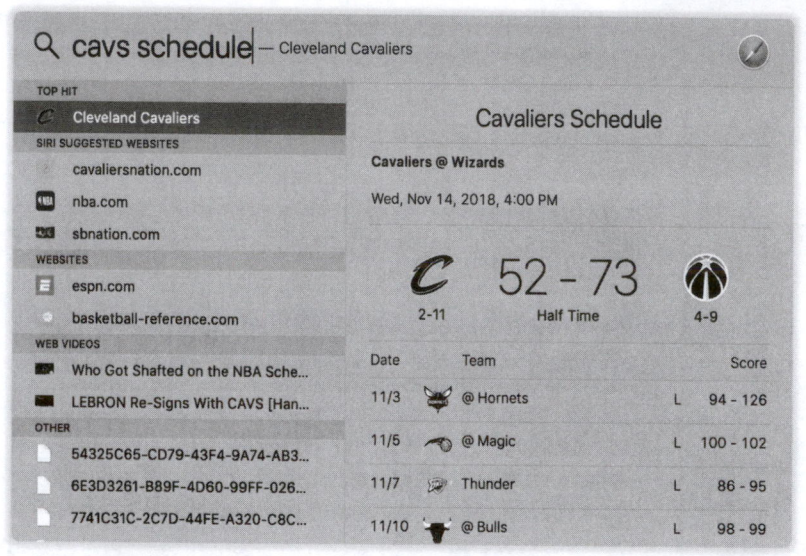

Figure 3-3:
You can search for team scores or schedules (sf giants schedule), team lineups (knicks roster), league standings (marlins standings), or player stats (lebron james). You can double-click within the preview pane to open a web page with further details.

- **Web videos.** Spotlight can find a video from YouTube or Vimeo. You generally get only a single result, and you can't actually play the video in the Spotlight box, so it's not as handy as it could be.

- **Flight info.** Spotlight can find you the latest information about any flight. Just type in the airline and the flight number to get a map of the flight, status, and other details.

Calculations and Conversions

Yes, Spotlight is great for searching your Mac and the internet. But it also has a third skill: It can do math for you. Get into the habit of hitting ⌘-space when you have a quick question about any of the following:

- **Calculations.** Spotlight is a tiny pocket calculator, always at the ready. Press ⌘-space, type or paste 38*48.2-7+55, and marvel at the first result in the Spotlight menu: 1879.6. There's your answer—and you didn't even have to fire up the Calculator.

(Use the asterisk, *, to mean "times" and the slash, /, as "divided by.")

And Spotlight is not just a four-function calculator, either. It works with square roots: Type *sqrt(25),* and you'll get the answer 5. It also works with functions like log(x), exp(x), sin(x), sinh(x), and e. You can even type *pi* to represent, you know, pi.

- **Music.** Spotlight can find a song in your own iTunes music collection. Type the name of a performer, album, or song to find it.

- **Restaurants, businesses, points of interest.** Spotlight is hooked into macOS's Maps program and everything it knows about the world. You can quickly look up landmarks like *empire state building* or *washington monument*, business names like *home depot*, and business categories like *sushi, pizza,* or *gas station*.

 In each case, the preview pane shows you a snippet of the map of that location, plus handy buttons like Directions, Website, and Share. Most of these buttons hand you off to the Maps app to complete the task. (Spotlight finds only the biggest-name businesses. It can't find addresses, coordinates, or smaller companies.)

 If you search for the name of a nearby restaurant, the results include driving directions, photos, hours of operation, Yelp reviews, and contact information.

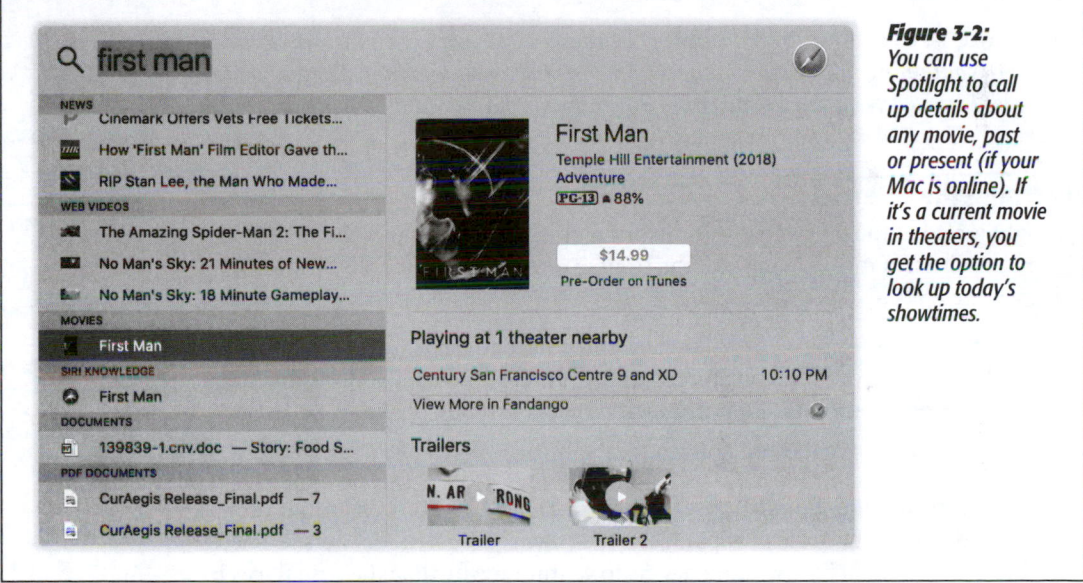

Figure 3-2:
You can use Spotlight to call up details about any movie, past or present (if your Mac is online). If it's a current movie in theaters, you get the option to look up today's showtimes.

- **Stocks.** Type a stock abbreviation (*AAPL* or *NFLX*) or a wordier phrase (*Microsoft stock*) to see an info panel of its current price, its rise or fall today, and its 52-week high and low.

- **Weather.** Need a forecast? Type "weather" plus the city name (*weather boston*).

- **Tweets and hashtags.** You can type Twitter hashtags to see the latest tweets. (A hashtag is a searchable keyword preceded by a # symbol, like #firstworldproblems or #StanleyCup.) When you search for one, Spotlight shows you a few matching tweets—a great way to find out what's happening in the world.

- **The iTunes Store.** Want to know if Apple sells or rents a certain movie or TV show? Use Spotlight. It searches Apple's online store without your having to open

you use Messages (Chapter 19), Spotlight can also find the lucky members of your buddies lists.

Tip: The Spotlight menu is a full-blown English dictionary, too. Or, more specifically, it's wired directly into macOS's own dictionary, which sits in your Applications folder.

So if you type a word—say, *myrmecophile*—into the search box, you see the Dictionary definition in the results. Click it to see the full-blown entry in the preview pane. (In this example, that would be "n: an invertebrate or plant that has a symbiotic relationship with ants.")

You can also type out, in plain English, a description of files you're trying to find. You can use any combination of file types (*documents, movies, images, presentations, email*), dates and times (*2019, last year, this week, last month, in February*), the names of email senders or recipients (*simon jary, halle franklin*), plus the words and phrases inside each file.

In other words, you can search for things like these: *files I worked on last week, slides from 2018 containing EduMotion, images from last year, messages from Xerxes, photos of tia, files I created yesterday, emails from Bob last year that contain documents,* or *the presentation I was working on yesterday.*

Searching the Internet

Spotlight is also a Google wannabe. It can bring up results from the web for all kinds of common information, saving you the trouble of opening your web browser and doing a search.

You'll often find, for example, a Wikipedia entry in the results, or Twitter results, along with matches from the App Store, the iTunes music/movie/TV store, the Maps app's database of restaurants and businesses, movies currently playing, and so on.

Here are the kinds of things it knows about:

- **General information.** Spotlight uses Google to provide lists of web links it thinks you'll find useful. The beauty of Spotlight is that, often, you get the answers you need right in the Spotlight box, without having to venture any further afield on the web.

- **Movies.** Spotlight is seamlessly integrated with its software cousin, iTunes. When you type the name of a movie—past or present—the preview panel shows you a handy dossier about that flick: its year of release; genre; rating (like PG-13 or R); its rating by viewers (like four stars); plot summary, cast and crew lists; and even a button or two that allow you to rent, buy, or preorder the movie on iTunes (Figure 3-2).

Tip: For recent movies, you see the critical rating from *RottenTomatoes.com*, a popular movie-rating site. This rating is expressed as a percentage (like 66 percent, meaning that's how many people liked the movie), as well as with icons. The red tomato indicates a good movie (more than 60 percent liked it); the green splatter means a bad one.

Tip: You can make this results window taller—drag downward on its bottom edge—or move it around the screen (drag its top bar). Bonus tip: To restore the Spotlight window to its original size and position, hold the cursor down on the Q icon at the top of your screen.

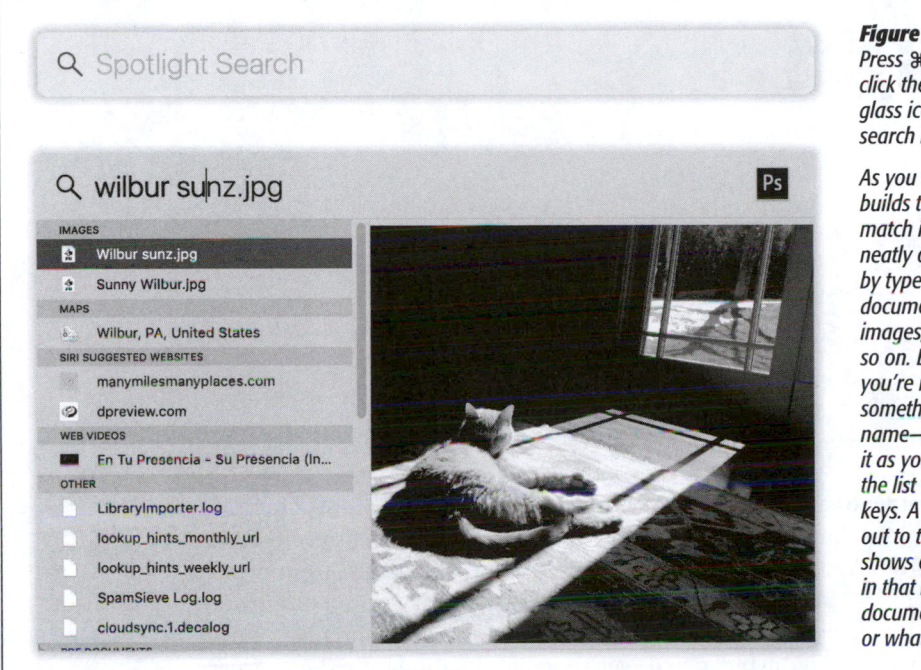

Figure 3-1:
Press ⌘-space bar, or click the magnifying-glass icon, to make the search box appear.

As you type, Spotlight builds the list of every match it can find, neatly organized by type: programs, documents, folders, images, PDFs, and so on. Better yet, if you're not sure what something is, click its name—or pause on it as you walk down the list with the arrow keys. A preview pops out to the right. It shows exactly what's in that movie, picture, document, web page, or whatever.

Searching Your Mac

As you'd expect, Spotlight can round up anything with an icon on your Mac. Any file, folder, program, picture, movie, PDF document, music file, Microsoft Office document, and even font, regardless of its name or folder location. Spotlight can also find things according to their file types (type *.docx* to find Word files), download source (type *cnet.com* to find programs you downloaded from that site), sender (a name or email address), or Finder tag (page 92).

In the Spotlight search box, you can type part of its name or some text that appears *inside* the document you want. For example, if you're trying to find a file called *Pokémon Fantasy League.doc,* then typing just *pok* or *leag* would probably suffice. (The search box doesn't find text in the *middles* of words, though; it searches from the beginnings of words.)

Spotlight also finds matching information within many of your Mac programs: every email message, Contacts entry, calendar appointment, web bookmark, System Preferences panel, To Do item, chat transcript, dictionary definition, and website in your History list. Spotlight can even find photos according to *who's in them* (using the Faces feature in Photos) or where they were taken (using its Places feature). If

Spotlight

Every computer offers a way to find files. But Spotlight, a star feature of macOS, shows matches for your search beyond your Mac; it can fetch results from the web, from Apple's app and music stores, from the Maps app, from movie theaters, and so on. It's also the world's most flexible calculator. It can not only do math, but it can also *convert* things: kilometers to miles, Celsius to Fahrenheit, euros to dollars, and so on. And it can pull down even more information from the internet, like sports scores, Twitter handles (and hashtags), weather, stock quotes, and lists of Vimeo and YouTube videos.

Even better, it understands "natural language" searches. That is, you can type out plain-English queries that describe what you're looking for, like "files I worked on in January," "slides from 2018 containing WidgeTech," or "images from last year."

Note: Spotlight also understands plain French, Italian, German, Simplified Chinese, and Spanish, if one of those is more your thing.

The Spotlight Menu

See the little Q in your menu bar? That's the mousey way to open the Spotlight search box. The other way is to press ⌘-space bar. If you can memorize only one keystroke on your Mac, that's the one to learn. It works both at the desktop and in apps.

In any case, the Spotlight text box appears just below your menu bar (Figure 3-1). Feel free to drag it around your screen. As soon as you begin typing what you're looking for, a list of results appears below the search box. This is a live, interactive search; that is, Spotlight modifies the menu of search results *as you type*.

- **Mail** simply shows you the grand total of all your email and attachments. From here, it's up to you to use one of the file-attachment removal options described already.

- **Trash.** Here's all the stuff sitting in your Trash. You can look over these things—you even get to see how long they've been in the Trash, so you know how close to their 30-day expiration date you are—and delete them individually or all at once.

- **System.** It might come as a surprise to see that macOS itself eats up 66 gigabytes of your drive—that's over half the space on base-model MacBooks! Unfortunately, there's nothing you can do about it; the Mac needs all those bits. That's why this item is listed in gray.

You can also press the space bar for a Quick Look at it (page 58).

Tip: You can also delete a selected item by pressing ⌘-Delete.

- **Downloads.** Here's everything in your Downloads folder. Chances are pretty good that you've got some installers and other junk you don't need anymore. Once again, it's quick work to delete them, right from here.

- **File Browser.** This column-view list shows the entire contents of your drive, with the biggest folders listed at the top. It's now pretty easy to spot the things that are eating up space unnecessarily.

Note: No ❌ appears in this list when you point to a file. To delete one, you have to right-click or two-finger click its name and, from the shortcut menu, choose Move to Trash.

More to Delete

The left side of the Manage Storage window lists other categories of large files. Click one of these headings to see, in the main window, the gunk within. In many cases, you can point to a list item to reveal the ❌ that lets you delete it on the spot.

- **Applications.** Most programs you've downloaded or installed yourself (but not the built-in macOS apps) appear here, presented for instant deletion. Really, now: When's the last time you ran BeeKeeper Pro?

- **Documents.** This view is identical to the File Browser described in the previous section.

- **GarageBand.** The instrument sounds and music-instruction videos in GarageBand, Apple's music-creation program, take up many gigabytes of storage. This option offers a Remove GarageBand Sound Library file, so that you can delete them all in a swoop. (You can always re-download them later.)

- **Books app books.** A typical ebook eats up only 5 or 10 megabytes, but they do add up.

- **iCloud Drive.** Here's another road into the Store in iCloud option, where everything on your desktop and in your Documents folder gets copied to iCloud. When your drive fills up, the originals get deleted from your Mac. (See page 224 for more on iCloud Desktop & Documents.)

- **iOS Files.** This item (Figure 2-18, top) really should be called "iOS Backups." Each time you back up an iPhone, iPad, or iPod Touch on your Mac, it creates a huge backup file. You might be surprised to find ancient backups still clogging up your drive—duplicate backups, or backups of i-devices you sold long ago.

- **iTunes.** Here are all the apps you've downloaded to iTunes for transferring to your iPhone or iPad. Some of them are pretty huge. And some are probably so old that you don't use them anymore.

on their servers, instead of downloading to your Mac as usual. (You can grab them whenever you need them, just by opening those older messages and clicking the attachment button.)

- **Don't automatically download attachments.** This choice is even more drastic. It tells your Mac not to download *any* file attachments until you try to open them. You'll save a ton of disk space, although you won't be able to open (download) those attachments without an internet connection.

Tip: The master on/off switch for this feature is in Mail→Preferences→Accounts.

Empty Trash Automatically

This item does just what it says—it's another way to turn on the feature described on page 98. (The master switch is in Finder→Preferences→Advanced.)

Reduce Clutter

Clicking Review Files auto-clicks the Documents category (in the left-side panel), which opens a fairly amazing set of lists (Figure 2-18):

- **Large Files.** On this tab, the Mac lists all the biggest files on your drive. You're supposed to look them over, scanning for whoppers that you don't really need anymore.

 If you point to something, you get two buttons. If you click the ⊗ button, the Mac asks if you're sure and then deletes the file forever—bypassing the safety net of the Trash. If you click ⊙, the Mac reveals the file in its native Finder window habitat.

Figure 2-18:
The left-side category list offers various files that, once deleted, can restore a lot of disk space. For example, iOS Files (top) lists iPhone and iPad backups, some of which might be duplicated or very old. And the Documents category (bottom) presents three tabs. Some, like Large Files, offer buttons for each item that let you insta-delete them or find them in the Finder.

Store in iCloud

If you click this button, you're offered two checkboxes:

- **Store files from Desktop and Documents in iCloud Drive.** If you turn this item on, the Mac copies everything on your desktop and in your Documents folder to Apple's iCloud servers online. (See page 224 for more on iCloud Desktop & Documents.)

- **Store photos and videos in iCloud Photo Library.** This item copies all your original photos and videos to Apple's iCloud servers.

Later, as your Mac begins to run out of space, it quietly and automatically *deletes the originals* of these files to free up room. You can download your originals, which are safely stored online, whenever you need them—but in the meantime, you're not carrying around a bunch of huge files that you never use.

When iCloud has deleted a desktop or Documents-folder file, for example, it leaves behind an icon marked with a ☁ badge. If you ever need that file, just double-click its icon as usual to download it (and open it). Seamless as could be.

Similarly, what you'll see in Photos are screen-sized versions of your pictures— maybe 1 megapixel instead of 20. But if you ever want the original, just double-click to open it. (To be clear: No files are deleted from your Mac *until you're running low on space*.)

Of course, using these options requires a lot more space on the iCloud service than the measly 5 GB you get for free. You'll have to sign up for one of Apple's more expensive plans, like $12 a year for 50 GB of storage, or $120 a year for a terabyte.

It's a solid, if pricey, way to be free of storage worries.

Note: Once you've turned on these options, you can't turn them off again here. Instead, open System Preferences→iCloud to change the settings for Desktop and Documents, and Photos→Preferences to control iCloud Photo Library.

Optimize

The Optimize button, too, presents you with some checkboxes:

- **Automatically remove watched iTunes movies and TV shows.** When your drive gets low on space (under 10 GB), this feature zaps movie and TV-show files on your Mac that you've already watched. (You're always free to re-download them at no charge.) Video files are huge, so you may find some real gold here.

Note: The Mac will continue to delete these video files after you've watched them—at least until you turn the feature off in iTunes (choose Preferences→Advanced).

- **Download only recent attachments.** The two options in this pop-up menu refer to files attached to incoming email messages (in the Mail app). This first one means that file attachments on older messages, still sitting in your inbox, will stay online,

Note: Purgeable means "expendable." These are files that are on your Mac but don't need to be. They're files that you can download again whenever you need them, like photos and email attachments that are backed up on iCloud; Asian-language fonts and dictionaries you've never used; and movies you've already watched. This notion of "purgeable" will become clearer once you read "Store in iCloud," next.

By the way: When you see the Finder report how much free space is available on your drive, it's *including* the purgeable space. If you actually try to copy a file onto your nearly full drive, the Mac will nuke the purgeable files instantly to make room.

Figure 2-17:
Top: Point to a bar without clicking to see its label. Everything that the Mac thinks you can probably do without is marked here with striped lines, labeled Purgeable.

Bottom: The Mac now comes with a heavy-duty arsenal of tools to help you find and destroy big or ancient files.

If, in that dialog box, you click Manage, you arrive at the impressive window shown at bottom in Figure 2-17. It's the Manage Storage dialog box—a blessing to anyone whose hard drive has ever been full. It contains no fewer than five tools for freeing up space. Ready?

Note: The Manage Storage dialog box duplicates several on/off switches that sit in the Preferences of various apps. In the following sections, you'll see where to find them.

But now you don't have to budge from your current window. Click the file(s) you want to send, click Share→AirDrop, click the name of the nearby destination Mac, iPhone, or iPad, and click Send. Off it goes!

- **Notes** adds the contents of the file to a new page in your Notes app. (A note can hold graphics, movies, sounds—and even icons from the Finder. See page 446.)

- **Messages** sends the file to somebody's iPhone. Type a little message and then click Send. Off it goes, just as though you'd sent it from the Messages app (Chapter 19).

- **Twitter, Facebook, Flickr, Vimeo.** These options no longer appear in Mojave—to protect your security and privacy, according to Apple.

- **Add to Photos, Add to Aperture.** If you've selected a photo (or several), these commands send your masterpieces directly into your favorite photo-organizing program.

- **More.** This command opens up a dialog box where you can rearrange the commands in your Share menu, turn off the ones you don't use, and so on; see page 265.

Optimized Storage

Your Mac sits at the unhappy pinch point between two opposing trends: the growing size of today's files (videos, photos, music) and the shrunken size of our available storage (the non-hard disks on today's Mac laptops).

But macOS can solve that problem rather neatly, by reclaiming huge swaths of wasted space on your drive.

It begins with the window shown in Figure 2-17. To see it, choose ←→About This Mac; in the dialog box, click Storage. You get a handsome graph that shows the breakdown of the junk that's clogging up your drive(s): Apps, Documents, System, and so on (Figure 2-17, top).

UP TO SPEED

Compressing, Zipping, and Archiving

MacOS comes with a built-in command that compresses a file or folder down to a single, smaller icon—an archive—suitable for storing or emailing. It creates .zip files, the same compression format used in Windows. That means you can now send .zip files back and forth to PC owners without worrying that they won't be able to open them.

To compress something, right-click or two-finger click a file or folder and choose "Compress [the icon's name]" from the shortcut menu. (Of course, you can use the File menu or the ✿ menu instead.) MacOS thoughtfully creates a .zip archive, but it leaves the original behind so you can continue working with it. Behind the scenes, the Mac relies on a little app called Archive Utility. Sometimes it remains open after the unzipping process; don't be alarmed. Just scold it and then quit it.

Opening a .zip file somebody sends you is equally easy: Just double-click it. Zip!—it opens.

Note: If your Mac has a Touch Bar, there's a New Folder with Selection button available to install there (see page 237).

With a cool animation, the Finder throws the selected icons into a brand-new folder. It's initially named New Folder With Items (duh), but the hard part is over. All you have to do is rename it—and be grateful that you were spared the 736 steps it would have taken you to do the same job manually.

Share ⬆

Here's a handy menu of ways to send whatever's highlighted to somebody else.

Note: You don't actually have to open a shortcut menu to find the ⬆ button; it's also sitting right there in every Finder window toolbar. And if your Mac has a Touch Bar, there's a Share button available to install there, too (page 237).

In the case of selected Finder icons, you can use these methods (see Figure 2-16):

- **Mail** whips open and creates a new, outgoing message with the selected file(s) already attached. Address and send, and make a sacrifice to the right-clicky gods.

- **AirDrop.** AirDrop is a slick, simple way to shoot a file from one Mac to another—or even to or from an iPhone or iPad—without involving any setup, network settings, or user accounts; see page 313.

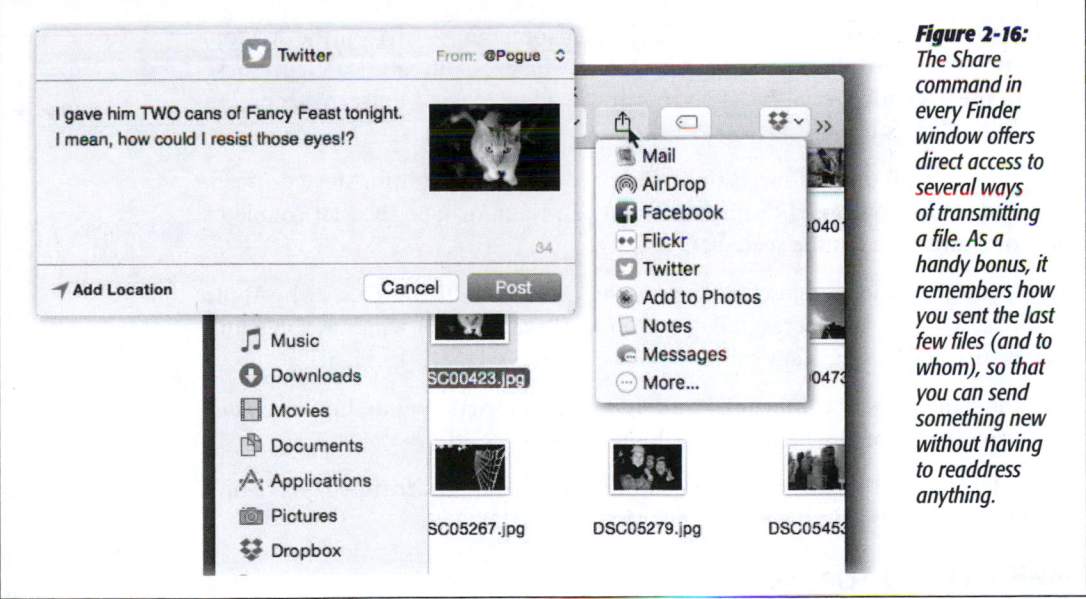

Figure 2-16:
The Share command in every Finder window offers direct access to several ways of transmitting a file. As a handy bonus, it remembers how you sent the last few files (and to whom), so that you can send something new without having to readdress anything.

But as in rival operating systems, you can shave seconds and steps off your workload if you master *shortcut menus:* short menus that sprout out of things you click, offering commands the software thinks you might want to invoke at the moment, as shown in Figure 2-15.

Figure 2-15:
These pop-up entities used to be called contextual menus, but Apple started calling them "shortcut menus" several years ago, perhaps because that's what they're called in Windows and Unix.

To summon one, just right-click or two-finger click something—an icon, the desktop, a window, a link in Safari, text in a word processor, whatever. You can also trigger these shortcut menus with special clicks on your trackpad or Magic Mouse; see page 239 for additional options.

In any case, a menu drops down listing relevant commands: Get Info, Move to Trash, Copy, and so on. You can click the command you want, or type the first couple of letters of it and then tap the space bar.

These menus become more useful the more you get to know them. That's why Apple provided a second way to access them. At the top of every Finder window, you'll find a ✿ pop-up menu, technically called the *Action menu* (Figure 2-15, right).

It lists the same sorts of commands you'd find in the shortcut menus, but it's *visible,* so novices stand a better chance of stumbling onto it.

The Finder shortcut menus offer some of the most useful Mac features ever. Don't miss the two described in the next sections in particular.

New Folder with Selection

Imagine this: You've got a bunch of icons scattered on your desktop, or a mass of related files in a window. You can highlight all of them; right-click or two-finger click any one of them; and from the shortcut menu, choose "New Folder with Selection (12 items)" (or whatever the number of icons is).

Depending on whether you clicked a document, program, disk, alias, or whatever, the various panels may include the following:

- **Tags.** Yes, here's yet another place where you can add or delete tags for a file.

- **Comments.** Here you can type in comments for your own reference. Later, you can view these remarks in any list view if you display the Comments column—and you can find them when you conduct Spotlight searches (Chapter 3).

- **General.** Here's where you can view the name of the icon and also see its size, creation date, most recent change date, locked status, and so on.

 If you click a disk, this info window shows you its capacity and how full it is. If you click the Trash, you see how much stuff is in it. If you click an alias, this panel shows you a Select New Original button and reveals where the original file is. The General panel always opens the first time you summon the Get Info window.

- **More Info.** Just as the name implies, here you'll find more info, most often the dimensions and color format (graphics only) and when the icon was last opened. These morsels are also easily Spotlight-searchable.

- **Name & Extension.** On this panel, you can read and edit the name of the icon in question. The "Hide extension" checkbox refers to the suffix on macOS file names (the last three letters of Letter to Congress.doc, for example).

 Many macOS documents, behind the scenes, have file name extensions of this kind—but macOS comes factory-set to hide them. By turning off this checkbox, you can make the suffix reappear for an individual file. (Conversely, if you've elected to have macOS *show* all file name suffixes, then this checkbox lets you hide the extensions on individual icons.)

- **Open with.** This section is available for documents only. Use the controls on this screen to specify which program will open when you double-click this document, or any document of its type.

- **Preview.** When you're examining pictures, text files, PDF files, Microsoft Office files, sounds, clippings, and movies, you see a magnified thumbnail version of what's actually *in* that document. This preview is like a tiny version of Quick Look (Chapter 1). A controller lets you play sounds and movies where appropriate.

- **Sharing & Permissions.** This panel is available for all kinds of icons. If other people have access to your Mac (either from across the network or when logging in, in person), this panel lets you specify who is allowed to open or change this particular icon. See Chapter 13 for a complete discussion of this hairy topic.

Shortcut Menus, Action Menus

It's part of the Mac's user-friendly heritage: You can do practically everything using only the mouse. Everything is out front, unhidden, and clickable, whether it's an icon, a button, or a menu.

Note: What's App Nap? Well, when a program's window is completely covered up by other windows, the Mac slows down that background app—ditto for Safari background tabs. Slower means less power-hungry—as much as 23 percent, Apple says. But the instant you bring the program to the foreground, it snaps back to full speed.

- **For a disk icon,** you get statistics about its capacity and how much of it is full.

- **If *nothing* is selected,** you get information about the desktop itself (or the open window), including the amount of disk space consumed by everything on or in it.

- **If you highlight so many icons** simultaneously that their Get Info windows would overwhelm your screen, macOS thoughtfully tallies up their information into a single summary window. It shows you how many icons you highlighted, breaks them down by type ("23 documents, 3 folders," for example), and adds up their file sizes. That's a great opportunity to change certain file characteristics on numerous files simultaneously, such as locking or unlocking them, hiding or showing their file name suffixes, changing their ownership or permissions (page 578), and so on.

 How many icons do you have to highlight to trigger this Multiple Item Info box? That depends on the size of your screen; bigger monitors can hold more Get Info boxes. If you highlight fewer than that magic number of icons, macOS opens up individual Get Info windows for each one.

Tip: You can force the Multiple Item Info dialog box to appear, though, even if you've highlighted only a couple of icons. Just press Control-⌘-I. (The Option-⌘-I trick described next works for this purpose, too.)

Uniwindow vs. Multiwindow

Ordinarily, when you click an icon and then choose File→Get Info, a new dialog box appears for each icon (unless you've highlighted a lot of icons, as just described).

But there's a useful variation on the Get Info dialog box called the Inspector. It's a single Get Info window that *changes,* even though it remains open on the screen, as you click different icons. It's a clutter-free way to explore different files, icons, and disks.

To open the Inspector, select an icon and then press Option-⌘-I (or hold down Option and choose File→Show Inspector). The Get Info Inspector window that appears looks slightly different (it has a smaller title bar and a dimmed Minimize button), and it changes to reflect whatever icons you now click.

The Get Info Panels

Apple built the Get Info window out of a series of collapsed "flippy triangles," as shown in Figure 2-14. Click a triangle to expand a corresponding information panel.

Tip: The title-bar hierarchical menu described on page 21 works in the Get Info dialog box, too. That is, ⌘-click the Get Info window's title bar to reveal where this icon is in your folder hierarchy.

Get Info

By clicking an icon and then choosing File→Get Info (or pressing ⌘-I, or touching Get Info on the Touch Bar [page 233], if you've installed one there), you open an important window like the one shown in Figure 2-14. It's a collapsible, multipanel screen that provides a wealth of information about a highlighted icon. For example:

- **For a document icon,** you see when it was created and modified, and what programs it "belongs" to.

- **For an alias,** you learn the location of the actual icon it refers to.

- **For a program,** you can turn on Prevent App Nap.

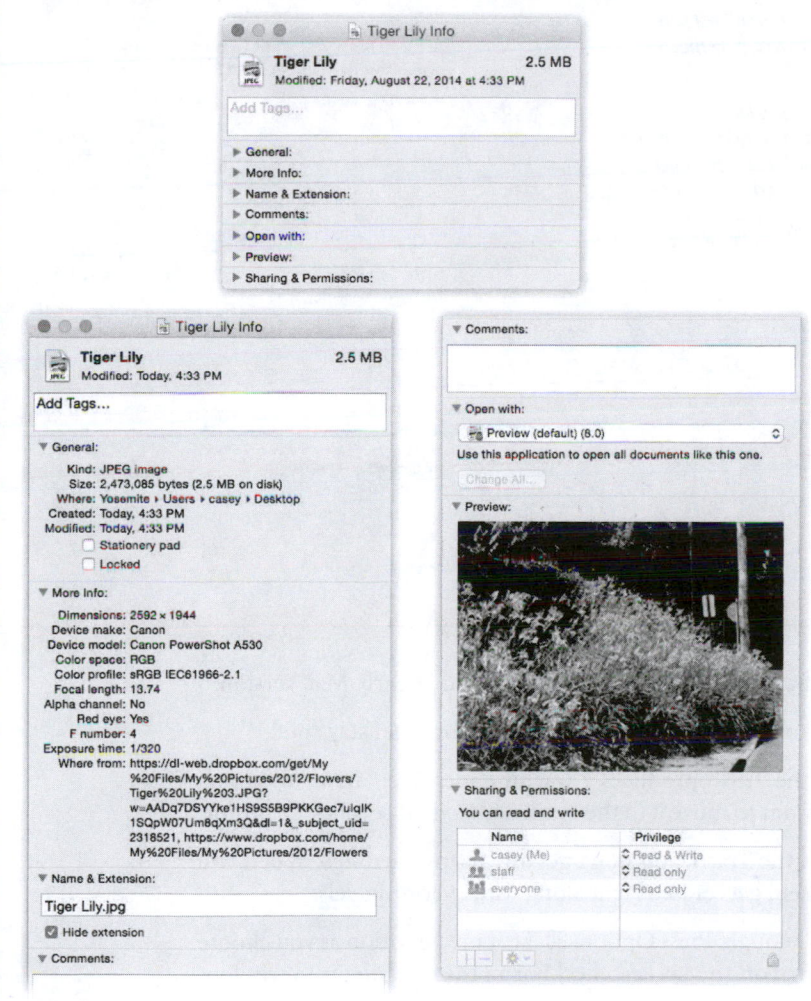

Figure 2-14:

Top: The Get Info window can be as small as this, with all its information panes collapsed.

Bottom: Or, if you click each flippy triangle to open its corresponding panel of information (or Option-click to expand them all at once), it can be as huge as this—shown here split in two because the book isn't tall enough to show the whole thing. The resulting dialog box can easily grow taller than your screen, which is a good argument for either (a) closing the panels you don't need at any given moment or (b) running out to buy a really gigantic monitor.

And as long as you're taking the trouble to read this caption, here's a tasty bonus: There's a secret command called Get Summary Info. Highlight a group of icons, press Control-⌘-I, and marvel at the special Get Info box that tallies up their sizes and other characteristics.

If you turn on this option in Finder→Preferences→Advanced ("Remove items from the Trash after 30 days"), then you can forget about having to empty the Trash manually. You can just think of it as a 30-day safety net for things you're pretty sure you want to ditch.

Locked Files: The Next Generation

By highlighting a file or folder, choosing File→Get Info, and turning on the Locked checkbox, you protect that file or folder from accidental deletion (see Figure 2-13 at bottom). A little 🔒 appears on the corner of the full-size icon, also shown in Figure 2-13.

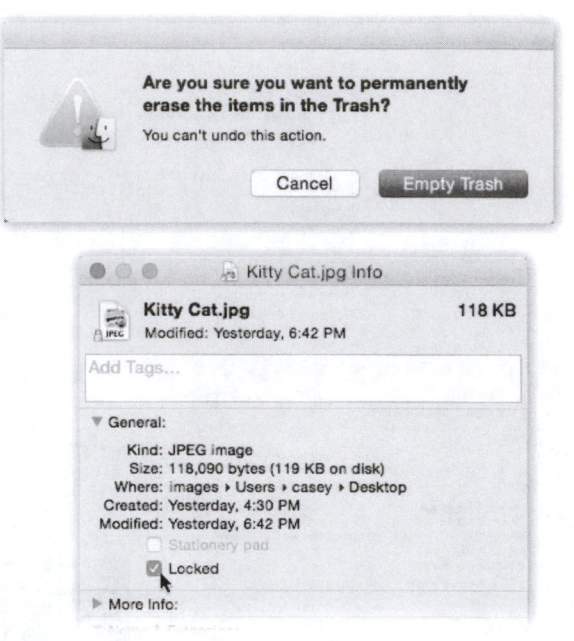

Figure 2-13:
Top: Your last warning. MacOS doesn't tell you how many items are in the Trash or how much disk space they take up.

Bottom: The Get Info window for a locked file. Locking a file in this way isn't military-level security by any stretch—any passing evildoer can unlock the file in the same way you locked it. But it does trigger a warning when you try to put it into the Trash, providing at least one layer of protection against losing or deleting it.

Locked files these days behave quite differently than they did in early Mac versions:

- **Dragging the file into another folder makes a copy;** the original stays put.

- **Putting the icon into the Trash produces a warning message:** "Item 'Shopping List' is locked. Do you want to move it to the Trash anyway?" If so, click Continue.

- **Once a locked file is in the Trash, you don't get any more warnings.** When you empty the Trash, that item gets erased right along with everything else.

You can unlock files easily enough. Press Option-⌘-I (or press Option as you choose File→Show Inspector). Turn off the Locked checkbox in the resulting Info window. (Yes, you can lock or unlock a mass of files at once.)

You'll find the Put Back command wherever fine shortcut menus are sold. For example, it appears when you two-finger click the icon, right-click it, or click the icon and then open the ⚙ menu.

Tip: The same keystroke you use to hurl something *into* the trash (⌘-Delete) also works to hurl it *out* again. That is, you can highlight something in the Trash and press ⌘-Delete to put it back where it once belonged.

- **Hit Undo.** If dragging a file to the Trash was something you just did, you can press ⌘-Z—the keyboard shortcut for the Edit→Undo command. (The Finder offers a five-level Undo, meaning that you can retrace your last five actions.)

 Undo not only removes a file from the Trash, but it also returns it to the folder from which it came. This trick works even if the Trash window isn't open.

- **Drag it manually.** Of course, you can also drag any icon out of the Trash with the mouse, which gives you the option of putting it somewhere new (as opposed to back in the folder it started from).

Tip: Here's a secret method of trashing something that *bypasses* its visit to the Trash can—and instead deletes it instantly. While pressing the Option key, choose File→Delete Immediately (or press Option-⌘-Delete). When it's all over, that icon is gone—and the Trash was never even involved.

Emptying the Trash I: Quick and Easy

If you're confident that the items in the Trash window are worth deleting, use any of these three options to empty it:

- **Choose Finder→Empty Trash.**

- **Press Shift-⌘-Delete.** Or, if you'd just as soon not bother with the "Are you sure?" message, throw the Option key in there, too.

- **Right-click the wastebasket icon** (or two-finger click it, or just click it and hold the mouse button down for a moment); choose Empty Trash from the shortcut menu.

The Mac asks you to confirm your decision. (Figure 2-13 shows this message.) If you click Empty Trash (or press Return), macOS deletes those files from your hard drive.

Tip: If you'd rather not be interrupted for confirmation every time you empty the Trash, you can suppress this message permanently. To do that, choose Finder→Preferences, click Advanced, and then turn off "Show warning before emptying the Trash."

Emptying the Trash II: Even Easier

The Mac can empty the Trash automatically after 30 days, just as Windows has been able to do for years. (Well, technically, it removes *individual items* from the trash after each has sat there for 30 days.)

The Trash

No single element of the Macintosh interface is as recognizable or famous as the Trash can icon, which appears at the end of the Dock. (It's actually a wastebasket, not a can.)

You can discard almost any icon by dragging it into the Trash can. When the tip of your arrow cursor touches the Trash icon, the little wastebasket turns black. When you release the mouse, you're well on your way to discarding whatever it was you dragged. As a convenience, macOS even replaces the empty-wastebasket icon with a wastebasket-filled-with-crumpled-up-papers icon, to let you know there's something in there.

It's worth learning the keyboard alternative to dragging something into the Trash: Highlight the icon, and then press ⌘-Delete (which corresponds to the File→Move to Trash command).

Or, if your Mac has a Touch Bar (page 233), you can install a Move to Trash button on it, so that one tap there does the trick.

The keyboard and Touch Bar techniques are not only far faster than dragging, but they also require far less precision. MacOS does all the Trash-targeting for you.

Note: If a file is locked, a message appears to let you know; it offers you the chance to fling it into the Trash anyway. That's a better solution than in older versions of macOS, when you were forced to unlock the file before you could trash it.

Rescuing Files and Folders from the Trash

File and folder icons sit in the Trash forever—or until you choose Finder→Empty Trash, whichever comes first.

If you haven't yet emptied the Trash, you can open its window by clicking the wastebasket icon once. Now you can review its contents: icons you've placed on the waiting list for extinction. Here's how you can change your mind about one of them:

- **Use the Put Back command.** This feature flings the trashed item back into whatever folder it came from, even if that was weeks ago.

GEM IN THE ROUGH

Opening Things in the Trash

Now and then, it's useful to see what some document in the Trash *is* before committing it to oblivion—and the only way to do that is to open it. Trouble is, you can't open it by double-clicking; you'll get nothing but an error message.

Or at least that's what Apple *wants* you to think.

First of all, you can use Quick Look (page 58) to inspect something in the Trash.

But if Quick Look can't open the file—or if you want to *edit* it instead of just reading it—then drag the document onto the icon of a program that can open it. That is, if a file called Don't Read Me.txt is in the Trash, you can drag it onto, say, the Word or TextEdit icon in your Dock.

The document dutifully pops open on the screen. Inspect, close, and *then* empty the Trash (or rescue the document).

Figure 2-12:
A tag doesn't change the background color of an icon's name, as labels once did. That's because you can now apply more than one tag to a single icon.

Instead, tags show up as colored dots—and if you've applied more than one, they show up as stacked, side-by-side colored dots.

- **Find them all using the Find box.** Type a few letters of the tag's name in the Find box at the top-right corner of any Finder window. Use the "Tags" search token.

- **Find them all with Spotlight.** Into the Spotlight box (Chapter 3), type *tag:orange* (or whatever the tag name is). The results list shows you all the icons you've tagged that way.

The beauty of these last two methods is that you can combine search criteria. In the Spotlight box, you could search for *tag:orange* and *kind:movie*, for example.

Detagging Files

To remove a tag from an icon, use any of the same menu commands you used to apply the tag in the first place (right-click or two-finger click, File→Tags, click the ⬭ menu). In the Tags panel, just delete the tag name.

So how do you choose which tags get these exalted positions? In the dialog box shown in Figure 2-11 (center), drag each favored tag's name into the Favorite Tags box at bottom. (You can remove one by dragging its dot *out* of that box.)

Applying Tags

To apply a tag to a file, highlight the file(s), and then do one of the following:

- **Choose from a menu.** Right-click or two-finger click an icon in the Finder or click the ⬭ button at the top of the Finder window (Figure 2-10, middle). Or choose File→Tags.

 In each case, you get to see colored dots representing the "menu favorite" tags in your arsenal, as described already. Or you can click Show All to see the complete scrolling list of dozens. (You can apply multiple tags to a single icon.)

- **Use the Sidebar.** You can drag Finder icons *onto* the names of tags in the Sidebar.

- **Apply while saving.** You can tag a file as you're saving it (Figure 2-10, bottom).

- **Apply in the Get Info box.** See page 100.

- **Apply with the Tag button on the Touch Bar (page 233).** If your laptop has the Touch Bar above the keyboard, then a ⬭ button appears whenever you've selected an icon (or several). Tap the ⬭ to view your list of tags on the Touch Bar; tap the one you want to apply.

- **Apply within the app.** Certain Apple programs, like TextEdit, Pages, Numbers, and Keynote, bear a tiny triangle next to the document's name on the title bar (page 21). You can click it to open a Tags box, which lets you edit a document's tags while you're still working on it.

- **Hit a keystroke.** Page 210 describes how you can assign keystrokes to common Mac menu commands. As it turns out, the File→Tags command is available for assignment, too. Give it, say, Control-T, and from now on you can call up the Tags dialog box without even taking your fingers off the keyboard.

 For the application name, use Finder; for the menu title, type *Tags…* (press Option-semicolon to produce that three-dot ellipsis, not three periods).

Once you've applied a tag, you can see it in the Finder. It's represented as a colored dot next to the file's name; see Figure 2-12.

Using Tags

OK. So you sat up all weekend, painstakingly tagging your thousands of files. Now comes the payoff: *using* tags.

- **Find them all with a click.** Click one of the tag names in the Sidebar (Figure 2-11, left). You've instantly performed a Mac-wide search for all files with that tag. They appear in a single search-results window, regardless of where they're actually sitting on your computer.

But to create a *new* tag, use one of the techniques shown in Figure 2-10. You're simultaneously creating a new tag and applying it to the file(s) in question. The new tag will be available later in the regular Tags menus.

Editing Tag Names and Colors

To change a tag's name, reassign it to a different color, or delete the tag entirely, open the Tags tab of the Preferences dialog box, as shown in Figure 2-11.

Tip: Actually, an identical set of controls appears when you right-click or two-finger click one of the tags that appears in the Sidebar of any Finder window. And if you have a Touch Bar (page 233), keep in mind you can add an Edit Tags button to it, too, as described on page 237.

Figure 2-11:
Middle: In Finder→Preferences→Tags, you can right-click or two-finger click a tag for the shortcut menu shown here. It lets you rename a tag, delete it, or choose a different color.

Left: You can install some favored tags in the Sidebar.

Right: An even smaller set of favorites appears in Finder menus and shortcut menus.

Two Sets of Favorites Tags

Apple is prepared for Tagageddon; it's created a system that could lead some people to create *hundreds* of tags. That number, of course, is a bit unwieldy. Fortunately, Apple also has equipped you with not one but two sets of "favorites."

- **Sidebar favorites.** The Sidebar at the left side of each Finder window has a section reserved exclusively for displaying the tags you use the most (Figure 2-11, left). To choose which tags you want installed here, open the Preferences dialog box shown in Figure 2-11, center, and make your selections.

- **Menu favorites.** As shown in Figure 2-11 at right, there's room for only a few favorite tags—their colored dots, anyway—right in the File→Tags menu, or the shortcut menu that appears when you right-click or two-finger click an icon.

- **You have more than seven tags available;** in fact, you can have dozens (although you can choose from only seven colors).

- **You can create, assign, and use tags in many more ways,** in many more places, than you could labels. For example, you can assign a tag or two to a new document *as you're naming and saving it.*

- **Tags** *sync.* That is, if you have more than one Mac, and they're signed into the same iCloud account, the same tags are available on all your machines.

What Tags Are Good For

After you've applied tags to icons, you can perform some unique file-management tasks—in some cases on all of them simultaneously, even if they're scattered across multiple hard drives. For example:

- **Round up files with Find.** Using the Spotlight search command described in Chapter 3, you can round up all the icons with a particular tag, no matter which folders they're in.

- **Sort a list view by tag.** No other Mac sorting method lets you create an arbitrary order for the icons in a window. When you sort by tag, the Mac creates alphabetical clusters *within* each tag grouping.

This technique might be useful when, for example, your job is to process several different folders of documents; for each folder, you're supposed to convert graphics files, throw out old files, or whatever. As soon as you finish working your way through one folder, flag it with a tag called Done. The folder jumps to the top (or bottom) of the window, safely marked for your reference pleasure, leaving the next unprocessed folder at your fingertips, ready to go.

Tip: In a list view, the quickest way to sort by tag is to first make the tag column visible. Do so by choosing View→Show View Options and then turning on the Tags checkbox.

- **Track progress.** Use different-colored tags to track the status of files in a certain project. For example, the first drafts have no tags at all. Once they've been edited and approved, make them blue. Once they've been sent to the home office, make them purple.

(Heck, you could have all kinds of fun with this: Money-losing projects get red tints; profitable ones get green; things that make you sad get blue. Or not.)

Creating Tags

Apple starts you out with a few handy tags, ready to apply to any files you like. They come with ingenious names like Red, Yellow, Blue, and Gray.

If you upgraded your Mac from an earlier version of the operating system, you'll find your old Finder labels magically reincarnated as tags, too.

Finder Tags

Finder tags offer a way to color-code, or apply a keyword to, your icons (Figure 2-10). They're a lot like the Finder labels that have been on the Mac for decades, with a few differences:

- **You can apply more than one tag** to an icon, in effect letting it be in more than one place, or sortable in more than one way. A photo of Aunt Edna in her early days on the farm could be tagged Relatives, Photos, *and* Ancient History.

Figure 2-10:
Use the File menu,
⌐ menu, or shortcut
menu to apply tags to
highlighted icons. You
can even apply a tag
within an icon's Get Info
dialog box.

Middle: The same menu
is your opportunity to
create (and simultane-
ously apply) a new tag.


Bottom: You can also
apply a tag—or even
create a new one—at the
moment you're saving a
new document. Just type
the new tag names into
the Tags box that appears
just below the Save As
box.

Tip: MacOS makes it easy to find the file an alias "points to" without actually having to open it. Just highlight the alias and then choose File→Show Original (⌘-R), or choose Show Original from the ⚙ menu. MacOS immediately displays the actual, original file, sitting patiently in its folder, wherever that may be.

Broken Aliases

Don't email an alias to the Tokyo office and then depart for the airport, hoping to give the presentation upon your arrival in Japan. When you double-click the alias, now separated from its original, you'll get the message shown in the dialog box at the bottom of Figure 2-9.

Be grateful the Mac doesn't just show you an error message that says " 'NSA Institutional Ethics Handbook' can't be found." Instead, you can click the Fix Alias button. It opens the Fix Alias dialog box, which you can use to navigate the folders on your Mac. When you click a new icon and then click Choose, you associate the orphaned alias with a different file. From now on, double-clicking the alias opens the new file.

Or you can click Delete Alias (to delete the orphan alias) or OK (to do nothing, leaving it where it is).

Tip: You don't have to wait until the original file no longer exists before choosing a new original for an alias. You can perform alias reassignment surgery anytime you like. Just highlight the alias icon and then choose File→Get Info. In the Get Info dialog box, click Select New Original. In the resulting window, find and double-click the file you'd now like to open whenever you double-click the alias.

POWER USERS' CLINIC

Designing Your Own Icons

You don't have to be content with the icons provided by Microsoft, Apple, or whatever company wrote your software. You can paste new icons onto your file, disk, and folder icons to help you pick them out at a glance.

The easiest way to replace an icon is to copy it from *another* icon. To do so, highlight the icon you want to copy, hold down the Option key, and choose File→Show Inspector. In the resulting window, click the icon, and then choose Edit→Copy.

Next, click the icon to which you want to transfer the copied picture. Its icon now appears in the Info dialog box that's still open on the screen. Click the icon in the dialog box, and this time choose Edit→Paste.

If you'd rather introduce all-new icons, you're welcome to steal some of the beautifully designed ones waiting at *iconfactory.com* and the icon sites linked to it. Once you've

downloaded these special icon files, you can copy their images from the Get Info window as you would any icon.

To design a macOS icon from scratch, use a graphics program like Photoshop or a shareware app like Pixelmator or GraphicConverter. Once you've saved your icon file, select it, and then copy and paste its icon using the Show Inspector method just described.

Note that you can't change certain folder icons that macOS considers important, like Applications or System. You're also not allowed to change icons that belong to other people who share your Mac and sign in under a different name (Chapter 12).

You can, however, change the special macOS folder icons in your Home folder—Pictures, Documents, and so on—and your hard drive icon.

You can create as many aliases as you want of a single file; therefore, in effect, aliases let you stash that file in many different folder locations simultaneously. Double-click any one of them, and you open the original file, wherever it may be on your system.

Tip: You can also create an alias of an icon by Option-⌘-dragging it out of its window. (Aliases you create this way lack the word *alias* on the file name—a delight to those who find the suffix redundant and annoying.) You can also create an alias by right-clicking or two-finger clicking a normal icon and choosing Make Alias from the shortcut menu that appears, or by highlighting an icon and then choosing Make Alias from the ✿ menu.

Figure 2-9:
Top: You can identify an alias by the tiny arrow badge on the lower-left corner. (Mac old-timers should note that the name no longer appears in italics.)

Bottom: If the alias can't find the original file, you're offered the chance to hook it up to a different file.

What's Good About Aliases

An alias takes up very little disk space, even if the original file is enormous. Aliases are smart, too: Even if you rename the alias, rename the original file, move the alias, and move the original around on the disk, double-clicking the alias still opens the original file.

And that's just the beginning of alias intelligence. Suppose you make an alias of a file that's on a removable disc, like a DVD. When you double-click the alias on your hard drive, the Mac requests that particular disc by name. And if you double-click the alias of a file on a different machine on the network, your Mac attempts to connect to the appropriate machine, prompting you for a password—even if the other machine is thousands of miles away and your Mac must go online to connect.

Here are a couple of ways you can put aliases to work:

- **You can file a document you're working on** in several different folders, or place a particular folder in several different locations, for convenience.

- **You can use the alias feature** to save you some of the steps required to access another hard drive on the network. (Details on this trick are in Chapter 12.)

- **You can turn off this feature entirely** by choosing System Preferences→ Accessibility→Mouse & Trackpad, and turning off the "Spring-loading delay" checkbox.

- **Tap the space bar to make the folder spring open at your command.** That is, even with the slider set to the Long delay setting, you can force each folder to spring open when *you* are ready by tapping the space bar as you hold down the mouse button. True, you need two hands to master this one, but the control you regain is immeasurable.

Tip: The space bar trick works even when the "Spring-loading delay" checkbox (in System Preferences→ Accessibility→Mouse & Trackpad) is turned off. That's a handy arrangement, because it means folder windows never pop open accidentally.

- **Whenever a folder springs open into a window,** twitch your mouse up to the newly opened window's title bar or down to its information strip. Doing so ensures that your cursor won't wind up hovering on, and accidentally opening, an inner folder. With the cursor parked on the gradient gray, you can take your time to survey the newly opened window's contents, and plunge into an inner folder only after gaining your bearings.

Tip: Email programs like Outlook and Mail have spring-loaded folders, too. You can drag a message out of the list and into one of your filing folders, wait for the folder to spring open and reveal its subfolders, and then drag it directly into one of them.

Aliases: Icons in Two Places at Once

Highlighting an icon and then choosing File→Make Alias (or pressing ⌘-L) generates an *alias*, a specially branded duplicate of the original icon (Figure 2-9). It's not a duplicate of the *file*—just of the *icon*—so it requires negligible storage space. When you double-click the alias, the original file opens. (A Macintosh alias is essentially the same as a Windows *shortcut*.)

FREQUENTLY ASKED QUESTION

Dragging to Copy a Disk

Help! I'm trying to copy a CD onto my hard drive. When I drag it onto the hard drive icon, I get only an alias—not a copy of the CD.

Sure enough, dragging a disk onto a disk creates an alias. But producing a copy of the dragged icon is easy enough: Just press Option or ⌘ as you drag.

Honestly, though: Why are you trying to copy a CD this way in the first place?

Using Disk Utility (page 504) instead saves space, lets you assign a password, and usually fools whatever software was on the CD into thinking that it's still *on* the original CD.

When you finally release the mouse, you're left facing the final window. All the previous windows closed along the way. You've placed the icon into the depths of the nested folders.

Figure 2-8:
Top: To make spring-loaded folders work, start by dragging an icon onto a folder or disk icon. Don't release the mouse button. Wait for the window to open automatically around your cursor.

Bottom: Now you can either let go of the mouse button to release the file in its new window or drag it onto yet another, inner folder. It, too, will open. As long as you don't release the mouse button, you can continue until you've reached your folder-within-a-folder destination.

Making Spring-Loaded Folders Work

That spring-loaded folder technique sounds good in theory, but it can be disconcerting in practice. For most people, the long wait before the first folder opens is almost enough wasted time to negate the value of the feature altogether. Furthermore, when the first window finally does open, you're often caught by surprise. Suddenly your cursor—mouse button still down—is inside a window, sometimes directly on top of another folder you never intended to open.

Fortunately, you can regain control of spring-loaded folders using these tricks:

- **Choose System Preferences→Accessibility.** In the Mouse & Trackpad pane, adjust the "Spring-loading delay" slider to a setting that drives you less crazy. For example, if the first folder takes too long to open, then drag the slider toward the Short setting.

outgoing message is already open in that program, then you can drag the file directly into its window, too.) In either case, use the ⌘-Tab app switcher (page 177) in mid-drag to switch programs.

- **Launch from a Dock icon.** By dragging this title-bar icon onto another program's *Dock icon,* you open your document in that other program. For example, if you're in TextEdit working on a memo and you decide you'll need the full strength of Microsoft Word to dress it up, you can drag its title-bar icon directly onto the Word icon in the Dock. Word then launches and opens up the TextEdit document, ready for editing.

Note to struggling writers: Unfortunately, you can't drag an open document directly into the Trash.

Spring-Loaded Folders: Dragging Icons into Closed Folders

You want to drag an icon not just into a folder, but into a folder *inside* that folder. This challenge would ordinarily require you to open the folder, open the inner folder, drag the icon in, and then close both windows. As you can imagine, the process is even messier if you want to drag an icon into a sub-subfolder or a *sub*-sub-subfolder.

Instead of fiddling around with all those windows, you can instead use the *spring-loaded folders* feature. Figure 2-8 shows you how it's done.

Tip: You can even drag icons onto disks or folders whose icons appear in the Sidebar (Chapter 1). When you do so, the main part of the window flashes to reveal the contents of the disk or folder you've dragged onto. When you let go of the mouse, the main window changes back to reveal the contents of the disk or folder where you *started* dragging.

In short, the Sidebar and spring-loaded folders make a terrific drag-and-drop way to file an icon from anywhere to anywhere—without having to open or close any windows at all.

GEM IN THE ROUGH

Icon's Progress: The Least-Marketed Feature

Here's an unsung little feature: When you're copying a file or a folder, a tiny progress bar appears right on the icons as they sit in their new location. Animated and everything!

Doesn't matter if it's list view, icon view, or what—you'll see the progress bar.

You'll also see the little ⊗ button at the top-left corner. That, of course, means "Click me to cancel this

Blurbs, Brochures, Notes 2

copying job, since you obviously don't know about the ⌘-period keystroke."

Think of it as a little bit of mistake-recovery insurance, finally on the Mac after almost 30 years.

Oh, and one more happy bit of news: If the Mac happens to get shut down before the copying is complete, the process resumes automatically when it comes to life again.

Dragging from the Title Bar

You may remember from Chapter 1 that the title bar of every Finder window harbors a secret pop-up menu. When you ⌘-click it, you're shown a little ladder that delineates your current position in the folder hierarchy. You may also remember that the tiny icon just to the left of the window's name is actually a handle that you can drag to move a folder into a different window.

In many programs, you get the same features in *document* windows, as shown in Figure 2-7. For example, by dragging the tiny document icon next to the document's name, you can perform these three interesting stunts:

- **Create an alias on the desktop or the Dock.** By dragging this icon to the desktop or onto a folder or disk icon, you create an instant alias of the document you're working on. (If you drag into the right end of the Dock, you can park the document's icon there, too.) Before the Resume Windows feature came along, this was useful when, for example, you were about to knock off for the night and wanted easy access to the file you'd been working on when you returned the next day.

- **Attach a file to an email message.** You can drag a document (using its proxy icon as a handle) onto the icon of an email program like Mail or Outlook. That process creates a new, outgoing message with the file you dragged already attached. (If an

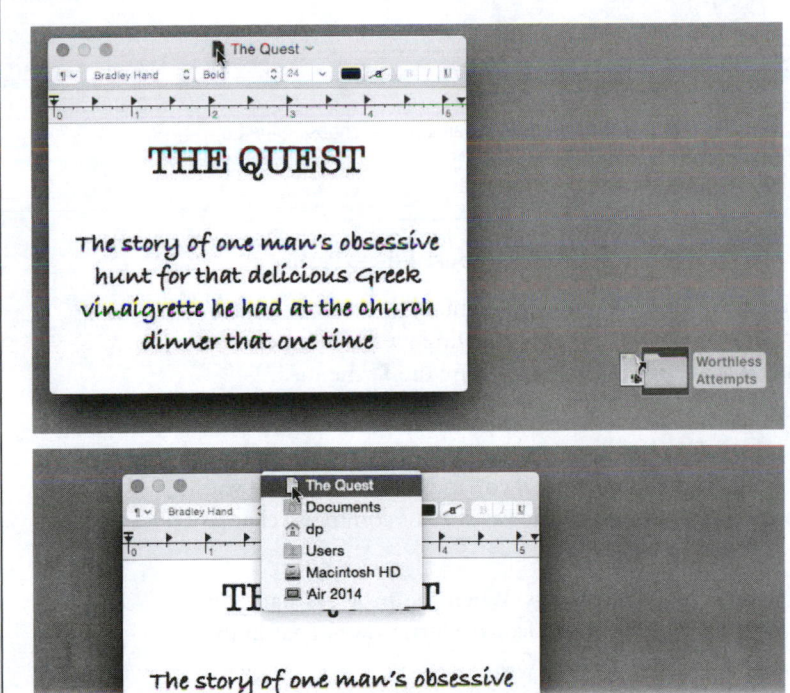

Figure 2-7:

Top: By dragging the document-window proxy icon, you can create an alias of your document on the desktop or anywhere else. (Make sure the icon has darkened before you begin to drag.)

Bottom: If you ⌘-click the name of the document in its title bar, you get to see exactly where this document sits on your hard drive. (Choosing the name of one of these folders opens that folder and switches you to the Finder.)

Note: This business of pressing Option or ⌘ *after* you begin dragging is a tad awkward, but it has its charms. For example, it means you can change your mind about the purpose of your drag in mid-movement, without having to drag back and start over.

And if it turns out you just dragged something into the wrong window or folder, a quick ⌘-Z (the shortcut for Edit→Undo) puts it right back where it came from.

Copying or Moving with Copy and Paste

Dragging icons to copy or move them feels good because it's so direct: You actually see your arrow cursor pushing the icons into the new location.

But you pay a price for this satisfying illusion. You may have to spend a moment or two fiddling with your windows to create a clear "line of drag" between the icon to be moved and the destination folder. (A background window will courteously pop to the foreground to accept your drag. But if it wasn't open to begin with, you're out of luck.)

There's a better way. Use Copy and Paste to move or copy icons from one window into another. The routine goes like this:

1. **Highlight the icon or icons you want to move.**

 Use any of the techniques described starting on page 81.

2. **Choose Edit→Copy.**

 Or press the keyboard shortcut: ⌘-C.

Tip: You can combine steps 1 and 2 by right-clicking or two-finger clicking an icon and choosing the Copy command from the shortcut menu that appears—or by using the ✿ menu. If you've selected several icons, say five, then the command says "Copy 5 items."

3. **Open the window where you want to put the icons. Choose Edit→Paste.**

 Once again, you may prefer to use the keyboard equivalent: ⌘-V. And once again, you can also right-click or two-finger click inside the window and then choose Paste from the shortcut menu that appears, or you can use the ✿ menu.

 If you add the Option key—press Option-⌘-V—you *move* the icons to the new window instead of copying them. That is, the originals disappear after they appear in the new location. (This might make more sense if you use the menu way: If you open the Edit menu and press Option, you'll see the Paste Items command change to say Move Items Here.)

 You can press ⌘-period to interrupt the process. When the progress bar goes away, it means you've successfully transferred the icons, which now appear in the new window.

drag any *one* of them; the others tag along.) As you drag, you see the ghostly images of all the selected icons moving with your cursor. And the cursor itself sprouts a circled number that reminds you how many files you're moving.

Tip: You can tell the copying is underway even if the progress bar is hidden. A tiny progress bar appears right on the icon of the copied material in its new home. You can cancel the process either by pressing ⌘-period or by clicking the ⊗ in the progress window.

Understanding when the Mac *copies* a dragged icon and when it *moves* it bewilders many a beginner. However, the scheme is fairly simple:

- **On a single disk,** dragging from one folder to another *moves* the icon.

- **Dragging from one disk** (or disk partition) to another *copies* the folder or file. (You can drag icons either into an open window or directly onto a disk or folder icon.)

- **If you press the Option key** as you release an icon you've dragged, you *copy* the icon instead of moving it. Doing so within a single folder produces a duplicate of the file called "[Whatever its name was] copy."

- **If you press the ⌘ key** as you release an icon you've dragged from one disk to another, you *move* the file or folder, in the process deleting it from the original disk.

GEM IN THE ROUGH

Smart Handling of Identically Named Icons

What if you're dragging a file or folder into some window—and there's already a file or folder there with the same name?

In operating systems in days of yore, a warning appeared. It let you Stop (the whole operation) or Replace (the existing items with the ones you were moving). MacOS today is much smarter. It offers a third option: Keep Both. If you click it, macOS adds the number 2 (or 3, or 4...) to the end of each incoming file's name.

Tip 1: If you press Option, the Keep Both button changes to say Skip (meaning "Don't copy *this* file, but keep going with the others I dragged").

Tip 2: If you're dragging *several* files whose names match existing files, macOS asks you about each one (Stop, Replace, Keep Both?). If you intend to answer the same way for every single file, save yourself the insanity by turning on the "Apply to all" checkbox before answering the question.

There's another, related feature that comes into play when you paste a *folder* into a spot where there's another folder with the same name. In this case, the Mac offers to *merge the contents* of the two folders.

It might say: "An item named 'Notes' already exists in this location. Do you want to replace it with the one you're moving? Each folder has unique items such as 'Salary Projections' and 'Stealth Projects.doc.' " And your choices are Stop, Keep Both, or Replace All. (These options appear only when you're *pasting* a folder into a new window—not dragging it. They also appear when you Option-drag a folder into a new window to copy it there or when you drag it to a different disk.)

If you click Keep Both, the Finder *combines the contents* of the two folders. The folder you're pasting disappears, but its contents join the contents of the other folder (the one in the destination window) in blissful harmony.

Tip: In icon view, you can either Shift-click *or* ⌘-click to select multiple individual icons. But you may as well just learn to use the ⌘ key when selecting individual icons. That way you won't have to use a different key in each view.

Once you've highlighted multiple icons, you can manipulate them all at once. For example, you can drag them en masse to another folder or disk by dragging any *one* of the highlighted icons. All other highlighted icons go along for the ride. This technique is especially useful when you want to back up a bunch of files by dragging them onto a different disk, delete them all by dragging them to the Trash, and so on.

When multiple icons are selected, the commands in the File and Edit menus—like Duplicate, Open, and Make Alias—apply to all of them simultaneously.

Tip: Don't forget that you can instantly highlight all the files in a window (or on the desktop) by choosing Edit→Select All (⌘-A)—no icon-clicking required.

Selecting Icons from the Keyboard

For the speed fanatic, using the mouse to click an icon is a hopeless waste of time. Fortunately, you can also select an icon by typing the first few letters of its name.

When looking at your Home window, for example, you can type *M* to select the Movies folder. And if you actually intended to select the Music folder instead, then press the Tab key to select the next icon in the window alphabetically. Shift-Tab highlights the *previous* icon alphabetically. Or use the arrow keys to highlight a neighboring icon.

(The Tab-key trick works only in icon, list, and gallery views—not in column view, alas. You can always use the ◄ and ► keys to highlight adjacent columns, however.)

After highlighting an icon this way, you can manipulate it using the commands in the File menu or their keyboard equivalents: Open (⌘-O), put it into the Trash (⌘-Delete), Get Info (⌘-I), Duplicate (⌘-D), or make an alias (⌘-L), as described later in this chapter. By turning on the special accessibility features described on page 324, you can even *move* the highlighted icon using only the keyboard.

If you're a first-time Mac owner, you may find it excessively nerdy to memorize keystrokes for jobs the mouse can do. If you make your living using the Mac, however, memorizing these keystrokes will reward you immeasurably with speed and efficiency.

Moving and Copying Icons

In macOS, there are two ways to move or copy icons from one place to another: by dragging them and by using the Copy and Paste commands.

Copying by Dragging

You can drag icons from one folder to another, from one drive to another, from a drive to a folder on another drive, and so on. (When you've selected several icons,

to drag over the icons themselves—your cursor can touch any part of a file's row, like its modification date or file size.

Tip: If you include a particular icon in your diagonally dragged group by mistake, ⌘-click it to remove it from the selected cluster.

- **To highlight consecutive icons in a list.** If you're looking at the contents of a window in list view or column view, you can drag vertically over the file and folder names to highlight a group of consecutive icons, as described already. (Begin the drag in a blank spot.)

There's a faster way to do the same thing; see Figure 2-6.

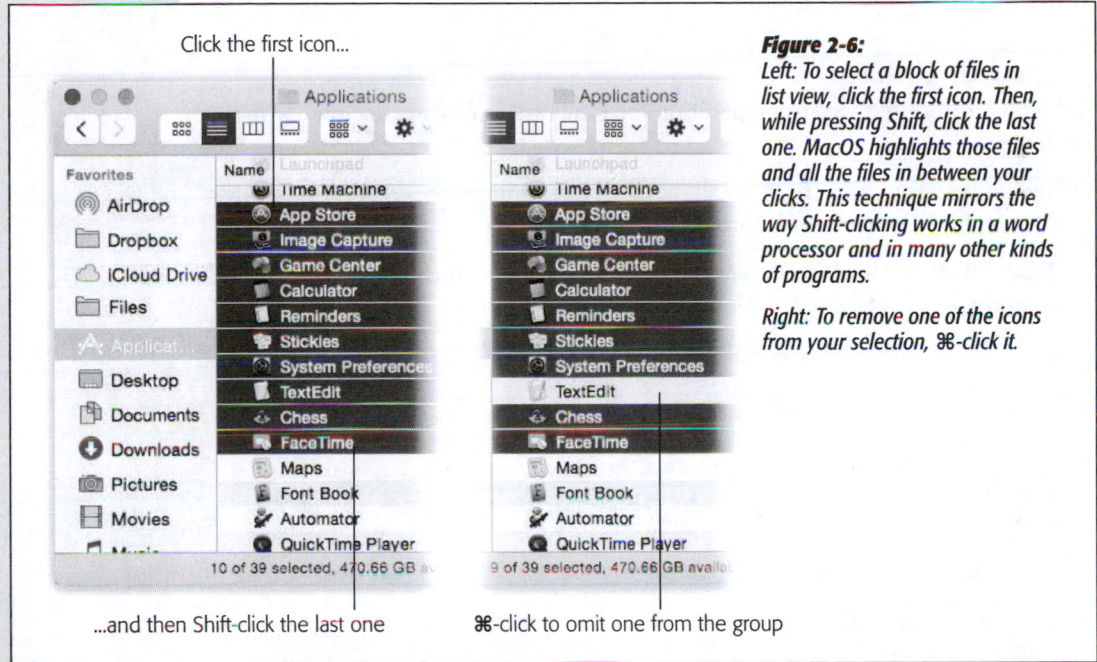

Click the first icon...

Figure 2-6:
Left: To select a block of files in list view, click the first icon. Then, while pressing Shift, click the last one. MacOS highlights those files and all the files in between your clicks. This technique mirrors the way Shift-clicking works in a word processor and in many other kinds of programs.

Right: To remove one of the icons from your selection, ⌘-click it.

...and then Shift-click the last one ⌘-click to omit one from the group

- **To highlight arbitrary icons.** If you want to highlight only the first, third, and seventh icons in a window, for example, start by clicking icon #1. Then ⌘-click each of the others (or ⌘-drag new rectangles around them). Each icon darkens to show that you've selected it.

If you're highlighting a long string of icons and click one by mistake, you don't have to start over. Instead, just ⌘-click it again so the dark highlighting disappears. (If you do want to start over, you can deselect all selected icons by clicking any empty part of the window—or by pressing the Esc key.) The ⌘ key trick is especially handy if you want to select almost all the icons in a window. Press ⌘-A to select everything in the folder, and then ⌘-click any unwanted icons to deselect them.

Selecting Icons

To highlight a single icon in preparation for printing, opening, duplicating, or deleting, click the icon once. (In a list or column view, as described in Chapter 1, you can also click on any visible piece of information about that file—its size, kind, date modified, and so on.) Both the icon and the name darken in a uniquely macOSish way.

Tip: You can change the color of the oval highlighting that appears around the name of a selected icon. Choose →System Preferences, click General, and use the Highlight Color pop-up menu.

That much may seem obvious. But most first-time Mac owners have no idea how to manipulate *more* than one icon at a time—an essential survival skill in a graphic interface like the Mac's.

Selecting by Clicking

To highlight multiple files in preparation for moving or copying, use one of these techniques:

- **Highlight all the icons.** To select all the icons in a window, press ⌘-A (the equivalent of the Edit→Select All command).

- **Highlight several icons by dragging.** You can drag diagonally to highlight a group of nearby icons, as shown in Figure 2-5. In a list view, in fact, you don't even have

Figure 2-5:
You can highlight several icons simultaneously by dragging a box around them. To do so, drag from outside the target icons diagonally, creating a translucent gray rectangle as you go. Any icons or icon names touched by this rectangle are selected when you release the mouse. If you press the Shift or ⌘ key as you do this, then any previously highlighted icons remain selected.

casey
4 of 9 selected, 474.89 GB available

Desktop Documents Downloads

Dropbox For the Taxidermist Movies

Music Pictures Public

- **Add Text** tacks some text onto the files' original names; use the second pop-up menu to specify *where* (beginning or end). *Example:* Change "Mom's Recipes—Fish," "Mom's Recipes—Desserts"… into "My Mom's Recipes—Fish," "My Mom's Recipes—Desserts"…

- **Format** is complicated but powerful. It completely obliterates whatever the files are called now; instead, it gives them all the same base name (like "Recipes"), differentiating them with a number or the date, either before or after their base names.

 Suppose, for example, that you type "Recipes" into the Custom Format box. That's the base name.

 Now, if you choose "Name and Index" from the second pop-up menu and click Rename, you'll get files named "Recipes 1," "Recipes 2," and so on. You can specify that you want the number (what macOS calls the *index*) either before or after the base name, and what number should begin the sequence. Name and Counter is the same, except that each number is padded out to five digits ("Recipes 00001," "Recipes 00002"…).

 Finally, Name and Date adds the current time and date to the end of every file's name, in the form "2018-3-19 at 20.20.05 PM" (which means "March 19, 2018, at 8:20 p.m."). Of course, that means every selected file will have exactly the *same* name ("Recipes 2018-3-19 at 20.20.05 PM"). The Mac will give you an instant error message, therefore, *unless* the original files are in different folders or have different file name extensions (like .jpg, .doc, and so on).

The batch-renaming feature is delicious and awesome, but there is some fine print. Don't search and replace the file name extensions (like .jpg or .doc); you might not be able to open the files afterward. Don't rename system files or your Home folder.

And use a shareware program like A Better Finder Rename if you want even more power and flexibility in mass-renaming files.

Printing a Window—or a List of Files

In Mac OS 9, I could print a Finder window. I'd get a neat list of the files, which I could use as a label for a CD I was going to burn, or whatever. How do I print a Finder window in macOS? (The File→Print command prints a selected document, not the list of files in a window.)

It's easy enough to make a list of files for printing. Once the window is open on your screen, choose Edit→Select All. Choose Edit→Copy. Now switch to a word processor and paste. (If you're using TextEdit, use Edit→Paste and Match Style instead.) You get a tidy list of all the files in that window, ready to format and print.

This simple file name list isn't the same as printing a window; you don't get the status bar showing how many items are on the disk and how full the disk is. For that purpose, you could always make a screenshot of the window (page 626) and print that. Of course, that technique is no good if the list of files is taller than the screen itself.

Really, what you want is Print Window, a handy shareware program dedicated to printing out your Finder windows, without these workarounds and limitations. You can download it from this book's "Missing CD" page at *missingmanuals.com*.

- **In addition to letters and numbers,** macOS also assigns punctuation marks an "alphabetical order," which is this: ` (the accent mark above the Tab key), ^, _, -, space, –, —, comma, semicolon, !, ?, ', ", (,), [,], {, }, @, *, /, &, #, %, +, <, =, ≠, >, |, ~, and $.

Numbers come after punctuation; letters come next; and bringing up the rear are these characters: μ (Option-M), π (Option-P), Ω (Option-Z), and (Shift-Option-K).

Renaming Batches of Files

It's one of macOS's most useful features, and hardly anyone knows it exists: You can rename a whole windowful of files at once—numbering them, correcting spelling in dozens of files at once, deleting a certain phrase from their names, and so on.

To perform this kind of simultaneous name surgery, begin by selecting all the files whose names you want to edit, as described in the next section. Then right-click or two-finger click any one of them; from the shortcut menu, choose "Rename 12 Items" (or whatever the number is).

Now you get the dialog box shown in Figure 2-4. Its pop-up menu offers three ways to rename the icons en masse:

- **Replace Text.** This, ladies and gents, is search and replace for text in your files' names. Fill in the "Find" and "Replace with" boxes; click Rename. *Example:* Change "Mom's Recipes—Fish," "Mom's Recipes—Desserts"…into "My Own Recipes— Fish," "My Own Recipes—Desserts"…

Figure 2-4:
MacOS offers a range of sophisticated batch-renaming options. There's search and replace within file names; there's "add the same text to the beginning or end of the file names"; and there's the option shown here, Format.

Here you completely replace the existing file names with new, consecutively numbered names, available in various creative styles.

In any case, a rectangle appears around the name (Figure 2-3). At this point, the existing name is highlighted; just begin typing to replace it. If you type a very long name, the rectangle grows vertically to accommodate new lines of text.

Tip: If you simply want to add letters to the beginning or end of the file's existing name, press the ◀ or ▶ key after pressing Return. The insertion point jumps to the beginning or end of the file name.

Figure 2-3:
Click an icon's name (top left) to produce the renaming rectangle (top right), in which you can edit the file's name. MacOS is kind enough to highlight only the existing name, and not the suffix (like .jpg or .doc).

Now begin typing to replace the existing name (bottom left). When you're finished typing, press Return or Tab to seal the deal, or just click somewhere else.

You can give more than one file or folder the same name, as long as they're not in the same folder. For example, you can have as many files named "Chocolate Cake Recipe" as you like, provided that each is in a different folder. And, of course, files called Recipe.doc and Recipe.xls can coexist in a folder, too.

As you edit a file's name, remember that you can use the Cut, Copy, and Paste commands in the Edit menu to move selected bits of text around, just as though you were word processing. The Paste command can be useful when, for instance, you're renaming many icons in sequence (Quarterly Estimate 1, Quarterly Estimate 2...).

And now, a few tips about renaming icons:

- **When the Finder sorts files,** a space is considered alphabetically *before* the letter A. To force a particular file or folder to appear at the top of a list view window, insert a space (or an underscore) before its name.

- **Older operating systems sort files** so that the numbers 10 and 100 come before 2, the numbers 30 and 300 come before 4, and so on. You wind up with alphabetically sorted files like this: "1. Big Day," "10. Long Song," "2. Floppy Hat," "20. Dog Bone," "3. Weird Sort," and so on. Generations of people have learned to put zeros in front of their single-digit numbers just to make the sorting look right. In macOS, though, you get exactly the list you'd hope for: "1. Big Day," "2. Floppy Hat," "3. Weird Sort," "10. Long Song," and "20. Dog Bone."

When you turn on the new View→Use Stacks command, your desktop icons auto-clump into related piles (Figure 2-2, bottom), auto-sorted by date created, date last opened, date modified, tag, or kind (for example, Documents and Images). The result: far fewer icons on your desktop, and far less clutter. You've created more order without expending any time or effort.

Note: Folders never get clumped—only stray icons.

So how do you find what you need? Just click one of the stacks to expand its contents, pushing the others out of the way if necessary (Figure 2-2, bottom right). Now that your inner icons are exposed, you can use them as usual: Double-click to open, tap the space bar for Quick Look (page 58), and so on.

Close the stack again by clicking it.

Note, by the way, that the View→Group Stacks By command lets you change *how* macOS creates the stacks:

- **Kind** clumps them by file type: Images, Documents, Music, PDF Documents, Spreadsheets, Presentations, and so on.

- **Date Last Opened, Date Created, Date Added** [to the desktop], and **Date Modified** create Stacks for Today, Yesterday, Last 7 Days, Last 30 Days, and so on.

- **Tags,** of course, creates a Stack for each of your colored tags (page 92).

If you're a soldier in the Leave-Stuff-Out-on-the-Desktop Army, rejoice. After all, why should your real-world desktop be the only surface with piles of stuff?

Icon Names

Every document, program, folder, and disk on your Mac is represented by an *icon:* a colorful little picture that you can move, copy, or double-click to open. In macOS, you can scale them to practically any size.

An icon's name can have up to 255 letters and spaces. If you're accustomed to the 31-character or even 8-character limits of older computers, that's quite a luxurious ceiling.

If you're used to Windows, you may be delighted to discover that in macOS you can name your files using letters, numbers, punctuation—in fact, any symbol except the colon (:), which the Mac uses behind the scenes for its own folder-hierarchy designation purposes. And you can't use a period to *begin* a file's name.

Rename One File

To rename a file, click its name or icon (to highlight it) and then press Return. (Or, if you have time to kill, click once on the name, wait a moment, and then click a second time. Or right-click or two-finger click the icon; from the shortcut menu, choose Rename.)

have your password. Details on sharing the Mac are in Chapter 12, and those on networking are in Chapter 13.

- **Sites.** MacOS used to have a built-in *web server,* software that turns your Mac into a website that people on your network—or, via the internet, all over the world—can connect to. This macOS feature relied on a program called the Apache web server, which is so highly regarded in the Unix community that programmers lower their voices when they mention it.

 The web server is gone now, as described in Chapter 20. If you have a Sites folder, it's where you put the actual web pages you wanted to make available to the internet at large—in a previous version of the Mac operating system.

Desktop Stacks

It doesn't matter that Apple has provided us with folders, windows, and other organizational tools; some of us will always use the *desktop* as our organizational structure (Figure 2-2, top). We leave our icons there, sometimes dozens of them in a seething chaotic array, with the vague rationalization that it takes too much effort to file them away in folders (and the vague fear that we'll never find them again).

In macOS Mojave, Apple, with a big corporate sigh, has given in. "OK, fine," it seems to say. "You insist upon leaving everything strewn across your desktop? Then at least let us help you tidy it all up."

Figure 2-2:
There's a huge difference between a messy desktop (top) and one with Desktop Stacks turned on (bottom left). Click one of the stacks—PDF Documents, in this example—to expand the contents of that folder for easier access (bottom right).

Note: Your own Library folder starts out invisible. But as you'll soon learn from this book, having access to it is frequently useful. That's why Apple gave you a sneaky way to open it even when it's invisible: Press the Option key as you open the Go menu in the Finder; choose Library (which doesn't appear in the menu until you press Option). Or make it stay unhidden permanently; see page 41.

Once again, this setup may seem redundant if you're the only person who uses your Mac. But it makes perfect sense in the context of families, schools, or offices where many people share a single machine. Because you have your own Library folder, you can have a font collection that's "installed" on the Mac only when *you're* using it. Each person's program preference files (the files that determine where Photoshop's palettes appear and so on) are stored independently, too. And each person, of course, sees her own email when launching macOS's Mail program—because mail, too, is generally stored in your personal Library folder.

Other Library folders store your Bookmarks, web browser plug-ins, cached web pages, keyboard layouts, sound files, and so on.

- **Movies, Music, Pictures.** The various macOS programs that deal with movies, music, and pictures will propose these specialized folders as storage locations. For example, when you plug a digital camera into a Mac, the Photos program automatically begins to download the photos on it—and stores them in the Pictures folder. Similarly, iMovie is programmed to look for the Movies folder when saving its files, and iTunes stores its audio files in the Music folder.

- **Public.** If you're on a network, or if others use the same Mac when you're not around, this folder can be handy: It's the "Any of you guys can look at these files" folder. Other people on your network, as well as other people who sit down at this machine, are allowed to see whatever you've put in here, even if they don't

UP TO SPEED

The Computer Window

In your explorations of the Finder's Go menu, you may have wondered about the command called Computer (Shift-⌘-C). ("Go to Computer? Jeez, I thought I was already *at* my computer!")

As in Microsoft Windows, the Computer window holds the icons for all the disks connected to your machine—the hard drive, a CD that you've inserted, a flash drive, another external hard drive, and so on—as well as an icon called Network. (The Network icon appears even if you're not, in fact, on a network.) This is the topmost level of your Mac. This is the stuff that can't be put into any folder at all.

So what's it for? In some ways, the Computer window is redundant. After all, macOS displays your disk icons on the desktop *and* in the Sidebar. But some people, particularly Windows refugees, don't care for that icons-on-the-desktop feature. In the interest of creating a neater, cleaner desktop, they turn it off (by choosing Finder→Preferences and turning off the three checkboxes under "Show these items on the Desktop").

Furthermore, in the interest of creating neater windows, some people also *hide* the Sidebar. In that case, the Computer window still provides access to all your disks.

Otherwise, the Computer window really doesn't serve much purpose except as a familiar landmark to Windows veterans and Mac fans who grew used to it in the era before the Sidebar came along.

- **Library.** This folder bears more than a passing resemblance to the System Folder subfolders of Macs gone by, or the Windows folder on PCs. It stores components for the operating system and your programs (sounds, fonts, preferences, help files, printer drivers, modem scripts, and so on).

- **System.** This is Unix, baby. These are the actual files that turn on your Mac and control its operations. You'll rarely have any business messing with this folder.

- **Users.** As noted earlier, this folder stores the Home folders for everyone who uses this machine.

What's in Your Home Folder

Within the folder that bears your name, you'll find another set of standard Mac folders. (The Mac considers them holy: They have special logos on their folder icons, and you can't rename them.) MacOS creates these folders solely as a convenience:

- **Desktop.** When you drag an icon out of a window and onto your macOS desktop, it may *appear* to show up on the desktop. But that's just an optical illusion, a visual convenience. In truth, nothing in macOS is really *on* the desktop. It's in this Desktop folder and mirrored on the desktop area.

 The reason is simple enough: Everyone who shares your machine will, upon logging in, see his own stuff sitting on the desktop. Now you know how macOS does it: There's a separate Desktop folder in every person's Home folder.

Tip: The fact that the desktop is actually a folder is handy, because it gives you a sneaky way to jump to your Home folder from anywhere. Simply click the desktop background and then press ⌘-▲ (which is the keystroke for Go→Enclosing Folder). Because that keystroke means "Open whatever folder contains the one I'm examining," it instantly opens your Home folder. (Your Home folder is, of course, the "parent" of your Desktop folder.)

- **Documents.** Apple suggests you keep your actual work files in this folder. Sure enough, whenever you save a new document (when you're working in Keynote or Word, for example), the Save As box proposes storing the new file in this folder.

 Your programs may also create folders of their own here. For example, you may find a Microsoft User Data folder for your Outlook email, a Virtual Machines folder for use with VMware Fusion, and so on.

- **Downloads.** All the files you download—from your web browser, from AirDrop, and so on—wind up here, for easy finding later.

- **Library.** As noted earlier, the *main* Library folder (the one in your main hard drive window) contains folders for fonts, preferences, help files, and so on.

 You have your own Library folder, too, in your Home folder. It stores the same kinds of things—but they're *your* fonts, *your* preferences.

Like it or not, macOS considers you one of these people. If you're the only one who uses this Mac, fine—simply ignore the sharing features. (You can also ignore all that business at the beginning of Chapter 1 about logging in.) But in its little software head, macOS still considers you an account holder and stands ready to accommodate any others who should come along.

In any case, now you should see the importance of the Users folder in the main hard drive window. Inside are folders—the Home folders—named for the different people who use this Mac. In general, nobody is allowed to touch what's inside anybody else's folder.

If you're the sole proprietor of the machine, of course, there's only one Home folder in the Users folder—named for you. (The Shared folder doesn't count; it's described on page 548.)

Yes, macOS imposes a fairly rigid folder structure. But by keeping such tight control over which files go where, macOS keeps itself pure—and very, very stable. Furthermore, keeping all your stuff in a single folder makes it easy for you to back up your universe. It also makes life easier when you try to connect to your machine from elsewhere in the office (over the network) or elsewhere in the world (over the internet), as described in Chapter 20.

What's on Your Hard Drive

If you *did* want to explore the entirety of macOS, to examine the contents of your hard drive (choose Go→Computer and double-click "Macintosh HD"), you'd find the following folders in the main hard drive window:

- **Applications.** This folder contains the complete collection of macOS programs on your Mac (not counting the invisible Unix ones). Even so, you'll rarely open programs by opening this folder; the Dock is a far more efficient launcher, as described in Chapter 4.

UP TO SPEED

The Wacky Keystrokes of macOS

MacOS offers a glorious assortment of predefined keystrokes for jumping to the most important locations on your Mac: your Home folder, the Applications folder, the Utilities folder, the Computer window, your iDisk, the Network window, and so on.

Better yet, the keystrokes are incredibly simple to memorize: Just press Shift-⌘ and the first letter of the location you want. Shift-⌘-H opens your Home folder, Shift-⌘-A opens the Applications folder, and so on. You learn one,

you've learned 'em all. The point here is that Shift-⌘ means *places*.

The other system-wide key combo, Option-⌘, means *functions*. For example, Option-⌘-D hides or shows the Dock, Option-⌘-H is the Hide Others command, Option-⌘-+ magnifies the screen (if you've turned on this feature in System Preferences→Accessibility), Option-⌘-Esc brings up the Force Quit dialog box, and so on. You can find the full list in Appendix D, but consistency is always nice.

Your Home Folder

So where is your nest of files, folders, and so on? All of it, everything of yours on this computer, lives in the *Home folder*. That's a folder bearing your name (or whatever name you typed in when you installed macOS).

MacOS is rife with shortcuts for opening this all-important folder:

- **Choose Go→Home,** or press Shift-⌘-H.

- **In the Sidebar** (page 17), click the ⌂ icon that bears your name.

You might also consider adding your Home folder to the Dock (page 139) or making it the window that appears when you press ⌘-N or choose File→New Finder Window (see page 28).

All these steps open your Home folder directly.

If you're the compulsive sort, you can also navigate to it the long way: Double-click the Users folder and then double-click the folder inside it that bears your name and looks like a house (see Figure 2-1).

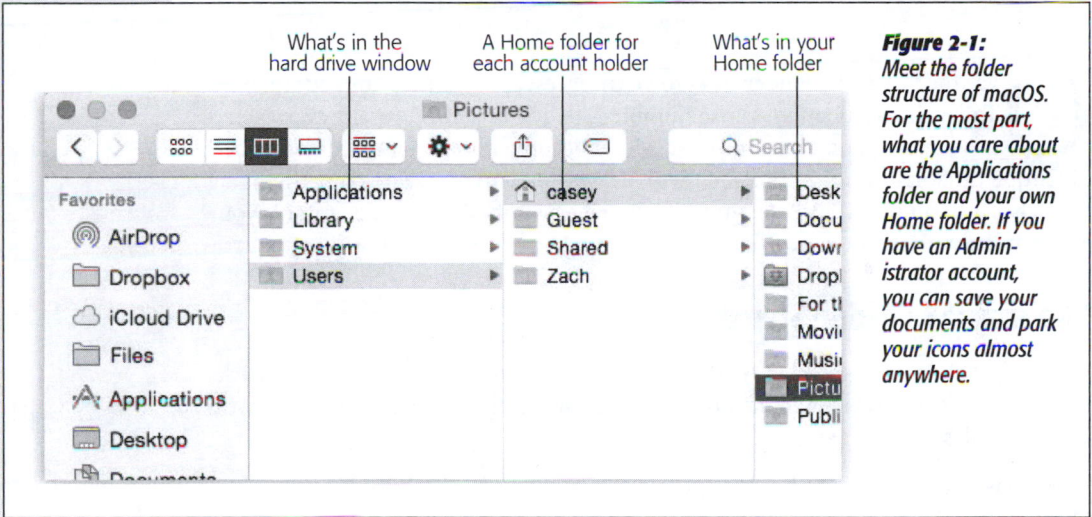

What's in the hard drive window A Home folder for each account holder What's in your Home folder

Figure 2-1:
Meet the folder structure of macOS. For the most part, what you care about are the Applications folder and your own Home folder. If you have an Administrator account, you can save your documents and park your icons almost anywhere.

So why has Apple demoted your files to a folder three levels deep? The answer may send you through the five stages of grief—denial, anger, bargaining, depression, and finally acceptance—but if you're willing to go through it, much of the mystery surrounding macOS will fade away.

MacOS has been designed from the ground up for *computer sharing*. It's ideal for any situation where different family members, students, or workers share the same Mac.

Each person who uses the computer will turn on the machine to find her own separate desktop picture, set of files, web bookmarks, font collection, and preference settings. (You'll find much more about accounts in Chapter 12.)

Organizing Your Stuff

Over the years, the Finder has grown in size, scope, features, and complexity. Today, its occupants—those humble little icons that represent every scrap of your work on that computer—have become more talented than the cast of Cirque du Soleil. You can rename them, delete them, move them, copy them, tag them, get info on them, and of course file them away in folders. This chapter is your guide to life with icons.

The macOS Folder Structure

For the first 20 years of the Mac's existence, you began your workday by double-clicking the Macintosh HD icon in the upper-right corner of the screen. That's where you kept your files.

These days, though, you'd be disappointed if you did that. All you'll find in the Macintosh HD window is a set of folders called Applications, Library, Users, and so on—folders *you* didn't put there.

Most of these folders aren't very useful to you, the Mac's human companion. They're there for macOS's own use—which is why, today, the Macintosh HD icon doesn't even appear on the screen. (At least not at first; you can choose Finder→Preferences and turn the "Hard disks" checkbox back on if you really want to.)

Think of your main hard drive window as storage for the operating system itself, which you'll access only for occasional administrative purposes.

and "Protect your data and your Mac"—presumably the issues that trigger the most help-hotline calls to Apple. Keep clicking text headings until you find a topic you want to read.

Or click "Table of Contents" to see the left-side list of topics, which you can use to drill down to the subject you need (Figure 1-32, bottom).

You can backtrack by clicking the < button at the top of the window.

Tip: Annoyingly, the help window insists on floating in front of all other windows; you can't send it to the back like you can any normal program. Therefore, consider making the help window tall and skinny, so you can put it alongside the program you're working in. Drag any edge of the box to change the window's shape.

• **Use the search box in the Help program.** Type the phrase you want, like *printing* or *switching applications,* into the search box at the top of the window, and then press Return. As you type, a list of proposed matches drops down from the search box. When you click the closest match, you're shown a list of help-screen topics that may pertain to what you need; see Figure 1-32 for details.

Tip: You can also hit Shift-⌘-/ (that is, ⌘-?) to open the help search box. And you can change that keystroke, if you like, in System Preferences→Keyboard→Shortcuts→App Shortcuts.

After a moment, the menu becomes a list of Apple help topics pertaining to your search. Click one to open the Help browser described next; you've just saved some time and a couple of steps.

Tip: The results menu does not, however, show all of Help's results—only the ones Apple thinks are most relevant. If you choose Show All Help Topics at the bottom of the menu, the Help browser opens. It shows a more complete list of Help search results.

- **Drill down.** Alternatively, you can begin your quest for assistance the old-fashioned way: by opening the Help browser first. To do that, choose Help→macOS Help. (In other programs, it might say, for example, "Mail Help." Either way, this command appears only when nothing is typed in the search box.)

After a moment, you arrive at the Help browser shown at top in Figure 1-32. The starting screen offers several "quick click" topics like "Do more on the desktop"

Figure 1-32:
Mac Help likes to help with big-ticket tasks like joining a network, setting up email, or browsing the web. Once you perform a search for some topic, or use the left-side topic list to drill down (bottom), you get a details page that offers a list of finely grained step-by-steps.

You're expected to find the topic you want in one of these three ways:

- **Use the search box.** The first "command" in the Help menu is, in fact, a search box (Figure 1-31). You can type a few words here to specify what you want help with: "setting up printer," "disk space," whatever.

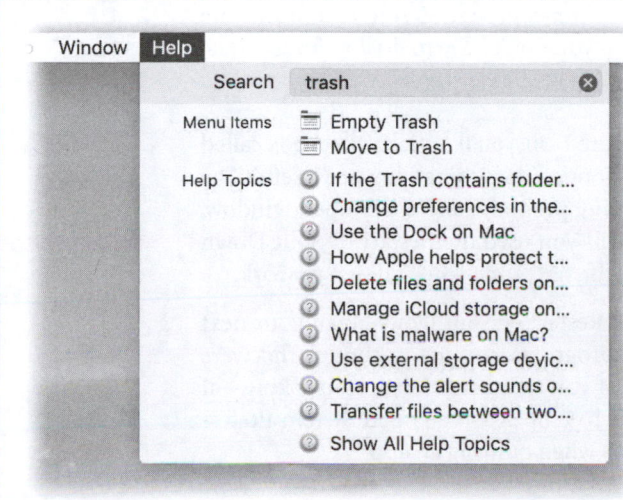

Figure 1-31:
You don't have to open the Help program to begin a search. No matter what program you're in, typing a search phrase into the box shown here produces an instantaneous list of help topics, ready to read.

GEM IN THE ROUGH

Menu Help in the Help Menu

MacOS contains a weird, wonderful little enhancement to its online help system. It helps you find menu commands.

You're floundering in some program. You're *sure* there's a page-numbering command. But there are 11 menus, and 143 submenus, hiding in those menus, and you

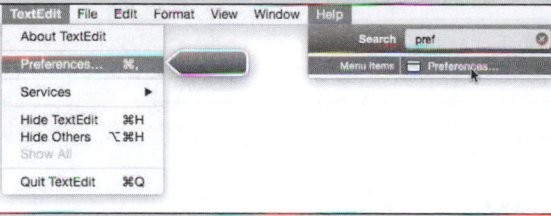

haven't got time for the pain. That's when you should think of using the Help menu. When you type *page number* (or whatever) into its search box, the results menu lists, at the top, the names of any menu commands that contain the words you typed. Better still, it actually *opens that menu* for you, and displays a big, blue, animated, floating arrow pointing to the command you wanted. Slide your cursor over, click the command you wanted, and get on with your life.

Supertip: This feature is especially helpful in web browsers like Safari and Firefox, because it even finds entries in your Bookmarks and History menus! In Safari, for example, you can pluck a recently visited site out of the hundreds in the daily History submenus. You've just saved yourself a *lot* of poking around menus, trying to find the name of a site you know you've seen recently.

Ultratip: If you think about it, this feature also means that you have complete keyboard power over every menu in every program in the world. Hit Shift-⌘-/ (that is, ⌘-?) to open the Help search box, type a bit of the command's name, and then use the arrow keys to walk down the results. Hit Return to trigger the command you want.

- **Press Control-Option-⌘-⏏.** (It's not as complex as it looks—the first three keys are all in a tidy row to the left of the space bar.)

- **Press Control-⏏** (or hold down the ⏻ button) to summon the dialog box shown in Figure 1-30. Click Shut Down (or press Return).

- **Wait.** If you've set up the Energy Saver preferences (page 353) to shut down the Mac automatically at a specified time, then you don't have to do anything.

The "Reopen Windows" Option

In the Shut Down dialog box illustrated in Figure 1-30, you'll notice a checkbox called "Reopen windows when logging back in." That option does something very useful: The next time you start up your Mac, every running program, and every open window, will reopen exactly as they were at the moment you used the Restart or Shut Down command. This saves you a lot of reopening the next time you sit down to work.

If you turn off that checkbox when you click Restart or Shut Down, then your next startup will take you to the desktop, with no programs running, as though this were still some year between 1984 and 2010. And if you want the Mac to stop asking—if you never want your programs and windows to reopen—then open System Preferences→General, and turn on "Close windows when quitting an app."

Log Out

If you share your Mac, then you should log out when you're done. Doing so ensures that your stuff is safe from the evil and the clueless, even when you're out of the room. To do it, choose →Log Out [your name], or press Shift-⌘-Q.

When the confirmation dialog box appears, click Log Out (or press Return) or just wait for one minute (a message performs the countdown for you). The Mac hides your world from view and displays the Log In dialog box, ready for its next victim.

Tip: One more time: If you press Option as you release the mouse on the →Log Out command, you squelch the "Are you sure?" box.

Logging out is described in much more detail in Chapter 12.

Getting Help in macOS

It's a good thing you've got a book about macOS in your hands, because the only manual you get with it is the Help menu, a browser-like program that reads a set of help files that reside in your System→Library folder.

Note: In fact, you may not even be that lucky. The general-information help page about each topic is on your Mac, but thousands of the more technical pages reside online and require an internet connection to read.

- **Tap the Sleep button on your Touch Bar,** if you have one (and if you've installed the Sleep button there; see page 237).

- **Just walk away,** confident that the Energy Saver setting in System Preferences will send the machine off to dreamland automatically at the specified time.

Tip: Ordinarily, closing your MacBook's lid means cutting it off from the world. But the Power Nap feature lets your Mac stay connected to your network and to the internet, even while it's otherwise sleeping. It can download email, back up your stuff, download software updates, and so on. For details, see page 355.

Figure 1-30:
Once the Shut Down dialog box appears, you can press the S key instead of clicking Sleep, R for Restart, Esc for Cancel, or Return for Shut Down.

Restart

You shouldn't have to restart the Mac very often—only in times of severe trouble-shooting mystification, in fact. Here are a few ways to do it:

- **Choose →Restart.** A confirmation dialog box appears; click Restart (or press Return).

Tip: If you press Option as you release the mouse on the →Restart command, you won't be bothered by an "Are you sure?" confirmation box.

- **Press Control-⌘-⏏.**

- **Press Control-⏏** (or hold down the ⏻ button) to summon the dialog box shown in Figure 1-30; click Restart (or type *R*).

Shut Down

To shut down your machine completely (when you don't plan to use it for more than a couple of days, when you plan to transport it, and so on), do one of the following:

- **Choose →Shut Down.** A simple confirmation dialog box appears; click Shut Down (or press Return).

Tip: Once again, if you press Option as you release the mouse, no confirmation box appears.

Tabs in Other Apps

Apparently, you just can't keep a good idea down. Tabbed windows, which did so well in web browsers, eventually made their way to the Finder—and now they're in six *other* Apple programs: Mail, Maps, TextEdit, Pages, Keynote, and Numbers. Some non-Apple apps that are "document-based" (you work in multiple windows, each containing a different document) also have tabs.

For one reason or another, you *don't* get tabbed windowing in any other built-in Apple apps. And you don't get it in Microsoft programs.

If you're using one of the anointed apps, start by opening at least two windows. (Some apps, like Mail, create a new tab when you choose File→New Tab.) Choose Window→Merge All Windows to turn them into tabs. At this point, a + button appears at the top right of the window, so that you can create a new blank tab.

Tip: If you like, those apps can open a new tab, rather than a separate window, every time you create a new document. In System Preferences→Dock, the "Prefer tabs when opening documents" pop-up menu offers three choices. "Always" means *every* new document will appear in a tab. "In Full Screen Only" means that new documents become tabs only when you're in Full Screen mode (page 178). And "Manually" means that new tabs appear only when you use the New Tab command.

At that point, you can switch tabs, rearrange them, close them, and separate them exactly as described already.

Logging Out, Shutting Down

If you're the only person who uses your Mac, finishing up a work session is simple. You can either turn off the machine or simply let it go to sleep, in any of several ways.

Sleep Mode

If you're still shutting down your Mac every night, you may be doing a lot more waiting than necessary. Sleep mode consumes very little power, keeps everything you were doing open and available, and wakes up almost immediately.

To make your machine sleep, do one of the following:

- **Close the lid.** (Hint: This works primarily on laptops.)

- **Press the power button (⏻) on your Mac.** Tapping that button (for about a half-second) makes any kind of Mac drop off to sleep instantly.

- **Hold down the power button (⏻) for two seconds.** You get the box shown in Figure 1-30; hit Sleep (or type *S*).

- **Choose →Sleep.** Or press Option-⌘-⏏.

- **Press Control-⏏.** In the dialog box shown in Figure 1-30, click Sleep (or type *S*).

Tip: And what will it show? Whatever you've chosen in the Finder→Preferences→General→"New Finder windows show" pop-up menu. It's usually your Recents window, or maybe the desktop's contents.

• **A New Tab button is also available to install onto your Touch Bar,** if you have one of those on your MacBook Pro (page 237).

Using Tabs

So why bother opening tabs? Because you can perform a few power-usery stunts now that you couldn't before. Like this:

• **Move files around.** You can drag a file or folder icon into another tab, as shown in Figure 1-29.

• **View the same window twice.** Put one copy of the window in list view, another in icon view. Or view different sections of a long list of files in two side-by-side tabs.

• **Live in a desktop-free world.** Click the green ⊙ button (upper-left corner) to put your Finder window into Full Screen mode. (See page 178 for more on Full Screen mode.)

Now you can work in tabs, manipulating your files, without ever seeing the desktop.

Tab Management

Once you've got some tabs adorning your window, you can operate them thusly:

• **To switch tabs,** click one, or press Control-Tab. (Add the Shift key to cycle through the tabs in reverse.) If you forget these important keystrokes, they're listed for you as commands in the Window menu.

• **Rearrange tabs** by dragging them horizontally.

• **Turn a tab into a stand-alone window** by dragging it away from the other tabs. (Or choose Window→Move Tab to New Window.)

Tip: There's no built-in keyboard shortcut for the Window-menu commands like Move Tab to New Window and Merge All Windows. But it's easy enough to add a shortcut of your own, as described on page 210.

• **Move a tab into a different window** by dragging it. That is, you can drag a tab from one window to another.

• **Round up a bunch of open windows** into a single tabbed window: Choose Window→Merge All Windows. That's a good one.

• **To close a tab,** press the usual "close window" keystroke, ⌘-W. (Or, if it's a slow day at work, choose File→Close Tab. Or move your cursor onto the tab itself and click the tiny ✖ that appears.)

• **To close all tabs,** add the Option key. For example, press Option-⌘-W or Option-click the Close button on one of the tabs.

makes it easy to move icons back and forth between them (Figure 1-29), or even to view the same window twice in different views.

As a convenience, Apple designed the commands, keystrokes, and clicks to work exactly as they do in Safari.

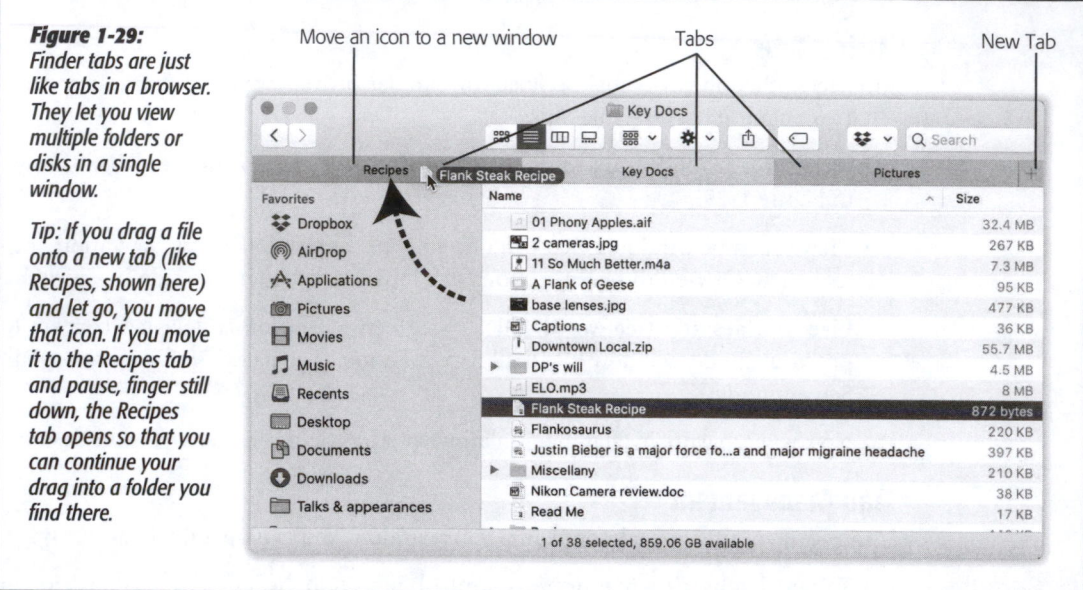

Figure 1-29:
Finder tabs are just like tabs in a browser. They let you view multiple folders or disks in a single window.

Tip: If you drag a file onto a new tab (like Recipes, shown here) and let go, you move that icon. If you move it to the Recipes tab and pause, finger still down, the Recipes tab opens so that you can continue your drag into a folder you find there.

Move an icon to a new window Tabs New Tab

Creating Tabs

There are almost as many ways to open new tabs as there are people:

- **Press the ⌘ key as you open a folder or disk.** (That shouldn't come as a shock; you ⌘-click a link to open a new tab in Safari, too.)

Tip: You can ⌘-click the names of places in the Sidebar of a Finder window, too, like Documents or Pictures.

- **Right-click or two-finger click a folder or disk.** From the shortcut menu, choose Open in New Tab.

- **If you already have some tabs, then click the + button at the far right.** (Even if you haven't created any tabs yet, that button appears if you've made the tab bar visible; choose View→Show Tab Bar.)

- **Drag a disk or folder icon onto the + button at the far right of the tab bar.**

- **Select a folder or disk (or several).** From the ✿ menu, choose Open in New Tab(s)—or press Control-⌘-O.

- **Choose File→New Tab,** or press ⌘-T.

otherwise. (When you're finished with the close-up, click the ⊕ button in the control bar to restore the original Quick Look window, or the ✖ button to exit Quick Look altogether.)

Tip: How's this for an undocumented shortcut? If you highlight an icon and then press Option-space bar, or Option-click the eyeball icon, you go straight into Full Screen mode without having to open the smaller Quick Look window first. Kewl.

(OK, this is actually part of the slideshow feature, but it's also good for super-enlarging a single icon.)

- **Share it.** Click the ⬆ in the title bar to open the Share pop-up menu—a quick way to send this document on to somebody or to post it online.

- **Open with [program name].** This button shows up at the top-right corner of your Quick Look window. It might say, for example, Open with Preview.

 Handy, really. It says: "Oh, so you've been Quick Looking to find a particular document, and this is the one you wanted? Click me to jump directly into the program that opens it, so you can get to work reading or editing. I've just saved your having to close the window and double-click the icon."

Tip: Actually, you have a much bigger target than the "Open with" button in the corner. You can double-click *anywhere in the Quick Look window* to open the document (in whatever program is named on the "Open with" button).

 Better yet: If you click and hold your cursor on that "Open with" button, then you get a secret pop-up menu of other programs that could open the file you're looking at.

- **Keep it going.** Once you've opened Quick Look for one icon, you don't have to close it before inspecting another icon. Just keep clicking different icons (or pressing the arrow keys to walk through them); the Quick Look window changes instantly with each click to reflect the new document.

- **Fix the size.** Quick Look tries to display an entire picture or document in a single small window. To view it at actual size, hold down the Option key.

Finder Tabs

The world discovered the miracle of tabs in *web browsers* years ago. It was a simple software design idea, modeled after the tabs of paper file folders, that let you keep multiple web pages open at once in a single window. What convenience! What cleanliness!

But it took until 2013 for someone to realize that tabs might be useful at the desktop, too. That's when Apple added tabs to Finder windows.

They do exactly the same job they do in Safari: They let you keep open the windows of several different containers—folders or disks—in a single window frame. That

Nothing. But in macOS, you can highlight any icon and then tap the space bar for an instant preview.

- **Press ⌘-Y.** Another keystroke for the same function. The space bar is still better.

- **Click the ◉ icon at the top of the window.** But who uses the mouse anymore?

- **Choose File→Quick Look.**

- **Choose Quick Look from the Action menu (✿) at the top of every Finder window.**

- **Right-click or two-finger click an icon; from the shortcut menu, choose Quick Look.**

- **Tap the ◉ icon on your Touch Bar (page 233),** if you have one.

You exit Quick Look in any one of these same ways.

Note: Whenever Quick Look appears in a menu or shortcut menu, its wording changes to reflect the name of the icon. For example, it might say "Quick Look 'Secret Diary.doc.' "

In any case, the Quick Look window now opens, showing a gigantic preview of the document (Figure 1-27). Rather nice, eh?

The idea here is that you can check out a document without having to wait for it to open in the traditional way—at full size. For example, you can read the text in a Word or PowerPoint document without actually having to open Word or PowerPoint, which saves you about 45 minutes.

In Mojave, in fact, you may even be able to edit your document right in the Quick Look pane. Tucked along the top of the window, you'll find the same Quick Actions buttons described on page 56: for pictures, Rotate and Markup; for PDF documents, Markup; and so on.

Tip: You can use the usual "next page" gesture (two-finger swipe up or down on a trackpad, one-finger swipe on the Magic Mouse) to page through PDF or iWork documents, or to move among photos if you've highlighted a whole bunch.

It's astonishing how few Mac fans are aware of this incredibly useful feature. Learn it!

What Quick Look Knows

Quick Look doesn't recognize all documents. If you try to preview, for example, a Final Cut Pro video project, a sheet-music file, a .zip archive, or a database file, all you'll see is a 6-inch-tall version of its generic icon. You won't see what's inside.

People can write plug-ins for those nonrecognized programs. For example, plug-ins that let you see what's inside folders and .zip files await at *quicklookplugins.com.* In the meantime, here's what Quick Look recognizes right out of the box:

- **Graphics files and photos.** This is where Quick Look can really shine, because it's often useful to get a quick look at a photo without having to haul Photos or

- **On Desktop.** This option, new in macOS Mojave, applies the same idea to icons on your desktop: Folders appear first, and then loose files after them. (The checkbox has no effect if you have *not* opted to sort your desktop icons.)

Quick Look

As the preceding several thousand pages make clear, there are lots of ways to view and manage the teeming mass of files and folders on a typical hard drive. Some of them actually let you see what's in a document without having to open it—the preview column in column view, the giant icons in gallery, the preview pane, and so on.

Quick Look takes this idea to another level. It lets you open and browse a document at nearly full size—without switching window views or opening any new programs (see Figure 1-27). You highlight an icon (or several) and then do one of these things:

- **Press the space bar.** This is by far the best technique to learn. After all, unless you're editing a file's name, what has the space bar ever done for you in the Finder?

Figure 1-27:
Once the Quick Look window is open, you can play a file (movies and sounds), study it in more detail (most kinds of graphics files), or even read it (PDF, Word, and Excel documents). You can also click another icon, and another, and another, without ever closing the preview; the contents of the window simply change to reflect whatever you've just clicked.

Bonus tip: Quick Look works even on icons in the Trash, so you can figure out what something is before you nuke it forever.

Tip: These Quick Actions commands also show up in the shortcut menu that appears when you right-click or two-finger click an icon. They're also on the MacBook Pro's Touch Bar, and in every Quick Look window.

In every case, the More ☺ menu offers a Customize command. In the resulting box, you're treated to a master list of every Quick Actions button the preview pane can display. At the outset, it's not such a big list: Rotate, Markup, Create PDF, and Trim.

Fortunately, other apps can add to this list, and so can you, if you're handy with Automator. (See the Automator.pdf appendix on this book's page at *missingmanuals.com*; when you create your new workflow in Automator, choose Contextual Workflow as the file type.)

In general, you'll probably wind up using the preview pane, and those Quick Actions buttons, mostly for working through folders of photos, and maybe PDF files.

To turn off the pane, choose View→Hide Preview.

Keep Folders on Top

Hiding away in Finder→Preferences→Advanced, "Keep folders on top" awaits. It turns out to be incredibly useful (see Figure 1-26).

- **In windows when sorting by name.** When you've sorted a window's contents alphabetically, all the folders now appear at the top of the list, in their own little alphabetical grouping. (Otherwise they appear mixed in with the loose files, all in one alphabetical list.) This "folders first" arrangement is how things work in Windows—and, although Apple may not have wanted to admit it for 30 years, it's pretty handy.

Figure 1-26:
Left: Ordinarily, folders (highlighted here for clarity) appear sorted alphabetically into lists of loose files.

Right: But the "Keep folders on top in windows when sorting by name" option places them into their own neighborhood above the list.

The Preview Pane

In any of the four Finder views, there's yet another way to see instant previews of what's in each file you highlight (the words in a Word file, the image in a JPEG photo, the numbers in an Excel spreadsheet, and so on). It's called the preview pane (Figure 1-25).

Figure 1-25:
Bottom: You can make this preview pane appear in any Finder window, no matter what view it's in. It shows both the contents of the selected file and some handy details about it. At the bottom, you get one-click processing buttons like Rotate and Markup.

Top: The Markup window offers an array of tools for annotating a photo or PDF document. You can add text boxes, lines, shapes, freehand marker or highlighting marks—or your signature.

To see it, choose View→Show Preview (or press Shift-⌘-P). Now there's a full-height preview pane at the right side of the window. It shows the contents of the highlighted file, along with a dossier of details about it. Depending on the kind of file it is, you may see its name, date, and size; author (Word documents); number of pages and level of security (PDF files); album name, audio channels, and duration (music files); aperture, shutter speed, resolution, lens, and focal length (photos); and so on.

In Mojave, at the bottom, you'll find Quick Actions buttons, relevant to the kind of file you've clicked. For a photo, the buttons are Rotate, Markup, and (when you click the More ⊙ button) Create PDF. For a PDF document, it's Markup and maybe Add Password. For an audio or video file, there's a Trim button.

In any case, gallery view is ideal for perusing folders full of pictures. It lets you get a good clear view of each file without actually having to open it.

To fire up gallery view, open a window. Then click the Gallery button (⌨️) in the toolbar. Or choose View→as Gallery, or press ⌘-4.

Now the window splits. On the bottom: a scrolling row of icons. On the top: the giant preview of whichever one is highlighted. It's probably not something you'd want to set up for every folder, because browsing is a pretty inefficient way to find something. But in folders that contain photos or movies (and aren't filled with hundreds of files), gallery view can be a handy and satisfying way to browse.

Figure 1-24:
The top half of a gallery window shows a giant preview of the highlighted document. It's especially useful for photos, videos, PDF files, Office documents, and text documents. When a PDF or presentation document comes up here, you can scroll vertically through it; for a movie, click the little ▶ button to play the video, right in place.

And now, notes on gallery view:

- **Multipage documents, presentation files, movies, and sounds are special.** When you point to one, you get the ▶ button and a scrubber bar. For a Keynote or PowerPoint file, you get a vertical scroll bar to move through the slides. If it's a PDF document, you can use your trackpad or mouse wheel to move through the pages vertically.

- **The previews are actual icons.** When you're looking at a gallery view mini-document, you can drag it with your mouse—you've got the world's biggest target—anywhere you'd like: another folder, the Trash, wherever.

Grouping the Column Contents

The Group commands are available to column view, too; you can add those category headings to the clumps of files in each window. It all works exactly as described starting on page 41.

View Options

Just as in icon and list views, you can choose View→Show View Options to open a dialog box—a spartan one, in this case—offering additional control over your column views.

- **Always open in column view.** Once again, this option lets you override your system-wide preference setting for all windows. See page 36 for details.

- **Browse in column view.** Ensures that any folder inside this one will open up in column view when double-clicked.

- **Group By, Sort By.** You can put column-view icons into arranged groups—and sort them within those groups—just as described starting on page 41.

- **Text size** affects the type used for icons in all column views.

- **Show icons.** For maximum speed, turn off this option. Now you see only file names—not the tiny icons next to them—in all column views. Weird!

- **Show icon preview.** Turn off this option if you don't want the tiny icons in column view to display their actual contents—photos showing their images, Word and PDF documents showing their first pages, and so on. You get generic, identical icons for each file type (text, photo, or whatever).

- **Show preview column.** The far-right preview column can be handy when you're browsing graphics, sounds, or movie files. Feel free to enlarge this final column when you want a better view of the picture or movie; you can make it really big.

 The rest of the time, though, the preview column can get in the way, slightly slowing down the works and pushing other, more useful columns off to the left side of the window. If you turn off this checkbox, then the preview column will be empty.

Tip: No matter what view you're in, remember this: If you ever start dragging an icon and then change your mind, just press the Esc key or ⌘-period, even while the mouse button is still down. The icon flies back to its precise starting place. Or, if you've already dragged something to a new window and now you regret it, press ⌘-Z (for Undo). Too bad real life doesn't have a similar feature.

Gallery View

The old Cover Flow view has received a tweak in Mojave. It still displays a jumbo preview of each icon as you arrow-key your way through the items in a folder. But now the icons themselves appear in a horizontal row instead of in a list view (Figure 1-24). And you no longer get to see the icons' names (unless you're pointing to one).

- **Within a highlighted column,** press the ▲ or ▼ keys to highlight successive icons in the list. Or type the first couple of letters of an icon's name to jump directly to it.

- **When you finally highlight the icon you've been looking for,** press ⌘-O or ⌘-▼ to open it (or double-click it, of course). You can open anything in any column; you don't have to wait until you've reached the rightmost column.

Manipulating the Columns

The number of columns you can see without scrolling depends on the width of the window. That's not to say, however, that you're limited to four columns (or whatever fits on your monitor). You can make the columns wider or narrower—either individually or all at once—to suit the situation, according to this scheme:

- **To make a single column wider or narrower,** drag the vertical dividing line at its right edge (see Figure 1-23). To adjust all the columns simultaneously, press the Option key as you drag the handle.

Figure 1-23:
When you move your cursor close to the divider line between columns, you get a double-headed arrow. That's a sign that you can now drag that line to adjust the width of the column to its left.

- **To make a column precisely as wide as necessary** to reveal all the names of its contents, double-click the handle on its right side.

- **To make *all* columns as wide as required**—when you absolutely, positively don't want any names truncated—Option-double-click a column's right-side handle.

Tip: If you're having trouble remembering all those key and click combinations, you're not alone. Fortunately, if you right-click or two-finger click the handle at the right side of a column, you get a shortcut menu that offers these commands: Right Size This Column (make it exactly as wide as necessary), Right Size All Columns Individually (make *every* column exactly as wide as necessary), and Right Size All Columns Equally (make all columns *the same width,* based on whatever width is necessary to see all the names in the *narrowest* one).

horizontal scroll bar to bring them back.) You can keep clicking until you're looking at the file icons inside the most deeply nested folder.

If you discover that your hunt for a particular file has taken you down a blind alley, it's not a big deal to backtrack, since the trail of folders you've followed to get here is still sitting before you on the screen. As soon as you click a different folder in one of the earlier panes, the panes to its right suddenly change, so that you can burrow down a different rabbit hole.

Figure 1-22:
If the rightmost folder contains pictures, sounds, Office documents, or movies, then you can look at them or play them right there in the Finder. You can drag this jumbo preview icon anywhere—into another folder or to the Trash, for example.

The beauty of column view is that, first of all, it keeps your screen tidy. It effectively shows you several simultaneous folder levels but contains them within a single window. With a quick ⌘-W, you can close the window, panes and all. Second, column view provides an excellent sense of where you are. Because your trail is visible at all times, it's much harder to get lost—wondering what folder you're in and how you got there—than in any other window view.

Column View by Keyboard

Efficiency fans can operate this entire process by keyboard alone. For example:

- **You can jump from one column** to the next by pressing the ◀ or ▶ keys.

- **You can use the Go menu,** or the icons in the Sidebar, to fill your columns with the contents of the corresponding folder—Home, Favorites, Applications, and so on.

- **The Back command** (clicking the ‹ button on the toolbar, pressing ⌘-[, or choosing Go→Back) works as it does in a web browser: It retraces your steps backward. Once you've gone back, in fact, you can then go forward again; choose Go→Forward, click the › button on the toolbar, or press ⌘-].

Rearranging Columns

You're stuck with the Name column at the far left of a window. However, you can rearrange the other columns just by dragging their gray column headers horizontally. If the Mac thinks you intend to drop a column to, say, the left of the column it overlaps, you'll actually see an animated movement—indicating a column reshuffling—even before you release the mouse button.

Adjusting Column Widths

If you place your cursor carefully on the dividing line between two column headings, you'll find that you can drag the divider line horizontally. Doing so makes the column to the left of your cursor wider or narrower.

What's delightful about this activity is watching macOS scramble to rewrite its information to fit the space you give it. For example, as you make the Date Modified (or Created) column narrower, "March 7, 2019 at 2:22 PM" shrinks first to "Mar 7, 2019 at 2:22 PM," then to "3/7/19, 2:22 PM," and finally to a terse "3/7/19."

If you make a column too narrow, macOS shortens the file names by removing text from the middle. An ellipsis (…) appears to show you where the missing text would have appeared. (Apple reasoned that truncating the ends of file names would hide useful information, like the numbers at the end of "Letter to Marge 1," "Letter to Marge 2," and so on. It would also hide the extensions, such as Thesis.doc, that may appear on file names in macOS.)

For example, suppose you've named a Word document "Justin Bieber—A Major Force for Righteousness and Cure for Depression, Acne, and Migraine Headache." (Yes, file names really can be that long.) If the Name column is too narrow, you might see only "Justin Bieber—A Major…Migraine Headache."

Tip: You don't have to make the column mega-wide to read the full text of a file whose name has been shortened. Just point to the icon's name without clicking. After a moment, a floating balloon appears—something like a tooltip in Microsoft programs—to identify the full name.

In fact, you can hover your mouse up or down a list over truncated file names, and their tooltip balloons appear instantaneously. (This trick works in list, column, and gallery views—and in Save and Open dialog boxes, for that matter.)

Column View

The goal of column view is simple: to let you burrow down through nested folders without leaving a trail of messy, overlapping windows in your wake. The solution is shown in Figure 1-22. It's a list view that's divided into vertical panes. The first pane (not counting the Sidebar) shows whatever disk or folder you first opened.

When you click a disk or folder in this list (once), the second pane shows a list of everything in it. Each time you click a folder in one pane, the pane to its right shows what's inside. The other panes slide to the left, sometimes out of view. (Use the

- **Icon size.** These two buttons offer you a choice of icon sizes for the current window: either tiny or standard. Unlike icon view, list view doesn't give you a size slider.

 Fortunately, even the tiny icons aren't so small that they show up blank. You still get a general idea of what they're supposed to look like.

- **Text size.** You can change the type size for your icon labels, either globally or one window at a time.

- **Show columns.** Turn on the columns you'd like to appear in the current window's list view, as described in the previous section.

- **Use relative dates.** In a list view, the Date Modified, Date Added, Date Last Opened, and Date Created columns generally display information in a format like this: "December 24, 2018 at 11:01 AM." (The Mac uses shorter date formats as the column gets narrower.) But when the "Use relative dates" option is turned on, it substitutes the words "Yesterday" or "Today" where appropriate, making recent files easier to spot.

- **Calculate all sizes.** See the box below.

- **Show icon preview.** Exactly as in icon view, this option turns the icons of graphics files into miniatures of the photos or images within.

- **Use as Defaults.** Click to make your changes in the View Options box apply to all windows in that view on your Mac. (Option-click this button to restore a wayward window back to your defaults.)

FREQUENTLY ASKED QUESTION

Calculate All Sizes

When I sort my list view by size, I see only dashes for folder sizes. What am I doing wrong?

Nothing at all; that's normal. When viewing a Finder window, you see a Size statistic for each file. For folders and disks, however, you sometimes see only uninformative dashes.

Most Mac fans study this anomaly momentarily, scratch their chins, and then get back to their work. (Former Windows people don't even scratch their chins; Windows PCs *never* show folder-size or disk-size information in list views.)

Here's what's going on: In the olden days (like 2016), it could take a computer a long time to add up the sizes of all files inside a folder. Your System→Library folder alone, for example, contains over 100,000 files. Instead of making you wait while it did all the addition, the Mac simply showed you dashes in the folder's Size column.

On occasion, however, you really did want to see how big your folders were. In such cases, you could choose View→Show View Options and turn on "Calculate all sizes." You'd see the folder sizes slowly begin to pop onto the screen, from the top of the window down, as the Mac crunched the numbers on the files within.

In fact, you could even turn on the "Calculate all sizes" option *globally*—that is, for all windows.

The "Calculate all sizes" option is still there in macOS Mojave, and you can still turn it on or off. But a lot has changed now, thanks to the Apple File System (page 505). Among the virtues of this filing system, it makes turning on "Calculate all sizes" instantaneous for all but the largest folders. There's really no reason not to have it turned on for all folders, all the time.

Tip: For disks and folders, you see only dashes—at first. You can, however, instruct the Mac to reveal their sizes, as described on page 50.

- **Kind.** In this column, you can read what kind of file each icon represents. You may see, for example, Folder, JPEG Image, Application, and so on.

- **Version.** This column displays the version numbers of your programs. For folders and documents, you just see dashes.

- **Comments.** This rarely seen column (Figure 1-21) can actually be among the most useful. Suppose you're a person who uses the Comments feature (highlight an icon, choose File→Get Info, type notes about that item into the Comments box). This column displays the first line of those comments about each icon, which comes in handy when tracking multiple versions of your documents.

Figure 1-21:
If your screen is big enough, you can expand the Comments column to show several paragraphs, all in a single line. (To enter some comments about an icon, type into the Comments box in its Get Info, as shown here at bottom.)

- **Tag.** Tags are colors and identifying phrases that you can slap onto icons, wherever they appear, to help you categorize and group them. For details, see page 92.

 Even with this column turned off, you can still see an icon's color, of course. But only by turning on this column do you get to see the text phrase you've associated with each label.

Other View Options

The View Options for a list view include several other useful settings; choose View→Show View Options or press ⌘-J.

- **Always open in list view.** Turn on this option to override your system-wide preference setting for all windows. See page 36 for details.

- **Browse in list view.** Ensures that any folder inside this one will also open up in list view, even if its regularly scheduled view is something else.

Your Choice of Columns

Choose View→Show View Options. In the dialog box that appears, you're offered on/off checkboxes for the different columns of information macOS can show you, as illustrated in Figure 1-20:

- **iCloud Status.** This checkbox is dimmed for every folder except what's in your iCloud Drive folder (page 221). If you turn it on, you'll get a column that indicates whether or not each file has been downloaded from iCloud to your Mac.

- **Date Modified.** This date-and-time stamp indicates when a document was last saved. Its accuracy, of course, depends on the accuracy of your Mac's built-in clock.

Note: Many an up-to-date file has been lost because someone spotted a very old date on a folder and assumed that the files inside were equally old. That's because the modification date shown for a folder doesn't reflect the age of its contents. Instead, the date on a folder indicates only when items were last moved into or out of that folder. The actual files inside may be much older, or much more recent.

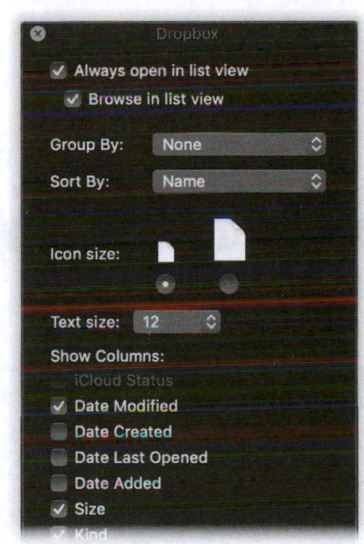

Figure 1-20:
The checkboxes you turn on in the View Options dialog box determine which columns of information appear in a list-view window. Many people live full and satisfying lives with only the three default columns—Date Modified, Kind, and Size—turned on. But the other columns can be helpful in special circumstances; the trick is knowing what information appears there.

- **Date Created.** This date-and-time stamp shows when a document was *first* saved.

- **Date Last Opened.** Just what it sounds like.

- **Date Added.** This option shows when a file was added to this folder or window.

- **Size.** With a glance, you can tell from this column how much disk space each of your files and folders is taking up in kilobytes, megabytes, gigabytes, or terabytes—whichever the Mac thinks you'll find most helpful.

Tip: Once you've expanded a folder by clicking its flippy triangle, you can even drag a file icon out of the folder so that it's loose in the list-view window. To do so, drag it directly upward onto the column headings area (where it says Name, for example). When you release the mouse, you see that the file is no longer inside the expanded folder.

Figure 1-19:
Click a "flippy triangle" (left) to see the list of the folders and files inside that folder (right). Or press the equivalent keystrokes: ▶ (to open) and ◀ (to close).

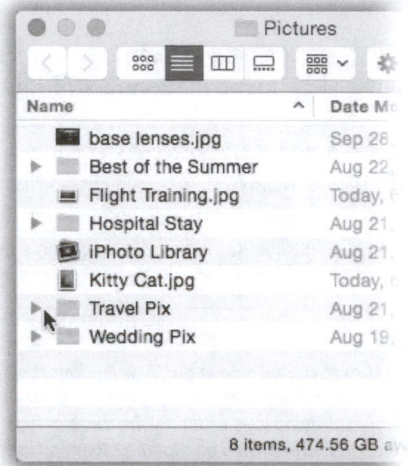

GEM IN THE ROUGH

Flippy Triangle Keystrokes

The keystrokes that let you open and close flippy triangles in a list view are worth committing to memory.

First, pressing the Option key when you click a flippy triangle lets you view a folder's contents *and* the contents of any folders inside it. The result, in other words, is a longer list that may involve several levels of indentation.

If you prefer to use the keyboard, substitute ▶ (to expand a selected folder's flippy triangle) or ◀ (to collapse the folder listing again). Here again, adding the Option key expands or collapses *all* levels of folders within the selected one.

Suppose, for example, that you want to find out how many files are in your Pictures folder. The trouble is, you've organized your graphics files within that folder in several category folders. And you realize that the "how many items" statistic in the status bar shows only how many icons are

visible in the window. In other words, you won't know your total photo count until you've expanded all the folders within the Pictures folder.

You could perform the entire routine from the keyboard like this: Get to your Home folder by pressing Shift-⌘-H. Select the Pictures folder by typing the letter P. Open it by pressing ⌘-O (the shortcut for File→Open) or ⌘-▼. Switch to list view, if necessary, with a quick ⌘-2. Highlight the entire contents by pressing ⌘-A (short for Edit→Select All).

Now that all folders are highlighted, press Option-▶. You may have to wait a moment for the Mac to open every subfolder of every subfolder. But, eventually, the massive list appears, complete with many levels of indentation. At last, the "items" statistic in the status bar gives you a complete, updated tally of how many files and folders, combined, are in the window.

Sorting the List

Most of the world's list-view fans like their files listed alphabetically. It's occasionally useful, however, to view the newest files first, largest ones first, or whatever.

When a desktop window displays its icons in list view, a convenient strip of column headings appears. These headings aren't just signposts; they're buttons, too. Click Name for alphabetical order, Date Modified to view the newest first, Size to view the largest files at the top, and so on.

Don't miss the tiny ∧ or ∨ that appears in the column you've most recently clicked. It shows you which way the list is being sorted. When it's ∧, then the oldest files, smallest files, or files beginning with numbers (or the letter A) appear at the top of the list, depending on which sorting criterion you selected (see Figure 1-18).

Tip: It may help you to remember that when the smallest portion of the triangle is at the top (∧), the smallest files are listed first when viewed in size order.

To reverse the sorting order, click the column heading a second time. Now the ∨ shows you that the newest files, largest files, or files beginning with the letter Z appear at the top of the list.

Note: You can also change the sorting order using the Sort By command described earlier. But, honestly, clicking the column headings is much faster.

Grouping the List

You can arrange your list view into groups by name, date, kind, and so on, with tidy headings that help you make sense of it all. This unsung feature is described under "Group By and Sort By" on page 41.

Flippy Triangles

One of the Mac's most attractive features is the tiny triangle that appears to the left of a folder's name in a list view. In its official documents, Apple calls these buttons *disclosure triangles;* internally, the programmers call them *flippy triangles.* (They don't appear if you've sorted the window using the View→Group By menu.)

When you click one, the list view turns into an outline, showing the contents of the folder in an indented list, as shown in Figure 1-19. Click the triangle again to collapse the folder listing. You're saved the trouble and clutter of opening a new window just to view the folder's contents.

By selectively clicking flippy triangles, you can in effect peer inside two or more folders simultaneously, all within a single list-view window. You can move files around by dragging them onto the tiny folder icons.

Note: There's only one View Options dialog box. Once it's open, you can adjust the icon sizes or arrangement options of other windows just by clicking them. Each time you click inside a window, the View Options dialog box remains in front, changing to reflect the settings of the window you just clicked.

Incidentally, you can get rid of the View Options box the same way you summoned it: by pressing ⌘-J.

List View

In windows that contain a lot of icons, list view is a powerful weapon in the battle against chaos. It shows you a tidy table of your files' names, dates, sizes, and so on (Figure 1-18). You get to decide how wide your columns should be, which of them should appear, and in what order (except that Name is always the first column). Here's how to master these columns.

Figure 1-18:
You control the sorting order of a list view by clicking the column headings (top). Click a second time to reverse the sorting order (bottom). You'll find the ∧ or ∨ triangles—indicating the identical information—in email programs, iTunes, and anywhere else where reversing the sorting order of a list can be useful.

Tip: In icon view, you get an additional option: Snap to Grid. It means "Let me drag these icons into any sequence I want." When you release each drag, the icon jumps into the nearest position on the underlying spacing grid (unless you press the ⌘ key, which gives you full manual control over the icon's position).

In general, this option disappears if you're using one of the Group By options. After all, if you've asked the Mac to arrange your icons into groups, then you've relinquished control of their grid spacing. (The exception: You can still move icons when they're grouped by name–but only if you're dragging into gaps that maintain alphabetical order.)

Free dragging–and grid spacing

Whenever you've applied a Group or Sort to an icon view, the icons remain rooted to an invisible underlying rows-and-columns grid. You can't budge them.

Tip: You can, however, control how tight or loose that grid is, using the "Grid spacing" slider described on page 36.

But there are two situations when you're allowed to drag icons freely into any order you want:

- **Icons never snap to the grid.** If both Group By and Sort By are set to None, then you can go nuts, freely dragging icons into sloppy, off-the-grid positions.

 If, later, you become overwhelmed by shame at your untidiness, you can choose View→Clean Up. Now all the icons in the window jump to the closest positions on the invisible underlying grid.

 This same command appear in the shortcut menu when you right-click or two-finger click anywhere inside an icon-view window, which is handier if you have a huge monitor. There's even a Clean Up By submenu in the View menu and the shortcut menu. These commands don't just put icons back onto the closest grid positions; they put the icons into their proper sorted positions among the other icons—by name, size, date, and so on.

- **Icons always snap to the grid.** If Group By is set to None but Sort By is set to Snap to Grid, then you can drag icons into any order you like (that is, not in any particular sorted order)—but they'll snap to the grid when you let go of the mouse button.

Tip: If you press the ⌘ key as you release the drag, you can reverse the snapping logic. That is, the icons *will* snap to the grid if Sort By is set to None, but you can drag them freely if it's set to Snap to Grid. (Don't press the key until after you've begun to drag.)

Although it doesn't occur to most people, you can also apply any of the commands described in this section—Clean Up, Group, Sort—to icons lying loose on your desktop. Even though they don't seem to be in any window at all, you can specify small or large icons, automatic alphabetical arrangement, and so on. Just click the desktop before using the View menu or the View Options dialog box.

- **In the View Options palette (seen in Figure 1-14), use the Group By pop-up menu.** Yes, it's a fourth place to find the same options.

In each case, you can choose None to turn off the grouping altogether.

Tip: On the desktop, macOS Mojave offers a supercharged way to group your icons: desktop stacks, described on page 76.

Remember, grouping (clumping) is not sorting. You can, in fact, sort the icons differently within each arranged group; read on.

Sorting

Sorting means just what it says: You can sort your files alphabetically (by Name), chronologically (by Date), in order of hugeness (by Size), and so on. See Figure 1-17.

Figure 1-17:
You can use either the View menu or the View Options window (right) to turn on permanent cleanliness mode. You've told the Mac to keep these icons on the invisible grid, sorted the way you requested. Just don't get frustrated when you try to drag an icon and discover that it won't budge.

You can sort a window whether or not you've also grouped it. You can even sort by different criteria. For example, you might have the programs in your Applications folder grouped by category but sorted alphabetically within each category.

Once again, Apple gives you four ways to sort:

- **Option-click the ⊞ icon in the toolbar of the Finder window.**

- **Choose View→Sort By.**

- **Right-click or two-finger click an empty spot in an icon-view window.**

- **In the View Options palette, use the Sort By pop-up menu.**

In each case, you've opened a menu of sorting criteria: Name, Kind, Date, Size, and so on.

Apple wants to make extra, extra sure you're aware of the Group commands. It gives you four different ways to find them:

- **Choose View→Group By.** Choose one of the criteria from the submenu. Your options are Name (alphabetically); Kind (type of file, like Images, Movies, and Documents); Application (which program opens which documents); Date (Last Opened, Added [to the window], Modified, or Created); Size; or Tags (Finder Tag colors, described on page 92). Marvel as the Finder puts your files into tidy categorized groups.

Note: When you're looking at the Applications folder, you get a special choice: Application Category. It clumps your programs by what they do: Productivity, Social Networking, Music, Video, Board Games, Entertainment, Utilities, Reference, Photography, and so on. Pretty cool, actually.

Figure 1-16:
You can view your Finder-window files in neat little groups, separated by headings.

Top: The Applications window, in icon view, grouped by Application Category.

Middle: The Documents folder, in list view, grouped by Application (meaning "which program opens this document").

Bottom: A pictures folder, in column view, grouped by Date Added.

- **Choose from the ▦ icon.** This icon appears in the toolbar of every Finder window. It contains the same options listed in the previous bullet.

- **Right-click or two-finger click** an empty spot in an icon-view window; choose from the Group By shortcut menu. Yep, it's those same commands again.

frontmost window). If you set up the frontmost window with a colored background, big icons, small text, and a tight grid, and then you click Use as Defaults, you'll see that look in every disk or folder window you open. You've been warned.

Fortunately, there are two auxiliary controls that can give you a break from all the sameness:

- **First, you can set up individual windows** to be weirdo exceptions to the rule; see page 36.

- **Second, you can remove any departures** from the default window view—after a round of disappointing experimentation on a particular window, for example—using a secret button. Choose View→Show View Options to open the View Options dialog box. Now hold down the Option key. The Use as Defaults button magically changes to Restore to Defaults, which means "Abandon all the changes I've foolishly made to the look of this window."

Tip: In the View Options for your Home folder, a checkbox appears: Show Library Folder. The Library folder is usually hidden, to prevent clueless newbies from wreaking havoc on important files. But macOS is willing to give it back to you—if you know about this sneaky little trick.

Group By and Sort By

You can wield two different kinds of control over the layout of files in a Finder window: grouping and sorting.

Note: You can perform all these obsessive reorganizations in *any view:* icon view, list view, column view, or gallery view.

Grouping

Grouping files means "Put my files into related clumps, separated by headings that identify them." For example, you can arrange your documents into Application groups (meaning which program opens each one); now you can see at a glance which files will open in, say, iTunes when you double-click them. Or you can organize your Pictures folder into Date Added groups, with headings like "Today," "Last 7 Days," and "Earlier."

To use groups, turn on View→Use Groups. Then use the View→Group By submenu to specify how you want your icons grouped. There are some incredibly useful options here; Figure 1-16 shows a few examples.

Tip: In icon view, the icons under each heading appear in a *single row*, scrolling off endlessly to the right. Use the usual sideways-scrolling gesture to flip through a row. (That is, swipe to the left on a trackpad with two fingers, or with one finger on a Magic Mouse.)

If you're not into gestures, or if you don't have a swipeable input device, then click the tiny Show All button at the right end of a row. Now you've turned off that one-row-per-heading thing, and all the icons under that heading appear in the usual rows and columns; scroll down to see them all.

use a graphics program to scale the picture down to something smaller than your screen resolution.

Use as Defaults

This harmless-looking button can actually wreak havoc on your kingdom—or restore order to it—with a single click. It applies the changes you've just made in the View Options dialog box to all icon-view windows on your Mac (instead of only the

The Color Picker

Here and there—in System Preferences, iMovie, TextEdit, Microsoft Office, and many other programs—macOS offers you the opportunity to choose a *color* for some element: your desktop background, a window, and so on.

The dialog box that appears offers a miniature color lab that lets you dial in any color in the Mac's rainbow—several color labs, actually, arrayed across the top, each designed to make color choosing easier in certain circumstances:

Color wheel. Drag the scroll bar horizontally to adjust the brightness, and then drag your cursor around the ball to pick the shade.

Color sliders. From the pop-up menu, choose the color-mixing method you prefer. CMYK stands for cyan, magenta, yellow, and black. People in the printing industry will feel immediately at home, because these four colors are the component inks for color printing. (These people may also be able to explain why K stands for black.)

RGB is how a TV or computer monitor thinks of colors: as proportions of red, green, and blue light. Grayscale means shades of gray, like a black-and-white TV. And HSB stands for hue, saturation, and brightness—a favorite color-specifying scheme in scientific circles.

In each case, just drag the sliders to mix up the color you want, or type in the percentages of each component.

Color palettes. This option presents canned sets of color swatches. They're primarily for programmers who want

quick access to the standard colors in macOS. The Web Safe Colors list is useful for web designers, too; they can use it to ensure that the colors they choose will display properly on other computers.

Image palettes. Here's the visible rainbow arrayed yet another way: in cloudy, color-arranged streaks. (Cool tip: If you drag a graphics file directly into the dialog box, it appears in the spectrum's place. That's a handy trick if you're trying to identify the color of a certain spot on an image, for example.)

Colored pencils. Now this is a good user interface. You can click each pencil to see its color name: Mocha, Fern, Cayenne, and so on. (Some interior decorator in Cupertino had a field day naming these things.)

In any of these color pickers, you can also "sample" a color that's outside the dialog box—a color you found on a web page, for example. Just click the eyedropper icon and then move your cursor around the screen. You'll see the sliders and numbers change inside the dialog box automatically when you click.

Finally, note that you can store frequently used (or frequently admired) colors in the tiny palette squares at the bottom. To do that, drag the big rectangular color swatch (next to the eyedropper) directly over into one of the little squares, where it will stay fresh for weeks.

If you don't have space for all the colors you want at the bottom of the window, you can grab the line above the eyedropper and drag it up to make room for more.

Once a window is open, choose View→Show View Options (⌘-J). The bottom of the resulting dialog box offers three choices:

- **Default.** This is the standard option (white).

- **Color.** When you click this button, you see a small rectangular button beside the word "Color." Click it to open the Color Picker, which you can use to choose a new background color for the window (Figure 1-15, top). Unless it's April Fools' Day, pick a light color. If you choose a dark one—like black—you won't be able to make out the lettering of the icons' names.

Figure 1-15:
The View Options for an icon-view window let you create colored backgrounds (top) or even use photos as window wallpaper (bottom). Using a photo may have a soothing, comic, or annoying effect—like making the icon names completely unreadable. (Note, by the way, how the icons' names have been set to appear beside the icons, rather than underneath, in the lower illustration. That provides all the handy, freely draggable convenience of an icon view, along with the more compact vertical spacing of a list view.)

- **Picture.** If you choose this option, a "Drag image here" square appears. Now find a graphics file—one of Apple's in the Desktop Pictures folder, or one of your own, whatever—and drag it into that "well."

You see that macOS has superimposed the window's icons on the photo. As you can see in Figure 1-15, bottom, low-contrast or light-background photos work best for legibility.

Incidentally, the Mac has no idea what sizes and shapes your window may assume in its lifetime. Therefore, it makes no attempt to scale down a selected photo to fit neatly into the window. If you have a high-res digital camera, therefore, you may see only the upper-left corner of your photo in the window. For better results,

- **Graphics files.** Certain other kinds of files may show a helpful info line, too. For example, graphics files display their dimensions in pixels.

- **Sounds and QuickTime movies.** The light-blue bonus line tells you how long the sound or movie takes to play. An MP3 file might say "03' 08" " (three minutes, eight seconds).

- **.zip files.** On compressed archives like .zip files, you get to see an archive's total size on disk (like "48.9 MB").

Show icon preview

This option is what makes icons display their contents. If you turn it off, then icons no longer look like miniature versions of their contents (tiny photos, tiny PDF files, and so on). Everything takes on generic icons.

You might prefer this arrangement when, for example, you want to be able to pick out all the PDF files in a window full of mixed document types. Thanks to the matching icons, it's easy now.

Background

Here's a luxury that other operating systems can only dream about: You can fill the background of any icon-view window on your Mac with a certain color—or even a photo.

Color coordinating or "wallpapering" certain windows is more than just a gimmick. In fact, it can serve as a time-saving visual cue. Once you've gotten used to the fact that your main Documents folder has a sky-blue background, you can look at a screen filled with open windows and pick it out like a sharpshooter. Color-coded Finder windows are also especially easy to distinguish at a glance when you've minimized them to the Dock.

Note: Background colors and pictures show up only in icon view.

GEM IN THE ROUGH

Multiple Views, Same Folder

If you've read this chapter carefully, you may have discovered a peculiar quirk of the macOS Finder: By choosing File→New Finder Window, you open a second, completely independent Finder window. Therefore, if you stop to think about it, there's nothing to stop you from opening a third, fourth, or fifth copy of *the same folder window.* Once they're open, you can even switch them into different views.

Try this, for example: Choose Go→Applications. Choose File→New Finder Window (⌘-N), and then choose Go→Applications *again.* Using the View menu or the controls in the toolbar, put one of these windows into list view and the other into icon view.

This ability has its advantages. For example, you might decide to open the same window twice while doing some hard-drive housekeeping. By keeping a list view open, you can check the Size column as you move your files into different folders (so you can make sure the folders fit onto a blank CD, for example). By keeping a *column* view open, on the other hand, you gain quicker navigational access to the stuff on your drive.

But for your Pictures folder, it probably makes more sense to set up icon view, so you can see a thumbnail of each photo without having to open it.

That's the idea here. Open Pictures, change it to icon view, and then turn on "Always open in icon view." Now every folder on your Mac is in list view except Pictures.

Browse in icon view

This option makes sure that any folders inside the current window open up into icon view, too, even if you'd previously set them to open into some other view. So if you're looking at your Pictures folder in icon view and you open the Grand Canyon Jaw-Droppers folder inside it, then that folder also will be in icon view.

Group By, Sort By

For a discussion of these pop-up menus, see page 41.

Icon size

It's super-easy to make all your icons bigger or smaller; just drag the "Icon size" slider in the lower-right corner of the window. (To make the slider appear, turn on View→Show Status Bar.) But for the benefit of old-timers who expect to find that slider in the View Options window, well, there's an identical slider there.

Grid spacing

You can control how closely icons are spaced in a window. Figure 1-14 shows all.

Text size

Your choices range only from 10 to 16 points, and you can't choose a different font for your icons' names. But using this pop-up menu, you can adjust the type size. And for people with especially big or especially small screens—or for people with aging retinas—this feature is much better than nothing.

In fact, you can actually specify a different type size for every window on your machine. (Why would you want to adjust the point size independently in different windows? Well, because you might want smaller type to fit more into a crammed list view without scrolling, while you can afford larger type in less densely populated windows.)

Label position

Click either Bottom or Right to indicate where you want an icon's name to appear, relative to its icon. As shown in Figure 1-15 at bottom, this option lets you create, in effect, a multiple-column list view in a single window.

Show item info

While you've got the View Options palette open, try turning on "Show item info." Suddenly you get a new line of information (in tiny blue type) for certain icons, saving you the effort of opening up the folder or file to find out what's in it. For example:

- **Folders.** The info line lets you know how many icons are inside each without having to open it up. Now you can spot empties at a glance.

(⌘-J). (You can put a View Options button onto your Touch Bar, if you have one, too; see page 237.)

The dialog box shown in Figure 1-14 appears.

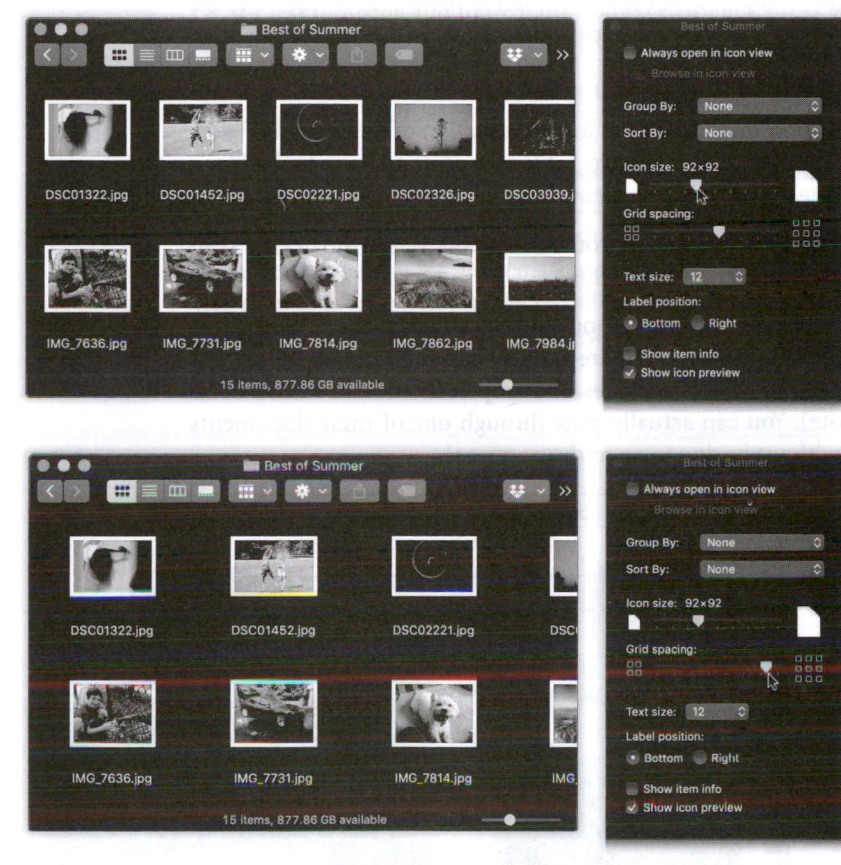

Figure 1-14:
Drag the "Grid spacing" slider to specify how tightly packed you want your icons to be. At the minimum setting, they're so crammed it's almost ridiculous; you may not even be able to see their full names. But sometimes you don't really need to. At a more spacious setting (bottom), you get a lot more white space.

Always open in icon view

It's easy—almost scarily easy—to set up your preferred look for all folder windows on your entire system. With one click on the Use as Defaults button (described on page 40), you can change the window view of 20,000 folders at once—to icon view, list view, or whatever you like.

Note: The wording of this item in the View Options dialog box changes according to the view you're in at the moment. In a list-view window, it says "Always open in list view." In a gallery–view window, it's "Always open in gallery view." And so on. But the function is the same: to override the default (master) setting.

The "Always open in icon view" option lets you override that master setting, just for one window. For example, you might generally prefer a neat list view with large text.

Tip: Each tiny folder icon in this display is fully operational. You can double-click it to open it, right-click or two-finger click it to open a shortcut menu, or even drag things into it.

Status Bar

MacOS hides yet another information strip at the bottom of a window: the status bar, which tells you how many icons are in the window ("14 items," for example) and the free space remaining on the disk. To make it appear, choose View→Show Status Bar.

Figure 1-10:

Top: Suppose you've got a window. Hey–it could happen. You double-click the right edge of it, and boom: You've extended the window all the way to the right edge of the screen (middle).

Bottom: If you press Option at the same time, you extend the window all the way to both edges of the screen. This feature works in Apple's own programs (Finder, Mail, TextEdit, and so on), but not in programs that have their own weird ways of doing things (Microsoft Word, for example).

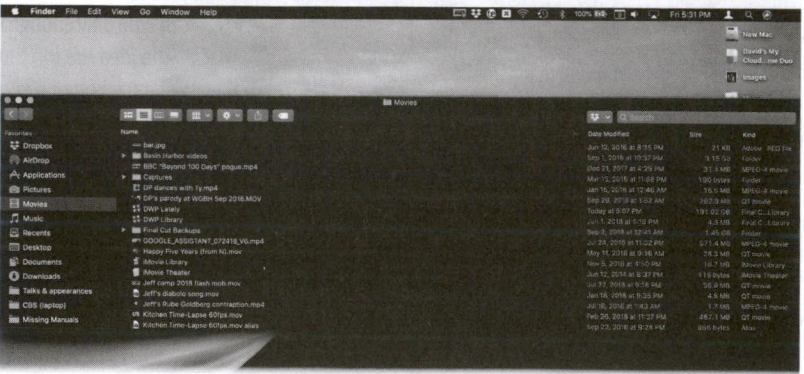

That's a long-winded way of explaining why, in most programs, the scroll bars are hidden. See Figure 1-9 for details.

Note: If the missing scroll bars leave you jittery and disoriented, you can bring them back. Open System Preferences→General and then turn on "Show scroll bars: Always."

Insta–Full Screen

Why drag a window manually? That's so 2015! Now you can let the software do the dragging for you.

Turns out that if you *double-click* any edge of a window, it snaps to the full width of your screen in that direction: left, right, top, or bottom (see Figure 1-10).

And if you double-click any edge while pressing Option, the window expands to the full height or width of the monitor in both directions (Figure 1-10, bottom).

Resizable Edges

For the first 28 years of its existence, the Mac offered only one way to make a window bigger or smaller: Drag the ribbed-looking lower-right corner. These days, you can drag *any* edge of a window to change its shape. Just move the pointer carefully to the exact top, bottom, left, or right edge; once the pointer changes to a double-headed arrow, you can drag to move that window's edge in or out.

Tip: There are a few cool, totally undocumented variations on the window-edge-dragging business. First, if you press the Option key while dragging, you resize the *opposite edge* simultaneously. For example, if you Option-drag the bottom edge upward, the top edge simultaneously collapses downward. If you press Shift as you drag, you resize the *entire* window, retaining its proportions. And if you Shift-Option-drag, you resize the window around its center, rather than from its edges.

Snappable Windows

It's easy to position windows tightly against each other, side by side, for comparison or copying. As you slowly drag a window (by its title bar, for example), you'll notice that its edge *sticks* momentarily to any other window edge it passes.

This feature works only in Apple's own programs—and it doesn't happen if you're dragging *quickly*.

Tip: If you're pressing the Option key as you drag, you eliminate that moment of stickiness. Use this trick when you're in a real, *real* hurry.

Path Bar

Choose View→Show Path Bar to see a tiny map at the bottom of the window, showing where you are in the folder hierarchy. If it says Casey→Pictures→Picnic, well, then, by golly, you're looking at the contents of the Picnic folder, which is inside Pictures, which is inside your Home folder (assuming your name is Casey).

you were moving into a document, because the window itself went pure white when you dragged the handle. Today, though, you can manipulate the contents of a window and see where you are. Nobody questions the absence of scroll bars on an iPad, right? Because you just push the contents of a window around with your fingers to scroll.

In macOS, you scroll by pushing two fingers up the trackpad (or one finger up the Magic Mouse) or by turning your mouse's scroll wheel. You almost never use the antiquated method of dragging the scroll bar's handle manually, with the mouse.

Tip: You can also scroll using the keyboard. Your Page Up and Page Down keys let you scroll up and down, one screen at a time, without ever having to take your hands off the keyboard. The Home and End keys are generally useful for jumping directly to the top or bottom of your document (or Finder window). And, if you've bought a mouse that has a scroll wheel on the top, you can use it to scroll windows without pressing any keys at all.

Figure 1-9:
Scroll bars don't appear at all while you're working (right); you have more screen area dedicated to your work. If you begin to scroll by sliding your fingers up or down the trackpad or Magic Mouse, the scroll-bar handle appears, so you know where you are (middle).

At that point, if you point to the scroll bar, it fattens up so you can grab it (left).

NOSTALGIA CORNER

How the Scroll Bar Used to Work

If you are that rare, special individual who still operates the scroll bar by clicking it with the mouse, the old-style controls are still around.

For example: Ordinarily, when you click in the scroll bar track above or below the dark-gray handle bar, the window scrolls by one screenful. But another option awaits when you choose System Preferences→General and turn on "Jump to the spot that's clicked." Now when you click the scroll-bar track, the Mac considers the entire scroll bar a proportional

map of the document and jumps precisely to the spot you clicked. That is, if you click the very bottom of the scroll-bar track, you see the very last page.

No matter which scrolling option you choose, you can always override your decision on a case-by-case basis by *Option*-clicking the scroll-bar track. In other words, if you've selected the "Jump to the spot that's clicked" option, you can produce a "Jump to the next page" scroll by Option-clicking in the scroll-bar track.

- Press ⌘-▲ (up arrow).

- Choose Go→Enclosing Folder.

None of that helps you, however, if you want to move a file from one folder into the other, or to compare the contents of two windows. In that case, you probably want to see both windows open at the same time.

You can open a second window using any of these techniques:

- Choose File→New Finder Window (⌘-N).

Tip: What folder contents fill the "new" window that appears when you use this command? Usually, it's the Recents folder (page 18)—but it can be any window you want. Choose Finder→Preferences→General. Change the "New Finder windows show" pop-up menu to whatever folder you'd like to use as the starting point for your computing life. Your Home folder (page 72) is a good choice. But you're also free to choose your Documents folder, your iDisk, or any folder at all. Now every new Finder window shows you that specified folder, which is a useful arrangement.

- Double-click a folder or disk icon on your desktop.

The Finder Toolbar

Chapter 4 describes this fascinating desktop-window element in great detail.

Old Finder Mode

Old Finder Mode (not the official Apple term) was designed for people who came to the Mac from a much older version, like Mac OS 9, and lost half their hair when they discovered how different things were. In this mode, there are two big differences that make macOS more like its predecessors:

- **The Sidebar and the toolbar** blink out of sight.

- **Double-clicking a folder** now works like it did back in 2000. Every time you double-click a folder, you open a new window for it.

The Old Finder Mode button no longer appears, but the mode itself is still available. Press Option-⌘-T, the equivalent for the View→Hide Toolbar command. (Repeat that keystroke or command to turn Old Finder Mode off again.) This won't work if your Finder window has multiple tabs open, but that's not going to be a problem if you're yearning for the days of yore.

Scroll Bars

On the modern Mac, scroll bars don't appear nearly as often as they used to. A scroll bar, of course, is the traditional window-edge slider that lets you move through a document that's too big for the window. Without scroll bars, for example, you'd never be able to write a letter that's taller than your screen.

On the very first Macs, scroll bars were a necessary evil; those computers were too underpowered to manage visibly moving the contents of the window. That's why scroll bars were invented in the first place: to give you some feedback about how far

Two Clicks, One Window

Double-clicking a folder in a window doesn't leave you with two open windows. Instead, double-clicking a folder makes the contents of the original window disappear (Figure 1-8).

Tip: If you Option-double-click a folder, you don't simply replace the contents of a fixed window that remains onscreen; you actually switch windows, as evidenced by their changing sizes and shapes.

Figure 1-8:
To help you avoid window clutter, Apple has designed macOS windows so that double-clicking a folder in a window (top) doesn't actually open another window (bottom). Every time you double-click a folder in an open window (except in column view), its contents replace whatever was previously in the window. If you double-click three folders in succession, you still wind up with just one open window.

So what if you've now opened Inner Folder B, and you want to backtrack to Outer Folder A? In that case, just click the tiny ‹ button—the Back button—in the upper-left corner of the window, or use one of these alternatives:

- Choose Go→Back.

- Press ⌘-[(left bracket).

If you miss those hazy, happy days, just press the Option key as you click. The button sprouts a ⊕ button like it used to. Now you'll get a zoomed window instead of a full-screen one. (A second Option-click restores the window to its previous size.)

Note: Not all programs permit you to full-screenize their windows. In those apps, this green button displays the ⊕ button and, when clicked, merely zooms the window.

The Folder Proxy Icon

In the Finder, there's a tiny icon next to the window's name (Figure 1-7). It's a stand-in—a proxy—for that window's folder itself. By dragging this tiny icon, you can move or copy the folder into a different folder or disk, into the Sidebar, into the Trash, or into the Dock without having to first close the window.

Tip: You have to hold down the mouse button on the folder proxy icon until the icon darkens before dragging. (It darkens in a fraction of a second.)

Figure 1-7:
When you find yourself in a Finder window that contains useful stuff, consider dragging its proxy icon to the Dock. That will install its folder or disk icon there for future use. It's not the same as minimizing the window, which puts the icon into the Dock only temporarily.

(Note: Most document windows also offer a proxy-icon feature, but it usually produces only an alias when you drag the proxy to a different folder or disk.)

When you drag this proxy icon to a different place on the same disk, the usual folder-dragging rules apply: Hold down the Option key if you want to copy the original disk or folder; ignore the Option key to move it. (You'll find details on moving and copying icons in the next chapter.)

Many programs, including Microsoft Word, Preview, TextEdit, and others, offer the same mini-icon in open document windows. Once again, you can use it as a handle to drag a document into a new folder or onto a new disk. Sometimes, doing that really does move the document—but more often you just get an alias of it in the new location.

Nowadays, your document windows can minimize themselves into their programs' Dock icons, rather than creating new Dock icons for themselves. That way, your Dock doesn't get any more crowded, and the icons on it don't keep shrinking away to atoms.

To turn on this feature, choose System Preferences→Dock. Turn on "Minimize windows into application icon."

So how do you get those windows back out of the Dock icon? You use Dock Exposé, which is described on page 198.

Figure 1-6:
Clicking the Minimize button sends a window sliding down to the Dock, collapsing in on itself as though being forced through a tiny, invisible funnel. A little icon appears on the lower-right corner of its minimized image to identify the program it's running in.

Full Screen Button

A click on the third dot, the green one, on every window's title bar (in most programs, anyway), throws the window into *Full Screen mode*, in which the menu bars and window edges disappear, in the name of making your window fill your screen edge to edge. See page 178 for details.

As your cursor approaches this green dot, a little indicator appears inside it: ⊗. That's the hint that you're about to enter Full Screen mode.

And once you're in Full Screen mode, you can push your cursor to the top of the screen to reveal the window controls. When it passes over the green dot, it changes to this: ⊕. That's right: It's the universal symbol for "Click me to *leave* Full Screen mode."

In OS X versions before Yosemite, this button was called the Zoom button. It made a desktop window just large enough to reveal all the icons inside it—or, in programs, large enough to reveal all the text, graphics, or music. (The Window→Zoom command does the same thing, and so does double-clicking the title bar of a Finder window.)

you hide a window that has to remain open (because you're waiting for some task to finish) so you can read something else in the meantime.

And now, some Minimize button micro-goodies:

- **If you enjoy the ability to roll up your windows in this way,** remember that you actually have a bigger target than the tiny Minimize button. (You can make the entire title bar a giant Minimize button, as described on page 22.)

 Better yet, you can also minimize the frontmost window of almost any program (including the Finder) from the keyboard by pressing ⌘-M. That's a keystroke worth memorizing on your first day with the Mac.

- **Option-clicking one minimized window on the Dock** un-minimizes all a program's windows—at least for Cocoa programs (page 227).

Tip: MacOS can change menu commands as you press modifier keys. For example, open a couple of Finder windows and then click the Window menu. Focus on the Minimize Window command. Now press Option and watch both the wording and the listed keyboard equivalent change instantly to Minimize All (Option-⌘-M).

The Option key works wonders on the File menu, too.

- **In the bad old days (up to late 2009),** minimizing a bunch of documents could get really messy. Each one flew onto the Dock, putting a new icon there, creating a tighter and tighter squeeze, shrinking the Dock's icons until they were the size of Tic Tacs.

POWER USERS' CLINIC

Adjusting the Genie Speed

Apple has a name for the animation you see when you minimize, open, or close a window: the *genie effect*, because it so closely resembles the way Barbara Eden, Robin Williams, and other TV and movie genies entered and exited their magic lamps and bottles.

You don't have to watch the "genie" animation in precisely the same way, day in and day out. There's no keystroke for making the animation go faster, but you can substitute a faster *style* of minimizing animation.

To do so, choose System Preferences→Dock. From the "Minimize windows using" pop-up menu, choose Scale Effect, and then close the window. Now, instead of collapsing through an invisible funnel, minimized windows simply shrink as they fly down to the Dock, remaining rectangular. The time you save isn't going to get you home an hour earlier each day, but at least you have the illusion of greater speed.

There's a third animation style, too, but there's a trick to unleashing it: You need the free utility called TinkerTool. It's available from this book's "Missing CD" page at *missingmanuals.com.*

Nostalgia moment: When Steve Jobs first demonstrated Mac OS X, one of his favorite bits was slowing down the animation so everyone could see it in graceful slow motion. How did he do that?

For years, you could Shift-click a window's Minimize button to make it collapse into the Dock at about one-tenth its usual speed. The Shift key also slowed the un-minimizing animation, the one you see when you click a window icon in the Dock to restore it to full size.

Alas, Apple's No Fun Committee removed this feature from macOS Mojave. Ah, the cost of progress.

Close Button

As the tip of your cursor crosses the three buttons at the upper-left corner of a window, tiny symbols appear inside them: ⊗, ⊖, and ⊙. Ignore the gossip that these symbols were added to help color-blind people who can't distinguish the colors red, yellow, and green. Color-blind people are perfectly capable of distinguishing the buttons by their positions, just as they do with traffic lights.

But for people who aren't paying attention to button position, these cues distinguish the buttons even further. They also signal when it's time to click. For example, as described in the previous section, you can use these three buttons even when the window is not at the front. You know the buttons are ripe for the clicking when you see the little symbols appear under your cursor.

The most important window gadget is the Close button, the red, droplet-like button in the upper-left corner (see Figure 1-4). Clicking it closes the window, which collapses back into the icon from which it came.

Tip: If, while working on a document, you see a tiny dot in the center of the Close button, macOS is trying to tell you that you haven't yet saved your work. (It doesn't appear in Auto Save programs like TextEdit.) The dot goes away when you save the document.

The universal keyboard equivalent of the Close button is ⌘-W (for window)—a keystroke well worth memorizing. If you get into the habit of dismissing windows with that deft flick of your left hand, you'll find it far easier to close several windows in a row, because you won't have to aim for successive Close buttons.

In many programs, something special happens if you're pressing the Option key when using the Close button or its ⌘-W equivalent: You close all open windows. This trick is especially useful in the Finder, where a quest for a particular document may have left your screen plastered with open windows for which you have no further use. Option-clicking the Close button of any one window (or pressing Option-⌘-W) closes all of them.

The Option-key trick doesn't close all windows in *every* program—only those in the *current* program. Option-closing a Microsoft Word document closes all Word windows, but your Finder windows remain open.

Moreover, Option-closing doesn't work in all programs.

Minimize Button

Click this yellow dot to minimize any Mac window, sending it shrinking, with a genie-like animated effect, into the right end of the Dock, where it then appears as an icon. The window isn't gone. It's just out of your way for the moment, as though you've set it on a shelf. To bring it back, click the newly created Dock icon; see Figure 1-6. Chapter 4 has more on the Dock.

Minimizing is a great window-management tool. In the Finder, minimizing a window lets you see whatever icons were hiding behind it. In a web browser, minimizing lets

the main hard drive window by right-clicking or two-finger clicking the folder name "Users" and then choosing Macintosh HD from the menu.

Tip: Keyboard lovers, take note. Instead of using the title bar menu, you can also jump to the enclosing window by pressing ⌘-▲ (up arrow), which is the shortcut for the Go→Enclosing Folder command. Pressing ⌘-▼ (down arrow) takes you back into the folder you started in, assuming that it's still highlighted. (This makes more sense when you try it than when you read it.)

Figure 1-5:
Right-click or two-fin-ger click a Finder window's title bar to summon the folder hierarchy menu. This trick also works in most other programs. For example, you can right-click a docu-ment window's title to find out where the document is saved on your hard drive.

Once you've mastered dragging, you're ready for these title bar tips:

- **Pressing the ⌘ key** lets you drag the title bar of an inactive window—one that's partly covered by a window in front—without bringing it to the front. (Drag any empty part of the title bar—not the title itself.)

 By the way, you can close, minimize, or full-screenize a background window without the help of the ⌘ key. Just click one of those three corresponding title-bar buttons normally, even if the window you're working on is in front of it.

- **Double-clicking the title bar** is a special technique: It *zooms* the window, enlarging it enough to reveal all the icons inside it (or, in programs, large enough to reveal all the text, graphics, or music). If your monitor isn't big enough to show all the icons in a window, then the window grows to show as many as possible.

 With a quick visit to System Preferences→Dock, though, you can change things up. You can turn on "Double-click a window's title bar to minimize." Now dou-ble-clicking the title bar makes the window collapse into the Dock, exactly as though you had clicked the Minimize button.

Tip: If you've turned on that "minimize" option, then you can minimize *all* desktop windows, sending them flying to the Dock, when you double-click the title bar while pressing the Option key.

Title Bar

The title bar (Figure 1-4) has several functions. First, when a bunch of windows are open, the darkened title bar, window name, mini-icon, and colored left-corner buttons tell you which window is active—in front. (In background windows, these elements appear dimmed and colorless.) Second, the title bar acts as a handle that lets you move the window around on the screen.

Figure 1-4:
When Steve Jobs unveiled the new Mac operating system at Macworld Expo in 2000, he said his goal was to oversee the creation of an interface so attractive "you just want to lick it." Desktop windows, with their juicy, fruit-flavored controls, are a good starting point.

You can also move a window by dragging the solid gray strip on the bottom, assuming you've made it appear (choose View→Show Status Bar).

Tip: Here's a nifty keyboard shortcut: You can cycle through the different open windows in one program without using the mouse. Just press ⌘-~ (that is, the tilde key, to the left of the number 1 key on U.S. keyboards). With each press, you bring a different window forward within the current program. It works both in the Finder and in your everyday programs, and it beats the pants off using the mouse to choose a name from the Window menu. (Note the difference from ⌘-Tab, which cycles through different open *programs*.)

After you've opened one folder that's inside another, the title bar's secret folder hierarchy menu is an efficient way to backtrack—to return to the enclosing window. Get into the habit of right-clicking (or two-finger clicking, or Control-clicking, or ⌘-clicking) the name of the window to access the menu shown in Figure 1-5. (You can release the Control or ⌘ key immediately after clicking.)

By choosing the name of a folder from this menu, you open the corresponding window. When browsing the contents of the Users folder, for example, you can return to

- **Adjust the width** of the Sidebar by dragging its right edge—either the skinny divider line or the extreme right edge of the vertical scroll bar, if there is one. You "feel" a snap at the point where the line covers up about half of each icon's name. Any covered-up names sprout ellipses (…) to let you know there's more (as in "Secret Salaries Spreadsh…").

- **Hide the Sidebar** by pressing Option-⌘-S, which is the shortcut for the View→Hide Sidebar command. Bring the Sidebar back into view by pressing the same key combination (or by using the Show Sidebar command).

Tip: You can hide and show the Sidebar manually, too: To hide it, drag its right edge all the way to the left edge of the window. Unhide it by dragging the left edge of the window to the right again.

Then again, why would you ever want to hide the Sidebar? It's one of the handiest navigation aids since the invention of the steering wheel. For example:

- **It takes a lot of pressure off the Dock.** Instead of filling up your Dock with folder icons (all of which look frustratingly alike and are unlabeled), use the Sidebar to store them. You leave the Dock that much more room for programs and documents.

- **It's better than the Dock.** In some ways, the Sidebar is a lot like the Dock, in that you can stash favorite icons of any sort there. But the Sidebar reveals the names of these icons, and the Dock doesn't until you use the mouse to point there.

- **It makes ejecting easy.** Just click the ⏏ button next to any removable disk to make it pop out.

- **You can drag onto its folders and disks.** That is, you can drag icons onto Sidebar icons, just as though they were the real disks, folders, and programs they represent.

- **It simplifies connecting to networked disks.** Park your other computers' shared folder and disk icons here, as described in Chapter 13, to shave several steps off the usual connecting-via-network ritual.

Fixing the Sidebar

Anything you drag out of the Sidebar can be dragged back in again, including the big-ticket items like Applications and Pictures. That's good to know if you drag something important out of the Sidebar and then change your mind.

Even so, there's a quicker way to restore the Sidebar to its factory settings.

If you choose Finder→Preferences and then click the Sidebar button, you discover

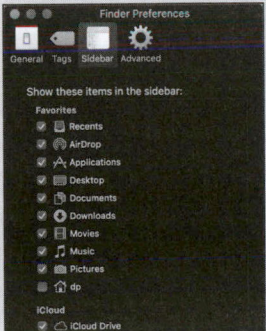

the checkboxes shown here. They let you put back the Apple-installed icons you may have removed in haste. Just turn on a checkbox to restore its icon to your Sidebar. So if something you expect to see in your Sidebar isn't there, check back here.

On the other hand, you may as well streamline your computing life by turning *off* the checkboxes of icons you *never* want to see filling your Sidebar.

Fine-tuning the Sidebar

The beauty of this parking lot for containers is that it's so easy to set up with your favorite places. For example:

- **Remove an icon** by dragging it out of the Sidebar. It vanishes. You haven't actually removed anything from your Mac; you've just unhitched its alias from the Sidebar.

Tip: If you drag a Locations item out of the list, you'll have to choose Finder→Preferences→Sidebar and then turn on the appropriate checkbox to put it back in.

Figure 1-3:
Good things to put in the Sidebar: favorite programs, disks on a network you often connect to, a document you're working on every day, and so on. You can drag a document onto a folder icon to file it there, drag a document onto a program's icon to open it with the "wrong" program, and so on.

Drag this divider to shrink or widen the Sidebar

Sidebar

- **Rearrange the icons** by dragging them up or down in the list. For example, hard drives don't appear at the top of the Sidebar as in the olden days, but you're free to drag them back into those coveted spots.

- **Rearrange the sections** by dragging *them* up or down. For example, you can drag Favorites to the bottom but promote the Locations category.

- **Install a new icon** by dragging it off your desktop (or out of a window) into any spot in the Favorites list of the Sidebar; a horizontal line shows where it will land after you let go. You can't drag icons into any section of the Sidebar—just Favorites.

Tip: You can also highlight an icon wherever it happens to be and then choose File→Add to Sidebar, or just press Control-⌘-T.

- **iCloud.** This heading offers the fantastic iCloud Drive, a Dropbox-like feature that's described on page 221.

- **Locations.** Here's a complete list of *containers*: other computers on your network (Chapter 13), hard drives, iPhones, iPads, CDs, DVDs, memory cards, USB flash drives, and so on. (Your main hard drive doesn't usually appear, but you can drag it here, or turn it on in Finder→Preferences→Sidebar.) The removable ones (like memory cards, flash drives, and disks) bear a ⏏ logo, which you can click to eject that disk.

- **Tags.** This section lists all your Finder *tags* (color-coded keywords). See page 92 for more on tags.

Note: If you remove everything listed under one of these headings, the heading itself disappears to save space. It reappears the next time you put something in its category back into the Sidebar.

What Happened to "All My Files"?

It was there for years on the Mac, at the top of the Sidebar: the All My Files folder. It was a super-convenient, massive, searchable, sortable list of every human-useful file on the computer: documents, pictures, movies, music. No matter what folders they were *actually* in, they appeared in this single window.

People could use All My Files to find, for example, all the presentation files on the Mac, just by sorting the list by Kind. Or, when running out of disk space, they could sort it by file size, making it easy to see which files were eating up the most space.

What's with the past tense? The All My Files folder is gone. The Mysterious Minds of Apple decided to replace it with a folder called Recents.

You might expect that this Recents folder lists every file that you've recently interacted with. In fact, though, it lists only files you've *opened* recently. Files you just *created or downloaded* don't appear here (because you haven't *opened* them), much to the confusion of everyone.

If you miss All My Files, it's easy to recreate the effect. The trick is to create a smart folder, as described on page 138. But you'll want to set it up as shown here, where the Kind is "Document" and the sub-criteria rows list anything opened, modified, or created in the past 90 days (or whatever time you specify). (See page 128 for details on setting up this kind of query, and remember to Option-click the **+** button to open the "Any of the following are true" rows.)

Save this Smart Folder, name it "All My Files," turn on "Add to Sidebar," and boom—you're back in business.

Oh—and then choose Finder→Preferences→Sidebar and *turn off* Recents.

Disk icons on the desktop

For years, Apple has encouraged its flock to keep a clean desktop, to get rid of all the icons that many of us leave strewn around. Especially the hard drive icon, which had appeared in the upper-right corner of the screen since the original 1984 Mac.

Today, the Macintosh HD icon doesn't normally appear on the screen. "Look," Apple seems to be saying, "if you want access to your files and folders, just open them directly—from the Dock or your Home folder (page 72). Most of the stuff on the hard drive is system files of no interest to you, so let's just get that icon out of your way."

If you'd prefer that the disk icons return to your desktop, then choose Finder→ Preferences, click General, and turn on the checkboxes of the disks whose icons you want on the desktop: hard disks, external disks, CDs, and so on.

Windows and How to Work Them

In designing macOS, one of Apple's key goals was to address the window-proliferation problem. As you create more files, stash them in more folders, and launch more programs, it's easy to wind up paralyzed before a screen awash with overlapping rectangles.

That's the problem admirably addressed by Mission Control, described in detail on page 183. Some handy clutter and navigation controls are built into the windows themselves, too. For example:

The Sidebar

The Sidebar (Figure 1-3) is the pane at the left side of every Finder window, unless you've hidden it. (It's also at the left side of every Open dialog box and every full-sized Save dialog box.) It's slightly translucent—your desktop picture shines through just a little bit.

The Sidebar has as many as four sections, each preceded by a collapsible heading.

Tip: If you point to a heading without clicking, a tiny Hide or Show button appears. Click it to collapse or expand that heading's contents.

Here are the headings you'll soon know and love:

- **Favorites.** This primary section of the Sidebar is the place to stash things for easy access. You can stock this list with the icons of disks, files, programs, folders, and the virtual, self-updating folders called *saved searches.*

 Each icon is a shortcut. For example, click the Applications icon to view the contents of your Applications folder in the main part of the window. And if you click the icon of a file or a program, it opens.

 Here, too, you'll find the icon for AirDrop, the instant file-sharing feature described on page 572. (The All My Files "folder" is gone; see the box on the next page.)

The menu bar

Every popular operating system saves space by concealing its most important commands in menus that drop down. MacOS's menus are especially refined:

- **They stay down.** MacOS menus stay open until you click the mouse, trigger a command from the keyboard, or buy a new computer, whichever comes first.

Tip: Actually, menus are even smarter than that. If you give the menu name a quick click, the menu opens and stays open. If you click the menu name and hold the mouse button down for a moment, the menu opens but closes again when you release the button. Apple figures that, in that case, you're just exploring, reading, or hunting for a certain command.

- **They're consistently arranged.** The first menu in every program, which appears in bold lettering, tells you at a glance what program you're in (Safari, Microsoft Word, whatever). The commands in this Application menu include About (which indicates what version of the program you're using), Preferences, and Quit, as well as commands like Hide Others and Show All (which control window clutter, as described on page 202). In short, all the Application menu's commands actually pertain to the application you're using.

 The File and Edit menus come next. The File menu contains commands for opening, saving, and closing files. (See the logic?) The Edit menu contains the Cut, Copy, and Paste commands.

 The last menu is almost always Help. It opens a miniature web browser that lets you search the online Mac help files for explanatory text.

- **You can operate them from the keyboard.** Once you've clicked open a menu, you can highlight any command in it just by typing the first letter (*g* for Get Info, for example). It's especially great for "Your country" pop-up menus on websites, where "United States" is about 200 countries down in the list. You can type *united s* to jump right to it.

 You can also press Tab to open the next menu, Shift-Tab to open the previous one, and Return to "click" the highlighted command.

- **They can hide themselves.** You can set things up so that the menu bar disappears completely when you're not using it. You get a little more room on your screen. Particularly if you use keyboard shortcuts for menu commands, why should the menu bar just sit there all day, eating up space?

 The on/off switch for this menu-hiding feature is in System Preferences→General; turn on "Automatically hide and show the menu bar." Then, when you do want to open a menu manually, just move your cursor to the top edge of the screen; the menu bar reappears.

- **You can add a new icon to the Dock by dragging it there.** Rearrange Dock icons by dragging them. Remove a Dock icon by dragging it away from the Dock.

- **Click something once to open it.** When you click a program's icon, a tiny black dot appears under it to let you know it's open.

 When you click a folder's icon, you get a *stack*—an arcing row of icons, or a grid of them, that indicates what's inside. See page 141 for more on stacks.

- **Each Dock icon sprouts a pop-up menu.** To see the menu, hold the mouse button down on a Dock icon—or right-click or two-finger click it. A shortcut menu of useful commands pops right out.

- **If you have a trackpad, you can view miniatures of all open windows in a program by pointing to its Dock icon and then swiping down with three fingers.** Details on how to turn on this feature are on page 196.

Figure 1-2:
The macOS landscape looks like a more futuristic version of the operating systems you know and love. This is just a starting point, however. You can dress it up with a different background picture, adjust your windows in a million ways, and of course fill the Dock with only the programs, disks, folders, and files you need.

Apple menu · Menu bar · Desktop · Menulets · Dock · Trash

Because the Dock is such a critical component of macOS, Apple has decked it out with enough customization controls to keep you busy experimenting for months. You can change its size, move it to the sides of your screen, hide it entirely, and so on. Chapter 4 contains complete instructions for using and understanding the Dock.

The menu

The menu houses important Mac-wide commands like Sleep, Restart, and Shut Down. They're always available, no matter which program you're using.

Chapter 12 offers much more on this business of accounts and logging in.

> **Note:** In certain especially paranoid workplaces, you may not see the rogues' gallery shown in Figure 1-1. You may just get two text boxes, where you're supposed to type in your name and password. Without the icons of known account holders, an evil hacker's job is that much more difficult.

Figure 1-1:
On Macs used by multiple people, this is one of the first things you see upon turning on the computer. Click your name. (If the list is long, you may have to swipe the trackpad to find your name—or just type its first few letters.)

Inset: At this point, you're asked to type in your password. Type it, and then click Log In (or press Return). If you type the wrong password, the box vibrates, in effect shaking its little dialog-box head, suggesting that you guess again.

The Elements of the macOS Desktop

The desktop is the shimmering, three-dimensional macOS landscape shown in Figure 1-2. On a new Mac, it's covered by a photo of a spectacular, massive sand dune—California's Sierra Nevada Mojave Desert (get it?). If you upgraded from an earlier version of macOS, you keep whatever desktop picture you had before.

If you've ever used a computer before, most of the objects on your screen are nothing more than updated versions of familiar elements. Here's a quick tour.

The Dock

This translucent row of colorful icons (Figure 1-2, bottom) is a launcher for the programs, files, folders, and disks you use often—and an indicator to let you know which programs are already open. They appear to rest on a sheet of transparent, smoked glass.

In principle, the Dock is very simple:

- **It has three sections.** Programs are the left side. In Mojave, the icons of some recently opened programs live in the middle. Everything else goes on the right, including documents, folders, and disks.

Folders, Windows & Finder Tabs

T hese days, the graphic user interface (icons, windows, trash cans) is standard. MacOS, Windows, Chrome OS, Android, iOS—every operating system is fundamentally the same, and a very long way from the lines of typed commands that defined the earliest computers.

That's not to say that the graphic interface hasn't evolved, though; it has. Herewith: a grand tour of the state of the art in computer desktops—the one in Mojave.

Getting into macOS

When you first turn on a Mac running macOS, an Apple logo greets you, soon joined by a skinny progress bar that lets you know how much longer you have to wait.

Logging In

What happens next depends on whether you're the Mac's sole proprietor or have to share it with other people in an office, school, or household.

- **If it's your own Mac,** and you've already been through the setup process described in Appendix A, no big deal. You arrive at the macOS desktop.

- **If it's a shared Mac,** you may encounter the Login screen, shown in Figure 1-1. It's like a portrait gallery, set against a blurry version of your usual desktop picture. Click your icon.

 If the Mac asks for your password, type it and then click Log In (or press Return). You arrive at the desktop. Or, if your Mac has a Touch Bar (page 233) and you've registered your fingerprint, then touch that finger to the sensor at the right end of the bar.

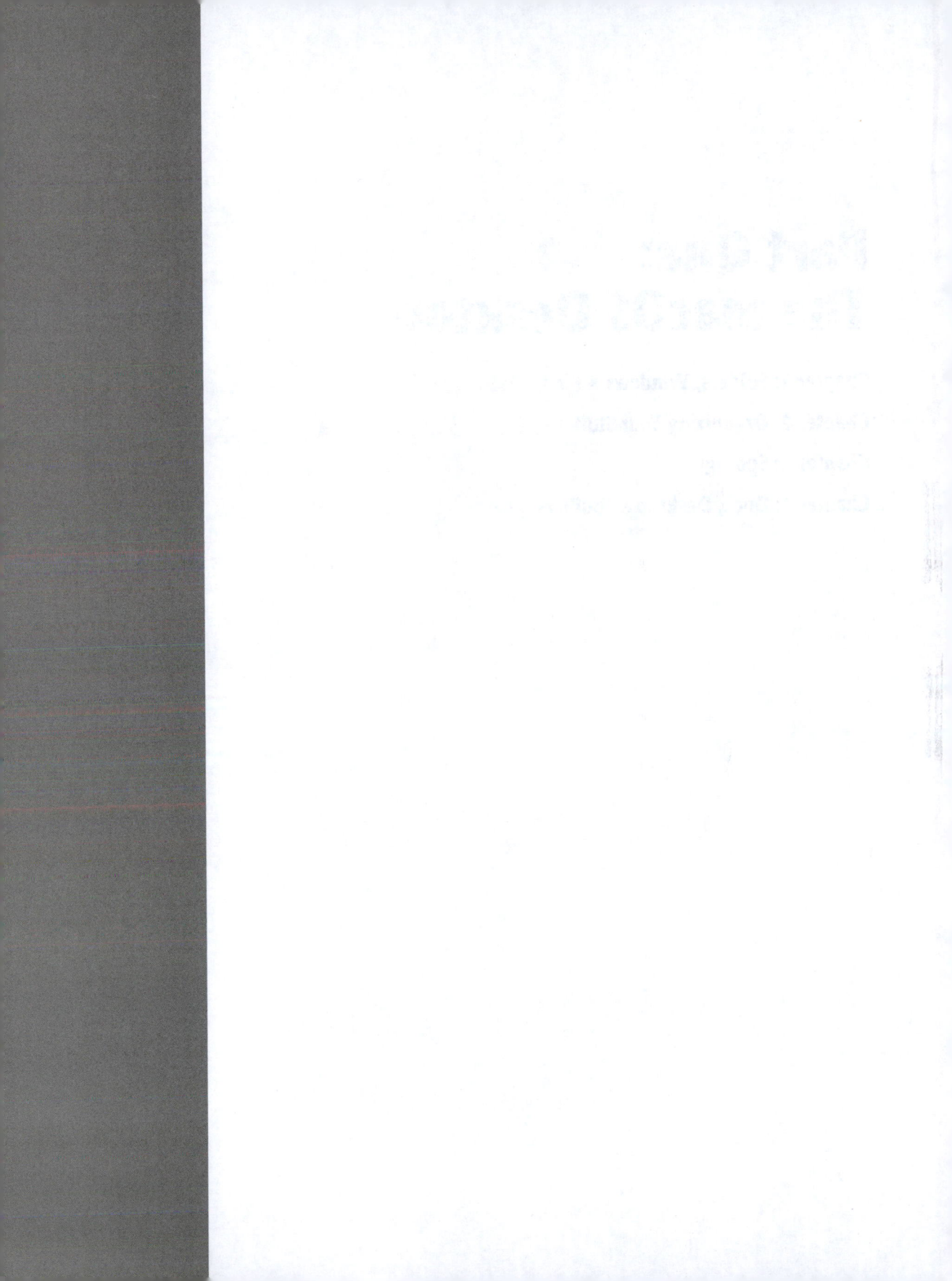

Part One:
The macOS Desktop

1

- **Icons.** The colorful inch-tall pictures that appear in your various desktop folders are the graphic symbols that represent each program, disk, and document on your computer. If you click an icon one time, it darkens, indicating that you've just *highlighted* or *selected* it. Now you're ready to manipulate it by using, for example, a menu command.

A few more tips on using the Mac keyboard appear at the beginning of Chapter 6. Otherwise, if you've mastered this much information, then you have all the technical background you need to enjoy *macOS Mojave: The Missing Manual.*

(There's also *right-clicking*. That very important topic is described in depth on page 239.)

- **Menus.** The *menus* are the words at the top of your screen: , File, Edit, and so on. Click one to make a list of commands appear.

 Some people click once to open a menu and then, after reading the choices, click again on the one they want. Other people like to press the mouse button continuously after the initial click on the menu title, drag down the list to the desired command, and only then release the mouse button. Either method works fine.

- **Dialog boxes.** See Figure I-2 for a tour of the onscreen elements you'll frequently be asked to use, like checkboxes, radio buttons, tabs, and so on.

Figure I-2:
Knowing what you're doing on the Mac often requires knowing what things are called. Here are some of the most common onscreen elements. They include checkboxes (turn on as many as you like) and radio buttons (only one can be turned on in each grouping).

Pressing Return is usually the same as clicking the default button—the lower-right button that almost always means "OK, I'm done here."

- **Keyboard shortcuts.** If you're typing along in a burst of creative energy, it's disruptive to have to grab the mouse to use a menu. That's why many Mac fans prefer to trigger menu commands by pressing key combinations. For example, in word processors, you can press ⌘-B to produce a boldface word. When you read an instruction like "Press ⌘-B," start by pressing the ⌘ key, and then, while it's down, type the letter B, and finally release both keys.

Tip: You know what's really nice? The keystroke to open the Preferences dialog box in every Apple program—Mail, Safari, iMovie, Photos, TextEdit, Preview, and on and on—is always the same: ⌘-comma. Better yet, that standard is catching on in other apps, too, like Word, Excel, and PowerPoint.

- **Gestures.** A *gesture* is a swipe across your trackpad (on your laptop, or on an external Apple trackpad) or across the top surface of the Apple Magic Mouse. Gestures have been given huge importance in macOS. Page 827 contains a handy list of them.

"On your hard drive, you'll find a folder called System. Open that. Inside the System folder window is a folder called Libraries; double-click to open it. Inside *that* folder is yet another one called Fonts. Double-click to open it, too." See Figure I-1.

Figure I-1:
If this book says "Choose View→Sort By→Name," it's describing a logical sequence of steps.

In this example, that would mean clicking the View menu, choosing the Sort By command from it, and then choosing Name from the submenu.

About MissingManuals.com

To get the most out of this book, visit *missingmanuals.com*. Click the "Missing CDs" link—and then this book's title—to reveal a neat, organized, chapter-by-chapter list of the shareware and freeware mentioned in this book.

The website also offers book corrections and updates. (To see them, click the book's title, and then click View/Submit Errata.) In fact, please submit such corrections and updates yourself! In an effort to keep the book as up-to-date and accurate as possible, each time we print more copies of this book, I'll make any confirmed corrections you've suggested. I'll also note such changes on the website so you can mark important corrections into your own copy of the book, if you like. And I'll keep the book current as Apple releases more macOS 10.14 updates.

The Very Basics

To use this book, and indeed to use a Mac, you need to know some basics. This book assumes you're familiar with a few terms and concepts:

- **Clicking.** To *click* means to point the arrow cursor at something on the screen and then—without moving the cursor—press and release the clicker button on the mouse or trackpad. To *double-click,* of course, means to click twice in rapid succession, again without moving the cursor at all. And to *drag* means to move the cursor while holding down the mouse button.

 When you're told to ⌘-*click* something, you click while pressing the ⌘ key (which is next to the space bar). *Shift-clicking, Option-clicking,* and *Control-clicking* work the same way—just click while pressing the corresponding key.

Even so, some chapters come with free downloadable appendixes—PDF documents, available on this book's "Missing CD" page at *missingmanuals.com*—that go into further detail on some of the tweakiest features. (You'll see references to them sprinkled throughout the book.)

Maybe this idea will save a few trees—and a few back muscles when you try to pick this book up.

About the Outline

MacOS Mojave: The Missing Manual is divided into six parts, each containing several chapters:

- **Part One: The macOS Desktop** covers everything you see on the screen when you turn on a Mac: folders, windows, icons, the Dock, the Sidebar, Spotlight, Dashboard, Spaces, Mission Control, Launchpad, Time Machine, menus, scroll bars, the Trash, aliases, the menu, and so on.

- **Part Two: Programs in macOS** is dedicated to the proposition that an operating system is little more than a launchpad for *programs*—the actual applications you use: email programs, web browsers, word processors, graphics suites, and so on. These chapters describe how to work with applications—how to open them, switch among them, swap data between them, and use them to create and open files. And there's also, of course, a chapter about Siri.

- **Part Three: The Components of macOS** is an item-by-item discussion of the software nuggets that make up this operating system—the 30-ish panels of System Preferences and the 50-some programs in your Applications and Utilities folders.

- **Part Four: The Technologies of macOS** treads in more advanced territory, like networking and file sharing. These chapters also cover the visual talents of the Mac (fonts, printing, graphics) and its multimedia gifts (sound, movies).

- **Part Five: macOS Online** covers all the internet features, including the Mail email program and the Safari web browser; Messages for instant messaging and audio or video chats; internet sharing; Apple's free, online iCloud services; and connecting to and controlling your Mac from across the wires—FTP, SSH, VPN, and so on.

- **Part Six: Appendixes.** This book's appendixes include guidance on installing this operating system, a troubleshooting handbook, a Windows-to-Mac dictionary (to help Windows refugees find the new locations of familiar features in macOS), and a master list of all the keyboard shortcuts and trackpad/mouse gestures on your Mac.

About→These→Arrows

Throughout this book, you'll find sentences like this one: "Open the System folder→Libraries→Fonts folder." That's shorthand for a much longer instruction that directs you to open three nested folders in sequence, like this:

- **Seventy new emoji.** At last, the little cartoon emoji symbols include characters with red, curly, or gray hair—or no hair at all. There are new emoji for superheroes, cold face, party face, pleading face, face with hearts, kangaroo, parrot, lobster, mango, lettuce, cupcake, and more. How did we *live...?*

- **Siri knows a little more.** Siri can now answer questions about celebrities, food nutrition, motorsports, and your own passwords. ("Hey Siri: Show me my Hulu password!")

- **Favicons on your tabs.** In Safari's Preferences, you can turn on favicons (those little website-logo icons) so they appear on each of your tabs.

- **A couple of removals.** The Mac used to let you store your account details for Twitter, Facebook, LinkedIn, Vimeo, and Flickr right in System Preferences. And they were options in the Share menu, too, so you could post photos and tweets directly from your Mac apps. But no longer.

 Back to My Mac is gone, too. Apple says these removals make the Mac more secure from hackers.

 Oh, and stationery templates are no longer part of the Mail app.

True, that's not a very long list of new stuff in macOS. But look at the bright side: With changes this minor, it means you won't have many app glitches to get over.

About This Book

To find your way around macOS Mojave, you're expected to use Apple's online help system. And as you'll quickly discover, these help pages are tersely written, offer very little technical depth, lack useful examples, and provide no tutorials whatsoever. You can't mark your place, underline, or read them in the bathroom.

The purpose of this book, then, is to serve as the manual that should have accompanied macOS—version 10.14 in particular. Whether you have an antique, hand-cranked 2012 iMac or one of the shiny new 2018 models, like the sleek updated MacBook Air or the compact, screenless Mac mini, this is your user guide.

MacOS Mojave: The Missing Manual is designed to accommodate readers at every technical level. The primary discussions are written for advanced-beginner or intermediate Mac fans. But if you're a Mac first-timer, miniature sidebar articles called "Up to Speed" provide the introductory information you need to understand the topic at hand. If you're a Mac veteran, on the other hand, keep your eye out for similar shaded boxes called "Power Users' Clinic." They offer more-technical tips, tricks, and shortcuts.

When you write a book like this, you do a lot of soul-searching about how much to cover. Of course, a thinner book, or at least a thinner-looking one, is always preferable; plenty of readers are intimidated by a book that dwarfs the Tokyo White Pages.

On the other hand, Apple keeps adding features and rarely takes them away. So this book isn't getting any skinnier.

- **Configuration fingerprinting.** Cookies aren't the only tools that advertising networks have for tracking your online activity. They also use *fingerprinting*: following you by identifying the particular characteristics of your Mac, such as its hardware configuration, the plug-ins it uses, and even the fonts it has installed. But in macOS Mojave, all the Macs in the world look alike to the advertisers, making it dramatically harder for them to track you.

Lots of Misc.

Some of the smaller tweaks:

- **Gallery view.** The old Cover Flow view has received a weird, minor tweak. It still displays a large thumbnail of each icon as you arrow-key your way through the items in a folder. But now, the icons themselves appear in a horizontal row, instead of in a list view. And now it's called gallery view.

- **More permission granting.** You know how the Mac asks for permission every time an app wants to use your location, contacts, or calendar? Now it also asks you when an app wants to access your camera, microphone, Mail database, Messages history, Time Machine backups, or Safari data.

- **Recent Apps on the Dock.** For the first time, the Dock displays a mini-bank of icons representing the programs you've used most recently. (You can turn that off in System Preferences→Dock.)

- **Group FaceTime.** Yep: Video calls with up to 32 people simultaneously (on Macs with Mojave or iPhones/iPads running iOS 12). You see the other participants on floating tiles, which get big and pop to the fore when somebody speaks. This, of course, isn't a novel invention (hi, Google Hangouts!). But for the tens of millions of Apple fans, it's welcome.

- **Redesigned Mac App Store.** The Mac App Store gains features from the iOS App Store, like video previews, app ranking, and Editor's Choice selections. (Apple says Microsoft Office and Adobe Lightroom will be coming to the Mac App Store for the first time, too.)

- **Auto-text-code entry.** You know that system where, when you try to log into a website (your bank's, for example), they send a six-digit number code to your cellphone, which you're supposed to type into the login screen? Now the Mac can automatically "see" that texted code and offer to type it in with one click.

- **Reused password spotting.** If you view your passwords in Safari's Preferences, you'll see special symbols to indicate passwords you've used more than once. Safari offers to change them to much stronger passwords (which, of course, it memorizes for you).

- **A revamped Save panel.** The controls for changing your view of the "Mini-Finder" in a Save As dialog box (list, column, icon view; grouping commands; sorting commands) are now consolidated into a single pop-up menu.

- **Voice Memos** is the iPhone's traditional audio-recording (and basic editing) app. The presence of this app on the Mac means there's no more figuring out how to transfer your recordings from the phone to the computer; they appear on the Mac automatically.

- **Home.** HomeKit is Apple's home-automation standard. This app lets you control any product whose box says "Works with HomeKit"—all those "smart" or "connected" door locks, security cameras, power outlets, thermostats, doorbells, light bulbs, leak/freeze/temperature/humidity/air-quality sensors, and so on.

All of this, Apple says, is the first phase in its long-term plan to let software companies bring their iOS apps to the Mac with very little rewriting. ("Almost every year, people ask us the question, 'Are you merging iOS and macOS?'" says Apple VP Craig Federighi. "No! Of course not.")

Safari Defenses

Last year, Apple introduced a technology in its Safari browser that prevents advertisers from tracking you as you move from site to site. This year, it has tripled down on that promise. Apple says that it's slamming shut privacy holes you didn't even realize you had:

- **Like buttons, Share buttons, Comment buttons.** Little do most people realize: Those buttons allow social-media sites to track you, too, whether you use those them or not. Now, Safari blocks them from sending information about you and your actions—until you actually use those controls. And even then, it warns you that "This information will be shared with Facebook," for example.

UP TO SPEED

Upside-Down Scrolling

If you haven't upgraded your Mac in long time, you might discover something alarming when you try to scroll using your laptop's trackpad: When you slide your fingers *upward*, the page scrolls *down*. That's backward, isn't it?

For your entire computing career so far, you've always dragged the scroll bar down to move the contents of the page up—and now Apple has swapped the directions. Why would Apple throw such a monkey wrench into your life?

The main reason is to make the Mac match the iPad, where you drag your finger *up* to move the page *up*.

Anyway, you have two choices: You can spend a couple of days getting used to the new arrangement—or you can put things back to the way they've always been. To do that, open

System Preferences. For a trackpad: Click Trackpad, click Scroll & Zoom, and then turn off "Scroll direction: natural." For a Magic Mouse: Click Mouse, click Point & Click, and then turn off "Scroll direction: natural."

Note: If you have a non-Apple mouse that has a scroll wheel, then the Mouse pane may not offer this scroll-direction option. You can still reverse the scroll-direction logic, though, if you're handy in Terminal (macOS's command line program).

Just open Terminal and type *defaults write ~/Library/ Preferences/.GlobalPreferences com.apple.swipescrolldirection -bool false.* When you press Return and log out, you'll find that the time-honored scroll directions have been restored.

Screenshot Tools

When you capture the screen image using the age-old keystroke Shift-⌘-3 (whole screen) or Shift-⌘-4 (portion of the screen), it now works as it does on iOS: It shrinks down into a thumbnail in the corner of the screen. If you click it before it disappears, you can open it up, edit it, crop it, mark it up, delete it, or share it. You're spared the whole business of finding and editing and sending the shot after creating it.

Even better: The new keystroke Shift-⌘-5 opens a master screen-capture utility panel. It offers buttons for capturing still images of your screen (whole screen or a portion) and also for capturing *videos* of your screen activity (whole screen or a portion). An Options menu lets you choose whether or not the cursor should be included, whether or not you need a timer (a few seconds to get the screen set up properly), and where you want the resulting screenshot sent.

Not everyone needs to capture photos and videos of the screen every day. But if you do, this enhancement is awesome.

Continuity Camera

This cool feature turns your iPhone or iPad into a detached, handheld, wireless camera for your Mac. When you snap a photo, it appears on the Mac a moment later, for incorporating into whatever app you're using. (It requires that iOS 12 be running on your phone or tablet.) Page 315 has the details.

The iPhone's document-scanning module is available, too, using the same mechanism. It comes complete with auto-straightening and -clarifying magic for whatever piece of paper you're scanning. Insta-PDF!

These features can be brilliant time-savers for researchers and students. If you use Messages on your Mac to do your texting, it's life-changing: Now you can pop a photo into the conversation without any file-transferring nonsense.

Four New Apps

Four apps that have been on iOS for years are now full-blown Mac apps. All four take great advantage of your Mac's large screen. And, maybe more important, all four sync wirelessly with your phone, so the news (or stocks, or voice recordings, or home-automation settings) are identical on all your Apple gadgets. Here's what you'll get:

- **News** is Apple's news app. It culls articles from hundreds of publications, online and off (*The New York Times*, *The Wall Street Journal*, *The Washington Post*, *Esquire*, *NPR*, *HuffPost*, and so on), and then presents them in gorgeous, ad-free magazine-like layout. Some of the sections are curated by Apple editors, chosen for fairness and neutrality; other sections are For You, algorithmically determined based on your interests.

- **Stocks** tracks your stocks and bonds. When you click a stock's name, you see the latest news about that company, brought to you by the same headline engine that drives News.

The changes in macOS Mojave are either "thoughtful and strategic" or "ridiculously minor," depending on your generosity of thought toward Apple products.

Herewith: a list of what's new.

Dark Mode

Dark Mode is a dark-gray color scheme (page 158); you're offered the chance to turn it on during the installation process, and you can turn it on and off at will in System Preferences→General. Once you turn it on, most of Apple's built-in apps—Finder, Mail, Calendar, Messages, iTunes, Notes, Xcode, and so on—match that white-on-black appearance.

Apple says that, by making menus and panels darker, Dark Mode helps to emphasize your document or photo, making it pop more. Dark Mode may also be less disturbing to someone sleeping next to you in bed, because it radiates less light from the screen.

As a bonus, Mojave comes with two new desktop wallpapers, called Dynamic Desktop, that actually change their look as the day wears on, as though the sun is moving through the sky.

Accent Colors

For 10 years, your list of accent color options—used in progress bars, OK buttons, highlighted menu names and menu commands—was pretty short: blue or gray.

MacOS Mojave offers a choice of *eight* accent colors. You might be surprised to see what a difference a new accent color makes to the experience of using the Mac.

Desktop Stacks

Desktop stacks (View→Use Stacks) is designed for people who leave their desktops strewn with icons. When you turn on stacks, your desktop icons auto-clump into related piles, sorted by date created, date last opened, date modified, tag, or kind (for example, Documents and Images). Each icon auto-expands when you click it. Why should your real-world desktop be the only one with stuff in piles?

Preview Sidebar

The Preview sidebar column (View→Show Preview) shows what's inside any icon you select: a thumbnail of a photo, for example, or the first page of a Word document. It also shows the file's *metadata*—your choice of data bits like size, date, camera model, number of pages, and so on.

But this one's got Quick Actions buttons at the bottom, relevant to the kind of file you've clicked. For a photo, the buttons include Rotate and Mark Up. For a PDF document, it's Mark Up or Add Password. If you're handy with Apple's Automator app, you can make your own Quick Actions buttons, too.

Introduction

MacOS Mojave is the 14th major version of Apple's Unix-based operating system. It's got very little in common with the original Mac operating system, the one that saw Apple through the 1980s and 1990s. Apple dumped that in 2001, when CEO Steve Jobs decided it was time for a change. Apple had spent too many years piling new features onto a software foundation originally poured in 1984. Programmers and customers complained of the "spaghetti code" the Mac OS had become.

So today, underneath macOS's classy, shining desktop is Unix, the industrial-strength, rock-solid OS that drives many a website and university. It's not new by any means; in fact, it's decades old and has been polished by generations of programmers.

Note: Beginning with Sierra in 2016, Apple stopped calling the Mac operating system "OS X." It's now "macOS." That's partly because Apple sought consistency with the software in its other products—iOS and watchOS—and partly, no doubt, because it was tired of hearing people pronounce it "oh ess sex."

What's New in Mojave

Having run out of big cat species (Lion, Jaguar, Panther, Tiger, Leopard, Snow Leopard), Apple has begun naming its Mac operating systems after rock formations in California. There was Yosemite, and then El Capitan, and then Sierra and High Sierra, after the Sierra Nevada mountain range. And now there's Mojave, named after the California desert.

Acknowledgments

Over the years, over the many editions of this book, many friends and colleagues have contributed enthusiasm, expertise, and even prose to this Missing Manual. They include Tom Gewecke, Zachary Brass, Kirill Voronin, Dan Pourhadi, Rich Koster, J.D. Biersdorfer, Teresa Noelle Roberts, Ben Waldie, Brian Sawyer, Phil Simpson, and Lesa Snider.

I owe debts of thanks to O'Reilly's Missing Manuals editor-in-chief, Nan Barber; to Apple's Todd Benjamin and Bill Evans for going beyond the call of duty to chase down tweaky tech answers; to my assistant Jan Carpenter, whose help made my survival possible; and to Julie Van Keuren, whose Missing Manual role over the past decade has grown from humble copy editor to full-blown editorial and design factory.

I also wish I could send out an "I Made the Book Better!" T-shirt to every reader who ever took the time to write with corrections, suggestions, tips, and tricks. And thanks, as always, to David Rogelberg for believing in the idea.

Above all, this book owes its existence to the patience and affection of Nicki, Kelly, Tia, and Jeffrey. They make these books—and everything else—possible.

—*David Pogue*

About The Missing Manuals

Missing Manuals are witty, well-written guides to computer products that don't come with printed manuals (which is just about all of them). Each book features a hand-crafted index; cross-references to specific page numbers (not just "see Chapter 14"); and an ironclad promise never to put an apostrophe in the possessive pronoun "its."

Also by David Pogue:

- *iPhone: The Missing Manual*
- *Windows 10: The Missing Manual*
- *David Pogue's Digital Photography: The Missing Manual*
- *Pogue's Basics: Tech*
- *Pogue's Basics: Money*
- *Pogue's Basics: Life*

The Missing Credits

About the Author

 David Pogue (author, illustrator) has been a *New York Times* columnist since 2000 (although somewhere in there, he took a five-year detour at Yahoo Finance).

He's also a four-time Emmy-winning correspondent for *CBS News Sunday Morning,* the host of several *NOVA* miniseries on PBS, and the creator of the Missing Manual series. He's written or co-written more than 100 books, including dozens in this series, six in the *For Dummies* line (including *Macs, Magic, Opera,* and *Classical Music*), two novels (one for middle-schoolers), *The World According to Twitter,* and three books of essential tips and shortcuts: *Pogue's Basics: Tech, Pogue's Basics: Life,* and *Pogue's Basics: Money.* In his other life, David is a former Broadway show conductor, a magician, and a funny public speaker. He lives in Connecticut with his wife, Nicki, and three awesome children.

You can find a complete list of David's columns and videos, and sign up to get them by email, at *authory.com/davidpogue.* His website is *davidpogue.com.* He welcomes feedback about his books by email at *david@pogueman.com.*

About the Creative Team

Julie Van Keuren (editor, indexer, interior book designer) spent 14 years in print journalism before deciding to upend her life, move to Montana, and live the freelancing dream. She now works for a variety of terrific clients who understand that skilled editing, writing, book layout, and indexing don't have to come from inside a cubicle. She and her husband, sci-fi writer M.H. Van Keuren, have two adult sons. Email: *JulieVanK@gmail.com.*

Diana D'Abruzzo (proofreader) is a Virginia-based freelance editor with more than 20 years of experience in the journalism and book publishing industries. More information on her life and work can be found at *dianadabruzzo.com.*

Kellee Katagi (proofreader) has devoted most of her 20-plus-year writing and editing career to covering fitness, nutrition, travel, and outdoor sports. A former managing editor of SKI magazine, she now smiths words from her Colorado home, where she lives with her husband and three kids. Email: *kelkatagi@gmail.com.*

Judy Le (proofreader) is an editor based in Virginia, where she lives with her husband and their son. In her spare time she pursues interests with great fervor just before dropping them entirely.

Part Four: The Technologies of macOS

Chapter 12: Accounts, Security & Gatekeeper 521

Chapter 13: Networking, File Sharing & AirDrop 567

Table of Contents

macOS Mojave: The Missing Manual
by David Pogue

Copyright © 2018 David Pogue. All rights reserved.
Printed in the United States of America.

Editor: Julie Van Keuren
Proofreaders: Diana D'Abruzzo, Kellee Katagi, and Judy Le
Illustrator: David Pogue
Interior book designer: Julie Van Keuren (based on a design by Phil Simpson)
Indexer: Julie Van Keuren

Published by O'Reilly Media, Inc.,
1005 Gravenstein Highway North, Sebastopol, CA 95472.

O'Reilly Media books may be purchased for educational, business, or sales
promotional use. Online editions are also available for most titles: *safari@oreilly.
com*. For more information, contact our corporate/institutional sales department:
800-998-9938 or *corporate@oreilly.com*.

December 2018: First Edition.

ISBN: 978-1-492-04040-8
[LSC]

macOS Mojave

the missing manual®
The book that should have been in the box®

David Pogue

O'REILLY®

Beijing | Boston | Farnham | Sebastopol | Tokyo

macOS Mojave

the missing manual®

The book that should have been in the box®